INTRODUCTION TO CONTEMPORARY

CIVILIZATION IN THE WEST

A SOURCE BOOK

Introduction to Contemporary Civilization in the West

A SOURCE BOOK

PREPARED BY THE CONTEMPORARY CIVILIZATION

STAFF OF COLUMBIA COLLEGE, COLUMBIA UNIVERSITY

VOLUME I • THIRD EDITION • 1960 • NEW YORK

Columbia University Press

COPYRIGHT © 1946, 1954, 1960, COLUMBIA UNIVERSITY PRESS, NEW YORK

THIRD EDITION 1960

First printing 1960
Second printing 1961

PUBLISHED IN GREAT BRITAIN, INDIA, AND PAKISTAN
BY THE OXFORD UNIVERSITY PRESS
LONDON, BOMBAY, AND KARACHI

MANUFACTURED IN THE UNITED STATES OF AMERICA

PREFACE TO THE FIRST EDITION

T HE PURPOSE of these volumes of readings is to enable the student to approach the making of contemporary civilization through the ideas and institutions which helped make it. An important aspect of any historical event or movement is the interpretation and justification of it by those who participated in it. Reflection by the student upon society and history supplies both a pattern and a perspective for intelligent control. Such reflection is impossible apart from the traditions of human thinking. A civilized person has a past and must be conscious of his own roots and growth in order to participate intelligently in his society. Each of the readings that follow has been chosen because it is a genuine source of contemporary civilization. These readings embody not historical curiosities but ideas that have persisted.

There has been little attempt to make the selections present the entire thought of an individual, or to present literary masterpieces as works of art or unified wholes. In view of the primary aim to develop the student's critical understanding of his society, the selections for the most part present specific, important arguments. Many great names and documents do not appear. A source book, of any kind, must discriminate in the light of its purpose. In deciding what to use, and what to exclude, the editors have tried constantly to keep to the forefront the limitations of time and the teachability of the material. These readings are not designed to polish off an education, but rather to help the student lay the groundwork for his more advanced courses in the social sciences. It is important to emphasize that, in Columbia College, the *Source Book* is used in conjunction with a guiding *Manual* and appropriate textbook assignments, which help to supply the necessary historical context and continuity.

Although the course in Contemporary Civilization has been required of all freshmen in Columbia College for more than twenty-five years, the present degree of emphasis on the reading of original source materials was first introduced, on a trial basis, in the spring of 1941. Results were so encouraging that the readings soon came to be regarded, by staff and students alike, as one of the most valuable features of the course. To facilitate revision, the selections were at first published in twenty-four separate fascicles, corresponding to the organizational division of the subject matter. Supplementary fascicles, embodying the first fruits of practice, appeared in 1943. These earlier readings were in large part prepared by Charles Frankel. Collaborators on the original or supplementary fascicles were Jacques Barzun, Paul Beik, J. B. Brebner, Harry J. Carman, George Crothers, Charles W. Cole, Eugene O. Golob, Louis M. Hacker, G. Adolph Koch, Dwight C. Miner, Ernest Nagel, Donald W. O'Connell, John H. Randall, Jr., Herbert W. Schneider, William O. Shanahan, and Robert E. Tschan.

The present edition constitutes a major revision of the content and organization of the readings, based upon five years of classroom experience. Every part of the work has undergone thorough re-editing. Many of the selections previously used have been omitted, while those retained have been carefully re-examined. Abbreviations have been made where it seemed advisable, and better translations used where possible. A large number of new selections have been added after consideration of the needs which have emerged in this type of course, including much valuable material not elsewhere available in English.

Because the advantages of the separate fascicles have largely disappeared with the success and solidification of the source-readings enterprise, the present edition is offered in two bound volumes. In this more substantial and attractive form, it is hoped that students will find the *Source Book* a work of useful reference in their later college studies and that it will become a welcome addition to their permanent libraries. While the *Source Book* has been constructed with the requirements of the Columbia College course primarily in view, the Committee is aware that the material can be abbreviated or in other ways adapted to the needs of various types of courses in other colleges and universities.

The emphasis in these volumes has been deliberately placed on the specifically European institutions and ideas which have helped to shape the character of contemporary civilization. The impress of these institutions and ideas on the United States and its place in international affairs, together with the distinctively American contribution to contemporary civilization, are studied in the second year of the course, and analogous source-readings are designed to accompany this part of the work.

For permission to reprint material from their publications, thanks and acknowledgments are hereby extended to the publishers mentioned in the selections that follow.

The Committee whose work this edition of the *Source Book* represents consisted of the undersigned and, for a shorter period, John R. Everett.

JUSTUS BUCHLER, *Chairman*
PAUL BEIK

Columbia University
January, 1946

EUGENE O. GOLOB
K. WILLIAM KAPP

PREFACE TO THE SECOND EDITION

THE PRESENT REVISION of the 1946 edition of the *Source Book* is not a radical one so far as method and principles are concerned. But both volumes have been intensively re-examined, and many modifications have been made in the light of six more years of practical classroom experience. Most of the changes are designed to further existing aims of the first-year course in Contemporary Civilization at Columbia College and, more generally, the several additional functions which the book is known to serve elsewhere. The Contemporary Civilization staff does not pretend to have "solved" the problems of general education (indeed, the very notion would be self-contradicting); but it has been gratified to find how effectively the bulk of the 1946 material was serving the purposes of the Columbia and many other programs.

Though the two volumes of the *Source Book* independently meet a number of needs, they can be used to particular advantage in connection with the new two-volume edition of *Chapters in Western Civilization*. Each of the "Chapters" now corresponds to a subdivision of the *Source Book*, supplying a background for the topic in question. "Chapters" and "Sources" are thus mutually illuminating.

The structure of the *Source Book* (both volumes) has been partially altered; certain chapter headings have been re-formulated; extensive and important new material has been specially translated for this edition; many of the introductions to the readings have been revised; and foreign phrases occurring in the readings have been translated. These changes—along with the specific changes enumerated below for Volume One—have been made in the interests of scholarship, clarity, and classroom effectiveness. In Volume One:

1. New source-readings have been introduced,
   (a) from authors and documents hitherto unrepresented: Las Siete Partidas, Goliard Poets, Plato, Plotinus, Camoens, Sepúlveda and Las Casas (The New World), Boccaccio, The Thirty-nine Articles, Bossuet, Diderot, Helvétius.
   (b) from (and sometimes replacing the previous material of) authors or movements already represented: various medieval documents, Fugger (News-Letter), Hus, Galileo, Kant, Cahier.
2. Certain existing source-readings have been amplified, contracted, or re-

edited for one reason or another—*e.g.,* greater fullness, greater conciseness, better continuity, the insertion of significant passages: Machiavelli, Pico della Mirandola, Veronese Inquisition, More, Calvin, Newton, Hobbes, Harrington, Locke, Condorcet, Montesquieu, Rousseau, Young.

3. One author represented by a selection that did not prove useful in the classroom has been omitted: Mandeville.

The Committee is indebted to Benjamin N. Nelson for fertile suggestions and extraordinary scholarly aid. Harold Barger has contributed various editorial services unstintingly. To Eleanor W. Blau, Nora Louise Magid, Lewis Morris, and Samuel L. Sochis the Committee is grateful for assistance in preparing the manuscript, and to Susan H. Bowen, Anita S. Gelber, and Merton L. Reichler for their contribution to the task of reading proof. To the publishers acknowledged in the individual selections thanks are extended for their permission to reprint copyrighted material.

In connection specifically with Volume One of the *Source Book,* Harold D. Hantz and Robert C. Stover were of great assistance in solving certain editorial problems. New translations have been contributed by Arthur C. Danto and Gregory L. Rabassa, as well as by members of the Committee. New introductions have been written and old ones revised by Louis Cohn-Haft, Arthur C. Danto, Irwin Edman, Paul O. Kristeller, Fritz R. Stern, Horace S. Thayer, Robert K. Webb, and members of the Committee.

The Committee wishes to record the invaluable chairmanship of one of its members, George T. Matthews, up to the end of 1952. John Kotselas of Columbia University Press has displayed unfailing patience, cooperation, and efficiency in supervising the process of publication. Dean Lawrence H. Chamberlain of Columbia College, a long-time participant in the Contemporary Civilization Program, has contributed generously toward the solution of many problems facing the Committee. It would be impossible to exaggerate the extent to which the Committee relied upon the experience, judgment, and high editorial discrimination of Justus Buchler, Chairman of the Program. Whatever range, perspective, and insight the *Source Book* has come to exhibit can be in large measure attributed to his inspiration as scholar and teacher.

Editorial Committee
JOSEPH L. BLAU
RALPH H. BOWEN
PETER J. GAY
SIDNEY GELBER
GEORGE T. MATTHEWS
Columbia University RICHARD M. MORSE, *Chairman*
May, 1954 STEPHEN W. ROUSSEAS

PREFACE TO THE THIRD EDITION

THE THIRD REVISION of this *Source Book* appears during the fortieth year of the Contemporary Civilization course at Columbia College. Although it is more extensively revised than the second edition, the traditions of the course at Columbia and the expectations of the many schools using the book have by now established a nearly inviolable format. The changes, then, in few significant ways alter the basic purposes and outlines of the previous editions.

Nearly every introduction has been shortened and revised so as to provide merely background information and to leave more to the student in analyzing the documents. There also has been some rearrangement of the sections and of documents within sections. In line with the forthcoming complete revision of the two volumes of *Chapters in Western Civilization,* the background essays used in conjunction with the *Source Book* at Columbia College, a number of section titles have been revised.

The new readings from documents and authors previously unrepresented include:

Paul of Tarsus, Maimonides, Pope Gregory VII, Frederick Barbarossa, Marsilius of Padua, Truce of God, Francis Bacon (on Henry VII of England), Coluccio Salutati, Giorgio Vasari, Pope Pius II, Blaise Pascal, Fénelon, Count de Saint-Simon.

The following writers or topics have been re-edited to include additional material or to provide a shorter or fresher selection of ideas:

Plato, Augustine, Thomas Aquinas, The Manor (Annals of Xanten), The Town (Autobiography of Guibert), Las Siete Partidas, Jean Bodin (on the Commonwealth), Overseas Expansion (retitled Christopher Columbus), The New World, Thomas More, Francis Bacon, Galileo Galilei, Jacques Bénigne Bossuet, John Locke, Immanuel Kant, Voltaire, Denis Diderot, David Hume, Jean Jacques Rousseau, Baron de Montesquieu.

Considerations of space in this volume and of usefulness in our course have made it necessary to drop these readings:

Plotinus, Papal Revenues, The Reign of Henry VII, Luis Vaz de Camoens, Fugger News-Letter, Monopolistic Trade Practices, The Thirty-nine Articles, The French Woolens Regulation of 1669, The Navigation Act of 1651, Daniel Defoe, Baron d'Holbach, Florentine Merchants, Jean Bodin (Reply to Monsieur de Malestroit), Boccaccio, Diderot (The Encyclopedia), Mercier de la Rivière. The selections on the French Revolution will now be found in the third edition of Volume Two.

In completing this revision the editorial Committee has been put heavily in debt to certain individuals. Patricia Moyer, now at the University of Nottingham, England, as a Marshall Fellow, did extensive general editorial work as did Raymond Lubitz, currently a Kellett Fellow at Oriel College, Oxford. Professor Robert Benson, now at Wesleyan University, was a member of the editorial committee for one year. His suggestions at committee meetings helped especially in revising the documents on the Middle Ages.

Professor John A. Hutchison of the Department of Religion of Columbia University gave us much of his time and advice on various theologians. Dr. Stephen J. Gendzier of the French Department at Columbia supplied us with translations from Diderot and Condorcet. The taxing job of typing the extracts was shared cheerfully among Carol Kooi, Leni Kroul, Lalitha Nayagam, Jane Slater, and Joseph Plut.

A number of Columbia College students gave many hours to help complete this volume in its last stages. Thanks go especially to Barry S. Augenbraun, Bruce H. Bank, William R. Bishin, Alan H. Feld, Nathan Gross, and Stephen C. Lerner.

The Bible text in this publication is from the *Revised Standard Version of the Bible,* copyrighted 1946 and 1952 by the Division of Christian Education, National Council of Churches and used by permission.

A special word of thanks is due Elinor Stoneman, whose knowledge and taste as senior editorial secretary were invaluable. Were it not for her diligence during many months of hard work it would have been impossible to meet our deadline and match the standards set for us by our predecessors on the editorial committee.

The cooperation and interest of John G. Palfrey, Dean of Columbia College, have immeasurably helped the committee overcome problems of staff and finances. It is hoped that this volume will reflect well on his constant efforts to aid us.

Editorial Committee
MARVIN HARRIS
SIDNEY MORGENBESSER
JOSEPH ROTHSCHILD
BERNARD WISHY, *Chairman*

Columbia University
June, 1960

CONTENTS

I THE MEDIEVAL HERITAGE: CLASSICAL INFLUENCES

PLATO

PLATO (427?–347? B.C.) was born in Athens, the son of noble parents. As the pupil and friend of Socrates (469–399 B.C.), Plato adopted his tutor's technique of conversational questioning (dialectic); indeed, it is largely through the writings of Plato that we have any records at all of Socrates, for he left no known manuscripts and perhaps expressed himself only in talk with his students. Socrates was condemned to death for alleged impiety. Probably this was one of several reasons that influenced Plato to avoid an active political career and instead to found, in 388 B.C., his Academy in Athens, where he taught mathematics and philosophy. His work there was interrupted by two abortive efforts late in life to achieve a practical realization of his political ideals in Syracuse, a Greek city-state on the island of Sicily.

Plato wrote nearly thirty works in forty years, using the dialectical method. Among his early works are the *Apology* and *Crito,* concerning Socrates, and *Ion,* an investigation of the source of poetic ability. As he began to develop his views more explicitly, Plato wrote *Phaedrus,* a treatise on rhetoric, which contains his principal notions on the contemplation of the ideal. There followed *Gorgias,* on absolute morality, and *Meno,* on the acquisition of knowledge. Other works continued to dramatize opposing arguments as in the early Socratic dialogues. *Symposium* is on the love of beauty; *Phaedo* on immortality; *The Republic* an attempt to reconcile moral theory and political practice in the concepts of the ideal of justice and the rule of philosopher-kings.

In his *Seventh Epistle* Plato says that his philosophy has never been put into words and never will be. It is, indeed, difficult to summarize Plato's philosophy, or even briefly to sketch the system of thought he created as a setting for the moral faith of his older friend Socrates. Plato's writings include some of the boldest speculation in the history of philosophy; and his theories of knowledge, of love, nature, and human destiny; his political, moral, and psychological constructions; and his doctrine of Forms—implying as it does a vision of the universe at once moral and mathematical, esthetic and rational—have stimulated, and often intoxicated, a hundred generations of thinkers. One such thinker, Alfred North Whitehead, has said, "The safest general characterization of the European philosophical tradition is that it consists of a series of footnotes to Plato."

The following selections are from *The Republic* (translated from the Greek by John Llewelyn Davies and David James Vaughan).

THE REPUBLIC

Book VI

THUS, Glaucon, I said, after pursuing a lengthened inquiry we have, not without difficulty, discovered who are true philosophers and who are not.

Yes, he replied; probably it was not easy to abridge the inquiry.

Apparently not, I said. However that may be, I think, for my part, that the result would have been brought out still more clearly, if we had to speak of this only, without discussing the many points that still await our notice, if we wish to ascertain wherein the superiority of a righteous over an unrighteous life consists.

Then what are we to do next?

We have only to take the step next in order. Since those who are able to apprehend the eternal and immutable, are philosophers, while those who are incapable of this and who wander in the region of change and multiformity, are not philosophers, which of the two, tell me, ought to be governors of a state?

What must I reply, if I am to do justice to the question?

Ask yourself which of the two are to be thought capable of guarding the laws and customs of states, and let these be appointed guardians.

You are right.

Can there be any question as to whether a blind man, or one with quick sight, is the right person to guard and keep any thing?

There can be no question about it.

Then do you think that there is a particle of difference between the condition of blind persons, and the state of those who are absolutely destitute of the knowledge of things as they really are, and who possess in their soul no distinct exemplar, and cannot, like painters, fix their eyes on perfect truth as a perpetual standard of reference, to be contemplated with the minutest care, before they proceed to deal with earthly canons about things beautiful and just and good, laying them down where they are required, and where they already exist watching over their preservation?

No, indeed, there is not much difference.

Shall we then appoint such persons to the office of guardians, in preference to those who not only have gained a knowledge of each thing in its reality, but in practical skill are not inferior to the former, and come behind them in no other department of excellence?

Why, if these latter are not wanting in the other qualifications, it would be perfectly absurd to choose any others. For just the point in which they are superior may be said to be the most important of all. . . .

Well then, I continued, the causes of the prejudice against philosophy, and the injustice of this prejudice, have in my opinion been satisfactorily disposed of, unless you have anything to add.

No, I have nothing more to say on this head: but which of the constitutions of our time is the one that you call suited to philosophy?

There is not one that I can call so: nay, what I complain of is precisely this, that no state, as now constituted, is a worthy sphere for a philosophic nature. Hence that nature becomes warped and deteriorated. For just as the seed of a rare exotic when sown in a foreign soil, habitually becomes enfeebled and loses its essential character, and eventually passes into a common plant of the country; so this kind of character at the present day, failing to preserve its peculiar virtues, degenerates into tendencies that are not its own: but if it could only find the most perfect constitution, answering to itself as the most perfect of characters, it will then give proof that it is the true divine type; whereas all other kinds of character and of vocation are merely human. Now I make no doubt you will proceed to ask me what this constitution is.

You are mistaken, he said; what I was going to ask was, whether you were thinking of this constitution, whose organization we have discussed, or of another.

The same, I replied, in all points but one; and this one point was alluded to during the discussion, when we said that it would be necessary to have constantly present in the state some authority, that should view the constitution in the very light in which you, the legislator, viewed it, when you framed the laws.

True, it was alluded to.

But it was not sufficiently developed, because I was alarmed by your objections, which shewed that the demonstration of it would be tedious and difficult: for it is by no means the easiest part of the discussion that is left.

What is that part?

To shew in what way a state may handle philosophy without incurring utter destruction. For we know that all great things are hazardous, and, according to the proverb, beautiful things are indeed hard of attainment.

Nevertheless, he said, let this point be cleared up, in order that the demonstration may be complete.

The hindrance, if any, will arise, not from want of will, but from want of power. My zeal, at any rate, you shall see with your own eyes. For observe at once with what reckless zeal I proceed to assert, that a state ought to deal with the pursuit of philosophy on a plan the very reverse of that now in vogue.

How so?

At present, those who pursue philosophy at all are mere striplings just emerged from boyhood, who take it up in the intervals of housekeeping and business; and, after just dipping into the most abstruse part of the study, (by which I mean Dialectic), abandon the pursuit altogether, and these are the most advanced philosophers; and ever afterwards, if, on being invited, they consent to listen to others whose attention is devoted to it, they think it a great condescension, because they imagine that philosophy ought to be made a mere secondary occupation; and on the approach of old age, all but a very few are extinguished far more effectually than the sun of Heracleitus,[1] inasmuch as they are not, like it, rekindled.

And pray what is the right plan? he asked.

Just the opposite. In youth and boyhood they ought to be put through a course of training in philosophy, suited to their years; and while their bodies are growing up to manhood, especial attention should be paid to them, as a serviceable acquisition in the cause of philosophy. At the approach of that period, during which the mind begins to attain its maturity, the mental exercises ought to be rendered more severe. Finally, when their bodily powers begin to fail, and they are released from public duties and military service, from that time forward they ought to lead a dedicated life, and consecrate themselves to this one pursuit, if they are to live happily on earth, and after death to crown the life they have led with a corresponding destiny in another world.

Well, indeed, Socrates, I do not doubt your zeal. But I expect most of your hearers, beginning with Thrasymachus, to oppose you with still greater zeal, and express their unqualified dissent.

Do not make a quarrel between me and Thrasymachus, when we have just become friends;—though I do not mean to say that we were enemies before. I shall leave nothing untried, until I have either won him over to my way of thinking, along with the rest, or have achieved something for their good in that future state, should they ever happen, in a second existence, to encounter similar discussions.

Truly a trifling adjournment! he exclaimed.

Rather speak of it as a nothing, compared with all time. However, it need not surprise us that most people disbelieve in my doctrines; for they have never yet seen our present theory realized. No, what is much more likely is,

[1] Heracleitus is said to have believed that the sun was extinguished every evening and rekindled every morning.

that they have met with proposals somewhat resembling ours, but forced expressly into appearing of a piece with one another, instead of falling spontaneously into agreement, as in the present case. They have never yet seen,
in either one or more instances, a man moulded into the most perfect possible conformity and likeness to virtue, both in words and in works, reigning
in a state as perfect as himself. Or do you think they have?

No, indeed I do not.

And further, my dear friend, they have not listened often enough to discussions of an elevated and liberal tone, confined to the strenuous investigation of truth by all possible means, simply for the sake of knowing it; and
which therefore will, both in private disquisitions and in public trials, keep
at a respectful distance from those subtleties and special pleadings, whose
sole aim it is to prolong debate, and elicit applause.

You are right again.

It was for these reasons, and in anticipation of these results, that, notwithstanding my fears, I was constrained by the force of truth on a former occasion to assert, that no state, or constitution, or individual either, can ever
become perfect, until these few philosophers, who are at present described
as useless though not depraved, find themselves accidentally compelled,
whether they like it or not, to accept the charge of a state, which in its turn
finds itself compelled to be obedient [2] to them; or until the present sovereigns
and kings, or their sons, are divinely inspired with a genuine love of genuine
philosophy. Now to assert the impossibility of both or either of these con-
tingencies, I for my part pronounce irrational. If they are impossible, we
may fairly be held up to derision as mere visionary theorists. Am I not right?

You are.

If, then, persons of first-rate philosophical attainments, either in the countless ages that are past have been, or in some foreign clime, far beyond the
limits of our horizon, at the present moment are, or hereafter shall be, constrained by some fate to undertake the charge of a state, I am prepared to
argue to the death in defence of this assertion, that the constitution described
has existed, does exist, yea and will exist, wherever the Muse aforesaid has
become mistress of a state. For its realization is no impossibility, nor are
our speculations impracticable; though their difficulty is even by us acknowledged.

I am of the same opinion, said he.

But are you prepared to say, that the majority, on the contrary, entertain
a different opinion?

Perhaps so.

[2] Reading Κατηκόῳ.

My excellent friend, beware how you bring so heavy a charge against the multitude. No doubt they will change their minds, if you avoid controversy, and endeavour with all gentleness to remove their prejudice against the love of learning, by shewing them whom you understand by philosophers, and defining, as we have just done, their nature and cultivation, that they may not suppose you to mean such characters as are uppermost in their own thoughts; or shall you venture to maintain that, even if they look at them from your point of view, they will entertain a different opinion from yours, and return another sort of answer? In other words, do you think that an unmalicious and gentle person can quarrel with one who is not quarrelsome, or feel malice towards one who is not malicious? I will anticipate you with the declaration that, in my opinion, a disposition so perverse may be found in some few cases, but not in the majority of mankind.

I am myself entirely of your opinion, he replied.

Then are you not also of my opinion on just this point, that the ill-will which the multitude bear to philosophy is to be traced to those who have forced their way in, like tipsy men, where they had no concern, and who abuse one another and delight in picking quarrels, and are always discoursing about persons,—conduct peculiarly unsuitable to philosophy?

Very unsuitable.

For surely, Adeimantus, he who has his thoughts truly set on the things that really exist, cannot even spare time to look down upon the occupations of men, and, by disputing with them, catch the infection of malice and hostility. On the contrary, he devotes all his time to the contemplation of certain well-adjusted and changeless objects; and beholding how they neither wrong nor are wronged by each other, but are all obedient to order and in harmony with reason, he studies to imitate and resemble them as closely as he can. Or do you think it possible for a man to avoid imitating that with which he reverently associates?

No, it is impossible.

Hence the philosopher, by associating with what is godlike and orderly, becomes, as far as is permitted to man, orderly and godlike himself: though here, as everywhere, there is room for misconstruction.

Indeed, you are right.

So that, if he ever finds himself compelled to study how he may introduce into the habits of men, both in public and in private life, the things that draw his notice in that higher region, and to mould others as well as himself, do you think that he will prove an indifferent artist in the production of temperance and justice and all public virtue?

Certainly not.

Well, but if the multitude are made sensible that our description is a correct one, will they really be angry with the philosophers, and will they discredit our assertion, that a state can only attain to true happiness, if it be delineated by painters who copy the divine original?

They will not be angry, if they are made sensible of the fact. But pray how do you mean them to sketch it?

They will take for their canvas, I replied, a state and the moral nature of mankind, and begin by making a clean surface; which is by no means an easy task. However you are aware, that at the very outset they will differ from all other artists in this respect, that they will refuse to meddle with man or city, and hesitate to pencil laws, until they have either found a clear canvas, or made it clear by their own exertions.

Yes, and they are right.

In the next place, do you not suppose that they will sketch in outline the form of their constitution?

Doubtless they will.

Their next step, I fancy, will be to fill up this outline; and in doing this they will often turn their eyes to this side and to that, first to the ideal forms of justice, beauty, temperance, and the like, and then to the notions current among mankind; and thus, by mingling and combining the results of their studies, they will work in the true human complexion, guided by those realizations of it among men, which, if you remember, even Homer has described as godly and godlike.

You are right.

And, I imagine, they will go on rubbing out here and repainting there, until they have done all in their power to make the moral character of men as pleasing as may be in the eye of heaven.

Well, certainly their picture will be a very beautiful one.

Do we then, I continued, make any progress in persuading those assailants, who by your account were marching stoutly to attack us, that such a painter of constitutions is to be found in the man whom we praised lately in their hearing, and who occasioned their displeasure, because we proposed to deliver up our cities into his hands? And do they feel rather less exasperation at being told the same thing now?

Yes, much less, if they are wise.

I think so too; for pray, how will they be able to dispute our position? Can they deny that philosophers are enamoured of real existence and of truth?

No, it would be indeed ridiculous to do that.

Well; can they maintain that their character, such as we have described it, is not intimately allied to perfection?

No, they cannot.

Once more; will they tell us that such a character, placed within reach of its appropriate studies, will fail to become as thoroughly good and philosophical as any character can become? Or will they give the preference to those whom we discarded?

Surely not.

Will they then persist in their anger, when I assert that, till the class of philosophers be invested with the supreme authority in a state, such state and its citizens will find no deliverance from evil, and the fabulous constitution which we are describing will not be actually realized?

Probably they will grow less angry.

What do you say to our assuming, not merely that they are less angry, but that they are perfectly pacified and convinced, in order that we may shame them into acquiescence, if nothing else will do?

By all means assume it.

Well then, let us regard these persons as convinced so far. But, in the next place, will anybody maintain that kings and sovereigns cannot by any possibility beget sons gifted with a philosophic nature?

No one in the world will maintain that.

And can any one assert, that, if born with such a nature, they must necessarily be corrupted? I grant that their preservation is a difficult matter; but I ask, is there any one who will maintain that in the whole course of time not one of all the number can ever be preserved from contamination?

Who could maintain that?

Well but, I continued, one such person, with a submissive state, has it in his power to realize all that is now discredited.

True, he has.

For, surely, if a ruler establishes the laws and customs which we have detailed, it is, I presume, not impossible for the citizens to consent to carry them out.

Certainly not.

And, pray, would it be a miracle, beyond the verge of possibility, if what we think right were thought right by others also?

For my part I think not.

But I believe we have quite convinced ourselves, in the foregoing discussion, that our plan, if possible, is the best.

Yes, quite.

So that the conclusion, apparently, to which we are now brought with regard to our legislation, is, that what we propose is best, if it can be realized; and that to realize it is difficult, but certainly not impossible.

True, that is our conclusion, he said.

Well, then, this part of the subject having been laboriously completed, shall we proceed to discuss the questions still remaining, in what way, and by the help of what pursuits and studies, we shall secure the presence of a body of men capable of preserving the constitution unimpaired, and what must be the age at which these studies are severally undertaken?

Let us do so by all means.

I have gained nothing, I continued, by my old scheme of omitting the troublesome questions involved in the treatment of the women and children, and the appointment of the magistrates; which I was induced to leave out from knowing what odium the perfectly correct method would incur, and how difficult it would be to carry into effect. Notwithstanding all my precautions, the moment has now arrived when these points must be discussed. It is true the question of the women and children has been already settled, but the inquiry concerning the magistrates must be pursued quite afresh. In describing them, we said, if you recollect, that, in order to place their patriotism beyond the reach of suspicion, they must be tested by pleasure and by pain, and proved never to have deserted their principles in the midst of toil and danger and every vicissitude of fortune, on pain of forfeiting their position if their powers of endurance fail; and that whoever comes forth from the trial without a flaw, like gold tried in the fire, must be appointed to office, and receive, during life and after death, privileges and rewards. This was pretty nearly the drift of our language, which, from fear of awakening the question now pending, turned aside and hid its face.

Your account is quite correct, he said; I remember perfectly.

Yes, my friend, I shrank from making assertions which I have since hazarded; but now let me venture upon this declaration, that we must [3] make the most perfect philosophers guardians.

We hear you, he replied.

Now consider what a small supply of these men you will, in all probability, find. For the various members of that character, which we described as essential to philosophers, will seldom grow incorporate: in most cases that character grows disjointed.

What do you mean?

You are aware that persons endowed with a quick comprehension, a good memory, sagacity, acuteness, and their attendant qualities, do not readily grow up to be at the same time so noble and lofty-minded, as to consent to live a regular, calm, and steady life: on the contrary, such persons are drifted by their acuteness hither and thither, and all steadiness vanishes from their life.

True.

[3] Transposing φύλακας and φιλοσόφους.

On the other hand, those steady and invariable characters, whose trustiness makes one anxious to employ them, and who in war are slow to take alarm, behave in the same way when pursuing their studies; that is to say, they are torpid and stupid, as if they were benumbed, and are constantly dozing and yawning, whenever they have to toil at anything of the kind.

That is true.

But we declare that, unless a person possesses a pretty fair amount of both qualifications, he must be debarred all access to the strictest education, to honour, and to government.

We are right.

Then do you not anticipate a scanty supply of such characters?

Most assuredly I do.

Hence we must not be content with testing their behaviour in the toils, dangers, and pleasures, which we mentioned before; but we must go on to try them in ways which we then omitted, exercising them in a variety of studies, and observing whether their character will be able to support the highest subjects, or whether it will flinch from the trial, like those who flinch under other circumstances.

No doubt, it is proper to examine them in this way. But pray which do you mean by the highest subjects?

I presume you remember, that, after separating the soul into three specific parts, we deduced the several natures of justice, temperance, fortitude, and wisdom?

Why, if I did not remember, I should deserve not to hear the rest of the discussion.

Do you also remember the remark which preceded that deduction?

Pray what was it?

We remarked, I believe, that to obtain the best possible view of the question, we should have to take a different and a longer route, which would bring us to a thorough insight into the subject: still that it would be possible to subjoin a demonstration of the question, flowing from our previous conclusions. Thereupon you said that such a demonstration would satisfy you; and then followed those investigations, which, to my own mind, were deficient in exactness; but you can tell me whether they contented you.

Well, to speak for myself, I thought them fair in point of measure; and certainly the rest of the party held the same opinion.

But, my friend, no measure of such a subject, which falls perceptibly short of the truth, can be said to be quite fair: for nothing imperfect is a measure of anything: though people sometimes fancy that enough has been done, and that there is no call for further investigation.

Yes, he said, that is a very common habit, and arises from indolence.

Yes, but it is a habit remarkably undesirable in the guardian of a state and its laws.

So I should suppose.

That being the case, my friend, such a person must go round by that longer route, and must labour as devotedly in his studies as in his bodily exercises. Otherwise, as we were saying just now, he will never reach the goal of that highest science, which is most peculiarly his own.

What! he exclaimed, are not these the highest? Is there still something higher than justice and those other things which we have discussed?

Even so, I replied: and here we must not contemplate a rude outline, as we have been doing: on the contrary, we must be satisfied with nothing short of the most complete elaboration. For would it not be ridiculous to exert one-self on other subjects of small value, taking all imaginable pains to bring them to the most exact and spotless perfection; and at the same time to ignore the claim of the highest subjects to a corresponding exactitude of the highest order?

The sentiment is a very just one. But do you suppose that any one would let you go without asking what that science is which you call the highest, and of what it treats?

Certainly not, I replied; so put the question yourself. Assuredly you have heard the answer many a time; but at this moment either you have forgotten it, or else you intend to find me employment by raising objections. I incline to the latter opinion; for you have often been told that the essential Form of the Good is the highest object of science, and that this essence, by blending with just things and all other created objects, renders them useful and advantageous. And at this moment you can scarcely doubt that I am going to assert this, and to assert, besides, that we are not sufficiently acquainted with this essence. And if so,—if, I say, we know everything else perfectly, without knowing this,—you are aware that it will profit us nothing; just as it would be equally profitless to possess everything without possessing what is good. Or do you imagine it would be a gain to possess all possessible things, with the single exception of things good; or to apprehend every conceivable object, without apprehending what is good,—in other words, to be destitute of every good and beautiful conception?

Not I, believe me.

Moreover, you doubtless know besides, that the chief good is supposed by the multitude to be pleasure,—by the more enlightened, insight? [4]

Of course I know that.

---

[4] φρόνησις. Practical wisdom, or insight.

And you are aware, my friend, that the advocates of this latter opinion are unable to explain what they mean by insight, and are compelled at last to explain it as insight into that which is good.

Yes, they are in a ludicrous difficulty.

They certainly are: since they reproach us with ignorance of that which is good, and then speak to us the next moment as if we knew what it was. For they tell us that the chief good is insight into good, assuming that we understand their meaning, as soon as they have uttered the term "good."

It is perfectly true.

Again: are not those, whose definition identifies pleasure with good, just as much infected with error as the preceding? For they are forced to admit the existence of evil pleasures, are they not?

Certainly they are.

From which it follows, I should suppose, that they must admit the same thing to be both good and evil. Does it not?

Certainly it does.

Then is it not evident that this is a subject often and severely disputed?

Doubtless it is.

Once more: is it not evident, that though many persons would be ready to do and seem to do, or to possess and seem to possess, what seems just and beautiful, without really being so; yet, when you come to things good, no one is content to acquire what only seems such; on the contrary, everybody seeks the reality, and semblances are here, if nowhere else, treated with universal contempt?

Yes, that is quite evident.

This good, then, which every soul pursues, as the end of all its actions, divining its existence, but perplexed and unable to apprehend satisfactorily its nature, or to enjoy that steady confidence in relation to it, which it does enjoy in relation to other things, and therefore doomed to forfeit any advantage which it might have derived from those same things;—are we to maintain that, on a subject of such overwhelming importance, the blindness we have described is a desirable feature in the character of those best members of the state in whose hands everything is to be placed?

Most certainly not.

At any rate, if it be not known in what way just things and beautiful things come to be also good, I imagine that such things will not possess a very valuable guardian in the person of him who is ignorant on this point. And I surmise that none will know the just and the beautiful satisfactorily till he knows the good.

You are right in your surmises.

Then will not the arrangement of our constitution be perfect, provided it be overlooked by a guardian who is scientifically acquainted with these subjects?

Unquestionably it will. But pray, Socrates, do *you* assert the chief good to be science or pleasure or something different from either?

Ho, ho, my friend! I saw long ago that you would certainly not put up with the opinions of other people on these subjects.

Why, Socrates, it appears to me to be positively wrong in one who has devoted so much time to these questions, to be able to state the opinions of others, without being able to state his own.

Well, I said, do you think it right to speak with an air of information on subjects on which one is not well-informed?

Certainly not with an air of information; but I think it right to be willing to state one's opinion for what it is worth.

Well, but have you not noticed that opinions divorced from science are all ill-favoured? At the best they are blind. Or do you conceive that those who, unaided by the pure reason, entertain a correct opinion, are at all superior to blind men, who manage to keep the straight path?

Not at all superior, he replied.

Then is it your desire to contemplate objects that are ill-favoured, blind, and crooked, when it is in your power to learn from other people about bright and beautiful things?

I implore you, Socrates, cried Glaucon, not to hang back, as if you had come to the end. We shall be content even if you only discuss the subject of the chief good in the style in which you discussed justice, temperance, and the rest.

Yes, my friend, and I likewise should be thoroughly content. But I distrust my own powers, and I feel afraid that my awkward zeal will subject me to ridicule. No, my good sirs: let us put aside, for the present at any rate, all inquiry into the real nature of the chief good. For, methinks, it is beyond the measure of this our enterprize to find the way to what is, after all, only my present opinion on the subject. But I am willing to talk to you about that which appears to be an off-shoot of the chief good, and bears the strongest resemblance to it, provided it is also agreeable to you; but if it is not, I will let it alone.

Nay, tell us about it, he replied. You shall remain in our debt for an account of the parent.

I wish that *I* could pay, and you receive, the parent sum, instead of having to content ourselves with the interest springing from it. However, here I present you with the fruit and scion of the essential good. Only take care that I do not involuntarily impose upon you by handing in a forged account of this offspring.

We will take all the care we can; only proceed.

I will do so, as soon as we have come to a settlement together, and you have been reminded of certain statements made in a previous part of our conversation, and renewed before now again and again.

Pray what statements?

In the course of the discussion we have distinctly maintained the existence of a multiplicity of things that are beautiful, and good, and so on.

True, we have.

And also the existence of an essential beauty, and an essential good, and so on;—reducing all those things which before we regarded as manifold, to a single form and a single entity in each case, and addressing each as an independent being.

Just so.

And we assert that the former address themselves to the eye, and not to the pure reason; whereas the forms address themselves to the reason, and not to the eye.

Certainly.

Now with what part of ourselves do we see visible objects?

With the eyesight.

In the same way we hear sounds with the hearing, and perceive everything sensible with the other senses, do we not?

Certainly.

Then have you noticed with what transcendent costliness the architect of the senses has wrought out the faculty of seeing and being seen?

Not exactly, he replied.

Well then, look at it in this light. Is there any other kind of thing, which the ear and the voice require, to enable the one to hear, and the other to be heard, in the absence of which third thing the one will not hear, and the other will not be heard?

No, there is not.

And I believe that very few, if any, of the other senses require any such third thing. Can you mention one that does?

No, I cannot.

But do you not perceive that, in the case of vision and visible objects, there is a demand for something additional?

How so?

Why, granting that vision is seated in the eye, and that the owner of it is attempting to use it, and that colour is resident in the objects, still, unless there be present a third kind of thing, devoted to this especial purpose, you are aware that the eyesight will see nothing, and the colours will be invisible.

Pray what is the third thing to which you refer?

Of course I refer to what you call light.

You are right.

Hence it appears, that of all the pairs aforesaid, the sense of sight, and the faculty of being seen, are coupled by the noblest link, whose nature is anything but insignificant, unless light is an ignoble thing.

No, indeed; it is very far from being ignoble.

To whom, then, of the gods in heaven can you refer as the author and dispenser of this blessing? And whose light is it that enables our sight to see so excellently well, and makes visible objects appear?

There can be but one opinion on the subject, he replied: your question evidently alludes to the sun.

Then the relation subsisting between the eyesight and this deity is of the following nature, is it not?

Describe it.

Neither the sight itself, nor the eye, which is the seat of sight, can be identified with the sun.

Certainly not.

And yet, of all the organs of sensation, the eye, methinks, bears the closest resemblance to the sun.

Yes, quite so.

Further, is not the faculty which the eye possesses dispensed to it from the sun, and held by it as something adventitious?

Certainly it is.

Then is it not also true, that the sun, though not identical with sight, is nevertheless the cause of sight, and is moreover seen by its aid?

Yes, quite true.

Well then, I continued, believe that I meant the sun, when I spoke of the offspring of the chief good, begotten by it in a certain resemblance to itself,—that is to say, bearing the same relation in the visible world to sight and its objects, which the chief good bears in the intellectual world to pure reason and its objects.

How so? Be so good as to explain it to me more at length.

Are you aware, that whenever a person makes an end of looking at objects, upon which the light of day is shedding colour, and looks instead at objects coloured by the light of the moon and stars, his eyes grow dim and appear almost blind, as if they were not the sea of distinct vision?

I am fully aware of it.

But whenever the same person looks at objects on which the sun is shining, these very eyes, I believe, see clearly, and are evidently the seat of distinct vision?

Unquestionably it is so.

Just in the same way understand the condition of the soul to be as follows. Whenever it has fastened upon an object, over which truth and real existence are shining, it seizes that object by an act of reason, and knows it, and thus proves itself to be possessed of reason: but whenever it has fixed upon objects that are blent with darkness,—the world of birth and death,—then it rests in *opinion,* and its sight grows dim, as its opinions shift backwards and forwards, and it has the appearance of being destitute of reason.

True, it has.

Now, this power, which supplies the objects of real knowledge with the truth that is in them, and which renders to him who knows them the faculty of knowing them, you must consider to be the essential Form of Good, and you must regard it as the origin of science, and of truth, so far as the latter comes within the range of knowledge: and though knowledge and truth are both very beautiful things, you will be right in looking upon good as something distinct from them, and even more beautiful. And just as, in the analogous case, it is right to regard light and vision as resembling the sun, but wrong to identify them with the sun; so, in the case of science and truth, it is right to regard both of them as resembling good, but wrong to identify either of them with good; because, on the contrary, the quality of the good ought to have a still higher value set upon it.

That implies an inexpressible beauty, if it not only is the source of science and truth, but also surpasses them in beauty; for, I presume, you do not mean by it pleasure.

Hush! I exclaimed, not a word of that. But you had better examine the illustration further, as follows.

Shew me how.

I think you will admit that the sun ministers to visible objects, not only the faculty of being seen, but also their vitality, growth, and nutriment, though it is not itself equivalent to vitality.

Of course it is not.

Then admit that, in like manner, the objects of knowledge not only derive from the good the gift of being known, but are further endowed by it with a real and essential existence; though the good, far from being identical with real existence, actually transcends it in dignity and power.

Hereupon Glaucon exclaimed with a very amusing air, Good heavens! what a miraculous superiority!

Well, I said, you are the person to blame, because you compel me to state my opinions on the subject.

Nay, let me entreat you not to stop, till you have at all events gone over again your similitude of the sun, if you are leaving anything out.

Well, to say the truth, I am leaving out a great deal.

Then pray do not omit even a trifle.

I fancy I shall leave much unsaid; however, if I can help it under the circumstances, I will not intentionally make any omission.

Pray do not.

Now understand that, according to us, there are two powers reigning, one over an intellectual, and the other over a visible region and class of objects;— if I were to use the term "firmament" [5] you might think I was playing on the word. Well then, are you in possession of these as two kinds,—one visible, the other intellectual?

Yes, I am.

Suppose you take a line divided into two unequal parts,—one to represent the visible class of objects, the other the intellectual,—and divide each part again into two segments on the same scale. Then, if you make the lengths of the segments represent degrees of distinctness or indistinctness, one of the two segments of the part which stands for the visible world will represent all images:—meaning by images, first of all, shadows; and, in the next place, reflections in water, and in close-grained, smooth, bright substances, and everything of the kind, if you understand me.

Yes, I do understand.

Let the other segment stand for the real objects corresponding to these images,—namely, the animals about us, and the whole world of nature and of art.

Very good.

Would you also consent to say that, with reference to this class, there is, in point of truth and untruthfulness, the same distinction between the copy and the original, that there is between what is matter of opinion and what is matter of knowledge?

Certainly I should.

Then let us proceed to consider how we must divide that part of the whole line which represents the intellectual world.

How must we do it?

Thus: one segment of it will represent what the soul is compelled to in-

[5] The play upon τὸ ὁρατὸν, "the visible," and οὐρανὸς, "heaven," cannot be represented in English. The meaning apparently is,—"I do not use the term οὐρανὸς, lest you should suppose that I wish to connect it etymologically with ὁράω."

vestigate by the aid of the segments of the other part, which it employs as images, starting from hypotheses, and travelling not to a first principle, but to a conclusion. The other segment will represent the objects of the soul, as it makes its way from an hypothesis to a first principle [6] which is not hypothetical, unaided by those images which the former division employs, and shaping its journey by the sole help of real essential forms.

I have not understood your description so well as I could wish.

Then we will try again. You will understand me more easily when I have made some previous observations. I think you know that the students of subjects like geometry and calculation, assume by way of materials, in each investigation, all odd and even numbers, figures, three kinds of angles, and other similar data. These things they are supposed to know, and having adopted them as hypotheses, they decline to give any account of them, either to themselves or to others, on the assumption that they are self-evident; and, making these their starting point, they proceed to travel through the remainder of the subject, and arrive at last, with perfect unanimity, at that which they have proposed as the object of investigation.

I am perfectly aware of the fact, he replied.

Then you also know that they summon to their aid visible forms, and discourse about them, though their thoughts are busy not with these forms, but with their originals, and though they discourse not with a view to the particular square and diameter which they draw, but with a view to the absolute square and the absolute diameter, and so on. For while they employ by way of images those figures and diagrams aforesaid, which again have their shadows and images in water, they are really endeavouring to behold those abstractions which a person can only see with the eye of thought.

True.

This, then, was the class of things which I called intellectual; but I said that the soul is constrained to employ hypotheses while engaged in the investigation of them,—not travelling to a first principle, (because it is unable to step out of, and mount above, its hypotheses,) but using, as images, just the copies that are presented by things below,—which copies, as compared with the originals, are vulgarly esteemed distinct and valued accordingly.

I understand you to be speaking of the subject-matter of the various branches of geometry and the kindred arts.

Again, by the second segment of the intellectual world understand me to mean all that the mere reasoning process apprehends by the force of dialectic, when it avails itself of hypotheses not as first principles, but as genuine hypotheses, that is to say, as stepping-stones and impulses, whereby it may

---

[6] Omitting τὸ before ἐπ'αρχήν.

force its way up to something that is not hypothetical, and arrive at the first principle of every thing, and seize it in its grasp; which done, it turns round, and takes hold of that which takes hold of this first principle, till at last it comes down to a conclusion, calling in the aid of no sensible object whatever, but simply employing abstract, self-subsisting forms, and terminating in the same.

I do not understand you so well as I could wish, for I believe you to be describing an arduous task; but at any rate I understand that you wish to declare distinctly, that the field of real existence and pure intellect, as contemplated by the science of dialectic, is more certain than the field investigated by what are called the arts, in which hypotheses constitute first principles, which the students are compelled, it is true, to contemplate with the mind and not with the senses; but, at the same time, as they do not come back, in the course of inquiry, to a first principle, but push on from hypothetical premises, you think that they do not exercise pure reason on the questions that engage them, although taken in connexion with a first principle these questions come within the domain of the pure reason. And I believe you apply the term understanding, not pure reason, to the mental habit of such people as geometricians,—regarding understanding as something intermediate between opinion and pure reason.

You have taken in my meaning most satisfactorily; and I beg you will accept these four mental states, as corresponding to the four segments,—namely pure reason corresponding to the highest, understanding to the second, belief to the third, and conjecture to the last; and pray arrange them in gradation, and believe them to partake of distinctness in a degree corresponding to the truth of their respective objects.

I understand you, said he. I quite agree with you, and will arrange them as you desire.

Book VII

Now THEN, I proceeded to say, go on to compare our natural condition, so far as education and ignorance are concerned, to a state of things like the following. Imagine a number of men living in an underground cavernous chamber, with an entrance open to the light, extending along the entire length of the cavern, in which they have been confined, from their childhood, with their legs and necks so shackled, that they are obliged to sit still and look straight forwards, because their chains render it impossible for them to turn their heads round: and imagine a bright fire burning some way off, above and behind them, and an elevated roadway passing between the fire and the prisoners, with a low wall built along it, like the screens which conjurors put up in front of their audience, and above which they exhibit their wonders.

I have it, he replied.

Also figure to yourself a number of persons walking behind this wall, and carrying with them statues of men, and images of other animals, wrought in wood and stone and all kinds of materials, together with various other articles, which overtop the wall; and, as you might expect, let some of the passers-by be talking, and others silent.

You are describing a strange scene, and strange prisoners.

They resemble us, I replied. For let me ask you, in the first place, whether persons so confined could have seen anything of themselves or of each other, beyond the shadows thrown by the fire upon the part of the cavern facing them?

Certainly not, if you suppose them to have been compelled all their lifetime to keep their heads unmoved.

And is not their knowledge of the things carried past them equally limited?

Unquestionably it is.

And if they were able to converse with one another, do you not think that they would be in the habit of giving names to the objects which they saw before them?

Doubtless they would.

Again: if their prison-house returned an echo from the part facing them, whenever one of the passers-by opened his lips, to what, let me ask you, could they refer the voice, if not to the shadow which was passing?

Unquestionably they would refer it to that.

Then surely such persons would hold the shadows of those manufactured articles to be the only realities.

Without a doubt they would.

Now consider what would happen if the course of nature brought them a release from their fetters, and a remedy for their foolishness, in the following manner. Let us suppose that one of them has been released, and compelled suddenly to stand up, and turn his neck round and walk with open eyes towards the light; and let us suppose that he goes through all these actions with pain, and that the dazzling splendour renders him incapable of discerning those objects of which he used formerly to see the shadows. What answer should you expect him to make, if some one were to tell him that in those days he was watching foolish phantoms, but that now he is somewhat nearer to reality, and is turned towards things more real, and sees more correctly; above all, if he were to point out to him the several objects that are passing by, and question him, and compel him to answer what they are? Should you not expect him to be puzzled, and to regard his old visions as truer than the objects now forced upon his notice?

Yes, much truer.

And if he were further compelled to gaze at the light itself, would not his eyes, think you, be distressed, and would he not shrink and turn away to the things which he could see distinctly, and consider them to be really clearer than the things pointed out to him?

Just so.

And if some one were to drag him violently up the rough and steep ascent from the cavern, and refuse to let him go till he had drawn him out into the light of the sun, would he not, think you, be vexed and indignant at such treatment, and on reaching the light, would he not find his eyes so dazzled by the glare as to be incapable of making out so much as one of the objects that are now called true?

Yes, he would find it so at first.

Hence, I suppose, habit will be necessary to enable him to perceive objects in that upper world. At first he will be most successful in distinguishing shadows; then he will discern the reflections of men and other things in water, and afterwards the realities; and after this he will raise his eyes to encounter the light of the moon and stars, finding it less difficult to study the heavenly bodies and the heaven itself by night, than the sun and the sun's light by day.

Doubtless.

Last of all, I imagine, he will be able to observe and contemplate the nature of the sun, not as it *appears* in water or on alien ground, but as it *is* in itself in its own territory.

Of course.

His next step will be to draw the conclusion, that the sun is the author of the seasons and the years, and the guardian of all things in the visible world, and in a manner the cause of all those things which he and his companions used to see.

Obviously, this will be his next step.

What then? When he recalls to mind his first habitation, and the wisdom of the place, and his old fellow-prisoners, do you not think he will congratulate himself on the change, and pity them?

Assuredly he will.

And if it was their practice in those days to receive honour and commendations one from another, and to give prizes to him who had the keenest eye for a passing object, and who remembered best all that used to precede and follow and accompany it, and from these data divined most ably what was going to come next, do you fancy that he will covet these prizes, and envy those who receive honour and exercise authority among them? Do you not rather imagine that he will feel what Homer describes, and wish extremely

> To drudge on the lands of a master,
> Under a portionless wight,

and be ready to go through anything, rather than entertain those opinions, and live in that fashion?

For my own part, he replied, I am quite of that opinion. I believe he would consent to go through anything rather than live in that way.

And now consider what would happen if such a man were to descend again and seat himself on his old seat? Coming so suddenly out of the sun, would he not find his eyes blinded with the gloom of the place?

Certainly, he would.

And if he were forced to deliver his opinion again, touching the shadows aforesaid, and to enter the lists against those who had always been prisoners, while his sight continued dim, and his eyes unsteady,—and if this process of initiation lasted a considerable time,—would he not be made a laughing-stock, and would it not be said of him, that he had gone up only to come back again with his eyesight destroyed, and that it was not worth while even to attempt the ascent? And if any one endeavoured to set them free and carry them to the light, would they not go so far as to put him to death, if they could only manage to get him into their power?

Yes, that they would.

Now this imaginary case, my dear Glaucon, you must apply in all its parts to our former statements, by comparing the region which the eye reveals, to the prison-house, and the light of the fire therein to the power of the sun: and if, by the upward ascent and the contemplation of the upper world, you understand the mounting of the soul into the intellectual region, you will hit the tendency of my own surmises, since you desire to be told what they are; though, indeed, God only knows whether they are correct. But, be that as it may, the view which I take of the subject is to the following effect. In the world of knowledge, the essential Form of Good is the limit of our inquiries, and can barely be perceived; but, when perceived, we cannot help concluding that it is in every case the source of all that is bright and beautiful,—in the visible world giving birth to light and its master, and in the intellectual world dispensing, immediately and with full authority, truth and reason;—and that whosoever would act wisely, either in private or in public, must set this Form of Good before his eyes.

To the best of my power, said he, I quite agree with you.

That being the case, I continued, pray agree with me on another point, and do not be surprised, that those who have climbed so high are unwilling to take a part in the affairs of men, because their souls are ever loath to desert that upper region. For how could it be otherwise, if the preceding simile is indeed a correct representation of their case?

True, it could scarcely be otherwise.

Well: do you think it a marvellous thing, that a person, who has just quitted the contemplation of divine objects for the study of human infirmities, should betray awkwardness, and appear very ridiculous, when with his sight still dazed, and before he has become sufficiently habituated to the darkness that reigns around, he finds himself compelled to contend in courts of law, or elsewhere, about the shadows of justice, or images which throw the shadows, and to enter the lists in questions involving the arbitrary suppositions entertained by those who have never yet had a glimpse of the essential features of justice?

No, it is anything but marvellous.

Right: for a sensible man will recollect that the eyes may be confused in two distinct ways and from two distinct causes,—that is to say, by sudden transitions either from light to darkness, or from darkness to light. And, believing the same idea to be applicable to the soul, whenever such a person sees a case in which the mind is perplexed and unable to distinguish objects, he will not laugh irrationally, but he will examine whether it has just quitted a brighter life, and has been blinded by the novelty of darkness, or whether it has come from the depths of ignorance into a more brilliant life, and has been dazzled by the unusual splendour; and not till then will he congratulate the one upon its life and condition, and compassionate the other; and if he chooses to laugh at it, such laughter will be less ridiculous than that which is raised at the expense of the soul that has descended from the light of a higher region.

You speak with great judgment.

Hence, if this be true, we cannot avoid adopting the belief, that the real nature of education is at variance with the account given of it by certain of its professors, who pretend, I believe, to infuse into the mind a knowledge of which it was destitute, just as sight might be instilled into blinded eyes.

True; such are their pretensions.

Whereas, our present argument shews us that there is a faculty residing in the soul of each person, and an instrument enabling each of us to learn; and that, just as we might suppose it to be impossible to turn the eye round from darkness to light without turning the whole body, so must this faculty, or this instrument, be wheeled round, in company with the entire soul, from the perishing world, until it be enabled to endure the contemplation of the real world and the brightest part thereof, which, according to us, is the Form of Good. Am I not right?

You are.

Hence, I continued, this very process of revolution must give rise to an art, teaching in what way the change will most easily and most effectually be brought about. Its object will not be to generate in the person the power of seeing. On the contrary, it assumes that he possesses it, though he is turned in a wrong direction, and does not look towards the right quarter; and its aim is to remedy this defect.

So it would appear.

Hence, while, on the one hand, the other so-called virtues of the soul seem to resemble those of the body, inasmuch as they really do not pre-exist in the soul, but are formed in it in the course of time by habit and exercise; the virtue of wisdom, on the other hand, does most certainly appertain, as it would appear, to a more divine substance, which never loses its energy, but by change of position becomes useful and serviceable, or else remains useless and injurious. For you must, ere this, have noticed how keen-sighted are the puny souls of those who have the reputation of being clever but vicious, and how sharply they see through the things to which they are directed, thus proving that their powers of vision are by no means feeble, though they have been compelled to become the servants of wickedness, so that the more sharply they see, the more numerous are the evils which they work.

Yes, indeed it is the case.

But, I proceeded, if from earliest childhood these characters had been shorn and stripped of those leaden, earthborn weights, which grow and cling to the pleasures of eating and gluttonous enjoyments of a similar nature, and keep the eye of the soul turned upon the things below;—if, I repeat, they had been released from these snares, and turned round to look at objects that are true, then these very same souls of these very same men would have had as keen an eye for such pursuits as they actually have for those in which they are now engaged.

Yes, probably it would be so.

Once more: is it not also probable, or rather is it not a necessary corollary to our previous remarks, that neither those who are uneducated and ignorant of truth, nor those who are suffered to linger over their education all their life, can ever be competent overseers of a state,—the former because they have no single mark in life, which they are to constitute the end and aim of all their conduct both in private and in public; the latter, because they will not act without compulsion, fancying that, while yet alive, they have been translated to the islands of the blest.

That is true.

It is, therefore, our task, I continued, to constrain the noblest characters in our colony to arrive at that science which we formerly pronounced the highest, and to set eyes upon the good, and to mount that ascent we spoke of; and, when they have mounted and looked long enough, we must take care to refuse them that liberty which is at present permitted them.

Pray what is that?

The liberty of staying where they are, and refusing to descend again to those prisoners, or partake of their toils and honours, be they mean or be they exalted.

Then are we to do them a wrong, and make them live a life that is worse than the one within their reach?

You have again forgotten, my friend, that law does not ask itself how some one class in a state is to live extraordinarily well. On the contrary, it tries to bring about this result in the entire state; for which purpose it links the citizens together by persuasion and by constraint, makes them share with one another the benefit which each individual can contribute to the common weal, and does actually create men of this exalted character in the state, not with the intention of letting them go each on his own way, but with the intention of turning them to account in its plans for the consolidation of the state.

True, he replied; I had forgotten.

Therefore reflect, Glaucon, that far from wronging the future philosophers of our state, we shall only be treating them with strict justice, if we put them under the additional obligation of watching over their fellow-citizens, and taking care of them. We shall say; It is with good reason that your compeers elsewhere refuse to share in the labours of their respective states. For they take root in a city spontaneously, in defiance of the prevailing constitution; and it is but fair that a self-sown plant, which is indebted to no one for support, should have no inclination to pay to anybody wages for attendance. But in your case, it is we that have begotten you for the state as well as for yourselves, to be like leaders and kings of a hive,—better and more perfectly trained than the rest, and more capable of playing a part in both modes of life. You must therefore descend by turns, and associate with the rest of the community, and you must habituate yourselves to the contemplation of these obscure objects. For, when habituated, you will see a thousand times better than the residents, and you will recognize what each image is, and what is its original, because you have seen the realities of which beautiful and just

and good things are copies. And in this way you and we shall find that the
life of the state is a substance, and not a phantom like the life of our present
states, which are mostly composed of men who fight among themselves for
shadows, and are at feud for the administration of affairs, which they regard
as a great boon. Whereas I conceive the truth stands thus: That city in which
the destined rulers are least eager to rule, will inevitably be governed in the
best and least factious manner, and a contrary result will ensue if the rulers
are of a contrary disposition.

ARISTOTLE

ARISTOTLE (384–322 B.C.) was born in Stagira on the Thracian peninsula, the son of a physician (Nicomachus) attached to the Macedonian court. His early training was in medicine, and when he came to Athens at 17 to study at Plato's Academy (366–347), he balanced his tutor's emphasis on theory with a concern for the biological and practical. After tutoring Alexander the Great for seven years in the Macedonian court (343–336) he returned to Athens as the leader of the famous school, the Lyceum. Most of his extant writings, which survive in loose form, perhaps as lecture notes of his students or preliminary drafts, were composed during the twelve years he conducted the Lyceum. When Alexander's death evoked anti-Macedonian agitations in Athens in 323 B.C., Aristotle fled to Chalcis, where he died.

Aristotle's most important works cover a wide variety of subjects. *Organum* presents his scientific method with its emphasis on the logic inherent in man's mind but realized only through experience. His work on the physical universe (*Physics, On the Heavens*) foreshadows Ptolemy in its theory of concentric spheres and fixed stars. His biological treatises (*History of Animals, On the Parts of Animals*) are fairly accurate. *On the Soul* is a psychological study of the soul that had wide influence on medieval Christian thinkers. *Nicomachean Ethics* deals with moral issues in the broader context of politics. *Rhetoric* and *Poetics,* which presents the famous definition of tragedy, are further examples of his varied interests. His *Constitution of Athens,* rediscovered in the late nineteenth century, is an examination of that city's political system.

Aristotle's investigations embraced practically the entire range of knowledge of his day, and in defining the specific fields to be surveyed by the separate disciplines he cut the paths that were followed, on the whole, by later scientific inquiry. Aristotle's *Politics* presents an idea of political science which has been a basis of practically all later political philosophies. In contrast to his predecessor Plato, who was concerned to construct an ideal state as a standard of moral life, Aristotle places upon political science the additional obligation of canvassing the materials with which the statesman has to work and of estimating the limitations as well as the possibilities of existing situations. The fruitful combination of empirical investigation of the facts and the critical inquiry into their ideal possibilities forms Aristotle's distinctive idea of what political science ought to be. Aristotle considers the subject of his *Politics* and that of his *Ethics* to be closely interrelated, the problem of the individual good life culminating naturally in the problems of good citizenship and the statesman's art. The *Ethics* begins by introducing moral problems into political considerations and ends with remarks concerning the effect of public laws upon private moral issues. The *Politics* follows the program that is laid down for it in the last paragraph of the *Ethics* and never loses sight of the fact that the state is justified in so far as it produces the highest attainable moral life. Aristotle's opening discussion of the state as the highest form of community, aiming at the best life possible, reflects the attempt of the tightly knit Greek city-state to serve as the self-sufficient and ultimate source and guarantor of distinctively human virtues.

In his discussion of the ideal state Aristotle criticizes Plato sharply and somewhat ironically for overlooking "the wisdom of ages" and insists that political wisdom is to be found, not in the impeccable dialectic of the professional philosopher or ruler, but in the growing stock of insights that accrues to public opinion in the course of time. Constitutional rule is the defining characteristic of the good state, not simply a makeshift meant to function in the absence of benevolent despots or philosopher kings. For good government is not the special province of the expert, but is the enterprise of a community of equals sharing a common fund of tradition and aspiration. In so conceiving politics as a function of general cultural conditions, not simply as a business of governmental administration, Aristotle lays down a program for political science which has been tremendously influential in subsequent political thought. Aristotle's *Politics* have exerted their great influence not only through the work of his student Alexander the Great but also by the transformation in Roman law and philosophy of the city-state into a world-wide state or cosmopolis governed by natural law.

The following selections from the *Politics* are in J. E. C. Welldon's translation from the Greek (London, 1883).

❡

POLITICS

[Book I]

CHAPTER I

SEEING THAT EVERY STATE is a sort of association and every association is formed for the attainment of some Good—for some presumed Good is the end of all action—it is evident that, as some Good is the object of all associations, so in the highest degree is the supreme Good the object of that association which is supreme and embraces all the rest, in other words, of the State or political association.

Now it is wrong to confound, as some do, the functions of the constitutional statesman, king, householder and slavemaster. They hold that the difference between them is not one of kind, but depends simply upon the number of persons ruled, i.e. that a man is a slavemaster, if he has but few subjects; if he has more, a householder; if still more, a constitutional statesman or king, there being no distinction between a large household and a small State; also that a man is either a king or a constitutional statesman according as he governs absolutely or in conformity to the laws of political science, being alternately ruler and subject. Such an opinion is erroneous. Our meaning will be clear,

however, if we follow our usual method of investigation. For as in other cases
we have to analyse a compound whole into the uncompounded elements which
are its least parts, so in examining the constituents of a State we shall incidentally best ascertain the points of difference between the above-mentioned
forms of government and the possibility of arriving at a scientific conclusion
in regard to each of them.

CHAPTER II

Here, as elsewhere, the best system of examination will be to begin at the
beginning and observe things in their growth.

There are certain primary essential combinations of those who cannot exist
independently one of another. Thus male and female must combine in order
to procreate children, nor is there anything deliberate or arbitrary in their
so doing; on the contrary, the desire of leaving an offspring like oneself
is natural to man as to the whole animal and vegetable world. Again, natural
rulers and subjects combine for safety—*and when I say "natural,"* I mean that
there are some persons qualified intellectually to form projects, and these are
natural rulers or natural masters; while there are others qualified physically
to carry them out, and these are subjects or natural slaves, so that the interests
of master and slave are coincident.

Now Nature has differentiated females from slaves. None of Nature's
products wears a poverty-stricken look like the Delphian knife [1] as it is called
that cutlers make; each has a single definite object on the principle that any
instrument admits of the highest finish, only if it subserves a single purpose
rather than several. Among non-Greek peoples on the other hand females
and slaves stand on one and the same footing. The reason is that natural rulers
do not exist among them, and the association they form consists of none but
slaves male and female; hence the poets say

'Tis meet Greeks rule barbarians,[2]

implying the natural identity of barbarians or non-Greeks and slaves.

But to resume: the associations of male and female, master and slave constitute the primary form of household, and Hesiod was right when he wrote

Get thee
First house and wife and ox to plough withal,

for an ox is to the poor what a servant is to the rich.

Thus the association naturally formed for the supply of everyday wants is a
household; its members, according to Charondas, are "those who eat of the

1 [The Delphian knife was a knife intended to serve more purposes than one, and therefore
not especially suited to any.]
2 [Euripides, *Iphigenia in Aulis,* 1400.]

same store," or, according to the Cretan Epimenides "those who sit around the same hearth."

Again, the simplest association of several households for something more than ephemeral purposes is a village. It seems that the village in its most natural form is derived from the household, including all the children of certain parents and the children's children, or, as the phrase sometimes is, "all who are suckled upon the same milk."

This is the reason why States were originally governed by kings as is still the case with uncivilized peoples; they were composed of units accustomed to this form of government. For as each household is under the kingly government of its eldest member, so were also the offshoot-households as comprising none but blood-relations. It is this condition of things that Homer means when he describes *the Cyclopes* as

> law-givers each
> Of his own wives and children,

in allusion to their want of corporate life. This patriarchal government was universal in primitive times; in fact the reason why all nations represent the polity of the Gods as monarchical is that such originally was, if it is not still, their own polity, and men assimilate the lives no less than the bodily forms of the Gods to their own.

Lastly, the association composed of several villages in its complete form is the State, in which the goal of full independence may be said to be first attained. For as the State was formed to make life possible, so it exists to make life good. Consequently if it be allowed that the simple associations, *i.e. the household and the village,* have a natural existence, so has the State in all cases; for in the State they attain complete development, and Nature implies complete development, as the nature of anything, e.g. of a man, a house or a horse, may be defined to be its condition when the process of production is complete. Or *the naturalness of the State may be proved in another way:* the object proposed or the complete development of a thing is its highest Good; but independence *which is first attained in the State* is a complete development or the highest Good *and is therefore natural.*

Thus we see that the State is a natural institution, that Man is naturally a political animal and that one who is not a citizen of any State, if the cause of his isolation be natural and not accidental, is either a superhuman being or low *in the scale of civilization,* as he stands alone like a "blot" on the backgammon board. The "clanless, lawless, heartless" man so bitterly described by Homer [3] is a case in point; for he is naturally a citizen of no state and a lover

[3] [*Iliad,* ix, 63, 64.]

of war. Also that Man is a political animal in a higher sense than a bee or any other gregarious creature is evident from the fact that Nature, as we are fond of asserting, creates nothing without a purpose and Man is the only animal endowed with speech. Now mere sounds serve to indicate sensations of pain and pleasure and are therefore assigned to other animals as well as to Man; for their nature does not advance beyond the point of perceiving pain and pleasure and signifying these perceptions to one another. The object of speech on the other hand is to indicate advantage and disadvantage and therefore also justice and injustice. For it is a special characteristic which distinguishes Man from all other animals that he alone enjoys perception of good and evil, justice and injustice and the like. But these are the principles of that association which constitutes a household or a State.

Again, in the order of Nature the State is prior to the household or the individual. For the whole must needs be prior to its part. For instance, if you take away *the body which is* the whole, there will not remain any such thing as a foot or a hand, unless we use the same word in a different sense as when we speak of a stone hand as a hand. For a hand separated from the body will be a disabled hand; whereas it is the function or faculty of a thing which makes it what it is, and therefore when things lose their function or faculty it is not correct to call them the same things but rather homonymous, *i.e. different things having the same name.*

We see then that the State is a natural institution, and also that it is prior to the individual. For if the individual as a separate unit is not independent, he must be a part and must bear the same relation to the State as other parts to their wholes; and one who is incapable of association with others or is independent and has no need of such association is no member of a State, in other words he is either a brute or a God. Now the impulse to political association is innate in all men. Nevertheless the author of the first combination whoever he was was a great benefactor of human kind. For man, as in his condition of complete development, *i.e. in the State,* he is the noblest of all animals, so apart from law and justice he is the vilest of all. For injustice is always most formidable when it is armed; and Nature has endowed Man with arms which are intended to subserve the purposes of prudence and virtue but are capable of being wholly turned to contrary ends. Hence if Man be devoid of virtue, no animal is so unscrupulous or savage, none so sensual, none so gluttonous. Just action on the other hand is bound up with the existence of a State; for the administration of justice is an ordinance of the political association and the administration of justice is nothing else than the decision of what is just.

CHAPTER III

Having now ascertained the constituent elements of the State, as every State is composed of households we must begin with a discussion of Domestic Economy.

There are various parts of Domestic Economy corresponding to the constituent parts of a household, which in its complete form comprises slaves and free persons. But as the right method of investigating anything is to reduce it to its elements and the primary or elementary parts of a household are master and slave, husband and wife, parent and children, we have to examine the true nature and character of these three relations, i.e. the relations of a slave-master to his slaves, of a husband to his wife and of a parent to his children. These three we may lay down as certain. But there is another part which is sometimes regarded as equivalent to the whole of Domestic Economy and sometimes as its principal part, and the truth is well worthy of investigation. I mean the so-called Art of Finance.

We will first consider the relations of master and slave in order to arrive at a practical conclusion and also, if possible, to frame some theory of the subject better than those now in vogue. There are some thinkers, as I said at the beginning of this treatise, who hold that the ownership of slaves is a science and identify the functions of the householder, the slavemaster, the constitutional statesman and the king. Others again regard slaveowning as doing violence to Nature on the ground that the distinction of slave and free man is wholly conventional and has no place in Nature, and is therefore void of justice, as resting on mere force.

CHAPTER IV

Property then is a part of the household and the Art of acquiring property a part of Domestic Economy, inasmuch as without certain necessaries it is impossible to live happily or indeed to live at all. Nor can the art of the householder any more than any definite art dispense with its proper instruments, if its work is to be adequately performed. Instruments however may be animate or inanimate. In the case e.g. of a pilot, the tiller is an inanimate instrument, the "lookout" an animate one; in fact in every art an assistant is virtually an instrument. Thus we conclude that any given property is an instrument conducing to life, property as a whole is a mass of instruments, a slave is an animate property, and every assistant may be described as a single instrument doing the work of several. For suppose that every instrument could obey a person's orders or anticipate his wishes and so fulfil its proper function like the legendary figures of Daedalus or the tripods of Hephaestus which, if we may believe the poet,

> Entered self-moved the conclave of the Gods,

suppose, I say, that in like manner combs were in the habit of combing and quills of playing the cithern of themselves, mastercraftsmen would have no need of assistants nor masters of slaves. While then instruments in the common use of the term are instruments of production, a property is an instrument of action; that is to say, while a comb is not only used but produces something else, a coat or a bed can only be used. And as there is this difference of kind between production and action and instruments are necessary to both, it follows that there must be a corresponding difference in the instruments. Now life consists not in production but in action; and as *every property is an instrument conducing to existence, and a slave is an animate property,* it follows that a slave is an assistant in the sphere of action.

The term "property" may be compared to the term "member," in that a member is not only a member of something else but belongs wholly to that something, and the same is true of a property. Thus while a master is master of his slave but in no sense belongs to him, a slave is not only the slave of a certain master but belongs wholly to his master.

These facts clearly prove the nature and faculty of the slave. A natural slave is one who, although a human being, is naturally not his own master but belongs to someone else. Now this is the case with a human being when he is nothing more than a property, and a property means any instrument of action which has a separate existence, *i.e. is not a mere part of the person who uses it.*

[Book III]

CHAPTER I

In any inquiry into the nature and character of particular polities we may say that the first point to be considered is the nature of the State. At present there is often a difference of opinion, as one party asserts that it is the State which has done a certain action, and another that it is not the State but the Oligarchy or the Tyrant *by whom it was governed.* Also *it is necessary to settle this point, as* a State is the sphere in which all the activity of a statesman or legislator is displayed, and the polity itself is nothing more than a certain order of the inhabitants of the State. But as the State belongs to the category of compound things, like anything else which is a whole but composed of many parts, it is clear that we must first investigate the conception of the citizen; for the State is composed of a number of citizens. We have to inquire then to whom the title "citizen" belongs, or, in other words, what is the nature of a citizen. For the conception of the citizen as of the State is often disputed, nor is the world agreed in recognizing the same person as a citizen. Thus it often happens that one who is a citizen in a Democracy is not a citizen in an Oligarchy.

Now putting out of sight persons who acquire the title of citizen in some exceptional way, e.g. honorary citizens, we may lay it down that it is not residence which constitutes a citizen, as the qualification of residence belongs equally to aliens settled in the country and to slaves. Nor again does citizenship consist simply in the participation in legal rights to the extent of being party to an action as defendant or plaintiff, for this is a qualification possessed equally by the members of different States who associate on the basis of commercial treaties. (It may be observed that in many places resident aliens are not admitted to the full enjoyment even of these legal rights, but are obliged to put themselves under the protection of a patron. It is only in a certain imperfect sense then that they are members of an association so constituted.) Such persons on the contrary are much in the same position as children who are too young to be entered upon the register of the deme or old men who are exempted from civil duties; for although these classes are to be called citizens in a certain sense, it is not in a sense quite absolute and unlimited, but with some such qualifying word as "immature" or "superannuated" or the like, it does not matter what. Our meaning at least is plain; we want a definition of the citizen in the absolute sense, one to whom no such exception can be taken as makes it necessary to correct our definition. For difficulties of a similar kind may be discussed and settled respecting persons who have been disfranchised or exiled. There is nothing whereby a citizen in the absolute sense is so well defined as by participation in judicial power and public office. But the offices of State are of two kinds. Some are determinate in point of time; thus there are certain offices which may never in any circumstances or may only after certain definite intervals be held a second time by the same person. Other officers again are perpetual, e.g. jurors and members of the public Assembly. It will be objected perhaps that jurors and members of the public Assembly are not officers of State at all and that their functions do not invest them with an official status; although it is ridiculous to deny the title of "officers" to the supreme authorities in the State. But this matter we may regard as unimportant; it is a mere question of name. The fact is that there is no word to express rightly the common function of a juror and a member of the public Assembly. Let us call it for distinction's sake a perpetual office. Citizens then we may define as those who participate in judicial and deliberative office.

This is perhaps the definition of a citizen which is most appropriate to all who are so called. It is to be observed however that, where things included under a general head are specifically different and one is conceived of as first, another as second and another as third, there is either no characteristic whatever common to them all as such, or the common characteristic exists only in a slight degree. But polities, as we see, differ specifically from each other, some are later and others earlier; for the corrupt or perverted forms are necessarily later than the uncorrupted. What we mean by perverted forms will appear hereafter. It follows then that the citizen in each polity must also be different. Accordingly it is principally to the citizen in a Democracy that our definition applies; it is possibly true in the other polities, but not necessarily. For in some there is no democratical element, nor are there any regular public assemblies but only extraordinary ones, and the administration of justice is divided among various boards, as e.g. at Lacedaemon, where different civil cases are decided by different Ephors, cases of homicide by the Senate and no doubt other cases by some other magistracy. It is the same at Carthage, where all suits are tried by certain magistrates. However, *we need not give up* our definition of a citizen, as it admits of correction. For in all polities except Democracy the right of voting in the Assembly and of acting as jurors belongs not to perpetual officers but to persons whose term of office is strictly defined; as it is either to such officers collectively or to some of them that judicial and deliberative functions, whether upon all or upon certain matters only, are assigned.

Thus we see clearly the nature of the citizen. One who enjoys the privilege of participation in deliberative or judicial office—he and he only is, according to our definition, a citizen of the State in question, and a State is in general terms such a number of persons thus qualified as is sufficient for an independent life.

CHAPTER IV

. . . We have now to consider whether the virtue of a good man and of a virtuous citizen is to be regarded as identical or different.

But if we are to investigate this point, we must first ascertain roughly the virtue of a citizen. A citizen then like a sailor may be described as a member of a society. And although the sailors have different faculties, one being an oarsman, another a pilot, a third a "look-out" man, and a fourth having some other similar title, it is evident that, while the most exact definition of the virtue or excellence of each will be exclusively appropriate to the individual, there will at the same time be a common definition applicable to all. For safety in navigation is the object they all have in view; it is this that every sailor strives for. Similarly then in the case of the citizens, although they are different, yet it is the safety of the association or in other words of the polity which is their object; and hence the virtue of the citizen is necessarily relative to the polity.

Assuming then that there are several kinds of polity, we see that the virtuous citizen *in all polities* cannot have a uniform perfect virtue, whereas it is a uniform perfect virtue which in our theory is characteristic of the good man. It is therefore clearly possible to be a virtuous citizen without possessing the virtue characteristic of a virtuous man. However we may investigate and discuss the same question in a different way by taking the case of the best polity. If we assume the possibility of a State consisting solely of virtuous members, still each of them is bound to perform his own work well, and this is itself a result implying virtue; but as all the citizens cannot be alike, it follows that *in this case as in others* the virtue of a good citizen and a good man cannot be one and the same. For the virtue of the virtuous citizen must be possessed by all the citizens of this State, as otherwise it cannot be the best possible; but it is impossible that they should all possess the virtue of the good man, unless the citizens of the virtuous State must all be alike, *which is contrary to the conception of a State*. Again *we may put the matter thus:* Since the members of the State are dissimilar, and, as an animal e.g. consists of soul and body, soul of reason and appetite, and a household of husband and wife, master and slave, so too a State consists of all these and of other dissimilar elements besides, it follows that the virtue of all the citizens can no more be one and the same than the virtue of a leader and a subordinate member of a chorus.

That the virtue of a virtuous citizen and a virtuous man is not absolutely the same is evident from these considerations. But will there be certain cases in which they are the same? We say that the virtuous ruler combines goodness and prudence, whereas prudence is not indispensable to the citizen. Nay it is sometimes said that the very education of a ruler is different *from that of a subject,* as in fact we see that the sons of kings, *unlike ordinary citizens,* are educated in horsemanship and strategy, and Euripides

> No fineries be theirs
> But only the State's needs,[4]

where, *as speaking of young princes,* he implies that there is a special education suitable to a ruler. If then the virtue of a good ruler and a good man is identical, and the subject as well as the ruler a citizen, it follows that the virtue of a citizen and a man will be identical, not absolutely but only in the case of certain citizens; for the virtue of a ruler *who can never be a subject* and of an ordinary citizen is not the same, and it is this fact probably which gave rise to the saying of Jason *of Pherae* that he was hungry whenever he was not a

---

[4] [A line from the lost play of Euripides, *Aeolus.*]

tyrant, meaning that he did not understand how to live as a private person. It must be confessed however that the capacity for rule and subjection alike is generally lauded, and that the virtue of a citizen is held to consist in the ability to be both an excellent ruler and an excellent subject. If then we define the virtue of the good man as suited to a position of rule, and that of the good citizen as equally suited to rule and subjection, the union of the two qualities cannot be so laudable as is supposed. *Perhaps however the difficulty may be solved in this way.* As it appears that there are some cases where ruler and subject ought to learn both rule and subjection, and other cases where they ought to learn one only, it may be seen from the following considerations that the citizen understands and participates in both. There is such a thing as the rule of a slave-master over slaves; its sphere, as we understand it, is the bare necessaries of life, the use rather than the production of which must necessarily be understood by the ruler. The other side of this relation is absolutely slavish; I mean the capacity for performing acts of menial service. But under the term "slave" we recognize various species, as the occupations of a slave are various. One class of slaves consists wholly of manual labourers, i.e., as the name itself implies, of those who live by the work of their hands, among whom is the mechanical artisan. It is on this account, *i.e. because artisans are necessarily slavish,* that in some States the handicraftsmen were of old excluded from public office until the extreme development of Democracy. The functions proper to subjects of this description are not such as should be learnt by any good man or statesman or citizen, except occasionally for the satisfaction of his personal wants; else the relation of master and slave ceases to exist. On the other hand, there is a species of rule where the subjects are the equals of the ruler in birth and free persons, viz. constitutional rule, as we define it, which the ruler must needs learn by being a subject, as e.g., Cavalry-generalship by first serving under a Cavalry general, or Infantry-generalship by first serving under an Infantry general and holding the command of a company *as at Athens,* or a corps *as at Lacedaemon.* Hence it is said and said with truth that the only way to be a good ruler is to be a subject first. But as there is a difference in the virtue of rulers and subjects, the good citizen should possess the knowledge and ability to be both; in fact the virtue of a citizen may be defined as a practical acquaintance both as ruler and subject with the rule characteristic of a free community. Also a good man is capable of rule and subjection alike, although the temperance and justice proper to rule are different in kind from those which are proper to subjection. For in the case of one who being a subject is still a free man, *and therefore enjoys his share of rule,* it is clear that his virtue, if he is good, e.g., his justice will not be uniform but will comprise a variety of species corresponding to the position which he will hold now as ruler and now as subject, in the same way as there are differences between the temperance and courage of a man and a woman. Thus a man would be considered a coward who was only as brave as a brave woman, and a woman as a chatterbox, who was only as modest as a good man. For the domestic duties of man and woman are distinct, the function of the man being to acquire and of the woman to preserve. But *of all the virtues* prudence is the only one which belongs exclusively to a ruler; all the rest must, as it seems, belong equally to rulers and subjects. Whereas, if we consider the case of subjects, it is not prudence but true opinion which is a virtue proper to them; for the subject may be compared to a flute-maker and the ruler to a flute-player who uses the instrument.

These considerations furnish an answer to the question whether the virtue of a good man and a virtuous citizen is the same or different, and in what sense it is either one or the other.

CHAPTER VI [5]

This being determined, we have next to consider whether it is right to assume a single polity or several, and, if several, what is the nature of each, and how many there are, and what are the points of distinction between them. A polity may be defined as an order of the State in respect of its offices generally and especially of the supreme office. For the governing class is everywhere supreme in the State, and the nature of the polity is determined by the governing class. I mean e.g. that it is the commons who are supreme in a Democracy and the Few on the other hand in an Oligarchy, and *accordingly* we call their polities distinct. The same remark may be extended to all the rest; *if the governing class is different, so is the polity.*

We must begin by laying down (1) the object for which a State is framed and (2) the various kinds of rule which may be exercised over man in his social existence.

It has been stated at the very outset of our treatise in the discussion of Domestic Economy and the government of slaves that Man is naturally a political animal, and consequently, even where there is no need of mutual service, men are none the less anxious to live together. Still it cannot be denied that the common advantage of all is also a motive of union, *more or less operative* according to the degree in which each individual is capable of the higher life. Although to the citizens, both collectively and individually, this higher

---

[5] [In the preceding chapter Aristotle determines that eligibility to the honors of the state and to public office are the most exact marks of citizenship.]

life is emphatically the end proposed, yet life itself is also an object for which they unite and maintain the corporate political association; for it is probable that some degree of the higher life is necessarily implied in merely living, unless there is a great preponderance of hardship in the life. Certain it is that the majority of men endure much suffering without ceasing to cling to life—a proof that a certain happiness or natural sweetness resides in it.

But *to proceed to the second point:* it is not difficult to distinguish the forms of rule which are generally recognized; for even in our unscientific discourses we often discuss and determine their character. In the government of slaves, although the interests of natural slave and natural master are really identical, yet the object of the rule is nevertheless the interest of the master and is that of the slave only incidentally, because, if the slave is destroyed, it is impossible that the master's government should be maintained. On the other hand, in the rule of children or a wife or a whole household, which in our terminology is economic rule, the end is either the good of the subjects or some common good of rulers and subjects alike, i.e. it is essentially the good of the subjects, as we see in the other arts such as Medicine and Gymnastic, although it may perhaps incidentally be also the good of the rulers themselves. For there is no reason why the gymnastic trainer should not himself be occasionally one of the gymnasts, as the pilot is invariably one of the crew. And thus while the trainer or pilot has in view *not his own interest but* the interest of those who are under him, yet in any case where he himself shares their position he enjoys incidentally the same benefit as they do; for the one becomes a sailor and the other one of the gymnasts, although he is a trainer. *It is because the object of political rule is the benefit of the subjects* that in any State framed on the principle of equality and similarity among the citizens a claim is put forward for an alteration of rule. It was originally claimed, as is natural enough, that all should serve the State in turn, and that, as each citizen during his period of rule or office had already paid regard to the interest of another, so that other should in turn pay regard to his. But nowadays the profits derivable from the public service and an official status create a desire for perpetuity of office; it is as though the officers of State, being invalids, were to enjoy good health *during all their term of power,* in which case it is probable that they would be equally eager for office.

It is evident then that all such polities as regard the good of the community are really normal according to the principle of abstract justice, while such as regard the private good of the rulers are all corruptions or perversions of the normal polities; for the relations of rulers to the subjects in them are like the relations of a master to his slaves, whereas the State is *properly* a society of free persons.

CHAPTER VII

Having now settled these points, we have next to consider the number of different polities and their nature. We will begin with the normal polities; for when they are determined the perverted forms will be evident at once.

As in any State the polity and the governing class are virtually the same, *i.e. the polity is determined by the governing class,* as the governing class is the supreme authority in a State, and as supreme power must be vested either in an individual or in a Few or in the Many, it follows that, when the rule of the individual or the Few or the Many is exercised for the benefit of the community at large, the polities are normal, whereas the polities which subserve the private interest either of the individual or the Few or the masses are perversions; for either the members of the State do not deserve the name of citizens, or they ought to have a share in its advantages. The form of Monarchy in which regard is paid to the interest of the community is commonly known as Kingship, and the government of the Few, although of a number exceeding one, for the good of all, as Aristocracy, whether because the rule is in the hands of the best citizens (οἱ ἄριστοι) or because they exercise it for the best interests (τὸ ἄριστον) of the State and all its members; while when it is the masses who direct public affairs for the interest of the community, the government is called by the name which is common to all the polities, viz. a Polity. The result in this case is such as might have been expected. For although it is possible to find an individual or a few persons of eminent virtue, it can hardly be the case that a larger number are perfectly accomplished in every form of virtue; at the best they will be accomplished only in military virtue, as it is the only one of which the masses are capable. The consequence is that in this polity, *viz. the Polity proper,* the military class is supreme, and all who bear arms enjoy full political privileges.

As perverted forms of the polities just mentioned we have Tyranny by the side of Kingship, Oligarchy of Aristocracy and Democracy of Polity. For Tyranny is monarchical rule for the good of the monarch, Oligarchy *the rule of a Few* for the good of the wealthy, and Democracy *the rule of the Many* for the good of the poor; none of them subserves the interest of the community at large.

CHAPTER VIII

But we ought to describe at rather greater length the nature of these several polities, as the matter is one which presents certain difficulties, and it is proper that a philosophical inquirer in any subject, who looks at something more than the merely practical side, should not ignore or omit any point but should bring to light the actual truth in all.

Tyranny is, as has been said, a form of Monarchy corresponding in the political association to the rule of a master over his slaves; Oligarchy a government where the supreme power in the polity is vested in the propertied classes; Democracy, on the contrary, a government where it is vested in those who possess no considerable property, i.e. the poor. But there is an initial difficulty in this definition. Democracy being defined as a polity in which the masses are supreme, suppose the supreme authority in the State were to reside in the majority who are rich; or similarly, to take the converse case, the polity being called an Oligarchy where a small number of persons are supreme, suppose it happens somewhere or other that the supreme power is in the hands of the poor who are stronger although less numerous than the rich; it would seem that our definition of the polities is unsatisfactory in these cases. On the other hand, if we combine numerical minority with wealth and numerical majority with poverty, and designate the polities accordingly as an Oligarchy where the offices of State are in the hands of the rich being a minority, and a Democracy where they are in the hands of the poor being a majority, there is here another difficulty. How are we to describe the polities we mentioned just now, viz. where the rich being a majority or the poor being a minority are respectively supreme in the State? For there is no other polity besides those we have named. It seems then to be proved by our argument that the small or large number of the class which is supreme in the State is only an accident of Oligarchies on the one hand and Democracies on the other, owing to the fact that the rich are few and the poor numerous all the world over. Accordingly the polities above mentioned, *viz. where the rich are a majority or the poor a minority,* do not in fact constitute exceptions. The really distinctive characteristics of Democracy and Oligarchy are poverty and wealth; and it is a necessary law that wherever wealth constitutes the title to rule, whether the rulers are a minority or a majority, the polity is an Oligarchy, whereas, if the poor are rulers, it is a Democracy. But as a matter of fact it happens, as we said, that in the one case the rulers are few and in the other many; for there are only few people who are wealthy, whereas liberty is enjoyed by all alike, and wealth and liberty are the grounds upon which the two parties respectively base their claim to be masters of the polity.

CHAPTER IX

In endeavouring to estimate the claims of the two parties, we must first ascertain what are the definitions they give of Oligarchy and Democracy, and what is the principle of justice characteristic of the one or the other. For Oligarchs and Democrats agree in this, that they both adhere to a certain principle of justice; but they do not advance beyond a certain point or put forward a full statement of justice in the proper sense of the word. Thus the one party, *i.e,* *the Democrats,* hold that justice is equality; and so it is, but not for all the world but only for equals. The others, i.e. *the Oligarchs,* hold that inequality is just, as indeed it is, but not for all the world but only for unequals. Both put out of sight one side of the relation, viz. the persons *who are to enjoy the* *equality or inequality,* and *consequently* form a wrong judgment. The reason is that they are judging of matters which affect themselves, and we are all sorry judges when our personal interests are at stake. And thus whereas justice is a relative term and, as has been already stated in the Ethics,[6] implies that the ratio of distribution is constant in respect of the things distributed and the persons who receive them, the two parties, while they are of one mind about the equality of the thing, differ as to what constitutes equality in the recipients, principally for the reason just alleged, viz. that they are bad judges where their own interests are concerned, but secondly also because the fact that each maintains a certain principle of justice up to a certain point is one which itself leads them to suppose that they are maintaining a principle of justice in the absolute sense. For the Oligarchs, if they are superior in a partic- ular point, viz. in money, assume themselves to be superior altogether; while the Democrats, if they are equal in a particular point, viz. in personal liberty, assume themselves to be equal altogether. But they omit the point of capital importance. If a multitude of possessions was the sole object of their associa- tion or union, then their share in the State is proportionate to their share in the property, and in this case there would seem to be no resisting the argu- ment of the oligarchical party that, where there is, e.g. a capital of one hun- dred minae, the contributor of a single mina ought not in justice to enjoy the same share either of the principal or of the profits accruing as a person who has given the remaining ninety-nine. But the truth is that the object of their association is to live well—not merely to live; otherwise slaves and the lower animals might form a State, whereas this is in fact impossible, as they are in- capable of happiness or of a life regulated by a definite moral purpose, i.e. *of* *the conditions necessary to a State.* Nor is the object military alliance and security against injury from any quarter. Nor again is the end proposed barter and intercommunion; for, if it were, the Tyrrhenians and Carthaginians and all such nations as are connected by commercial treaties might be regarded as citizens of a single State. Among them there certainly exist contracts in regard to Customs, covenants against mutual injury and formal articles of alliance. But there are no magistracies common to all the contracting parties instituted

6 [Book V, chap. vi.]

to secure these objects, but different magistracies exist in each of the States; nor do the members of the one feel any concern about the right character of members of the other or about the means of preserving all who come under the treaties from being unjust and harbouring any kind of wickedness or indeed about any point whatever, except the prevention of mutually injurious actions. Virtue and vice on the other hand are matters of earnest consideration to all whose hearts are set upon good and orderly government. And from this fact it is evident that a State which is not merely nominally but in the true sense of the word a State should devote its attention to virtue. To neglect virtue is to convert the political association into an alliance differing in nothing except in the local contiguity of its members from the alliances formed between distant States, to convert the law into a mere covenant, or, as the sophist Lycophron said, a mere surety for the mutual respect of rights, without any qualification for producing goodness or justice in the citizens. But it is clear that this is the true view *of the State, i.e. that it promotes the virtue of its citizens.* For if one were to combine different localities in one, so that e.g. the walls of Megara and Corinth were contiguous, yet the result would not be a single State. Nor again does the practice of intermarriage *necessarily imply a single State,* although intermarriage is one of the forms of association which are especially characteristic of States. So too if we suppose the case of certain persons living separately, although not so far apart as to prevent association, but under laws prohibitive of mutual injury in the exchange of goods, if we suppose e.g. *A* to be a carpenter, *B* a husbandman, *C* a cobbler, *D* something else, and the total to amount to ten thousand, but their association to be absolutely confined to such things as barter and military alliance, here again there would certainly not be a State. What then is the reason? It is assuredly not the absence of local contiguity in the association. For suppose the members were actually to form a union upon such terms of association as we have described, suppose at the same time that each individual were to use his own household as a separate State, and their intercourse were limited as under the conditions of a defensive alliance to rendering mutual assistance against aggression, still the conception of a State in the strict view would not even then be realized, if their manner of social dealings after the union were to be precisely the same as when they lived apart.

It is clear then that the State is not merely a local association or an association existing to prevent mutual injury and to promote commercial exchange. So far is this from being the case that, although these are indispensable conditions, if a State is to exist, yet all these conditions do not necessarily imply a State. *A State on the contrary is first realized when there is* an association of households and families in well living with a view to a complete and independent existence. (This will not be the case, however, unless the members inhabit one and the same locality and have the practice of intermarriage.) It is for this reason that there were established in the different States matrimonial connexions, clanships, common sacrifices and such amusements as promote a common life. But all this is the work of friendship, for the choice of a common life implies *no more than* friendship. And thus while the end of a State is living well, these are only means to the end. A State on the contrary is the association of families and villages in a complete and independent existence or in other words, according to our definition,[7] in a life of felicity and noble-ness. We must assume then that the object of the political association is not merely a common life but noble action. And from this it follows that they who contribute most to the association, as so conceived, possess a larger interest in the State than they who are equal or superior in personal liberty or birth but inferior in political virtue, or than they who have the superiority in wealth but the inferiority in virtue.

CHAPTER X

It is evident then from our observations that in the controversy respecting the different polities each party is the representative of a certain partial justice. It is difficult however to decide what ought to be the supreme authority in the State. It must be either the masses or the rich or the respectable classes or an individual of preeminent merit or a tyrant. But all these suppositions appear to involve awkward consequences. For suppose the poor, as being a majority, distribute among themselves the property of the rich, is such action not unjust? *No,* it may be said, for it was decreed by the supreme authority in the State and *therefore* justly decreed. What then are we to describe as the height of in-justice, *if not this?* Or again, take the whole body of citizens and suppose that the majority distribute among themselves the property of the minority, it is evident that they thereby destroy the State. But it is certainly not the virtue of anything which destroys its possessor, nor can justice be destructive to a State. It is evident then that such a law as we have supposed cannot be just. Again, the same hypothesis would inevitably justify all the actions of a tyrant, as his oppression depends upon superior strength, like the oppression of the wealthy by the masses. Well then, is it just that rule should be in the hands of the minority or the propertied class? But on that hypothesis, if the minority adopt the same line of action, if they plunder the masses and despoil them in their possessions, is such action just? If it is, so was the action of the majority in the former case. That all such conduct then is wrong and unjust is indis-putable. Ought then the respectable classes to enjoy rule and supreme power?

[7] [The definition given in Book X of the *Ethics*.]

But if so, it is a necessary consequence that all the rest of the citizens are excluded from honours, as they do not enjoy the honour of political office. For we regard the offices of State as public honours; and if they are always in the hands of the same persons, it follows that all others are excluded from honour. Is then the rule of the most virtuous individual to be preferred? It may be objected that this is a system still more oligarchical than the last, as it involves the exclusion of a still larger number from honour.

Perhaps however it will be urged that there is an evil in the supremacy of any human being with his liability to the emotions incident to the soul, and that the law ought rather to be supreme. But on that hypothesis, if the law is oligarchical or democratical, what difference will it make to the difficulties we have raised? The difficulties already described will still meet us.

CHAPTER XI

We may defer for the present the discussion of all these cases except one. But the theory that supreme power should be vested in the masses rather than in a few persons, although they are the best, is one which would seem to be refuted *by the remarks we have made;* and indeed there is a certain difficulty involved in it, although there is probably also a certain degree of truth. For it is possible that the Many, of whom each individual is not a virtuous man, are still collectively superior to the few best persons, i.e. *superior* not as individuals but as a body, as picnics are superior to feasts supplied at the expense of a single person. For as the total number is large, it is possible that each has a fractional share of virtue and prudence and that, as the multitude collectively may be compared to an individual with many feet, hands and senses, so the same is true of their character and intelligence. It is thus that the Many are better judges *than the Few* even of musical and poetical compositions; for some judge one part, some another, and all of them collectively the whole. But the point in which virtuous men are superior to any ordinary persons is the same in which handsome people, it is said, are superior to those who are not handsome and the representations of art to the realities, viz. that the features which *in real life* are distributed among a number of objects are *in the works of art* collected into one; for, if we take each feature by itself, the eye of one *living person* and another part of another are more beautiful than those in the painting. Whether the superiority of the Many to the few virtuous persons is possible, whatever be the character of the commons or the masses, is uncertain, or perhaps in some cases it is plainly impossible. For the same line of argument would be equally applicable to the lower animals. *It would be absurd however to pretend that a number of the lower animals are superior to a few men;* yet there are human beings who may be described as not appreciably superior to the lower animals. At the same time there do exist masses of people in whose case our theory is open to no objection.

These considerations then supply us with an answer to the question which was raised before, *viz. what ought to be the supreme authority in the State,* as well as to one closely connected with it, viz. what should be the limits set to the authority of the free citizens or the masses, i.e. of all who are not wealthy and do not enjoy any especial reputation for virtue? There is a certain danger in their eligibility to the highest offices of State, a danger that injustice on the one hand will lead them into crime, and folly on the other hand into error; whereas their exclusion in theory and practice from all office is a condition of things which may well inspire alarm, as there never exists a large body of persons excluded from all honours or of poor, but the State of which they are members is sure to have a large number of enemies within its pale. It remains then that they should participate in deliberative and judicial functions. It is in accordance with this view that various law-givers, and Solon among the number, empower the commons to elect officers of State and to hold them responsible, but deny them all individual tenure of office. For in their collective capacity they possess an adequate perceptive power and by admixture with their superiors subserve the interests of the State, in the same way as adulterated food if mixed with unadulterated makes the whole more nutritious than the small amount *of unadulterated food* would have been, although individually each has but an imperfect faculty of judgment.

There are however difficulties incident to this system of polity; first, that the faculty of judging, e.g., who has adopted a right course of medical treatment would seem to belong exclusively to the person who is also capable of treating the patient medically and restoring him from his actual malady to health, in other words to the physician. The same is true of any other art empirical or scientific. It may be argued then that, as a physician should be responsible to physicians, so should any other class of persons be responsible to their peers. The answer is that the word "physician" may mean either the ordinary medical practitioner or the scientific student of medicine, or, thirdly, one who has just mastered the principles of the art; there is hardly any art in which we do not find persons answering to these three classes, and the right of judgment is assigned as much to those who have merely mastered the principles as to those who possess a scientific knowledge of the subject. And secondly the same appears to be the case in regard to the election of officers. The right exercise of the elective power, *it may be urged,* as well as of the power of scrutiny is the function exclusively of those who are masters of the science. Thus a geometrician or a pilot ought to be elected solely by persons who understand geometry or navigation. Even granted that there are some occupations and arts in which certain non-professional persons have a vote in the election, they certainly do not exercise a greater influence than the experts. According to this theory then it is inadvisable to entrust the masses with final authority either in electing officers of State or in holding them responsible. It is probable however that there is some mistake in this mode of argument, partly—unless the character of the masses is absolutely slavish—for the reason already alleged, that, although individually they are worse judges than the experts, yet in their collective capacity they are better or at least as good, and partly because there are some subjects in which the artist himself is not the sole or best judge, viz. all subjects in which the results produced are criticized equally well by persons who are not masters of the art. Thus it is not the builder alone whose function it is to criticize the merits of a house; the person who uses it, i.e. the householder, is actually a better judge, and similarly a pilot is a better judge of a helm than a carpenter or one of the company of a dinner than the cook.

This difficulty we may perhaps regard as being thus satisfactorily settled. There is another however closely connected with it. Is it not an absurdity, it is often said, to invest the lower orders with supreme authority in matters of higher moment than the respectable classes? Yet there are no more momentous duties than those of electing officers of State and holding them responsible, and it is just these which in some polities, as has been already remarked, are conferred upon the commons. For the Public Assembly is supreme in all such matters, although the members of the Assembly, the Council and the Law-courts need not be persons of large property or of suitable age, whereas a higher property qualification is required for lords of the treasury, generals and the highest officers of State. Yet this difficulty admits of a similar solution. It may reasonably be argued that the existing state of things is right. For it is not the individual juror or the individual member of the Council or Assembly who exercises official power but the whole Court or Council or body of commons, of which the individuals specified are but fractions. It is as a mere fraction *of the whole and so deriving all importance from the whole* that I conceive of the individual member of the Council, Assembly or Law-court. Hence it is right that the masses should control greater interests *than the Few,* as there are many members of the commons, the Council or the Law-court, and the actual collective property of them all exceeds the property of those who hold high offices of State as individuals or in limited bodies.

With this discussion of these points we must be content. But the initial difficulty we mentioned *as to the supreme authority in the State* brings out nothing so clearly as that it is the laws, if rightly enacted, which should be supreme, and that the officers of State, whether one or many, should have supreme au-

thority only in those matters upon which it is wholly impossible for the laws
to pronounce exactly because of the difficulty of providing in a general statement for all cases. What should be the character of the laws if rightly enacted
has not yet been ascertained; on the contrary our old difficulty still remains.
This only is indisputable, that the laws enacted are necessarily relative to the
polity in which they exist. But if this is the case, it is evident that the laws
adapted to the normal polities are necessarily just, whereas those adapted to
the perverted polities are unjust.

CHAPTER XII

We have seen that in all sciences and arts the end proposed is some Good,
that in the supreme of all sciences and arts, i.e. the political faculty, the end
is preeminently the highest Good and that justice or in other words the interest of the community is the political Good. We have seen too that justice
is universally regarded as a species of equality, and that up to a certain point,
if not further, the conclusions of the philosophical arguments, in which ethical
questions have been discussed and determined, are accepted on all hands, in
so far as it is admitted that the notion of justice implies a thing to be given
and persons to receive it, and that equals ought to receive an equal share. We
have therefore to ascertain the characteristics which constitute personal equality
or inequality—a difficult question which can be settled only by the aid of
political philosophy.

It may perhaps be urged that superiority in respect of any and every Good
should be a ground for an unequal distribution of public offices, if the persons were absolutely alike in all other respects, as any difference in the persons
constitutes a difference in their rights and deserts. Yet, if this is true, complexion, stature or any other Good will equally entitle persons to a preference
in political rights. But the falsity of this position is apparent on the surface,
as may be seen in any other science or faculty. For instance, if there are several
flute-players of equal skill, it is not right to give the persons of higher birth a
preference in the flutes, for their birth will not make them better flute-players,
and the superior instruments ought to be given to the superior perform-
ers. If our point is still obscure, it will be plain if we carry the illustration a little further. Suppose there is a person superior to others in
the art of flute-playing, but far inferior in nobility of birth or beauty, even
granting that nobility and beauty are severally greater Goods than skill upon
the flute, and that their superiority to skill upon the flute is proportionally
greater than the superiority of our supposed individual *to others* in flute-
playing, still it is to him that we must give the finest flutes. For, *if we are to
have regard to wealth and nobility in assigning the flutes,* superiority in these

respects ought to contribute in some degree to the excellence of the performance; whereas they do not contribute at all. And further, the theory is one
which would lead us to regard any Good whatever as comparable with any
other Good. For if a certain amount of stature is preferable *to a certain amount
of wealth or freedom,* it follows that stature generally may be weighed in the
scales against wealth or freedom. Hence, if one person has a greater superiority
in stature than another in virtue, and the distinction of stature generally is
greater than that of virtue, all things in the world will be comparable with each
other. For if a certain amount of stature is more valuable than a certain amount
of something else, it is obvious that there is a certain amount of stature which
is equal to a certain amount of that something. But as this *universal com-
mensurability* is out of the question, it is evidently reasonable in the realm
of politics not to regard any and every inequality as constituting a title to the
offices of State. For the fact that some persons are slow and others swift is no
reason why they should enjoy a less or greater measure *of official power;* it is
rather in the gymnastic games that superiority of this kind receives its appropriate honour. The claim to office on the other hand must be confined to
those elements which enter into the constitution of a State. Accordingly it
is reasonable enough that noble or free-born or wealthy persons should lay
claim to political honour. For a State necessarily contains free persons and
tax-payers *or a propertied class,* as it can no more consist exclusively of paupers
than of slaves. But if these elements are indispensable, the same is obviously
true of justice and military virtue, both of which are essential to the good
administration of a State, although not, as were the elements before mentioned,
to its very existence.

CHAPTER XIII

If we look then to the mere existence of a State, it would seem that all or
at least some of the elements named are rightful claimants *to political supremacy,* whereas if we look to a good life, it would seem that culture and virtue
have the justest claims, as has been already remarked. But as it is not right
that persons who are equal in one point only should have an equal share or
persons who are unequal in one point only an unequal share of everything, it
is a necessary consequence that all such polities as are characterized by this
sort of equality or inequality are perversions.

It has been already observed that the different claimants *to political power*
have all in a certain sense, although not all absolutely, justice on their side.
Thus the claim of the wealthy is that they have a larger interest in the soil,
and the soil is national property, and also that they are generally more to be
trusted in commercial transactions. The claims of free persons and of nobles

on the other hand are closely related to each other. For, *if the title of the free consists in their citizenship,* the nobler classes are citizens in a higher sense than commoners, and nobility is always honoured in any country. Another argument *in favour of the nobles* is the probability that the children of better parents will themselves be better; for nobility is hereditary virtue. The same principles will lead us to regard the claim of virtue *to political supremacy* as also just on the ground that justice, as we assert,[8] is a virtue essential to an association *like the State,* and all the other virtues are necessary concomitants of justice. Again, if we compare the numerical majority with the minority, the former *may put in a claim;* for they are stronger and richer and better, when the majority as a whole are set against the minority.

The question arises then: If in a single State there exist all these classes, i.e. the Good, the Wealthy and the Noble, and besides them a mass of mere citizens, will there or will there not be a controversy as to the persons who ought to be rulers? It is true that in the several polities we have mentioned the decision of the rulers does not give rise to controversy. For it is in respect of the bodies in which the supreme power resides that they differ from each other, one being in the hands of the wealthy, another of the men of virtuous character, and so on throughout the list. Still the point we are considering is this, When all these elements exist simultaneously *in a State,* how is the polity to be defined? Suppose that the persons possessed of virtue are extremely few in number, upon what principle is the line to be drawn? It would seem right to consider the question of fewness relatively to the task to be performed, *i.e. to consider* whether they are capable of administering a State or are sufficiently numerous to constitute a State of themselves. There is a certain difficulty however which may be raised in regard to all the claimants to the honours of State. The plea of those who claim rule in virtue of their wealth and similarly that of those who claim it on the score of birth would appear to be quite devoid of justice; for it is evident that, if we go further and suppose an individual wealthier than all the rest of the citizens together, the same principle of justice will entitle this individual to be ruler of all the rest, and similarly will entitle an individual of preeminent nobility to be ruler of all whose claim depends upon personal freedom. The same will be the case in aristocracies with virtue. If there is an individual morally superior to all the members of the governing class who are assumed to be virtuous, the same principle of justice, *which entitles them to govern,* entitles this individual to be supreme. Or again, if the masses are entitled to be supreme as being stronger than the Few, then in any case where an individual or several persons, although not so many as the mass of the population, are stronger than the rest, it is they rather than the masses

---

[8] [Ethics, Book V.]

who would be entitled to supremacy. All these considerations seem to prove that none of the principles, upon which *certain classes of people* claim to be rulers themselves and to have all others in subjection under them, is right. For even against those who claim supremacy in the governing class on the score of virtue, and similarly against those who claim it on the score of wealth, the masses would be able to advance a just plea, as there is no reason why on certain occasions the masses, not indeed individually but collectively, should not be better and wealthier than the Few.

Accordingly it is possible in this way to meet the difficult question or problem sometimes suggested. Some people find it difficult to determine whether the legislator, if he desires to enact the most absolutely right laws, should have regard in his legislation to the interest of the better classes or of the majority in cases where the conditions are such as we have described, *i.e. where the majority are collectively richer or more virtuous than the Few*. But rightness *in regard to laws* must be conceived as implying equality and, so conceived, it has reference to the interest of the State as a whole, or in other words to the common interest of the citizens. But while a citizen in general is one who is capable of being a ruler and a subject, yet in each several polity he is different; and relatively to the best polity he is one who has the ability and purpose so to live both as subject and ruler as will conduce to the life which is according to virtue. If however there is an individual or more persons than one, although not enough to constitute the full complement of a State, so preeminent in their excess of virtue that neither the virtue of all the other citizens nor their political capacity is comparable to theirs, if they are several, or, if it is an individual, to his alone, such persons are not to be regarded any more as part of a State. It will be a wrong to them to treat them as worthy of mere equality when they are so vastly superior in virtue and political capacity, for any person so exceptional may well be compared to a deity upon the earth. And from this it clearly follows that legislation can be applicable to none but those who are equals in race and capacity; while for persons so exceptional there is no law, as they are a law in themselves. For any attempt to legislate for them would be ridiculous; they would probably make the same reply as did the lions in Antisthenes's story to the declamation of the hares when they demanded universal equality. . . .

[Book IV]

CHAPTER I

In all the roll of arts and sciences, which are not restricted to a single branch of a subject but are complete treatments of some one subject as a whole, it is the province of one and the same art or science to consider all the questions appropriate to a given subject, e.g. *if we take the case of Gymnastic, to consider firstly* the sort of discipline which is beneficial to particular physical constitutions; secondly the nature of the best discipline, as it is certain that the best discipline is such as is appropriate to the person who enjoys the finest consitution and is endowed with the richest natural advantages; and thirdly the discipline which is uniformly beneficial to the great majority of people taken collectively; for this is equally a function of Gymnastic. And further if a person is content with aspiring to something short of his proper physical condition or scientific expertness in athletic exercises, it is none the less the business of the trainer or gymnastic master to produce even this inferior measure of capacity. Similarly we find this to be the case in Medicine or Shipbuilding or Tailoring or any other art. It is evidently therefore the business of the self-same science to consider the nature of the best polity or in other words the character of polity which would best satisfy our ideal, if there were no impediment in external circumstances, and *secondly* the nature of the polity appropriate to particular classes of persons. For as the best polity is probably out of the reach of large numbers of people, it is right that the good legislator and the true statesman should keep his eyes open not only to the absolutely best polity but also to the polity which is best under the actual conditions. We may add thirdly an assumed polity; for it is right that in the case of any given polity he should be competent to consider the means of calling it into existence and, when it has come into existence, the method of endowing it with the longest life. I am referring to the case where the conditions of a particular State are such that the polity under which it exists is not the best *nor indeed can ever be the best, as* it is unprovided with the very essentials *of the best polity,* nor again is the best which is possible in the circumstances, but some polity of an inferior kind. And besides all this it is right that he should understand the polity which is most appropriate to the mass of states, *especially* as the great majority of political writers, even if successful in their treatment of the other points, utterly miss the mark of practical utility. For it is not only the *absolutely* best polity which is the proper subject of consideration, but also that which is possible *in any given case* and similarly that which is comparatively easy of attainment and has a closer affinity to the polities of all existing States. But our modern writers either aspire to the highest polity, for which a number of external advantages are indispensable, or, if they describe a form more generally attainable, put out of sight all existing forms *except the favoured one* and pronounce a panegyric upon the Lacedaemonian or some other polity. What we want however is to introduce some system which the world will easily be induced and enabled to accept as an innovation upon the existing forms; for it is quite as troublesome a task to amend a polity as to establish it in the first instance, just as the task of correcting one's knowledge is quite as troublesome as that of acquiring it at first. . . .

CHAPTER II

As at the beginning of our treatise we divided polities into the normal polities, which are three in number, viz. Kingship, Aristocracy and Polity, and the perversions of these which are also three, viz. Tyranny the perversion of Kingship, Oligarchy of Aristocracy and Democracy of Polity; as Aristocracy and Kingship have been already discussed—for the consideration of the best polity is nothing else than a discussion of the polities which bear these names, as in theory each of them is constituted on the basis of virtue furnished with external means—and as further the points of difference between Aristocracy and Kingship and the occasions when a polity is to be regarded as regal have been determined, it remains to describe the form which is called by the general name of all polities, *viz. the Polity,* and the remaining forms, Oligarchy, Democracy and Tyranny.

It is evident, if we consider these perversions, which is the worst and which is the next worst. For the perversion of the primary or most divine form must be the worst; and as Kingship must either be a mere name and not a reality or must have its justification in the vast superiority of the reigning king, it follows that Tyranny is the form which is worst and farthest removed from a constitutional government, Oligarchy the next worst—for Aristocracy, *it must be remembered,* is widely different from Oligarchy—and Democracy the least bad. An earlier writer [9] has already expressed himself in this sense, although not from the same point of view as ours. For *he recognized a good and a bad form of each of these polities and* held that of all the polities when they are good, i.e. of good Oligarchy and the like, Democracy is the worst, but that when they are bad it is the best. We maintain on the contrary that these polities are wholly vitiated, and it is not right to speak of one Oligarchy as being better than another but only as being less bad. . . .

CHAPTER XI

But what is the best polity and the best life for the great majority of States and persons, as tested by the standard not of a virtue which is beyond the attainment of ordinary human beings, nor of such an education as requires natural advantages and the external resources which Fortune alone can give, nor again of the ideally constructed polity, but of such a life as the majority of people are capable of realizing in a political association and such a polity

[9] [Plato, *The Statesman.*]

as the majority of States are capable of enjoying? For as the so-called Aristocracies of which we recently spoke lie in some respects beyond the reach of ordinary States and in others approximate to the Polity in the limited sense of the term, we may speak of the two forms, *viz. Aristocracy and Polity,* as one and the same.

In the determination of all these questions we may start from the same principles. If it has been correctly stated in the *Ethics* that the happy life is a life which is unimpeded in the exercise of virtue, and that virtue is a mean between two extremes, it follows that the mean life, viz. the attainment of the mean condition possible to the citizens of any State, is the best. And further the same canons of virtue and vice necessarily hold good for a State and for its polity, as the polity is, so to say, the life of a State.

In every State without exception there are three parts, viz. the very rich, the very poor and thirdly the intermediate class. As it is admitted then that the moderate or intermediate condition is best, it is evident that the possession of Fortune's gifts in an intermediate degree is the best thing possible. For this is the condition in which obedience to reason is easiest; whereas one who is excessively beautiful, strong, noble or wealthy, or on the contrary excessively poor or weak or deeply degraded cannot easily live a life conformable to reason. Such persons are apt in the first case to be guilty of insolence and criminality on a large scale, and in the second to become rogues and petty criminals. But all crimes are the results either of insolence or of roguery, both which are conditions prejudicial to the interests of States. And further persons, who are in the enjoyment of an extraordinary amount of Fortune's gifts, strength, wealth, friends and so on, have neither the disposition nor the knowledge necessary for submission to authority—a fault which they derive from their home-training in early years, as they are educated amidst such indulgence that they do not get the habit of submitting even to their masters—while persons who suffer from too great deficiency of these blessings are reduced to a state of mental degradation. Thus while the latter do not understand how to rule, but only how to be ruled like slaves, the former do not understand how to submit to any rule, but only to exercise the rule of slave-masters. The result is a State composed exclusively of slaves and slave-masters instead of free men, with sentiments of envy on the one side and of contempt on the other. But such sentiments are the very negation of friendship and political association; for all association implies friendship, as is proved by the fact that people do not choose even to walk on the same road with their enemies. But in theory at least the State is composed as far as possible of persons who are equal and similar, and this is especially the condition of the middle class. And from this it follows that, if we take the parts of which the State in our conception is composed, it is a State of this kind, *viz. composed largely of the middle class,* which enjoys the best political constitution. Further it is this middle class of citizens which runs the least risk of destruction in a State. For as they do not like paupers lust after the goods of others, nor do others lust after theirs, as paupers after the property of the rich, they pass an existence void of peril, being neither the objects nor the authors of conspiracies. Hence it was a wise prayer of Phocylides

> The middle class within the State
> Fares best, I ween;
> May I be neither low nor great
> But e'en between.

It is clear then that the best political association is the one which is controlled by the middle class, and that the only States capable of a good administration are those in which the middle class is numerically large and stronger, if not than both the other classes, yet at least than either of them, as in that case the addition of its weight turns the scale and prevents the predominance of one extreme or the other. Accordingly it is an immense blessing to a State that the active citizens should possess an intermediate and sufficient amount of property; for where there is a class of extremely wealthy people on the one hand and a class of absolute paupers on the other, the result is either an extreme Democracy or an untempered Oligarchy, or, as the outcome of the predominance of either extreme, a Tyranny. For Tyranny results from the most violent form of Democracy or from Oligarchy, but is far less likely to result from a polity in which the middle class is strong and the citizens all stand much on the same level. The reason of this we will state hereafter when we treat of the revolutions of polities. It is evident however that the intermediate form of polity is best, as it is the only one which is free from political disturbances. For it is where the middle class is large that there is the least danger of disturbances and dissensions among the citizens. And this too, viz. the largeness of the middle class, is the reason why great States are comparatively little liable to political disturbances; whereas in small States it is easy to divide the whole population into two camps, leaving no intermediate class, and all the citizens in them are practically either poor or rich. It is the middle class too which imparts to Democracies a more secure and permanent character than to Oligarchies, as the middle class are more numerous and enjoy a larger share of the honours of State in Democracies than in Oligarchies; for if there is no middle class, and the poor in virtue of their numbers are preponderant, the consequence is failure and speedy destruction of the State.

We may fairly regard it as an indication *of the same fact, viz. of the superiority of the middle class,* that the best legislators belong to the middle class of citizens, e.g. Solon, as is evident from his poems, Lycurgus—for he was not king—Charondas and most others.

We see too from these facts why it is that the great majority of polities are either democratical or oligarchical. The reason is that, as the middle class is generally small in them, whichever of the two other classes enjoys the superiority in any case, whether it be the propertied class or the commons, it is a party which transgresses the rule of the mean that imparts its own bias to the polity, and thereby produces either Democracy or Oligarchy. And there is the further fact that in consequence of the political disturbances and contentions between the commons on the one hand and the rich on the other whichever party happens to get the better of its opponents, instead of establishing a polity of a broad and equal kind, assumes political supremacy as a prize of the victory and sets up either a Democracy or an Oligarchy. We may add that the two States, which have attained an imperial position in Greece, having regard solely to their own respective polities always established either Democracies or Oligarchies in the different States, not out of any consideration for the interests of the States in question, but simply for their own interest. And the result of all these circumstances is that the intermediate polity is either never realized at all or only seldom and in a few States; for among all who have hitherto attained a commanding position there has been only a single individual who was prevailed upon to restore this political system, *viz. a Polity*. And indeed it has become a settled habit among the citizens of Greek States not even to desire the principle of equality but to seek a position either of rule or of patient submission to a dominant power.

The nature of the best polity and the reason why it is the best are now clear. But taking the general list of polities and remembering that according to our former statement there are several varieties of Democracy and Oligarchy, we shall not after our determination of the best polity find a difficulty in discerning what kind of polity is to be placed first, second and so on in due order according to their comparative excellence and inferiority. For the nearer a polity is to the best polity, the better of course it will be, and the further it is removed from the mean, the worse it will be, unless indeed it is tried with reference to an arbitrary standard. And when I speak of an arbitrary standard, I mean that there are many cases in which one of two polities is preferable *in itself,* but the other may well be more advantageous to a certain State.

CHAPTER XII

The nature and character of the polities suited to particular natures and characters is the next question which we have to consider.

It is necessary to begin by assuming a principle of general application, viz.

that the part of the State which desires the continuance of the polity ought to be stronger than that which does not. But in every State there is a qualitative and a quantitative element. By the former I mean freedom, wealth, culture and nobility; by the latter mere numerical superiority. But it is possible that of the parts of which the State is composed the quality may belong to one and the quantity to another, e.g. that the ignoble classes may be numerically larger than the noble or the poor than the rich, but that their superiority in quantity may not be commensurate with their inferiority in quality. It is necessary therefore to institute a comparison between the two elements.

Where the numerical superiority of the poor bears the proportion we have indicated *to the qualitative superiority of the rich, i.e. is vastly superior to it,* it is natural that the polity established should be a Democracy, and that the species of Democracy should be determined by the character of the commons to whom the superiority belongs, i.e. that, if it is the agricultural population which is predominant, it should be the primary form of Democracy, if the mechanical and wage-earning population, the latest development of Democracy, and so for all the intermediate forms. Where on the other hand the superiority of the rich or upper classes in quality is greater than its inferiority in quantity, it is natural that the polity should be an Oligarchy, and as in the last case that the species of Oligarchy should be determined by the character of the oligarchical population in whom the superiority resides.

But the legislator in his political system ought always to secure the support of the middle class. For if the laws which he enacts are oligarchical, he should aim at *the satisfaction of* the middle class; if democratical, he should engage their support in behalf of the laws. But it is only where the numbers of the middle class preponderate either over both the extremes or over only one of them that there is a possibility of a permanent polity. For there is no danger of a conspiracy among the rich and the poor against the middle class, as neither rich nor poor will consent to a condition of slavery, and if they try to find a polity which is more in the nature of a compromise, they will not discover any other than this, *viz. the polity which rests upon the middle class.* For the mutual distrustfulness *of the Oligarchs and Democrats* will prevent them from consenting to an alternation of rule. All the world over on the other hand there is nobody so thoroughly trusted as an arbitrator, and the middle class occupies a position of arbitration *between the rich and the poor.*

But the permanence of the polity will depend upon the excellence of the fusion. It is a common and serious mistake made even by those who desire to set up aristocratical polities not only to give an undue share of power to the rich but to endeavour to deceive the commons. For the spurious advantages are sure in time to produce a real evil, as the usurpations of the rich are more fatal to the polity than those of the commons.

CICERO

THE IDEA OF NATURAL LAW dealt with in this selection has been one of the most powerful intellectual forces, serving recurrently as an instrument for the criticism of custom, convention, and legislation. There is a continuous tradition of appeal to the law of nature from the Greeks to the eighteenth century.

The most important early formulation of natural law came from the Stoics, notably Panaetius (c.100 B.C.), who gave to Stoic theory the shape in which it came to the Roman statesman Cicero (106–43 B.C.). His writings were for centuries the most widely used textbooks in all Europe. Rarely an original thinker, Cicero's importance lies in his influence upon Roman law and political theory. His concern with the rule of law and his emphasis upon "the people" as the ultimate source of authority was often revived and became a chief source of the social contract theory. Roman lawyers continually appealed to it in the form which it took in the Digest of Justinian (A.D. 533).

The Church Fathers used Cicero's statement of natural law as a basis for belief in a universal community of all men and for natural theology and divine law. His emphasis upon the equality of all men before the law, the moral obligation of the state to do justice, and the absolute authority of legally constituted governments has echoes in many medieval writers, particularly Thomas Aquinas.

The two books in which Cicero developed these principles were *The Republic* (*De republica*) and *The Laws* (*De legibus*). The selections that follow have been taken from the latter book. The original dialogue form has been eliminated from the passages that follow. The translation from the Latin was made by Francis Barham in 1841.

THE LAWS

THE SUBJECT of our present discussion . . . comprehends the universal principles of equity and law. In such a discussion therefore on the great moral law of nature, the practice of the civil law can occupy but an insignificant and subordinate station. For according to our idea, we shall have to explain the true nature of moral justice, which is congenial and correspondent with the true nature of man. We shall have to examine those principles of legislation by which all political states should be governed. And last of all, shall we have to speak of those laws and customs which are framed for the use and convenience of particular peoples, which regulate the civic and municipal affairs of the citizens, and which are known by the title of civil laws.

It is not so much the science of law that produces litigation, as the ignorance of it (*potius ignoratio juris litigiosa est quam scientia*). But more of this bye-and-bye.

With respect to the true principle of justice, many learned men have maintained that it springs from Law. I hardly know if their opinion be not correct, at least, according to their own definition; for "Law(say they) is the highest reason, implanted in nature, which prescribes those things which ought to be done, and forbids the contrary." This, they think, is apparent from the converse of the proposition; because this same reason, when it is confirmed and established in men's minds, is the law of all their actions.

They therefore conceive that the voice of conscience is a law, that moral prudence is a law, whose operation is to urge us to good actions, and restrain us from evil ones. They think, too, that the Greek name for law (νομος), which is derived from νέμω, to distribute, implies the very nature of the thing, that is, to give every man his due. For my part, I imagine that the moral essence of law is better expressed by its Latin name, (*lex*), which conveys the idea of selection or discrimination. According to the Greeks, therefore, the name of law implies an equitable distribution of goods: according to the Romans, an equitable discrimination between good and evil.

The true definition of law should, however, include both these characteristics. And this being granted as an almost self-evident proposition, the origin of justice is to be sought in the divine law of eternal and immutable morality. This indeed is the true energy of nature, the very soul and essence of wisdom, the test of virtue and vice. But since every discussion must relate to some subject, whose terms are of frequent occurrence in the popular language of the citizens, we shall be sometimes obliged to use the same terms as the vulgar, and to conform to that common idiom which signifies by the word law, all the arbitrary regulations which are found in our statute books, either commanding or forbidding certain actions.

We should seek for justice in its native source, which being discovered, we shall afterwards be able to speak with more authority and precision respecting our civil laws, that come home to the affairs of our citizens.

I shall endeavour to describe a system of Laws adapted to that Commonwealth, which Scipio declares to be most desirable in those Six Books which I have written under that title. All our laws, therefore, are to be accommodated to that mixed kind of political government there recommended. We shall also treat of the general principles of morals and manners, which appear most appropriate to such a constitution of society, but without descending to particular details.

Grant me that the entire universe is overruled by the power of God, that by his nature, reason, energy, mind, divinity, or some other word of clearer signification, all things are governed and directed. . . . Since you grant me the existence of God, and the superintendence of Providence, I maintain that he has been especially beneficent to man. This human animal—prescient, sagacious, complex, acute, full of memory, reason and counsel, which we call man,—is generated by the supreme God in a more transcendent condition than most of his fellow-creatures. For he is the only creature among the earthly races of animated beings endued with superior reason and thought, in which the rest are deficient. And what is there, I do not say in man alone, but in all heaven and earth, more divine than reason, which, when it becomes ripe and perfect, is justly termed wisdom?

There exists, therefore, since nothing is better than reason, and since this is the common property of God and man, a certain aboriginal rational inter-course between divine and human natures. This reason, which is common to both, therefore, can be none other than right reason; and since this *right reason* is what we call *Law,* God and men are said by Law to be consociated. Be-tween whom, since there is a communion of law, there must be also a com-munication of Justice.

Law and Justice being thus the common rule of immortals and mortals, it follows that they are both the fellow-citizens of one city and commonwealth. And if they are obedient to the same rule, the same authority and denomina-tion, they may with still closer propriety be termed fellow-citizens, since one celestial regency, one divine mind, one omnipotent Deity then regulates all their thoughts and actions.

This universe, therefore, forms one immeasurable Commonwealth and city, common alike to gods and mortals. And as in earthly states, certain particular laws, which we shall hereafter describe, govern the particular relationships of kindred tribes; so in the nature of things doth an universal law, far more magnificent and resplendent, regulate the affairs of that universal city where gods and men compose one vast association.

When we thus reason on universal nature, we are accustomed to reason after this method. We believe that in the long course of ages and the uninterrupted succession of celestial revolutions, the seed of the human race was sown on our planet, and being scattered over the earth, was animated by the divine gift of souls. Thus men retained from their terrestrial origin, their perishable and mortal bodies, while their immortal spirits were ingenerated by Deity. From which consideration we are bold to say that we possess a certain consan-guinity and kindred fellowship with the celestials. And so far as we know, among all the varieties of animals, man alone retains the idea of the Divinity. And among men there is no nation so savage and ferocious as to deny the necessity of worshipping God, however ignorant it may be respecting the nature of his attributes. From whence we conclude that every man must recognize a Deity, who considers the origin of his nature and the progress of his life.

Now the law of virtue is the same in God and man, and cannot possibly be diverse. This virtue is nothing else than a nature perfect in itself, and developed in all its excellence. There exists therefore a similitude between God and man; nor can any knowledge be more appropriate and sterling than what relates to this divine similitude.

Nature, attentive to our wants, offers us her treasures with the most graceful profusion. And it is easy to perceive that the benefits which flow from her are true and veritable gifts, which Providence has provided on purpose for human enjoyment, and not the fortuitous productions of her exuberant fecundity. Her liberality appears, not only in the fruits and vegetables which gush from the bosom of the earth, but likewise in cattle and the beasts of the field. It is clear that some of these are intended for the advantage of mankind, a part for propagation, and a part for food. Innumerable arts have likewise been discovered by the teaching of nature; for her doth reason imitate, and skilfully discover all things necessary to the happiness of life.

With respect to man this same bountiful nature hath not merely allotted him a subtle and active spirit, but moreover favoured him with physical senses, like so many guardians and messengers. Thus has she improved our understanding in relation to many obscure principles, and laid the foundation of practical knowledge; and in all respects moulded our corporeal faculties to the service of our intellectual genius. For while she has debased the forms of other animals, who live to eat rather than eat to live, she has bestowed on man an erect stature, and an open countenance, and thus prompted him to the contemplation of heaven, the ancient home of his kindred immortals. So exquisitely, too, hath she fashioned the features of the human race, as to make them symbolic of the most recondite thoughts and sentiments. As for our too eloquent eyes (*oculi nimis arguti*), do they not speak forth every impulse and passion of our souls? And that which we call *expression,* in which we infinitely excel all the inferior animals, how marvellously it delineates all our speculations and feelings! Of this the Greeks well knew the meaning, though they had no word for it.

I will not enlarge on the wonderful faculties and qualities of the rest of the body, the modulation of the voice, and the power of oratory, which is perhaps the greatest instrument of our influence over human society. These matters do not belong to the occasion of our present discourse, and I think that Scipio has already sufficiently explained them in those books of mine which you have read.

As the Deity, therefore, was pleased to create man as the chief and president of all terrestrial creatures, so it is evident, without further argument, that human nature has made the greatest advances by its intrinsic energy; that nature, which without any other instruction than her own, has developed the first rude principles of the understanding, and strengthened and perfected reason to all the appliances of science and art.

You may well describe these topics as grand, which we are now briefly discussing. For of all the questions on which our philosophers argue, there is none which it is more important thoroughly to understand than this, *that man is born for justice, and that law and equity are not a mere establishment of opinion, but an institution of nature.* This truth will become still more apparent if we investigate the nature of human association and society.

There is no one thing more like to another, more homogeneous and analogous, than man is to man. And if the corruption of customs, and the variation of opinions, had not induced an imbecility of minds, and turned them aside from the course of nature, no one would more nearly resemble himself than all men would resemble all men. Therefore whatever definition we give of man, it must include the whole human race. And this is a good argument, that no portion of mankind can be heterogeneous or dissimilar from the rest; because, if this were the case, one definition could not include all men.

In fact, reason, which alone gives us so many advantages over beasts, by means of which we conjecture, argue, refute, discourse, and accomplish and conclude our designs, is assuredly common to all men; for the faculty of acquiring knowledge is similar in all human minds, though the knowledge itself may be endlessly diversified. By the same senses we all perceive the same objects, and that which strikes the sensibilities of the few, cannot be indifferent to those of the many. Those first rude elements of intelligence which, as I before observed, are the earliest developments of thought, are similarly exhibited by all men; and that faculty of speech which is the soul's interpreter, agrees in the ideas it conveys, though it may differ in the syllables that express them. And therefore there exists not a man in any nation, who, adopting his true nature for his true guide, may not improve in virtue.

Nor is this resemblance which all men bear to each other remarkable in those things only which accord to right reason. For it is scarcely less conspicuous in those corrupt practices by which right reason is most cruelly violated. For all men alike are captivated by voluptuousness, which is in reality no better than disgraceful vice, though it may seem to bear some natural relations to goodness; for by its delicious delicacy and luxury it insinuates error into the mind, and leads us to cultivate it as something salutary, forgetful of its poisonous qualities.

An error, scarcely less universal, induces us to shun death, as if it were annihilation; and to cling to life, because it keeps us in our present stage of existence, which is perhaps rather a misfortune than a desideratum. Thus, likewise, we erroneously consider pain as one of the greatest evils, not only on account of its present asperity, but also because it seems the precursor of mortality. Another common delusion obtains, which induces all mankind to associate renown with honesty, as if we are necessarily happy when we are renowned, and miserable when we happen to be inglorious.

In short, our minds are all similarly susceptible of inquietudes, joys, desires and fears; and if opinions are not the same in all men, it does not follow, for example, that the people of Egypt who deify dogs and cats, do not labour under superstition in the same way as other nations, though they may differ from them in the forms of its manifestation.

But in nothing is the uniformity of human nature more conspicuous than in its respect for virtue. What nation is there, in which kindness, benignity, gratitude, and mindfulness of benefits are not recommended? What nation in which arrogance, malice, cruelty, and unthankfulness, are not reprobated and detested! This uniformity of opinions, invincibly demonstrates that mankind was intended to compose one fraternal association. And to affect this, the faculty of reason must be improved till it instructs us in all the arts of well-living. . . .

It follows, then, in the line of our argument, *that nature made us just that we might participate our goods with each other, and supply each other's wants.* You observe in this discussion whenever I speak of nature, I mean *nature in its genuine purity,* and not in the corrupt state which is displayed by the depravity of evil custom, which is so great, that the natural and innate flame of virtue is often almost extinguished and stifled by the antagonist vices, which are accumulated around it.

But if our true nature would assert her rights, and teach men the noble lesson of the poet, who says, "I am a man, therefore no human interest can be indifferent to me,"—then would justice be administered equally by all and to all. For nature hath not merely given us reason, but right reason, and consequently that law, which is nothing else than right reason enjoining what is good, and forbidding what is evil.

Now if nature hath given us law, she hath also given us justice,—for as she has bestowed reason on all, she has equally bestowed the sense of justice on all. And therefore did Socrates deservedly execrate the man who first drew a distinction between the law of nature and the law of morals, for he justly conceived that this error is the source of most human vices.

It is to this essential union between the naturally honourable, and the politically expedient, that this sentence of Pythagoras refers:—"Love is universal: let its benefits be universal likewise." From whence it appears that when a wise man is attached to a good man by that friendship whose rights are so extensive, that phenomenon takes place which is altogether incredible to worldlings, and yet it is a necessary consequence, that he loves himself not more dearly than he loves his friend. For how can a difference of interests arise where all interests are similar? If there could be such a difference of interests, however minute, it would be no longer a true friendship, which vanishes immediately when, for the sake of our own benefit, we would sacrifice that of our friend. . . .

[I will add a few considerations] in conformity with the method of the philosophers. I do not mean the older sages of philosophy, but those modern philosophers who keep a magazine of arguments in reserve, on every imaginable topic, and who, instead of discussing questions freely and unconstrainedly, will permit us to speak only in accordance with their logical arrangements and dialectical distinctions. These gentlemen will never allow that we have done justice to our subject, unless we demonstrate that nature is just, and justice is natural, in a distinct and scientific disputation. . . .

Was it the fear of punishment, and not the nature of the thing itself that ought to restrain mankind from wickedness, what, I would ask, could give villains the least uneasiness, abstracting from all fears of this kind? And yet none of them was ever so audaciously impudent, but he endeavoured to justify what he had done by some law of nature, denied the fact, or else pretended a just sorrow for it. Now if the wicked have the confidence to appeal to these laws, with what profound respect ought good men to treat them?

There is the greater need, therefore, of insisting on the natural and unavoidable penalties of conscience. For if either direct punishment, or the fear of it, was what deterred from a vicious course of life, and not the turpitude of the thing itself, then none could be guilty of injustice, in a moral sense, and the greatest offenders ought rather to be called imprudent than wicked.

On the other hand, if we are determined to the practice of goodness, not by its own intrinsic excellence, but for the sake of some private advantage, we are cunning, rather than good men. What will not that man do in the dark who fears nothing but a witness and a judge? Should he meet a solitary individual in a desert place, with a large sum of money about him, and altogether unable to defend himself from being robbed, how would he behave? In such a case the man whom we have represented to be honest from principle, and the nature of the thing itself, would converse with the stranger, assist him, and show him the way. But as to the man who does nothing for the sake of another, and measures everything by the advantage it brings to himself, it is obvious, I suppose, how such a one would act; and should he deny that he would kill the man or rob him of his treasure, his reason for this cannot be that he apprehends there is any moral turpitude in such actions, but only because he is afraid of a discovery, and the bad consequences that would thence ensue. A sentiment this, at which not only learned men, but even clowns must blush.

It is therefore an absurd extravagance in some philosophers to assert that all things are necessarily just, which are established by the civil laws and the institutions of the people. Are then the laws of tyrants just, simply because they are laws? If the thirty tyrants of Athens imposed certains laws on the Athenians, and if these Athenians were delighted with these tyrannical laws, are we therefore bound to consider these laws as just? For my own part, I do not think such laws deserve any greater estimation than that passed during our own interregnum, which ordained, that the dictator should be empowered to put to death with impunity, whatever citizens he pleased, without hearing them in their own defence.

There can be but one essential justice, which cements society, and one law which establishes this justice. This law is right reason, which is the true rule of all commandments and prohibitions. Whoever neglects this law, whether written or unwritten, is necessarily unjust and wicked.

But if justice consists in submission to written laws and national customs, and if, as the Epicureans persist in affirming, everything must be measured by utility alone, he who wishes to find an occasion of breaking such laws and customs, will be sure to discover it. So that real justice remains powerless if not supported by nature, and this pretended justice is overturned by that very utility which they call its foundation.

But this is not all. If nature does not ratify law, all the virtues lose their sway. What becomes of generosity, patriotism, or friendship? Where should we find the desire of benefitting our neighbours, or the gratitude that acknowledges kindness? For all these virtues proceed from our natural inclination to love and cherish our associates. This is the true basis of justice, and without this, not only the mutual charities of men, but the religious services of the gods, would become obsolete; for these are preserved, as I imagine, rather by the natural sympathy which subsists between divine and human beings, than by mere fear and timidity.

If the will of the people, the decrees of the senate, the adjudications of magistrates, were sufficient to establish justice, the only question would be how to gain suffrages, and to win over the votes of the majority, in order that corruption and spoliation, and the falsification of wills, should become lawful. But if the opinions and suffrages of foolish men had sufficient weight to outbalance the nature of things, might they not determine among them, that what is essentially bad and pernicious should henceforth pass for good and beneficial? Or why should not a law able to enforce injustice, take the place of equity? Would not this same law be able to change evil into good, and good into evil?

As far as we are concerned, we have no other rule capable of distinguishing between a good or a bad law, than our natural conscience and reason. These, however, enable us to separate justice from injustice, and to discriminate between the honest and the scandalous. For common sense has impressed in our minds the first principles of things, and has given us a general acquaintance with them, by which we connect with Virtue every honourable and excellent quality, and with Vice all that is abominable and disgraceful.

Now we must entirely take leave of our senses, ere we can suppose that law and justice have no foundation in nature, and rely merely on the transient opinions of men. We should not venture to praise the virtue of a tree or a horse, in which expression there is an abuse of terms, were we not convinced that this virtue was in their nature, rather than in our opinion. For a stronger reason, it is mainly with respect to the moral nature of things, that we ought to speak of honour and shame among men.

If opinion could determine respecting the character of universal virtue, it might also decide respecting particular or partial virtues. But who will dare to determine that a man is prudent and cautious in his moral disposition, from any external appearances? For virtue evidently lies in perfect rationality, and this resides in the inmost depths of our nature. The same remark applies to all honour and honesty, for we judge of true and false, creditable and discreditable, rather by their essential qualities, than their external relations. Thus we judge according to their intrinsic nature, that rationality of life, which is virtue, must be ever constant and perpetual, and that inconstancy must necessarily be vicious.

We form an estimate of the opinions of youths, but not by their opinions. Those virtues and vices which reside in their moral natures, must not be measured by opinions. And so of all moral qualities, we must discriminate between honourable and dishonourable by reference to the essential nature of the things themselves.

The good we commend, must needs contain in itself something commendable. For as I before stated, goodness is not a mode of opinion: it is what it is, by the force of its very essence. If it were otherwise, opinion alone might constitute virtue and happiness, which is the most absurd of suppositions. And since we judge of good and evil by their nature, and since good and evil are the true constituents of honour and shame, we should judge in the same manner all honourable and all shameful qualities, testing them by the law of nature, without prejudice or passion. But our steady attention to this moral law of nature is often too much disturbed by the dissension of men and the variation of opinions. We might perhaps obey this law of nature more exactly, if we attended more accurately to the evidence of our senses, which being absolutely natural, are less likely to be deceived by artificial objects. Those objects, indeed, which sometimes present to us one appearance, sometimes another, we term fictions of the senses; but it is far otherwise. For neither parent, nor nurse, nor master, nor poet, nor drama, deceive our senses; nor do popular prejudices seduce them. But our delusions are connected with corruption of our mental opinions. And this corruption is either superinduced by those causes of error I have enumerated, which, taking possession of the young and uneducated, betray them into a thousand perversities, or by that voluptuousness which is the mimic of goodness, implicated and interfused through all our senses—the prolific mother of all human disasters. For she so corrupts us by her bewitching blandishments that we no longer perceive that things may be essentially excellent, though they have none of this deliciousness and pruriency.

From what I have said on this subject, it may then easily be concluded, that Justice and Equity are desirable for their own sake. For all virtuous men love Justice and Equity, for what they are in themselves; and we cannot believe that such virtuous men should delude themselves by loving something which does not deserve their affection. Justice and Right are therefore desirable and amiable in themselves; and if this is true of Right, it must be true of all the moral virtues with which it is connected. What then shall we say of liberality? Is it to be exercised gratuitously, or does it covet some reward and recompense? If a man does good without expecting any recompense for his kindness, then it is gratuitous: if he does expect compensation, it is a mere matter of traffic. Doubtless, he who truly deserves the reputation of a generous and good-natured man, performs his philanthropical duties without consulting his secular interests. In the same way the virtue of justice demands neither emolument nor salary, and therefore we desire it for its own sake, because it is its own reward. And for this reason we should entertain the same estimate of all moral virtues.

Besides this, if we weigh virtue by the mere utility and profit that attend it, and not by its own merit, the virtue which results will be in fact a species of vice (*malitia rectissime decitur*). For the more a man's views are self-interested, the further he recedes from probity. It therefore necessarily happens, that those who measure virtue by profit, acknowledge no other virtue than this usurious vice. For who could be called benevolent, if none endeavoured to do good for the love of others? Where could we find the grateful person, if those who are disposed to gratitude could meet no benefactor disinterested enough to deserve it? What would become of sacred friendship, if we were not to love our friends for their own sake with all our heart and soul? In pursuance of this pseudo-benevolence, we must desert our friend, as soon as we can derive no further assistance from him. What can be more inhuman! But if friendship ought rather to be cultivated on its own account, for the same reason are society, equality, and justice, desirable for themselves. If this were not so, there could be no justice at all, since nothing is more opposite to the very essence of virtue than selfish interest.

What then shall we say of temperance, sobriety, continence, modesty, bashfulness, and chastity? Is it the fear of laws, or the dread of judgments and penalties, which restrain intemperance and dissoluteness? Do we then live in innocence and moderation, only to acquire a certain secular reputation? And when we blush at licentious discourse, is it only through a squeamish prudery, lest our reputation should be stained? How I am ashamed at those philosophers, who assert that there are no vices to be avoided but those which the laws have branded with infamy. Can it be said that those are truly chaste, who abstain from adultery, merely for the fear of public exposure, and that disgrace which is only one of its many evil consequences? Indeed, what can you praise or blame with reason, if you depart from that great law and rule of nature, which makes the difference between right and wrong? Shall corporal defects, if they are remarkable, shock our sensibilities, and shall those of the soul make no impression on us?—Of the soul, I say, whose turpitude is so evidently proved by its vices. For what is there more hideous than avarice, more ferocious than lust, more contemptible than cowardice, more base than stupidity and folly? Well, therefore, may we style unhappy, those persons in whom any one of these vices is conspicuous, not on account of the disgraces or losses to which they are exposed, but on account of the moral baseness of their sins.

We may apply the same ethical test to those who are distinguished for their virtue. For if virtue be not the highest excellence to which we aspire, it necessarily follows that there is something better than virtue. Is it money, fame, beauty, health? All these appear of little value to us when we possess them, especially when we consider that the duration of their enjoyment is altogether uncertain. Is it that basest of all things, voluptuousness? Certainly not; for nothing gives so much dignity to virtue, as its capacity of overruling and despising all the gratifications of secular and sensual life. . . .

I should say, that Cato, and municipal citizens like him, have two countries, one, that of their birth, and the other, that of their choice. Cato being born at Tusculum, was elected a citizen of Rome, so that a Tusculan by extraction, and a Roman by election, he had, besides his native country, a rightful one. So among your Athenians, before Theseus urged them to quit their rural territories, and assembled them at Athens, those that were natives of Sunium, were reckoned as Sunians and Athenians at the same time. In the same way, we may justly entitle as our country, both the place from where we originated, and that to which we have been associated. It is necessary, however, that we should attach ourselves by a preference of affection to the latter, which, under the name of the Commonwealth, is the common country of us all. For this country it is, that we ought to sacrifice our lives; it is to her that we ought to devote ourselves without reserve; and it is for her that we ought to risk and hazard all our riches and our hopes. Yet this universal patriotism does not prohibit us from preserving a very tender affection for the native soil that was the cradle of our infancy and our youth.

Therefore I will never disown Arpinum as my country, at the same time acknowledging that Rome will always secure my preference, and that Arpinum can only deserve the second place in my heart. . . .

Let us once more examine, before we descend to particulars, what is the essence and moral obligation of law; lest, when we come to apply it to its subordinate relations, we should not exactly understand each other for want of explanation; and lest we should be ignorant of the force of those terms which are usually employed in jurisprudence.

This . . . hath been the decision of the wisest philosophers; that law was neither excogitated by the genius of men, nor is it anything discovered in the progress of society; but a certain eternal principle, which governs the entire universe; wisely commanding what is right, and prohibiting what is wrong. Therefore, that aboriginal and supreme law is the Spirit of God himself; enjoining virtue, and restraining vice. For this reason it is, that this law, which the gods have bestowed on the human race, is so justly applauded. For it is the reason and mind of Wisdom, urging us to good, and deterring us from evil.

From little children have we learned such phrases as this, "that a man appeals to justice, and goes to law;" and a great many municipal laws have we heard mentioned; but we should not understand that such commandments and prohibitions have sufficient moral power to make us practise virtue and avoid vice.

The moral power of law, is not only far more ancient than these legal institutions of states and peoples, but it is coeval with God himself, who beholds and governs both heaven and earth. For it is impossible that the divine mind should exist without reason; and divine reason must necessarily be possessed of a power to determine what is virtuous and what is vicious. Nor, because it was nowhere written, that one man should maintain the pass of a bridge against the enemy's whole army, and that he should order the bridge behind him to be cut down, are we therefore to imagine that the valiant Cocles did not perform this great exploit, agreeably to the laws of nature and the dictates of true bravery. Again, though in the reign of Tarquin there was no written law concerning adultery, it does not therefore follow that Sextus Tarquinius did not offend against the eternal law when he committed a rape on Lucretia, daughter of Tucipitinus. For, even then he had the light of reason deduced from the nature of things, that incites to good actions and dissuades from evil ones. And this has the force of a law, not from the time it was written, but from the first moment it began to exist. Now, this existence of moral obligation is coeternal with that of the divine mind. Therefore the true and supreme law, whose commands and prohibitions are equally infallible, is the right reason of the Sovereign Deity.

Therefore, as the Divine Mind, or reason, is the supreme law, so it exists in the mind of the sage, so far as it can be perfected in man. With respect to civil laws, which differ in all ages and nations, the name of law belongs to them not so much by right as by the favour of the people. For every law which deserves the name of a law ought to be morally good and laudable, as we might demonstrate by the following arguments. It is clear, that laws were originally made for the security of the people, for the preservation of cities, for the peace and benefit of society. Doubtless, the first legislators persuaded the people that they would write and publish such laws only as should conduce to the general morality and happiness, if they would receive and obey them. Such were the regulations, which being settled and sanctioned, they justly entitled *Laws*. From which we may reasonably conclude, that those who made unjustifiable and pernicious enactments for the people, counteracted their own promises and professions; and established anything rather than *laws*, properly so called, since it is evident that the very signification of the word *law*, comprehends the essence and energy of justice and equity.

I would therefore interrogate you on this point like our inquisitive philosophers. If a state wants something, wanting which it is reckoned no state, must not that something be something good? [And furthermore, if] a state has no law, is it not for that reason to be reckoned no state? We must therefore reckon law among the very best things.

If then in the majority of nations, many pernicious and mischievous enactments are made, as far removed from the law of justice we have defined as the mutual engagements of robbers, are we bound to call them laws? For as we cannot call the recipes of ignorant empirics, who give poisons instead of medicines, the prescriptions of a physician, we cannot call that the true law of the people, whatever be its name, if it enjoins what is injurious, let the people receive it as they will. For law is the just distinction between right and wrong, conformable to nature, the original and principal regulator of all things, by which the laws of men should be measured, whether they punish the guilty or protect the innocent. [Consequently] no law but that of justice should either be proclaimed as a law or enforced as a law. [Therefore] regard as nullable and voidable the laws of Titius and Apuleius, because they are unjust. You may say the same of the laws of Livius, so much the more, since a single vote of the senate would be sufficient to abrogate them in an instant. But that law of justice, which I have explained, can never be rendered obsolete or inefficacious.

[Therefore, we require the] laws of justice the more ardently, because they would be durable and permanent, and would not require those perpetual alterations which all injudicious enactments demand. . . .

Let this, therefore, be a fundamental principle in all societies, that the gods are the supreme lords and governors of all things,—that all events are directed by their influence and wisdom, and that they are loving and benevolent to mankind. They likewise know what every person really is; they observe his actions, whether good or bad; they discern whether our religious professions are sincere and heart-felt, and are sure to make a difference between good men and the wicked.

When once our minds are confirmed in these views, it will not be difficult to inspire them with true and useful sentiments,—such as this, that no man should be so madly presumptuous as to believe that he has either reason or intelligence, if he does not believe that the heaven and the world possess them likewise, or in other words, that there is no Supreme Mind which keeps the universe in motion. The presumption is the more excessive in man, who with his best philosophy, can hardly understand what the universe means.

In truth, we can scarcely reckon him a man, whom neither the regular courses of the stars, nor the alternations of day and night, nor the temperature of the seasons, nor the productions that nature displays for his use, do not urge to gratitude towards heaven.

As the beings furnished with reason are incomparably superior to those who want it, and we cannot say, without impiety, that anything transcends the universal Nature, we must therefore confess that divine reason is contained within her. Who will dispute the utility of these sentiments, when he shall reflect how many cases of the greatest importance are decided by oaths; how much the sacred rites performed in making treaties tend to assure peace and tranquility; also, what numbers the fear of divine punishment has reclaimed from a vicious course of life; and how sacred the social rights must be in a society where a firm persuasion obtains of the immediate intervention of the immortal gods, both as witnesses and judges of our actions? Such is the "preamble of the law," to use the expression of Plato.

II THE MEDIEVAL HERITAGE: CHRISTIAN AND JEWISH CONCEPTIONS OF LIFE

PAUL OF TARSUS

Born in Tarsus, Cilicia (present-day Turkey), of an orthodox Jewish family who were also Roman citizens, Saul or Paul (in the latinized version of his name) was as a youth trained as a tentmaker and sent to Jerusalem to study rabbinic law under the sage Gamaliel. Initially a zealous, nationalistic Jew, Paul assisted and applauded at a riot against the young Christian community of Jerusalem after the first post-crucifixion Pentecost. The Jewish High Priest thereupon commissioned him in the year 35 to suppress incipient Christianity in Damascus. As he approached that Syrian city Paul experienced a vision of Jesus and was converted to Christianity, subsequently becoming its energetic missionary throughout the Mediterranean world and the leading formulator of its theology. Vigorously attacking those apostles who wished to retain the Judaic character of the young Christian community, Paul successfully insisted that it not commit itself to Jewish law and ritual. His victory in this controversy enabled the Christian church, spearheaded by his proselytizing activities, to convert to its doctrine vast numbers of gentiles. His doctrine stated that Jesus was and is God's son, whose crucifixion made possible forgiveness of sin and salvation to all true believers. Paul was executed during the persecutions of Nero, c.67.

These letters of Paul come from the Revised Standard Version of the Bible. (New York, Thomas Nelson & Sons, 1952).

❧

THE LETTER OF PAUL TO THE ROMANS

CHAPTER I

1. Paul, a servant of Jesus Christ, called to be an apostle, set apart for the gospel of God which he promised beforehand through his prophets in the holy scriptures, the gospel concerning his Son, who was descended from David according to the flesh and designated Son of God in power according to the Spirit of holiness by his resurrection from the dead, Jesus Christ our Lord, through whom we have received grace and apostleship to bring about obedience to the faith for the sake of his name among all the nations, including yourselves who are called to belong to Jesus Christ;

7. To all God's beloved in Rome, who are called to be saints:

Grace to you and peace from God our Father and the Lord Jesus Christ.

8. First, I thank my God through Jesus Christ for all of you, because your faith is proclaimed in all the world. For God is my witness, whom I serve with my spirit in the gospel of his Son, that without ceasing I mention you

always in my prayers, asking that somehow by God's will I may now at last succeed in coming to you. For I long to see you, that I may impart to you some spiritual gift to strengthen you, that is, that we may be mutually encouraged by each other's faith, both yours and mine. I want you to know, brethren, that I have often intended to come to you (but thus far have been prevented), in order that I may reap some harvest among you as well as among the rest of the Gentiles. I am under obligation both to Greeks and to barbarians, both to wise and to the foolish: so I am eager to preach the gospel to you also who are in Rome.

16. For I am not ashamed of the gospel: it is the power of God for salvation to every one who has faith, to the Jew first and also to the Greek. For in it the righteousness of God is revealed through faith for faith; as it is written, "He who through faith is righteous shall live."

18. For the wrath of God is revealed from heaven against all ungodliness and wickedness of men who by their wickedness suppress the truth. For what can be known about God is plain to them, because God has shown it to them. Ever since the creation of the world his invisible nature, namely, his eternal power and deity, has been clearly perceived in the things that have been made. So they are without excuse; for although they knew God they did not honor him as God or give thanks to him, but they became futile in their thinking and their senseless minds were darkened. Claiming to be wise, they became fools, and exchanged the glory of the immortal God for images resembling mortal man or birds or animals or reptiles.

24. Therefore God gave them up in the lust of their hearts to impurity to the dishonoring of their bodies among themselves, because they exchanged the truth about God for a lie and worshiped and served the creature rather than the Creator, who is blessed forever! Amen.

26. For this reason God gave them up to dishonorable passions. Their women exchanged natural relations for unnatural, and the men likewise gave up natural relations with women and were consumed with passion for one another, men committing shameless acts with men and receiving in their own persons the due penalty for their error.

28. And since they did not see fit to acknowledge God, God gave them up to a base mind and to improper conduct. They were filled with all manner of wickedness, evil, covetousness, malice. Full of envy, murder, strife, deceit, malignity, they are gossips, slanderers, haters of God, insolent, haughty, boastful, inventors of evil, disobedient to parents, foolish, faithless, heartless, ruthless. Though they know God's decree that those who do such things deserve to die, they not only do them but approve those who practice them.

CHAPTER II

Therefore you have no excuse, O man, whoever you are, when you judge another; for in passing judgment upon him you condemn yourself, because you, the judge, are doing the very same things. We know that the judgment of God rightly falls upon those who do such things. Do you suppose, O man, that when you judge those who do such things and yet do them yourself, you will escape the judgment of God? Or do you presume upon the riches of his kindness and forbearance and patience? Do you not know that God's kindness is meant to lead you to repentance? But by your hard and impenitent heart you are storing up wrath for yourself on the day of wrath when God's righteous judgment will be revealed. For he will render to every man according to his works: to those who by patience in well-doing seek for glory and honor and immortality, he will give eternal life; but for those who are factious and do not obey the truth, but obey wickedness, there will be wrath and fury. There will be tribulation and distress for every human being who does evil, the Jew first and also the Greek, but glory and honor and peace for every one who does good, the Jew first and also the Greek. For God shows no partiality.

12. All who have sinned without the law will also perish without the law, and all who have sinned under the law will be judged by the law. For it is not the hearers of the law who are righteous before God, but the doers of the law who will be justified. When Gentiles who have not the law do by nature what the law requires, they are a law to themselves, even though they do not have the law. They show that what the law requires is written on their hearts, while their conscience also bears witness and their conflicting thought accuse or perhaps excuse them on that day when, according to my gospel, God judges the secrets of men by Christ Jesus.

17. But if you call yourself a Jew and rely upon the law and boast of your relation to God and know his will and approve what is excellent, because you are instructed in the law, and if you are sure that you are a guide to the blind, a light to those who are in darkness, a corrector of the foolish, a teacher of children, having in the law the embodiment of knowledge and truth—you then who teach others, will you not teach yourself? While you preach against stealing, do you steal? You who say that one must not commit adultery, do you commit adultery? You who abhor idols, do you rob temples? You who boast in the law, do you dishonor God by breaking the law? For, as it is written,

"The name of God is blasphemed among the Gentiles because of you."

25. Circumcision indeed is of value if you obey the law; but if you break

the law, your circumcision becomes uncircumcision. So, if a man who is un-circumcised keeps the precepts of the law, will not his uncircumcision be regarded as circumcision? Then those who are physically uncircumcised but keep the law will condemn you who have the written code and circumcision but break the law. For he is not a real Jew who is one outwardly, nor is true circumcision something external and physical. He is a Jew who is one inwardly, and real circumcision is a matter of the heart, spiritual and not literal. His praise is not from men but from God.

CHAPTER III

Then what advantage has the Jew? Or what is the value of circumcision? Much in every way. To begin with, the Jews are entrusted with the oracles of God. What if some were unfaithful? Does their faithlessness nullify the faithfulness of God? By no means! Let God be true though every man be false, as it is written,

"That thou mayest be justified in thy words, and prevail when thou art judged."

5. But if our wickedness serves to show the justice of God, what shall we say? That God is unjust to inflict wrath on us? (I speak in a human way.) By no means! For then how could God judge the world? But if through my falsehood God's truthfulness abounds to his glory, why am I still being condemned as a sinner? And why not do evil that good may come?—as some people slanderously charge us with saying. Their condemnation is just.

9. What then? Are we Jews any better off? No, not at all; for I have already charged that all men, both Jews and Greeks, are under the power of sin, as it is written:

"None is righteous, no, not one; no one understands, no one seeks for God.

12. All have turned aside, together they have gone wrong; no one does good, not even one."

13. "Their throat is an open grave, they use their tongues to deceive." "The venom of asps is under their lips."

14. "Their mouth is full of curses and bitterness."

15. "Their feet are swift to shed blood,

16. in their paths are ruin and misery,

17. and the way of peace they do not know."

18. "There is no fear of God before their eyes."

19. Now we know that whatever the law says it speaks to those who are under the law, so that every mouth may be stopped, and the whole world

may be held accountable to God. For no human being will be justified in his sight by works of the law since through the law comes knowledge of sin.

21. But now the righteousness of God has been manifested apart from law, although the law and the prophets bear witness to it, the righteousness of God through faith in Jesus Christ for all who believe. For there is no distinction; since all have sinned and fall short of the glory of God, they are justified by his grace as a gift, through the redemption which is in Christ Jesus, whom God put forward as an expiation by his blood, to be received by faith. This was to show God's righteousness, because in his divine forbearance he had passed over former sins; it was to prove at the present time that he himself is righteous and that he justifies him who has faith in Jesus.

27. Then what becomes of our boasting? It is excluded. On what principle? On the principle of works? No, but on the principle of faith. For we hold that a man is justified by faith apart from works of law. Or is God the God of Jews only? Is he not the God of Gentiles also? Yes, of Gentiles also, since God is one; and he will justify the circumcised on the ground of their faith and the uncircumcised because of their faith. Do we then overthrow the law by this faith? By no means! On the contrary, we uphold the law.

CHAPTER IV

What then shall we say about Abraham, our forefather according to the flesh? For if Abraham was justified by works, he has something to boast about, but not before God. For what does the scripture say? "Abraham believed God, and it was reckoned to him as righteousness." Now to one who works, his wages are not reckoned as a gift but as his due. And to one who does not work but trusts him who justifies the ungodly, his faith is reckoned as righteousness. So also David pronounces a blessing upon the man to whom God reckons righteousness apart from works:

7. "Blessed are those whose iniquities are forgiven, and whose sins are covered; blessed is the man against whom the Lord will not reckon his sin."

9. Is this blessing pronounced only upon the circumcised, or also upon the uncircumcised? We say that faith was reckoned to Abraham as righteousness. How then was it reckoned to him? Was it before or after he had been circumcised? It was not after, but before he was circumcised. He received circumcision as a sign or seal of the righteousness which he had by faith while he was still uncircumcised. The purpose was to make him the father of all who believe without being circumcised and who thus have righteousness reckoned to them, and likewise the father of the circumcised who are

not merely circumcised but also follow the example of the faith which our father Abraham had before he was circumcised.

13. The promise to Abraham and his descendants, that they should inherit the world, did not come through the law but through the righteousness of faith. If it is the adherents of the law who are to be the heirs, faith is null and the promise is void. For the law brings wrath, but where there is no law there is no transgression.

16. That is why it depends on faith, in order that the promise may rest on grace and be guaranteed to all his descendants—not only to the adherents of the law but also to those who share the faith of Abraham, for he is the father of us all, as it is written, "I have made you the father of many nations"—in the presence of the God in whom he believed, who gives life to the dead and calls into existence the things that do not exist. In hope he believed against hope, that he should become the father of many nations; as he had been told, "So shall your descendants be." He did not weaken in faith when he considered his own body, which was as good as dead because he was about a hundred years old, or when he considered the barrenness of Sarah's womb. No distrust made him waver concerning the promise of God, but he grew strong in his faith as he gave glory to God, fully convinced that God was able to do what he had promised. That is why his faith was "reckoned to him as righteousness." But the words, "it was reckoned to him," were written not for his sake alone, but for ours also. It will be reckoned to us who believe in him that raised from the dead Jesus our Lord, who was put to death for our trespasses and raised for our justification.

CHAPTER V

Therefore, since we are justified by faith, we have peace with God through our Lord Jesus Christ. Through him we have obtained access to this grace in which we stand, and we rejoice in our hope of sharing the glory of God. More than that, we rejoice in our sufferings, knowing that suffering produces endurance, and endurance produces character, and character produces hope, and hope does not disappoint us, because God's love has been poured into our hearts through the Holy Spirit which has been given to us.

6. While we were yet helpless, at the right time Christ died for the ungodly. Why, one will hardly die for a righteous man—though perhaps for a good man one will dare even to die. But God shows his love for us in that while we were yet sinners Christ died for us. Since, therefore, we are now justified by his blood, much more shall we be saved by him from the wrath of God. For if while we were enemies we were reconciled to God

by the death of his Son, much more, now that we are reconciled, shall we be saved by his life. Not only so, but we also rejoice in God through our Lord Jesus Christ, through whom we have now received our reconciliation.

12. Therefore as sin came into the world through one man and death through sin, and so death spread to all men because all men sinned—sin indeed was in the world before the law was given, but sin is not counted where there is no law. Yet death reigned from Adam to Moses, even over those whose sins were not like the transgression of Adam, who was a type of the one who was to come.

15. But the free gift is not like the trespass. For if many died through one man's trespass, much more have the grace of God and the free gift in the grace of that one man Jesus Christ abounded for many. And the free gift is not like the effect of that one man's sin. For the judgment following one trespass brought condemnation, but the free gift following many trespasses brings justification. If, because of one man's trespass, death reigned through that one man, much more will those who receive the abundance of grace and the free gift of righteousness reign in life through the one man Jesus Christ.

18. Then as one man's trespass led to condemnation for all men, so one man's act of righteousness leads to acquittal and life for all men. For as by one man's disobedience many were made sinners, so by one man's obedience many will be made righteous. Law came in, to increase the trespass; but where sin increased, grace abounded all the more, so that, as sin reigned in death, grace also might reign through righteousness to eternal life through Jesus Christ our Lord.

CHAPTER VI

What shall we say then? Are we to continue in sin that grace may abound? By no means! How can we who died to sin still live in it? Do you not know that all of us who have been baptized into Christ Jesus were baptized into his death? We were buried therefore with him by baptism into death, so that as Christ was raised from the dead by the glory of the Father, we too might walk in newness of life.

5. For if we have been united with him in a death like his, we shall certainly be united with him in a resurrection like his. We know that our old self was crucified with him so that the sinful body might be destroyed, and we might no longer be enslaved to sin. But if we have died with Christ, we believe that we shall also live with him. For we know that Christ being raised from the dead will never die again; death no longer has dominion over him. The death he died he died to sin, once for all, but the life he

lives he lives to God. So you also must consider yourselves dead to sin and alive to God in Christ Jesus.

12. Let not sin therefore reign in your mortal bodies, to make you obey their passions. Do not yield your members to sin as instruments of wickedness, but yield yourselves to God as men who have been brought from death to life, and your members to God as instruments of righteousness. For sin will have no dominion over you, since you are not under law but under grace.

15. What then? Are we to sin because we are not under law but under grace? By no means! Do you not know that if you yield yourselves to any one as obedient slaves, you are slaves of the one whom you obey, either of sin, which leads to death, or of obedience, which leads to righteousness? But thanks be to God, that you who were once slaves of sin have become obedient from the heart to the standard of teaching to which you were committed, and, having been set free from sin, have becomes slaves of righteousness. I am speaking in human terms, because of your natural limitations. For just as you once yielded your members to impurity and to greater and greater iniquity, so now yield your members to righteousness for sanctification.

20. When you were slaves of sin, you were free in regard to righteousness. But then what return did you get from the things of which you are now ashamed? The end of those things is death. But now that you have been set free from sin and have become slaves of God, the return you get is sanctification and its end, eternal life. For the wages of sin is death, but the free gift of God is eternal life in Christ Jesus our Lord.

CHAPTER VII

Do you not know, brethren—for I am speaking to those who know the law—that the law is binding on a person only during his life? Thus a married woman is bound by law to her husband as long as he lives; but if her husband dies she is discharged from the law concerning the husband. Accordingly, she will be called an adulteress if she lives with another man while her husband is alive. But if her husband dies she is free from that law, and if she marries another man she is not an adulteress.

4. Likewise, my brethren, you have died to the law through the body of Christ, so that you may belong to another, to him who has been raised from the dead in order that we may bear fruit for God. While we were living in the flesh, our sinful passions, aroused by the law, were at work in our members to bear fruit for death. But now we are discharged from the law,

dead to that which held us captive, so that we serve not under the old written code but in the new life of the Spirit.

7. What then shall we say? That the law is sin? By no means! Yet, if it had not been for the law, I should not have known sin. I should not have known what it is to covet if the law had not said, "You shall not covet." But sin, finding opportunity in the commandment, wrought in me all kinds of covetousness. Apart from the law sin lies dead. I was once alive apart from the law, but when the commandment came, sin revived and I died; the very commandment which promised life proved to be death for me. For sin, finding opportunity in the commandment, deceived me and by it killed me. So the law is holy and the commandment is holy and just and good.

13. Did that which is good, then, bring death to me? By no means! It was sin, working death in me through what is good, in order that sin might be shown to be sin, and through the commandment might become sinful beyond measure. We know that the law is spiritual; but I am carnal, sold under sin. I do not understand my own actions. For I do not do what I want, but I do the very thing I hate. Now if I do what I do not want, I agree that the law is good. So then it is no longer I that do it, but sin which dwells within me. For I know that nothing good dwells within me, that is, in my flesh. I can will what is right, but I cannot do it. For I do not do the good I want, but the evil I do not want is what I do. Now if I do what I do not want, it is no longer I that do it, but sin which dwells within me.

21. So I find it to be a law that when I want to do right, evil lies close at hand. For I delight in the law of God, in my inmost self, but I see in my members another law at war with the law of my mind and making me captive to the law of sin which dwells in my members. Wretched man that I am! Who will deliver me from this body of death? Thanks be to God through Jesus Christ our Lord! So then, I of myself serve the law of God with my mind, but with my flesh I serve the law of sin.

CHAPTER VIII

There is therefore now no condemnation for those who are in Christ Jesus. For the law of the Spirit of life in Christ Jesus has set me free from the law of sin and death. For God has done what the law, weakened by the flesh, could not do: sending his own Son in the likeness of sinful flesh and for sin, he condemned sin in the flesh and for sin, in order that the just requirement of the law might be fulfilled in us, who walk not according

to the flesh but according to the Spirit. For those who live according to the flesh set their minds on the things of the flesh, but those
who live according to the Spirit set their minds on the things of the
Spirit. To set the mind on the flesh is death, but to set the mind on the
Spirit is life and peace. For the mind that is set on the flesh is hostile to
God; it does not submit to God's law, indeed it cannot; and those who are
in the flesh cannot please God.

9. But you are not in the flesh, you are in the Spirit, if the Spirit of God
really dwells in you. Any one who does not have the Spirit of Christ does
not belong to him. But if Christ is in you, although your bodies are dead
because of sin, your spirits are alive because of righteousness. If the Spirit of
him who raised Jesus from the dead dwells in you, he who raised Christ
Jesus from the dead will give life to your mortal bodies also through his
Spirit which dwells in you.

12. So then, brethren, we are debtors, not to the flesh, to live according to
the flesh—for if you live according to the flesh you will die, but if by the
Spirit you put to death the deeds of the body you will live. For all who are
led by the Spirit of God are sons of God. For you did not receive the spirit
of slavery to fall back into fear, but you have received the spirit of sonship.
When we cry, "Abba! Father!" it is the Spirit himself bearing witness with
our spirit that we are children of God, and if children, then heirs, heirs of
God and fellow heirs with Christ, provided we suffer with him in order
that we may also be glorified with him.

18. I consider that the sufferings of this present time are not worth comparing with the glory that is to be revealed to us. For the creation awaits
with eager longing for the revealing of the sons of God; for the creation
was subjected to futility, not of its own will but by the will of him who
subjected it in hope; because the creation itself will be set free from its
bondage to decay and obtain the glorious liberty of the children of God.
We know that the whole creation has been groaning in travail together until
now; and not only the creation, but we ourselves, who have the first fruits
of the Spirit, groan inwardly as we wait for adoption as sons, the redemption
of our bodies. For in this hope we were saved. Now hope that is seen is not
hope. For who hopes for what he sees? But if we hope for what we do not
see, we wait for it with patience.

26. Likewise the Spirit helps us in our weakness; for we do not know
how to pray as we ought, but the Spirit himself intercedes for us with sighs
too deep for words. And he who searches the hearts of men knows what is
the mind of the Spirit, because the Spirit intercedes for the saints according
to the will of God.

28. We know that in everything God works for good with those who love him, who are called according to his purpose. For those whom he fore-knew he also predestined to be conformed to the image of his Son, in order that he might be the first-born among many brethren. And those whom he predestined he also called; and those whom he called he also justified; and those whom he justified he also glorified.

31. What then shall we say to this? If God is for us, who is against us? He who did not spare his own Son but gave him up for us all, will he not also give us all things with him? Who shall bring any charge against God's elect? It is God who justifies; who is to condemn? Is it Christ Jesus, who died, yes, who was raised from the dead, who is at the right hand of God, who indeed intercedes for us? Who shall separate us from the love of Christ? Shall tribulation, or distress, or persecution, or famine, or nakedness, or peril, or sword? As it is written,

"For thy sake we are being killed all the day long; we are regarded as sheep to be slaughtered."

No, in all these things we are more than conquerors through him who loved us. For I am sure that neither death, nor life, nor angels, nor prin-cipalities, nor things present, nor things to come, nor powers, nor height, nor depth, nor anything else in all creation, will be able to separate us from the love of God in Christ Jesus our Lord.

CHAPTER IX

I am speaking the truth in Christ, I am not lying; my conscience bears me witness in the Holy Spirit, that I have great sorrow and unceasing anguish in my heart. For I could wish that I myself were accursed and cut off from Christ for the sake of my brethren, my kinsmen by race. They are Israelites, and to them belong the sonship, the glory, the covenants, the giving of the law, the worship, and the promises; to them belong the patriarchs, and of their race, according to the flesh, is the Christ. God who is over all be blessed for ever. Amen.

6. But it is not as though the word of God had failed. For not all who are descended from Israel belong to Israel, and not all are children of Abra-ham because they are his descendants; but "Through Isaac shall your de-scendants be named." This means that it is not the children of the flesh who are the children of God, but the children of the promise are reckoned as descendants. For this is what the promise said, "About this time I will re-turn and Sarah shall have a son." And not only so, but also when Rebecca had conceived children by one man, our forefather Isaac, though they were not yet born and had done nothing either good or bad, in order that God's

purpose of election might continue, not because of works but because of his call, she was told, "The elder will serve the younger." As it is written, "Jacob I loved, but Esau I hated."

14. What shall we say then? Is there injustice on God's part? By no means! For he says to Moses, "I will have mercy on whom I have mercy, and I will have compassion on whom I have compassion." So it depends not upon man's will or exertion, but upon God's mercy. For the scripture says to Pharaoh, "I have raised you up for the very purpose of showing my power in you, so that my name may be proclaimed in all the earth." So then he has mercy upon whomever he wills, and he hardens the heart of whomever he wills.

19. You will say to me then, "Why does he still find fault? For who can resist his will?" But, who are you, a man, to answer back to God? Will what is molded say to its molder, "Why have you made me thus?" Has the potter no right over the clay, to make out of the same lump one vessel for beauty and another for menial use? What if God, desiring to show his wrath and to make known his power, has endured with much patience the vessels of wrath made for destruction, in order to make known the riches of his glory for the vessels of mercy, which he has prepared beforehand for glory, even us whom he has called, not from the Jews only but also from the Gentiles? As indeed he says in Hosea, "Those who were not my people I will call 'my people,' and her who was not beloved I will call 'my beloved.'" "And in the very place where it was said to them, 'You are not my people,' they will be called 'sons of the living God.'"

27. And Isaiah cries out concerning Israel: "Though the number of the sons of Israel be as the sand of the sea, only a remnant of them will be saved; for the Lord will execute his sentence upon the earth with rigor and dispatch." And as Isaiah predicted, "If the Lord of hosts had not left us children, we would have fared like Sodom and have been made like Gomorrah."

30. What shall we say, then? That Gentiles who did not pursue righteousness have attained it, that is, righteousness through faith; but that Israel who pursued the righteousness which is based on law did not succeed in fulfilling that law. Why? Because they did not pursue it through faith, but as if it were based on works. They have stumbled over the stumbling-stone, as it is written, "Behold I am laying in Zion a stone that will make men stumble, a rock that will make them fall; and he who believes in him will not be put to shame."

CHAPTER X

Brethren, my heart's desire and prayer to God for them is that they may be saved. I bear them witness that they have a zeal for God, but it is not enlightened. For, being ignorant of the righteousness that comes from God, and seeking to establish their own, they did not submit to God's righteousness. For Christ is the end of the law, that every one who has faith may be justified.

5. Moses writes that the man who practices the righteousness which is based on the law shall live by it. But the righteousness based on faith says, Do not say in your heart, "Who will ascend into heaven?" (that is, to bring Christ down) or "Who will descend into the abyss?" (that is, to bring Christ up from the dead). But what does it say? The word is near you, on your lips and in your heart (that is, the word of faith which we preach); because, if you confess with your lips that Jesus is Lord and believe in your heart that God raised him from the dead, you will be saved. For man believes with his heart and so is justified, and he confesses with his lips and so is saved. The scripture says, "No one who believes in him will be put to shame." For there is no distinction between Jew and Greek; the same Lord is Lord of all and bestows his riches upon all who call upon him. For, "every one who calls upon the name of the Lord will be saved."

14. But how are men to call upon him in whom they have not believed? And how are they to believe in him of whom they have never heard? And how are they to hear without a preacher? And how can men preach unless they are sent? As it is written, "How beautiful are the feet of those who preach good news!" But they have not all heeded the gospel; for Isaiah says, "Lord, who has believed what he has heard from us?" So faith comes from what is heard, and what is heard comes by the preaching of Christ.

18. But I ask, have they not heard? Indeed they have; for

"Their voice has gone out to all the earth, and their words to the ends of the world."

Again I ask, did Israel not understand? First Moses says,

"I will make you jealous of those who are not a nation; with a foolish nation I will make you angry."

Then Isaiah is so bold as to say,

"I have been found by those who did not seek me; I have shown myself to those who did not ask for me."

21. But of Israel he says, "All day long I have held out my hands to a disobedient and contrary people."

CHAPTER XI

I ask, then, has God rejected his people? By no means! I myself am an Israelite, a descendant of Abraham, a member of the tribe of Benjamin. God has not rejected his people whom he foreknew. Do you not know what the scripture says of Elijah, how he pleads with God against Israel? "Lord, they have killed thy prophets, they have demolished thy altars, and I alone am left, and they seek my life." But what is God's reply to him? "I have kept for myself seven thousand men who have not bowed the knee to Baal." So too at the present time there is a remnant, chosen by grace. But if it is by grace, it is no longer on the basis of works; otherwise grace would no longer be grace.

7. What then? Israel failed to obtain what it sought. The elect obtained it, but the rest were hardened, as it is written,

"God gave them a spirit of stupor, eyes that should not see, and ears that should not hear, down to this very day."

And David says, "Let their feast become a snare and a trap, a pitfall and a retribution for them; let their eyes be darkened so that they cannot see, and bend their backs for ever."

11. So I ask, have they stumbled so as to fall? By no means! But through their trespass salvation has come to the Gentiles, so as to make Israel jealous. Now if their trespass means riches for the world, and if their failure means riches for the Gentiles, how much more will their full inclusion mean!

13. Now I am speaking to you Gentiles. Inasmuch then as I am an apostle to the Gentiles, I magnify my ministry in order to make my fellow Jews jealous, and thus save some of them. For if their rejection means the reconciliation of the world, what will their acceptance mean but life from the dead? If the dough offered as first fruits is holy, so is the whole lump; and if the root is holy, so are the branches.

17. But if some of the branches were broken off, and you, a wild olive shoot, were grafted in their place to share the richness of the olive tree, do not boast over the branches. If you do boast, remember it is not you that support the root, but the root that supports you. You will say, "Branches were broken off so that I might be grafted in." That is true. They were broken off because of their unbelief, but you stand fast only through faith. So do not become proud, but stand in awe. For if God did not spare the natural branches, neither will he spare you. Note then the kindness of and the severity of God: severity toward those who have fallen, but God's kindness to you, provided you continue in his kindness; otherwise you too will be cut off. And even the others, if they do not persist in their unbelief, will

be grafted in, for God has the power to graft them in again. For if you have been cut from what is by nature a wild olive tree, and grafted, contrary to nature, into a cultivated olive tree, how much more will these natural branches be grafted back into their own olive tree.

25. Lest you be wise in your own conceits, I want you to understand this mystery, brethren: a hardening has come upon part of Israel, until the full number of the Gentiles come in, and so all Israel will be saved; as it is written,

"The Deliverer will come from Zion, he will banish ungodliness from Jacob"; "and this will be my covenant with them when I take away their sins."

As regards the gospel they are enemies of God, for your sake; but as regards election they are beloved for the sake of their forefathers. For the gifts and the call of God are irrevocable. Just as you were once disobedient to God but now have received mercy because of their disobedience, so they have now been disobedient in order that by the mercy shown to you they also may receive mercy. For God has consigned all men to disobedience, that he may have mercy upon all.

33. O the depth of the riches and wisdom and knowledge of God! How unsearchable are his judgments and how inscrutable his ways!

"For who has known the mind of the Lord, or who has been his counselor?"

"Or who has given a gift to him that he might be repaid?"

For from him and through him and to him are all things. To him be glory forever. Amen.

CHAPTER XII

I appeal to you therefore, brethren, by the mercies of God, to present your bodies as a living sacrifice, holy and acceptable to God, which is your spiritual worship. Do not be conformed to this world but be transformed by the renewal of your mind, that you may prove what is the will of God, what is good and acceptable and perfect.

3. For by the grace given to me I bid every one among you not to think of himself more highly than he ought to think, but to think with sober judgment, each according to the measure of faith which God has assigned him. For as in one body we have many members, and all the members do not have the same function, so we, though many, are one body in Christ, and individually members one of another. Having gifts that differ according to the grace given to us, let us use them: if prophecy, in proportion to our faith; if service, in our serving; he who teaches, in his teaching; he who ex-

horts, in his exhortation; he who contributes, in liberality; he who gives aid, with zeal; he who does acts of mercy, with cheerfulness.

9. Let love be genuine; hate what is evil, hold fast to what is good; love one another with brotherly affection; outdo one another in showing honor. Never flag in zeal, be aglow with the Spirit, serve the Lord. Rejoice in your hope, be patient in tribulation, be constant in prayer. Contribute to the needs of the saints, practice hospitality.

14. Bless those who persecute you; bless and do not curse them. Rejoice with those who rejoice, weep with those who weep. Live in harmony with one another; do not be haughty, but associate with the lowly; never be conceited. Repay no one evil for evil, but take thought for what is noble in the sight of all. If possible, so far as it depends upon you, live peaceably with all. Beloved, never avenge yourselves, but leave it to the wrath of God; for it is written, "Vengeance is mine, I will repay, says the Lord." No, "if your enemy is hungry, feed him; if he is thirsty, give him drink; for by so doing you will heap burning coals upon his head." Do not be overcome by evil, but overcome evil with good.

CHAPTER XIII

Let every person be subject to the governing authorities. For there is no authority except from God, and those that exist have been instituted by God. Therefore he who resists the authorities resists what God has appointed, and those who resist will incur judgment. For rulers are not a terror to good conduct, but to bad. Would you have no fear of him who is in authority? Then do what is good, and you will receive his approval, for he is God's servant for your good. But if you do wrong, be afraid, for he does not bear the sword in vain; he is the servant of God to execute his wrath on the wrongdoer. Therefore one must be subject, not only to avoid God's wrath but also for the sake of conscience. For the same reason you also pay taxes, for the authorities are ministers of God, attending to this very thing. Pay all of them their dues, taxes to whom taxes are due, revenue to whom revenue is due, respect to whom respect is due, honor to whom honor is due.

8. Owe no one anything, except to love one another; for he who loves his neighbor has fulfilled the law. The commandments, "You shall not commit adultery, You shall not kill, You shall not steal, You shall not covet," and any other commandment, are summed up in this sentence, "You shall love your neighbor as yourself." Love does no wrong to a neighbor; therefore love is the fulfilling of the law.

11. Besides this you know what hour it is, how it is full time now for you to wake from sleep. For salvation is nearer to us now than when we first

believed; the night is far gone, the day is at hand. Let us then cast off the works of darkness and put on the armor of light; let us conduct ourselves becomingly as in the day, not in reveling and drunkenness, not in debauchery and licentiousness, not in quarreling and jealousy. But put on the Lord Jesus Christ, and make no provision for the flesh, to gratify its desires.

CHAPTER XIV

As for the man who is weak in faith, welcome him, but not for disputes over opinions. One believes he may eat anything, while the weak man eats only vegetables. Let not him who eats despise him who abstains, and let not him who abstains pass judgment on him who eats; for God has welcomed him. Who are you to pass judgment on the servant of another? It is before his own master that he stands or falls. And he will be upheld, for the Master is able to make him stand.

5. One man esteems one day as better than another, while another man esteems all days alike. Let every one be fully convinced in his own mind. He who observes the day, observes it in honor of the Lord. He also who eats, eats in honor of the Lord, since he gives thanks to God; while he who abstains, abstains in honor of the Lord and gives thanks to God. None of us lives to himself, and none of us dies to himself. If we live, we live to the Lord, and if we die, we die to the Lord; so then, whether we live or whether we die, we are the Lord's. For to this end Christ died and lived again, that he might be Lord both of the dead and of the living.

10. Why do you pass judgment on your brother? Or you, why do you despise your brother? For we shall all stand before the judgment seat of God; for it is written,

"As I live, says the Lord, every knee shall bow to me, and every tongue shall give praise to God."

So each of us shall give account of himself to God.

13. Then let us no more pass judgment on one another, but rather decide never to put a stumbling-block or hindrance in the way of a brother. I know and am persuaded in the Lord Jesus that nothing is unclean in itself; but it is unclean for any one who thinks it unclean. If your brother is being injured by what you eat, you are no longer walking in love. Do not let what you eat cause the ruin of one for whom Christ died. So do not let what is good to you be spoken of as evil. For the kingdom of God does not mean food and drink but righteousness and peace and joy in the Holy Spirit; he who thus serves Christ is acceptable to God and approved by men. Let us then pursue what makes for peace and for mutual upbuilding. Do not, for the sake of food, destroy the work of God. Everything is indeed clean, but it

is wrong for any one to make others fall by what he eats; it is right not to eat meat or drink wine or do anything that makes your brother stumble. The faith that you have, keep between yourself and God; happy is he who has no reason to judge himself for what he approves. But he who has doubts is condemned, if he eats, because he does not act from faith; for whatever does not proceed from faith is sin.

CHAPTER XV

We who are strong ought to bear with the failings of the weak, and not to please ourselves; let each of us please his neighbor for his good, to edify him. For Christ did not please himself; but, as it is written, "The reproaches of those who reproached thee fell on me." For whatever was written in former days was written for our instruction, that by steadfastness and by the encouragement of the scriptures we might have hope. May the God of steadfastness and encouragement grant you to live in such harmony with one another, in accord with Christ Jesus, that together you may with one voice glorify the God and Father of our Lord Jesus Christ.

7. Welcome one another, therefore, as Christ has welcomed you, for the glory of God. For I tell you that Christ became a servant to the circumcised to show God's truthfulness, in order to confirm the promises given to the patriarchs, and in order that the Gentiles might glorify God for his mercy. As it is written,

"Therefore I will praise thee among the Gentiles, and sing to thy name"; and again it is said, "Rejoice, O Gentiles, with his people"; and again, "Praise the Lord, all Gentiles, and let all the peoples praise him";

and further Isaiah says, "The root of Jesse shall come, he who rises to rule the Gentiles; and in him shall the Gentiles hope."

May the God of hope fill you with all joy and peace in believing, so that by the power of the Holy Spirit you may abound in hope.

14. I myself am satisfied about you, my brethren, that you yourselves are full of goodness, filled with all knowledge, and able to instruct one another. But on some points I have written to you very boldly by way of reminder, because of the grace given me by God to be a minister of Christ Jesus to the Gentiles in the priestly service of the gospel of God, so that the offering of the Gentiles may be acceptable, sanctified by the Holy Spirit. In Christ Jesus, then, I have reason to be proud of my work for God. For I will not venture to speak of anything except what Christ has wrought through me to win obedience from the Gentiles, by word and deed, by the power of signs and wonders, by the power of the Holy Spirit, so that from

Jerusalem and as far round as Illyricum I have fully preached the gospel of Christ, thus making it my ambition to preach the gospel, not where Christ has already been named, lest I build on another man's foundation, but as it is written, "They shall see who have never been told of him, and they shall understand who have never heard of him."

22. This is the reason why I have so often been hindered from coming to you. But now, since I no longer have any room for work in these regions, and since I have longed for many years to come to you, I hope to see you in passing as I go to Spain, and to be sped on my journey there by you, once I have enjoyed your company for a little. At present, however, I am going to Jerusalem with aid for the saints. For Macedonia and Achaia have been pleased to make some contribution for the poor among the saints at Jerusalem; they were pleased to do it, and indeed they are in debt to them, for if the Gentiles have come to share in their spiritual blessings, they ought also to be of service to them in material blessings. When therefore I have completed this, and have delivered to them what has been raised, I shall go on by way of you to Spain; and I know that when I come to you I shall come in the fulness of the blessing of Christ.

30. I appeal to you, brethren, by our Lord Jesus Christ and by the love of the Spirit, to strive together with me in your prayers to God on my behalf, that I may be delivered from the unbelievers in Judea, and that my service for Jerusalem may be acceptable to the saints, so that by God's will I may come to you with joy and be refreshed in your company. The God of peace be with you all. Amen. . . .

THE LETTER OF PAUL TO THE GALATIANS

CHAPTER I

Paul an apostle—not from men nor through man, but through Jesus Christ and God the Father, who raised him from the dead—and to all the brethren who are with me,

To the churches of Galatia:

3. Grace to you and peace from God the Father and our Lord Jesus Christ, who gave himself for our sins to deliver us from the present evil age, according to the will of our God and Father; to whom be the glory for ever and ever. Amen.

6. I am astonished that you are so quickly deserting him who called you in the grace of Christ and turning to a different gospel—not that there is another gospel, but there are some who trouble you and want to pervert the

gospel of Christ. But even if we, or an angel from heaven, should preach to you a gospel contrary to that which we preached to you, let him be accursed. As we have said before, so now I say again, If any one is preaching to you a gospel contrary to that which you received, let him be accursed.

10. Am I now seeking the favor of men, or of God: Or am I trying to please men? If I were still pleasing men, I should not be a servant of Christ.

11. For I would have you know, brethren, that the gospel which was preached by me is not man's gospel. For I did not receive it from man, nor was I taught it, but it came through a revelation of Jesus Christ. For you have heard of my former life in Judaism, how I persecuted the church of God violently and tried to destroy it, and I advanced in Judaism beyond many of my own age among my people, so extremely zealous was I for the traditions of my fathers. But when he who had set me apart before I was born, and had called me through his grace, was pleased to reveal his Son to me, in order that I might preach him among the Gentiles, I did not confer with flesh and blood, nor did I go up to Jerusalem to those who were apostles before me, but I went away into Arabia; and again I returned to Damascus.

18. Then after three years I went up to Jerusalem to visit Cephas, and remained with him fifteen days. But I saw none of the other apostles except James the Lord's brother. (In what I am writing to you, before God, I do not lie!) Then I went into the regions of Syria and Cili'cia. And I was still not known by sight to the churches of Christ in Judea; they only heard it said, "He who once persecuted us is now preaching the faith he once tried to destroy." And they glorified God because of me.

CHAPTER II

Then after fourteen years I went up again to Jerusalem with Barnabas, taking Titus along with me. I went up by revelation; and I laid before them (but privately before those who were of repute) the gospel which I preach among the Gentiles, lest somehow I should be running or had run in vain. But even Titus, who was with me, was not compelled to be circumcised, though he was a Greek. But because of false brethren secretly brought in, who slipped in to spy out our freedom which we have in Christ Jesus, that they might bring us into bondage—to them we did not yield submission even for a moment, that the truth of the gospel might be preserved for you. And from those who were reputed to be something (what they were makes no difference to me; God shows no partiality)—those, I say, who were of repute added nothing to me; but on the contrary, when they saw that I had been entrusted with the gospel to the uncircumcised, just as Peter had been entrusted with the gospel to the circumcised (for he who worked through Peter for the mission to the circumcised worked through me also for the Gentiles), and when they perceived the grace that was given to me, James and Cephas and John, who were reputed to be pillars, gave to me and Barnabas the right of fellowship, that we should go to the Gentiles and they to the circumcised; only they would have us remember the poor, which very thing I was eager to do.

11. But when Cephas came to Antioch I opposed him to his face, because he stood condemned. For before certain men came from James, he ate with the Gentiles; but when they came he drew back and separated himself, fearing the circumcision party. And with him the rest of the Jews acted insincerely, so that even Barnabas was carried away by their insincerity. But when I saw that they were now straightforward about the truth of the gospel, I said to Cephas before them all, "If you though a Jew, live like a Gentile and not like a Jew, how can you compel the Gentiles to live like Jews?" We ourselves, who are Jews by birth and not Gentile sinners, yet who know that a man is not justified by works of the law but through faith in Jesus Christ, even we have believed in Christ Jesus, in order to be justified by faith in Christ, and not by works of the law, because by works of the law shall no one be justified. But if, in our endeavor to be justified in Christ, we ourselves were found to be sinners, is Christ then an agent of sin? Certainly not! But if I build up again those things which I tore down, then I prove myself a transgressor. For I through the law died to the law, that I might live to God. I have been crucified with Christ; it is no longer I who live, but Christ who lives in me; and the life I now live in the flesh I live by faith in the Son of God, who loved me and gave himself for me. I do not nullify the grace of God; for if justification were through the law, then Christ died to no purpose.

CHAPTER III

O foolish Galatians! Who has bewitched you, before whose eyes Jesus Christ was publicly portrayed as crucified? Let me ask you only this: Did you receive the Spirit by works of the law, or by hearing with faith? Are you so foolish? Having begun with the Spirit, are you now ending with the flesh? Did you experience so many things in vain?—if it really is in vain. Does he who supplies the Spirit to you and works miracles among you do so by works of the law, or by hearing with faith?

6. Thus Abraham "believed God, and it was reckoned to him as righteousness." So you see that it is men of faith who are the sons of Abraham. And the scripture, foreseeing that God would justify the Gentiles by faith, preached the gospel beforehand to Abraham, saying, "In thee shall all the

nations be blessed." So then, those who are men of faith are blessed with Abraham who had faith.

10. For all who rely on works of the law are under a curse; for it is written, "Cursed be every one who does not abide by all things written in the book of the law, and do them." Now it is evident that no man is justified before God by the law; for "He who through faith is righteous shall live"; but the law does not rest on faith, for "He who does them shall live by them." Christ redeemed us from the curse of the law, having become a curse for us— for it is written, "Cursed be everyone who hangs on a tree"—that in Christ Jesus the blessing of Abraham might come upon the Gentiles, that we might receive the promise of the Spirit through faith.

15. To give a human example, brethren: no one annuls even a man's will, or adds to it, once it has been ratified. Now the promises were made to Abraham and to his offspring. It does not say, "And to offsprings," referring to many; but, referring to one, "And to your offspring," which is Christ. This is what I mean: the law, which came four hundred and thirty years afterward, does not annul a covenant previously ratified by God, so as to make the promise void. For if the inheritance is the law, it is no longer by promise; but God gave it to Abraham by a promise.

19. Why then the law? It was added because of transgressions, till the offspring should come to whom the promise had been made; and it was ordained by angels through an intermediary. Now an intermediary implies more than one; but God is one.

21. Is the law then against the promises of God? Certainly not; for if a law had been given which could make alive, then righteousness would in-deed be by the law. But the scripture consigned all things to sin, that what was promised to faith in Jesus Christ might be given to those who believe.

23. Now before faith came, we were confined under the law, kept under restraint until faith should be revealed. So that the law was our custodian until Christ came, that we might be justified by faith. But now that faith has come, we are no longer under a custodian; for in Christ Jesus you are all sons of God, through faith. For as many of you as were baptized into Christ have put on Christ. There is neither Jew nor Greek, there is neither slave nor free, there is neither male nor female; for you are all one in Christ Jesus. And if you are Christ's, then you are Abraham's offspring, heirs ac-cording to promise.

CHAPTER IV

I mean that the heir, so long as he is a child, is no better than a slave, though he is the owner of all the estate; but he is under guardians and trustees until the date set by the father. So with us; when we were children, we were slaves to the elemental spirits of the universe. But when the time had fully come, God sent forth his Son, born of woman, born under the law, to redeem those who were under the law, so that we might receive adoption as sons. And because you are sons, God has sent the Spirit of his Son into our hearts, crying, "Abba! Father!" So through God you are no longer a slave but a son, and if a son then an heir.

8. Formerly, when you did not know God, you were in bondage to beings that by nature are no gods; but now that you have come to know God, or rather to be known by God, how can you turn back again to the weak and beggarly elemental spirits, whose slaves you want to be once more? You observe days, and months, and seasons, and years! I am afraid I have labored over you in vain.

12. Brethren, I beseech you, become as I am, for I also have become as you are. You did me no wrong; you knew it was because of a bodily ailment that I preached the gospel to you at first; and though my condition was a trial to you, you did not scorn or despise me, but received me as an angel of God, as Christ Jesus. What has become of the satisfaction you felt? For I bear you witness that, if possible, you would have plucked out your eyes and given them to me. Have I then become your enemy by telling you the truth? They make much of you, but for no good purpose; they want to shut you out, that you may make much of them. For a good purpose it is always good to be made much of, and not only when I am present with you. My little children, with whom I am again in travail until Christ be formed in you! I could wish to be present with you now and to change my tone, for I am perplexed about you.

21. Tell me, you who desire to be under law, do you not hear the law? For it is written that Abraham had two sons, one by a slave and one by a free woman. But the son of the slave was born according to the flesh, the son of the free woman through promise. Now this is an allegory: these women are two covenants. One is from Mount Sinai, bearing children for slavery; she is Hagar. Now Hagar is Mount Sinai in Arabia; she corresponds to the present Jerusalem, for she is in slavery with her children. But the Jerusalem above is free, and she is our mother. For it is written,

> "Rejoice, O barren one that dost not bear;
>   break forth and shout, thou who are not in travail;
>   for the desolate hath more children than she who hath a husband."

Now we, brethren, like Isaac, are children of promise. But as at that time he who was born according to the flesh persecuted him who was born according to the Spirit, so it is now. But what does the scripture say? "Cast out the slave and her son; for the son of the slave shall not inherit with the son of the free woman." So, brethren, we are not children of the slave but of the free woman.

CHAPTER V

For freedom Christ has set us free; stand fast therefore, and do not submit again to a yoke of slavery.

2. Now I, Paul, say to you that if you receive circumcision, Christ will be of no advantage to you. I testify again to every man who receives circumcision that he is bound to keep the whole law. You are severed from Christ, you who would be justified by the law; you have fallen away from grace. For through the Spirit, by faith, we wait for the hope of righteousness. For in Christ Jesus neither circumcision nor uncircumcision is of any avail, but faith working through love. You were running well; who hindered you from obeying the truth? This persuasion is not from him who called you. A little yeast leavens the whole lump. I have confidence in the Lord that you will take no other view than mine; and he who is troubling you will bear his judgment, whoever he is. But if I, brethren, still preach circumcision, why am I still persecuted? In that case the stumbling-block of the cross has been removed. I wish those who unsettle you would mutilate themselves!

13. For you were called to freedom, brethren; only do not use your freedom as an opportunity for the flesh, but through love be servants of one another. For the whole law is fulfilled in one word, "You shall love your neighbor as yourself." But if you bite and devour one another take heed that you are not consumed by one another.

16. But I say, walk by the Spirit, and do not gratify the desires of the flesh. For the desires of the flesh are against the Spirit, and the desires of the Spirit are against the flesh, for these are opposed to each other, to prevent you from doing what you would. But if you are led by the Spirit you are not under the law. Now the works of the flesh are plain: immorality, impurity, licentiousness, idolatry, sorcery, enmity, strife, jealousy, anger, selfishness, dissension, party spirit, envy, drunkenness, carousing, and the like. I warn you, as I warned you before, that those who do such things shall not inherit the kingdom of God. But the fruit of the Spirit is love, joy, peace, patience, kindness, goodness, faithfulness, gentleness, self-control; against such there is no law. And those who belong to Christ Jesus have crucified the flesh with its passions and desires.

25. If we live by the Spirit, let us also walk by the Spirit. Let us have no self-conceit, no provoking of one another, no envy of one another.

CHAPTER VI

Brethren, if a man is overtaken in any trespass, you who are spiritual should restore him in a spirit of gentleness. Look to yourself, lest you too be tempted. Bear one another's burdens, and so fulfil the law of Christ. For if any one thinks he is something, when he is nothing, he deceives himself. But let each one test his own work, and then his reason to boast will be in himself alone and not in his neighbor. For each man will have to bear his own load.

6. Let him who is taught the word share all good things with him who teaches.

7. Do not be deceived; God is not mocked, for whatever a man sows, that he will also reap. For he who sows to his own flesh will from the flesh reap corruption; but he who sows to the Spirit will from the Spirit reap eternal life. And let us not grow weary in well-doing, for in due season we shall reap, if we do not lose heart. So then, as we have opportunity, let us do good to all men, and especially to those who are of the household of faith.

11. See with what large letters I am writing to you with my own hand. It is those who want to make a good showing in the flesh that would compel you to be circumcised, and only in order that they may not be persecuted for the cross of Christ. For even those who receive circumcision do not themselves keep the law, but they desire to have you circumcised that they may glory in your flesh. But far be it from me to glory except in the cross of our Lord Jesus Christ, by which the world has been crucified to me, and I to the world. For neither circumcision counts for anything, nor uncircumcision, but a new creation. Peace and mercy be upon all who walk by this rule, upon the Israel of God.

17. Henceforth let no man trouble me; for I bear on my body the marks of Jesus.

18. The grace of our Lord Jesus Christ be with your spirit, brethren. Amen.

MOSES MAIMONIDES

M OSES BEN MAIMON (1135–1204) was born in Cordova. He was instructed by his father in the Bible, the Talmud, and mathematics; Arab teachers gave him his education in philosophy and the natural sciences, especially medicine.

About 1160 his family, with most of the rest of the Jewish community of Cordova, fled to Fez, in Morocco, to escape the pressure to convert to Islam. In Fez, too, the Jews were forced to attend the mosques, and in 1165 the family emigrated to Palestine and then to Egypt.

Maimonides set up as a physician in Old Cairo and gave public lectures on philosophy. In 1171 Sultan Saladin made Egypt a refuge for persecuted Jews. Maimonides' fame grew, both as a physician and, on the strength of his commentary on the *Mishnah* (1168), as a rabbinical authority. In 1180 appeared the great religious code, the *Mishnah Torah,* which unified the Talmud and explained the Law from the standpoint of Aristotelianism; in 1190 he finished his masterpiece, the *Moreh Nebuchim,* a philosophical defense of Judaism.

During the remainder of his life Maimonides was personal physician to Alafdel, the eldest son of Saladin, and he did much medical work, including treatises used for many generations in European medical schools.

Maimonides' philosophical writings are among those works which attempted to reconcile traditional religious teachings with reason, that is, with Aristotle; and like Averroës and Thomas Aquinas, his counterparts in Islam and the Christian world, he was bitterly opposed by many of his own faith. Nevertheless, all subsequent attempts to fix the basic doctrines of Judaism have proceeded from his work.

Although Maimonides lived a thousand years later than Paul, his Letter to Yemen is one of the clearest statements of the central beliefs of Judaism as answers to the claims of Christianity. It draws the distinction between Jew and Christian much more sharply and more directly than most previous Jewish literature. It makes clear the Jewish conceptions of righteousness and of the moral law that Pauline Christianity at various times claimed to have canceled, subsumed into itself, or universalized into a call for faith in Christ as the Messiah and for love for all men as equals before God.

The following selection is taken from Maimonides' *Epistle to Yemen,* translated by Boaz Cohen (New York, American Academy for Jewish Research, 1952).

THIS IS THE TEXT OF THE EPISTLE OF
R. MOSES b. MAIMON, RABBI
AND DAYYAN OF BLESSED MEMORY,
IN REPLY TO A LETTER FROM R. JACOB
OF YEMEN

To the honored, great, and holy Master and Teacher, Jacob, wise and genial, dear and revered sage, son of the honored, great, and holy Master and Teacher, Nathaniel Fayyumi, distinguished Prince of Yemen, president of its congregations, leader of its communities of Yemen. May the Lord keep and protect them. From a loving friend who never saw him but knows him only by reputation, Moses b. Maimon b. Joseph b. Isaac b. Obadiah of blessed memory.

Blessed be the Lord that He has suffered Jews to remain who observe the Torah and obey its injunctions in the most distant peninsulas, as we were graciously assured through Isaiah, His servant, for it is you the people of Yemen he was alluding to when he prophesied "From the uttermost part of the earth have we heard songs."

When your communication arrived in Egypt, dearly beloved friend, our ears were pleased at hearing it read, and the mere view of it was a feast to the eyes. It revealed that you were one of the ministers of the Lord who dwell in His fane, and are pitched at His standard; that you pursue the study of the Torah, love its laws, and watch at its gates. May the Lord divulge unto you its secrets, and stock you abundantly with the knowledge of its treasures, make its crown your chief crown, place its necklace upon your neck, and may its words be a lamp unto your feet, and a light unto your path, and through them may you become celebrated. "When all the people of the land will see that the name of the Lord is upon you they shall fear you."

You write that the rebel leader in Yemen decreed compulsory apostasy for the Jews by forcing the Jewish inhabitants of all the places he had subdued to desert the Jewish religion just as the Berbers had compelled them to do in Maghreb. Verily, this news has broken our backs and has astounded and dumbfounded the whole of our community. And rightly so. For these are evil tidings, "and whosoever heareth of them, both his ears tingle." Indeed, our hearts are weakened, our minds are confused, and the powers of the body wasted because of the dire misfortunes which brought religious persecutions upon us from the two ends of the world, the East and the West, "so that the enemies were in the midst of Israel, some on this side, and some on that side." The prophet upon learning of such difficult and dreadful times prayed and interceded in our behalf, as we read, "Then said I, O Lord God, cease, I beseech Thee: How shall Jacob stand? for he is small." Indeed, this is a subject which no religious man dare take lightly, nor any one who believes in Moses put aside. There can be no doubt that these are the Messianic travails concerning which the sages invoked God that they be spared seeing and experiencing them. Similarly the prophets trembled when they envisioned them as we learn from the words of Isaiah, "My heart panteth, fearfulness affrighteth me, the twilight I have longed for hath been turned for me into trembling." Note also the divine exclamation in the Torah expressing sympathy for those who will experience them, as we read, "Alas, who shall live when God doeth this!"

You write that the hearts of some people have turned away, uncertainty befalls them and their beliefs are weakened, while others have not lost faith nor have they become disquieted. Concerning this matter we have a divine premonition through Daniel who predicted that the prolonged stay of Israel in the Diaspora, and the continuous persecutions will cause many to drift away from our faith, to have misgivings, or to go astray, because they witnessed our feebleness, and noted the triumph of our adversaries and their dominion over us, while others would neither oscillate in their belief, nor be shaken in their convictions. This may be gathered from the verse, "Many shall purify themselves, make themselves white, and be refined, but the wicked shall do wickedly, and none of the wicked shall understand; but they that are wise shall understand." Further on he foretells that even men of understanding and intelligence who would have brooked milder misfortunes and remained firm in their belief in God and in His servant Moses, will yield to distrust and will err, when they are visited by sterner and harsher afflictions, while only a few will remain pure in faith as we read, "And some of them that are wise shall stumble."

And now, my co-religionists, it is essential for you all to give attention and consideration to that which I am going to point out to you. You should impress it upon the minds of your women and children, so that their faith which may be enfeebled and impaired may be strengthened, and that they be re-established in an unceasing belief. May the Lord deliver us and you from religious doubt!

Remember, that ours is the true and authentic Divine religion, revealed to us through Moses, the master of the former as well as the later prophets, by means of which God has distinguished us from the rest of mankind, as Scripture says, "Only the Lord had a delight in thy fathers to love them and He chose their seed after them, even you above all peoples." This did not happen because of our merits, but rather as an act of Divine grace, and on account of our forefathers who were cognizant of God and submitted to Him as we read, "The Lord did not set His love upon you, nor choose you because ye were more in number than any people . . . but because the Lord loved you, and because He would keep the oath which He swore unto your fathers." God has made us unique by His laws and precepts, and our pre-eminence is manifested in His rules and statutes, as Scripture says, in narrating God's mercies to us, "And what great nation is there, that hath statutes and ordinances so righteous as all this law, which I set before you this day?" Therefore all the nations instigated by envy and impiety rose up against us, and all the kings of the earth motivated by injustice and enmity applied themselves to persecute us. They wanted to thwart God, but He cannot be thwarted. Ever since the time of Revelation, every despot or slave that has attained to power, be he violent or ignoble, has made it his first aim and his final purpose to destroy our law, and to vitiate our religion, by means of the sword, by violence, or by brute force, such as Amalek, Sisera, Sennacherib, Nebuchadnezzar, Titus, Hadrian, may their bones be ground to dust, and others like them. This is one of the two classes which attempt to foil the divine will.

The second class consists of the most intelligent and educated among the nations, such as the Syrians, Persians, and Greeks. These also endeavor to demolish our law and to vitiate it by means of arguments which they invent, and by means of controversies which they institute. They seek to render the Law ineffectual and to wipe out every trace thereof by means of their polemical writings, just as the despots plan to do it with the sword. But neither the one nor the other shall succeed. We possess the divine assurance given to Isaiah concerning any tyrant that will wish to undermine our Law and to annihilate it by weapons of war, that the Lord will demolish them so that they will have no effect. This is only a metaphorical way of saying that his efforts will be of no avail, and that he will not accomplish his purpose. In like manner whenever a disputant shall attempt to demonstrate the falsity of our Law, the Lord will shatter his arguments and prove them absurd, untenable and ineffective. This divine promise is contained in the following verse, "No weapon that is formed against thee shall prosper; and every tongue that shall rise against thee in judgment thou shalt condemn."

Although the exponents of both methods persuade themselves that this is a structure which can be demolished, and they exert themselves to undermine its firmly established foundations, they only increase their pain and toil. The structure remains as firmly planted as ever, while the God of Truth mocks and derides them, because they endeavor, with their feeble intelligence, to achieve a goal that is beyond the powers of mortal man. The inspired writer describes their attempt and God's scorn of them in the following verses: "Let us break their bonds asunder, and cast away their words from us. He that sitteth in heaven laugheth, the Lord hath them in derision." Both of these parties have harassed and afflicted us incessantly throughout the epoch of our political independence, and partly during the period of our dispersion.

After that there arose a new sect which combined the two methods, namely, conquest and controversy, into one, because it believed that this procedure would be more effective in wiping out every trace of the Jewish nation and religion. It, therefore, resolved to lay claim to prophecy and to found a new faith, contrary to our Divine religion, and to contend that it was equally God-given. Thereby it hoped to raise doubts and to create confusion, since one is opposed to the other and both supposedly emanate from a Divine source, which would lead to the destruction of both religions. For such is the remarkable plan contrived by a man who is envious and querulous. He will strive to kill his enemy and to save his own life, but when he finds it impossible to attain his objective, he will devise a scheme whereby they both will be slain.

The first one to have adopted this plan was Jesus the Nazarene, may his bones be ground to dust. He was a Jew because his mother was a Jewess although his father was a Gentile. For in accordance with the principles of our law, a child born of a Jewess and a Gentile, or of a Jewess and a slave, is legitimate. Jesus is only figuratively termed an illegitimate child. He impelled people to believe that he was a prophet sent by God to clarify perplexities in the Torah, and that he was the Messiah that was predicted by each and every seer. He interpreted the Torah and its precepts in such a fashion as to lead to their total annulment, to the abolition of all its commandments and to the violation of its prohibitions. The sages, of blessed memory, having become aware of his plans before his reputation spread among our people, meted out fitting punishment to him.

Daniel had already alluded to him when he presaged the downfall of a wicked one and a heretic among the Jews who would endeavor to destroy the Law, claim prophecy for himself, make pretenses to miracles, and allege that he is the Messiah, as it is written, "Also the children of the impudent among thy people shall make bold to claim prophecy, but they shall fall."

Quite some time after, a religion appeared the origin of which is traced to him by the descendants of Esau, albeit it was not the intention of this person to establish a new faith. For he was innocuous to Israel, as neither individual nor groups were unsettled in their beliefs because of him, since his inconsistencies were so transparent to every one. Finally he was overpowered and put a stop to by us when he fell into our hands, and his fate is well known.

After him arose the Madman who emulated his precursor since he paved the way for him. But he added the further objective of procuring rule and submission, and he invented his well known religion. All of these men purposed to place their teachings on the same level with our divine religion. But only a simpleton who lacks knowledge of both would liken divine institutions to human practices. Our religion differs as much from other religions for which there are alleged resemblances as a living man endowed with the faculty of reason is unlike a statue which is ever so well carved out of marble, wood, bronze or silver. When a person ignorant of divine wisdom or of God's works sees the statue that superficially resembles a man in its contours, form, features, and color, he believes that the structure of the parts of a statue is like the constitution of a man, because he is deficient in understanding concerning the inner organization of both. But the informed person who knows the interior of both, is cognizant of the fact that the internal structure of the statue betrays no skillful workmanship at all, whereas the inward parts of man are truly marvellously made, a testimony to the wisdom of the Creator, such as the prolongation of the nerves in the muscles and their ramifications, the branching out of the sinews and their intersections and the network of their ligaments and their manner of growth, the articulations of the bones and the joints, the pulsating and non-pulsating blood vessels and their ramifications, the setting of the limbs into one another, the uncovered and covered parts, every one of these in proportion, in form and proper place.

Likewise, a person ignorant of the secret meaning of Scripture and the deeper significance of the Law, would be led to believe that our religion has something in common with another if he makes a comparison between the two. For he will note that in the Torah there are prohibitions and commandments, just as in other religions there are permitted and interdicted acts. Both contain a system of religious observances, positive and negative precepts, sanctioned by reward and punishment.

If he could only fathom the inner intent of the Law, then he would realize that the essence of the true divine religion lies in the deeper meaning of its positive and negative precepts, every one of which will aid man in his striving after perfection, and remove every impediment to the attainment of excellence. These commands will enable the throng and the élite to acquire moral and intellectual qualities each according to his ability. Thus the godly community becomes pre-eminent, reaching a twofold perfection. By the first perfection, I mean man's spending his life in this world under the most agreeable and congenial conditions. The second perfection would constitute the achievement of intellectual objectives, each in accordance with his native powers.

The tenets of the other religions which resemble those of Scripture have no deeper meaning, but are superficial imitations, copied from and patterned after it. They modelled their religions upon ours in order to glorify themselves, and indulge the fancy that they are similar to so and so. However, their counterfeiting is an open secret to the learned. Consequently they became objects of derision and ridicule just as one laughs and smiles at an ape when it imitates the actions of men.

This event was predicted in the divinely inspired prophecy of Daniel, according to which, in some future time a person would appear with a religion similar to the true one, with a book of Scripture and oral communications, who will arrogantly pretend that God had vouchsafed him a revelation, and that he held converse with Him, besides making other extravagant claims. Thus Daniel in his description of the rise of the Arabic kingdom after the fall of the Roman Empire, alluded to the appearance of the Madman and his victories over the Roman, Persian, and Byzantine empires in the vision concerning a horn which grew, became long and strong. This is clearly indicated in a verse that can be understood by the masses as well as by the select few. Since this interpretation is borne out by the facts of history, no other meaning can be given to the following verse: "I considered the horns, and, behold, there came among them another horn, a little one, before which three of the first horns were plucked up by the roots; and, behold, in this horn were eyes like the eyes of a man, and a mouth speaking great things."

Now consider how remarkably apt the symbolism is. Daniel says that he saw a small horn that was going up. When it became longer, even marvellously longer, it cast down before it three horns and behold in the side of the horn there were two eyes similar to the two eyes of man, and a mouth speaking wanton words. This obviously alludes to the person who will found a new religion similar to the divine law, and makes claims to a revelation of a Scripture, and to prophecy. He will furthermore endeavor to alter and abolish the Law, as it is said, "and he shall seek to change the seasons and the law."

Daniel was divinely informed that He would destroy this person notwithstanding his greatness and his long endurance together with the remaining adherents of his predecessors. For the three parties that warred
against us will ultimately perish, i.e., the one that sought to overpower us
with the sword, the second which strove to conquer us by arguments, as well
the third that founded a religion similar to ours.

Though they shall appear to be triumphant for a while, and be in the
ascendancy for a longer or shorter period of time, they shall not last nor
endure. We have a divine assurance from time immemorial that whenever
a decree of apostasy is passed against us, God will ultimately terminate it.
When King David inspired by the Holy Spirit and speaking in the name of
the community reflected, how many peoples ruled over Israel in the past,
and how many trials and tribulations they had undergone from the beginning of their history, and nevertheless were not exterminated, he was moved
to exclaim, "Much have they afflicted me from youth up; but they have not
prevailed against me."

My brethren, you all know that in the time of Nebuchadnezzar the
Wicked, the Jews were compelled to worship idols and none was spared
save Hananiah, Mishael and Azariah. Ultimately God destroyed Nebuchadnezzar, and put an end to his laws, and the religion of Truth came back
to its own.

Similarly during the Second Commonwealth when the wicked Greek
rulers gained control of Palestine, they instituted severe persecutions against
Israel in order to abolish the Torah. The Jews were compelled to profane
the Sabbath, and were forbidden to observe the rite of circumcision. Every
Jew was forced to write on his garment the words "we have no portion in
the Lord God of Israel," and also to engrave this sentence on the horns of
his ox and then plough with it. This state of affairs lasted about fifty-two
years. Finally, God brought to an end simultaneously their empire and
their laws.

The sages, of blessed memory, frequently allude to persecutions in the
following manner: "once the wicked government passed the following decree of persecution," or, "they decreed so and so." After a while God would
make the decree null and void by destroying the power which issued it.
It was this observation that led the rabbis of blessed memory to affirm that
persecutions are of short duration.

The divine assurance was given to Jacob our father, that his descendants
would survive the people who degraded and discomfited them as it is
written: "And thy seed shall be like the dust of the earth." That is to say,
although his offspring will be abased like dust that is trodden under foot,

they will ultimately emerge triumphant and victorious, and as the simile implies, just as the dust settles finally upon him who tramples upon it, and remains after him, so shall Israel outlive its persecutors.

The prophet Isaiah has long ago predicted that various peoples will succeed in vanquishing Israel and lording over them for some time. But that ultimately God will come to Israel's assistance and will put a stop to their woes and affliction as is suggested in the following verse: "A grievous vision is declared unto me; the treacherous one will deal treacherously, and the spoiler will spoil; Go up O Elam, besiege O Media! but ultimately the sighing thereof I shall make cease."

We are in possession of the divine assurance that Israel is indestructible and imperishable, and will always continue to be a pre-eminent community. As it is impossible for God to cease to exist, so is Israel's destruction and disappearance from the world unthinkable, as we read, "For I the Lord change not, and ye, O sons of Jacob, will not be consumed." Similarly He has avowed and assured us that it is unimaginable that He will reject us entirely even if we disobey Him, disregard His behests, as the prophet Jeremiah avers, "Thus saith the Lord: If heaven above can be measured, and the foundations of the earth searched out beneath, Then will I also cast off all the seed of Israel for all that they have done, saith the Lord." Indeed this very promise has already been given before through Moses our Teacher who says, "And yet for all that, when they are in the land of their enemies, I will not reject them, neither will I abhor them, to destroy them utterly, and to break My covenant with them; for I am the Lord their God."

Put your trust in the true promises of Scripture, brethren, and be not dismayed at the series of persecutions or the enemy's ascendency over us, or the weakness of our people. These trials are designed to test and purify us so that only the saints and the pious ones of the pure and undefiled lineage of Jacob will adhere to our religion and remain within the fold, as it is written, "And among the remnant are those whom the Lord shall call." This verse makes it clear that they are not numerous, being the descendants of those who were present on Mount Sinai, witnessed the divine Revelation, entered into the covenant of God, and undertook to do and obey as is signified in their saying, "we will do, and obey." They obligated not only themselves but also their descendants, as it is written, "to us and to our children forever." We have been given adequate divine assurance that not only did all the persons who were present at the Sinaitic Revelation believe in the prophecy of Moses in his Law, but that their descendants likewise would do so, until the end of time, as it is written, "Lo, I come unto thee in a thick cloud, that the people may hear when I speak with thee, and may also believe thee forever."

Consequently it is manifest that he who spurns the religion that was revealed at that theophany, is not an offspring of the folk who witnessed it. For our sages of blessed memory have insisted that they who entertain scruples concerning the divine message are not scions of the race that were present on Mount Sinai. May God guard us and you from doubt, and banish from our midst confusion, suspicion, which lead to it.

Now, my co-religionists in the Diaspora, it behooves you to hearten one another, the elders to guide the youth, and the leaders to direct the masses. Give your assent to the Truth that is immutable and unchangeable, and to the following postulates of a religion that shall never fail. God is one in a unique sense of the term, and Moses is His prophet and spokesman, and the greatest and most perfect of the seers. To him was vouchsafed by God what has never been vouchsafed to any prophet before him, nor will it be in the future. The entire Torah was divinely revealed to Moses of whom it was said, "with him do I speak mouth to mouth." It will neither be abrogated nor superseded, neither supplemented nor abridged. Never shall it be supplanted by another divine revelation containing positive and negative duties. Keep well in mind the Revelation on Sinai in accordance with the divine precept to perpetuate the memory of this occasion and not to allow it to fall into oblivion. Furthermore we were enjoined to impress this event upon the minds of our children, as it is written, "Only take heed to thyself, and keep thy soul diligently, lest thou forget the things which thine eyes saw, and lest they depart from thy heart all the days of thy life; but make them known unto thy children and thy children's children."

When a man finds it arduous to gain a livelihood in one country he emigrates to another. All the more is it incumbent upon a Jew who is restricted in the practice of his religion, to depart to another place. If he finds it impossible to leave that locality for the time being, he must not become careless and indulge with abandon in the desecration of the Sabbath and the dietary laws on the assumption that he is exempt from all religious obligation. It is the eternally inescapable duty, willy-nilly, of every one belonging to the stock of Jacob to abide by the Law. Nay, he exposes himself to punishment for the violation of each and every positive and negative precept. Let no man conclude that he may freely disregard the less important ceremonies without liability to penalty because he has committed under duress some major sins. For Jeroboam, son of Nebat, may his bones be ground to dust, was chastised not only for the sin of worshipping the calves and inciting Israel to do the same, but also for his failure to construct a booth on the Feast of Tabernacles. This is one of the fundamental principles of our religion. Understand it aright, teach it, and apply the principle widely.

In your letter you mention that the apostle has spurred on a number of people to believe that several verses in Scripture allude to the Madman, such as "bimeod meod," "be shined forth from Mount Paran," "a prophet from the midst of thee," and the promise to Ishmael "I will make him a great nation." These arguments have been rehearsed so often that they have become nauseating. It is not enough to declare that they are altogether feeble; nay, to cite as proofs these verses is ridiculous and absurd in the extreme. For these are not matters that can confuse the minds of anyone. Neither the untutored multitude nor the apostates themselves who delude others with them, believe in them or entertain any illusions about them. Their purpose in citing these verses is to win favor in the eyes of the Gentiles by demonstrating that they believe the statement of the Koran that Mohammed was mentioned in the Torah. But the Muslims themselves put no faith in their arguments, they neither accept nor cite them, because they are manifestly so fallacious. Inasmuch as the Muslims could not find a single proof in the entire Bible nor a reference or possible allusion to their prophet which they could utilize, they were compelled to accuse us saying, "You have altered the text of the Torah, and expunged every trace of the name of Mohammed therefrom." They could find nothing stronger than this ignominious argument the falsity of which is easily demonstrated to one and all by the following facts. First, Scripture was translated into Syriac, Greek, Persian and Latin hundreds of years before the appearance of Mohammed. Secondly, there is a uniform tradition as to the text of the Bible both in the East and the West, with the result that no differences in the text exist at all, not even in the vocalization, for they are all correct. Nor do any differences affecting the meaning exist. The motive for their accusation lies therefore, in the absence of any allusion to Mohammed in the Torah.

The phrase "a great nation" cited above does not connote a people in possession of prophecy or a Law, but merely one large in numbers just as in reference to idolaters Scripture says "nations greater and mightier than yourselves." Similarly, the phrase "bimeod meod" simply signifies "exceedingly." Were there any allusion in the verse to Mohammed, then it would have read "and I shall bless him bimeod meod," and whoever likes to hang on to a spider's web might then discover a reference to Mohammed therein. As it is, since Scripture says "I shall increase him bimeod meod," it can only denote an extravagant increment in numbers.

There is no question that the Divine assurance to Abraham to bless his descendants, to reveal the Torah to them, and to make them the Chosen People, refers only to the offspring of Isaac. For Ishmael is mentioned as an adjunct and appendage in the blessing of Isaac, which reads "and also of the

son of the bond-woman will I make a nation." This verse suggests that
Isaac holds a primary position and Ishmael a subordinate place. This point
is made even more explicit in the blessing which ignores Ishmael entirely.
"For in Isaac shall seed be called in thee." The meaning of God's promise
to Abraham is that the issue of Ishmael will be vast in numbers but neither
pre-eminent nor the object of divine favor, nor distinguished for the attainment of excellence. Not because of them will Abraham be famed or celebrated, but by the noted and illustrious scions of Isaac. The phrase "shall be
called" simply means, shall be renowned, as it does in the verse, "Let thy
name be called in them, and the name of my fathers Abraham and Isaac."
Other verses also indicate that when God promised Abraham that His law
would be vouchsafed to his children as is implied in the words "And I will be
their God," He meant Isaac to the exclusion of Ishmael as is intimated in the
declaration "But My covenant will I establish with Isaac." Similarly, Isaac
by bestowing the blessing of Abraham upon Jacob exclusively, debarred
Esau from it, as we read in his benediction "And may He give you the blessing of Abraham." To sum up, the Divine covenant made with Abraham to
grant the sublime Law to his descendants referred exclusively to those who
belonged to the stock of both Isaac and Jacob. Hence the prophet expresses
his gratitude to God for "the covenant which He made with Abraham, and
his oath unto Isaac, which He established unto Jacob for a statute, and to
Israel for an everlasting covenant."

Scripture prohibits us from making any amendments to the Law or
eliminating anything, for we read "Thou shalt not add thereto, nor diminish
from it." We pledged and obligated ourselves to God to abide by His Law,
we, our children, and our children's children, until the end of time as
Scripture says "The secret things belong to the Lord Our God, but the things
which are revealed belong unto us and to our children forever." Any
prophet, therefore, no matter what his pedigree is, be he priest, Levite, or
Amalekite, is perfidious even if he asserts that only one of the precepts of
the Torah is void, in view of the Mosaic pronouncement "unto us and
unto our children forever." Such a one we would declare a false prophet and
would execute him if we had jurisdiction over him. We would take no
notice of the miracles that he might perform, just as we would disregard
the wonder-working of one who seeks to lure people to idolatry, as we are
enjoined in the verse "And the sign or wonder came to pass . . . thou shalt
not hearken unto the words of that prophet." Since Moses, of blessed
memory, has prohibited image worship for all the time, we know that the
miracles of a would-be-seducer to idolatry are wrought by trickery and

sorcery. Similarly, since Moses has taught us that the Law is eternal, we stamp definitely as a prevaricator any one who argues that it was destined to be in force for a fixed duration of time, because he contravenes Moses. Consequently we pay no attention to his assertions or supernatural performances.

If a Jewish or Gentile prophet urges and encourages people to follow the religion of Moses without adding thereto or diminishing therefrom, like Isaiah, Jeremiah, and the others, we demand a miracle from him. If he can perform it we recognize him and bestow upon him the honor due to a prophet, but if he fails to do so, he is put to death. We require only a miracle as his credentials, although it may be wrought by stratagem or magic, just as we accept the evidence of witnesses although there is a possibility of perjury. For we are divinely commanded through Moses to render judgment in a suit at law in accordance with the testimony of two witnesses, the possibility of false swearing notwithstanding. Similarly we are enjoined to yield obedience to one who asserts that he is a prophet provided he can substantiate his claims by miracle or proofs, although there is a possibility that he is an impostor. However, if the would-be-prophet teaches tenets that negate the doctrines of Moses, then we must repudiate him. This point was made abundantly clear in the introduction to our large work on the commentary of the Mishnah, where you will find some useful information concerning principles which form the foundation of our religion, and the pillars of our faith.

It is incumbent upon you to know that the rule that nothing may ever be added to or diminished from the Laws of Moses, applies equally to the oral law, that is the traditional interpretation transmitted through the sages of blessed memory. Be cautious and on your guard lest any of the heretics, may they speedily perish! mingle among you, for they are worse than apostates. For although this country is, as you know, a place of scholars, students and schools, they indulge in bombastic talk and we warn our people against their occasional errors, heresies and mistakes. As for you, in this distant country, although you are scholars, learned in the law, and pious, you are few in number, may God increase your number and hasten the time of gathering you all together. If any of the heretics rises up to corrupt the people, they will undermine the faith of the young folks and they will not find a savior. Beware of them and know that it is permitted to slay them in our opinion for they repudiate the statement in the prophecy of

Moses who commanded us to act "According to the law which they shall teach thee, and according to the judgment which they shall tell thee thou shalt do." They assert in wicked defiance that they believe most firmly in the prophecy of Moses, as the Arabs and Byzantines say, yet they destroy and nullify his law and kill the adherents thereof. Whoever joins them is just like his seducer. We deemed it imperative to call your attention to these facts, and to raise the young generation on these tenets, because they are a pillar of faith!

It is, my co-religionists, one of the fundamental articles of the faith of Israel, that the future redeemer of our people will spring only from the stock of Solomon, son of David. He will gather our nation, assemble our exiles, redeem us from our degradation, propagate the true religion, and exterminate his opponents as is clearly stated in Scripture "I see him but not now, I behold him but not nigh, there shall step forth a star out of Jacob, and a sceptre shall arise out of Israel. And shall smite through the corners of Moab, and break down all the sons of Seth. And Edom shall be a possession, Seir also, even his enemies, shall be a possession, while Israel doeth valiantly." He will be sent by God at a time of great catastrophe and dire misfortune for Israel as was predicted in the verse "There will be none remaining, shut up or left at large." And when he appears, he will fulfill the promises made in his behalf. A later prophet too was alluding to the Messianic tribulations when he declared "But who can endure the day of his coming." This is the proper understanding of this article of faith.

How odd is your remark about this man [the false messiah of Yemen], that he is renowned for his meekness and a little wisdom as if these were indeed the attributes of the Messiah. Do these characteristics make him a Messiah? You were beguiled by him because you have not considered the pre-eminence of the Messiah, the manner and place of his appearance, and the marks whereby he is to be identified. The Messiah, indeed, ranks after Moses in eminence and distinction, and God has bestowed some gifts upon him which he did not bestow upon Moses, as may be gathered from the following verses: "His delight shall be in the fear of the Lord." "The Spirit of the Lord shall rest upon him." "And Righteousness shall be the girdle of his loins." Six appellations were divinely conferred upon him, as the following passage indicates: "For a child is born unto us, and a son is given unto us, and the government is upon his shoulder, and he is called Pele, Yoetz, El, Gibbor, Abiad, Sar-Shalom." And another verse alluding to the Messiah culminates in the following manner "Thou art my son, this day have I begotten thee." All these statements demonstrate the pre-eminence of the Messiah.

Transcendent wisdom is a sine qua non for inspiration. It is an article of our faith that the gift of prophecy is vouchsafed only to the wise, the strong, and the rich. Strong is defined as the ability to control one's passions. Rich signifies wealthy in knowledge. Now if we dare not put trust in a man's pretensions to prophecy, if he does not excel in wisdom, how much less must we take seriously the claims of an ignoramus to be the Messiah. That the man in question is a sciolist is evident from the order he issued, as you state, to the people to give away all their possessions for eleemosynary purposes. They did right in disobeying him, and he was wrong inasmuch as he disregarded the Jewish law concerning alms-giving. For Scripture says, "If a man will devote anything of all that he has" and the rabbis explain in their comment on this verse, "part of all that he has, but not all that he has," (Sifra ad locum). The sages accordingly set bounds to the bounty of the beneficent in an explicit statement which reads "He who is inclined to be liberal with the poor, may not part with more than a fifth of his possessions." There is no doubt that the process of reasoning which led him to claim that he is the Messiah, induced him to issue a command to his fellowmen to give away their property and distribute it to the poor. But then the affluent would become destitute and vice-versa. According to his ordinance, it would be necessary for the nouveaux riches to return their recently-acquired property to the newly impoverished. Such a regulation, which would keep property moving in a circle, is the acme of folly.

As to the place where the Messiah will make his first appearance, Scripture intimates that he will first present himself only in the Land of Israel, as we read, "He will suddenly appear in His Temple." As for the advent of the Messiah, nothing at all will be known about it before it occurs. The Messiah is not a person concerning whom it may be predicted that he will be the son of so and so, or of the family of so and so. On the contrary he will be unknown before his coming, but he will prove by means of miracles and wonders that he is the true Messiah. Scripture in allusion to his mysterious lineage says, "His name is the Shoot, and he will shoot up out of his place." Similarly, Isaiah referring to the arrival of the Messiah implies that neither his father nor mother, nor his kith nor kin will be known, "For he will shoot up right forth as a sapling, and as a root out of the dry ground." After his manifestation in Palestine, Israel will be gathered in Jerusalem and the other cities of Palestine. Then will the tidings spread to the East and the West until it will reach you in Yemen and those beyond you in India as we learn from Isaiah, "That sendeth ambassadors by the sea, even in vessels of papyrus upon the waters, go, ye swift messengers, to a nation that has been pulled and plucked to a people that suffered terribly from their beginning onward." The process of the final redemption will not be reversed so that it will first appear in distant lands, and ultimately reach Palestine.

You know that the Christians falsely ascribe marvelous powers to Jesus the Nazarene, may his bones be ground to dust, such as the resurrection of the dead and other miracles. Even if we would grant them for the sake of argument, we should not be convinced by their reasoning that Jesus is the Messiah. For we can bring a thousand proofs or so from the Scripture that it is not so even from their point of view. Indeed, will anyone arrogate this rank to himself unless he wishes to make himself a laughing stock?

AUGUSTINE

AUGUSTINE (354–430) was born in North Africa; his mother, Monica, represented a strong Christian influence in his life. He went to school in Carthage and during his youth became an advocate of Manichaeism. After teaching rhetoric at Rome, he went to Milan where, under the tutelage of Ambrose, bishop of Milan, he was converted to Christianity. As a priest and bishop of Hippo, Augustine devoted himself for most of his life to the practical and theoretical problems of attaining unity within the Christian Church. He died during the attack of the Vandals on Hippo.

Augustine wrote many treatises on the dogmas of Christian theology: the concept of the Trinity; the doctrine of apostolic succession; the duties of monastic orders; and the opposition to Pelagianism, which denies the concept of original sin that was basic in Augustinian theology. His *Confessions* (c.400) explains his conversion to Christianity and is an influential guide for the Christian mystic. The *City of God* (after 412) interprets history as the conflict between the eternal City of God and the temporal kingdom of Satan or the City of Earth (e.g., Rome), which is temporary as well as temporal.

The Augustinian philosophy is a compound of ideas taken from the teachings of Jesus of Nazareth, from the interpretation of the gospel by Paul of Tarsus, "the apostle to the Gentiles," from the theology of Manichaeism, and from the philosophy of Neoplatonism. Paul conceived the victory of the spirit to be possible only through the power of a transforming faith, and the brotherhood of all men in Christ was signalized, in the final analysis, by common initiation into the death and resurrection of the Savior and by mystic participation in Christ. The "errors" of Augustine's youth enriched this conception of Christianity. In the first place, he interpreted God in a Neoplatonic fashion as the One in Whom alone spirits can find rest, peace, and happiness. All Being emanates from Him and to Him all true beings return. Material bodies are the negation of being. This Neoplatonic doctrine is retained by Augustine side by side with vestiges of the Manichaean "error" of interpreting the universe as the struggle between two competing forces —good and evil.

For Augustine, the Church was the body ministering in this life to the needs revealed for the heavenly life. One part of his importance in the history of social and political institutions rests upon his formulation of the theory with which the Christian Church through subsequent centuries operated. It was the supreme authority for attaining salvation, and exercised through the sacraments almost a monopoly on the means of grace.

The following selections are from the *Enchiridion* (*Handbook*), translated by J. F. Shaw, and from the *City of God,* translated by Marcus Dods (Edinburgh, 1872). Both translations are from the Latin.

ENCHIRIDION

CHAPTER IX: WHAT WE ARE TO BELIEVE. IN REGARD TO NATURE IT IS NOT NECESSARY FOR THE CHRISTIAN TO KNOW MORE THAN THAT THE GOODNESS OF THE CREATOR IS THE CAUSE OF ALL THINGS

WHEN . . . THE QUESTION is asked what we are to believe in regard to religion, it is not necessary to probe into the nature of things, as was done by those whom the Greeks call *physici;* nor need we be in alarm lest the Christian should be ignorant of the force and number of the elements,—the motion, and order, and eclipses of the heavenly bodies; the form of the heavens; the species and the natures of animals, plants, stones, fountains, rivers, mountains; about chronology and distances; the signs of coming storms; and a thousand other things which those philosophers either have found out, or think they have found out. For even these men themselves, endowed though they are with so much genius, burning with zeal, abounding in leisure, tracking some things by the aid of human conjecture, searching into others with the aids of history and experience, have not found out all things; and even their boasted discoveries are oftener mere guesses than certain knowledge. It is enough for the Christian to believe that the only cause of all created things, whether heavenly or earthly, whether visible or invisible, is the goodness of the Creator, the one true God; and that nothing exists but Himself that does not derive its existence from Him; and that He is the Trinity—to wit, the Father, and the Son begotten of the Father, and the Holy Spirit proceeding from the same Father, but one and the same Spirit of Father and Son.

CHAPTER XXV: GOD'S JUDGMENTS UPON FALLEN MEN AND ANGELS. THE DEATH OF THE BODY IS MAN'S PECULIAR PUNISHMENT

. . . There is one form of punishment peculiar to man—the death of the body. God had threatened him with this punishment of death if he should sin, leaving him indeed to the freedom of his own will, but yet commanding his obedience under pain of death; and He placed him amid the happiness of Eden, as it were in a protected nook of life, with the intention that, if he preserved his righteousness, he should thence ascend to a better place.

CHAPTER XXVI: THROUGH ADAM'S SIN HIS WHOLE POSTERITY WERE COR-
RUPTED, AND WERE BORN UNDER THE PENALTY OF DEATH, WHICH HE
HAD INCURRED

Thence, after his sin, he was driven into exile, and by his sin the whole race of which he was the root was corrupted in him, and thereby subjected to the penalty of death. And so it happens that all descended from him, and from the woman who had led him into sin, and was condemned at the same time with him,—being the offspring of carnal lust on which the same punishment of disobedience was visited,—were tainted with the original sin, and were by it drawn through divers errors and sufferings into that last and endless punishment which they suffer in common with the fallen angels, their corrupters and masters, and the partakers of their doom. And thus "by one man sin entered into the world, and death by sin; and so death passed upon all men, for that all have sinned." By "the world" the apostle, of course, means in this place the whole human race.

CHAPTER XXVII: THE STATE OF MISERY TO WHICH ADAM'S SIN REDUCED
MANKIND, AND THE RESTORATION EFFECTED THROUGH THE MERCY OF
GOD

Thus, then, matters stood. The whole mass of the human race was under condemnation, was lying steeped and wallowing in misery, and was being tossed from one form of evil to another, and, having joined the faction of the fallen angels, was paying the well-merited penalty of that impious rebellion. For whatever the wicked freely do through blind and unbridled lust, and whatever they suffer against their will in the way of open punishment, this all evidently pertains to the just wrath of God. But the goodness of the Creator never fails either to supply life and vital power to the wicked angels (without which their existence would soon come to an end); or, in the case of mankind, who spring from a condemned and corrupt stock, to impart form and life to their seed, to fashion their members, and through the various seasons of their life, and in the different parts of the earth, to quicken their senses, and bestow upon them the nourishment they need. For He judged it better to bring good out of evil, than not to permit any evil to exist. And if He had determined that in the case of men, as in the case of the fallen angels, there should be no restoration to happiness, would it not have been quite just, that the being who rebelled against God, who in the abuse of his freedom spurned and transgressed the command of his Creator when he could so easily have kept it, who defaced in himself the image of his Creator by stubbornly turning away from His light, who by an evil use of his free-will broke away from his wholesome bondage to the Creator's laws, —would it not have been just that such a being should have been wholly and to all eternity deserted by God, and left to suffer the everlasting punishment he had so richly earned? Certainly so God would have done, had He been only just and not also merciful, and had He not designed that His unmerited mercy should shine forth the more brightly in contrast with the unworthiness of its objects.

CHAPTER XXX: MEN ARE NOT SAVED BY GOOD WORKS, NOR BY THE FREE DETERMINATION OF THEIR OWN WILL, BUT BY THE GRACE OF GOD THROUGH FAITH

But this part of the human race to which God has promised pardon and a share in His eternal kingdom, can they be restored through the merit of their own works? God forbid. For what good work can a lost man perform, except so far as he has been delivered from perdition? Can they do anything by the free determination of their own will? Again I say, God forbid. For it was by the evil use of his free-will that man destroyed both it and himself. For, as a man who kills himself must, of course, be alive when he kills himself, but after he has killed himself ceases to live, and cannot restore himself to life; so, when man by his own free-will sinned, then sin being victorious over him, the freedom of his will was lost. "For of whom a man is overcome, of the same is he brought in bondage." This is the judgment of the Apostle Peter. And as it is certainly true, what kind of liberty, I ask, can the bond-slave possess, except when it pleases him to sin? For he is freely in bondage who does with pleasure the will of his master. Accordingly, he who is the servant of sin is free to sin. And hence he will not be free to do right, until, being freed from sin, he shall begin to be the servant of righteousness. And this is true liberty, for he has pleasure in the righteous deed; and it is at the same time a holy bondage, for he is obedient to the will of God. But whence comes this liberty to do right to the man who is in bondage and sold under sin, except he be redeemed by Him who has said, "If the Son shall make you free, ye shall be free indeed?" And before this redemption is wrought in a man, when he is not yet free to do what is right, how can he talk of the freedom of his will and his good works, except he be inflated by that foolish pride of boasting which the apostle restrains when he says, "By grace are ye saved, through faith."

CHAPTER XXXI: FAITH ITSELF IS THE GIFT OF GOD; AND GOOD WORKS WILL NOT BE WANTING IN THOSE WHO BELIEVE

And lest men should arrogate to themselves the merit of their own faith at least, not understanding that this too is the gift of God, this same apostle, who says in another place that he had "obtained mercy of the Lord to be faithful," here also adds: "and that not of yourselves; it is the gift of God: not of works, lest any man should boast." And lest it should be thought that good works will be wanting in those who believe, he adds further: "For we are His workmanship, created in Christ Jesus unto good works, which God hath before ordained that we should walk in them." We shall be made truly free, then, when God fashions us, that is, forms and creates us anew, not as men—for He has done that already—but as good men, which His grace is now doing, that we may be a new creation in Christ Jesus, according as it is said: "Create in me a clean heart, O God." For God had already created his heart, so far as the physical structure of the human heart is concerned; but the psalmist prays for the renewal of the life which was still lingering in his heart.

CHAPTER XXXII: THE FREEDOM OF THE WILL IS ALSO THE GIFT OF GOD, FOR GOD WORKETH IN US BOTH TO WILL AND TO DO

And further, should any one be inclined to boast, not indeed of his works, but of the freedom of his will, as if the first merit belonged to him, this very liberty of good action being given to him as a reward he had earned, let him listen to this same preacher of grace, when he says: "For it is God which worketh in you, both to will and to do of His own good pleasure"; and in another place: "So, then, it is not of him that willeth, nor of him that runneth, but of God that showeth mercy." Now as, undoubtedly, if a man is of the age to use his reason, he cannot believe, hope, love, unless he will to do so, nor obtain the prize of the high calling of God unless he voluntarily run for it; and what sense is it "not of him that willeth, nor of him that runneth, but of God that showeth mercy," except that, as it is written, "the preparation of the heart is from the Lord?" . . . The true interpretation of the saying, "It is not of him that willeth, nor of him that runneth, but of God that showeth mercy," is that the whole work belongs to God, who both makes the will of man righteous, and thus prepares it for assistance, and assists it when it is prepared. For the man's righteousness of will precedes many of God's gifts, but not all; and it must itself be included among those which it does not precede. We read in Holy Scripture, both that God's mercy "shall meet me," and that His mercy "shall follow me." It goes before the un-

willing to make him willing; it follows the willing to make his will effectual.
Why are we taught to pray for our enemies, who are plainly unwilling to
lead a holy life, unless that God may work willingness in them? And why
are we ourselves taught to ask that we may receive, unless that He who has
created in us the wish, may Himself satisfy the wish? We pray, then, for our
enemies, that the mercy of God may prevent them, as it has prevented us:
we pray for ourselves that His mercy may follow us.

CHAPTER XLV: IN ADAM'S FIRST SIN, MANY KINDS OF SIN WERE INVOLVED

However, even in that one sin, which "by one man entered into the world,
and so passed upon all men," and on account of which infants are baptized,
a number of distinct sins may be observed, if it be analyzed as it were
into its separate elements. For there is in it pride, because man chose to be
under his own dominion, rather than under the dominion of God; and
blasphemy, because he did not believe God; and murder, for he brought
death upon himself; and spiritual fornication, for the purity of the human
soul was corrupted by the seducing blandishments of the serpent; and theft,
for man turned to his own use the food he had been forbidden to touch; and
avarice, for he had a craving for more than should have been sufficient for
him; and whatever other sin can be discovered on careful reflection to be involved in this one admitted sin.

CHAPTER L: CHRIST TOOK AWAY NOT ONLY THE ONE ORIGINAL SIN, BUT
ALL THE OTHER SINS THAT HAVE BEEN ADDED TO IT

. . . The first man brought one sin into the world, but this man took
away not only that one sin, but all that He found added to it. Hence the
apostle says: "And not as it was by one that sinned, so is the gift: for the
judgment was by one to condemnation, but the free gift is of many offenses
unto justification." For it is evident that the one sin which we bring with us
by nature would, even if it stood alone, bring us under condemnation; but the
free gift justifies man from many offenses: for each man, in addition to the
one sin which, in common with all his kind, he brings with him by nature,
has committed many sins that are strictly his own. . . .

CHAPTER LVI: THE HOLY SPIRIT AND THE CHURCH. THE CHURCH IS THE
TEMPLE OF GOD

And now, having spoken of Jesus Christ, the only Son of God, our Lord,
with the brevity suitable to a confession of our faith, we go on to say that we
believe also in the Holy Ghost,—thus completing the Trinity which constitutes the Godhead. Then we mention the Holy Church. And thus we are

made to understand that the intelligent creation, which constitutes the free Jerusalem, ought to be subordinate in the order of speech to the Creator, the Supreme Trinity: for all that is said of the man Christ Jesus has reference, of course, to the unity of the person of the Onlybegotten. Therefore the true order of the Creed demanded that the Church should be made subordinate to the Trinity, as the house to Him who dwells in it, the temple to God who occupies it, and the city to its builder. And we are here to understand the whole Church, not that part of it only which wanders as a stranger on the earth, praising the name of God from the rising of the sun to the going down of the same, and singing a new song of deliverance from its old captivity; but that part also which has always from its creation remained steadfast to God in heaven, and has never experienced the misery consequent upon a fall. This part is made up of the holy angels, who enjoy uninterrupted happiness; and (as it is bound to do) it renders assistance to the part which is still wandering among strangers: for these two parts shall be one in the fellowship of eternity, and now they are one in the bonds of love, the whole having been ordained for the worship of the one God. Wherefore, neither the whole Church, nor any part of it, has any desire to be worshipped instead of God, nor to be God to any one who belongs to the temple of God —that temple which is built up of the saints who were created by the uncreated God. . . . The temple of God, then, that is, of the Supreme Trinity as a whole, is the Holy Church, embracing in its full extent both heaven and earth.

CHAPTER LXV: GOD PARDONS SINS, BUT ON CONDITION OF PENITENCE, CERTAIN TIMES FOR WHICH HAVE BEEN FIXED BY THE LAW OF THE CHURCH

. . . Crimes themselves, however great, may be remitted in the Holy Church; and the mercy of God is never to be despaired of by men who truly repent, each according to the measure of his sin. And in the act of repentance, where a crime has been committed of such a nature as to cut off the sinner from the body of Christ, we are not to take account so much of the measure of time as of the measure of sorrow; for a broken and a contrite heart God does not despise. But as the grief of one heart is frequently hid from another, and is not made known to others by words or other signs, when it is manifest to Him of whom it is said, "My groaning is not hid from Thee," those who govern the Church have rightly appointed times of penitence, that the Church in which the sins are remitted may be satisfied; and outside the Church sins are not remitted. For the Church alone has received the pledge of the Holy Spirit, without which there is no remission of sins—such, at least, as brings the pardoned to eternal life.

CHAPTER LXI: THE PARDON OF SIN HAS REFERENCE CHIEFLY TO THE FU-
TURE JUDGMENT

Now the pardon of sin has reference chiefly to the future judgment. For, as far as this life is concerned, the saying of Scripture holds good: "A heavy yoke is upon the sons of Adam, from the day that they go out of their mother's womb, till the day that they return to the mother of all things." So that we see even infants, after baptism and regeneration, suffering from the infliction of divers evils: and thus we are given to understand, that all that is set forth in the sacraments of salvation refers rather to the hope of future good, than to the retaining or attaining of present blessings. For many sins seem in this world to be overlooked and visited with no punishment, whose punishment is reserved for the future (for it is not in vain that the day when Christ shall come as Judge of quick and dead is peculiarly named the day of judgment); just as, on the other hand, many sins are punished in this life, which nevertheless are pardoned, and shall bring down no punishment in the future life.

CHAPTER XCVIII: PREDESTINATION TO ETERNAL LIFE IS WHOLLY OF GOD'S
FREE GRACE

And, moreover, who will be so foolish and blasphemous as to say that God cannot change the evil wills of men, whichever, whenever, and wheresoever He chooses, and direct them to what is good? But when He does this, He does it of mercy; when He does it not, it is of justice that He does it not; for "He hath mercy on whom He will have mercy, and whom He will He hardeneth." And when the apostle said this, he was illustrating the grace of God, in connection with which he had just spoken of the twins in the womb of Rebecca, "who being not yet born, neither having done any good or evil, that the purpose of God according to election might stand, not of works, but of Him that calleth, it was said unto her, The elder shall serve the younger." And in reference to this matter he quotes another prophetic testimony: "Jacob have I loved, but Esau have I hated." But perceiving how what he had said might affect those who could not penetrate by their understanding the depth of this grace: "What shall we say then?" he says: "Is there unrighteousness with God? God forbid." For it seems unjust that, in the absence of any merit or demerit, from good or evil works, God should love the one and hate the other. Now, if the apostle had wished us to understand that there were future good works of the one, and evil works of the other, which of course God foreknew, he would never have said, "not of works," but, "of future works," and in that way would have solved the difficulty, or rather there would then have been no difficulty to solve. As it is, however, after answering, "God forbid"; that is, God forbid that there should be unrighteousness with God; he goes on to prove that there is no unrighteousness in God's doing this, and says: "For He saith to Moses, I will have mercy on whom I have mercy, and I will have compassion on whom I will have compassion." Now, who but a fool would think that God was unrighteous, either in inflicting penal justice on those who had earned it, or in extending mercy to the unworthy? Then he draws his conclusion: "So then it is not of him that willeth, nor of him that runneth, but of God that showeth mercy." Thus both the twins were born children of wrath, not on account of any works of their own, but because they were bound in the fetters of that original condemnation which came through Adam. But He who said, "I will have mercy on whom I will have mercy," loved Jacob of His undeserved grace, and hated Esau of His deserved judgment. And as this judgment was due to both, the former learnt from the case of the latter that the fact of the same punishment not falling upon himself gave him no room to glory in any merit of his own, but only in the riches of the divine grace; because "it is not of him that willeth, nor of him that runneth, but of God that showeth mercy." And indeed the whole face, and, if I may use the expression, every lineament of the countenance of Scripture conveys by a very profound analogy this wholesome warning to every one who looks carefully into it, that he who glories should glory in the Lord.

CHAPTER XCIX: AS GOD'S MERCY IS FREE, SO HIS JUDGMENTS ARE JUST, AND CANNOT BE GAINSAID

Now after commending the mercy of God, saying, "So it is not of him that willeth, nor of him that runneth, but of God that showeth mercy," that he might commend His justice also (for the man who does not obtain mercy finds, not iniquity, but justice, there being no iniquity with God), he immediately adds: "For the scripture saith unto Pharaoh, Even for this same purpose have I raised thee up, that I might show my power in thee, and that my name might be declared throughout all the earth." And then he draws a conclusion that applies to both, that is, both to His mercy and His justice: "Therefore hath He mercy on whom He will have mercy, and whom He will He hardeneth." "He hath mercy" of His great goodness, "He hardeneth" without any injustice; so that neither can he that is pardoned glory in any merit of his own, nor he that is condemned complain of anything but his own demerit. For it is grace alone that separates the redeemed from the lost, all having been involved in one common perdition through their common origin. Now if any one, on hearing this, should say, "Why doth He yet find

fault? for who hath resisted His will?" as if a man ought not to be blamed
for being bad, because God hath mercy on whom He will have mercy, and
whom He will He Hardeneth, God forbid that we should be ashamed to
answer as we see the apostle answered: "Nay, but, O man, who art thou
that repliest against God? Shall the thing formed say to Him that formed it,
Why hast Thou made me thus? Hath not the potter power over the clay, of
the same lump to make one vessel unto honor, and another unto dishonor?"
Now some foolish people think that in this place the apostle had no answer
to give; and for want of a reason to render, rebuked the presumption of his
interrogator. But there is great weight in this saying: "Nay, but, O man, who
art thou?" and in such a matter as this it suggests to a man in a single word
the limits of his capacity, and at the same times does in reality convey an
important reason. For if a man does not understand these matters, who is he
that he should reply against God? And if he does understand them, he finds
no further room for reply. For then he perceives that the whole human race
was condemned in its rebellious head by a divine judgment so just, that if not
a single member of the race had been reedeemed, no one could justly have
questioned the justice of God; and that it was right that those who are redeemed should be redeemed in such a way as to show, by the greater number who are unredeemed and left in their just condemnation, what the whole
race deserved, and whither the deserved judgment of God would lead even
the redeemed, did not His undeserved mercy interpose, so that every mouth
might be stopped of those who wish to glory in their own merits, and that he
that glorieth might glory in the Lord."

CHAPTER CXVII: LOVE, WHICH IS GREATER THAN FAITH AND HOPE, IS SHED
    ABROAD IN OUR HEARTS BY THE HOLY GHOST

And now as to *love,* which the apostle declares to be greater than the other
two graces, that is, than faith and hope, the greater the measure in which it
dwells in a man, the better is the man in whom it dwells. For when there
is a question as to whether a man is good, one does not ask what he believes,
or what he hopes, but what he loves. For the man who loves aright no doubt
believes and hopes aright; whereas the man who has not love believes in
vain, even though his beliefs are true; and hopes in vain, even though the
objects of his hope are a real part of true happiness; unless, indeed, he believes and hopes for this, that he may obtain by prayer the blessing of love.
For, although it is not possible to hope without love, it may yet happen that a
man does not love that which is necessary to the attainment of his hope; as,
for example, if he hopes for eternal life (and who is there that does not desire
this?) and yet does not love righteousness, without which no one can attain

to eternal life. Now this is the true faith of Christ which the apostle speaks of, "which worketh by love"; and if there is anything that it does not yet embrace in its love, asks that it may receive, seeks that it may find, and knocks that it may be opened unto it. For faith obtains through prayer that which the law commands. For without the gift of God, that is, without the Holy Spirit, through whom love is shed abroad in our hearts, the law can command, but it cannot assist; and, moreover, it makes a man a transgressor, for he can no longer excuse himself on the plea of ignorance. Now carnal lust reigns where there is not the love of God. . . .

CHAPTER CXXI: LOVE IS THE END OF ALL THE COMMANDMENTS, AND GOD
HIMSELF IS LOVE

All the commandments of God, then, are embraced in love, of which the apostle says: "Now the end of the commandment is charity, out of a pure heart, and of a good conscience, and of faith unfeigned." Thus the end of every commandment is charity, that is, every commandment has love for its aim. But whatever is done either through fear of punishment or from some other carnal motive, and has not for its principle that love which the Spirit of God sheds abroad in the heart, is not done as it ought to be done, however it may appear to men. For this love embraces both the love of God and the love of our neighbor, and "on these two commandments hang all the law and the prophets." We may add the Gospel and the apostles. For it is from these that we hear this voice: The end of the commandment is charity, and God is love. Wherefore, all God's commandments, one of which is "Thou shalt not commit adultery," and all those precepts which are not commandments but special counsels, one of which is, "It is good for a man not to touch a woman," are rightly carried out only when the motive principle of action is the love of God, and the love of our neighbor in God. And this applies both to the present and the future life. We love God now by faith, then we shall love Him through sight. Now we love even our neighbor by faith; for we who are ourselves mortal know not the hearts of mortal men. But in the future life, the Lord "both will bring to light the hidden things of darkness, and will make manifest the counsels of the hearts, and then shall every man have praise of God"; for every man shall love and praise in his neighbor the virtue which, that it may not be hid, the Lord Himself shall bring to light. Moreover, lust diminishes as love grows, till the latter grows to such a height that it can grow no higher here. For "greater love hath no man than this, that a man lay down his life for his friends." Who then can tell how great love shall be in the future world, when there shall be no lust for it to restrain and conquer? For that will be the perfection of health when there shall be no struggle with death.

THE CITY OF GOD

Book I

PREFACE

The glorious city of God is my theme in this work, which you, my dearest son Marcellinus, suggested, and which is due to you by my promise. I have undertaken its defence against those who prefer their own gods to the Founder of this city—a city surpassingly glorious, whether we view it as it still lives by faith in this fleeting course of time, and sojourns as a stranger in the midst of the ungodly, or as it shall dwell in the fixed stability of its eternal seat, which it now with patience waits for, expecting until "righteousness shall return unto judgment," and it obtain, by virtue of its excellence, final victory and perfect peace. A great work this, and an arduous; but God is my helper. For I am aware what ability is requisite to persuade the proud how great is the virtue of humility, which raises us, not by a quite human arrogance, but by a divine grace, above all earthly dignities that totter on this shifting scene. For the King and Founder of this city of which we speak, has in Scripture uttered to His people a dictum of the divine law in these words: "God resisteth the proud, but giveth grace unto the humble." But this, which is God's prerogative, the inflated ambition of a proud spirit also affects, and dearly loves that this be numbered among its attributes, to

"Show pity to the humbled soul.
And crush the sons of pride." [1]

And therefore, as the plan of this work we have undertaken requires, and as occasion offers, we must speak also of the earthly city, which, though it be mistress of the nations, is itself ruled by its lust of rule.

CHAPTER I

For to this earthly city belong the enemies against whom I have to defend the city of God. Many of them, indeed, being reclaimed from their ungodly error, have become sufficiently creditable citizens of this city; but many are so inflamed with hatred against it, and are so ungrateful to its Redeemer for His signal benefits, as to forget that they would now be un-

[1] Virgil *Aeneid* vi.854. The renderings of Virgil are from Conington.

able to utter a single word to its prejudice, had they not found in its sacred places, as they fled from the enemy's steel, that life in which they now boast themselves. Are not those very Romans, who were spared by the barbarians through this respect for Christ, become enemies to the name of Christ? The reliquaries of the martyrs and the churches of the apostles bear witness to this; for in the sack of the city they were open sanctuary for all who fled to them, whether Christian or Pagan. To their very threshold the bloodthirsty enemy raged; there his murderous fury owned a limit. Thither did such of the enemy as had any pity convey those to whom they had given quarter, lest any less mercifully disposed might fall upon them. And, indeed, when even those murderers who everywhere else showed themselves pitiless came to those spots where that was forbidden which the licence of war permitted in every other place, their furious rage for slaughter was bridled, and their eagerness to take prisoners was quenched. Thus escaped multitudes who now reproach the Christian religion, and impute to Christ the ills that have befallen their city; but the preservation of their own life—a boon which they owe to the respect entertained for Christ by the barbarians—they attribute not to our Christ, but to their own good luck. They ought rather, had they any right perceptions, to attribute the severities and hardships inflicted by their enemies, to that divine providence which is wont to reform the depraved manners of men by chastisement, and which exercises with similar afflictions the righteous and praiseworthy—either translating them, when they have passed through the trial, to a better world, or detaining them still on earth for ulterior purposes. And they ought to attribute it to the spirit of these Christian times, that, contrary to the custom of war, these bloodthirsty barbarians spared them, and spared them for Christ's sake, whether this mercy was actually shown in promiscuous places, or in those places specially dedicated to Christ's name, and of which the very largest were selected as sanctuaries, that full scope might thus be given to the expansive compassion which desired that a large multitude might find shelter there. Therefore ought they to give God thanks, and with sincere confession flee for refuge to His name, that so they may escape the punishment of eternal fire—they who with lying lips took upon them this name, that they might escape the punishment of present destruction. For of those whom you see insolently and shamelessly insulting the servants of Christ, there are numbers who would not have escaped that destruction and slaughter had they not pretended that they themselves were Christ's servants. Yet now, in ungrateful pride and most impious madness, and at the risk of being punished in everlasting darkness, they perversely oppose that name under which they fraudulently protected themselves for the sake of enjoying the light of this brief life.

CHAPTER II

There are histories of numberless wars, both before the building of Rome and since its rise and the extension of its dominion: let these be read, and let one instance be cited in which, when a city had been taken by foreigners, the victors spared those who were found to have fled for sanctuary to the temples of their gods; [2] or one instance in which a barbarian general gave orders that none should be put to the sword who had been found in this or that temple. Did not Aeneas see

> "Dying Priam at the shrine,
> Staining the hearth he made divine?" [3]

Did not Diomedes and Ulysses

> "Drag with red hands, the sentry slain,
> Her fateful image from your fane,
> Her chaste locks touch, and stain with gore
> The virgin coronal she wore?" [4]

Neither is that true which follows, that

> "Thenceforth the tide of fortune changed,
> And Greece grew weak." [5]

For after this they conquered and destroyed Troy with fire and sword; after this they beheaded Priam as he fled to the altars. Neither did Troy perish because it lost Minerva. For what had Minerva herself first lost, that she should perish? Her guards perhaps? No doubt; just her guards. For as soon as they were slain, she could be stolen. It was not, in fact, the men who were preserved by the image, but the image by the men. How, then, was she invoked to defend the city and the citizens, she who could not defend her own defenders?

CHAPTER III

And these be the gods to whose protecting care the Romans were delighted to entrust their city! O too, too piteous mistake! And they are enraged at us when we speak thus about their gods, though, so far from being enraged at their own writers, they part with money to learn what they say; and, indeed, the very teachers of these authors are reckoned worthy of a

[2] The Benedictine remind us that Alexander and Xenophon, at least on some occasions, did so.
[3] Virgil *Aeneid* ii.501–2.   [4] *Aeneid* ii.166.   [5] *Ibid.*

salary from the public purse, and of other honours. There is Virgil, who is read by boys, in order that this great poet, this most famous and approved of all poets, may impregnate their virgin minds, and may not readily be forgotten by them, according to that saying of Horace,

> "The fresh cask long keeps its first tang." [6]

Well, in this Virgil, I say, Juno is introduced as hostile to the Trojans, and stirring up Aeolus, the king of the winds, against them in the words,

> "A race I hate now ploughs the sea,
> Transporting Troy to Italy,
> And home-gods conquered . . ." [7]

And ought prudent men to have entrusted the defence of Rome to these conquered gods? But it will be said, this was only the saying of Juno, who, like an angry woman, did not know what she was saying. What, then, says Aeneas himself—Aeneas who is so often designated "pious"? Does he not say,

> "Lo! Panthus, 'scaped from death by flight,
> Priest of Apollo on the height,
> His conquered gods with trembling hands
> He bears, and shelter swift demands?" [8]

Is it not clear that the gods (whom he does not scruple to call "conquered") were rather entrusted to Aeneas than he to them, when it is said to him,

> "The gods of her domestic shrines
> Your country to your care consigns?" [9]

If, then, Virgil says that the gods were such as these, and were conquered, and that when conquered, they could not escape except under the protection of a man, what madness is it to suppose that Rome had been wisely entrusted to these guardians, and could not have been taken unless it had lost them! Indeed, to worship conquered gods as protectors and champions, what is this but to worship, not good divinities, but evil omens? Would it not be wiser to believe, not that Rome would never have fallen into so great a calamity had not they first perished, but rather that they would have perished long since had not Rome preserved them as long as she could? For who does not see, when he thinks of it, what a foolish assumption it is that they could not be vanquished under vanquished defenders, and that they only perished because they had lost their guardian gods, when, indeed, the only cause of their perishing was that they chose for their protectors gods condemned to perish? The poets, therefore, when they com-

[6] Horace *Epistles* I.ii.69.   [7] *Aeneid* i.71.   [8] *Aeneid* ii.319.   [9] *Aeneid* ii.293.

posed and sang these things about the conquered gods, had no intention
to invent falsehoods, but uttered, as honest men, what the truth extorted
from them. This, however, will be carefully and copiously discussed in
another and more fitting place. Meanwhile I will briefly, and to the best of
my ability, explain what I meant to say about these ungrateful men who
blasphemously impute to Christ the calamities which they deservedly suffer
in consequence of their own wicked ways, while that which is for Christ's
sake spared them in spite of their wickedness they do not even take the
trouble to notice; and in their mad and blasphemous insolence, they use
against His name those very lips wherewith they falsely claimed that same
name that their lives might be spared. In the places consecrated to Christ,
where for His sake no enemy would injure them, they restrained their
tongues that they might be safe and protected; but no sooner do they emerge
from these sanctuaries, than they unbridle these tongues to hurl against Him
curses full of hate.

CHAPTER IV

Troy itself, the mother of the Roman people, was not able, as I have said,
to protect its own citizens in the sacred places of their gods from the fire and
sword of the Greeks, though the Greeks worshipped the same gods. Not only
so, but

> "Phoenix and Ulysses fell
> In the void courts by Juno's cell
>   Were set the spoil to keep;
> Snatched from the burning shrines away,
> There Ilium's mighty treasure lay,
> Rich altars, bowls of massy gold,
> And captive raiment, rudely rolled
>   In one promiscuous heap;
> While boys and matrons, wild with fear,
> In long array were standing near." [10]

In other words, the place consecrated to so great a goddess was chosen, not
that from it none might be led out a captive, but that in it all the captives
might be immured. Compare now this "asylum"—the asylum not of an
ordinary god, not of one of the rank and file of gods, but of Jove's own sister
and wife, the queen of all the gods—with the churches built in memory of
the apostles. Into it were collected the spoils rescued from the blazing
temples and snatched from the gods, not that they might be restored to the
vanquished, but divided among the victors; while into these was carried

[10] Virgil *Aeneid* ii.761.

back, with the most religious observance and respect, everything which belonged to them, even though found elsewhere. There liberty was lost; here preserved. Their bondage was strict; here strictly excluded. Into that temple men were driven to become the chattels of their enemies, now lording it over them; into these churches men were led by their relenting foes, that they might be at liberty. In fine, the gentle Greeks appropriated that temple of Juno to the purposes of their own avarice and pride; while these churches of Christ were chosen even by the savage barbarians as the fit scenes for humility and mercy. But perhaps, after all, the Greeks did in that victory of theirs spare the temples of those gods whom they worshipped in common with the Trojans, and did not dare to put to the sword or make captive the wretched and vanquished Trojans who fled thither; and perhaps Virgil, in the manner of poets, has depicted what never really happened? But there is no question that he depicted the usual custom of an enemy when sacking a city. . . .

Book IV

CHAPTER III

Now, therefore, let us see how it is that they dare to ascribe the very great extent and duration of the Roman empire to those gods whom they contend that they worship honourably, even by the obsequies of vile games and the ministry of vile men: although I should like first to inquire for a little what reason, what prudence, there is in wishing to glory in the greatness and extent of the empire, when you cannot point out the happiness of men who are always rolling, with dark fear and cruel lust, in warlike slaughters and in blood, which, whether shed in civil or foreign war, is still human blood; so that their joy may be compared to glass in its fragile splendour, of which one is horribly afraid lest it should be suddenly broken in pieces. That this may be more easily discerned, let us not come to nought by being carried away with empty boasting, or blunt the edge of our attention by loud-sounding names of things, when we hear of people, kingdoms, provinces. But let us suppose a case of two men; for each individual man, like one letter in a language, is as it were the element of a city or kingdom, however far-spreading in its occupation of the earth. Of these two men let us suppose that one is poor, or rather of middling circumstances; the other very rich. But the rich man is anxious with fears, pining with discontent, burning with covetousness, never secure, always uneasy, panting from the perpetual strife of his enemies, adding to his patrimony indeed by these miseries to an immense degree, and by these additions also heaping up most bitter cares. But that other man of moderate wealth is contented with a small and compact estate, most dear to his own family, enjoying the sweetest peace with his kindred neighbours and friends, in piety religious, benignant in mind, healthy in body, in life frugal, in manners chaste, in conscience secure. I know not whether any one can be such a fool, that he dare hesitate which to prefer. As, therefore, in the case of these two men, so in two families, in two nations, in two kingdoms, this test of tranquillity holds good; and if we apply it vigilantly and without prejudice, we shall quite easily see where the mere show of happiness dwells, and where real felicity. Wherefore if the true God is worshipped, and if He is served with genuine rites and true virtue, it is advantageous that good men should long reign both far and wide. Nor is this advantageous so much to themselves, as to those over whom they reign. For, so far as concerns themselves, their piety and probity, which are great gifts of God, suffice to give them true felicity, enabling them to live well the life that now is, and afterwards to receive that which is eternal. In this world, therefore, the dominion of good men is profitable, not so much for themselves as for human affairs. But the dominion of bad men is hurtful chiefly to themselves who rule, for they destroy their own souls by greater licence in wickedness; while those who are put under them in service are not hurt except by their own iniquity. For to the just all the evils imposed on them by unjust rulers are not the punishment of crime, but the test of virtue. Therefore the good man, although he is a slave, is free; but the bad man, even if he reigns, is a slave, and that not of one man, but, what is far more grievous, of as many masters as he has vices; of which vices when the divine Scripture treats, it says, "For of whom any man is overcome, to the same he is also the bond-slave."

CHAPTER IV

Justice being taken away, then, what are kingdoms but great robberies? For what are robberies themselves, but little kingdoms? The band itself is made up of men; it is ruled by the authority of a prince, it is knit together by the pact of the confederacy; the booty is divided by the law agreed on. If, by the admittance of abandoned men, the evil increases to such a degree that it holds places, fixes abodes, takes possession of cities, and subdues people, it assumes the more plainly the name of a kingdom, because the reality is now manifestly conferred on it, not by the removal of covetousness, but by the addition of impunity. Indeed, that was an apt and true reply which was given to Alexander the Great by a pirate who had been seized. For when that king had asked the man what he meant by keeping hostile possession of the sea, he answered with bold pride, "What thou meanest by seizing the whole earth; but because I do it with a petty ship, I am called a robber, whilst thou who dost it with a great fleet art styled emperor.". . .

CHAPTER XXXIV

. . . That it might be known that these earthly good things, after which those pant who cannot imagine better things, remain in the power of the one God Himself, not of the many false gods whom the Romans have formerly believed worthy of worship, He multiplied His people in Egypt from being very few, and delivered them out of it by wonderful signs. Nor did their women invoke Lucina when their offspring was being incredibly multiplied; and that nation having increased incredibly, He Himself delivered, He Himself saved them from the hands of the Egyptians, who persecuted them, and wished to kill all their infants. Without the goddess Rumina they sucked; without Cunina they were cradled; without Educa and Potina they took food and drink; without all those puerile gods they were educated; without the nuptial gods they were married; without the worship of Priapus they had conjugal intercourse; without invocation of Neptune the divided sea opened up a way for them to pass over, and overwhelmed with its returning waves their enemies who pursued them. Neither did they consecrate any goddess Mannia when they received manna from heaven; nor, when the smitten rock poured forth water to them when they thirsted, did they worship Nymphs and Lymphs. Without the mad rites of Mars and Bellona they carried on war; and while, indeed, they did not conquer without victory, yet they did not hold it to be a goddess, but the gift of their God. Without Segetia they had harvests; without Bubona, oxen; honey without Mellona; apples without Pomona: and, in a word, everything for which the Romans thought they must supplicate so great a crowd of false gods, they received much more happily from the one true God. And if they had not sinned against Him with impious curiosity, which seduced them like magic arts, and drew them to strange gods and idols, and at last led them to kill Christ, their kingdom would have remained to them, and would have been, if not more spacious, yet more happy, than that of Rome. And now that they are dispersed through almost all lands and nations, it is through the providence of that one true God; that whereas the images, altars, groves, and temples of the false gods are everywhere overthrown, and their sacrifices prohibited, it may be shown from their books how this has been foretold by their prophets so long before; lest, perhaps, when they should be read in ours, they might seem to be invented by us. But now, reserving what is to follow for the following book, we must here set a bound to the prolixity of this one. . . .

Book V

CHAPTER I

The cause, then, of the greatness of the Roman empire is neither fortuitous nor fatal, according to the judgment or opinion of those who call those things *fortuitous* which either have no causes, or such causes as do not proceed from some intelligible order, and those things *fatal* which happen independently of the will of God and man, by the necessity of a certain *order*. In a word, human kingdoms are established by divine providence. And if any one attributes their existence to fate, because he calls the will or the power of God itself by the name of fate, let him keep his opinion, but correct his language. For why does he not say at first what he will say afterwards, when some one shall put the question to him, What he means by *fate?* For when men hear that word, according to the ordinary use of the language, they simply understand by it the virtue of that particular position of the stars which may exist at the time when any one is born or conceived, which some separate altogether from the will of God, whilst others affirm that this also is dependent on that will. But those who are of opinion that, apart from the will of God, the stars determine what we shall do, or what good things we shall possess, or what evils we shall suffer, must be refused a hearing by all, not only by those who hold the true religion, but by those who wish to be the worshippers of any gods whatsoever, even false gods. For what does this opinion really amount to but this, that no god whatever is to be worshipped or prayed to? Against these, however, our present disputation is not intended to be directed, but against those who, in defence of those whom they think to be gods, oppose the Christian religion. They, however, who make the position of the stars depend on the divine will, and in a manner decree what character each man shall have, and what good or evil shall happen to him, if they think that these same stars have that power conferred upon them by the supreme power of God, in order that they may determine these things according to their will, do a great injury to the celestial sphere, in whose most brilliant senate, and most splendid senate-house, as it were, they suppose that wicked deeds are decreed to be done—such deeds as that if any terrestrial state should decree them, it would be condemned to overthrow by the decree of the whole human race. What judgment, then, is left to God concerning the deeds of men, who is Lord both of the stars and of men, when to these deeds a celestial necessity is attributed? . . .

CHAPTER IX

The manner in which Cicero addresses himself to the task of refuting the Stoics, shows that he did not think he could effect anything against them in argument unless he had first demolished divination. And this he attempts to accomplish by denying that there is any knowledge of future things, and maintains with all his might that there is no such knowledge either in God or man, and that there is no prediction of events. Thus he both denies the foreknowledge of God, and attempts by vain arguments, and by opposing to himself certain oracles very easy to be refuted, to overthrow all prophecy, even such as is clearer than the light (though even these oracles are not refuted by him).

But, in refuting these conjectures of the mathematicians, his argument is triumphant, because truly these are such as destroy and refute themselves. Nevertheless, they are far more tolerable who assert the fatal influence of the stars than they who deny the foreknowledge of future events. For, to confess that God exists, and at the same time to deny that He has foreknowledge of future things, is the most manifest folly. This Cicero himself saw, and therefore attempted to assert the doctrine embodied in the words of Scripture, "The fool hath said in his heart, There is no God." That, however, he did not do in his own person, for he saw how odious and offensive such an opinion would be; and, therefore in his book on the nature of the gods, he makes Cotta dispute concerning this against the Stoics, and preferred to give his own opinion in favour of Lucilius Balbus, to whom he assigned the defence of the Stoical position, rather than in favour of Cotta, who maintained that no divinity exists. However, in his book on divination, he in his own person most openly opposes the doctrine of the prescience of future things. But all this he seems to do in order that he may not grant the doctrine of fate, and by so doing destroy free will. For he thinks that, the knowledge of future things being once conceded, fate follows as so necessary a consequence that it cannot be denied.

But, let these perplexing debatings and disputations of the philosophers go on as they may, we, in order that we may confess the most high and true God Himself, do confess His will, supreme power, and prescience. Neither let us be afraid lest, after all, we do not do by will that which we do by will, because He, whose foreknowledge is infallible, foreknew that we would do it. It was this which Cicero was afraid of, and therefore opposed foreknowledge. The Stoics also maintained that all things do not come to pass by necessity, although they contended that all things happen according to destiny. What is it, then, that Cicero feared in the prescience of future things? Doubtless it was this—that if all future things have been foreknown, they will happen in the order in which they have been foreknown; and if they come to pass in this order, there is a certain order of things foreknown by God; and if a certain order of things, then a certain order of causes, for nothing can happen which is not preceded by some efficient cause. But if there is a certain order of causes according to which everything happens which does happen, then by fate, says he, all things happen which do happen. But if this be so, then is there nothing in our own power, and there is no such thing as freedom of will; and if we grant that, says he, the whole economy of human life is subverted. In vain are laws enacted. In vain are reproaches, praises, chidings, exhortations had recourse to; and there is no justice whatever in the appointment of rewards for the good, and punishments for the wicked. And that consequences so disgraceful, and absurd, and pernicious to humanity may not follow, Cicero chooses to reject the foreknowledge of future things, and shuts up the religious mind to this alternative, to make choice between two things; either that something is in our own power, or that there is foreknowledge—both of which cannot be true; but if the one is affirmed, the other is thereby denied. He, therefore, like a truly great and wise man, and one who consulted very much and very skillfully for the good of humanity, of those two chose the freedom of the will, to confirm which he denied the foreknowledge of future things; and thus, wishing to make men free, he makes them sacrilegious. But the religious mind chooses both, confesses both, and maintains both by the faith of piety. But how so? says Cicero; for the knowledge of future things being granted, there follows a chain of consequences which ends in this, that there can be nothing depending on our own free wills. And further, if there is anything depending on our wills, we must go backwards by the same steps of reasoning till we arrive at the conclusion that there is no foreknowledge of future things. For we go backwards through all the steps in the following order:—If there is free will, all things do not happen according to fate; if all things do not happen according to fate, there is not a certain order of causes; and if there is not a certain order of causes, neither is there a certain order of things foreknown by God—for things cannot come to pass except they are preceded by efficient causes—but, if there is no fixed and certain order of causes foreknown by God, all things cannot be said to happen according as He foreknew that they would happen. And further, if it is not true that all things happen just as they have been foreknown by Him, there is not, says he, in God any foreknowledge of future events.

Now, against the sacrilegious and impious darings of reason, we assert both that God knows all things before they come to pass, and that we do by our free will whatsoever we know and feel to be done by us only because we will it. But that all things come to pass by fate, we do not say; nay we affirm that nothing comes to pass by fate; for we demonstrate that the name of fate, as it is wont to be used by those who speak of fate, meaning thereby the position of the stars at the time of each one's conception or birth, is an unmeaning word, for astrology itself is a delusion. But an order of causes in which the highest efficiency is attributed to the will of God, we neither deny nor do we designate it by the name of fate, unless, perhaps, we may understand fate to mean that which is spoken, deriving it from *fari,* to speak; for we cannot deny that it is written in the sacred Scriptures, "God hath spoken once; these two things have I heard, that power belongeth unto God. Also unto Thee, O God, belongeth mercy: for Thou wilt render unto every man according to his works." Now the expression, "Once hath He spoken," is to be understood as meaning *"immovably,"* that is, unchangeably hath He spoken, inasmuch as He knows unchangeably all things which shall be, and all things which He will do. We might, then, use the word fate in the sense it bears when derived from *fari,* to speak, had it not already come to be understood in another sense, into which I am unwilling that the hearts of men should unconsciously slide. But it does not follow that, though there is for God a certain order of all causes, there must therefore be nothing depending on the free exercise of our own wills, for our wills themselves are included in that order of causes which is certain to God, and is embraced by His foreknowledge, for human wills are also causes of human actions; and He who foreknew all the causes of things would certainly among those causes not have been ignorant of our wills. For even that very concession which Cicero himself makes is enough to refute him in this argument. For what does it help him to say that nothing takes place without a cause, but that every cause is not fatal, there being a fortuitous cause, a natural cause, and a voluntary cause? It is sufficient that he confesses that whatever happens must be preceded by a cause. For we say that those causes which are called fortuitous are not a mere name for the absence of causes, but are only latent, and we attribute them either to the will of the true God, or to that of spirits of some kind or other. And as to natural causes, we by no means separate them from the will of Him who is the author and framer of all nature. But now as to voluntary causes. They are referable either to God, or to angels, or to men, or to animals of whatever description, if indeed those instinctive movements of animals devoid of reason, by which, in accordance with their own nature, they seek or shun various things are to be called wills. And when I speak of the wills of angels, I mean either the wills of good angels, whom we call the angels of God, or of the wicked angels, whom we call the angels of the devil, or demons. Also by the wills of men I mean the wills either of the good or of the wicked. And from this we conclude that there are no efficient causes of all things which come to pass unless voluntary causes, that is, such as belong to that nature, which is the spirit of life. For the air or wind is called spirit, but, inasmuch as it is a body, it is not the spirit of life. The spirit of life, therefore, which quickens all things, and is the creator of every body, and of every created spirit, is God Himself, the uncreated spirit. In His supreme will resides the power which acts on the wills of all created spirits, helping the good, judging the evil, controlling all, granting power to some, not granting it to others. For, as He is the creator of all natures, so also is He the bestower of all powers, not of all wills; for wicked wills are not from Him, being contrary to nature, which is from Him. As to bodies, they are more subject to wills; some to our wills, by which I mean the wills of all living mortal creatures, but more to the wills of men than of beasts. But all of them are most of all subject to the will of God, to whom all wills also are subject, since they have no power except what He has bestowed upon them. The cause of things, therefore, which makes but is not made, is God; but all other causes both make and are made. Such are all created spirits, and especially the rational. Material causes, therefore, which may rather be said to be made than to make, are not to be reckoned among efficient causes, because they can only do what the wills of spirits do by them. How, then, does an order of causes which is certain to the foreknowledge of God necessitate that there should be nothing which is dependent on our wills, when our wills themselves have a very important place in the order of causes? Cicero, then, contends with those who call this order of causes fatal, or rather designate this order itself by the name of fate; to which we have an abhorrence, especially on account of the word, which men have become accustomed to understand as meaning what is not true. But, whereas he denies that the order of all causes is most certain, and perfectly clear to the prescience of God, we detest his opinion more than the Stoics do. For he either denies that God exists—which, indeed, in an assumed personage, he has laboured to do, in his book *De Natura Deorum*—or if he confesses that He exists, but denies that He is prescient of future things, what is that but just "the fool saying in his heart there is no God"? For one who is not prescient of all future things is not God. Wherefore our wills also have just so much power as God willed and foreknew that they should have; and therefore whatever power they have, they have it within most certain limits; and whatever they are to do, they are most assuredly to do, for He whose foreknowledge is infallible foreknew that they would have the power to do it, and would do it. Wherefore, if I should choose to apply the name of fate to anything at all, I should rather say that fate belongs to the weaker of two parties, will to the stronger, who has the other in his power, than that the freedom of our will is excluded by that order of causes, which, by an unusual application of the word peculiar to themselves, the Stoics call *Fate*. . . .

Book XI

CHAPTER I

The city of God we speak of is the same to which testimony is borne by that Scripture, which excels all the writings of all nations by its divine authority, and has brought under its influence all kinds of minds, and this not by a casual intellectual movement, but obviously by an express providential arrangement. For there it is written, "Glorious things are spoken of thee, O city of God." And in another psalm we read, "Great is the Lord, and greatly to be praised in the city of our God, in the mountain of His holiness, increasing the joy of the whole earth." And a little after, in the same psalm, "As we have heard, so have we seen in the city of the Lord of hosts, in the city of our God. God has established it for ever." And in another, "There is a river the streams whereof shall make glad the city of our God, the holy place of the tabernacles of the Most High. God is in the midst of her, she shall not be moved." From these and similar testimonies, all of which it were tedious to cite, we have learned that there is a city of God, and its Founder has inspired us with a love which makes us covet its citizenship. To this Founder of the holy city the citizens of the earthly city prefer their own gods, not knowing that He is the God of gods, not of false, i.e. of impious and proud gods, who, being deprived of His unchangeable and freely communicated light, and so reduced to a kind of poverty-stricken power, eagerly grasp at their own private privileges, and seek divine honours from their deluded subjects; but of the pious and holy gods, who are better pleased to submit themselves to one, than to subject many to themselves, and who would rather worship God than be worshipped as God. But to the enemies of this city we have replied in the ten preceding books, according to our ability and the help afforded by our Lord and King. Now, recognizing what is expected of me, and not unmindful of my promise, and relying, too, on the same succour, I will endeavor to treat of the origin, and progress, and deserved destinies of the two cities (the earthly and the heavenly, to wit), which, as we said, are in this present world commingled, and as it were entangled together. And, first, I will explain how the foundations of these two cities were originally laid, in the difference that arose among the angels.

CHAPTER II

It is a great and very rare thing for a man, after he has contemplated the whole creation, corporeal and incorporeal, and has discerned its mutability, to pass beyond it, and, by the continued soaring of his mind, to attain to the unchangeable substance of God, and, in that height of contemplation, to learn from God Himself that none but He has made all that is not of the divine essence. For God speaks with a man not by means of some audible creature dinning in his ears, so that atmospheric vibrations connect Him that makes with him that hears the sound, nor even by means of a spiritual being with the semblance of a body, such as we see in dreams or similar states; for even in this case He speaks as if to the ears of the body, because it is by means of the semblance of a body He speaks, and with the appearance of a real interval of space—for visions are exact representations of bodily objects. Not by these, then, does God speak, but by the truth itself, if any one is prepared to hear with the mind rather than with the body. For He speaks to that part of man which is better than all else that is in him, and than which God Himself alone is better. For since man is most properly understood (or, if that cannot be, then, at least, *believed*) to be made in God's image, no doubt it is that part of him by which he rises above those lower parts he has in common with the beasts, which brings him nearer to the Supreme. But since the mind, itself, though naturally capable of reason and intelligence, is disabled by besotting and inveterate vices not merely from delighting and abiding in, but even from tolerating His unchangeable light, until it has been gradually healed, and renewed, and made capable of such felicity, it had, in the first place, to be impregnated with faith and so purified. And that in this faith it mght advance the more confidently towards the truth, the truth itself, God, God's Son, assuming humanity without destroying His divinity, established and founded this faith, that there might be a way for man to man's God through a God-man. For this is the Mediator between God and men, the man Christ Jesus. For it is as man that He is the Mediator and the way. Since, if the way lieth between him who goes, and the place whither he goes, there is hope of his reaching it; but if there be no way, or if he know not where it is, what boots it to know whither he should go? Now the only way that is infallibly secured against all mistakes, is when the very same person is at once God and man, God our end, man our way. . . .

CHAPTER IV

Of all visible things, the world is the greatest; of all invisible, the greatest is God. But that the world is, we see; that God is, we believe. That God made the world, we can believe from no one more safely than from God Himself. But where have we heard Him? Nowhere more distinctly than in the Holy Scriptures, where His prophet said, "In the beginning God created the heavens and the earth." Was the prophet present when God made the heavens and the earth? No; but the wisdom of God, by whom all things were made, was there, and wisdom insinuates itself into holy souls, and makes them the friends of God and His prophets, and noiselessly informs them of His works. They are taught also by the angels of God, who always behold the face of the Father, and announce His will to whom it befits. Of these prophets was he who said and wrote, "In the beginning God created the heavens and the earth." And so fit a witness was he of God, that the same Spirit of God, who revealed these things to him, enabled him also so long before to predict that our faith also would be forthcoming.

But why did God choose then to create the heavens and earth which up to that time He had not made? If they who put this question wish to make out that the world is eternal and without beginning, and that consequently it has not been made by God, they are strangely deceived, and rave in the incurable madness of impiety. For, though the voices of the prophets were silent, the world itself, by its well-ordered changes and movements, and by the fair appearance of all visible things, bears a testimony of its own, both that it has been created, and also that it could not have been created save by God, whose greatness and beauty are unutterable and invisible. As for those who own, indeed, that it was made by God, and yet ascribe to it not a temporal but only a creational beginning, so that in some scarcely intelligible way the world should always have existed a created world, they make an assertion which seems to them to defend God from the charge of arbitrary hastiness, or of suddenly conceiving the idea of creating the world as a quite new idea, or of casually changing His will, though He be unchangeable. But I do not see how this supposition of theirs can stand in other respects, and chiefly in respect of the soul; for if they contend that it is co-eternal with God, they will be quite at a loss to explain whence there has accrued to it new misery, which through a previous eternity had not existed. For if they said that its happiness and misery ceaselessly alternate, they must say, further, that this alternation will continue for ever; whence will result this absurdity, that, though the soul is called blessed, it is not so in this, that it foresees its own misery and disgrace. And yet, if it does not foresee it, and supposes that it will be neither disgraced nor wretched, but always blessed, then it is blessed because it is deceived; and a more foolish statement one cannot make. But if their idea is that the soul's misery has alternated with its bliss during the ages of the past eternity, but that now, when once the soul has been set free, it will return henceforth no more to misery, they are nevertheless of opinion that it has never been truly blessed before, but begins at last to enjoy a new and uncertain happiness; that is to say, they must acknowledge that some new thing, and that an important and signal thing, happens to the soul which never in a whole past eternity happened to it before. And if they deny that God's eternal purpose included this new experience of the soul, they deny that He is Author of its blessedness, which is unspeakable impiety. If, on the other hand, they say that the future blessedness of the soul is the result of a new decree of God, how will they show that God is not chargeable with that mutability which displeases them? Further, if they acknowledge that it was created in time, but will never perish in time—that it has, like number, a beginning but no end—and that, therefore, having once made trial of misery, and been delivered from it, it will never again return thereto, they will certainly admit that this takes place without any violation of the immutable counsel of God. Let them, then, in like manner believe regarding the world that it too could be made in time, and yet that God, in making it, did not alter His eternal design.

CHAPTER V

Next, we must see what reply can be made to those who agree that God is the Creator of the world, but have difficulties about the time of its creation, and what reply, also, they can make to difficulties we might raise about the place of its creation. For, as they demand why the world was created then and no sooner, we may ask why it was created just here where it is, and not elsewhere. For if they imagine infinite spaces of time before the world, during which God could not have been idle, in like manner they may conceive outside the world infinite realms of space, in which, if any one says that the Omnipotent cannot hold His hand from working, will it not follow that they must adopt Epicurus' dream of innumerable worlds? with this difference only, that he asserts that they are formed and destroyed by the fortuitous movements of atoms, while they

will hold that they are made by God's hand, if they maintain that, throughout the boundless immensity of space, stretching interminably in every
direction round the world, God cannot rest, and that the worlds which
they suppose Him to make cannot be destroyed. For here the question
is with those who, with ourselves, believe that God is spiritual, and the
Creator of all existences but Himself. As for others, it is a condescension
to dispute with them on a religious question, for they have acquired a
reputation only among men who pay divine honours to a number of gods,
and have become conspicuous among the other philosophers for no other
reason than that, though they are still far from the truth, they are near it
in comparison with the rest. While these, then, neither confine in any
place, nor limit, nor distribute the divine substance, but, as is worthy of
God, own it to be wholly though spiritually present everywhere, will they
perchance say that this substance is absent from such immense spaces outside the world, and is occupied in one only, (and that a very little one compared with the infinity beyond,) the one, namely, in which is the world?
I think they will not proceed to this absurdity. Since they maintain that
there is but one world, of vast material bulk, indeed, yet finite, and in its
own determinate position, and that this was made by the working of God,
let them give the same account of God's resting in the infinite times before the world as they give of His resting in the infinite spaces outside of it.
And as it does not follow that God set the world in the very spot it occupies
and no other by accident rather than by divine reason, although no human
reason can comprehend why it was so set, and though there was no
merit in the spot chosen to give it the precedence of infinite others, so
neither does it follow that we should suppose that God was guided by
chance when He created the world in that and no earlier time, although
previous times had been running by during an infinite past, and though
there was no difference by which one time could be chosen in preference
to another. But if they say that the thoughts of men are idle when they
conceive infinite places, since there is no place beside the world, we reply
that, by the same showing, it is vain to conceive of the past times of God's
rest, since there is no time before the world. . . .

Book XII

CHAPTER V

All natures, . . . inasmuch as they are, and have therefore a rank and
species of their own, and a kind of internal harmony, are certainly good.
And when they are in the places assigned to them by the order of their

nature, they preserve such being as they have received. And those things which have not received everlasting being, are altered for better or for worse, so as to suit the wants and motions of those things to which the Creator's law has made them subservient; and thus they tend in the divine providence to that end which is embraced in the general scheme of the government of the universe. So that, though the corruption of transitory and perishable things brings them to utter destruction, it does not prevent their producing that which was designed to be their result. And this being so, God, who supremely is, and who therefore created every being which has not supreme existence (for that which was made of nothing could not be equal to Him, and indeed could not be at all had He not made it), is not to be found fault with on account of the creature's faults, but is to be praised in view of the natures He has made. . . .

CHAPTER VI

. . . the true cause of the blessedness of the good angels is found to be this, that they cleave to Him who supremely is. And if we ask the cause of the misery of the bad, it occurs to us, and not unreasonably, that they are miserable because they have forsaken Him who supremely is, and have turned to themselves who have no such essence. And this vice, what else is it called than pride? For "pride is the beginning of sin." They were unwilling, then, to preserve their strength for God; and as adherence to God was the condition of their enjoying an ampler being, they diminished it by preferring themselves to Him. This was the first defect, and the first impoverishment, and the first flaw of their nature, which was created, not indeed supremely existent, but finding its blessedness in the enjoyment of the Supreme Being; whilst by abandoning Him it should become, not indeed no nature at all, but a nature with a less ample existence, and therefore wretched.

If the further question be asked, What was the efficient cause of their evil will? there is none. For what is it which makes the will bad, when it is the will itself which makes the action bad? And consequently the bad will is the cause of the bad action, but nothing is the efficient cause of the bad will. For if anything is the cause, this thing either has or has not a will. If it has, the will is either good or bad. If good, who is so left to himself as to say that a good will makes a will bad? For in this case a good will would be the cause of sin; a most absurd supposition. On the other hand, if this hypothetical thing has a bad will, I wish to know what made it so; and that we may not go on for ever, I ask at once, what made the *first* evil will bad? For that is not the first which was itself corrupted by an evil will, but that is the first which was made evil by no other will. For if it were preceded by that which made it evil, that will was first which made the other evil. But if it is replied, "Nothing made it evil; it always was evil," I ask if it has been existing in some nature. For if not, then it did not exist at all; and if it did exist in some nature, then it vitiated and corrupted it, and injured it, and consequently deprived it of good. And therefore the evil will could not exist in an evil nature, but in a nature at once good and mutable, which this vice could injure. For if it did no injury, it was no vice; and consequently the will in which it was, could not be called evil. But if it did injury, it did it by taking away or diminishing good. And therefore there could not be from eternity, as was suggested, an evil will in that thing in which there had been previously a natural good, which the evil will was able to diminish by corrupting it. If, then, it was not from eternity, who, I ask, made it? The only thing that can be suggested in reply is, that something which itself had no will, made the will evil. I ask, then, whether this thing was superior, inferior, or equal to it? If superior, then it is better. How, then, has it no will, and not rather a good will? The same reasoning applies if it was equal; for so long as two things have equally a good will, the one cannot produce in the other an evil will. Then remains the supposition that that which corrupted the will of the angelic nature which first sinned, was itself an inferior thing without a will. But that thing, be it of the lowest and most earthly kind, is certainly itself good, since it is a nature and being, with a form and rank of its own in its own kind and order. How, then, can a good thing be the efficient cause of an evil will? How, I say, can good be the cause of evil? For when the will abandons what is above itself, and turns to what is lower, it becomes evil—not because that is evil to which it turns, but because the turning itself is wicked. Therefore it is not an inferior thing which has made the will evil, but it is itself which has become so by wickedly and inordinately desiring an inferior thing. For if two men, alike in physical and moral constitution, see the same corporal beauty, and one of them is excited by the sight to desire an illicit enjoyment, while the other steadfastly maintains a modest restraint of his will, what do we suppose brings it about, that there is an evil will in the one and not in the other? What produces it in the man in whom it exists? Not the bodily beauty, for that was presented equally to the gaze of both, and yet did not produce in both an evil will. Did the flesh of the one cause the desire as he looked? But why did not the flesh of the other? Or was it the disposition? But why not the disposition of both? For we are supposing that both were of a like temperament of body and soul. Must we, then, say that the one was tempted by a secret suggestion of the evil spirit? As if it was not by his own will that he consented to this suggestion and to any inducement whatever! This consent, then, this evil will which he presented to the evil suasive influence—what was the cause of it, we ask? For, not to delay on such a difficulty as this, if both are tempted equally, and one yields and consents to the temptation, while the other remains unmoved by it, what other account can we give of the matter than this, that the one is willing, the other unwilling, to fall away from chastity? And what causes this but their own wills, in cases at least such as we are supposing, where the temperament is identical? The same beauty was equally obvious to the eyes of both; the same secret temptation pressed on both with equal violence. However minutely we examine the case, therefore, we can discern nothing which caused the will of the one to be evil. For if we say that the man himself made his will evil, what was the man himself before his will was evil but a good nature created by God, the unchangeable good? Here are two men who, before the temptation, were alike in body and soul, and of whom one yielded to the tempter who persuaded him, while the other could not be persuaded to desire that lovely body which was equally before the eyes of both. Shall we say of the successfully tempted man that he corrupted his own will, since he was certainly good before his will became bad? Then, why did he do so? Was it because his will was a nature, or because it was made of nothing? We shall find that the latter is the case. For if a nature is the cause of an evil will, what else can we say than that evil arises from good, or that good is the cause of evil? And how can it come to pass that a nature, good though mutable, should produce any evil—that is to say, should make the will itself wicked?

CHAPTER VII

Let no one, therefore, look for an efficient cause of the evil will; for it is not efficient, but deficient, as the will itself is not an effecting of something, but a defect. For defection from that which supremely is, to that which has less of being—this is to begin to have an evil will. Now, to seek to discover the causes of these defections—causes, as I have said, not efficient, but deficient—is as if someone sought to see darkness, or hear silence. Yet both of these are known by us, and the former by means only of the eye, the latter only by the ear; but not by their positive actuality, but by their want of it. Let no one, then, seek to know from me what I know that I do not know; unless he perhaps wishes to learn to be ignorant of that of which all we know is, that it cannot be known. For those things which are known not by their actuality, but by their want of it, are known, if our expression may be allowed and understood, by not knowing them, that by knowing them they may be not known. For when the eyesight surveys objects that strike the sense, it nowhere sees darkness but where it begins not to see. And so no other sense but the ear can perceive silence, and yet it is only perceived by not hearing. Thus, too, our mind perceives intelligible forms by understanding them; but when they are deficient, it knows them by not knowing them; for "who can understand defects?"

CHAPTER VIII

This I do know, that the nature of God can never, nowhere, nowise be defective, and that natures made of nothing can. These latter, however, the more being they have, and the more good they do (for then they do something positive), the more they have efficient causes; but in so far as they are defective in being, and consequently do evil (for then what is their work but vanity?) they have deficient causes. And I know likewise, that the will could not become evil, were it unwilling to become so; and therefore its failings are justly punished, being not necessary, but voluntary. For its defections are not to evil things, but are themselves evil; that is to say, are not towards things that are naturally and in themselves evil, but the defection of the will is evil, because it is contrary to the order of nature, and an abandonment of that which has supreme being for that which has less. For avarice is not a fault inherent in gold, but in the man who inordinately loves gold, to the detriment of justice, which ought to be held in incomparably higher regard than gold. Neither is luxury the fault of lovely and charming objects, but of the heart that inordinately loves sensual pleasures, to the neglect of temperance, which attaches us to objects more lovely in their spirituality, and more delectable by their incorruptibility. Nor yet is boasting the fault of human praise, but of the soul that is inordinately fond of the applause of men, and that makes light of the voice of conscience. Pride, too, is not the fault of him who delegates power, nor of power itself, but of the soul that is inordinately enamoured of its own power, and despises the more just dominion of a higher authority. Consequently he who inordinately loves the good which any nature possesses, even though he obtain it, himself becomes evil in the good, and wretched because deprived of a greater good.

CHAPTER XXI

Now that we have solved, as well as we could, this very difficult question about the eternal God creating new things, without any novelty of will, it is easy to see how much better it is that God was pleased to pro-

duce the human race from the one individual whom He created, than if
He had originated it in several men. For as to the other animals, He created
some solitary, and naturally seeking lonely places—as the eagles, kites, lions,
wolves, and such like; others gregarious, which herd together, and prefer
to live in company—as pigeons, starlings, stags, and little fallow deer, and
the like: but neither class did He cause to be propagated from individuals,
but called into being several at once. Man, on the other hand, whose
nature was to be a mean between the angelic and bestial, He created in
such sort, that if he remained in subjection to His Creator as his rightful
Lord, and piously kept His commandments, he should pass into the company of the angels, and obtain, without the intervention of death, a blessed
and endless immortality; but if he offended the Lord his God by a proud
and disobedient use of his free will, he should become subject to death,
and live as the beasts do—the slave of appetite, and doomed to eternal
punishment after death. And therefore God created only one single man,
not, certainly, that he might be a solitary bereft of all society, but that by
this means the unity of society and the bond of concord might be more
effectually commended to him, men being bound together not only by
similarity of nature, but by family affection. And indeed He did not even
create the woman that was to be given him as his wife, as he created the
man, but created her out of the man, that the whole human race might
derive from one man.

CHAPTER XXII

And God was not ignorant that man would sin, and that, being himself
made subject now to death, he would propagate men doomed to die, and
that these mortals would run to such enormities in sin, that even the
beasts devoid of rational will, and who were created in numbers from the
waters and the earth, would live more securely and peaceably with their
own kind than men, who had been propagated from one individual for
the very purpose of commending concord. For not even lions or dragons
have ever waged with their kind such wars as men have waged with one
another. But God foresaw also that by His grace a people would be called
to adoption, and that they, being justified by the remission of their sins,
would be united by the Holy Ghost to the holy angels in eternal peace,
the last enemy, death, being destroyed; and He knew that this people
would derive profit from the consideration that God has caused all men
to be derived from one, for the sake of showing how highly He prizes unity
in a multitude.

CHAPTER XXIII

God, then, made man in His own image. For He created for him a soul endowed with reason and intelligence, so that he might excel all the creatures of earth, air, and sea, which were not so gifted. And when He had formed the man out of the dust of the earth, and had willed that his soul should be such as I have said—whether He had already made it, and now by breathing imparted it to man, or rather made it by breathing, so that that breath which God made by breathing (for what else is "to breathe" than to make breath?) is the soul—He made also a wife for him, to aid him in the work of generating his kind, and her He formed of a bone taken out of the man's side, working in a divine manner. For we are not to conceive of this work in a carnal fashion, as if God wrought as we commonly see artisans, who use their hands, and material furnished to them, that by their artistic skill they may fashion some material object. God's hand is God's power; and He, working invisibly, effects visible results. But this seems fabulous rather than true to men, who measure by customary and everyday works the power and wisdom of God, whereby He understands and produces without seeds even seeds themselves; and because they cannot understand the things which at the beginning were created, they are sceptical regarding them—as if the very things which they do know about human propagation, conceptions and births, would seem less incredible if told to those who had no experience of them; though these very things, too, are attributed by many rather to physical and natural causes than to the work of the divine mind.

CHAPTER XXIV

But in this book we have nothing to do with those who do not believe that the divine mind made or cares for this world. As for those who believe their own Plato, that all mortal animals—among whom man holds the pre-eminent place, and is near to the gods themselves—were created not by that most high God who made the world, but by other lesser gods created by the Supreme, and exercising a delegated power under His control—if only those persons be delivered from the superstition which prompts them to seek a plausible reason for paying divine honours and sacrificing to these gods as their creators, they will easily be disentangled also from this their error. For it is blasphemy to believe or to say (even before it can be understood) that any other than God is creator of any nature, be it never so small and mortal. And as for the angels, whom those Platonists prefer to call gods, although they do, so far as they are permitted and commissioned, aid in the production of the things around us, yet not on that account are we to call them creators, any more than we call gardeners the creators of fruits and trees. . . .

Book XIII

CHAPTER XII

When, therefore, it is asked what death it was with which God threatened our first parents if they should transgress the commandment they had received from Him, and should fail to preserve their obedience— whether it was the death of soul, or of body, or of the whole man, or that which is called second death—we must answer, It is all. For the first consists of two; the second is the complete death, which consists of all. For, as the whole earth consists of many lands, and the Church universal of many churches, so death universal consists of all deaths. The first consists of two, one of the body, and another of the soul. So that the first death is a death of the whole man, since the soul without God and without the body suffers punishment for a time; but the second is when the soul, without God but with the body, suffers punishment everlasting. When, therefore, God said to that first man whom he had placed in Paradise, referring to the forbidden fruit, "In the day that thou eatest thereof thou shalt surely die," that threatening included not only the first part of the first death, by which the soul is deprived of God; nor only the subsequent part of the first death, by which the body is deprived of the soul; nor only the whole first death itself, by which the soul is punished in separation from God and from the body;—but it includes whatever death there is, even to that final death which is called second, and to which none is subsequent.

CHAPTER XIII

For, as soon as our first parents had transgressed the commandment, divine grace forsook them, and they were confounded by their own wickedness; and therefore they took fig-leaves (which were possibly the first that came to hand in their troubled state of mind), and covered their shame; for though their members remained the same, they had shame now where they had none before. They experienced a new motion of their flesh, which had become disobedient to them, in strict retribution of their own disobedience to God. For the soul, revelling in its own liberty, and scorning to serve God, was itself deprived of the command it had formerly maintained over the body. And because it had wilfully deserted its superior Lord, it no longer held its own inferior servant; neither could it hold the flesh subject, as it would always have been able to do had it remained itself subject to God. Then began the flesh to lust against the Spirit, in which strife we are born, deriving from the first transgression a seed of death, and bearing in our members, and in our vitiated nature, the contest or even victory of the flesh.

CHAPTER XIV

For God, the author of natures, not of vices, created man upright; but man, being of his own will corrupted, and justly condemned, begot corrupted and condemned children. For we all were in that one man, since we all were that one man who fell into sin by the woman who was made from him before the sin. For not yet was the particular form created and distributed to us, in which we as individuals were to live, but already the seminal nature was there from which we were to be propagated; and this being vitiated by sin, and bound by the chain of death, and justly condemned, man could not be born of man in any other state. And thus, from the bad use of free will, there originated the whole train of evil, which, with its concatenation of miseries, convoys the human race from its depraved origin, as from a corrupt root, on to the destruction of the second death, which has no end, those only being excepted who are freed by the grace of God. . . .

Book XIV

CHAPTER I

We have already stated in the preceding books that God, desiring not only that the human race might be able by their similarity of nature to associate with one another, but also that they might be bound together in harmony and peace by the ties of relationship, was pleased to derive all men from one individual, and created man with such a nature that the members of the race should not have died, had not the two first (of whom the one was created out of nothing, and the other out of him) merited this by their disobedience; for by them so great a sin was committed, that by it the human nature was altered for the worse, and was transmitted also to their posterity, liable to sin and subject to death. And the kingdom of death so reigned over men, that the deserved penalty of sin would have hurled all headlong even into the second death, of which there is no end, had not the undeserved grace of God saved some therefrom. And thus it has come to pass, that though there are very many and great nations all over the earth, whose rites and customs, speech, arms, and dress, are distinguished by marked differences, yet there are no more than two kinds of human society, which we may justly call two cities, according to the language of our Scriptures. The one consists of those who wish to live after the flesh, the other of those who wish to live after the spirit; and when they severally achieve what they wish, they live in peace, each after their kind.

CHAPTER II

First, we must see what it is to live after the flesh, and what to live after the spirit. For any one who either does not recollect, or does not sufficiently weigh, the language of sacred Scripture, may, on first hearing what we have said, suppose that the Epicurean philosophers live after the flesh, because they place man's highest good in bodily pleasure; and that those others do so who have been of opinion that in some form or other bodily good is man's supreme good; and that the mass of men do so who, without dogmatizing or philosophizing on the subject, are so prone to lust that they cannot delight in any pleasure save such as they receive from bodily sensations; and he may suppose that the Stoics, who place the supreme good of men in the soul, live after the spirit; for what is man's soul, if not spirit? But in the sense of the divine Scripture both are proved to live after the flesh. For by flesh it means not only the body of a ter-restrial and mortal animal, as when it says, "All flesh is not the same flesh, but there is one kind of flesh of men, another flesh of beasts, another of fishes, another of birds," but it uses this word in many other significations; and among these various usages, a frequent one is to use flesh for man himself, the nature of man taking the part for the whole, as in the words, "By the deeds of the law there shall no flesh be justified"; for what does he mean here by "no flesh" but "no man"? And this, indeed, he shortly after says more plainly: "No man shall be justified by the law"; and in the Epistle to the Galatians, "Knowing that a man is not justified by the works of the law." And so we understand the words, "And the Word was made flesh"—that is, man, which some not accepting in its right sense, have supposed that Christ had not a human soul. For as the whole is used for the part in the words of Mary Magdalene in the Gospel, "They have taken away my Lord, and I know not where they have laid Him," by which she meant only the flesh of Christ, which she supposed had been taken from the tomb where it had been buried, so the part is used for the whole, flesh being named, while man is referred to, as in the quotations above cited.

Since, then, Scripture uses the word flesh in many ways, which there is not time to collect and investigate, if we are to ascertain what it is to live after the flesh (which is certainly evil, though the nature of flesh is not itself evil), we must carefully examine that passage of the epistle which the Apostle Paul wrote to the Galatians, in which he says, "Now the works of the flesh are manifest, which are these: adultery, fornication, uncleanness, lasciviousness, idolatry, witchcraft, hatred, variance, emulations, wrath, strife, seditions, heresies, envyings, murders, drunkenness, revellings, and such like: of the which I tell you before, as I have also told you in time past that they which do such things shall not inherit the kingdom of God." This whole passage of the apostolic epistle being considered, so far as it bears on the matter in hand, will be sufficient to answer the question, what it is to live after the flesh. For among the works of the flesh which he said were manifest, and which he cited for condemnation, we find not only those which concern the pleasure of the flesh, as fornications, uncleanness, lasciviousness, drunkenness, revellings, but also those which, though they be remote from fleshly pleasure, reveal the vices of the soul. For who does not see that idolatries, witchcrafts, hatreds, variance, emulations, wrath, strife, heresies, envyings, are vices rather of the soul than of the flesh? For it is quite possible for a man to abstain from fleshly pleasures for the sake of idolatry or some heretical error; and yet, even when he does so, he is proved by this apostolic authority to be living after the flesh; and in abstaining from fleshly pleasure, he is proved to be practising damnable works of the flesh. Who that has enmity has it not in his soul? or who would say to his enemy, or to the man he thinks his enemy, You have a bad flesh towards me, and not rather, You have a bad spirit towards me? In fine, if any one heard of what I may call "carnalities," he would not fail to attribute them to the carnal part of man; so no one doubts that "animosities" belong to the soul of man. Why then does the doctor of the Gentiles in faith and verity call all these and similar things works of the flesh, unless because, by that mode of speech whereby the part is used for the whole, he means us to understand by the word flesh the man himself?

CHAPTER III

But if any one says that the flesh is the cause of all vices and ill conduct, inasmuch as the soul lives wickedly only because it is moved by the flesh, it is certain he has not carefully considered the whole nature of man. For "the corruptible body, indeed, weigheth down the soul." Whence, too, the apostle, speaking of this corruptible body, of which he had shortly before said, "though our outward man perish," says, "We know that if our earthly house of this tabernacle were dissolved, we have a building of God, an house not made with hands, eternal in the heavens. For in this we groan, earnestly desiring to be clothed upon with our house which is from heaven: if so be that being clothed we shall not be found naked. For we that are in this tabernacle do groan, being burdened: not for that we would be unclothed, but clothed upon, that mortality might be swallowed up in life." We are then burdened with this corruptible body; but knowing that the cause of this burdensomeness is not the nature and substance of the body, but its corruption, we do not desire to be deprived of the body, but to be clothed with its immortality. For then, also, there will be a body, but it shall no longer be a burden, being no longer corruptible. At present, then, "the corruptible body presseth down the soul, and the earthly tabernacle weigheth down the mind that museth upon many things," nevertheless they are in error who suppose that all the evils of the soul proceed from the body.

Virgil, indeed, seems to express the sentiments of Plato in the beautiful lines, where he says—

> "A fiery strength inspires their lives,
> An essence that from heaven derives,
> Though clogged in part by limbs of clay,
> And the dull 'vesture of decay;' " [11]

but though he goes on to mention the four most common mental emotions —desire, fear, joy, sorrow—with the intention of showing that the body is the origin of all sins and vices, saying—

> "Hence wild desires and groveling fears,
> And human laughter, human tears,
> Immured in dungeon-seeming night,
> They look abroad, yet see no light," [12]

yet we believe quite otherwise. For the corruption of the body, which weighs down the soul, is not the cause but the punishment of the first sin; and it was not the corruptible flesh that made the soul sinful, but the sinful soul that made the flesh corruptible. And though from this corruption of the flesh there arise certain incitements to vice, and indeed vicious desires, yet we must not attribute to the flesh all the vices of a wicked life, in case we thereby clear the devil of all these, for he has no flesh. For though we cannot call the devil a fornicator or drunkard, or ascribe to him any sensual indulgence (though he is the secret instigator and prompter of those who sin in these ways), yet he is exceedingly proud and

[11] *Aeneid* vi.730–32.　　　　[12] *Aeneid* vi.733, 734.

envious. And this viciousness has so possessed him, that on account of it he is reserved in chains of darkness to everlasting punishment. Now these vices, which have dominion over the devil, the apostle attributes to the flesh, which certainly the devil has not. For he says "hatred, variance, emulations, strife, envying" are the works of the flesh; and of all these evils pride is the origin and head, and it rules in the devil though he has no flesh. For who shows more hatred to the saints? Who is more at variance with them? Who more envious, bitter, and jealous? And since he exhibits all these works, though he has no flesh, how are they works of the flesh, unless because they are the works of man, who is, as I said, spoken of under the name of flesh? For it is not by having flesh, which the devil has not, but by living according to himself—that is, according to man—that man became like the devil. For the devil too, wished to live according to himself when he did not abide in the truth; so that when he lied, this was not of God, but of himself, who is not only a liar, but the father of lies, he being the first who lied, and the originator of lying as of sin.

CHAPTER IV

When, therefore, man lives according to man, not according to God, he is like the devil. Because not even an angel might live according to an angel, but only according to God, if he was to abide in the truth, and speak God's truth and not his own lie. And of man, too, the same apostle says in another place, "If the truth of God hath more abounded through my lie"; —"my lie," he said, and "God's truth." When, then, a man lives according to the truth, he lives not according to himself, but according to God; for He was God who said, "I am the truth." When, therefore, man lives according to himself—that is, according to man, not according to God—assuredly he lives according to a lie; not that man himself is a lie, for God is his author and creator, who is certainly not the author and creator of a lie, but because man was made upright, that he might not live according to himself, but according to Him that made him—in other words, that he might do His will and not his own; and not to live as he was made to live, that is a lie. For he certainly desires to be blessed even by not living so that he may be blessed. And what is a lie if this desire be not? Wherefore it is not without meaning said that all sin is a lie. For no sin is committed save by that desire or will by which we desire that it be well with us, and shrink from it being ill with us. That, therefore, is a lie which we do in order that it may be well with us, but which makes us more miserable than we were. And why is this, but because the source of man's happiness lies only in God, whom he abandons when he sins, and not in himself, by living according to whom he sins?

In enunciating this proposition of ours, then, that because some live according to the flesh and others according to the spirit there have arisen two diverse and conflicting cities, we might equally well have said, "because some live according to man, others according to God." For Paul says very plainly to the Corinthians, "For whereas there is among you envying and strife, are ye not carnal, and walk according to man?" So that to walk according to man and to be carnal are the same; for by *flesh,* that is, by a part of man, man is meant. For before he said that those same persons were animal whom afterwards he calls carnal, saying "For what man knoweth the things of a man, save the spirit of man which is in him? even so the things of God knoweth no man, but the Spirit of God. Now we have received not the spirit of this world, but the Spirit which is of God; that we might know the things which are freely given to us of God. Which things also we speak, not in the words which man's wisdom teacheth, but which the Holy Ghost teacheth; comparing spiritual things with spiritual. But the animal man perceiveth not the things of the Spirit of God; for they are foolishness unto him." It is to men of this kind, then, that is, to animal men, he shortly after says, "And I, brethren, could not speak unto you as unto spiritual, but as unto carnal." And this is to be interpreted by the same usage, a part being taken for the whole. For both the soul and the flesh, the component parts of man, can be used to signify the whole man; and so the animal man and the carnal man are not two different things, but one and the same thing, viz. man living according to man. In the same way it is nothing else than men that are meant either in the words, "By the deeds of the law there shall no *flesh* be justified"; or in the words, "Seventy-five *souls* went down into Egypt with Jacob." In the one passage, "no flesh" signifies "no man"; and in the other, by "seventy-five souls" seventy-five men were meant. And the expression, "not in words which man's wisdom teacheth" might equally be "not in words which fleshly wisdom teacheth"; and the expression, "ye walk according to man," might be "according to the flesh." And this is still more apparent in the words which followed: "For while one saith, I am of Paul, and another, I am of Apollos, are ye not men?" The same thing which he had before expressed by "ye are animal," "ye are carnal," he now expresses by "ye are men"; that is, ye live according to man, not according to God, for if you lived according to Him, you should be gods.

CHAPTER V

There is no need, therefore, that in our sins and vices we accuse the nature of the flesh to the injury of the Creator, for in its own kind and degree the flesh is good; but to desert the Creator good, and live according to the created good, is not good, whether a man choose to live according to the flesh, or according to the soul, or according to the whole human nature, which is composed of flesh and soul, and which is therefore spoken of either by the name flesh alone, or by the name soul alone. For he who extols the nature of the soul as the chief good, and condemns the nature of the flesh as if it were evil, assuredly is fleshly both in his love of the soul and hatred of the flesh; for these his feelings arise from human fancy, not from divine truth. The Platonists, indeed, are not as foolish as, with the Manichaeans, to detest our present bodies as an evil nature; for they attribute all the elements of which this visible and tangible world is compacted, with all their qualities, to God their Creator. Nevertheless, from the death-infected members and earthly construction of the body they believe the soul is so affected, that there are thus originated in it the diseases of desires, and fears, and joy, and sorrow, under which four perturbations, as Cicero calls them, or passions, as most prefer to name them with the Greeks, is included the whole viciousness of human life. But if this be so, how is it that Aeneas in Virgil, when he had heard from his father in Hades that the souls should return to bodies, expresses surprise at this declaration, and exclaims:

> "O father! and can thought conceive
> That happy souls this realm would leave,
> And seek the upper sky,
> With sluggish clay to reunite?
> This direful longing for the light,
> Whence comes it, say, and why?" [13]

This direful longing, then, does it still exist even in that boasted purity of the disembodied spirits, and does it still proceed from the death-infected members and earthly limbs? Does he not assert that, when they begin to long to return to the body, they have already been delivered from all these so-called pestilences of the body? From which we gather that, were this endlessly alternating purification and defilement of departing and returning souls as true as it is most certainly false, yet it could not be averred that all culpable and vicious motions of the soul originate in the earthly body; for, on their own showing, "this direful longing," to use the words

[13] *Aeneid* vi.719-21.

of their noble exponent, is so extraneous to the body, that it moves the soul that is purged of all bodily taint, and is existing apart from any body whatever, and moves it, moreover, to be embodied again. So that even they themselves acknowledge that the soul is not only moved to desire, fear, joy, sorrow, by the flesh, but that it can also be agitated with these emotions at its own instance.

CHAPTER VI

But the character of the human will is of moment; because, if it is wrong, these motions of the soul will be wrong, but if it is right, they will be not merely blameless, but even praiseworthy. For the will is in them all; yea, none of them is anything else than will. For what are desire and joy but a volition of consent to the things we wish? And what are fear and sadness but a volition of aversion from the things which we do not wish? But when consent takes the form of seeking to possess the things we wish, this is called desire; and when consent takes the form of enjoying the things we wish, this is called joy. In like manner, when we turn with aversion from that which we do not wish to happen, this volition is termed fear; and when we turn away from that which has happened against our will, this act of will is called sorrow. And generally in respect of all that we seek or shun, as a man's will is attracted or repelled, so it is changed and turned into these different affections. Wherefore the man who lives according to God, and not according to man, ought to be a lover of good, and therefore a hater of evil. And since no one is evil by nature, but whoever is evil is evil by vice, he who lives according to God ought to cherish towards evil men a perfect hatred, so that he shall neither hate the man because of his vice, nor love the vice because of the man, but hate the vice and love the man. For the vice being cursed, all that ought to be loved, and nothing that ought to be hated, will remain. . . .

Book XIX

CHAPTER I

As I see that I have still to discuss the fit destinies of the two cities, the earthly and the heavenly, I must first explain, so far as the limits of this work allow me, the reasonings by which men have attempted to make for themselves a happiness in this unhappy life, in order that it may be evident, not only from divine authority, but also from such reasons as can be adduced to unbelievers, how the empty dreams of the philosophers differ from the hope which God gives to us, and from the substantial fulfilment of it which He will give us as our blessedness. Philosophers have expressed a great variety of diverse opinions regarding the ends of goods and of evils, and this question they have eagerly canvassed, that they might, if possible, discover what makes a man happy. For the end of our good is that for the sake of which other things are to be desired, while it is to be desired for its own sake; and the end of evil is that on account of which other things are to be shunned, while it is avoided on its own account. Thus, by the *end of good,* we at present mean, not that by which good is destroyed, so that it no longer exists, but that by which it is finished, so that it becomes complete; and by the *end of evil* we mean, not that which abolishes it, but that which completes its development. These two ends, therefore, are the supreme good and the supreme evil; and, as I have said, those who have in this vain life professed the study of wisdom have been at great pains to discover these ends, and to obtain the supreme good and avoid the supreme evil in this life. And although they erred in a variety of ways, yet natural insight has prevented them from wandering from the truth so far that they have not placed the supreme good and evil, some in the soul, some in the body, and some in both. From this tripartite distribution of the sects of philosophy, Marcus Varro, in his book *De Philosophia,* has drawn so large a variety of opinions, that, by a subtle and minute analysis of distinctions, he numbers without difficulty as many as 288 sects—not that these have actually existed, but sects which are possible.

To illustrate briefly what he means, I must begin with his own introductory statement in the above-mentioned book, that there are four things which men desire, as it were by nature without a master, without the help of any instruction, without industry or the art of living which is called virtue, and which is certainly learned: either pleasure, which is an agreeable stirring of the bodily sense; or repose, which excludes every bodily inconvenience; or both these, which Epicurus calls by the one name, pleasure; or the primary objects of nature, which comprehend the things already named and other things, either bodily, such as health and safety, and integrity of the members, or spiritual, such as the greater and less mental gifts that are found in men. Now these four things—pleasure, repose, the two combined, and the primary objects of nature—exist in us in such sort that we must either desire virtue on their account, or them for the sake of virtue, or both for their own sake; and consequently there arise from this distinction twelve sects, for each is by this consideration tripled. I will illustrate this in one instance, and having done so, it will not be difficult to understand the others. According, then, as bodily pleasure is subjected, preferred, or united to virtue, there are three sects. It is subject to virtue when it is chosen as subservient to virtue. Thus it is a duty of virtue to live for one's country, and for its sake to beget children, neither of which can be done without bodily pleasure. For there is pleasure in eating and drinking, pleasure also in sexual intercourse. But when it is preferred to virtue, it is desired for its own sake, and virtue is chosen only for its sake, and to effect nothing else than the attainment or preservation of bodily pleasure. And this, indeed, is to make life hideous; for where virtue is the slave of pleasure it no longer deserves the name of virtue. Yet even this disgraceful distortion has found some philosophers to patronize and defend it. Then virtue is united to pleasure when neither is desired for the other's sake, but both for their own. And therefore, as pleasure, according as it is subjected, preferred, or united to virtue, makes three sects, so also do repose, pleasure and repose combined, and the prime natural blessings, make their three sects each. For as men's opinions vary, and these four things are sometimes subjected, sometimes preferred, and sometimes united to virtue, there are produced twelve sects. But this number again is doubled by the addition of one difference, viz. the social life; for whoever attaches himself to any of these sects does so either for his own sake alone, or for the sake of a companion, for whom he ought to wish what he desires for himself. And thus there will be twelve of those who think some one of these opinions should be held for their own sakes, and [an]other twelve who decide that they ought to follow this or that philosophy not for their own sakes only, but also for the sake of others whose good they desire as their own. These twenty-four sects again are doubled, and become forty-eight by adding a difference taken from the New Academy. For each of these four and twenty sects can hold and defend their opinion as certain, as the Stoics defended the position that the supreme good of man consisted solely in virtue; or they can be held as probable, but not certain, as the New Academics did. There are, therefore, twenty-four who hold their philosophy as certainly true, [and an]other twenty-four who hold their opinions as probable, but not certain. Again, as each person who attaches himself to any of these sects may adopt the mode of life either of the Cynics or of the other philosophers, this distinction will double the number, and so make ninety-six sects. Then, lastly, as each of these sects may be adhered to either by men who love a life of ease, as those who have through choice or necessity addicted themselves to study, or by men who live a busy life, as those who, while philosophizing, have been much occupied with state affairs and public business, or by men who choose a mixed life, in imitation of those who have apportioned their time partly to erudite leisure, partly to necessary business: by these differences the number of the sects is tripled, and becomes 288.

I have thus, as briefly and lucidly as I could, given in my own words the opinions which Varro expresses in his book. But how he refutes all the rest of these sects, and chooses one, the Old Academy, instituted by Plato, and continuing to Polemo, the fourth teacher of that school of philosophy which held that their system was certain; and how on this ground he distinguishes it from the New Academy, which began with Polemo's successor Arcesilaus, and held that all things are uncertain; and how he seeks to establish that the Old Academy was as free from error as from doubt—all this, I say, were too long to enter upon in detail, and yet I must not altogether pass it by in silence. Varro then rejects, as a first step, all those differences which have multiplied the number of sects; and the ground on which he does so is that they are not differences about the supreme good. He maintains that in philosophy a sect is created only by its having an opinion of its own different from other schools on the point of the ends-in-chief. For man has no other reason for philosophizing than that he may be happy; but that which makes him happy is itself the supreme good. In other words, the supreme good is the reason of philosophizing; and therefore that cannot be called a sect of philosophy which pursues no way of its own towards the supreme good. Thus, when it is asked whether a wise man will adopt the social life, and desire and be interested in the supreme good of his friend as in his own, or will, on the contrary, do all that he does merely for his own sake, there is no question here about the supreme good, but only about the propriety of associating or not associating a friend in its participation: whether the wise man will do this not for his own sake, but for the sake of his friend in whose good he delights as in his own. So, too, when it is asked whether all things about which philosophy is concerned are to be considered uncertain, as by the New Academy, or certain, as the other philosophers maintain, the question here is not what end should be pursued, but whether or not we are to believe in the substantial existence of that end; or, to put it more plainly, whether he who pursues the supreme good must maintain that it is a true good, or only that it appears to him to be true, though possibly it may be delusive—both pursuing one and the same good. The distinction, too, which is founded on the dress and manners of the Cynics, does not touch the question of the chief good, but only the question whether he who pursues that good which seems to himself true should live as do the Cynics. There were, in fact, men who, though they pursued different things as the supreme good, some choosing pleasure, others virtue, yet adopted that mode of life which gave the Cynics their name. Thus, whatever it is which distinguishes the Cynics from other philosophers, this has no bearing on the choice and pursuit of that good which constitutes happiness. For if it had any such bearing, then the same habits of life would necessitate the pursuit of the same chief good, and diverse habits would necessitate the pursuit of different ends. . . .

CHAPTER XII

Whoever gives even moderate attention to human affairs and to our common nature, will recognise that if there is no man who does not wish to be joyful, neither is there any one who does not wish to have peace. For even they who make war desire nothing but victory—desire, that is to say, to attain to peace with glory. For what else is victory than the conquest of those who resist us? and when this is done there is peace. It is therefore with the desire for peace that wars are waged, even by those who take pleasure in exercising their warlike nature in command and battle. And hence it is obvious that peace is the end sought for by war. For every man seeks peace by waging war, but no man seeks war by making peace. For even they who intentionally interrupt the peace in which they are living have no hatred of peace, but only wish to change it into a peace that suits them better. They do not, therefore, wish to have no peace, but only one more to their mind. And in the case of sedition, when men have separated themselves from the community, they yet do not effect what they wish, unless they maintain some kind of peace with their fellow-conspirators. And therefore even robbers take care to maintain peace with their comrades, that they may with greater effect and greater safety invade the peace of other men. And if an individual happens to be of such unrivalled strength, and to be so jealous of partnership, that he trusts himself with no comrades, but makes his own plots, and commits depredations and murders on his own account, yet he maintains some shadow of peace with such persons as he is unable to kill, and from whom he wishes to conceal his deeds. In his own home, too, he makes it his aim to be at peace with his wife and children, and any other members of his household; for unquestionably their prompt obedience to his every look is a source of pleasure to him. And if this be not rendered, he is angry, he chides and punishes; and even by this storm he secures the calm peace of his own home, as occasion demands. For he sees that peace cannot be maintained unless all the members of the same domestic circle be subject to one head, such as he himself is in his own house. And therefore if a city or nation offered to submit itself to him, to serve him in the same style as he had made his household serve him, he would no longer lurk in a brigand's hiding-places, but lift his head in open day as a king, though the same covetousness and wickedness should remain in him. And thus all men desire to have peace with their own circle whom they wish to govern as suits themselves. For even those whom they make war against they wish to make their own, and impose on them the laws of their own peace.

But let us suppose a man such as poetry and mythology speak of—a man so insociable and savage as to be called rather a semi-man than a man. Although, then, his kingdom was the solitude of a dreary cave, and he himself was so singularly bad-hearted that he was named Κακός, which is the Greek word for *bad;* though he had no wife to soothe him with endearing talk, no children to play with, no sons to do his bidding, no friend to enliven him with intercourse, not even his father Vulcan (though in one respect he was happier than his father, not having begotten a monster like himself); although he gave to no man, but took as he wished whatever he could, from whomsoever he could, when he could; yet in that solitary den, the floor of which, as Virgil [14] says, was always reeking with recent slaughter, there was nothing else than peace sought, a peace in which no one should molest him, or disquiet him with any assault or alarm. With his own body he desired to be at peace; and he was satisfied only in proportion as he had this peace. For he ruled his members, and they obeyed him; and for the sake of pacifying his mortal nature, which rebelled when it needed anything, and of allaying the sedition of hunger which threatened to banish the soul from the body, he made forays, slew, and devoured, but used the ferocity and savageness he displayed in these actions only for the preservation of his own life's peace. So that, had he been willing to make with other men the same peace which he made with himself in his own cave, he would neither have been called bad, nor a monster, nor a semi-man. Or if the appearance of his body and his vomiting smoky fires frightened men from having any dealings with him, perhaps his fierce ways arose not from a desire to do mischief, but from the necessity of finding a living. But he may have had no existence, or, at least, he was not such as the poets fancifully describe him, for they had to exalt Hercules, and did so at the expense of Cacus. It is better, then, to believe that such a man or semi-man never existed, and that this, in common with many other fancies of the poets, is mere fiction. For the most savage animals (and he is said to have been almost a wild beast) encompass their own species with a ring of protecting peace. They cohabit, beget, produce, suckle, and bring up their young, though very many of them are not gregarious, but solitary— not like sheep, deer, pigeons, starlings, bees, but such as lions, foxes, eagles, bats. For what tigress does not purr over her cubs, and lay aside her ferocity to fondle them? What kite, solitary as he is when circling over

[14] *Aeneid* viii.195.

his prey, does not seek a mate, build a nest, hatch the eggs, bring up the
young birds, and maintain with the mother of his family as peaceful a
domestic alliance as he can? How much more powerfully do the laws of
man's nature move him to hold fellowship and maintain peace with all
men so far as in him lies, since even wicked men wage war to maintain
the peace of their own circle, and wish that, if possible, all men belonged
to them, that all men and things might serve but one head, and might,
either through love or fear, yield themselves to peace with him! It is thus
that pride in its perversity apes God. It abhors equality with other men
under Him; but, instead of His rule, it seeks to impose a rule of its own
upon its equals. It abhors, that is to say, the just peace of God, and loves
its own unjust peace; but it cannot help loving peace of one kind or other.
For there is no vice so clean contrary to nature that it obliterates even
the faintest traces of nature.

He, then, who prefers what is right to what is wrong, and what is well-
ordered to what is perverted, sees that the peace of unjust men is not
worthy to be called peace in comparison with the peace of the just. And
yet even what is perverted must of necessity be in harmony with, and in
dependence on, and in some part of the order of things, for otherwise it
would have no existence at all. Suppose a man hangs with his head downwards, this is certainly a perverted attitude of body and arrangement of
its members; for that which nature requires to be above is beneath, and
vice versa. This perversity disturbs the peace of the body, and is therefore
painful. Nevertheless, the spirit is at peace with its body, and labours for
its preservation, and hence the suffering; but if it is banished from the
body by its pains, then, so long as the bodily framework holds together,
there is in the remains a kind of peace among the members, and hence
the body remains suspended. And inasmuch as the earthly body tends towards the earth, and rests on the bond by which it is suspended, it tends
thus to its natural peace, and the voice of its own weight demands a place
for it to rest; and though now lifeless and without feeling, it does not
fall from the peace that is natural to its place in creation, whether it already has it, or is tending towards it. For if you apply embalming preparations to prevent the bodily frame from mouldering and dissolving, a kind
of peace still unites part to part, and keeps the whole body in a suitable
place on the earth—in other words, in a place that is at peace with the
body. If, on the other hand, the body receive no such care, but be left to
the natural course, it is disturbed by exhalations that do not harmonize
with one another, and that offend our senses; for it is this which is perceived in putrefaction until it is assimilated to the elements of the world,

and particle by particle enters into peace with them. Yet throughout this process the laws of the most high Creator and Governor are strictly observed, for it is by Him the peace of the universe is administered. For although minute animals are produced from the carcase of a larger animal, all these little atoms, by the law of the same Creator, serve the animals they belong to in peace. And although the flesh of dead animals be eaten by others, no matter where it be carried, nor what it be brought into contact with, nor what it be converted and changed into, it still is ruled by the same laws which pervade all things for the conservation of every mortal race, and which brings things that fit one another into harmony.

CHAPTER XIII

The peace of the body then consists in the duly proportioned arrangement of its parts. The peace of the irrational soul is the harmonious repose of the appetites, and that of the rational soul the harmony of knowledge and action. The peace of body and soul is the well-ordered and harmonious life and health of the living creature. Peace between man and God is the well-ordered obedience of faith to eternal law. Peace between man and man is well-ordered concord. Domestic peace is the well-ordered concord between those of the family who rule and those who obey. Civil peace is a similar concord among the citizens. The peace of the celestial city is the perfectly ordered and harmonious enjoyment of God, and of one another in God. The peace of all things is the tranquillity of order. Order is the distribution which allots things equal and unequal, each to its own place. And hence, though the miserable, in so far as they are such, do certainly not enjoy peace, but are severed from that tranquillity of order in which there is no disturbance, nevertheless, inasmuch as they are deservedly and justly miserable, they are by their very misery connected with order. They are not, indeed, conjoined with the blessed, but they are disjoined from them by the law of order. And though they are disquieted, their circumstances are notwithstanding adjusted to them, and consequently they have some tranquillity of order, and therefore some peace. But they are wretched because, although not wholly miserable, they are not in that place where any mixture of misery is impossible. They would, however, be more wretched if they had not that peace which arises from being in harmony with the natural order of things. When they suffer, their peace is in so far disturbed; but their peace continues in so far as they do not suffer, and in so far as their nature continues to exist. As, then, there may be life without pain, while there cannot be pain without some kind of life, so there may be peace without war, but there cannot be war without some kind of peace, because war supposes the existence of some natures to wage it, and these natures cannot exist without peace of one kind or another.

And therefore there is a nature in which evil does not or even cannot exist; but there cannot be a nature in which there is no good. Hence, not even the nature of the devil himself is evil, in so far as it is nature, but it was made evil by being perverted. Thus he did not abide in the truth, but could not escape the judgment of the Truth; he did not abide in the tranquillity of order, but did not therefore escape the power of the Ordainer. The good imparted by God to his nature did not screen him from the justice of God by which order was preserved in his punishment; neither did God punish the good which He had created, but the evil which the devil had committed. God did not take back all He had imparted to his nature, but something He took and something He left, that there might remain enough to be sensible of the loss of what was taken. And this very sensibility to pain is evidence of the good which has been taken away and the good which has been left. For, were nothing good left, there could be no pain on account of the good which had been lost. For he who sins is still worse if he rejoices in his loss of righteousness. But he who is in pain, if he derives no benefit from it, mourns at least the loss of health. And as righteousness and health are both good things, and as the loss of any good thing is a matter of grief, not of joy—if, at least, there is no compensation, as spiritual righteousness may compensate for the loss of bodily health—certainly it is more suitable for a wicked man to grieve in punishment than to rejoice in his fault. As, then, the joy of a sinner who has abandoned what is good is evidence of a bad will, so his grief for the good which he has lost when he is punished is evidence of a good nature. For he who laments the peace his nature has lost is stirred to do so by some relics of peace which makes his nature friendly to itself. And it is very just that in the final punishment the wicked and godless should in anguish bewail the loss of the natural advantages they enjoyed, and should perceive that they were most justly taken from them by that God whose benign liberality they had despised. God, then, the most wise creator and most just Ordainer of all natures, who placed the human race upon earth as its greatest ornament, imparted to men some good things adapted to this life, to wit, temporal peace, such as we can enjoy in this life from health and safety and human fellowship, and all things needful for the preservation and recovery of this peace, such as the objects which are accommodated to our outward senses, light, night, the air, and waters suitable for us, and everything the body requires to sustain, shelter, heal, or beautify it: and all under this most equitable condition, that every man

who made a good use of these advantages suited to the peace of his mortal
condition, should receive ampler and better blessings, namely, the peace
of immortality, accompanied by glory and honour in an endless life made
fit for the enjoyment of God and of one another in God; but that he who
used the present blessings badly should both lose them and should not
receive the others.

CHAPTER XIV

The whole use, then, of things temporal has a reference to this result
of earthly peace in the earthly community, while in the city of God it is
connected with eternal peace. And therefore, if we were irrational animals,
we should desire nothing beyond the proper arrangement of the parts of
the body and the satisfaction of the appetites—nothing, therefore, but bodily
comfort and abundance of pleasures, that the peace of the body might
contribute to the peace of the soul. For if bodily peace be awanting, a bar
is put to the peace even of the irrational soul, since it cannot obtain the
gratification of its appetites. And these two together help out the mutual
peace of soul and body, the peace of harmonious life and health. For as
animals, by shunning pain, show that they love bodily peace, and by pursuing pleasure to gratify their appetites, show that they love peace of the
soul, so their shrinking from death is a sufficient indication of their intense
love of that peace which binds soul and body in close alliance. But, as man
has a rational soul, he subordinates all this which he has in common with
the beasts to the peace of his rational soul, that his intellect may have
free play and may regulate his actions, and that he may thus enjoy the
well-ordered harmony of knowledge and action which constitutes, as we
have said, the peace of the rational soul. And for this purpose he must
desire to be neither molested by pain, nor disturbed by desire, nor extinguished by death, that he may arrive at some useful knowledge by which
he may regulate his life and manners. But, owing to the liability of the
human mind to fall into mistakes, this very pursuit of knowledge may
be a snare to him unless he has a divine Master, whom he may obey
without misgiving, and who may at the same time give him such help
as to preserve his own freedom. And because, so long as he is in this mortal
body, he is a stranger to God, he walks by faith, not by sight; and he
therefore refers all peace, bodily or spiritual or both, to that peace which
mortal man has with the immortal God, so that he exhibits the well-
ordered obedience of faith to eternal law. But as this divine Master inculcates two precepts—the love of God and the love of our neighbour—
and as in these precepts a man finds three things he has to love—God,

himself, and his neighbour—and that he who loves God loves himself thereby, it follows that he must endeavour to get his neighbour to love God, since he is ordered to love his neighbour as himself. He ought to make this endeavour in behalf of his wife, his children, his household, all within his reach, even as he would wish his neighbour to do the same for him if he needed it; and consequently he will be at peace, or in well-ordered concord, with all men, as far as in him lies. And this is the order of this concord, that a man, in the first place, injure no one, and, in the second, do good to every one he can reach. Primarily, therefore, his own household are his care, for the law of nature and society gives him readier access to them and greater opportunity of serving them. And hence the apostle says, "Now, if any provide not for his own, and specially for those of his own house, he hath denied the faith, and is worse than an infidel." This is the origin of domestic peace, or the well-ordered concord of those in the family who rule and those who obey. For they who care for the rest rule—the husband the wife, the parents the children, the masters the servants; and they who are cared for obey—the women their husbands, the children their parents, the servants their masters. But in the family of the just man who lives by faith and is as yet a pilgrim journeying on to the celestial city, even those who rule serve those whom they seem to command; for they rule not from a love of power, but from a sense of the duty they owe to others—not because they are proud of authority, but because they love mercy. . . .

CHAPTER XXIV

But if we discard this definition of a people, and, assuming another, say that a people is an assemblage of reasonable beings bound together by a common agreement as to the objects of their love, then, in order to discover the character of any people, we have only to observe what they love. Yet whatever it loves, if only it is an assemblage of reasonable beings and not of beasts, and is bound together by an agreement as to the objects of love, it is reasonably called a people; and it will be a superior people in proportion as it is bound together by higher interests, inferior in proportion as it is bound together by lower. According to this definition of ours, the Roman people is a people, and its weal is without doubt a commonwealth or republic. But what its tastes were in its early and subsequent days, and how it declined into sanguinary seditions and then to social and civil wars, and so burst asunder or rotted off the bond of concord in which the health of a people consists, history shows, and in the preceding books I have related at large. And yet I would not on this account say either that it was not a people, or that its administration was not a republic, so long as there remains an assemblage of reasonable beings bound together by a common agreement as to the objects of love. But what I say of this people and of this republic I must be understood to think and say of the Athenians or any Greek state, of the Egyptians, of the early Assyrian Babylon, and of every other nation, great or small, which had a public government. For, in general, the city of the ungodly, which did not obey the command of God that it should offer no sacrifice save to Him alone, and which, therefore, could not give to the soul its proper command over the body, nor to the reason its just authority over the vices, is void of true justice.

CHAPTER XXV

For though the soul may seem to rule the body admirably, and the reason the vices, if the soul and reason do not themselves obey God, as God has commanded them to serve Him, they have no proper authority over the body and the vices. For what kind of mistress of the body and the vices can that mind be which is ignorant of the true God, and which, instead of being subject to His authority, is prostituted to the corrupting influences of the most vicious demons? It is for this reason that the virtues which it seems to itself to possess, and by which it restrains the body and the vices that it may obtain and keep what it desires, are rather vices than virtues so long as there is no reference to God in the matter. For although some suppose that virtues which have a reference only to themselves, and are desired only on their own account, are yet true and genuine virtues, the fact is that even then they are inflated with pride, and are therefore to be reckoned vices rather than virtues. For as that which gives life to the flesh is not derived from flesh, but is above it, so that which gives blessed life to man is not drived from man, but is something above him; and what I say of man is true of every celestial power and virtue whatsoever.

CHAPTER XXVI

Wherefore, as the life of the flesh is the soul, so the blessed life of man is God, of whom the sacred writings of the Hebrews say, "Blessed is the people whose God is the Lord." Miserable, therefore, is the people which is alienated from God. Yet even this people has a peace of its own which is not to be lightly esteemed, though, indeed, it shall not in the end enjoy it, because it makes no good use of it before the end. But it is our interest that it enjoy this peace meanwhile in this life; for as long as the two cities are commingled, we also enjoy the peace of Babylon. For from Babylon the people of God is so freed that it meanwhile sojourns in its company. And therefore the apostle also admonished the Church to pray for kings and those in authority, assigning as the reason, "that we may live a quiet and tranquil life in all godliness and love." And the prophet Jeremiah, when predicting the captivity that was to befall the ancient people of God, and giving them the divine command to go obediently to Babylonia, and thus serve their God, counselled them also to pray for Babylonia, saying, "In the peace thereof shall ye have peace"—the temporal peace which the good and the wicked together enjoy.

CHAPTER XXVII

But the peace which is peculiar to ourselves we enjoy now with God by faith, and shall hereafter enjoy eternally with Him by sight. But the peace which we enjoy in this life, whether common to all or peculiar to ourselves, is rather the solace of our misery than the positive enjoyment of felicity. Our very righteousness, too, though true in so far as it has respect to the true good, is yet in this life of such a kind that it consists rather in the remission of sins than in the perfecting of virtues. Witness the prayer of the whole city of God in its pilgrim state, for it cries to God by the mouth of all its members, "Forgive us our debts as we forgive our debtors." And this prayer is efficacious not for those whose faith is "without works and dead," but for those whose faith "worketh by love." For as reason, though subjected to God is yet "pressed down by the corruptible body," so long as it is in this mortal condition, it has not perfect authority over vice, and therefore this prayer is needed by the righteous. For though it exercises authority, the vices do not submit without a struggle. For however well one maintains the conflict, and however thoroughly he has subdued these enemies, there steals in some evil thing, which, if it do not find ready expression in act, slips out by the lips, or insinuates itself into the thought; and therefore his peace is not full so long as he is at war with his vices. For it is a doubtful conflict he wages with those that resist, and his victory over those that are defeated is not secure, but full of anxiety and effort. Amidst these temptations, therefore, of all which it has been summarily said in the divine oracles, "Is not human life upon earth a temptation?" who but a proud man can presume that he so lives that he has no need to say to God, "Forgive us our debts?" And such a man is not great, but swollen and puffed up with vanity, and is justly resisted by Him who abundantly gives grace to the humble. Whence it is said, "God resisteth the proud, but giveth grace to the humble." In this, then, consists the righteousness of a man, that he submit himself to God, his body to his soul, and his vices, even when they rebel, to his reason, which either defeats or at least resists them; and also that he beg from God grace to do his duty, and the pardon of his sins, and that he renders to God thanks for all the blessings he receives. But, in that final peace to which all our righteousness has reference, and for the sake of which it is maintained, as our nature shall enjoy a sound immortality and incorruption, and shall have no more vices, and as we shall experience no resistance either from ourselves or from others, it will not be necessary that reason should rule vices which no longer exist, but God shall rule the man, and the soul shall rule the body, with a sweetness and facility suitable to the felicity of a life which is done with bondage. And this condition shall there be eternal, and we shall be assured of its eternity; and thus the peace of this blessedness and the blessedness of this peace shall be the supreme good.

CHAPTER XXVIII

But, on the other hand, they who do not belong to this city of God shall inherit eternal misery, which is also called the second death, because the soul shall then be separated from God its life, and therefore cannot be said to live, and the body shall be subjected to eternal pains. And consequently this second death shall be the more severe, because no death shall terminate it. But war being contrary to peace, as misery to happiness, and life to death, it is not without reason asked what kind of war can be found in the end of the wicked answering to the peace which is declared to be the end of the righteous? The person who puts this question has only to observe what it is in war that is hurtful and destructive, and he shall see that it is nothing else than the mutual opposition and conflict of things. And can he conceive a more grievous and bitter war than that in which the will is so opposed to passion, and passion to the will, that their hostility can never be terminated by the victory of either, and in which the violence of pain so conflicts with the nature of the body, that neither yields to the other? For in this life, when this conflict has arisen, either pain conquers and death expels the feeling of it, or nature conquers and health expels the pain. But in the world to come the pain continues that it may torment, and the nature endures that it may be sensible of it; and neither ceases to exist, lest punishment also should cease. Now, as it is through the last judgment that men pass to these ends, the good to the supreme good, the evil to the supreme evil, I will treat of this judgment in the following book.

BENEDICT

THE CLERGY of the Middle Ages were divided between the *secular*—those who administered the parishes and the more worldly affairs of the Church —and the *regular*—those who lived under the *regula* of a monastery. The monastic life was necessarily available to only a few, but it was nevertheless looked upon as the ideal existence by the philosophers of the Middle Ages. Monastic institutions were established in the Near East during the fourth century and spread rapidly to the West. Their aim was to regularize and discipline an exclusive dedication to God.

In the sixth century, Benedict of Nursia (c.480–c.553) developed the system of government under which the famous monastery of Monte Cassino operated and which was adopted by most Western monasteries through the medieval period. It is probable that the Rule of St. Benedict was formulated at the behest of high authorities in the Church, perhaps Pope Hormisdas, in the effort to reform monastic practice. Originally regarded as having a relatively limited sphere of application, the Rule constituted by the time of Charlemagne the well-established practice of Western monks, and later became the basis of new orders like those at Cluny and Citeaux.

The *Rule of St. Benedict* has a prologue and seventy-three chapters. It is based on the experience of Benedict and his order and codifies the principles of their lives, chiefly centered around doctrines of poverty, chastity, obedience, piety, and labor.

The following translation by E. F. Henderson appears in his *Select Historical Documents of the Middle Ages* (London, George Bell and Sons, 1896). The *Rule* was originally written in Low Latin, the vernacular of the time; whether it was drawn up gradually in response to the needs of the monks or written at one time cannot be determined, but 530 is a likely date of its composition.

THE RULE OF ST. BENEDICT

Prologue. . . . We are about to found, therefore, a school for the Lord's service; in the organization of which we trust that we shall ordain nothing severe and nothing burdensome. But even if, the demands of justice dictating it, something a little irksome shall be the result, for the purpose of amending vices or preserving charity—thou shalt not therefore, struck by fear, flee the way of salvation, which can not be entered upon except through a narrow entrance. But as one's way of life and one's faith progresses, the heart becomes broadened, and, with the unutterable sweetness of love, the way of the mandates of the Lord is traversed. Thus, never departing from His guidance, continuing in the monastery in His teaching until death, through patience we are made partakers in Christ's passion, in order that we may merit to be companions in His kingdom.

Concerning the kinds of monks and their manner of living. It is manifest that there are four kinds of monks. The cenobites are the first kind; that is, those living in a monastery, serving under a rule or an abbot. Then the second kind is that of the anchorites; that is, the hermits—those who, not by the new fervour of a conversion but by the long probation of life in a monastery, have learned to fight against the devil, having already been taught by the solace of many. They, having been well prepared in the army of brothers for the solitary fight of the hermit, being secure now without the consolation of another, are able, God helping them, to fight with their own hand or arm against the vices of the flesh or of their thoughts.

But a third very bad kind of monks are the sarabites, approved by no rule, experience being their teacher, as with the gold which is tried in the furnace. But, softened after the manner of lead, keeping faith with the world by their works, they are known through their tonsure to lie to God. These being shut up by twos or threes, or, indeed, alone, without a shepherd, not in the Lord's but in their own sheep-folds—their law is the satisfaction of their desires. For whatever they think good or choice, this they call holy; and what they do not wish, this they consider unlawful. But the fourth kind of monks is the kind which is called gyratory. During their whole life they are guests, for three or four days at a time, in the cells of the different monasteries, throughout the various provinces; always wandering and never stationary, given over to the service of their own pleasures and the joys of the palate, and in every way worse than the sarabites. Concerning the most wretched way of living of all such monks it is better to be silent than to speak. These things therefore being omitted, let us proceed, with the aid of God, to treat of the best kind, the cenobites.

What the Abbot should be like. An abbot who is worthy to preside over a monastery ought always to remember what he is called, and carry out with his deeds the name of a Superior. For he is believed to be Christ's representative, since he is called by His name, the apostle saying: "Ye have received the spirit of adoption of sons, whereby we call Abba, Father." And so the abbot should not—grant that he may not—teach, or decree, or order, any thing apart from the precept of the Lord; but his order or teaching should be sprinkled with the ferment of divine justice in the minds of his disciples. Let the abbot always be mindful that, at the tremendous judgment of God, both things will be weighed in the balance: his teaching and the obedience of his disciples. And let the abbot know that whatever the father of the family finds of less utility among the sheep is laid to the fault of the shepherd. Only in a case where the whole diligence of their pastor shall have been bestowed on an unruly and disobedient flock, and his whole care given to their morbid actions, shall that pastor, absolved in the judgment of the Lord, be free to say to the Lord with the prophet: "I have not hid Thy righteousness within my heart, I have declared Thy faithfulness and Thy salvation, but they despising have scorned me." And then at length let the punishment for the disobedient sheep under his care be death itself prevailing against them. Therefore, when anyone receives the name of abbot, he ought to rule over his disciples with a double teaching; that is, let him show forth all good and holy things by deeds more than by words. So that to ready disciples he may propound the mandates of God in words; but, to the hard-hearted and the more simple-minded, he may show forth the divine precepts by his deeds. But as to all the things that he has taught to his disciples to be wrong, he shall show by his deeds that they are not to be done; lest, preaching to others, he himself shall be found worthy of blame, and lest God may say at some time to him a sinner: "What hast thou to do to declare my statutes or that thou should'st take my covenant in thy mouth. Seeing that thou hatest instruction and casteth my words behind thee; and why beholdest thou the mote that is in thy brother's eye, but considerest not the beam that is in thine own eye?" He shall make no distinction of persons in the monastery. One shall not be more cherished than another, unless it be the one whom he finds excelling in good works or in obedience. A free-born man shall not be preferred to one coming from servitude, unless there be some other reasonable cause. But if, justice demanding that it should be thus, it seems good to the abbot, he shall do this no matter what the rank shall be. But otherwise they shall keep their own places; for whether we be bond or free we are all one in Christ; and, under one God, we perform an equal service of subjection; for God is no respecter of persons. Only in this way is a distinction made by Him concerning us: if we are found humble and surpassing others in good works. Therefore let him (the abbot) have equal charity for all: let the same discipline be administered in all cases according to merit. In his teaching indeed the abbot ought always to observe that form laid down by the apostle when he says: "reprove, rebuke, exhort." That is, mixing seasons with seasons, blandishments with terrors, let him display the feeling of a severe yet devoted master. He should, namely, rebuke more severely the unruly and the turbulent. The obedient, moreover, and the gentle and the patient, he should exhort, that they may progress to higher things. But the negligent and scorners, we warn him to admonish and reprove. Nor let him conceal the sins of the erring: but, in order that he may prevail, let him pluck them out by the roots as soon as they begin to spring up; being mindful of the danger of Eli the priest of Shiloh. And the more honest and intelligent minds, indeed, let him rebuke with words, with a first or second admonition; but the wicked and the hard-hearted and the proud, or the disobedient, let him restrain at the very beginning of their sin by castigation of the body, as it were, with whips: knowing that it is written: "A fool is not bettered by words." And again: "Strike thy son with the rod and thou shalt deliver his soul from death." The abbot ought always to remember what he is, to remember what he is called, and to know that from him to whom more is committed, the more is demanded. And let him know what a difficult and arduous thing he has undertaken—to rule the soul and aid the morals of many. And in one case indeed with blandishments, in another with rebukes, in another with persuasion—according to the quality or intelligence of each one—he shall so conform and adapt himself to all, that not only shall he not suffer detriment to come to the flock committed to him, but shall rejoice in the increase of a good flock. Above all things, let him not, dissimulating or undervaluing the safety of the souls committed to him, give more heed to transitory and earthly and passing things: but let him always reflect that he has undertaken to rule souls for which he is to render account. And, lest perchance he enter into strife for a lesser matter, let him remember that it is written: "Seek ye first the kingdom of God and His righteousness; and all these things shall be added unto you." And again: "They that fear Him shall lack nothing." And let him know that he who undertakes to rule souls must prepare to render account. And, whatever number of brothers he knows that he has under his care, let him know for certain that at the day of judgment he shall render account to God for all their souls; his own soul without doubt being included. And thus, always fearing the future interrogation of the shepherd concerning the flocks

entrusted to him, while keeping free from foreign interests he is rendered
careful for his own. And when, by his admonitions, he administers correction
to others, he is himself cleansed from his vices.

About calling in the brethren to take council. As often as anything especial is
to be done in the monastery, the abbot shall call together the whole congregation, and shall himself explain the question at issue. And, having heard the
advice of the brethren, he shall think it over by himself, and shall do what he
considers most advantageous. And for this reason, moreover, we have said
that all ought to be called to take counsel: because often it is to a younger person that God reveals what is best. The brethren, moreover, with all subjection
of humility, ought so to give their advice, that they do not presume boldly to
defend what seems good to them; but it should rather depend on the judgment of the abbot; so that whatever he decided to be the more salutary, they
should all agree to it. But even as it behooves the disciples to obey the master,
so it is fitting that he should providently and justly arrange all matters. In
all things, indeed, let all follow the Rule as their guide; and let no one rashly
deviate from it. Let no one in the monastery follow the inclination of his own
heart; and let no one boldly presume to dispute with his abbot, within or without the monastery. But, if he should so presume, let him be subject to the discipline of the Rule. The abbot, on the other hand, shall do all things fearing
the Lord and observing the Rule; knowing that he, without a doubt, shall
have to render account to God as to a most impartial judge, for all his decisions.
But if any lesser matters for the good of the monastery are to be decided upon,
he shall employ the counsel of the elder members alone, since it is written:
"Do all things with counsel, and after it is done thou wilt not repent." . . .

Concerning obedience. The first grade of humility is obedience without
delay. This becomes those who, on account of the holy service which they have
professed, or on account of the fear of hell or the glory of eternal life consider
nothing dearer to them than Christ: so that, so soon as anything is commanded
by their superior, they may not know how to suffer delay in doing it, even
as if it were a divine command. Concerning whom the Lord said: "As soon as
he heard of me he obeyed me." And again he said to the learned men: "He
who heareth you heareth me." Therefore let all such, straightway leaving their
own affairs and giving up their own will, with unoccupied hands and leaving
incomplete what they were doing—the foot of obedience being foremost—
follow with their deeds the voice of him who orders. And, as it were, in the
same moment, let the aforesaid command of the master and the perfected
work of the disciple—both together in the swiftness of the fear of God—be
called into being by those who are possessed with a desire of advancing to
eternal life. And therefore let them seize the narrow way of which the Lord

says: "Narrow is the way which leadeth unto life." Thus, not living according to their own judgment nor obeying their own desires and pleasures, but walking under another's judgment and command, passing their time in monasteries, let them desire an abbot to rule over them. Without doubt all such live up to that precept of the Lord in which he says: "I am not come to do My own will but the will of Him that sent Me." . . .

Concerning humility. . . . The sixth grade of humility is, that a monk be contented with all lowliness or extremity, and consider himself, with regard to everything which is enjoined on him, as a poor and unworthy workman; saying to himself with the prophet: "I was reduced to nothing and was ignorant; I was made as the cattle before thee, and I am always with thee." The seventh grade of humility is, not only that he, with his tongue, pronounce himself viler and more worthless than all; but that he also believe it in the innermost workings of his heart; humbling himself. . . . The eighth degree of humility is that a monk do nothing except what the common rule of the monastery, or the example of his elders, urges him to do. The ninth degree of humility is that a monk restrain his tongue from speaking; and, keeping silence, do not speak until he is spoken to. The tenth grade of humility is that he be not ready, and easily inclined, to laugh. . . . The eleventh grade of humility is that a monk, when he speaks, speak slowly and without laughter, humbly with gravity, using few and reasonable words; and that he be not loud of voice. . . . The twelfth grade of humility is that a monk shall, not only with his heart but also with his body, always show humility to all who see him: that is, when at work, in the oratory, in the monastery, in the garden, on the road, in the fields. And everywhere, sitting or walking or standing, let him always be with head inclined, his looks fixed upon the ground; remembering every hour that he is guilty of his sins. Let him think that he is already being presented before the tremendous judgment of God, saying always to himself in his heart what that publican of the gospel, fixing his eyes on the earth, said: "Lord I am not worthy, I a sinner, so much as to lift up mine eyes unto Heaven." . . .

How the monks shall sleep. They shall sleep separately in separate beds. They shall receive positions for their beds, after the manner of their characters, according to the dispensation of their abbot. If it can be done, they shall all sleep in one place. If, however, their number do not permit it, they shall rest by tens or twenties, with elders who will concern themselves about them. A candle shall always be burning in that same cell until early in the morning. They shall sleep clothed, and girt with belts or with ropes; and they shall not have their knives at their sides while they sleep, lest perchance in a dream they should wound the sleepers. And let the monks be always on the alert; and, when the signal is given, rising without delay, let them hasten to mutually prepare themselves for the service of God—with all gravity and modesty, however. The younger brothers shall not have beds by themselves, but interpersed among those of the elder ones. And when they rise for the service of God, they shall exhort each other mutually with moderation, on account of the excuses that those who are sleepy are inclined to make. . . .

What care the abbot should exercise with regard to the excommunicated. With all solicitude the abbot shall exercise care with regard to delinquent brothers: "They that be whole need not a physician, but they that are sick." And therefore he ought to use every means, as a wise physician, to send in as it were secret consolers—that is, wise elder brothers who, as it were secretly, shall console the wavering brother and lead him to the atonement of humility. And they shall comfort him lest he be swallowed up by overmuch sorrow. On the contrary, as the same apostle says, charity shall be confirmed in him, and he shall be prayed for by all. For the abbot should greatly exert his solicitude, and take care with all sagacity and industry, lest he lose any of the sheep entrusted to him. For he should know that he has undertaken the care of weak souls, not the tyranny over sound ones. And he shall fear the threat of the prophet through whom the Lord says: "Ye did take that which ye saw to be strong, and that which was weak ye did cast out." And let him imitate the pious example of the good Shepherd, who, leaving the ninety and nine sheep upon the mountains, went out to seek the one sheep that had gone astray: and He had such compassion upon its infirmity, that He deigned to place it upon His sacred shoulders, and thus to carry it back to the flock. . . .

Whether the monks should have anything of their own. More than anything else is this special vice to be cut off root and branch from the monastery, that one should presume to give or receive anything without the order of the abbot, or should have anything of his own. He should have absolutely not anything: neither a book, nor tablets, nor a pen—nothing at all. For indeed it is not allowed to the monks to have their own bodies or wills in their own power. But all things necessary they must expect from the Father of the monastery; nor is it allowable to have anything which the abbot did not give or permit. All things shall be common to all, as it is written: "Let not any man presume or call anything his own." But if any one shall have been discovered delighting in this most evil vice: being warned once and again, if he do not amend, let him be subjected to punishment.

Whether all ought to receive necessaries equally. As it is written: "It was divided among them singly, according as each had need": whereby we do not say—far from it—that there should be an excepting of persons, but a consideration for infirmities. Wherefore he who needs less, let him thank God and not be dismayed; but he who needs more, let him be humiliated on account of his infirmity, and not exalted on account of the mercy that is shown him. And thus all members will be in peace. Above all, let not the evil of murmuring appear, for any cause, through any word or sign whatever. But, if such a murmurer is discovered, he shall be subjected to stricter discipline. . . .

Although human nature itself is prone to have pity for these ages—that is, old age and infancy—nevertheless the authority of the Rule also has regard for them. Their weakness shall always be considered, and in the matter of food, the strict tenor of the Rule shall by no means be observed, as far as they are concerned; but they shall be treated with pious consideration, and may anticipate the canonical hours. . . .

We believe, moreover, that, for the daily refection of the sixth as well as of the ninth hour, two cooked dishes, on account of the infirmities of the different ones, are enough for all tables: so that whoever, perchance, can not eat of one may partake of the other. Therefore let two cooked dishes suffice for all the brothers: and, if it is possible to obtain apples or growing vegetables, a third may be added. One full pound of bread shall suffice for a day, whether there be one refection, or a breakfast and a supper. But if they are going to have supper, the third part of that same pound shall be reserved by the cellarer, to be given back to those who are about to sup. But if, perchance, some greater labour shall have been performed, it shall be in the will and the power of the abbot, if it is expedient, to increase anything; surfeiting above all things being guarded against, so that indigestion may never seize a monk: for nothing is so contrary to every Christian as surfeiting. . . . But the eating of the flesh of quadrupeds shall be abstained from altogether by every one, excepting alone the weak and the sick. . . .

Concerning the daily manual labour. Idleness is the enemy of the soul. And therefore, at fixed times, the brothers ought to be occupied in manual labours; and again, at fixed times, in sacred reading. Therefore we believe that, according to this disposition, both seasons ought to be arranged: so that, from Easter until the Calends of October, going out early, from the first until the fourth hour they shall do what labour may be necessary. Moreover, from the fourth hour until about the sixth, they shall be free for reading. After the meal of the sixth hour, moreover, rising from table, they shall rest in their beds with all silence; or, perchance, he that wishes to read may so read to himself that he do not disturb another. And the nona (the second meal) shall be gone through with more moderately about the middle of the eighth hour; and again they shall work at what is to be done until Vespers. But, if the exigency or poverty of the place demands that they be occupied by themselves in picking fruits, they shall not be dismayed: for then they are truly monks if they live by the labours of their hands; as did also our fathers and the apostles. Let all things be done with moderation, however, on account of the faint-hearted. From the Calends of October, moreover, until the beginning of Lent they shall be free for reading until the second full hour. At the second hour the tertia (morning service) shall be held, and all shall labour at the task which is enjoined upon them until the ninth. The first signal, moreover, of the ninth hour having been given, they shall each one leave off his work: and be ready when the second signal strikes. Moreover after the refection they shall be free for their readings or for psalms. But in the days of Lent, from dawn until the third full hour, they shall be free for their readings; and, until the tenth full hour, they shall do the labour that is enjoined on them. In which days of Lent they shall all receive separate books from the library: which they shall read entirely through in order. These books are to be given out on the first day of Lent. Above all there shall certainly be appointed one or two elders, who shall go round the monastery at the hours in which the brothers are engaged in reading, and see to it that no troublesome brother chance to be found who is open to idleness and trifling, and is not intent on his reading; being not only of no use to himself, but also stirring up others. If such a one—may it not happen—be found, he shall be admonished once and a second time. If he do not amend, he shall be subject under the Rule to such punishment that the others may have fear. Nor shall brother join brother at unsuitable hours. Moreover on Sunday all shall engage in reading: excepting those who are deputed to various duties. But if anyone be so negligent and lazy that he will not or can not read, some task shall be imposed upon him which he can do; so that he be not idle. On feeble or delicate brothers such a labour or art is to be imposed, that they shall neither be idle, nor shall they be so oppressed by the violence of labour as to be driven to take flight. Their weakness is to be taken into consideration by the abbot.

Although at all times the life of the monk should be such as though Lent were being observed: nevertheless, since few have that virtue, we urge that, on those said days of Lent, he shall keep his life in all purity; and likewise wipe out, in those holy days, the negligencies of other times. This is then worthily done if we refrain from all vices, if we devote ourselves to prayer with weeping, to reading and compunction of heart, and to abstinence. Therefore, on these days, let us add of ourselves something to the ordinary amount of our service: special prayers, abstinence from food and drink; so that each one, over and above the amount allotted to him, shall offer of his own will something to God with rejoicing of the Holy Spirit. That is, he shall restrict his body in food, drink, sleep, talkativeness, and merry-making; and, with the joy of a spiritual desire, shall await the holy Easter. The offering, moreover, that each one makes, he shall announce to his abbot; that it may be done with his prayers and by his will. For what is done without the permission of the spiritual Father, shall be put down to presumption and vain-glory, and not to a monk's credit. Therefore all things are to be done according to the will of the abbot. . . .

Whether a monk should be allowed to receive letters or anything. By no means shall it be allowed to a monk—either from his relatives, or from any man, or from one of his fellows—to receive or to give, without order of the abbot, letters, presents or any gift, however small. But even if, by his relatives, anything has been sent to him: he shall not presume to receive it, unless it have first been shown to the abbot. But if he order it to be received, it shall be in the power of the abbot to give it to whomever he may will. And the brother to whom it happened to have been sent shall not be chagrined; that an opportunity be not given to the devil. Whoever, moreover, presumes otherwise, shall be subject to the discipline of the Rule. . . .

Concerning the manner of receiving brothers. When any new comer applies for conversion, an easy entrance shall not be granted him: but, as the apostle says, "Try the spirits if they be of God." Therefore, if he who comes perseveres in knocking, and is seen after four or five days to patiently endure the insults inflicted upon him, and the difficulty of ingress, and to persist in his demand: entrance shall be allowed him, and he shall remain for a few days in the cell of the guests. After this, moreover, he shall be in the cell of the novices, where he shall meditate and eat and sleep. And an elder shall be detailed off for him who shall be capable of saving souls, who shall altogether intently watch over him, and make it a care to see if he reverently seek God, if he be zealous in the service of God, in obedience, in suffering shame. And all the harshness and roughness of the means through which God is approached shall be told him in advance. If he promise perseverance in his steadfastness, after the lapse of two months this Rule shall be read to him in order, and it shall be said to him: "Behold the law under which thou dost wish to serve; if thou canst observe it, enter; but if thou canst not, depart freely." If he have stood firm thus far, then he shall be led into the aforesaid cell of the novices; and again he shall be proven with all patience. And, after the lapse of six months, the Rule shall be read to him; that he may know upon what he is entering. And, if he stand firm thus far, after four months the same Rule shall again be re-read to him. And if, having deliberated with himself, he shall promise to keep everything, and to obey all the commands that are laid upon him: then he shall be received in the congregation; knowing that it is decreed, by the law of the Rule, that from that day he shall not be allowed to depart from the monastery, nor to shake free his neck from the yoke of the Rule, which, after such tardy deliberation, he was at liberty either to refuse or receive. He who is to be received, moreover, shall, in the oratory, in the presence of all, make promise concerning his steadfastness and the change in his manner of life and his obedience to God and to His saints; so that if, at any time, he act contrary, he shall know that he shall be condemned by Him whom he mocks. Concerning which promise he shall make a petition in the name of the saints whose relics are there, and of the abbot who is present. Which petition he shall write with his own hand. Or, if he really be not learned in letters, another, being asked by him, shall write it. And that novice shall make his sign; and with his own hand shall place it (the petition) above the altar. And when he has placed it there, the novice shall straightway commence this verse: "Receive me oh Lord according to thy promise and I shall live, and do not cast me down from my hope." Which verse the whole congregation shall repeat three times, adding: "Glory be to the Father." Then that brother novice shall prostrate himself at the feet of each one, that they may pray for him. And, already, from that day, he shall be considered as in the congregation. If he have any property, he shall either first present it to the poor, or, making a solemn donation, shall confer it on the monastery, keeping nothing at all for himself: as one, forsooth, who from that day, shall know that he shall not have power even over his own body. Straightway, therefore in the oratory, he shall take off his own garments in which he was clad, and shall put on the garments of the monastery. Moreover those garments which he has taken off shall be placed in the vestiary to be preserved; so that if, at any time, the devil persuading him, he shall consent to go forth from the monastery—may it not happen—then, taking off the garments of the monastery, he may be cast out. That petition of his, nevertheless, which the abbot took from above the altar, he shall not receive again; but it shall be preserved in the monastery.

Concerning the sons of nobles or of poor men who are presented. If by chance any one of the nobles offers his son to God in the monastery: if the boy himself is a minor in age, his parents shall make the petition which we spoke of above. And, with an oblation, they shall enwrap that petition and the hand of the boy in the linen cloth of the altar; and thus they shall offer him. Concerning their property, moreover, either they shall promise in the present petition, under an oath, that they never, either through some chosen person, or in any way whatever, will give him anything at any time, or furnish him with the means of possessing it. Or, indeed, if they be not willing to do this, and wish to offer something as alms to the monastery for their salvation, they shall make a donation of the things which they wish to give to the monastery; retaining for themselves, if they wish, the usufruct. And let all things be so observed that no suspicion may remain with the boy; by which being deceived he might perish—which God forbid—as we have learned by experience. The poorer ones shall also do likewise. Those, however, who have nothing at all shall simply make their petition; and, with an oblation, shall offer their son before witnesses. . . .

If any abbot seek to ordain for himself a priest or deacon, he shall elect from among his fold one who is worthy to perform the office of a priest. He who is ordained, moreover, shall beware of elation or pride. Nor shall he presume to do anything at all unless what he is ordered to by the abbot; knowing that he is all the more subject to the Rule. Nor, by reason of the priesthood, shall he forget obedience and discipline; but he shall advance more and more towards God. But he shall always expect to hold that position which he had when he entered the monastery: except when performing the service of the altar, and if, perchance, the election of the congregation and the will of the abbot inclines to promote him on account of his merit of life. He shall, nevertheless, know that he is to observe the Rule constituted for him by the deans or provosts: and that, if he presume otherwise, he shall be considered not a priest but a rebel. And if, having often been admonished, he do not amend: even the bishop shall be called in in testimony. But if, even then, he do not amend, his faults being glaring, he shall be thrust forth from the monastery. That is, if his contumaciousness shall have been of such a kind, that he was not willing to be subject to or to obey the Rule.

Concerning rank in the congregation. They shall preserve their rank in the monastery according as the time of their conversion and the merit of their life decrees; and as the abbot ordains. And the abbot shall not perturb the flock committed to him; nor, using as it were an arbitrary power, shall he unjustly dispose anything. But he shall always reflect that he is to render account to God for all his judgments and works. Therefore, according to the order which he has decreed, or which the brothers themselves have held: thus they shall go to the absolution, to the communion, to the singing of the psalm, to their place in the choir. And in all places, altogether, age does not decide the rank or affect it; for Samuel and Daniel, as boys, judged the priests. Therefore excepting those who, as we have said, the abbot has, for a higher reason, preferred, or, for certain causes, degraded: all the rest, as they are converted, so they remain. Thus, for example, he who comes to the monastery at the second hour of the day, may know that he is younger than he who came at the first hour of the day, of whatever age or dignity he be. And, in the case of boys, discipline shall be observed in all things by all. The juniors, therefore, shall honour their seniors; the seniors shall love their juniors. In the very calling of names, it shall be allowed to no one to call another simply by his name: but the seniors shall call their juniors by the name of brothers. The juniors, moreover, shall call their seniors "nonni," which indicates paternal reverence. The abbot, moreover, because he is believed to be Christ's representative, shall be called Master and Abbot; not by his assumption, but through honour and love for Christ. His thoughts moreover shall be such, and he shall show himself such, that he may be worthy of such honour. Moreover, wherever the brothers meet each other, the junior shall seek a blessing from the senior. When the greater one passes, the lesser one shall rise and give him a place to sit down. Nor shall the junior presume to sit unless his senior bid him; so that it shall be done as is written: "Vying with each other in honour." Boys, little ones or youths, shall obtain their places in the oratory or at table with discipline as the end in view. Out of doors, moreover, or wherever they are, they shall be guarded and disciplined; until they come to an intelligent age.

Concerning the ordination of an abbot. In ordaining an abbot this consideration shall always be observed: that such a one shall be put into office as the whole congregation, according to the fear of God, with one heart— or even a part, however small, of the congregation with more prudent counsel —shall have chosen. He who is to be ordained, moreover, shall be elected for merit of life and learnedness in wisdom; even though he be the lowest in rank in the congregation. But even if the whole congregation with one consent shall have elected a person consenting to their vices—which God forbid—and those vices shall in any way come clearly to the knowledge of the bishop to whose diocese that place pertains, or to the neighbouring abbots or Christians: the latter shall not allow the consent of the wicked to prevail, but shall set up a dispenser worthy of the house of God; knowing that they will receive a good reward for this, if they do it chastely and with zeal for God. Just so they shall know, on the contrary, that they have sinned if they neglect. The abbot who is ordained, moreover, shall reflect always what a burden he is undertaking, and to whom he is to render account of his stewardship. He shall know that he ought rather to be of help than to command. He ought, therefore, to be learned in the divine law, that he may know how to give forth both the new and the old; chaste, sober, merciful. He shall always exalt mercy over judgment, that he may obtain the same. He shall hate vice, he shall love the brethren. In his blame itself he shall act prudently and do nothing excessive; lest, while he is too desirous of removing the rust, the vessel be broken. And he shall always suspect his own frailty; and shall remember that a bruised reed is not to be crushed. By which we do not say that he shall permit vice to be nourished; but prudently, and with charity, he shall remove it, according as he finds it to be expedient in the case of each one, as we have already said. And he shall strive rather to be loved than feared. He shall not be troubled and anxious; he also shall not be too obstinate; he shall not be jealous and too suspicious; for then he will have no rest. In his commands he shall be provident, and shall consider whether they be of God or of the world. He shall use discernment and moderation with regard to the labours which he enjoins, thinking of the discretion of St. James who said: "if I overdrive my flocks they will die all in one day." Accepting therefore this and other testimony of discretion the mother of the virtues, he shall so temper all things that there may be both what the strong desire, and the weak do not flee. And, especially, he shall keep the present Rule in all things; so that, when he hath ministered well, he shall hear from the Lord what that good servant did who obtained meat for his fellow servants in his day: "Verily I say unto you," he said, "that he shall make him ruler over all his goods. . . ."

That they shall be mutually obedient. The virtue of obedience is not only to be exhibited by all to the abbot, but also the brothers shall be thus mutually obedient to each other; knowing that they shall approach God through this way of obedience. The command therefore of the abbot, or of the provosts who are constituted by him, being given the preference—since we do not allow private commands to have more weight than his—for the rest, all juniors shall obey their superiors with all charity and solicitude. But if any one is found contentious, he shall be punished. If, moreover, any brother, for any slight cause, be in any way rebuked by the abbot or by any one who is his superior; or if he feel, even lightly, that the mind of some superior is angered or moved against him, however little: straightway, without delay, he shall so long lie prostrate at his feet, atoning, until, with the benediction, that anger shall be appeased. But if any one scorn to do this, he shall either be subjected to corporal punishment; or, if he be contumacious, he shall be expelled from the monastery. . . .

Concerning the fact that not every just observance is decreed in this Rule. We have written out this Rule, indeed, that we may show those observing it in the monasteries how to have some honesty of character, or beginning of conversion. But for those who hasten to the perfection of living, there are the teachings of the holy Fathers: the observance of which leads a man to the heights of perfection. For what page, or what discourse, of Divine authority of the Old or the New Testament is not a most perfect rule for human life? Or what book of the holy Catholic Fathers does not trumpet forth how by the right path we shall come to our Creator? Also the reading aloud of the Fathers, and their decrees, and their lives; also the Rule of our holy Father Basil—what else are they except instruments of virtue for well-living and obedient monks? We, moreover, blush with confusion for the idle, and the evilly living and the negligent. Thou, therefore, whoever doth hasten to the celestial fatherland, perform with Christ's aid this Rule written out as the least of beginnings: and then at length, under God's protection, thou wilt come to the greater things that we have mentioned; to the summits of learning and virtue.

BONAVENTURE

BONAVENTURE (1221–74) was born in Italy and was christened Johannes Fidanza. While still a young man he entered the Franciscan order. At Paris, where he went to study, he was initiated into the Augustinian theology by Alexander of Hales (d. 1245), and Bonaventure always considered himself a continuator of Alexander's teachings. His teaching career at the University of Paris was terminated when he became General of the Franciscan order in 1257. He spent the rest of his life in the administration of the delicate affairs of the Franciscans and died at the Second Council of Lyons, to which he was a papal legate.

The philosophy of Bonaventure represents a culminating point in the tradition of Christian mysticism stemming from Augustine and practiced distinctively by the Franciscan order. The philosophy of Thomas Aquinas, with its devotion to the ideal of intellectual contemplation, is complemented by that of Bonaventure, with its preeminent dedication to the attainment of union with God through mystic love, by which man gradually learns to center his desire in the eternal.

The Journey of the Mind to God is not itself primarily a philosophical work. It was written in 1259 during Bonaventure's stay on Mount Alvernia and is a study in the attainment of a peace that passeth understanding. As such, it is devoted primarily to the nature of Christian love rather than Christian understanding.

This enterprise lies at the summit, if not at the base, of monasticism. The life of a *religiosus* was the systematic turning of love from sensible objects, an ideal which even the secular Christian professed but found impossible to embody.

The following selections were translated from the Latin by Father James and published as *The Franciscan Vision* (London: Burns, Oates, and Washbourne, 1937).

THE JOURNEY OF THE MIND TO GOD

PROLOGUE

AT THE OUTSET I invoke the Source whence all enlightenment descends to man, the Father of light from whom is "every best gift and every perfect gift." Through the Son of God, our Lord Jesus Christ, I appeal to the Eternal Father that by the intercession of the most holy Virgin Mary, Mother of the same God and Lord, Christ Jesus, and by that of Blessed Francis, our guide and father, He might impart to us the "spirit of wisdom and revelation" so as to direct our feet in the ways of that peace which surpasseth all understanding. It was the gospel of this peace our Lord Jesus Christ preached; it was peace such as this He gave to men. Following in the footsteps of the Master, our father St. Francis, went through life preaching peace at the beginning and end of every discourse, wishing peace to all whom he met on the way, and sighing after ecstatic peace in every elevation of his mind like a citizen of that Jerusalem, whereof it is said by that Man of Peace who was peaceful with them that hated peace: "Seek ye those things which are for the peace of Jerusalem." For he knew that only in peace stands the throne of Solomon, as it is written: "in peace is his dwelling-place, and his habitation is in Sion."

Inspired by the example of the Blessed Francis, I sought after this peace with ardent longing—I, a sinner, who, though in all respects unworthy, have succeeded, the seventh in the order of time, to the general ministry of the brethren. It happened that as this desire came vehemently to me, and I longed for peace, God led me, in the thirty-third year after the death of Francis, to Mount Alvernia as to a place of quiet. While I abode there and was pondering over certain elevation of the human mind to God, the associations of the place brought before me that miracle which on this very spot had happened to the Blessed Francis when he saw a winged Seraph in the image of the Crucified. It occurred to me that the vision vouchsafed to St. Francis typified the uplifting of our father in contemplation and the manner of his rapture suggested itself to my mind. . . .

DEGREES OF THE SOUL'S ASCENT: GOD'S FOOTPRINTS IN CREATION

"Happy the man whose help is from Thee, when he hath set pilgrimages in his heart through the Valley of Tears, to the goal he hath fixed." Since happiness is nothing else but the enjoyment of the Supreme Good, and the Supreme Good is above us, no one can be happy who does not rise beyond himself. This raising up of man is to be understood, of course, of mind and heart and not of body, and since there is question of reaching above himself on the part of man, he must be helped by supernatural strength and be lifted up by a higher power than stoops to raise him. However much then a man's inward steps are ordered and progress made, it is of no avail unless accompanied by help from on high. But divine aid is at hand for those who seek it with a devout and humble heart, and sigh for it in this Valley of Tears; this is done by fervent prayer. Prayer is, therefore, the source and origin of every upward progress that has God for goal. Wherefore, Dionysius in his "Mystical Theology," wishing to instruct us in these transcendent workings of the soul sets down prayer as the first condition. Let us each, therefore, have recourse to prayer and say to our Lord God: "Lead me, O Lord, on Thy path, that I may walk in Thy truth. Let my heart rejoice that it feareth Thy name."

By so praying we are led to discern the degrees of the soul's ascent to God.

For, inasmuch as, in our present condition, this universe of things is a ladder whereby we may ascend to God, since among these things some are God's footprints, some God's image, some corporeal, some spiritual, some temporal, some eternal, and, hence, some outside of us, and some inside, it follows that if we are to attain to the contemplation of the First Principle and Source of all things, in Himself altogether spiritual, eternal, and above us, we must begin with God's footprints which are corporeal, temporal and outside us and so enter on the Way that leads to God. We enter in within our own souls, which are images of the eternal God, spiritual and interior to us, and this is to enter into the Truth of God. Finally, we must reach out beyond and above ourselves to the region of the eternal and supereminently spiritual and look to the First Principle of all, and that is to enjoy the knowledge of God in reverential contemplation of His Majesty. . . .

In direct relation with this threefold progress of the soul to God, the human mind has three fundamental attitudes or outlooks. The first is towards corporeal things without, and in this respect it is designated as animal or simply sensual; the next is where it enters in within itself to contemplate itself, and here it ranks as spirit; the third is where its upward glance is beyond itself, and then it is designated "mens" or mind. In all three ways the human soul must prepare to raise itself to God so that it may love Him with the whole mind, with all its heart, and with its whole soul, for in this consists the fullness of the Law and the highest Christian Wisdom.

But since every one of the aforesaid modes is doubled, according as we come to consider God as Alpha, and as Omega, or according as we come to contemplate God in each as in and through a mirror, or because each of these modes of contemplation may be joined with another, or operative simply and purely in itself, so it is necessary that these three primary grades should be raised to the number six; whence, as God completed the universal world in six days, and rested on the seventh, so the smaller world of man is led in the most orderly way, by six successive grades of illumination, to the quiet of contemplation. A symbol of this may be seen in the six steps that led to the throne of Solomon; in the six-winged Seraphim which Isaiah beheld in vision; in the six days after which God called Moses from the midst of darkness; and in the six days after which, as we read in Matthew, Christ led His disciples up into a mountain, and was transfigured before them.

Corresponding to the six degrees of the soul's ascent to God there are within the soul six kinds of faculties or powers by which we rise from depths to the heights, from external to things internal, from things of time to those of eternity, to wit, sense, imagination, reason, intellect, intelligence, and the fine point or apex of the soul. These powers we have implanted in us by nature;

by sin deformed, they are reformed through grace; and they must be purified by justice, exercised by knowledge, and made perfect by wisdom. . . .

Since it is imperative first to make the ascent of Jacob's Ladder before we can hope to descend, let us place the first step of the ascent at the bottom holding up this whole sensible world before us as a mirror, through which we may rise to God, the supreme Craftsman. In that way we shall be true Israelites passing forth from the land of Egypt to the land of promise, and also true Christians going forth from this world to the Father, and lovers of Wisdom who answer the Call which says: "Come unto me all ye that desire me, and be ye filled with mine offspring." "For from the greatness and beauty of created things, their Creator may be seen and known."

The supreme wisdom, power and benevolence of the Creator are reflected in all created things. This is intimated in a threefold manner by the adjustment of external and internal senses in man. The bodily senses minister to the mind, whether it be engaged in rational investigation, in docile faith, or in intellectual contemplation. In contemplation it considers the actual existence of things; in faith it examines the unfolding of events; and in reasoning it surmises their potential pre-excellence.

The first point of view, which is that of contemplation, considering things in themselves, discerns in them weight, number, and measure: weight which marks the point to which they tend, number whereby they are distinguished, and measure whereby they are limited. Hereby it sees in things mode, species, order, as well as substance, virtue and action, from which the mind may arise, as from footprints, to the knowledge of the power, wisdom and boundless goodness of the Creator.

The second point of view, which is that of faith, when it considers the universe goes on to reflect upon its origin, its course, and its end. For "by faith we understand that the world was framed by the word of God." By faith we know that the three epochs—of nature, of the law, and of grace—have succeeded one another in order. By faith we know that the world will terminate with a final judgment. In the first, we observe God's power; in the second, His providence; and in the third, His justice.

The third point of view, that of reason, when it investigates the universe recognises that some things have only being, others being and life, and others possess not only being and life but knowledge and discernment. This gives us three levels of reality, ranging from lowest to highest. From this viewpoint, also, it is clear that some things are merely corporeal, and some partly corporeal and partly spiritual, while others, ranking highest in perfection and dignity, are purely spiritual. Likewise some things, it is seen, are mutable and corruptible, such as terrestrial things; others are mutable and incorruptible, such as celestial bodies; whence it may be concluded that some things are both immutable and incorruptible, such as supercelestial things. From these visible things, therefore, the human mind rises up to consider the power and goodness and wisdom of God in whom reside Being and Life and Intelligence, in a purely spiritual, incorruptible, and immutable state. . . .

GOD'S IMAGE RECONSTRUCTED BY GRACE IN THE SOUL

Where a man falls, there must he lie, unless someone intervenes to raise him up. In the same way man must have lain, chained by the life of the senses and unable to come to the contemplation of his soul and of eternal truth within it, were it not for the intervention of Truth Itself. Taking unto Itself a human form in Jesus Christ, becoming, as it were, a ladder between earth and heaven, Truth repaired God's original ladder smashed in Adam. No matter how enlightened a man may be either by nature or by acquired knowledge, he cannot come to the contemplation of his inmost self or experience delight in the Lord except it be through the mediation of Jesus Christ, who says: "I am the door; by me if any man enter in he shall be saved and shall go in and out and shall find pastures." But the approach to this door is conditioned by our faith in Him, our hope in Him, and our love: by faith, hope, and charity. If, therefore, we are to re-enter in within ourselves, as into a long-lost paradise, and come to a fruition of the truth, we must enter by the door of faith, hope, and charity, virtues that are based on the mediation between God and man of His Son, Christ Jesus, who is, as it were, the Tree of Life in the garden of Paradise.

God's Image in the soul of man, then, must be re-constituted by means of the three theological virtues, faith, hope and charity. These virtues purify, enlighten and perfect the soul, thus repairing God's broken Image, fitting out the soul for the heavenly Jerusalem and constituting it a unit of the Church militant which is the offspring of the heavenly Jerusalem as is suggested by the Apostle: "That Jerusalem which is above is free, which is our mother." The soul, therefore, that has faith and hope in Christ, and is adorned with Charity in Him, the Word of the Father, incarnate, uncreated and inspired, "the way, the truth and the life," has advanced in its quest in a threefold manner. By faith in Christ, the uncreated Word and Splendour of the Father, the soul recaptures two mystical senses of hearing and vision: hearing, to accept the sayings of Christ, and vision, with which to contemplate the splendours of His light. By the virtue of hope, the soul sighs for the coming of the Word proceeding from the Father, and in this longing and attachment begins anew to experience the sweet odour of Christ as by a veritable sense of smell. Finally, by love for Christ, hastening to embrace the Word Incarnate who comes, the soul receives in return from Him such heavenly delight that in a very ecstasy of love it finds itself anew experiencing such a relish and feeling of intimacy as can be only compared with the physical senses of taste and touch. The soul adorned with these new mystical senses is like the Spouse in the Canticle of Canticles, delighting with all its senses in the presence of its Bridegroom, celebrating in song its union with God, and for its purpose employing the medium of this Canticle of Canticles composed for those who reach the fourth degree of contemplation. The understanding of all this is beyond the grasp of people who have not actually experienced it; the experience itself is something ineffable and cannot be expressed in rational terms or exhausted by reflective considerations. In this degree of contemplation the soul is equipped with mystical senses for no other purpose than this experimental knowledge of God whereby it may behold that which is supremely beautiful, hear that which is deepest harmony, sense the most transcendent odour, taste a sweetness source of all other sweetness, and experience the intimacies of contact with the Source of all delights. Possessed of these mystic senses, the soul is disposed for ecstatic raptures of devotion, exultation and delight, as is suggested by three sets of phrases from the Canticle of Canticles. Of these, the first is uttered in a fullness of devotion and the soul is likened to a rod of smoke from the perfumes of myrrh and frankincense. The second, in an excess of exultation, sees the soul as like the dawn, like the moon, like the sun itself, raised up mystically to receive its Bridegroom. The third suggests the rapture when the soul in an ecstasy of joy leans upon its Beloved, gently breathing in the delight of Him.

At this stage the soul in its hierarchical character is prepared for the goal of its efforts which is that heavenly Jerusalem, with its divinely ordered hierarchy, into which it must enter. The very prime condition of this ultimate issue is that this supernal Jerusalem first descend into the heart of man, as John in his Apocalypse saw, and bestow upon the soul its own ordered and hierarchical character. This is brought about by the reconstitution of God's Image in the soul by grace and the theological virtues, by the addition of those mystic senses to which we have referred and by the rapturous elevations of the soul which follow, so that the human spirit now reflects the hierarchic order of the heavenly Jerusalem, being purified, enlightened and perfected. But if this hierarchy of heaven is to be reflected in the soul, it must, in addition, show forth the presence of heaven's nine choirs in an ordered series which will consist of vocation, communication, persuasion, ordination, invigoration, command, acceptance, revelation and unction. The three first-named of these have regard to the nature of the human soul; the three following grades to the soul's industry and activity; the last three bear a direct relation to grace.

Possessing these, the soul when it enters in within itself finds itself in presence of the heavenly Jerusalem, where it beholds the orders of the angels and reflected in these orders God who, dwelling in them, is the Source of all their actions. Little wonder that St. Bernard should write to Eugenius:

> God in the Seraphim loves as charity; God in the Cherubim knows as truth; in the Thrones He sits in equity; in the Dominations He prevails as majesty; He rules in Principalities as power; in the Virtues He reflects His virtue; in the Archangels He spreads His light; in the Angels His piety shines.

Thus entering within ourselves to find God as He is present to us in all those gifts which are the outcome of His most generous bounty we begin to learn how truly God is "all in all."

To attain to this degree of contemplation the indispensable and principal aid is the divinely-inspired Sacred Scripture, just as for the preceding degree philosophy was the chief pre-requisite. For the Scriptures inculcate chiefly the necessity of repairing what was lost by sin and of re-constructing the broken order of things. The virtues of faith, hope, and charity occupy accordingly a prominent place therein. This is especially true of charity. Of this St. Paul says: "The end of the law is charity from a pure heart, and a good conscience, and an unfeigned faith." He also declares that charity is "the fulfilment of the law." Our Saviour inculcates the same truth when He says that "the whole law and the prophets" depend upon the two precepts, the love of God and the love of one's neighbour. These two forms of love are found united in the one true Bridegroom of the Church, Christ Jesus, who is at once our Neighbour and our God, who is our Brother and Lord, at once our Friend and our King, the uncreated Word Incarnate, our Creator and Re-Creator, Alpha and Omega. Christ is also the supreme High Priest who purifies, enlightens and perfects His Spouse, the Church, in its entirety and in every individual holy soul.

It is with Christ in this sense, and with His Church in its saintly hierarchy, that Scripture is chiefly concerned, urging men to be purified, enlightened and perfected according to the threefold law, the natural law, the written law, and the law of grace. Thus by the Mosaic law men may be said to be purified, by the prophetic revelations they are enlightened, and by the evangelical message they are brought to perfection. We may put it in another way. There is in Scripture a threefold meaning or significance: the metaphorical, by which men are purified and led to a more upright life; the allegorical, which illuminates the understanding; the anagogical, which intoxicates the soul with deep draughts of wisdom. All this is brought about by the different preparations we have just been describing. We began with the three theological virtues, then came the mystical senses, followed in turn by three forms of rapture, and finally came the many acts of the mind which fall into a hierarchical design.

By these, indeed, as by so many steps, we enter in within our souls to behold God in the glories of the saints, and to rest therein, as in a bridal chamber, docile to the bidding of the divine Bridegroom not to stir until the impulse to awaken arises.

We have ascended two of the intermediary steps in the soul's progress towards the contemplation of God within it. In this there is the suggestion of the two wings, extending from the body, and poised as if for flight. In the first place, recall how we can pass to the contemplation of God when we regard our souls in their natural powers, with their activities, their inclinations and acquired habits, as mirrors wherein God's perfection is reflected: this constituted the third degree or gradient in the soul's ascent to God. Secondly, we reached the fourth degree when we came to consider the soul, no longer in its mere natural state but as perfected by the life of grace, when we saw in turn the infused virtues, the mystical senses and supernatural raptures. The path stretches out before us, definitely marked and ordered, passing from purification to enlightenment and finally to perfection. The Scriptures light the way in partial revelations that pass from angel to man according to the dictum of St. Paul, "the law was ordained by angels in the hand of a mediator." In fine, the order and hierarchy that had to be introduced into the disposition of the soul for its ascent reflected the hierarchic choirs which are found in the heavenly Jerusalem.

The effect of all this progressive enlightenment on the soul is that it becomes the dwelling-place of divine Wisdom. The daughter and spouse and friend of God, a member of Christ the Head, and sister and co-heir with Him, the soul is made the sanctuary of the Holy Spirit, a temple grounded in faith, raised on hope, and dedicated to God in its own sanctity as well as in that of its conjoint body. All this is accomplished by the perfectly sincere love of Christ which is "poured forth in our hearts by the Holy Ghost who is given to us" and without which we can not know the secret things of God. For as "no one can know the things of a man save the spirit of man, which is in him, even so the things of God none knoweth save the Spirit of God." Let us, therefore, be rooted and grounded in love, so that we may be able to comprehend, with all the saints, what is the length of eternity, the breadth of liberality, the height of majesty, and the depth of discerning Wisdom.

THE QUIET OF CONTEMPLATION

In its progress towards the possession of God the soul has now passed through six stages. The number of these gradients in the journey of the soul is not without its own significance. Six steps led up to the throne of Solomon and to peace where, as in some inner Jerusalem, the true man of peace reposed in peace of soul. Six wings, too, enveloped the Seraph thereby suggesting to us a picture of the true contemplative raised up from things of earth and enlightened by supernal wisdom. And in six days was the labour of creation completed before the rest of the Sabbath supervened. Recall these six stages of human progress towards the quiet of contemplation. In the first, the soul was led to God by going out to external things to admire in them the work of God's creative power. Then, looking at creation, the soul beheld God's footprints upon the world's surface: the material world became a mirror in which it beheld its God. Next, turning its attention inwards to itself, the soul began to reach God from a consideration of itself as God's created image, and then a further step was made when it began to behold God in the mirror of its renovated being. Whereupon, the soul was led to raise its gaze above and beyond itself, seeking, as it were, the light of God's countenance and rejoicing in its own progress. But no rest was possible until it found God in His own reflected light, for all this progress was achieved in a degree suitable for those who are still pilgrims on the way to God and who must depend upon their own efforts to scale the heights of contemplation. But when the soul shall have reached the sixth step and begun to contemplate the First and Highest Principle of all and Jesus Christ, the Mediator of God and man, then it shall have contact with spiritual things, so sublime that any comparison with created things becomes impossible, and so deeply mysterious that all intellectual keenness is unavailing. Then it will be swept up not only beyond the wonders of all creation but out of its very self and above it. By means of Jesus Christ, the Way, the Door, the Ladder, shall this transition be affected, for He is as it were, the Seat of Mercy, placed over the ark of God, and the Sacrament hidden from the ages.

With face fully turned towards this Seat of Mercy, seeing Him hanging on the Cross, in faith, hope, charity, devotion, delight, exaltation, appreciation, praise and jubilation, the soul is ready to celebrate its Passover, that is, its transition from things of time to the eternal, passing over, by the power of the Cross, the Red Sea into the desert where it will begin to taste the hidden manna, there to rest in the tomb of Christ to all appearance dead yet experiencing, in so far as a pilgrim may, what was promised on the hill of Calvary to the good thief: "This day thou shalt be with Me in paradise."

This was the vision of Blessed Francis on the lofty mountain where he was raised into an ecstasy of contemplation and upon which I thought out the things here written. To him appeared a six-winged Seraph fastened to a Cross. From the companion who was with him when these things happened and when he was taken up by God in ecstasy, I and many others have gathered this account. In this. Blessed Francis, another Jacob become Israel, is for us a perfect model of the contemplative life, just as hitherto he had proved himself outstanding in the life of action, so that more by the force of his example than by word, God invited the truly spiritual to seek after such quiet of contemplation and ecstasy of soul as was experienced by him on Mount Alvernia.

If this transition, however, is to be genuine and perfect, then must all labour on the part of the soul's reasoning faculty cease and the soul's deep affection be centered in God and transformed, as it were, into Him. So mysterious and sublime is this experience that none save he to whom it has been given knows anything of it, that nobody receives except he who desires it, and this desire comes to him only whose whole being is inflamed by the fire of the Holy Spirit sent by Christ upon the earth. Hence it is that the "hidden things" of God were revealed, as the Apostle says, by the Holy Ghost.

Since, therefore, to arrive at this rapturous state of soul nature is of no avail and human industry of comparatively little value, little heed must be paid to inquiry but much to unction, little account must be taken of human language but much of internal experience of joy, attention must be weaned away from words and writing so as to concentrate on God's Gift to man, His Holy Spirit. In a word, the human soul must turn away its eyes from all created essences to fix them on the uncreated Essence of the Father, the Son and the Holy Ghost; the words of Dionysius must well up within it and address themselves to the Triune God: "O supereminent and transcendent Holy Trinity, Inspiration of all Christian philosophy, direct our steps to the unknown, sublime, and re-splendent heights of mystic utterances. On these heights are to be found the new, the absolutely unquestionable and unchanging mysteries of theology hid-den away, as it were, in the obscurity of excessively lightsome darkness and illuminating silence. Here on these heights, so resplendent in their excessive light, men are enlightened and spiritual souls are filled with the splendours of the true good." These things we address to God. But to the friend to whom this writing is directed we also speak and say: Do thou, O friend, push on boldly to the mystic vision, abandon the work of the senses and the operations of the reasoning faculty, leave aside all things visible and invisible, being and non-being, and cleave as far as possible, and imperceptibly, to the Unity of Him who transcends all essences and all knowledge. In this immeasurable and absolute elevation of soul, forgetting all created things and liberated from them, thou shalt rise above thyself and beyond all creation to find thyself within the shaft of light that flashes out from the divine, mysterious darkness.

But if thou wouldst know how such things are accomplished, then ask grace, not learning; desire, not understanding; the groanings of prayer, not industry in study; the Spouse, not the master; God, not man; obscurity, not clarity. Seek not so much light as fire which inflames one totally, filling the soul with unction and ardent desires, and raising it out of its very self aloft to God. This fire is indeed God whose "furnace is in Jerusalem." It was kindled on earth by the Man, Jesus, in the fervour of His most ardent passion. In this fervour he participates who can say: "My soul hath chosen strangling and my bones death." He shall see God who chooses such a death, for it is undoubtedly true that "Man shall not see me and live." Let us die, therefore, and by the door of death enter into this darkness. Let us impose silence on our anxieties, our concupiscences, and upon the working of our imagination. Let us, with Christ crucified, pass from this world to the Father, that when He shall be revealed to us we may say with Philip: "It is enough for us." Let us listen with St. Paul to the words: "My grace is sufficient for thee." Let us cry out exultingly with David: "My flesh and my heart faileth, but God is the strength of my heart and my portion for ever." "Blessed be the Lord for evermore; and let all the people say: Amen and Amen."

THOMAS AQUINAS

THE GREATEST NAME in the notable upsurge of intellectual activity in the thirteenth century is that of the "Angelic Doctor," Thomas Aquinas (1225–74). Born near Naples of noble parents, he entered the Dominican order and studied under Albert the Great (Albertus Magnus), whose encyclopedic productivity was surpassed only by Thomas himself. Teaching at Naples, Cologne, and Paris, Thomas was the foremost of those Dominicans who dominated university life in the thirteenth century.

As a student Aquinas wrote many commentaries on the scriptures and on such philosophers as Boethius and Aristotle. Most of the doctrines he explored are treated in his first major work, *Summa contra Gentiles* (1261–64), the chief medieval treatment of the relationship between faith and natural reason. *Summa Theologica,* begun in 1265 and left incomplete at the time of Aquinas' death, is his effort to deal systematically with the entire body of knowledge. Its three major divisions include: (a) the conception of God, the problems of existence, creation, and God's jurisdiction over the world; (b) mankind, a system of morals based on Aristotelian ethics, and another based on theology; (c) and the relationship between God and man, chiefly embodied in the person of Christ.

Thomas took the materials for his reconstruction of traditional Augustinian supernaturalism from the resurgent Aristotelian philosophy, employing Aristotle's logic, much of his language, and many of his observations on human life. Some of the works of Aristotle had been banned at Paris in 1210, and Thomas' attempt to reformulate Aristotle met with much opposition during his life and after his death. Many of his doctrines were condemned at Paris and at Oxford, despite the intercession of his aged teacher Albert. Nevertheless, within a century Thomism had become the orthodox basis of Christian philosophy.

Faith and reason complement each other in the Thomistic philosophy; there is nothing in reason which goes against faith and there is nothing in faith which contradicts reason. Faith extends beyond reason, however. In cases where reason is impotent to arrive at a conclusive answer, that is, where reason can produce equally cogent arguments on both sides of a question, Thomas holds we must depend upon the Revelation, which is given to mankind by the grace of God in order to help it out of such an *impasse.*

A characteristic example of the way in which Thomism could be applied to specific situations requiring the adjustment of old values and new interests is Thomas' treatment of the questions of just price and usury. The traditional view of the Church toward such commercial affairs had been represented by this dictum of Augustine: "Business is in itself an evil, for it turns men from seeking true rest, which is God." Again, a passage such as the following, incorporated in canon law by Gratian, is representative: "The man who buyeth a thing in order that he may gain by selling it again unchanged and as he bought it, that man is of the buyers and sellers who are cast forth from God's temple." This attitude persisted in the Middle Ages. The growing extent of capitalist forms of production and exchange had made this attitude less practical by the time of Thomas, especially since the Church itself was a great borrower and lender and property holder. Thomas' formulations of these issues were representative attempts to govern a new set of institutions with an enduring or practical Christian ethic. And if the regulations he set forth were not everywhere easy to define or to apply, nevertheless, Thomas was able to reconstruct traditional beliefs in a way that made them command attention in a changing world.

The following selections are from the *Summa Theologica*. The whole work contains thirty-eight treatises, and a definitive edition was published at Basel in 1485. The translation from the Latin used here is by the English Dominican fathers (London: Burns, Oates, and Washbourne, 2d rev. ed., 1920–29). The selection from the *Governance of Rulers* (written about 1265) was translated from the Latin by G. B. Phelan (London, Sheed and Ward, 1938).

SUMMA THEOLOGICA

FIRST ARTICLE: WHETHER, BESIDES THE PHILOSOPHICAL SCIENCES, ANY FURTHER DOCTRINE IS REQUIRED?

We proceed thus to the First Article.

Objection 1. It seems that, besides the philosophical sciences, we have no need of any further knowledge. For man should not seek to know what is above reason: *Seek not the things that are too high for thee.* But whatever is not above reason is sufficiently considered in the philosophical sciences. Therefore any other knowledge besides the philosophical sciences is superfluous.

Obj. 2. Further, knowledge can be concerned only with being, for nothing can be known, save the true, which is convertible with being. But everything, that is, is considered in the philosophical sciences—even God Himself; so that there is a part of philosophy called theology, or the divine science, as is clear from Aristotle. Therefore, besides the philosophical sciences, there is no need of any further knowledge.

On the contrary, It is written: *All Scripture inspired of God is profitable to teach, to reprove, to correct, to instruct in justice.* Now Scripture, inspired of God, is not a part of the philosophical sciences discovered by human reason. Therefore it is useful that besides the philosophical sciences there should be another science—*i.e.*, inspired of God.

I answer that, It was necessary for man's salvation that there should be a knowledge revealed by God, besides the philosophical sciences investigated by human reason. First, because man is directed to God as to an end that surpasses the grasp of his reason: *The eye hath not seen, O God, besides Thee, what things Thou hast prepared for them, that wait for Thee.* But the end must first be known by men who are to direct their thoughts and actions to the end. Hence it was necessary for the salvation of man that certain truths which exceed human reason should be made known to him by divine revelation. Even as regards those truths about God which human reason can investigate, it was necessary that man be taught by a divine revelation. For the truth about God, such as reason can know it, would only be known by a few, and that after a long time, and with the admixture of many errors; whereas man's whole salvation, which is in God, depends upon the knowledge of this truth. Therefore, in order that the salvation of men might be brought about more fitly and more surely, it was necessary that they be taught divine truths by divine revelation. It was therefore necessary that, besides the philosophical sciences investigated by reason, there should be a sacred science by way of revelation.

Reply Obj. 1. Although those things which are beyond man's knowledge may not be sought for by man through his reason, nevertheless, what is revealed by God must be accepted through faith. Hence the sacred text continues, *For many things are shown to thee above the understanding of man.* And in such things sacred science consists.

Reply Obj. 2. Sciences are diversified according to the diverse nature of their knowable objects. For the astronomer and the physicist both prove the same conclusion—that the earth, for instance, is round; the astronomer by means of mathematics (*i.e.,* abstracting from matter), but the physicist by means of matter itself. Hence there is no reason why those things which are treated by the philosophical sciences, so far as they can be known by the light of natural reason, may not also be treated by another science so far as they are known by the light of the divine revelation. Hence the theology included in sacred doctrine differs in genus from that theology which is part of philosophy.

SECOND ARTICLE: WHETHER SACRED DOCTRINE IS A SCIENCE?

We proceed thus to the Second Article.

Objection 1. It seems that sacred doctrine is not a science. For every science proceeds from self-evident principles. But sacred doctrine proceeds from articles of faith which are not self-evident, since their truth is not admitted by all; *For all men have not faith.* Therefore sacred doctrine is not a science.

Obj. 2. Further, science is not of individuals. But sacred doctrine treats of individual facts, such as the deeds of Abraham, Isaac and Jacob, and the like. Therefore sacred doctrine is not a science.

On the contrary, Augustine says that *to this science alone belongs that whereby saving faith is begotten, nourished, protected and strengthened.* But this can be said of no science except sacred doctrine. Therefore sacred doctrine is a science.

I answer that, Sacred doctrine is a science. We must bear in mind that there are two kinds of sciences. There are some which proceed from principles known by the natural light of the intellect, such as arithmetic and geometry and the like. There are also some which proceed from principles known by the light of a higher science: thus the science of optics proceeds from principles established by geometry, and music from principles established by arithmetic. So it is that sacred doctrine is a science because it proceeds from principles made known by the light of a higher science, namely, the science of God and the blessed. Hence, just as music accepts on authority the principles taught by the arithmetician, so sacred science accepts the principles revealed by God.

Reply Obj. 1. The principles of any science are either in themselves self-evident, or reducible to the knowledge of a higher science; and such, as we have said, are the principles of sacred doctrine.

Reply Obj. 2. Individual facts are not treated in sacred doctrine because it is concerned with them principally; they are rather introduced as examples to be followed in our lives (as in the moral sciences), as well as to establish the authority of those men through whom the divine revelation, on which this sacred scripture or doctrine is based, has come down to us.

THIRD ARTICLE: WHETHER SACRED DOCTRINE IS ONE SCIENCE?

We proceed thus to the Third Article.

Objection 1. It seems that sacred doctrine is not one science, for according to the Philosopher *that science is one which treats only of one class of subjects.* But the creator and the creature, both of whom are treated in sacred doctrine, cannot be grouped together under one class of subjects. Therefore sacred doctrine is not one science.

Obj. 2. Further, in sacred doctrine we treat of angels, corporeal creatures and human morality. But these belong to separate philosophical sciences. Therefore sacred doctrine cannot be one science.

On the contrary, Holy Scripture speaks of it as one science; *Wisdom gave him the knowledge [scientiam] of holy things.*

I answer that, Sacred doctrine is one science. The unity of a power or habit is to be gauged by its object, not indeed, in its material aspect, but as regards the formality under which it is an object. For example, man, ass, stone, agree in the one formality of being colored; and color is the formal object of sight. Therefore, because Sacred Scripture (as we have said) considers some things under the formality of being divinely revealed, all things which have been divinely revealed have in common the formality of the object of this science. Hence, they are included under sacred doctrine as under one science.

Reply Obj. 1. Sacred doctrine does not treat of God and creatures equally, but of God primarily, and of creatures only so far as they are referable to God as their beginning or end. Hence the unity of this science is not impaired.

Reply Obj. 2. Nothing prevents inferior powers or habits from being diversified by objects which yet agree with one another in coming together under a higher power or habit; because the higher power or habit regards its own object under a more universal formality. Thus, the object of the *common sense* is the sensible, including, therefore, whatever is visible or audible. Hence the *common sense,* although one power, extends to all the objects of the five senses. Similarly, objects which are the subject-matter of different philosophical sciences can yet be treated by this one single sacred science under one aspect, namely, in so far as they can be included in revelation. So that in this way sacred doctrine bears, as it were, the stamp of the divine science, which is one and simple, yet extends to everything.

FOURTH ARTICLE: WHETHER SACRED DOCTRINE IS A PRACTICAL SCIENCE?

We proceed thus to the Fourth Article.

Objection 1. It seems that sacred doctrine is a practical science, for a practical science is that which ends in action, according to the Philosopher. But sacred doctrine is ordained to action: *Be ye doers of the word, and not hearers only.* Therefore sacred doctrine is a practical science.

Obj. 2. Further, sacred doctrine is divided into the Old and the New Law. But law belongs to moral science, which is a practical science. Therefore sacred doctrine is a practical science.

On the contrary, Every practical science is concerned with the things man can do; as moral science is concerned with human acts, and architecture with buildings. But sacred doctrine is chiefly concerned with God, Who is rather the Maker of man. Therefore it is not a practical but a speculative science.

I answer that, Sacred doctrine, being one, extends to things which belong to the different philosophical sciences, because it considers in each the same formal aspect, namely, so far as they can be known through the divine light. Hence, although among the philosophical sciences some are speculative and others practical, nevertheless, sacred doctrine includes both; as God, by one and the same science, knows both Himself and His works.

Still, it is more speculative than practical, because it is more concerned with divine things than with human acts; though even of these acts it treats inasmuch as man is ordained by them to the perfect knowledge of God, in which consists eternal beatitude.

This is a sufficient answer to the Objections.

FIFTH ARTICLE: WHETHER SACRED DOCTRINE IS NOBLER THAN OTHER SCIENCES?

We proceed thus to the Fifth Article.

Objection 1. It seems that sacred doctrine is not nobler than other sciences, for the nobility of a science depends on its certitude. But other sciences, the principles of which cannot be doubted, seem to be more certain than sacred doctrine; for its principles—namely, articles of faith—can be doubted. Therefore, other sciences seem to be nobler.

Obj. 2. Further, it is the part of a lower science to draw upon a higher; as music draws upon arithmetic. But sacred doctrine does draw upon the philosophical sciences; for Jerome observes, in his Epistle to Magnus, that the *ancient doctors so enriched their books with the doctrines and thoughts of the philosophers, that thou knowest not what more to admire in them, their profane erudition or their scriptural learning?* Therefore sacred doctrine is inferior to other sciences.

On the contrary, Other sciences are called the handmaidens of this one: *Wisdom sent her maids to invite to the tower.*

I answer that, Since this science is partly speculative, and partly practical, it transcends all other sciences, speculative and practical. Now one speculative science is said to be nobler than another either by reason of its greater certitude, or by reason of the higher dignity of its subject-matter. In both these respects this science surpasses other speculative sciences; in point of greater certitude, because other sciences derive their certitude from the natural light of human reason, which can err, whereas this derives its certitude from the light of the divine knowledge, which cannot err; in point of the higher dignity of its subject-matter, because this science treats chiefly of those things which by their sublimity transcend human reason, while other sciences consider only those things which are within reason's grasp. Of the practical sciences, that one is nobler which is ordained to a more final end, as political science is nobler than military science; for the good of the army is directed to the good of the state. But the purpose of this science, in so far as it is practical, is eternal beatitude, to which as to an ultimate end the ends of all the practical sciences are directed. Hence it is clear that from every standpoint it is nobler than other sciences.

Reply Obj. 1. It may well happen that what is in itself the more certain may seem to us the less certain because of the weakness of our intellect, *which is dazzled by the clearest objects of nature; as the owl is dazzled by the light of the sun.* Hence the fact that some happen to doubt about the articles of faith is not due to the uncertain nature of the truths, but to the weakness of the human intellect; yet the slenderest knowledge that may be obtained of the highest things is more desirable than the most certain knowledge obtained of the lowest things, as is said in *De Animalibus* xi.

Reply Obj. 2. This science can draw upon the philosophical sciences, not as though it stood in need of them, but only in order to make its teaching clearer. For it accepts its principles, not from the other sciences, but immediately from God, by revelation. Therefore it does not draw upon the other sciences as upon its superiors, but uses them as its inferiors and handmaidens: even so the master sciences make use of subordinate sciences, as political science of military science. That it thus uses them is not due to its own defect or insufficiency, but to the defect of our intellect, which is more easily led by what is known through natural reason (from which proceed the other sciences), to that which is above reason, such as are the teachings of this science.

SIXTH ARTICLE: WHETHER THIS DOCTRINE IS A WISDOM?

We proceed thus to the Sixth Article.

Objection 1. It seems that this doctrine is not a wisdom. For no doctrine which borrows its principles is worthy of the name of wisdom, seeing that the wise man directs, and is not directed. But this doctrine borrows its principles. Therefore it is not a wisdom.

Obj. 2. Further, it is a part of wisdom to prove the principles of other sciences. Hence it is called the chief of sciences, as is clear in *Ethics* vi. But this doctrine does not prove the principles of other sciences. Therefore it is not a wisdom.

Obj. 3. Further, this doctrine is acquired by study, whereas wisdom is acquired by God's inspiration, and is accordingly numbered among the gifts of the Holy Spirit. Therefore this doctrine is not a wisdom.

On the contrary, It is written: *This is your wisdom and understanding in the sight of nations.*

I answer that, This doctrine is wisdom above all human wisdoms not merely in any one order, but absolutely. For since it is the part of a wise man to order and to judge, and since lesser matters can be judged in the light of some higher cause, he is said to be wise in any genus who considers the highest cause in that genus. Thus in the realm of building, he who plans the form of the house is called wise and architect, in relation to the subordinate laborers who trim the wood and make ready the stones: thus it is said, *as a wise architect I have laid the foundation.* Again, in the order of all human life, the prudent man is called wise, inasmuch as he directs his acts to a fitting end; thus it is said, *Wisdom is prudence to a man.* Therefore, he who considers absolutely the highest cause of the whole universe, namely God, is most of all called wise. Hence wisdom is said to be the knowledge of divine things, as Augustine says. But sacred doctrine essentially treats of God viewed as the highest cause, for it treats of Him not only so far as He can be known through creatures just as philosophers knew Him—*That which is known of God is manifest in them* —but also so far as He is known to Himself alone and revealed to others. Hence sacred doctrine is especially called a wisdom.

Question II: The Existence of God
(In Three Articles)

BECAUSE the chief aim of sacred doctrine is to teach the knowledge of God not only as He is in Himself, but also as He is the beginning of things and their last end, and especially of rational creatures, as is clear from what has been already said, therefore, in our endeavor to expound this science, we shall treat: (1) of God; (2) of the rational creature's movement towards God; (3) of Christ Who as man is our way to God.

In treating of God there will be a threefold division:

For we shall consider (1) whatever concerns the divine essence. (2) Whatever concerns the distinctions of Persons. (3) Whatever concerns the procession of creatures from Him.

Concerning the divine essence, we must consider:

(1) Whether God exists? (2) The manner of His existence, or, rather, what is *not* the manner of His existence. (3) Whatever concerns His operations—namely, His knowledge, will, power.

Concerning the first, there are three points of inquiry:

(1) Whether the proposition *God exists* is self-evident? (2) Whether it is demonstrable? (3) Whether God exists?

FIRST ARTICLE: WHETHER THE EXISTENCE OF GOD IS SELF-EVIDENT?

We proceed thus to the First Article.

Objection 1. It seems that the existence of God is self-evident. For those things are said to be self-evident to us the knowledge of which exists naturally in us, as we can see in regard to first principles. But as Damascene says, *the knowledge of God is naturally implanted in all.* Therefore the existence of God is self-evident.

Obj. 2. Further, those things are said to be self-evident which are known as soon as the terms are known, which the Philosopher says is true of the first principles of demonstration. Thus, when the nature of a whole and of a part is known, it is at once recognized that every whole is greater than its part. But as soon as the signification of the name *God* is understood, it is at once seen that God exists. For by this name is signified that thing than which nothing greater can be conceived. But that which exists actually and mentally is greater than that which exists only mentally. Therefore, since as soon as the name *God* is understood it exists mentally, it also follows that it exists actually. Therefore the proposition *God exists* is self-evident.

Obj. 3. Further, the existence of truth is self-evident. For whoever denies the existence of truth grants that truth does not exist; and, if truth does not exist, then the proposition *Truth does not exist* is true; and if there is anything true, there must be truth. But God is truth itself; *I am the way, the truth, and the life.* Therefore *God exists* is self-evident.

On the contrary, No one can mentally admit the opposite of what is self-evident, as the Philosopher states concerning the first principles of demonstration. But the opposite of the proposition *God is* can be mentally admitted: *The fool said in his heart, There is no God.* Therefore, that God exists is not self-evident.

I answer that, A thing can be self-evident in either of two ways; on the one hand, self-evident in itself, though not to us; on the other, self-evident in itself, and to us. A proposition is self-evident because the predicate is included in the essence of the subject: *e.g., Man is an animal,* for animal is contained in the essence of man. If, therefore, the essence of the predicate and subject be known to all, the proposition will be self-evident to all; as is clear with regard to the first principles of demonstration, the terms of which are certain common notions that no one is ignorant of, such as being and non-being, whole and part, and the like. If, however, there are some to whom the essence of the predicate and subject is unknown, the proposition will be self-evident in itself, but not to those who do not know the meaning of the predicate and subject of the proposition. There-fore, it happens, as Boethius says, that there are some notions of the mind which are common and self-evident only to the learned, as that incorporeal substances are not in space. Therefore I say that this proposition, *God exists,* of itself is self-evident, for the predicate is the same as the subject, because God is His own existence, as will be hereafter shown. Now because we do not know the essence of God, the proposition is not self-evident, to us, but needs to be demonstrated by things that are more known to us, though less known in their nature—namely, by His effects.

Reply Obj. 1. To know that God exists in a general and confused way is implanted in us by nature, inasmuch as God is man's beatitude. For man naturally desires happiness and what is naturally desired by man is naturally known by him. This, however, is not to know absolutely that God exists; just as to know that someone is approaching is not the same as to know that Peter is approaching, even though it is Peter who is approaching; for there are many who imagine that man's perfect good, which is happi-ness, consists in riches, and others in pleasures, and others in something else.

Reply Obj. 2. Perhaps not everyone who hears this name *God* understands it to signify something than which nothing greater can be thought, seeing that some have believed God to be a body. Yet, granted that everyone under-stands that by this name God is signified something than which nothing greater can be thought, nevertheless, it does not therefore follow that he understands that what the name signifies exists actually, but only that it exists mentally. Nor can it be argued that it actually exists, unless it be admitted that there actually exists something than which nothing greater can be thought; and this precisely is not admitted by those who hold that God does not exist.

Reply Obj. 3. The existence of truth in general is self-evident, but the existence of a Primal Truth is not self-evident to us.

SECOND ARTICLE: WHETHER IT CAN BE DEMONSTRATED THAT GOD EXISTS?

We proceed thus to the Second Article.

Objection 1. It seems that the existence of God cannot be demonstrated. For it is an article of faith that God exists. But what is of faith cannot be demonstrated, because a demonstration produces scientific knowledge, whereas faith is of the unseen, as is clear from the Apostle. Therefore it cannot be demonstrated that God exists.

Obj. 2. Further, essence is the middle term of demonstration. But we cannot know in what God's essence consists, but solely in what it does not consist, as Damascene says. Therefore we cannot demonstrate that God exists.

Obj. 3. Further, if the existence of God were demonstrated, this could only be from his effects. But His effects are not proportioned to Him, since He is infinite and His effects are finite, and between the finite and infinite there is no proportion. Therefore, since a cause cannot be demonstrated by an effect not proportioned to it, it seems that the existence of God cannot be demonstrated.

On the contrary, The Apostle says: *The invisible things of Him are clearly seen, being understood by the things that are made.* But this would not be unless the existence of God could be demonstrated through the things that are made; for the first thing we must know of anything is, whether it exists.

I answer that, Demonstration can be made in two ways: One is through the cause, and is called *propter quid,* and this is to argue from what is prior absolutely. The other is through the effect, and is called a demonstration *quia*; this is to argue from what is prior relatively only to us. When an effect is better known to us than its cause, from the effect we proceed to the knowledge of the cause. And from every effect the existence of its proper cause can be demonstrated, so long as its effects are better known to us; because, since every effect depends upon its cause, if the effect exists, the cause must pre-exist. Hence the existence of God, in so far as it is not self-evident to us, can be demonstrated from those of His effects which are known to us.

Reply Obj. 1. The existence of God and other like truths about God, which can be known by natural reason, are not articles of faith, but are preambles to the articles; for faith presupposes natural knowledge, even as grace presupposes nature and perfection the perfectible. Nevertheless, there is nothing to prevent a man, who cannot grasp a proof, from accepting, as a matter of faith, something which in itself is capable of being scientifically known and demonstrated.

Reply Obj. 2. When the existence of a cause is demonstrated from an effect, this effect takes the place of the definition of the cause in proving the cause's existence. This is especially the case in regard to God, because, in order to prove the existence of anything, it is necessary to accept as a middle term the meaning of the name, and not its essence, for the question of its essence follows on the question of its existence. Now the names given to God are derived from His effects, as will be later shown. Consequently, in demonstrating the existence of God from His effects, we may take for the middle terms the meaning of the name of *God.*

Reply Obj. 3. From effects not proportioned to the cause no perfect knowledge of that cause can be obtained. Yet, from every effect the existence of the cause can be clearly demonstrated, and so we can demonstrate the existence of God from His effects; though from them we cannot know God perfectly as He is in His essence.

THIRD ARTICLE: WHETHER GOD EXISTS?

We proceed thus to the Third Article.

Objection 1. It seems that God does not exist; because if one of two contraries be infinite, the other would be altogether destroyed. But the Name *God* means that He is infinite goodness. If, therefore, God existed, there would be no evil discoverable; but there is evil in the world. Therefore God does not exist.

Obj. 2. Further, it is superfluous to suppose that what can be accounted for by a few principles has been produced by many. But it seems that everything we see in the world can be accounted for by other principles, supposing God did not exist. For all natural things can be reduced to one principle, which is nature; and all voluntary things can be reduced to one principle, which is human reason, or will. Therefore there is no need to suppose God's existence.

On the contrary, It is said in the person of God: *I am Who am.*

I answer that, The existence of God can be proved in five ways.

The first and more manifest way is the argument from motion. It is certain, and evident to our senses, that in the world some things are in motion. Now whatever is moved is moved by another, for nothing can be moved except it is in potentiality to that towards which it is moved; whereas a thing moves inasmuch as it is an act. For motion is nothing else than the reduction of something from potentiality to actuality. But nothing can be reduced from potentiality to actuality, except by something in a state of actuality. Thus that which is actually hot, as fire, makes wood, which is potentially hot, to be actually hot, and thereby moves and changes it. Now it is not possible that the same thing should be at once in actuality and potentiality in the same respect, but only in different respects. For what is actually hot cannot simultaneously be potentially hot; but it is simultaneously potentially cold. It is therefore impossible that in the same respect and in the same way a thing should be both mover and moved, i.e., that it should move itself. Therefore, whatever is moved must be moved by another. If that by which it is moved be itself moved, then this also must needs be moved by another, and that by another again. But this cannot go on to infinity, because then there would be no first mover, and, consequently, no other mover, seeing that subsequent movers move only inasmuch as they are moved by the first mover; as the staff moves only because it is moved by the hand. Therefore it is necessary to arrive at a first mover, moved by no other; and this everyone understands to be God.

The second way is from the nature of efficient cause. In the world of sensible things we find there is an order of efficient causes. There is no case known (neither is it, indeed, possible) in which a thing is found to be the efficient cause of itself; for so it would be prior to itself, which is impossible. Now in efficient causes it is not possible to go on to infinity, because in all efficient causes following in order, the first is the cause of the intermediate cause, and the intermediate is the cause of the ultimate cause, whether the intermediate cause be several, or one only. Now to take away the cause is to take away the effect. Therefore, if there be no first cause among efficient causes, there will be no ultimate, nor any intermediate, cause. But if in efficient causes it is possible to go on to infinity, there will be no first efficient cause, neither will there be an ultimate effect, nor any intermediate efficient causes; all of which is plainly false. Therefore it is necessary to admit a first efficient cause, to which everyone gives the name of God.

The third way is taken from possibility and necessity, and runs thus. We find in nature things that are possible to be and not to be, since they are found to be generated, and to be corrupted, and consequently, it is possible for them to be and not to be. But it is impossible for these always to exist, for that which can not-be at some time is not. Therefore, if everything can not-be, then at one time there was nothing in existence. Now if this were true, even now there would be nothing in existence, because that which does not exist begins to exist only through something already existing. Therefore, if at one time nothing was in existence, it would have been impossible for anything to have begun to exist; and thus even now nothing would be in existence—which is absurd. Therefore, not all beings are merely possible, but there must exist something the existence of which is necessary. But every necessary thing either has its necessity caused by another, or not. Now it is impossible to go on to infinity in necessary things which have their necessity caused by another, as has been already proved in regard to efficient causes. Therefore we cannot but admit the existence of some being having of itself its own necessity, and not receiving it from another, but rather causing in others their necessity. This all men speak of as God.

The fourth way is taken from the gradation to be found in things. Among beings there are some more and some less good, true, noble, and the like. But *more* and *less* are predicted of different things according as they resemble in their different ways something which is the maximum, as a thing is said to be hotter according as it more nearly resembles that which is hottest; so that there is something which is truest, something best, something noblest, and consequently, something which is most being, for those things that are greatest in truth are greatest in being, as it is written in

Metaph. ii. Now the maximum in any genus is the cause of all in that genus, as fire, which is the maximum of heat, is the cause of all hot things, as is said in the same book. Therefore there must also be something which is to all beings the cause of their being, goodness, and every other perfection; and this we call God.

The fifth way is taken from the governance of the world. We see that things which lack knowledge, such as natural bodies, act for an end, and this is evident from their acting always, or nearly always, in the same way, so as to obtain the best result. Hence it is plain that they achieve their end, not fortuitously, but designedly. Now whatever lacks knowledge cannot move towards an end, unless it be directed by some being endowed with knowledge and intelligence; as the arrow is directed by the archer. Therefore some intelligent being exists by whom all natural things are directed to their end; and this being we call God.

Reply Obj. 1. As Augustine says: *Since God is the highest good, He would not allow any evil to exist in His works, unless His omnipotence and goodness were such as to bring good even out of evil.* This is part of the infinite goodness of God, that He should allow evil to exist, and out of it produce good.

Reply Obj. 2. Since nature works for a determinate end under the direction of a higher agent, whatever is done by nature must be traced back to God as to its first cause. So likewise whatever is done voluntarily must be traced back to some higher cause other than human reason and will, since these can change and fail; for all things that are changeable and capable of defect must be traced back to an immovable and self-necessary first principle, as has been shown.

Question XC: On the Essence of Law
(In Four Articles)

CONCERNING LAW, we must consider (1) law itself in general; (2) its parts. Concerning law in general three points offer themselves for our consideration: (1) its essence; (2) the different kinds of law; (3) the effects of law.

Under the first head there are four points of inquiry: (1) Whether law is something pertaining to reason? (2) Concerning the end of law. (3) Its cause. (4) The promulgation of law.

FIRST ARTICLE: WHETHER LAW IS SOMETHING PERTAINING TO REASON?

We proceed thus to the First Article.

Objection 1. It would seem that law is not something pertaining to reason. For the Apostle says: *I see another law in my members,* etc. But nothing pertaining to reason is in the members, since the reason does not make use of a bodily organ. Therefore law is not something pertaining to reason.

Obj. 2. Further, in the reason there is nothing else but power, habit and act. But law is not the power itself of reason. In like manner, neither is it a habit of reason, because the habits of reason are the intellectual virtues, of which we have spoken above. Nor again is it an act of reason, because then law would cease when the act of reason ceases, for instance, while we are asleep. Therefore law is nothing pertaining to reason.

Obj. 3. Further, the law moves those who are subject to it to act rightly. But it belongs properly to the will to move to act, as is evident from what has been said above. Therefore law pertains, not to the reason, but to the will, according to the words of the Jurist: *Whatsoever pleaseth the sovereign has the force of law.*

On the contrary, It belongs to the law to command and to forbid. But it belongs to reason to command, as was stated above. Therefore law is something pertaining to reason.

I answer that, Law is a rule and measure of acts, whereby man is induced to act or is restrained from acting; for *lex* [law] is derived from *ligare* [to bind], because it binds one to act. Now the rule and measure of human acts is the reason, which is the first principle of human acts, as is evident from what has been stated above. For it belongs to the reason to direct to the end, which is the first principle in all matters of action, according to the Philosopher. Now that which is the principle in any genus is the rule and measure of that genus: for instance, unity in the genus of numbers, and the first movement in the genus of movements. Consequently, it follows that law is something pertaining to reason.

Reply Obj. 1. Since law is a kind of rule and measure, it may be in something in two ways. First, as in that which measures and rules; and since this is proper to reason, it follows that, in this way, law is in the reason alone. —Secondly, as in that which is measured and ruled. In this way, law is in all those things that are inclined to something because of some law; so that any inclination arising from a law may be called a law, not essentially, but by participation as it were. And thus the inclination of the members to concupiscence is called *the law of the members.*

Reply Obj. 2. Just as, in external acts, we may consider the work, and the work done, for instance, the work of building and the house built, so in the acts of reason, we may consider the act itself of reason, *i.e.,* to understand and to reason, and something produced by this act. With regard to the speculative reason, this is first of all the definition; secondly, the proposition; thirdly, the syllogism or argument. And since the practical reason also makes use of the syllogism in operable matters, as we have stated above and as the Philosopher teaches, hence we find in the practical reason something that holds the same position in regard to operations as, in the speculative reason, the proposition holds in regards to conclusions. Such universal propositions of the practical reason that are directed to operations have the nature of law. And these propositions are sometimes under our actual consideration, while sometimes they are retained in the reason by means of a habit.

Reply Obj. 3. Reason has its power of moving from the will, as was stated above; for it is due to the fact that one wills the end, that the reason issues its commands as regards things ordained to the end. But in order that the volition of what is commanded may have the nature of law, it needs to be in accord with some rule of reason. And in this sense is to be understood the saying that the will of the sovereign has the force of law; or otherwise the sovereign's will would savor of lawlessness rather than of law.

SECOND ARTICLE: WHETHER LAW IS ALWAYS DIRECTED TO THE COMMON GOOD?

We proceed thus to the Second Article.

Objection 1. It would seem that law is not always directed to the common good as to its end. For it belongs to law to command and to forbid. But commands are directed to certain individual goods. Therefore the end of law is not always the common good.

Obj. 2. Further, law directs man in his actions. But human actions are concerned with particular matters. Therefore law is directed to some particular good.

Obj. 3. Further, Isidore says: *If law is based on reason, whatever is based on reason will be a law.* But reason is the foundation not only of what is ordained to the common good, but also of that which is directed to private good. Therefore, law is not directed only to the good of all, but also to the private good of an individual.

On the contrary, Isidore says that *laws are enacted for no private profit, but for the common benefit of the citizens.*

I answer that, As we have stated above, law belongs to that which is a principle of human acts, because it is their rule and measure. Now as reason is a principle of human acts, so in reason itself there is something which is the principle in respect of all the rest. Hence to this principle chiefly and mainly law must needs be referred. Now the first principle in practical matters, which are the object of the practical reason, is the last end: and the last end of human life is happiness or beatitude, as we have stated above. Consequently, law must needs concern itself mainly with the order that is in beatitude. Moreover, since every part is ordained to the whole as the imperfect to the perfect, and since one man is a part of the perfect community, law must needs concern itself properly with the order directed to universal happiness. Therefore the Philosopher, in the above definition of legal matters, mentions both happiness and the body politic, since he says that we call those legal matters *just which are adapted to produce and preserve happiness and its parts for the body politic.* For the state is a perfect community, as he says in *Politics* i.

Now, in every genus, that which belongs to it chiefly is the principle of the others, and the others belong to that genus according to some order towards that thing. Thus fire, which is chief among hot things, is the cause of heat in mixed bodies, and these are said to be hot in so far as they have a share of fire. Consequently, since law is chiefly ordained to the common good, any other precept in regard to some individual work must needs be devoid of the nature of a law, save in so far as it regards the common good. Therefore every law is ordained to the common good.

Reply Obj. 1. A command denotes the application of a law to matters regulated by law. Now the order to the common good, at which law aims is applicable to particular ends. And in this way commands are given even concerning particular matters.

Reply Obj. 2. Actions are indeed concerned with particular matters, but those particular matters are referable to the common good, not as to a common genus or species, but as to a common final cause, according as the common good is said to be the common end.

Reply Obj. 3. Just as nothing stands firm with regard to the speculative reason except that which is traced back to the first indemonstrable principles, so nothing stands firm with regard to the practical reason, unless it be directed to the last end which is the common good. Now whatever stands to reason in this sense has the nature of a law.

THIRD ARTICLE: WHETHER THE REASON OF ANY MAN IS COMPETENT TO MAKE LAWS?

We proceed thus to the Third Article.

Objection 1. It would seem that the reason of any man is competent to make laws. For the Apostle says that *when the Gentiles, who have not the law, do by nature those things that are of the law, . . . they are a law to themselves.* Now he says this of all in general. Therefore anyone can make a law for himself.

Obj. 2. Further, as the Philosopher says, *the intention of the lawgiver is to lead men to virtue.* But every man can lead another to virtue. Therefore the reason of any man is competent to make laws.

Obj. 3. Further, just as the sovereign of a state governs the state, so every father of a family governs his household. But the sovereign of a state can make laws for the state. Therefore every father of a family can make laws for his household.

On the contrary, Isidore says, and the *Decretals* repeat: *A law is an ordinance of the people, whereby something is sanctioned by the Elders together with the Commonalty.* Therefore not everyone can make laws.

I answer that, A law, properly speaking, regards first and foremost the order to the common good. Now to order anything to the common good belongs either to the whole people, or to someone who is the vicegerent of the whole people. Hence the making of a law belongs either to the whole people or to a public personage who has care of the whole people; for in all other matters the directing of anything to the end concerns him to whom the end belongs.

Reply Obj. 1. As was stated above, a law is in a person not only as in one that rules, but also, by participation, as in one that is ruled. In the latter way, each one is a law to himself, in so far as he shares the direction that he receives from one who rules him. Hence the same text goes on: *Who show the work of the law written in their hearts.*

Reply Obj. 2. A private person cannot lead another to virtue efficaciously; for he can only advise, and if his advice be not taken, it has no coercive power, such as the law should have, in order to prove an efficacious inducement to virtue, as the Philosopher says. But this coercive power is vested in the whole people or in some public personage to whom it belongs to inflict penalties, as we shall state further on. Therefore the framing of laws belongs to him alone.

Reply Obj. 3. As one man is a part of the household, so a household is a part of the state; and the state is a perfect community, according to *Politics* i. Therefore, just as the good of one man is not the last end, but is ordained to the common good, so too the good of one household is ordained to the good of a single state, which is a perfect community. Consequently, he that governs a family can indeed make certain commands or ordinances, but not such as to have properly the nature of law.

FOURTH ARTICLE: WHETHER PROMULGATION IS ESSENTIAL TO LAW?

We proceed thus to the Fourth Article.

Objection 1. It would seem that promulgation is not essential to law. For the natural law, above all, has the character of law. But the natural law needs no promulgation. Therefore it is not essential to law that it be promulgated.

Obj. 2. Further, it belongs properly to law to bind one to do or not to do something. But the obligation of fulfilling a law touches not only those in whose presence it is promulgated, but also others. Therefore promulgation is not essential to law.

Obj. 3. Further, the binding force of law extends even to the future, since *laws are binding in matters of the future,* as the jurists say. But promulgation concerns those who are present. Therefore it is not essential to law.

On the contrary, It is laid down in the *Decretals* that *laws are established when they are promulgated.*

I answer that, As was stated above, a law is imposed on others as a rule and measure. Now a rule or measure is imposed by being applied to those who are to be ruled and measured by it. Therefore, in order that a law obtain the binding force which is proper to a law, it must needs be applied to the men who have to be ruled by it. But such application is made by its being made known to them by promulgation. Therefore promulgation is necessary for law to obtain its force.

Thus, from the four preceding articles, the definition of law may be gathered. Law is nothing else than an ordinance of reason for the common good, promulgated by him who has the care of the community.

Reply Obj. 1. The natural law is promulgated by the very fact that God instilled it into man's mind so as to be known by him naturally.

Reply Obj. 2. Those who are not present when a law is promulgated are bound to observe the law, in so far as it is made known or can be made known to them by others, after it has been promulgated.

Reply Obj. 3. The promulgation that takes place in the present extends to future time by reason of the durability of written characters, by which means it is continually promulgated. Hence Isidore says that *lex* [law] *is derived from legere* [to read] *because it is written.*

Question XCI: On the Various Kinds of Law
(In Six Articles)

WE MUST NOW consider the various kinds of law, under which head there are six points of inquiry: (1) Whether there is an eternal law? (2) Whether there is a natural law? (3) Whether there is a human law? (4) Whether there is a divine law? (5) Whether there is one divine law, or several? (6) Whether there is a law of sin?

FIRST ARTICLE: WHETHER THERE IS AN ETERNAL LAW?

We proceed thus to the First Article.

Objection 1. It would seem that there is no eternal law. For every law is imposed on someone. But there was not someone from eternity on whom a law could be imposed, since God alone was from eternity. Therefore no law is eternal.

Obj. 2. Further, promulgation is essential to law. But promulgation could not be from eternity, because there was no one to whom it could be promulgated from eternity. Therefore no law can be eternal.

Obj. 3. Further, law implies order to an end. But nothing ordained to an end is eternal, for the last end alone is eternal. Therefore no law is eternal.

On the contrary, Augustine says: *That Law which is the Supreme Reason connot be understood to be otherwise than unchangeable and eternal.*

I answer that, As we have stated above, law is nothing else but a dictate of practical reason emanating from the ruler who governs a perfect community. Now it is evident, granted that the world is ruled by divine providence, as was stated in the First Part, that the whole community of the universe is governed by the divine reason. Therefore the very notion of the government of things in God, the ruler of the universe, has the nature of a law. And since the divine reason's conception of things is not subject to time, but is eternal, according to *Prov.* viii.23, therefore it is that this kind of law must be called eternal.

Reply Obj. 1. Those things that do not exist in themselves exist in God, inasmuch as they are known and preordained by Him, according to *Rom.* iv.17: *Who calls those things that are not, as those that are.* Accordingly, the eternal concept of the divine law bears the character of an eternal law in so far as it is ordained by God to the government of things foreknown by Him.

Reply Obj. 2. Promulgation is made by word of mouth or in writing, and in both ways the eternal law is promulgated, because both the divine Word and the writing of the Book of Life are eternal. But the promulgation cannot be from eternity on the part of the creature that hears or reads.

Reply Obj. 3. Law implies order to the end actively, namely, in so far as it directs certain things to the end; but not passively,—that is to say, the law itself is not ordained to the end, except accidentally, in a governor whose end is extrinsic to him, and to which end his law must needs be ordained. But the end of the divine government is God Himself, and His law is not something other than Himself. Therefore the eternal law is not ordained to another end.

SECOND ARTICLE: WHETHER THERE IS IN US A NATURAL LAW?

We proceed thus to the Second Article.

Objection 1. It would seem that there is no natural law in us. For man is governed sufficiently by the eternal law, since Augustine says that *the eternal law is that by which it is right that all things should be most orderly.* But nature does not abound in superfluities as neither does she fail in necessaries. Therefore man has no natural law.

Obj. 2. Further, by the law man is directed, in his acts, to the end, as was stated above. But the directing of human acts to their end is not a function of nature, as is the case in irrational creatures, which act for an end solely by their natural appetite; whereas man acts for an end by his reason and will. Therefore man has no natural law.

Obj. 3. Further, the more a man is free, the less is he under the law. But man is freer than all the animals because of his free choice, with which he is endowed indistinction from all other animals. Since, therefore, other animals are not subject to a natural law, neither is man subject to a natural law.

On the contrary, The *Gloss* on *Rom.* ii.14 (*When the Gentiles, who have not the law, do by nature those things that are of the law*) comments as follows: *Although they have no written law, yet they have the natural law, whereby each one knows, and is conscious of, what is good and what is evil.*

I answer that, As we have stated above, law, being a rule and measure, can be in a person in two ways: in one way, as in him that rules and measures; in another way, as in that which is ruled and measured, since a thing is ruled and measured in so far as it partakes of the rule or measure. Therefore, since all things subject to divine providence are ruled and measured by the eternal law, as was stated above, it is evident that all things partake in some way in the eternal law, in so far as, namely, from its being imprinted on them, they derive their respective inclinations to their proper acts and ends. Now among all others, the rational creature is subject to divine providence in a more excellent way, in so far as it itself partakes of a share of providence, by being provident both for itself and for others. Therefore it has a share of the eternal reason, whereby it has a natural inclination to its proper act and end; and this participation of the eternal law in the rational creature is called the natural law. Hence the Psalmist, after saying: *Offer up the sacrifice of justice,* as though someone asked what the works of justice are, adds: *Many say, Who showeth us good things?* in answer to which question he says: *The light of Thy countenance, O Lord, is signed upon us.* He thus implies that the light of natural reason, whereby we discern what is good and what is evil, which is the function of the natural law, is nothing else than an imprint on us of the divine light. It is therefore evident that the natural law is nothing else than the rational creature's participation of the eternal law.

Reply Obj. 1. This argument would hold if the natural law were something different from the eternal law; whereas it is nothing but a participation thereof, as we have stated above.

Reply Obj. 2. Every act of reason and will in us is based on that which is according to nature, as was stated above. For every act of reasoning is based on principles that are known naturally, and every act of appetite in respect of the means is derived from the natural appetite in respect of the last end. Accordingly, the first direction of our acts to their end must needs be through the natural law.

Reply Obj. 3. Even irrational animals partake in their own way of the eternal reason, just as the rational creature does. But because the rational creature partakes thereof in an intellectual and rational manner, therefore the participation of the eternal law in the rational creature is properly called a law, since a law is something pertaining to reason, as was stated above. Irrational creatures, however, do not partake thereof in a rational manner, and therefore there is no participation of the eternal law in them, except by way of likeness.

THIRD ARTICLE: WHETHER THERE IS A HUMAN LAW?

We proceed thus to the Third Article.

Objection 1. It would seem that there is not a human law. For the natural law is a participation of the eternal law, as was stated above. Now through the eternal law *all things are most orderly,* as Augustine states. Therefore the natural law suffices for the ordering of all human affairs. Consequently there is no need for a human law.

Obj. 2. Further, law has the character of a measure, as was stated above. But human reason is not a measure of things, but *vice versa,* as is stated in *Metaph.* x. Therefore, no law can emanate from the human reason.

Obj. 3. Further, a measure should be most certain, as is stated in *Metaph.* x. But the dictates of the human reason in matters of conduct are uncertain, according to *Wis.* ix.14: *The thoughts of mortal men are fearful, and our counsels uncertain.* Therefore no law can emanate from the human reason.

On the contrary, Augustine distinguishes two kinds of law, the one eternal, the other temporal, which he calls human.

I answer that, As we have stated above, a law is a dictate of the practical reason. Now it is to be observed that the same procedure takes place in the practical and in the speculative reason, for each proceeds from principles to conclusions, as was stated above. Accordingly, we conclude that just as in the speculative reason, from naturally known indemonstrable principles we draw the conclusions of the various sciences, the knowledge of which is not imparted to us by nature, but acquired by the efforts of reason, so too it is that from the precepts of the natural law, as from common and indemonstrable principles, the human reason needs to proceed to the more particular determination of certain matters. These particular determinations, devised by human reason, are called human laws, provided that the other essential conditions of law be observed, as was stated above. Therefore Tully says in his *Rhetoric* that *justice has its sources in nature; thence certain things came into custom by reason of their utility; afterwards these things which emanated from nature, and were approved by custom, were sanctioned by fear and reverence for the law.*

Reply Obj. 1. The human reason cannot have a full participation of the dictate of the divine reason, but according to its own mode, and imperfectly. Consequently, just as on the part of the speculative reason, by a natural participation of divine wisdom, there is in us the knowledge of certain common principles, but not a proper knowledge of each single truth, such as that contained in the divine wisdom, so, too, on the part of the practical reason, man has a natural participation of the eternal law, according to certain common principles, but not as regards the particular determinations of individual cases, which are, however, contained in the eternal law. Hence the need for human reason to proceed further to sanction them by law.

Reply Obj. 2. Human reason is not, of itself, the rule of things. But the principles impressed on it by nature are the general rules and measures of all things relating to human conduct, of which the natural reason is the rule and measure, although it is not the measure of things that are from nature.

Reply Obj. 3. The practical reason is concerned with operable matters, which are singular and contingent, but not with necessary things, with which the speculative reason is concerned. Therefore human laws cannot have that inerrancy that belongs to the demonstrated conclusions of the sciences. Nor is it necessary for every measure to be altogether unerring and certain, but according as it is possible in its own particular genus.

SUMMA THEOLOGICA

Of Cheating, Which Is Committed in Buying and Selling

First, we shall consider cheating, which is committed in buying and selling: secondly, we shall consider usury, which occurs in loans. In connection with the other voluntary commutations no special kind of sin is to be found distinct from rapine and theft.

Under the first head there are four points of inquiry: (1) Of unjust sales as regards the price; namely, whether it is lawful to sell a thing for more than its worth? (2) Of unjust sales on the part of the thing sold. (3) Whether the seller is bound to reveal a fault in the thing sold? (4) Whether it is lawful in trading to sell a thing at a higher price than was paid for it?

FIRST ARTICLE: WHETHER IT IS LAWFUL TO SELL A THING FOR MORE THAN ITS WORTH?

We proceed thus to the First Article.

Objection 1. It would seem that it is lawful to sell a thing for more than its worth. In the commutations of human life, civil laws determine that which is just. Now according to these laws it is just for buyer and seller to deceive one another: and this occurs by the seller selling a thing for more than its worth, and the buyer buying a thing for less than its worth. Therefore it is lawful to sell a thing for more than its worth.

Obj. 2. Further, that which is common to all would seem to be natural and not sinful. Now Augustine relates that the saying of a certain jester was accepted by all, *You wish to buy for a song and to sell at a premium,* which agrees with the saying, *It is naught, it is naught, saith every buyer: and when he is gone away, then he will boast.*[1] Therefore it is lawful to sell a thing for more than its worth.

Obj. 3. Further, it does not seem unlawful if that which honesty demands be done by mutual agreement. Now, according to the Philosopher [2] in the friendship which is based on utility, the amount of the recompense for a favour received should depend on the utility accruing to the receiver: and this utility sometimes is worth more than the thing given, for instance if the receiver be in great need of that thing, whether for the purpose of avoiding a danger, or of deriving some particular benefit. Therefore, in contracts of buying and selling, it is lawful to give a thing in return for more than its worth.

[1] Proverbs xx, 14.   [2] *Nicomachean Ethics,* VIII, 13.

On the contrary, it is written[3] *All things . . . whatsoever you would that men should do to you, do you also to them.* But no man wishes to buy a thing for more than its worth. Therefore no man should sell a thing to another man for more than its worth.

I answer that, it is altogether sinful to have recourse to deceit in order to sell a thing for more than its just price, because this is to deceive one's neighbour so as to injure him. Hence Tully [Cicero] says *Contracts should be entirely free from double-dealing; the seller must not impose upon the bidder, nor the buyer upon one that bids against him.*

But, apart from fraud, we may speak of buying and selling in two ways. First, as considered in themselves, and from this point of view, buying and selling seem to be established for the common advantage of both parties, one of whom requires that which belongs to the other, and vice versa, as the Philosopher states.[4] Now whatever is established for the common advantage, should not be more of a burden to one party than to another, and consequently all contracts between them should observe equality of thing and thing. Again, the quality of a thing that comes into human use is measured by the price given for it, for which purpose money was invented, as stated in the *Ethics*.[5] Therefore if either the price exceed the quantity of the thing's worth, or, conversely, the thing exceed the price, there is no longer the equality of justice: and consequently, to sell a thing for more than its worth, or to buy it for less than its worth, is in itself unjust and unlawful.

Secondly we may speak of buying and selling, considered as accidentally tending to the advantage of one party, and to the disadvantage of the other: for instance, when a man has great need of a certain thing, while another man will suffer if he be without it. In such a case the just price will depend not only on the thing sold, but on the loss which the sale brings on the seller. And thus it will be lawful to sell a thing for more than it is worth in itself, though the price paid be not more than it is worth to the owner. Yet if the one man derive a great advantage by becoming possessed of the other man's property, and the seller be not at a loss through being without that thing, the latter ought not to raise the price, because the advantage accruing to the buyer is not due to the seller, but to a circumstance affecting the buyer. Now no man should sell what is not his, though he may charge for the loss he suffers.

On the other hand if a man find that he derives great advantage from something he has bought, he may, of his own accord, pay the seller something over and above: and this pertains to his honesty.

Reply Obj. 1. Human law is given to the people among whom there are many lacking virtue, and it is not given to the virtuous alone. Hence human law

[3] Matthew vii, 12.   [4] *Politics*, II, 3.   [5] *Ethics*, V, 5.

was unable to forbid all that is contrary to virtue; and it suffices for it to prohibit whatever is destructive of human intercourse, while it treats other matters as though they were lawful, not by approving of them, but by not punishing them. Accordingly, if without employing deceit the seller disposes of his goods for more than their worth, or the buyer obtain them for less than their worth, the law looks upon this as licit, and provides no punishment for so doing, unless the excess be too great, because then even human law demands restitution to be made, for instance if a man be deceived in regard of more than half the amount of the just price of a thing.

On the other hand the Divine law leaves nothing unpunished that is contrary to virtue. Hence, according to the Divine law, it is reckoned unlawful if the equality of justice be not observed in buying and selling: and he who has received more than he ought must make compensation to him that has suffered loss, if the loss be considerable. I add this condition, because the just price of things is not fixed with mathematical precision, but depends on a kind of estimate, so that a slight addition or subtraction would not seem to destroy the equality of justice.

Reply Obj. 2. As Augustine says *this jester, either by looking into himself or by his experience of others, thought that all men are inclined to wish to buy for a song and sell at a premium. But since in reality this is wicked, it is in every man's power to acquire that justice whereby he may resist and overcome this inclination.* And then he gives the example of a man who gave the just price for a book to a man who through ignorance asked a low price for it. Hence it is evident that this common desire is not from nature but from vice, wherefore it is common to many who walk along the broad road of sin.

Reply Obj. 3. In commutative justice we consider chiefly real equality. On the other hand, in friendship based on utility we consider equality of usefulness, so that the recompense should depend on the usefulness accruing, whereas in buying it should be equal to the thing bought.

SECOND ARTICLE: WHETHER A SALE IS RENDERED UNLAWFUL THROUGH A FAULT IN THE THING SOLD?

We proceed thus to the Second Article.

Objection 1. It would seem that a sale is not rendered unjust and unlawful through a fault in the thing sold. For less account should be taken of the other parts of a thing than of what belongs to its substance. Yet the sale of a thing does not seem to be rendered unlawful through a fault in its substance: for instance, if a man sell instead of the real metal, silver or gold produced by some chemical process, which is adapted to all the human uses for which silver and gold are necessary, for instance in the making of vessels and the like. Much less therefore will it be an unlawful sale if the thing be defective in other ways.

Obj. 2. Further, any fault in the thing, affecting the quantity, would seem chiefly to be opposed to justice which consists in equality. Now quantity is known by being measured: and the measures of things that come into human use are not fixed, but in some places are greater, in others less, as the Philosopher states.[6] Therefore just as it is impossible to avoid defects on the part of the thing sold, it seems that a sale is not rendered unlawful through the thing sold being defective.

Obj. 3. Further, the thing sold is rendered defective by lacking a fitting quality. But in order to know the quality of a thing, much knowledge is required that is lacking in most buyers. Therefore a sale is not rendered unlawful by a fault (in the thing sold).

On the contrary, Ambrose says: *It is manifestly a rule of justice that a good man should not depart from the truth, nor inflict an unjust injury on anyone, nor have any connection with fraud.*

I answer that a threefold fault may be found pertaining to the thing which is sold. One, in respect of the thing's substance: and if the seller be aware of a fault in the thing he is selling, he is guilty of a fraudulent sale, so that the sale is rendered unlawful. Hence we find it written against certain people, *Thy silver is turned into dross, thy wine is mingled with water:* [7] because that which is mixed is defective in its substance.

Another defect is in respect of quantity which is known by being measured: wherefore if anyone knowingly make use of a faulty measure in selling, he is guilty of fraud, and the sale is illicit. Hence it is written: *Thou shalt not have divers weights in thy bag, a greater and a less: neither shall there be in thy house a greater bushel and a less,* and further on: *For the Lord . . . abhorreth him that doth these things, and He hateth all injustice.*[8]

A third defect is on the part of the quality, for instance, if a man sell an unhealthy animal as being a healthy one: and if anyone do this knowingly he is guilty of a fraudulent sale, and the sale, in consequence, is illicit.

In all these cases not only is the man guilty of a fraudulent sale, but he is also bound to restitution. But if any of the foregoing defects be in the thing sold, and he knows nothing about this, the seller does not sin, because he does that which is unjust materially, nor is his deed unjust. Nevertheless he is bound to compensate the buyer, when the defect comes to his knowledge. Moreover what has been said of the seller applies equally to the buyer. For sometimes it happens that the seller thinks his goods to be specifically of lower

[6] *Ibid.,* V, 7.   [7] Isaiah i, 22.   [8] Deuteronomy xxv, 13, 14, 16.

value, as when a man sells gold instead of copper, and then if the buyer be aware of this, he buys it unjustly and is bound to restitution: and the same applies to a defect in quantity as to a defect in quality.

Reply Obj. 1. Gold and silver are costly not only on account of the usefulness of the vessels and other like things made from them, but also on account of the excellence and purity of their substance. Hence if the gold or silver produced by alchemists has not the true specific nature of gold and silver, the sale thereof is fraudulent and unjust, especially as real gold and silver can produce certain results by their natural action, which the counterfeit gold and silver of alchemists cannot produce. Thus the true metal has the property of making people joyful, and is helpful medicinally against certain maladies. Moreover real gold can be employed more frequently, and lasts longer in its condition of purity than counterfeit gold. If however real gold were to be produced by alchemy, it would not be unlawful to sell it for the genuine article, for nothing prevents art from employing certain natural causes for the production of natural and true effects, as Augustine says [9] of things produced by the art of the demons.

Reply Obj. 2. The measures of saleable commodities must needs be different in different places, on account of the difference of supply: because where there is greater abundance, the measures are wont to be larger. However in each place those who govern the state must determine the just measures of things saleable, with due consideration for the conditions of place and time. Hence it is not lawful to disregard such measures as are established by public authority or custom.

Reply Obj. 3. As Augustine says [10] the price of things saleable does not depend on their degree of nature, since at times a horse fetches a higher price than a slave; but it depends on their usefulness to man. Hence it is not necessary for the seller or buyer to be cognizant of the hidden qualities of the thing sold, but only of such as render the thing adapted to man's use, for instance, that the horse be strong, run well and so forth. Such qualities the seller and buyer can easily discover.

THIRD ARTICLE: WHETHER THE SELLER IS BOUND TO STATE THE DEFECTS OF THE THINGS SOLD?

We proceed thus to the Third Article.

Objection 1. It would seem that the seller is not bound to state the defects of the thing sold. Since the seller does not bind the buyer to buy, he would seem to leave it to him to judge of the goods offered for sale. Now judgment about a thing and knowledge of that thing belong to the same person. Therefore

---

[9] *On the Trinity*, III, 8.   [10] *The City of God*, XI, 16.

it does not seem imputable to the seller if the buyer be deceived in his judgment, and be hurried into buying a thing without carefully inquiring into
its condition.

Obj. 2. Further, it seems foolish for anyone to do what prevents him carrying out his work. But if a man states the defects of the goods he has for sale,
he prevents their sale: wherefore Tully pictures a man as saying: *Could anything be more absurd than for a public crier, instructed by the owner, to cry:
"I offer this unhealthy house for sale"?* Therefore the seller is not bound to
state the defects of the thing sold.

Obj. 3. Further, man needs more to know the road of virtue than to know
the faults of things offered for sale. Now one is not bound to offer advice to
all or to tell them the truth about matters pertaining to virtue, though one
should not tell anyone what is false. Much less therefore is a seller bound to
tell the faults of what he offers for sale, as though he were counselling the
buyer.

Obj. 4. Further, if one were bound to tell the faults of what one offers for
sale, this would only be in order to lower the price. Now sometimes the price
would be lowered for some other reason, without any defect in the thing sold:
for instance, if the seller carry wheat to a place where wheat fetches a high
price, knowing that many will come after him carrying wheat; because if the
buyers knew this they would give a lower price. But apparently the seller
need not give the buyer this information. Therefore, in like manner, neither,
need he tell him the faults of the goods he is selling.

On the contrary, Ambrose says: *In all* contracts the defects of the saleable
commodity must be stated; *and unless the seller make them known, although
the buyer has already acquired a right to them, the contract is voided on account
of the fraudulent action.*

I answer that it is always unlawful to give anyone an occasion of danger or
loss, although a man need not always give another the help or counsel which
would be for his advantage in any way; but only in certain fixed cases, for
instance when someone is subject to him, or when he is the only one who can
assist him. Now the seller who offers goods for sale, gives the buyer an occasion
of loss or danger, by the very fact that he offers him defective goods, if such
defect may occasion loss or danger to the buyer: loss, if, by reason of this defect,
the goods are of less value, and he takes nothing off the price on that account:
danger, if this defect either hinder the use of the goods or render it hurtful,
for instance, if a man sells a lame for a fleet horse, a tottering house for a safe
one, rotten or poisonous food for wholesome. Wherefore if suchlike defects be
hidden, and the seller does not make them known, the sale will be illicit and
fraudulent, and the seller will be bound to compensation for the loss incurred.

On the other hand, if the defect be manifest, for instance if a horse have but one eye, or if the goods though useless to the buyer, be useful to someone else, provided the seller take as much as he ought from the price, he is not bound to state the defect of the goods, since perhaps on account of that defect the buyer might want him to allow a greater rebate than he need. Wherefore the seller may look to his own indemnity, by withholding the defect of the goods.

Reply Obj. 1. Judgment cannot be pronounced save on what is manifest: for *a man judges of what he knows.*[11] Hence if the defects of the goods offered for sale be hidden, judgment of them is not sufficiently left with the buyer unless such defects be made known to him. The case would be different if the defects were manifest.

Reply Obj. 2. There is no need to publish beforehand by the public crier the defects of the goods one is offering for sale, because if he were to begin by announcing its defects, the bidders would be frightened to buy, through ignorance of other qualities that might render the thing good and serviceable. Such defect ought to be stated to each individual that offers to buy: and then he will be able to compare the various points one with the other, the good with the bad: for nothing prevents that which is defective in one respect being useful in many others.

Reply Obj. 3. Although a man is not bound strictly speaking to tell everyone the truth about matters pertaining to virtue, yet he is so bound in a case when unless he tells the truth, his conduct would endanger another man in detriment to virtue: and so it is in this case.

Reply Obj. 4. The defect in a thing makes it of less value now than it seems to be: but in the case cited, the goods are expected to be of less value at a future time, on account of the arrival of other merchants, which was not foreseen by the buyers. Wherefore the seller, since he sells his goods at the price actually offered him, does not seem to act contrary to justice through not stating what is going to happen. If however he were to do so, or if he lowered his price, it would be exceedingly virtuous on his part: although he does not seem to be bound to do this as a debt of justice.

FOURTH ARTICLE: WHETHER, IN TRADING, IT IS LAWFUL TO SELL A THING AT A HIGHER PRICE THAN WHAT WAS PAID FOR IT?

We proceed thus to the Fourth Article.

Objection 1. It would seem that it is not lawful, in trading, to sell a thing for a higher price than we paid for it. For Chrysostom says in Matth. xxi, 12: *He that buys a thing in order that he may sell it, entire and unchanged, at a profit, is the trader who is cast out of God's temple.* Cassiodorus speaks in the

[11] *Nicomachean Ethics,* I, 3.

same sense in his commentary on Ps. lxx, 15, *Because I have not known learn-ing, or trading according to another version: What is trade, says he, but buying at a cheap price with the purpose of retailing at a higher price?* and he adds: *Such were the tradesmen whom Our Lord cast out of the temple.* Now no man is cast out of the temple except for a sin. Therefore suchlike trading is sinful.

Obj. 2. Further, it is contrary to justice to sell goods at a higher price than their worth, or to buy them for less than their value. Now if you sell a thing for a higher price than you paid for it, you must either have bought it for less than its value, or sell it for more than its value. Therefore this cannot be done without sin.

Obj. 3. Further, Jerome says: *Shun, as you would the plague, a cleric who from being poor has become wealthy, or who, from being a nobody has become a celebrity.* Now trading would not seem to be forbidden to clerics except on account of its sinfulness. Therefore it is a sin in trading, to buy at a low price and to sell at a higher price.

On the contrary, Augustine commenting on Ps. lxx, 15, *Because I have known learning,* says: *The greedy tradesman blasphemes over his losses; he lies and perjures himself over the price of his wares. But these are vices of the man, not of the craft, which can be exercised without these vices.* Therefore trading is not in itself unlawful.

I answer that a tradesman is one whose business consists in the exchange of things. According to the Philosopher [12] exchange of things is twofold; one, natural as it were, and necessary, whereby one commodity is exchanged for another, or money taken in exchange for a commodity, in order to satisfy the needs of life. Suchlike trading, properly speaking does not belong to trades-men, but rather to housekeepers or civil servants who have to provide the household or the state with the necessaries of life. The other kind of exchange is either that of money for money, or of any commodity for money, not on account of the necessities of life, but for profit, and this kind of exchange, properly speaking, regards tradesmen, according to the Philosopher.[13] The former kind of exchange is commendable because it supplies a natural need: but the latter is justly deserving of blame, because, considered in itself, it satisfies the greed for gain, which knows no limit and tends to infinity. Hence trading, considered in itself, has a certain debasement attaching thereto, in so far as, by its very nature, it does not imply a virtuous or necessary end. Nevertheless gain which is the end of trading, though not implying, by its nature, anything virtuous or necessary, does not, in itself, connote anything sinful or contrary to virtue: wherefore nothing prevents gain from being di-

[12] *Politics,* I, 3.   [13] *Ibid.*

rected to some necessary or even virtuous end, and thus trading becomes lawful. Thus, for instance, a man may intend the moderate gain which he seeks to acquire by trading for the upkeep of his household, or for the assistance of the needy: or again, a man may take to trade for some public advantage, for instance, lest his country lack the necessaries of life, and seek gain, not as an end, but as payment for his labour.

Reply Obj. 1. The saying of Chrysostom refers to the trading which seeks gain as a last end. This is especially the case where a man sells something at a higher price without its undergoing any change. For if he sells at a higher price something that has changed for the better, he would seem to receive the reward of his labour. Nevertheless the gain itself may be lawfully intended, not as a last end, but for the sake of some other end which is necessary or virtuous, as stated above.

Reply Obj. 2. Not everyone that sells at a higher price than he bought is a tradesman, but only he who buys that he may sell at a profit. If, on the contrary, he buys not for sale but for possession, and afterwards, for some reason wishes to sell, it is not a trade transaction even if he sell at a profit. For he may lawfully do this, either because he has bettered the thing, or because the value of the thing has changed with the change of place or time, or on account of the danger he incurs in transferring the thing from one place to another, or again in having it carried by another. In this sense neither buying nor selling is unjust.

Reply Obj. 3. Clerics should abstain not only from things that are evil in themselves, but even from those that have an appearance of evil. This happens in trading, both because it is directed to worldly gain, which clerics should despise, and because trading is open to so many vices, since *a merchant is hardly free from sins of the lips.* There is also another reason, because trading engages the mind too much with worldly cares, and consequently withdraws it from spiritual cares; wherefore the Apostle says: *No man being a soldier to God entangleth himself with secular businesses.*[14] Nevertheless it is lawful for clerics to engage in the first mentioned kind of exchange, which is directed to supply the necessaries of life, either by buying or by selling.

Of the Sin of Usury

We must now consider the sin of usury, which is committed in loans: and under this head there are four points of inquiry: (1) Whether it is a sin to take money as a price for money lent, which is to receive usury? (2) Whether it is lawful to lend money for any other kind of consideration, by way of pay-

[14] II Timothy ii, 4.

ment for the loan? (3) Whether a man is bound to restore just gains derived from money taken in usury? (4) Whether it is lawful to borrow money under a condition of usury?

FIRST ARTICLE: WHETHER IT IS A SIN TO TAKE USURY FOR MONEY LENT?

We proceed thus to the First Article.

Objection 1. It would seem that it is not a sin to take usury for money lent. For no man sins through following the example of Christ. But Our Lord said of Himself: *At My coming I might have exacted it,* i. e., the money lent, *with usury.*[15] Therefore it is not a sin to take usury for lending money.

Obj. 2. Further, *The law of the Lord is unspotted,* because, to wit, it forbids sin.[16] Now usury of a kind is allowed in the Divine law, *Thou shalt not lend to thy brother money, nor corn, nor any other thing, but to the stranger:* [17] nay more, it is even promised as a reward for the observance of the Law, *Thou shalt lend to many nations, and shalt not borrow of any one.*[18] Therefore it is not a sin to take usury.

Obj. 3. Further, in human affairs justice is determined by civil laws. Now civil laws allows usury to be taken. Therefore it seems to be lawful.

Obj. 4. Further, the counsels are not binding under sin. But, among other counsels we find: *Lend, hoping for nothing thereby.*[19] Therefore it is not a sin to take usury.

Obj. 5. Further, it does not seem to be in itself sinful to accept a price for doing what one is not bound to do. But one who has money is not bound in every case to lend it to his neighbour. Therefore it is lawful for him sometimes to accept a price for lending it.

Obj. 6. Further, silver made into coins does not differ specifically from silver made into a vessel. But it is lawful to accept a price for the loan of a silver vessel. Therefore it is also lawful to accept a price for the loan of a silver coin. Therefore usury is not in itself a sin.

Obj. 7. Further, anyone may lawfully accept a thing which its owner freely gives him. Now he who accepts the loan, freely gives the usury. Therefore he who lends may lawfully take the usury.

On the contrary, it is written: *If thou lend money to any of thy people that is poor, that dwelleth with thee, thou shalt not be hard upon them as an extortioner, nor oppress them with usuries.*[20]

I answer that to take usury for money lent is unjust in itself, because this is to sell what does not exist, and this evidently leads to inequality which is contrary to justice.

[15] Luke xix, 23.   [16] Psalms xix, 8.   [17] Deuteronomy xxiii, 19, 20.
[18] Deuteronomy xxviii, 12.   [19] Luke vi, 35.   [20] Exodus xxii, 25.

In order to make this evident, we must observe that there are certain things the use of which consists in their consumption: thus we consume wine when we use it for drink, and we consume wheat when we use it for food. Wherefore in suchlike things the use of the thing must not be reckoned apart from the thing itself, and whoever is granted the use of the thing, is granted the thing itself; and for this reason, to lend things of this kind is to transfer the ownership. Accordingly if a man wanted to sell wine separately from the use of the wine, he would be selling the same thing twice, or he would be selling what does not exist, wherefore he would evidently commit a sin of injustice. In like manner he commits an injustice who lends wine or wheat, and asks for double payment, viz., one, the return of the thing in equal measure, the other, the price of the use, which is called usury.

On the other hand there are things the use of which does not consist in their consumption: thus to use a house is to dwell in it, not to destroy it. Wherefore in such things both may be granted: for instance, one man may hand over to another the ownership of his house while reserving to himself the use of it for a time, or vice versa, he may grant the use of the house, while retaining the ownership. For this reason a man may lawfully make a charge for the use of his house, and, besides this, revendicate the house from the person to whom he has granted its use, as happens in renting and letting a house.

Now money, according to the Philosopher [21] was invented chiefly for the purpose of exchange: and consequently the proper and principal use of money is its consumption or alienation whereby it is sunk in exchange. Hence it is by its very nature unlawful to take payment for the use of money lent, which payment is known as usury: and just as a man is bound to restore other ill-gotten goods, so is he bound to restore the money which he has taken in usury.

Reply Obj. 1. In this passage usury must be taken figuratively for the increase of spiritual goods which God exacts from us, for He wishes us ever to advance in the goods which we receive from Him: and this is for our own profit not for His.

Reply Obj. 2. The Jews were forbidden to take usury from their brethren, i. e., from other Jews. By this we are given to understand that to take usury from any man is evil, simply because we ought to treat every man as our neighbour and brother, especially in the state of the Gospel, whereto all are called. Hence it is said without any distinction: *He that hath not put out his money to usury,* and *Who hath not taken usury.*[22] They were permitted, however, to take usury from foreigners, not as though it were lawful, but in order to avoid a greater evil, lest, to wit, through avarice to which they were prone ac-

---

[21] *Nichomachean Ethics,* V, 5; *Politics,* I, 3.   [22] Psalms xv, 5; Ezekiel xviii, 8.

cording to Isaiah lvi, II, they should take usury from the Jews who were worshippers of God.

Where we find it promised to them as a reward, *Thou shalt fenerate to many nations,* etc., fenerating is to be taken in a broad sense for lending, where we read: *Many have refused to fenerate, not out of wickedness,* i. e., they would not lend. Accordingly the Jews are promised in reward an abundance of wealth, so that they would be able to lend to others.

Reply Obj. 3. Human laws leave certain things unpunished, on account of the condition of those who are imperfect, and who would be deprived of many advantages, if all sins were strictly forbidden and punishments appointed for them. Wherefore human law has permitted usury, not that it looks upon usury as harmonizing with justice, but lest the advantage of many should be hindered. Hence it is that in civil law it is stated that *those things according to natural reason and civil law which are consumed by being used, do not admit of usufruct,* and that *the senate did not (nor could it) appoint a usufruct to such things, but established a quasi-usufruct,* namely by permitting usury. Moreover the Philosopher, led by natural reason, says that *to make money by usury is exceedingly unnatural.*[23]

Reply Obj. 4. A man is not always bound to lend, and for this reason it is placed among the counsels. Yet it is a matter of precept not to seek profit by lending: although it may be called a matter of counsel in comparison with the maxims of the Pharisees, who deemed some kinds of usury to be lawful, just as love of one's enemies is a matter of counsel. Or again, he speaks here not of the hope of usurious gain, but of the hope which is put in man. For we ought not to lend or do any good deed through hope in man, but only through hope in God.

Reply Obj. 5. He that is not bound to lend may accept repayment for what he has done, but he must not exact more. Now he is repaid according to equality of justice if he is repaid as much as he lent. Wherefore if he exacts more for the usufruct of a thing which has no other use but the consumption of its substance, he exacts a price of something non-existent: and so his exaction is unjust.

Reply Obj. 6. The principal use of a silver vessel is not its consumption, and so one may lawfully sell its use while retaining one's ownership of it. On the other hand the principal use of silver money is sinking it in exchange, so that it is not lawful to sell its use and at the same time expect the restitution of the amount lent. It must be observed, however, that the secondary use of silver vessels may be an exchange, and such use may not be lawfully sold. In like

[23] *Politics,* I, 3.

manner there may be some secondary use of silver money; for instance, a man might lend coins for show, or to be used as security.

Reply Obj. 7. He who gives usury does not give it voluntarily simply, but under a certain necessity, in so far as he needs to borrow money which the owner is unwilling to lend without usury.

SECOND ARTICLE: WHETHER IT IS LAWFUL TO ASK FOR ANY OTHER KIND OF CONSIDERATION FOR MONEY LENT?

We proceed thus to the Second Article.

Objection 1. It would seem that one may ask for some other kind of consideration for money lent. For everyone may lawfully seek to indemnify himself. Now sometimes a man suffers loss through lending money. Therefore he may lawfully ask for or even exact something else besides the money lent.

Obj. 2. Further, as stated in the *Ethics* [24] one is in duty bound by a point of honour, to repay anyone who has done us a favour. Now to lend money to one who is in straits is to do him a favour for which he should be grateful. Therefore the recipient of a loan, is bound by a natural debt to repay something. Now it does not seem unlawful to bind oneself to an obligation of the natural law. Therefore it is not unlawful, in lending money to anyone, to demand some sort of compensation as a condition of the loan.

Obj. 3. Further, just as there is real remuneration, so is there verbal remuneration, and remuneration by service, as a gloss says on Isaiah xxxiii, 15, *Blessed is he that shaketh his hands from all bribes.* Now it is lawful to accept service or praise from one to whom one has lent money. Therefore in like manner it is lawful to accept any other kind of remuneration.

Obj. 4. Further, seemingly the relation of gift to gift is the same as of loan to loan. But it is lawful to accept money for money given. Therefore it is lawful to accept repayment by loan in return for a loan granted.

Obj. 5. Further, the lender, by transferring his ownership of a sum of money removes the money further from himself than he who entrusts it to a merchant or craftsman. Now it is lawful to receive interest for money entrusted to a merchant or craftsman. Therefore it is also lawful to receive interest for money lent.

Obj. 6. Further, a man may accept a pledge for money lent, the use of which pledge he might sell for a price: as when a man mortgages his land or the house wherein he dwells. Therefore it is lawful to receive interest for money lent.

Obj. 7. Further, it sometimes happens that a man raises the price of his goods under guise of loan, or buys another's goods at a low figure; or raises his price through delay in being paid, and lowers his price that he may be paid the

[24] V, 5.

sooner. Now in all these cases there seems to be payment for a loan of money: nor does it appear to be manifestly illicit. Therefore it seems to be lawful to expect or exact some consideration for money lent.

On the contrary, among other conditions requisite in a just man it is stated that he *hath not taken usury and increase.*[25]

I answer that according to the Philosopher [26] a thing is reckoned as money *if its value can be measured by money.* Consequently, just as it is a sin against justice, to take money, by tacit or express agreement, in return for lending money or anything else that is consumed by being used, so also is it a like sin, by tacit or express agreement to receive anything whose price can be measured by money. Yet there would be no sin in receiving something of the kind, not as exacting it, nor yet as though it were due on account of some agreement tacit or expressed, but as a gratuity: since, even before lending the money, one could accept a gratuity, nor is one in a worse condition through lending.

On the other hand it is lawful to exact compensation for a loan, in respect of such things as are not appreciated by a measure of money, for instance, benevolence, and love for the lender, and so forth.

Reply Obj. 1. A lender may without sin enter an agreement with the borrower for compensation for the loss he incurs of something he ought to have, for this is not to sell the use of money but to avoid a loss. It may also happen that the borrower avoids a greater loss than the lender incurs, wherefore the borrower may repay the lender with what he has gained. But the lender cannot enter an agreement for compensation, through the fact that he makes no profit out of his money: because he must not sell that which he has not yet and may be prevented in many ways from having.

Reply Obj. 2. Repayment for a favour may be made in two ways. In one way, as a debt of justice; and to such a debt a man may be bound by a fixed contract: and its amount is measured according to the favour received. Wherefore the borrower of money or any such thing the use of which is its consumption is not bound to repay more than he received in loan: and consequently it is against justice if he be obliged to pay back more. In another way a man's obligation to repayment for favour received is based on a debt of friendship, and the nature of this debt depends more on the feeling with which the favour was conferred than on the greatness of the favour itself. This debt does not carry with it a civil obligation, involving a kind of necessity that would exclude the spontaneous nature of such a repayment.

Reply Obj. 3. If a man were, in return for money lent, as though there had been an agreement tacit or expressed, to expect or exact repayment in the shape of some remuneration of service or words, it would be the same as if he ex-

[25] Ezekiel xviii, 7.   [26] *Nicomachean Ethics,* IV, 1.

pected or exacted some real remuneration, because both can be priced at a money value, as may be seen in the case of those who offer for hire the labour which they exercise by work or by tongue. If on the other hand the remuneration by service or words be given not as an obligation, but as a favour, which is not to be appreciated at a money value, it is lawful to take, exact, and expect it.

Reply Obj. 4. Money cannot be sold for a greater sum than the amount lent, which has to be paid back: nor should the loan be made with a demand or expectation of aught else but of a feeling of benevolence which cannot be priced at a pecuniary value, and which can be the basis of a spontaneous loan. Now the obligation to lend in return at some future time is repugnant to such a feeling, because again an obligation of this kind has its pecuniary value. Consequently it is lawful for the lender to borrow something else at the same time, but it is unlawful for him to bind the borrower to grant him a loan at some future time.

Reply Obj. 5. He who lends money transfers the ownership of the money to the borrower. Hence the borrower holds the money at his own risk and is bound to pay it all back: wherefore the lender must not exact more. On the other hand he that entrusts his money to a merchant or craftsman so as to form a kind of society, does not transfer the ownership of his money to them, for it remains his, so that at his risk the merchant speculates with it, or the craftsman uses it for his craft, and consequently he may lawfully demand as something belonging to him, part of the profits derived from his money.

Reply Obj. 6. If a man in return for money lent to him pledges something that can be valued at a price, the lender must allow for the use of that thing towards the repayment of the loan. Else if he wishes the gratuitous use of that thing in addition to repayment, it is the same as if he took money for lending, and that is usury; unless perhaps it were such a thing as friends are wont to lend to one another gratis, as in the case of the loan of a book.

Reply Obj. 7. If a man wish to sell his goods at a higher price than that which is just, so that he may wait for the buyer to pay, it is manifestly a case of usury: because this waiting for the payment of the price has the character of a loan, so that whatever he demands beyond the just price in consideration of this delay is like a price for a loan, which pertains to usury. In like manner if a buyer wishes to buy goods at a lower price than what is just, for the reason that he pays for the goods before they can be delivered, it is a sin of usury; because again this anticipated payment of money has the character of a loan, the price of which is the rebate on the just price of the goods sold. On the other hand if a man wishes to allow a rebate on the just price in order that he may have his money sooner, he is not guilty of the sin of usury.

THIRD ARTICLE: WHETHER A MAN IS BOUND TO RESTORE WHATEVER PROFITS HE HAS MADE OUT OF MONEY GOTTEN BY USURY?

We proceed thus to the Third Article.

Objection 1. It would seem that a man is bound to restore whatever profits he has made out of money gotten by usury. For the Apostle says: [27] *If the root be holy, so are the branches.* Therefore likewise if the root be rotten so are the branches. But the root was infected with usury. Therefore whatever profit is made therefrom is infected with usury. Therefore he is bound to restore it.

Obj. 2. Further, it is laid down: *Property accruing from usury must be sold, and the price repaid to the persons from whom the usury was extorted.* Therefore, likewise, whatever else is acquired from usurious money must be restored.

Obj. 3. Further, that which a man buys with the proceeds of usury is due to him by reason of the money he paid for it. Therefore he has no more right to the thing purchased than to the money he paid. But he was bound to restore the money gained through usury. Therefore he is also bound to restore what he acquired with it.

On the contrary, a man may lawfully hold what he has lawfully acquired. Now that which is acquired by the proceeds of usury is sometimes lawfully acquired. Therefore it may be lawfully retained.

I answer that there are certain things whose use is their consumption, and which do not admit of usufruct, according to law. Wherefore if suchlike things be extorted by means of usury, for instance money, wheat, wine and so forth, the lender is not bound to restore more than he received (since what is acquired by such things is the fruit not of the thing but of human industry), unless indeed the other party by losing some of his own goods be injured through the lender retaining them: for then he is bound to make good the loss.

On the other hand there are certain things whose use is not their consumption: such things admit of usufruct, for instance house or land property and so forth. Wherefore if a man has by usury extorted from another his house or land, he is bound to restore not only the house or land but also the fruits accruing to him therefrom, since they are the fruits of things owned by another man and consequently are due to him.

Reply Obj. 1. The root has not only the character of matter, as money made by usury has; but has also somewhat the character of an active cause, in so far as it administers nourishment. Hence the comparison fails.

Reply Obj. 2. Further, property acquired from usury does not belong to the person who paid usury, but to the person who bought it. Yet he that paid usury has a certain claim on that property just as he has on the other goods of

[27] Romans xi, 16.

the usurer. Hence it is not prescribed that such property should be assigned to the persons who paid usury, since the property is perhaps worth more than what they paid in usury, but it is commanded that the property be sold, and the price be restored, of course according to the amount taken in usury.

Reply Obj. 3. The proceeds of money taken in usury are due to the person who acquired them not by reason of the usurious money as instrumental cause, but on account of his own industry as principal cause. Wherefore he has more right to the goods acquired with usurious money than to the usurious money itself.

FOURTH ARTICLE: WHETHER IT IS LAWFUL TO BORROW MONEY UNDER A CONDITION OF USURY?

We proceed thus to the Fourth Article.

Objection 1. It would seem that it is not lawful to borrow money under a condition of usury. For the Apostle says [28] that they *are worthy of death . . . not only they that do these sins, but they also that consent to them that do them.* Now he that borrows money under a condition of usury consents in the sin of the usurer, and gives him an occasion of sin. Therefore he sins also.

Obj. 2. Further, for no temporal advantage ought one to give another an occasion of committing a sin: for this pertains to active scandal, which is always sinful. Now he that seeks to borrow from a usurer gives him an occasion of sin. Therefore he is not to be excused on account of any temporal advantage.

Obj. 3. Further, it seems no less necessary sometimes to deposit one's money with a usurer than to borrow from him. Now it seems altogether unlawful to deposit's one's money with a usurer, even as it would be unlawful to deposit one's sword with a madman, a maiden with a libertine, or food with a glutton. Neither therefore is it lawful to borrow from a usurer.

On the contrary, he that suffers injury does not sin, according to the Philosopher,[29] wherefore justice is not a mean between two vices, as stated in the same book. Now a usurer sins by doing an injury to the person who borrows from him under a condition of usury. Therefore he that accepts a loan under a condition of usury does not sin.

I answer that it is by no means lawful to induce a man to sin, yet it is lawful to make use of another's sin for a good end, since even God uses all sin for some good, since He draws some good from every evil as stated in the *Enchiridion*.[30] Hence when Publicola asked whether it were lawful to make use of an oath taken by a man swearing by false gods (which is a manifest sin, for he gives Divine honour to them) Augustine answered that he who uses, not for a bad but for a good purpose, the oath of a man that swears by false gods, is a party,

---

[28] Romans i, 32.   [29] *Nicomachean Ethics*, V, 11.   [30] Augustine, *Enchiridion*, XI.

not to his sin of swearing by demons, but to his good compact whereby he kept his word. If however he were to induce him to swear by false gods, he would sin.

Accordingly he must also answer to the question in point that it is by no means lawful to induce a man to lend under a condition of usury: yet it is lawful to borrow for usury from a man who is ready to do so and is a usurer by profession; provided the borrower has a good end in view, such as the relief of his own or another's need. Thus too it is lawful for a man who had fallen among thieves to point out his property to them (which they sin in taking) in order to save his life, after the example of the ten men who said to Ismahel: *Kill us not: for we have stores in the field.*

Reply Obj. 1. He who borrows for usury does not consent to the usurer's sin but makes use of it. Nor is it the usurer's acceptance of usury that pleases him, but his lending, which is good.

Reply Obj. 2. He who borrows for usury gives the usurer an occasion, not for taking usury, but for lending; it is the usurer who finds an occasion of sin in the malice of his heart. Hence there is passive scandal on his part, while there is no active scandal on the part of the person who seeks to borrow. Nor is this passive scandal a reason why the other person should desist from borrowing if he is in need, since this passive scandal arises not from weakness or ignorance but from malice.

Reply Obj. 3. If one were to entrust one's money to a usurer lacking other means of practising usury; or with the intention of making a greater profit from his money by reason of the usury, one would be giving a sinner matter for sin, so that one would be a participator in his guilt. If, on the other hand, the usurer to whom one entrusts one's money has other means of practising usury, there is no sin in entrusting it to him that it may be in safer keeping, since this is to use a sinner for a good purpose.

ON THE GOVERNANCE OF RULERS

CHAPTER II: IT IS MORE EXPEDIENT THAT A MULTITUDE OF MEN LIVING TOGETHER BE RULED BY ONE MAN RATHER THAN BY MANY

HAVING SET FORTH . . . preliminary points we must now inquire what is better for a province or a city; whether to be ruled by one man or by many. Now this may be considered from the very purpose of government. For the aim of any ruler should be directed towards securing the welfare of whatever he undertakes to rule. The duty of the pilot, for instance, is to preserve his ship amidst the perils of the sea and to bring it unharmed to the port of safety. Now, the welfare and safety of a multitude formed into a society is the preservation of its unity, which is called peace, and which, if taken away, the benefit of social life is lost and moreover the multitude in its disagreement becomes a burden to itself. The chief concern of the ruler of a multitude, therefore, should be to procure the unity of peace: and it is not legitimate for him to deliberate whether he shall establish peace in the multitude subject to him, just as a physician does not deliberate whether he shall heal the sick man encharged to him. For no one should deliberate about an end which he is obliged to seek, but only about the means to attain that end. Wherefore, the Apostle, having commended the unity of the faithful people, says: "Be ye careful to keep the unity of the spirit in the bond of peace." [1] The more efficacious, therefore, a government is in keeping the unity of peace, the more useful it will be. For we call that more useful which leads the better to the end. Now it is manifest that what is itself one can more efficaciously bring about unity than several: just as the most efficacious cause of heat is that which is by its nature hot. Therefore the rule of one man is more useful than the rule of many.

Furthermore, it is evident that several persons could by no means keep a multitude from harm (*conservant*) if they totally disagreed. For a certain union is necessary among them if they are to rule at all: several men, for instance, could not pull a ship in one direction unless joined together in some fashion. Now several are said to be united according as they come closer to being one. So one man rules better than several who come near being one.

Again, whatever is in accord with nature is best: for in all things nature does what is best. Now, every natural governance is governance by one. In the multitude of bodily members there is one which moves them all, namely, the heart; and among the powers of the soul one power presides as chief, namely, the reason. Even among bees there is one queen (*rex*) and in the whole universe there is One God, Maker and Ruler of all things. And this is reasonable. For every multitude is derived from unity. Wherefore, artificial things imitate natural things and since a work of art is better according as it attains a closer likeness to what is in nature, it necessarily follows that it is best, in the case of a human multitude, that it be ruled by one person.

This is also evident from experience; for provinces or cities which are not ruled by one person are torn with dissensions and are tossed about without peace so that the complaint seems to be fulfilled which the Lord uttered through the Prophet: "Many pastors have destroyed my vineyard." [2] But, on the contrary, provinces and cities which are ruled under one king enjoy peace, flourish

---

[1] Eph. iv, 3.   [2] Jer. xii, 10.

in justice and delight in prosperity. Hence, the Lord by His prophets promises to His people as a great reward that He will give them one head and that one Prince will be in the midst of them.

CHAPTER V: THAT IN A GOVERNMENT BY MANY, TYRANNICAL GOVERNMENT OCCURS MORE FREQUENTLY THAN IN A GOVERNMENT BY ONE: THERE-FORE THE RULE OF ONE MAN IS BETTER

When a choice is to be made between two things from both of which danger impends, that one must by all means be chosen from which the lesser evil follows. Now, lesser evil follows from a monarchy if it be changed into a tyranny, than from the government of several nobles, when it becomes corrupt. For the dissension which commonly follows upon the government of several, runs counter to the good of peace, which is the principal thing in a social group; which good, indeed, is not done away with by a tyranny, unless there be an excess of tyranny which rages against the whole community, but certain goods of particular men are hindered. The rule of one man is therefore to be preferred to the rule of many, although perils follow from both. Further, that from which great dangers may more often follow is, it would seem, the more to be avoided; but the greatest dangers to the multitude follow more frequently from the rule of many than from the rule of one. For, it commonly happens that one out of the many turns from the pursuit of the common good more than does one man ruling alone. Now when any one among several leaders turns aside from the pursuit of the common good, danger of internal dissension threatens the multitude of subjects, because when the chiefs quarrel, the consequence is that dissension in the multitude follows. If, however, one man is in command, he usually, indeed, looks to the common good; or if he turn his attention away from the common good, it does not immediately follow that he turns his attention to the oppression of his subjects, which is an excess of tyranny and holds the highest degree of wickedness in government, as has been shown above. The dangers which arise from the government of many are more to be avoided, therefore, than those which arise from the government of one. Moreover, it happens that the rule of many is changed into a tyranny not less, but perhaps more, frequently than the rule of one. For once dissension arises through the rule of several, it often happens that one triumphs over the others and usurps the government of the multitude for himself alone; and this indeed may be clearly seen from what has come about in such circumstances. For the rule of almost all groups of many has ended in tyranny, as is plainly seen in the Roman Republic. When it had been administered for a long time by several magistrates, dissensions and civil wars arose and it fell into the power of the most cruel tyrants. And, in general, if one carefully considers what has happened in the past and what is happening in the present, he will discover that more men practised tyranny in lands ruled by many than in those governed by one. If, therefore, kingly rule, which is the best government, seems chiefly to be avoided because of tyranny, and, on the other hand, tyranny is wont to occur not less, but more, in the rule of many than in the rule of one, it follows that it is simply more expedient to live under one king than under the rule of several.

CHAPTER VI: CONCLUSION, THAT THE RULE OF ONE MAN IS SIMPLY THE BEST. IT SHOWS HOW THE MULTITUDE MUST BE DISPOSED IN REGARD TO HIM, BECAUSE THE OPPORTUNITY OF TYRANNIZING MUST BE REMOVED FROM HIM, AND THAT HE SHOULD BE TOLERATED EVEN IN HIS TYRANNY ON ACCOUNT OF THE GREATER EVIL TO BE AVOIDED

Therefore, since the rule of one man, which is the best, is to be preferred, and since it may happen that it be changed into a tyranny, which is the worst, it is clear from what has been said that diligent zeal must be exercised in order that the interests of the multitude be so safeguarded with regard to their king that they may not fall under a tyrant. First it is necessary that the man who is raised up to be king by those to whom this office belongs, should be of such character that it is improbable he should fall into tyranny. Wherefore, Daniel, commending the Providence of God with respect to the establishment of the king says: "The Lord hath sought him a man according to his own heart." [3] Then, once the king is established, the government of the kingdom must be so arranged that opportunity to tyrannize be removed. At the same time his power should be so tempered that he cannot easily fall into tyranny. How these things may be done we must consider in what follows. Finally, provision must be made for facing the situation should the king turn aside into tyranny.

Indeed, if there be not an excess of tyranny it is more expedient to tolerate for a while the milder tyranny than, by acting against the tyrant, to be involved in many perils which are more grievous than the tyranny itself. For it may happen that those who act against the tyrant are unable to prevail and the tyrant, thus provoked, rages the more. Even if one should be able to prevail against the tyrant, from this fact itself very grave dissensions among the people frequently ensue: the multitude may be broken up by factions either during their revolt against the tyrant, or, concerning the organization of the government, after the tyrant has been overthrown. It also happens that sometimes, while the multitude is driving out the tyrant by the help of some man, he, having received the power, seizes the tyranny, and fearing to suffer from another what he did to his predecessor, oppresses his subjects with a more grievous

[3] I Kings xiii, 14.

slavery. For this is wont to happen in tyranny, namely, that the second be-comes more grievous than the one preceding, inasmuch as, without abandon-ing the previous oppressions, he himself thinks up fresh ones from the malice of his heart: whence, in Syracuse, when there was a time that everybody de-sired the death of Dionysius, a certain old woman kept constantly praying that he might be unharmed and that he might survive her. When the tyrant learned this he asked why she did it. Then she said, "When I was a girl we had a harsh tyrant and I wished for his death; when he was killed, there suc-ceeded him one who was somewhat harsher: I was very eager to see the end of his dominion also: then we began to have a third ruler still more harsh—that was you. So if you should be taken away a worse would succeed in your place."

Now some have been of opinion that if the excess of tyranny is unbearable, it would be an act of virtue for strong men to slay the tyrant and to expose themselves to dangers of death in order to set the multitude free. An example of this occurs even in the Old Testament. For a certain Aioth (*Aod*) slew Eglon, King of Moab, who was oppressing the people of God under harsh slavery, with the dagger fastened to his thigh; and he was made a judge of the people. But this opinion is not in accord with apostolic teaching. For Peter admonishes us to be reverently subject to our masters, not only to the good and gentle but also to the froward: "For if one who suffers unjustly bear his trouble for conscience sake, this is a grace." [4] Wherefore, when many Roman emperors tyrannically persecuted the faith of Christ, a great multitude both of the nobility and of the populace was converted to the faith and they were praised, not for resisting, but for patiently and courageously bearing death for Christ. This is plainly manifested in the case of the holy legion of Thebans. Aioth (*Aod*), then, must be considered rather as having slain a foe, than as having assassinated a ruler of the people, though a tyrannical one. Hence even in the Old Testament we read that they who killed Joas, the king of Juda, although he had fallen away from the worship of God, were slain and their children spared according to the precept of the law. It would, moreover, be dangerous both for the multitude and for their rulers if certain persons should attempt on their own private presumption, to kill their governors, even tyrants. For to dangers of this kind, usually the wicked expose themselves more than the good. For the rule of a king, no less than that of a tyrant, is burdensome to the wicked because, according to the words of Solomon, [5] "A wise king scat-tereth the wicked." Consequently, by presumption of this kind, danger to the people from the loss of their king would be more imminent than relief through the removal of the tyrant.

[4] I Peter ii, 18, 19.   [5] Prov. xx, 26.

Furthermore it rather seems, that to proceed against the cruelty of tyrants is an action to be undertaken, not through the private presumption of a few, but by public authority. First of all, if to provide itself with a king belong to the right of any multitude, it is not unjust that the king set up by that multitude be destroyed or his power restricted, if he tyrannically abuse the royal power. It must not be thought that such a multitude is acting unfaithfully in deposing the tyrant, even though it had previously subjected itself to him in perpetuity; because he himself has deserved that the covenant with his subjects should not be kept, since, in ruling the multitude, he did not act faithfully as the office of a king demands. Thus did the Romans cast out from the kingship, Tarquin the Proud, whom they had accepted as their king, because of his tyranny and the tyranny of his sons; and they set up in their place a lesser power, namely, the consular power. So too Domitian, who had succeeded those most moderate Emperors, Vespasian, his father, and Titus, his brother, was slain by the Roman senate when he exercised tyranny, and all that he had wickedly done to the Romans, was justly and profitably, by a decree of the senate, declared null and void.

Thus it came about that Blessed John the Evangelist, the beloved disciple of God, who had been exiled to the island of Patmos by that very Domitian, was sent back to Ephesus by a decree of the senate.

If, however, it pertains to the right of some higher authority to provide a king for a certain multitude, a remedy against the wickedness of a tyrant is to be looked for from him. Thus when Archelaus, who had already begun to reign in Judaea in the place of Herod, his father, was imitating his father's wickedness, a complaint against him having been laid before Caesar Augustus by the Jews, his power was, first of all, diminished by depriving him of his title of king and by dividing one half of his kingdom between his two brothers; later, since he was not restrained from tyranny even by this means, Tiberius Caesar sent him into exile in Lyons, a city of Gaul.

Should no human aid whatsoever against a tyrant be forthcoming, recourse must be had to God, the King of all, who is a helper in due time in tribulation. "For, it lies within His power to turn the cruel heart of the tyrant to mildness." [6] In the words of Solomon: [7] "The heart of the king is in the hand of the Lord, whithersoever He will He shall turn it." He it was who turned into mildness the cruelty of King Assuerus, who was preparing death for the Jews. He it was who so transformed the cruel king Nabuchodonosor that he became a proclaimer of the divine power. "Therefore," he said, "I, Nabuchodonosor, do now praise and magnify and glorify the King of Heaven: because all his works are true and His ways judgments, and them that walk in pride He is

[6] Prov. ix, 10.   [7] Prov. xxi, 1.

able to abase." [8] Those tyrants, however, whom he deems unworthy of conversion he is able to put out of the way or reduce them to the lowest degree, according to the words of the Wise Man: "God hath overturned the thrones of proud princes: and hath set up the meek in their stead." He it was who, seeing the afflicting of his people in Egypt and hearing their cry, hurled the tyrant Pharaoh with his army into the sea. He it was who not only banished from his kingly throne the above mentioned Nabuchodonosor in his former pride, but also cast him from the fellowship of men and changed him into the likeness of a beast. For also His hand is not shortened that He cannot free His people from tyrants. For by Isaias He promises to give his people rest from their labour and trouble and harsh slavery in which they had formerly served; and by Ezechiel He says, "I will deliver my flock from their mouth," [9] that is from the mouth of shepherds who feed themselves. But to deserve to secure this benefit from God, the people must desist from sin; because by divine permission wicked men receive power to rule as a punishment for sin, as the Lord says by the Prophet Osee: [10] "I will give thee a king in my wrath"; and it is said in Job that he "maketh a man that is a hypocrite to reign for the sins of the people." [11] Sin must therefore be done away with that the scourge of tyrants may cease.

CHAPTER VIII: HERE THE DOCTOR DECLARES OF WHAT SORT IS THE TRUE END OF THE KING, THE END WHICH SHOULD MOVE HIM TO RULE WELL

Therefore, since worldly honour and human glory are not a sufficient reward for royal cares it remains to enquire what sort of reward is sufficient. Now, it is proper that a king look to God for his reward, for a servant looks to his master for the reward of his service. Now, in governing his people a king is the minister of God, as the Apostle says: All power is from the Lord God and God's minister is "an avenger to execute wrath upon him that doth evil"; [12] and in the Book of Wisdom, kings are described as being ministers of God. Consequently, kings ought to look to God for the reward of their ruling. Now, God sometimes rewards kings for their service by temporal goods. But such rewards are common to both the good and the wicked. Wherefore the Lord says: "Nabuchodonosor, king of Babylon, hath made his army to undergo hard service against Tyre . . . and there hath been no reward given him nor his army, for Tyre, for the service he rendered me against it," [13] for that service, namely, by which power is the minister of God, according to the Apostle, and the avenger to execute wrath upon him that doth evil: and

---

[8] Dan. iv, 34.   [9] Ez. xxxiv, 10.   [10] Hos. xiii, 11.
[11] Job xxxiv, 30.   [12] Rom. xiii, 1, 4.   [13] Ez. xxix, 18.

afterwards he adds, regarding the reward, "Therefore, thus saith the Lord God: 'I will set Nabuchodonosor the king of Babylon in the land of Egypt, and he shall rifle the spoils thereof . . . and it shall be wages for his army.'" Therefore, if God recompenses wicked kings who fight against the enemies of God, though not with the intention of serving God, but to execute their own hatred and cupidity, by giving them such great rewards as to yield them victory over their foes, to subject kingdoms to their sway and to grant them spoils to rifle, what will he do for good kings who rule the people of God and assail his enemies from a holy motive? He promises them not an earthly reward indeed but an everlasting one and in none other than in Himself, as Peter says, to the shepherds of the people, "Feed the flock of God that is among you and when the prince of pastors shall appear," that is the King of kings, Christ, "you shall receive a neverfading crown of glory," [14] concerning which Isaias says, "The Lord shall be a crown of glory and a garland of joy to his people." [15]

This is also clearly shown by reason. For it is implanted in the minds of all who have the use of reason that the reward of virtue is happiness. The virtue (*virtus*) of anything whatsoever is explained to be that which makes its possessor good and renders his deed good. Moreover, everyone strives by working well to attain that which is most deeply implanted in desire; namely, to be happy. This, no one is able not to will. It is therefore, fitting to expect as a reward for virtue that which makes man happy. Now, if to work well is a virtuous deed and the king's work is to rule his people well, then that which makes him happy will be the king's reward. But what that is has now to be considered.

Happiness we say is the ultimate end of our desires. Now the movement of desire does not go on to infinity, else natural desire would be vain for infinity cannot be traversed. Since, then, the desire of an intellectual nature is for universal good, that good alone can make it truly happy, which, when attained, leaves no further good to be desired. Whence, happiness is called the perfect good inasmuch as it comprises in itself all things desirable. But no earthly good is such a good. For they who have riches desire to have more, and the like is clear for the rest: and if they do not seek more, they at least desire that those they have should abide or that others should follow in their stead, for nothing permanent is found in earthly things. Consequently there is nothing earthly which can calm desire. And so nothing earthly can make man happy, that it may be a fitting reward for a king.

Again, the last perfection and perfect good of anything you choose depends upon something higher, for even bodily things are made better by the addition

[14] I Peter v, 2, 4.   [15] Isa. xiii, 5.

of better things, but worse by being mixed with baser things. For if gold is mingled with silver, the silver is made better, while by an admixture of lead it is rendered impure. Now, it is manifest that all earthly things are beneath the human mind; but happiness is the last perfection and the perfect good of man, which all men desire to reach. Therefore, there is no earthly thing which could make man happy, nor is any earthly thing a sufficient reward for a king. For, as Augustine says,[16] we do not call Christian princes happy merely because they have reigned a long time, or because after a peaceful death they have left their sons to rule or because they subdued the enemies of the state, or because they were able to guard against or to suppress citizens who rose up against them; but we call them happy if they rule justly, if they prefer to rule their passions rather than any nations whatsoever, if they do all things not through the ardour of vain glory but for the love of eternal happiness. Such Christian rulers we say are happy, now in hope, afterwards in very fact when that which we await shall come to pass. But there is not any other created thing which would make a man happy and which could be set up as the reward for a king. For the desire of each thing tends toward its source, whence is the cause of its being. But the cause of the human soul is none other than God who made it to His own image. Therefore, it is God alone Who can still the desires of man and make man happy and be the fitting reward for a king.

Furthermore, the human mind knows universal good through understanding and desires it through will: but universal good is not found except in God. Therefore there is nothing which could make man happy, fulfilling his every desire, but God, of whom it is said in the Psalm, "Who satisfieth thy desire with good things." [17] In this therefore, should the king place his reward. Accordingly King David, with this in mind, said, "What have I in heaven? And besides Thee what do I desire upon earth?" [18] and he afterwards adds in answer to this question, "It is good for me to adhere to my God and to put my hope in the Lord God." For it is He who gives salvation to kings, not merely temporal salvation by which He saves both men and beasts together, but also that salvation of which He says by the mouth of Isaias, "But my salvation shall be for ever," that salvation by which He saves men and makes them equal to the angels. Therefore, it can thus be verified that the reward of the king is honour and glory. But what worldly and frail honour can be likened to this honour that a man be made a citizen and a kinsman of God, numbered among the sons of God and obtain the inheritance of the heavenly kingdom with Christ? This is the honour of which King David in desire and wonder says, "Thy friends, O God, are made exceedingly honourable." [19] And further, what glory of human praise can be compared to this, not uttered by the false

16 *City of God*, V, 24.   17 Ps. cii, 5.   18 Ps. lxxii, 25.   19 Ps. xvii, 138.

tongue of flatterers nor the fallacious opinion of men, but issuing from the witness of our inmost conscience and confirmed by the testimony of God, who promises to those who confess Him that he will confess them before the Angels of God in the glory of the Father? They who seek this glory will find it and they will win the glory of men which they do not seek; witness Solomon, who not only received from the Lord wisdom which he sought, but was made glorious above other kings.

CHAPTER XII: HE PROCEEDS TO SHOW THE OFFICE OF A KING, WHEREIN
    ACCORDING TO THE WAYS OF NATURE, HE POINTS OUT THAT THE KING
    IS IN THE KINGDOM, AS THE SOUL IS IN THE BODY, IN THE SAME MAN-
    NER AS GOD IS IN THE UNIVERSE

The next point to be considered is the nature of the kingly office and what sort of man a king must be. Now, because things which are in accordance with art imitate the things which are in accordance with nature (from which, in fact, we must receive in order that we may work according to reason), it appears that the best kingly administration will be one which is patterned after the regime of nature. In things of nature, however, there is found to be both a universal and a particular rulership; universal, by the fact that every-thing is embraced under the rulership of God, who governs all things by His providence. The particular rulership which is found in man is most like the Divine rulership. For this reason man is called a smaller world, since in him there is found the form of universal rulership. For, just as the universe of corporeal creatures and all spiritual powers come under the Divine govern-ment, in like manner are the members of the body and the other powers of the soul controlled by reason, and thus, in a certain proportionate manner, reason is to man what God is to the world. Since man is by nature a social animal living in a group, as we have pointed out above, a likeness of the divine rulership is found in him, not only in this, that a single man is ruled by reason, but also in that a multitude is governed through the reason of one man. This appertains above all to the office of a king, although among certain animals that live socially a likeness of this rulership is to be found. For example, we likewise say there are queens (*reges*) among bees, not that among them ruler-ship is exercised through reason, but through natural instinct implanted in them by the Great Ruler, who is the author of nature. Therefore let the king recognize that such is the office which he undertakes, namely, that he is to be in the kingdom what the soul is in the body, and what God is in the world. If he reflect seriously upon this, from one motive, a zeal for justice will be enkindled in him, when he contemplates that he has been appointed to this position in place of God, to exercise judgment in his kingdom; from another, he acquires the gentleness of clemency and mildness, when he considers as his own members, those individuals who are subject to his rulership.

CHAPTER XIV: WHAT MANNER OF GOVERNMENT IS POSSIBLE FOR A KING, SEEING THAT IT IMITATES THE DIVINE PROVIDENCE; THIS METHOD OF GOVERNMENT HAD ITS ORIGIN IN THE GUIDANCE OF A SHIP; AND A COMPARISON IS SET UP BETWEEN SACERDOTAL AND ROYAL DOMINION

Just as the founding of a city or a kingdom may suitably be learned from the way the world was created, so too the way to govern may be learned from the governing of the world. Before going into that, however, we should consider that to govern is to bring the thing governed in a suitable way to its proper end. Thus a ship is said to be governed, when, through the skill of the sailor, it is brought by a direct route and unharmed to harbour. Consequently, if anything is ordained to an end outside itself (as a ship to a harbour), it is the governor's duty, not only to preserve the thing unharmed, but further to bring it to its end. If on the contrary, there should be anything whose end is not outside itself, then the governor's endeavours would merely tend to preserve the thing itself undamaged in its proper perfection. Although nothing of this kind is found in the world, except God Himself, Who is the end of all, yet the care of that which is ordained to something outside itself, is hindered by many things and in different ways. For, perhaps, one person may have the duty of preserving a thing in existence, and another the duty of bringing it to a higher state of perfection. This is clearly the case in the example of the ship, from which the idea (*ratio*) of government is derived. For it is the carpenter's duty to repair anything that is broken in the ship, but the sailor bears the anxiety of bringing the ship to port. It is the same with man. The doctor sees to it that a man's life is preserved in health, the tradesman supplies the necessities of life, the teacher takes care that he learns the truth, and the tutor sees that he lives according to reason. If a man were not ordained to any other end outside himself, the above mentioned cares would be sufficient for him.

But as long as a man's mortal life endures there is some good extraneous to him, namely, final beatitude which is looked for after death, in the enjoyment of God, for as the Apostle says: [20] "As long as we are in the body we are far from the Lord." Consequently the Christian man, for whom that beatitude has been purchased by the blood of Christ, and who in order to attain it, has received the earnest of the Holy Ghost, needs an additional spiritual care to direct him to the harbour of eternal salvation, and this care is provided for the faithful by the ministers of the Church of Christ.

[20] II Cor. v, 6.

We must form the same judgment about the end of society as a whole as we do concerning the end of one man. If, therefore, the end of man were some good that exists in himself, then the ultimate end of the multitude to be governed would likewise be for the multitude to acquire such good and persevere in its possession. If such an ultimate end either of an individual man or a multitude, were a corporeal one, namely, life and health of body, to govern would then be a physician's charge. If that ultimate end were an abundance of wealth, then some financier would be king of the multitude. If the good of the knowledge of truth were of such a kind that the multitude might attain to it, the king would have the duty of teacher. But it is clear, that the end of any multitude gathered together, is to live virtuously. For, men form groups for the purpose of living well together, a thing which the individual man living alone could not attain. But a good life is a virtuous life. Therefore a virtuous life is the end for which men form groups.

The evidence for this lies in the fact that only those who render mutual assistance to one another in living well truly form part of an assembled multitude. For if men assembled merely to *live,* then animals and serfs would form a part of the civil body. And if men assembled only to acquire wealth, then all those who traded together, would belong to one city. Thus we see that only those are regarded as forming one society who are directed by the same laws and the same government, to live well. Therefore, since man, by living virtuously, is ordained to a higher end, which consists of the enjoyment of God, as we have said above, then human society must have the same end as the individual man. Therefore, it is not the ultimate end of an assembled multitude to live virtuously, but through virtuous living to attain to the possession of God. Furthermore if it could attain this end by the power of human nature, then the duty of a king would have to include the direction of men to this end. We are supposing that he is called "king" to whom the supreme power of governing in human affairs is entrusted. Now the higher the end to which a government is ordained, the loftier is that government; for we always find that the one to whom it pertains to achieve the final end, commands those who execute the things that are ordained to that end. For example, the captain, whose business it is to regulate navigation, tells the man who builds the ship what kind of a ship he must build in order that it be suitable to navigation; and the citizen who bears arms, tells the blacksmith what kind of arms to make. But, because a man does not attain his end which is the possession of God, by human power, but by Divine power, according to the words of the Apostle: "By the grace of God life everlasting," [21] therefore the task of leading him to that end does not pertain to human government but to divine.

[21] Rom. vi, 23.

Consequently, government of this kind pertains to that king who is not only a man, but also God, namely to our Lord Jesus Christ, Who by making men sons of God, brought them to the glory of Heaven.

This then is the government which has been delivered to Him and which shall not be destroyed, on account of which He is called, in Holy Writ, not Priest only, but King, as Jeremias says: "The king shall reign and he shall be wise." [22] Hence a royal priesthood is derived from Him, and what is more, all those who believe in Christ, in so far as they are His members, are called kings and priests. Consequently, in order that spiritual things might be distinguished from earthly things, the ministry of this kingdom has been entrusted not to earthly kings, but to priests, and in the highest degree to the chief priest, the successor of St. Peter, the Vicar of Christ, the Roman Pontiff, to whom all the kings of Christian peoples are to be subject as to our Lord Jesus Christ Himself. For those to whom pertains the care of intermediate ends should be subject to him to whom pertains the care of the ultimate end, and be directed by his rule. Because the priesthood of the gentiles, and the whole worship of their Gods existed merely for the acquisition of temporal goods (which were all ordained to the common good of the multitude, whose care devolved upon a king), the priests of the gentiles were very properly subject to the kings. Similarly, because in the old law earthly goods were promised to a religious people (not indeed by demons but by the true God), the priests of the old law, we read, were also subject to the kings. But in the new law there is a higher priesthood by which men are guided to heavenly goods. Consequently in the law of Christ, kings must be subject to priests.

Therefore, it was a marvelous effect of Divine Providence that in the city of Rome, which God had foreseen would be the principal seat of the Christian people, the custom was gradually established that the rulers of the city should be subject to the priests, for as Valerius Maximus relates: "Our City has always considered that everything should yield precedence to religion, even those things in which it aimed to display the splendor of supreme majesty. Wherefore our governments did not hesitate to minister to religion, considering that they would thus hold control of human affairs if they faithfully and constantly were submissive to divine authority." Because it was to come to pass that the religion of the Christian priesthood should especially thrive in France, God permitted that among the Gauls too, their tribal priests, called Druids, should lay down the law of all Gaul, as Julius Caesar relates in the book which he wrote about the Gallic war.[23]

[22] Jer. xxiii, 5.   [23] De Bello Gallico, VI, 13.

CHAPTER XV: . . . HERE WE NOTE THOSE THINGS WHICH DISPOSE TOWARDS
A PROPER LIFE, AND THOSE WHICH HINDER, AND ALSO THE REMEDY WHICH
THE KING MUST APPLY AGAINST THESE HINDRANCES

. . . For an individual man to lead a good life two things are required. The first and most important is to act in a virtuous manner (for virtue is that by which one lives well); the second, which is secondary, and, as it were, instrumental, is a sufficiency of those bodily goods whose use is necessary for an act of virtue. Yet the unity of man is brought about by nature, while the unity of a society, which we call peace, must be procured through the efforts of the ruler. Therefore, to establish virtuous living in a multitude three things are necessary. First of all, that the multitude be established in the unity of peace. Second, that the multitude thus united in the bond of peace, be guided to good deeds. For just as a man can do nothing well unless unity within his members be presupposed, so a multitude of men which lacks the unity of peace, is hindered from virtuous action, by the fact that it fights against its very existence as a group. In the third place, it is necessary that there be at hand a sufficient supply of the things required for proper living, procured by the ruler's efforts. Then, when virtuous living is set up in society by the efforts of the king, it remains for him to look to its conservation.

Now there are three things which prevent permanence in public virtue. One of these arises from nature. For the good of society should not be established for one time only; it should be in a sense perpetual. Men, on the other hand, cannot abide forever because they are mortal. Even while they are alive they do not always preserve the same vigor, for the life of man is subject to many changes. So a man is not equally suited to the performance of the same duties throughout the whole span of his life. A second impediment to the preservation of public good which comes from within, consists in the perversity of the wills of man, inasmuch as they are either too lazy to perform what the state demands, or, still further, they are harmful to the peace of society, because, by transgressing justice, they disturb the peace of their neighbors. The third hindrance to the preservation of the state comes from without, namely, when peace is destroyed through the attacks of enemies, or, as it sometimes happens, the kingdom or city is completely blotted out. In regard to these three dangers, a triple charge is laid upon the king. First of all, he must take care of the appointment of men to succeed or replace others in charge of the various offices, just as, by the providence of God, provision is made for the succession and replacement of corruptible things, which cannot last forever the same, by the generation of things to take their place. Thus just as the integrity of the universe is maintained so too, the good of the multitude subject to the king will be maintained by his care, provided he carefully attend to the appointment of new men to fill the place of those who drop out. In the second place, by his law and orders, punishments and rewards, he restrains the men subject to him from wickedness, and encourages them to works of virtue, following the example of God, Who gave His law to man and requites those who observe it with rewards, and those who transgress it with punishments. The king's third charge is to keep the multitude entrusted to him safe from the enemy. For it would be useless to prevent internal dangers if the multitude could not be defended against external dangers.

So, for the proper direction of the multitude, there remains the third duty of the kingly office, namely, that he be solicitous for its improvement. He performs this duty when, in each of the things we have mentioned, he corrects what is out of order, and supplies what is lacking, and, if any of them can be done better he tries to do it. This is why the Apostle [24] exhorts the faithful to be zealous for the better gifts. These then are the duties of the kingly office, each of which must now be treated in greater detail.

[24] I Cor. xii, 31.

BERNARD GUI

THE INQUISITION played an important role in the Middle Ages, but one so out of keeping with modern concepts of civil liberty and toleration that its purpose and nature have often been grossly misunderstood. While it is true that the Inquisition was turned to political or economic ends, as when King Philip the Fair used it to expropriate the Templars (1307–14), to sincere inquisitors such as Bernard Gui its object was primarily the salvation of wayward souls. The philosophical basis for an institution such as the Inquisition is stated clearly by St. Thomas Aquinas as follows:

". . . With regard to heretics, two considerations are to be kept in mind: (1) on their side, (2) on the side of the Church.

"(1) There is the sin, whereby they deserve not only to be separated from the Church by excommunication, but also to be shut off from the world by death. For it is a much more serious matter to corrupt faith, through which comes the soul's life, than to forge money, through which temporal life is supported. Hence if forgers of money or other malefactors are straightway justly put to death by secular princes, with much more justice can heretics, immediately upon convictions, be not only excommunicated but also put to death.

"(2) But on the side of the Church there is mercy, with a view to the conversion of them that are in error; and therefore the Church does not straightway condemn, but *after a first and second admonition,* as the Apostle teaches [Tit. iii, 10]. After that, if he be found still stubborn, the Church gives up hope of his conversion and takes thought for the safety of others, by separating him from the Church by sentence of excommunication; and, further, leaves him to the secular court, to be exterminated from the world by death. . . ."

Procedure against heresy was always one of the tasks that befell a bishop, but, being one task among many, was not well done when heresy was rife and heretics numerous. Thus it was handed over to the mendicant friars, the Franciscans and the Dominicans (except in England and Scandinavia, where it remained in the hands of the bishops), the latter being the more prominently associated with the Inquisition. Bernard Gui (c.1261–1331) was one of the Dominican monks who devoted himself to this work, mostly in southeastern France, and wrote for the guidance of his colleagues and successors a *Manual* (c.1321), itself partly based on earlier manuals and inquisitorial experiences. The following selections from this work, translated from the Latin text given by G. Mollat (ed., Bernard Gui, *Manuel de l'inquisiteur,* 2 vols., Paris, 1926–27), are intended to illustrate some of the objects, methods, and beliefs of the inquisitors, and to cast light on a particular heresy, the Waldensian, as one of those they fought.

MANUAL OF THE INQUISITOR

GENERAL INSTRUCTIONS

. . . IF A PERSON spoke openly and clearly against the faith, offering the arguments and authorities upon which heretics usually rely, it would be very easy
for the faithful learned of the Church to convict him of heresy, since he would
be deemed a heretic by the very fact that he tried to defend error. But since
present day heretics attempt and seek to conceal their errors rather than to avow
them openly, men trained in the learning of the Scriptures cannot convict
them, because they escape in verbal trickery and wily thinking. Learned men
are even apt to be confounded by them, and the heretics congratulate themselves and are all the stronger therefore, seeing that they can thus delude the
learned to the point of escaping artfully by the twists and turns of their crafty,
cheating and underhanded replies.

It is, indeed, all too difficult to bring heretics to reveal themselves when,
instead of frankly avowing their error they conceal it, or when there is not
sure and sufficient testimony against them. Under these circumstances difficulties rise on all sides for the investigator. On the one hand his conscience
will torment him if he punishes without having obtained a confession or
conviction of heresy; on the other hand, all that repeated experience has taught
him of the falseness, guile and malice of such people will cause him still greater
anguish. If they escape punishment owing to their fox-like craftiness it is to
the great harm of the faith, for they become even stronger, more numerous
and more wily than before. Moreover, lay persons devoted to the faith find it
scandalous that an inquisitorial case, once begun, should be abandoned more
or less for lack of method. Seeing that the learned are fooled by common, base
people, they are thereby weakened in their faith to a certain degree, for they
believe that we always have at our disposal convincing and clear arguments
against which no one can contend, without our immediately being able to
convince him, and in such a way that the laity themselves would clearly understand these arguments. Thus, under such circumstances it is inexpedient, in
the presence of laity, to discuss the faith with heretics who are so guileful.

Just as a single remedy is not suitable to all diseases, and medication varies
according to the particular case, so one cannot use for all the heretics of the
different sects the same method of questioning, investigation and examination,
but should employ a method particular and appropriate to each case or group.
Therefore the inquisitor, as a wise doctor of souls, will proceed with caution
in the investigation and questioning, according to the persons he is questioning

or in whose company he is conducting the investigation, taking into account their rank, condition, status, malady and with due regard for local conditions. . . .

OF THE SECT OF THE WALDENSES AND FIRST OF ITS ORIGINS AND BEGINNINGS

The sect or heresy of the Waldenses or the Poor of Lyon came into being about the year of the Lord 1170. The man responsible for its creation was an inhabitant of Lyon, Waldes or Waldo, whence the name of its devotees. He was wealthy, but, after giving up all his property, determined to practice poverty and evangelic perfection in the manner of the apostles. He had had the Gospels and several other books of the Bible translated into vulgar tongue for his use, as well as several maxims of Saints Augustine, Jerome, Ambrose and Gregory, grouped under titles, which he and his followers called sentences. They read them very often, although they hardly understood them; nevertheless, infatuated with themselves, although they had little learning, they usurped the role of the apostles and dared to preach the Gospel in the streets and public squares. The said Waldes or Waldo drew into this presumption numerous accomplices of both sexes whom he sent out preaching as disciples.

These people, although stupid and unlearned, traveled through the villages, men and women, and entered homes, and, preaching in the squares and even in the churches, the men especially, spread about them a mass of errors.

Summoned by the Archbishop of Lyon, the lord Jean aux Blanches-Mains, who forbade them such a presumption, they refused obedience, declaring, in order to excuse their madness, that one should obey God rather than man. God ordered the apostles to preach the Gospel to all beings, they said, applying to themselves that which had been said of the apostles, whose followers and successors they boldly declared themselves to be, by a false profession of poverty and by masquerading under an appearance of holiness. Indeed they despised the prelates and clergy because, they said, they owned great wealth and lived in pleasures.

Owing to this arrogant usurpation of the function of preaching, they became teachers of error. Summoned to renounce preaching, they disobeyed and were declared in contempt, and consequently excommunicated and banished from their town and country. Finally, as they persisted, a council held at Rome before the Lateran Council [reference is to fourth Lateran Council, 1215] declared them schismatic and condemned them as heretics. Thus multiplied upon the earth they scattered through the provinces, into neighboring regions and unto the borders of Lombardy. Separated and cut off from the Church, and joining, on the other hand, with other heretics and drinking in their errors, they blended with their own concoctions the errors and heresies of earlier heretics.

THE ERRORS OF THE PRESENT WALDENSES (THEY PREVIOUSLY HELD SEVERAL OTHERS)

Disdain for ecclesiastical authority was and still is the prime heresy of the Waldenses. Excommunciated for this reason and delivered over to Satan, they have fallen into innumerable errors, and have blended the errors of earlier heretics with their own concoctions.

The misled believers and sacrilegious masters of this sect hold and teach that they are in no way subject to the lord Pope or Roman Pontiff, or to the other prelates of the Roman Church, and that the latter persecute and condemn them unjustly and improperly. Moreover, they declare that they cannot be excommunicated by this Roman Pontiff and these prelates, and that obedience is owed to none of them when they order and summon the followers and masters of the said sect to abandon or abjure this sect, although this sect be condemned as heretical by the Roman Church. . . .

Moreover, the sect does not accept canonical authority, or the decretals or constitutions of the Sovereign Pontiffs, any more than the regulations concerning fasts and the observance of the feasts or the decrees of the Fathers. Straying from the straight road, they recognize no authority therein, scorn them, reject and condemn them.

Moreover, the followers of the sect are even more perniciously mistaken concerning the sacrament of penance and the power of the keys. They declare they have received—this is their doctrine and their teaching—from God and none other, like the apostles who held it of Christ, the power of hearing the confessions of men and women who desire to confess to them, of granting them absolution and of prescribing penance. Thus they hear confessions, grant absolution and prescribe penance, although they have not been ordained as priests or clerics by a bishop of the Roman Church and although they are just laymen. They in no way claim to hold this power from the Roman Church, on the contrary, they deny it; and in fact, they hold it neither from God nor from His Church, since they have been cast out from the Church by this very Church, outside which there is neither true penance nor salvation.

Moreover, this same sect hold up to ridicule the indulgences established and granted by the prelates of the Church, saying they are worthless.

Moreover, they are in error with respect to the sacrament of the Eucharist. They claim, not publicly but secretly, that in the sacrament of the altar the bread and wine do not become body and blood of Christ when the priest who celebrates or consecrates is a sinner; and by sinner they mean any man who does not belong to their sect. Moreover, they claim, on the contrary, that any upright man, even a layman, without having received priestly ordination from the hands of a Catholic bishop, may consecrate the body and blood of Christ, provided he be of their sect. They believe that women too can do this, subject to the same condition. Thus they hold that any holy man is a priest.

OF THE FALSE AND CRAFTY REPLIES IN WHICH THEY HIDE

It is very difficult to question and examine the Waldenses; to such an extent do they hide in duplicity and tricks of words, in order not to be discovered, that one cannot draw from them the truth about their errors. Thus it is necessary at this point to say a few words about their deceit and guile.

They act in the following manner. When one of them is arrested for investigation, he usually presents himself fearlessly, as if his conscience were tranquil and without remorse. Ask him if he knows the cause of his arrest, and he will answer softly and with a smile: "My lord, I would be happy to learn it from your lips." Asked about his faith and beliefs: "I believe all that a good Christian believes," he declares. Try to learn what he means by a good Christian: "He who believes what is taught by the Holy Church." What does he call the Holy Church: "My lord," he replies, "what you yourself say and believe to be the Holy Church." If you say, "I believe it is the Roman Church ruled by the Pope and the other prelates under his authority," he replies: "And I too believe it," meaning "I am convinced that that is indeed your belief."

SPECIAL QUESTIONS FOR MEMBERS OF THE SECT OF WALDENSES

The following questions are to be put to one who confesses belonging to the sect of the Waldenses: has he seen or heard one or more members of the sect, society or brotherhood which we call Waldenses or the Poor of Lyon (among their group they call themselves Brothers or the Poor of Christ)?

Also, where, when, with whom did he see them and who were they?

Also, has he heard their preachings, teachings, pronouncements or words?

Also, what has he learned of them and of their doctrine?

Also, what have they said to him on the subject of oaths? Is it always and in all cases a sin?

Also, what have they said to him with respect to the purgatory of souls after death or after this life?

Also, with respect to prayers for the dead?

Also with respect to the indulgences granted by the Pope and the prelates of the Roman Church, although the Waldenses do not speak indiscriminately and openly about the last three points in the presence of the simplest of their believers, but only before the best informed and most learned in their secrets. . . .

Also, had he already appeared before an inquisitor on a charge of Waldensianism? Had he been notified to appear, summoned or arrested? Had he confessed? Had he been absolved? Had a penance been imposed upon him? Had he in law abjured the heresy and Waldensianism and other similar things? . . .

SPECIAL FORM FOR ABJURING THE SECT AND HERESY OF THE WALDENSES

I, —, of — place, of — diocese, brought in judgment before you, —, inquisitor, in the presence of the most sacred Gospels of the Lord, do completely abjure all heresy contrary to the faith of Our Lord Jesus Christ and of the Holy Roman Church, and particularly the sect and heresy of those who are called Waldenses or the Poor of Lyon, with whom I had relations and of whom I was one, whose errors I believed in and whose propositions I believed to be true, and especially such or such an error (specify). I abjure their whole doctrine and renounce being among their supporters, those who harbor them, defenders and believers, under the penalty of the law for those who, having judicially abjured heresy, fall back therein.

Moreover, I swear and promise to prosecute heretics and especially the Waldenses and their believers, as far as I am able, and to seek out, denounce, have them arrested and brought before the inquisitors. . . .

INSTRUCTIONS CONCERNING THE PROCEDURE TO BE FOLLOWED WITH PERSONS WHO HAVE CONFESSED THE TRUTH IN COURT AND WITH THOSE WHO HAVE BEEN CHARGED AND ARE SUSPECT WHO REFUSE TO DO SO

If having stated in court the truth concerning the infractions committed by himself or by another person, having abjured all heresy and been reconciled with the unity of the Church, an accused shows repentance that seems sincere; and if, moreover, there is no fear that he may flee, be corrupted or relapse, and if there are no other objections, he shall be released with another person as bond for him until the time of the general sermon in the course of which penance for his crimes will be imposed on him, among others.

On the other hand, when a person who is suspected of, denounced or reported for or accused of the crime of heresy has been charged and refuses to confess, he shall be held in prison until the truth comes to light; the status and station of the person, as well as the nature of the suspicion and of the crime should, however, be taken into account. He may be released with another person as bond for him, especially when proof of his guilt is not conclusive, when the accusation was not direct but incidental and when suspicion was not clear-cut, until such time as a new charge shall be raised against him. Nevertheless, those who benefit from this leniency shall, instead of imprisonment, take a position before the door of the home of the inquisitor each day until the mid-day meal, and after this meal until the supper hour, and shall not depart there-from without permission of the inquisitor.

Stationing in this fashion, it should be noted, has sometimes proved more harmful than beneficial, especially when there were several such persons to-gether and they advised each other and, this has been observed and proved, were confirmed in their errors.

When an accused is strongly suspect and in all likelihood and probability guilty, and when the inquisitor is thoroughly convinced thereof; in such a case, when the person is obdurate in his testimony and persists in his denials, as I have observed time and time again, he should not be released for any rea-son whatever, but should be held for a number of years, in order that his trials may open his mind. Many have I seen who, thus subjected for a number of years to this regime of vexations and confinement, end by admitting not only recent but even long-standing and old crimes, going back thirty and forty years or more.

OF THE INQUISITORS' GENERAL SERMON

After receiving the statements and testimony of the accused concerning the accused themselves or other persons with respect to heresy, the harboring or protection of heretics or other matters within the jurisdiction of the office of the Inquisition, after recording and closing the dossiers of the defense of per-sons living or dead, after a detailed and conscientious study of all records in the case, confessions or evidence for the defense, the inquisitors will secure the opinion of prelates and jurists; they will then hold the sermon with fitting solemnity; it is on this occasion that they will grant clemency, impose penance or issue sentences, according to the merit or fault of each.

At a proper time before the sermon, the inquisitors will seek the opinion of the said counselors. A summary and short extract concerning the crimes will be made, indicating the essence of the confession of each accused with respect to the misdeed in question, with no names mentioned, and this through prudence, in order that the counselors be able more freely to judge the penance to be imposed, without regard to person. There would, it is true, be a better established opinion if the dossiers were made available in their entirety; this is to be done, moreover, when and where the discretion of the counselors can be relied upon and when there is no danger of a breach of secrecy. Such a method would also be less prejudicial. From the beginning, however, such has not been the custom of the Inquisition, because of the aforementioned danger; nevertheless, the complete confessions of the accused will be laid before the diocesan or his vicar, in the presence of a few experts, secretaries and jurors.

One or two days before the sermon, the inquisitor, with a notary and several other persons present, will read the above mentioned extract in vulgar tongue to each of the interested parties separately; the same extract will likewise be read during the public sermon, and the person concerned will be addressed in the following terms: "Thou, so-and-so, of such-and-such a place, as it appears from thy confession, hast done thus and so."

Moreover, on the eve of the sermon, the inquisitor, either himself or through another person as he judges best, will summon each and every one of the accused to appear at a specified place for the public sermon the next day. There they will receive penance or hear sentence, according to the nature of the case. The next day, early in the morning, the sermon will be held.

Here is the order to be followed in an inquisitor's general sermon in the Toulouse and Carcassonne regions:

First: a brief sermon will be delivered, in view of the large number of cases, after which the usual indulgence will be pronounced.

Second: the oath of the officers of the royal court, consuls and others present holding temporal jurisdiction will be received.

Third: those persons who have received this clemency will be dispensed from wearing crosses.

Fourth: those men and women for whom it is judged proper will be released from prison, and will be assigned to wear crosses and undertake pilgrimages.

Fifth: the misdeeds of those who are to receive penances or be sentenced will be listed and read in the following order: first those who are to receive arbitrary penalties such as pilgrimages, wearing of crosses and the observation of general rules of conduct; then those who are simply to be imprisoned; then those who are to be subjected to a penalty and be imprisoned as false witnesses; next, priests or clergy who are to be unfrocked and imprisoned; next come those deceased who should have been imprisoned in life, which should be stated; then heretics who died impenitent and whose bodies are to be exhumed; then fugitives thereby to be condemned as heretics and those who have relapsed into heresy following legal abjuration, who are to be handed over to the secular arm, laymen first and then clergy, if there are any; advanced heretics who refuse to abandon heresy and return to the unity of the Church, whether they be Manicheans [Albigenses] or Waldenses, whether they belong to the sect and heresy of those who, calling themselves Beguines or the Poor of Christ, withdraw from the community of the faithful and weaken the power of the Pope and the Church. Finally come those who, after legally confessing their heresy, have subsequently retracted these confessions or those who, having been convicted of heresy on the basis of crushing testimony, refuse to confess the truth and who, moreover, fail to defend themselves at law and purge themselves of their crime, all classes of accused who, as unrepentant heretics, are to be handed over to the secular court.

Sixth: after the listing of misdeeds, and before the imposition of penances on repentant persons, these shall abjure heresy and swear to obey the orders of the Church and of the inquisitors; they will then be relieved of the sentences of excommunication they have incurred, as is known, for their crimes in heresy, and which are generally promulgated by virtue of the law.

Seventh: sentences will first be proclaimed in Latin, and then summarized in vulgar tongue. The same order will be followed as in listing the misdeeds, if this can be conveniently done. Indeed, at times the number of persons who are to receive penances, penalties and sentences makes it hardly possible to follow this order, and one may be compelled to follow another. The judge will decide this at his discretion and will do what seems to him most fitting and expedient. . . .

THE MANNER OF ACTING TOWARD HERETICS WHO REPENT AT THE MOMENT OF EXECUTION

Should it happen, as it already has on several occasions, that a condemned person abandoned and handed over to the secular arm, taken by said court and brought to the place of execution, should bespeak and affirm a desire to repent and renounce the said errors, he should be spared and returned to the inquisitors. And they should receive him, unless he had perhaps already relapsed into heresy, for here equity is to be preferred to severity, and that shock to the weak should be avoided that comes when the Church refuses the sacrament of penance to him who requests it. The office of the Inquisition formerly acted in this fashion at times.

In such a case, the inquisitors should take all necessary precautions, for those who are converted in such an extremity are rightfully suspect of acting in fear of punishment, and the inquisitors should carefully consider whether the conversion is genuine or feigned. Let them test the convert to see if he walks in the shadows or in the light, lest he be a wolf beneath a lamb's appearance.

And this may be brought out in several ways and according to several signs: if, for example, he promptly and spontaneously reveals and denounces all his accomplices to the inquisitors; if he attacks his sect in gesture, words and deeds; if he admits his former errors humbly and one by one; if he detests and abjures them; and all of these things can be known with certainty through the questioning he will undergo and the confession he will sign.

When he has thus been readmitted to trial and has therein confessed, he should then retract and detest, with his own lips, all his old errors, publicly and legally abjure these same errors in particular and all heresy in general, confess the Catholic faith, and promise and swear all other things usually required of those who abjure. And then will he be subjected to life imprisonment, there to do penance, the right to commute the penalty being reserved, as is the custom.

As has already been said, this clemency and admission to penance after pronouncement of sentence is not, in truth in common law; but the office of the Inquisition, holding very broad powers, has introduced this procedure in many cases of this kind. And since what it has in view and seeks above all is the salvation of souls and purity of the faith, it admits to penance, the first time, heretics who wish to be converted and return to the unity of the Church. Moreover, the confessions of these converts frequently lead to the discovery of accomplices and of errors: the truth is brought to light, falsehood is uncloaked, and the office benefits thereby.

Once a conversion of this type appears to the inquisitors probably to be feigned and simulated, everything is brought to a halt and the sentence is carried out.

CHURCH AND STATE

THE BATTLE for supremacy between popes and temporal monarchs was perhaps inevitable in an age in which the popes not only were interested in religious matters but had a large number of ecclesiastic vassals and also held temporal power in Italy and, through the ecclesiastical hierarchy, the other lands of central and western Europe.

The initial relations between the Roman state and the Christian church were hostile. Despite persecution, however, Christianity spread with such rapidity throughout the Mediterranean world that in 313 it was granted toleration by the Edict of Milan through the cordial influence of the Emperor Constantine I (reigned 307–37), who was himself baptized on his deathbed. By the end of the century, Christianity had become the one legal religion of the empire. In the Eastern or Byzantine half of the Roman heritage, with its capital at Constantinople, the church early came to be closely supervised by the state, a relationship generally termed caesaropapism. In the West, on the other hand, the Catholic Church, led by the bishops of Rome, or popes, successfully asserted its claims to greater autonomy from state control, particularly after emperors ceased to be resident in Rome. Developing the theory of the two powers, or two swords, the Church insisted that while the sword of temporal authority was admittedly held by the state, it must nevertheless be wielded in the interest and at the direction of the Church, for the spiritual sword was declared the superior one. Pope Gelasius I (reigned 492–96) first developed the classic formulation of this theory in a letter to the Byzantine Emperor Anastasius (reigned 491–518).

The extreme secular position in the battle for supremacy between popes and temporal monarchs in the late Middle Ages maintained the right of the emperor to have a voice in the election of popes and to appoint bishops and other ecclesiastical lords through the ceremony of investiture. The extreme clerical position maintained the right of the pope to name emperors and other lay rulers.

The dramatic struggle over investiture produced the celebrated pilgrimage to Canossa of the Holy Roman Emperor Henry IV to seek absolution from the great reforming Pope Gregory VII, who after serving as chief guide, advisor, and administrator for twenty-four years to five different popes, had himself been elected pontiff in 1073. Gregory's insistence on maintaining the prerogative of the Church against secular rulers had brought him into conflict with Henry, who had seized Church lands and invested his own bishops. Called upon to answer for his conduct in 1075, Henry retorted by summoning a council of his supporters at Worms (Germany) in 1076 which declared the pope deposed. Gregory VII responded by excommunicating Henry and absolving the imperial subjects from their oaths of allegiance. The resulting sedition and revolts in Germany obliged the emperor to humble himself to the pope at Canossa in northern Italy (1077) in order to be readmitted into the Church. In 1080 the dispute was resumed. Gregory made his position in the controversy clearest in a letter at the time to Hermann, bishop of Metz. Henry IV, again excommunicated, appointed an antipope and in 1083 captured Rome. Gregory VII died two years later in exile at Salerno after a lifetime in which, more than any other person, he established the character and power of the late medieval papacy.

The investiture controversy itself was settled by the Concordat of Worms (1122), substantially a victory for the papacy. It provided for ecclesiastical investiture of bishops in their religious authority and secular investiture of bishops in their temporal authority as feudal vassals. But the battle for control continued and gradually became a contest for world supremacy in the political field. Frederick Barbarossa (= red beard; 1123?–1190), Holy Roman Emperor and German king (1152–90), viewed himself as the heir and restorer of the classic Roman empire and tradition. He regarded as part of his political mission the suppression of feudal unrest in Germany and of the self-ruling cities of Italy. Frederick's interventions in the latter country strained his relations with the papacy to such an extent that Pope Adrian IV sent him a letter implying that the empire was held by Frederick as a fief from the papacy (1156). Frederick, supported by the German bishops, replied by claiming the imperial title "through the election of the princes from God alone." There followed nearly twenty years of intermittent and unsuccessful war in Italy. Upon the restoration of peace in Italy, Frederick returned to Germany where he confiscated the fiefs and brought about the downfall of his most powerful feudal vassal. In May, 1189, Frederick set out on the Third Crusade, in the course of which he was drowned while crossing a river in Cilicia (Turkey).

The papacy seemed to have triumphed fully under Innocent III (1198–1216); his voice was heard in royal councils, and to him King John gave England, holding his kingdom in return as the pope's vassal. But the underlying trend toward secularization continued. It was dramatized by the struggle between Pope Boniface VIII (1294–1303) and King Philip the Fair of France (1285–1314). The king brought a bishop to trial before a lay court, and the pope, after several skirmishes, issued the bull *Unam Sanctam* (1302). Philip replied by having the pope seized at Anagni; Boniface was soon released, but died soon thereafter. With his successor, Clement V, began the papal residence at Avignon, under the domination of the French kings, that lasted till 1377.

In the next part of the campaign against the pope, Emperor Louis IV (1314–47), gave sanctuary to Marsilius of Padua (c.1275–c.1342), who, with John of Jandun, had written a notable work, *Defensor Pacis* (*The Defender of the Peace*). Marsilius was an Italian theologian, physician, and political theorist. He studied at the universities of Padua and Paris, becoming rector of the latter c.1312. As a propagandist in the service of the Emperor Louis against Pope John XXII, Marsilius developed the most radically secularist political theory of the Middle Ages. *Defensor Pacis,* published in 1326, argues that all political power, lay as well as ecclesiastical, is derived from the people and that the church is therefore properly subordinate to the state, which expresses the people's will. The book's author was excommunicated by the pope within a year of its publication, and Marsilius was obliged to spend his later life in Germany under the protection of the emperor. Unlike Barbarossa, Marsilius considered neither the Empire nor Germany central to his political thought. It is based, instead, primarily on the governmental theory and practice of the Italian city-states, whose political tradition stimulated in Marsilius, as it was to inspire two centuries later in Machiavelli, a profound bitterness toward the papacy as the alleged corruptor of Italy and the cause of the country's disunion.

Licet Juris (1338), the enactment of the electors of the Holy Roman Empire, is another statement of the secular position in the last great struggle for supremacy between pope and German emperor. When Pope Benedict XII (1334–42) summoned Emperor Louis IV to renounce his rights and title, the German electors replied with *Licet Juris*.

The texts of *Unam Sanctam* and *Licet Juris*, originally in Latin, are taken from E. F. Henderson, *Select Historical Documents of the Middle Ages* (London, George Bell and Sons, 1896). The extract from *The Deeds of Frederick Barbarossa* by Otto, bishop of Freising, and his secretary, Rahewin, is from the translation by Charles C. Mierow (New York, Columbia University Press, "Records of Civilization" Series, 1953). The selection from Marsilius is from the translation by Alan Gewirth in Volume II of *Marsilius of Padua: the Defender of Peace* (New York, Columbia University Press, "Records of Civilization" Series, 1956). The text of the letter of Gregory VII to Hermann of Metz can be found in Henry J. Bettenson, ed., *Documents of the Christian Church* (New York, Oxford University Press, 1947).

GREGORY VII ON INVESTITURE

BISHOP GREGORY, servant of the servants of God, to his beloved brother in Christ, Hermann bishop of Metz, greeting and apostolic benediction. It is doubtless owing to a dispensation of God that, as we learn, thou art ready to endure trials and dangers in defense of the truth. For such is His ineffable grace and wonderful mercy that He never allows His chosen ones completely to go astray—never permits them utterly to fall or to be cast down. For after they have been afflicted by a period of persecution—a useful term of probation as it were,—He makes them, even if they have been for a time faint-hearted, stronger than before. Since, moreover, manly courage impels one strong man to act more bravely than another and to press forward more boldly—even as among cowards fear induces one to flee more disgracefully than another—we wish, beloved, with the voice of exhortation, to impress this upon thee: thou shouldst the more delight to stand in the army of the Christian faith among the first, the more thou art convinced that the conquerors are the most worthy and the nearest to God. Thy request, indeed, to be aided, as it were, by our writings and fortified against the madness of those who babble forth with impious tongue that the authority of the holy and apostolic see had no authority to excommunicate Henry—a man who despises the Christian law; a destroyer of the churches and of the empire; a patron and companion of heretics—or to absolve anyone from the oath of fealty to him, seems to us to be hardly necessary when so many and such absolutely decisive warrants are to be found in the pages of Holy Scripture. Nor do we believe, indeed, that those who (heaping up for themselves damnation) impudently detract from the truth and contradict it have added these assertions to the audacity of their defense so much from ignorance as from a certain madness.

For, to cite a few passages from among many, who does not know the words of our Lord and Saviour Jesus Christ who says, in the gospel: "Thou art Peter and upon this rock will I build my church, and the gates of hell shall not prevail against it; and I will give unto thee the keys of the kingdom of Heaven; and whatsoever thou shalt bind upon earth shall be bound also in Heaven, and whatsover thou shalt loose upon earth shall be loosed also in Heaven"? Are kings excepted here? Or are they not included among the sheep which the Son of God committed to St. Peter? Who, I ask, in view of this universal concession of the power of binding and loosing, can think that he is withdrawn from the authority of St. Peter, unless, perhaps, that unhappy man who is unwilling to bear the yoke of the Lord and subjects himself to the burden of the devil, refusing to be among the number of Christ's sheep? It will help him little to his wretched liberty that he shake from his proud neck the divinely granted power of Peter. For the more anyone, through pride, refuses to bear it, the more heavily shall it press up on him unto damnation at the judgment.

The holy Fathers, as well in general councils as in their writings and doings, have called the Holy Roman Church the universal mother, accepting and serving with great veneration this institution founded by the divine will, this pledge of a dispensation to the church, this privilege entrusted in the beginning and confirmed to St. Peter the chief of the apostles. And even as they accepted its statements in confirmation of their faith and of the doctrines of holy religion, so also they received its judgments—consenting in this, and agreeing as it were with one spirit and one voice: that all greater matters and exceptional cases, and judgments over all churches, ought to be referred to it as to a mother and a head; that from it there was no appeal; that no one should or could retract or reverse its decisions. . . .

. . . Shall not an authority founded by laymen—even by those who do not know God,—be subject to that authority which the providence of God Almighty has for His own honor established and in His mercy given to the world? For His Son, even as He is undoubtedly believed to be God and man, so is He considered the highest priest, the head of all priests, sitting on the right hand of the Father and always interceding for us. Yet He despised a secular kingdom which makes the sons of this world swell with pride, and came of His own will to the priesthood of the cross. Who does not know that kings and leaders are sprung from men who were ignorant of God, who by pride, robbery, perfidy, murders—in a word, by almost every crime at the prompting of the devil, who is the prince of this world—have striven with blind cupidity and intolerable presumption to dominate over their equals, that is, over mankind? To whom, indeed, can we better compare them, when they seek to make the priests of God bend to their feet, than to him who is head over all the sons of pride and who, tempting the Highest Pontiff Himself, the Head of priests, the Son of the Most High, and promising to Him all the kingdoms of the world said: "All these I will give unto Thee if Thou wilt fall down and worship me"? Who can doubt but that the priests of Christ are to be considered the fathers and masters of kings and princes and of all the faithful? Is it not clearly pitiful madness for a son to attempt to subject to himself his father, a pupil his master; and for one to bring into his power and bind with iniquitous bonds him by whom he believes that he himself can be bound and loosed not only on earth but also in Heaven? This the Emperor Constantine the Great, lord of all the kings and princes of nearly the whole world, plainly understood—as the blessed Gregory reminds us in a letter to the Emperor Maurice, when, sitting last after all the bishops in the holy council of Nicaea, he presumed to give no sentence of judgment over them, but addressed them as gods and decreed that they should not be subject to his judgment but that he should be dependent upon their will . . . .

Many pontiffs have excommunicated kings or emperors. For, if particular examples of such princes is needed, the blessed pope Innocent excommunicated the emperor Arcadius for consenting that St. John Chrysostom should be expelled from his see. Likewise another Roman pontiff, Zacchary, deposed a king of the Franks, not so much for his iniquities as because he was not fitted to exercise so great power. And in his stead he set up Pepin, father of the emperor Charles the Great, in his place—releasing all the Franks from the oath of fealty which they had sworn him. As, indeed, the holy Church frequently does by its authority when it absolves servitors from the fetters of an oath sworn to such bishops as, by apostolic sentence, are deposed from their pontifical rank. And the blessed Ambrose—who, although a saint, was still not bishop over the whole Church—excommunicated and excluded from the Church the Emperor Theodosius the Great for a fault which, by other priests, was not regarded as very grave. He shows, too, in his writings, that gold does not so much excel lead in value as the priestly dignity transcends the royal power; speaking thus towards the beginning of his pastoral letter: "The honor and sublimity of bishops, brethren, is beyond all comparisons. If one should compare them to resplendent kings and diademed princes it would be far less worthy than if one compared the base metal lead to gleaming gold. For indeed one can see how the necks of kings and princes are bowed before the knees of priests; and how, having kissed their right hands, they believe themselves strengthened by their prayers." And a little later, "Ye should know, brethren, that we have mentioned all this to show that nothing can be found in this world more lofty than priests or more sublime than bishops."

Furthermore every Christian king, when he comes to die, seeks as a pitiful suppliant the aid of a priest, that he may escape hell's prison, may pass from the darkness into the light, and at the judgment of God may appear absolved from the bondage of his sins. Who, in his last hour (what layman, not to speak of priests), has ever implored the aid of an earthly king for the salvation of his soul? And what king or emperor is able, by reason of the office he holds, to rescue a Christian from the power of the devil through holy baptism, to number him among the sons of God, and to fortify him with the divine unction? Who of them can by his own words make the body and blood of our Lord,—the greatest act in the Christian religion? Or who of them possesses the power of binding and loosing in heaven and on earth? From all of these considerations it is clear how greatly the priestly office excels in power.

Who of them can ordain a single clerk in the Holy Church, much less depose him for any fault? For in the orders of the Church a greater power is needed to depose than to ordain. Bishops may ordain other bishops, but can by no means depose them without the authority of the apostolic see. Who, therefore, of even moderate understanding, can hesitate to give priests the precedence over kings? Then, if kings are to be judged by priests for their sins, by whom can they be judged with better right than by the Roman pontiff?

In short, any good Christians may far more properly be considered kings than may bad princes. For the former, seeking the glory of God, strictly govern themselves, whereas the latter, seeking the things which are their own and not the things of God, are enemies to themselves and tyrannical oppressors of others. Faithful Christians are the body of the true king, Christ; evil rulers, that of the devil. The former rule themselves in the hope that they will eternally reign with the Supreme Emperor, but the sway of the latter ends in their destruction and eternal damnation with the prince of darkness, who is king over all the sons of pride.

It is certainly not strange that wicked bishops are of one mind with a bad king, whom they love and fear for the honors which they have wrongfully obtained from him. Such men simoniacally ordain whom they please and sell God even for a paltry sum. As even the elect are indissolubly united with their Head, so also the wicked are inescapably leagued with him who is the head of evil, their chief purpose being to resist the good. But surely we ought not so much to denounce them as to mourn for them with tears and lamentations, beseeching God Almighty to snatch them from the snares of Satan in which they are held captive, and after their peril to bring them at last to a knowledge of the truth.

We refer to those kings and emperors who, too much puffed up by worldly glory, rule not for God but for themselves. Now, since it belongs to our office to admonish and encourage everyone according to the rank or dignity which he enjoys, we endeavor, by God's grace, to arm emperors and kings and other princes with the weapon of humility, that they may be able to allay the waves of the sea and the floods of pride. For we know that earthly glory and the cares of this world usually tempt men to pride, especially those in authority; so that they neglect humility and seek their own glory, desiring to lord it over their brethren. Therefore it is of especial advantage for emperors and kings, when their minds tend to be puffed up and to delight in their own glory, to discover a way of humbling themselves, and to realize that what causes their complacency is the thing which should be feared above all else. Let them, therefore, diligently consider how perilous and how much to be feared is the royal or imperial dignity. For very few are saved of those who enjoy it; and those who, through the mercy of God, do come to salvation are not so glorified in the Holy Church by the judgment of the Holy Spirit as are many poor people. For, from the beginning of the world until our own times, in the whole of authentic history we do not find seven emperors or kings whose lives were as distinguished for religion and so adorned by miracles of power as those of an innumerable multitude who despised the world—although we believe many of them to have found mercy in the presence of God Almighty. For what emperor or king was ever so distinguished by miracles as were St. Martin, St. Antony, and St. Benedict—not to mention the apostles and martyrs? And what emperor or king raised the dead, cleansed lepers, or healed the blind? See how the Holy Church praises and venerates the Emperor Constantine of blessed memory, Theodosius and Honorius, Charles and Louis as lovers of justice, promoters of the Christian religion, defenders of the churches: it does not, however, declare them to have been resplendent with such glorious miracles. Moreover, to how many kings or emperors has the Holy Church ordered chapels or altars to be dedicated, or masses to be celebrated in their honor? Let kings and other princes fear lest the more they rejoice at being placed over other men in this life, the more they will be subjected to eternal fires. For of them it is written: "The powerful shall powerfully suffer torments." And they are about to render account to God for as many men as they have had subjects under their dominion. But if it be no little task for any private religious man to guard his own soul: how much labor will there be for those who are rulers over many thousands of souls? Moreover, if the judgment of the Holy Church severely punishes a sinner for the slaying of one man, what will become of those who, for the sake of worldly glory, hand over many thousands to death? And such persons, although after having slain many they often say with their lips "I have sinned," nevertheless rejoice in their hearts at the extension of their (so-called) fame. They do not regret what they have done. Nor are they grieved at having sent their brethren down to Tartarus. As long as they do not repent with their whole heart, nor agree to give up what they have acquired or kept through bloodshed, their repentance remains without the true fruit of penitence before God.

Therefore they should greatly fear and often call to mind what we have said above, that out of the innumerable host of kings in all countries from the beginning of the world, very few are found to have been holy; whereas in one single see—the Roman—of the successive bishops from the time of blessed Peter the Apostle, nearly one hundred are counted amongst the most holy. And why is this, unless because kings and princes, enticed by vain glory, prefer, as has been said, their own things to things spiritual, whereas the bishops of the Church, despising vain glory prefer God's will to earthly things? The former are quick to punish offenses against themselves, but lightly tolerate those who sin against God. The latter readily pardon those who sin against themselves, but do not readily forgive offenders against God. The former, too bent on earthly achievements, think little of spiritual ones; the latter, earnestly meditating on heavenly things, despise the things of earth.

Therefore let those whom Holy Church, of its own will and after proper counsel, not for transitory glory but for the salvation of many, calls to have rule or dominion, humbly obey. And let them always beware in that point as to which St. Gregory in that same pastoral book bears witness: "Indeed, when a man disdains to be like to men, he is made like to an apostate angel." Thus Saul, after having possessed the merit of humility, came to be swollen with pride when at the summit of power. Through humility, indeed, he was advanced; through pride, rejected—God being witness who said: "When thou wast small in thine own eyes, did I not make thee head over the tribes of Israel?" And a little further on: "Moreover, strange to say, when he was small in his own eyes he was great in the eyes of God; but when he seemed great in his own eyes he was small in the eyes of God." Let them also carefully retain what God says in the gospel: "I seek not my own glory"; and, "He who will be the first among you shall be the servant of all." Let them always prefer the honor of God to their own; let them cherish and guard justice by observing the rights of every man; let them not walk in the counsel of the ungodly but, with an assenting heart, always consort with good men. Let them not seek to subject to themselves or to subjugate the Holy Church as a handmaid; but above all let them strive, by recognizing the teachers and fathers, to render due honor to the eyes of the Church—the priests of God. For if we are ordered to honor our fathers and mothers after the flesh—how much more our spiritual ones! And if he who has cursed his father or mother after the flesh is to be punished with death—what does he merit who curses his spiritual father or mother? Let them not, led astray by worldly love, strive to place one of their own sons over the flock for which Christ poured forth His blood, if they can find someone who is better and more useful than he: lest, loving their son more than God, they inflict the greatest damage on the Holy Church. For he who neglects to provide to the best of his ability for such a want—and, one might say, necessity—of Holy Mother Church is openly convicted of not loving God and his neighbor as a Christian should.

For if this virtue, love, has been neglected, no matter what good anyone does he shall be without any fruit of salvation. And so by humbly doing these things, and by observing the love of God and of their neighbor as they ought, they may hope for the mercy of Him who said: "Learn of Me, for I am meek and lowly of heart." If they have humbly imitated Him they shall pass from this servile and transitory kingdom to a true kingdom of liberty and eternity.

THE DEEDS OF FREDERICK BARBAROSSA

In the middle of the month of October [1157] the emperor set out for Burgundy to hold a diet at Besançon. Now Besançon is the metropolis of one of the three parts into which the renowned Charles the Great divided his empire for distribution among his three sons, all enjoying the royal title. It is situated on the river Doubs. In this city practically all the chief men of that land had assembled, and also many ambassadors from foreign lands, namely, Romans, Apulians, Tuscans, Venetians, Franks, English, and Spaniards, awaited the emperor's arrival. He was received with the most festive display and solemn acclaim. For the whole world recognized him as the most powerful and most merciful ruler, and undertook, with mingled love and fear, to honor him with new tokens of respect, to extol him with new praises.

But before our pen addresses itself to an account of the affairs of this province and its management, we must speak of the ambassadors of the Roman pontiff, Hadrian—why they came and how they departed—because the authority of this delegation was very great and their errand very serious. No one will complain at the prolixity of this account who considers carefully the importance of the matter and the length of time that this tempest has raged and still rages. The personnel of the embassy consisted of Roland, cardinal priest of the title of St. Mark and chancellor of the Holy Roman Church, and Bernard, cardinal priest of the title of St. Clement, both distinguished for their wealth, their maturity of view, and their influence, and surpassing in prestige almost all others in the Roman Church.

Now the cause of their coming seemed to have an air of sincerity; but it was afterward clearly discerned that unrest and an occasion for mischief lay beneath the surface. One day, upon the prince's retiring from the uproar and tumult of the people, the aforesaid messengers were conducted into his presence in the more secluded retreat of a certain oratory and—as was fitting—were received with honor and kindness, claiming (as they did) to be the bearers of good tidings.

But the beginning of their speech appeared notable at the very outset. It is said to have been as follows: "Our most blessed father, Pope Hadrian, salutes you, and the College of Cardinals of the Holy Roman Church, he as father, they as brethren." After a brief interval they produced the letter that they bore. Copies of this and other letters which passed back and forth in this time of confusion, I have taken pains to insert in this work that any reader who may wish to judge, attracted and summoned not by my words or assertions but by the actual writings of the parties themselves, may choose freely the side to which he desires to lend his favor. Now the content of the letter was as follows:

ix. "Bishop Hadrian, the servant of the servants of God, to his beloved son Frederick, the illustrious emperor of the Romans, greeting and apostolic benediction.

"We recollect having written, a few days since, to the Imperial Majesty, of that dreadful and accursed deed, an offense calling for atonement, committed in our time, and hitherto, we believe, never attempted in the German lands. In recalling it to Your Excellency, we cannot conceal our great amazement that even now you have permitted so pernicious a deed to go unpunished with the severity it deserves. For how our venerable brother E[skil], archbishop of Lund, while returning from the apostolic see, was taken captive in those parts by certain godless and infamous men—a thing we cannot mention without great and heartfelt sorrow—and is still held in confinement; how in taking him captive, as previously mentioned, those men of impiety, a seed of evildoers, children that are corrupters, drew their swords and violently assaulted him and his companions, and how basely and shamefully they treated them, stripping them of all they had, Your Most Serene Highness knows, and the report of so great a crime has already spread abroad to the most distant and remote regions. To avenge this deed of exceptional violence, you, as a man to whom we believe good deeds are pleasing but evil works displeasing, ought with great determination to arise and bring down heavily upon the necks of the wicked the sword which was entrusted by divine providence to you 'for the punishment of evildoers and for the praise of them that do well,' and should most severely punish the presumptuous. But you are reported so to have ignored and indeed been indifferent to this deed, that there is no reason why those men should be repentant at having incurred guilt, because they have long since perceived that they have secured immunity for the sacrilege which they have committed.

"Of the reason for this indifference and negligence we are absolutely ignorant, because no scruple of conscience accuses our heart of having in aught offended the glory of Your Serenity. Rather have we always loved, with sincere affection, and treated with an attitude of due kindness, your person as that of our most dear and specially beloved son and most Christian prince, who, we doubt not, is by the grace of God grounded on the rock of the apostolic confession.

"For you should recall, O most glorious son, before the eyes of your mind, how willingly and how gladly your mother, the Holy Roman Church, received you in another year, with what affection of heart she treated you, what great dignity and honor she bestowed upon you, and with how much pleasure she conferred the emblem of the imperial crown, zealous to cherish in her most kindly bosom the height of Your Sublimity, and doing nothing at all that she knew was in the least a variance with the royal will.

"Nor do we regret that we fulfilled in all respects the ardent desires of your heart; but if Your Excellency had received still greater benefits at our hand (had that been possible), in consideration of the great increase and advantage that might through you accrue to the Church of God and to us, we would have rejoiced, not without reason.

"But now, because you seem to ignore and hide so heinous a crime, which is indeed known to have been committed as an affront to the Church universal and to your empire, we both suspect and fear that perhaps your thoughts were directed toward this indifference and neglect on this account: that at the suggestion of an evil man, sowing tares, you have conceived against your most gracious mother the Holy Roman Church and against ourselves—God forbid!—some displeasure or grievance.

"On this account, therefore, and because of all the other matters of business which we know to impend, we have thought best to dispatch at this time from our side to Your Serenity two of the best and dearest of those whom we have about us, namely, our beloved sons, Bernard, cardinal priest of St. Clement's, and Roland, cardinal priest of St. Mark's and our chancellor, men very notable for piety and wisdom and honor. We very earnestly beseech Your Excellency that you receive them with as much respect as kindness, treat them with all honor, and that whatever they themselves set forth before Your Imperial Dignity on our behalf concerning this and concerning other matters to the honor of God and of the Holy Roman Church, and pertaining also to the glory and exaltation of the empire, you accept without any hesitation as though proceeding from our mouth. Give credence to their words, as if we were uttering them." [September 20, 1157.]

x. When this letter had been read and carefully set forth by Chancellor Rainald in a faithful interpretation, the princes who were present were moved to great indignation, because the entire content of the letter appeared to have no little sharpness and to offer even at the very outset an occasion for future trouble. But what had particularly aroused them all was the fact that in the aforesaid letter it had been stated, among other things, that the fullness of dignity and honor had been bestowed upon the emperor by the Roman pontiff, that the emperor had received from his hand the imperial crown, and that he would not have regretted conferring even greater benefits (*beneficia*) upon him, in consideration of the great gain and advantage that might through him accrue to the Roman Church. And the hearers were led to accept the literal meaning of these words and to put credence in the aforesaid explanation because they knew that the assertion was rashly made by some Romans that hitherto our kings had possessed the imperial power over the City, and the kingdom of Italy, by gift of the popes, and that they made such representations and handed them down to posterity not only orally but also in writing and in pictures. Hence it is written concerning Emperor Lothar, over a picture of this sort in the Lateran palace:

> Coming before our gates, the king vows to safeguard the City,
> Then, liegeman to the Pope, by him he is granted the crown.

Since such a picture and such an inscription, reported to him by those faithful to the empire, had greatly displeased the prince when he had been near the City in a previous year [1155], he is said to have received from Pope Hadrian, after a friendly remonstrance, the assurance that both the inscription and the picture would be removed, lest so trifling a matter might afford the greatest men in the world an occasion for dispute and discord.

When all these matters were fully considered, and a great tumult and uproar arose from the princes of the realm at so insolent a message, it is said that one of the ambassadors, as though adding sword to flame, inquired: "From whom then does he have the empire, if not from our lord the pope?" Because of this remark, anger reached such a pitch that one of them, namely, Otto, count palatine of Bavaria (it was said), threatened the ambassador with his sword. But Frederick, using his authority to quell the tumult, commanded that the ambassadors, being granted safe-conduct, be led to their quarters and that early in the morning they should set forth on their way; he ordered also that they were not to pause in the territories of the bishops and abbots, but to return to the City by the direct road, turning neither to the right nor to the left. And so they returned without having accomplished their purpose, and what had been done by the emperor was published throughout the realm in the following letter [October, 1157]:

xi. "Whereas the Divine Sovereignty, from which is derived all power in heaven and on earth, has entrusted unto us, His anointed, the kingdom and the empire to rule over, and has ordained that the peace of the churches is to be maintained by the imperial arms, not without the greatest distress of heart are we compelled to complain to Your Benevolence that from the head of the Holy Church, on which Christ has set the imprint of his peace and love, there seem to be emanating causes of dissensions and evils, like a poison, by which, unless God avert it, we fear the body of the Church will be stained, its unity shattered, and a schism created between the temporal and spiritual realms.

"For when we were recently at the diet in Besançon and were dealing with the honor of the empire and the security of the Church with all due solicitude, apostolic legates arrived asserting that they bore to Our Majesty such tidings that the honor of the empire should receive no small increase.

After we had honorably received them on the first day of their arrival, and on the second, as is customary, had seated ourself with our princes to hear their tidings, they, as though inspired by the Mammon of unrighteousness, by lofty pride, by arrogant disdain, by execrable haughtiness, presented a message in the form of a letter from the pope, the content of which was to the effect that we ought always to remember the fact that the lord pope had bestowed upon us the imperial crown and would not even regret it if Our Excellency had received greater benefits (*beneficia*) from him.

"This was the message of fatherly kindness, which was to foster the unity of Church and empire, which was to bind them together in the bonds of peace, which was to bring the hearts of its hearers to harmony with both and obedience to both! Certain it is that at that impious message, devoid of all truth, not only did Our Imperial Majesty conceive a righteous indignation, but all the princes who were present were filled with so great fury and wrath that they would undoubtedly have condemned those two wicked priests to death, had not our presence averted this.

"Moreover, because many copies of this letter were found in their possession, and blank parchments with seals affixed that were still to be written on at their discretion, whereby—as has been their practice hitherto—they were endeavoring to scatter the venom of their iniquity throughout the churches of the Teutonic realm, to denude the altars, to carry off the vessels of the house of God, to strip crosses of their coverings, we obliged them to return to the City by the way they had come, lest an opportunity be afforded them of proceeding further.

"And since, through election by the princes, the kingdom and the empire are ours from God alone, Who at the time of the passion of His Son Christ subjected the world to dominion by the two swords, and since the apostle Peter taught the world this doctrine: 'Fear God, honor the king,' whosoever says that we received the imperial crown as a benefice (*pro beneficio*) from the lord pope contradicts the divine ordinance and the doctrine of Peter and is guilty of a lie. But because we have hitherto striven to snatch from the hand of the Egyptians the honor and freedom of the churches, so long oppressed by the yoke of undeserved slavery, and are intent on preserving to them all their rights and dignities, we ask Your University to grieve at so great an insult to us and to the empire, hoping that your unwavering loyalty will not permit the honor of the empire, which has stood, glorious and undiminished, from the founding of the City and the establishment of the Christian religion even down to your days, to be disparaged by so unheard-of a novelty, such presumptuous arrogance, knowing that—all ambiguity aside—we would prefer to encounter the risk of death rather than to endure in our time the reproach of so great a disorder."

xvi (xv). Meanwhile, the legates of the apostolic see, Roland and Bernard, had returned [to Rome] and set forth the great insults they had sustained, the great danger they had undergone, adding even more serious charges to what was serious enough, in order to provoke the bishop of the Roman city to seek vengeance for the things they said they had endured. In this matter the Roman clergy were divided among themselves, so that a number of them favored the party of the emperor and blamed the thoughtlessness or inexperience of those who had been sent; however, a certain group upheld the wishes of their pontiff. Now, being about to speak of this commotion, we desire (as we said above) that the reader shall not depend on our words, but that, as we place on record the letters sent back and forth, he may decide from them what side he should favor or to whom he wishes to remain loyal. But we seek indulgence for ourself, who venerate with due respect both persons, namely, the priestly and the royal, too much to venture to make a rash judgment concerning one of them. And so the following is a copy of a letter sent by the supreme pontiff to the archbishops and bishops concerning these matters:

"As often as any attempt is made in the Church directed against the honor of God and welfare of the faithful, the solicitude of our brothers and fellow bishops, and of those in particular who are led by the spirit of God, must be aroused, that matters which have been wrongly done may receive the correction that is pleasing to God.

"Now at this time, a matter of which we cannot speak without the deepest sorrow, our very dear son Frederick, emperor of the Romans, has done such a thing as we do not know to have been done in the times of our predecessor. For when we had sent to his presence two of our very good brothers, Bernard, of the title of St. Clement, and Roland, our chancellor, of the title of St. Mark, cardinal priests, he seems to have received them gladly when first they came into his presence. But on the following day, when they returned to him and our letter was read in his hearing, taking umbrage at a certain expression therein employed, namely, 'we have bestowed upon you the benefice (*beneficium*) of the imperial crown,' he blazed forth with such great anger that it was disgraceful to hear and would be painful to repeat the insults that he is said to have hurled at us and our legates, and to recall in how humiliating a fashion he obliged them to retire from his presence and with all speed from his land. And as they departed from his presence, he issued an edict that no one from your realm should approach the apostolic see, and is said to have set guards throughout all the bounds of that same realm who should forcibly detain those who desired to come to the apostolic see.

"Although we are somewhat disturbed by this act, yet at heart we draw very great consolation from the fact that he did not do this on your advice and that of the princes. Hence we are confident that by your counsel and persuasion his wrath may easily be calmed.

"Wherefore, brethren, inasmuch as your own interests, and those of all the churches—not our interest only—are clearly at stake in this matter, we admonish and exhort Your Love and in the Lord to interpose yourselves as a wall before the house of the Lord, and strive to lead back our aforesaid son to the right way as soon as possible. See especially that he cause his chancellor Rainald and the count palatine, who had the presumption to spew forth great blasphemies against our aforesaid legates and your very holy mother, the Roman Church, to offer such apology and to do it so openly that, as the bitterness of their speech has offended the ears of many, so also their apology may tend to recall many to the right way.

"Let not our same son give heed to the counsels of the ungodly, let him consider what is behind and before, and walk in that way in which Justinian and other Catholic emperors are known to have walked. For by imitating the example of those men he will be able to lay up for himself both honor on earth and blessedness in heaven.

"You also, if you lead him back to the right way, will both serve the blessed Peter, prince of apostles, and will preserve your own liberty and that of your churches. Otherwise may our aforesaid son learn from your admonition, may he learn from the truth of the Gospel promise, that the Holy Roman Church founded by God on an immovable rock will be steadfast forever, under the Lord's protection, by whatsoever tempests it may be shaken.

"Moreover, as you know, it was not seemly for him to have attempted so steep a path without your counsel, hence we believe that upon hearing your admonitions he can the more easily be brought back—like a man of discretion and a Catholic emperor—to a more reasonable frame of mind."

xvii (xvi). Upon the receipt of this letter and an embassy to the same purport, the bishops of Germany took counsel and replied to the apostolic see in the following words:

"Although we know and are sure that neither wind nor storm can overthrow the Church of God, founded upon a firm rock, yet we, being weak and faint-hearted, are shaken and tremble whenever blows of this kind befall. Hence we are, of course, gravely disturbed and alarmed at these developments which seem likely to prove—unless God avert it—the source of great evil between Your Holiness and your most devoted son, our lord, the emperor. Indeed, in consequence of those words which were contained in your letter, which you sent by your messengers, those most prudent and honorable men, the Lord Bernard and the Lord Roland, the chancellor, venerable cardinal priests, our whole empire has been thrown into confusion. Neither the ears of the emperor nor those of the princes could endure to hear them. All have so stopped their ears that—saving Your Holiness' grace —we dare not and cannot uphold or approve in any way those words, by reason of their unfortunate ambiguity of meaning, because they were hitherto unknown and unheard of. We received and welcomed, however, with due reverence your letter, and have advised your son, our lord the emperor, as you ordered, and—thanks be to God!—have received from him the following reply, worthy of a Catholic prince, namely:

" 'There are two things by which our realm should be governed, the sacred laws of the emperors, and the good customs of our predecessors and our fathers. The limits set by them on the Church we do not wish to overstep, nor can we; whatever is not in accord with them, we reject. We gladly accord to our father the reverence that is his due. The free crown of empire we ascribe solely to the divine beneficence (*beneficium*). We recognize first in the election the vote of the archbishop of Mainz, then those of the other princes, according to their rank; the anointing as king we recognize as the prerogative of the archbishop of Cologne; the final anointing, as emperor, indeed pertains to the supreme pontiff. "Whatsoever is more than these cometh of evil."

" 'It is not to show disrespect for our most beloved and reverend father and consecrator that we obliged the cardinals to depart from our land. But we did not wish to permit them to proceed further, to the disgrace and shame of our empire, with their letters, written or blank. We have not closed the way in and out of Italy by edict, nor do we wish in any way to close it to those going to the Roman see as pilgrims or on their own necessary business, in reasonable fashion, with testimonials from their bishops and prelates. But we intend to resist those abuses by which all the churches of our realm have been burdened and weakened, and almost all the discipline of the cloisters killed and buried. In the chief city of the world God has, through the power of the empire, exalted the Church; in the chief city of the world the Church, not through the power of God, we believe, is now destroying the empire. It began with a picture, the picture became an inscription, the inscription seeks to become an authoritative utterance. We shall not endure it, we shall not submit to it; we shall lay down the crown before we consent to have the imperial crown and ourself thus degraded. Let the pictures be destroyed, let the inscriptions be withdrawn, that they may not remain as eternal memorials of enmity between the empire and the papacy.'

"These and other matters—for instance, concerning the agreement between the Ro[mans] and W[illiam] of Sicily, and other pacts made in Italy —which we do not venture to recount in detail, we heard from the lips of our lord the emperor. In the absence of the count palatine, who has already been sent ahead to make preparations for the expedition into Italy, we have heard nothing from the chancellor, who is still present here, save that he was of meek and peaceful bearing, except when he defended the ambassadors with all his might when their lives were threatened by those present, as everyone there could attest.

"As for the rest, we humbly ask and beseech Your Sanctity to pardon our weakness and, like a good shepherd, calm the high spirits of your son with a letter more conciliatory than that former one, that the Church of God may rejoice in tranquil devotion and that the empire may glory in its sublimity, with the mediation and aid of the 'Mediator between God and man, the man Christ Jesus.'"

xviii (xvii). The emperor began his expedition propitiously, and pitching camp at Augsburg, a city of Rhaetia, on the river Lech, he awaited for seven days the soldiery who poured in from various directions [June, 1158].

Meanwhile the Roman bishop, being informed of the coming of the prince—for his legates, the above-mentioned Chancellor Rainald and Count Palatine Otto, had entered Italy long before—now changed his attitude for the better and sent ambassadors to calm Frederick's spirit, namely, Henry, cardinal priest of the title of Saints Nereus and Achilles, and Hyacinth, cardinal deacon of St. Mary-in-the-Greek-School, men of prudence in secular matters, and much better qualified for dealing with affairs of state than those previously sent.

xxii. Accordingly, when Frederick had pitched his camp in the plains of Augsburg (as has already been said), he admitted to his presence those same legates and, receiving them graciously, asked the cause of their coming. With due reverence and downcast eyes they began their mission in these words: "The bishop of the Holy Roman Church, Your Excellency's most devoted father in Christ, salutes you as the very dear and spiritual son of St. Peter. Salutations also from our venerable brothers, your clergy, all the cardinals, to you as lord and emperor of the City and of the world. With what great love the Holy Roman Church esteems the dignity and honor of your empire, how she has—though unwillingly enough—endured your anger without consciousness of guilt, both this present writing and the words placed upon our lips shall declare."

They then produced a letter which was given to the venerable Bishop Otto of Freising to read and to interpret—a man who felt a peculiar grief at the controversy between the state and the Church. This is a copy of the letter:

xxiii. "Since we assumed the care of the Church Universal by God's will and pleasure, we have been careful to do honor to Your Magnificence in all matters, that your love of us and veneration for the apostolic see might daily increase. When we heard that your feelings had been roused against us by certain people, we sent to you, to ascertain your will, two of our best and most distinguished brothers, the Cardinal Priest R[oland], the chancellor, of the title of St. Mark, and B[ernard], of the title of St. Clement, who had always been solicitous in the Roman Church for the honor of Your Majesty. Hence we learned with great astonishment that they were treated otherwise than behooved the imperial dignity. For your heart was stirred to anger, it is said, by the use of a certain word, namely *beneficium*. Yet this should not have vexed the heart of even one in lowly station, to say nothing of so great a man. For although this word *beneficium* is by some interpreted in a different significance than it has by derivation, it should nevertheless have been understood in the meaning which we ourselves put upon it, and which it is known to have possessed from the beginning. For this word is formed of *bonus* (good) and *factum* (deed), and among us *beneficium* means not a fief but a good deed. In this sense it is found in the entire body of Holy Scripture, wherein we are said to be ruled and supported *ex beneficio Dei,* not as by a fief (*feudum*) but as by His benediction and His 'good deed' (*bono facto*). And indeed Your Highness clearly recognizes that we placed the emblem of imperial dignity upon your head in so good and honorable a fashion that it merits recognition by all as a good deed. Hence when certain people have tried to twist that word and the following formula, namely, 'we have conferred upon you the imperial crown,' from its proper meaning to another, they have done this not on the merits of the case, but of their own desire and at the instigation of those who by no means love the concord of Church and state. For by 'we have conferred' (*contulimus*) we meant nothing else than when we said before 'we have placed' (*imposuimus*). As for the report that you afterward ordered the turning back of ecclesiastical persons on due visitation to the sacrosanct Roman Church, if it be so, we believe that Your Discretion, O very dear son in Christ, must realize how unseemly an act that was. For if you harbored any bitterness toward us, it should have been intimated to us by your envoys and letters, and we would have taken care to safeguard your honor, as that of our very dear son. Now therefore, as we have, at the advice of your beloved son H[enry], duke of Bavaria and Saxony, sent into your presence two of our brothers, Henry, cardinal priest of the title of Saints Nereus and Achilles, and Hyacinth, cardinal deacon of St. Mary in Cosmedin, truly wise and estimable men, we urge and exhort Your Highness in the Lord that you receive them with honor and kindness. Know also that what is imparted to Your Magnificence by them on our behalf has proceeded from the sincerity of our heart. And therefore may Your Highness so strive to reach an agreement with these our sons, through the mediation of our aforesaid son, the duke, that there may remain no seed of discord between you and your mother, the Holy Roman Church."

xxiv (xxiii). When the letter had been read and set forth with favorable interpretation, the emperor was mollified, and becoming more gracious he indicated to the legates certain specific matters to be considered later which might lead to dispute unless properly corrected. When to this they made answer agreeable to the prince and in all respects satisfactory, and promised that the bishop of Rome would do nothing derogatory to the royal dignity, but would always preserve inviolate the honor and the just claims of empire, he guaranteed peace and friendship both to the supreme pontiff and to all the Roman clergy, and certified it for the absent by giving them also, through those who were present, a kiss in token of peace. So the ambassadors were gladdened and enriched with royal gifts, and set forth for the City.

THE BULL "UNAM SANCTAM"

WE ARE COMPELLED, our faith urging us, to believe and to hold—and we do firmly believe and simply confess—that there is one holy catholic and apostolic church, outside of which there is neither salvation nor remission of sins; her Spouse proclaiming it in the canticles: "My dove, my undefiled is but one, she is the choice one of her that bare her"; which represents one mystic body, of which body the head is Christ; but of Christ, God. In this church there is one Lord, one faith and one baptism. There was one ark of Noah, indeed, at the time of the flood, symbolizing one church; and this being finished in one cubit had, namely, one Noah as helmsman and commander. And, with the exception of this ark, all things existing upon the earth were, as we read, destroyed. This church, moreover, we venerate as the only one, the Lord saying through His prophet: "Deliver my soul from the sword, my darling from the power of the dog." He prayed at the same time for His soul—that is, for Himself the Head—and for His body,—which body, namely, he called the one and only church on account of the unity of faith promised, of the sacraments, and of the love of the church. She is that seamless garment of the Lord which was not cut but which fell by lot. Therefore of this one and only church there is one body and one head—not two heads as if it were a monster:—Christ, namely, and the vicar of Christ, St. Peter, and the successor of Peter. For the Lord Himself said to Peter, Feed my sheep. My sheep, He said, using a general term, and not designating these or those particular sheep; from which it is plain that He committed to him *all* His sheep. If, then, the Greeks or others say that they were not committed to the care of Peter and his successors, they necessarily confess that they are not of the sheep of Christ; for the Lord says, in John, that there is one fold, one shepherd and one only. We are told by the word of the gospel that in this His fold there are two swords,—a spiritual, namely, and a temporal. For when the apostles said "Behold here are two swords"— when, namely, the apostles were speaking in the church—the Lord did not reply that this was too much, but enough. Surely he who denies that the temporal sword is in the power of Peter wrongly interprets the word of the Lord when He says: "Put up thy sword in its scabbard." Both swords, the spiritual and the material, therefore, are in the power of the church; the one, indeed, to be wielded for the church, the other by the church; the one by the hand of the priest, the other by the hand of kings and knights, but at the will and sufferance of the priest. One sword, moreover, ought to be under the other, and the temporal authority to be subjected to the spiritual. For when the apostle says "there is no power but of God, and the powers that are of God are ordained," they would not be ordained unless sword were under sword and the lesser one, as it were, were led by the other to great deeds. For according to St. Dionysius the law of divinity is to lead the lowest through the intermediate to the highest things. Not therefore, according to the law of the universe, are all things reduced to order equally and immediately; but the lowest through the intermediate, the intermediate through the higher. But that the spiritual exceeds any earthly power in dignity and nobility we ought the more openly to confess the more spiritual things excel temporal ones. This also is made plain to our eyes from the giving of tithes, and the benediction and the sanctification; from the acceptation of this same power, from the control over those same things. For, the truth bearing witness, the spiritual power has to establish the earthly power, and to judge it if it be not good. Thus concerning the church and the ecclesiastical power is verified the prophecy of Jeremiah: "See, I have this day set thee over the nations and over the kingdoms," and the other things which follow. Therefore if the earthly power err it shall be judged by the spiritual power; but if the lesser spiritual power err, by the greater. But if the greatest, it can be judged by God alone, not by man, the apostle bearing witness. A spiritual man judges all things, but he himself is judged by no one. This authority, moreover, even though it is given to man and exercised through man, is not human but rather divine, being given by divine lips to Peter and founded on a rock for him and his successors through Christ himself whom he has confessed; the Lord himself saying to Peter: "Whatsoever thou shalt bind," etc. Whoever, therefore, resists this power thus ordained by God, resists the ordination of God, unless he makes believe, like the Manichean, that there are two beginnings. This we consider false and heretical, since by the testimony of Moses, not "in the beginnings," but "in the beginning" God created the Heavens and the earth. *Indeed we declare, announce and define, that it is altogether necessary to salvation for every human creature to be subject to the Roman pontiff.* The Lateran, Nov. 14, in our 8th year. As a perpetual memorial of this matter.

DEFENSOR PACIS

Discourse One

CHAPTER IV: ON THE FINAL CAUSE OF THE STATE AND OF ITS CIVIL REQUIREMENTS, AND THE DIFFERENTIATION IN GENERAL OF ITS PARTS

The state, according to Aristotle in the *Politics,* Book I, Chapter 1, is "the perfect community having the full limit of self-sufficiency, which came into existence for the sake of living, but exists for the sake of living well." This phrase of Aristotle—"came into existence for the sake of living but exists for the sake of living well"—signifies the perfect final cause of the state, since those who live a civil life not only live, which beasts or slaves do too, but live well, having leisure for those liberal functions in which are exercised the virtues of both the practical and the theoretic soul.

3. But the living and living well which are appropriate to men fall into two kinds, of which one is temporal or earthly, while the other is usually called eternal or heavenly. However, this latter kind of living, the eternal, the whole body of philosophers were unable to prove by demonstration, nor was it self-evident, and therefore they did not concern themselves

with the means thereto. But as to the first kind of living and living well or good life, that is, the earthly, and its necessary means, this the glorious philosophers comprehended almost completely through demonstration. Hence for its attainment they concluded the necessity of the civil community, without which this sufficient life cannot be obtained. Thus the foremost of the philosophers, Aristotle, said in his *Politics,* Book 1, Chapter 1: "All men are driven toward such an association by a natural impulse." Although sense experience teaches this, we wish to bring out more distinctly that cause of it which we have indicated, as follows: Man is born composed of contrary elements, because of whose contrary actions and passions some of his substance is continually being destroyed; moreover, he is born "bare and unprotected" from excess of the surrounding air and other elements, capable of suffering and of destruction, as has been said in the science of nature. As a consequence, he needed arts of diverse genera and species to avoid the aforementioned harms. But since these arts can be exercised only by a large number of men, and can be had only through their association with one another, men had to assemble together in order to attain what was beneficial through these arts and to avoid what was harmful.

4. But since among men thus assembled there arise disputes and quarrels which, if not regulated by a norm of justice, would cause men to fight and separate and thus finally would bring about the destruction of the state, there had to be established in this association a standard of justice and a guardian or maker thereof. And since this guardian has to restrain excessive wrongdoers as well as other individuals both within and outside the state who disturb or attempt to oppress the community, the state had to have within it something by which to resist these. Again, since the community needs various conveniences, repairs, and protection of certain common things, and different things in time of peace and in time of war, it was necessary that there be in the community men to take care of such matters, in order that the common necessity might be relieved when it was expedient or needful. But beside the things which we have so far mentioned, which relieve only the necessities of the present life, there is something else which men associated in a civil community need for the status of the future world promised to the human race through God's supernatural revelation, and which is useful also for the status of the present life. This is the worship and honoring of God and the giving of thanks both for benefits received in this world and for those to be received in the future one. For the teaching of these things and for the directing of men in them, the state had to designate certain teachers. The nature and qualities

of all these and the other matters mentioned above will be treated in detail in the subsequent discussions.

5. Men, then, were assembled for the sake of the sufficient life, being able to seek out for themselves the necessaries enumerated above, and exchanging them with one another. This assemblage, thus perfect and having the limit of self-sufficiency, is called the state, whose final cause as well as that of its many parts has already been indicated by us in some measure, and will be more fully distinguished below. For since diverse things are necessary to men who desire a sufficient life, things which cannot be supplied by men of one order or office, there had to be diverse orders or offices of men in this association, exercising or supplying such diverse things which men need for sufficiency of life. But these diverse orders or offices of men are none other than the many and distinct parts of the state.

Let it suffice, then, to have covered thus in outline what the state is, why there came about such an association, and the number and division of its parts.

CHAPTER XVII: ON THE NUMERICAL UNITY OF THE SUPREME GOVERNMENT OF THE CITY OR STATE, AND THE NECESSITY FOR THAT UNITY; WHENCE THERE APPEARS ALSO THE NUMERICAL UNITY OF THE CITY OR STATE ITSELF, AND OF EACH OF ITS PRIMARY PARTS OR OFFICES

We must now discuss the unity of the ruler or government. To begin with, let us say that in a single city or state there must be only a single government; or if there is more than one government in number or in species, as seems expedient in large cities and especially in a state (*regno*) taken in its first sense, then there must be among them one in number which is supreme, to which all the other governments are reduced, by which they are regulated, and which corrects any errors arising in them.

2. Now I maintain, with respect to this supreme government alone, that it must necessarily be one in number, not many, if the state or city is to be rightly ordered. And I say the same with regard to the ruler, not that the ruler is to be one in number with respect to person but rather with respect to office. For there may be some supreme, well-tempered government which is one in number, but in which more than one man rules; such are the aristocracy and the polity, of which we spoke in Chapter VIII. These several men, however, are numerically one government with respect to office, because of the numerical unity of every action, judgment, sentence or command forthcoming from them. For no such action can emerge from any one of them separately, but only from the common decree and consent of

them all or of their weightier part, in accordance with the laws established on such matters. And it is because of such numerical unity of the action thus forthcoming from them that the government is and is called one in number, whether it be ruled by one man or by many. Such unity of action is not, however, required in any of the other offices or parts of the state; for in each of them there can and must be forthcoming separately, from the diverse individuals in them, many actions similar or diverse in species. Indeed, such unity of action in these offices would be unbearable and harmful both to the community and to the individuals.

3. Such being the meaning of the numerical unity of the government or ruler, we wish to prove that the government or ruler of the city or state is to be only one in number, or, if more than one, that the supreme government of them all is to be only one in number, not more. We shall demonstrate this first as follows. If there were several governments in the city or state, and they were not reduced or ordered under one supreme government, then the judgment, command, and execution of matters of benefit and justice would fail, and because men's injuries would therefore be unavenged the result would be fighting, separation, and finally the destruction of the city or state. But this consequence is the evil which is most to be avoided; and that it is a consequence of the given antecedent, that is, of a plurality of governments, can be clearly shown. For, in the first place, transgressors of the laws cannot reasonably be brought to justice unless they are called before the ruler for examination of the charges against them. But if we assume a plurality of governments not reduced to some one supreme government, as our opponent says, then no one called before the ruler will be able sufficiently to obey the summons. For suppose, as frequently happens, that because of some transgression of the law a man is called by several rulers not ordered one below another, to answer charges at the same time. One ruler is bound and able to summon the accused man for the same reason as the other ruler; and the man who is summoned is bound to appear before one of the rulers, lest he be regarded as being in contempt, for the same reason as before the other ruler, or rulers, if there be more than two. Either, therefore, he will appear before all the rulers at once, or before none of them, or else before a certain one and not before the other or others. But he will not appear before all the rulers at one and the same time, since this is impossible by nature and by art, for the same body cannot be in different places at the same time, or reply or speak at the same time to many persons who are perhaps asking different questions at the same time. Moreover, even though it is impossible, let us assume that the person summoned

does appear before several rulers, and is silent or replies to different questions at the same time. Yet he will perhaps be convicted by one ruler and be acquitted by another, of the same crime; or if convicted by both, with different penalties. Hence he will be both required and not required to make amends; or if required by both, it will be to such a large degree by one, and to a greater or lesser degree by another, and thus both to such a degree and not to such a degree. Hence he will either do contradictory things at the same time, or else will make no amends at all. For he must obey one ruler's command for the same reason as another's. He has no more reason for appearing before one ruler than before the other or others. If, however, he appears before one of them, ignoring the others, and is perhaps absolved by him of civil guilt and punishment, he will nevertheless be convicted by the others for contempt. Therefore the man summoned will neither appear before all the rulers at once nor be able properly to appear before a certain one and not before another. The only remaining course, consequently, is for the man who is summoned to appear before no ruler at all; therefore justice will be incapable of being done in his case. It is impossible, therefore, for the city or state to have a plurality of such governments not subordinated one to another, if civil justice and benefit are to be conserved.

4. Moreover, if there were a plurality of such governments, the common utility would be completely disturbed. For the rulers must frequently command the assemblage of the citizens, especially of those who have leisure, to inquire into and to decide matters relating to the common benefit, or to avoid harmful impending dangers such as are presented by external or internal enemies who intend to oppress the community and to take away its freedom. Now the citizens or subjects who must obey the command of one ruler to assemble at a certain place and time must for the same reason obey the command of another ruler to assemble at the place and time which he selects; and each ruler might select the same time but different places; and again, what one of the rulers wishes to propose may perhaps be different from what the other wants. But it does not seem possible to be in different places at the same time, or to have different aims at the same time.

5. Again, from this there would result the division and opposition of the citizens, their fighting and separation, and finally the destruction of the state, for some of the citizens would wish to obey one government, and some another. There would also be strife between the governments themselves because one of them would want to be superior to the other; in addition, the governments would war against the citizens who refused to be

subject to them. Moreover, when the rulers disagreed or quarreled among themselves, since they would lack a superior judge, the above-mentioned scandals would also arise.

6. Again, if this plurality of governments is assumed, one of the greatest effects of human reason and art will be useless and superfluous. For all the civil utility which would be had from many supreme governments can be perfectly had through one government or one supreme government without the harms resulting from a plurality of them.

7. Moreover, if such a plurality is assumed, no state or city will be one. For states are one, and are called one, because of the unity of the government to which and by which all the other parts of the state are ordered, as will appear also from what follows. And again there will be no order of the parts of the city or state, since they will be ordered to no first part, because they are required to be subjected to none, as is clear from the previous arguments. And there will be a confusion both of them and of the whole state; for each man will choose for himself whatever office he wishes, one or more, with no one regulating or separating such offices. So many are the evils which would follow upon this that it is difficult or impossible to enumerate them all. . . .

Discourse Two

CHAPTER II: ON THE DISTINCTION OF THE MEANINGS OF THE WORDS OR TERMS WHICH COMPOSE THE QUESTIONS TO BE DECIDED

. . . . .

8. It now remains to distinguish the meanings of the words "judge" and "judgment," which signifies the action of the judge. For these are among the terms which have many meanings, and that multiplicity introduces ambiguity which impedes the determination of questions. In one sense, "judge" means anyone who discerns or knows, especially in accordance with some theoretic or practical habit; and so the word "judgment" means such men's knowledge or discernment. In this sense, the geometer is a judge, and judges concerning figures and their attributes; and the physician judges concerning the healthy and the sick, and the prudent man concerning what should be done and what should be avoided, and the housebuilder concerning how to build houses. Thus, every knower or expert is called a judge, and judges about things which can be known or done by him. It was in this sense that Aristotle used these words in the *Ethics*, Book I, Chapter 1, when he said: "Everyone judges well the things which he knows, and is a good judge of them."

In another sense, this word "judge" means the man who has the science of political or civil law, and who is usually called an "advocate," although in many provinces, and particularly in Italy, he is called a "judge."

In a third sense, this word "judge" means the ruler, and "judgment" means the sentence of the ruler who has the authority to judge concerning the just and beneficial in accordance with the laws or customs, and to command and execute through coercive force the sentences made by him. In this sense, a certain book is called Judges, being one part of the holy canon or Bible. It was in this sense, too, that Aristotle spoke of the judge or ruler in the *Rhetoric,* Book I, Chapter 1, when he said: "But the magistrate and the judge make judgments concerning the present and the determinate." So, too, referring to the judgment of the ruler, he continues: "They," that is, the magistrate or judge, "are often involved in personal likes and dislikes, so that they cannot see the truth sufficiently well, but instead have regard in their judgments to their own pleasure and displeasure."

There are perhaps other meanings of the above words; we think, however, that we have indicated those which are more familiar and more necessary for our proposed inquiry.

CHAPTER IV: ON THE CANONIC SCRIPTURES, THE COMMANDS, COUNSELS, AND
    EXAMPLES OF CHRIST AND OF THE SAINTS AND APPROVED DOCTORS WHO
    EXPOUNDED THE EVANGELIC LAW, WHEREBY IT IS CLEARLY DEMONSTRATED
    THAT THE ROMAN OR ANY OTHER BISHOP OR PRIEST, OR CLERGYMAN,
    CAN BY VIRTUE OF THE WORDS OF SCRIPTURE CLAIM OR ASCRIBE TO HIM-
    SELF NO COERCIVE RULERSHIP OR CONTENTIOUS JURISDICTION, LET ALONE
    THE SUPREME JURISDICTION OVER ANY CLERGYMAN OR LAYMAN; AND
    THAT, BY CHRIST'S COUNSEL AND EXAMPLE, THEY OUGHT TO REFUSE SUCH
    RULERSHIP, ESPECIALLY IN COMMUNITIES OF THE FAITHFUL, IF IT IS
    OFFERED TO THEM OR BESTOWED ON THEM BY SOMEONE HAVING THE
    AUTHORITY TO DO SO; AND AGAIN, THAT ALL BISHOPS, AND GENERALLY
    ALL PERSONS NOW CALLED CLERGYMEN, MUST BE SUBJECT TO THE CO-
    ERCIVE JUDGMENT OR RULERSHIP OF HIM WHO GOVERNS BY THE AU-
    THORITY OF THE HUMAN LEGISLATOR, ESPECIALLY WHERE THIS LEGISLATOR
    IS CHRISTIAN

We now wish from the opposite side to adduce the truths of the holy Scripture in both its literal and its mystical sense, in accordance with the interpretations of the saints and the expositions of other approved doctors of the Christian faith, which explicitly command or counsel that neither the

Roman bishop called pope, nor any other bishop or priest, or deacon, has or ought to have any rulership or coercive judgment or jurisdiction over any priest or non-priest, ruler, community, group, or individual of whatever condition; understanding by "coercive judgment" that what we said in Chapter II of this discourse to be the third sense of "judge" or "judgment."

2. The more clearly to carry out this aim, we must not overlook that in this inquiry it is not asked what power and authority is or was had in this world by Christ, who was true God and true man, nor what or how much of this power he was able to bestow on St. Peter and the other apostles and their successors, the bishops or priests; for Christian believers have no doubts on these points. But we wish to and ought to inquire what power and authority, to be exercised in this world, Christ wanted to bestow and in fact (*de facto*) did bestow on them, and from what he excluded and prohibited them by counsel or command. For we are bound to believe that they had from Christ only such power and authority as we can prove to have been given them through the words of Scripture, no other. For it is certain to all the Christian believers that Christ, who was true God and true man, was able to bestow, not only on the apostles but also on any other men, coercive authority or jurisdiction over all rulers or governments and over all the other individuals in the world; and even more perhaps, as for example the power to create things, to destroy or repair heaven and earth and the things therein, and even to be in complete command of the angels; but these powers Christ neither bestowed nor determined to bestow on them. Hence Augustine, in the tenth sermon *On the Words of the Lord in Matthew,* wrote the following: "'Learn of me' not how to make a world, not how to create all visible and invisible things, nor how to do miracles in the world and revive the dead; but: 'because I am meek and humble of heart.'"

3. Therefore for the present purpose it suffices to show, and I shall first show, that Christ himself came into the world not to dominate men, nor to judge them by judgment in the third sense, nor to wield temporal rule, but rather to be subject as regards the status of the present life; and moreover, that he wanted to and did exclude himself, his apostles and disciples, and their successors, the bishops or priests, from all such coercive authority or worldly rule, both by his example and by his words of counsel or command. I shall also show that the leading apostles, as Christ's true imitators, did this same thing and taught their successors to do likewise; and moreover, that both Christ and his apostles wanted to be and were continuously subject in property and in person to the coercive jurisdiction of secular rulers,

and that they taught and commanded all others, to whom they preached or wrote the law of truth, to do likewise, under pain of eternal damnation. Then I shall write a chapter on the power or authority of the keys which Christ gave to the apostles and their successors in office, bishops and priests, so that it may be clear what is the nature, quality, and extent of such power, both of the Roman bishop and of the others. For ignorance on this point has hitherto been and still is the source of many questions and damnable controversies among the Christian faithful, as was mentioned in the first chapter of this discourse.

4. And so in pursuit of these aims we wish to show that Christ, in his purposes or intentions, words, and deeds, wished to exclude and did exclude himself and the apostles from every office of rulership, contentious jurisdiction, government, or coercive judgment in this world. This is first shown clearly beyond any doubt by the passage in the eighteenth chapter of the gospel of John. For when Christ was brought before Pontius Pilate, vicar of the Roman ruler in Judaea, and accused of having called himself king of the Jews, Pontius asked him whether he had said this, or whether he did call himself a king, and Christ's reply included these words, among others: "My kingdom is not of this world," that is, I have not come to reign by temporal rule or dominion, in the way in which worldly kings reign. And proof of this was given by Christ himself through an evident sign when he said: "If my kingdom were of this world, my servants would certainly fight, that I should not be delivered to the Jews," as if to argue as follows: If I had come into this world to reign by worldly or coercive rule, I would have ministers for this rule, namely, men to fight and to coerce transgressors, as the other kings have; but I do not have such ministers, as you can clearly see. Hence the interlinear gloss: "It is clear that no one defends him." And this is what Christ reiterates: "But now my kingdom is not from hence," that is, the kingdom about which I have come to teach.

5. Expounding these evangelic truths, the saints and doctors write as follows, and first St. Augustine:

If he had answered Pilate's question directly, he would have seemed to be answering not the Jews but only the Gentiles who thought this of him. But after answering Pilate, he answered the Jews and the Gentiles more opportunely and fitly, as if to say: Hear ye, Jews and Gentiles, I do not impede your rule in this world. What more do you want? Through faith approach ye the kingdom which is not of this world. For what is his kingdom but those who believe in him?

This, then, is the kingdom concerning which he came to teach and order, a kingdom which consists in the acts whereby the eternal kingdom is attained, that is, the acts of faith and the other theological virtues; not, however, by coercing anyone thereto, as will be made clear below. For when there are two coercive dominions in respect of the same multitude, and neither is subordinated to the other, they impede one another, as was shown in Chapter XVII of Discourse I. But Christ had not come to impede such dominion, as Augustine said. Hence on the passage in the same chapter of John: "Thy own nation and the chief priests have delivered thee up to me. What hast thou done?" Augustine wrote: "He sufficiently shows that the act is looked upon as a crime, as if to say: If you deny you are a king, what then have you done to be delivered up to me; as if it would not be strange if he who called himself king were delivered up to the judge to be punished." So, then, Augustine thought that it would be nothing strange if Christ had been punished, had he called himself secular king, especially before those who did not know he was God; and that he denied he would be king of such a kingdom or with such authority, namely, to coerce transgressors of the law. Hence on the words in the same chapter of John: "Sayest thou this thing of thyself, or did others tell it thee of me?" Theophylact wrote: "Christ spoke to Pilate as if to say: If you say this on your own, show the signs of my rebellion, but if you have heard it from others, then make the ordinary inquiry." But if the opinion of our adversaries were correct, Christ should never have said what Theophylact states, namely, that Pilate should make the ordinary inquiry about him; indeed, were they correct, he should rather have said that it did not pertain to Pilate to make this inquiry, inasmuch as he, Christ, of right (*de jure*) was not and did not wish to be subject to him in jurisdiction or coercive judgment.

9. It now remains to show that not only did Christ himself refuse rulership or coercive judgment in this world, whereby he furnished an example for his apostles and disciples and their successors to do likewise, but also he taught by words and showed by example that all men, both priests and nonpriests, should be subject in property and in person to the coercive judgment of the rulers of this world. By his word and example, then, Christ showed this first with respect to property, by what is written in the twenty-second chapter of Matthew. For when the Jews asked him: "Tell us therefore, what dost thou think? Is it lawful to give tribute to Caesar or not?" Christ, after looking at the coin and its inscription, replied: "Render therefore to Caesar the things that are Caesar's, and to God the things that are God's." Whereon the interlinear gloss says, "that is, tribute and money." And on the words: "Whose image and inscription is this?" Ambrose wrote as follows: "Just as Caesar demanded the imprinting of his image, so too does God demand that

the soul be stamped with the light of his countenance." Note, therefore, what it was that Christ came into the world to demand. Furthermore, Chrysostom writes as follows: "When you hear: 'Render to Caesar the things that are Caesar's,' know that he means only those things which are not harmful to piety, for if they were, the tribute would be not to Caesar but to the devil." So, then, we ought to be subject to Caesar in all things, so long only as they are not contrary to piety, that is, to divine worship or commandment. Therefore, Christ wanted us to be subject in property to the secular rule. This too was plainly the doctrine of St. Ambrose, based upon this doctrine of Christ, for in his epistle against Valentinian, entitled *To the People,* he wrote: "We pay to Caesar the things that are Caesar's and to God the things that are God's. That the tribute is Caesar's is not denied."

CHAPTER IX: ON THE RELATION OF HUMAN ACTS TO DIVINE LAW AND TO THE JUDGE OF THE OTHER WORLD, NAMELY CHRIST; AND ALSO HOW THESE ACTS ARE RELATED TO THE TEACHER OF THE SAME LAW, THE BISHOP OR PRIEST, IN THIS WORLD

According to this reasoning, therefore, there is also a certain judge who has coercive authority over transgressors of divine law, which we have called the coercive standard of some human acts both immanent and transient. But this judge is one alone, Christ, and no one else. Whence in the fourth chapter of James: "There is one lawmaker and judge, that is able to destroy and to deliver." But this judge's coercive power is not exercised over anyone in this world, to punish or reward transgressors or observers of the law made immediately by him, which we have often called the evangelic law. For in his mercy Christ wished to give every person the opportunity to become deserving up to the very end of his life and to repent of sins committed against Christ's law, as will be shown below by the authorities of the holy Scripture.

2. But there is also another judge according to the evangelic Scripture, who is analogous to the human law's judge in the first sense. This other judge is the priest, who is the teacher in this world of divine law and of its commands concerning what must be done or shunned in order to attain eternal life and avoid punishment. However, he has no coercive power in this world to compel anyone to observe these commands. For it would be useless for him to coerce anyone to observe them, since the person who observed them under coercion would be helped not at all toward eternal salvation, as we showed clearly in Chapter V of this discourse, paragraph 6, through Chrysostom, or rather through the Apostle. Hence this judge is properly likened to the physician, who is given the authority to teach, com-

mand, and predict or judge about the things which it is useful to do or omit in order to attain bodily health and avoid illness or death. It was for this reason, too, that Christ called himself a physician in and for the status of the present life, and not a ruler or a judge. Hence in the fifth chapter of Luke, which we also quoted in a preceding chapter, Christ spoke of himself to the Pharisees as follows: "They that are well do not need a physician, but they that are sick." For Christ did not ordain that anyone should be forced to observe in this world the law made by him, and for this reason he did not appoint in this world a judge having coercive power over transgressors of this law.

3. Hence it must be noted that the evangelic law can stand in a twofold relation to men, over whom it was made by Christ. In one way, it can be related to them in and for the status of the present life; and in this way it has in its various parts the nature more of a doctrine, theoretic or practical or both, than of a law taken in its last and proper sense, although the word "law" can also be taken in other senses, like the second and the third, which we discussed in Chapter X of Discourse I. And the reason for what we have said is that law, taken in its last and proper sense, is a coercive standard, that is, a standard in accordance with which its transgressor is punished by the coercive force which is given to the man who must judge in accordance with it. But now the evangelic doctrine, or the maker of that law, does not command that anyone be compelled in this world to observe the things which it commands men to do or omit in this world. Consequently, in its relation to man's status in and for this world, it ought to be called a doctrine, not a law, except in the way we have said. This was also the view of the Apostle in the second epistle to Timothy, Chapter 3, when he said: "All scripture divinely inspired is useful for teaching, for reproof, for correction, for instruction in righteousness." But never did the Apostle say: for coercion or punishment in this world. Hence in the second epistle to the Corinthians, Chapter 1: "Not because we exercise dominion over your faith, but we are the helpers of your joy; for by faith ye stand." Whereon Ambrose wrote what we quoted above in Chapter V of this discourse, and it bears repeating: "And lest they," that is, the Corinthians, "resent what might appear almost as dominion, in that he," the Apostle, "had said 'to spare you I did not come,' he," the Apostle, "adds: But I do not say 'to spare you' 'because we exercise dominion over your faith,' that is, because your faith undergoes dominion and coercion, for faith is of the will, not of necessity; but I say it rather 'because we are the helpers,' if you wish to co-operate." Note, then, they are helpers, that is, by teaching, and "if you wish

to cooperate." "For 'by faith,' which works through choice, 'ye stand,' not by dominion."

But the evangelic Scripture or law can also stand in another relation to men, for their status in the other world, in which alone, and not in this one, those men will be punished who have transgressed this law in the present life. And viewed in this other relation it is most properly given the name of law, and he who will then judge in accordance with it is most properly called a judge, in the third sense as having coercive power. But inasmuch as the priest or bishop, whoever he be, guides and regulates men in accordance with this law in the status of the present life alone, although with reference to the future life, and since the immediate maker of that law, Christ, has not granted to the priest the authority to coerce anyone in accordance with it in this world, it follows that the priest is not properly called a judge, in the third sense as having coercive power, and he neither can nor should coerce anyone in this world by such judgment through punishment in property or in person. Analogous to this is the relation of any practical teacher, such as a physician, to the judgment of men's bodily health, without coercive power over anyone, as we said near the beginning of this chapter.

7. According to the truth, therefore, and the clear intention of the Apostle and the saints, who were the foremost teachers of the church or faith, it is not commanded that anyone, even an infidel, let alone a believer, be compelled in this world through pain or punishment to observe the commands of the evangelic law, especially by a priest; and hence the ministers of this law, the bishops or priests, neither can nor should judge anyone in this world by a judgment in the third sense, or compel an unwilling person, by any pain or punishment, to observe the commands of divine law, especially without authorization by the human legislator; for such coercive judgment in accordance with divine law must not be exercised or executed in this world, but only in the future one. Hence in the nineteenth chapter of Matthew: "But Jesus said to them," that is, to the apostles: "Verily I say unto you, that ye which have followed me, in the regeneration when the son of man shall sit on the throne of his glory, ye also shall sit upon twelve thrones, judging the twelve tribes of Israel." See, then, when it was that the apostles were going to sit with Christ as judges in the third sense, namely, in the other world, not in this one. Whereon the gloss: "'in the regeneration,' that is, when the dead will rise up alive again." Hence, according to the gloss: "There are two regenerations, the first from water and the holy spirit, the second in resurrection." Hence "ye also shall sit," and

the gloss according to Augustine says: "When he who was in the guise of a servant and who was judged," that is, Christ, who was in this world judged by coercive judgment, and did not himself judge, "will exercise judiciary power," that is, in the resurrection, "you shall be judges with me." See, then, that according to Christ's words in the gospel and the exposition of the saints, Christ did not in this world exercise judiciary, that is, coercive, power, which we call judgment in the third sense, but rather, in the guise of a servant, he underwent such judgment by another man; and when he will exercise such coercive judiciary power in the other world, then, and not before, will the apostles sit with him to make judgments.

THE LAW "LICET JURIS"

ALTHOUGH THE PROOFS of both kinds of law (civil and canon) manifestly declare that the imperial dignity and power proceeded from of old directly through the Son of God, and that God openly gave laws to the human race through the emperor and the kings of the world; and since the emperor is made true emperor by the election alone of those to whom it pertains, and needs not the confirmation or approbation of any one else, since on earth he has no superior as to temporal things, but to him peoples and nations are subject, and our Lord Jesus Christ Himself ordered to be rendered unto God the things that are God's, and unto Caesar the things that are Caesar's; because, nevertheless, some, led by the blindness of avarice and ambition, and having no understanding of Scripture, but turning away from the path of right feeling into certain iniquitous and wicked deceptions, and, breaking forth into detestable assertions, do wage war against the imperial power and authority and against the prerogatives of the emperors, electors, and other princes, and of the faithful subjects of the empire, falsely asserting that the imperial dignity and power come from the pope and that he who is elected emperor is not true emperor or king unless he be first confirmed and crowned through the pope or the apostolic see; and since, through such wicked assertions and pestiferous dogmas the ancient enemy moves discord, excites quarrels, prepares dissensions and brings about seditions:—therefore, for the purpose of averting such evil, by the counsel and consent of the electors and of the other princes of the empire we declare that the imperial dignity and power comes directly from God alone; and that, by the old and approved right and custom of the empire, after any one is chosen as emperor or king by the electors of the empire concordantly, or by the greater part of them, he is, in consequence of the election alone, to be considered and called true king and emperor of the Romans, and he ought to be obeyed by all the subjects of the empire. And he shall have full power of administering the laws of the empire and of doing the other things that pertain to a true emperor; nor does he need the approbation, confirmation, authority or consent of the apostolic see or of any one else.

And therefore we decree by this law, to be forever valid, that he who is elected emperor concordantly or by the majority of the electors, shall, in consequence of the election alone, be considered and regarded by all as the true and lawful emperor; and that he ought to be obeyed by all the subjects of the empire, and that he shall have, and shall be considered and firmly asserted by all to have and to hold, the imperial administration and jurisdiction and the plenitude of the imperial power.

Moreover, whatever persons shall presume to assert or say anything contrary to these declarations, decrees or definitions, or any one of them; or to countenance those who assert or say anything; or to obey their mandates or letters or precepts: we deprive them from now on, and decree them to be deprived by the law and by the act itself, of all the fiefs which they hold from the empire, and of all the favours, jurisdictions, privileges and immunities granted to them by us or our predecessors. Moreover, we decree that they have committed the crime of high treason and are subject to all the penalties inflicted on those committing the crime of high treason. Given in our town of Frankfort on the 8th day of the month of August A.D. 1338.

DANTE

D ANTE ALIGHIERI (1265–1321) was born in Florence and studied with Brunetto Latini; he probably participated in military journeys during his youth. He was active in Florentine politics as a prior, a participant in an embassy to Rome, and a leader of the group combating the extension of papal domination to Florence. Dante was turned aside from his career in the public affairs of Florence by the success of Pope Boniface VIII in extending his secular authority to that city. Indeed, sentenced to exile under pain of death, Dante spent the rest of his life away from his native city. He died in Ravenna at the court of Guido da Polenta.

Among Dante's Latin prose works is *De Monarchia,* a late medieval attempt to restate the "two swords" theory in order to bring peace to Europe by establishing a united Christendom under emperor and pope, each supreme in his own way.

Dante's argument was neither original nor effective, but it marks the culmination of a long controversy. Like Thomas Aquinas, he adopted the Aristotelian view of human society or "civilization" as the fulfillment of human nature and reason. The renewed interest in Roman law in the late Middle Ages is exhibited especially in the second book of the *De Monarchia,* where Dante reformulates with a pronouncedly theological turn the Roman lawyers' arguments for the independence of the emperor. The *De Monarchia* may well seem, as Lord James Bryce once said, to be more an epitaph than a prophecy. Indeed, the empire to which Dante turned wielded its power during the Middle Ages more as a tradition than as a political actuality, and the universal peace which he hoped the empire might bring seems to be largely a nostalgic idealization of the *Pax Romana* of antiquity. Indirectly, however, the *De Monarchia* was influential, and in a sense prophetic. The ideal of a unified Christendom as the agency of universal peace has been an intellectual and emotional force of the first magnitude. On the other hand, Dante's argument also has importance for those modern churches that believe in a radical separation of political and religious bodies.

De Monarchia was probably made public in or shortly after 1310; it was first printed in 1559 and was then placed on the Church's Index of Forbidden Books. The following translation from the Latin is by A. G. Ferrers Howell and P. H. Wicksteed (London, J. M. Dent, 1904).

DE MONARCHIA

[*Book I*]

CHAPTER II

. . . THE TEMPORAL monarchy . . . which is called empire is "a unique princedom extending over all persons in time," or, "in and over those things which are measured by time"; and there rise three main inquiries concerning the same: for in the first place we may inquire and examine whether it is needful for the well-being of the world; in the second, whether the Roman people rightfully assumed to itself the function of monarchy; and in the third, whether the authority of the monarchy depends immediately upon God, or upon some other minister or vicar of God.

But inasmuch as every truth which is not a first principle is demonstrated by reference to one that is, it behooves us in every inquiry to be clear as to the first principle to which we are to return by analysis, in order to establish the certainty of all such propositions as may afterwards be laid down. . . .

That thing, then, if there is any, which is the goal of the entire civilisation of the human race, will give us this first principle, a reduction to which will be held a sufficient explanation of everything to be proved hereafter. But it would be folly to suppose that there is a goal of this civilisation and a goal of that, but no one goal of all civilisations.

CHAPTER III

So now we must consider what is the goal of human civilisation as a whole, which, when we see, more than half our work will be done, according to the Philosopher *Ad Nicomachum*.[1] And to understand the point in question we must note that like as there is an end for which nature produces the thumb, and another than this for which she produces the whole hand, and again another than either for which the arm, and another than all of these for which the whole man, so there is one end for which she produces the individual man, another for which the domestic group, another for which the district, another for which the city-state, and another for which the kingdom; and lastly, there is an ultimate goal for which the eternal God, by his art, which is nature, brings into being the human race in its universality. And it is this last for which we are now seeking as the first principle to direct our inquiry.

Wherefore be it known in the first place that God and nature makes naught superfluous, but all that comes into being is for some function. For no created being is a final goal in the intention of the Creator, as Creator; but rather is the proper function of that being the goal. Wherefore it comes to pass that the proper function does not come into existence for the sake of the being, but the latter for the sake of the former.

There is, then, some function proper to humanity as a whole for which that same totality of men is ordained in so great multitude, to which function neither one man nor one family, nor one district nor one city-state, nor any individual kingdom may attain. And what this function is will be obvious if the specific potentiality of mankind generally be made clear. I say, then, that

[1] [Aristotle's *Nicomachean Ethics*.]

no capacity which is shared by many beings, differing in species, is the specific capacity of any one of them. For since that which is specific constitutes a species, it would follow that one essence would be specifically assigned to several species, which is impossible. The specific capacity, then, which differentiates man is not merely *being,* taken without qualification, for this he shares with the elements; neither *compound being,* for this we find in the minerals; nor *animated being,* for this is in plants; nor *apprehension,* for this is shared by the brutes; but *apprehension by means of the potential intellect,* which mode of being is not competent to any other save man, either above him or below. . . .

CHAPTER IV

. . . The work proper to the human race, taken as a whole, is to keep the whole capacity of the potential intellect constantly actualised, primarily for speculation, and secondarily (by extension, and for the sake of the other) for action.

And since it is with the whole as it is with the part, and it is the fact that in sedentary quietness the individual man is perfected in knowledge and in wisdom, it is evident that in the quiet or tranquillity of peace the human race is most freely and favourably disposed towards the work proper to it (which is almost divine, even as it is said "Thou hast made him a little lower than the angels"). Whence it is manifest that universal peace is the best of all those things which are ordained for our blessedness. And that is why there rang out to the shepherds from on high, not riches, not pleasures, not honours, not length of life, not health, not strength, not beauty, but peace. For the celestial soldiery proclaims, "Glory to God in the highest; and, on earth, peace to men of good will." Hence, also, "Peace be with you" was the salutation of him who was the salvation of man. For it was meet that the supreme saviour should utter the supreme salutation. And likewise his disciples saw good to preserve this custom, and amongst them Paul, as all may see in his salutations.

Our exposition, then, has made clear what is the better means (or rather the best) whereby the human race attains to its proper work. And thus we perceive the directest means of approach to that whereto as to their ultimate goal all our doings are directed, which directest means is universal peace. Therefore let this underlie the following arguments, as that first principle which we needed (as aforesaid) for a mark, set up in advance; into which, as into the most manifest truth, whatsoever is to be proved must be resolved.

CHAPTER V

And now, to resume what we said at the outset, three main questions are raised and discussed about the temporal monarchy, more commonly called the empire; concerning which, as already declared, we purpose to make inquiry, in the order indicated above, under the first principle now laid down. Let us therefore first discuss whether a temporal monarchy is needful for the well-being of the world.

Now against its being needful there is no force either of argument or of authority, whereas most powerful and most patent arguments establish that it is. Of which let the first be drawn from the authority of the philosopher in his *Politics*. For there his venerable authority asserts that when more things than one are ordained for a single purpose, needs must one of them guide or rule, and the others be guided or ruled. And to this not only the glorious name of the author, but inductive argument also forces assent.

For if we consider an individual man, we shall see that this is true of him; since whereas all his faculties are ordained for felicity, the intellectual faculty is the guide and ruler of all the others, else he cannot attain to felicity. If we consider the family, the goal of which is to prepare its members to live well, there must needs be one to guide and rule whom they call the pater-familias, or his representative; according to the philosopher when he says, "Every house is ruled by the oldest." And it is his task, as Homer says, to rule over all the rest, and to impose laws on his housemates; whence the proverbial curse, "May you have a peer in your house." If we consider a district, the end of which is helpful co-operation both in persons and in appliances, one must needs be the guide of the rest, whether he be imposed upon them by another or rise to eminence out of themselves, with the consent of the rest. Else not only do they fail to attain the mutual support they aim at, but sometimes when several strive for pre-eminence, the whole district is brought to ruin. And if we consider a city, the end of which is to live well and suitably, there must be a single rule, and this not only in a rightly ordained polity, but even in a wrong one. For if it be otherwise not only is the end of civil life missed, but the very city itself ceases to be what it was. If finally we consider a special kingdom, the end of which is the same as that of the city, only with bitter assurance of tranquillity, there must be one king to rule and govern, else not only do they in the kingdom fail to reach the goal, but the kingdom itself lapses into ruin, according to that saying of the infallible truth, "every kingdom divided against itself shall be laid waste." If, then, this is so in these cases and in every other case in which a single end is aimed at, the proposition laid down above is true.

Now it is admitted that the whole human race is ordained for a single end, as was set forth before. Therefore there must be one guiding or ruling power. And this is what we mean by monarch or emperor. Thus it appears that for the well-being of the world there must be a monarchy or empire.

CHAPTER IX

. Likewise every son is well and best disposed when he follows the track of a perfect father, in so far as his proper nature allows. The human race is the son of heaven, which is most perfect in all its work, for "man is begotten by man and the sun" according to the philosopher in the second *De Naturali Auditu*.[2] Wherefore the human race is best disposed when it follows the track of heaven in so far as its proper nature allows. And since the whole heaven, in all its parts, motions, and movers, is regulated by a single motion (to wit of the *primum mobile*), and a single motor, God (as human reason apprehends in philosophy with the utmost clearness), it follows, if our syllogising is sound, that the human race is then best disposed when it is ruled on its motors and motions by a single prince as single motor, and by a single law as single motion. Wherefore it appears necessary to the well-being of the world that there should be a monarchy or single princedom, which is called empire. This reasoning Boethius sighed forth when he said:—

> *O felix hominum genus,*
> *Si vestros animos amor*
> *Quo cœlum regitur, regat!* [3]

CHAPTER XII

And the human race when most free is best disposed. This will be clear if the principle of freedom be understood. Wherefore be it known that the first principle of our freedom is freedom of choice, which many have on their lips but few in their understanding. For they get as far as saying that free choice is free judgment in matters of will; and herein they say the truth; but the import of the words is far from them, just as is the case with our teachers of logic in their constant use of certain propositions, given by way of example in logic; for instance, "A triangle has three angles equal to two right angles."

Therefore I say that judgment is the link between apprehension and appetite. For first a thing is apprehended, then when apprehended it is judged to be good or bad, and finally he who has so judged it pursues or shuns it. If, then, the judgment altogether sets the appetite in motion, and is in no measure anticipated by it, it is free. But if the judgment is moved by the appetite, which to some extent anticipates it, it cannot be free, for it does not move of itself, but is drawn captive by another. And hence it is that brutes cannot have free judgment because their judgments are always anticipated by appetite. And

---

[2] [Aristotle's *On the Nature of Hearing.*]
[3] [*Oh happy race of men, were your minds ruled by heaven-ruling love!*]

hence too it may be seen that the intellectual substances whose wills are immutable, and separated souls departing from this life in grace, do not lose their freedom of choice because of the immutability of their wills, but retain it in its most perfect and potent form.

When we see this we may further understand that this freedom (or this principle of all our freedom) is the greatest gift conferred by God on human nature; for through it we have our felicity here as men, through it we have our felicity elsewhere as deities. And if this be so, who would not agree that the human race is best disposed when it has fullest use of this principle? But it is under a monarch that it is most free. As to which we must know that this is free which exists "for the sake of itself and not of some other," as the Philosopher has it in his work, *De Simpliciter Ente*.[4] For that which exists for the sake of something else is conditioned by that for the sake of which it exists, as a road is conditioned by the goal. It is only when a monarch is reigning that the human race exists for its own sake, and not for the sake of something else. For it is only then that perverted forms of government are made straight, to wit democracies, oligarchies, and tyrannies, which force the human race into slavery (as is obvious to whosoever runs through them all), and that government is conducted by kings, aristocrats (whom they call *optimates*), and zealots for the people's liberty. For since the monarch has love of men in the highest degree, as already indicated, he will desire all men to be made good, which cannot be under perverted rulers. Whence the Philosopher in his *Politics* says, "Under a perverted government a good man is a bad citizen, but under a right one, a good man and a good citizen are convertible terms." And such right governments purpose freedom, to wit that men should exist for their own sakes. For the citizens are not there for the sake of the consuls, nor the nation for the sake of the king, but conversely, the consuls for the sake of the citizens, the king for the sake of the nation. For just as the body politic is not established for the benefit of the laws, but the laws for the benefit of the body politic, so too they who live under the law are not ordained for the benefit of the legislator, but rather he for theirs, as saith the Philosopher again in what has been left by him on the present matter. Hence it is clear that, albeit the consul or king be masters of the rest as regards the way, yet as regards the end they are their servants; and the monarch most of all, for he must assuredly be regarded as the servant of all. Hence it may begin to appear at this point how the monarch is conditioned in laying down the laws by the end set before him.

Therefore the human race is best disposed when under a monarchy. Whence it follows that for the well-being of the world the existence of a monarchy is necessary.

---

[4] [Roughly translated "On Being, as Such." That is, Aristotle's *Metaphysics*.]

CHAPTER XV

. . . It is clear, then, that everything which is good, is good in virtue of consisting in unity. And since concord, as such, is a good, it is manifest that it consists in some unity, as in its proper root. . . .

The human race when best disposed is a concord. For as a single man when best disposed both as to mind and body is a concord, and so also a house, a city, and a kingdom, so likewise is the whole human race. Therefore the human race when best disposed depends upon a unity in wills. But this unity cannot be unless there is one will dominating and ruling all the rest to oneness; inasmuch as the wills of mortals, because of the seductive delights of youth, have need of a directive principle, as the philosopher teaches in the last *Ad Nicomachum*. Nor can that one will exist unless there be a single prince of all, whose will may be the mistress and ruler of all others. Now if all the above deductions are sound, which they are, it is necessary for the best disposition of the human race that there should be a monarch in the world, and therefore for the well-being of the world that there should be a monarchy.

CHAPTER XVI

All the reasons set forth above are confirmed by a memorable experience; namely, of that state of mortal things which the Son of God, when about to become man for man's salvation, either awaited, or, when he would, produced. For if we go through all the states and periods of man, even from the fall of our first parents, which was the point at which we turned aside on our wanderings, we shall find that the world was never quiet on every side except under divus Augustus, the monarch, when there was a perfect monarchy. And that in truth the human race was then blessed in the tranquillity of universal peace is witnessed by all the historians, witnessed by illustrious poets. To this the scribe of the gentleness of Christ has likewise deigned to bear witness; and finally Paul has called that most happy state the "fulness of time." Verily the time and all temporal things were full, for no ministry to our felicity was then vacant of its minister.

But what the state of the world has been since that seamless garment first suffered rending by the nail of covetousness we may read—would that we might not also see! O race of men in what storms and losses, in what ship-wrecks must thou needs be tossed, so long as, transformed into a beast of many heads, thou strivest after many things! Thou art sick in either intellect, sick in affection. Thou dost not minister to the higher intellect by reasonings that cannot be gainsaid, nor to the lower by the aspect of experience, nor even to thy affection by the sweetness of divine persuasion, when there sounds to thee through the trumpet of the Holy Spirit, "Behold how good and how pleasant it is for brethren to dwell together in unity."

[Book II]

CHAPTER II

Whereas we have inquired concerning the truth of the first matter in dispute with such adequacy as the subject-matter allows, the truth of the second now presses for inquiry—to wit, whether it was by right that the Roman people acquired for itself the dignity of empire; and the first step of this investigation is to ascertain that truth to which the arguments of the present investigation must be reduced as to their proper principle.

Be it known then that like as art exists in three grades—in the mind of the artificer, in the instrument, and in the material informed by art—so too we may regard nature in three grades. For nature is in the mind of the first mover, which is God, and further in the heaven as in the instrument by means of which the likeness of the eternal excellence is spread over fluctuating matter. And as when the artificer is perfect and the instrument is in perfect order, any flaw that may occur in the form of art must be imputed to the material alone, so, since God realises the supreme perfection, and his instrument, the heaven, falls no way short of its due perfection (as is evident from our studies in philosophy concerning the heaven) it remains that whatsoever flaw there is in things below is a flaw on the part of the material submitted to the action of God and the heaven, and is beside the intention both of God and the active principle of nature, and of the heaven; and that whatsoever good there is in things below, since it cannot come from the matter itself, which only exists as potentiality, must come primarily from the artificer, God, and secondarily from heaven, which is the instrument of that divine art which men commonly call nature.

Hence it is clear that right, since it is good, exists, primarily, in the mind of God. And since everything that is in the mind of God is God (according to that word "What was made was life in him"), and since God supremely wills himself, it follows that right is willed by God, inasmuch as it is in him. And since in God the will and what is willed are identical, it follows further that the divine will is right itself, and hence it follows again that right as manifested in things is naught else than the similitude of the divine will. Whence it comes to pass that whatever is not consonant with the divine will cannot be right, and whatever is consonant with the divine will is right. Wherefore to ask whether anything takes place by right, though the words differ, is yet naught else than to inquire whether it takes place according to what God wills. Let this, then, be our underlying principle: that whatever God wills in the society of men is to be regarded as true and pure right.

Moreover we must remember that, as the philosopher teaches in the first *Ad Nicomachum,* "Certainty is not to be looked for in the same degree in every case, but according as the nature of the subject admits it." Wherefore it will be sufficient ground for the arguments to proceed on, under the principle we have reached, if we investigate the right of that glorious people by the aid of manifest signs and the authorities of the sages. In sooth the will of God is in itself invisible, but the invisible things of God are understood and perceived by means of things which are made. For though the seal be hidden yet does the wax stamped by it yield patent knowledge of it, hidden though it be. Nor is it marvellous if the divine will must be sought through signs, since even the human will is no otherwise perceived than by signs, save to the man himself who wills.

CHAPTER III

I affirm, then, with respect to this matter, that it was by right and not by usurpation that the Roman people vindicated to itself the office of monarch, which is called empire, over all mortals. And the first proof thereof is this. It was meet for the noblest people to be set above all others. The Roman people was the noblest. Therefore it was meet for it to be set above all others . . .

Nobilitas animi sola est atque unica virtus.[5]

CHAPTER VII

And what nature has ordained, it is right to maintain. For nature in the provision she makes does not fall short of the providence of man, else the effect would surpass the cause in excellence, which is impossible. But we perceive that when colleges are instituted, not only is the order of the colleagues with respect to each other considered by him who institutes them, but also the capacity for exercising their office. And this amounts to a consideration of the limitation of the right of the college or ordered institution, for right does not extend beyond power. Therefore nature, in what she ordains, does not fall short of this provision. Whence it is clear that nature orders things with reference to their faculties, which reference is the foundation of right laid down in things by nature. Hence it follows that the natural order in things cannot be preserved without right, since the basis of right is inseparably bound up with that order. Necessarily, therefore, the preservation of such order is right.

The Roman people was ordained by nature to command. Which is thus made clear: Just as he would fall short of the perfection of art who should

5 [*Virtue is the sole and only nobility of mind.*]

consider the final form alone, but should take no heed for the means by which
to attain to the form, so would nature if she contemplated only the universal
form of the divine similitude in the universe, and neglected the means thereto.
But nature lacks no perfection, since she is the work of the divine intelligence.
Therefore she contemplates all the means by which the final goal of her intention is approached.

Since, then, there exists a goal of the human race, which is, in its turn, a
necessary means to the accomplishment of the universal goal of nature, it
follows that nature contemplates it. Wherefore the philosopher does well to
show in the second *De Naturali Auditu* that nature always acts with a view to
the end. And since nature cannot attain this goal by means of a single man
(since the operations needful thereto are many, requiring multiplicity in the
operators), nature must of necessity produce a multiplicity of men, ordained
for diverse operations; to which, in addition to the influence from above, the
virtues and properties of places here below do much contribute. Thus we see
that not only individual men, but peoples, are some of them apt by nature
to rule and others to be subject and to serve, as the Philosopher sets forth in
what he has written *de Politicis*. And for such as these last, even as he says,
it is not only expedient to be ruled, but also just, even though they be forced
thereto.

And if these things are so, it is not to be doubted that nature ordained in the
world a place and a people for universal command; else she would have been
lacking to herself, which is impossible. Now what this place and what this
people were is sufficiently manifest from what has been said above and what
will be said below, to wit, Rome and her citizens or people. . . .

[Book III]

CHAPTER I

. . . The present question, . . . concerning which we are to make inquiry,
lies between two great lights, to wit the Roman pontiff and the Roman prince;
and we are to ask whether the authority of the Roman monarch, who is monarch of the world by right, as proved in the second book, is immediately dependent upon God; or rather on some vicar or minister of God, by whom
I understand the successor of Peter, who in very truth bears the keys of the
kingdom of heaven.

CHAPTER III

On the threshold of this investigation we must note that the truth about
the first question required explanation rather to remove ignorance than to

quell contentiousness; whereas the investigation of the second question is concerned equally with ignorance and contentiousness. For there are many things of which we are ignorant, but on which we do not dispute; for instance, the geometrician knows not how to square the circle, but does not dispute thereon; and the theologian knows not the number of the angels, yet does not dispute about it; nor does the Egyptian know aught of the civilisation of the Scythians, but he does not therefore dispute as to their civilisation.

Now the truth of this third question has to deal with such contentiousness that whereas in other cases ignorance is wont to be the cause of contentiousness, here it is rather contentiousness which is the cause of ignorance. For to men whose wills insist on flying ahead of the inspection of their reason it ever befalls that if their affections are wrong they put the light of reason behind their backs, and are led like blind men by their affections, while obstinately denying that they are blind. Whence it comes right often to pass not only that falsehood has a patrimony of her own, but that many [of her subjects] issuing from her boundaries o'errun the encampments of others, and there, understanding naught themselves are naught understood, and thus stir the wrath of some, the indignation of others, and of certain the laughter.

Well, then, there are three classes of men who chiefly fight against the truth which we are seeking.

For the supreme pontiff, the vicar of our Lord Jesus Christ and successor of Peter (to whom we owe not what is due to Christ but what is due to Peter), in zeal perchance for the keys, together with certain pastors of Christian flocks, and others who, I believe, are moved solely by zeal for mother church, oppose the truth which I am about to demonstrate; perhaps, as I have said, in zeal and not in insolence.

But there are others, whose stubborn greed has put out the light of reason, who declare themselves sons of the church, whereas they are of their father the devil, who not only stir up contentiousness with respect to this question, but hating the very name of the most sacred princedom, would impudently deny the first principles of the former investigations and of this.

There is also a third set whom they call the Decretalists, strangers and ignorant in every kind of theology and philosophy, who carp at the empire, laying all their weight upon their Decretals (which, for the matter of that, I hold to be worthy of reverence), and setting their hopes, I take it, on the supremacy of the same. And no wonder; for I have heard one of them declare and volubly maintain that the traditions of the church are the foundation of the faith; may which impious thought be extirpated from the minds of men by those whom the world doubts not to have believed, before the traditions of the church were, in Christ the Son of God, either to come or present or having already suffered; and believing to have hoped, and hoping to have glowed with love, and so glowing to have become co-heirs with him.

And that such may be utterly excluded from the present wrestling ground be it noted that there is certain scripture, antecedent to the church, certain contemporaneous with the church and certain posterior to the church.

Before the church are the Old and New Testaments, which were "given for eternity," as the prophet says; for this is what the church means when she says to the Bridegroom, "Draw me after thee."

With the church came those venerable chief councils with which no believer doubts that Christ was present, since we have it that he himself, when about to ascend to heaven, said to his disciples, "Behold, I am with you through all the days until the end of the world," as Matthew bears witness. There are likewise the scriptures of the doctors, Augustine and others; and he who doubts that they were aided by the Holy Spirit has either never seen their fruits, or if he has seen, has by no means tasted them.

After the church came those traditions which they call Decretals, which, indeed, though they are to be revered because of the apostolic authority, should indubitably be held inferior to the fundamental scripture, since Christ blamed the priests for the contrary. For when they asked him, "Why do your disciples transgress the tradition of the elders?" (for they neglected the washing of hands), Christ as Matthew testifies, answered them, "And why do ye transgress the commandment of God for the sake of your tradition?" Wherein he sufficiently indicates that the tradition was of less account.

But if the traditions of the Church are subsequent of the church, as has been set forth, then of necessity authority accrues not to the church from the traditions, but to the traditions from the church. And they who have naught save the traditions to allege must be shut out, as already said, from this wrestling ground. For they who are pursuing this truth must proceed, as they track it, on ground of those scriptures from which the authority of the church flows.

These, then, being thus excluded, we must likewise exclude others, who, though covered with the feathers of crows, yet prank themselves as white sheep in the flock of the Lord. These are the sons of impiety who, that they may follow up their own infamies, prostitute their mother, drive out their brethren, and will not hear of a judge. For why should arguments be sought for them when their greed prevents them from seeing even the first principles?

Wherefore there remains only the struggle with those who are led by a certain zeal towards mother church to overlook the precise truth which we are investigating. And with them, relying upon the reverence which a dutiful son owes to his father, which a dutiful son owes to his mother, I—in duty towards Christ, in duty towards the church, in duty towards the pastor, in duty towards all who profess the Christian religion—enter in the cause of truth upon the contention of this book.

CHAPTER IX

They also take that word in Luke which Peter utters to Christ when he says, "Lo here are two swords," and they say that by those two swords the two regimens aforesaid are meant; and since Peter said they were where he was, that is with him, they argue that, in authority, those two regimens abide with Peter's successor.

And we must proceed against this by denying the sense on which the argument is built; for they say that those two swords which Peter produced import the two aforesaid regimens, which must be flatly denied, in the first place because such an answer would not have agreed with the meaning of Christ, and secondly because Peter, after his impulsive manner, answered merely to the obvious aspect of things.

Now that his answer would not have agreed with the meaning of Christ will be manifest if we consider the words that precede and the occasion of the words. For it must be borne in mind that this saying was on the day of the supper, wherefore, higher up, Luke begins thus: "Now the day of unleavened bread was come, on which the passover must needs be slain"; and at this supper Christ had already spoken of his approaching passion in which he must be parted from his disciples. It must also be noted that when those words were spoken all the twelve disciples were together; whence, shortly after the words just quoted, Luke says, "And when the hour was come he lay down to meat and the twelve apostles with him." And thence without a break in the conversation he comes to these words, "When I sent you forth without scrip and purse and sandals, was aught lacking to you? And they said, no. Wherefore he said to them: But now whosoever has a scrip let him take it, and likewise his purse; and whosoever has not a sword, let him sell his coat and buy one." Wherein the meaning of Christ is clear enough, for he did not say "buy (if we have them not) two swords" but rather "twelve," since it was to the twelve disciples that he said "let him who has not buy," that each of them might have one. And he said this, moreover, forewarning them of the oppression and contempt that was to come upon them; as though he should say, "As long as I was with you ye were received. Now ye will be chased away. Wherefore it behoves you to make ready even those things which I erst forbade you, for there is need." Therefore if the answer of Peter, made to those words, had borne the meaning they assign to it, it would at any rate not have corresponded to the meaning of Christ; and Christ would have rebuked him for it, as he often did when he answered beside the mark. Here, however, he did not so, but acquiesced, saying to him "it is enough," as though he should say, "I mention it, because of your need; but if you cannot have one each, then two may suffice. . . ."

But if, after all, those words of Christ and Peter are to be taken typically, they must not be applied to the point which these of whom I speak would have, but must be taken to refer to that sword of which Matthew writes as follows: "Think not that I am come to send peace upon the earth. I am come not to send peace, but a sword; for I am come to set a man against his father," and the rest. And this, indeed, comes to pass both in word and deed; wherefore Luke said *ad Theophilum* "What Jesus began to do and to teach." Such was the sword which Christ bid them buy, and which Peter answered was already there twofold. For they were ready both for words and deeds, whereby to do what Christ declared that he himself had come to do with the sword, as we have shown.

CHAPTER X

It is further urged by some that the Emperor Constantine, when cleansed of his leprosy at the intercession of Sylvester, who was then supreme pontiff, granted the seat of empire, to wit Rome, to the church, together with many other dignities of the empire. Whence they argue that no one can assume those dignities thenceforth except he receive them from the church, whose they say they are. And from this it would certainly follow that the one authority is dependent on the other, as they would have it.

Having therefore set out and refuted the arguments which seemed to have their roots in the divine utterances, it remains to set forth and refute those which are rooted in the doings of the Romans and in human reason; the first of which is the one that stands above, the syllogism running thus: "The things that are the church's none may have by right save from the church," and this is granted. "The Roman regimen is the church's. Therefore none may have it of right save from the church." And the minor they prove by what has been indicated above as to Constantine.

This minor, then, I deny; and as to their proof, I say that it has no force, because Constantine had no power to alienate the imperial dignity, nor had the church power to receive it.

And if they persist in their objection, my contention may be thus proved. No one is at liberty to do, in virtue of the office deputed to him, things that are counter to that office, else the same thing in the same capacity would be counter to itself, which is impossible. But it is counter to the office deputed to the emperor to rend the empire, since it is his office to hold the human race subject to unity in willing and diswilling, as may easily be seen in the first of this present. Wherefore to rend the empire is not competent to the emperor. If therefore certain dignities were (as they say) alienated from the empire by Constantine and ceded to the power of the church, the seamless tunic was rent, which not even they durst rend who pierced Christ, very God, with the lance.

Moreover, like as the church hath its own foundation, so too hath the empire; for the foundation of the church is Christ, whence the Apostle, *Ad Corinthos,* "Other foundation can no man lay than that is laid, which is Christ Jesus." He is the rock on which the church is built; but the foundation of the empire is human right. Now I say that like as the church may not contradict its own foundation, but must ever rest upon it, according to that passage of the *Canticles,* "Who is this that cometh up from the desert, flowing with delights, leaning on her beloved?" so neither may the empire do anything counter to human right. But it were counter to human right should the empire destroy itself. Therefore the empire may not destroy itself. Since, then, to rend the empire were to destroy it (inasmuch as the empire consists in the unity of universal monarchy), it is manifest that he who wields the authority of the empire may not rend the empire. And that it is counter to human right to destroy the empire is manifest from what has gone before.

Moreover, every jurisdiction is prior to its judge, for the judge is appointed to the jurisdiction, and not conversely. But the empire is a jurisdiction embracing every temporal jurisdiction in its scope, therefore it is prior to its judge, who is the emperor, because the emperor is appointed to it, and not conversely. Whence it is clear that the emperor, as emperor, cannot change it, since it is the source of his being what he is. Now I say thus: Either he was emperor when he is said to have made the grant to the church, or he was not. And if not, it is obvious that he had no power of making grants with respect to the empire. If he was, then, since such a grant was to the prejudice of his jurisdiction, he, as emperor, had no power to make it.

Further, if one emperor had power to tear never so little a piece from the jurisdiction of the empire, so on the same showing had another also. And since the temporal jurisdiction is finite, and any finite thing can be used up by finite subtractions, it would follow that the prime jurisdiction might be reduced to nothing, which is contrary to reason.

And again, since he who "confers" is in the relation of agent, and he on whom "it is conferred" in the relation of patient (as the philosopher has it in the fourth *Ad Nicomachum*), in order for a grant to be legitimate there must be the due disposition not only of him who grants but of him to whom the grant is made. For it seems that the acts of the agents inhere in a suitably disposed patient. But the church was entirely undisposed for receiving temporal things, in virtue of express prohibitive command, as we learn from Matthew, thus: "Possess not gold nor silver, nor money in your girdles, nor purse for your journey," and the rest. For, although we find in Luke a relaxation of the precept with respect to certain things, yet nowhere have I been able to find that permission was given to the church, after that prohibition, to possess gold and silver. Wherefore if the church had no power to receive, then even if Constantine, as far as he was concerned, had power to give, still the action was impossible because the patient had not the due disposition. It is evident, therefore, that neither could the church receive by way of possession, nor could the other grant by way of alienation. The emperor, however, had power to depute a patrimony or the like to the guardianship of the church, the superior dominion always remaining intact, its unity not admitting of division. The vicar of God, too, might receive, not as possessor, but as dispenser of the fruits for the poor of Christ, on behalf of the church; as it is known the apostles did.

CHAPTER XIV

Further, if the church had power to give the Roman prince his authority, she would either have it from God, or from herself, or from some emperor, or from the universal consent of mortals, or at least the majority of them. There is no other crevice through which this power could have flowed to the church. But she has it not from any of these. Therefore she has not the said power at all.

Now that she has it not from any of these is shown as follows. If she had received it from God, it would have been either by divine or by natural law (for what is received from nature is received from God, though the proposition cannot be converted). But it is not by natural law; for nature imposes laws only on her own effects, since God cannot be insufficient where he produces aught into being without secondary agents. Wherefore since the church is not an effect of nature but of God, who says, "On this rock will I build my church," and elsewhere, "I have finished the work thou gavest me to do," it is manifest that nature did not give laws to her.

But neither is it by divine law, for every divine law is held in the bosom of the two Testaments. In which bosom I cannot find that anxiety or care concerning temporal things was commended to the priesthood, either former or latter. Nay, rather I find that the former priests were expressly excluded therefrom, as is plain from those of God *Ad Moysen,* and the like of the latter priests by those of Christ *Ad Discipulos.* But they could not have been relieved of this care if the authority of the temporal regimen had been derived from the priesthood, since at any rate anxiety would press upon them concerning due provision in granting the authorisation, and afterwards in continuous watching lest he whom they had authorised should wander from the path of right.

Now that she did not receive it from herself is easily shown. There is naught that can give what it has not got. Wherefore everything that effects anything must already be in act that which it contemplates effecting, as is seen in what is written *De Simpliciter Ente*. But it is clear that if the church gave herself that virtue she cannot have had it before she gave it; and thus she would have given herself what she had not got, which is impossible.

And that she did not receive it from any emperor is sufficiently plain from what has been set forth above.

And that she had it not from the consent of all, or of the majority of men, who doubts? since not only all the Asiatics and Africans but the greater part of those dwelling in Europe would repudiate the thought. Nay! it is wearisome to bring proofs of things absolutely manifest.

CHAPTER XV

Again, that which is against the nature of anything is not in the number of its virtues, since the virtues of each thing follow its nature, for the attainment of its end. But virtue to authorise rule over our mortality is contrary to the nature of the church. Therefore it is not of the number of her virtues.

To prove the minor be it known that the nature of the church is the form of the church. For though nature is predicated of material and of form, yet it is more properly predicated of form as is shown in the *De Naturali Auditu*. But the form of the church is no other than the life of Christ, embraced both in his words and in his deeds. For his life was the idea and exemplar of the church militant, especially of pastors, and most of all of the supreme pastor, whose it is to feed the lambs and sheep. Whence he himself in John, when bequeathing the form of his life, says, "I have given you an example that as I have done to you so should ye also do." And specifically to Peter when he had committed to him the office of pastor, as we learn from the same source, he said, "Peter, follow thou me." But Christ in the presence of Pilate renounced any such regimen as that in question. "My kingdom," said he, "is not of this world. If my kingdom were of this world, my servants would fight that I should not be given over to the Jews. But now my kingdom is not hence."

Which is not so to be understood as though Christ, who is God, were not lord of this kingdom; since the Psalmist says, "For the sea is his and he made it. And his hands established the dry land"; but that as the exemplar of the church he had no charge of this kingdom. As though a golden seal were to say of itself, "I am not the standard in any class," which saying would not hold concerning it in as far as it is gold, since as gold it is the standard in the class of metals; but it holds concerning it in so far as it is a definite stamp capable of being received by impression.

It is therefore the formal principle of the church to say and to feel that same. And to say or feel the opposite is obviously counter to its form, or to its nature, which is the same thing. Whence we gather that the power of authorising this kingdom is counter to the nature of the church, for contrariety in an opinion or a saying follows from contrariety in the thing said or opined; even as truth or falsehood in speech is caused by the being or non-being of the thing, as the teaching of the *Predicaments* shows us. It has therefore been sufficiently shown by the preceding arguments, which lead to an incongruity, that the authority of the empire by no means depends on the church.

CHAPTER XVI

Although in the preceding chapter it has been shown by reduction to an incongruity that the authority of the empire is not caused by the authority of the supreme pontiff, yet it has not been altogether proved that it depends immediately on God, save by consequential inference; for the consequential inference is that if it does not depend on the vicar of God it depends on God. And, therefore, for the perfect establishment of the proposition, we must prove by direct demonstration that the emperor or monarch of the world is in immediate relation to the Prince of the universe, who is God.

Now to understand this be it known that man alone of beings holds a midplace between corruptible and incorruptible; wherefore he is rightly likened by the philosophers to the horizon which is between two hemispheres. For man, if considered after either essential part, to wit soul and body, is corruptible if considered only after the one, to wit the body, but if after the other, to wit the soul, he is incorruptible. Wherefore the Philosopher says well of the soul (in that it is incorruptible), in the second *De Anima*,[6] "And it alone is capable of being separated from the corruptible as perpetual."

If man, then, is a kind of mean between corruptible and incorruptible things, since every mean savours of the nature of the extremes, it is necessary that man should savour of either nature. And since every nature is ordained to a certain end it follows that there must be a twofold end of man, so that like as he alone amongst all beings partakes of corruptibility and incorruptibility, so he alone amongst all beings should be ordained for two final goals, of which the one should be his goal as a corruptible being, and the other as an incorruptible.

That unutterable providence, then, has set two ends before man to be contemplated by him; the blessedness, to wit. of this life. which consists in the

[6] [Aristotle's *On the Soul*.]

exercise of his proper power and is figured by the terrestrial paradise, and the blessedness of eternal life, which consists in the fruition of the divine aspect, to which his proper power may not ascend unless assisted by the divine light. And this blessedness is given to be understood by the celestial paradise.

Now to these two as to diverse ends it behoves him to come by diverse means. For to the first we attain by the teachings of philosophy, following them by acting in accordance with the moral and intellectual virtues. To the second by spiritual teachings which transcend human reason, as we follow them by acting according to the theological virtues; faith, hope, to wit, and charity. Now albeit these ends and means are made plain to us, the one by human reason (which the philosophers have wholly brought to our knowledge), the other by the Holy Spirit (which hath revealed the truth that is beyond our nature, but yet needful to us, by means of the prophets and sacred writers and by Jesus Christ the Son of God co-eternal with the said Spirit, and by his disciples), yet would human greed cast them behind were not men, like horses going astray in their brutishness, held in the way by bit and rein.

Wherefore man had need of a twofold directive power according to his twofold end, to wit, the supreme pontiff, to lead the human race, in accordance with things revealed, to eternal life; and the emperor, to direct the human race to temporal felicity in accordance with the teachings of philosophy. And since none, or few (and they with extremest difficulty) could reach this port, were not the waves of seductive greed assuaged and the human race left free to rest in the tranquillity of peace, this is that mark on which he who has charge of the world and is called the Roman prince should chiefly fix his mind, to wit, that on this threshing floor of mortality life should be lived in freedom and in peace. And since the disposition of this world follows the disposition that inheres in the circulation of the heavens, in order to accomplish this end, namely, that the charters which conduce to liberty and peace should be applied by the ruler in question with due reference to time and place, it is needful that they should be dispensed by him who looks upon the whole disposition of the heavens presently. And that is he only who so preordained that disposition that by it he in his providence might weave all things together, each in its due order.

But if this be so, God alone chooses, he alone confirms, since he hath no superior. Whence we may further gather that neither they who now are, nor such others of any kind as have ever been called the electors, should so be called; but rather should they be reckoned the heralds of divine providence. Whence it comes to pass that they to whom is granted the honour of making the proclamation, are subject from time to time to dissent; because either all or some of them are clouded by the mists of greed, and discern not the face of the divine dispensation.

Thus, then, it is plain that the authority of the temporal monarch descends upon him without any mean from the fountain of universal authority. Which fountain, one in the citadel of its simplicity, flows into manifold channels out of the abundance of its excellence.

And now already methinks I have sufficiently reached the mark I set before myself. For the truth of that question has been searched out in which was asked whether the office of monarch were necessary to the well-being of the world, and of that in which was asked whether the Roman people acquired empire for itself by right, and also of that last question in which was asked whether the monarch's authority depended from God, or immediately from some other. The truth concerning which last question is not to be received in such narrow sense as that the Roman prince is subordinate in naught to the Roman pontiff; inasmuch as mortal felicity is in a certain sense ordained with reference to immortal felicity. Let Cæsar, therefore, observe that reverence to Peter which a first-born son should observe to a father, so that illuminated by the light of paternal grace he may with greater power irradiate the world, over which he is set by him alone who is ruler of all things spiritual and temporal.

III THE MEDIEVAL HERITAGE: ECONOMY, SOCIETY, POLITY

THE MANOR

I N RECENT YEARS economic historians have turned increasingly to local studies
to correct the old notion of the "typical" manor, and it has come to be realized
that these agrarian units of the Middle Ages displayed wide variations in
extent, layout, practice, and internal relationships. Geographical factors or racial
origins were important determinants, and much might depend on the nature of
the lordship—whether it rested with, say, an ecclesiastical corporation, a great
baron, or a poor and relatively unintelligent knight. All or most of these diverse
estates, however, exhibited certain common features and practices which the following documents will help to illustrate.

After the death of Charlemagne in 814 the vigorous, united, and relatively
civilized empire of western (Catholic) Christendom which he had established was
rent by internal fissures and exposed to external attacks which threatened to over-
whelm it. The pagan Northmen of Scandinavia, a new horde of Magyar-Huns
from the east, a confident Islam all subjected the western empire to an ordeal
which to its contemporaries appeared catastrophic and which made more grave
the chaotic conditions, illustrated below in *The Annals of Xanten,* that constantly
threatened the attempts to use the manor as a basis for security and order in the
ninth century.

The *Capitulare de Villis,* probably composed by Louis the Pious, king of
Aquitaine, shortly before 800, is a list of instructions for the use of stewards on
the royal properties of Carolingian Gaul. It reveals such persistent manorial concerns as the insuring of justice and fair and accustomed treatment for the inhabitants, the proper maintenance of supply for the lord, and the ever-present danger
of the defaulting or dishonest steward.

This care for administration was probably not matched in Europe for many
years after the collapse of the highly centralized Carolingian empire. It was on
the ecclesiastical estates that the highest efficiency was first attained—with a
probable corollary of a harder life for the serf—and, because the records for the
earlier Middle Ages come almost exclusively from such estates, our views of that
period are probably distorted. In England it is not until the thirteenth century
that one begins to find, under royal pressure for increased contributions in military
service or money, an equivalent concern for estate management among the lay
lords. One finds in this period an increasing number of surveys and records of
administration, drawn up to give the lord a means of calculating his resources and
of checking his subordinates. The fourteenth-century survey, or "extent," given
below is from the manor of Bernehorne, Sussex, in the south of England. A group
of inhabitants especially likely to know the facts gave sworn testimony as to the
extent, types, and value of the land; this was set down, followed by a record of
the tenants and of the land held by each with the payments and services due the
lord. The wide variation in status and dues indicates the difficulty of generalization
in a situation which was becoming continually more complex.

Like every unit of society in the Middle Ages, the manor centered in a court, which dealt not only with economic questions like the possession and use made of a holding or a default on services, but with police matters as well. Like the public courts of the local government areas of hundred and shire in England, the manor courts for centuries kept no records; lords began, however, also in the thirteenth century, to require that proceedings be set down in rolls. The examples given here comes from the rolls of the Abbey of Bec.

The *Capitulare de Villis* has been translated from the text given in the *Monumenta Germaniae Historica: Leges II* (1883), Vol. I. J. H. Robinson's translation of *The Annals of Xanten* is from his *Readings in European History,* Vol. I (Boston, Ginn and Co., 1904). The translation of the Bernehorne extent is published in the University of Pennsylvania *Translations and Reprints,* III, No. 5 (1897), 7–11. F. W. Maitland's translation of the pleas of the manor of the Abbey of Bec is from his edition for the Selden Society of *Select Pleas in Manorial and Other Seignorial Courts* (1889), I, 19–20, 43–46. In each case the original text is in Latin.

CAPITULARE DE VILLIS

1. WE WISH that our estates which we have instituted to serve our needs discharge their services to us entirely and to no other men.

2. Our people shall be well taken care of and reduced to poverty by no one.

3. Our stewards shall not presume to put our people to their own service, either to force them to work, to cut wood, or to do any other task for them. And they shall accept no gifts from them, either horse, ox, cow, pig, sheep, little pig, lamb, or anything else excepting bottles of wine or other beverage, garden produce, fruits, chickens, and eggs.

4. If any of our people does injury to us either by stealing or by some other offense he shall make good the damage and for the remainder of the legal satisfaction he shall be punished by whipping, with the exception of homicide and arson cases which are punishable by fines. The stewards, for injuries of our people to other men, shall endeavor to secure justice according to the practices which they have, as is the law. Instead of paying fines our people, as we have said, shall be whipped. Freemen who live in our domains or estates shall make good the injuries they do according to their law and the fines which they have incurred shall be paid for our use either in cattle or in equivalent value.

5. When our stewards ought to see that our work is done—the sowing, plowing, harvesting, cutting of hay, or gathering of grapes—let each one at the proper season and in each and every place organize and oversee what is to be done that it may be done well. If a steward shall not be in his district

or can not be in some place let him choose a good substitute from our people or another in high repute to direct our affairs that they may be successfully accomplished. And he shall diligently see to it that a trustworthy man is delegated to take care of this work.

6. We wish our stewards to give a tithe of all our products to the churches on our domains and that the tithe not be given to the churches of another except to those entitled to it by ancient usage. And our churches shall not have clerics other than our own, that is, of our people or our palace.

7. Each steward shall perform his services fully, just as it has been prescribed, and if the necessity should arise that more must be done then he shall determine whether he should increase the service or the day-work.

8. Our stewards shall take care of our vines in their district and cultivate them well. And they shall put the wine in good vessels and carefully see to it that none is lost. And other required wine which is not from our vines they shall buy for provisioning the royal estates. And when they have bought more than is needed for this provisioning they shall inform us that we can let them know what is to be done with it. For they shall put the product of our vines to our use. The wine which those persons on our estates pay as rent shall be put in our cellars.

9. We wish that each steward in his district have measures of the *modius, sextarius,* the *situla* of eight *sextarii,* and the *corbus,* the same as we have in our palace.

10. Our mayors, foresters, stablemen, cellarers, deans, toll-collectors, and other officers shall do the regular and fixed labor and pay the due of pigs for their holdings and fulfill well their offices in return for the manual labor remitted them. And if any mayor holds a benefice he shall send his representative so that the manual labor and other services will be performed for him.

11. No steward shall take lodging for his own need or for his dogs from our people or from those in the forests.

12. No steward shall maintain at the expense of anyone else our hostages placed on our estates.

13. The stewards shall take good care of the stallions and not allow them to remain in one pasture too long lest they damage it. And if there should be any unsound or too old or about to die they shall inform us in good time before the season for putting them with the mares.

14. They shall take good care of our mares and separate them from the colts at the right time. And when the fillies increase in number they shall also be separated to form a new herd.

15. Our stewards shall have our foals sent to the palace in the winter at the Feast of Saint Martin.

16. We wish that our stewards fully perform in the manner established for them whatever we or the queen or our officers, the seneschal or the butler, in our name or that of the queen command. If anyone shall not do this through negligence he shall abstain from drink from the time that it is made known to him until he comes into our presence or that of the queen and seeks pardon from us. And if the steward is with the army, on guard duty, or on a mission or otherwise engaged and he commands his assistants to do something and they fail to do it, then they shall come afoot to the palace and abstain from food and drink until they have given their reasons for not doing it. Then they shall receive their sentence, a whipping or whatever we or the queen deem appropriate.

17. Each steward shall have as many men taking care of the bees for our use as he has estates in his district.

18. At our mills the stewards shall have hens and geese according to the nature of the mill or as many more as is possible.

19. In our barns on the chief estates they shall have at least 100 chickens and 30 geese and on our lesser estates at least 50 chickens and 12 geese.

20. Each steward shall have the produce [of the fowl] brought always in abundance to the manor every year and besides shall inspect it three or four or more times.

21. Each steward shall have fish-ponds on our estates where they were before and if it is possible to enlarge them, he shall do so. Where there were none before and it is now possible to have them let them be constructed.

22. Those who hold vines from us shall have no less than three or four circles of grapes for our use.

23. On each of our estates the stewards shall have cow-barns, pigsties, sheep folds, and stables for goats, as many as possible, and never be without them. And they shall further have for performing their services cows furnished by our serfs so that our barns and teams are not in the least diminished by the services of work on our demesne. And when they are charged with furnishing food they shall have lame but healthy oxens and cows, and horses that are not mangy, and other healthy animals. They shall not on that account strip, as we have said, the cow-barns or the plough-beasts.

24. Each steward shall be responsible that whatever ought to be supplied for our table is all good and excellent and prepared carefully and cleanly. And each steward shall have grain for two meals for each day of the service that he is charged with supplying our table. Similarly the other provisions shall be good in all respects, the flour as well as the meat.

25. The stewards shall make known on the first of September whether or not there is pasturage for the hogs.

26. The mayors shall not have more land in their administration than they can get about and oversee in one day.

27. Our houses shall constantly have fire and watch service that they may be safe. And when royal envoys or legates are coming to or leaving the palace, in no wise shall they exercise the right of bed and board in our manor houses except by our special order or that of the queen. But the count in his district or those persons who have been accustomed of old to caring for envoys and legates shall continue to do so as before. And pack-horses and other necessary things shall be provided in the customary fashion that they may come to the palace or depart in a fashion befitting them.

28. We wish that every year in Lent on Palm Sunday, which is called Hosanna Sunday, our stewards carefully render according to our instructions the money arising from the products of our land after we know for the particular year what our income is.

29. Each steward shall see to it that anyone of our people who have cases to plead shall not of necessity have to come to us so that he will not lose through negligence days on which he ought to be working. And if one of our serfs has some rights to claim outside our lands, his master shall do all that he can to secure justice for him. In case the serf shall not be able to get justice his master shall not permit him to exhaust himself in his efforts but shall see to it that the matter is made known to us by himself or by his representative.

30. Of those things that our stewards ought to provide for our needs, we wish them to put aside all the products due us from them, and what must be placed in the wagons for the army, taking it from the homes as well as from the herdsmen and that they know how much they have reserved for this purpose.

31. They shall set aside each year what they ought to give as food and maintenance to the workers entitled to it and to the women working in the women's quarters and shall give it fully at the right time and make known to us what they have done with it and where they got it.

32. Each steward shall see to it that he always has the very best seed by purchase or otherwise.

33. After the above things have been set aside and after the sowing and other works have been done, all that remains of all the products shall be preserved until we give word to what extent they shall be sold or stored according to our order.

34. At all times it is to be seen to with diligence that whatever is worked upon or made with the hands such as lard, smoked meat, salted meat, newly salted meat, wine, vinegar, mulberry wine, cooked wine, fermentations,

mustard, cheese, butter, malt, beer, mead, honey, wax, and flour shall be prepared or made with the greatest cleanliness.

35. We wish that fat be made of the fat sheep and pigs. Moreover the stewards shall have in each estate not less than two fattened oxen either there to be made into fat or to be sent to us.

36. Our woods and forests shall be well taken care of and where there shall be a place for a clearing let it be cleared. Our stewards shall not allow the fields to become woods and where there ought to be woods they shall not allow anyone to cut too much or damage them. And they shall look carefully after our wild beasts in the forests and also take care of the gos-hawks and sparrow-hawks reserved for our use. They shall collect diligently our tax for the use of our forests and if our stewards or our mayors or their men put their pigs for fattening in our forests they shall be the first to pay the tenth of them to give a good example so that thereafter the other men will pay the tenth in full.

37. The stewards shall keep our fields and cultivated lands in good shape and care for the meadows at the right time.

38. They shall always have sufficient fat geese and chickens for our use when they ought to provide it or send it to us.

39. We wish that the stewards collect the chickens and eggs which the lesser officials and the holders of *mansi* pay each year and when they are not needed that they have them sold.

40. Each steward shall always have on our estates for the sake of adorn-ment unusual birds, peacocks, pheasants, ducks, pigeons, partridges, and turtledoves.

41. The buildings on our estates and the fences which enclose them shall be well taken care of and the stables and kitchens, bake-houses and presses shall be carefully ordered so that the workers in our service can perform their duties fittingly and very cleanly.

42. Each manor shall have in the store-room counterpanes, bolsters, pillows, bedclothes, table and bench covers, vessels of brass, lead, iron, and wood, andirons, chains, pot-hooks, adzes, axes, augurs, knives, and all sorts of tools so that it will not be necessary to seek them elsewhere or to borrow them. And the stewards shall be responsible that the iron instruments sent to the army are in good condition and when they are returned that they are put back into the store-room.

43. For our women's work-shops the stewards shall provide the materials at the right time as it has been established, that is flax, wool, woad, vermilion dye, madder, wool-combs, teasels, soap, grease, vessels and the other lesser things which are necessary there.

44. Of the minor foods two-thirds shall be sent for our service each year, vegetables as well as fish, cheese, butter, honey, mustard, vinegar, millet, panic, dried and fresh herbs, radishes, and turnips; similarly wax, soap, and other lesser things. Whatever is left shall be made known to us in an inventory as we have said above. The stewards shall by no means neglect to do this as they have up to now because we wish to check by the two-thirds sent to us what that third is which remains.

45. Each steward shall have good workmen in his district—iron-workers, goldsmiths, silversmiths, leather-workers, turners, carpenters, shield-makers, fishermen, fowlers or falconers, soap-makers, brewers who know how to make beer, cider, perry or any other beverage fit to drink, bakers who can make bread for our needs, net-makers who are skilled in making nets for hunting as well as fishing or for taking birds, and other workmen whose listing would be a lengthy matter.

46. They shall take good care of our walled game preserves which the people call parks and always repair them in time and on no account delay so that it becomes necessary to rebuild them. They shall do the same for all the buildings.

47. Our hunters and falconers and other servitors who attend us zealously in the palace shall receive assistance on our estates in carrying out what we or the queen have ordered by our letters when we send them on any of our affairs, or when the seneschal or butler instructs them to do anything on our authority.

48. The wine-presses on our estates shall be well taken care of. The stewards shall see to it that no one presumes to press our grapes with his feet but that all is done cleanly and honestly.

49. The women's quarters, that is, their houses, heated rooms, and sitting-rooms, shall be well ordered and have good fences around them and strong gates that our work may be done well.

50. Each steward shall see to it that there are as many horses in one stable as ought to be there and as many attendants as should be with them. And those stablemen who are free and hold benefices in that district shall live off their benefices. Similarly if they are men of the domain who hold *mansi* they shall live off them. Those who do not have such shall receive maintenance from the demesne.

51. Each steward shall see to it that in no manner wicked men conceal our seed under the ground or do otherwise with the result that our harvests are smaller. And likewise, concerning other misdeeds, they shall watch them so that they can do no harm.

52. We wish that our stewards render justice to our *coloni* and serfs and to

the *coloni* living on our estates, to the different men fully and entirely such as they are due.

53. Each steward shall see to it that our men in their districts in no way become robbers or evil-doers.

54. Each steward shall see to it that our people work well at their tasks and do not go wandering off to markets.

55. We wish that whatever our stewards have sent, supplied, or set aside for our use they shall record in an inventory; whatever they have dispensed in another; and what is left they shall also make known to us in an inventory.

56. Each steward shall hold frequent audiences in his district, administer justice, and see to it that our peoples live uprightly.

57. If any of our serfs wishes to say anything to us about our affairs over and above his steward, the steward shall not obstruct the means of his coming to us. If the steward knows that his assistants wish to come to the palace to speak against him then he shall make known to the palace the arguments against them so that their denunciations in our ears may not engender disgust. Accordingly we wish to know whether they come from necessity or without sufficient cause.

58. When our pups are committed to the stewards to be raised, the steward shall feed them at his own expense or entrust them to his assistants, that is to the mayors and deans or to the cellarers, who shall feed them well at their own expense unless it happens that by our order or that of the queen they are to be fed on our estate at our expense. In that case the steward shall send a man for this work who will feed them well. And he shall set aside what is to be fed them so that it will not be necessary for him to go to the kennels every day.

59. Each steward when he should give service shall send every day three *librae* of wax and eight *sextaria* of soap; besides this he shall do his best to send six *librae* of wax wherever we shall be with out attendants on the Feast of Saint Andrew; he shall do likewise at Mid-Lent.

60. On no account shall mayors be selected from the powerful men but from those of middling estate who are trustworthy.

61. Each steward when he should give service shall have his malt brought to the palace and at the same time have the master brewers come who are to make good beer there.

62. That we may know what and how much of everything we have, each steward every year at Christmas shall report those of our revenues which they hold, everything differentiated clearly and orderly. That is, an accounting of the land cultivated with the oxen which our ploughmen drive and that which is cultivated by the holders of *mansi* who owe us labor-service; of

the payments of pigs, the taxes, the income from judgments and fines and from the beasts taken in our forests without our permission and from the other compositions; an accounting of the mills, forests, fields, bridges, and ships; of the free men and the hundred-men who owe service for parts of our domain; of the markets, vineyards and of those who pay us wine; of the hay, firewood, torches, planks and other lumber; of the income from the waste-land; of the vegetables, millet, panic, wool, flax, and hemp; of the fruit of the trees, of the big and little nuts, of the graftings of various trees, of the gardens, turnips, fishponds, hides, skins and horns; of the honey, wax, fat, tallow, and soap; of the mulberry wine, cooked wine, mead, and vinegar; of the beer, new and old wine, new and old grain, chickens and eggs, and geese; of the fishermen, smiths, shield-makers and leather-workers; of the troughs, boxes, and cases; of the turners and saddlers; of the forges and mines, that is iron, lead, and other mines; of those paying taxes; and of the colts and fillies.

63. Of all the above mentioned things nothing that we require shall seem hard to our stewards for we wish the stewards to require them from their assistants in the same fashion without any hardship. And all things which any man shall have in his house or on his estates our stewards ought also to have on our estates.

64. Our carts which accompany the army, that is, the war-carts, shall be well-constructed, and their coverings be good, with hides on top and so sown together that if the necessity of swimming waters should arise they can cross rivers without any water getting to the provisions inside and in this fashion our things may, as we said, get across without damage. And we wish that flour for our use be put in each cart, that is 12 *modii,* and that they put in those in which wine is sent 12 *modii* of our measure. In each cart let them have a shield, a lance, a quiver, and a bow.

65. The fish in our fish-ponds shall be sold and others put in their place so that they may always have fish in them. However, when we are not coming to our estates they shall be sold and our stewards shall dispose of them to our advantage.

66. The stewards shall report to us the number of male and female goats and their horns and skins; and they shall bring to us annually newly salted cuts of fat goats.

67. The stewards shall inform us about any vacant *mansi* or any newly acquired serfs if they have any in their district for whom they have no place.

68. We wish that each steward always have ready good barrels bound with iron which they can send to the army or to the palace and that the stewards do not make containers of leather.

69. The stewards at all times shall report to us how many wolves each one has taken and shall send the skins to us. And in the month of May they shall hunt down and destroy the whelps with poison, traps, pits, and dogs.

70. We wish that the stewards have all sorts of plants in the garden, namely, lilies, roses, fenugreek, costmary, sage, rue, southernwood, cucumbers, pumpkins, squash, kidney-beans, cumin, rosemary, caraway, chick-peas, squill, gladiolus, dragon-arum, anise, colosynth, heliotrope, spicknel, seseli, lettuce, fennel-flower, rocket, garden cress, burdock, penny-royal, horse-parsley, parsley, celery, lovage, juniper, dill, sweet-fennel, endive, dittany, mustard, savory, water-mint, garden mint, apple-mint, tansy, catnip, centaury, garden-poppy, beets, hazel-wort, marshmallows, tree-hibiscus, mallows, carrots, parsnip, garden-orach, amaranth, kohlrabi, cabbages, onions, chives, leeks, radishes, shallots, cibols, garlic, madder, teasel, garden beans, Moorish peas, coriander, chervil, capers, clary. And the gardener shall have house-leek growing on his house.

As for trees, we wish that they have various kinds of apple, pear, and plum trees, sorb, medlar, chestnut, peach trees of different kinds, quince, filbert, almond, mulberry, laurel, pine, fig, walnut, and cherry trees of various kinds.

Names of apple trees: *gozmaringa, geroldinga, crevedella, spirauca,* sweet ones and sour ones, and all the kind that keep, as well as those which are eaten when picked and those that are forced.

They shall have three or four kinds of pears which will keep, sweet ones, cooking, and late pears.

THE ANNALS OF XANTEN

(844) POPE GREGORY departed this world and Pope Sergius followed in his place. Count Bernhard was killed by Charles. Pippin, king of Aquitaine together with his son and the son of Bernhard, routed the army of Charles, and there fell the abbot Hugo. At the same time King Louis advanced with his army against the Wends, one of whose kings, Gestimus by name, was killed; the rest came to Louis and pledged him their fidelity, which, however, they broke as soon as he was gone. Thereafter Lothaire, Louis, and Charles came together for council in Diedenhofen, and after a conference they went their several ways in peace.

(845) Twice in the canton of Worms there was an earthquake; the first in the night following Palm Sunday, the second in the holy night of Christ's Resurrection. In the same year the heathen broke in upon the Christians at many points, but more than twelve thousand of them were killed by

the Frisians. Another party of invaders devastated Gaul; of these more than six hundred men perished. Yet owing to his indolence Charles agreed to give them many thousand pounds of gold and silver if they would leave Gaul, and this they did. Nevertheless the cloisters of most of the saints were destroyed and many of the Christians were led away captive.

After this had taken place King Louis once more led a force against the Wends. When the heathen had learned this they sent ambassadors, as well as gifts and hostages, to Saxony, and asked for peace. Louis then granted peace and returned home from Saxony. Thereafter the robbers were afflicted by a terrible pestilence, during which the chief sinner among them, by the name of Reginheri, who had plundered the Christians and the holy places, was struck down by the hand of God. They then took counsel and threw lots to determine from which of their gods they should seek safety; but the lots did not fall out happily, and on the advice of one of their Christian prisoners that they should cast their lot before the God of the Christians, they did so, and the lot fell happily. Then their king, by the name of Rorik, together with all the heathen people, refrained from meat and drink for fourteen days, when the plague ceased, and they sent back all their Christian prisoners to their country.

(846) According to their custom the Northmen plundered Eastern and Western Frisia and burned the town of Dordrecht, with two other villages, before the eyes of Lothaire, who was then in the castle of Nimwegen, but could not punish the crime. The Northmen, with their boats filled with immense booty, including both men and goods, returned to their own country.

In the same year Louis sent an expedition from Saxony against the Wends across the Elbe. He personally, however, went with his army against the Bohemians, whom we call Beu-winitha, but with great risk. . . . Charles advanced against the Britons, but accomplished nothing.

At this same time, as no one can mention or hear without great sadness, the mother of all churches, the basilica of the apostle Peter, was taken and plundered by the Moors, or Saracens, who had already occupied the region of Beneventum. The Saracens, moreover, slaughtered all the Christians whom they found outside the walls of Rome, either within or without this church. They also carried men and women away prisoners. They tore down, among many others, the altar of the blessed Peter, and their crimes from day to day bring sorrow to Christians. Pope Sergius departed life this year.

(847) After the death of Sergius no mention of the apostolic see has come in any way to our ears. Rabanus [Maurus], master and abbot of Fulda, was solemnly chosen archbishop as the successor of Bishop Otger, who had died.

Moreover the Northmen here and there plundered the Christians and engaged in a battle with the counts Sigir and Liuthar. They continued up the Rhine as far as Dordrecht, and nine miles farther to Meginhard, when they turned back, having taken their booty.

(848) On the fourth of February, towards evening, it lightened and there was thunder heard. The heathen, as was their custom, inflicted injury on the Christians. In the same year King Louis held an assembly of the people near Mayence. At this synod a heresy was brought forward by a few monks in regard to predestination. These were convicted and beaten, to their shame, before all the people. They were sent back to Gaul whence they had come, and, thanks be to God, the condition of the church remained uninjured.

(849) While King Louis was ill his army of Bavaria took its way against the Bohemians. Many of these were killed and the remainder withdrew, much humiliated, into their own country. The heathen from the North wrought havoc in Christendom as usual and grew greater in strength, but it is revolting to say more of this matter.

(850) On January 1st of that season, in the octave of the Lord, towards evening, a great deal of thunder was heard and a mighty flash of lightning seen; and an overflow of water afflicted the human race during this winter. In the following summer an all too great heat of the sun burned the earth. Leo, pope of the apostolic see, an extraordinary man, built a fortification round the church of St. Peter the apostle. The Moors, however, devasted here and there the coast towns in Italy. The Norman Rorik, brother of the above-mentioned younger Heriold, who earlier had fled dishonored from Lothaire, again took Dordrecht and did much evil treacherously to the Christians. In the same year so great a peace existed between the two brothers—Emperor Lothaire and King Louis—that they spent many days together in Osning [Westphalia] and there hunted, so that many were astonished thereat; and they went each his way in peace.

(851) The bodies of certain saints were sent from Rome to Saxony,— that of Alexander, one of seven brethren, and those of Romanus and Emerentiana. In the same year the very noble empress, Irmingard by name, wife of the emperor Lothaire, departed this world. The Normans inflicted much harm in Frisia and about the Rhine. A mighty army of them collected by the river Elbe against the Saxons, and some of the Saxon towns were besieged, others burned, and most terribly did they oppress the Christians. A meeting of our kings took place on the Maas.

(852) The steel of the heathen glistened; excessive heat; a famine followed. There was not fodder enough for the animals. The pasturage for the swine was more than sufficient.

(853) A great famine in Saxony so that many were forced to live on horse meat.

(854) The Normans, in addition to the very many evils which they were everywhere inflicting upon the Christians, burned the church of St. Martin, bishop of Tours, where his body rests.

(855) In the spring, Louis, the eastern king, sent his son of the same name to Aquitaine to obtain possession of the heritage of his uncle Pippin.

(856) The Normans again chose a king of the same name as the preceding one, and related to him, and the Danes made a fresh incursion by sea, with renewed forces, against the Christians.

(857) A great sickness, accompanied by swelling of the bladder, prevailed among the people. This produced a terrible foulness, so that the limbs were separated from the body even before death came.

(858) Louis, the eastern king, held an assembly of the people of his territory in Worms.

(859) On the first of January, as the early mass was being said, a single earthquake occurred in Worms and a triple one in Mayence before daybreak.

(860) On the fifth of February thunder was heard. The king returned from Gaul after the whole empire had gone to destruction, and was in no way bettered.

(861) The holy bishop Luitbert piously furnished the cloister which is called the Freckhorst with many relics of the saints, namely, of the martyrs Boniface and Maximus, and of the confessors Eonius and Antonius, and added a portion of the manger of the Lord and of his grave, and likewise of the dust of the Lord's feet as he ascended to heaven. In this year the winter was long and the above-mentioned kings again had a secret consultation on the above-mentioned island near Coblenz, and they laid waste everything round about.

HOW THE NORTHMEN HARRIED FRANKLAND [AND] LAID SIEGE TO PARIS

(882) . . . The Northmen in the month of October intrenched themselves at Condé, and horribly devastated the kingdom of Carloman, while King Charles with his army took his stand on the Somme at Barleux. The Northmen ceased not from rapine and drove all the inhabitants who were left beyond the Somme. . . .

[King Carloman gave them battle] and the Franks were victorious and killed nigh a thousand of the Northmen, Yet they were in no wise discomfited by this battle. . . . They went from Condé back to their ships, and thence laid waste the whole kingdom with fire and sword as far as the Oise.

They destroyed houses, and razed monasteries and churches to the ground, and brought to their death the servants of our holy religion by famine and sword, or sold them beyond the sea. They killed the dwellers in the land and none could resist them.

Abbot Hugo, when he heard of these calamities, gathered an army and came to aid the king. When the Northmen came back from a plundering expedition . . . he, in company with the king, gave them chase. They, however, betook themselves to a wood, and scattered hither and yon, and finally returned to their ships with little loss. In this year died Hinckmar, archbishop of Rheims, a man justly esteemed by all.

(883) . . . In the spring the Northmen left Condé and sought the country along the sea. Here they dwelt through the summer; they forced the Flemings to flee from their lands, and raged everywhere, laying waste the country with fire and sword. As autumn approached, Carloman, the king, took his station with his army in the canton of Vithman at Mianai, opposite Lavier, in order to protect the kingdom. The Northmen at the end of October came to Lavier with cavalry, foot soldiers, and all their baggage. Ships, too, came from the sea up the Somme and forced the king and his whole army to flee and drove them across the river Oise. The invaders went into winter quarters in the city of Amiens and devastated all the land to the Seine and on both sides of the Oise, and no man opposed them; and they burned with fire the monasteries and churches of Christ. . . .

(884) At this time died Engelwin, bishop of Paris, and the abbot Gauzelin was put in his stead. The Northmen ceased not to take Christian people captive and to kill them, and to destroy churches and houses and burn villages. Through all the streets lay bodies of the clergy, of laymen, nobles, and others, of women, children, and suckling babes. There was no road nor place where the dead did not lie; and all who saw Christian people slaughtered were filled with sorrow and despair.

Meanwhile, because the king was still a child, all the nobles came together in the city of Compiegne to consider what should be done. They took counsel, and decided to send to the Northmen the Dane Sigfried, who was a Christian and faithful to the king, and the nephew of Heorie, the Dane, that he might treat with the nobles of his people and ask them to accept tribute money and leave the kingdom.

He accordingly undertook to carry out the task assigned to him, went to Amiens, and announced his mission to the leaders of the Northmen. After long consultations and much going to and fro, these decided to impose upon the king and the Franks a tribute of twelve thousand pounds of silver, according to their manner of weighing. After both parties had given hostages, the people who dwelt beyond the Oise were secure in some degree. They enjoyed this security from the day of the Purification of St. Mary until the month of October.

The Northmen, however, made raids in their accustomed manner beyond the Scheldt, and laid waste all things with fire and sword, and totally destroyed churches, monasteries, cities and villages, and put the people to slaughter. After the holy Easter festival the collection of the tribute began, and churches and church property were ruthlessly plundered. At last, the whole sum being finally brought together, the Franks assembled with a view of resisting the Northmen should they break their pledges, but the Normans burned their camp and retreated from Amiens. . . .

(885) [In December of this same year Carloman was accidentally killed while on a boar hunt.] As soon as Emperor Charles received tidings of this, he made a hasty journey and came to Pontion; and all the men of Carloman's kingdom went to him there and submitted to his sway. . . .

On the twenty-fifth of July the whole host of the Northmen forced their way to Rheims. Their ships had not yet come, so they crossed the Seine in boats they found there, and quickly fortified themselves. The Franks followed them. All those who dwelt in Neustria and Burgundy gathered to make war upon the Northmen. But when they gave battle it befell that Ragnold, duke of Maine, was killed, with a few others. Therefore all the Franks retreated in great sorrow and accomplished nothing.

Thereupon the rage of the Northmen was let loose upon the land. They thirsted for fire and slaughter; they killed Christian people and took them captive and destroyed churches; and no man could resist them.

Again the Franks made ready to oppose them, not in battle, but by building fortifications to prevent the passage of their ships. They built a castle on the river Oise at the place which is now called Pontoise, and appointed Aletramus to guard it. Bishop Gauzelin fortified the city of Paris. . . .

Elated with victory, the Northmen appeared before Paris, and at once attacked a tower, confident that they could take it quickly because it was not yet fully fortified. But the Christians defended it manfully and the battle raged from morning till evening. The night gave a truce to fighting and the Northmen returned to their ships. Bishop Gauzelin and Count Odo worked with their men all night long to strengthen the tower against assaults. The next day the Northmen returned and tried to storm the tower, and they fought fiercely till sunset. The Northmen had lost many of their men and they returned to their ships. They pitched a camp before the city and laid siege to it and bent all their energies to capture it. But the Christians fought bravely and stood their ground.

(886) On the sixth of February those in the city suffered a severe reverse. The river rose and washed away the Little Bridge. When the bishop heard of this disaster he sent brave and noble men to guard the tower, so that they might begin to rebuild the broken bridge when morning broke. The Northmen knew all that had happened. They arose before sunrise, hurried with all their forces to the tower, surrounded it on all sides so that no reenforcements could reach the garrison, and tried to take the tower by storm.

The guard resisted valiantly, and the clamor of the multitude arose to heaven. The bishop was on the city wall with all the inhabitants. The people wept and groaned because they could not aid their own. The bishop commended them all to Christ because there was nothing else that he could do. The Northmen tried to break in the gate of the tower and finally set fire to it. Those who were within, weakened by wounds, were conquered by fire; and to the shame of Christianity, they were killed in divers ways and cast into the river. The Northmen then destroyed the tower; and afterward they ceased not to assault the city itself.

The bishop was heartbroken over this heavy loss. He straightway sent to Count Herkenger and begged him to go at once to Germany and ask Henry, duke of Austrasia, to aid him and the Christian people. Herkenger hastened to carry out the mission entrusted him, and persuaded Henry to come with an army to Paris. He, however, accomplished nothing there and soon returned to his own country.

Then Gauzelin, who sought in all possible ways to help the Christian people, decided to come to a friendly understanding with Sigfried, king of the Danes, to secure the deliverance of the city from siege.

Unhappily, while negotiations were going on, the bishop fell into sore infirmity. He ended his life and was buried in his city. The Northmen were aware of his death; and before it was announced to the citizens, the Northmen proclaimed from the gates that the bishop was dead. The people were exhausted by the siege and overwhelmed by the death of their father; and they lost courage and abandoned themselves to sorrow. But Odo, the illustrious count, gave them renewed strength with his brave words.

The Northmen ceased not to attack the city daily; many were killed and still more were disabled by wounds, and food began to give out in the city. At this time Hugo, the venerable abbot, departed his life and was buried in the Monastery of St. German Antisdoro. Odo saw how the people were falling into despair, and he went forth secretly to seek aid from the nobles of the kingdom, and to send word to the emperor that the city would soon be lost unless help came. When Odo returned to Paris he found the people lamenting his absence. Nor did he reenter the city without a remarkable incident. The Northmen had learned that he was coming back, and they blocked his way to the gate. But Odo, though his horse was killed, struck down his enemies right and left, forced his way into the city, and brought joy to the anxious people. . . .

The siege had lasted eight months when the emperor came to relieve the city. It was in the autumn that he appeared before Paris with a very strong army. . . . But he did not force them to raise the siege. He made terms with them and signed a shameful treaty, He promised to pay a ransom for the city, and gave them leave to march unopposed into Burgundy, to plunder it during the winter.

A MANOR OF THE FOURTEENTH CENTURY, A.D. 1307

EXTENT OF the manor of Bernehorne, made on Wednesday next after the feast of St. Gregory the Pope, in the thirty-fifth year of the reign of King Edward, in the presence of Brother Thomas, keeper of Marley, John de la More, and Adam de Thruhlegh, clerks, on the oath of William de Gocecoumbe, Walter le Parker, Richard le Knyst, Richard the son of the latter, Andrew of Estone, Stephen Morsprich, Thomas Brembel, William de Swynham, John Pollard, Roger le Glide, John Syward and John de Lillingewist, who say etc., that there are there all the following things:

The jurors [1] say that the principal messuage [2] and its garden with the herbage [3] and curtilage [4] are worth yearly 6s. 8d.; and the dovecote is worth yearly 5s.; and the windmill is worth yearly 20s.

And there are there 12 acres of thick undergrowth whence the pannage and herbage are worth yearly 2s.

And there are there 42 acres of maritime land [5] in a certain place called Scotsmarsh, each acre of which is worth yearly 12d., the sum being 42s.

And there are 7 acres and 1 rood of maritime land in a certain place called Aldithewisse; and 47 acres and 3 roods of maritime land in a certain place called Flittermarsh, each acre of which is worth yearly 12d., the sum being 55s.

---

[1] [That is, those who gave sworn testimony.]   [2] [Dwelling site.]
[3] [Pasture.]   [4] [Yard.]
[5] [Apparently land that was close to the salt marsh but yet capable of being cultivated, since agricultural services of the villein tenants are mentioned subsequently. Bernehorne is quite near the sea.]

And there are there 22 acres of maritime land in two places called Pundfold and Longrech; and 7 acres of maritime land in a certain place called Wyssh, and 8 acres and 3 roods of maritime land in a certain place called Upcroft marsh, and 3 acres and a half of maritime land in a certain place called Rede-wysshe; and each acre is worth yearly 12d., the sum being 41s. 3d. [Various numbers of acres of land situated in different places and at values from 3d. to 18d. per acre a year are here named.] . . .

The total of the acres of woods is 12 acres.

The total of the acres of arable land is 444 acres and 3 roods, of which 147 acres 4 roods are maritime land, 101 acres marshy land, and 180 acres waste ground.

The total of the acres of meadow is 13 acres 1 rood.

The total of the whole preceding extent 18£ 10s. 4d.

John Pollard holds a half acre in Aldithewisse and owes 18d. at the four terms, and owes from it relief and heriot.

John Suthinton holds a house and 40 acres of land and owes 3s. 6d. at Easter and Michaelmas.

William of Swynhamme holds 1 acre of meadow in the thicket of Swyn-hamme and owes 1d. at the feast of Michaelmas.

Ralph of Leybourne holds a cottage and 1 acre of land in Pinden and owes 3s. at Easter and Michaelmas, and attendance at the court in the manor every three weeks, relief and heriot.

Richard Knyst of Swynhamme holds two acres and a half of land and owes yearly 4s.

William at Knelle holds 2 acres of land in Aldithewisse and owes yearly 4s.

Roger le Glede holds a cottage and 3 roods of land and owes 2s. 6d. at Easter and Michaelmas.

Alexander Hamound holds a little piece of land near Aldithewisse and owes 1 goose, of the value of 2d.

The sum of the whole rent of the free tenants, with the value of the goose, is 18s. 9d.

They say moreover that John of Cayworth holds a house and 30 acres of land, and owes yearly 2s. at Easter and Michaelmas; and he owes a cock and two hens of Christmas, of the value of 4d.

And he ought to harrow for 2 days at the Lenten sowing with one man and his own horse and his own harrow, the value of the work being 4d.; and he is to receive from the lord on each day three meals, of the value of 5d., and then the lord will be at a loss of 1d. Thus his harrowing is of no value to the service of the lord.

And he ought to carry the manure of the lord for 2 days with 1 cart, with his own 2 oxen, the value of the work being 8d.; and he is to receive from the lord each day 3 meals of the price as above. And thus the service is worth 3d. clear.

And he shall find 1 man for 2 days for mowing the meadow of the lord, who can mow, by estimation 1 acre and a half, the value of the mowing of an acre being 6d.; the sum is therefore 9d.; and he is to receive each day 3 meals of the value given above; and thus that mowing is worth 4d. clear.

And he ought to gather and carry that same hay which he has cut, the price of the work being 3d.

And he shall have from the lord 2 meals for 1 man, of the value of 1½d. Thus the work will be worth 1½d. clear.

And he ought to carry the hay of the lord for 1 day with a cart and 3 animals of his own, the price of the work being 6d. And he shall have from the lord 3 meals of the value of 2½d. And thus the work is worth 3½d. clear.

And he ought to carry in autumn beans or oats for 2 days with a cart and 3 animals of his own, the value of the work being 12d. And he shall receive from the lord each day 3 meals of the value given above; and thus the work is worth 7d. clear.

And he ought to carry wood from the woods of the lord as far as the manor for two days in summer with a cart and 3 animals of his own, the value of the work being 9d. And he shall receive from the lord each day 3 meals of the price given above; and thus the work is worth 4d. clear.

And he ought to find 1 man for 2 days to cut heath, the value of the work being 4d., and he shall have 3 meals each day of the value given above; and thus the lord will lose, if he receives the service, 3d. Thus that mowing is worth nothing to the service of the lord.

And he ought to carry the heath which he has cut, the value of the work being 5d. And he shall receive from the lord 3 meals at the price of 2½d. And thus the work will be worth 2½d. clear.

And he ought to carry to Battle twice in the summer season, each time half a load of grain, the value of the service being 4d. And he shall receive in the manor each time 1 meal of the value of 2d. And thus the work is worth 2d. clear.

The total of the rents, with the value of the hens, is 2s. 4d.

The total of the value of the works is 2s. 3½d; owed from the said John yearly.

William of Cayworth holds a house and 30 acres of land and owes at Easter and Michaelmas 2s. rent. And he shall do all customs just as the foresaid John of Cayworth.

William atte Grene holds a house and 30 acres of land and owes in all things just as the said John.

Alan atte Felde holds a house and 16 acres of land (for which the sergeant pays to the court of Bixley 2s.),[6] and he owes at Easter and Michaelmas 4s., attendance at the manor court, relief and heriot.

John Lyllingwyst holds a house and 4 acres of land and owes at the two terms 2s., attendance at the manor court, relief and heriot.

The same John holds 1 acre of land in the fields of Hoo and owes at the two periods 2s., attendance, relief and heriot.

Reginald atte Denne holds a house and 18 acres of land and owes at the said periods 18d., attendance, relief and heriot.

Robert of Northehou holds 3 acres of land at Saltcote and owes at the said periods attendance, relief and heriot.

Total of the rents of the villeins, with the value of the hens, 20s.

Total of all the works of these three villeins, 6s. 10½d.

And it is to be noted that none of the above named villeins can give their daughters in marriage nor cause their sons to be tonsured,[7] nor can they cut down timber growing on the lands they hold, without license of the bailiff or sergeant of the lord, and then for building purposes and not otherwise. And after the death of any one of the foresaid villeins the lord shall have as a heriot his best animal, if he had any; if however he have no living beast the lord shall have no heriot, as they say. The sons or daughters of the foresaid villeins shall give for entrance into the holding after the death of their predecessors as much as they give of rent per year.

Silvester the priest holds 1 acre of meadow adjacent to his house, and owes yearly 3s.

Total of the rent of tenants for life, 3s.

Petronilla atte Holme holds a cottage and a piece of land and owes at Easter and Michaelmas . . . attendance, relief and heriot.

Walter Herying holds a cottage and a piece of land and owes at Easter and Michaelmas 18d., attendance, relief and heriot.

Isabella Mariner holds a cottage and owes at the feast of St. Michael 12d., attendance, relief and heriot. [Eleven other cotters are named holding cottages and amounts of land varying from a rood to three and a half acres and giving payments up to three shillings, and the other services.] . . .

---

[6] [Bixley was a neighboring manor, held by the bishop of Chichester, having certain claims over some of the land in the manor of Bernehorne.]

[7] [That is, to let them enter the clergy. This was not only a common prohibition according to the custom of many manors but was enacted in statute law. "Sons of rustics ought not to be ordained without the assent of the lord on whose land they are known to have been born." Constitutions of Clarendon, c. 16. (A.D. 1164.)]

Total of the rents of the said cotters, with the value of the hens, 34s. 6d.

And it is to be noted that all the said cotters shall do as regards giving their daughters in marriage, having their sons tonsured, cutting down timber, paying heriot, and giving fines for entrance just as John of Cayworth, and the rest of the villeins formerly mentioned.

Note, fines [8] and penalties, with heriots and reliefs, are worth yearly 5s.

PLEAS OF THE MANORS OF THE ABBEY OF BEC

OGBOURNE [WILTSHIRE]. Thursday in Whitsun week. [A.D. 1249.]

William Blackbeard in mercy for not coming with his law as he was bound to do. Pledges, Geoffrey of Wick and Geoffrey Payn. Fine, 6d.

It was presented that Stephen Shepherd by night struck his sister with a knife and grievously wounded her. Therefore let him be committed to prison. Afterwards he made fine with 2s. Pledge, Geoffrey of Wick.

It was presented that Robert Carter's son by night invaded the house of Peter Burgess and in felony threw stones at his door so that the said Peter raised the hue. Therefore let the said Robert be committed to prison. Afterwards he made fine with 2s.

Nicholas Drye, Henry le Notte (fine, 12d.) and Thomas Hogue (fine, 12d.) were convicted for that they by night invaded the house of Sir Thomas the Chaplain and forcibly expelled thence a man and woman who had been taken in there as guests. Therefore they are in mercy. Pledges of the said Thomas, Richard of Lortemere and Jordan of Paris. Pledges of the said Henry, Richard Pen . . . and Richard Butry.

Adam Moses gives half a sextary of wine to have an inquest as to whether Henry Ayulf accused him of the crime of larceny and used opprobrious and contumelious words of him. Afterwards they made accord and Henry finds security for an amercement. Fine, 12d.

Isabella Sywards in mercy for having sold to Richard Bodenham land that she could not warrant him.

All the ploughmen of great Ogbourne are convicted by the oath of twelve men . . . because by reason of their default [the land] of the lord was ill ploughed whereby the lord is damaged to the amount of 9s. . . . And Walter

---

[8] [A "fine" was a payment made to the lord by any one who acquired land in the manor in any other way than by inheritance, in which case the payment was relief. The usual word for a penalty was not "fine" but "amerciament"; or it was recorded that a person was "in mercy."]

Reaper is in mercy for concealing [that is, not giving information as to] the said bad ploughing. Afterwards he made fine with the lord with 1 mark.

From Ralph Joce 6s. 8d. for his son, because he [the son] unlawfully carried off corn from the lord's court. Pledge, Geoffrey Joce.

From Henry Pink 12d. for a trespass by waylaying.

From Eve Corner 6d. for a trespass of her pigs.

From Ralph Scales 6d. for timber carried off.

From William Cooper 12d. for ploughing his own land with the lord's plough without licence.

From Hugh Newman 12d. for trespass in the wood.

From Richard Penant 12d. for the same.

From Helen widow of Little Ogbourne 6d. for the same.

From Nicholas Siward 6d. for a false complaint against William Pafey.

From William Pafey 12d. for fighting with the said Nicholas.

From the widow of Ralph Shepherd 6d. for a trespass in Pencombe.

RUISLIP [MIDDLESEX]. Court holden on Friday next after the feast of S. Barnabas in the twenty-fourth year of Edward I. [A.D. 1296.]

Adam of Ramsey was attached to answer the lord at the suit of William Forester and William Reaper on the pledge of William of the Exchequer and Robert Aliz in a plea of trespass, why when the said Adam together with persons unknown had at Ruislip on the Friday in Whitsunweek come with a cart upon the fee and franchise of the lord to the house of Hugh Marleward the born bondman of the said lord and there had caused to be carried away in the said cart certain timber cut down by the said Hugh Marleward against the lord's prohibition (the said prohibition so issued by the lord being known to the said Adam), in order that against the lord's will the said timber might be removed from the lord's franchise to the damage of the lord 100s., and when the said William Forester and William Reaper as bailiffs of the lord had come up and found the transport taking place and had on behalf of our lord the king and of his [Adam's] lord commanded him not to remove the said timber thus placed under the lord's prohibition from the said place against the lord's will and to find pledges to answer the lord in his court as to his having thus attempted to remove the said timber from the lord's franchise against the lord's will, and had taken a horse from the said Adam's cart by way of gage in order to attach him to answer the lord for the said trespass, he the said Adam together with persons unknown made an assault upon them [the two Williams] by force and arms and would not permit himself to be attached in manner aforesaid according to the law and custom of the realm, but to the utmost of his power made rescue of the said horse which had been attached, whereupon the said two Williams raised the hue against the said Adam and his adherents who were thus making assault, and to the hue there came Walter Savage tithingman of Eastcot with his whole tithing,[9] and the said Adam himself raising the hue bade them in the king's name follow him with the hue saying that he while acting as serjeant of our lord the king had been robbed of his horse by the said two Williams against his will and against the king's peace, whereupon the said Walter the tithingman with his whole tithing affrighted by the command thus given in the king's name raised the hue and along with Adam pursued after the said two Williams as though they were felons unto the manor [house] of the lord, and moreover at the gate of the said manor [house] the said Adam with those who were following him raised the hue against the lord and his men, saying as aforesaid that he had been robbed of his said horse by the said two Williams; [all of which was] to the damage and dishonour of the lord to the amount of 100s. and more; all of which things the said Adam did. Of all of which trespasses thus in full court charged against him, the said Adam confesses himself in all respects guilty, and he puts himself in the lord's mercy and finds pledges, to wit, Walter Savage, Robert Nothel, John Kevere and Hugh Marleward. Afterwards the amercement was affeered [10] at two marks by Roger of Southcote William of the Exchequer and Hugh of Combe free suitors of the court.

Henry White demands one acre of land which was holden by John his brother whose heir he is, as he says. And Cristina Trice comes and says that she has greater right to hold the said acre for her life than Henry to demand it, for she says that the said John purchased the said acre after his marriage with her and according to the custom of the manor of Ruislip a wife after her husband's death should hold the whole of any purchase made by him after his marriage with her; and this she offers to verify by the court, and she gives the lord 6d. to have an inquest. And the inquest says that the custom of the manor is as Cristina pleads it, so that she has greater right to hold than Henry to demand the said land. Therefore it is considered that she do hold as she now holds and that Henry be in mercy etc.; [fine,] 3d.

The chief pledges present that Robert of Chiltern, William called the Clerk, Henry called Prust, Henry Cook, John Maleville, Elias Smith, William Leper,

[9] [A "tithing" refers to a group, usually ten in number, under a "tithingman" responsible for the behavior of its members and for pursuing criminals.]
[10] [Fixed.]

Robert Redhead and Peter Steven made default. It is commanded that they be attached etc.

It is presented that William Forester raised the hue against Adam of Ramsey and rightfully. Therefore let Adam find gage for an amercement.

Also it is presented that Walter Savage, John Blackmere, William Field, William Marleward, John ate Hatche, Robert Wrenche, Richard ate Forde, Amicia of Pinner, Juliana ate Hulle, Richard Sherewind, Richard Wheeler, William Edelot and Ralph Fountain levied the hue against the lord and his servants wrongfully and kept it up for a long time before the lord's gate and wrongfully. Therefore they are adjudged to the pillory [?] and put in the stocks etc.

Also it is presented that Geoffrey of Reygate raised the hue against John Payn and rightfully. Therefore let John find gage for an amercement.

Also it is presented that John Fige raised the hue and that rightfully against certain men who by night with force and arms were carrying off the lord's sparrow-hawks, of which men nothing is as yet known.

John Robin offered the lord a mark of silver for leave to retire from the office of reeve.[11] It is commanded that the money be levied.

John Kevere raised the hue against the lord and his servants wrongfully, and denied in full court that he was the lord's born bondman, wherefore his land was seized into the lord's hand. Afterwards he comes and in full court confesses himself the lord's born bondman and is put back in seisin of his land and places himself altogether in the lord's mercy etc. The case is respited.

[11] [Bailiff.]

THE TOWN

THE RAPID GROWTH of towns—in number, size, and wealth—is perhaps the most striking phenomenon in late medieval Europe. Whatever their origins, the guarantee of their continued existence and the stimulus to their growth were found in trade. The volume of European trade had never fallen so low as people have been accustomed to think, although its character and direction changed considerably after the break-up of the Mediterranean economy of the ancient world. From the tenth century, however, there was a rapid acceleration, radiating from the great entrepôts in northern Italy and the Low Countries.

The early towns were not very attractive. Life expectancy was short, and the risks of medieval trading were great; but fortunes were made, and a new society was produced in which were to be found ultimately the most effective solvents of the old order. In the earlier centuries, the distinction between towns and countryside was not great; but the needs of commerce, notably for freedom from tolls and arbitrary exactions and for special laws, courts, and administration, soon led to insistence by the townsmen on autonomy and a fight to keep a similar economy from developing in country villages. Some lords, among them many ecclesiastics, opposed these town developments and gave way only to heavy pressure or even force; others, notably the kings, associated themselves with the movements, sold charters for handsome sums, and in the long run profited both financially and politically from their foresight. Often charters were drawn up in imitation of grants to other towns; thus the "Laws of Breteuil," a small town in Normandy, were widely copied in England. King John's charter to Gloucester, granted in 1200 and confirmed in 1227 and 1328, is illustrative of the privileges which townsmen wanted. The term "borough" in England was applied to towns of widely varying privileges characterized by a certain form of free, heritable, and alienable tenure known as burgage, although in time the use of the term became confused. The uniqueness of the boroughs is reflected in the separate summoning of and consultation with their representatives in early parliaments.

Within the towns trade and industry were frequently organized by guilds, groups of merchants or craftsmen devoted to the maintenance of monopoly, some protection and assurance of quality for the consumer, regulation of production and common commercial policy, and the provision of social and welfare facilities for their members. The patterns of guild organization and control varied greatly, and it is difficult in the present state of research in economic history to speak confidently about their origins or procedures, but the documents printed here reflect certain typical activities and concerns. The Southampton ordinances, a fourteenth-century document many of whose provisions long antedate 1300, apply to a merchant guild, a type in existence very early but by no means universal, London being a striking example of a city which never had a merchant guild. The articles of the London hatters of 1347, on the other hand, illustrate the guild principle as applied in a particular trade, with a special emphasis on the rules governing production. Although masters in the so-called craft guilds often carried through the whole process of production from the purchase of raw material to the sale of the finished product, it must not be assumed that, at least in large cities, there were no merchant capitalists who could influence both supply and sale and so limit the craftsman's independence.

Despite their concern for monopoly, guilds should not be compared to trade unions; they are rather more like modern trade associations concerned with the position and reputation of their members and which at times have tendencies to set common policies and prices. But guild regulation could not easily prevent a man with capital from grasping opportunities offered by an expanding economy; and indeed in many instances guilds were perverted to serve the interests of more important and wealthy members who were able to seize control. As guilds grew more wealthy and elaborate, with special uniforms, sumptuous banquets, and luxurious guildhalls, they fell away from their original economic purposes into exclusiveness and lethargy.

The relation between guilds and town governments was close. Often only freemen of a guild had the right to chose officials or to hold office; and the town governments found the guilds useful organs for supervising industry and trade. Municipal control, direct or indirect, was aimed at maintaining quality and reasonable prices and at enforcing the dominant commercial morality which condemned such sharp practices as the buying of goods before they came to market, cornering the market, or buying simply to sell again at a profit—the famous abuses of forestalling, engrossing, and regrating. A good illustration of such a municipal code is the Grimsby Provision, agreed to before a representative of King Henry III and approved by him in 1258.

That the sense of order and propriety in these various charters can give a misleading idea of town life in the Middle Ages is illustrated in the selection from *The Autobiography of Guibert*. Guibert (1053–1124), historian and theologian, was born of noble parents and dedicated from infancy to the Church. In 1104 he was chosen head of the abbey of Notre Dame de Nogent, and he took a prominent part in ecclesiastical affairs from that time onward.

He wrote several works, the only one of any importance his autobiography. This work, modeled after the *Confessions* of Augustine, is valuable primarily as a historical source, although it also conveys the flavor of the period very well, particularly in this description of a twelfth-century communal revolt.

The translations of the Gloucester charter and Grimsby Provision have been compiled from the topical presentations edited by A. Ballard, *British Borough Chapters* (2 vols., Cambridge University Press, 1913 and 1923). The Southampton ordinances appear in the University of Pennsylvania *Translations and Reprints,* II, No. 1 (1895), 12–17. The articles of the London hatters are taken from H. T. Riley, *Memorials of London and London Life, 1276–1419* (London, 1868). The selection from Guibert is from *The Autobiography of Guibert,* translated by C. C. Swinton Bland (New York, Dutton, 1926). The guild documents are from the French, and the others from the Latin.

CHARTER TO THE BURGESSES
OF GLOUCESTER

JOHN, BY THE GRACE OF GOD KING ETC. Know ye that we have granted and by this charter confirmed to our burgesses of Gloucester the whole borough of Gloucester with its appurtenances to be held of us and our heirs for ever at farm, rendering every year fifty-five pounds sterling as they were wont to render and ten pounds by tale as increment of the farm at our Exchequer in the Easter term and in the Michaelmas term.

We also grant to our burgesses of Gloucester of the Merchant Guild that none of them shall plead outside the walls of the borough of Gloucester on any plea except pleas of foreign tenures and except the minters and our ministers.

We also grant to them that none of them shall fight a duel. And that concerning pleas pertaining to our crown they shall clear themselves according to the ancient custom of the borough.

We also grant this to them that all the burgesses of the Merchant Guild shall be quit of toll, lastage, pontage, and stallage in and out of fairs and throughout the seaports of all our lands both on this and the other side of the sea, saving in all things the liberties of the city of London.

And that none shall be judged of an amercement of money except according to the ancient law of the borough which they had in the time of our ancestors.

And that they shall justly have their lands and tenures and mortgages and all debts, whosoever owes them to them.

And concerning their lands and tenures which are within the borough, right shall be done to them according to the custom of the borough.

And of all their debts which are lent in Gloucester and of mortgages there made pleas shall be held at Gloucester.

And if any in all our land take toll or custom from the men of Gloucester of the Merchant Guild, after he has failed to redress, the sheriff of Gloucester or the reeve of Gloucester shall take distress therefor at Gloucester, saving in all things the liberties of the city of London.

Moreover, for the improvement of the borough we have granted them that they all shall be quit of Year's gift and of Scotale if our sheriff or any other bailiff exacts Scotale.

These aforesaid customs we grant to them and all other liberties and free customs which they had in the time of our ancestors when they better or more freely had the same.

And if any customs were unjustly raised during the war, they shall be disallowed.

And whoever shall seek the borough of Gloucester with his merchandise, whether foreigners or others, of whatever place they may be, they may come, sojourn, and depart in our safe peace on paying the due customs, and no one shall unjustly disturb them against this our charter.

And we forbid anyone to commit wrong or damage or molestation against them on pain of forfeiture of ten pounds to us.

Wherefore we wish and firmly ordain that the aforesaid burgesses and their heirs have and hold in inheritance from us and our heirs all the aforementioned things, well and in peace, freely and quietly, and honorably, just as it is written above.

We also will and grant that our same burgesses of Gloucester by the common counsel of their borough shall elect two of the more legal and discreet burgesses of the borough of Gloucester and present them to our chief justice at Westminster, and these men or one of them shall well and faithfully keep the provostship of the borough and shall not be removed so long as they administer things well in their bailiwick, except by the common counsel of the borough.

We will also that in the same borough of Gloucester there shall be elected by the common counsel of the burgesses four of the more legal and discreet men of the borough to keep the pleas of the crown and the other matters which pertain to us and our crown in the same borough. And to see that the reeves or the reeve of that borough justly and lawfully treat both poor and rich.

Witness: . . . etc.

ORDINANCES OF THE GUILD MERCHANT OF SOUTHAMPTON

1. In the first place, there shall be elected from the Gild Merchant, and established, an alderman, a steward, a chaplain, four skevins,[1] and an usher. And it is to be known that whosoever shall be alderman shall receive from each one entering into the Gild fourpence, the steward, twopence; the chaplain, twopence; and the usher, one penny. And the Gild shall meet twice a

---

[1] [Bailiffs.]

year: that is to say, on the Sunday next after St. John the Baptist's day, and on the Sunday next after St. Mary's day.

2. And when the Gild shall be sitting no one of the Gild is to bring in any stranger, except when required by the alderman or steward. And the alderman shall have a sergeant to serve before him, the steward another sergeant, and the two skevins a sergeant, and the other two skevins a sergeant, and the chaplain shall have his clerk.

3. And when the Gild shall sit, the alderman is to have, each night, so long as the Gild sits, two gallons of wine and two candles, and the steward the same; and the four skevins and the chaplain, each of them one gallon of wine and one candle, and the usher one gallon of wine.

4. And when the Gild shall sit, the lepers of La Madeleine shall have of the alms of the Gild, two sesters of ale, and the sick of God's House and of St. Julian shall have two sesters of ale. And the Friar's Minors shall have two sesters of ale and one sester of wine. And four sesters of ale shall be given to the poor wherever the Gild shall meet.

5. And when the Gild is sitting, no one who is of the Gild shall go outside of the town for any business, without the permission of the steward. And if any one does so, let him be fined two shillings, and pay them.

6. And when the Gild sits, and any gildsman is outside of the city so that he does not know when it will happen, he shall have a gallon of wine if his servants come to get it. And if a gildsman is ill and is in the city, wine shall be sent to him, two loaves of bread and a gallon of wine and a dish from the kitchen; and two approved men of the Gild shall go to visit him and look after his condition.

7. And when a gildsman dies, all those who are of the Gild and are in the city shall attend the service for the dead, and gildsmen shall bear the body and bring it to the place of burial. And whoever will not do this shall pay according to his oath, two pence, to be given to the poor. And those of the ward where the dead man shall be ought to find a man to watch over the body the night that the dead shall lie in his house. And so long as the service of the dead shall last, that is to say, the vigil and the mass, there ought to burn four candles of the Gild, each candle of two pounds weight or more, until the body is buried. And these four candles shall remain in the keeping of the steward of the Gild.

8. The steward ought to keep the rolls and the treasure of the Gild under the seal of the alderman of the Gild.

9. And when a gildsman dies, his eldest son or his next heir shall have the seat of his father, or of his uncle, if his father was not a gildsman, and of no other one; and he shall give nothing for his seat. No husband can have a seat

in the Gild by right of his wife, nor demand a seat by right of his wife's ancestors.

10. And no one has the right or power to sell or give his seat in the Gild to any man; and the son of a gildsman, other than his eldest son, shall enter into the Gild on payment of ten shillings, and he shall take the oath of the Gild.

11. And if a gildsman shall be imprisoned in England in time of peace, the alderman with the steward, and with one of the skevins shall go, at the cost of the Gild, to procure the deliverance of the one who is in prison.

12. And if any gildsman strikes another with his fist and is convicted thereof, he shall lose the Gild until he shall have bought it back for ten shillings, and taken the oath of the Gild again like a new member. And if a gildsman strikes another with a stick, or a knife, or any other weapon, whatever it may be, he shall lose the Gild and the franchise, and shall be held as a stranger until he shall have been reconciled to the good men of the Gild and has made recompense to the one whom he has injured; and has paid a fine to the Gild of twenty shillings, and this shall not be remitted.

13. If any one does an injury, who is not of the Gild, and is of the franchise or strikes a gildsman and is reasonably convicted he shall lose his franchise and go to prison for a day and a night.

14. And if any stranger, or any other who is not of the Gild nor of the franchise, strikes a gildsman, and is reasonably convicted thereof, let him be in prison two days and two nights, unless the injury is such that he should be more severely punished.

15. And if a gildsman reviles or slanders another gildsman, and a complaint of it comes to the alderman, and, if he is reasonably convicted thereof, he shall pay two shillings fine to the Gild, and if he is not able to pay he shall lose the Gild.

16. And if anyone, who is of the franchise, speaks evil of a gildsman, and is convicted of this before the alderman, he shall pay five shillings for a fine, or lose the franchise.

17. And no one shall come to the council of the Gild if he is not a gildsman.

18. And if anyone of the Gild forfeits the Gild by any act or injury, and is excluded by the alderman and the steward and the skevins and the twelve sworn men of the city; and he wishes to have the Gild again, he shall do all things anew just as one who has never been of the Gild, and shall made amends for his injury according to the discretion of the alderman and the aforesaid approved men. And if anyone of the Gild or of the franchise brings a suit against another outside of the city, by a writ or without a writ, he shall lose the Gild and the franchise if he is convicted of it.

19. And no one in the city of Southampton shall buy anything to sell again

in the same city, unless he is of the Gild Merchant or of the franchise. And if anyone shall do so and is convicted of it, all which he has so bought shall be forfeited to the king; and no one shall be quit of custom unless he proves that he is in the Gild or in the franchise, and this from year to year.

20. And no one shall buy honey, fat, salt herrings, or any kind of oil, or millstones, or fresh hides, or any kind of fresh skins, unless he is a gildsman; nor keep a tavern for wine, nor sell cloth at retail, except in market or fair days; nor keep grain in his granary beyond five quarters, to sell at retail, if he is not a gildsman; and whoever shall do this and be convicted, shall forfeit all to the king.

21. No one of the Gild ought to be partner or joint dealer in any of the kinds of merchandise before mentioned with anyone who is not of the Gild, by any manner of coverture, or art, or contrivance, or collusion, or in any other manner. And whosoever shall do this and be convicted, the goods in such manner bought shall be forfeited to the king, and the gildsman shall lose the Gild.

22. If any gildsman falls into poverty and has not the wherewithal to live, and is not able to work or to provide for himself, he shall have one mark from the Gild, to relieve his condition when the Gild shall sit. No one of the Gild nor of the franchise shall avow another's goods for his by which the custom of the city shall be injured. And if any one does so and is convicted, he shall lose the Gild and the franchise; and the merchandise so avowed shall be forfeited to the king.

23. And no private man nor stranger shall bargain for or buy any kind of merchandise coming into the city before a burgess of the Gild Merchant, so long as the gildsman is present and wishes to bargain for and buy this merchandise; and if any one does so and is convicted, that which he buys shall be forfeited to the king.

24. And anyone who is of the Gild Merchant shall share in all merchandise which another gildsman shall buy or any other person, whoever he is, if he comes and demands part and is there where the merchandise is bought, and also if he gives satisfaction to the seller and gives security for his part. But no one who is not a gildsman is able or ought to share with a gildsman, without the will of the gildsman.

25. And if any gildsman or other of the city refuse a part to the gildsman in the manner above said, he shall not buy or sell in that year in the town, except his victuals.

26. And if any merchant of the town buys wine or grain so that all the risk shall be on the buyer, he shall not pay custom for this merchandise. And if any risk is upon the seller, he shall pay.

27. It is provided that the chief alderman of the town, or the bailiffs and the

twelve sworn men, shall give attention to the merchants as well strangers as private men, as often as it shall be required, to see that they have sufficient security for their debts, and recognisance from their debtors; and the day of this shall be enrolled before them, so that if that day is not kept, on proof by the creditor, the debtor should be then distrained according to the recognisance which he has made, in lands and chattels, to give satisfaction according to the usage of the town, without any manner of pleading, so that the men of the town should not have damage by the default of payment of the debtors aforesaid.

28. And if any gildsman for any debt which he may owe, will not suffer himself to be distrained, or when he has been distrained, shall break through, or make removal or break the king's lock, and be convicted thereof, he shall lose his gildship until he has bought it again for twenty shillings, and this each time that he offends in such manner. And he shall be none the less distrained until he has made satisfaction for the debt he owes; and if he will not submit to justice as aforesaid and be thereof convicted, he shall go to prison for a day and a night like one who is against the peace; and if he will not submit to justice let the matter be laid before the king, and his council in manner aforesaid.

29. And the chief alderman, and the twelve sworn men, or the bailiffs, each month, or at least four times a year shall see that the assize [2] of bread and ale be well kept in all points according to the price of corn.

32. Every year, on the morrow of St. Michael, shall be elected by the whole community of the town, assembled in a place provided, to consider the estate and treat of the common business of the town—then shall be elected by the whole community, twelve discreet men to execute the king's commands, together with the bailiffs, and to keep the peace and protect the franchise, and to do and keep justice to all persons, as well poor as rich, natives or strangers, all that year; and to this they shall be sworn in the form provided. And these twelve discreet men shall choose the same day two discreet men from among themselves and the other profitable and wise men to be bailiffs for the ensuing year, who shall take care that the customs shall be well paid; and they shall receive their jurisdiction the day after St. Michael's, as has been customary. And this shall be done from year to year, so that the bailiffs shall be renewed every year, and the twelve men aforesaid, if there is occasion. The same shall be done as to clerk and sergeants of the city, in making and removing.

35. The common-chest shall be in the house of the chief alderman or of the steward, and the three keys of it shall be lodged with three discreet men of the aforesaid twelve sworn men, or with three of the skevins, who shall loyally

[2] [A statute regulating prices.]

take care of the common seal, and the charters, and the treasure of the town; and no letter shall be sealed with the common seal, nor any charter taken out of the common-chest but in the presence of six or twelve sworn men, and of the alderman and steward; and nobody shall sell by any kind of measure or weight that is not sealed under forfeiture of two shillings.

63. No one shall go out to meet a ship bringing wine or other merchandise coming to the town, in order to buy anything, before the ship be arrived and come to anchor for unlading; and if any one does so and is convicted, the merchandise which he shall have bought shall be forfeited to the king.

ARTICLES OF THE GUILD OF LONDON HATTERS

The points of the Articles touching the trade of Hat-makers, accepted by Thomas Leggy, Mayor, and the Aldermen of the City of London, at the suit, and at the request, of the folks of the said trade:

In the first place, that six men of the most lawful and most befitting of the said trade shall be assigned and sworn to rule and watch the trade, in such manner as other trades of the said city are ruled and watched by their Wardens.

Also, that no one shall make or sell any manner of hats within the franchise of the city aforesaid, if he be not free of the same city; on pain of forfeiting to the Chamber the hats which he shall have made and offered for sale.

Also, that no one shall be made apprentice in the said trade for a less term than seven years, and that, without fraud or collusion. And he who shall receive any apprentice in any other manner, shall lose his freedom, until he shall have bought it back again.

Also, that no one of the said trade shall take any apprentice, if he be not himself a freeman of the said city.

Also, that the Wardens of the said trade shall make their searches for all manner of hats that are for sale within the said franchise, so often as need shall be. And that the aforesaid Wardens shall have power to take all manner of hats that they shall find defective and not befitting, and to bring them before the Mayor and Aldermen of London, that so the defaults which shall be found may be punished by their award.

Also, whereas some workmen in the said trade have made hats that are not befitting, in deceit of the common people, from which great scandal, shame, and loss have often arisen to the good folks of the said trade, they pray that no workman in the said trade shall do any work by night touching the same, but only in clear daylight; that so, the aforesaid Wardens may openly inspect their work. And he who shall do otherwise, and shall be convicted thereof before the Mayor and Aldermen, shall pay to the Chamber of the Guildhall, the first time forty pence, the second time half a mark, and the third time he shall lose his freedom.

Also, that no one of the said trade shall be admitted to be free of the City, or to work in the said trade, or to sell any manner of hats within the said franchise, if he be not attested by the aforesaid Wardens as being a good and lawful person, and as a proper workman.

Also, that no one of the said trade shall receive the apprentice or serving-man of another, until he has fully completed his term, or his master has given him a proper dismissal; on pain of paying, for every time, to the said Chamber half a mark, down to the fourth time, when he shall lose his freedom, until he shall have bought it back again.

Also, that no one of the said trade shall receive the serving-man of another to work, so long as he is in debt to his master; but he is to remain in the service of his master, until he shall have made satisfaction for the debt which he owes him. And he who shall receive such serving-man otherwise, shall pay to the said Chamber for every time forty pence; but only down to the fourth time, when he shall lose his freedom, until he shall have bought it back again.

Also, whereas foreign folks of divers Counties do bring to the said city divers manners of hats to sell, and carry them about the streets, as well before the houses of freemen of the said trade, as elsewhere; and thereby bar them of their dealings and of their sale, so that the freemen of the said trade in the City are greatly impoverished thereby; it is agreed that no strange person bringing hats to the said city for sale, shall sell them by retail, but only in gross, and that, to the freemen of the City; on pain of losing the same.

THE GRIMSBY PROVISION

KNOW YE that whereas strife had arisen between the rich men of our town of Grimsby and the poor men of the same town on the purchase of merchandise there, and whereas We for the common benefit of the said town had sent thither our beloved and loyal servant, Gilbert of Preston, to hear the said quarrel and amend the wrongs arising therefrom, We have learnt from the said Gilbert that by the common consent of the community of the said town it has been provided and agreed in the presence of the said Gilbert that the underwritten provision shall be held and observed there, to wit:

That no merchant of Grimsby buy herrings, fish or any other wares coming to the said port, or deliver the same, before sunrise nor after sunset, nor before the ship has touched land and the yard of the ship bearing those wares or some other gangway is placed from the ship to the land on which men may enter that ship.

That all sales be made openly and not in secret and in the port where the ships touch or in the marsh or on the ship and not elsewhere.

No merchant of the said town shall be denied a share in any merchandise, so long as he was present at the purchase.

If any merchant with any merchandise whatsoever enter the port of Grimsby with his ship, and is unwilling to sell his merchandise except to one or more of his friends who have been wont to make loans to him from their own chattels, he or they for whom the said merchant reserved his merchandise shall have only the third part of such merchandise and the neighbouring burgesses who were present at the purchase shall have two parts of such merchandise, provided that they hold land in burgage which they can sell and give; and this shall be the law concerning all ships that enter the port with any merchandise except the ships of fishermen from France and Flanders.

That he or they for whom the said fishermen of France and Flanders reserve their merchandise, shall not sell it except to their neighbours, being fellow burgesses, and this they shall do in common and not specially.

And if they sell that merchandise otherwise, that merchandise shall be taken by the bailiffs and the community of the said town into our hand, and they shall sell it to our profit, and nevertheless the said vendors shall be distrained to pay the said fishers for the merchandise so reserved for them, and shall have for their trouble twelve pence from each last of herrings and twelve pence from every hundred of cod, and no more.

That all tenants in the country shall buy herring, fish and other victuals of this kind without hindrance, provided that they or their servants are present at the unloading of the ship bearing those victuals.

That no one go by ship or boat to meet ships bearing any wares to the said town to fix prices or speak with the merchants of those wares on any sale before those ships touch in the port of the said town or in the port of Freshney, and if they do so the boatmen and all others who were with them shall be placed in the stocks for eight days fully without any deliverance, and if they do this a second time all and singular shall be placed in the stocks and kept there for eight days fully, and each shall pay half a mark to the common good of the said town; and if they do it a third time they shall be put out of the community of the said town for a whole year.

That no man nor the servant of any man of Grimsby shall accost any ships entering the said ports to bargain with the merchants about making any reservation of wares, and if he do so, he shall pay half a mark to the common good of the said town, and if he have not whence he can pay it, he shall be placed in the stocks for fully seven days without any deliverance.

That no fisherman of the Humber shall sell in houses or boats or in any place except our common market of the said town, and if he does so, he shall pay half a mark to the common good of the said town, or shall sit in the stocks for fully seven days without deliverance.

That no male or female regrater shall buy flesh or fish or any other victuals in the said town before the first hour, under penalty of half a mark to be paid to the common good of the said town. And if any of them have no means whence he can pay the money he shall sit in the stocks for seven days without deliverance and shall lose the victuals so purchased beforehand.

That no baker buy corn in the said town before the first hour, and if he does so, he shall lose the corn so bought, and it shall be given to the community of the said town.

That no one shall make bargains by handclasp for herring or other fish or for corn, except burgesses of the said town, and that handclasp bargains shall hold unless the merchandise, for which the bargains were made, is worse than was agreed, and of this a reasonable valuation shall be made by men worthy of credit.

That on the day agreed between merchants the buyer pay without any delay the money he owes to his creditor, and if he does not, the creditor shall complain to the bailiffs of the said town who shall immediately send for the buyer and if he admits the debt, the bailiffs shall order him to pay it within three tides, if the debt be owed for herring or any other kind of fish; and if the debt be owed for corn or other wares, the debtor shall pay within three days, and if the buyer do not pay within that term, the bailiffs shall pay out of the common purse of the said town, and shall take double the debt from the buyer, and if the buyer have nothing whence to pay the debt, his house shall be taken into our hand and detained until there has been received therefrom double the value of the said debt, and then it shall be restored to him. And if the buyer does not admit the debt, he shall enjoy the law and custom of the said town.

That every baker of the said town have his own seal for marking the bread which he makes.

If any burgess of the said town is distrained for his neighbour comburgess within Lincolnshire, he shall show it to the bailiffs of the said town, who shall forthwith order him for whom he was distrained to deliver the pledges so taken within eight days, under penalty of twenty shillings to be paid to the common good of the said town, and if he was distrained without the shire, the said bailiffs shall order him for whom he was distrained to deliver the pledges within forty days, under penalty of forty shillings to be paid to the common good of the town, and if he was distrained without the realm of England and has made this known to the said bailiffs, they shall forthwith order him for whom the distraint was made to satisfy the distrained man on his distraint within forty days, or within three days to start his journey to him who took the said distresses so as to deliver the distresses, and this under penalty of sixty shillings to be paid to the common good of the said town.

Now We, holding the said provision to be valid and pleasing in all and singular its articles, as far as we are concerned, at the request of the burgesses of the said town, and by the advice of the nobles who are of our council, do grant and confirm it for us and our heirs, so far as the aforesaid articles are reasonably provided.

THE AUTOBIOGRAPHY OF GUIBERT, ABBOT OF NOGENT SOUS COUCY

• • • • • •

AFTER HIM Enguerrand succeeded, who surpassed the aforesaid bishop both in birth and learning, but in guarding the rights of the Church he was very poor in comparison with the other. For certain revenues of the bishop, of which royal violence had at one time robbed that See, had been extracted from King Philip by Helinandus himself with entreaties and gifts and their restoration had been confirmed by the king's letters and seal; but this man on his entry, to his own ruin, gave back everything to the king, and during the rule of the three succeeding bishops they have been lost to the church and perhaps will be for ever. Hence in my opinion he has made parties to this simony all succeeding bishops, who shall take up the office with such fear of the king as to shrink from demanding restitution of that which he to his damnation gave for being made bishop.

Now a certain man with the same surname, Enguerrand, that is, of Boves, closely related to him, was very liberal, bountiful and agreeable, treating the churches with very great respect and munificence, those at least where he knew religion was observed, but, on the other hand, so abandoned in his love of women, that he kept all sorts, bondwomen and harlots, about him and hardly did anything except at the dictation of their wantonness. Now being most unlucky in his matrimonial fortunes and beginning to stray amongst other men's wives, he secretly possessed himself of the wife of his kinsman, the Count of Namur, and the woman whom he had tempted

in secret, he then united to himself openly in marriage. This union, condemned by many as anathema and declared accursed by the protests of
councils, they would both have readily renounced on the approach of
shame, had not the relationship of the husband and the craft of the woman's
flatteries softened the bishop. This gentleness so far encouraged their
adulterous embraces, as to give secret absolution for a tie that had been
made in the face of the world and publicly excommunicated. Oh, shame!
Surely those to whom he falsely gave assurance of absolution never dared
to consider themselves absolved.

After his death . . . when the bishopric had been vacant for two years,
at last we met together to choose a successor. Amongst those present was
the same Enguerrand, who, when the former bishop was rejected by the
king because of his frivolity, had by his appeal to the king obtained his
election. It was plain that he was using every effort of his influence to obtain the election of one who would be under his hand. One who had
the favour of the king and the clergy as a candidate, would not for that
reason dare to oppose his marriage. To the ruin, therefore, of the city and
of the whole province they chose a certain Gaudry, recommended by the
King of England, who by report was rich in silver and gold.

The aforesaid person being chosen by the clergy in a vain hope of profit,
by the efforts of Enguerrand in the first place with the aid of the rest
to their own harm, request for his election is made by the King of England
at the court contrary to canon law. He, although by no means doubtful of
the man's election, because he had no title from any church and had been
admitted to no holy orders except those of a clerk, used his influence to
have him made a sub-deacon and to procure him a canonry in the church
of Rouen, although up to this time he had lived the life of a soldier only.
When all, therefore, had given their assent to his election, Master Anselm,
the light of all France, ay, of the whole Latin world in learning and serenity
of character, alone opposed it. He, on certain information, was aware of
his character, whereas we were unwillingly supporting a stranger. There
were some of us, it is true, who did not approve of him, but amongst the
others cowards who followed the lead of our powerful rulers.

Being accepted, therefore, and coming into the city with empty pomp,
not long after he begged me to go with him to Rome. The Abbot of St.
Vincent, Adalberon, a native of Soissons, a good scholar, with the Abbot
of Remiremont, also not unlearned, and myself, junior to them both in

knowledge and years, he induced to go with him, paying the expenses himself. Setting out, therefore, and arriving at Langres, we were informed
that the Lord Pope Pascal had just before left Rome and was drawing
near to the borders of that diocese. In that town we stayed eight days.

And when the Lord Pope had come to Dijon, the clergy of Laon, a great
number of whom the bishop-elect had brought with him, go out to meet
the Pope and plead the cause of their elect before him in the castle where
he was staying. With many to tell him, the Pope was soon acquainted with
the facts and promised to act in accordance with the wishes of his peti-
tioners. Now their plea was that he had been duly elected, if the other
charges made by Anselm and conveyed to the ears of the Pope were
withdrawn. But the Pope's palace advisers, discovering how wealthy the
man was, made themselves agreeable to him and flattered him. For it is the
way of the world to become pleasant on the mention of gold.

The Pope, therefore, being received into the city, dealt next day with
the matter of our choice. And after I had read before him the report on
the election in which more than enough was said about his life and character, the Pope summoning us Abbots, who were present, and certain
priests of the church who had come with the bishop-elect, began to address us, taking for his subject the report of the election brought to him.
Now the assembly was full of very distinguished persons, Italian bishops
and our own, besides cardinals, and other very learned men. The Pope
then first asked why we had chosen a stranger. As none of the priests
made any reply to that (for hardly any of them knew the rudiments of
Latin), he turned to the Abbots. Now I was sitting between the other
two. They remaining silent when addressed, began on either side to urge
me to speak, and I, my youth making me abashed, and afraid to be branded
with rashness in a place and matter of such consequence, was with difficulty
induced to open my mouth. . . . In careful phrases I expressed myself
with moderate warmth and not deviating very far from the truth, that
we had not an intimate personal knowledge of the man, but had accepted
as true the testimony of others who had spoken of him with goodwill.

Finally, he asked what orders he had, and I replied that he was a sub-
deacon. Then he enquired in what church he had served, whereat I hesitated, fearing to lie, but it was suggested by my fellow-abbots that it was
in the church of Rouen. To this, however, I added truly that it was recently. Lastly, he asked whether he was of legitimate birth. He had clearly
been told that he was a bastard. On that head, as I was more certain than

on other points and spoke without hesitation, the Pope said, "Do you bring proof of this?" And I said, "On the other points I am silent, but on this I confidently affirm that he is neither bastard nor base-born." This objection the Pope, as we have said, withdrew. But the reason why he raised these points one after the other, was not to prevent his appointment, but because Anselm, who had made the charges against him, was present, so that what he had said privately, he might have the opportunity to bring up before the man's face.

But the Master having seen more deeply into the corruption of the palace party (I do not say of the Lord Pope), thought it a difficult matter to wrest the club from the hand of Hercules; therefore the great scholar, seeing the lords relying on the Lord Pope and myself, if I may dare to say so in jest, omitted to give any direct contradiction. And so the debate fell to the ground, the bishop-elect was brought forward, and the Pope's permission for his appointment granted. The meeting therefore having broken up and the Pope being gone, a group of cardinals approached me with great warmth saying, "Your speech gave us much pleasure." Which pleasure, Thou knowest, my Lord God, arose not so much from the fineness of my speech as from the very good hope they had of money, with which he had come stuffed. For both I and my fellow-abbot, Adalberon of St. Vincent, were each of us carrying twenty pounds of that money, with which perhaps the wide gape of their expectations was filled, and for that reason they were glad to back him and his backers.

Now when he received the sacrament of the anointing at St. Rufin, a gloomy omen was discovered in the Gospel of the day. For it was this; "A sword hath pierced through her soul." . . . In word and in conduct he was wonderfully unstable, wonderfully light. He took delight in talking about military affairs, dogs and hawks, which he had learnt to do among the English. Hence on one occasion when he had dedicated a church, and I with a young clerk of good disposition was riding in attendance, he came on a countryman with a lance. Snatching this up, with the mitre still on his head, which he should have held sacred, and spurring his horse, he couched it as if to strike an opponent. To him we said, the clerk in plain, but I in poetic fashion, "They agree not well and stay not together, the mitre and the lance."

Meanwhile that great wealth of English money, of cups and vessels, which had been wickedly gathered together, was quickly squandered. I have certainly heard from Master Anselm, who had travelled with him, when now Bishop, to revisit England, that when he came there, so great complaints broke out for restitution of vessels here and money there, wherever he turned, that it was plain to the Master, that his much paraded riches had been stolen from others or acquired by dishonest means.

About three years after his appointment he gave the following sign, as it were, to his time. One of the nobles of the city was the castellan of a nun's convent, named Gerard, a man of great energy. He, although of small stature and of lean frame, had so lively a mind and tongue, such energy in the pursuit of war, that he compelled the provinces of Soissons, Laon and Nijons, to fear him and won the respect of most men. Although he was known far and wide as one of sterling character, sometimes he made biting jests in coarse language against those about him, but never against people of good character. Hence he took upon himself both to speak ill in private and to shew open displeasure against that Countess of whom mention has been made before, acting very perversely in so doing, because he was attacking Enguerrand, this woman's besieger, who had with his great wealth advanced Gerard's fortunes. But before taking a wife Gerard had himself been too intimate with the woman of whom we are speaking. After he had been her lover for some time, on his marriage he drew in the rein of his wanton connection. Then the women too began to attack one another with foul words. For they were mutually aware of one another's lightness and the more they secretly knew of one another, the worse was their abuse. The Countess was therefore enraged against the other woman's husband, because she had been jilted by him and against his wife because she knew that from her lips frequently fell insulting remarks on herself, and being more venomous than any serpent, her determination to ruin the man waxed greater every day.

But because God puts a stumbling block in the way of those who would wilfully fall, an opportunity of destroying him suddenly occurred in the outbreak of enmity between Gerard and the Bishop Gaudry in consequence of offensive words used by Gerard about the Bishop and his household, which the Bishop endured neither patiently nor in silence. For having plotted with his friends and almost all the nobles of the city for the death of Gerard, after exchanging with them mutual oaths of assistance, to which certain rich women were parties, he left the matter in the hands of his fellow-conspirators and went on a journey to the Apostolic See, taken there by the basest designs, not to seek the Apostles, Thou knowest, O God, but that he might by his absence protect himself from any suspicion of complicity in such a crime. And so setting out about Martinmas, he arrived at Rome and stayed there until he learnt that the murder of his enemy had been carried out; who was as much hated by the bad as he was beloved by the good.

Now there were in that conspiracy with the Bishop himself two archdeacons of the church, Walter and Guy. . . .

Armed with seals and the Apostolic rescripts the Lord Prelate returned from Rome. . . .

Now after some time when he had set out for England to extract money from the English king, whom he had served, and who had formerly been his friend, the Archdeacons Walter and Guy, with the nobles of the city, devised the following plan: Of old time such ill-fate had settled upon that city that neither God nor any lord was feared therein, but according to each man's power and lust the state was involved in rapine and murder. For to begin with the source of the plague, whenever it happened that the king came there, he who ought to have exacted respect for himself with royal severity, was himself first shamefully fined on his own property. When his horses were led to the water morning or evening, his grooms were beaten and the horses carried off. It was known that the very clergy were held in such contempt, that neither their persons nor their goods were spared, as it is written, "Like as the people, so the priest." But what shall I say about the baser people? No one of the countrymen came into the city, no one except under the safest conduct approached it, who was not thrown into prison and held to ransom, or was not, as opportunity served, drawn without cause into a lawsuit. . . .

The clergy with the archdeacons considering this, and the nobles catching at pretexts for exacting money from the people, offer them through agents the choice of making composition by paying a sum to cover them. Now Commune is a new and a bad name of an arrangement for all the poorest classes to pay their usual due of servitude to their lords only once in the year, and to make good any breach of the laws they have committed by the payment fixed by law, and to be entirely free from all other exactions usually imposed on serfs. The people seizing on this opportunity for freeing themselves gathered huge sums of money to fill the gaping mouths of so many greedy men. And they, pleased with the shower poured upon them, took oaths binding themselves in the matter.

A pledge of mutual aid had been thus exchanged by the clergy and nobles with the people, when the Bishop returned with much wealth from England and being moved to anger against those responsible for this innovation, for a long time kept away from the city. But a quarrel full of honour and glory began between him and Walter, the archdeacon, his accomplice. The Archdeacon made very unbecoming remarks about his Bishop on the subject of the death of Gerard. . . .

Saying therefore that he was moved with relentless wrath against those who had taken that oath and the principals in the transaction, in the end his loud-sounding words were suddenly quieted by the offer of a great heap of silver and gold. Therefore he swore that he would maintain the rights of the Commune according to the terms duly drawn up at Noyon and Saint-Quintin. The King too was induced by a bribe from the people to confirm the same by oath. O my God, who could say how many disputes arose when the gifts of the people were accepted, how many after oath had been sworn to reverse what they had agreed to, whilst they sought to bring back the serfs who had been freed from the oppression of their yoke, to their former state. At least there was implacable hate by the Bishop and nobles against the citizens, and whereas he has not the power to crush the freedom of the French, after the fashion of Normandy and England, the pastor is weak and forgetful of his sacred calling through his insatiable greed. Whenever one of the people entered a court of law, where he was dependent not on the justice of God, but on his ability to please his judges, if I may say so, he was drained of his substance to the last penny.

Hence because the taking of gifts is wont to be attended by the sub-version of all justice, the coiners of the currency, knowing that if they did wrong in their office, they could save themselves by money bribes, cor-rupted the coinage with so much base metal that through this very many were reduced to poverty. For as they made coins of the cheapest bronze, which in a moment of certain dishonest arts they made brighter than silver, (shame on them!) fond men were deceived, and giving up their goods of great or little value, got in exchange nothing but dross. And the patient suffering of this by the Lord Bishop was well rewarded, and thus not only within the province of Laon but in all directions the ruin of many was hastened. And when he was deservedly powerless to uphold the value of his own currency wickedly debased by himself, he instituted pence of Amiens, also most debased, to be current in the city for some time; but when he could by no means keep that up, he struck an impression of his own time, on which he had stamped a pastoral staff to represent him-self. This was received with such laughter and scorn, that it had less value than the debased coinage.

Meantime, since on the issue of each of these new coins, proclamation was made that no one should criticise the wretched impression, there ensued frequent occasion for accusing the people of speaking evil of the Bishop's ordinances, and hence exaction of all sorts of heavy fines could be carried out. Moreover a certain monk of the very worst reputation in every respect, named Theodorus of Thorn, of which place he was a native, brought very large quantities of silver from Flanders. Bringing all this down to the false standard of the Laon mint, he scattered it all over the surrounding province. By appealing to the greed of the rich with his hateful presents and bringing in lies, perjury and want, he robbed his country of truth, justice and wealth. No act of an enemy, no plunderings, no burnings have hurt the province more ever since the Roman walls contained the ancient mint of the city.

Having therefore summoned the nobles and certain of the clergy on the last day of Lent in the holy days of the Passion of our Lord, he determined to urge the annulment of the Commune, to which he had sworn, and had by bribes induced the King to swear, and the day before the Passover, that is to say on the day of the Lord's Supper, he summoned the King to this pious duty and instructed the King and all his people to break their oaths. . . . He was intriguing with the King's courtiers for the annulment of the Commune and for the restoration by the King of the laws of the city to their former state. But the citizens fearing their overthrow, promised four hundred (perhaps more) pounds to the King and his courtiers. In reply the Bishop begged the nobles to go with him to interview the King. They promised on their part seven hundred pounds, and King Louis, son of Philip, of conspicuous person and a mighty warrior, hating sloth in business, of dauntless courage in adversity, and in other respects a good man, in this was not very just that he gave ear and attention too much to worthless persons debased by greed. And this redounded to his own great loss and blame and the ruin of many, which it is certain took place here and elsewhere.

The King's craving for money being turned therefore, as I have said, to feed upon the larger promise, through his consent the oaths of the Bishop and the nobles became void without any regard for honour or the sacred season. That night because of the outbreak of disorder caused by his most unjust blow, although the King had a lodging elsewhere, he was afraid to sleep outside the Bishop's palace. Very early in the morning the King departed and the Bishop assured the nobles they need have no fear about the agreement to pay so much money, knowing that he himself would pay whatever they had promised. "And," said he, "if I do not perform my promise, hand me over to the king's prison for ransom."

The compact of the Commune being broken, such rage, such amazement seized the citizens that all the officials abandoned their duties and the stalls of the craftsmen and cobblers were closed and nothing was exposed for sale by the innkeepers and hucksters, who expected to have nothing left when the lords began plundering. For at once the property of all was calculated by the Bishop and nobles, and whatever any man was known to have given to arrange the Commune, so much was demanded of him to procure its annulment. These events took place on the day of the Passover, which is called the preparation, and on the holy Sabbath when their minds were being prepared to receive the body and blood of the Lord, they were made ready for murders only here, for perjury there. Why say more? All the efforts of the prelate and the nobles in these days were reserved for fleecing their inferiors. But those inferiors were no longer moved by mere anger, but goaded into a murderous lust for the death of the Bishop and his accomplices and bound themselves by oath to effect their purpose. Now they say that four hundred took the oath. Such a mob could not be secret and when it came to the ears of Anselm towards evening of the holy Sabbath, he sent word to the Bishop, as he was retiring to rest, not to go out to the early morning service, knowing that if he did he must certainly be killed. But he, infatuated with excessive pride said, "Fie, surely I shall not perish at the hands of such." Yet notwithstanding his scornful words, he did not dare to rise for matins or to enter the church. The next day, as he followed the clergy in procession, he ordered his household people and all the soldiers coming behind him to carry short swords under their garments. In this procession, when a little disorder, as is likely in a crowd, began to arise, one of the citizens coming out of the crypt and thinking the time had come for the murder, to which they were sworn, began to cry out in a loud voice as a signal, "Commune, Commune!" over and over again. And because it was a feast day, this was easily stopped, yet it brought suspicion on the other party. And so, when the service of the mass was over, the Bishop summoned a great number of countrymen from the episcopal manors and manned the towers of the church and gave orders that his palace should be guarded, although he was almost as much hated by them, as they knew that the piles of money, which he had promised the King, must be drained from their own purses.

Now on the second day after Easter it is the custom for the clergy to assemble at St. Vincent's. Since therefore the conspirators had been anticipated the day before, they had decided to act on this day, and would have done so, if they had seen that all the nobles were with the Bishop. For they had found one of the nobles in the suburb, a harmless man, who

had recently married a young cousin of mine, a woman of modest character. But they were unwilling to attack him fearing to put others on their
guard. Having therefore reached the third day of Easter and feeling more
secure the Bishop allows those men to depart, whom he had put in the
towers and palace to protect him.

The next day, that is, the fifth in Easter week, after midday, as he was
engaged in business with Archdeacon Walter about the getting of money,
behold there arose a disorderly noise throughout the city. . . .

Next the outrageous mob attacking the Bishop and howling before the
walls of his palace, he with some who were succouring him fought them
off by hurling of stones and shooting of arrows. For he now, as at all times,
shewed great spirit as a fighter; but because he had wrongly and in vain
taken up another sword, by the sword he perished. Therefore being unable
to stand against the reckless assaults of the people, he put on the clothes
of one of his servants and flying to the vaults of the church hid himself in
a cask, shut up in which with the head fastened on by a faithful follower
he thought himself safely hidden. And as they ran hither and thither demanding where, not the Bishop, but the hangdog, was, they seized one
of his pages, but through his faithfulness could not get what they wanted.
Laying hands on another, they learn from the traitor's nod where to look
for him. Entering the vaults, therefore, and searching everywhere, at last
they found him in the following manner.

There was a pestilent fellow, a bondman of the church of the Blessed
Vincent, but for a long time an official and overseer of Enguerrand of
Coucy, who being set over the collection of tolls paid for crossing the
bridge called Soord, sometimes watched there until there were only a few
travellers passing, and having robbed them of all their property, in order
that they might make no complaint against him, threw them into the river
with a weight round their necks. How often he had done this, God only
knows. The number of the thefts and robberies being more than any
one could count, the unchecked wickedness of his heart, and one as might
say, was displayed also in the truculence of his looks. This man having
incurred the displeasure of Enguerrand, went over wholly to the party of
the Commune in Laon. He who had spared neither monk nor clerk nor
stranger, in fact no sex, was last of all to be the slayer of a bishop. He the
leader and instigator of this attack searched most diligently for the Bishop,
whom he hated more bitterly than the rest.

And so, as they sought for him in every vessel, this fellow halted in
front of that cask, where the man was hiding, and having broken in the

head, asked again and again who was there. And he, hardly able to move his frozen lips under his blows, said "A prisoner." Now the Bishop was wont in mockery to call him Isengrin, I suppose, because of his wolfish look, for so many people call wolves. The wretch, therefore, says to the Bishop, "Is this my Lord Isengrin stored away?" Renulf therefore, sinner though he was, yet the Lord's anointed, was dragged forth from the cask by the hair, beaten with many blows and brought out into the open air in the narrow lane of the clergy's cloister before the house of the chaplain Godfrey. And as he piteously implored them, ready to take oath that he would henceforth cease to be their Bishop, that he would give them un-limited riches, that he would leave the country, and as they with hardened hearts jeered at him, one named Bernard and surnamed de Brueys, lifting his battle-axe brutally dashed out the brains of that sacred, though sinner's, head, and he slipped between the hands of those who held him, was dead before he reached the ground stricken by another thwart blow under the eye-sockets and across the middle of the nose. There brought to his end, his legs were cut off and many another wound inflicted. But Thibaut seeing the ring on the finger of the erstwhile prelate and not being able to draw it off, cut off the dead man's finger and took it. And so stripped to his skin he was thrown into a corner in front of his chaplain's house. My God, who shall recount the mocking words that were thrown at him by passersby, as he lay there, and with what clods and stones and dirt his corpse was covered?

THE ORDINANCE OF LABORERS

IN THE SUMMER of 1348 the Black Death, coming from the distant East by way of the Continent, raged in western England. It spread in the winter to London and thence to the eastern coast. Many authorities describe the scourge as a bubonic plague, although others point out the similarity of its symptoms to those of the influenza epidemic of 1918. In England, in any case, between a quarter and a third of the population died.

The plague brought about a scarcity of laborers. Higher wages, in some cases fantastic ones, were asked and had to be given. Prices rose. There had been government regulation of such economic concerns before. Now the king issued the far-reaching Ordinance of Laborers of June, 1349, and Parliament at its next session passed the somewhat more specific Statute of Laborers in February, 1351. Both king and Parliament sought to set some limit to the runaway conditions which were threatening to bring English society to ruin.

A serious attempt was made to enforce the regulations, and the justices of laborers were created to administer them. Many violators were punished, and there can be little doubt that some lowering of the demands of workers was effected. It was, nevertheless, impossible to keep wages and prices at the statutory level. England was left to find economic balance by a continued, if accelerated, transference of villein holdings to rented ones and by the commutation of services to money payments. Although it should be kept in mind that conditions were not the same throughout all England, the landlord was the one who suffered most, economically, during this period. He regained his position only in time, and then as the recipient of extensive rents. Many villeins gained from their changed tenure, as many more were to do in the future, and wage earners found many a lord willing to violate the Statute despite the possible penalties.

The effects of the plague upon economic and social life, though sudden and dramatic, should be estimated in their true historic perspective. Undoubtedly there had already set in a pronounced movement away from labor services toward money rents, from servile holding to renting, and an increase in the number of hired workingmen. On the Continent this movement had been especially evident. It was merely accelerated by the conditions brought about by the pestilence.

The Ordinance of Laborers, which follows, has been put into English more nearly approaching present-day usage on the basis of the translation in the *Statutes of the Realm* (1810), Vol. I, and by comparison with the Latin and Old French texts, respectively, in B. H. Putnam, *The Enforcement of the Statutes of Labourers* (New York, Columbia University Press, 1908), Appendix.

AN ORDINANCE CONCERNING LABORERS AND SERVANTS

THE KING TO THE SHERIFF OF KENT. Greeting. Because a great part of the people and especially of workmen and servants late died of the pestilence, many seeing the necessity of lords and the scarcity of servants will not serve unless they receive excessive wages, and others preferring to beg in idleness rather than get their living by labor, we, considering the serious inconvenience which may hereafter arise from the lack especially of ploughmen and such laborers, have held deliberation and consultation on this matter with the prelates and the nobles and other experienced men assisting us, and by their unanimous counsel have ordained:

That every man and woman of our kingdom of England of whatever condition, free or bond, ablebodied, and within the age of sixty years, not living by trade or practicing a certain craft, or having of his own by which he may live, or his own land in the tillage of which he may occupy himself, and not serving another, if, his station considered, he be needed to serve in appropriate service, he shall be bound to serve him who so requires him. And he shall receive only the wages, liveries, hire, or salary, which were accustomed to be given in the places where he ought to serve, in the twentieth year of our reign of England or in the five or six common years immediately preceding, with the provision that the lords be preferred before others in the bondmen or the tenants holding their land thus to be retained in their service. Nevertheless the said lords in this shall retain no more than are necessary for them. And if any such man or woman, being required to serve, will not do the same and it is proved by two true men before the sheriff, the bailiff, lord, or constable of the town where this happens, he shall immediately be taken by them or one of them and put in the nearest jail there to remain under strict custody until he finds surety to serve in the aforesaid manner.

And if any reaper, mower, or other workman or servant of whatever status or condition, retained in any man's service, leaves the said service without reasonable cause or permission before the term agreed, he shall undergo the penalty of imprisonment. And no one shall presume to receive or to retain any such in his service under the same penalty.

And no man shall pay or promise to pay anyone any more wages, liveries, hire, or salary than the accustomed one as aforementioned. Nor shall anyone in any other manner demand or receive the same under penalty of double that which shall be so paid, promised, demanded, or received to be given to him who thereby shall feel himself injured. And if none such is willing to prosecute then it shall go to any of the people who will prosecute. And such prosecution shall be in the court of the lord of the place where such case happens. And if the lords of the towns or manors shall presume in any way to act contrary to our present ordinance either by themselves or by their servants, then prosecution shall be made in the aforementioned manner against them in the counties, wapentakes, ridings, or in our other courts of this kind under penalty of three times that paid or promised them or their servants. And if by chance any before this present ordinance shall have contracted with anyone for such service at higher wages, by no means shall he be bound by reason of the said contract to pay more than otherwise was accustomed to be paid to such person. On the contrary he shall not presume to pay any more under the aforementioned penalty.

And saddlers, pelterers, whittawyers, cordwainers, tailors, smiths, carpenters, masons, tilers, shipwrights, carters, and all other artisans and laborers shall not take for their labor and workmanship more than what was accustomed to be paid to such persons in the twentieth year and other common years preceding, as aforementioned, in the places where they shall happen to work. And if anyone shall receive more, he shall be committed to the nearest jail in the aforementioned manner.

And butchers, fishmongers, hostelers, brewers, bakers, poulterers, and all other sellers of all sorts of victuals shall be bound to sell the same victuals for a reasonable price having regard for the price that such victuals are sold in nearby places so that such sellers have moderate profit—not excessive ones but those to be reasonably required by the distance of the places whence the said victuals are carried. And if any sell such victuals in any other manner, and be convicted thereof in the aforementioned manner he shall pay double what he so received to the injured party or in default of him to any other that will prosecute in this matter. And the mayor and the bailiffs of the cities, boroughs, merchant-towns, and others, and of ports and maritime places shall have power to inquire of each and everyone who shall in any way trangress against this and to levy the aforementioned penalty to the use of those by whose suits such transgressors shall have been convicted. And in case the same mayor and bailiffs shall neglect to execute these premises, and be convicted of it before the justices to be appointed by us, then the same mayor and bailiffs shall be compelled by the same justices to pay to the injured party, or to any other prosecuting in his default, three times the value of the thing thus sold. And nevertheless they shall be grievously punished on our part.

And because many sturdy beggars, as long as they can live by begging, refuse to labor and give themselves up to idleness and sin and sometimes to theft and other infamies, no one under the aforementioned penalty of imprisonment shall presume in the guise of piety or alms to give anything to such who are well able to labor or to aid them in their slothfulness, so that by this they may be compelled to labor for the necessities of life.

We order you, firmly enjoining, that you cause each and every of these premises to be publicly proclaimed and to be observed and duly put in execution as aforementioned in the cities, boroughs, merchant-towns, sea-ports, and other places in your bailiwick where you shall think fit, within liberties as well as without. And by no means omit to do this as you regard us and the common advantage of our realm, and as you wish to keep yourself unharmed.

Witness the King at Westminster, the eighteenth day of June, by the King himself and the whole Council.

Like writs are directed to each of the sheriffs throughout England.

THE KING, TO THE REVEREND FATHER IN CHRIST, W., BY THE SAME GRACE [OF GOD], BISHOP OF WINCHESTER. Greeting. "Because a great part of the people," as before, until "for the necessities of life" and then thus: And therefore we request that you make public these premises in every one of the churches and other places of your diocese where you think fit, directing the rectors, the vicars of such churches, the priests and others under you to exhort and to lead their parishioners by salutary admonitions to labor and to observe the aforesaid ordinance as the particular need may require. And that you also restrain the stipendiary chaplains of your diocese aforementioned who, as it is said, in like manner now refuse to serve without an excessive salary. And compel them to serve for the accustomed salary, as befits them, under pain of suspension and interdict. And by no means omit to do this as you regard us and the common advantage of our realm.

Witness, as before, by the King himself and the whole Council.

Like letters of request are directed to the several bishops of England, and to the guardian of the spiritualities of the Archbishopric of Canterbury during the vacancy of the See, under the same date.

GRANT OF TWO FAIRS AT
AIX-LA-CHAPELLE

IN THE MIDDLE AGES markets and fairs were important for the exchange of goods. They stimulated production and provided an effective means of distributing raw materials and finished products. The granting of rights to hold markets and fairs was a valuable source of income to both lords and localities. Competition developed to see who could attract more merchants through the granting of better conditions.

Markets were principally concerned with the exchange of local produce. Commonly held once a week, they were, of course, a basis for larger trading activity and may well be considered the foundation of the hierarchy of medieval exchange institutions.

Fairs were on a grander scale and were held seasonally and for longer periods. To them came merchants from distant places to engage in larger transactions and to distribute finished products and raw materials which were then further distributed by lesser traders. Because of their advantageous geographical situation and because of the privileges granted by higher authorities, certain localities became the sites of famous fairs. Perhaps the best known in western Europe were the fairs of the province of Champagne, an important production center for woolens—and, of course, wine—situated at the most important crossroads in western Europe, roughly halfway between the Mediterranean (reached via the Rhone and Marseille, or via the Alpine passes and the Po Valley) and the Atlantic (reached via the Seine and Paris, or via the Escant and Bruges, or via the Rhine and Cologne).

No fair could be successful without an abundant local supply of money. The coins struck at the Champagne fairs of Provins became world famous; so did the standard weights of the Champagne center of Troyes. The excessive variety of moneys in use was partly compensated by the tendency of local coinages to conform with better-known standards. There was a Provins block and a Cologne block (to which Aix-la-Chapelle adhered from the beginning); moreover, the royal coinage of Paris, the imperial coinage of Pavia, and the coins of the prosperous cities of Venice (ducate) and Florence (florins) were widely imitated. On the other hand, operations of change in the fairs led to speculation on the anticipated fluctuations of foreign coins and, through a devious channel, also to the introduction of the bill of exchange.

The Champagne fairs declined in the later thirteenth century, owing to a combination of circumstances including the appearance of Genoese and Venetian ships in the North Sea, which was reached by way of the Gibraltar Strait. Furthermore, with the growth of semipermanent commercial companies, most of the functions of the fairs were provided for by a network of agencies (*fattorie*) which each company kept in the main centers of international trade.

The following has been taken from R. C. Cave and H. H. Coulson, eds., *A Source Book for Medieval Economic History* (St. Paul, Minn., Bruce Publishing Co., 1936).

GRANT OF TWO FAIRS AT AIX-LA-CHAPELLE, 1166

IN THE NAME of the Holy and Indivisible Trinity, Frederick, by favor of divine clemency, Emperor Augustus of the Romans. Since the royal palace of Aix-la-Chapelle excels all provinces and cities in dignity and honor, both for the praise given there to the body of the most blessed Emperor Charlemagne, which that city alone is known to have, and because it is a royal seat at which the Emperors of the Romans were first crowned, it is fitting and reasonable that we, following the example of the holy lord Charlemagne and of other predecessors of ours, should fortify that same place, which is a pillar of support to the empire, with lavish gifts of liberty and privileges, as if with walls and towers. We have therefore decreed that there should be held twice a year the solemn and universal fairs of Aix-la-Chapelle. And this we have done on the advice of the merchants. Moreover, we have preserved the rights of neighboring cities, so that these fairs may not only not be a hindrance to their fairs but may rather increase their profits. And so, on the advice of our nobles, we have given, out of respect for the most holy lord, the Emperor Charlemagne, this liberty to all merchants—that they may be quit and free of all toll throughout the year at these fairs in this royal place, and may buy and sell goods freely just as they wish. No merchant, nor any other person, may take a merchant to court for the payment of any debt during these fairs, nor take him there for any business that was conducted before the fairs began; but if anything be done amiss during the fairs, let it be made good according to justice during the fairs. Moreover, the first fair shall begin on Quadragesima Sunday, which is six weeks before Easter, and it shall last for fifteen days. The second fair shall begin eight days before the feast of St. Michael and shall continue for eight days after that feast. And all people coming to, staying at, or going from the fairs shall have peace for their persons and goods. And lest the frequent changing of coins, which are sometimes light and sometimes heavy, should redound to the hurt of so glorious a place at any time in the future, on the advice of our court, we have ordered money to be struck there of the same purity, weight, and form, and in the same quantity, and to be kept to the same standard. Twenty-four solidi shall be struck from a mark, always having the value of twelve solidi of Cologne, so that twelve Cologne solidi may always be made from twenty-four of these solidi, just as twenty-four solidi may always be struck from twelve solidi of Cologne. The form of the coins will be such that on one side will be the image of St. Charles the Great and his superscription, and on the obverse our own image with the superscription of our own name. And a certain abuse has prevailed for a long time in the courts of Aix-la-Chapelle so that if he, who was impleaded for calumny or for any other thing, could not offer satisfaction by compensation for his offense, except he flee from the country at once, he incurred the full penalty of composition; therefore, we, condemning this bad law forever, have decreed that any one may offer in this our royal town of Aix-la-Chapelle, for any cause for which he has been impleaded, compensation by whatever small thing he is able to take off with his hands while standing upright, without bending his body, such thing as a cloak, tunic, hat, shirt, or other garment. And because the taking and exchanging of money, other than the money of Aix-la-Chapelle, has been condemned by an unjust law, we have decreed to the contrary, that all money shall be current in our city according to its quality, and it shall be accepted by everyone according to what it has been declared to be worth. Moreover, we grant and confirm to the merchants of that city that they may have a mint and a house for exchanging their silver and money whenever they decide to go away on business. Whoever out of boldness decides to oppose our decree, or by temerity to break it, shall be in our mercy and will pay a hundred pounds of gold to our court. And in order that all the things we have decreed may be accepted as genuine and be faithfully observed we have ordered this charter to be written and to be sealed by the impression of our seal.

THE KING'S MIRROR

THE ELEMENTS of a flourishing commercial and manufacturing economy, in the literal sense of the word manufacturing, "hand-made," were generally present in favored parts of western Europe by the eleventh century. The Crusades and the colonization in eastern Europe bear witness to growing economic activity. Land was being reclaimed from the forests, stockades were appearing on the frontiers, pilgrims and merchants were moving afar, and the amenities of life were sought after. Certainly agriculture was of the greatest importance, as it was to continue to be well into the eighteenth century; but in the eleventh and succeeding centuries trade and manufacturing gained in importance and contributed to changes in economic, political, and social institutions and in the accepted principles of conduct.

The attitude of the foremost men of the Middle Ages toward life in general and daily commerce in particular, was that the individual's every action should be guided by his concern for his immortal soul and for the good of his fellow men. The social consciousness of that period, which was firmly founded in religion, encouraged the development of institutions which could check those who thought less of salvation and of the community than of their own immediate gain.

The *King's Mirror* was written between 1240 and 1247 by a learned Norseman who remains anonymous. The translation from the old Norse has been taken from L. M. Larson's edition, published by The American-Scandinavian Foundation (New York, 1917).

THE KING'S MIRROR

"THE FEAR OF THE LORD IS THE BEGINNING OF WISDOM"

Son. Good day, sire! I have come to see you as it behooves a humble and obedient son to approach a loving and renowned father; and I pray you to listen with patience to the questions that I have in mind to ask and kindly to vouchsafe an answer to each one.

Father. Inasmuch as you are my only son, I am pleased to have you come often to see me, for there are many subjects which we ought to discuss. I shall be glad to hear what you wish to inquire about and to answer such questions as are discreetly asked.

Son. I have heard the common report (which I believe is true) as to your wisdom, that in all the land it would be difficult to find a man who has greater insight into every form of knowledge than you have; for all those who have difficult matters to settle are eager to get your decision. I have also been told that the same was true when you were at the royal court, and that the entire government, lawmaking, treaty making, and every other sort of business, seemed to be guided by your opinion. Now as I am the lawful heir to your worldly possessions, I should also like to share somewhat in the heritage of your wisdom. Wherefore I wish to have you point out to me the beginnings and the alphabet of wisdom, as far as I am able to learn them from you, so that I may later be able to read all your learned writings, and thus follow in your footsteps. For I am sure that after your decease many will rely on your having trained me after your own ways.

Father. It pleases me to hear you speak in this wise, and I shall be glad to answer; for it is a great comfort to me that I shall leave much wealth for my own true son to enjoy after my days; but I should scarcely regard him as a son, though I had begotten him, if he were a fool. Now if you seek understanding, I will show you the basis and the beginning of all wisdom, as a great and wise man once expressed it: to fear Almighty God, this is the beginning of wisdom. But He is not to be feared as an enemy, but rather with the fear of love, as the Son of God taught the man who asked him what the substance of the law was. For the Son of God referred him to the Scripture that reads as follows: Thou shalt love God with all thy heart and with all thy strength and with all thy might. Now one should love God above everything else and fear Him at all times when evil desires arise; he should banish evil longings for God's sake, though he were bold enough to cherish them for men's sake. Now if you wish to know what are the beginnings and the first steps in the pursuit of wisdom, this is the true beginning, and there is none other. And whoever learns this and observes it shall not be wanting in true knowledge or in any form of goodness.

Son. This is indeed loving counsel, such as one might expect from you; besides, it is good and easily learned by every one whom fortune follows. Still, if one is to be reputed a wise man, it will surely be necessary to take up many things that pertain to the various crafts.

Father. This is the beginning and the alphabet of every good thing. But through the alphabet one learns to read books, and in the same way, it is always better the more crafts are added to this art. For through the crafts a man gains wisdom whatever the calling that he intends to follow, whether that of kingsman, yeoman, or merchant.

THE ACTIVITIES AND HABITS OF A MERCHANT

Son. I am now in my most vigourous years and have a desire to travel abroad; for I would not venture to seek employment at court before I had observed the customs of other men. Such is my intention at present, unless you should give me other advice.

Father. Although I have been a kingsman rather than a merchant, I have no fault to find with that calling, for often the best of men are chosen for it. But much depends on whether the man is more like those who are true merchants, or those who take the merchant's name but are mere frauds and foisterers, buying and selling wrongfully.

Son. It would be more seemly for me to be like the rightful ones; for it would be worse than one might think likely, if your son were to imitate those who are not as they ought. But whatever my fate is to be, I desire to have you inform me as to the practices of such men as seem to be capable in that business.

Father. The man who is to be a trader will have to brave many perils, sometimes at sea and sometimes in heathen lands, but nearly always among alien peoples; and it must be his constant purpose to act discreetly wherever he happens to be. On the sea he must be alert and fearless.

When you are in a market town, or wherever you are, be polite and agreeable; then you will secure the friendship of all good men. Make it a habit to rise early in the morning, and go first and immediately to church wherever it seems most convenient to hear the canonical hours, and hear all the hours and mass from matins on. Join in the worship, repeating such psalms and prayers as you have learned. When the services are over, go out to look after your business affairs. If you are unacquainted with the traffic of the town, observe carefully how those who are reputed the best and most prominent merchants conduct their business. You must also be careful to examine the wares that you buy before the purchase is finally made to make sure that they are sound and flawless. And whenever you make a purchase, call in a few trusty men to serve as witnesses as to how the bargain was made.

You should keep occupied with your business till breakfast or, if necessity demands it, till midday; after that you should eat your meal. Keep your table well provided and set with a white cloth, clean victuals, and good drinks. Serve enjoyable meals, if you can afford it. After the meal you may either take a nap or stroll about a little while for pastime and to see what other good merchants are employed with, or whether any new wares have come to the borough which you ought to buy. On returning to your lodgings examine your wares, lest they suffer damage after coming into your hands. If they are found to be injured and you are about to dispose of them, do not conceal the flaws from the purchaser: show him what the defects are and make such a bargain as you can; then you cannot be called a deceiver. Also put a good price on your wares, though not too high, and yet very near what you see can be obtained; then you cannot be called a foisterer.

Finally, remember this, that whenever you have an hour to spare you should give thought to your studies, especially to the law books; for it is clear that those who gain knowledge from books have keener wits than others, since those who are the most learned have the best proofs for their knowledge. Make a study of all the laws, but while you remain a merchant there is no law that you will need to know more thoroughly than the Bjarkey code. If you are acquainted with the law, you will not be annoyed by quibbles when you have suits to bring against men of your own class, but will be able to plead according to law in every case.

But although I have most to say about laws, I regard no man perfect in knowledge unless he has thoroughly learned and mastered the customs of the place where he is sojourning. And if you wish to become perfect in knowledge, you must learn all the languages, first of all Latin and French, for these idioms are most widely used; and yet, do not neglect your native tongue or speech.

Son. May God reward you, sire, for the love of kinship that you show in pointing out so many things that I may find needful,—if I have the good fortune to learn them and to remember them after they are learned. And if you think there are any other important matters that ought to be taken up in this discussion, I shall be glad to listen attentively.

Father. There are, indeed, certain matters which should not be omitted from this discourse, but they can be stated in a few words, if that seems best. Train yourself to be as active as possible, though not so as to injure your health. Strive never to be downcast, for a downcast mind is always morbid; try rather to be friendly and genial at all times, of an even temper and never moody. Be upright and teach the right to every man who wishes to learn from you; and always associate with the best men. Guard your tongue carefully; this is good counsel, for your tongue may honor you, but it may also condemn you. Though you be angry speak few words and never in passion; for unless one is careful, he may utter words in wrath that he would later give gold to have unspoken. On the whole, I know of no revenge, though many employ it, that profits a man less than to bandy heated words with another, even though he has a quarrel to settle with him. You shall know of a truth that no virtue is higher or stronger than the power to keep one's tongue from foul or profane speech, tattling, or slanderous talk in any form. If children be given to you, let them not grow up without learning a trade; for we may expect a man to keep closer to knowledge and business when he comes of age, if he is trained in youth while under control.

And further, there are certain things which you must beware of and shun like the devil himself: these are drinking, chess, harlots, quarreling, and throwing dice for stakes. For upon such foundations the greatest calamities are built;

and unless they strive to avoid these things, few only are able to live long without blame or sin.

Observe carefully how the sky is lighted, the course of the heavenly bodies, the grouping of the hours, and the points of the horizon. Learn also how to mark the movements of the ocean and to discern how its turmoil ebbs and swells; for that is knowledge which all must possess who wish to trade abroad. Learn arithmetic thoroughly, for merchants have great need of that.

If you come to a place where the king or some other chief who is in authority has his officials, seek to win their friendship; and if they demand any necessary fees on the ruler's behalf, be prompt to render all such payments, lest by holding too tightly to little things you lose the greater. Also beware lest the king's belongings find their way into your purse; for you cannot know but that he may be covetous who has those things in charge, and it is easier to be cautious beforehand than to crave pardon afterwards. If you can dispose of your wares at suitable prices, do not hold them long; for it is the wont of merchants to buy constantly and to sell rapidly.

If you are preparing to carry on trade beyond the seas and you sail your own ship, have it thoroughly coated with tar in the autumn and, if possible, keep it tarred all winter. But if the ship is placed on timbers too late to be coated in the fall, tar it when spring opens and let it dry thoroughly afterwards. Always buy shares in good vessels or in none at all. Keep your ship attractive, for then capable men will join you and it will be well manned. Be sure to have your ship ready when summer begins and do your traveling while the season is best. Keep reliable tackle on shipboard at all times, and never remain out at sea in late autumn, if you can avoid it. If you attend carefully to all these things, with God's mercy you may hope for success. This, too, you must keep constantly in mind, if you wish to be counted a wise man, that you ought never to let a day pass without learning something that will profit you. Be not like those who think it beneath their dignity to hear or learn from others such things even as might avail them much if they knew them. For a man must regard it as great an honor to learn as to teach, if he wishes to be considered thoroughly informed.

There remain a few minor matters that ought to be mentioned. Whenever you travel at sea, keep on board two or three hundred ells of wadmal of a sort suitable for mending sails, if that should be necessary, a large number of needles, and a supply of thread and cord. It may seem trivial to mention these things, but it is often necessary to have them on hand. You will always need to carry a supply of nails, both spikes and rivets, of such sizes as your ship demands; also good boat hooks and broadaxes, gouges and augers, and all such other tools as ship carpenters make use of. All these things that I have now named you must remember to carry with you on shipboard, whenever you sail on a trading voyage and the ship is your own. When you come to a market town where you expect to tarry, seek lodgings from the innkeeper who is reputed the most discreet and the most popular among both kingsmen and boroughmen. Always buy good clothes and eat good fare if your means permit; and never keep unruly or quarrelsome men as attendants or messmates. Keep your temper calm though not to the point of suffering abuse or bringing upon yourself the reproach of cowardice. Though necessity may force you into strife, be not in a hurry to take revenge; first make sure that your effort will succeed and strike where it ought. Never display a heated temper when you see that you are likely to fail, but be sure to maintain your honor at some later time, unless your opponent should offer a satisfactory atonement.

If your wealth takes on rapid growth, divide it and invest it in a partnership trade in fields where you do not yourself travel; but be cautious in selecting partners. Watch with care over the property which the saints are to share with you and always bring it faithfully to the place to which it was originally promised.

If you have much capital invested in trade, divide it into three parts: put one-third into partnerships with men who are permanently located in market boroughs, are trustworthy, and are experienced in business. Place the other two parts in various business ventures; for if your capital is invested in different places, it is not likely that you will suffer losses in all your wealth at one time: more likely it will be secure in some localities, though frequent losses be suffered. But if you find that the profits of trade bring a decided increase to your funds, draw out the two-thirds and invest them in good farm land, for such property is generally thought the most secure, whether the enjoyment of it falls to one's self or to one's kinsmen. With the remaining third you may do as seems best,—continue to keep it in business or place it all in land.

However, though you decide to keep your funds invested in trade, discontinue your own journeys at sea or as a trader in foreign fields, as soon as your means have attained sufficient growth and you have studied foreign customs as much as you like. Keep all that you see in careful memory, the evil with the good; remember evil practices as a warning, and the good customs as useful to yourself and to others who may wish to learn from you.

ROBERT OF CLARI

A LESS UPLIFTING PICTURE of commerce in the medieval period than that furnished by the *King's Mirror* is offered by the history of the conventionally numbered "Fourth" Crusade. The Italian city-states were in a favorable position to maintain a thriving sea-borne trade. This was more marked after the Mohammedans had been driven into Africa from the Continent (with the exception of Spain) and from many strategic western islands, and when the Crusades carried the war into the eastern littoral of the Mediterranean. The paramount interest of commerce did not, however, foster any great spirit of cooperation among the city-states against the Mohammedan enemy. When it served their mercantile purposes they might ally to fight the Mohammedans if fighting was necessary; otherwise they drove their bargains and let crusading idealism bob along in the wake. No more than many of the kings and the feudal nobility could they, for other reasons, set aside their own bitter rivalries, even when they actually undertook crusading ventures. From the complexity of the religious, political, and economic motives behind them the Crusades gain much of their lasting interest. Here only the more narrowly economic interests of the city-states, and more particularly those of Venice, will be treated.

Venice, founded only in the fifth century, when refugees fled to her lagoons and islands before the barbarian invaders, was favored by early and continuous connections with Constantinople, and in fact was nominally a part of the Eastern empire. Until the Crusades, Venice was the great middle-man between the East and the West, just as Constantinople was the entrepôt for wares from the Orient. There were, to be sure, other cities, and among them Pisa and Genoa became important, especially in the western Mediterranean, by driving the Mohammedans from Corsica and Sardinia and, in the case of Pisa, by striking out to share in the trade with the Eastern empire. When the Normans conquered southern Italy and Sicily, the assistance given by Genoa and Pisa was rewarded. More importantly, however, the Mohammedans had lost the key to the straits between the eastern and the western Mediterranean. Norman designs to control this trade and to bottle up the Adriatic as well, and even to conquer as far east as Constantinople, were thwarted by Venice, who thus preserved her commercial interests as well as the position of the Eastern empire. From the emperor, Venice secured almost a monopoly of western trade with Constantinople.

When the Crusades opened to the Italian cities larger opportunities in Asia Minor, Syria, and Palestine, rivalry mounted in the same proportion. Venice with her considerable fleet, which could be used for offense as well as for peaceful pursuits, got her good share of territory and trading privileges in the new ports. This situation was not to last, for the Holy Land, except for a few remnants, was lost to Saladin between 1187 and 1190. Venice now turned her thoughts toward an actual conquest of the Eastern empire, an undertaking which with the assistance of the Crusaders was shortly successful.

When Pope Innocent III planned a new Crusade he thought in terms of the conquest of a territory which might serve strategically as a sound base for striking at the Mohammedans in the Holy Land. How this intention was perverted by the Venetians to the conquest of Zara—a Christian city but nonetheless a rival to Venice's supremacy in the Adriatic—is told in Robert of Clari's *Conquest of Constantinople*. Thereafter the crusade was turned against Constantinople, where a revolution had worked against the Venetian interests in favor of the Pisans. Constantinople fell on April 13, 1204, and in apportioning the war's spoils Venice received three-eighths of the city and the church of Santa Sophia. She further made her seapower secure in the Aegean by the acquisition of the more important ports and islands. She also had a monopoly of the rich Black Sea trade through her control of the Bosporus. The Genoese were now her bitter rivals, and it was they who helped Michael Palaeologus regain Constantinople in 1261. The Venetians, in turn, were excluded and turned to other fields, such as Egypt, where they made more extensive treaties with the Sultan than they had previously enjoyed. Against Genoa, however, Venice could not prevail in Constantinople and the Black Sea.

The increasing political importance of the Ottoman Turks in the fourteenth century led at times to cooperation between the two rivals but never for long. In 1381 Genoa carried the war against the city of Venice itself and succeeded only in wearing herself out by the prodigious effort. Torn by civil strife at home, Genoa was easily occupied by the French in 1396. When in 1453 the Turks took Constantinople, lamentations resounded throughout western Europe, comparable only to those which followed the taking of Rome by the Visigoths in 410.

The following selection is taken from E. N. McNeal's translation from the Old French in *The Conquest of Constantinople* (New York, Columbia University Press, "Records of Civilization" series, 1936).

THE CONQUEST OF CONSTANTINOPLE

PREPARATIONS FOR THE CRUSADE

Afterwards, when the marquis had taken the cross, he said to the barons: "Lords," said the marquis, "where will you want to pass oversea, and to what land of the Saracens will you want to go?" The barons answered that they did not want to go to the land of Syria, for they would not be able to accomplish anything there, but they had thought of going to Babylon [Cairo] or to Alexandria, there in the very midst of things, where they would be able to do most, and had planned to hire a fleet which could transport them there all together. Then the marquis said that this was a good plan and he was right well agreed to it, and that they should send good messengers from among their best knights to Pisa or Genoa or Venice. To this plan the barons all agreed.

Then they chose their messengers, and they all agreed that Conon of Béthune should go and the marshal of Champagne. Then when they had chosen their messengers, the barons parted from one another, and the marquis went away to his own country and each of the others likewise. They commanded the messengers to hire vessels to transport four thousand knights and their harness and one hundred thousand men on foot. The messengers got ready their gear and went straight on until they came to Genoa, and they spoke to the Genoese and told them what they were seeking, and the Genoese said they could not help them in it at all. Then they went to Pisa and spoke to them of Pisa, and they answered them that they did not have so many vessels and could not do anything for them. Then they went on to Venice and spoke to the doge of Venice and told him what they were seeking: that they wanted to hire passage for four thousand knights and their harness and for one hundred thousand men on foot. When the doge heard of this, he said he would think on it, for so great an affair ought to be well considered. Then the doge summoned all the high councilors of the city and spoke to them and showed them what had been asked of him. And when they had counseled together the doge answered the messengers and said to them: "Lords, we are willing to make a bargain with you. We will find you a navy large enough for your needs for one hundred thousand marks, if you agree, on the understanding that I shall go along with half of those who are able to bear arms from all of Venice and that we shall have half of all the gains that are made there. And we will add fifty galleys at our own cost. And within a year from the day we shall name we will set you in whatever land you wish, whether at Babylon or at Alexandria." When the messengers heard this, they replied that a hundred thousand marks would be too much, and they talked together until they made a bargain for eighty and seven thousand marks, and the doge and the Venetians and the messengers swore to keep this bargain. Then the doge said that he wanted to have twenty-five thousand marks as advance payment, in order to begin building the navy. The messengers replied that he should send messengers back with them to France, and they would gladly see to it that the twenty-five thousand marks were paid to them. Then the messengers took leave and went on back, and the doge sent a high man of Venice along with them to receive the advance payment.

Then the doge had his ban cried through all Venice, that no Venetian should be so bold as to engage in any business, but rather they should all help to build the navy, and they did so. So they began to build the richest navy that ever was seen.

When the messengers came to France, they made it known that they were come. Then word was sent to all the barons who had taken the cross that they were to come straightway to Corbie. When they were all come together, the messengers told what they had done. When the barons heard it, they were greatly pleased and they approved right well what they had done. And they did great honor to the messengers of the doge of Venice, and they gave them some of the money left by the count of Champagne and some of the money which Master Fulk had collected, and the count of Flanders put in some of his money, until there were twenty-five thousand marks. So they gave this money to the messenger of the doge of Venice and they gave him safe-conduct to go with it to his own country.

Then word was sent to all the crusaders through all the lands, that they should all set out at Easter to go to Venice, so as to be there between Pentecost and August, without fail, and they did so. So when Easter was past they all came together. Many there were of fathers and mothers, sisters and brothers, wives and children, who made great lamenting over their loved ones.

THE CRUSADERS IN VENICE

When the pilgrims were all assembled at Venice and saw the rich navy that had been made, the rich ships, the great freighters, the transports to carry the horses, and the galleys, they marveled at it greatly and at the great riches which they found in the city. When they saw that they could not all find quarters in the city, they decided among them to go and quarter themselves on the Isle of St. Nicholas, which was entirely surrounded by sea and was a league away from Venice. So the pilgrims went there and set up their tents and quartered themselves the best they could.

When the doge of Venice saw that all the pilgrims were come, he sent for all those of his land of Venice. And when they were all come, the doge commanded that half of them should equip themselves and make ready to go along in the fleet with the pilgrims. When the Venetians heard this, some of them were glad, but others said they could not go; and they were not able to decide how the half of them should be chosen to go. Finally they made a drawing of lots in this way: balls of wax were made in pairs and in one of the two they put a slip of paper. Then they came to the priest and gave them to him and he made the sign of the cross over them and gave one of the two balls to each of two Venetians and the one who had the ball with the writing in it had to go with the fleet. So they were divided. Now when the pilgrims had taken quarters on the Isle of St. Nicholas, the doge of Venice and the Venetians went to talk with them, and they demanded their pay for the navy which they had prepared. And the doge said to them that they had done ill in this, that they had sent word by their messengers to have a navy prepared for four thousand knights and their harness and for one hundred thousand men on foot, and of these four thousand knights there were not more than a thousand, because some had gone to other ports, and of these hundred thousand men on foot there were not more than fifty thousand or sixty. "So," said the doge, "we want you to pay us the covenanted price that was agreed on between us." When the crusaders heard this, they talked together and agreed among them that each knight should give four marks and each horse four and each mounted sergeant two, and that he who gave less should give at least one mark. When they had gathered this money, they gave it to the Venetians and there still remained fifty thousand marks to pay. When the doge and the Venetians saw that the pilgrims had not paid them more than this, they were all very angry. Finally the doge said to them: "Lords," said he, "you have used us ill, for as soon as your messengers had made the bargain with me I commanded through all my land that no trader should go a-trading, but that all should help prepare this navy. So they have waited ever since and have not made any money for a year and a half past. Instead, they have lost a great deal, and therefore we wish, my men and I, that you should pay us the money you owe us. And if you do not do so, then know that you shall not depart from this island before we are paid, nor shall you find anyone to bring you anything to eat or to drink." The doge was a right worthy man, and so he did not cease from having brought to them enough to eat and to drink.

When the counts and the crusaders heard what the doge said, they were sorely grieved and greatly dismayed. Then they made another collection and borrowed as much money as they could from those who they thought had any, and they paid this to the Venetians, and when they had paid it, there still remained thirty-six thousand marks to pay. And they told them that they were in an evil plight and that the host was impoverished by this collection which they had made and that they could not raise any more money to pay them, but rather had scarcely enough for the host to live on. When the doge saw that they could not pay all the money, but were indeed in very hard straits because of it, he spoke to his own people and said: "Lords," said he, "if we let these men go back to their own land, we shall always be held for rogues and cheats. Rather let us go to them and tell them that if they will pay us the thirty-six thousand marks they owe us, out of the first gains which they shall make for themselves, we will put them overseas." The Venetians agreed willingly to what the doge said. So they went to the pilgrims where they were quartered, and when they were come there the doge said to them: "Lords," said he, "we have taken counsel, I and my people, to this effect, that if you are willing to promise faithfully to pay us the thirty-six thousand marks you owe us, out of the first gains that you shall make for yourselves, we will put you oversea." When the crusaders heard what the doge said and proposed, they were right glad, and they fell at his feet for joy and promised faithfully that they would do what the doge had devised. And there was such rejoicing that night that there was no one so poor as not to make a great illumination, and they carried great torches on the end of their lances around their lodges and inside of them, so that it seemed as if the whole camp were on fire.

Afterwards the doge came to them and said: "Lords, it is now winter and we cannot cross oversea. The fault cannot be laid on me, for I would have had you make the crossing long ago if it had not been for you. But let us make the best of it," said the doge. "There is a city near here, Zara is its name. They of the city have done us much harm, and I and my men want to be avenged on them if we can. If you will trust me, we will go there and stay there this winter until toward Easter, and then we will make ready our fleet and go oversea to the service of God. For Zara is a very fine city and plenteous in all good things." The barons and the high men of the crusaders agreed to what the doge had said, but the host as a whole did not know anything of this plan, save only the highest men. Then they all got ready their gear and their navy and put to sea. And each of the high men had his own ship for himself and his people and his transport to carry his horses, and the doge had with him fifty galleys all at his own cost. The galley he was in was all vermilion and it had a canopy of vermilion samite spread over him, and there were four silver trumpets trumpeting before him and drums making a great noise. And all the high men, and the clerks and laymen, and great and small, displayed so much joy at the departure that never yet was there such rejoicing, nor was ever such a fleet seen or heard of. And the pilgrims had all the priests and clerks mount on the high poops of the ships to chant the *Veni creator spiritus*.[1] And everyone, great and small, wept with emotion and for the great joy they had. When the fleet set out from the harbor of Venice . . . [A half-line blank in the manuscript] . . . freighters and these rich ships and so many other vessels, that it was the finest thing to see that has ever been since the beginning of the world. For there were fully a hundred pairs of trumpets, of silver and of brass, all sounding at the departure, and so many drums and tabors and other instruments that it was a fair marvel. When they were on that sea and had spread their sails and had their banners set high on the poops of the ships and their ensigns, it seemed indeed as if the sea were all a-tremble and all on fire with the ships they were sailing and the great joy they were making. Then they went on until they came to a city, Pola was its name. There they made land and refreshed themselves and stayed there a little, until they were well restored and had bought new provisions to put in their ships. Afterwards they put to sea again. And if they had made much joy and festivity before, now they made as much or even more, so that the people of the city were amazed at the great joy and at the mighty fleet and at the noble display they made. And they said, and it was true, that never had so fair a fleet or so rich been seen or assembled in any land as there was there.

THE CRUSADING HOST AT ZARA

The Venetians and the pilgrims sailed until they came to Zara on the eve of the feast of St. Martin. Now they of the city of Zara were sore afraid when they saw these ships and this mighty fleet approaching, so they had the gates of the city closed and took arms to defend themselves as best they could. When they were armed, the doge spoke to all the high men of the host and said to them: "Lords, this city has done much harm to me and to my people, and I would gladly avenge myself on it. So I pray you to help me." And the barons and the high men answered that they would gladly help him. Now the people of Zara knew right well that the Venetians hated them, so they had secured a letter from Rome, saying that anyone who should make war on them or do them any harm would be excommunicated. And they sent this letter by good messengers to the doge and the pilgrims who had landed there. When the messengers came to the camp, the letter was read before the doge and the pilgrims, and when the letter was read and the doge had heard it, he said that he would not give over having his revenge on those of the city, not even for the excommunication of the apostolic. At that the messengers went away.

---

[1] [*"Come, Creator Spirit."* This was a favorite hymn in the Roman Breviary.]

Then the doge spoke again to the barons and said: "Lords, know you well that I will not in any degree give over being avenged on them, no, not even for the apostolic." And he prayed the barons to help him. The barons all answered that they would gladly help him, save only Count Simon of Montfort and my lord Enguerrand of Boves. These said that they would not go against the commandments of the apostolic, nor did they want to be excommunicated. So they made themselves ready and went to Hungary to stay there all the winter. When the doge saw that the barons would help him, he had his engines set up to assault the city, until they of the city saw that they could not long hold out. So they threw themselves on their mercy and surrendered the city to them. Then the pilgrims and the Venetians entered in, and the city was divided into two halves so that the pilgrims had one half and the Venetians the other. . . .

In the meantime, while the crusaders and the Venetians were staying there that winter, the crusaders bethought them that they had spent a great deal. And they talked with one another and said that they could not go to Babylon or to Alexandria or to Syria, because they had neither provisions nor money for going there. For they had spent nearly everything, on the long delay they had made as well as on the great price they had given for the hire of the fleet. So they said they could not go, and if they went they would not be able to do anything, because they had neither money nor provisions to maintain themselves.

The doge of Venice saw right well that the pilgrims were in sore straits, and he spoke to them and said: "Lords, in Greece there is a land that is very rich and plenteous in all good things. If we could have a reasonable excuse for going there and taking provisions and other things in the land until we were well restored, it would seem to me a good plan. Then we should be well able to go oversea." Then the marquis rose and said "Lords, last year at Christmas I was in Germany at the court of my lord the emperor. There I saw a youth who was brother to the wife of the emperor of Germany. This youth was the son of the emperor Isaac of Constantinople, whose brother had taken the empire of Constantinople from him by treason. Whoever could get hold of this youth," said the marquis, "would be well able to go to Constantinople and get provisions and other things, for this youth is the rightful heir."

[The main account continues with the Crusaders sending for Alexius and their going to Constantinople, and then with the taking of the city.]

POPE INNOCENT III

THE PREOCCUPATION of the Italian cities with commerce even at the expense of the successful prosecution of the Crusades did not escape the intelligent contemporary observer. Treatises written as programs for the recovery of the Holy Land refer to the necessity of cutting off trade relations with the enemy; the popes issued prohibitions and employed excommunication and the interdict where the spiritual objectives of the Crusade were being ignored.

The selection which follows is Pope Innocent III's revision of the decree of the Third Lateran Council of 1179, which excommunicated Christians who furnished weapons, iron, and timber, or served on Saracen ships warring on Christians, took their fellow navigators prisoner, robbed them, or plundered shipwrecked Christians instead of lending aid. The selection has been translated from the Register of Innocent III for the year 1198 and in accordance with the Latin text, the *Patrologia Latina,* edited by J. P. Migne (1855).

ON VENETIAN TRADE WITH THE MOHAMMEDANS

TO THE DOGE AND THE PEOPLE OF VENICE

In behalf of the eastern province, besides the forgiveness of sins which we promise those setting out thither at their own expense, and besides the favor of apostolic protection which we bestow on those aiding the land, we have renewed that decree of the Lateran Council which ordered cut off from the communion of the Church those Christians who presume to furnish the Saracens with weapons, iron, or timbers for their galleys, and to serve as helmsmen or navigators on their galleys and other piratical craft, and which ordered their property to be confiscated by all secular princes and consuls of cities, and that, if any were taken prisoner they should be the slaves of their captors. According to the example of Pope Gregory, our predecessor of happy memory, we have placed under sentence of excommunication all those who in the future shall have relations with the Saracens either directly or indirectly, or shall attempt to supply or transport by ships anything by way of assistance, as long as the war between us and them shall last.

Nevertheless, our beloved sons, the noble men Andrew Donatus and Benedict Grilion, your envoys, recently approaching the Holy See caused to be explained to us that your city was suffering great loss by our decree because Venice does not engage in agriculture but rather in shipping and commerce. We, therefore, moved by the paternal affection in which we especially hold you, forbid you to presume under pain of anathema to aid the Saracens by selling, giving, or exchanging with them iron, oakum, pitch, sharp instruments, rope, weapons, galleys, ships, and timbers, hewn or in the rough. For the present and until we give you other instructions on this matter by command, we permit those of you going into the realm of Egypt or Cairo to transport other goods when it shall be necessary. We do this in the hope that for this favor you should be more strongly inspired to go to the aid of the province of Jerusalem. And you should see to it that you undertake nothing against our apostolic commandment. For there can be no doubt that he who attempts anything fraudulently in evasion of this mandate against his own conscience is bound by divine condemnation.

GENOESE SHIPPING

THE FORTUNES of Genoa as a trade center began much later than those of Venice. In the ninth and tenth centuries the latter was already the main channel for the thinned-out trade of the Byzantine and Moslem countries with central and western Europe. Genoa shared the economic decline of the Continent until an Arab raid, in which the city was plundered and many prisoners were carried away, forced the population to plan a counteroffensive. Under the leadership of their bishop and, above all, of the land-owning families, the Genoese gradually cleared the Moslem invaders from the main islands of the western Mediterranean and carried out successful expeditions in northwest Africa and in Arab Spain. These wars opened the sea for navigation and showed to the Genoese themselves and their maritime allies (especially the Pisans) the opportunity of trading with the Arabs. The loot gained in the first incursions supplied the initial capital to build up the maritime and commercial strength of Genoa, and the returns of trade rapidly increased the sums first risked in overseas commerce.

The most widely used contract in Genoese trade was a sort of partnership called "accomendatio." One of the partners remained at home and lent money or goods to another partner, who carried along the investment in a business trip by sea or land. The traveling partner was not held to invest capital of his own. Both the risks and the profits were shared, the investor getting three fourths or (in overland ventures) one half of the profits, while the remainder was the reward of management. Theoretically the investor who stayed at home kept the right of giving detailed instructions on the use of his money in trade, but in practice the traveling partner had the control of the venture. Again, in theory each of the partners in a contract was liable with all of his goods, but in practice no partner was asked to refund shares lost by the others in unsuccessful enterprises. Often the ownership of vessels was also divided into shares, with the dual purpose of pooling the capital of many men in such a costly enterprise as the construction and equipment of a large ship and of distributing the risks among many shareholders.

The following translations from the Latin are made from the texts in E. H. Byrne, *Genoese Shipping in the Twelfth and Thirteenth Centuries* (Cambridge, Mass., Medieval Academy of America, 1930), and G. L. Bratianu, *Actes des notaires génois de Péra et de Caffa de la fin du treizième siècle, 1281–1290* (Bucharest, Cultura Naţională, 1927).

SHIPPING CONTRACT, GENOA,

February 23, 1250

WE Conrad Guarco, Pontius Riccio, Peter D'Oria, Guy Spinola, and Lanfranc Riccio, *share-holders* of the "navis" sail-ship called Great Paradise, each of us being liable for all the share-holders and for the entire investment, charter to you Ido Lercari jr., Ottolino di Negro (in your name and in name of Lanfranc Dugo), Willy Tartaro (in your name and in name of Jimmy Spinola), Benedict Castagna, Nicholas D'Oria (in your name and in name of Ansaldino D'Oria), Philip di Stazione, Bartholomew de Mari, Jimmy of Verdun, Hugh Lomello, James Rosso, and Diotisalvi Buonaventura, *merchants,* said ship for this present voyage overseas (to Syria), making a freight charge as stated below, and with sailors and sailing equipment as described below. In fact, we promise and agree with you, said merchants . . . that we shall have said ship ready and prepared with six cotton sails, three of which must be new, and with a hemp sail, and with nine pieces of mast, fit and in good condition, and with twenty-two anchors—and, in the voyage home, twenty-five anchors—and with twenty cables in new springs, besides other retted cables, and with ten springs, and with all other shrouds and equipment sufficient for said ship in said voyage. And we shall have a hundred sailors, among whom there are to be twenty bow-men and two experienced warrant officers, in whose number no servant or share-holder must be counted, except for the pilot personally. Also we promise to you merchants . . . that we shall have that ship, with sailors and everything described above, ready and prepared to sail from the harbor of Genoa, and to engage in said trip, within the middle of next March; and that we shall go with said ship to Monaco or Antibo in order to take aboard there the cargo of said ship, and thence engage in said trip with the purpose of carrying it through. And after said ship has called at Monaco or Antibo in order to take aboard said cargo, we promise that within ten days we shall have her ready and prepared to hoist her sails, and to carry through said trip with said ship. If, however—may this not happen—we should hear reports that some armament is being made in the Sicilian area or else-where, which would prevent us from going safely with said ship and your merchandise to the area of Acre, we promise you that we shall go with said ship and your merchandise to Tripoli, in conformity with your wish (as you merchants will be on said ship), or with the wish of your majority in proportion to your share in the cargo. Also we promise to you, said merchants . . . that we shall not allow more than a hundred pilgrims—among whom there are to be no women—to come aboard said ship, either in going or in coming back; this, provided that no pilgrim will be allowed to stay from the middle mast to the stern. And we shall take aboard in said ship one merchant per cargo of ten *cantaria* of Acre after we have laden said ship. And we shall not allow any merchant to come aboard in Genoa in said ship on better conditions than any of you without your permission and wish, or the permission and wish of your majority. We may lade, however, up to 200 bales between the two decks of said ship in the voyage overseas. In coming back with said ship from overseas to Genoa, however, we promise that we shall not lade nor allow to be laden any merchandise between the two decks of said ship. Neither shall we allow any to be laden in any place where we may call with said ship while coming back to Genoa from overseas areas. Besides, we promise and agree with you said merchants . . . that we shall have said ship, with everything described above, ready and prepared within the middle of next September in the Acre area or in the place where she will have been laden, with the purpose of hoisting sails and going back to Genoa with the cargo of said ship. If, however, you should prefer to pay, and be in agreement about paying, according to the weight of Acre for said ship, we promise to you said merchants . . . that we shall discount, in the payment of the freight which you shall have to make for your things and merchandise, all that you have paid us in Genoa for the freight of your bales and merchandise, at the rate of three Saracenic besants of Syria per pound paid in Genoa; and we shall carry in said ship all of your things and merchandise and luggage, up to twenty bales per thousand of Genoese pounds.

In turn, we said merchants . . . promise and agree with you said shareholders that we shall go aboard said ship with all of our merchandise and bales within said date, in order to engage in said trip and carry it through as described above. And we shall give you in said ship ten *cantaria* of Acre per thousand Genoese pounds for such quantity of merchandise, things, and bales, which we shall take along and lade in said ship. And we shall give and pay you for the freight eleven Saracenic besants of Syria per *cantarium* of Acre of such cargo as we shall lade in said ship. If, however, within four days of our arrival with said ship in the area of Syria (wherever we shall call with said ship in order to unload), we merchants should choose and agree to pay according to the weight of Genoa, then we promise that we said merchants shall give and pay to you share-holders ten pounds of Genoese money per *cantarium* of such bales and merchandise as we shall lade in said ship, according to the use and practice of Genoese weight; and we shall pay you the whole freight in Genoa for those bales and merchandise, at said rate which each one of us is to give for the cargo. And for such freight as shall remain to be paid to you by some of us for our bales and merchandise laden in said ship as described above, we promise you . . . that we shall give and pay three Saracenic besants of Syria per pound of such freight as shall remain to be paid to you by some of us merchants, within fifteen days of our decision to pay according to the weight of Genoa as described above. If, however, we should decide to pay according to the weight of Syria, then we promise you that we shall give and pay said freight and the cargo of said ship according to Genoese law, in Acre or wherever she will lade in order to go back to Genoa; and we shall lade no other merchandise and things in said ship but ours only and those of the merchants mentioned above. Besides, we said merchants promise . . . that we shall observe each one of the aforesaid stipulations without exception.

We share-holders on our own behalf, and we said merchants on our behalf and on behalf of the others mentioned above, promise to fulfill and execute each and all of the said stipulations, under penalty of paying 1,000 pounds of Genoese money to the other party. We reciprocally offer as security our goods, both present and future, for the fine and for the execution of the promise; and each of us merchants and share-holders is to be liable for everyone and for the entire sum with respect to the aforesaid obligations, waiving the benefit of the New Constitution concerning the co-defendants, and of the epistle of the divine Hadrian, and of the right of the principal debtor.

Executed in Genoa, in the church of St. Maria of the Vineyards, in 1250, seventh indiction, on the twenty-third of February, between terce and nones [canonical] hour. Witnesses: Marino of Parma, Nicholas son of Judge Guarnerius, and Tommy D'Oria. And they asked two copies to be made of it. This was made on behalf of said share-holders and merchants. Notary Palodino of Sestri Ponente.

"PARTNERSHIP" AGREEMENT, PERA,

June 28, 1281

I Johnny, son of Ambrose Zaccaria, acknowledge that I have gotten and received in "accomendatio" ("partnership") from you, Percival of Arenzano, hyperpers 140 of gold, of Constantinople alloy, invested in Lombard cloth; and I waive the exception of not getting and receiving the hyperpers, and all other rights. That "accomendatio" I am to carry in the [Eastern] Roman Empire, in exchange for one half of the profit, and I am to include it in my general reckoning of expenses and profits, in proportion to each hyperper of investment, having the right to send back [the outcome of the transaction] ahead of me. Then, upon my return, I promise that I shall hand over and place in your hands or in the hands of your accredited messenger, personally or through a messenger, the capital and profit of said "accommendatio," such as the Lord will give unto me, keeping back one half of the profit. In case of failure I promise you, who are entering this stipulation, a fine of twice as much as I have received, plus all damages and expenses which you incur in order to recover said sum. And on account of this I offer to you as security all my goods both present and future.

Executed in Pera opposite Constantinople, under the porch of the Genoese, the year of the Nativity of Our Lord 1281, on the twenty-eighth day of June, between terce and nones hour. Witnesses: John of Cremona, banker, and William Gandolfi, notary. Notary Simone of Albaro.

LAS SIETE PARTIDAS

IN THE KINGDOMS of Leon and Castile, which were united in 1230 and can for convenience be called Spain, the long centuries of "Reconquest" from the Moors had entailed the granting of a multitude of *fueros* (privileges) by the kings within successively recovered domains. In the thirteenth century, however, Spanish monarchs, anxious to broaden the base of nationhood, began to make uniform the laws of the realm. This task was facilitated, first, by the fact that a seventh-century Christian-Visigothic compilation of principles for tribunals of justice (the *Liber Iudiciorum*) was still in general acceptance and, second, by the fact that jealousies among cities and within estates had led the crown partly to recognize, in essence if not in form, various classes of *fueros*. In 1265 the definitive codification appeared as the *Libro de las Leyes* (Book of the Laws), usually called *Las Siete Partidas* for "the seven parts" into which it was for mystical reasons divided.

The literary rendition of the *Partidas* was principally the work of Alfonso X (1221–84), whose devotion to poetry, historiography, geometry, astronomy, and occult sciences prejudiced his statecraft but won him the epithet Alfonso the Wise. The sources were ancient Visigothic customs, Church decretals, and more recent usages of the changing economy—compiled under the influence of jurists whose studies in Paris and Bologna had acquainted them with the order, simplicity, and broad scope of the Justinian Digest and Code of sixth-century Rome. Despite their threat to local privileges, however, which delayed promulgation until 1348, the spirit of the *Partidas* is medieval and Christian rather than statist and neo-Roman. Their primary concern is not with creating a homogeneous citizenry, or imperium, subject to easy manipulation by the crown, but with making the various orders of the realm susceptible to notions of Christian justice. As one writer has said, the *Partidas* contain principles *of* conduct, not rules *for* conduct. By the sixteenth century the *Partidas* came to be supplemented extensively by restrictive, regulatory codes of imperial Spain, a trend then active throughout Europe. But such was their vigor that they furnished an effective body of jurisprudence into the nineteenth century, and some of their provisions even became law in the United States in the statutes of Louisiana and Florida. Emphasizing the estates of the knight and prelate, they exemplify an ideal of society which, in broad outline, prevailed throughout late-medieval western Europe.

The following selections have been adapted from Samuel Scott Parsons's translation from the Spanish (taken, by permission, from *Las Siete Partidas*, published by and copyright 1931, Commerce Clearing House, Inc., Chicago 1, Illinois).

LAS SIETE PARTIDAS

Partida II, Title X

LAW I: WHAT THE WORD "PEOPLE" MEANS

Some think that the word "people" refers to the common people, such as artisans and laborers, but this is not the case, for in ancient Babylon, Troy and Rome, famous cities which did things in a reasonable and orderly fashion, each thing was called by an appropriate name. In these cities the word "people" was used to designate all classes together, upper, middle and lower, for all are necessary, and none can be excepted. In order for them to live well and be protected and supported, they all must assist one another.

Partida IV, Title XXIII (On the Status of Men)

LAW I: WHAT THE STATUS OF MEN MEANS; ITS VARIOUS TYPES AND ITS BENEFITS

Status hominum means . . . the state, condition or manner in which men live or find themselves. . . . It is quite worthwhile to be able to recognize and know the condition of men, for by this means one can better distinguish and render a decision in conflicts which occur with respect to their persons.

LAW II: HOW THE QUALITY WHICH ATTACHES TO THE CONDITION OF MEN IS DISTINGUISHED

The quality of the status of men has several divisions, for according to law the person of a freeman is judged differently from that of a slave, even though no distinction may exist between them according to nature. In like manner men of noble descent are honored and judged in another way from those of inferior rank, and priests from laymen, and legitimate children from bastards, and Christians from Moors and Jews. Moreover, the status of a man is superior to that of a woman in many things and in many respects. . . .

Title XXIV (Concerning the Obligation Existing between Men and Their Lords by Reason of Natural Feeling)

LAW I: WHAT NATURAL FEELING MEANS AND WHAT DISTINCTION EXISTS BETWEEN IT AND NATURE

Natural feeling means a mutual obligation of men to love and cherish one another for some just reason. The following distinction exists between it and nature, namely: nature is a force which causes everything to remain in the condition directed by the hand of God; natural feeling is something which resembles nature and assists everything derived from it to exist and be preserved.

LAW III: THE OBLIGATIONS OF INDIVIDUALS TO THEIR PARENTS

The obligation which man owes God is greater than anything else which can possibly exist. This debt has a natural origin, because He caused man to be born and preserves his life and affords him the hope of a perpetual existence according to his merit in the other world; and he should know, love and fear God for these reasons. . . . Moreover, men owe a great natural obligation to their fathers and mothers. The obligation a man owes his father is very great, because he begot him at the proper time and diminished his own substance in order that the other might exist, and also because his father's property will belong to him. He is also under deep obligation to his mother for the reason that she had her share in his origin, and underwent severe hardships before he was born, serious danger at the time, and encountered much trouble rearing him. He is indebted to the nurse who brought him up, because she gave him her milk at a time when he required it and nourished him as his mother would have done. He is also under a great obligation to his tutor, because he formed him and guided him when he had need of it, and was as a father to him. . . .

LAW IV: CONCERNING THE OBLIGATIONS WHICH INDIVIDUALS OWE THEIR LORDS AND THE COUNTRY IN WHICH THEY LIVE, AND HOW THIS RELATION SHOULD BE MAINTAINED BETWEEN THEM

All dependents should love their lords because of the natural obligation which they owe them, and should serve them because of the benefits they receive from them and those which they expect to receive. They should honor them because of the honor which they obtain from them, and protect them because they and their property are protected by them, and increase their property because their own will be increased for the same reason, and cheerfully suffer death for their lords, if it should be necessary, because of the good and honorable life which they have lived with them. They owe a great debt to their country, for they should love it and add to it and die for it, whenever this becomes necessary. . . .

LAW V: HOW NATURAL RELATIONSHIP MAY BE LOST

To denaturalize himself . . . is for a man to abandon the relationship maintained with his lord or with the country in which he lives. Since it is a sort of natural obligation, this relation cannot be dissolved except for some just reason. The lawful reasons by which individuals can do this are four in number. One of them arises from a fault of the dependent and three from a fault of the lord. This would be the case where the dependent commits treason against his lord or his country and by this act alone is deprived of the property and honors coming from his lord and his country. The first of the three which arises from a fault of the lord is when he attempts to cause the death of his dependent without reason and without justice; the second, when he dishonors him through his wife; the third, when he wrongfully disinherits him and is unwilling to treat him with justice, either by the decision of friends or of his court.

Title XXV (Concerning Vassals)

LAW I: WHAT A LORD IS, AND WHAT A VASSAL IS

A lord, properly speaking, is one who has command of and authority over all persons living on his lands. All should call a person of this kind lord, not only those who are his dependents, but also those who visit him and his holdings. Moreover, every man is called a lord who by reason of nobility of birth has power to arm knights and hold serfs, but a person of this kind should not be styled lord except by those who are his vassals and receive benefits from him. Vassals are those who receive honors and benefits from their lords, such as knighthood, land or money, in return for special services which they are obliged to render.

LAW II: HOW MANY KINDS OF LORDSHIP AND VASSALAGE THERE ARE

There are five different kinds of lordship and vassalage. The first, and most important, is that which the king maintains over all persons in his reign, called in Latin *merum imperium,* which means the clear and absolute right to judge and command the people of his country. The second is that which lords exercise over their vassals in consideration of the benefits and honors which the latter receive from them, as we have explained above. The third is that which lords enjoy over their estates, whether this refers to free towns therein or to their own patrimony, according to the *fueros* of Castile. The fourth is the authority which fathers have over their children. . . . The fifth is the power which masters possess over their slaves, as previously stated in the laws which treat of this subject.

Partida II, Title XXI (*Concerning Knights and the Things Which it is Proper for Them to Do*)

DEFENDERS constitute one of the three means through which God desired the world to be sustained. Just as those who pray to God for the people are called preachers, and those who cultivate the earth and perform the work by means of which men must live and be supported are called laborers, those, on the other hand, whose duty is to protect all are called defenders; and hence it was considered proper by the ancients that the men who have such duties to perform should be carefully selected. This is the case because three things are implied by defense, namely: energy, honor and power.

In [another] Title we have shown how the people should act toward the country in which they live, by begetting offspring which may inhabit it; by cultivating it in order to enjoy its fruits; by obtaining control of the objects which it contains; and by protecting it and defending it from its enemies as the common duty of all. These things, however, are the particular duty of knights, whom the ancients called defenders: first, because they are of higher rank; second, because they are especially appointed to defend the country and aggrandize it. . . .

LAW IV: KNIGHTS SHOULD POSSESS FOUR CHIEF VIRTUES

Excellent qualities which men possess naturally are called good habits and are styled *virtutes* in Latin. Four of these are superior, namely, prudence, fortitude, temperance and justice. Although every man who desires to be good should endeavor to acquire these virtues . . . among them there are none to whom this is more proper than to the defenders, since it is their duty to protect Church, monarchs and all others. Prudence will enable them to do this to their advantage and without injury; fortitude will cause them to be firm and not irresolute in what they do; moderation will induce them to perform their duties as they should and not be guilty of excess; and justice will enable them to act according to the right. For this reason the ancients, by way of commemoration, caused arms of four kinds to be made for the knights: first, such as they put on their bodies and feet; second, those with which they gird themselves; third, those which they bear in front of them; fourth, those with which they strike. Although these are of many forms, nevertheless they are all designed for two purposes: some for the protection of the body, which are called armor, others for inflicting blows, which are called weapons. Since the defenders did not ordinarily possess these weapons and, even if they had them, might not always be able to carry them, the ancients deemed it proper to contrive one which should be emblematic of all these, and this is the sword. For, as the arms which men put on for the purpose of defense indicate prudence, which is a virtue that protects them from all evils which can come upon them through their own fault, so the hilt of a sword which a man holds in his grasp is also suggestive of this, for as long as he holds it, he has the power to raise or lower it, or strike with it or abandon it; and as the arms which a man carries before him to defend himself denote fortitude, which is a virtue that renders him steadfast in the midst of dangers which may come upon him, so all the fortitude of the sword lies in its pommel, for to it is attached the hilt, the guard and the blade.

Since the armor which a man girds on is intermediate between that with which he is clothed and the weapons with which he strikes, and thus resembles the virtue of moderation between things which are excessive and those which are less than they should be, with great similarity to this the guard is placed between the handle and the blade of the sword. Furthermore, as the arms which a man holds ready to strike with, whenever it is advisable, symbolize justice, which includes right and equality, so the blade of the sword, which is straight and sharp and cuts the same with both edges, represents the same thing. On account of all this the ancients ordained that noble defenders should always wear the sword, and that by means of it and with no other weapon they should receive the honor of knighthood, in order that they might always be reminded of the four virtues which they should possess; for, without them, they could not perfectly maintain the condition of defense for which they were appointed.

LAW V: DEFENDERS SHOULD BE INTELLIGENT

There are still other excellent qualities, in addition to those we mentioned in the preceding law, which knights should possess. One of these is that they be intelligent. For intelligence is the one thing in the world which best directs a man to be accomplished in his actions, and which causes him to differ most from other creatures. For this reason the knights who have to defend themselves and others, as we have stated, should be intelligent. For if they are not so, they will fail in the duties which they are required to perform, because ignorance will prevent them from showing their power against those whom they should acquaint with it; and, on the other hand, it will make them treat those badly whom they are bound to protect. Moreover, it will cause them to be cruel toward those to whom they should show pity, and merciful when they should be relentless; and will induce them to commit a still greater offense which could lead to disloyalty, for it may make them love those whom they should hate and hate those whom they should love. It may also make them bold where they should not be so and weak where they should have courage, and cause them to covet what they should not possess and forget what they ought to covet; and, in this way, ignorance will cause them to err in everything which they have to do.

LAW VII: KNIGHTS SHOULD BE WELL MANNERED

When *hidalgos* practice things which are of a contrary nature, it causes them in the end to acquire good habits. This signifies that on the one hand they may be powerful and brave, and on the other gentle and humble. For as it becomes them to use strong and bold language in order to frighten their enemies and cause them to retire when they are among them, they should also have quiet and unassuming manners, in order to allure and attract those who are with them, and be courteous to them in both word and deed, for it is natural that he who uses kindness when it is not suitable will afterwards experience the want of it when he most needs it.

LAW XVIII: HOW KNIGHTS SHOULD BE CLOTHED

The ancients established the rule that knights should wear clothes of colored cloth so long as they were young, as, for instance, red, yellow, green or purple, because these gave them an appearance of cheerfulness; but they did not deem it proper for them to wear black, gray or any other drab color which might impart to them an appearance of sadness. They did this in order that their dress might be elegant, and that they might be cheerful and their hearts be emboldened, rendering them more valiant. Although their clothes might be cut in many ways according to the different customs and practices of the country, all were required to make and wear their cloaks in the following manner; namely, they should be cut wide and long, and cover them as far as their feet, and enough cloth should be taken from both sides for a knot to be made above the left shoulder, contrived in such a way that the head could be inserted and withdrawn without hindrance. This was called the knightly cloak, and it was given this name because no other man but a knight had a right to wear it in this manner. The cloak was cut after this pattern as a sign that knights should be covered with humility, in order to obey their superiors. The knot was used because it represents, as it were, the tie of religion and admonishes them to be obedient, not only to their lords but also to their commanders. For this reason they wore the cloak not only while they ate and drank, but also while they sat, walked and rode. All their other clothing was clean and very elegant, each wearing what was prescribed by the custom of his locality. They did this in order that whoever saw them might be able to distinguish them from other people so as to show them honor. They established the same regulation with regard to armor that they did concerning the weapons which they bore, that is, that it should be handsome and richly adorned.

LAW XIX: KNIGHTS SHOULD BE TEMPERATE IN FOOD, DRINK AND SLEEP

Eating, drinking and sleeping are natural activities without which men cannot exist. Knights should indulge in them, however, in three ways: first, according to the time; second, with moderation; third, with propriety. Knights were formerly quite accustomed to observe these conditions, for, as in time of peace it was their practice to eat at appointed times so that they could go to the table twice a day and eat good, well-cooked and commonplace food, so also when they went to war they ate but once in the morning and very little, and took their principal meal in the evening. This was done for the reason that they might not be very hungry or very thirsty, and that if they should be wounded they might be more readily cured. In those times they were given coarse and strong meat abounding in fat in order that they might eat but little of it and that it might greatly benefit them and make their flesh strong and hard. They were also given to drink weak wine mixed with much water so that it might not interfere with their understanding or their prudence. When fever was prevalent they were given a little vinegar mixed with much water to quench their thirst and prevent the fever from attacking them and making them ill; and this they drank during the day when they were very thirsty in order to lengthen their lives and improve their health and preserve the latter by not eating and drinking too much.

In addition to all this they derived another great benefit since their daily expenses were lessened, so that they could better accomplish daring deeds, which is something very proper for those whose duty it is to make war. In addition, they were trained not to be heavy sleepers, because this is very injurious to such as have important duties to perform, and especially so to knights who are engaged in hostilities. For this reason, just as they were permitted in time of peace to wear soft and smooth linen when they took their rest, so in time of war they were not permitted to lie down except in scanty and coarse cloth or in their pourpoints. This was done in order that they might sleep less and be accustomed to the endurance of hardship, for it was maintained that no vice which they might have would offset their being victorious.

LAW XXIII: IN WHAT WAY KNIGHTS SHOULD BE HONORED

Knights should be greatly honored, and there are three reasons for this: first, on account of the nobility of their descent; second, on account of their excellent qualities; third, on account of the benefits of which they are the source. Kings should honor them as persons through whom they must act by protecting and honoring themselves along with them and by contributing to their power and their distinction. All others together should show them honor, because they are to them as a shield and a defense and for their protection have to encounter all dangers which arise. Since knights expose themselves to many forms of peril in order to perform the aforesaid acts, they should be respected in many ways. Hence no one should be in front of them in church when they are present at services, except the prelates and other priests who conduct them or kings or great lords whom they are obliged to obey and serve. Nor should anyone else take precedence of them in making an offering or in receiving the salute of peace; nor while they are at their meals should any squire or any other person except a knight, or some man who merits it on account of his rank or his excellent qualities, sit down with them; nor ought anyone but a knight or some other eminent man use abusive language to them. They should, moreover, be honored in their own houses, and no one should enter them with violence except by command of the king or by order of a court in cases where they have deserved it; nor should their horses or arms be taken in execution, where any other movable or immovable can be found liable to seizure. And, although nothing else may be found for this purpose, their war-horses should not be taken or they be compelled to dismount while they are riding other animals; nor should their houses be entered for the purpose of making a levy while they or their wives are there. There are special cases, however, in which they can appoint a certain time within which to leave their houses and surrender them and their contents.

The ancients also attached so much importance to the honor of knights that they avoided seizing property not only where they and their wives were but also where their cloaks and shields were found. They conferred upon them another mark of distinction, for wherever men met knights they humbled themselves before them, and it is still customary in Spain in our day to say to good and eminent men: "We humble ourselves." After a knight has been created he is entitled to still another honor, for he is eligible to the dignity of emperor or king, which he was not before, just as no priest can be a bishop if he has not previously been ordained to say Mass.

LAW XXIV: WHAT SUPERIORITY KNIGHTS HAVE APART FROM OTHER MEN

Knights are, above other men, entitled to recognized and separate marks of honor, not only in those matters mentioned in the preceding law, but also in others which we shall state here. . . . [When] a knight is prosecuted for an offense which he has committed, although such indications or suspicions may arise against him which, in the case of another man, would cause him to be tortured, the knight should not be put to torture except for an act of treason which concerns the king whose subject or vassal he is, or the kingdom in which he lives by reason of the privilege of birth which he there enjoys. We also decree that even though the crime were proved against him, he ought not to suffer an ignominious death, as for instance being dragged, hanged or mutilated. He should, instead, be decapitated according to law or starved to death when it is desired to manifest great severity against him on account of some offense of which he is guilty.

The ancients of Spain, when knights employed themselves in stealing or robbing others of their property or committed perfidy or treason (which are deeds which render men vile in heart and deprive them of goodness) and were convicted of such serious offenses, ordered that they be thrown down from some lofty place to be dashed to pieces, or drowned in the sea or in some other body of water so as never to be seen again, or delivered up as a prey to wild beasts. . . .

LAW XXV: WHY AND HOW KNIGHTS LOSE THE HONOR OF KNIGHTHOOD

For knights to forfeit the honor of knighthood by their own fault is the greatest degradation which they can undergo. The ancients, however, considered that this could justly happen in two ways: first, when they were merely deprived of the order of knighthood with no corporal punishment inflicted upon them; second, when they commited such offenses as to deserve death. In the latter instance they should be deprived of knighthood before being executed. The reasons for which they can be deprived of knighthood are the following: for instance, when a knight is with the army or on the frontier by command of his lord and sells or disposes of his horse or his arms, or loses them while throwing dice, or gives them away to prostitutes, or leaves them in pledge in some drinking house, or steals those of his companions or has them stolen, or when he knowingly makes a man a knight when he does not deserve it, or when he engages openly in trade, or labors with his hands in any vile employment to obtain money when he is not a captive.

The other reasons for which he should lose the honor of knighthood before he is put to death are as follows: for instance, when a knight flees in the battlefield, or abandons his lord or castle or any other place under his command, when he sees his lord taken prisoner or killed and does not hasten to his assistance, or does not provide him with a horse if his own is killed, or does not liberate him from prison in any way he can when able to do so. Although sentence must be executed for these reasons and for others which relate to perfidy or treason, he must nevertheless be degraded before he is put to death. He must be deprived of knighthood in the following manner, namely: the king should order a squire to put on his spurs and gird on his sword and cut his baldric with a knife at the shoulder and also to cut the straps of his spurs while he is still wearing them. After this is done he should no longer be called a knight, and he loses the honor and the privileges of knighthood; and he may not be appointed to any office for the king or the Council; nor has he the right to accuse or challenge any knight.

Partida I, Title V (On the Prelates of the Holy Church, whose Duty it is to Expound the Faith and Administer the Sacraments)

LAW I: WHAT "BISHOP" MEANS AND WHAT POSITIONS PRELATES OCCUPY IN THE HOLY CHURCH

"Prelate" means a person of high rank in the Holy Church, and the most honored of these are the bishops, for while there is the pope and there are patriarchs, archbishops and primates . . . nevertheless all these are bishops, although they may have other names. A bishop means a keeper. For without doubt they are appointed to guard the Catholic Faith, since they occupy the place of the Apostles and have the same power which Our Lord Jesus Christ conferred upon the latter when he said to them: "What you bind on earth shall be bound in heaven, and what you loose on earth shall be loosed in heaven." These are, as it were, the pillars of the Holy Church, by means of which the Faith is sustained, for they more than other prelates are required to preach and expound it to the people and to defend it by argument against heretics and all such as desire to oppose it. . . .

Thus we should consider bishops as saints and obey and honor them as persons who occupy the place of the Apostles.

LAW XXX: WHAT QUALIFICATIONS THOSE ELECTED BISHOPS MUST ESPECIALLY POSSESS

The Apostle St. Paul established the rule governing ordination, in which he stated what habits and qualifications a prelate of superior rank must possess in order to be eligible. He held that since this man had been elected by the choice of God it was necessary that he should surpass all other men in excellence. The rule which he established declares that such a one must be without mortal sin, have no impediment by reason of marriage, must be temperate in eating and drinking, wise, chaste, polite, hospitable, competent to explain the faith, not quarrelsome, violent or avaricious, and know how to keep his church in order.

LAW XXXVI: PRELATES MUST BE TEMPERATE IN EATING AND DRINKING

One who is elected to offices of high ecclesiastical rank should be temperate in eating and drinking, having a care not to eat immoderately or drink so as to become intoxicated, since this is one of the greatest sins of which he can be guilty, for because of it man fails to recognize God, himself and all other things as well, more than in the case of any other sin. As the ancient sages declared, wine is the way which leads men to all sins. For this reason intemperance is the first thing that should be forbidden to a prelate, for it is necessary that one who must give advice to many people should always have a clear and functioning brain. Therefore if one of them, after he has been reprimanded for this error, should not be willing to reform, his superior must deprive him of his office and benefices. Moreover, eating too much is forbidden to every man, and especially to the prelate, because chastity cannot be easily preserved where there is inordinate indulgence in food and great excesses prevail. For this reason the saints declared that it is not proper that those whose duty it is to preach poverty and the hardships which Our Lord Jesus Christ suffered for us in this world should do so with faces that are red from eating and drinking to excess. Leaving this out of consideration, serious illnesses—in consequence of which men die before their time or perish from the result of some injury—naturally result from immoderate eating.

LAW XXXVII: CONCERNING MATTERS WHICH PRELATES SHOULD UNDERSTAND

A prelate should be well informed and intelligent, and especially so in these three things: first, in the Faith, so that he may know how to instruct the souls which are given unto his care to be saved, and for this reason he must understand the science of Divinity; second, he must be acquainted with those branches of knowledge called arts, and with four of them especially, namely, grammar, which is the art of learning the Latin language; and logic, which explains how to distinguish truth from falsehood; and rhetoric, which is a science that explains how to arrange words elegantly and properly; and also music, which is the knowledge of notes necessary for the chants of Holy Church. . . . As for the other branches of knowledge,[1] the Holy Fathers did not consider it advisable that prelates should endeavor to know much about them. Although these branches of knowledge are noble and very excellent, still in themselves they are not suitable for churchmen, for they do not induce them to perform works of piety, as, for instance, preaching and hearing confessions and other things of this kind which they are required to do by virtue of their office. The third thing that prelates should be acquainted with relates to temporal matters and is the knowledge of governing their bishoprics properly and keeping their houses in order.

LAW XXXIX: PRELATES SHOULD BE REFINED

The Holy Church requires prelates to be refined, and in two ways: first, with regard to themselves, second, in their relations with others. As to what concerns themselves, this is divided into two things, good thoughts and good habits. That which concerns their relations with others is divided into four things, namely: eating and drinking, as has been mentioned above, and the matter of dress and manners. By dress many things are understood, as, for instance, they must wear their garments long and not short, with sleeves which are not sewed, and shoes without strings. They must not use gilt bridles, saddles or suspended or gilt breast-leathers or gilded spurs or other things indicative of pomp, or wear cloaks with sleeves, unless they change their dress through fear. Nor should they wear jewels or belts with gilded buckles. The Holy Church also deemed it proper that they should not go without the Roman surplice over their other garments, unless they had formerly been friars or monks, for the latter cannot lay aside their habit. They should also wear their robes buttoned or fastened in front as a sign of chastity, but this they must do so as not to display hypocrisy. Moreover, they should have broad tonsures and wear their hair so short that their ears can be seen. This was established as a token of the kingdom of God, which they hope to attain and where, if they perform their duties as they should, they will be crowned. For just as kings must govern men in temporal matters, so must churchmen in spiritual matters,

[1] [Geometry, arithmetic, and astronomy.]

and for this reason the Church calls them rectors. From their shaven crowns it is understood that they must remove their minds from the pleasures of this world, abandon temporal affairs and consider themselves sufficiently provided for if they have food to eat and clothes to wear. They should also be refined in their behavior, conducting themselves properly and modestly, as befits them. The outward behavior and comportment that men exhibit in their deeds naturally make clear their desires and achievements.

LAW XLI: HOW PRELATES SHOULD PREACH AND EXPLAIN THE FAITH

Churchmen of superior rank should be expounders and preachers of the religion of Our Lord Jesus Christ, as they occupy the place of the Apostles. Their instruction and preaching should be of two kinds: one of words, the other of deeds, because the Scriptures of Our Lord Jesus Christ declare that He first began to act and afterwards to teach. This agrees also with what St. Jerome said, namely: that the wolves should be frightened away by the barking of the dogs and the staff of the shepherd. By barking is understood preaching, which arouses fear through speech, and by the staff the punishment which results from the good works which prelates themselves do and exhort others to do. Punishment by deed, however, should be imposed with moderation and great prudence, and with love and not ill will, in order that men may understand that it issues from a love of God and that they are chastised so that they may obtain good and not so that they may be done harm. Prelates should not despise men on account of the sins they commit nor do them injury on that account, but should rescue them from their sins as far as they can; for true justice should be administered with sorrow and for lawful reasons, just as injustice is inflicted rudely and without right.

LAW XLII: WHAT QUALIFICATIONS A PRELATE SHOULD POSSESS IN ORDER TO PREACH AND EXPOUND THE FAITH PROPERLY

A prelate should preach to the people of his bishopric, to priests as well as laymen. . . . Preaching must be done in one of the following ways, namely: either by explaining how the people may know and understand the belief in the Faith and how to avoid committing sin after they have understood it, or by explaining how they can perform penance for their sins after they have committed them. In order to do this properly, one who preaches must possess three qualifications: first, charity, which means the love of God, more than anything else, and love for his neighbor as for himself; second, he must lead a good life; third, he must preach well. . . . He who preaches well and lives an evil life shows the way to God in a manner to cause injury, and offers an example of sin to those who hear him. A preacher of this kind may be compared to ashes from which lye oozes and washes other things while the ashes themselves remain unclean. He may also be compared to a stone aqueduct through which clear and clean waters flow, by means of which the land is irrigated and the plains are made to bring forth crops but which do no good to the stone nor soften it, the stone remaining as rough and hard as it was before. He may also be compared to a lighted taper which burns itself up and lights others but receives no benefit from its own brightness. . . .

LAW LXV: WHAT SUPERIORITY IN DIGNITY PRELATES HAVE OVER OTHER PRIESTS

Prelates, through the dignity of the Holy Church, have superiority over other priests in seven respects. First, upon the day that they are made bishops the power of their confessors, or of any other superior which exists if they belonged to any religious order, ceases to exist. Second, they cannot be appointed the guardians of orphans. Third, if the prelate was a slave or the vassal of some noble family, or is decended from any of these, he will for the future be free, and no one can again reduce him to servitude or cause him to render to his lord the service which he formerly was bound to perform. If, however, he was an official of the court of the king and among those required to render accounts, he is still not free because of the above reason, unless he surrenders three-fourths of his possessions at the time he was elected. Fourth, he cannot be compelled to testify before any judge or anywhere else if he does not wish to do so, but he must inform a judge that he will tell the truth, as far as he knows it, in the way stated in the Title on witnesses. Fifth, he is not required to attend nor can he be compelled to appear in person in a lawsuit before any secular judge, unless the king commands him to appear before him. Sixth, he cannot be compelled to give security in any lawsuit. Seventh, he must not give anything to the judges out of the property concerning which the lawsuit arose, as other men do. . . .

LAW LXVI: ALL CHRISTIANS, IN WORD AND DEED, MUST OBEY THE WILL OF PATRIARCHS, PRIMATES, ARCHBISHOPS, AND BISHOPS

Patriarchs, primates, archbishops and bishops deserve to be honored and respected on account of the positions which they occupy, concerning which we have already spoken in preceding laws. This honor should be manifested in three ways: first, in thought, second, in word, third, in deed. In thought, it should be believed that prelates occupy the places of the Apostles, as stated above, and that they are intermediaries between God and the people and pray for the latter, and that their prayers will be heard with respect to such things as they ask for with justice; for thus Our Lord Jesus Christ spoke to the Apostles: "What you ask of me in prayer believe that I will grant it to you, and that you will obtain it." The honor due by word is that prelates should be called lords, because of the honorable positions of the Apostles which they fill, as has been stated, and because they are guardians of the soul. The honor in deed to which they are entitled is that persons should rise in their presence and receive them kindly and show them reverence in other things, according to the customs of the country.

MAGNA CARTA

THE PROCESS of royal centralization in England went against many assumptions and practices of feudalism. After the death of Henry II, the conservative baronage was certain in time to come to open conflict with the king and his advisers, who were often churchmen or "upstarts" of no family and reputation and so distrusted by the barons. The demands of the crusader king Richard I (1189–99) led to a further tightening of administrative procedures; the reign of John (1199–1216) brought a considerable consolidation of novelties and a number of important legal and administrative reforms. Distrusting the assumptions and ideals of feudalism and impatient with the limitations imposed by custom, John could with good reason be accused of undermining rights guaranteed by feudal law. The barons, newly conscious of the common interests of their class and beginning to think of themselves as representatives of the nation, were determined that a stop should be put to royal aggression. Outmaneuvered and unable to satisfy his opponents by partial concessions, John was forced to set his seal to the Great Charter at Runnymede (on the Thames near Windsor) on June 19, 1215. Still neither side trusted the other. John was released from his obligations by Pope Innocent III, whose vassal he had earlier become out of purely political considerations. England was invaded by the son of Philip Augustus of France, Prince Louis, to whom the rebellious barons had offered the crown. But the virtual civil war was ended by the sudden death of John; and on the accession of the infant Henry III the royal advisers voluntarily accepted the major provisions of the Charter.

The Charter was reissued with changes in 1216, 1217, and 1225. It very early came to be considered a fundamental law of the kingdom, and is the first entry in the *Statutes of the Realm*. To contemporaries, John's charter was unique only in size; hence its name, whatever significance the word "great" (*Magna*) may have acquired since.

By making specific certain feudal obligations—such as aids and feudal incidents—which had formerly rested on custom, it forced the royal administrators into a circumscribed position from which they could escape only by the use of nonfeudal devices and procedures. But the Charter also accepts many of the reforms of the king, notably in the field of law, and a number of provisions look to the better government of England.

The translation of the Latin text has been taken from W. S. McKechnie, *Magna Carta* (Glasgow, J. Maclehose and Sons, 1914).

MAGNA CARTA

JOHN, by the grace of God, king of England, lord of Ireland, duke of Normandy and Aquitaine, and count of Anjou, to the archbishops, bishops, abbots, earls, barons, justiciars, foresters, sheriffs, stewards, servants, and to all his bailiffs and liege subjects, greeting. Know that, having regard to God and for the salvation of our souls, and those of all our ancestors and heirs, and unto the honour of God and the advancement of holy Church, and for the reform of our realm, [we have granted as underwritten] by advice of our venerable fathers, Stephen, archbishop of Canterbury, primate of all England and cardinal of the holy Roman Church, Henry archbishop of Dublin, William of London, Peter of Winchester, Jocelyn of Bath and Glastonbury, Hugh of Lincoln, Walter of Worcester, William of Coventry, Benedict of Rochester, bishops; of master Pandulf, subdeacon and member of the household of our lord the Pope, of brother Aymeric, master of the Knights of the Temple in England, and of the illustrious men William Marshal, earl of Pembroke, William, earl of Salisbury, William, earl Warenne, William, earl of Arundel, Alan of Galloway, constable of Scotland, Waren Fitz Gerald, Peter Fitz Herbert, Hubert de Burgh, seneschal of Poitou, Hugh de Neville, Matthew Fitz Herbert, Thomas Basset, Alan Basset, Philip d'Aubigny, Robert of Roppesley, John Marshal, John Fitz Hugh, and others, our liegemen.

1. In the first place we have granted to God, and by this our present charter confirmed for us and our heirs for ever that the English church shall be free, and shall have her rights entire, and her liberties inviolate; and we will that it be thus observed; which is apparent from this that the freedom of elections, which is reckoned most important and very essential to the English church, we, of our pure and unconstrained will, did grant, and did by our charter confirm and did obtain the ratification of the same from our lord, Pope Innocent III, before the quarrel arose between us and our barons: and this we will observe, and our will is that it be observed in good faith by our heirs for ever. We have also granted to all freemen of our kingdom, for us and our heirs forever, all the underwritten liberties, to be had and held by them and their heirs, of us and our heirs forever.

2. If any of our earls or barons, or others holding of us in chief by military service shall have died, and at the time of his death his heir shall be full of age and owe "relief" he shall have his inheritance on payment of the ancient relief, namely the heir or heirs of an earl, £100 for a whole earl's barony; the heir or heirs of a baron, £100 for a whole barony; the heir or heirs of a knight, 100s. at most for a whole knight's fee; and whoever owes less let him give less, according to the ancient custom of fiefs.

3. If, however, the heir of any one of the aforesaid has been under age and in wardship, let him have his inheritance without relief and without fine when he comes of age.

4. The guardian of the land of an heir who is thus under age, shall take

from the land of the heir nothing but reasonable produce, reasonable customs, and reasonable services, and that without destruction or waste of men or goods; and if we have committed the wardship of the lands of any such minor to the sheriff, or to any other who is responsible to us for its issues, and he has made destruction or waste of what he holds in wardship, we will take of him amends, and the land shall be committed to two lawful and discreet men of that fee, who shall be responsible for the issues to us or to him to whom we shall assign them; and if we have given or sold the wardship of any such land to anyone and he has therein made destruction or waste, he shall lose that wardship, and it shall be transferred to two lawful and discreet men of that fief, who shall be responsible to us in like manner as aforesaid.

5. The guardian, moreover, so long as he has the wardship of the land, shall keep up the houses, parks, fishponds, stanks,[1] mills, and other things pertaining to the land, out of the issues of the same land; and he shall restore to the heir, when he has come to full age, all his land, stocked with ploughs and "waynage," [2] according as the season of husbandry shall require, and the issues of the land can reasonably bear.

6. Heirs shall be married without disparagement, yet so that before the marriage takes place the nearest in blood to that heir shall have notice.[3]

7. A widow, after the death of her husband, shall forthwith and without difficulty have her marriage portion and inheritance; nor shall she give anything for her dower, or for her marriage portion, or for the inheritance which her husband and she held on the day of the death of that husband; and she may remain in the house of her husband for forty days after his death, within which time her dower shall be assigned to her.

8. No widow shall be compelled to marry, so long as she prefers to live without a husband; provided always that she gives security not to marry without our consent, if she holds of us, or without the consent of the lord of whom she holds, if she holds of another.

9. Neither we nor our bailiffs shall seize any land or rent for any debt, so long as the chattels of the debtor are sufficient to repay the debt; nor shall the sureties of the debtor be distrained so long as the principal debtor is able to satisfy the debt; and if the principal debtor shall fail to pay the debt, having nothing wherewith to pay it, then the sureties shall answer for the debt; and let them have the lands and rents of the debtor, if they desire them, until they are indemnified for the debt which they have paid for him, unless the principal debtor can show proof that he is discharged thereof as against the said sureties.

---

[1] [Other ponds, especially millponds.]   [2] [Meaning uncertain; probably, "tools."]

[3] [Disparagement meant forced marriage with one not an equal. The king might regulate the marriage of his wards, but John had made a practice of selling female wards (with their estates) to favorites and others. Some took refuge in the veil.]

10. If one who has borrowed from the Jews any sum, great or small, die before that loan be repaid, the debt shall not bear interest while the heir is under age, of whomsoever he may hold; and if the debt fall into our hands, we will not take anything except the principal sum contained in the bond.

11. And if anyone die indebted to the Jews, his wife shall have her dower and pay nothing of that debt; and if any children of the deceased are left under age, necessaries shall be provided for them in keeping with the holding of the deceased; and out of the residue the debt shall be paid, reserving, however, service due to feudal lords; in like manner let it be done touching debts due to others than Jews.

12. No scutage nor aid shall be imposed on our kingdom, unless by common counsel of our kingdom, except for ransoming our person, for making our eldest son a knight, and for once marrying our eldest daughter; and for these there shall not be levied more than a reasonable aid.[4] In like manner it shall be done concerning aids from the city of London.

13. And the city of London shall have all its ancient liberties and free customs, as well by land as by water; furthermore, we decree and grant that all other cities, boroughs, towns, and ports shall have all their liberties and free customs.[5]

14. And for obtaining the common counsel of the kingdom anent the assessing of an aid, except in the three cases aforesaid, or of a scutage, we will cause to be summoned the archbishops, bishops, abbots, earls, and greater barons, severally by our letters; and we will moreover cause to be summoned generally, through our sheriffs and bailiffs, all others who hold of us in chief, for a fixed date, namely, after the expiry of at least forty days, and at a fixed place; and in all letters of such summons we will specify the reason of the summons. And when the summons has thus been made, the business shall proceed on the day appointed, according to the counsel of such as are present, although not all who were summoned have come.

15. We will not for the future grant to any one licence to take an aid from his own free tenants, except to ransom his body, to make his eldest son a knight, and once to marry his eldest daughter; and on each of these occasions there shall be levied only a reasonable aid.

16. No one shall be distrained for performance of greater [military] service for a knight's fee, or for any other free tenement, than is due therefrom.

4 [Scutage was paid in place of military service. Aids were levies (in theory voluntary) collected by the king on special occasions; such occasions traditionally were confined to the three mentioned.]

5 [Cherished were the right to local self-government, and the right to levy tolls and to place oppressive restrictions on merchants from neighboring towns.]

17. Common pleas shall not follow our court, but shall be held in some fixed place.

18. Inquests of *novel disseisin,* of *mort d'ancestor,* and of *darrein present-ment,*[6] shall not be held elsewhere than in their own county-courts, and that in manner following,—We, or, if we should be out of the realm, our chief justiciar, will send two justiciars through every county four times a year, who shall, along with four knights of the county chosen by the county, hold the said assizes in the county court, on the day and in the place of meeting of that court.

19. And if any of the said assizes cannot be taken on the day of the county court, let there remain of the knights and freeholders, who were present at the county court on that day, as many as may be required for the efficient making of judgments, according as the business be more or less.

20. A freeman shall not be amerced [7] for a slight offence, except in accord-ance with the degree of the offence; and for a grave offence he shall be amerced in accordance with the gravity of the offence, yet saving always his "contene-ment"; [8] and a merchant in the same way, saving his "merchandise"; and a villein shall be amerced in the same way, saving his "waynage"—if they have fallen into our mercy: and none of the aforesaid amercements shall be imposed except by the oath of honest men of the neighbourhood.

21. Earls and barons shall not be amerced except through their peers, and only in accordance with the degree of the offence.

22. A clerk shall not be amerced in respect of his lay holding except after the manner of the others aforesaid; further, he shall not be amerced in ac-cordance with the extent of his ecclesiastical benefice.

23. No village or individual shall be compelled to make bridges at river banks, except those who from of old were legally bound to do so.

24. No sheriff, constable, coroners, or others of our bailiffs, shall hold pleas of our Crown.[9]

25. All counties, hundreds, wapentakes, and trithings, except our demesne manors, shall remain at the old rents, and without any additional payment.[10]

26. If any one holding of us a lay fief shall die, and our sheriff or bailiff shall exhibit our letters patent of summons for a debt which the deceased owed to us, it shall be lawful for our sheriff or bailiff to attach and catalogue chattels of the deceased, found upon the lay fief, to the value of that debt, at the sight

---

[6] [Such "inquests" were forms of legal action for remedying recent wrongful eviction, denial of inheritance, and wrongful appointment to a church office, respectively.]

[7] [Fined.]   [8] ["Sustenance," that is, enough to live on.]

[9] [That is, criminal cases shall be tried by the king's judges, and not by local officials.]

[10] [The three quaint items mentioned each were county subdivisons. In this context "rents" meant mainly revenues from royal manors and from local courts of justice; often the king sold the right to collect these revenues to the sheriff of the county.]

of law-worthy men, provided always that nothing whatever be thence removed until the debt which is evident shall be fully paid to us; and the residue shall be left to the executors to fulfil the will of the deceased; and if there be nothing due from him to us, all chattels shall go to the deceased, saving to his wife and children their reasonable shares.

27. If any freeman shall die intestate, his chattels shall be distributed by the hands of his nearest kinsfolk and friends, under supervision of the church, saving to everyone the debts which the deceased owed to him.

28. No constable or other bailiff of ours shall take corn or other provisions from anyone without immediately tendering money therefor, unless he can have postponement thereof by permission of the seller.

29. No constable shall compel any knight to give money in lieu of castle-guard, when he is willing to perform it in his own person, or if he himself cannot do it from any reasonable cause then by another responsible man. Further, if we have led or sent him upon military service, he shall be relieved from guard in proportion to the time during which he has been on service because of us.

30. No sheriff or bailiff of ours, or other person, shall take the horses or carts of any freeman for transport duty, against the will of the said freeman.

31. Neither we nor our bailiffs shall take, for our castles or for any other work of ours, wood which is not ours, against the will of the owner of that wood.

32. We will not retain beyond one year and one day, the lands of those who have been convicted of felony, and the lands shall thereafter be handed over to the lords of the fiefs.

33. All kydells [11] for the future shall be removed altogether from Thames and Medway, and throughout all England, except upon the sea shore. [12]

34. The writ which is called *praecipe* shall not for the future be issued to anyone, regarding any tenement whereby a freeman may lose his court. [13]

35. Let there be one measure of wine throughout our whole realm; and one measure of ale; and one measure of corn, to wit, "the London quarter"; and one width of cloth whether dyed, or russet, or "halberget," to wit, two ells within the selvedges; of weights also let it be as of measures. [14]

36. Nothing in future shall be given or taken for a writ of inquisition of life or limbs, but freely it shall be granted, and never denied. [15]

---

[11] [Fish weirs.]   [12] [The purpose was to aid navigation.]

[13] [The king had used this writ to transfer cases involving feudal tenure from feudal (or seignorial) to royal courts.]

[14] ["Halberget" may have meant thick cloth worn under a coat of mail. An "ell" was 45 inches.]

[15] [This writ enabled someone challenged to a duel (trial by combat) to have the dispute tried in court.]

37. If anyone holds of us by fee-farm, by socage, or by burgage, and holds also land of another lord by knight's service, we will not by reason of that fee-farm, socage, or burgage, have the wardship of the heir, or of such land of his as is of the fief of that other; nor shall we have wardship of that fee-farm, socage, or burgage, unless such fee-farm owes knight's service.[16] We will not by reason of any small serjeanty which anyone may hold of us by the service of rendering to us knives, arrows, or the like, have wardship of his heir or of the land which he holds of another lord by knight's service.

38. No bailiff for the future shall, upon his own unsupported complaint, put anyone to his "law," without credible witnesses brought for this purpose.[17]

39. No freeman shall be taken or [and] imprisoned or disseised [18] or exiled or in any way destroyed, nor will we go upon him nor send upon him, except by the lawful judgment of his peers or [and] by the law of the land.

40. To no one will we sell, to no one will we refuse or delay, right or justice.

41. All merchants shall have safe and secure exit from England, and entry to England, with the right to tarry there and to move about as well by land as by water, for buying and selling by the ancient and right customs, quit from all evil tolls, except in time of war such merchants as are of the land at war with us. And if such are found in our land at the beginning of the war, they shall be detained, without injury to their bodies or goods, until information be received by us, or by our chief justiciar, how the merchants of our land found in the land at war with us are treated; and if our men are safe there, the others shall be safe in our land.

42. It shall be lawful in future for anyone excepting always those imprisoned or outlawed in accordance with the law of the kingdom, and natives of any country at war with us, and merchants, who shall be treated as is above provided to leave our kingdom and to return, safe and secure by land and water, except for a short period in time of war, on grounds of public policy—reserving always the allegiance due to us.

43. If anyone holding of some escheat, such as the honour of Wallingford, Nottingham, Boulogne, Lancaster, or of other escheats which are in our hands and are baronies, shall die, his heir shall give no other relief, and perform no other service to us than he would have done to the baron, if that barony had been in the baron's hand; and we shall hold it in the same manner in which the baron held it.[19]

---

[16] [In theory the king claimed wardship as a substitute for military service that a minor obviously could not perform. Since the three forms of tenure did not involve military service, the right to wardship in such cases is denied.]

[17] [The purpose of this provision is unknown.]　　　　　[18] [Expropriated.]

[19] [A barony escheated (reverted) to the king when the baron left no heir. This clause protects the subtenants.]

44. Men who dwell without the forest [20] need not henceforth come before our justiciars of the forest upon a general summons, except those who are impleaded, or who have become sureties for any person or persons attached for forest offences.

45. We will appoint as justices, constables, sheriffs, or bailiffs only such as know the law of the realm and mean to observe it well.

46. All barons who have founded abbeys, concerning which they hold charters from the kings of England, or of which they have long-continued possession, shall have the wardship of them, when vacant, as they ought to have.

47. All forests that have been made such in our time shall forthwith be disafforested; and a similar course shall be followed with regard to river-banks that have been placed "in defence" [21] by us in our time.

48. All evil customs connected with forests and warrens,[22] foresters and warreners, sheriffs and their officers, river-banks and their wardens, shall immediately be inquired into in each county by twelve sworn knights of the same county chosen by the honest men of the same county, and shall, within forty days of the said inquest, be utterly abolished, so as never to be restored, provided always that we previously have intimation thereof, or our justiciar, if we should not be in England.

49. We will immediately restore all hostages and charters delivered to us by Englishmen, as sureties of the peace or of faithful service.

50. We will entirely remove from their bailiwicks,[23] the relations of Gerard of Athée so that in future they shall have no bailiwick in England; namely, Engelard of Cigogné, Peter, Guy, and Andrew of Chanceaux, Guy of Cigogné, Geoffrey of Martigny with his brothers, Philip Mark with his brothers and his nephew Geoffrey, and the whole brood of the same.

51. As soon as peace is restored, we will banish from the kingdom all foreign-born knights, cross-bowmen, serjeants, and mercenary soldiers, who have come with horses and arms to the kingdom's hurt.

52. If anyone has been dispossessed or removed by us, without the legal judgment of his peers, from his lands, castles, franchises, or from his right, we will immediately restore them to him; and if a dispute arise over this, then let it be decided by the five-and-twenty barons of whom mention is made below in the clause for securing the peace. Moreover, for all those possessions, from which anyone has, without the lawful judgment of his peers, been disseised or removed, by our father, King Henry, or by our brother, King Richard, and

---

[20] [The king's game preserve, inside which the common law had no validity.]
[21] [That is, in which the hunting of wildfowl had been reserved.]
[22] [Areas where there existed hunting rights less exclusive than in the "forests."]
[23] ["Bailiwick" was a local magistracy; the persons named were royal favorites.]

which we retain in our hand or which are possessed by others, to whom we are bound to warrant them we shall have respite until the usual term of crusaders; excepting those things about which a plea has been raised, or an inquest made by our order, before our taking of the cross; but as soon as we return from our expedition or if perchance we desist from the expedition we will immediately grant full justice therein.

53. We shall have, moreover, the same respite and in the same manner in rendering justice concerning the disafforestation or retention of those forests which Henry our father and Richard our brother afforested, and concerning the wardship of lands which are of the fief of another, namely, such wardships as we have hitherto had by reason of a fief which anyone held of us by knight's service, and concerning abbeys founded on other fiefs than our own, in which the lord of the fee claims to have right; and when we have returned, or if we desist from our expedition, we will immediately grant full justice to all who complain of such things.

54. No one shall be arrested or imprisoned upon the appeal of a woman, for the death of any other than her husband.

55. All fines made with us unjustly and against the law of the land, and all amercements imposed unjustly and against the law of the land, shall be entirely remitted, or else it shall be done concerning them according to the decision of the five-and-twenty barons of whom mention is made below in the clause for securing the peace, or according to the judgment of the majority of the same, along with the aforesaid Stephen, archbishop of Canterbury, if he can be present, and such others as he may wish to bring with him for this purpose, and if he cannot be present the business shall nevertheless proceed without him, provided always that if any one or more of the aforesaid five-and-twenty barons are in a similar suit, they shall be removed as far as concerns this particular judgment, others being substituted in their places after having been selected by the rest of the same five-and-twenty for this purpose only, and after having been sworn.

56. If we have disseised or removed Welshmen from lands or liberties, or other things, without the legal judgment of their peers in England or in Wales, they shall be immediately restored to them; and if a dispute arise over this, then let it be decided in the marches by the judgment of their peers; for tenements in England according to the law of England, for tenements in Wales according to the law of Wales, and for tenements in the marches according to the law of the marches. Welshmen shall do the same to us and ours.

57. Further, for all those possessions from which any Welshman has, without the lawful judgment of his peers, been disseised or removed by King Henry our father, or King Richard our brother, and which we retain in our hand or

which are possessed by others, to whom we are bound to warrant them we shall have respite until the usual term of crusaders; excepting those things about which a plea has been raised or an inquest made by our order before we took the cross; but as soon as we return, or if perchance we desist from our expedition, we will immediately grant full justice in accordance with the laws of the Welsh and in relation to the foresaid regions.

58. We will immediately give up the son of Llywelyn and all the hostages of Wales, and the charters delivered to us as security for the peace.

59. We will do towards Alexander, King of Scots, concerning the return of his sisters and his hostages, and concerning his franchises, and his right, in the same manner as we shall do towards our other barons of England, unless it ought to be otherwise according to the charters which we hold from William his father, formerly King of Scots; and this shall be according to the judgment of his peers in our court.

60. Moreover, all these aforesaid customs and liberties, the observance of which we have granted in our kingdom as far as pertains to us towards our men, shall be observed by all of our kingdom, as well clergy as laymen, as far as pertains to them towards their men.

61. Since, moreover, for God and the amendment of our kingdom and for the better allaying of the quarrel that has arisen between us and our barons, we have granted all these concessions, desirous that they should enjoy them in complete and firm endurance for ever, we give and grant to them the underwritten security, namely, that the barons choose five-and-twenty barons of the kingdom, whomsoever they will, who shall be bound with all their might, to observe and hold, and cause to be observed, the peace and liberties we have granted and confirmed to them by this our present Charter, so that if we, or our justiciar, or our bailiffs or any one of our officers, shall in anything be at fault towards any one, or shall have broken any one of the articles of the peace or of this security, and the offence be notified to four barons of the foresaid five-and-twenty, the said four barons shall repair to us or our justiciar, if we are out of the realm, and, laying the transgression before us, petition to have that transgression redressed without delay. And if we shall not have corrected the transgression or, in the event of our being out of the realm, if our justiciar shall not have corrected it within forty days, reckoning from the time it has been intimated to us or to our justiciar, if we should be out of the realm, the four barons aforesaid shall refer that matter to the rest of the five-and-twenty barons, and those five-and-twenty barons shall, together with the community of the whole land, distrain and distress us in all possible ways, namely, by seizing our castles, lands, possessions, and in any other way they can, until redress has been obtained as they deem fit, saving harmless our own person, and the

persons of our queen and children; and when redress has been obtained, they shall resume their old relations towards us. And let whoever in the country desires it, swear to obey the orders of the said five-and-twenty barons for the execution of all the aforesaid matters, and along with them, to molest us to the utmost of his power, and we publicly and freely grant leave to every one who wishes to swear, and we shall never forbid any one to swear. All those, moreover, in the land who of themselves and of their own accord are un-willing to swear to the twenty-five to help them in constraining and molesting us, we shall by our command compel the same to swear to the effect foresaid. And if any one of the five-and-twenty barons shall have died or departed from the land, or be incapacitated in any other manner which would prevent the foresaid provisions being carried out, those of the said twenty-five barons who are left shall choose another in his place according to their own judgment, and he shall be sworn in the same way as the others. Further, in all matters, the execution of which is intrusted to these twenty-five barons, if perchance these twenty-five are present and disagree about anything, or if some of them, after being summoned, are unwilling or unable to be present, that which the majority of those present ordain or command shall be held as fixed and es-tablished, exactly as if the whole twenty-five had concurred in this; and the said twenty-five shall swear that they will faithfully observe all that is afore-said, and cause it to be observed with all their might. And we shall procure nothing from any one, directly or indirectly, whereby any part of these con-cessions and liberties might be revoked or diminished; and if any such thing has been procured, let it be void and null, and we shall never use it personally or by another.[24]

62. And all the ill-will, hatreds, and bitterness that have arisen between us and our men, clergy and lay, from the date of the quarrel, we have completely remitted and pardoned to every one. Moreover, all trespasses occasioned by the said quarrel, from Easter in the sixteenth year of our reign till the restoration of peace, we have fully remitted to all, both clergy and laymen, and com-pletely forgiven, as far as pertains to us. And, on this head, we have caused to be made for them letters testimonial patent of the lord Stephen, archbishop of Canterbury, of the lord Henry, archbishop of Dublin, of the bishops afore-said, and of Master Pandulf as touching this security and the concessions aforesaid.

63. Wherefore it is our will, and we firmly enjoin, that the English Church be free, and that the men in our kingdom have and hold all the aforesaid

---

[24] [These provisions illustrate the ultimately contractual nature of the feudal relation between lord and vassal. They anticipate the modern notion of a limited monarchy, but the whole plan is so crudely drawn that it is perhaps fortunate that it was not put into practice as it stands.]

liberties, rights, and concessions, well and peaceably, freely and quietly, fully and wholly, for themselves and their heirs, of us and our heirs, in all respects and in all places for ever, as is aforesaid. An oath, moreover, has been taken, as well on our part as on the part of the barons, that all these conditions aforesaid shall be kept in good faith and without evil intent. Given under our hand—the above-named and many others being witnesses—in the meadow which is called Runnymede, between Windsor and Staines, on the fifteenth day of June, in the seventeenth year of our reign.

THE TRUCE OF GOD

THE MEDIEVAL CHURCH instituted the Truce of God in an attempt to curb private warfare by penalizing with excommunication those who resorted to arms during such times of the year as the clergy had declared a closed season on feuds. The Truce of God developed from the earlier institution known as the Peace of God, which had been developed by the Church in France in the tenth century to protect the lives and property of the clergy and other presumed noncombatants such as pilgrims, peasants, women, and merchants.

Beginning in 1027 in the French diocese of Elne in the eastern Pyrenees with a prohibition against fighting between 9:00 P.M. Saturday and 1:00 A.M. Monday, the institution of the Truce of God was soon extended until by decision of the Lateran Council of 1139 only some ninety days in the year, excluding all holy days, were open for fighting throughout Christendom. In spite of the threat of excommunication and the occasional establishment of peace militias, private warfare was not brought under reasonable control until medieval monarchies developed reasonably effective police powers.

This selection is taken from J. H. Robinson, *Readings in European History*, Vol. I (Boston, Ginn and Co., 1904).

THE TRUCE OF GOD ISSUED BY A SYNOD HELD AT COLOGNE IN 1083

INASMUCH as in our own times the Church, through its members, has been extraordinarily afflicted by tribulations and difficulties, so that tranquillity and peace were wholly despaired of, we have endeavored with God's help to come to its aid, in the midst of its sufferings and perils. And by the advice of our faithful subjects we have at length provided this remedy, so that we might to some extent reestablish, on certain days at least, the peace which, because of our sins, we could not make enduring. Accordingly, we have enacted and set forth the following:

Having called together those under us to a legally summoned council, which was held at Cologne, the chief city of our provinces, in the church of St. Peter, in the 1083d year of our Lord's Incarnation, in the sixth indiction, on the twelfth day before the Kalends of May, after arranging other business, we have caused to be read in public what we proposed to do in this matter. After this had been fully discussed by all, both clergy and people with God's aid reached an agreement, and we set forth in what manner and during what parts of the year the peace should be observed, namely:

That from the first day of the Advent of our Lord through Epiphany, and from the beginning of Septuagesima to the eighth day after Pentecost and through that whole day, and throughout the year on every Sunday, Friday, and Saturday, and on the fast days of the four seasons, and on the eve and the day of all the apostles, and on all days canonically set apart —or which shall in future be set apart—for fasts or feasts, this decree of peace shall be observed; so that both those who travel and those who remain at home may enjoy security and the most entire peace, so that no one may commit murder, arson, robbery, or assault, no one may injure another with a sword, club, or any kind of weapon. Let no one, however irritated by wrong, presume to carry arms, shield, sword, or lance, or any kind of armor, from the Advent of our Lord to the eighth day after Epiphany, and from Septuagesima to the eighth day after Pentecost. On the remaining days, indeed, namely, on Sundays, Fridays, apostles' days, and the vigils of the apostles, and on every day set aside, or to be set aside, for fasts or feasts, arms may be carried, but on this condition, that no injury shall be done in any way to any one.

If it shall be necessary for any one, during the period of the peace,—i.e. from the Advent of our Lord to the eighth day after Epiphany, and from Septuagesima to the eighth day after Pentecost,—to go from one bishopric into another in which the peace is not observed, he may bear arms, but on the condition that he shall not injure any one, except in self-defense if he is attacked; and when he returns into our diocese he shall immediately lay aside his arms. If it shall happen that any castle is besieged during the days which are included within the peace, the besiegers shall cease from attack unless they are set upon by the besieged and compelled to beat the latter back.

And in order that this statute of peace should not be violated by any one rashly or with impunity, a penalty was fixed by the common consent of all, namely: If a free man or noble violates it, i.e. commits homicide, or wounds any one or is at fault in any manner whatever, he shall be expelled from his lands, without any indulgence on account of the payment of money or the intercession of friends and his heirs shall take all the property. If he holds a fief, the lord to whom it belongs shall receive it again. Moreover, if it appear that his heirs after his expulsion have furnished him any support or aid, and if they are convicted of it, the estate shall be taken from them and revert to the king. But if they wish to clear themselves of the charge against them, they shall take oath, with twelve who are equally free or equally noble.

If a slave kills a man, he shall be beheaded; if he wounds a man, he shall lose a hand; if he does an injury in any other way with his fist or a club, or by striking with a stone, he shall be shorn and flogged. If, however, he is accused and wishes to prove his innocence, he shall clear himself by the ordeal of cold water, but he must himself be put into the water and no one else in his place. If, however, fearing the sentence decreed against him, he flees, he shall be under a perpetual excommunication; and if he is known to be in any place, letters shall be sent thither, in which it shall be announced to all that he is excommunicated, and that it is unlawful for any one to associate with him. In the case of boys who have not yet completed their twelfth year, the hand ought not to be cut off; but only in the case of those who are twelve years or more of age. Nevertheless, if boys fight, they shall be whipped and prevented from fighting.

It is not an infringement of the peace if any one orders his delinquent slave, pupil, or any one in any way under his charge, to be chastised with rods or sticks. It is also an exception to this constitution of peace if the lord king publicly orders an expedition to attack the enemies of the kingdom, or is pleased to hold a council to judge the enemies of justice. The peace is not violated if, during the times specified, a duke, or other counts, magistrates, or their substitutes, hold courts and inflict punishment legally on thieves, robbers, and other criminals.

The statute of this noble peace is especially enacted for the safety of those engaged in feuds; but after the end of the peace they are not to dare to rob and plunder in the villages and houses, since the laws and penalties enacted before the institution of the peace are still legally valid to restrain them from crime, and, moreover, because robbers and highwaymen are excluded from this divine peace, and indeed from any peace.

If any one attempts to oppose this pious institution and is unwilling to promise peace to God with the others, or to observe it, no priest in our diocese shall presume to say a mass for him, or shall take any care for his salvation; if he is sick, no Christian shall dare to visit him; on his deathbed he shall not receive the Eucharist, unless he repents. The supreme authority of the peace pledged to God and generally extolled by all will be so great that it will be observed not only in our times, but forever among our posterity, because if any one shall presume to infringe or violate it, either now or ages hence, until the end of the world, he is irrevocably excommunicated by us.

The responsibility for carrying out the above-mentioned penalties against the violators of the peace rests no more with the counts, local judges, or officials than with the whole people in general. They are to be especially careful not to show friendship or hatred, nor to do anything contrary to justice in punishing, nor to conceal crimes, which may be hidden, but to bring them to light. No one is to receive money for the release of those taken in fault, or to attempt to aid the guilty by any favor of any kind, because whoever does this incurs the intolerable damnation of his soul; and all the faithful ought to remember that this peace has not been promised to men, but to God, and therefore must be observed so much the more rigidly and firmly. Wherefore we exhort all in Christ to guard inviolably this necessary contract of peace, and if any one hereafter presumes to violate it, let him be damned by the ban of irrevocable excommunication and by the anathema of eternal perdition.

THE GOLIARD POETS

THE MIDDLE AGES were not all manorial drudgery and monastic piety. The rise of the universities, accompanied by a revived interest in the pagan Latin classics, resulted in the twelfth century in a great burst of intellectual and creative activity. A part of that new and essentially secular spirit was expressed in the sudden flowering of vernacular literatures all over Europe. Latin literature also shared in the renaissance. One variety of Latin lyric that appeared expressed a revived paganism.

The authors, the so-called Goliard poets, represent—for the most part anonymously—the convention of student rebellion against accepted authority. Their medieval label derives from Goliath, the enemy of David, the ancestor of Jesus, and hence a kind of Antichrist. Their Latin lyrics include earnest praises of natural forces and physical desires, parodies of religious literature (often blasphemous, if not obscene), and serious satires of the corruption of the clergy. The importance of their work, or perhaps the organized nature of their protest, can be seen in the frequent directions for their suppression in the Church councils of the thirteenth century. Educated but vagabond participants in the university world of their era, the Goliards gave vitality to the profane strain in the medieval world. By the fourteenth century, however, they had dispersed as a definable group.

The "Song of the Vagrant Order" is an impudent Goliardic invention in which the rules and customs of a fanciful, very unmonastic Order of Goliards are set forth. The translation is from *The Goliard Poets* (Norfolk, New Directions; copyright 1949 by George F. Whicher) and is here reprinted by kind permission of the publisher and of the translator, Professor Whicher.

SONG OF THE VAGRANT ORDER

When through all the realms of earth
"Go ye out" resounded,
Priests began to gad about,
Monks with rapture bounded,
Deacons from the Evangels rose,
Weary of redundance—
One and all our order join,
Seeking life's abundance.

In our order it is writ:
"Take all things and try them,

Seek for the best things of life,
See you profit by them.
Wicked priests must rouse your zeal,
Be their stern despisers
If when you demand a dole
They behave like misers."

Austrians, Bavarians,
Saxons, ay, and Mark-men,
Good companions as ye are,
I entreat ye, hark, men!

Hear these new decretals, then
Be their staunch defenders:
Death to penny-pinching men
And not liberal spenders.

We ourselves are fountains where
Bounty never stagnates,
Since we welcome to our ranks
Lesser men and magnates;
We relieve the rich of care,
Give the poor a fresh hold,
Lazars such as godly monks
Banish from their threshold.

We receive the shaven skull
Gladly as the hairy,
When a priest elopes or monk
Bolts the monastery;
Boys from school and masters too,
Parsons, clerks—we're flattered!
But your scholar is our prize,
Clad in robes untattered.

Righteous or unrighteous, we
In our corps enlist them,
Lame and feeble, brave and strong,
All alike subsist them;
Some are in the flower of youth,
Some with age are stricken,
Some are cold of heart, and some,
Warmed by Venus, quicken.

Warmongers and pacifists,
Mild men and demonic,
Roman and Bohemian,
Slavic and Teutonic:
Men of medium size we take,
Likewise dwarfs and giants,
Humble folk, and those who still
Bid the gods defiance.

Truly then our order ranks
As a sect or nation,
Since so many kinds of men
Find here a vocation.
Hic, haec, hoc, he, she, and it,
Here can take their places,
Hospitality like ours
Joins all creeds and races.

Of the vagrant order's laws
These are fundamental:
Generous must we be in life,
In demeanor gentle;
Also we must love a roast,
Dripping unctuous juices,
More than pecks of barley-meal
Fit for a hermit's uses.

Matins next our rule forbids,
Fie on early waking!
Eerie phantoms always prowl
Just as day is breaking,
Causing visions that entail
Direful consequences;
He who rises with the dawn
Hardly has his senses.

So our order interdicts
Matins now and ever;
When we rise, the chimney nook
Claims our first endeavor,
There let serve a bird with wine,
Mixing pleasant prattle,
We have nought to fear from fate
Till the dice-cups rattle.

Last, our order interdicts
All superfluous clothing;
One who sports an overcoat
We must view with loathing.

Let him pledge his needless wrap
At the shrine of Decius,
Soon his vest will follow too—
Dice are avaricious.

What I've said of outer clothes
Holds as well of inner:
Stake your drawers if you've a shirt—
Courage makes a winner;
Why, if boots go up the spout,
For your socks be heedful?
You will certainly be damned
If you lack the needful.

None of us must leave an inn
Till his hunger's sated,
Let him beg a penny too
If necessitated;
There's a chance the small, despised
Coin your needs importune

May, if played by skillful hands,
Swell into a fortune.

None must ever take the road
When the wind's contrary,
Nor present a doleful face
If his prospects vary.
Let him keep a cheerful heart,
Hopes are sure to brighten,
When the sky is darkest, then
It can only lighten.

Give to any folk you meet
Reasons for your questing,
As that men's peculiar ways
Seem in need of testing:
"Probity from pravity
Seeking to unravel,
Reprobates to reprobate,
That is why I travel."

IV CENTRALIZED GOVERNMENT AND THE SECULAR POLITICAL SPIRIT

PHILIPPE DE COMMINES

THE STRENUOUS CAREER of Louis XI, king of France from 1461 to 1483, is illustrative of the process of dynastic state building in the period of feudalism's decay. Born during the Hundred Years War—he was five years old when Joan of Arc appeared—Louis as a young man led troops against the English and against rebellious French nobles, plotted against his father, King Charles VII, and eventually ran away to the court of neighboring Burgundy, where he impatiently awaited the day of his succession to the throne. Crowned king in 1461, he asserted his authority with such vigor that most of France's great nobles formed a league against him and accepted the aid of the powerful Charles the Bold of Burgundy, whose father's hospitality to Louis had gone unrewarded. That Louis XI triumphed over this coalition, after many years, and succeeded in unifying and extending the territories under control of the French crown, was the result of his ruthless diplomacy and shrewdness in choosing means which enhanced royal absolutism at the expense of feudal restraints. Supported by the lesser nobles and upper bourgeoisie, who were not averse to seeing their social superiors disciplined and who judged correctly that the king would keep the peasantry and artisans in their place, Louis XI taxed harshly, increased the royal budget, and with the aid of dependable officials governed in a manner which may be said to foreshadow the later and greater absolutism of Louis XIV.

Among Louis XI's most intimate advisers was the Flemish nobleman Philippe de Commines (c.1445–1509), who after the death of his master described the reign in a part of his *Mémoires,* the *Cronique et hystoire du roy Louis onziesme,* with such skill that he has been called the finest historian of his day. Philippe de Commines had been educated at the Burgundian court and had been one of Charles the Bold's officers for a number of years before entering the service of Louis XI. To his natural talents was therefore added an unusual opportunity to observe and reflect upon the subject matter of his history, a part of which appears below in a translation from the French by Andrew R. Scoble (*Memoirs of Philippe de Commines,* London, 1856).

MEMOIRS

IN THE YEAR 1470, the king, having a fair opportunity, as he thought, resolved to be revenged of the Duke of Burgundy, and secretly endeavoured to persuade the towns upon the River Somme, as Amiens, St. Quentin, and Abbeville, to forsake the duke, and admit some of his troops into their garrisons; for it is always the custom of great princes (especially if they be wise), to seek out some fair pretence or other to cover their designs. In order to your better under-

standing the intrigues and artifices of the French court in this kind of transactions, I will give a relation of the whole management of this affair; for the
king and duke were both of them deceived, and a very bloody and cruel war
commenced upon it, which lasted thirteen or fourteen years. The king indeed
had a great desire to excite those towns to rebel, and set up his standard, upon
pretence that the Duke of Burgundy had extended the bounds of his dominions
farther than the treaty would bear. Upon this account several envoys and
ambassadors were sent from one court to the other, backward and forward,
who passed and re-passed through these towns, and proposed and drove on
their several bargains very securely, there being no garrisons in these towns;
for the whole kingdom of France, as well on that side towards the Duke of
Burgundy's dominions, as on the other towards the Duke of Bretagne's, was
in perfect peace, and the Duke of Guienne was to all appearance in great
friendship with the king. However, the king had no design to commence a
war purely to repossess himself of one or two of those towns, and no more;
but his intention was to raise a universal rebellion in the Duke of Burgundy's
dominions, hoping, by that means, to make himself master of all his country.

Many persons, to ingratiate themselves with the king, undertook the management of these secret negotiations, and reported them much forwarder than
he really found them; one promised him one town, and another another town,
and that they had bargained for them all; but had the king's designs reached no
farther than the events which succeeded . . . he would not have violated the
peace, nor involved himself in a new war; for he had published the peace at
Paris three months after his return into his kingdom; and he began his enterprise not without some fear and caution; but the violent desires he had to it,
at last prevailed over his timorousness, and he was spurred on to it by some
of his courtiers.

The Count of St. Paul, a very wise man, and Constable of France, with
several of the Duke of Guienne's servants and others, earnestly desired a war
between those two great princes, rather than peace, and that for two reasons:
—The first was, that they were afraid their great revenues would be lessened,
if the peace should continue; for the constable had 400 men-at-arms or lances,
paid every muster, without any comptroller, and above 30,000 francs a-year,
besides the salary of his office, and the profits of several good places which he
had in his possession. The other was, because they had observed and talked
among themselves, that the nature of the king was such, that unless he was
at war with some foreign prince, he would certainly find some quarrel or
other at home with his servants, domestics, and officers; for his mind must
always be working. Prompted by these specious arguments, they endeavoured

to persuade the king to commence the war; and the constable promised to take St. Quentin whenever he pleased, for his lands lay near it; and he boasted much of his great intelligence in Brabant and Flanders, and that he could induce several of those towns to revolt against the Duke of Burgundy.

The Duke of Guienne being of the same opinion, all his principal governors offered the king their services, and promised him to bring along with them 400 or 500 men-at-arms, whom the Duke of Guienne kept constantly in pay; but their design was not as the king took it, but quite contrary, as you will see hereafter.

The king was always wont to proceed gravely and solemnly in all actions of importance, and therefore he convoked the three Estates at Tours in the months of March and April, 1470 (a thing which he had never done before, nor ever did afterwards), but he summoned only such persons as he thought would not oppose his designs. In this assembly he complained of several of the Duke of Burgundy's enterprises and practices against his crown; he ordered the Count d'Eu to bring in a complaint against the duke for detaining from him St. Vallery and other towns belonging to the jurisdiction of Abbeville and the county of Ponthieu. . . . In this assembly there were present several lawyers, as well of the parliament as elsewhere; by all of whom it was concluded, according to the intention of the king, that a day should be appointed, and the Duke of Burgundy summoned to appear in person before the Parliament at Paris. The king knew very well his answer would be insolent, or that he would do something or other against the authority of that court, which would give him a more plausible pretence of declaring war against him.

The Duke of Burgundy received his summons in Ghent from the hands of one of the officers of the Parliament, as he was going to mass; he was much surprised, and highly offended at it, and ordered the officer to be taken into custody, where he remained several days, but at length he was dismissed.

You see the measures that were concerted for the invasion of the Duke of Burgundy's territories; who, having intelligence of it, immediately enlisted great numbers of men, but at half-pay (as they called it), who were to be ready in arms at their houses upon the first summons. However, they were mustered constantly once a month, and received their pay.

In this posture affairs continued for three or four months; but the duke growing weary of the expense, disbanded his soldiers; for the king having sent several embassies to him, he began to think the storm was blown over, and retired into Holland. He had now no soldiers in pay, ready to be employed upon any occasion, nor garrisons in his frontier towns, which was greatly to his disadvantage, by reason of the designs on foot for bringing over Amiens, Abbeville, and St. Quentin to the king. While the Duke of Burgundy was in Holland, John, late Duke of Bourbon, gave him notice, that in a short time a war would break out against him, as well in Burgundy as Picardy, for the king had great intelligence both in those provinces and in his household. The Duke of Burgundy being wholly unprovided with troops (having disbanded his army, as I said before), was much alarmed at this news; upon which he passed immediately into Artois by sea, and went straight to Hesdin. There he began to find out the secret intrigues of some of his officers, and the trans- actions which were being managed privately in the above-mentioned towns. At first he could not be persuaded of the truth of it, so that it was some time before he would be convinced of their treachery; but at length he sent for two of the principal citizens of Amiens, whom he suspected to have a hand in those secret negotiations; yet they excused themselves so handsomely, that he suf- fered them to depart. Not long after this some of the duke's household revolted from him, and went over to the king, as the Bastard Baudouin, and several others; which made him fearful lest more should follow their example. To prevent the worst, he issued a proclamation, requiring all his people to be immediately in arms; but few obeyed it, for winter was approaching, and the duke had not been many days arrived from Holland. . . .

But it is now high time for me to declare what it was that moved the con- stable, the Duke of Guienne, and their principal ministers (notwithstanding the many good offices, the supplies, and honourable dealing which the Duke of Guienne had received from the Duke of Burgundy), and what advantage they proposed to themselves by fomenting the war between these two great princes, who were then in peace in their several provinces. I have said some- thing of it before, that it was to secure their pensions and employments, lest the king, having no wars abroad, should either take them away, or retrench them. But this was not the chief cause. The Duke of Guienne and his party had passionately desired a match between him and the sole daughter and heiress of the Duke of Burgundy (for the Duke of Burgundy had no sons). The Duke of Burgundy had been often solicited in this business, and always gave them hopes, but would never suffer it to be concluded, and indeed enter- tained propositions from other persons. . . .

By the messages which were sent, first from the Duke of Guienne, and afterwards from the constable, it is plain the whole business was premeditated . . . so that it may be easily concluded this war was undertaken to force the Duke of Burgundy to consent to that match. The king was deceived when he was put upon it; and the story of their intelligence in the Duke of Bur- gundy's country was utterly, or to a great extent, false. However, during this whole expedition, the king was served faithfully by the constable, who mortally hated the Duke of Burgundy, because he knew that the duke had no affection for him. The Duke of Guienne also served the king very honestly in this war, with a considerable body of troops, and the Duke of Burgundy's affairs were in a dangerous condition; yet if, in the beginning of this rupture, the duke (as I said before) would have consented to the marriage of his daughter with the Duke of Guienne, all the above-mentioned great lords would have abandoned the king, and employed all their power and interest against him; but it is in vain for man to determine in these cases, for God Almighty ever executes as he pleases. . . .

The king was overjoyed to see himself rid of all those whom he hated, and who were his chief enemies; on some of them he had been personally revenged, as on the constable of France, the Duke of Nemours, and several others. His brother, the Duke of Guienne, was dead, and his majesty came to the succession of the duchy. The whole house of Anjou was extinct; both René, King of Sicily, John and Nicholas, Dukes of Calabria, and since them their cousin, the Count du Maine, afterwards made Count of Provence. The Count d'Armagnac had been killed at Lestore, and the king had got the estates and moveables of all of them. But the house of Burgundy, being greater and more powerful than the rest, having maintained war with Charles VII, our master's father, for two and thirty years together without any cessation, by the assistance of the English; and having their dominions bordering upon the king's, and their subjects always inclinable to invade his kingdom; the king had reason to be more than ordinarily pleased at the death of that duke, and he triumphed more in his ruin than in that of all the rest of his enemies, as he thought that nobody, for the future, either of his own subjects, or his neighbours, would be able to oppose him, or disturb the tranquillity of his reign. He was at peace with England, as you have heard, and made it his chief business to continue so. . . .

I cannot understand why God has preserved the city of Ghent so long, which has occasioned so much mischief, and which is no good either to the public, or the country wherein it is seated, and much less to its prince. It is not like Bruges, which indeed is a place of trade, and of great resort for foreigners of all nations, in which more commodities and merchandise are disposed of than in any other town in Europe, so that to have had that town destroyed, would have been an irreparable loss; but it seems to me, that God has not made any created being in this world, neither man nor beast, nor anything else, but He has set up some other thing in opposition to it, to keep it within just bounds of fear and humility. In this respect Ghent is admirably well situated, for certainly the countries round about it are the most luxurious, the most splendid, and the most addicted to those pleasures to which man is inclined, of any country in Christendom; yet they are good Christians, and to outward appearance God is religiously honoured and served. But it is not the house of Burgundy alone that has a thorn in its side; France has England as a check; England has Scotland; and Spain, Portugal (I will not mention Granada, for they are enemies to the true faith, though otherwise Granada has given the kingdom of Castile much trouble to this very day). The princes of Italy, who generally have no other title to their territories but what they derive from Heaven (and of that we can have no certain knowledge), and who rule their subjects with cruelty, violence, and oppression in respect to their taxes, are curbed and kept in check by the commonwealth and free states in Italy, namely, Venice, Florence, Genoa, Bologna, Siena, Pisa, Lucca, and others; which are in a great many respects diametrically opposite, they to the princes, and the princes to them; and all keep a watchful eye over one another, that neither of them may grow too powerful for his neighbour. But to come to particulars in relation to the state of Italy. The house of Aragon has that of Anjou to curb it; the Visconti Dukes of Milan have the house of Orleans, and though they be feeble abroad, their subjects hold them in great dread. The Venetians (as I said before) have the princes of Italy, but more especially the Florentines, in opposition against them; and the Florentines, the neighbouring commonwealths of Sienna and Genoa. The Genoese are sufficiently plagued with their own bad government and treachery towards each other, not to mention their factions and parties, the Fregosi, the Adorni, the Dorias, and others; but this everybody knows so well, that I shall insist no longer on it.

In Germany you are well acquainted with the animosity that rages between the houses of Austria and Bavaria, and how the house of Bavaria is subdivided within itself. The house of Austria again has the Swiss for its enemy, upon the account only of a small village called Switz (not able to raise 600 men), but now the whole country takes its denomination from it, and is so increased in power and riches that two of the best towns belonging to the house of Austria are Zurich and Fribourg, both of which are in Switzerland. Besides, they have won several memorable battles, and slain several of the Dukes of Austria in the field. There are also many other factions and private animosities in Germany; the house of Cleves against the house of Guelders, and the Dukes of Guelders against the Dukes of Juliers. The Easterlings (that remote people in the north) withstand the Kings of Denmark; and, to speak in general of all Germany, there are so many fortified places, and so many people in them ready for all manner of mischief (as plundering, robbing, and killing) upon every trivial occasion, that it is a wonder to think of it. A private person, with only one servant to wait on him, will defy a whole city, and declare war against a duke, that he may have a pretence to rob and plunder him; especially if he has a little castle, perched upon a rock, to retreat to, where he can keep twenty or thirty horses, to scour the country, and plunder according to his directions.

Robbers of this kind are seldom punished by the German princes, who employ them upon all occasions; but the towns and free states punish them severely whenever they catch any of them, and have often besieged and blown up their castles, for which purpose they have generally a certain number of forces in pay, who are always in readiness to defend them. So that these princes and towns in Germany are placed in this opposition and discord, that no one may encroach upon his neighbour—which is absolutely necessary, not only in Germany, but all the world over. . . .

It is therefore to be concluded, that neither natural reason, nor our own knowledge, nor the fear of God, nor love of our neighbour, nor anything else, is always sufficient to restrain us from doing violence to one another, or to withhold us from retaining what we have got already, or to hinder us from usurping the possessions of other people by all possible ways. For if great princes once get possession of any towns or castles, though they belong to their nearest relations or neighbours, all the reasons above mentioned will not prevail with them to restore them; and after they have once published some artful reasons or specious pretence for keeping them, everybody applauds their reasons, especially those who are nearest about them, and desirous of being in their favour. I am not speaking here of disputes between inferior persons, for they have superiors above them who sometimes do them justice; at least, if a man's cause be at all good, his pockets full, and he willing to part with his money, and unless the court (that is the prince under whose authority he lives) opposes him. So that it would seem probable that God is as it were constrained to show many signs, and to chastise us with many rods for our indolence and perverseness; but the brutishness and ignorance of princes are very dangerous and dreadful, because the happiness or misery of their subjects depends wholly upon them. Wherefore, if a prince is powerful and has a large standing army, by the help of which he can raise money to pay his troops, or to spend in a luxurious way of living, or in anything that does not directly tend to the advancement of the common good, and if he will not retrench his outrageous extravagances himself, and those courtiers that are about him rather endeavour to flatter and applaud him in everything he does, than to dissuade him from doing ill (for fear of incurring his displeasure), who can apply any remedy in this case but God alone?

God indeed does not now converse with mankind after the same manner as He did of old, nor are there any prophets to declare His pleasure, but His word is sufficiently known and declared, and clear enough to any that are willing to understand it; so that there will be none excused for ignorance, especially if they have had time and natural sense to consider these matters. How, then, shall those great princes escape who keep their people in such subjection, that they raise what taxes they please by force, by which they compel their subjects to obedience, and enforce the least of their commands with penalty of life? Some of them punish under pretence of justice and have those about them who are always ready to comply with their wishes, and make a capital crime of what in itself is a venial offense. If they want sufficient evidence to condemn a man, they have ways of multiplying interrogatories, and falsifying the examinations of the witnesses, to weary the defendant, and destroy him with expenses, delaying his trial, and by that means giving encouragement to any that will bring a fresh information against him. If that will not do, and answers not their intentions, they have a shorter method, by stating the case as they please themselves, and giving out it was necessary the culprit should be made an example of. To others that are of a higher quality, and depend upon them, they say, "You have disobeyed and done contrary to the duty and allegiance you owe me": and upon that bare pretence and allegation they proceed, if they can, to seize upon their estates by force, and reduce them to extreme poverty and distress. If they have a neighbour that is of martial temper, they will be sure not to disturb him: but if his kingdom is in a poor weak condition, he will never be left at rest: they will assert he has assisted their enemies, or levied contributions on their countries; or else they will excite quarrels to give them occasion to ruin him. If that will not do, they will support their enemies secretly against him, and will supply them with troops. They think their own subjects live too long, though they have served their predecessors never so faithfully, and will displace them to make room for new creatures of their own. They will molest and quarrel with the clergy upon the score of their benefices, in order to extort compositions for the enriching of some person recommended to them by such as are subservient to their looser pleasures, and who often have great influence upon them. They exhaust their nobility in preparations for war, which they undertake at their pleasure, without consulting their council, or such as they ought to advise with before they enter upon action, though they have employed both their persons and estates to enable them to undertake it. To the common people they leave little or nothing, though their taxes be greater than they ought; nor do they take any care to restrain the licentiousness of their soldiers, who are constantly quartered throughout the country without paying anything; and commit all manner of excesses and insolencies, as everybody knows; for not contented with the ordinary provisions for which they are paid, they beat and abuse the poor country people, and force them to buy bread, wine, and other dainties, on purpose for their eating; and if the good man's wife or daughter happens to be handsome, his wisest course is to keep them out of their sight. And yet, where money is plenty, it would be no hard matter to prevent this disorder and confusion, by paying them every two months at farthest, which would obviate their pretence of want of pay, and leave them without excuse, and cause no inconvenience to the prince, because his money is raised punctually every year. . . .

But to proceed in my design. Is there any king or prince upon earth who has power to raise one penny of money, except on his own demesnes, without the consent of the poor subject who is to pay it, unless it be by tyranny and violence? It may be objected, that there are some times in which the assembling of great councils cannot be waited for, and that their debates would be too tedious. The preparations and beginnings of war are never so sudden but kings have time enough to consider of it; and when it is begun with the consent and concurrence of his subjects, the prince is always more strong and formidable to his enemy. If it be a defensive war, the storm is seen afar off, especially if it be an invasion, and then the good subject cannot complain, or refuse anything that is demanded: nor can any case happen so suddenly, but some important persons may be called together, to show the necessity of the war, which is much better than to commence hostilities arbitrarily and feignedly, with a design only to raise money. Money, I am sensible, is necessary at all times to secure the frontiers, in times of peace as well as war, that they may not be surprised; but all should be done with moderation, and depends much upon the wisdom of the prince; for if he be a good man he knows what God is, what the world is, what he ought to do, and what he ought to avoid. In my opinion, of all the countries in the world with which I was ever acquainted, the government is no where so well managed, the people no where less obnoxious to violence and oppression, nor their houses less liable to be destroyed and demolished by war than in England, for there the calamities fall only upon the authors of them.

Of all the kings in the world our sovereign has the least reason to use this expression, "I have the privilege to raise what money I please upon my subjects"; for that is a power neither he nor any prince else has; and they do him no honour who say so in order to make him appear greater, for they make him only more terrible and odious to his neighbours, who would never consent to live under his government. But, if our king or his courtiers, who are desirous of augmenting his reputation and grandeur, were to say thus: "My subjects are so good and loyal, that they refuse me nothing I ask them; I am the most feared, best obeyed, and best served by my subjects of any prince in the world; my subjects are the most patient under injury and affliction, and most forgetful of all past sufferings"; this, in my judgment, is more honourable (and I am sure it is true) than to say, "I take what I will; I have privilege to do it, and I will keep it." . . .

As an instance of the affections of the French to their prince, we need look no further back than our own times. At the meeting of the three Estates at Tours, upon the death of our good master Louis XI (whom God pardon!), who died in 1483, that assembly in such a juncture might be thought dangerous; and some there were (but considerable neither for their quality nor virtue) who said then, and have often repeated it since, that it was a diminution of the king's prerogative, and no less than treason against him to talk of assembling the Estates; but it is such as these who commit treason against God, the king, and their country; and those who use these expressions are in undeserved authority and reputation, and are wholly unfit for anything but flattery, whispering lies and stories into the ears of their masters, which make them afraid of these assemblies, lest they should take notice of them and their manners, and call them to an account for their villainous practices. This kingdom was at that time accounted very weak by all people, having endured for twenty years and upwards, such great and horrible taxes as exceeded all precedent by above 3,000,000 of francs per annum. . . .

And yet, in this weak, oppressed, and impoverished kingdom, upon the death of our king, was there any sedition among the people against the prince who now reigns? Did either nobles or commons take arms to oppose him? Was there any one else whom they desired to place on the throne? Did they endeavour either to deprive, or so much as to restrain him in his authority, that he should not have the power of a king? Not at all! and indeed if any had been so conceited as to say yes, they would have had none to help them, for his subjects acted quite contrary; and all the nobility, gentry, commons, and citizens, obeyed his summons, made their personal appearance before him, recognized his power, and swore allegiance to him. The princes and nobles delivered in their petitions humbly upon their knees, and a council of twelve were appointed to take them into consideration, and according to the advice of that council, the king (being then but thirteen years old) did either grant or refuse them. In the assembly of the Estates, the king and his council being present, some requests and remonstrances were made for the good of the kingdom, with all possible humility and deference to the good pleasure of the king and his council.

They who shall read these Memoirs hereafter, and have a better knowledge of the affairs of this kingdom and its neighbouring States than I have, may perhaps wonder that, from the Duke of Burgundy's death to this time, which is little less than a year, I have not said a word of the English, nor of their suffering the king to seize upon those towns which were near them, as Arras, Boulogne, Hesdin, Ardres and several other castles, and to lie so many days before St. Omer. The reason of it was, because, in cunning and artifice, our king was much superior to King Edward, who was indeed a brave prince, and had won eight or nine battles in England, in which he had been always present himself, and had fought constantly on foot, which redounded much to his honour; but the two kings were placed in different circumstances, and the English king depended not so much upon his diligence or understanding, for upon the success of one battle he was absolute master till another rebellion disturbed him. In England, when any disputes arise, and occasion a war, the controversy is generally decided in eight or ten days, when one party or other gains the victory; but with us, on this side of the water, affairs are managed quite otherwise. Our king is obliged, whilst he is carrying on any war, to keep a watchful eye upon his neighbours, as well as over the rest of his kingdom; and particularly to satisfy the King of England above all, who must be quieted at any cost, and cajoled with ambassadors, promises, and presents, lest he should attempt anything that might interrupt our king's designs. For our master was well aware that the nobility, commons, and clergy of England, are always ready to enter upon a war with France, being incited thereunto, not only upon the account of their old title to its crown, but by the desire of gain, for it pleased God to permit their predecessors to win several memorable battles in this kingdom, and to continue in the possession of Normandy and Guienne for the space of three hundred and fifty years, before Charles VII gave them the first blow; during which time they carried over enormous booty into England, not only in plunder, which they had taken in the several towns, but in the richness and quality of their prisoners, who were many of them great princes and lords, who paid them vast ransoms for their liberty; so that every Englishman afterwards hoped to do the same thing, and return home laden with spoils. . . .

The king accordingly found himself under an absolute necessity to caress and pacify the King of England, and the rest of his neighbours, whom he perceived inclinable to peace, in hopes of receiving his money; and therefore he paid a pension of fifty thousand crowns punctually in London, and allowed it to be called tribute by the English. He also distributed sixteen thousand more among the King of England's officers that were about his person, particularly to the Chancellor, the Master of the Rolls (who is now chancellor), the High Chamberlain, the Lord Hastings (a man of honour and prudence, and of great authority with his master, and deservedly, upon account of the faithful service he had done him), Sir Thomas Montgomery, the Lord Howard (who afterwards espoused King Richard's interest, and was created Duke of Norfolk), the Lord Cheney, master of the horse, Mr. Chalenger, and a certain marquis, who was the Queen of England's son, by her first husband. Besides these great presents, he was also very generous to ambassadors; and all who were sent to him from the English court, though their messages were never so harsh and displeasing, he dispatched with such fair words and large presents, that they went away very well satisfied with him; and though they were certainly assured (at least some of them), that what he did was only to gain time to effect his designs, yet their private interest prevailed with them to wink at it, highly to the detriment and disadvantage of their public affairs. . . .

In this posture were affairs between the King of England and our master: however, the King of England was earnestly solicited and urged to assist the young princess, and he sent several embassies to our master to remonstrate with him, and to press him either for a peace, or a cessation of arms. For some of the privy council of England, and of the Parliament (which is of the same nature as our three Estates), were persons of wisdom and penetration, who came out of the country, and were not pensioners of France like the rest, and these pressed hard, that the King of England would interpose vigorously for the Princess of Burgundy; urging, that we did but dissemble with them, and amuse them with hopes of a marriage, as it very plainly appeared: for at the treaty of Picquigny the two kings had mutually sworn, that within the space of a year, the King of England's daughter should be sent for; but though the King of France had permitted her to be styled the dauphiness, yet the time was elapsed, and the lady had not been sent for. But all the arguments his subjects made use of could not prevail with King Edward, for several reasons. King Edward was a voluptuous prince, wholly addicted to his pleasures and ease; and having been, in his former expeditions, reduced to great straits and necessities, he had no mind to involve himself in a new war on this side of the water: the fifty thousand crowns, too, which were punctually paid him in the Tower, softened his heart, and hindered him from concerning himself in this affair. Besides, his ambassadors were always bribed, and entertained so nobly, that they left the French court well satisfied, though the king's answers were always uncertain, in order to gain time; for they were always told that in a few days the king would send ambassadors of his own, who would satisfy their master in every point which had been left in doubt.

As soon as the King of England's ambassadors were returned, about three weeks or a month later, sometimes more, sometimes less (which in such cases is a great matter), the king our master would send his envoys; but always new persons, and such as had not been employed in any overture with the English before, to the end that if anything had been promised by their predecessors, but not afterwards performed, they might pretend ignorance, and not be obliged to give an answer. The ambassadors, therefore, who were sent into England, used their utmost endeavours to persuade King Edward of the good inclinations of the King of France, so that he might remain quiet, and not give the least assistance to the Princess of Burgundy: for both the King and the Queen of England were so desirous of the match with their daughter, that upon that account, not to mention several other reasons, the king was willing to wink at these proceedings, and take no notice of the remonstrances that were made to him by some of his privy council, who represented to him how prejudicial it would be to the interest of the whole nation. . . .

. . . For certainly, had it not been in hopes of this marriage, the King of England would never so tamely have suffered our king to have taken so many towns, without endeavouring to have defended them; and had he declared at the outset for the young Princess of Burgundy, as our king was so fearful of bringing anything to a hazard, he would not have encroached so far upon the dominions of the House of Burgundy, nor have weakened it so much. . . .

After this manner (as I have said before), transactions were managed between the two kings for no other purpose but to gain time, by which means the Princess of Burgundy's affairs began visibly to decay; for of the few soldiers that remained after her father's death, many revolted from her to the king, especially after the Lord des Cordes had quitted her service, and carried several others along with him. Some were forced to leave her because their estates or abodes lay very near or within the towns which had declared for the king; others left her in hopes of preferment; for in that respect no prince was so noble and generous to his servants as our master. Besides, commotions and factions discovered themselves daily in the great towns, and particularly in Ghent, which wanted to have everything its own way, as you have already heard. Several husbands were proposed to the Princess of Burgundy, and every one was of opinion there was a necessity of her marrying to defend those territories that she had left to her, or (by marrying the dauphin), to recover what she had lost. Several were entirely for this match. . . . Some opposed the match, and urged the disproportion of their age, the dauphin being but nine years old, and besides engaged to the King of England's daughter; and these suggested the son of the Duke of Cleves. Others recommended Maximilian, the emperor's son, who is at present King of the Romans. . . .

I am verily persuaded, that if the king had been inclined to have had her marry the Count of Angoulesme, who is now living, she would have consented to it, so desirous was she to continue her alliance with France. God, however, thought fit to appoint her another husband, for reasons unknown perhaps to us, unless it were, that it might occasion greater wars and confusions on both sides than could possibly have happened, had she married the Count of Angoulesme, for by this match the provinces of Flanders and Brabant sustained great miseries and afflictions. The Duke of Cleves was at this time in Ghent with the princess, making friends, and trying all arts to effect a marriage between the princess and his son, but she had no inclination to it, for the character of the young gentleman pleased neither her nor any person about her court. At last a marriage was again proposed between her and the emperor's son, the present King of the Romans, of which there had formerly been some overtures between the Emperor and Duke Charles, and a match concluded between them. The emperor had in his custody a letter written by the young lady, at her father's command, under her own hand, and a diamond ring of considerable value. The purport of the letter was to acquaint his imperial majesty, that, in obedience to her father's commands, she promised to accomplish the marriage with his son the Duke of Austria, in the same form and manner as her father the Duke of Burgundy should think fit to prescribe. . . .

This aforesaid marriage was performed with great pomp and solemnity, but affairs were not placed by it in a much better posture; for they were both very young. Duke Maximilian was a person of no great knowledge, both in consequence of his youth, and of his being in a foreign country. Besides, his education had been but indifferent, and not serviceable for the management of great affairs; nor, if it had been better, had he a sufficient body of troops ready to have attempted anything considerable: so that his poor countries were involved in great troubles, which have continued to this day, and are like to continue. For which reasons, as I said before, it is a great misfortune to any country to have to seek a foreign sovereign; and God has been very merciful to France in establishing that law against the inheritance of the crown by a daughter. A private or insignificant family may be much aggrandised by it; but a great kingdom, like ours, will always be greatly inconvenienced, and incommoded. A few days after the consummation of this marriage (if not at the very time of its negotiation), the whole country of Artois was lost. (It will be sufficient for me to narrate the substance of events, and if I fail in terms, or the just computation of times, I hope the reader will excuse me.) The king's affairs went on prosperously, without any manner of opposition, during the winter; only now and then some overture or proposition was made, which came to nothing; for both sides being high in their demands, the war could not but continue. Duke Maximilian and the Princess of Burgundy had a son the first year, namely, the Archduke Philip, who is now reigning. . . .

In Hainault the king was possessed of two towns, Quesnoy le Comte and Bouchain, both which he restored; at which several persons were highly astonished, knowing his aversion to any peace, and how desirous he was to take all, and leave the house of Burgundy nothing; and my opinion is, if he could have done it undisturbedly, and destroyed or divided those territories at his ease, he would not have failed to have done so. But, as he told me afterwards himself, he surrendered those towns in Hainault for two reasons: the first was, because he thought a prince had more strength and importance in his own country, where he was anointed and crowned, than he could have out of his dominions; and these towns were not in his territory. The other was, because there had been solemn oaths and great confederacies between the emperors and the kings of France, not to invade or usurp upon one another's dominions; and those above-mentioned places belonging to the empire were restored in the year 1478.

. . . Factions and parties are very perilous and fatal, especially to the nobility, who are too prone to propagate and foment them. If it be alleged that by this means both parties are kept in awe, and the secret minds of his subjects are discovered to the prince, I agree that a young prince may encourage faction among his ladies, and it may be pleasant and diverting enough, and may give him opportunity of finding out some of their intrigues; but nothing is so dangerous to a nation as to nourish such factions and partialities among men of courage and magnanimity; it is no less than setting one's own house on fire; for immediately some or other cry out, "The king is against us," seize upon some fortified town, and correspond with his enemies. And certainly the factions of Orleans and Burgundy ought to make us wise on this point; for they began a war which lasted seventy-two years, in which the English were concerned, and thought by those unhappy divisions to have conquered the kingdom.

HENRY VII OF ENGLAND

Henry VII (reigned 1485-1509), first of the Tudor line which was to include the better-known English monarchs Henry VIII and Elizabeth, ruled at a time when there was opportunity for the crown to play a large part in the direction of a strong central government. Driven from the Continent at the close of the Hundred Years War, England in the mid-fifteenth century was already well along the road to national unity, but, despite the considerable powers which it had already won, Parliament appeared unable to provide security and order without the guidance of a determined king. Powerful nobles, supported by armed retainers, were still capable of pursuing their ambitions in private wars; lawlessness was too often unpunished, with the result that in many districts life and property were unsafe. In the period preceding the reign of Henry VII these conditions were emphasized by the so-called "Wars of the Roses," a struggle for the crown carried on by the rival houses of Lancaster and York.

Distantly related on his mother's side to the House of Lancaster, Henry Tudor was able to claim the throne when the unpopularity of his predecessor, Richard III of the House of York, made rebellion possible. The doubtfulness of Henry's right to the succession was in part overcome by military victory and by parliamentary recognition, but his real success in consolidating the dynasty lay in his ability to satisfy large numbers of the English people, particularly the lesser nobles and the middle class. Once in power, Henry VII had to face the problems—to a large extent common to the heads of other dynastic states—of taming the great nobles, filling the treasury, finding reliable officials, avoiding parliamentary interference, and charting a careful course in international affairs. The extent of his success is indicated by the following portrait by Francis Bacon in his *History of the Reign of King Henry VII* in *The Works of Francis Bacon* (London, Longmans and Co., 1890).

HISTORY OF THE REIGN OF KING HENRY VII

This king (to speak of him in terms equal to his deserving) was one of the best sort of wonders; a wonder for wise men. He had parts (both in his virtues and his fortune) not so fit for a commonplace as for observation. Certainly he was religious, both in his affection and observance. But as he could see clear (for those times) through superstition; so he would be blinded now and then by human policy. He advanced churchmen. He was tender in the privilege of sanctuaries, though they wrought him much mischief. He built and endowed many religious foundations, besides his memorable hospital of the Savoy: and yet was he a great almsgiver in secret; which showed that his works in public were dedicated rather to God's glory than his own. He professed always to love and seek peace; and it was his usual preface in his treaties, that when Christ came into the world peace was sung, and when he went out of the world peace was bequeathed. And this virtue could not proceed out of fear or softness, for he was valiant and active; and therefore no doubt it was truly Christian and moral. Yet he knew the way to peace was not to seem to be desirous to avoid wars. Therefore would he make offers and fames of wars, till he had mended the conditions of peace. It was also much, that one that was so great a lover of peace should be so happy in war. For his arms, either in foreign or civil wars, were never infortunate; neither did he know what a disaster meant. The war of his coming in, and the rebellions of the Earl of Lincoln and the Lord Audley, were ended by victory. The wars of France and Scotland by peaces sought at his hands. That of Brittaine by accident of the duke's death. The insurrection of the Lord Lovell, and that of Perkin at Exeter and in Kent, by flight of the rebels before they came to blows. So that his fortune of arms was still inviolate. The rather sure, for that in the quenching of the commotions of his subjects he ever went in person; sometimes reserving himself to back and second his lieutenants, but ever in action. And yet that was not merely forwardness, but partly distrust of others.

He did much maintain and countenance his laws; which (nevertheless) was no impediment to him to work his will. For it was so handled that neither prerogative nor profit went to diminution. And yet as he would sometimes strain up his laws to his prerogative, so would he also let down his prerogative to his Parliament. For mint and wars and martial discipline (things of absolute power) he would nevertheless bring to Parliament. Justice was well administered in his time, save where the king was party; save also that the counsel table intermeddled too much with *meum* and *tuum*. For it was a very court of justice during his time; especially in the beginning. But in that part both of justice and policy which is the durable part, and cut as it were in brass or marble, which is the making of good laws, he did excel. And with his justice he was also a merciful prince: as in whose time there were but three of the nobility that suffered—the Earl of Warwick; the Lord Chamberlain; and the Lord Audley; though the first two were instead of numbers in the dislike and obloquy of the people. But there were never so great rebellions expiated with so little blood drawn by the hand of justice as the two rebellions of Blackheath and Exeter. As for the severity used upon those which were taken in Kent, it was but upon a scum of people. His pardons went ever both before and after his sword. But then he had withal a strange kind of interchanging of large and inexpected pardons with severe executions: which (his wisdom considered) could not be imputed to any inconstancy or inequality; but either to some reason which we do not now know, or to a principle he had set unto himself, that he would vary and try both ways in turn. But the less blood he drew the more he took of treasure; and as some construed it, he was the more sparing in the one that he might be the more pressing in the other; for both would have been intolerable. Of nature assuredly he coveted to accumulate treasure; and was a little poor in admiring riches. The people (into whom there is infused for the preservation of monarchies a natural desire to discharge their princes, though it be with the unjust charge of their councillors and ministers) did impute this unto Cardinal Morton and Sir Reignold Bray; who as it after appeared (as councillors of ancient authority with him) did so second his humours, as nevertheless they did temper them. Whereas Empson and Dudley that followed, being persons that had no reputation with him otherwise than by the servile following of his bent, did not give way only (as the first did) but shape his way to those extremities, for which himself was touched with remorse at his death; and which his successor renounced, and sought to purge. This excess of his had at that time many glosses and interpretations. Some thought the continual rebellions wherewith he had been vexed had made him grow to hate his people: Some thought it was done to pull down their stomachs and to keep them low: Some, for that he would leave his son a golden fleece: Some suspected he had some high design upon foreign parts. But those perhaps shall come nearest the truth that fetch not their reasons so far off; but rather impute it to nature, age, peace, and a mind fixed upon no other ambition or pursuit: whereunto I should add, that having every day occasion to take notice of the necessities and shifts for money of other great princes abroad, it did the better by comparison set off to him the felicity of full coffers. As to his expending of treasure, he never spared charge which his affairs required: and in his buildings was magnificent; but his rewards were very limited. So that his liberality was rather upon his own state and memory than upon the deserts of others. He was of an high mind, and loved his own will and his own way; as one that revered himself, and would reign indeed. Had he been a private man he would have been termed proud; but in a wise prince, it was but keeping of distance; which indeed he did towards all, not admitting any near or full approach either to his power or to his secrets. For he was governed by none. His queen (notwithstanding she had presented him with divers children; and with a crown also, though he would not acknowledge it) could do nothing with him. His mother he reverenced much, heard little. For any person agreeable to him for society (such as was Hastings to King Edward the Fourth, or Charles Brandon after to King Henry the Eighth), he had none; except we should account for such persons Foke and Bray and Empson, because they were so much with him. But it was but as the instrument is much with the workman. He had nothing in him of vainglory, but yet kept state and majesty to the height; being sensible that majesty maketh the people bow, but vainglory boweth to them.

To his confederates abroad he was constant and just; but not open. But rather such was his inquiry and such his closeness, as they stood in the light towards him, and he stood in the dark to them; yet without strangeness, but with a semblance of mutual communication of affairs. As for little envies or emulations upon foreign princes (which are frequent with many kings), he had never any, but went substantially to his own business. Certain it is, that though his reputation was great at home, yet it was greater abroad. For foreigners that could not see the passages of affairs, but made their judgments upon the issues of them, noted that he was ever in strife and ever aloft. It grew also from the airs which the princes and states abroad received from their ambassadors and agents here; which were attending the court in great number, whom he did not only content with courtesy, reward, and privateness; but (upon such conferences as passed with them) put them in admiration to find his universal insight into the affairs of the world: which though he did suck chiefly from themselves, yet that which he had gathered from them all seemed admirable to every one. So that they did write ever to their superiors in high terms concerning his wisdom and art of rule. Nay when they were returned, they did commonly maintain intelligence with him; such a dexterity he had to impropriate to himself all foreign instruments.

He was careful and liberal to obtain good intelligence from all parts abroad; wherein he did not only use his interest in the liegers here, and his pensioners which he had both in the court of Rome and the other courts of Christendom, but the industry and vigilancy of his own ambassadors in foreign parts. For which purpose his instructions were ever extreme curious and articulate; and in them more articles touching inquisition than touching negotiation: requiring likewise from his ambassadors an answer, in particular distinct articles, respectively to his questions.

As for his secret spials which he did employ both at home and abroad, by them to discover what practices and conspiracies were against him; surely his case required it; he had such moles perpetually working and casting to undermine him. Neither can it be reprehended; for if spials be lawful against lawful enemies, much more against conspirators and traitors. But indeed to give them credence by oaths or curses, that cannot be well maintained; for those are too holy vestments for a disguise. Yet surely there was this further good in his employing of these flies and familiars; that as the use of them was cause that many conspiracies were revealed, so the fame and suspicion of them kept (no doubt) many conspiracies from being attempted.

Towards his queen he was nothing uxorious; nor scarce indulgent; but companiable and respective, and without jealousy. Towards his children he was full of paternal affection, careful of their education, aspiring to their high advancement, regular to see that they should not want of any due honour and respect; but not greatly willing to cast any popular lustre upon them.

To his council he did refer much, and sat oft in person; knowing it to be the way to assist his power and inform his judgment; in which respect also he was fairly patient of liberty both of advice and of vote, till himself were declared.

He kept a strait hand on his nobility, and chose rather to advance clergymen and lawyers, which were more obsequious to him, but had less interest in the people, which made for his absoluteness, but not for his safety. Insomuch as I am persuaded it was one of the causes of his troublesome reign. For that his nobles, though they were loyal and obedient, yet did not cooperate with him, but let every man go his own way. He was not afraid of an able man, as Lewis [Louis] the Eleventh was. But contrariwise he was served by the ablest men that then were to be found; without which his affairs could not have prospered as they did. For war, Bedford, Oxford, Surrey, Dawbeny, Brooke, Poynings. For other affairs, Morton, Foxe, Bray, the Prior of Lanthony, Warham, Urswick, Hussey, Frowick, and others. Neither did he care how cunning they were that he did employ: for he thought himself to have the master-reach. And as he chose well, so he held them up well. For it is a strange thing, that though he were a dark prince, and infinitely suspicious, and his times full of secret conspiracies and troubles; yet in twenty-four years' reign he never put down or discomposed councillor or near servant, save only Stanley the Lord Chamberlain. As for the disposition of his subjects in general towards him, it stood thus with him; that of the three affections which naturally tie the hearts of the subjects to their sovereign—love, fear, and reverence—he had the last in height; the second in good measure; and so little of the first, as he was beholding to the other two.

He was a prince, sad, serious, and full of thoughts and secret observations; and full of notes of memorials of his own hand, especially touching persons; as whom to employ, whom to reward, whom to inquire of, whom to beware of, what were the dependencies, what were the factions, and the like; keeping (as it were) a journal of thoughts. There is to this day a merry tale, that his monkey (set on, as it was thought, by one of his chamber) tore his principal notebook all to pieces, when by chance it lay forth: whereat the court which liked not those pensive accounts was almost tickled with sport.

He was indeed full of apprehensions and suspicions. But as he did easily take them, so he did easily check them and master them; whereby they were not dangerous, but troubled himself more than others. It is true, his thoughts were so many, as they could not well always stand together; but that which did good one way, did hurt another. Neither did he at some times weigh them aright in their proportions. Certainly that rumour which did him so much mischief (that the Duke of York should be saved and alive) was (at the first) of his own nourishing, because he would have more reason not to reign in the right of his wife. He was affable, and both well and fair spoken; and would use strange sweetness and blandishments of words, where he desired to effect or persuade any thing that he took to heart. He was rather studious than learned, reading most books that were of any worth in the French tongue. Yet he understood the Latin, as appeareth in that Cardinal Hadrian and others, who could very well have written French, did use to write to him in Latin.

For his pleasures, there is no news of them. And yet by his instructions to Marsin and Stile touching the Queen of Naples, it seemeth he could interrogate well touching beauty. He did by pleasures as great princes do by banquets, come and look a little upon them, and turn way. For never prince was more wholly given to his affairs, nor in them more of himself; insomuch as in triumphs of justs and tourneys and balls and masks (which they then called disguises) he was rather a princely and gentle spectator than seemed much to be delighted.

No doubt, in him as in all men (and most of all in kings) his fortune wrought upon his nature, and his nature upon his fortune. He attained to the crown, not only from a private fortune, which might endow him with moderation; but also from the fortune of an exiled man, which had quickened in him all seeds of observation and industry. And his times being rather prosperous than calm, had raised his confidence by success, but almost marred his nature by troubles. His wisdom, by often evading from perils, was turned rather into a dexterity to deliver himself from dangers when they pressed him, than into a providence to prevent and remove them afar off. And even in nature, the sight of his mind was like some sights of eyes; rather strong at hand than to carry afar off. For his wit increased upon the occasion; and so much the more if the occasion were sharpened by danger. Again, whether it were the shortness of his foresight, or the strength of his will, or the dazzling of his suspicions, or what it was; certain it is that the perpetual troubles of his fortunes (there being no more matter out of which they grew) could not have been without some great defects and main errors in his nature, customs, and proceedings, which he had enough to do to save and help with a thousand little industries and watches. But those do best appear in the story itself. Yet take him with all his defects, if a man should compare him with the kings his concurrents in France and Spain, he shall find him more politic than Lewis the Twelfth of France, and more entire and sincere than Ferdinando of Spain. But if you shall change Lewis the Twelfth for Lewis the Eleventh, who lived a little before, then the consort is more perfect. For that Lewis the Eleventh, Ferdinando, and Henry, may be esteemed for the *tres magi* of kings of those ages. To conclude, if this king did no greater matters, it was long of himself; for what he minded he compassed.

He was a comely personage, a little above just stature, well and straight limbed, but slender. His countenance was reverend, and a little like a churchman: and as it was not strange or dark, so neither was it winning or pleasing, but as the face of one well disposed. But it was to the disadvantage of the painter, for it was best when he spake.

His worth may bear a tale or two, that may put upon him somewhat that may seem divine. When the Lady Margaret his mother had divers great suitors for marriage, she dreamed one night that one in the likeness of a bishop in pontifical habit did tender her Edmund Earl of Richmond (the king's father) for her husband. Neither had she ever any child but the king, though she had three husbands. One day when King Henry the Sixth (whose innocency gave him holiness) was washing his hands at a great feast, and cast his eyes upon King Henry, then a young youth, he said, "This is the lad that shall possess quietly that that we now strive for." But that that was truly divine in him, was that he had the fortune of a true Christian as well as of a great king, in living exercised and dying repentant. So as he had an happy warfare in both conflicts, both of sin and the cross.

He was born at Pembroke Castle, and lieth buried at Westminster, in one of the stateliest and daintiest monuments of Europe, both for the chapel and for the sepulchre. So that he dwelleth more richly dead, in the monument of his tomb, than he did alive in Richmond or any of his palaces, I could wish he did the like in this monument of his fame.

NICCOLÒ MACHIAVELLI

Niccolò Machiavelli (1469–1527) was a Florentine who came from the class of impoverished gentry that was losing caste before the rapid rise of the bourgeoisie. He served Florence in various diplomatic posts for fourteen years, serving on missions requiring at once the utmost in finesse and in tough-mindedness. When in 1512 the pope was victorious over France and its Florentine ally and the antirepublican Medici were returned to power, Machiavelli was one of those forced into exile. It was during this period of exile that he wrote *The Prince* (1513), the *Discourses on Livy* (1513), and his other books. Machiavelli's energies found no adequate release merely in writing books, however, and like that other Florentine exile, Dante, he was ill at ease away from his native city. He made many attempts to get back into public life. The victorious revolution of the popular party in Florence in 1527 seemed to Machiavelli to be his opportunity. He returned to Florence, but the Florentine Council, some of whom had read *The Prince,* decided against trusting him as a public official. Machiavelli, however, died before he had heard of this decision.

Machiavelli's *The Prince* (1513), written while he was in exile, describes the nature of the strong ruler and the methods best calculated to keep him in office. The *Discourses on Livy* (1513) reveal Machiavelli's republicanism, his belief that widespread public virtue is necessary to preserve the state. Machiavelli also wrote a *History of Florence, On the Art of War,* poetry, and some sardonic drama.

The translation of sections of *The Prince* from the Italian is by Luigi Ricci (1903), revised by E. R. P. Vincent.

THE PRINCE

CHAPTER I: THE VARIOUS KINDS OF GOVERNMENT
AND THE WAYS BY WHICH
THEY ARE ESTABLISHED

All states and dominions which hold or have held sway over mankind are either republics or monarchies. Monarchies are either hereditary in which the rulers have been for many years of the same family, or else they are of recent foundation. The newly founded ones are either entirely new, as was Milan to Francesco Sforza, or else they are, as it were, new members grafted on to the hereditary possessions of the prince that annexes them, as is the kingdom of Naples to the King of Spain. The dominions thus acquired have either been previously accustomed to the rule of another prince, or else have been free states, and they are annexed either by force of arms of the prince himself, or of others, or else fall to him by good fortune or special ability.

CHAPTER II: OF HEREDITARY MONARCHIES

I will not here speak of republics, having already treated of them fully in another place. I will deal only with monarchies, and will discuss how the various kinds described above can be governed and maintained. In the first place, the difficulty of maintaining hereditary states accustomed to a reigning family is far less than in new monarchies; for it is sufficient not to transgress ancestral usages, and to adapt one's self to unforeseen circumstances; in this way such a prince, if of ordinary assiduity, will always be able to maintain his position, unless some very exceptional and excessive force deprives him of it; and even if he be thus deprived, on the slightest mischance happening to the new occupier, he will be able to regain it.

We have in Italy the example of the Duke of Ferrara, who was able to withstand the assaults of the Venetians in 1484 and of Pope Julius in 1510, for no other reason than because of the antiquity of his family in that dominion. In as much as the legitimate prince has less cause and less necessity to give offence, it is only natural that he should be more loved; and, if no extraordinary vices make him hated, it is only reasonable for his subjects to be naturally attached to him, the memories and causes of innovations being forgotten in the long period over which his rule has extended; whereas one change always leaves the way prepared for the introduction of another.

CHAPTER III: OF MIXED MONARCHIES

But it is in the new monarchy that difficulties really exist. First, if it is not entirely new, but a member as it were of a mixed state, its disorders spring at first from a natural difficulty which exists in all new dominions, because men change masters willingly, hoping to better themselves; and this belief makes them take arms against their rulers, in which they are deceived, as experience later proves that they have gone from bad to worse. This is the result of another very natural cause, which is the inevitable harm inflicted on those over whom the prince obtains dominion, both by his soldiers and by an infinite number of other injuries caused by his occupation.

Thus you find enemies in all those whom you have injured by occupying that dominion, and you cannot maintain the friendship of those who have helped you to obtain this possession, as you will not be able to fulfil their expectations, nor can you use strong measures with them, being under an obligation to them; for which reason, however strong your armies may be, you will always need the favour of the inhabitants to take possession of a province. It was from these causes that Louis XII of France, though able to occupy Milan without trouble, immediately lost it, and the forces of Ludovico alone were sufficient to take it from him the first time, for the inhabitants who had willingly opened their gates to him, finding themselves deluded in the hopes they had cherished and not obtaining those benefits they had anticipated, could not bear the vexatious rule of their new prince.

It is indeed true that, after reconquering rebel territories they are not so easily lost again, for the ruler is now, by the fact of the rebellion, less averse to secure his position by punishing offenders, unmasking suspects, and strengthening himself in weak places. So that although the mere appearance of such a person as Duke Ludovico on the frontier was sufficient to cause France to lose Milan the first time, to make her lose her grip of it the second time was only possible when all the world was against her, and after her armies had been defeated and driven out of Italy; which was the result of the causes above mentioned. Nevertheless it was taken from her both the first and the second time. The general causes of the first loss have been already discussed; it remains now to be seen what were the causes of the second loss and by what means France could have avoided it, or what measures might have been taken by another ruler in that position which were not taken by the King of France. Be it observed, therefore, that those states which on annexation are united to a previously existing state may or may not be of the same nationality and language. If they are, it is very easy to hold them, especially if they are not accustomed to freedom; and to possess them securely it suffices that the family of the princes which formerly governed them be extinct. For the rest, their old condition not being disturbed, and there being no dissimilarity of customs, the people settle down quietly under their new rulers, as is seen in the case of Burgundy, Brittany, Gascony, and Normandy, which have been so long united to France; and although there may be some slight differences of language, the customs of the people are nevertheless similar, and they can get along well together. Whoever obtains possession of such territories and wishes to retain them must bear in mind two things: the one, that the blood of their old rulers be extinct; the other, to make no alteration either in their laws or in their taxes; in this way they will in a very short space of time become united with their old possessions and form one state.

But when dominions are acquired in a province differing in language, laws, and customs, the difficulties to be overcome are great, and it requires good fortune as well as great industry to retain them; one of the best and most certain means of doing so would be for the new ruler to take up his residence there. This would render possession more secure and durable, and it is what the Turk has done in Greece. In spite of all the other measures taken by him to hold that state, it would not have been possible to retain it had he not gone to live there. Being on the spot, disorders can be seen as they arise and can quickly be remedied, but living at a distance, they are only heard of when they get beyond remedy. Besides which, the province is not despoiled by your officials, the subjects being able to obtain satisfaction by direct recourse to their prince; and wishing to be loyal they have more reason to love him, and should they be otherwise inclined they will have greater cause to fear him. Any external Power who wishes to assail that state will be less disposed to do so; so that as long as he resides there he will be very hard to dispossess.

The other and better remedy is to plan colonies in one or two of those places which form as it were the keys of the land, for it is necessary either to do this or to maintain a large force of armed men. The colonies will cost the prince little; with little or no expense on his part, he can send and maintain them; he only injures those whose lands and houses are taken to give to the new inhabitants, and these form but a small proportion of the state, and those who are injured, remaining poor and scattered, can never do any harm to him, and all the others are, on the one hand, not injured and therefore easily pacified; and, on the other, are fearful of offending lest they should be treated like those who have been dispossessed. To conclude, these colonies cost nothing, are more faithful, and give less offence; and the injured parties being poor and scattered are unable to do mischief, as I have shown. For it must be noted that men must either be caressed or else annihilated; they will revenge themselves for small injuries, but cannot do so for great ones; the injury therefore that we do to a man must be such that we need not fear his vengeance. But by maintaining a garrison instead of colonists, one will spend much more, and consume all the revenues of that state in guarding it, so that the acquisition will result in a loss, besides giving much greater offence, since it injures every one in that state with the quartering of the army on it; which being an inconvenience felt by all, every one becomes an enemy, and these are enemies which can do mischief, as, though beaten, they remain in their own homes. In every way, therefore, a garrison is as useless as colonies are useful. . . .

CHAPTER V: THE WAY TO GOVERN CITIES OR DOMINIONS
THAT, PREVIOUS TO BEING OCCUPIED,
LIVED UNDER THEIR OWN LAWS

When those states which have been acquired are accustomed to live at liberty under their own laws, there are three ways of holding them. The first is to despoil them; the second is to go and live there in person; the third is to allow them to live under their own laws, taking tribute of them, and creating within the country a government composed of a few who will keep it friendly to you. Because this government, being created by the prince, knows that it cannot exist without his friendship and protection, and will do all it can to keep them. What is more, a city used to liberty can be more easily held by means of its citizens than in any other way, if you wish to preserve it.

There is the example of the Spartans and the Romans. The Spartans held Athens and Thebes by creating within them a government of a few; nevertheless they lost them. The Romans, in order to hold Capua, Carthage, and Numantia, ravaged them, but did not lose them. They wanted to hold Greece in almost the same way as the Spartans held it, leaving it free and under its own laws, but they did not succeed; so that they were compelled to lay waste many cities in that province in order to keep it, because in truth there is no sure method of holding them except by despoiling them. And whoever becomes the ruler of a free city and does not destroy it, can expect to be destroyed by it, for it can always find a motive for rebellion in the name of liberty and of its ancient usages, which are forgotten neither by lapse of time nor by benefits received; and whatever one does or provides, so long as the inhabitants are not separated or dispersed, they do not forget that name and those usages, but appeal to them at once in every emergency, as did Pisa after being so many years held in servitude by the Florentines. But when cities or provinces have been accustomed to live under a prince, and the family of that prince is extinguished, being on the one hand used to obey, and on the other not having their old prince, they cannot unite in choosing one from among themselves, and they do not know how to live in freedom, so that they are slower to take arms, and a prince can win them over with greater facility and establish himself securely. But in republics there is greater life, greater hatred, and more desire for vengeance; they do not and cannot cast aside the memory of their ancient liberty, so that the surest way is either to lay them waste or reside in them.

CHAPTER IX: OF THE CIVIC PRINCIPALITY

But we now come to the case where a citizen becomes prince not through crime or intolerable violence, but by the favour of his fellow-citizens, which may be called a civic principality. To attain this position depends not entirely on worth or entirely on fortune, but rather on cunning assisted by fortune. One attains it by help of popular favour or by the favour of the aristocracy. For in every city these two opposite parties are to be found, arising from the desire of the populace to avoid the oppression of the great, and the desire of the great to command and oppress the people. And from these two opposing interests arises in the city one of the three effects: either absolute government, liberty, or licence. The former is created either by the populace or the nobility, depending on the relative opportunities of the two parties; for when the nobility see that they are unable to resist the people they unite in exalting one of their number and creating him prince, so as to be able to carry out their own designs under the shadow of his authority. The populace, on the other hand, when unable to resist the nobility, endeavour to exalt and create a prince in order to be protected by his authority. He who becomes prince by help of the nobility has greater difficulty in maintaining his power than he who is raised by the populace, for he is surrounded by those who think themselves his equals, and is thus unable to direct or command as he pleases. But one who is raised to leadership by popular favour finds himself alone, and has no one, or very few, who are not ready to obey him. Besides which, it is impossible to satisfy the nobility by fair dealing and without inflicting injury on others, whereas it is very easy to satisfy the mass of the people in this way. For the aim of the people is more honest than that of the nobility, the latter desiring to oppress, and the former merely to avoid oppression. It must also be added that the prince can never insure himself against a hostile populace on account of their number, but he can against the hostility of the great, as they are but few. The worst that a prince has to expect from a hostile people is to be abandoned, but from hostile nobles he has to fear not only desertion but their active opposition, and as they are more far-seeing and more cunning, they are always in time to save themselves and take sides with the one who they expect will conquer. The prince is, moreover, obliged to live always with the same people, but he can easily do without the same nobility, being able to make and unmake them at any time, and improve their position or deprive them of it as he pleases.

And to throw further light on this part of my argument, I would say, that the nobles are to be considered in two different manners; that is, they are either to be ruled so as to make them entirely dependent on your fortunes, or else not. Those that are thus bound to you and are not rapacious, must be honoured and loved; those who stand aloof must be considered in two ways, they either do this through pusillanimity and natural want of courage, and in this case you ought to make use of them, and especially such as are of good counsel, so that they may honour you in prosperity and in adversity you have not to fear them. But when they are not bound to you of set purpose and for ambitious ends, it is a sign that they think more of themselves than of you; and from such men the prince must guard himself and look upon them as secret enemies, who will help to ruin him when in adversity.

One, however, who becomes prince by favour of the populace, must maintain its friendship, which he will find easy, the people asking nothing but not to be oppressed. But one who against the people's wishes becomes prince by favour of the nobles, should above all endeavour to gain the favour of the people; this will be easy to him if he protects them. And as men, who receive good from whom they expected evil, feel under a greater obligation to their benefactor, so the populace will soon become even better disposed towards him than if he had become prince through their favour. Their prince can win their favour in many ways, which vary according to circumstances, for which no certain rule can be given, and will therefore be passed over. I will only say, in conclusion, that it is necessary for a prince to possess the friendship of the people; otherwise he has no resource in times of adversity.

Nabis, prince of the Spartans, sustained a siege by the whole of Greece and a victorious Roman army, and defended his country against them and maintained his own position. It sufficed when the danger arose for him to make sure of a few, which would not have sufficed if the populace had been hostile to him. And let no one oppose my opinion in this by quoting the trite proverb, "He who builds on the people, builds on mud"; because that is true when a private citizen relies upon the people and persuades himself that they will liberate him if he is oppressed by enemies or by the magistrates; in this case he might often find himself deceived, as were in Rome the Gracchi and in Florence Messer Georgio Scali. But when it is a prince who founds himself on this basis, one who can command and is a man of courage, and does not get frightened in adversity, and does not neglect other preparations, and one who by his own valour and measures animates the mass of the people, he will not find himself deceived by them, and he will find that he has laid his foundations well.

Usually these principalities are in danger when the prince from the position of a civil ruler changes to an absolute one, for these princes either command themselves or by means of magistrates. In the latter case their position is weaker and more dangerous, for they are at the mercy of those citizens who are appointed magistrates, who can, especially in times of adversity, with great facility deprive them of their position, either by acting against them or by not obeying them. The prince is not in time, in such dangers, to assume absolute authority, for the citizens and subjects who are accustomed to take their orders from the magistrates are not ready in these emergencies to obey his, and he will always in difficult times lack men whom he can rely on. Such a prince cannot base himself on what he sees in quiet times, when the citizens have need of the state; for then every one is full of promises and each one is ready to die for him when death is far off; but in adversity, when the state has need of citizens, then he will find but few. And this experience is the more dangerous, in that it can only be had once. Therefore a wise prince will seek means by which his subjects will always and in every possible condition of things have need of his government, and then they will always be faithful to him.

CHAPTER X: HOW THE STRENGTH OF ALL STATES SHOULD BE MEASURED

In examining the character of these principalities it is necessary to consider another point, namely, whether the prince has such a position as to be able in case of need to maintain himself alone, or whether he has always need of the protection of others. The better to explain this I would say, that I consider those capable of maintaining themselves alone who can, through abundance of men or money, put together a sufficient army, and hold the field against any one who assails them; and I consider to have need of others, those who cannot take the field against their enemies, but are obliged to take refuge within their walls and stand on the defensive. We have already discussed the former case and will speak of it in future as occasion arises. In the second case there is nothing to be said except to encourage such a prince to provision and fortify his own town, and not to trouble about the surrounding country. And whoever has strongly fortified his town and, as regards the government of his subjects, has proceeded as we have already described and will further relate, will be attacked with great reluctance, for men are always averse to enterprises in which they foresee difficulties, and it can never appear easy to attack one who has his town stoutly defended and is not hated by the people.

The cities of Germany are absolutely free, have little surrounding country, and obey the emperor when they choose, and they do not fear him or any other potentate that they have about them. They are fortified in such a manner that every one thinks that to reduce them would be tedious and difficult, for they all have the necessary moats and bastions, sufficient artillery, and always keep food, drink, and fuel for one year in the public storehouses. Beyond which, to keep the lower classes satisfied, and without loss to the commonwealth, they have always enough means to give them work for one year in these employments which form the nerve and life of the town, and in the industries by which the lower classes live. Military exercises are still held in high reputation, and many regulations are in force for maintaining them.

A prince, therefore, who possesses a strong city and does not make himself hated, cannot be assaulted; and if he were to be so, the assailant would be obliged to retire shamefully; for so many things change, that it is almost impossible for any one to maintain a siege for a year with his armies idle. And to those who urged that the people, having their possessions outside and seeing them burnt, will not have patience, and the long siege and self-interest will make them forget their prince, I reply that a powerful and courageous prince will always overcome those difficulties by now raising the hopes of his subjects that the evils will not last long, now impressing them with fear of the enemy's cruelty, now by dextrously assuring himself of those who appear too bold. Besides which, the enemy would naturally burn and ravage the country on first arriving and at the time when men's minds are still hot and eager to defend themselves, and therefore the prince has still less to fear, for after some time, when people have cooled down, the damage is done, the evil has been suffered, and there is no remedy, so that they are the more ready to unite with their prince, as it appears that he is under an obligation to them, their houses having been burnt and their possessions ruined in his defence.

It is the nature of men to be as much bound by the benefits that they confer as by those they receive. From which it follows that, everything considered, a prudent prince will not find it difficult to uphold the courage of his subjects both at the commencement and during a state of siege, if he possesses provisions and means to defend himself.

CHAPTER XI: OF ECCLESIASTICAL PRINCIPALITIES

It now only remains to us to speak of ecclesiastical principalities, with regard to which the difficulties lie wholly before they are possessed. They are acquired either by ability or by fortune; but are maintained without either, for they are sustained by ancient religious customs, which are so powerful and of such quality, that they keep their princes in power in whatever manner they proceed and live. These princes alone have states without defending them, have subjects without governing them, and their states, not being defended, are not taken from them; their subjects not being governed do not resent it, and neither think nor are capable of alienating themselves from them. Only these principalities, therefore, are secure and happy. But as they are upheld by higher causes, which the human mind cannot attain to, I will abstain from speaking of them; for being exalted and maintained by God, it would be the work of a presumptuous and foolish man to discuss them. However, I might be asked how it has come about that the Church has reached such great temporal powers, when, previous to Alexander VI, the Italian potentates—and not merely the really powerful ones, but every lord or baron, however insignificant—held it in slight esteem as regards temporal power; whereas now it is dreaded by a king of France, whom it has been able to drive out of Italy, and has also been able to ruin the Venetians. . . .

CHAPTER XIV: THE DUTIES OF A PRINCE WITH REGARD TO THE MILITIA

A prince should therefore have no other aim or thought, nor take up any other thing for his study, but war and its organisation and discipline, for that is the only art that is necessary to one who commands, and it is of such virtue that it not only maintains those who are born princes, but often enables men of private fortune to attain to that rank. And one sees, on the other hand, that when princes think more of luxury than of arms, they lose their state. The chief cause of the loss of states, is the contempt of this art, and the way to acquire them is to be well versed in the same.

Francesco Sforza, through being well armed, became, from private status, Duke of Milan; his sons, through wishing to avoid the fatigue and hardship of war, from dukes became private persons. For among other evils caused by being disarmed, it renders you contemptible; which is one of those disgraceful things which a prince must guard against, as will be explained later. Because there is no comparison whatever between an armed and a disarmed man, it is not reasonable to suppose that one who is armed will obey willingly one who is unarmed, or that any unarmed man will remain safe among armed servants. For one being disdainful and the other suspicious, it is not possible for them to act well together. And therefore a prince who is ignorant of military matters, besides the other misfortunes already mentioned, cannot be esteemed by his soldiers, nor have confidence in them.

He ought, therefore, never to let his thoughts stray from the exercise of war; and in peace he ought to practise it more than in war, which he can do in two ways: by action and by study. As to action, he must, besides keeping his men well disciplined and exercised, engage continually in hunting, and thus accustom his body to hardships; and meanwhile learn the nature of the land, how steep the mountains are, how the valleys debouch, where the plains lie, and understand the nature of rivers and swamps. To all this he should devote great attention. This knowledge is useful in two ways. In the first place, one learns to know one's country, and can the better see how to defend it. Then by means of the knowledge and experience gained in one locality, one can easily understand any other that it may be necessary to observe; for the hills and valleys, plains and rivers of Tuscany, for instance, have a certain resemblance to those of other provinces, so that from a knowledge of the country in one province one can easily arrive at a knowledge of others. And that prince who is lacking in this skill is wanting in the first essentials of a leader; for it is this which teaches how to find the enemy, take up quarters, lead armies, plan battles and lay siege to towns with advantage. . . .

But as to exercise for the mind, the prince ought to read history and study the actions of eminent men, see how they acted in warfare, examine the causes of their victories and defeats in order to imitate the former and avoid the latter, and above all, do as some men have done in the past, who have imitated some one, who has been much praised and glorified, and have always kept his deeds and actions before them, as they say Alexander the Great imitated Achilles, Cæsar Alexander, and Scipio Cyrus. And whoever reads the life of Cyrus written by Xenophon, will perceive in the life of Scipio how gloriously he imitated the former, and how, in chastity, affability, humanity, and liberality Scipio conformed to those qualities of Cyrus as described by Xenophon.

A wise prince should follow similar methods and never remain idle in peaceful times, but industriously make good use of them, so that when fortune changes she may find him prepared to resist her blows, and to prevail in adversity.

CHAPTER XV: OF THE THINGS FOR WHICH MEN, AND ESPECIALLY PRINCES, ARE PRAISED OR BLAMED

It now remains to be seen what are the methods and rules for a prince as regards his subjects and friends. And as I know that many have written of this, I fear that my writing about it may be deemed presumptuous, differing as I do, especially in this matter, from the opinions of others. But my intention being to write something of use to those who understand, it appears to me more proper to go to the real truth of the matter than to its imagination; and many have imagined republics and principalities which have never been seen or known to exist in reality; for how we live is so far removed from how we ought to live, that he who abandons what is done for what ought to be done, will rather learn to bring about his own ruin than his preservation. A man who wishes to make a profession of goodness in everything must necessarily come to grief among so many who are not good. Therefore it is necessary for a prince, who wishes to maintain himself, to learn how not to be good, and to use this knowledge and not use it, according to the necessity of the case.

Leaving on one side, then, those things which concern only an imaginary prince, and speaking of those that are real, I state that all men, and especially princes, who are placed at a greater height, are reputed for certain qualities which bring them either praise or blame. Thus one is considered liberal, another *misero* or miserly (using a Tuscan term, seeing that *avaro* with us still means one who is rapaciously acquisitive and *misero* one who makes grudging use of his own); one a free giver, another rapacious; one cruel, another merciful; one a breaker of his word, another trustworthy; one effeminate and pusillanimous, another fierce and high-spirited; one humane, another haughty; one lascivious, another chaste; one frank, another astute; one hard, another easy; one serious, another frivolous; one religious, another an unbeliever, and so on. I know that every one will admit that it would be highly praiseworthy in a prince to possess all the above-named qualities that are reputed good, but as they cannot all be possessed or observed, human conditions not permitting of it, it is necessary that he should be prudent enough to avoid the scandal of those vices which would lose him the state, and guard himself if possible against those which will not lose it him, but if not able to, he can indulge them with less scruple. And yet he must not mind incurring the scandal of those vices, without which it would be difficult to save the state, for if one considers well, it will be found that some things which seem virtues would, if followed, lead to one's ruin, and some others which appear vices result in one's greater security and wellbeing.

CHAPTER XVII: OF CRUELTY AND CLEMENCY, AND WHETHER IT IS BETTER TO BE LOVED OR FEARED

Proceeding to the other qualities before named, I say that every prince must desire to be considered merciful and not cruel. He must, however, take care not to misuse this mercifulness. Cesare Borgia was considered cruel, but his cruelty had brought order to the Romagna, united it, and reduced it to peace and fealty. If this is considered well, it will be seen that he was really much more merciful than the Florentine people, who, to avoid the name of cruelty, allowed Pistoia to be destroyed. A prince, therefore, must not mind incurring the charge of cruelty for the purpose of keeping his subjects united and faithful; for, with a very few examples, he will be more merciful than those who, from excess of tenderness, allow disorders to arise, from whence spring bloodshed and rapine; for these as a rule injure the whole community, while the executions carried out by the prince injure only individuals. And of all princes, it is impossible for a new prince to escape the reputation of cruelty, new states being always full of dangers. . . .

Nevertheless, he must be cautious in believing and acting, and must not be afraid of his own shadow, and must proceed in a temperate manner with prudence and humanity, so that too much confidence does not render him incautious, and too much diffidence does not render him intolerant.

From this arises the question whether it is better to be loved more than feared, or feared more than loved. The reply is, that one ought to be both feared and loved, but as it is difficult for the two to go together, it is much safer to be feared than loved, if one of the two has to be wanting. For it may be said of men in general that they are ungrateful, voluble, dissemblers, anxious to avoid danger, and covetous of gain; as long as you benefit them, they are entirely yours; they offer you their blood, their goods, their life, and their children, as I have before said, when the necessity is remote; but when it approaches, they revolt. And the prince who has relied solely on their words, without making other preparations, is ruined; for the friendship which is gained by purchase and not through grandeur and nobility of spirit is bought but not secured, and at a pinch is not to be expended in your service. And men have less scruple in offending one who makes himself loved than one who makes himself feared; for love is held by a chain of obligation which, men being selfish, is broken whenever it serves their purpose; but fear is maintained by a dread punishment which never fails.

Still, a prince should make himself feared in such a way that if he does not gain love, he at any rate avoids hatred; for fear and the absence of hatred may well go together, and will be always attained by one who abstains from interfering with the property of his citizens and subjects or with their women. And when he is obliged to take the life of any one, let him do so when there is a proper justification and manifest reason for it; but above all he must abstain from taking the property of others, for men forget more easily the death of their father than the loss of their patrimony. Then also pretexts for seizing property are never wanting, and one who begins to live by rapine will always find some reason for taking the goods of others, whereas causes for taking life are rarer and more fleeting.

But when the prince is with his army and has a large number of soldiers under his control, then it is extremely necessary that he should not mind being thought cruel; for without this reputation he could not keep an army united or disposed to any duty. Among the noteworthy actions of Hannibal is numbered this, that although he had an enormous army, composed of men of all nations and fighting in foreign countries, there never arose any dissension either among them or against the prince, either in good fortune or in bad.

This could not be due to anything but his inhuman cruelty, which together with his infinite other virtues, made him always venerated and terrible in the sight of his soldiers, and without it his other virtues would not have sufficed to produce that effect. Thoughtless writers admire on the one hand his actions, and on the other blame the principal cause of them.

And that it is true that his other virtues would not have sufficed may be seen from the case of Scipio (famous not only in regard to his own times, but all times of which memory remains), whose armies rebelled against him in Spain, which arose from nothing but his excessive kindness, which allowed more license to the soldiers than was consonant with military discipline. He was reproached with this in the senate by Fabius Maximus, who called him a corrupter of the Roman militia. Locri having been destroyed by one of Scipio's officers was not revenged by him, nor was the insolence of that officer punished, simply by reason of his easy nature; so much so, that some one wishing to excuse him in the senate said that there were many men who knew rather how not to err, than how to correct the errors of others. This disposition would in time have tarnished the fame and glory of Scipio had he persevered in it under the empire, but living under the rule of the senate this harmful quality was not only concealed but became a glory to him.

I conclude, therefore, with regard to being feared and loved, that men love at their own free will, but fear at the will of the prince, and that a wise prince must rely on what is in his power and not on what is in the power of others, and he must only contrive to avoid incurring hatred, as has been explained.

CHAPTER XVIII: IN WHAT WAY PRINCES MUST KEEP FAITH

How laudable it is for a prince to keep good faith and live with integrity, and not with astuteness, every one knows. Still the experience of our times shows those princes to have done great things who have had little regard for good faith, and have been able by astuteness to confuse men's brains, and who have ultimately overcome those who have made loyalty their foundation.

You must know, then, that there are two methods of fighting, the one by law, the other by force: the first method is that of men, the second of beasts; but as the first method is often insufficient, one must have recourse to the second. It is therefore necessary for a prince to know well how to use both the beast and the man. This was covertly taught to rulers by ancient writers, who relate how Achilles and many others of those ancient princes were given to Chiron the centaur to be brought up and educated under his discipline. The parable of this semi-animal, semi-human teacher is meant to indicate that a prince must know how to use both natures, and that the one without the other is not durable.

A prince being thus obliged to know well how to act as a beast must imitate the fox and the lion, for the lion cannot protect himself from traps, and the fox cannot defend himself from wolves. One must therefore be a fox to recognize traps, and a lion to frighten wolves. Those that wish to be only lions do not understand this. Therefore, a prudent ruler ought not to keep faith when by so doing it would be against his interest, and when the reasons which made him bind himself no longer exist. If men were all good, this precept would not be a good one; but as they are bad, and would not observe their faith with you, so you are not bound to keep faith with them. Nor have legitimate grounds ever failed a prince who wished to show colourable excuse for the non-fulfilment of his promise. Of this one could furnish an infinite number of modern examples, and show how many times peace has been broken, and how many promises rendered worthless, by the faithlessness of princes, and those that have been best able to imitate the fox have succeeded best. But it is necessary to be able to disguise this character well, and to be a great feigner and dissembler; and men are so simple and so ready to obey present necessities, that one who deceives will always find those who allow themselves to be deceived.

I will only mention one modern instance. Alexander VI did nothing else but deceive men, he thought of nothing else, and found the occasion for it; no man was ever more able to give assurances, or affirmed things with stronger oaths, and no man observed them less; however, he always succeeded in his deceptions, as he well knew this aspect of things.

It is not, therefore, necessary for a prince to have all the above-named qualities, but it is very necessary to seem to have them. I would even be bold to say that to possess them and always to observe them is dangerous, but to appear to possess them is useful. Thus it is well to seem merciful, faithful, humane, sincere, religious, and also to be so; but you must have the mind so disposed that when it is needful to be otherwise you may be able to change to the opposite qualities. And it must be understood that a prince, and especially a new prince, cannot observe all those things which are considered good in men, being often obliged, in order to maintain the state, to act against faith, against charity, against humanity, and against religion. And, therefore, he must have a mind disposed to adapt itself according to the wind, and as the variations of fortune dictate, and, as I said before, not deviate from what is good, if possible, but be able to do evil if constrained.

A prince must take great care that nothing goes out of his mouth which is not full of the above-named five qualities, and, to see and hear him, he should seem to be all mercy, faith, integrity, humanity, and religion. And nothing is more necessary than to seem to have this last quality, for men in general judge more by the eyes than by the hands, for every one can see, but very few have to feel. Everybody sees what you appear to be, few feel what you are, and those few will not dare to oppose themselves to the many, who have the majesty of the state to defend them; and in the actions of men, and especially of princes, from which there is no appeal, the end justifies the means. Let a prince therefore aim at conquering and maintaining the state, and the means will always be judged honourable and praised by every one, for the vulgar is always taken by appearances and the issue of the event; and the world consists only of the vulgar, and the few who are not vulgar are isolated when the many have a rallying point in the prince. A certain prince of the present time, whom it is well not to name, never does anything but preach peace and good faith, but he is really a great enemy to both, and either of them, had he observed them, would have lost him state or reputation on many occasions.

CHAPTER XXV: HOW MUCH FORTUNE CAN DO IN HUMAN AFFAIRS AND HOW IT MAY BE OPPOSED

It is not unknown to me how many have been and are of opinion that worldly events are so governed by fortune and by God, that men cannot by their prudence change them, and that on the contrary there is no remedy whatever, and for this they may judge it to be useless to toil much about them, but let things be ruled by chance. This opinion has been more held in our day, from the great changes that have been seen, and are daily seen, beyond every human conjecture. When I think about them, at times I am partly inclined to share this opinion. Nevertheless, that our freewill may not be altogether extinguished, I think it may be true that fortune is the ruler of half our actions, but that she allows the other half or thereabouts to be governed by us. I would compare her to an impetuous river that, when turbulent, inundates the plains, casts down trees and buildings, removes earth from this side and places it on the other; every one flees before it, and everything yields to its fury without being able to oppose it; and yet though it is of such a kind, still when it is quiet, men can make provision against it by dykes and banks, so that when it rises it will either go into a canal or its rush will not be so wild and dangerous. So it is with fortune, which shows her power where no measures have been taken to resist her, and directs her fury where she knows that no dykes or barriers have been made to hold her. And if you regard Italy, which has been the seat of these changes, and who has given the impulse to them, you will see her to be a country without dykes or banks of any kind. If she had been protected by proper measures, like Germany, Spain, and France, this inundation would not have caused the great changes that it has, or would not have happened at all.

This must suffice as regards opposition to fortune in general. But limiting myself more to particular cases, I would point out how one sees a certain prince to-day fortunate and to-morrow ruined, without seeing that he has changed in character or otherwise. I believe this arises in the first place from the causes that we have already discussed at length; that is to say, because the prince who bases himself entirely on fortune is ruined when fortune changes. I also believe that he is happy whose mode of procedure accords with the needs of the times, and similarly he is unfortunate whose mode of procedure is opposed to the times. For one sees that men in those things which lead them to the aim that each one has in view, namely, glory and riches, proceed in various ways; one with circumspection, another with impetuosity, one by violence, another by cunning, one with patience, another with the reverse; and each by these diverse ways may arrive at his aim. One sees also two cautious men, one of whom succeeds in his designs, and the other not, and in the same way two men succeed equally by different methods, one being cautious, the other impetuous, which arises only from the nature of the times, which does or does not conform to their method of procedure. From this it results, as I have said, that two men, acting differently, attain the same effect, and of two others acting in the same way, one attains his goal and not the other. On this depend also the changes in prosperity, for if it happens that time and circumstances are favourable to one who acts with caution and prudence he will be successful, but if time and circumstances change he will be ruined, because he does not change his mode of procedure. No man is found so prudent as to be able to adapt himself to this, either because he cannot deviate from that to which his nature disposes him, or else because having always prospered by walking in one path, he cannot persuade himself that it is well to leave it; and therefore the cautious man, when it is time to act suddenly, does not know how to do so and is consequently ruined; for if one could change one's nature with time and circumstances, fortune would never change.

Pope Julius II acted impetuously in everything he did and found the times and conditions so in conformity with that mode of procedure, that he always obtained a good result. Consider the first war that he made against Bologna while Messer Giovanni Bentivogli was still living. The Venetians were not pleased with it, neither was the King of Spain, France was conferring with him over the enterprise, notwithstanding which, owing to his fierce and impetuous disposition, he engaged personally in the expedition. This move caused both Spain and the Venetians to halt and hesitate, the latter through fear, the former through the desire to recover the entire kingdom of Naples. On the other hand, he engaged with him the King of France, because seeing him make this move and desiring his friendship in order to put down the Venetians, that king judged that he could not refuse him his troops without manifest injury. Thus Julius by his impetuous move achieved what no other pontiff with the utmost human prudence would have succeeded in doing, because, if he had waited till all arrangements had been made and everything settled before leaving Rome, as any other pontiff would have done, it would never have succeeded. For the King of France would have found a thousand excuses, and the others would have inspired him with a thousand fears. I will omit his other actions, which were all of this kind and which all succeeded well, and the shortness of his life did not suffer him to experience the contrary, for had times followed in which it was necessary to act with caution, his ruin would have resulted, for he would never have deviated from these methods to which his nature disposed him.

I conclude then that fortune varying and men remaining fixed in their ways, they are successful so long as these ways conform to circumstances, but when they are opposed then they are unsuccessful. I certainly think that it is better to be impetuous than cautious, for fortune is a woman, and it is necessary, if you wish to master her, to conquer her by force; and it can be seen that she lets herself be overcome by the bold rather than by those who proceed coldly. And therefore, like a woman, she is always a friend to the young, because they are less cautious, fiercer, and master her with greater audacity.

CHAPTER XXVI: EXHORTATION TO LIBERATE ITALY FROM THE
BARBARIANS

Having now considered all the things we have spoken of, and thought within myself whether at present the time was not propitious in Italy for a new prince, and if there was not a state of things which offered an opportunity to a prudent and capable man to introduce a new system that would do honour to himself and good to the mass of the people, it seems to me that so many things concur to favour a new ruler that I do not know of any time more fitting for such an enterprise. And if, as I said, it was necessary in order that the power of Moses should be displayed that the people of Israel should be slaves in Egypt, and to give scope for the greatness and courage of Cyrus that the Persians should be oppressed by the Medes, and to illustrate the preeminence of Theseus that the Athenians should be dispersed, so at the present time, in order that the might of an Italian genius might be recognised, it was necessary that Italy should be reduced to her present condition, and that she should be more enslaved than the Hebrews, more oppressed than the Persians, and more scattered than the Athenians; without a head, without order, beaten, despoiled, lacerated, and overrun, and that she should have suffered ruin of every kind.

And although before now a gleam of hope has appeared which gave hope that some individual might be appointed by God for her redemption, yet at the highest summit of his career he was thrown aside by fortune, so that now, almost lifeless, she awaits one who may heal her wounds and put a stop to the pillaging of Lombardy, to the rapacity and extortion in the Kingdom of Naples and in Tuscany, and cure her of those sores which have long been festering. Behold how she prays God to send some one to redeem her from this barbarous cruelty and insolence. Behold her ready and willing to follow any standard if only there be some one to raise it. There is nothing now she can hope for but that your illustrious house may place itself at the head of this redemption, being by its power and fortune so exalted, and being favoured by God and the Church, of which it is now the ruler. Nor will this be very difficult, if you call to mind the actions and lives of the men I have named. And although those men were rare and marvellous, they were none the less men, and each of them had less opportunity than the present, for their enterprise was not juster than this, nor easier, nor was God more their friend than He is yours. Here is a just cause; *"iustum enim est bellum quibus necessarium, et pia arma ubi nulla nisi in armis spes est."* [1] Here is the greatest willingness, nor can there be great difficulty where there is great willingness, provided that the measures are adopted of those whom I have set before you as examples. Besides this, unexampled wonders have been seen here performed by God, the sea has been opened, a cloud has shown you the road, the rock has given forth water, manna has rained, and everything has contributed to your greatness, the remainder must be done by you. God will not do everything, in order not to deprive us of freewill and the portion of the glory that falls to our lot.

It is no marvel that none of the before-mentioned Italians have done that which it is to be hoped your illustrious house may do; and if in so many revolutions in Italy and so many warlike operations, it always seems as if military capacity were extinct, this is because the ancient methods were not good, and no one has arisen who knew how to discover new ones. Nothing does so much honour to a newly-risen man than the new laws and measures which he introduces. These things, when they are well based and have greatness in them, render him revered and admired, and there is not lacking scope in Italy for the introduction of every kind of new organisation. Here there is great virtue in the members, if it were not wanting in the heads. Look how in duels and in contests of a few the Italians are superior in strength, dexterity, and intelligence. But when it comes to armies they make a poor show; which proceeds entirely from the weakness of the leaders, for those that know are not obeyed, and every one thinks that he knows, there being hitherto nobody who has

---

[1] [*For war is just when it is necessary, and arms are holy where there is no hope but in arms.*]

raised himself so high both by valour and fortune as to make the others yield. Hence it comes about that for so long a time, in all the wars waged during the last twenty years, whenever there has been an entirely Italian army it has always been a failure, as witness first Taro, then Alexandria, Capua, Genoa, Vailà, Bologna, and Mestri.

If your illustrious house, therefore, wishes to follow those great men who redeemed their countries, it is before all things necessary, as the true foundation of every undertaking, to provide yourself with your own forces, for you cannot have more faithful, or truer and better soldiers. And although each one of them may be good, they will united become even better when they see themselves commanded by their prince, and honoured and favoured by him. It is therefore necessary to prepare such forces in order to be able with Italian prowess to defend the country from foreigners. And although both the Swiss and Spanish infantry are deemed terrible, none the less they each have their defects, so that a third method of array might not only oppose them, but be confident of overcoming them. For the Spaniards cannot sustain the attack of cavalry, and the Swiss have to fear infantry which meets them with resolution equal to their own. From which it has resulted, as will be seen by experience, that the Spaniards cannot sustain the attack of French cavalry, and the Swiss are overthrown by Spanish infantry. And although a complete example of the latter has not been seen, yet an instance was furnished in the battle of Ravenna, where the Spanish infantry attacked the German battalions, which are organised in the same way as the Swiss. The Spaniards, through their bodily agility and aided by their bucklers, had entered between and under their pikes and were in a position to attack them safely without the Germans being able to defend themselves; and if the cavalry had not charged them they would have utterly destroyed them. Knowing therefore the defects of both these kinds of infantry, a third kind can be created which can resist cavalry and need not fear infantry, and this will be done by the choice of arms and a new organisation. And these are the things which, when newly introduced, give reputation and grandeur to a new prince.

This opportunity must not, therefore, be allowed to pass, so that Italy may at length find her liberator. I cannot express the love with which he would be received in all those provinces which have suffered under these foreign invasions, with what thirst for vengeance, with what steadfast faith, with what love, with what grateful tears. What doors would be closed against him? What people would refuse him obedience? What envy could oppose him? What Italian would withhold allegiance? This barbarous domination stinks in the nostrils of every one. May your illustrious house therefore assume this task with that courage and those hopes which are inspired by a just cause, so that under its banner our fatherland may be raised up, and under its auspices be verified that saying of Petrarch:

> Valour against fell wrath
> Will take up arms; and be the combat quickly sped!
> For, sure, the ancient worth,
> That in Italians stirs the heart, is not yet dead.

JEAN BODIN

WITH THE GROWTH of the national dynastic state came its theorists. One of the most important of these, rooted in the traditions of Roman law, was Jean Bodin (1530–96), lawyer and social philosopher. After completing his legal training at Toulouse, Bodin was given positions by Henry III and the duke of Alençon; in 1576 he was a delegate to the States General at Blois. France during his lifetime, before the reestablishment of strong central government by Henry IV, the first Bourbon king, was torn by civil and religious strife; and Bodin's work is very much in touch with contemporary events.

His principal work is *Six Books on the Commonwealth* (1576). His other works include *Method for the Easy Comprehension of History* (1566) and the famous economic treatise, *Reply to the Paradox of Monsieur Malestroit* (1568), which contains one of the earliest statements of the quantity theory of money.

The selections from the *Six Books on the Commonwealth* are taken from M. J. Tolley's translation (New York, Macmillan, 1955).

SIX BOOKS ON THE COMMONWEALTH

Concerning the Citizen

．　．　．　．　．

When the head of the family leaves the household over which he presides and joins with other heads of families in order to treat of those things which are of common interest, he ceases to be a lord and master, and becomes an equal and associate with the rest. He sets aside his private concerns to attend to public affairs. In so doing he ceases to be a master and becomes a citizen, and a citizen may be defined as a free subject dependent on the authority of another.

Before such things as cities and citizens, or any form of commonwealth whatsoever, were known among men, each head of a family was sovereign in his household, having power of life and death over his wife and children. But force, violence, ambition, avarice, and the passion for vengeance, armed men against one another. The result of the ensuing conflicts was to give victory to some, and to reduce the rest to slavery. Moreover the man who had been chosen captain and leader by the victors, under whose command success had been won, retained authority over his followers, who became his loyal and faithful adherents, and imposed it on the others, who became his slaves. Thus was lost the full and entire liberty of each man to live according to his own free will, without subjection to anyone. It was completely lost to the vanquished and converted into unmitigated servitude; it was qualified in the case of the victors in that they now rendered obedience to a sovereign leader. Anyone who did not wish to abandon part of his liberty, and live under the laws and commands of another, lost it altogether. Thus the words, hitherto unknown, of master and servant, ruler and subject, came into use.

Reason and common sense alike point to the conclusion that the origin and foundation of commonwealths was in force and violence. If this is not enough, it can be shown on the testimony of such historians as Thucydides, Plutarch, Caesar, and even by the laws of Solon, that the first generations of men were unacquainted with the sentiments of honour, and their highest endeavour was to kill, torture, rob, and enslave their fellows. So says Plutarch. We also have the evidence of sacred history, where it is said that Nimrod, the youngest son of Ham, was the first to subject his followers by force and violence. Wherefore he was called the mighty hunter, which to the Hebrews suggests the robber and despoiler. Demosthenes, Aristotle, and Cicero laboured under a misapprehension in repeating the error of Herodotus, who held that the first kings were chosen for their justice and their virtue, in what were believed to be heroic times. I have rebutted this view elsewhere on the grounds that in the first commonwealths, and for a long time after Abraham, there were innumerable slaves, as indeed was also found to be the case in the West Indies. This could hardly be unless there had been some violent forcing of the laws of nature.

Such being the origin of commonwealths, it is clear why a citizen is to be defined as a free subject who is dependent on the sovereignty of another. I use the term *free subject,* because although a slave is as much, or more, subject to the commonwealth as is his lord, it has always been a matter of common agreement that the slave is not a citizen, and in law has no personality. This is not the case with women and children, who are free of any servile dependence, though their rights and liberties, especially their power of disposing of property, is limited by the domestic authority of the head of the household. We can say then that every citizen is a subject since his liberty is limited by the sovereign power to which he owes obedience. We cannot say that every subject is a citizen. This is clear from the case of slaves. The same applies to aliens. Being subject to the authority of another, they have no part in the rights and privileges of the community. . . .

Concerning Sovereignty

SOVEREIGNTY is that absolute and perpetual power vested in a common-wealth which in Latin is termed *majestas*. . . . The term needs careful definition, because although it is the distinguishing mark of a common-wealth, and an understanding of its nature fundamental to any treatment of politics, no jurist or political philosopher has in fact attempted to de-fine it. . . .

I have described it as *perpetual* because one can give absolute power to a person or group of persons for a period of time, but that time expired they become subjects once more. Therefore even while they enjoy power, they cannot properly be regarded as sovereign rulers, but only as the lieutenants and agents of the sovereign ruler, till the moment comes when it pleases the prince or the people to revoke the gift. The true sovereign remains always seized of his power. Just as a feudal lord who grants lands to another retains his eminent domain over them, so the ruler who delegates authority to judge and command, whether it be for a short period, or during pleasure, remains seized of those rights of jurisdiction actually exercised by another in the form of a revocable grant, or precarious tenancy. For this reason the law requires the surrender of the authority committed to him, at the expiration of his term of office. In this respect there is no differ-ence between the highest officer of state and his humblest subordinate. If it were otherwise, and the absolute authority delegated by the prince to a lieutenant was regarded as itself sovereign power, the latter could use it against his prince who would thereby forfeit his eminence, and the subject could command his lord, the servant his master. This is a manifest absurdity, considering that the sovereign is always excepted personally, as a matter of right, in all delegations of authority, however executive. However much he gives there always remains a reserve of right in his own person, whereby he may command, or intervene by way of prevention, confirmation, evoca-tion, or any other way he thinks fit, in all matters delegated to a subject, whether in virtue of an office or a commission. Any authority exercised in virtue of an office or a commission can be revoked, or made tenable for as long or short a period as the sovereign wills.

These principles accepted as the foundations of sovereignty, it follows that neither the Roman Dictator, the Harmost of Sparta, the Esymnete of Salonika, the Archus of Malta, nor the ancient Balia of Florence (who had the same sort of authority), nor regents of kingdoms, nor holders of any other sort of commission, nor magistrates whatsoever, who have absolute power to govern the commonwealth for a certain term only, are possessed of sovereign authority. . . .

But supposing the king grants absolute power to a lieutenant for the terms of his life, is not that a perpetual sovereign power? For if one confines *perpetual* to that which has no termination whatever, then sovereignty cannot subsist save in aristocracies and popular states, which never die. If one is to include monarchy too, sovereignty must be vested not in the king alone, but in the king and the heirs of his body, which supposes a strictly hereditary monarchy. In that case there can be very few sovereign kings, since there are only a very few strictly hereditary monarchies. Those especially who come to the throne by election could not be included.

A perpetual authority therefore must be understood to mean one that lasts for the lifetime of him who exercises it. If a sovereign magistrate is given office for one year, or for any other predetermined period, and continues to exercise the authority bestowed on him after the conclusion of his term, he does so either by consent or by force and violence. If he does so by force, it is manifest tyranny. The tyrant is a true sovereign for all that. The robber's possession by violence is true and natural possession although contrary to the law, for those who were formerly in possession have been disseized. But if the magistrate continues in office by consent, he is not a sovereign prince, seeing that he only exercises power on sufferance. Still less is he a sovereign if the term of his office is not fixed, for in that case he has no more than a precarious commission. . . .

What bearing have these considerations on the case of the man to whom the people has given absolute power for the term of his natural life? One must distinguish. If such absolute power is given him simply and unconditionally, and not in virtue of some office or commission, nor in the form of a revocable grant, the recipient certainly is, and should be acknowledged to be, a sovereign. The people has renounced and alienated its sovereign power in order to invest him with it and put him in possession, and it thereby transfers to him all its powers, authority, and sovereign rights, just as does the man who gives to another possessory and proprietary rights over what he formerly owned. The civil law expressed this in the phrase "all power is conveyed to him and vested in him."

But if the people give such power for the term of his natural life to anyone as its official or lieutenant, or only gives the exercise of such power, in such a case he is not a sovereign, but simply an officer, lieutenant, regent, governor, or agent, and as such has the exercise only of a power inhering in another. When a magistrate institutes a perpetual lieutenant, even if he abandons all his rights of jurisdiction and leaves their exercise entirely to his lieutenant, the authority to command and to judge nevertheless does not reside in the lieutenant, nor the action and force of the law derive from him. If he exceeds his authority his acts have no validity, unless approved and confirmed by him from whom he draws his authority. For this reason King John, after his return from captivity in England, solemnly ratified all the acts of his son Charles, who had acted in his name as regent, in order, as was necessary, to regularize the position.

Whether then one exercises the power of another by commission, by institution, or by delegation, or whether such exercise is for a set term, or in perpetuity, such a power is not a sovereign power, even if there is no mention of such words as representative, lieutenant, governor, or regent, in the letters of appointment, or even if such powers are a consequence of the normal working of the laws of the country. In ancient times in Scotland, for instance, the law vested the entire governance of the realm in the next of kin, if the king should be a minor, on condition that everything that was done, was done in the king's name. But this law was later altered because of its inconvenient consequences.

Let us now turn to the other term of our definition and consider the force of the word *absolute*. The people or the magnates of a commonwealth can bestow simply and unconditionally upon someone of their choice a sovereign and perpetual power to dispose of their property and persons, to govern the state as he thinks fit, and to order the succession, in the same way that any proprietor, out of his liberality, can freely and unconditionally make a gift of his property to another. Such a form of gift, not being qualified in any way, is the only true gift, being at once unconditional and irrevocable. Gifts burdened with obligations and hedged with conditions are not true gifts. Similarly sovereign power given to a prince charged with conditions is neither properly sovereign nor absolute, unless the conditions of appointment are only such as are inherent in the laws of God and of nature.

If we insist however that absolute power means exemption from all law whatsoever, there is no prince in the world who can be regarded as sovereign, since all the princes of the earth are subject to the laws of God and of nature, and even to certain human laws common to all nations. On the other hand, it is possible for a subject who is neither a prince nor a ruler, to be exempted from all the laws, ordinances, and customs of the commonwealth. We have an example in Pompey the Great who was dispensed from the laws for five years, by express enactment of the Roman people, at the instance of the Tribune Gabinius. . . . But notwithstanding such exemptions from the operations of the law, the subject remains under the authority of him who exercises sovereign power, and owes him obedience.

On the other hand, it is the distinguishing mark of the sovereign that he cannot in any way be subject to the commands of another, for it is he who makes law for the subject, abrogates law already made, and amends obsolete law. No one who is subject either to the law or to some other person can do this. That is why it is laid down in the civil law that the prince is above the law, for the word law in Latin implies the command of him who is invested with sovereign power. Therefore we find in all statutes the phrase "notwithstanding all edicts and ordinances to the contrary that we have infringed, or do infringe by these present." This clause applied both to former acts of the prince himself, and to those of his predecessors. For all laws, ordinances, letters patent, privileges, and grants whatsoever issued by the prince, have force only during his own lifetime, and must be expressly, or at least tacitly, confirmed by the reigning prince who has cognizance of them. . . . In proof of which, it is the custom of this realm for all corporations and corporate bodies to ask for the confirmation of their privileges, rights, and jurisdictions, on the accession of a new king. Even Parlements and high courts do this, as well as individual officers of the crown.

If the prince is not bound by the laws of his predecessors, still less can he be bound by his own laws. One may be subject to laws made by another, but it is impossible to bind oneself in any matter which is the subject of one's own free exercise of will. As the law says, "there can be no obligation in any matter which proceeds from the free will of the undertaker." It follows of necessity that the king cannot be subject to his own laws. Just as, according to the canonists, the Pope can never tie his own hands, so the sovereign prince cannot bind himself even if he wishes. For this reason edicts and ordinances conclude with the formula "for such is our good pleasure," thus intimating that the laws of a sovereign prince, even when founded on truth and right reason, proceed simply from his own free will.

It is far otherwise with divine and natural laws. All the princes of the earth are subject to them, and cannot contravene them without treason and rebellion against God. His yoke is upon them, and they must bow their heads in fear and reverence before His divine majesty. The absolute power of princes and sovereign lords does not extend to the laws of God and of nature. He who best understood the meaning of absolute power, and made kings and emperors submit to his will, defined his sovereignty as a power to override positive law; he did not claim power to set aside divine and natural law.

But supposing the prince should swear to keep the laws and customs of his country, is he not bound by that oath? One must distinguish. If a prince promises in his own heart to obey his own laws, he is nevertheless not bound to do so, any more than anyone is bound by an oath taken to himself. Even private citizens are not bound by private oaths to keep agreements. The law permits them to cancel them, even if agreements are in themselves reasonable and good. But if one sovereign prince promises another sovereign prince to keep the agreements entered into by his predecessors, he is bound to do so even if not under oath, if that other prince's interests are involved. If they are not, he is not bound either by a promise, or even by an oath.

The same holds good of promises made by the sovereign to the subject, even if the promises were made prior to his election (for this does not make the difference that many suppose). It is not that the prince is bound either by his own laws or those of his predecessors. But he is bound by the just covenants and promises he has made, whether under oath to do so or not, to exactly the same extent that a private individual is bound in like case. A private individual can be released from a promise that was unjust or unreasonable, or beyond his competence to fulfil, or extracted from him by misrepresentations or fraud, or made in error, or under restraint and by intimidation, because of the injury the keeping of it does him. In the same way a sovereign prince can make good any invasion of his sovereign rights, and for the same reasons. So the principle stands, that the prince is not subject to his own laws, or those of his predecessors, but is bound by the just and reasonable engagements which touch the interests of his subjects individually or collectively.

Many have been led astray by confusing the laws of the prince with covenants entered into by him. This confusion has led some to call these covenants contractual laws. This is the term used in Aragon when the king issues an ordinance upon the petition of the Estates, and in return receives some aid or subsidy. It is claimed that he is strictly bound by these laws, even though he is not by any of his other enactments. It is however admitted that he may override even these when the purpose of their enactment no longer holds. All this is true enough, and well-founded in reason and authority. But no bribe or oath is required to bind a sovereign prince to keep a law which is in the interests of his subjects. The bare word of a prince should be as sacred as a divine pronouncement. It loses its force if he is ill-thought of as one who cannot be trusted except under oath, nor relied on to keep a promise unless paid to do so. Nevertheless it remains true in principle that the sovereign prince can set aside the laws which he has promised or sworn to observe, if they no longer satisfy the requirements of justice, and he may do this without the consent of his subjects. It should however be added that the abrogation must be express and explicit in its reference, and not just in the form of a general repudiation. But if on the other hand there is no just cause for breaking a law which the prince has promised to keep, the prince ought not to do so, and indeed cannot contravene it, though he is not bound to the same extent by the promises and covenants of his predecessors unless he succeeds by strict hereditary right.

A law and a covenant must therefore not be confused. A law proceeds from him who has sovereign power, and by it he binds the subject to obedience, but cannot bind himself. A covenant is a mutual undertaking between a prince and his subjects, equally binding on both parties, and neither can contravene it to the prejudice of the other, without his consent. The prince has no greater privilege than the subject in this matter. But in the case of laws, a prince is no longer bound by his promise to keep them when they cease to satisfy the claims of justice. Subjects however must keep their engagements to one another in all circumstances, unless the prince releases them from such obligations. Sovereign princes are not bound by oath to keep the laws of their predecessors. If they are so bound, they are not properly speaking sovereign.

The constitutional laws of the realm, especially those that concern the king's estate being, like the salic law, annexed and united to the Crown, cannot be infringed by the prince. Should he do so, his successor can always annul any act prejudicial to the traditional form of the monarchy, since on this is founded and sustained his very claim to sovereign majesty.

As for laws relating to the subject, whether general or particular, which do not involve any question of the constitution, it has always been usual only to change them with the concurrence of the three estates, either assembled in the States-General of the whole of France, or in each bailliwick separately. Not that the king is bound to take their advice, or debarred from acting in a way quite contrary to what they wish, if his acts are based on justice and natural reason. At the same time the majesty of the prince is most fully manifested in the assembly of the three estates of the whole realm, humbly petitioning and supplicating him, without any power of commanding or determining, or any right to a deliberative voice. Only that which it pleases the prince to assent to or dissent from, to command or to forbid, has the force of law and is embodied in his edict or ordinance.

Those who have written books about the duties of magistrates and such like matters are in error in maintaining that the authority of the Estates is superior to that of the prince. Such doctrines serve only to encourage subjects to resist their sovereign rulers. Besides, such views bear no relation to the facts, except when the king is in captivity, lunatic or a minor. If he were normally subject to the Estates, he would be neither a prince nor a sovereign, and the commonwealth would not be a kingdom or a monarchy, but a pure aristocracy where authority is shared equally between the members of the ruling class. . . .

Although in the Parliaments of the kingdom of England, which meet every three years, all three orders use great freedom of speech, as is characteristic of northern peoples, they still must proceed by petitions and supplications. . . . Moreover Parliaments in England can only assemble, as in this kingdom and in Spain, under letters patent expressly summoning them in the king's name. This is sufficient proof that Parliaments have no independent power of considering, commanding or determining, seeing that they can neither assemble nor adjourn without express royal command. . . . It may be objected that no extraordinary taxes or subsidies can be imposed without the agreement and consent of Parliament. King Edward I agreed to this principle in the Great Charter, which is always appealed to by the people against the claims of the king. But I hold that in this matter no other king has any more right than has the King of England, since it is not within the competence of any prince in the world to levy taxes at will on his people, or seize the goods of another arbitrarily, as Philippe de Comines very wisely argued at the Estates at Tours, as we may read in his *Memoirs*.

We must agree then that the sovereignty of the king is in no wise qualified or diminished by the existence of Estates. On the contrary his majesty appears more illustrious when formally recognized by his assembled subjects, even though in such assemblies princes, not wishing to fall out with their people, agree to many things which they would not have consented to, unless urged by the petitions, prayers, and just complaints of a people burdened by grievances unknown to the prince. After all, he depends for his information on the eyes and ears and reports of others.

From all this it is clear that the principal mark of sovereign majesty and absolute power is the right to impose laws generally on all subjects regardless of their consent. . . . And if it is expedient that if he is to govern his state well, a sovereign prince must be above the law, it is even more expedient that the ruling class in an aristocracy should be so, and inevitable in a popular state. A monarch in a kingdom is set apart from his subjects, and the ruling class from the people in an aristocracy. There are therefore in each case two parties, those that rule on the one hand,

and those that are ruled on the other. This is the cause of the disputes about sovereignty that arise in them, but cannot in a popular state. . . . There the people, rulers and ruled, form a single body and so cannot bind themselves by their own laws. . . .

When edicts are ratified by Estates or Parlements, it is for the purpose of securing obedience to them, and not because otherwise a sovereign prince could not validly make law. As Theodosius said with reference to the consent of the Senate, "it is not a matter of necessity but of expediency." He also remarked that it was most becoming in a sovereign prince to keep his own laws, for this is what makes him feared and respected by his subjects, whereas nothing so undermines his authority as contempt for them. As a Roman Senator observed "it is more foolish and ill-judged to break your own laws than those of another."

But may it not be objected that if the prince forbids a sin, such as homicide, on pain of death, he is in this case bound to keep his own law? The answer is that this is not properly the prince's own law, but a law of God and nature, to which he is more strictly bound than any of his subjects. Neither his council, nor the whole body of the people, can exempt him from his perpetual responsibility before the judgement-seat of God, as Solomon said in unequivocal terms. Marcus Aurelius also observed that the magistrate is the judge of persons, the prince of the magistrates, and God of the prince. Such was the opinion of the two wisest rulers the world has ever known. Those who say without qualification that the prince is bound neither by any law whatsoever, nor by his own express engagements, insult the majesty of God, unless they intend to except the laws of God and of nature, and all just covenants and solemn agreements. Even Dionysius, tyrant of Syracuse, said to his mother that he could exempt her from the laws and customs of Syracuse, but not from the laws of God and of nature. For just as contracts and deeds of gift of private individuals must not derogate from the ordinances of the magistrate, nor his ordinances from the law of the land, nor the law of the land from the enactments of a sovereign prince, so the laws of a sovereign prince cannot override or modify the laws of God and of nature.

There is one other point. If the prince is bound by the laws of nature, and the civil law is reasonable and equitable, it would seem to follow that the prince is also bound by the civil law. As Pacatius said to the Emperor Theodosius "as much is permitted to you as is permitted by the laws." In answer to this I would point out that the laws of a sovereign prince concern either public or private interests or both together. All laws moreover can be either profitable at the expense of honour, or profitable without involving honour at all, or honourable without profit, or neither honourable nor profitable. When I say "honour" I mean that which conforms with what is natural and right, and it has already been shown that the prince is bound in such cases. Laws of this kind, though published by the prince's authority, are properly natural laws. Laws which are profitable as well as just are even more binding on him. One need hardly concern oneself about the sanctity of laws which involve neither profit nor honour. But if it is a question of weighing honour against profit, honour should always be preferred. Aristides the Just said of Themistocles that his advice was always very useful to the people but shameful and dishonourable.

But if a law is simply useful and does not involve any principle of natural justice, the prince is not bound by it, but can amend it or annul it altogether as he chooses, provided that with the alteration of the law the profit to some does not do damage to others without just cause. The prince then can annul an ordinance which is merely useful in order to substitute one more or less advantageous, for profit, honour, and justice all have degrees of more and less. And just as the prince can choose the most useful among profitable laws, so he can choose the most just among equitable laws, even though while some profit by them others suffer, provided it is the public that profits, and only the private individual that suffers. It is, however, never proper for the subject to disobey the laws of the prince under the pretext that honour and justice require it. . . .

Edicts and ordinances therefore do not bind the ruler except in so far as they embody the principles of natural justice; that ceasing, the obligation ceases. But subjects are bound till the ruler has expressly abrogated the law, for it is a law both divine and natural that we should obey the edicts and ordinances of him whom God has set in authority over us, providing his edicts are not contrary to God's law. For just as the rear-vassal owes an oath of fealty in respect of and against all others, saving his sovereign prince, so the subject owes allegiance to his sovereign prince in respect of and against all others, saving the majesty of God, who is lord of all the princes of this world. From this principle we can deduce that other rule, that the sovereign prince is bound by the covenants he makes either with his subjects, or some other prince. Just because he enforces the covenants and mutual engagements entered into by his subjects among themselves, he must be the mirror of justice in all his own acts. . . . He has a double obligation in this case. He is bound in the first place by the principles of natural equity, which require that conventions and solemn promises should be kept, and in the second place in the interests of his own good faith, which he ought to preserve even to his own disadvantage, because he is the formal guarantor to all his subjects of the mutual faith they owe one another.

A distinction must therefore be made between right and law, for one implies what is equitable and the other what is commanded. Law is nothing else than the command of the sovereign in the exercise of his sovereign power. A sovereign prince is not subject to the laws of the Greeks, or any other alien power, or even those of the Romans, much less to his own laws, except in so far as they embody the law of nature which, according to Pindar, is the law to which all kings and princes are subject. Neither Pope nor Emperor is exempt from this law, though certain flatterers say they can take the goods of their subjects at will. But both civilians and canonists have repudiated this opinion as contrary to the law of God. They err who assert that in virtue of their sovereign power princes can do this. It is rather the law of the jungle, an act of force and violence. For as we have shown above, absolute power only implies freedom in relation to positive laws, and not in relation to the law of God. God has declared explicitly in His Law that it is not just to take, or even to covet, the goods of another. Those who defend such opinions are even more dangerous than those who act on them. They show the lion his claws, and arm princes under a cover of just claims. The evil will of a tyrant, drunk with such flatteries, urges him to an abuse of absolute power and excites his violent passions to the pitch where avarice issues in confiscations, desire in adultery, and anger in murder.

Since then the prince has no power to exceed the laws of nature which God Himself, whose image he is, has decreed, he cannot take his subjects' property without just and reasonable cause, that is to say by purchase, exchange, legitimate confiscation, or to secure peace with the enemy when it cannot be otherwise achieved. Natural reason instructs us that the public good must be preferred to the particular, and that subjects should give up not only their mutual antagonisms and animosities, but also their posssessions, for the safety of the commonwealth. . . .

It remains to be determined whether the prince is bound by the covenants of his predecessors, and whether, if so, it is a derogation of his sovereign power . . . A distinction must be made between the ruler who succeeds because he is the natural heir of his predecessor, and the ruler who succeeds in virtue of the laws and customs of the realm. In the first case the heir is bound by the oaths and promises of his predecessors just as is any ordinary heir. In the second case he is not so bound even if he is sworn, for the oath of the predecessor does not bind the successor. He is bound however in all that tends to the benefit of the kingdom.

There are those who will say that there is no need of such distinctions since the prince is bound in any case by the law of nations, under which covenants are guaranteed. But I consider that these distinctions are necessary nevertheless, since the prince is bound as much by the law of nations, but no more, than by any of his own enactments. If the law of nations is iniquitous in any respect, he can disallow it within his own kingdom, and forbid his subjects to observe it, as was done in France in regard to slavery. He can do the same in relation to any other of its provisions, so long as he does nothing against the law of God. If justice is the end of the law, the law the work of the prince, and the prince the image of God, it follows of necessity that the law of the prince should be modelled on the law of God.

The True Attributes of Sovereignty

Because there are none on earth, after God, greater than sovereign princes, whom God establishes as His lieutenants to command the rest of mankind, we must enquire carefully into their estate, that we may respect and revere their majesty in all due obedience, speak and think of them with all due honour. He who contemns his sovereign prince, contemns God whose image he is. . . . Aristotle, Polybius, and Dionysius Halicarnassus alone among the Greeks discussed the attributes of sovereignty. But they treated the subject so briefly that one can see at a glance that they did not really understand the principles involved. I quote Aristotle. "There are," he says, "three parts of a commonwealth. There must be provision for the taking and giving of counsel, for appointing to office and assigning to each citizen his duties, for the administration of justice." If he did not mean by *parts* attributes of sovereignty, he never treated of the subject at all, since this is the only passage which has any bearing. Polybius does not define the rights and duties of sovereignty either, but he says of the Romans that their constitution was a mixture of monarchy, aristocracy, and popular government, since the people made law and appointed to office, the Senate administered the provinces and conducted great affairs of state, the consuls enjoyed the pre-eminence of honour accorded to kings, especially in the field, where they exercised supreme command. This passage appears to imply a treatment of sovereign rights, since he says that those who enjoyed those rights had sovereign power. Dionysius Halicarnassus however had a clearer and better understanding of the matter than the others. When he was explaining how the King Servius deprived the Senate of authority, he observed that he transferred to the people the power to make and unmake law, to determine war and peace, to institute and deprive magistrates, and the right of hearing appeals from all courts whatsoever. In another passage, when describing the third conflict between the nobles and the people, he reported how the Consul Marcus Valerius rebuked the people and said that they should be content with the powers of making law, appointing to office and hearing appeals. Other matters should be left to the senate.

Since ancient times civilians, and especially those of more recent years, have elaborated these rights, especially in their treatises on what they call regalian rights. Under this heading they have collected an immense number of particular rights and privileges enjoyed by dukes, counts, bishops, and various officials, and even subjects of sovereign princes. As a result they describe dukes, such as those of Milan, Mantua, Ferrara, and Savoy, and even counts, as sovereign princes. However reasonable it may appear, this is an error. How can these rulers be regarded as anything but sovereign, they argue, when they make law for their subjects, levy war and conclude peace, appoint to all office in their dominions, levy taxes, make a free man of whom they please, pardon those who have forfeited their lives. What other powers has any sovereign prince?

But we have already shown above that the Dukes of Milan, Mantua, Ferrara, Florence, and Savoy hold of the Empire. Their most honourable title is that of Imperial Vicar and Prince of the Empire. . . . We have also pointed out the absurdities that ensue if one makes sovereigns of vassals, since the lord and his subject, the master and his servant, the man who makes the law and the man who obeys them, are thereby placed on an equal footing. Since this cannot be, it follows that dukes, counts, and all those who hold of another, or are bound by his laws and subject to his commands, whether of right or by constraint, are not sovereign. The same holds good of the highest officers of state, lieutenant-generals of the king, governors, regents, dictators, whatever the extent of their powers. They are not sovereigns since they are subject to the laws and commands of another and may be appealed against.

The attributes of sovereignty are therefore peculiar to the sovereign prince, for if communicable to the subject, they cannot be called attributes of sovereignty. . . . Just as Almighty God cannot create another God equal with Himself, since He is infinite and two infinities cannot co-exist, so the sovereign prince, who is the image of God, cannot make a subject equal with himself without self-destruction.

If this is so, it follows that rights of jurisdiction are not attributes of sovereignty since they are exercised by subjects as well as the prince. The same is true of the appointment and dismissal of officials, for this power also the prince shares with the subject, not only in regard to the lesser offices of justice, of police, of the armed forces, or of the revenues, but also in regard to responsible commanders in peace and war. . . . The infliction of penalties and the bestowing of awards is not an attribute of sovereignty either, for the magistrate has this power, though it is true he derives it from the sovereign. Nor is taking counsel about affairs of state an attribute of sovereignty, for such is the proper function of the privy council or senate in the commonwealth, a body always distinct from that in which sovereignty is vested. Even in the popular state, where sovereignty lies in the assembly of the people, so far from it being the function of the assembly to take counsel, it ought never be permitted to do so, as I shall show later.

It is clear therefore that none of the three functions of the state that Aristotle distinguishes are properly attributes of sovereignty. As for what Halicarnassus says about Marcus Valerius' speech to the people of Rome, when trying to pacify them, that they should be content with the prerogatives of making law and appointing magistrates, he does not make the point sufficiently clear. As I have already said, appointing to office is not an attribute of sovereignty. Moreover some further explanation is necessary of the nature of the law-making power. A magistrate can make laws binding on those subject to his jurisdiction, provided such laws do not conflict with the edicts and ordinances of his sovereign power.

Before going any further, one must consider what is meant by *law*. The word law signifies the right command of that person, or those persons, who have absolute authority over all the rest without exception, saving only the law-giver himself, whether the command touches all subjects in general or only some in particular. To put it another way, the law is the rightful command of the sovereign touching all his subjects in general, or matters of general application. . . . As to the commands of the magistrate, they are not properly speaking laws but only edicts. "An edict," says Varro, "is an order issued by a magistrate." Such orders are only binding on those subject to his jurisdiction, and are only in force for his terms of office.

The first attribute of the sovereign prince therefore is the power to make law binding on all his subjects in general and on each in particular. But to avoid any ambiguity one must add that he does so without the consent of any superior, equal, or inferior being necessary. If the prince can only make law with the consent of a superior he is a subject; if of an equal he shares his sovereignty; if of an inferior, whether it be a council of magnates or the people it is not he who is sovereign. The names of the magnates that one finds appended to a royal edict are not there to give force to the law, but as witnesses, and to make it more acceptable. . . . When I say that the first attribute of sovereignty is to give law to all in general and each in particular, I mean by this last phrase the grant of privileges. I mean by a privilege a concession to one or a small group of individuals, which concerns the profit or loss of those persons only. . . .

It may be objected however that not only have magistrates the power of issuing edicts and ordinances, each according to his competence and within his own sphere of jurisdiction, but private citizens can make law in the form of general or local custom. It is agreed that customary law is as binding as statute law. But if the sovereign prince is author of the law, his subjects are the authors of custom. But there is a difference between law and custom. Custom establishes itself gradually over a long period of years, and by common consent, or at any rate the consent of the greater part. Law is made on the instant and draws its force from him who has the right to bind all the rest. Custom is established imperceptibly and without any exercise of compulsion. Law is promulgated and imposed by authority, and often against the wishes of the subject. For this reason Dion Chrysostom compared custom to the king and law to the tyrant. Moreover law can break custom, but custom cannot derogate from the law, nor can the magistrate, or any other responsible for the administration of law, use his discretion about the enforcement of law as he can about custom. Law, unless it is permissive and relaxes the severity of another law, always carries penalties for its breach. Custom only has binding force by the sufferance and during the good pleasure of the sovereign prince, and so far as he is willing to authorize it. Thus the force of both statutes and customary law derives from the authorization of the prince . . . Included in the power of making and unmaking law is that of promulgating it and amending it when it is obscure, or when the magistrates find contradictions and absurdities.

All the other attributes and rights of sovereignty are included in this power of making and unmaking law, so that strictly speaking this is the unique attribute of sovereign power. It includes all other rights of sovereignty, that is to say of making peace and war, of hearing appeals from the sentences of all courts whatsoever, of appointing and dismissing the great officers of state; of taxing, or granting privileges of exemption to all subjects, of appreciating or depreciating the value and weight of the coinage, of receiving oaths of fidelity from subjects and liege-vassals alike, without exception of any other to whom faith is due. . . .

But because *law* is an unprecise and general term, it is as well to specify the other attributes of sovereignty comprised in it, such as the making of war and peace. This is one of the most important rights of sovereignty, since it brings in its train either the ruin or the salvation of the state. This was a right of sovereignty not only among the ancient Romans, but has always been so among all other peoples. . . . Sovereign princes are therefore accustomed to keep themselves informed of the smallest accidents and undertakings connected with warfare. Whatever latitude they may give to their representatives to negotiate peace or an alliance, they never grant the authority to conclude without their own express consent. This was illustrated in the negotiations leading up to the recent treaty of Câteaux-Cambrésis, when the king's envoys kept him almost hourly informed of all proposals and counterproposals. . . . In popular states and aristocracies the difficulty of assembling the people, and the danger of making public all the secrets of diplomacy has meant that the people have generally handed responsibility over to the council. Nevertheless it remains true that the commissions and the orders that it issues in discharge of this function proceed from the authority of the people, and are despatched by the council in the name of the people.

The third attribute of sovereignty is the power to institute the great officers of state. It has never been questioned that the right is an attribute of sovereignty, at any rate as far as the great officers are concerned. I confine it however to high officials, for there is no commonwealth in which these officers, and many guilds and corporate bodies besides, have not some power of appointing their subordinate officials. They do this in virtue of their office, which carries with it the power to delegate. For instance, those who hold feudal rights of jurisdiction of their sovereign prince in faith and homage have the power to appoint the judges in their courts, and their assistants. But this power is devolved upon them by the prince. . . . It is therefore not the mere appointment of officials that implies sovereign right, but the authorization and confirmation of such appointments. It is true however that in so far as the exercise of this right is delegated, the sovereignty of the prince is to that extent qualified, unless his concurrence and express consent is required.

The fourth attribute of sovereignty, and one which has always been among its principal rights, is that the prince should be the final resort of appeal from all other courts. . . . Even though the prince may have published a law, as did Caligula, forbidding any appeal or petition against the sentences of his officers, nevertheless the subject cannot be deprived of the right to make an appeal, or present a petition, to the prince in person. For the prince cannot tie his own hands in this respect, nor take from his subjects the means of redress, supplication, and petition, notwithstanding the fact that all rules governing appeals and jurisdictions are matters of positive law, which we have shown does not bind the prince. This is why the Privy Council, including the Chancellor de l'Hôpital, considered the action of the commissioners deputed to hold an enquiry into the conduct of the President l'Alemant irregular and unprecedented. They had forbidden him to approach within twenty leagues of the court, with the intention of denying him any opportunity of appeal. The king himself could not deny this right to the subject, though he is free to make whatsoever reply to the appeal, favourable or unfavourable, that he pleases. . . . Were it otherwise, and the prince could acquit his subjects or his vassals from the obligation to submit their causes to him in the last instance, he would make of them sovereigns equal with himself. . . . But if he would preserve his authority, the surest way of doing so is to avoid ever devolving any of the attributes of sovereignty upon a subject.

With this right is coupled the right of pardoning convicted persons, and so of overruling the sentences of his own courts, in mitigation of the severity of the law, whether touching life, property, honour, or domicile. It is not in the power of any magistrate, whatever his station, to do any of these things, or to make any revision of the judgement he has once given. . . . In a well-ordered commonwealth the right should never be delegated either to a special commission, or to any high officer of state, save in those circumstances where it is necessary to establish a regency, either because the king is abroad in some distant place, or in captivity, or incapable, or under age. For instance, during the minority of Louis IX, the authority of the Crown was vested in his mother Blanche of Castile as his guardian. . . . Princes however tend to abuse this right, thinking that to pardon is pleasing to God, whereas to exact the utmost punishment is displeasing to Him. But I hold, subject to correction, that the sovereign prince cannot remit any penalty imposed by the law of God, any more than he can dispense any one from the operation of the law of God, to which he himself is subject. If the magistrate who dispenses anyone from obedience to the ordinance of his king merits death, how much more unwarrantable is it for the prince to acquit a man of the punishment ordained by God's law? If a sovereign prince cannot deny a subject his civil rights, how can he acquit him of the penalties imposed by God, such as the death penalty exacted by divine law for treacherous murder?

It may be objected that the prince can never show the quality of mercy if he cannot remit punishments prescribed by divine law. But in my opinion there are other means of showing clemency, such as pardoning breaches of positive laws. For instance, if the prince forbids the carrying of arms, or the selling of foodstuffs to the enemy in time of war, on pain of death, he can very properly pardon the offence of carrying arms if it was done in self-defence, or the selling of provisions if done under the pressure of extreme poverty. Again, the penalty for larceny under the civil law is death. A merciful prince can reduce this to fourfold restitution, which is what is required by divine law. It has always been the custom among Christian kings to pardon unpardonable offences on Good Friday. But pardons of this kind bring in their train pestilences, famine, war, and the downfall of states. That is why it is said in the law of God that in punishing those who have merited death one averts the curse on the whole people. Of a hundred criminals only two are brought to justice, and of those brought to justice only one half are proved guilty. If the few proven cases of guilt are pardoned, how can punishment act as a deterrent to evil-doers? . . . The best way for a prince to exercise his prerogative of mercy is to pardon offences against his own person. Of all exercises of mercy none is more pleasing to God. But what can one hope of the prince who cruelly avenges all injuries to himself, but pardons those inflicted on others?

Faith and homage are also among the most important attributes of sovereignty, as was made clear when the prince was described as the one to whom obedience was due without exception.

As for the right of coinage, it is contained within the law-making power, for only he who can make law can regulate currency. This is illustrated in the very terms used by Greeks, Romans, and French alike, for the word *nummus* comes from the Greek *nomos* signifying both law and alloy. There is nothing of more moment to a country, after the law, than the denomination, the value, and the weight of the coinage, as we have already shown in a separate treatise. Therefore in every well-ordered commonwealth the prince reserves this right exclusively to himself. . . . And although in this kingdom many private persons, such as the Vicomte de Touraine, the Bishops of Meaux, Cahors, Agde, Ambrun and the Counts of St. Pol, de la Marche, Nevers, Blois, and others enjoyed this right, Francis I in a general edict cancelled all such rights whatsoever, declaring the concessions null and void. This right and attribute of sovereignty ought not ever to be granted to a subject. . . .

The right of levying taxes and imposing dues, or of exempting persons from the payment of such, is also part of the power of making law and granting privileges. Not that the levying of taxation is inseparable from the essence of the commonwealth, for as President Le Maître has shown, there was none levied in France till the time of Louis IX. But if any necessity should arise of imposing or withdrawing a tax, it can only be done by him who has sovereign authority. . . . It is true that many seigneurs have prescriptive rights of levying tallages, dues, and imposts. Even in this kingdom many seigneurs can levy tallage on four occasions in virtue of privileges confirmed by judgements in the courts, and by custom. Even seigneurs who have no rights of jurisdiction enjoy this privilege. But in my opinion the privilege started as an abuse which in consequence of long years of enjoyment acquired the dignity of a prescriptive right. But there is no abuse, of however long standing, that the law cannot amend, for the law exists to amend all abuses. Therefore, by the Edict of Moulins it was ordained that all rights of tallage claimed by seigneurs over their dependants could no longer be levied, notwithstanding immemorial prescription.

I have left out of this discussion those lesser prerogatives that individual sovereign princes claim in their own particular realms, as I have confined myself to those general attributes of sovereignty proper to all sovereign princes as such, but which, being inalienable and imprescriptible, cannot, of their very nature, be communicated to subordinate persons such as feudal lords, magistrates, or subjects of any degree whatsoever. Whatever grant a sovereign prince makes of lands or jurisdiction, the rights of the crown are always reserved. This was implied in a judgement of the High Court relating to appanages in France, that no passage of time could justify the usurpation of royal rights. If common lands cannot be acquired by prescription, how can the rights and attributes of sovereignty? It is certain, on the evidence of various edicts and ordinances, that the public domain is inalienable, and cannot be acquired by prescription. Over two thousand years ago Themistocles, in recovering common lands occupied by private persons, said in his speech to the people of Athens that men could acquire no prescriptive rights against God nor private citizens against the commonwealth.

Such are the principal characteristics of sovereign majesty, treated as briefly as possible, since I have already written at greater length on the subject in my book *De Imperio*. It is most expedient for the preservation of the state that the rights of sovereignty should never be granted out to a subject, still less to a foreigner, for to do so is to provide a stepping-stone whereby the grantee himself becomes the sovereign.

V EARLY MODERN CAPITALISM AND THE EXPANSION OF EUROPE

LUCAS PACIOLI

DOUBLE ENTRY BOOKKEEPING, developed in Italy in the course of the fourteenth century, was first published in systematic form by a Tuscan mathematician, Fra Lucas Pacioli (c.1445–c.1515). In 1494 appeared his *Suma de Arithmetica, Geometria, Proportione, et Proportionalita,* which included his treatise on bookkeeping.

The method outlined by Pacioli called for the keeping of an inventory and three books: the memorandum or daybook, in which all transactions were to be entered as they occurred; the journal, in which items were to be classified as to account and as debit or credit; and the ledger, in which items listed in the journal were to be entered as both credit and debit, the totals of which were, of course, always to be equal. A trial balance would bring any errors to light, and make it possible to ascertain the state of the business.

The following selection is from Pietro Crivelli's translation from the Italian, *An Original Translation of the Treatise on Double-Entry Book-keeping by Frater Lucas Pacioli* (New York, Harper and Brothers, 1924).

℃

TREATISE ON
DOUBLE ENTRY BOOKKEEPING

As IS KNOWN, three things are necessary to one who wishes to diligently carry on business. Of these the most important is cash, or any other substantial power . . . without which the carrying on of business is very difficult.

It has occurred that many, entering business with nothing but good faith, have yet carried on big business; and through their credit, faithfully served, have attained to greater wealth. In our conversations with persons throughout Italy, we have come across many of these; and in the great republics the word of a good merchant is considered sufficient, and oaths are taken on it saying: "it is the word of a real merchant." This cannot be admiration, as catholically (*catolicamente*), everybody is saved by faith, without which it is impossible to please God.

The second thing looked for in business is to be a good accountant and sharp bookkeeper and to arrive at this . . . we have regular rules and canons necessary to each operation, so that any diligent reader can understand all by himself. If one does not understand this well, the following would serve him in vain.

The third and last thing necessary is that all one's affairs be arranged in good order so that one may get, without loss of time, all particulars as to the debit and also the credit of all of them, as business does not deal with anything else. This is very useful, because it would be impossible to conduct business without due order of recording, for without rest, merchants would always be in great mental trouble. Therefore I have arranged this treatise wherein I give the method of recording all kinds of entries, proceeding chapter by chapter; and as I cannot put down all that ought to be written on the subject, nevertheless an industrious pilgrim will be able to apply it to any other required case.

We will here adopt the method employed in Venice which among others is certainly to be recommended, for with it one can carry on with any other. This work we shall divide into two principal parts: the one we shall call Inventory and the other we shall call Disposition (*dispone*). . . .

Let him, who, with due order wishes and expects to know how to keep a ledger and its journal well, be diligently attentive.

So that he may understand the process well, we will take the case of one who is starting in business and show how he must proceed in keeping his accounts and books, so that he will easily find each thing posted in its right place; because if he does not duly post them in their right place there would arise great trouble and confusion in all his affairs, as said: *"Ubi non est ordo ibi est confusio";*[1] but we will do as mentioned above and give to every merchant a perfect document, in two principal parts, which we will make quite clear separately so that they may bear healthy fruit.

It is first of all convenient to presuppose and imagine that each operator is working for an end, and so as to duly arrive at this he makes use of every effort in the process. The end or purpose of every business man being to make lawful, and fair enough profit to keep himself substantially; but he must always commence his affairs in the name of God, whose name must appear at the beginning of every manuscript, always bearing his Holy Name in mind.

He must then make his diligent inventory in the following way: He must first of all write on a sheet of paper or in a book aside, all that he has in the world, his personal belongings and household goods, estate, etc., and always begin with the things that are more valuable and easier to lose. These consist of ready cash, jewels, silver, etc., because estate, such as houses, lands, lakes, valleys, ponds, and the like, cannot be mislaid as are personal belongings and household goods. He must then write down, successively, the other things, always putting down first, in the said inventory, the day, the year, the place,

---

[1] [*Where order is not, there is confusion.*]

and his name. The whole inventory must be completed on the same day as otherwise it would give useless trouble in future handling. . . .

Having . . . diligently spoken of all the things that you have in belongings and estate one by one, as has been said, even if they numbered ten thousand, of their condition and nature if deposited in banks, or if placed in loans, all must be named in good order in the said Inventory giving all the counter-marks, names, surnames, as detailed as possible, because things can never be too clear to a merchant on account of an infinity of cases that might occur in business, as he who daily exercises in business knows. The proverb is right when it says that more points are required to make a good merchant, than to make a Doctor of Laws. Who can narrate the practices and cases that fall to the lot of a merchant, now by sea, now by land, now in times of peace and plenty, now in times of war and famine and in times of health and plague? During these times he must know what path to take in the markets, and at fairs, which are held now in one country or town, now in another. A merchant rightly resembles a cock, which, among other things, is the most watchful animal that exists. In winter or in summer it makes its nocturnal vigils, at no time resting. It is said of Philomene, i.e., of the nightingale, that it sings all through the night; this can be verified in summer during the hot weather; but not in winter, as experience is ready to show. A merchant's head is also compared to one that has a hundred eyes; yet these are not enough for him, either in words or in actions. Thus is said by those who know, that Venetians, Florentines, Genoese, Neapolitans, Milanese, Anconians, Brescians, Berga-menes, Aquileians, Sienese, Lucchesi, Perugians, Urbinians . . . represent in Italy, the principal cities of commerce. Much in excess of the others are the cities of Venice and Florence which must adopt rules and regulations for every need, as the municipal laws rightly say: *"Vigilantibus et non dormientibus jura subveniunt";* i.e., help comes to him who is watchful and not to him who sleeps. Thus in the divine offices of the Holy Church is sung that God has promised a crown to the watchful. This was Virgil's document given to Dante, as to his own son, when, in Canto 24 of *Inferno* he exhorts them to labour, by which means only, it is possible to arrive at the mount of Virtue. "Alas my son, it is necessary that you shake yourself; for one does not attain to fame in fine feathers and under quilts. He who wastes his life under these, leaves only a trace similar to that left by smoke in the air or by foam on the water." Another obscure poet comforts us about same by saying: "does fatigue not appear strange to you, that Mars never granted victory to those who resting, fed themselves." Also very convenient is the example of the sage when telling the lazy one to mirror himself on the ant. Paul the Apostle says that no one is worthy of the crown, but he who has legitimately fought for it. These reminders I have added for your own good, so that you give your daily attention to your affairs, chiefly in holding the pen to paper and writing day by day that which you require, as will be stated in the following;—but, above all first always keep God before your eyes and never miss hearing Mass in the morning, bearing in mind that because of it time is never lost, as by charity riches are not wasted; thus the following holy verse says: *"Nec caritas opes nec missa minuit iter,"* etc., and to this the Saviour exhorts us in St. Matthew, when he says: *"Primum quaerite regnum Dei, et haec omnia adjicientur vobis"*: seek you christians first the Kingdom of Heaven and then the other temporal and spiritual things you will easily obtain as your heavenly Father knows quite well what are your needs. I want this to be sufficient as instruction for the Inventory and for doing other good documents well.

1. All the creditors must be placed in the book at the right-hand side, and the debtors at the left-hand side.

2. All entries posted in the book must be double; that is, if you make one creditor you must make one debtor.

3. Each entry in the debit or in the credit must contain three things; viz., the day of the payment, the amount of the payment, and the reason for the entry.

4. The last name in the entry of the debit must be the first in the entry of the credit.

5. On the same day that the debit entry is made should also be made that of the credit.

6. By the balancing (Trial Balance) of the book is meant the folding of a sheet of paper lengthwise, on the right hand of which is copied down the names of the creditors of the book, and on the left-hand the debtors. It is then seen if the sum of the debits is equal to that of the credits, and if so the book is in order.

7. The balance (Trial Balance) of the book must be equal; that is, the sum of—I do not say creditors nor debtors—but I say the sum of the credits must be equal to that of the debits. If they should not be so then there would be an error in the book.

8. The cash account should always be a debtor or else equal. If it should be otherwise, then there would be an error in the book. . . .

10. The book should all be reckoned in one kind of money; though you may name within all sorts of money which may be used: ducats, *"denari,"* florins, gold *"scudi,"* or whatever they may be. But in reckoning up, it is best that it be all of one kind for as you begin the book so must you continue. . . .

12. If you have to make a new account, you must write it down on a new

page without going back to any previous pages, even if you have sufficient space to enter it therein. You must never go back to write; but always forward in order as the days go, which never return. If such a thing were done the book (ledger) would be deemed to be false.

All the cash that you may find and which properly belongs to you, that is, which you may have earned at different times in the past, or may have been left to you by your dead relatives, or given to you by some Prince, you shall make yourself creditor and cash debtor for same.

All the jewels and merchandise which properly belong to you and which you have earned, or may have been left to you under a will, or given to you as gifts, should be kept and valued in cash separately one from the other; and as many things as there are, you shall make as many accounts in the book (ledger), debiting each item saying:—For so many of which I have valued on this day: so many *"denari,"* etc., posted as a credit in this book on page, etc.; and then you will make your account creditor, viz., you yourself with each entry. But take note that these entries should not be of less value than 10 ducats each, as small things of little value are not placed in the book.

All the property which you may have and which properly belongs to you, such as houses, lands, shops, etc., shall be entered in the book. You will make the said houses debtors, have a cash value placed upon them according to your discretion, and make yourself creditor in your above-stated account. Then you will make the lands debtors separately, and estimate their value as said above, making yourself creditor in your above-stated account, and as I told you in the rules, every entry requires three things; viz., the day, the amount or value in cash, and the reason for the entry.

If you should make cash purchases of merchandise or of any other thing, you must debit such merchandise or other thing, and credit cash. If you should say I am buying for cash as stated, but a bank will pay for me, or a friend will do so, I will answer that in any case you must debit the merchandise thus bought as stated above; but where I told you to credit the cash, you should instead credit the bank or that friend of yours, who paid for you.

If you should make purchases of merchandise or of any other thing, for time payment of any period, you shall debit such merchandise or thing and credit the person from whom you made the time payment purchase. . . .

All the sales of merchandise or of other things shall be dealt with as above with the exception that you should put everything in the opposite way; viz., where I told you above to debit the merchandise you purchase, you shall always credit the merchandise you sell, and debit cash if it is sold for cash, or debit the bank that might have promised you the money. And if the sale has been made on time, you shall debit the person to whom you have made the sale on time, and if the sale was made partly for cash and partly on time you must do as I have shown you above in the two preceding paragraphs which deal with purchases on time.

Loans in cash made by you to some friend shall be debited to such friend, and credited to cash.

If you should receive a cash loan from some friend, you should debit the cash and credit your friend. . . .

All the merchandise expenses that you make in cash, for freights, duties, carriage, brokerage, porters, etc., shall be credited to cash, and debited to that merchandise for which you have incurred expenses.

JACOB FUGGER

Jacob Fugger (1459–1525) was one of three sons of Johann Fugger, the founder of the famous German merchant dynasty. Jacob's business activities were not confined to trade: he engaged in banking, finance, and manufacturing (mining); advanced loans to private individuals, kings, and the Pope; collected papal revenues from the sale of indulgences and transferred other taxes to Rome. He and his family financed the election of Charles V as Holy Roman Emperor (1519) by advancing the money required for the purchase of the votes of the electors.

Fugger was in every sense a capitalist entrepreneur. His business practices constituted an open challenge to the doctrine of just prices and the prohibition on lending money at interest. After the death of his brothers Ulrich and George, he attempted to gain complete control of their capital himself and made great efforts to ensure that the family partnership would continue after his own death. When, during his last years, relatives suggested to him that the time had come to enjoy his wealth, he is said to have replied that he had no intention of abandoning the business as long as he could make a profit.

The following selections are from Jacob Strieder, *Jacob Fugger the Rich* (New York, The Adelphi Company, 1931).

ARTICLES OF ASSOCIATION BETWEEN JACOB FUGGER AND HIS FOUR NEPHEWS

(December 30, 1512, Augsburg)

I, Jacob Fugger, burgher of Augsburg, hereby announce and make known to all and sundry that the former Ulrich and George Fugger, my beloved brothers, now deceased, and I for a period of several years carried on our fraternal trade together out of our common capital, and according to the property of each; and to that end we severally made contracts mutually binding upon ourselves. . . . These contracts were made in similar terms, and in them we bound ourselves mutually for ourselves and our various heirs in such a way that, if one or two among us three brothers died, the two or one remaining alive among us should determine for the heirs of the deceased what was their capital and their profit or gain. With this decision the heirs should be entirely satisfied, and should demand no further accounting, nor any other reckoning. Also, when one or two among us died, it should remain the same as though he or they still lived; and the same articles should continue to be in force, and the two or one among us who still lived should govern and act, according to these articles, exactly the same as though we all three still lived.

And it has now come to pass, in accordance with the will of the Almighty, that my two beloved brothers are deceased. . . . For that reason, I have now to make an accurate accounting, and an approximate estimate, in accordance with the above-named agreements and articles, to my two deceased brothers' heirs. . . . To all these I must make a distribution and a complete list on account of all the other property of my two above-named deceased brothers, and concerning all this arrange a complete transfer by quittance and in other ways.

For the fraternal association of myself and my two brothers Ulrich and George, in so far as it concerns the common trade, is now ended. In view of all this, and in order that the business begun by us three brothers might the longer continue, and so that our family and name be properly carried on, and my two brothers' sons become familiar with the trade, I have determined to carry on and manage the business myself, and to take industriously in hand my two brothers' sons, namely Ulrich and Hieronymus, sons of my brother Ulrich, and Raimund and Anton, sons of my brother George. I therefore invite them to join me in my common trade and in the Hungarian trade, and hereby do take them in with me in my business, for the six years next following the date of this document, and according to the terms of this agreement, but under no other conditions than the following:

The above-named four, my nephews, shall leave with me in my trade, for profit and loss during the specified time all their capital which is due and owing to them on account of the distribution and of the gain and profit of the trade which their two fathers and I formerly carried on, together with the noble and honorable Hansen and George Thurzo, our brothers-in-law, and otherwise. And this shall have reference to both the landed property and the "Preferred Share." And in my next accounting, which I shall give in the way determined upon by my two deceased brothers and myself in our agreements, they shall accept in their entirety the amounts which I shall allot to them or their heirs, and shall waive all further advances, and shall give me a complete quittance in the matter.

Furthermore shall my above-mentioned four nephews collectively and each in particular recognize and look upon me as the head of this my business, together with such trade as I give them to do and accomplish; they are also faithfully bound to be true and obedient in all things, in whatsoever form and for whatever things this may be required, and to further the trade and business, and to avoid damage and injury to it to the best of their ability, and to hold the business in complete secrecy and tell no one. And the association shall be called *Jacob Fugger und seine Gebrüder Söhne,* or in Italian, *Jacobo Fugger e nepoti.* They, my four above-mentioned nephews, shall also in unison and singly carry on such trade in accordance with my command, and shall do nothing but what I command and give them permission to do. And if I direct one or all of them to do something, and afterward recall it to myself, they shall not dispute it. And what I alone arrange, or bind the association to, to that shall they also none the less be committed, and shall be bound to its accomplishment along with me.

And what the above-named my four nephews collectively or singly shall do, that shall they or he in no way keep secret from me. To that end shall none of them conceal from me the record books or other writings, or their acts, but shall show me all faithfully and without contradiction. The same shall be done by their heirs, should one of them die; and they shall not have the power to enter into trade, nor to seize any writings, nor to conceal or keep them from me.

These my nephews shall further, neither collectively nor singly, carry on any kind of trade, enterprise, or association for themselves, neither among themselves nor with anyone else, without my knowledge and consent. To that end shall none of them, without my knowledge, consent, and desire undertake any kind of responsibility whatever, whether in money or landed property, neither orally, nor in writing, nor in any other way, neither for himself nor among themselves for me or for another outsider; and no matter in what fashion such might take place, it shall nevertheless be entirely void and without force.

Each of my above-named nephews shall also, in my business, render faithfully and truly an account of all his receipts and disbursements and his other dealings, and whatever is lacking in the accounting, he shall make good himself. And whatever any one of them shall for himself require, take, or need, that shall be charged to him. Nevertheless shall none of them without my permission and consent take any considerable amount of money to use for himself, nor take it in any way from the business. When, however, one or more desires money from the business for his need or nourishment, such money I will give and accord to him, but not more than the fourth part of his capital in the six years, but only at one time, and at a time when such payments seem to me to be least disadvantageous or harmful to the business. And the profit and gain for such sums shall then according to reckoning be withheld from him or them.

And since they, my nephews, have not contributed with me in two equal third parts to my Hungarian and other common trade, but I rather have had to contribute the larger share, it shall rest with me, and upon my pleasure, whether I grant and accord to them, for the gain and profit therefrom, anything in excess of their due, and their share in the capital.

And I reserve to myself, and have the right and the full power, in case any of the above-mentioned my four nephews, singly or in several conduct himself or themselves contrary to my pleasure and will or otherwise unfittingly, to dismiss him or them, before the expiration of the six years, or the extension thereof, in the business and the association, without being required to give any cause for my action; or to give them notice within the said six years and before the expiration of the same, or the extension thereof, or at any time that I choose. On the other hand, my nephews shall not have the power, singly or together, to do the same before the expiration of the six years or the extension thereof. And during the six years before the expiration of the same, or after the expiration of the six years, or as I may desire during the six years to dismiss from the trade, or give notice to one or more of my said nephews, or in case one or more dies during the six years or the extension thereof, then or otherwise, whenever I desire, for a long or short period, I shall and will have full power to close up all the business, affairs, and accounts that are then outstanding, and to reckon them up; and when I have thus done and reckoned, to say to them and their heirs how much belongs to each of them or their heirs. And with what I allot or reckon to each of them or the heirs of the same, they and their heirs shall be entirely satisfied, content, and appeased, without making any controversy, and shall accept that, and shall demand no further accounting nor anything else, but shall accord complete belief to my simple word. And the payment in the said case, both of capital and of profit, to whom it may belong, shall take place in six successive Frankfurt fairs, a sixth part at each fair; but in all the said cases, when the allotment and payment shall take place through me, it shall rest with me whether I divide and give over to them singly or together, or to the heirs of the same, debts or goods in making the payment, and how they shall be appraised or valued. And also after notice of the payment has been given, such money shall no longer lie for profit or for loss.

When then the six years have passed and expired, and in the meantime by me alone or after the six years by me and my nephews, the above-mentioned further contract has not been made, or I have not concluded another one with them, then this shall hold another three years after the expiration of the six years; and further, if after the expiration of the said three years, I have not further contracted with them, then it shall continue further. In case I should die in the six years, or during the time of the extension, then my two nephews,

Ulrich and Raimund, shall sign my name as it is now done, and shall have the power to carry on the business and the association, to handle money, debts, and goods, as though I were still living, and shall alone do and have all the power and the right which I have toward themselves, their brothers, and their and my heirs to make an accounting, statements, estimates, and deliveries; and shall not be disputed therein by my heirs nor by anyone else, but these shall trust and believe their simple word.

They, my two nephews, Ulrich and Raimund, shall not be hurried by my heirs for what is due to me from the business for capital and profit, but they, my two nephews, shall as stated above between themselves make an accounting and in one year or one and one-half years after my death shall make it known to my heirs, and then, in accordance with the announcement, in three years at six successive Frankfurt fairs shall make complete payment. . . .

I, Jacob Fugger, burgher of Augsburg, acknowledge in further confirmation all the above with this my own signature, and that this document is thus, with all its contents above described, by me declared, done, and arranged, and is sealed by me and others therein named, on account of my request.

EMPEROR MAXIMILIAN TO HIS GOVERNMENT AT INNSBRUCK

(May 20, 1515, Augsburg)

To my noble, honorable, learned, and faithful subjects. Several years since, for excellent reasons, we decided in secret, for our own good, and the good of our House and the House of Austria, upon two marriages between our son and daughter and the daughter and son of King Vladislaw of Hungary and Behaim. In connection therewith we procured a promise that, after the death of said King Vladislaw, until the time when his children came of age, the administration of the Crown of Hungary and Behaim should fall to us. We further determined to draw up the contracts necessary on both sides, and to exchange them; but still to keep the whole arrangement secret. And then we would both meet, so that the arrangement could be made public, and the betrothing of the children to one another be partially carried out, and all the above sworn to by the subjects of both of us. . . .

We have therefore concluded that our meeting should take place, and that in particular the daughter of the King of Hungary should be delivered into our hands. When we reached this conclusion, we sent our friend Von Gurgk again to both kings at Bresburg, so that he might make final arrangements with them, and provide for a meeting of all three of us with our children. . . .

Since, however, we require, as we noted above, for such a procedure a considerable sum of money, and since our treasury is almost exhausted, we must do what we can, and finance ourselves in whatever way is possible. For this reason, and on the above-mentioned grounds, we have made a financial deal with our counselor, Jacob Fugger, through two letters, which we herewith forward to you. . . .

Now as we know and realize with what considerable sums of money you have formerly helped us and how as a result our treasury is practically exhausted, we would gladly spare you; nevertheless, you are asked to consider of what importance these agreements are with Hungary, Behaim, and Poland, and in particular the marriage. And more especially since we are well informed that if we do not conclude this matter now, and meet with our royal brothers, that no arrangement will be possible in future, and the marriage will fall through, and the daughter will not be given to us; and furthermore that the two kings, as well as their kingdoms, lands, and people, will become declared enemies of our lands and people, and will ally themselves with the Venetians, strengthening and abetting the latter, so that we will be unable to conclude peace. In addition, we would certainly have the war in our Austrian lands at once; we are, indeed, unable to say to you how disadvantageous and weakening it would be to us if the above-mentioned dealings should fall through. But you can conceive it for yourselves. . . . And for these reasons, we request you to accept the proposed loan with the above-mentioned Fugger, . . . and not to refuse it nor delay it. For in the gracious trust which we repose in you, we have counted upon this in our financial plans, and have arranged our affairs and departure accordingly, and have so planned for us and our family, and have also sent word to the princes and arranged with them that, so soon as our friend, Cardinal von Gurgk writes that the main agreement with the two kings, and the fact of our meeting have been concluded, we are to move on immediately. But we cannot do this unless the loan from the Fuggers is carried through. For without this we cannot go on, but will have to drop all the above dealings with both kings, and abandon the plan for our and their children, and cancel all the arrangements; and it will probably bring about the disadvantages and injuries suggested above if we finally abandon our meeting with them. If we knew any other method of finance, we would have been only too glad to have spared you this; but we know of no other way.

CHRISTOPHER COLUMBUS

WHILE EUROPEAN COMMUNICATIONS with the Far East existed prior to the great burst of exploration in the late fifteenth and early sixteenth centuries, they were relatively scattered and minor compared to the rapid expansion for which they paved the way. Under the systematic leadership of Prince Henry the Navigator (1394–1460), the Portuguese pressed down to but did not round the great hump of Africa. In the next sixty years a new world was discovered, and Asia had been approached from both east and west.

The following selections are intended to throw light on the ideas and motives of the explorers and their backers, and on the shifts in state power that were inherent in the fact of European expansion overseas in the fifteenth and sixteenth centuries. They are translated by C. R. Markham in *The Journal of Christopher Columbus*, Vol. LXXXVI of the *Works Issued by the Hakluyt Society* (London, 1893). The letter of Paolo Toscanelli, a Florentine astronomer and the leading authority on navigation of his age, is from the Latin; the selections from the *Journal* are from the Spanish.

※

LETTER OF PAOLO TOSCANELLI TO COLUMBUS, 1474

PAUL, THE PHYSICIAN, to Cristobal Colombo greeting. I perceive your magnificent and great desire to find a way to where the spices grow, and in reply to your letter I send you the copy of another letter which I wrote, some days ago, to a friend and favourite of the most serene King of Portugal before the wars of Castille, in reply to another which, by direction of his Highness, he wrote to me on the said subject, and I send you another sea chart like the one I sent him, by which you will be satisfied respecting your enquiries: which copy is as follows:

Paul, the Physician, to Fernan Martins, Canon at Lisbon, greeting. It was pleasant to me to understand that your health was good, and that you are in the favour and intimacy with the most generous and most magnificent Prince, your King. I have already spoken with you respecting a shorter way to the places of spices than that which you take by Guinea, by means of maritime navigation. The most serene King now seeks from me some statement, or rather a demonstration to the eye, by which the slightly learned may take in and understand that way. I know this can be shown from the spherical shape of the earth, yet, to make the comprehension of it easier, and to facilitate the work, I have determined to show that way by means of a sailing chart. I, therefore, send to his Majesty a chart made by my own hands, on which are delineated your coasts and islands, whence you must begin to make your journey always westward, and the places at which you should arrive, and how far from the pole or the equinoctial line you ought to keep, and through how much space or over how many miles you should arrive at those most fertile places full of all sorts of spices and jewels. You must not be surprised if I call the parts where the spices are west, when they usually call them east, because to those always sailing west, those parts are found by navigation on the under side of the earth. But if by land and by the upper side, they will always be found to the east. The straight lines shown lengthways on the map indicate the distance from east to west, and those that are drawn across show the spaces from south to north. I have also noted on the map several places at which you may arrive for the better information of navigators, if they should reach a place different from what was expected, by reason of the wind or any other cause; and also that they may show some acquaintance with the country to the natives, which ought to be sufficiently agreeable to them. It is asserted that none but merchants live on the islands. For there the number of navigators with merchandise is so great that in all the rest of the world there are not so many as in one most noble port called Zaitun [in China]. For they affirm that a hundred ships laden with pepper discharge their cargoes in that port in a single year, besides other ships bringing other spices. That country is very populous and very rich, with a multitude of provinces and kingdoms, and with cities without number, under one prince who is called Great Kan, which name signifies *Rex Regum* in Latin, whose seat and residence is generally in the province Katay. His ancestors desired intercourse with Christians now 200 years ago. They sent to the Pope and asked for several persons learned in the faith, that they might be enlightened, but those who were sent, being impeded in their journey, went back. Also in the time of Eugenius one of them came to Eugenius, who affirmed their great kindness towards Christians, and I had a long conversation with him on many subjects, about the magnitude of their rivers in length and breadth, and on the multitude of cities on the banks of the rivers. He said that on one river there were near 200 cities with marble bridges great in length and breadth, and everywhere adorned with columns. This country is worth seeking by the Latins, not only because great wealth may be obtained from it, gold and silver, all sorts of gems, and spices, which never reach us; but also on account of its learned men, philosophers, and expert astrologers, and by what skill and art so powerful and magnificent a province is governed, as well as how their wars are conducted. This is for some satisfaction to his request, so far as the shortness of time and my occupations admitted: being ready in future more fully to satisfy his royal Majesty as far as he may wish.

Given at Florence, June 24th, 1474.

From the city of Lisbon due west there are 26 spaces marked on the map, each of which has 250 miles, as far as the most noble and very great city of Quinsay. For it is a hundred miles in circumference and has ten bridges, and its name signifies the city of Heaven; many wonders being related concerning it, touching the multitude of its handicrafts and resources. This space is almost a third part of the whole sphere. That city is in the province of Mangi, or near the province Katay, in which land is the royal residence. But from the island Antilia, known to you, to the most noble island of Cippangue [1] there are ten spaces. For that island is most fertile in gold, pearls, and precious stones, and they cover the temples and palaces with solid gold. Thus the spaces of sea to be crossed to the unknown parts are not great. Many things might perhaps have been declared more exactly, but a diligent thinker will be able to clear up the rest for himself. Farewell, most excellent one.

FROM THE JOURNAL OF THE FIRST VOYAGE OF COLUMBUS, 1492

Prologue: to the King and Queen of Spain

Because, O most Christian, and very high, very excellent, and puissant Princes, King and Queen of the Spains and of the islands of the Sea, our Lords, in this present year of 1492, after your Highnesses had given an end to the war with the Moors who reigned in Europe, and had finished it in the very great city of Granada, where in this present year, on the second day of the month of January, by force of arms, I saw the royal banners of your Highnesses placed on the towers of Alhambra, which is the fortress of that city, and I saw the Moorish King come forth from the gates of the city and kiss the royal hands of your Highnesses, and of the Prince my Lord, and presently in that same month, acting on the information that I had given to your Highnesses touching the lands of India, and respecting a Prince who is called *Gran Can,* which means in our language King of Kings, how he and his ancestors had sent to Rome many times to ask for learned men of our holy faith to teach him, and how the Holy Father had never complied, insomuch that many people believing in idolatries were lost by receiving doctrine of perdition: *Your Highnesses,* as Catholic Christians and Princes who love the holy Christian faith, and the propagation of it, and who are enemies to the sect of Mahoma and to all idolatries and heresies, resolved to send me, Cristobal Colon, to the said parts of India to see the said princes, and the cities and lands, and their disposition, with a view that they might be converted to our holy faith; and ordered that I should not go by land to the eastward, as had been customary, but that I should go by way of the west, whither up to this day, we do not know for certain that any one has gone.

Thus, after having turned out all the Jews from all your kingdoms and lord-

[1] [Japan.]

ships, in the same month of January, your Highnesses gave orders to me that with a sufficient fleet I should go to the said parts of India, and for this they made great concessions to me, and ennobled me, so that henceforward I should be called Don, and should be Chief Admiral of the Ocean Sea, perpetual Viceroy and Governor of all the islands and continents that I should discover and gain, and that I might hereafter discover and gain in the Ocean Sea, and that my eldest son should succeed, and so on from generation to generation for ever.

I left the city of Granada on the 12th day of May, in the same year of 1492, being Saturday, and came to the town of Palos, which is a seaport; where I equipped three vessels well suited for such service; and departed from that port, well supplied with provisions and with many sailors, on the 3d day of August of the same year, being Friday, half an hour before sunrise, taking the route to the islands of Canaria, belonging to your Highnesses, which are in the said Ocean Sea, that I might thence take my departure for navigating until I should arrive at the Indies, and give the letters of your Highnesses to those princes, so as to comply with my orders. As part of my duty I thought it well to write an account of all the voyage very punctually, noting from day to day all that I should do and see, and that should happen, as will be seen further on. Also, Lords Princes, I resolved to describe each night what passed in the day, and to note each day how I navigated at night. I propose to construct a new chart for navigating, on which I shall delineate all the sea and lands of the Ocean in their proper positions under their bearings; and further, I propose to prepare a book, and to put down all as it were in a picture, by latitude from the equator, and western longitude. Above all, I shall have accomplished much, for I shall forget sleep, and shall work at the business of navigation, that so the service may be performed; all which will entail great labour.

Monday, 12th of November. . . . The Admiral says that, on the previous Sunday, the 11th of November, it seemed good to take some persons from amongst those at *Rio de Mares,* to bring to the Sovereigns, that they might learn our language, so as to be able to tell us what there is in their lands. Returning, they would be the mouthpieces of the Christians, and would adopt our customs and the things of the faith, "I saw and knew (says the Admiral) that these people are without any religion, not idolaters, but very gentle, not knowing what is evil, nor the sins of murder and theft, being without arms, and so timid that a hundred would fly before one Spaniard, although they joke with them. They, however, believe and know that there is a God in heaven, and say that we have come from heaven. At any prayer that we say, they repeat, and make the sign of the cross. Thus your Highnesses should resolve to make them Christians, for I believe that, if the work was begun, in a little time a multitude of nations would be converted to our faith, with the acquisition of great lordships, peoples, and riches for Spain. Without doubt, there is in these lands a vast quantity of gold, and the Indians I have on board do not speak without reason when they say that in these islands there are places where they dig out gold, and wear it on their necks, ears, arms, and legs, the rings being very large. There are also precious stones, pearls, and an infinity of spices. In this river of Mares, whence we departed to-night, there is undoubtedly a great quantity of mastick, and much more could be raised, because the trees may be planted, and will yield abundantly. The leaf and fruit are like the mastick, but the tree and leaf are larger. As Pliny describes it, I have seen it on the island of Chios in the Archipelago. I ordered many of these trees to be tapped, to see if any of them would yield resin; but, as it rained all the time I was in that river, I could not get any, except a very little, which I am bringing to your Highnesses. It may not be the right season for tapping, which is, I believe, when the trees come forth after winter and begin to flower. But when I was there the fruit was nearly ripe. Here also there is a great quantity of cotton, and I believe it would have a good sale here without sending it to Spain, but to the great cities of the Gran Can, which will be discovered without doubt, and many others ruled over by other lords, who will be pleased to serve your Highnesses, and whither will be brought other commodities of Spain and of the Eastern lands; but these are to the west as regards us. There is also here a great yield of aloes, though this is not a commodity that will yield great profit. The mastick, however, is important, for it is only obtained from the said island of Chios, and I believe the harvest is worth 50,000 ducats, if I remember right. There is here, in the mouth of the river, the best port I have seen up to this time, wide, deep, and clear of rocks. It is an excellent site for a town and fort, for any ship could come close up to the walls; the land is high, with a temperate climate, and very good water.

Tuesday, 27th of November. . . . The Admiral also says:—"How great the benefit that is to be derived from this country would be, I cannot say. It is certain that where there are such lands there must be an infinite number of things that would be profitable. But I did not remain long in one port, because I wished to see as much of the country as possible, in order to make a report upon it to your Highnesses; and besides, I do not know the language, and these people neither understand me nor any other in my company; while the Indians I have on board often misunderstand. Moreover, I have not been able to see much of the natives, because they often take to flight. But now, if our Lord pleases, I will see as much as possible, and will proceed by little and little, learning and comprehending; and I will make some of my followers learn the language. For I have perceived that there is only one language up to this point. After they understand the advantages, I shall labour to make all these people Christians. They will become so readily, because they have no religion nor idolatry, and your Highnesses will send orders to build a city and fortress, and to convert the people. I assure your Highnesses that it does not appear to me that there can be a more fertile country nor a better climate under the sun, with abundant supplies of water. . . . If it will please God that your Highnesses should send learned men out here, they will see the truth of all I have said. I have related already how good a place *Rio de Mares* would be for a town and fortress, and this is perfectly true; but it bears no comparison with this place, nor with the *Mar de Nuestra Señora*. For here there must be a large population, and very valuable productions, which I hope to discover before I return to Castille. I say that if Christendom will find profit among these people, how much more will Spain, to whom the whole country should be subject. Your Highnesses ought not to consent that any stranger should trade here, or put his foot in the country, except Catholic Christians, for this was the beginning and end of the undertaking; namely, the increase and glory of the Christian religion, and that no other should come to these parts who was not a good Christian."

THE NEW WORLD

AMONG NEW WORLD COLONIZERS the Spaniards were those most dedicated to transplanting fully blown their metropolitan culture, and before long the grandeur of Mexico City and Lima outshone imperial Madrid. Spain was, therefore, the nation that most conscientiously endeavored to reconcile American conditions with enshrined European canons of government. The larger dimensions of the Spanish enterprise, Spain's evangelical mission in the New World (by the Papal Bull of 1493), and, in the sixteenth century, Spain's self-appointed role as defender of the faith against Lutheranism, made it urgent to legitimize formally the conquest. So too did the fact that the Aztecs and Incas, unlike Indians of forest and plain, were not to be driven away, exterminated, or summarily assimilated. Their complex social organization, already adapted for intensive economic production, had to be rendered intelligible in European terms and then fitted into the Spanish imperium.

Issues arising from the conquest were debated at Valladolid, Spain, in 1550–51 by Bartolomé de Las Casas—a Dominican friar, bishop of Chiapa (Guatemala), and official "Protector of the Indians"—and the learned humanist, Juan Ginés de Sepúlveda. Proceedings of the debate, which was convoked by Emperor Charles V to determine Spain's subsequent policy of conquest, are available only in a summary. The central points, however, appear in the selections which follow. Sepúlveda's *Democrates alter* (*The Second Democrates*, sequel to an earlier dialogue with "Democrates") was written in 1547 and immediately provoked the wrath of Las Casas. The latter had begun compiling his *Apologetic History of the Indies* in 1527; in 1550 this voluminous work, virtually completed, furnished his arguments for the polemic. The *Thirty Very Juridical Propositions,* published in 1552, are the most succinct statement of Las Casas's views regarding Spain's jurisdiction in the New World.

Sepúlveda (1490–1574), whose writings typified Renaissance elegance and erudition, studied in Bologna under the neo-Aristotelian, Pietro Pomponazzi. He was eminent as a theologian, jurist, philosopher, Hellenist, historian, and astronomer. Just before the debate he had published his translation of Aristotle's *Politics,* a source which both disputants freely interpreted. Las Casas (1474–1566) studied at Salamanca and in 1502 sailed to the West Indies; here he was ordained a priest and like any Spaniard of distinction received an allotment of Indians for labor. In a sudden conversion (1514) he found using such labor repugnant. The rest of his long and strenuous life he devoted to the Indian cause, writing treatises and histories in their defense, undertaking pacific missionary and colonizing ventures, making repeated appeals in person before the king and his councilors. From his highly exaggerated *Very Brief Relation of the Destruction of the Indies* (1552) derives much of the Spaniards' fame as brutal colonizers; the Spanish "New Laws" of 1542, however, promulgated largely at the behest of Las Casas himself, declared the Indian to be an unenslaveable freeman and are among the most humane codes of their kind.

The judges of the Las Casas–Sepúlveda debate rendered no formal decision. Las Casas, however, retained official favor; his opponent's *Democrates alter* was denied publication and reached print only in 1892. (The *Apologetic History* was not printed until 1909, but others of Las Casas's works circulated freely during his life.) Unlike Negroes, whose enslavement even Las Casas for a short time condoned, the Indians remained free vassals of the crown for two and a half centuries.

As might be expected, the humanitarianism of the Spanish crown was disingenuous. To enforce beneficent labor codes was to restrict the free action of privileged Spaniards in the New World, making the crown a final arbiter; and free Indians, unlike slaves, paid tribute to the royal treasury. It is difficult, however, to explain away the influence on Spanish policy of such men as Las Casas.

A "case study" of the effect of the meeting of Europeans and American natives can be found in the work of Bernal Díaz del Castillo, *The Conquest of New Spain.* Díaz (c.1492–c.1581), a Spanish soldier, conquistador, and historian, first arrived in the New World in 1514 with an expedition to Panama and three years later, after a stay in Cuba, participated in the discovery of Yucatan. In 1518 he enlisted with Hernan Cortés under whom he fought during the Spanish conquest of Mexico. Offended by the "official" history of this war written by Cortés' chaplain, Francisco López de Gómara, who had, in Díaz' opinion, given excessive credit to the commander and insufficient recognition to his officers and men, Díaz eventually settled in Guatemala where he wrote his own fresh and vivid account of the wars and colonization under the title *The True History of the Conquest of New Spain,* which carries the story to 1568.

The selection from Sepúlveda has been translated into English from the original Latin and the Spanish translation that are given in the *Boletín de la Real Academia de la Historia,* Vol. XXI (October, 1892). The Las Casas selections have been translated from the Spanish of the *Apologética historia de las Indias* (Madrid, 1909) and the *Treinta proposiciones muy jurídicas* (given in *Fray Bartolomé de las Casas: Doctrina,* ed. by Agustín Yáñez; Mexico City, 1941, pp. 33–51).

JUAN GINÉS DE SEPÚLVEDA: DEMOCRATES ALTER; OR, ON THE JUST CAUSES FOR WAR AGAINST THE INDIANS

To His Excellency Don Luis de Mendoza, Count of Tendilla and Marquis of Mondejar

Whether the war by means of which the rulers of Spain and our country-men have brought and are attempting to bring under their domination the barbarian inhabitants, commonly known as Indians, of the lands to the west and south is just or unjust and upon what legal right the domination of these peoples is based is, as you know, noble Marquis, a most important question. . . . And since I have said several things pertaining to this question in another dialogue, entitled *Democrates I*, . . . I thought it convenient to have the same characters carry on a discussion in my orchard on the banks of the Pisuerga, so that by repeating such opinions as are necessary they might cap the controversy which we have begun concerning the rights of waging war. One of these disputants, the German Leopold, somewhat contaminated by Lutheran errors, begins to speak in this manner:

L. I shall tell you a thousand and one times, Democrates, that there is no argument strong enough to convince me that war is lawful, much less among Christians. You surely remember that we have already argued this point for three long days in Rome, at the Vatican. . . .

D. Then, what new questions relating to this matter of the right to wage war do you wish to ask me?

L. Very few, but certainly not without merit. A few days ago, while I was strolling with some other friends in the palace of Prince Philip, Hernán Cortés, the Marquis del Valle, happened to pass, and upon seeing him, we began to speak at length about the deeds which he and others of the Emperor's cap-tains had accomplished in those lands to the west which were completely un-known to the ancient inhabitants of our world. These events surprised me mightily because of their grandeur and novelty and for being so unexpected; but thinking about them further, I was seized by a doubt, to wit, whether it was congruous with justice and Christian charity that the Spaniards should have made war on those innocent mortals who had caused them no harm. I wish to know, therefore, what you think about this and other similar wars which are waged without any reason or aim except for mere whim and greed. And I also want you to explain succinctly, with the clarity peculiar to your outstanding mind and subtle understanding, all the possible causes for a just war, and then to resolve the question in a few words.

D. . . . In the first place, one must keep in mind a principle which is the basis of this and many other questions: everything which is done in the name of natural rights or laws can also be done by virtue of divine rights or evangelical laws. When Christ tells us in the Gospels not to resist the evil-doer and, if someone strikes us upon one cheek, to turn the other . . . , we should not believe that he was attempting to do away with the laws of nature which permit one to resist force with force within the limits of a just defense. . . . Those words from the Bible are not laws in the obligatory sense of the word, but rather advice and exhortation which do not belong so much to everyday life as to apostolic perfection. . . .

I wish to make it clear that one should search not only in Christians and in the writings of the New Testament, but also in those philosophers whom we judge to have dealt most wisely with nature and the customs and governments of all societies, especially in the writings of Aristotle, whose precepts, except for a few opinions referring to matters beyond the capacity of human understanding, and which man can understand only through divine revelation, have been received by posterity with such unanimous approval that they no longer seem to be the words of a single philosopher, but the decisions and opinions held in common by all wise men.

L. Let us return, then, to the business at hand. Now show me the reasons, if there are any, by which you believe that war can be undertaken and waged in a just and pious manner.

D. A just war requires not only just causes for its undertaking, but also legitimate authority and upright spirit in whoever declares it and a proper manner in its conduct. . . .

L. . . . But what happens if a ruler, moved not by avarice or thirst for power, but by the narrowness of the borders of his state or by its poverty, should wage war upon his neighbors in order to seize their fields as an almost necessary prize?

D. That would not be war but theft. For a war to be just, the causes must be just. . . . Among the causes of a just war the most important, as well as the most natural, is that of repelling force with force when it is not possible to proceed in any other fashion. . . . The second cause of a just war is the recovery of things seized unjustly. . . . It is licit to recover not only one's own things which have been unjustly stolen, but also those of friends, and to defend them and keep them free from harm as much as if they were one's own. The third cause of a just war is to punish evil-doers who have not been punished in their own cities, or have been punished with negligence, so that . . . they will take heed and not commit their crimes a second time, and others will be frightened by their example. It would be easy to enumerate here the many wars waged by the Greeks and Romans for this reason, with much approval from the people, whose consensus must be considered to be a law of nature. . . .

There are other causes of just wars less clear and less frequent, but not therefore less just or based any less on natural and divine law, and one of them is the conquest by arms, if no other way is possible, of those who by natural condition must obey others and refuse to do so. The greatest philosophers state that this type of war is just according to the laws of nature. . . .

L. And who is born under such an unlucky star that nature condemned him to servitude? What difference do you find between having nature force one under the rule of another and being a slave by nature? Do you think that judges, who also pay much attention to natural law in many cases, are joking when they point out that all men since the beginning were born free, and that slavery was introduced contrary to nature and as a law of mere humans?

D. I believe that the jurist speaks with seriousness and great prudence, but this word slavery means quite a different thing for the jurist than for the philosopher. For the former slavery is an accidental thing, born of superior strength and from the laws of peoples, sometimes from civil laws, while philosophers see slavery as inferior intelligence along with inhuman and barbarous customs. . . .

Those who surpass the rest in prudence and talent, although not in physical strength, are by nature the masters. Those, on the other hand, who are retarded or slow to understand, although they may have the physical strength necessary for the fulfilment of all their necessary obligations, are by nature slaves, and it is proper and useful that they be so, for we even see it sanctioned in divine law itself, because it is written in the Book of Proverbs that he who is a fool shall serve the wise. . . . If they reject such rule, then it can be imposed upon them by means of arms, and such a war will be just according to the laws of nature. Aristotle said, "It seems that war arises in a certain sense from nature, since a part of it is the art of the hunt, which is properly used not only against animals, but also against those men who, having been born to obey, reject servitude: such a war is just according to nature. . . ."

L. If, by the laws of nature, the reign is to be reserved for the more prudent and virtuous men, suppose that the kingdom of Tunis (I wish to seek examples of misfortune among the infidels and not among our own peoples) were to fall, by virtue of patrimony and by rights of age, into the hands of a prince less prudent and virtuous than his younger brothers. Do you not think, according to your doctrine, that the kingdom should be given to the best of all of them and not to the least worthy?

D. If we seek the truth, Leopold, and heed only what is sought by reason and natural order, we shall have to say that sovereignty should always be in the hands of the wisest and most prudent, because the only true realm is one that is always governed by very prudent men and those who look after the welfare of the people. . . . But the happiness of man is not such that things which are in essence the best can always be accomplished without great inconveniences. According to physicians, it is of prime importance that the good humors dominate in the human body so that it will be maintained in its natural, healthy state, and when the contrary occurs, and the bad and corrupt humors dominate, they do not overlook any available means to remedy this disorder by purging the bad humors; but if there is the danger that in so doing there will be produced in the entire body a greater upheaval, doctors prudently abstain from undertaking so dangerous a cure, not because they are unaware that such a perversion of the humors is evil and contrary to nature, but because they prefer that the man live, even though in bad health, and not perish entirely. . . .

L. According to your opinion, Democrates, in order for a war to be considered just, a worthy aim and upright conduct are required, but this war against the barbarians, as I understand it, is not even undertaken with good intentions, since those who have started it have no other aim than that of acquiring, by right or wrong, the largest possible amount of gold and silver. . . . And since the Spanish do not wage this war justly or rationally, but with great cruelty and injury to the barbarians, and in the manner of a theft, there is no doubt that the Spanish are obliged to restore to the barbarians the things which they have seized, no less than must highwaymen what they have robbed from travelers.

D. One who condones the rule of a prince or nation over his or its citizens and subjects, Leopold, must not therefore have it thought that he approves of the sins of all their prefects and ministers. . . . And indeed it is not certain that everyone has waged war in this fashion if various reports which I have recently read concerning the conquest of New Spain [Mexico] are true. . . .

You can well understand, Leopold, if you know the customs and manners of different peoples, that the Spanish have a perfect right to rule these barbarians of the New World and the adjacent islands, who in prudence, skill, virtues, and humanity are as inferior to the Spanish as children to adults, or women to men, for there exists between the two as great a difference as between savage and cruel races and the most merciful, between the most intemperate and the moderate and temperate and, I might even say, between apes and men.

You surely do not expect me to recall at length the prudence and talents of the Spanish, since, as I believe, you have read Lucan, Silius Italicus, the two Senecas; and after these St. Isidore, inferior to no one in the field of theology, as in philosophy Averroes and Avempace excelled, and King Alfonso in astronomy, omitting many others who would be too many to enumerate. And who can ignore the other virtues of our people: strength, humanity, justice, and religion? . . . And what can I say of temperance, in greed as well as in lust, when there is hardly a nation in Europe which can be compared to Spain as concerns frugality and sobriety? And if it is true that in recent times I see that through commercial dealings with foreigners extravagance has invaded the tables of the mighty, nevertheless, just as good men reprove this, one must hope that in a short time there will be reestablished the pure and innate parsimony of our native customs. And as for that pertaining to the second part of temperance, even though the philosophers say that warlike men are quite taken with the pleasures of Venus, nonetheless, our soldiers, even in their personal vices and sins, are not accustomed to act contrary to the laws of nature. . . . And what can I say of the gentleness and humanity of our people, who, even in battle, after having gained the victory, put forth their greatest effort and care to save the greatest possible number of the conquered and to protect them from the cruelty of their allies?

Compare, then, these gifts of prudence, talent, magnanimity, temperance, humanity, and religion with those possessed by these half-men (*homunculi*), in whom you will barely find the vestiges of humanity, who not only do not possess any learning at all, but are not even literate or in possession of any monument to their history except for some obscure and vague reminiscences of several things put down in various paintings; nor do they have written laws, but barbarian institutions and customs. Well, then, if we are dealing with virtue, what temperance or mercy can you expect from men who are committed to all types of intemperance and base frivolity, and eat human flesh? And do not believe that before the arrival of the Christians they lived in that pacific kingdom of Saturn which the poets have invented; for, on the contrary, they waged continual and ferocious war upon one another with such fierceness that they did not consider a victory at all worthwhile unless they sated their monstrous hunger with the flesh of their enemies. This bestiality is among them even more prodigious for their great distance from the land of the Scythians, who also fed upon human bodies, and since furthermore these Indians were otherwise so cowardly and timid that they could barely endure the presence of our soldiers, and many times thousands upon thousands of them scattered in flight like women before Spaniards so few that they did not even number one hundred. . . . Although some of them show a certain ingenuity for various works of artisanship, this is no proof of human cleverness, for we can observe animals, birds, and spiders making certain structures which no human accomplishment can competently imitate. And as for the way of life of the inhabitants of New Spain and the province of Mexico, I have already said that these people are considered the most civilized of all, and they themselves take pride in their public institutions, because they have cities erected in a rational manner and kings who are not hereditary but elected by popular vote, and among themselves they carry on commercial activities in the manner of civilized peoples. But see how they deceive themselves, and how much I dissent from such an opinion, seeing, on the contrary, in these very institutions a proof of the crudity, the barbarity, and the natural slavery of these people; for having houses and some rational way of life and some sort of commerce is a thing which the necessities of nature itself induce, and only serves to prove that they are not bears or monkeys and are not totally lacking in reason. But on the other hand, they have established their nation in such a way that no one possesses anything individually, neither a house nor a field, which he can leave to his heirs in his will, for everything belongs to their masters whom, with improper nomenclature, they call kings, and by whose whims they live, more than by their own, ready to do the bidding and desire of these rulers and possessing no liberty. And the fulfilment of all this, not under the pressure of arms but in a voluntary and spontaneous way, is a definite sign of the servile and base soul of these barbarians. They have distributed the land in such a way that they themselves cultivate the royal and public holdings, one part belonging to the king, another to public feasts and sacrifices, with only a third reserved for their own advantage, and all this is done in such a way that they live as employees of the king, paying, thanks to him, exceedingly high taxes. . . . And if this type of servile and barbarous nation had not been to their liking and nature, it would have been easy for them, as it was not a hereditary monarchy, to take advantage of the death of a king in order to obtain a freer state and one more favorable to their interests; by not doing so, they have stated quite clearly that they have been born to slavery and not to civic and liberal life. Therefore, if you wish to reduce them, I do not say to our domination, but to a servitude a little less harsh, it will not be difficult for them to change their masters, and instead of the ones they had, who were barbarous and impious and inhuman, to accept the Christians, cultivators of human virtues and the true faith. . . .

When pagans are nothing more than pagans, and cannot be accused of anything more than not being Christians, which is what we call disbelief, there is no just reason to punish them or attack them with arms. Therefore, if there were to be found in the New World some enlightened people, civilized and humane, who worshiped not idols but the true God according to the law of nature, . . . even though they were not familiar with the Gospels or in possession of the Christian faith, it would seem that a war against this people would be illicit. . . .

L. I do not fully understand, Democrates, what you mean in this case by natural law, unless you say that it is observed by those who abstain from mortal sin and other like infamies, no matter how many other grave crimes they may commit. Even in this form you will find very few people who observe natural law. . . .

D. Do not worry uselessly, Leopold. The gravest sins are doubtless those committed against the law of nature, but be careful of drawing from this rash conclusions about nations in general; if in any of them there are some who sin against natural laws, this is no reason for saying that this nation does not observe natural law, because the public cause is to be considered not individually in each man but in public customs and institutions. . . .

L. Do you think, consequently, that pagans can be compelled to receive the faith in spite of the fact that St. Augustine denies this . . . ?

D. If I were so to believe there would be high authorities who would support my views, and I would still maintain that this was a great work of charity, for what greater benefit can one give a man than to communicate to him the faith of Christ? But since the will, as I have pointed out before, without which there is no room for faith, cannot be forced, it does not please St. Augustine and other great theologians to see undertaken this work, so great but sometimes so pernicious, of demanding the baptism of those who refuse it, or of their children, who, for the most part, are accustomed to follow the will of their fathers. I do not say, then, that they should be baptized by force, but that as far as it rests with us they be brought back from the edge of the precipice and be shown the way of truth by means of pious teachings and evangelical preachings, and as this does not seem possible to accomplish by any other way than first subjecting them to our rule, especially in times such as these, when preachers of the faith and miracles are so rare, I believe that the barbarians can be conquered within the same right which makes them compelled to hear the words of the Gospels. . . . These apostles are, then, the successors of the other apostles, that is, bishops and priests of the Church and preachers in all that pertains to the duties of preaching, and how can they preach to these barbarians if they are not sent to them, as St. Paul says, and how are they to be sent if these barbarians are not conquered first?

BARTOLOMÉ DE LAS CASAS: APOLOGETIC HISTORY OF THE INDIES

Apologetic and Summary History Treating the Qualities, Disposition, Description, Skies and Soil of These Lands; and the Natural Conditions, Governance, Nations, Ways of Life and Customs of the Peoples of These Western and Southern Indies, Whose Sovereign Realm Belongs to the Monarchs of Castile

ARGUMENT OF THE WORK

The ultimate cause for writing this work was to gain knowledge of all the many nations of this vast new world. They had been defamed by persons who feared neither God nor the charge, so grievous before divine judgment, of defaming even a single man and causing him to lose his esteem and honor. From such slander can come great harm and terrible calamity, particularly when large numbers of men are concerned and, even more so, a whole new world. It has been written that these peoples of the Indies, lacking human governance and ordered nations, did not have the power of reason to govern themselves—which was inferred only from their having been found to be gentle, patient and humble. It has been implied that God became careless in creating so immense a number of rational souls and let human nature, which He so largely determined and provided for, go astray in the almost infinitesimal part of the human lineage which they comprise. From this it follows that they have all proven themselves unsocial and therefore monstrous, contrary to the natural bent of all peoples of the world; and that He did not allow any other species of corruptible creature to err in this way, excepting a strange and occasional case. In order to demonstrate the truth, which is the opposite, this book brings together and compiles [certain natural, special and accidental causes which are specified below in Chapter CCLXIII]. . . . Not only have [the Indians] shown themselves to be very wise peoples and possessed of lively and marked understanding, prudently governing and providing for their nations (as much as they can be nations, without faith in or knowledge of the true God) and making them prosper in justice; but they have equalled many diverse nations of the world, past and present, that have been praised for their governance, politics and customs, and exceed by no small measure the wisest of all these, such as the Greeks and Romans, in adherence to the rules of natural reason. This advantage and superiority, along with everything said above, will appear quite clearly when, if it please God, the peoples are compared one with another. This history has been written with the aforesaid aim in mind by Fray Bartolomé de Las Casas, or Casaus, a monk of the Dominican Order and some-time bishop of Chiapa, who promises before the divine word that everything said and referred to is the truth, and that nothing of an untruthful nature appears to the best of his knowledge.

CHAPTER CXXVII. THE INDIANS POSSESSED MORE ENLIGHTENMENT AND NATURAL KNOWLEDGE OF GOD THAN THE GREEKS AND ROMANS

. . . These Indian peoples surpassed the Greeks and Romans in selecting for their gods, not sinful and criminal men noted for their great baseness, but virtuous ones—to the extent that virtue exists among people who lack the knowledge of the true God that is gained by faith. . . . The following argument can be formed for the proof of the above: The Indian nations seem to show themselves to be or to have been of better rational judgment and more prudent and upright in what they considered God to be. For nations which have reached the knowledge that there is a God hold in common the natural concept that God is the best of all things that can be imagined. Therefore the nation which has elected virtuous men as God or gods, though it might have erred in not selecting the true God, has a better concept and estimation of God and more natural purity than one which has selected and accepted for God or gods men known to be sinful and criminal. The latter was the case of the Greek and Roman states, while the former is that of all these Indian nations. . . . It seems probable that none of these Indian peoples will be more difficult of conversion than the ancient idolaters. First, because, as we have proved and are still proving, all these peoples are of good reason. Second, because they show less duplicity and more simplicity of heart than others. Third, because they are in their natural persons better adjusted, as has been proved above—a quality characteristic of men who may more easily be persuaded of the truth. Fourth, because an infinite number in their midst have already been converted (although some with certain difficulty, namely, those who worshiped many gods; for it is not possible except by a great miracle for a religion so aged, mellowed and time-honored to be abandoned suddenly, in a short time or with ease—as proven by all of the world's past and ancient idolaters). . . .

CHAPTER CCLXII. FROM ALL THAT HAS BEEN SAID IT IS INFERRED THAT THE INDIAN NATIONS EQUALLED AND EVEN SURPASSED ALL THE ANCIENT ONES IN GOOD LAWS AND CUSTOMS

. . . Let us compare [the ancients] with the people of the realms of Peru as concerns women, marriage and chastity. The [Peruvian] kings honored and favored marriages with their presence and performed them themselves or through their proconsuls and delegates. They themselves exhorted the newly-weds to live happily, and in this these people were superior to all nations. They were certainly superior to the Assyrians and Babylonians, . . . even to our own Spaniards of Cantabria, . . . more especially to the renowned isle of England . . . and to many others. . . . To whom were they not superior in the election and succession of kings and those who were to govern the country? They always chose the wisest, most virtuous and most worthy of ruling, those who had subordinated all natural and sensual affection and were free and clean of repugnant ambition and all private interest.

They were likewise more than moderate in exacting tribute of vassals and, so that the people should not be molested, in levying the costs of war. Their industries existed so that nations might communicate among each other and all live in peace. They had a frequent and meticulous census of all deaths and births and of the exact number of people in all estates of the realms. All persons had professions, and each one busied himself and worked to gain his necessary livelihood. They possessed abundant deposits of provisions which met all the necessities of their warriors, reduced the burden and trouble for the subjects and were distributed in the lean years. . . . Who of the peoples and kings of the world ever kept the men of their armies under such discipline that they would not dare to touch even a single fruit hanging over the road from a tree behind a wall? Not the Greeks, nor Alexander, nor the Romans, nor even our own Christian monarchs. Has anyone read of soldiers who, no matter where they were marching when not in battle, were as well commanded, trained, sober and orderly as good friars in a procession? They established order and laws for the obedience which vassals must show toward their immediate lords and for reverence between each other, the humble to the humble and the mighty to the mighty. The rearing of children, in which parents inculcate the obedience and faithfulness owed to superiors—where is it surpassed? . . . Has anyone read of any prince in the world among the ancient unbelievers of the past or subsequently among Christians, excepting St. Louis of France, who so attentively assisted and provided for the poor among his vassals—those not only of his own village or city but of all his large and extensive realms? They issued public edicts and personal commands to all nobles and provincial governors, of whom there were many, that all poor, widows and orphans in each province should be provided for from their own royal rents and riches, and that alms should be given according to the need, poverty and desert of each person. Where and among what people or nation was there a prince endowed with such piety and beneficence that he never dined unless three or four poor people ate from his plate and at his table? . . . Then, there is that miracle—such it may be called for being the most remarkable, singular and skilful construction of its kind, I believe, in the world—of the two highways . . . : across the mountains and along the coast. The finer and more admirable of these extends for at least six and perhaps eight hundred leagues and is said to reach the provinces of Chile. . . . In Spain and Italy I have seen portions of the highway said to have been built by the Romans from Spain to Italy, but it is quite crude in comparison with the one built by these peoples. . . .

CHAPTER CCLXIII. THE INDIANS ARE AS CAPABLE AS ANY OTHER
NATIONS TO RECEIVE THE GOSPEL

Thus it remains stated, demonstrated and openly concluded . . . throughout this book that all these peoples of the Indies possessed—as far as is possible through natural and human means and without the light of faith—nations, towns, villages and cities, most fully and abundantly provided for. With a few exceptions in varying degrees they lacked nothing, and some were endowed in full perfection for political and social life and for attaining and enjoying that civic happiness which in this world any good, rational, well provided and happy republic wishes to have and enjoy; for all are by nature of very subtle, lively, clear and most capable understanding. This they received (after the will of God, Who wished to create them in this way) from the favorable influence of the heavens, the gentle attributes of the regions which God gave them to inhabit, the clement and soft weather; from the composition of their limbs and internal and external sensory organs; from the quality and sobriety of their diet; from the fine disposition and healthfulness of the lands, towns and local winds; from their temperance and moderation in food and drink; from the tranquility, calmness and quiescence of their sensual desires; from their lack of concern and worry over the worldly matters that stir the passions of the soul, these being joy, love, wrath, grief and the rest; and also, *a posteriori,* from the works they accomplished and the effects of these. From all these causes, universal and superior, particular and inferior, natural and accidental, it followed, first by nature and then by their industry and experience, that they were endowed with the three types of prudence: the monastic, by which man knows how to rule himself; the economic, which teaches him to rule his house; and the political, which sets forth and ordains the rule of his cities. As for the divisions of this last type (which presupposes the first two types of prudence to be perfect) into workers, artisans, warriors, rich men, religion (temples, priests and sacrifices), judges and magistrates, governors, customs and into everything which concerns acts of understanding and will, . . . they were equal to many nations of the world outstanding and famous for being politic and reasonable. . . . We have, then, but slight occasion to be surprised at defects and uncouth and immoderate customs which we might find among our Indian peoples and to disparage them for these; for many and perhaps all other peoples of the world have been much more perverse, irrational and corrupted by depravity, and in their governments and in many virtues and moral qualities much less temperate and orderly. Our own forbears were much worse, as revealed in irrationality and confused government and in vices and brutish customs throughout the length and breadth of this our Spain, which has been shown in many places above. Let us, then, finish this book and give immense thanks to God for having given us enough life, strength and help to see it finished.

CHAPTER CCLXIV. THE MEANING OF THE WORD "BARBARIAN" AND THE SEVERAL CLASSES OF BARBARIAN PEOPLES

In certain places above we have referred to this term or word "barbarian," which many call and consider these Indian peoples and other nations to be. Sometimes in the Holy Scriptures and frequently in holy decrees and lay histories barbarians are named and referred to, especially since the Philosopher [Aristotle] makes particular mention in his *Politics* of barbarians. Many times I find the term wrongly used, owing to error or to confusion between some barbarians and others. In order therefore to avoid this error and confusion I wish to explain here what it is to be a barbarian and what nations can properly be called barbarian. For such a clarification one must make the following fourfold distinction. A nation or people or part thereof can be called barbarian for four reasons: first, considering the term broadly and improperly, for any strangeness, ferocity, disorder, exorbitance, degeneration of reason, of justice and of good customs and human benignity; or also for evincing opinion which is confused or flighty, furious, tumultuous or beyond reason. Thus, there are men who have deserted and forgotten the rules and order of reason and the gentleness and peacefulness which man should naturally possess; blind with passion, they change in some way, or are ferocious, harsh, severe, cruel, and are precipitated into acts so inhuman that fierce and wild beasts of the mountains would not commit them. They seem to have been divested of the very nature of man, and the word "barbarian" thus signifies a strangeness and exorbitance or novelty which is in discord with the nature and common reason of men. . . .

The second manner or species of barbarian is somewhat more limited; it includes those who lack a written language corresponding to their spoken one as the Latin language corresponds to our own. In short, people who lack the practice and study of letters are said to be barbarians *secundum quid*,[1] which

---

[1] [*Secundum quid* means *in some respect*. This is in contrast to *simpliciter*, or *absolutely*, which is used later on.]

means that they fall short by some measure or quality of not being barbarian, because in all else they can be wise, polished and lacking in ferocity, strangeness and harshness. Because the English lacked the practice of letters, the Venerable Bede, who was an Englishman, translated the liberal arts into the English language so that his people would not be considered barbarians. . . . In like manner, it is customary to call barbarian a man whose manner of speech is strange compared to another's, when one does not pronounce well the language of the other or when in conversation people do not manage to deal and converse with one another. According to Strabo, Book XIV, the first occasion the Greeks took to call other peoples barbarian was when the latter mispronounced the Greek language crudely and defectively. Hence there is no man or nation which is not considered barbarian by some other. . . . Just as we consider these peoples of the Indies barbarians, so they, since they do not understand us, also consider us barbarians and strangers. From this has arisen a great error in many of us, laymen, ecclesiastics and monks, concerning these Indian nations of diverse languages, which we neither understand nor penetrate, and of different customs. People of every profession and quality came to these lands from our nation after these people had lost their republics and their order of life and government, for we had put them in such great disorder and so reduced their numbers that they became almost completely annihilated. These arrivals find them in this state and think that the confusion and abasement in which they now live was always so and comes from their barbaric nature and disorderly government, while in truth we can affirm that in many ways they have seen in us no few customs which, with justifiable reason, might cause us to be taken for extreme barbarians by them—not so much barbarians of this second type, which means strangers, but of the first, for our being exceedingly ferocious, harsh, severe and abominable. . . .

CHAPTER CCLXV. OTHER MEANINGS WHICH THE NAME "BARBARIAN" MAY HAVE

The third species and manner of barbarians, interpreting the term or word most strictly and properly, comprises those who by their strange, harsh and evil customs, or by their evil and perverse inclination, turn out cruel and ferocious and, unlike other men, are not governed by reason. They are, on the contrary, stupid and foppish, and do not possess or administer law, justice or communities. Nor do they cultivate friendship or conversation with other men, for which they have no villages, townships or cities since they do not live in a society. Thus they do not possess or tolerate masters, laws, ordinances or a political regime. Nor do they maintain the communication necessary to mankind, such as buying, selling, trading, renting, directing and having gatherings among neighbors. They do not use deposits, loans and other contracts which are a part of the law of peoples, treated by the laws of the Digest and Institute and by the doctors. For the most part they live scattered through the wilderness, fleeing human contact, contenting themselves with only the company of their women, in the fashion of such animals as monkeys, wildcats and other nongregarious beasts. Such as these are, and are called, *simpliciter,* strictly and properly, barbarians. The inhabitants of the province called Barbary must have been like this, bereft of everything essential to the state of man, such as human reason and all those common and natural things which most men follow and use. Particular mention is made of them in the *Politics,* Book i, Chaps. ii and v, where it says that they are slaves by nature and worthy of always serving and being the subjects of others, because among them there is no natural dynasty, for they have no ordered government, nobility or subjects. . . . In this regard Aristotle says: "One who is not a citizen of any State, if the cause of his isolation be natural and not accidental, is either a superhuman being or low in the scale of civilization. The clanless, lawless, hearthless man so bitterly described by Homer is a case in point; for he is naturally a citizen of no state and a lover of war."

Such inclinations arise from many causes. Sometimes it is from the region in which they live and a type of sky which is unfavorable to them and intemperate; men who are born and live under these conditions are short of intelligence and show perverse inclinations toward the aforementioned evils. . . . The Philosopher adds in Chap. v that wise men can hunt or track them like animals in order to bring them under control and make use of them, causing the one who rules them to use his good judgment in attending to their welfare and keeping them from doing harm to others. In this way they can serve and profit their wise regent with their physical strength, because nature has made them robust for any work and chores which they might be ordered to do. Therefore to be *simpliciter,* properly and exactly, a barbarian is, as the Philosopher here concludes, to be a slave by nature. . . .

There are others in a state of slavery who are not barbarians, and they are not properly called slaves but will always be free. They can only in a very broad sense be called slaves, for the meaning here is merely that they must be ruled by others and told what to do, as if they were slaves. These are people who are born feeble-minded or half-witted, or almost so, or who lack the reasoning power to govern themselves. In this sense the children of freeborn men and gentlemen can at birth be called slaves, and this is what St. Paul means when he says: *Quanto tempore haeres parvulus est, nihil differt a servo,*[2] et cetera. The Philosopher deals with these in Book i of the *Politics,*

---

[2] [*As long as an heir is young, he is in no way different from a slave.*]

wherein he proves that servitude is as natural to some as is command to others, and that nature has produced some men apt and disposed to be governed by others and not to govern, and others to govern and rule their fellows and not to be commanded. It does not follow from this, however, that anyone who is wise and able to govern should then be the master of another who is not his equal; but it should be understood that nature has produced some to govern and others to be governed, and thus the question is one regarding aptitude and not the act of governing itself. In any other sense, kings would be slaves of any wise men in their kingdoms—just as they are in a fashion servants of their council and senate, to the extent that the latter determine and the king is guided by them and obliged by natural reason to obey and execute what they decide. . . . From what has been said, then, the distinction made by the Philosopher between the two types of barbarian seems clear. . . . Not all barbarians are either lacking in reason or slaves by nature, nor can they, for merely being barbarians, be subjugated by force if they possess kingdoms and are free.

CHAPTER CCLXVI. THE FOURTH TYPE OF BARBARIAN NATION

The fourth manner or species of barbarians, which can be inferred from the things said above, embraces all those who lack true religion and Christian faith—that is, all unbelievers, however wise and prudent they may be as philosophers and statesmen. The reason is that there is no nation (excepting that of the Christians) which does not possess and suffer many and great defects, and have barbarism in its laws, customs, way of life and government. The latter are not corrected nor is the manner of life cleansed or reformed through any ordering except by entry into the Church and acceptance of our holy Catholic faith; for this alone is the stainless law which converts souls and cleans away the filth of all evil customs by banishing idolatry and superstitious rites, from which originate all other infamies, vices and impurity, private and public. . . . But there is a clear distinction among unbelievers, as the doctors declare and as we too see from experience, for there are some unbelievers and barbarians whose lack of faith is purely negative. This means that they have never heard of Christ or our faith and doctrine, and thus are called unbelievers because they do not have the faith. They are like those whom we properly call Gentiles, meaning the offspring of people who have not yet been saved through holy baptism. They are like all nations (with the exception of the Jews), who in the beginning, before the advent of Christ, were allowed by the mysterious divine wisdom to fall into idolatry and the vices growing out of it, as appears in the *Acts of the Apostles,* XIV: "Who suffered all the nations to walk in their own ways." . . . The lack of faith of such people does not constitute a sin by reason of their not having faith in Christ, but rather is punishment for the sin of our parents, Adam and Eve. . . . Such unbelievers are not condemned except for other sins they commit, those which cannot be pardoned without faith; and this is the opinion of St. Thomas. Thus we call such unbelievers barbarians, and they are so, because through lack of doctrine, faith and the grace which goes with them they cannot but abound in many corrupt customs and suffer great defects in their laws and nations, as already proven for the Romans and others. We should not marvel at the vices and brutalities which they had and may have, but rather at those which they do not have. For according to St. Jerome every man who has no word of his Creator is not a man but a beast, and we should thank the One Who summoned us, before them, out of such dark shadows into the wondrous light of His faith; for our forbears suffered much greater shadows and darkness than do these people. . . .

CHAPTER CCLXVII. CONCLUSION OF THE EXPLANATION OF THE SEVERAL TYPES OF BARBARIAN NATIONS

There are other unbelievers and barbarians whose lack of faith is different from that of the foregoing; this is, and is called, the contrary species because of the perverseness shown toward the faith. They have heard the message of the Gospels, refuse to receive it and resist its preaching—it being known that they resist through the pure hatred they bear our faith and the name of Christ. They not only refuse to receive the faith and hear it but battle and persecute it, and were they able, they would destroy it by exalting and spreading their own sect. In these people real faithlessness and its sin achieve their full measure. . . .

EPILOGUE

From the whole discourse concerning barbarians the following differences seem clear. There are four types of barbarian. Three of them, the first, second, and fourth types, are barbarians *secundum quid,* which is to say, barbarian in that certain peoples have or suffer a certain defect or defects in their customs. This is especially so of those who lack our holy faith and applies to all unbelievers, however intelligent and wise they may be. The first two types may also include Christian nations whenever they stray from reason because of any cruel, harsh, disorderly and ferocious affairs or the furious impact of fearful ideas; this was well shown in Castile in 1520 at the time of the Communities.[3] . . . Only those barbarians contained in the third species are called and are

---

[3] [This refers to an unsuccessful series of outbreaks by the lower classes of the towns, or "Communities," against the nobles and bourgeoisie. The protest was against the privileges accorded to non-Spaniards in the realm under Emperor Charles V.]

simpliciter, properly and strictly, barbarians, because they are very remote from reason, neither living nor capable of living according to its rules, whether through lack of understanding or from excessive malice and depraved customs. It has been proved that it is expressly of those and not of the others that the Philosopher speaks in Book 1 of his *Politics* when he refers to barbarians.

. . . These peoples of the Indies are not of the first category, because all in that one are accidental and not natural (we will not explain here what is natural, or nearly so), and such defects cannot by nature befall a whole nation; for it would be a great monstrosity of human lineage if nature were to err to the extent of making men of one nation furious and foppish, foolish or blind with passion. We have indicated above at various times that nature cannot, for the most part, make mistakes as far as man is concerned; these peoples can, however, fall into this type accidentally like any others by conducting affairs with comparable disorder. Similarly, these nations do not belong to the third type, as is clear, because they have their kingdoms and kings, armies, well-ruled and orderly states, houses, treasuries and homes; they live under laws, codes and ordinances; in administering justice they prejudice no one. Hence they cannot belong to this type as they are completely the opposite. Nor do they belong to the second sub-group of the fourth type, for they have never harmed or done evil to the Church. They did not know or have word that the Church was in the world or what sort of people Christians were until we went seeking them. They had their lands, provinces, kingdoms and kings—how distant from ours everyone knows—each kingdom and province living among the others in peace. It follows, then, that all these peoples are barbarians in the broad sense, according to some quality; and the primary one is that they are unbelievers. This is only through their lack of our holy faith, which means a purely negative faithlessness, caused by mere ignorance, and is not a sin, as has been declared. Hence they belong, on these grounds, in the fourth category. They can also be included in the second one because of three qualities. One is that they are illiterate, or lack a written language as did the English. The second is that they are most humble peoples and obey their kings in a strange and admirable manner. The third is that they do not speak our language well nor understand us; but in this we are as barbarian to them as they to us. These, then, are the infinite peoples or nations that we call the western and southern Indies, which were populated for so many thousands of leagues and were discovered by that illustrious Don Christopher Columbus who first broke the isolation that had for so many thousands of years lain upon the Ocean Sea, of which he was most rightfully the first admiral.

THANKS BE TO GOD FOR EVER AND ALWAYS

BARTOLOMÉ DE LAS CASAS: THIRTY
VERY JURIDICAL PROPOSITIONS

Proposition I: The Pontiff of Rome, the canonically elected Vicar of Christ, successor of St. Peter, has the authority and power of Christ Himself, the Son of God, over all the people of the world, faithful or not, *insofar as he sees it necessary to guide men and set them upon the road to the eternal life, and to remove the impediments therefrom.* He uses and must use such power, however, in one way with the unfaithful who have never undergone holy baptism in the holy Church, particularly those who have never heard of Christ or His faith, and in another way with those who are faithful or once were so.

Proposition II: St. Peter and his successors are by divine law under the necessary obligation of attempting to see that the word and faith of Christ are preached throughout the world with the greatest diligence to all the unfaithful, *who it may be supposed will not resist the spread of the Gospels and Christian teachings.*

Proposition IV: Among ministers for the propagation and maintenance of the faith and Christian religion and for conversion of the unfaithful, the Christian monarchs occupy a position most necessary for the Church; for by means of their power, royal forces and worldly riches they can aid, shelter, preserve and defend the churchly and spiritual ministers, and the end mentioned above can be sought and obtained without confusion or hindrance.

Proposition VII: The Vicar of Christ, by divine authority and to avoid confusion, can and did most wisely, providently and justly divide among Christian princes the kingdoms and provinces of all the unfaithful of every disbelief or sect, thus committing and entrusting to the former the spreading of the holy faith, the extension of the Universal Church and the Christian faith and the conversion and spiritual welfare of those people as an ultimate aim.

Proposition VIII: The Supreme Pontiff did not make, nor does he or should he make, such a division, commission or concession *with the principal and final purpose of bringing the Christian princes into grace or enlarging with honor and more titles and riches their possessions.* His end is the spread of the divine religion, the honor of God and the conversion and salvation of the unfaithful, which is the intent and final aim of the King of Kings and Lord of Lords, Jesus Christ. *At the outset there is imposed upon the princes a most perilous duty and office,* for which they must give a complete accounting at the end of their days before the final judgment. *The aforesaid division and trust is therefore more for the good and benefit of the unfaithful than for that of the Christian princes.*

Proposition X: Among the unfaithful who live in distant kingdoms, who have never heard speak of Christ or received the faith, there are true kings and princes. *Royal dominion, dignity and preeminence belong to them by virtue of natural law and the law of peoples,* insofar as such dominion leads to the rule and governance of their kingdoms as sanctioned by divine and evangelical law and in the manner that superior persons have dominion over inferior things. With the advent of Jesus Christ, therefore, such dominions, honors, royal prerogatives and the rest were not abolished either universally or individually, *ipso facto nec ipso jure.*[4]

Proposition XI: An opinion contrary to the preceding proposition is erroneous and most pernicious and *whoever defends it vigorously will incur formal heresy.* It would at the same time be most impious, harmful and productive of innumerable thefts, acts of violence, tyrannies, ravages and robberies, irreparable damages and grievous sins, infamy, stench and hatred of the name of Christ and of the Christian religion, and a most effective impediment to our Catholic faith. It would be death, perdition and vainglory for the greater part of mankind, the most certain damnation of infinite souls and, finally, the cruel and foremost enemy of piety, meekness and Christian evangelical custom.

Proposition XII: For no sin of idolatry *or any other sin, grave as it may be,* are the said unfaithful, masters or subjects, to be deprived of their dominions, dignity or other possessions, *ipso facto vel ipso jure.*

Proposition XIII: Merely for the sin of idolatry or for any other sin, however enormous, grave and heinous, which was committed during the whole period of their unfaithfulness, before they had received holy baptism of their own free will, the unfaithful, particularly those whose lack of faith is simple ignorance, *cannot be punished by any judge in the world*—unless it be a case of those who directly impede the propagation of the faith and, having been sufficiently warned, maliciously persist in their actions.

Proposition XIX: All kings and natural rulers, cities, communities and villages in the Indies shall recognize the monarchs of Castile as their universal and sovereign rulers and emperors in the following manner: *after having received our holy faith and sacred baptism of their own free will; and if before receiving these they do not do so or wish to do so, they cannot be punished by any judge or court.*

Proposition XXII: The rulers of Castile are obliged by divine law to see that the faith of Christ is preached in the form which the Son of God left established in His Church. His apostles adhered to this form effectively and without any slack or failure; the universal Church has always by custom and de-

---

[4] [*Neither by deed nor by law.* The similar phrase in *Proposition XII* means, *Either by deed or by law.*]

crees ordained and constituted it, and the holy sages have explained and enlarged upon it in their books. The form consists in attracting the unfaithful and particularly the Indians, who are by nature very meek, humble and pacific, in a peaceful, loving, sweet and charitable manner, with gentleness, humility and good examples, and in giving them gifts and grants from our part rather than by taking anything of theirs away from them. In this way they will consider the God of the Christians to be a good, gentle and just God and will wish to belong to Him and to receive His Catholic faith and holy doctrine.

Proposition XXIII: To subject them first by warlike means is a form and procedure contrary to the law, gentle yoke, easy burden and gentleness of Jesus Christ. It was the same method used by Mahomet and the Romans to upset and despoil the world. It is that used today by the Turks and the Moors and which the Sherif is beginning to use. Therefore it is most evil, tyrannical, libelous of the sweet name of Christ, and the cause of infinite new blasphemies against the true God and the Christian religion. We have had very extensive experience with what has been done and is being done today in the Indies; because of it, the Indians consider God to be the most cruel, unjust and pitiless of gods, and consequently it impedes the conversion of many unfaithful, giving rise to the impossibility of infinite people in the new world ever to become Christians. This is, moreover, most clearly the infernal path to all the irreparable and distressing evils and damages set forth in *Proposition XI.*

Proposition XXVIII: Satan could not have invented any more effective pestilence with which to destroy the whole new world, to consume and kill off all its people and to depopulate it as such large and populous lands have been depopulated, than the inventions of the *repartimiento* and *encomiendas,*[5] by which those peoples were divided and assigned to Spaniards as if to all the devils put together, or like herds of cattle delivered to hungry wolves. (This means would have sufficed to depopulate the whole world.) By the *encomienda* or *repartimiento,* which was the cruelest form of tyranny and the one most worthy of hell-fire that could have been invented, all those peoples are prevented from receiving the Christian faith and religion, being held night and day by their wretched and tyrannical overlords, the Spaniards, in the mines, at personal labors and under incredible tributes; forced to carry loads one and two hundred leagues as if they were beasts or worse; and with clerics who preach the faith and give the Indians instruction and a knowledge of God persecuted and driven out of the Indian villages, leaving no witnesses to the acts of violence, cruelties and continual robberies and murders. Because of the

[5] [A *repartimiento* was an allocation of forced Indian labor. An *encomienda* was a conferred right to Indian tribute or labor; the grantee was responsible, though often only in theory, for the Indians' catechization and welfare.]

encomiendas and *repartimiento* the Indians have suffered and still suffer continual tortures, thefts and injustices to their persons and to their children, women and worldly goods. Because of the *encomiendas* and *repartimiento* there have perished in the space of forty-six years (and I was present) more than fifteen million souls without faith or sacraments, and more than three thousand leagues of land have been depopulated. I have been present, as I say, and as long as these *encomiendas* last, I ask that God be a witness and judge of what I say: the power of the monarchs, even were they on the scene, will not suffice to keep all the Indians from perishing, dying off and being consumed; and in this way a thousand worlds might end, without any remedy.

Proposition XXX and the last: From all the aforesaid, by dint of necessary consequence, it follows that, *without prejudice to the title and royal sovereignty which the monarchs of Castile exercise over the new world of the Indies, everything which has been done there—both by the unjust and tyrannical conquests and by the* repartimientos *and* encomiendas—*is null, void and without value or sanction of any right,* for everything has been done by absolute tyrants, without just cause or reason or the authority of their natural prince and monarch. . . .

MARTIN LUTHER

Economic changes and maladjustments played an important part in the religious upheaval of the sixteenth century. There is reason to believe that Zwingli, the Swiss reformer, was right in saying that the monopolistic practices of the large trading companies were one of the causes of the revolt against the Church. The rise in prices, the accumulation of enormous fortunes in the hands of a few, the spread of luxury, the growth of commercialism, the open violation of the laws against interest and usury, the progressive elimination of the smaller merchants from the competitive struggle, the impoverishment of the nobility—all these were developments which prepared the way for revolution and reform.

One man who was most insistent in giving expression to popular discontent was Martin Luther. (See Chapter VII below.) The selections from his pamphlet *On Trading and Usury* (1524) are taken from the translation from the German by C. M. Jacobs in *Works of Martin Luther* (Philadelphia, A. J. Holman, 1931), Vol. IV.

ON TRADING AND USURY

. . . I have wished to give a bit of warning and instruction to everyone about this great, nasty, widespread business of merchandising. If we were to accept the principle that everyone may sell his wares as dear as he can, and were to approve the custom of borrowing and forced lending and standing surety, and yet try to advise men how they could act the part of Christians and keep their consciences good and safe,—that would be the same as trying to teach men how wrong could be right and bad good, and how one could at the same time live and act according to the divine Scriptures and against the divine Scriptures. For these three errors,—that everyone may sell what is his own as dear as he will, borrowing, and becoming surety,—these, I say, are the three sources from which the stream of abomination, injustice, treachery and guile flows far and wide: to try to stem the flood and not stop up the springs, is trouble and labor lost.

At this point, therefore, I wish to tell of some of these tricks and evil doings which I have myself observed and which pious, good people have described to me, to make it apparent how necessary it is that the rules and principles which I have set down above be established and put in practice, if the consciences of merchants are to be counselled and aided; also in order that all the rest of their evil doings may be learned and measured by these; for how is it possible to tell them all? By the three aforementioned sources of evil, door and window are thrown wide to greed and to wicked, wily, self-seeking nature; room is made for them, occasion and power is given them to practice unhindered all sorts of wiles and trickery, and daily to think out more such schemes, so that everything stinks of avarice, nay, is drowned and drenched in avarice as in a great new Deluge.

First, there are some who have no conscientious scruples against selling their goods on credit for a higher price than if they were sold for cash: nay, there are some who wish to sell no goods for cash but everything on credit, so that they may make large profits. Observe that this way of dealing,—which is plainly against God's Word, against reason and all fairness, and springs from sheer wantonness and greed,—is a sin against one's neighbor, for it does not consider his loss, and robs and steals from him that which belongs to him; it is not a seeking for an honest living, but only for avaricious gain. According to divine law, goods should not be sold for a higher price on credit than for cash.

Again, there are some who sell their goods at a higher price than they command in the common market, or than is customary in the trade; and raise the price of their wares for no other reason than because they know that there is no more of that commodity in the country, or that the supply will shortly cease, and people must have it. That is a very rogue's eye of greed, which sees only one's neighbor's need, not to relieve it but to make the most of it and grow rich on one's neighbor's losses. All such people are manifest thieves, robbers and usurers.

Again, there are some who buy up the entire supply of certain goods or wares in a country or a city, so that they may have those goods solely in their own power and can then fix and raise the price and sell them as dear as they like or can. Now I have said above that the rule that a man may sell his goods as dear as he will or can is false and unchristian. It is far more abominable that one should buy up the whole commodity for that purpose. Even the imperial and temporal laws forbid this and call it "monopoly," i.e., purchase for self-interest, which is not to be tolerated in city or country, and princes and lords would stop it and punish it if they did their duty. Merchants who do this act just as though God's creatures and God's goods were made for them alone and given to them alone, and as though they could take them from other people and set on them whatever price they chose.

If anyone wishes to urge the example of Joseph in Genesis xli, how the holy man gathered all the grain in the country and afterwards, in the time of famine, bought with it for the king of Egypt all the money, cattle, land and people,—which seems, indeed, to have been a monopoly, or practice of self-interest,—this is the answer: This purchase of Joseph's was no monopoly, but a common and honest purchase, such as was customary in the country. He prevented no one else from buying during the good years, but it was his God-given wisdom which enabled him to gather the king's grain in the seven years of plenty, while others were accumulating little or nothing. For the text does not say that he alone bought in the grain, but that he "gathered it in the king's cities." If the others did not do likewise, it was their loss, for the common man usually devours his living unconcernedly and sometimes, too, he has nothing to accumulate. We see the same thing today. . . .

When some see that they cannot establish their monopolies in any other way because other people have the same goods, they proceed to sell their goods so cheap that the others can make no profit, and thus they compel them either not to sell at all, or else to sell as cheap as they themselves are selling and so be ruined. Thus they get their monopoly after all. These people are not worthy to be called men or to live among other men, nay they are not worth exhorting or instructing; for their envy and greed is so open and shameless that even at the cost of their own losses they cause loss to others, so that they may have the whole place to themselves. The authorities would do right if they took from such people everything they had and drove them out of the country. . . .

Again, it is a fine piece of sharp practice when one man sells to another, by means of promises, goods which he himself has not, as follows. A merchant from a distance comes to me and asks if I have such and such goods for sale. I say, Yes, though I have not, and sell them to him for ten or eleven gulden when they could otherwise be bought for nine or less, promising him to deliver them in two or three days. Meanwhile I go and buy the goods where I knew in advance that I could buy them cheaper; I deliver them and he pays me for them. Thus I deal with his,—the other man's,—money and property, without risk, trouble or labor, and I get rich. That is called "living off the street," on someone else's money; he who does this need not travel over land and sea. . . .

Here is another bit of self-seeking. Three or four merchants have in their control one or two kinds of goods that others have not, or have not for sale. When these men see that the goods are valuable and are advancing in price all the time because of war or of some disaster, they join forces and pretend to others that the goods are much in demand and that not many people have them on sale; if however there are some who have these goods for sale they put up a stranger to buy up all these goods, and when they have them entirely in their own control they make an agreement to this effect; Since there are no more of these goods to be had we will hold them at such and such a price, and whoever sells cheaper shall forfeit so and so much. This trick, I hear, is practiced chiefly and mostly by the English merchants in selling English or London cloth. It is said that they have a special council for this trade, like a city council, and all the Englishmen who sell English or London cloth must obey this council on penalty of a fine. The council decides at what price they are to sell their cloth and at what day and hour they are to have it on sale and when not. The head of this council is called the "court-master" and is regarded as little less than a prince. See what avarice can and dare do.

Again, I must report this little trick. I sell a man pepper or the like on six months' credit and know that he must sell it again by that time to get ready money. Then I go to him myself, or send someone else, and buy the pepper back for cash, but on these terms. What he bought from me for twelve gulden I buy back for eight, the market price is ten. So I make going and coming, so that he may get the money and maintain his credit; otherwise he might have the disgrace of having no one extend him credit in the future. . . .

Again there is another practice that is customary in the companies. A citizen deposits with a merchant one or two thousand gulden for six years. The merchant is to trade with this and pay the citizen annually two hundred gulden fixed interest, win or lose. What profit he makes above that is his own, but if he makes no profit he must still pay the charge. In this way the citizen is doing the merchant a great service, for the merchant expected with two thousand gulden to make at least three hundred; on the other hand, the merchant is doing the citizen a great service, for otherwise his money must lie idle and bring him no profit. That this common practice is wrong and is true usury I have shown sufficiently in the Discourse on Usury. . . .

Again, they have learned to store their goods in places where they increase in bulk. They put pepper, ginger and saffron in damp cellars or vaults so that they may gain in weight; woolen goods, silks, furs of martin and sable, they sell in dark vaults or booths, keeping them from the air, and this custom is so general that almost every kind of goods has its own kind of air, and there are no goods that some way is not known of taking advantage of the buyer, in the measure or the count or the yard or the weight. They know, too, how to give them a false color; or the best looking are put top and bottom and the worst in the middle. Of such cheating there is no end and no merchant dare trust another out of his sight and reach. . . .

Of the companies I ought to say much, but that whole subject is such a bottomless abyss of avarice and wrong that there is nothing in it that can be discussed with a clear conscience. For what man is so stupid as not to see that companies are nothing else than mere monopolies? Even the temporal law of the heathen forbids them as openly injurious, to say nothing of the divine law and Christian statutes. They have all commodities under their control and practice without concealment all the tricks that have been mentioned; they raise and lower prices as they please and oppress and ruin all the small merchants, as the pike the little fish in the water, just as though they were lords over God's creatures and free from all the laws of faith and love.

So it comes that all over the world spices must be bought at their price, which is alternating. This year they put up the price of ginger, next year of saffron, or vice versa, so that all the time the bend may be coming to the crook and they need suffer no losses and take no risks. If the ginger spoils or fails, they make it up on saffron and vice versa, so that they remain sure of their profit. All this is against the nature, not only of merchandise, but of all temporal goods, which God wills should be subject to risk and uncertainty. But they have found a way to make sure, certain, and perpetual profit out of insecure, unsafe, temporal goods, though all the world must be sucked dry and all the money sink and swim in their gullet. How could it ever be right and according to God's will that a man should in a short time grow so rich that he could buy out kings and emperors? But they have brought things to such a pass that the whole world must do business at a risk and at a loss, winning this year and losing next year, while they always win, making up their losses by increased profits, and so it is no wonder that they quickly seize upon the wealth of all the world, for a pfennig that is permanent and sure is better than a gulden that is temporary and uncertain. But these companies trade with permanent and sure gulden, and we with temporary and uncertain pfennigs. No wonder they become kings and we beggars!

Kings and princes ought to look into these things and forbid them by strict laws, but I hear that they have an interest in them, and the saying of Isaiah is fulfilled, "Thy princes have become companions of thieves." They hang thieves who have stolen a gulden or half a gulden and trade with those who rob the whole world and steal more than all the rest, so that the proverb may hold true: Big thieves hang the little ones, and as the Roman senator Cato said: Simple thieves lie in prisons and in stocks; public thieves walk abroad in gold and silk. But what will God say to this at last? He will do as He says by Ezekiel; princes and merchants, one thief with another, He will melt them together like lead and brass, as when a city burns, so that there shall be neither princes nor merchants any more. That time, I fear, is already at the door. We do not think of amending our lives, no matter how great our sin and wrong may be, and He cannot leave wrong unpunished.

No one need ask, then, how he can belong to the companies with a good conscience. The only advice to give him is: Let them alone, they will not change. If the companies are to stay, right and honesty must perish; if right and honesty are to stay, the companies must perish. "The bed is too narrow," says Isaiah, "one must fall out; the cover is too small, it will not cover both."

I know full well that this book of mine will be taken ill, and perhaps they will throw it all to the winds and remain as they are; but it will not be my fault, for I have done my part to show how richly we have deserved it if God shall come with a rod. If I have instructed a single soul and rescued it from the jaws of avarice, my labor will not have been in vain, though I hope, as I have said above, that this thing has grown so high and so heavy that it can no longer carry its own weight and they will have to stop at last.

Finally, let everyone look to himself. Let no one stop as a favor or a service to me, nor let anyone begin or continue to spite me or to cause me pain. It is your affair, not mine. May God enlighten us and strengthen us to do His good will. Amen.

THE GERMAN PEASANT WAR

THE SPIRIT OF REVOLT produced by the economic changes and maladjustments of the early sixteenth century found expression not only in the Protestant Revolution but in various secular reform programs drawn up in the form of "Articles" or "Constitutions." Many of these programs were utopian and visionary in character; others expressed the grievances of special groups of the population and advanced definite demands and clear-cut suggestions for reform. To the latter belong *The Twelve Articles* (c.1525). This famous document whose author is unknown, states the demands of the German peasantry during the Peasant War, which was ultimately suppressed with great cruelty. The grievances of the peasants were directed against the traditional forms of extortion and oppression from which they suffered at the hands of feudal lords and the Church.

Their condition had been steadily worsening for almost a century, and various risings of the peasants had already taken place. There has been much dispute over the extent of the responsibility of Luther and the reformers for the revolt; but it is certain in any case that the peasants had sufficient cause for revolt.

The translation from the German by J. S. Schapiro is based upon that of Professor J. H. Robinson in the University of Pennsylvania *Translations and Reprints,* Vol. II, and has been taken from Schapiro's *Social Reform and the Reformation* (New York, Columbia University Press, 1909).

THE TWELVE ARTICLES

THE FUNDAMENTAL AND RIGHTEOUS ARTICLES of the Peasants and Subjects of the Lay and Ecclesiastical Lords by whom They Consider Themselves Oppressed.

Peace to the Christian reader and the grace of God through Christ:

There are many evil writings put forth of late which take occasion, on account of the assembling of the peasants, to cast scorn upon the gospel, saying, "Is this the fruit of the new teaching, that no one should obey but that all should everywhere rise in revolt, and rush together to reform, or perhaps destroy altogether, the authorities, both ecclesiastic and lay?" The articles below shall answer these godless and criminal fault-finders, and serve, in the first place, to remove the reproach from the Word of God and, in the second place, to give a Christian excuse for the disobedience or even the revolt of the entire peasantry.

In the first place the gospel is not the cause of revolt and disorder, since it is the message of Christ, the promised Messiah; the word of life, teaching only love, peace, patience and concord. Thus all who believe in Christ should learn to be loving, peaceful, long-suffering and harmonious. This is the foundation of all the articles of the peasants (as will be seen), who accept the gospel and live according to it. How then can the evil reports declare the gospel to be a cause of revolt and disobedience? That the authors of the evil reports and the enemies of the gospel oppose themselves to these demands is due not to the gospel, but to the devil, the worst enemy of the gospel, who causes this opposition by raising doubts in the minds of his followers, and thus the Word of God, which teaches love, peace and concord, is overcome.

In the second place, it is clear that the peasants demand that this gospel be taught them as a guide in life, and they ought not to be called disobedient or disorderly. Whether or no, God grant the peasants, earnestly wishing to live according to His Word, their requests who shall find fault with the will of the Most High? Who shall meddle in His Judgments or oppose His Majesty? Did He not hear the Children of Israel when they called upon Him to save them out of the hands of Pharaoh? Can He not save His own to-day? Yea, He will save them and that speedily. Therefore, Christian reader, read the following article with care and then judge. Here follow the articles:

I. First, it is our humble petition and desire, as also our will and resolution, that in the future we shall have power and authority so that each community shall choose and appoint a pastor, and that we shall have the right to depose him should he conduct himself improperly. The pastor thus chosen should teach us the gospel pure and simple, without any additional doctrine or ordinance of man. For to teach us continually the true faith will lead us to pray God that through His grace this faith may increase within us and become part of us. For if His grace work not within us we remain flesh and blood, which availeth nothing; since the Scripture clearly teaches that only through faith can we come to God. Only through His mercy can we become holy. Hence such a guide and pastor is necessary and in this fashion grounded upon the Scriptures.

II. According as the just tithe is established by the Old Testament and fulfilled in the New, we are ready and willing to pay the fair tithe of grain. The word of God plainly provides that in giving rightly to God and distributing to His people the services of a pastor are required. We desire that for the future our church provost, whomsoever the community may appoint, shall gather and distribute this tithe. From this he shall give to the pastor, elected by the whole community, a decent and sufficient maintenance for him and his, as shall seem right to the whole community. What remains over shall be given to the poor of the place, as the circumstances and the general opinion demand. Should anything farther remain, let it be kept, lest anyone should have to leave the country on account of poverty. In case one or more villages themselves have sold the tithe on account of want, and formal testimony to this effect is given by an entire village, the claims of those to collect this tithe shall not be considered valid; but we will, as behooves us, make an agreement with such claimants to the end that we may repay the same in due time and manner. But those who have tithes which they have not purchased from a village, but which were appropriated by their ancestors, should not, and ought not to be paid any farther by the village, which shall apply its tithes to the support of the pastors elected as above indicated, or to assist the poor as is taught by the Scriptures. The small tithes, whether ecclesiastical or lay, we will not pay at all, for the Lord God created cattle for the free use of man. We will not, therefore, pay farther an unseemly tithe which is of man's invention.

III. It has been the custom hitherto for men to hold us as their own property, which is pitiable enough, considering that Christ has delivered and redeemed us all, the lowly as well as the great, without exception, by the shedding of His precious blood. Accordingly it is consistent with Scripture that we should be free and should wish to be so. Not that we would wish to be absolutely free and under no authority. God does not teach us that we should lead a disorderly life in the lusts of the flesh, but that we should love the Lord our God and our neighbor. We would gladly observe all this as God has commanded us in the celebration of the communion. He has not commanded us not to obey the authorities, but rather that we should be humble, not only towards those in authority, but towards every one. We are thus ready to yield obedience according to God's law to our elected and regular authorities in all proper things becoming a Christian. We therefore take it for granted that you will release us from serfdom as true Christians, unless it should be shown us from the Gospel that we are serfs.

IV. In the fourth place, it has been the custom heretofore that no poor man should be allowed to touch venison or wild fowl, or fish in flowing water, which seems to us quite unseemly and unbrotherly as well as selfish and not agreeable to the Word of God. In some places the authorities preserve the game to our great annoyance and loss, recklessly permitting the unreasoning animals to destroy to no purpose our crops, which God suffers to grow for the use of man; and yet we must submit quietly. This is neither godly nor neighborly; for when God created man He gave him dominion over all the animals, over the birds of the air and over the fish in the water. Accordingly it is our desire, if a man holds possession of waters, that he should prove from satisfactory documents that his right has been unwittingly acquired by purchase. We do not wish to take it from him by force, but his rights should be exercised in a Christian and brotherly fashion. But whosoever cannot produce such evidence should surrender his claim with good grace.

V. In the fifth place, we are aggrieved in the matter of wood-cutting, for the noble folk have appropriated all the woods to themselves alone. If a poor man requires wood, he must pay double price for it. It is our opinion in regard to a wood which has fallen into the hands of a lord, whether spiritual or temporal, that unless it was duly purchased it should revert again to the community. It should moreover, be free to every member of the community to help himself to such firewood as he needs in his home. Also, if a man requires wood for carpenter's purposes he should have it free, but with the knowledge of a person appointed by the community for that purpose. Should, however, no such forest be at the disposal of the community let that which has been duly bought be administered in a brotherly and Christian manner. If the forest, although unfairly appropriated in the first instance, was later duly sold, let the matter be adjusted in a friendly spirit and according to the Scriptures.

VI. Our sixth complaint is in regard to the excessive services which are demanded of us and which are increased from day to day. We ask that this matter be properly looked into so that we shall not continue to be oppressed in this way, but that some gracious consideration be given us, since our forefathers were required only to serve according to the Word of God.

VII. Seventh, we will not hereafter allow ourselves to be further oppressed by our lords, but will let them demand only what is just and proper according to the word of agreement between the lord and the peasant. The lord should no longer try to force more services or other dues from the peasant without payment, but should permit the peasant to enjoy his holding in peace and quiet. The peasant should, however, help the lord when it is necessary, and at proper times, when it will not be disadvantageous to the peasant, and for a suitable payment.

VIII. In the eighth place, we are greatly burdened by holdings which cannot support the rent exacted from them. The peasants suffer loss in this way and are ruined; and we ask that the lords may appoint persons of honor to inspect these holdings, and fix a rent in accordance with justice, so that the peasant shall not work for nothing, since the laborer is worthy of his hire.

IX. In the ninth place, we are burdened with a great evil in the constant making of new laws. We are not judged according to the offense, but sometimes with great ill-will and sometimes much too leniently. In our opinion, we should be judged according to the old written law, so that the case shall be decided according to its merits, and not with partiality.

X. In the tenth place, we are aggrieved by the appropriation by individuals of meadows and fields which at one time belonged to the community. These we will take again into our own hands. It may, however, happen that the land was rightfully purchased; when, however, the land has unfortunately been purchased in this way, some brotherly arrangement should be made according to the circumstances.

XI. In the eleventh place, we will entirely abolish the due called "heriot," and will no longer endure it, nor allow widows and orphans to be thus shamefully robbed against God's will, and in violation of justice and right, as has been done in many places, and by those who should shield and protect them. These lords have disgraced and despoiled us, and although they had little authority they assumed it. God will suffer this no more, and it shall be wholly done away with, and for the future no man shall be bound to give little or much.

XII. In the twelfth place, it is our conclusion and final resolution that if any one or more of the articles here set forth should not be in agreement with the Word of God, as we think they are, such article we will willingly retract if it is proved really to be against the Word of God by a clear explanation of the Scripture. Or if articles should now be conceded to us that are hereafter discovered to be unjust, from that hour they shall be void and null and without force. Likewise, if more complaints should be discovered which are based upon truth and the Scriptures and relate to offenses against God and our neighbor we are determined to reserve the right to present these also, and to exercise ourselves in all Christian teaching. For this we shall pray to God, since He can grant our demands, and He alone. The peace of Christ abide with us all.

VI

THE MORAL THOUGHT OF THE HUMANIST RENAISSANCE

PETRARCH

RANCESCO PETRARCA, or Petrarch (1304-74), is famous as a humanist poet and scholar, and to his own age he was no less renowned as a man of the world. An Italian by birth, Petrarch was educated in France and studied law in Italy. Although his interests centered around literature, he was the friend and political adviser of popes and princes and an educational reformer. Serving Cardinal Colonna, Petrarch became a canon and traveled throughout Europe. After a period of retirement writing at Vaucluse in southeastern France, he received the laurel crown at Rome in 1341 for his Italian poetry. Diplomatic services took him to Italy; he then spent time at Avignon. After the death of Cardinal Colonna, Petrarch served the Visconti family before his final retirement to Arquà, where he died.

A major figure in Italian literature and often called "the father of humanism," Petrarch shows the mutual attraction of ascetic and secular values so characteristic of modern man. His works in Latin, which he felt to be still the literary language *par excellence,* include: an epic, *Africa; Metrical Epistles; On Contempt for the Worldly Life; On Solitude;* and the *Letters.* His Italian works include the *Trionfi* (Triumphs) and the *Canzoniere* (Song Book). The latter is responsible for his fame as a love poet; inspired by a young girl, Laura, whom he first saw in 1327, Petrarch wrote the lyrics which, especially in the sonnet and ode forms, established a model for generations of European poets.

The following letter, originally in Latin (1336), is taken from Robinson and Rolfe, *Petrarch* (New York, G. P. Putnam's Sons, 1898; 2d ed., 1914).

THE ASCENT OF MOUNT VENTOUX

(Letter to Dionisio da Borgo San Sepolcro)

To-DAY I made the ascent of the highest mountain in this region, which is not improperly called Ventosum. My only motive was the wish to see what so great an elevation had to offer. I have had the expedition in mind for many years; for, as you know, I have lived in this region from infancy, having been cast here by that fate which determines the affairs of men. Consequently the mountain, which is visible from a great distance, was ever before my eyes, and I conceived the plan of some time doing what I have at last accomplished to-day. The idea took hold upon me with especial force when, in re-reading Livy's *History of Rome,* yesterday, I happened upon the place where Philip of Macedon, the same who waged war against the Romans, ascended Mount Haemus in Thessaly, from whose summit he was able, it is said, to see two seas, the Adriatic and the Euxine. Whether this be true or false I have not been able to determine, for the mountain is too far away, and writers disagree. Pomponius Mela, the cosmographer—not to mention others who have spoken of this occurrence—admits its truth without hesitation; Titus Livius, on the other hand, considers it false. I, assuredly, should not have left the question long in doubt, had that mountain been as easy to explore as this one. Let us leave this matter one side, however, and return to my mountain here,—it seems to me that a young man in private life may well be excused for attempting what an aged king could undertake without arousing criticism.

When I came to look about for a companion I found, strangely enough, that hardly one among my friends seemed suitable, so rarely do we meet with just the right combination of personal tastes and characteristics, even among those who are dearest to us. This one was too apathetic, that one over-anxious; this one too slow, that one too hasty; one was too sad, another over-cheerful; one more simple, another more sagacious, than I desired. I feared this one's taciturnity and that one's loquacity. The heavy deliberation of some repelled me as much as the lean incapacity of others. I rejected those who were likely to irritate me by a cold want of interest, as well as those who might weary me by their excessive enthusiasm. Such defects, however grave, could be borne with at home, for charity suffereth all things, and friendship accepts any burden; but it is quite otherwise on a journey, where every weakness becomes much more serious. So, as I was bent upon pleasure and anxious that my enjoyment should be unalloyed, I looked about me with unusual care, balanced against one another the various characteristics of my friends, and without committing any breach of friendship I silently condemned every trait which might prove disagreeable on the way. And— would you believe it?—I finally turned homeward for aid, and proposed the ascent to my only brother, who is younger than I, and with whom you are well acquainted. He was delighted and gratified beyond measure by the thought of holding the place of a friend as well as of a brother.

At the time fixed we left the house, and by evening reached Malaucène, which lies at the foot of the mountain, to the north. Having rested there a day, we finally made the ascent this morning, with no companions except two servants; and a most difficult task it was. The mountain is a very steep and almost inaccessible mass of stony soil. But, as the poet has well said, "Remorseless toil conquers all." It was a long day, the air fine. We enjoyed the advantages of vigour of mind and strength and agility of body, and everything else essential to those engaged in such an undertaking, and so had no other difficulties to face than those of the region itself. We found an old shepherd in one of the mountain dales, who tried, at great length, to dissuade us from the ascent, saying that some fifty years before he had, in the same ardour of youth, reached the summit, but had gotten for his pains nothing except fatigue and regret, and clothes and body torn by the rocks and briars. No one, so far as he or his companions knew, had ever tried the ascent before or after him. But his counsels increased rather than diminished our desire to proceed, since youth is suspicious of warnings. So the old man, finding that his efforts were in vain, went a little way with us, and pointed out a rough path among the rocks, uttering many admonitions, which he continued to send after us even after we had left him behind. Surrendering to him all such garments or other possessions as might prove burdensome to us, we made ready for the ascent, and started off at a good pace. But as usually happens, fatigue quickly followed upon our excessive exertion, and we soon came to a halt at the top of a certain cliff. Upon starting on again we went more slowly, and I especially advanced along the rocky way with a more deliberate step. While my brother chose a direct path straight up the ridge, I weakly took an easier one which really descended. When I was called back, and the right road was shown me, I replied that I hoped to find a better way round on the other side, and that I did not mind going farther if the path were only less steep. This was just an excuse for my laziness; and when the others had already reached a considerable height I was still wandering in the valleys. I had failed to find an easier path, and had only increased the distance and difficulty of the ascent. At last I became disgusted with the intricate way I had chosen, and resolved to ascend without more ado. When I reached my brother, who while waiting for me, had had ample opportunity for rest, I was tired and irritated. We walked along together for a time, but hardly had we passed the first spur when I forgot about the circuitous route which I had just tried, and took a lower one again. Once more I followed an easy, roundabout path through winding valleys, only to find myself soon in my old difficulty. I was simply trying to avoid the exertion of the ascent; but no human ingenuity can alter the nature of things, or cause anything to reach a height by going down. Suffice it to say that, much to my vexation and my brother's amusement, I made this same mistake three times or more during a few hours.

After being frequently misled in this way, I finally sat down in a valley and transferred my winged thoughts from things corporeal to the immaterial, addressing myself as follows:—"What thou hast repeatedly experienced to-day in the ascent of this mountain, happens to thee, as to many, in the journey toward the blessed life. But this is not so readily perceived by

men, since the motions of the body are obvious and external while those of
the soul are invisible and hidden. Yes, the life which we call blessed is to be
sought for on a high eminence, and strait is the way that leads to it. Many,
also, are the hills that lie between, and we must ascend, by a glorious stairway, from strength to strength. At the top is at once the end of our struggles
and the goal for which we are bound. All wish to reach this goal, but, as
Ovid says, 'To wish is little; we must long with the utmost eagerness to
gain our end.' Thou certainly dost ardently desire, as well as simply wish,
unless thou deceivest thyself in this matter, as in so many others. What,
then, doth hold thee back? Nothing, assuredly, except that thou wouldst
take a path which seems, at first thought, more easy, leading through low
and worldly pleasures. But nevertheless in the end, after long wanderings,
thou must perforce either climb the steeper path, under the burden of tasks
foolishly deferred, to its blessed culmination, or lie down in the valley of thy
sins, and (I shudder to think of it!), if the shadow of death overtake thee,
spend an eternal night amid constant torments." These thoughts stimulated
both body and mind in a wonderful degree for facing the difficulties which
yet remained. Oh, that I might traverse in spirit that other road for which I
long day and night, even as to-day I overcame material obstacles by my
bodily exertions! And I know not why it should not be far easier, since the
swift immortal soul can reach its goal in the twinkling of an eye, without
passing through space, while my progress to-day was necessarily slow, dependent as I was upon a failing body weighed down by heavy members.

One peak of the mountain, the highest of all, the country people call
"Sonny," why, I do not know, unless by antiphrasis, as I have sometimes
suspected in other instances; for the peak in question would seem to be the
father of all the surrounding ones. On its top is a little level place, and here
we could at last rest our tired bodies.

Now, my father, since you have followed the thoughts that spurred me on
in my ascent, listen to the rest of the story, and devote one hour, I pray you,
to reviewing the experiences of my entire day. At first, owing to the unac-
customed quality of the air and the effect of the great sweep of view spread
out before me, I stood like one dazed. I beheld the clouds under our feet, and
what I had read of Athos and Olympus seemed less incredible as I myself
witnessed the same things from a mountain of less fame. I turned my eyes
toward Italy, whither my heart most inclined. The Alps, rugged and snow-
capped, seemed to rise close by, although they were really at a great distance;
the very same Alps through which that fierce enemy of the Roman name
once made his way, bursting the rocks, if we may believe the report, by the
application of vinegar. I sighed, I must confess, for the skies of Italy, which

I beheld rather with my mind than with my eyes. An inexpressible longing came over me to see once more my friend and my country. At the same time I reproached myself for this double weakness, springing, as it did, from a soul not yet steeled to manly resistance. And yet there were excuses for both of these cravings, and a number of distinguished writers might be summoned to support me.

Then a new idea took possession of me, and I shifted my thoughts to a consideration of time rather than place. "To-day it is ten years since, having completed thy youthful studies, thou didst leave Bologna. Eternal God! In the name of immutable wisdom, think what alterations in thy character this intervening period has beheld! I pass over a thousand instances. I am not yet in a safe harbour where I can calmly recall past storms. The time may come when I can review in due order all the experiences of the past, saying with St. Augustine, 'I desire to recall my foul actions and the carnal corruption of my soul, not because I love them, but that I may the more love thee, O my God.' Much that is doubtful and evil still clings to me, but what I once loved, that I love no longer. And yet what am I saying? I still love it, but with shame, but with heaviness of heart. Now, at last, I have confessed the truth. So it is. I love, but love what I would not love, what I would that I might hate. Though loath to do so, though constrained, though sad and sorrowing, still I do love, and I feel in my miserable self the truth of the well known words, 'I will hate if I can; if not, I will love against my will.' Three years have not yet passed since that perverse and wicked passion which had a firm grasp upon me and held undisputed sway in my heart began to discover a rebellious opponent, who was unwilling longer to yield obedience. These two adversaries have joined in close combat for the supremacy, and for a long time now a harassing and doubtful war has been waged in the field of my thoughts."

Thus I turned over the last ten years in my mind, and then, fixing my anxious gaze on the future, I asked myself, "If, perchance, thou shouldst prolong this uncertain life of thine for yet two lustres, and shouldst make an advance toward virtue proportionate to the distance to which thou hast departed from thine original infatuation during the past two years, since the new longing first encountered the old, couldst thou, on reaching thy fortieth year, face death, if not with complete assurance, at least with hopefulness, calmly dismissing from thy thoughts the residuum of life as it faded into old age?"

These and similar reflections occurred to me, my father. I rejoiced in my progress, mourned my weaknesses, and commiserated the universal instability of human conduct. I had well-nigh forgotten where I was and our object in coming; but at last I dismissed my anxieties, which were better suited to other surroundings, and resolved to look about me and see what we had come to see. The sinking sun and the lengthening shadows of the mountain were already warning us that the time was near at hand when we must go. As if suddenly wakened from sleep, I turned about and gazed toward the west. I was unable to discern the summits of the Pyrenees, which form the barrier between France and Spain; not because of any intervening obstacle that I know of but owing simply to the insufficiency of our mortal vision. But I could see with the utmost clearness, off to the right, the mountains of the region about Lyons, and to the left the bay of Marseilles and the waters that lash the shores of Aigues Mortes, altho' all these places were so distant that it would require a journey of several days to reach them. Under our very eyes flowed the Rhone.

While I was thus dividing my thoughts, now turning my attention to some terrestrial object that lay before me, now raising my soul, as I had done my body, to higher planes, it occurred to me to look into my copy of St. Augustine's *Confessions,* a gift that I owe to your love, and that I always have about me, in memory of both the author and the giver. I opened the compact little volume, small indeed in size, but of infinite charm, with the intention of reading whatever came to hand, for I could happen upon nothing that would be otherwise than edifying and devout. Now it chanced that the tenth book presented itself. My brother, waiting to hear something of St. Augustine's from my lips, stood attentively by. I call him, and God too, to witness that where I first fixed my eyes it was written: "And men go about to wonder at the heights of the mountains, and the mighty waves of the sea, and the wide sweep of rivers, and the circuit of the ocean, and the revolution of the stars, but themselves they consider not." I was abashed, and, asking my brother (who was anxious to hear more), not to annoy me, I closed the book, angry with myself that I should still be admiring earthly things who might long ago have learned from even the pagan philosophers that nothing is wonderful but the soul, which, when great itself, finds nothing great outside itself. Then, in truth, I was satisfied that I had seen enough of the mountain; I turned my inward eye upon myself, and from that time not a syllable fell from my lips until we reached the bottom again. Those words had given me occupation enough, for I could not believe that it was by a mere accident that I happened upon them. What I had there read I believed to be addressed to me and to no other, remembering that St. Augustine had once suspected the same thing in his own case, when, on opening the book of the Apostle, as he himself tells us, the first words that he saw there were, "Not in rioting and drunkenness, not in chambering and wantonness, not in strife and envying. But put ye on the Lord Jesus Christ, and make not provision for the flesh, to fulfil the lusts thereof."

The same thing happened earlier to St. Anthony, when he was listening to the Gospel where it is written, "If thou wilt be perfect, go and sell that thou hast, and give to the poor, and thou shalt have treasure in heaven: and come and follow me." Believing this scripture to have been read for his especial benefit, as his biographer Athanasius says, he guided himself by its aid to the Kingdom of Heaven. And as Anthony on hearing these words waited for nothing more, and as Augustine upon reading the Apostle's admonition sought no farther, so I concluded my reading in the few words which I have given. I thought in silence of the lack of good counsel in us mortals, who neglect what is noblest in ourselves, scatter our energies in all directions, and waste ourselves in a vain show, because we look about us for what is to be found only within. I wondered at the natural nobility of our soul, save when it debases itself of its own free will, and deserts its original estate, turning what God has given it for its honour into dishonour. How many times, think you, did I turn back that day, to glance at the summit of the mountain, which seemed scarcely a cubit high compared with the range of human contemplation,—when it is not immersed in the foul mire of earth? With every downward step I asked myself this: If we are ready to endure so much sweat and labour in order that we bring our bodies a little nearer heaven, how can a soul struggling toward God, up the steeps of human pride and human destiny, fear any cross or prison or sting of fortune? How few, I thought, but are diverted from their path by the fear of difficulties or the love of ease! How happy the lot of those few, if any such there be! Is it of them, assuredly, that the poet was thinking, when he wrote:

> Happy the man who is skilled to understand
> Nature's hid causes; who beneath his feet
> All terrors casts, and death's relentless doom,
> And the loud roar of greedy Acheron.[1]

How earnestly should we strive, not to stand on mountain-tops, but to trample beneath us those appetites which spring from earthly impulses.

With no consciousness of the difficulties of the way, amidst these pre-occupations which I have so frankly revealed, we came, long after dark, but with the full moon lending us its friendly light, to the little inn which we had left that morning before dawn. The time during which the servants have been occupied in preparing our supper, I have spent in a secluded part

---

[1] *Georgics*, ii., 490 *sqq.*

of the house, hurriedly jotting down these experiences on the spur of the moment, lest, in case my task were postponed, my mood should change on leaving the place, and so my interest in writing flag.

You will see, my dearest father, that I wish nothing to be concealed from you, for I am careful to describe to you not only my life in general but even my individual reflections. And I beseech you, in turn, to pray that these vague and wandering thoughts of mine may some time become firmly fixed, and, after having been vainly tossed about from one interest to another, may direct themselves at last toward the single, true, certain, and everlasting good.

COLUCCIO SALUTATI

OLUCCIO SALUTATI (1331–1406) was a Tuscan, brought up in Bologna, a favorite of the Pepoli dynasty. At twenty he had completed his humanist studies and his training in law, after which he seems to have led a wandering life for some years. He later became official notary and then, in 1375, chancellor of Florence, an office he held until his death. He was known for his integrity, his eloquence, and his literary skill; his official letters were intended to bring honor upon the state by their elegant Latinity.

The present selection is not from Salutati the political theorist, author of *De tyranno* (1400), but from Salutati the humanist. The excerpts from his letters to Giuliano Zonarini, chancellor of Bologna, and to Brother John of San Miniato, have been taken from *Humanism and Tyranny,* edited by Ephraim Emerton (Cambridge, Mass., Harvard University Press, 1925).

❦

LETTER TO GIULIANO ZONARINI

October 25, 1378

AND NOW, my dear colleague, I will come to a matter in which you have stirred me up in no slight degree. I wrote to you asking you to buy for me a copy of Vergil, and you reply reproving me for not occupying myself with quite different matters and calling Vergil—to quote your own words—"a lying soothsayer." You say that, since it is forbidden in the Canon Law to concern oneself with books of that sort, I ought not to burden you with such an errand, and you generously offer me a number of volumes of pious literature. I beg you my dearest Giuliano, to pardon me if, in order that due supremacy of honor be maintained for the prince of Roman eloquence, the divinest of all poets, our own countryman, Vergil, and also that I may set you free from the error in which you seem to be involved, I address you in language rather more severe than is my wont.

I seem to feel a deep obligation to defend Vergil, of whom Horace says that earth never bore a purer spirit, lest he be shut out from the sanctuaries of Christians. I am bound also to clear up that error of yours which gives you such a horror of Vergil that you fear to be polluted by the mere purchase of the book.

How do you happen, my dear colleague, to have this dread of Vergil? You say that he records the monstrous doings of the gods and the vicious practices of men, and that, because he did not, as you say, walk in the way of the Lord, he leads his readers away from the straight path of the faith. But, if you think Vergil ought not to be touched because he was a heathen, why do you read Demosthenes, or Priscian, who was something far worse, an apostate? Or Job, to whom you yourself call attention, was he a Christian or was he of the circumcision? Or shall we give up Seneca and his writings because he was not renewed with the water of regeneration? If we throw aside the heritage of the Gentiles, whence shall we draw the rules of literary composition? Cicero is the fountain of eloquence, and everyone who since his day has handed on the art of rhetoric has drawn from that source. Read Augustine on Christian doctrine where he seems to touch (the heights of) eloquence, and certainly you will find the Ciceronian tradition renewed in the style of that great man. Not to read the inventions of the heathen out of devotion to the faith is a very weak foundation, especially when with their assistance you can the more easily combat the futilities of the Gentiles. Don't imagine that I have ever so read Vergil as to be led to accept his fables about the heathen gods! What I enjoy is his style, hitherto unequalled in verse, and I do not believe it is possible that human talent can ever attain to its loftiness and its charm.

I admire the majesty of his language, the appropriateness of his words, the harmony of his verses, the smoothness of his speech, the elegance of his composition and the sweetly flowing structure of his sentences. I admire the profundity of his thought and his ideas drawn from the depths of ancient learning and from the loftiest heights of philosophy.

In these days there is no mixture of heathenism among Christians throughout the civilized world:

> *Excessere omnes adytis arisque relictis*
> *Di. . . .*
>
> From every altar and protecting fire the gods are fled
> Which were the kingdom's stay,

(those gods) whom that accursed blind superstition worshipped have vanished from their altars and their shrines and have abandoned their glory to the true God, to Christ our Lord. It may have been worth while to warn Christians against the study of the poets at a time when heathens still lingered among them, but since that pest has been exterminated, what harm can it be for consecrated men to have read the poets who, even if they are of (no) profit for the moral conduct of life, nevertheless cannot spread such poison for the destruction of our faith that we shall cease humbly to adore our Creator. Was ever a girl so silly, an old wife so foolish, a man so demented as to imagine that Jupiter, Venus, Mars and all the rest of those divine monstrosities were either to be feared or worshipped? Believe me, we need have no fear of this in our day—I will not say among those who are learned enough to rise to the reading of the poets but even among the uneducated.

But you will say, that when we are reading these vain things we are wandering away from the study of sacred literature, since—to continue the Psalm which I began elsewhere—that man is blessed, "whose delight is in the law of the Lord and in his law doth he meditate day and night." I grant you, it is a more holy thing to apply oneself without ceasing to the reading of the sacred page; but these devices of the heathen, even the songs of the poets of which you have such a horror, if one reads them in a lofty spirit are of no little profit and incline us toward those writings which pertain to the faith and the reading of which you urge in your letters.

I might cite to you many passages from our own Vergil which you could readily see were drawn, not from any made-up fables or from the heathen learning, but from the very heights of a true doctrine of God. Perhaps it is in the nature of truth itself to rise above the floods of error; or perhaps God has willed to reveal himself to men through the witness of all sects and professions.

To recall some of the more evident of these passages: —Our poet says:

> *Terna tibi hec primum triplici diversa colore*
> *Licia circumdo terque hec altaria circum*
> *Effigiem duco: numero deus impare gaudet.*

> With triple threads of changeful colors three
> I wind thee round. Thrice round the altar then
> Thy image goes. Odd numbers please the gods.

How well these words may be applied to the mystery of the inexpressible Trinity if one looks at them aright, I leave to the judgment of yourself and all those who deal with theology. Nor is there wanting in Vergilian verse a further confirmation of the divine essence. When he said: *Nate, mee vires, mea magna potentia solus* (My son, who are alone my strength, my mighty power) he referred plainly enough to the unity of the Father and the Son. There is, further, this well-known reference to the institution of the Church: *Casti maneant in religione nepotes.* (Pure in this rite let thy descendants bide.) But why say more? Did he not assume the immortality of the soul and say that some would be punished forever, as for example:

> *sedet eternumque sedebit*
> *Infelix Theseus,—*

> There sits and aye shall sit
> Unhappy Theseus,—

while others who are to attain to glory are to be tried by various sufferings:

Quisque suos patimur manes; exinde per amplum
Mittimur Elysium,—

We bear each his own doom; thence we are sent through wide Elysium,—

adding, in harmony with the Gospel: *Pauci leta arva tenemus* (But few attain the joyous fields).

I admit that these truths are to be read more fully and more profitably in the writers of sacred books; but it is a part of the glory of Almighty God that he has revealed to future ages so many mysteries through the ignorant or through those who were aiming at other ends, even through those who knew him not.

I have dwelt upon this at such length that you may not suppose the reading of Vergil to be a mere idle occupation if one is willing to take the right view of it and to separate the wheat from the tares. Not, indeed, that I believe one should look there for the teachings of our faith or for the Truth: but, as Seneca says of himself, I go over into the enemy's camp, not as a guest or as a deserter, but as a spy. I, as a Christian, do not read my Vergil as if I were to rest in it forever or for any considerable time; but as I read I examine diligently to see if I can find anything that tends toward virtuous and honorable conduct, and as I run through the foreshadowings of his poetry, often with the aid of allegory and not without enjoyment, if I find something not compatible with the truth or obscurely stated, I try to make it clear by the use of reason. But, when it is my good fortune to find something in harmony with our faith, even though it be wrapped up in fiction, I admire it and rejoice in it, and since our poet himself thought it well to learn even from an enemy, I joyfully accept it and make a note of it.

Don't imagine that the holiest of men have been ignorant of poetry or of Vergil. Read the letters of Father Jerome: you will find almost every one of them adorned with verses from the poets. In his invective against Vigilantius Gallicus, not to mention others, he piles up so many poetical quotations in the prologue, that one might think it was not a Christian who was writing but some professor of the profane literature of the heathen. And what is still more remarkable, in the famous letter to Pope Damasus in which he expounds the parable of the Prodigal Son with divine genius, when he came to speak against poets and rhetoricians, he said:

The songs of the poets, the wisdom of this world, the display of rhetorical words are the food of demons. They delight everyone with their charm, they catch our ears with the modulation of sweetly-flowing verse, they enter into our souls and capture the secret places of the heart. Even when read carefully with the most devoted labor, they give us nothing but empty sound and noisy speech. In them is found no true satisfaction, no refreshment of righteousness; they who devote themselves to them remain starving for the truth and poverty-stricken for virtue.

While he said all this and much more in the sequel, nevertheless, bearing in mind the line of Vergil:

Matri longa decem tulerunt fastidia menses,

Begin, boy-babe! Give back thy mother's smile
Who ten long moons her weary sickness bore.
Begin, boy-babe!—

he says that he himself had borne the burden of ten months. And, writing to Augustine, he did not omit this verse:

Musica in luctu importuna narratio.

He recalls also the lines of Persius:

Ut nemo in sese tentat descendere, nemo
Sed precedenti spectatur mantica tergo

How utter, utter is the dearth of men
who venture down into their own
breasts, and how universally they stare
at the wallet on the back of the man
before them,—

and—not to turn aside from our Vergil—he adds: "Remember Dares and Entellus." Now, when a man in one short letter written to a most eminent Christian introduced so many poetic references, did he not give us an example that we should be careful by no means to neglect the poets? As to Jerome, on whose authority the sacred canons forbid the reading of Vergil and other poets, I would maintain without hesitation that if he had been ignorant of the poetry and rhetoric against which he inveighs so beautifully he would never have handed down to us the volumes of Holy Writ translated in his sweetly flowing style from both Greek and Hebrew into the Latin tongue. Never could he have spoken against his critics with such brilliancy of ideas and such charm of language. Nor, in his criticism of rhetoric—which I should regard as a fault in another man—would he have made use of the forces of rhetoric.

Furthermore, Aurelius Augustine, exponent and champion of the Christian faith, displayed such knowledge of the poets in all his writings that there is scarcely a single letter or treatise of his which is not crowded with poetic ornament. Not to speak of others, his "City of God" could never have been so strongly and so elaborately fortified against the vanity of the heathen if he had not been familiar with the poets and especially with Vergil. The theologians of our day confess they cannot understand these books, on account of their frequent references to Vergil and other poets—at least not their finer shades of meaning, and I have often known men of no mean ability and influence who have read Vergil and others for the sake of this knowledge and have eagerly gone a-begging to schoolboys who they thought could teach them.

Now, if you, through the power of your intellect, without a knowledge of the poets can understand grammar or most of the writings of the holy Fathers, filled as they are with poetical allusions, do not forbid the reading of Vergil to me and to others who delight in such studies, but who have not attained to the lofty heights of your genius. If you enjoy reading your books as by a most brilliant illumination, allow me, whose eyes do not admit so much light, in the midst of my darkness to gaze upon the stars of poetry, whereby the darkness of my night is brightened, and to search out a something for the upbuilding of truth and of our faith from amidst those fables whose bitter rind conceals a savor of exceeding sweetness. If you neither can nor will do this, then, with all good will on my part, leave the poets alone!

There remains one passage (of your letter) which really angered me. You called Vergil a "lying (*mentificus*) soothsayer." I understand you to mean by this word that he lies himself or causes others to lie. If any one else had said this I should have taken it quietly and merely said: "There are as many fools as there are people who try to rival Vergil with their verses!" But of you I do not venture to say this. One thing, however, I will say: that you could not have chosen a more appropriate word. I confess that Vergil may rightly be called a *vatis mentificus*, that is, "one who edifies the mind." He adorns Aeneas with every virtue and sets him forth as an example for us. He leads him in a marvellous progress fleeing from a corrupt city, a citadel of vice, the haughty Ilium—. . . *in Latium, sedes ubi fata quietas, ostendunt* (To Latium where the Fates show us a quiet resting-place), away from the fleshly lusts and mockeries of this present life to the peace of virtue, and there, as in a Troy renewed, he may do heroic battle with iniquity, and, fighting with better fortune at a more advanced age may win his triumph after traversing the errors of mortals by observation and noting the wretchedness of vice in the underworld. If one is willing to examine all this in a lofty spirit he will find in that author not merely a delightful outside with the fragrant perfume of flowers, but such food at the marrow that it may well be said to nourish the thinking mind.

There are many things I wanted to say to you on this subject, but the list of them would stretch out to such length that with my occupations, though my habit is to compose rapidly and to write quickly while composing, I could not develop my opinions, especially within the narrow limits of a letter.

So, good-bye! And according to that verse of Cato—for that apocryphal book has by usage come to be thus known—go right on reading your Vergil, secure, since you are not a priest, against any prohibition by your law. You will find in him delight for your eyes, food for your mind, refreshment for your thought, and you will gain from him no little instruction in the art of eloquence.

Fare you well again and again, my dearest friend and colleague! Don't forget me and do give me not only your approval, but your love!

Florence, October 25, 1378

LETTER TO GIULIANO ZONARINI

May 5, 1379

My dear Colleague:

It is now nearly a month since I was surprised to receive a letter of yours without address delivered by you in person to my servant. Not knowing for whom it was intended, and my servant being unable to read, I opened it, and when I found enclosed a letter of my excellent old friend Domenico Silvestri directed to you I was still more surprised and could not understand it until I had run through both letters, and then to my surprise were added both joy and pain. I was grieved, I must confess, to see what a controversy had arisen between you two, both of whom I love as my brothers, and that you had both gone into the fight with such unseemly bitterness. Neither of you showed any regard for learning nor any self-respect and you attacked each other with the "savage tooth of a Theon." From the merry war in which you and I had engaged about the praise of Vergil you descended to a regular battle and pommelled each other with cruel fists.

But after this grief there came an immense joy with the hope that, as my friend Domenico declared, this controversy would be for you both the beginning of a great and well founded affection. To conclude in the words of our Papirius

Non hec incassum, divisque absentibus, acta;
Forsan et has venturus amor premiserat iras.

These things were not done in vain or in the
absence of the gods; Perchance a love that is to
be sent this anger in advance.

It is no new thing that between the greatest of men strife and conflict have
been the prelude to a warm attachment. Not to mention others, I will speak
only of those two lights of the Christian faith, those rocks for heretics, approaching which the ships of error were either dashed to pieces or happily
sailing by reached the haven of salvation,—Aurelius Augustinus and Euse-
buis Hieronymus often in their correspondence made stinging attacks upon
each other and afterward found mutual excuses and exchanged most ami-
cable letters.

You commend the reading of Holy Scripture in such a way that you
seem to have a perfect horror of poetry; while he (Domenico) neither dis-
parages the sacred writings nor thinks that profane or heathen works should
be abandoned. This was and is my opinion also. It was, moreover, the
opinion of Jerome when he was bitterly attacked by a certain Magnus, an
orator at Rome, and I wish you would read his letter and see how many holy
men, both Greeks and Latins, he enumerates who made use of the poets
and philosophers even in their dogmatic writings. Now certainly they could
never have reproduced secular learning with such complete understanding
without daily practice in it.

Nor would I deny, since we live in a world of transient things, that it
is better to reach heaven by the straight way, through the study of the sacred
writings than through the twistings and turnings of the poets. But, seeing
that both roads properly followed lead to the same desired goal, though the
former is to be preferred, the latter is not to be neglected—and perhaps this
is not your contention.

Every creature and every device of created beings may, if we look at it
aright, invite us in some way toward our eternal Fatherland. What could
be more blasphemous if we consider the light of the divine teachings, what
more blameworthy or more futile if we reflect upon the darkness of human
reason, than to invent the worship of idols and to render, not even to a
creature, but to the devices and works of a creature the honor which we
owe in all humility to our Creator? And yet this invention had a useful
result. The gentile world, accustomed to adore these works of men's hands,
yet always saw in them a vision of some divine essence, and when they had
been taught by an easy process of reasoning, even in the very sanctuaries
of their temples, that these images of men and beasts were not gods they
were turned the more readily to the one true God.

If then the invention of idols, than which nothing could be more remote from or more contradictory to Almighty God, was of some profit toward salvation, what may we (not) hope for from the versus of the poets in which we seem to hear through the mystery of allegory or plainly in the very words themselves the echoes of the Holy Spirit of all truth.

But, lest I seem to be calling you away from sacred studies to these merely human affairs, I will say no more at present on this subject—if only this difference of opinion do not loosen the bonds of our former friendship, and also, if you will write kindly to me and my friend Domenico, who you see has written to apologize and even confesses himself in the wrong. I hope you will think of us both with affection and answer me in a fraternal spirit. . . .

But now, if agreeable to you I will impose silence upon myself in this discussion, leaving you, without further argument, to the books of orthodox scholars, provided you will allow me to browse in your writings and in those of the poets in a pleasant alternation of the serious and the entertaining.

Farewell, most excellent Colleague!

LETTER TO BROTHER JOHN
OF SAN MINIATO

I READ RECENTLY, Venerable Father in Christ, the letter which you wrote to that very dear son of mine, Angelo Corbinelli, and was greatly amused by it. You are trying, according to your habit, to draw him away from poetry and secular studies; or, to put it more exactly, to frighten him away from them. Whether you are right in so doing is your affair, and I leave you to the reproaches of my distinguished friend, John of Ravenna, and the many others who hold a contrary opinion.

As I read the beginning of your letter I was, to tell the truth, somewhat disturbed. You begin with these words: "The question I now bring forward for discussion with you I have only recently gone into at great length with my friend, the famous Coluccio, in several discourses back and forth, but the case is as yet not decided. I, however, as the saying is, remained alone upon the field, arms up and with my arguments not exhausted. I believe that I was undoubtedly the victor, and, though he is my superior in skill and diligence, yet I knew my man, and where his strength gives out he would not be ashamed to be beaten."

These are all your own words, and how can you believe yourself the victor when you confess that the case is as yet not decided? You might have alleged the passage of time and claimed that the limit was up; for the law does not permit a civil case to delay more than three years, but requires it to be settled within that time. In fact, I believe it is nearly five years since I received your last letter; but since on your own statement the case is still pending I will make use of the right which you grant me and will revive the slumbering dispute lest you convince yourself that I am beaten instead of being, as I am, the victor and (therefore) silent. I did reply to your objection at the time, briefly indeed but with solid argument and in such a way that the magic spell of your rejoinder did not, rightly considered, at all affect anything I had said. My line of battle stands firm, my opinion still unshaken, and up to the present moment, you have not knocked a single pebble out of my wall.

But I see you have not yet grasped the terms of the problem and are still caught in the simple-minded delusion that this Poetry of ours is a grave and unpardonable crime and a dangerous kind of humbug. If this be so, if under the cover of fictitious words there cannot be the purity and solidarity of truth, tell me, I conjure you, how is this true: "The Spirit of God moved upon the face of the waters?" or this: "God said: let there be light!" and hundreds of other similar sayings? How can a corporeal act be reported of the spirit of God, which is an incorporeal thing? How can it be said that "God said, let there be light!" when God has neither mouth nor tongue which are the members and implements necessary for speech? But of this later.

Now, that you may plainly perceive the truth, I will first show what we should understand by "poetry"; then I will make clear that the Holy Scriptures are not merely closely related thereto, but that in their form they are, in the truest and most complete sense, nothing else than poetry. Thirdly, I will try to show, as far as may be necessary, that the reading of the heathen poets is not forbidden to good Christians; and finally I will attempt to reply to what you have said, so that you may readily cease to imagine yourself the victor.

In the first place, every expression in speech is a concept of the mind before it is brought out in words, so that there can be no utterance which did not first exist in the mind. Whence it follows that the words we use have no meaning whatever except what is formed in our intellect. This we express through the agreements of grammar; we demonstrate it by the force of logic and drive it home by the arts of rhetoric. But when we desire to speak of God, since we do not comprehend him, the concept being wanting, there are no words in which we can suitably discourse of his unspeakable majesty, for if we could say the least thing about this, it would not be unspeakable,

To supply this need mortal men have been compelled to think out another and a most excellent way of speech. But this process of reflection could not be in terms of grammar, the function of which is merely to express mere concepts by mere names and words. Since men could not see God but could see many of his works, they could know him only by his works, that is, by a reverse process and so they began to speak of the divine being as if he were a kind of man, since they had nothing higher than man which they could understand and grasp through the senses whereby our knowledge is acquired. Whatever, therefore, we say about God is a human fiction borrowed from ourselves and from our actions. Alluding to this our Cicero says: "Homer imagined these things, ascribing human qualities to the gods," and he adds, as if wishing for something beyond human power: "I would prefer to ascribe divine qualities to ourselves."

And not only in speaking of God has this been done and is still done, but also, as Cicero says, men pretend that in the realms below things are done which without bodies can be neither done nor understood. They could not grasp with their minds the idea of pure, abstract living spirits but required some form or shape for them. He adds: "In our neighborhood is the Lake of Avernus

> *Unde anime excitantur obscura umbra, aperto ostio*
> *Alti Acherontis, falso sanguine, mortuorum imagines."*

Whence souls are called forth from the dark shades
through the opened gate of deep Acheron by false
(salted) blood—images of the dead.

"These images they represent as speaking, but that cannot be done without tongue or palate or the action and form of the throat, the sides and the lungs." Such are the words of Cicero, and they make plain, though it is clear enough of itself, that not only when we speak of God, but also when we discourse of incorporeal things, we are speaking figuratively, and what we say is, on the surface, false. This is the poetical manner of speaking, presenting outwardly what is false but containing within a hidden truth. Skill in this matter, the science or system of it is called "poetry" or "the poetic art"; the inventor or artificer is called "poet." Father Aristotle wrote a special treatise on this subject after his discussion of the whole *Trivium*.

Thus you can readily see that to this faculty belong especially all tropes, or metaphors, figures, turns of expression, transpositions, allegories, figurative expressions or parables. These, though they are treated in the science of grammar or rhetoric, are borrowed from the very essence of poetry—

just as, when logic treats of the concept it borrows this from the art of rhetoric of which the concept is the special instrument, as the syllogism is of dialectic; but when the rhetorician treats of this (qu. the syllogism), as they all do, he is trespassing on foreign ground.

You may, therefore, define poetry as that mode of speech which either in form or substance means something different from that which it presents. It was devised by necessity, accepted and amplified by practice, not merely when necessity required, but when adornment was desired. Poetry is distinct from every other type of discourse, and is defined in its own terms, and if you are willing to examine into it I cannot see what objection to it you could possibly find.

Now to come to my second point: Do you not see that sacred literature, the whole body of Holy Scripture, is, rightly considered, nothing else in its method of expression than poetry? For, when we are speaking of God or of incorporeal beings nothing is literally true, but beneath that surface of fiction there is nothing that is not true. And what other objection can you have to poetry? What is there about it that you can find to condemn? If you object to its method of expression you are beyond a doubt condemning sacred literature and the Holy Scriptures. For, what is Holy Scripture, so far as its form is concerned, but a fictitious thing, false as to its speech, although beneath this veil it hides the most absolute truth? Who could bear it if he were to take literally this passage of Scripture:

"And God saw that the wickedness of man was great in the earth, and that every imagination of the thoughts of his heart was only evil continually. And it repented the Lord that he had made man on the earth, and it grieved him at his heart. And the Lord said, I will destroy man whom I have created from the face of the earth."

First, as to the words, "When God saw." Since sight belongs to those who have eyes and God has no eyes, how can this phrase stand? But you will say: "We see both with our eyes and with our minds." That I admit. The one is spoken literally, the other figuratively. Literally we see with our eyes; figuratively, we see with our minds. Perhaps it would be more correct, more in accordance with the real meaning of the word, if in speaking of the mind we should say "perceive" rather than "see"; for "perceive" means both to see and to reflect. Let each be used in its proper sense. "When God saw" is not used in its strict sense, and cannot be true in the literal meaning of the words. . . .

From this has grown that mode of expression and that art of covering a zeal for truth with a surface of falsehood of which we are speaking. It was adopted by theologians, not only by those of the Gentiles, like Orpheus,

Museus and Linus, whom Augustine names among the first Gentile theologians, and all the rest who were led into error by that form of blindness, but also by all those chosen by nature or by circumcision from the people of God who have spoken piously and rationally of God. Finally it came also to Christians, who received it from all the prophets and sacred writings and found it mingled with the Holy Gospels by our Savior himself. Indeed, if there were in the Gospels nothing else but the countless parables which Christ put forth even though the Gospels lacked those other infinite mysteries in which they abound, it ought to be sufficiently clear to everyone that he did not disdain the art of poetic speech.

It follows, therefore, that this device is rather divine than human, and this is abundantly proved by the prophetic visions of dreams which, not to mention others and passing over the witness of the heathen lest I offend your ears, Joseph, the holiest of the patriarchs, set forth in his captivity to his companions and to the king's majesty, as he had done before to his father and his brethren and afterward interpreted to others. In these visions it is evident that God spoke many times in figures, so that we must admit that this marvellous mode of speaking in strange locutions is derived from God and not from men.

So it seems to me, my dear John, that you and the rest who have such an abhorrence of poetry are all too simple souls and are making a great mistake in trying to scare everyone away from imitating a divine form of speech as from a heinous crime. Forbid it if you please, and if you can, to yourselves in the cloister, but don't meddle with people outside. This is not within your province or your power. Forbid it to yourselves, as I have said, if you can, and see how many times a day you will be offending against your own law!

And now, to come more directly to my third point: What right have you, I beg you, to forbid my friend Angelo to indulge his taste of oratory, poetry and philosophy? What rights have you over any one outside your monastery? True, it is right for you and for everyone to encourage and even to command that which is honorable and to prohibit the contrary, but what is there in these things which makes it right to forbid them? I know and read daily in Jerome, Ambrose and Augustine splendid passages from philosophers and orators and verses from the poets which shine out like stars from those most sacred writings, and I do not suppose you condemn this as a crime. If things true and holy, decorous and beautiful, are found in those doctors and may be read there without harm, why should these same things be called profane and infamous in the original writings of their authors? Why are they forbidden to us if they were permitted to holy doctors? Or perhaps, are they false and wicked at the source and become true and virtuous when a little trickle of them occurs in the doctors? I cannot see why they became anathema on the lips of those who read them, when those holy men took them as true and sacred from the hands of their authors.

I beg you, my dear John, put an end to this and give up the fight. Do not have such confidence in your own purity and the judgment of a few persons as to forbid as unbecoming what the holiest and most universally approved doctors have done without hesitation, what is in the highest degree pious and generally commended, what makes those doctors admired by all for their learning and what gave them a far more powerful weapon against the heathen than Holy Scripture, which had influence among the Gentiles only in so far as they accepted it. . . .

Now I for my part have always thought there were three reasons for reading the poets: because they employ a peculiar vocabulary; because they abound in admirably adorned expressions and phrases, and because they illustrate our life as it ought to be by praising virtue and rebuking vice. For although they relate many scandalous things of both men and gods you will never find them praising these things. They are mentioned only to make vice hideous, so that everyone may see that such a judgment is passed upon them that neither the deeds nor the men who do them can at any time hope to escape reproof. Indeed it is, rightly considered, a mighty impulse and spur to do right and shun evil if men know that they are to be celebrated in song forever with their good and evil actions. Although this same thing is done by orators and historians, yet it is the very essence and special function of poets, since, as Father Aristotle says, "Every poem and every poetic expression is either praise or blame." And although orators and historians do this same thing, yet the former do it in order to persuade, to incriminate or to excuse, the latter in order to put in writing the truth of things as they happened, while it is the special function of poets to celebrate deeds in song in order that they may praise or blame them. So, if we would form a right judgment about poets, it is necessary to admit that when they write about immoral things they desire to bring reproach upon evil persons and evil deeds, but when they speak of virtuous things they desire to praise them and thus to warn their readers against the one as unseemly and incite them to the others as worthy of imitation.

The heathen doctrine of the gods is divided, according to a statement of Varro quoted by Augustine in his "City of God," into three parts, the physical, the political, and the mythical, which we call the fabulous. The first belongs to the philosophers, the second to the people and the rulers of the state, but the third is the affair of the poets. By the will of God it has come to pass that those gods which states have established by law are declared by philosophers to be naught; those which the people worship as gods in temples and at court are openly condemned by philosophers in their discussions in the schools, divine majesty being ascribed to I know not what incorporeal powers. Therefore arose rightfully the art of poetry which with its wonderful illusion showed that the gods civil and physical—for thus were they divided by Scaevola, most learned of pontiffs—with their fables and their foolish divinities, were no gods at all but men, and the worst kind of men at that, in whom not a trace of divinity could be found. Herein were the poets more sound than the philosophers, for they represented these gods as false and imaginary beings, so that all the crimes and vices which we read of in the poets are a libel upon the gods and are the clearest proof that these are false gods. Thus you in your simple-mindedness are condemning the very best thing there is in the poets.

But enough of this! There is nothing in human action so pure that a man may not turn it to evil if he thinks crosswise and finds his pleasure in evil speaking. Even if you consider the Song of Songs according to the letter, what can you find in the poets more erotic or more in the pastoral style—or even equally obscene or dealing more frankly with the nastiness of lust?—a book which, when you come to think of it, should relieve all poets from the charge of filthy language or of risky detail of invention. . . .

And now, to sum up all I have said, but not in detail: You have been able to see what Poetry is. You have learned not to deny that Holy Scripture, so far as its form is concerned, has the very closest relation to poetic diction and may well be compared with it as to its manner of speech. I have not urged or taught by argument but have most clearly set forth, that close attention should be given to poets, orators, and philosophers in accordance with the indications of the most holy doctors, so that we may not stand thunderstruck at some little verse quoted from a poet or at some opinion of a philosopher or an orator when they are only proving a point or adorning their style with their feathers or colors; also that we may learn how to oppose the heathen if we chance to be disputing with them or with any one who relies upon their authority, may answer their reasoning with our own and may adorn the truth with eloquence.

You have seen that the vices and crimes scattered through the verses of the poets are not, as you imagine, worthy of detestation, seeing that they are fictitious and composed in derision of fictitious deities. You have learned that Jerome and Augustine and Boethius, who never hesitated to quote poetry, did not exclude the works of the bards and the teachings of the heathen, but permitted them, provided only that they be not made an object in themselves. And many other things you now see which should cause you to change your opinion. Do not, therefore, henceforth oppose those who would engage in these studies, but teach them all to hasten on to other subjects and not to linger too long over the poets and other secular authors. It is not wrong to know evil, but it is wrong to do evil to one's ruin. Do you think it is wrong to learn the law of the Saracens in order to show its falsity or to dispute with those of an opposite opinion? Is any one such a mad fool as to think that the immoralities related in the poets are true and meant for imitation? Who would forbid us to learn things which furnish our equipment, which aid us in reproving what is false and help us to declare the truth? And since the reading of the poets is prescribed, on the authority of Quintilian, for students of rhetoric, will you shut us off also from the practice of oratory? . . . Be, therefore, of better counsel, lest you fall into error yourself and cause others to do so and through your ingratitude give offence to the poets to whom you owe so much. Remember that it is not a sign of holiness to deprive others of what is of daily use and profit to yourself.

Farewell, and pray for me!

Florence, January 24, 1406 A.D.

GIOVANNI PICO DELLA MIRANDOLA

G IOVANNI PICO, count of Mirandola (1463–94) was the youngest member
of an Italian family which claimed descent from the Emperor Constantine.
He was sent at fourteen to the University of Bologna, and after two years
he began to travel, going from one university to another and acquiring an enormous erudition. Seven years later, at the age of twenty-three, he came to Rome,
where he advertised that he would defend publicly against anyone in Europe a
list of nine hundred theses or conclusions relating to virtually every field of learning, offering even to pay the travel expenses of scholars coming from distant places.
The disputation and the book containing the theses were prohibited by Pope
Innocent VIII, though at a later date Pico was cleared of the charge of heresy by
Pope Alexander VI. Famous for his handsome appearance and polished manners
as well as for his brilliance and piety (he appears in Castiglione's *Book of the
Courtier*), Pico nevertheless planned to renounce the world and become a migrant
preacher, but a fever brought on his early death at the age of thirty-one.

Pico wrote *Heptaplus,* a mystical treatment of creation, and an unfinished
treatise opposing astrology. His *Oration on the Dignity of Man* was to have been
Pico's introductory speech for the disputation at Rome.

Pico's thought is a vast compound. Unlike most of the humanists, his intellectual
appetite was not bounded by classical antiquity. He sought to master and absorb
and harmonize the whole intellectual heritage of man: the Middle Ages and
antiquity, Aristotle and Plato, Christian, Arabian, and Jewish philosophy, early
Church Fathers and late scholastics, and a host of important individual thinkers
from the earliest times. He endeavored to reconcile Moses and Plato, Christianity
and paganism, mystical and theoretical thinking.

Walter Pater happily defines the character of Pico's humanism: "For the essence
of humanism is that belief of which he never seems to have doubted, that nothing
which has ever interested living men and women can wholly lose its vitality—no
language they have spoken, nor oracle beside which they have hushed their
voices, no dream which has once been entertained by actual human minds, nothing
about which they have ever been passionate, or expended time and zeal."

The following selection is from Elizabeth Livermoore Forbes's translation from
the Latin of Pico's *Oration,* which appeared in *The Renaissance Philosophy of
Man,* edited by Ernst Cassirer *et al.* (The University of Chicago Press; copyright
1948 by the University of Chicago).

☙

ORATION ON THE DIGNITY OF MAN

I HAVE READ in the records of the Arabians, reverend Fathers, that Abdala the Saracen,[1] when questioned as to what on this stage of the world, as it were, could be seen most worthy of wonder, replied: "There is nothing to be seen more wonderful than man." In agreement with this opinion is the saying of Hermes Trismegistus: "A great miracle, Asclepius, is man." But when I weighed the reason for these maxims, the many grounds for the excellence of human nature reported by many men failed to satisfy me —that man is the intermediary between creatures, the intimate of the gods, the king of the lower beings, by the acuteness of his sense, by the discernment of his reason, and by the light of his intelligence the interpreter of nature, the interval between fixed eternity and fleeing time, and (as the Persians say) the bond, nay, rather, the marriage song of the world, on David's testimony but little lower than the angels. Admittedly great though these reasons be, they are not the principal grounds, that is, those which may rightfully claim for themselves the privilege of the highest admiration. For why should we not admire more the angels themselves and the blessed choirs of heaven? At last it seems to me I have come to understand why man is the most fortunate of creatures and consequently worthy of all admiration and what precisely is that rank which is his lot in the universal chain of Being—a rank to be envied not only by brutes but even by the stars and by minds beyond this world. It is a matter past faith and a wondrous one. Why should it not be? For it is on this very account that man is rightly called and judged a great miracle and a wonderful creature indeed.

But hear, Fathers, exactly what this rank is and, as friendly auditors, conformably to your kindness, do me this favor. God the Father, the supreme Architect, had already built this cosmic home we behold, the most sacred temple of His godhead, by the laws of His mysterious wisdom. The region above the heavens He had adorned with Intelligences, the heavenly spheres He had quickened with eternal souls, and the excrementary and filthy parts of the lower world He had filled with a multitude of animals of every kind. But, when the work was finished, the Craftsman kept wishing that there were someone to ponder the plan of so great a work, to love its beauty, and to wonder at its vastness. Therefore, when everything was done (as Moses and Timaeus bear witness), He finally took thought concerning the creation of man. But there was not among His archetypes that from which He could fashion a new offspring, nor was there in His

---

[1] [*Abdala*, that is, *Abd Allah*, probably the cousin of Mohammed.]

treasure-houses anything which He might bestow on His new son as an inheritance, nor was there in the seats of all the world a place where the latter might sit to contemplate the universe. All was now complete; all things had been assigned to the highest, the middle, and the lowest orders. But in its final creation it was not the part of the Father's power to fail as though exhausted. It was not the part of His wisdom to waver in a needful matter through poverty of counsel. It was not the part of His kindly love that he who was to praise God's divine generosity in regard to others should be compelled to condemn it in regard to himself.

At last the best of artisans ordained that that creature to whom He had been able to give nothing proper to himself should have joint possession of whatever had been peculiar to each of the different kinds of being. He therefore took man as a creature of indeterminate nature and, assigning him a place in the middle of the world, addressed him thus: "Neither a fixed abode nor a form that is thine alone nor any function peculiar to thyself have we given thee, Adam, to the end that according to thy longing and according to thy judgment thou mayest have and possess what abode, what form, and what functions thou thyself shalt desire. The nature of all other beings is limited and constrained within the bounds of laws prescribed by Us. Thou, constrained by no limits, in accordance with thine own free will, in whose hand We have placed thee, shalt ordain for thyself the limits of thy nature. We have set thee at the world's center that thou mayest from thence more easily observe whatever is in the world. We have made thee neither of heaven nor of earth, neither mortal nor immortal, so that with freedom of choice and with honor, as though the maker and molder of thyself, thou mayest fashion thyself in whatever shape thou shalt prefer. Thou shalt have the power to degenerate into the lower forms of life, which are brutish. Thou shalt have the power, out of thy soul's judgment, to be reborn into the higher forms, which are divine."

O supreme generosity of God the Father, O highest and most marvelous felicity of man! To him it is granted to have whatever he chooses, to be whatever he wills. Beasts as soon as they are born (so says Lucilius) bring with them from their mother's womb all they will ever possess. Spiritual beings, either from the beginning or soon thereafter, become what they are to be for ever and ever. On man when he came into life the Father conferred the seeds of all kinds and the germs of every way of life. Whatever seeds each man cultivates will grow to maturity and bear in him their own fruit. If they be vegetative, he will be like a plant. If sensitive, he will become brutish. If rational, he will grow into a heavenly being. If intellectual, he will be an angel and the son of God. And if, happy in the lot of no created thing, he withdraws into the center of his own unity, his spirit, made one with God, in the solitary darkness of God, Who is set above all things, shall surpass them all. Who would not admire this our chameleon? Or who could more greatly admire aught else whatever? It is man who Asclepius of Athens, arguing from his mutability of character and from his self-transforming nature, on just grounds says was symbolized by Proteus in the mysteries. Hence those metamorphoses renowned among the Hebrews and the Pythagoreans.

For the occult theology of the Hebrews sometimes transforms the holy Enoch into an angel of divinity whom they call "Mal'akh Adonay Shebaoth"[2] and sometimes transforms others into other divinities. The Pythagoreans degrade impious men into brutes and, if one is to believe Empedocles, even into plants. Mohammed, in imitation, often had this saying on his tongue: "They who have deviated from divine law become beasts," and surely he spoke justly. For it is not the bark that makes the plant but its senseless and insentient nature; neither is it the hide that makes the beast of burden but its irrational, sensitive soul; neither is it the orbed form that makes the heavens but its undeviating order; nor is it the sundering from body but his spiritual intelligence that makes the angel. For if you see one abandoned to his appetites crawling on the ground, it is a plant and not a man you see; if you see one blinded by the vain illusions of imagery, as it were of Calypso, and, softened by their gnawing allurement, delivered over to his senses, it is a beast and not a man you see. If you see a philosopher determining all things by means of right reason, him you shall reverence: he is a heavenly being and not of this earth. If you see a pure contemplator, one unaware of the body and confined to the inner reaches of the mind, he is neither an earthly nor a heavenly being; he is a more reverend divinity vested with human flesh.

Are there any who would not admire man, who is, in the sacred writings of Moses and the Christians, not without reason described sometimes by the name of "all flesh," sometimes by that of "every creature," inasmuch as he himself molds, fashions, and changes himself into the form of all flesh and into the character of every creature? For this reason the Persian Euanthes, in describing the Chaldaean theology, writes that man has no semblance that is inborn and his very own but many that are external and foreign to him; whence this saying of the Chaldaeans: "Hanorish tharah sharinas," that is, "Man is a being of varied, manifold, and inconstant nature." But why do we emphasize this? To the end that after we have been born to this condition— that we can become what we will—we should understand that we ought to

[2] [*Angel of the Lord of Hosts.*]

have especial care to this, that it should never be said against us that, although born to a privileged position, we failed to recognize it and became like unto wild animals and senseless beasts of burden but that rather the saying of Asaph the prophet should apply: "Ye are all angels and sons of the Most High," and that we may not, by abusing the most indulgent generosity of the Father, make for ourselves that freedom of choice He has given into something harmful instead of salutary. Let a certain holy ambition invade our souls, so that, not content with the mediocre, we shall pant after the highest and (since we may if we wish) toil with all our strength to obtain it.

Let us disdain earthly things, contemn astral things, and, finally, esteeming less whatever is of the world, hasten to that court which is beyond the world and nearest to the Godhead. There, as the sacred mysteries relate, Seraphim, Cherubim, and Thrones hold the first places; let us, incapable of yielding to them, and intolerant of a lower place, emulate their dignity and their glory. If we have willed it, we shall be second to them in nothing. . . .

But by what means is one able either to judge or to love things unknown? Moses loved a God whom he saw and, as judge, administered among the people what he had first beheld in contemplation upon the mountain. Therefore, the Cherub as intermediary by his own light makes us ready for the Seraphic fire and equally lights the way to the judgment of the Thrones. This is the bond of the first minds, the Palladian order, the chief of contemplative philosophy. This is the one for us first to emulate, to court, and to understand; the one from whence we may be rapt to the heights of love and descend, well taught and well prepared, to the functions of active life. But truly it is worth while, if our life is to be modeled on the example of the Cherubic life, to have before our eyes and clearly understood both its nature and its quality and those things which are the deeds and the labor of Cherubs. But since it is not permitted us to attain this through our own efforts, we who are but flesh and know of the things of earth, let us go to the ancient fathers who, inasmuch as they were familiar and conversant with these matters, can give sure and altogether trustworthy testimony. Let us consult the Apostle Paul, the chosen vessel, as to what he saw the hosts of Cherubim doing when he was himself exalted to the third heaven. He will answer, according to the interpretation of Dionysius,[3] that he saw them being purified, then being illuminated, and at last being made perfect. Let us also, therefore, by emulating the Cherubic way of life on earth, by

---

[3] [Dionysius the Areopagite. The writings current under that name, composed by an unknown author probably about A.D. 500, were long attributed to Dionysius, the disciple of Paul, and hence enjoyed an enormous authority.]

taming the impulses of our passions with moral science, by dispelling the darkness of reason with dialectic, and by, so to speak, washing away the filth of ignorance and vice, cleanse our soul, so that her passions may not rave at random or her reason through heedlessness ever be deranged.

Then let us fill our well-prepared and purified soul with the light of natural philosophy, so that we may at last perfect her in the knowledge of things divine. And lest we be satisfied with those of our faith, let us consult the patriarch Jacob, whose form gleams carved on the throne of glory. Sleeping in the lower world but keeping watch in the upper, the wisest of fathers will advise us. But he will advise us through a figure (in this way everything was wont to come to those men) that there is a ladder extending from the lowest earth to the highest heaven, divided in a series of many steps, with the Lord seated at the top, and angels in contemplation ascending and descending over them alternately by turns. . . .

But indeed not only the Mosaic and Christian mysteries but also the theology of the ancients show us the benefits and value of the liberal arts, the discussion of which I am about to undertake. For what else did the degrees of the initiates observed in the mysteries of the Greeks mean? For they arrived at a perception of the mysteries when they had first been purified through those expiatory sciences, as it were, moral philosophy and dialectic. What else can that perception possibly be than an interpretation of occult nature by means of philosophy? Then at length to those who were so disposed came that ΕΠΟΠΤΕΙΑ,[4] that is to say, the observation of things divine by the light of theology. Who would not long to be initiated into such sacred rites? Who would not desire, by neglecting all human concerns, by despising the goods of fortune, and by disregarding those of the body, to become the guest of the gods while yet living on earth, and, made drunk by the nectar of eternity, to be endowed with the gifts of immortality though still a mortal being? Who would not wish to be so inflamed with those Socratic frenzies sung by Plato in the Phaedrus, that, by the oarage of feet and wings escaping speedily from hence, that is, from a world set on evil, he might be borne on the fastest of courses to the heavenly Jerusalem? Let us be driven, Fathers, let us be driven by the frenzies of Socrates, that they may so throw us into ecstasy as to put our mind and ourselves in God. Let us be driven by them, if we have first done what is in our power. For if through moral philosophy the forces of our passions have by a fitting agreement become so intent on harmony that they can sing together in undisturbed concord, and if through dialectic our reason has moved progressively in a rhythmical measure, then we shall be stirred by the frenzy of

[4] [*Initiation in the Eleusinian mysteries.*]

the Muses and drink the heavenly harmony with our inmost hearing. There-upon Bacchus, the leader of the Muses, by showing in his mysteries, that is, in the visible signs of nature, the invisible things of God to us who study philosophy, will intoxicate us with the fulness of God's house, in which, if we prove faithful, like Moses, hallowed theology shall come and inspire us with a doubled frenzy. For, exalted to her lofty heights, we shall measure therefrom all things that are and shall be and have been in indivisible eternity; and, admiring their original beauty, like the seers of Phoebus, we shall become her own winged lovers. And at last, roused by ineffable love as by a sting, like burning Seraphim rapt from ourselves, full of divine power we shall no longer be ourselves but shall become He Himself Who made us.

PIETRO POMPONAZZI

PIETRO POMPONAZZI (1462–1525), an important Italian interpreter of Aristotle, taught at Padua, Ferrara, and Bologna. His major work, *On the Immortality of the Soul* (1516), belongs from one point of view directly in the scholastic tradition. And yet Pomponazzi is a herald of new ways of thinking. Like the others of his age who sought to know the classics of the ancient world in a fresh light, he tried to rediscover, in text and in spirit, an Aristotle who lay buried beneath generations of commentary, translation, and assimilation to the Christian viewpoint.

When Aristotle discussed the nature of the soul, he approached it as a biological phenomenon in the natural world. The soul or psyche of a living thing he defined as its basic character, the way in which it functioned. The soul of man is the process of living and thinking, the process that makes him man and not just any animal at all. The soul is related to the body as the power of cutting to the knife, or the power of seeing to the eye. It can no more exist without the body than can seeing without the eyeball or cutting without the blade. The Arabian, Jewish, and Christian theologians of the Middle Ages, faced by the problem of reconciling Aristotle with dogma, developed a variety of interpretations of his psychology, all attempting to mitigate its suggestion of the mortality of the soul. Their efforts were largely based on certain obscure passages which seemed to depart from the naturalistic approach and to permit the conclusion that at least the rational part of the soul did not perish with the body. One tradition, developing under the influence of the Arabian philosopher Averroës, and subsequently known as Averroism, understood Aristotle to admit immortality for human reason in the abstract but to deny it to the individual human soul. Thomas Aquinas, on the other hand, found it possible to draw from Aristotle an argument for individual immortality.

Since the Church had condemned Averroism, accepted the Thomistic view, and begun to regard even a discussion of the problem as a dangerous heresy, Pomponazzi's book aroused a storm of controversy and criticism and was burned at Venice. The controversy centered more around the interpretation of Aristotle, who, as expounded by Aquinas, had become part of the foundation of Church doctrine, than around the problem of immortality in itself. Pomponazzi's work never faced trial; Pietro Bembo (later Cardinal Bembo), secretary to Pope Leo X, had the charges dismissed. Not long afterward Pomponazzi wrote two treatises in further elaboration of his position.

Of greater importance, perhaps, for modern thought than his views on the soul is his position on their ethical implications. The brief selection that follows is taken from the translation from the Latin by William Henry Hay (Haverford, Pa., Haverford College, 1938).

ON THE IMMORTALITY OF THE SOUL

IT MUST BE CONSIDERED that many men have thought that the soul was mortal, who nevertheless have written that it is immortal; but have done this on account of the proneness to evil of men who have little or no intellect, and neither recognizing nor loving the good things of the soul, spend their time only on bodily things. Wherefore it is necessary to correct them by this sort of device, just as a doctor behaves toward a sick man, and a nurse to a child lacking reason.

By these, as I think, other things also can be solved. For, although it is commonly said that, if the soul is mortal, man ought to give himself over completely to bodily pleasures, to commit all evils for his own use, and that it would be futile to worship God, to honor divine things, to pour forth prayers to God, to make sacrifices, and the rest of this sort, the answer is plain enough by what has been said. For since happiness is naturally sought and misery avoided, and by what has been said happiness consists in virtuous action, but misery in sinful action, since to worship God with the mind, to honor divine things, to pour out prayers to God, to sacrifice are actions particularly virtuous, therefore we ought to strive with all our strength to the acquisition of those. But on the contrary, thefts, robberies, murders, a life of pleasure are sins, which make man turn into a beast and cease to be a man; therefore we ought to abstain from these. And notice that one who works conscientiously, not expecting any reward other than virtue, seems to work far more virtuously and more ingenuously than he who expects some reward beyond virtue; and he who shuns sin on account of the foulness of sin, not because of the fear of punishment owed for sin, seems rather to be praised than he who avoids sin because of the fear of punishment, as in the verses:

> The good hate to sin from love of virtue,
> The evil hate to sin from fear of punishment.

Wherefore those more perfectly asserting that the soul is mortal seem better to preserve the principle of virtue than those who assert that it is immortal. For hope of reward and fear of punishment seem to bring a certain servility, which is contrary to the nature of virtue.

For a complement of this opinion it must be known that, as Aristotle teaches in the books *De generatione animalium*,[1] nature proceeds step by step, and in an orderly fashion, so that it does not join an extreme im-

[1] [*On the Generation of Animals.*]

mediately with an extreme, but an extreme with a mean. For we see that between grasses and trees mediate shrubs; between vegetables and animals are immoveable animate things, as oysters and the rest of this sort; and so on ascending further. The blessed Dionysius supports that in the seventh chapter of De divinis nominibus,[2] when he says that the divine wisdom joins the ends of things above to the beginnings of things below. Man, moreover, as has been said, is the most perfect of animals; wherefore since the human soul obtains first place among material things, therefore it will be joined with immaterial things, and is halfway between material and immaterial things. But a mean compared to the extremes is called the other of the extremes; wherefore compared to immaterial things it can be called material; and in respect to material things, immaterial. Nor does it deserve only those names, but also participates in the properties of the extremes: for green compared to white is not only called black; but also gathers sight like black, although not so intensely. Wherefore also the human soul has some of the properties of the intelligences and has some of the properties of all material things; whence it is that, when it performs functions with which it agrees with the intelligences, it is said to be divine and to be changed into Gods; but when it performs functions of the beasts, it is said to be changed into beasts; for on account of evil it is called a serpent or a fox, on account of cruelty a tiger, and so of the rest. For there is nothing in the world that on account of some property cannot agree with man himself; wherefore not undeservedly is man called the microcosm or the little world. Therefore some have said that man is a great marvel, since he is the whole world and convertible into every nature, since power has been given him to attain whatever property he may prefer. Therefore the ancients rightly mythologized when they said that some men had been made Gods, some lions, some wolves, some eagles, some fishes, some plants, some rocks, and so of the rest; since some men have attained intellect, some sense, some the powers of the vegetative soul: and so of the rest.

Therefore whoever place bodily pleasures before moral or intellectual virtues make man a beast rather than a God; those who put riches first make man gold: wherefore some are to be called beasts, some insensate. Therefore, although the soul is mortal, the virtues are not to be despised, and pleasures sought, unless one prefers to be a beast than a man, and insensate than sensate or knowing. Nevertheless one ought to know that however much man thus participates in the material and the immaterial, yet he is properly said to participate in the immaterial, because he lacks much of immateriality; but he is not properly said to participate in animals and

[2] [On Divine Names.]

vegetables, but to contain them, for he is below immaterial things and is above material. Wherefore he cannot arrive at the perfection of immaterial things: whence they are not called Gods, but god-like or divine. But man can not only make himself equal to a beast, nay even surpass a beast; for some men exist far crueller than any beasts, as Aristotle says in the seventh book of *Ethica:* "an evil man is ten thousand times worse than a beast." And just as it was said of cruelty, so it may be said of the other vices. Since, therefore, sin is so foul, the life of a sinful man so unjust, but the contrary with virtue, who, therefore, even if the soul be mortal, would rather choose sin than virtue, unless he preferred to be a beast or worse than a beast?

GIORGIO VASARI

Giorgio Vasari (1511–74), a Florentine architect, painter, and writer, spent his boyhood with the young Medici princes, by whose guardian he was apprenticed at the age of thirteen to Michelangelo and Andrea del Sarto, later coming under the influence of Raphael in Rome. Vasari traveled extensively in Italy and left several extant works of art in a number of her cities. His most famous work of architecture is the Uffizi palace in Florence; his best known efforts as a painter include portraits of the Medici family (to which he was court painter under Duke Alessandro), the allegorical decorations of the Great Hall in the Palazzo Vecchio of Florence, and the murals in the Vatican's Sala Regia. The frescoes in the cupola of the Duomo, or cathedral, of Florence, which Vasari intended to be the culmination of his artistic career, were unfinished at his death.

His personal contributions to art and architecture are overshadowed by Vasari's reputation as the classic biographer of other artists and as a pioneer of art history and art criticism. His *Lives of the Most Eminent Painters, Sculptors, and Architects* (1550, enlarged in 1568), though marred by errors and inaccuracies, is a classic of erudition and served for two centuries as a model of such books. It remains today the principal source of information on the lives and careers of the aristic predecessors and contemporaries of Vasari.

This selection is from the Foster translation of the mid-nineteenth century.

MICHELANGELO BUONARROTI

Painter, Sculptor, and Architect
1475–1564

While the artists who came after Giotto were doing their best to imitate and to understand nature, bending every faculty to increase that high comprehension sometimes called intelligence, the Almighty took pity on their often fruitless labor. He resolved to send to earth a spirit capable of supreme expression in all the arts, one able to give form to painting, perfection to sculpture, and grandeur to architecture. The Almighty Creator also graciously endowed this chosen one with an understanding of philosophy and with the grace of poetry. And because he had observed that in Tuscany men were more zealous in study and more diligent in labor than in the rest of Italy, He decreed that Florence should be the birthplace of this divinely endowed spirit.

In the Casetino, therefore, in 1475, a son was born to Signor Lodovico di Leonardo di Buonarroti Simoni, a descendant of the noble family of the counts of Canossa. The child's mother was also of a very good family. Lodovico was then mayor of Chiusi e-Caprese, near the spot where Saint Francis of Assisi received the stigmata. . . .

Because Lodovico had many children and was far from rich, he placed his boys as apprentices in the weaver's trade. At school, Michelangelo did more drawing than studying. A friend of his, Granacci, who, though just a boy, was working for Domenico Ghirlandaio, used to bring Michelangelo drawings made by his master, who was then one of the foremost painters of all Italy. The result was that Michelangelo became apprenticed to Ghirlandaio by the time he was fourteen years old.

He made great progress. One day he corrected the drawing of another and older disciple by a few strong lines. It is wonderful to see what a difference he made. I have the very sheet of paper, which Granacci gave me and which I treasure as a relic. I showed it to Michelangelo in Rome in the year 1550. He was most interested and pleased to see it and modestly remarked that evidently he knew more as a boy than now that he was old. One day when Ghirlandaio was painting the chapel in Santa Maria Novella, he went out, and while he was gone Michelangelo drew the scaffolding trestles, pots of paint, brushes and the apprentices at their tasks. When he returned, Domenico Ghirlandaio was amazed at the power and originality of the lad's work. "This boy knows more than I do!" he exclaimed.

Michelangelo made a Saint John in marble for Lorenzo di Pier Francesco de' Medici. He carved a sleeping cupid, life-size. A friend said, "I am certain that, if you bury this statue for a time and then send it to Rome as an antique, you will get more for it than if you sell it here in Florence." This Michelangelo is said to have done, though some say that the friend took it to Rome and buried it there. In any case the Cardinal of San Giorgio bought it for two hundred crowns. Others say that the friend delivered only thirty crowns to Michelangelo and told him that was all he could get and kept the difference. In the meanwhile the cardinal discovered that the cupid was no antique, and had, in fact, been made in Florence, and insisted on getting his money back. He was well laughed at, and even blamed for not being able to appreciate the merit of the work, which was really perfection. What matter, they laughed, whether it were modern or not? But there will always be men who value fashion rather than real worth. The whole affair increased Michelangelo's reputation. He was invited to Rome by Cardinal San Giorgio and stayed a year with him. But the cardinal had no understanding of art and did nothing to further Michelangelo's career.

Michelangelo now received letters from friends in Florence telling him that, if he came back, he might have the big piece of marble that Pier Soderini, then gonfaloniere of the city, had talked of giving to Leonardo da Vinci, but was now proposing to present to Andrea Sansovino, an excellent sculptor, who was making every effort to get it. Few people were courageous enough to attempt to carve this eighteen-foot block of stone, which had remained in the workshop of Santa Maria del Fiore ever since a certain Maestro Simone da Fiesole had marred it thirty-five years before.

No sooner had Michelangelo arrived in Florence than he set about securing the stone. He begged it of Soderini and received it as a worthless thing. He measured the mass and accommodated his design to the injury that had been done to it. He made a little model in wax of David, sling in hand. Then he built a boarding about the marble which hid it entirely from view. He let no one look at it until he had finished it.

The problem of moving the statue [the David] from Santa Maria del Fiore to the Piazza de' Signori now confronted him, but Giuliano da Sangallo and his brother Antonio made a stout framework of wood about it and suspended the figure by means of a clever slipknot that became tighter under tension. They moved it forward, gradually, by means of beams and windlasses.

Soderini was very pleased with it when it was in place. He watched Michelangelo retouch it and said he thought the nose too short. Michelangelo saw that Soderini was badly placed to view the head, but, to satisfy him, he took his chisel and a little loose marble dust in his hand and climbed the scaffolding. As he tapped lightly on the chisel, he let the marble dust drift down. "I like it better now," said Soderini, "You have given it life." Michelangelo came down, not without compassion for those who wish to appear good judges in matters about which they know nothing.

Then Michelangelo showed the statue. And we may say that it surpasses all others, both ancient and modern. Not even the treasures of Rome—the *Nile* and the *Tiber* in the Belvedere, or the *Giants* of Monte Cavallo—can compare with it. The whole form is divine. The outline of the legs is most beautiful. The connection of each limb to the body is faultless. Never since has a statue been produced with so fine an attitude, so perfect a grace, such beauty of hand, of foot, of brow. . . .

Michelangelo's fame, because of the *Pietà, il Gigante* [David], and the Cartoon was so great that in 1503, when he was twenty-nine years old, he was invited to Rome by Pope Julius II. His Holiness commissioned him to make his tomb. Months passed before the design was finally approved. Indeed, it outdid any monument, even the imperial tombs, in magnificence of superb ornament and wealth of figures. When it was accepted, Julius determined to rebuild the choir of Saint Peter's to make it a fit setting.

Michelangelo set to work with all his might excavating the marble at Carrara. He was provided with a fund of one thousand crowns and was assisted by two disciples. He toiled at Carrara for eight months without receiving any additional money or supply. He amused himself with the plan for a vast monument to himself that might be carved from the living rock. Finally he selected the blocks he needed and sent them to Rome by ship. There they filled fully half the piazza near Santa Caterina and all the space between Saint Peter's and the Castello where he had his studio. To make it easier for the Pope to watch him at work, a bridge was built from the corridor of the Vatican across to the studio. This intimacy between the Pope and his favorite made others envious and caused Michelangelo a great deal of trouble.

Michelangelo set up one portion of the tomb, that is the shorter sides of it. While he was doing this, more of his marble arrived from Carrara. Because Michelangelo found His Holiness engaged with important news just received from Bologna, he advanced the money out of his own pocket. A few days later he sought an audience with the Pope but was told to have patience by a groom of the chambers who added that he had orders not to admit him. A bishop who stood near observed that possibly the groom was unacquainted with the person whom he refused to admit. The groom replied that he knew him only too well. "I, however," he added, "am here to do as my superiors command, and to obey the orders of the Pope." Displeased with this reply, the master left, bidding the attendant tell His Holiness, when next he should inquire for Michelangelo that he had gone elsewhere. He went at once to his dwelling, where he left instructions that all his belongings should be sold to the Jews. He took horses that very night and left Rome.

Once in Poggibonsi, in Florentine territory, he made a halt. Five couriers followed him, one after another, with orders from the Pope, for him to return to Rome. No threat or entreaty could induce him to go back. But at last he wrote a letter, in which he complained of the treatment he had had and added that the Holy Father might seek someone who would serve him better.

In Florence, Michelangelo worked on the cartoon for the great hall. The Signoria received three briefs in which the Pope requested that he be sent back to Rome. But the very eagerness of these requests alarmed the artist, who is said to have considered placing himself in the service of the Grand Seigneur of Constantinople [the sultan]. Piero Soderini urged Michelangelo to go to the Pope, but finally prevailed by making him ambassador from the Florentine Republic and placing him in the care of his brother, Cardinal Soderini, and sending them both to Bologna, where the Pope then was.

When he arrived in Bologna, scarcely was his foot out of the stirrup before attendants hurried him to the Pope's presence. Michelangelo was accompanied by a bishop because Cardinal Soderini was ill. He knelt before the Pope, who merely glanced at him, saying angrily, "It seems that you would not come to us, but were waiting for us to come to you!" (He thus alluded to the fact that Bologna is nearer Florence than is Rome.) Michelangelo excused himself and admitted that he had acted in anger, but said that he could not bear to be ordered away. If he was wrong, he hoped the Pope would forgive him.

Now the bishop, in an effort to smooth things over, said that one should not expect artists to know anything outside their vocation, ignorant as they always were. This remark threw the Pope into a furious rage. He rushed at the bishop with a stick he happened to have in his hand, crying, "It is you who are the ignoramus, with your impertinences such as we would never think of uttering!" And he drove him out, the ushers hurrying the bishop along with blows. His rage thus spent upon the prelate, the Pope bestowed his benediction on Michelangelo. He then commissioned him to begin at once a bronze figure of himself, ten feet high. Of this figure we must say that the attitude was majestic and graceful, the draperies were rich and magnificent, and the countenance showed animation, force, resolution, and an imposing dignity. It was placed in a niche over the entrance of San Petronio in Bologna. . . .

. . . When the statue was almost finished in the clay, the Pope went to see it before he left Bologna. The Pope said he could not tell whether the figure was blessing or anathematizing the people. Michelangelo replied that he was admonishing the Bolognese to behave discreetly, and asked if he should not put a book in the left hand. "Put a sword," said the Pope, "for of letters I know but little."

The Pope left a thousand crowns on account with a banker for the completion of the figure, and after sixteen months of work it was set in place, as we have said. It was later torn down by the Bentivogli, and the bronze was sold to the duke of Ferrara, who made it into a cannon called the Julia.

The Pope returned to Rome; and while Michelangelo was still working on the statue, Bramante, who was the friend and kinsman of Raphael and hostile to Michelangelo, influenced the mind of the Pope to drop the work on the tomb and to employ Michelangelo instead on the painting of the chapel of Pope Sixtus [Sistine Chapel] in the Vatican. Bramante told the pontiff it was an invitation to death to build a tomb while one lived. Bramante and Michelangelo's other rivals hoped to thwart Michelangelo in his sculpture, in which he was perfect, and compel him to paint in fresco, in which they expected him to prove himself inferior to Raphael. Or, should he succeed at painting, it was almost certain that he would be so enraged as to secure the success of their main purpose, which was to be rid of him.

Michelangelo returned to Rome, therefore, and found the Pope no longer disposed to have the tomb finished. He was asked instead to paint the ceiling of the chapel, a great and difficult labor. Our artist, aware of his own inexperience, excused himself from the undertaking. He proposed that the work be given to Raphael. The more he refused, the more the impetuous Pope insisted. A quarrel threatened. Michelangelo saw that the Pope was determined, so he resolved to accept the task. His Holiness ordered Bramante to prepare the scaffolding. This he did by suspending the ropes through perforations in the ceiling. Michelangelo asked how the holes were going to be filled in when the painting was done. Bramante replied that they could think about it when the time came. Michelangelo saw that the architect was either incapable or unfriendly, and he went straight to the Pope to say that the scaffolding would not do and that Bramante did not know how to construct one. Julius, in the presence of Bramante, replied that Michelangelo might make it his own way. This he did by the use of a method that did not injure the walls, and which has since been pursued by Bramante and others. Michelangelo gave the ropes that were taken from Bramante's scaffolding to a poor carpenter, who sold them for a sum that made up his daughter's dowry.

For this work Michelangelo was paid three thousand crowns by the Pope. He may have spent twenty-five for colors. He worked under great personal inconvenience, constantly looking upward, so that he seriously injured his eyes. For months afterward he could read a letter only when he held it above his head. I can vouch for the pain of this kind of labor. When I painted the ceiling of the palace of Duke Cosimo, I never could have finished the work without a special support for my head. As it is, I still feel the effects of it, and I wonder that Michelangelo endured it so well. But, as the work progressed, his zeal for his art increased daily, and he grudged no labor and was insensible to all fatigue.

Down the center of the ceiling is the *History of the World,* from the Creation to the Deluge. The *Prophets* and the *Sibyls,* five on each side and one at each end, are painted on the corbels. The lunettes portray the genealogy of Christ. Michelangelo used no perspective, nor any one fixed point of sight, but was satisfied to paint each division with perfection of design. Truly this chapel has been, and is, the very light of our art. Everyone capable of judging stands amazed at the excellence of his work, at the grace and flexibility, the beautiful truth of proportion of the exquisite nude forms. These are varied in every way in expression and form. Some of the figures are seated, some are in motion, while others hold up festoons of oak leaves and acorns, the device of Pope Julius.

All the world hastened to behold this marvel and was overwhelmed, speechless with astonishment. The Pope rewarded Michelangelo with rich gifts and planned still greater works. Michelangelo sometimes remarked that he was aware that the pontiff really esteemed his abilities. When the Pope was sometimes rude and rough, he always soothed the injury by gifts and favors. Once, for example, Michelangelo asked leave to go to Florence for the festival of San Giovanni and begged also for some money for the journey. Pope Julius said, "Well! but when will this chapel be finished?" "When I can, Holy Father," said the artist. At that the Pope, who had a staff in his hand, struck Michelangelo and exclaimed, "When I can—when I can! I'll make thee finish it, and quickly." But no sooner had Michelangelo returned to his house to prepare for the journey than the pontiff's chamberlain brought five hundred crowns to pacify him. The chamberlain excused the Pope, declaring that these outbursts must be considered marks of His Holiness' favor. Michelangelo knew the Pope and was, after all, much attached to him. He laughed at what had happened, the more readily because things of this kind always turned out to his profit, and he saw that the Pope was anxious to keep him as a friend.

Pope Julius, before he felt the approaches of death, enjoined his nephews to see that his tomb should be constructed after a simpler design than that at first adopted. Michelangelo set to work with a will and he hoped to bring it to a conclusion without further obstacles. But Pope Julius died, and under Pope Leo [X] the work was laid aside. This pontiff was no less splendid in his undertakings than Julius. He was the first Florentine pope and he wished to leave some great memorial of himself and of that divine artist, Michelangelo, his fellow citizen, in his native city. He therefore commissioned Michelangelo to execute the façade of the church of San Lorenzo, which had been built by the house of Medici in Florence. He required Michelangelo to act as superintendent of the works. Michelangelo resisted as much as he dared, urging that he was pledged to do the tomb. But the Pope procured Michelangelo's release from the nephews of Pope Julius by promising that the artist should continue his preparations for the tomb by working on the figures for it in Florence, as he had formerly done. All this was much to the dissatisfaction of the cardinals [the nephews of Pope Julius] as well as to Michelangelo, who left Rome with tears in his eyes.

Back in Florence, the master erected the cupola of San Lorenzo. He had the goldsmith Piloto make a ball of seventy-two facets. His friends advised him to take care to have his lantern very different from Filippo Brunelleschi's. Michelangelo said, "Brunelleschi's would be difficult to imitate and impossible to surpass." He made monuments for the inside of the sacristy, for Giuliano and Lorenzo de' Medici. Michelangelo wished to imitate the old sacristy of Brunelleschi, but with new ornaments, and composed a decoration richer and more varied than any ever seen before. He boldly departed from the accepted rules. The unfortunate result has been that other artists have been encouraged to an injudicious imitation outside the wholesome rules of ornamentation. Artists, however, owe a great deal to Michelangelo, who freed them from the beaten path of convention. Boldness and grace are conspicuous in every part of his design, and the whole building is so unlike the usual treatment that one stands amazed at the sight of it.

Then came the sack of Rome and the exile of the Medici from Florence. Those who governed the city appointed Michelangelo to rebuild the fortifications. He prepared numerous plans to add to the defenses, fortifying San Miniato with bastions constructed after he had inspected the fortifications at Ferrara. While he was in Ferrara, Duke Alfonso I begged the master to execute some work of art for him at his leisure. This Michelangelo promised to do. He returned to Florence and proceeded with the fortifications. Yet he found time to paint a Leda, in tempera, for the duke of Ferrara, a divine performance. He also worked secretly on the statues for the tombs in San Lorenzo. He remained for six months at San Miniato, hastening the defenses, for the city would have been lost if the enemy had mastered that point. The sacristy was progressing and Michelangelo occupied a portion of his time in making seven statues for that place; one was a Madonna with the Infant astride her knee who turns as if entreating the breast, while the

Virgin holds him with one hand and supports herself with the other, bending forward to give it to the babe. The figures are not finished in every part, but in the imperfection of the sketch, perfection clearly shows. Still more amazing are the tombs of the dukes Giuliano and Lorenzo de' Medici. . . .

In 1534, Pope Clement died, and the work in San Lorenzo was at once laid aside. Michelangelo now believed himself free to give all his attention to the tomb of Pope Julius. But Pope Paul III soon summoned him, received him with great favor, and said he wished the master to enter his service. Michelangelo excused himself, saying he was under contract to the duke of Urbino to finish the tomb. Paul was much displeased. "For thirty years I have wished this! And now that I am Pope, will you disappoint me? That contract shall be torn up. I will have you work for me, come what may." Michelangelo was tempted to flee Rome and contrive to work on the tomb elsewhere, but he resolved to try to pacify the Pope, already so old, until something new happened.

Pope Paul, meanwhile, went with ten cardinals to Michelangelo's house to see the statues for the tomb of Julius. The cardinal of Mantua remarked that the Moses was sufficient of itself to do honor to the late pontiff. They also examined the cartoons for the wall of the chapel and were amazed at their beauty. His Holiness promised to persuade the duke of Urbino to be satisfied with three statues on condition that the other three be executed after Michelangelo's designs by other artists. But Michelangelo offered to pay for these three statues in order to be rid of this long and vexatious labor.

Michelangelo resolved, as he needs must, to enter the service of Pope Paul III and continue the painting of the chapel. The pontiff held the genius of Michelangelo in great respect and loved and admired him besides. The Pope wished to place his arms beneath the prophet Jonas where those of Julius II were, but he yielded at once with a good grace, when he saw that the suggestion gave Michelangelo pain.

I do not propose to describe the work [the *Last Judgment*], which has so often been reproduced. It will be enough to say that the purpose of the master was to render the human form in the absolute perfection of proportion and the greatest variety of attitude and to express the passions with force and truth. With this in mind he gave little attention to coloring and minutiae. . . .

When he was well, Michelangelo completed the painting. This great work may be described in the words of Dante, "Dead are the dead, the living

seem to live." Michelangelo surpassed himself. The seated figure of Our
Lord, terrible in his anger, turns toward the condemned, thundering anathema. Our Lady cowers in her mantle at the sight of that destruction. In a
word, we have here the true Last Judgment, the real Condemnation, the
effectual Resurrection. Those who thought they knew art are overcome by
this work. They gaze upon the evidence of power in these contours and
they tremble with fear as though some great spirit had possessed himself of
the art of design. The more they examine this work, the more they are
bewildered at the thought of a comparison of other paintings with this
paragon.

Fortunate is he, and happy are his memories, who has seen this wonder.
Thrice blessed art thou, O Paul, under whose protection was sheltered his
renown! A great happiness has been his birth for all artists, since Michelangelo has solved all the difficulties that previously obscured painting,
sculpture, and architecture.

Michelangelo worked at this painting for eight years and showed it to
the public on Christmas day in the year 1541. Not Rome only, but the
whole world, was filled with amazement and delight. For my part, I went
from Venice to Rome to see it and I was utterly astounded by it.

When Antonio da Sangallo died in 1546, a new director of the works of
St. Peter's was required, and at length the Pope was inspired to send for
Michelangelo. The master said that architecture was not his vocation, but
the Pope commanded him against his will, to accept the trust. One day
when he had gone to the building to examine it and to see Sangallo's wooden
model, he was met by a whole party of the Sangellicans who complimented
him on his appointment and remarked that the model before them was a
field on which he need never want pasture. "Well said," replied Michelangelo, thus implying, as he mentioned to a friend, that it was fit for sheep,
who knew nothing of art. He often declared publicly that Sangallo had
left the building without lights and that fifty years of work and three
hundred thousand crowns might be saved by a simplification of the design,
which he considered too elaborate with pinnacles, projections, and divisions
of members. He made a model to prove this and it is the one that has since
been used. This model cost twenty-five crowns and was finished in a fort-
night, while Sangallo's cost four thousand and was several years in the
making. It was easy to see that the church had become an endless source of
income rather than a building to be finished. Such a state of affairs could
not but displease so upright a man as Michelangelo, and he finally told
the contractors that he knew they were doing their best to hinder him, but

that, if he did undertake the charge, he would see to it that not one of them remained about the building. These words so publicly spoken aroused a great deal of ill feeling, and Michelangelo got no peace, since his adversaries constantly invented new ways of tormenting him.

At length the pontiff issued a decree that Michelangelo was to be in sole charge. Michelangelo inserted a clause that he was to receive no reward, but would perform his office for the love of God. Although Pope Paul more than once sent him money, Michelangelo would never accept any. . . .

In June 1557, the builder made a mistake in the vaulting of the apse of St. Peter's. Michelangelo sent Vasari his designs for the vaulting with this note:

This mistake has been committed because I am too old to visit the building as often as I could wish, although I had prepared an exact model of the work as I do of everything. I had thought that part finished, and now it will not be done this winter. If a man could die of shame and grief, I would not be alive now. I beg you to account to the duke for my not being at this moment in Florence.

The duke at last realized that the continuation of St. Peter's was the most important thing in the world to Michelangelo and he no longer pressed him to return to Florence. Whereupon the latter wrote to Vasari that he thanked the duke with all his heart for that great kindness and added, "God give me grace to serve him with my poor person, for my memory and understanding have gone to await him elsewhere." The date of this letter was August, 1557.

Our artist was now pressed to make his final arrangements known, and because he saw that little was done on the building, he was encouraged by his best friends to make at least a model of the cupola. Several months elapsed, however, before he could resolve on anything, but at length he made a beginning from which a much larger wooden one might be made later. Such a model was subsequently made by Maestro Giovanni Franzese, with all the parts executed with extreme nicety.

The completion of this model was a great satisfaction, not only to the friends of Michelangelo, but to all Rome. He continued to direct the work until the death of Pope Paul IV, when Pope Pius IV was chosen. That pontiff employed Piero Ligorio as his architect, yet he made many offers of service and showed much kindness to Michelangelo. His pension was continued, and some of the old allowances which our artist had lost in the pontificate of Paul IV were restored. The Pope employed him in many of his own buildings and during his reign the work of St. Peter's proceeded busily. Among other things, Michelangelo was required to design a monument to the memory of the Pope's brother, and the Cavaliere Leone Leoni of Arezzo was commissioned to construct it in the cathedral of Milan.

Now Duke Cosimo went that same year to Rome with his consort, the Duchess Leonora. Michelangelo went to see his excellency, who received him with much favor and out of respect for his great genius caused him to be seated near himself. Michelangelo then encouraged Cosimo anew to undertake the alteration of the great hall and he expressed his regret that he himself was no longer young enough to do him service. Michelangelo visited the duke several times, to the great satisfaction of both. When the most illustrious Don Francesco, Cosimo's son, was in Rome a short time afterward, the master visited him likewise. This prince always spoke to Michelangelo with uncovered head, so great was his reverence for that extraordinary man. To Vasari, Michelangelo wrote that he grieved that he was too infirm to do anything for his excellency. He went about Rome looking for some fine piece of antiquity to send to Florence as a present to that Signore.

Pope Pius asked Michelangelo for a design for the Porta Pia, and the master made three, all singularly beautiful. The pontiff chose the least costly and this has been erected. Finding that His Holiness would willingly have the other gates of Rome restored, he made numerous designs for them. He also made a design for the new church of Santa Maria degli Angeli, constructed in the Baths of Diocletian when that building was brought into the service of the Christians. The design of Michelangelo surpassed those of many other excellent architects. His Holiness, and all who have seen it, have been indeed amazed at his judgment and in the use he made of the whole skeleton of those baths. He designed a ciborium for the Sacrament, later executed by the artist in bronze, Jacopo Ciciliano, for this church.

Michelangelo had been working seventeen years on Saint Peter's, and the commissioners had more than once attempted to remove him. It chanced that Cesare da Castel Durante, overseer of the works, died, and Michelangelo put Luigi Gaeta, young but not inexperienced, in his place until he could find an overseer after his own heart. Some of the commissioners sent Luigi Gaeta away because they preferred Nanni di Baccio Bigio. Michelangelo, much displeased, would no longer go to St. Peter's. The commissioners announced that a substitute must be found since Michelangelo would and could do no more. When Michelangelo heard this, he sent to one of the commissioners, the bishop of Ferratino, who had spread the story that Michelangelo would have no more to do with the building, to say that he had no wish to give it up. Ferratino replied that he was sorry the master had not made his purpose known, but he added that a substitute was needed and that he would gladly accept Michelangelo's messenger as that substitute, a reply that appeared to satisfy Michelangelo. The bishop then told the other commissioners that a substitute was to be appointed and proposed Nanni Bigio, who was accepted and installed. Almost at once, Nanni Bigio had a great scaffolding built from the Pope's stable to the apse of Saint Peter's because, he declared, too many ropes were used in drawing up materials.

Michelangelo went to the Pope, whom he found on the piazza of the Capitol. His Holiness, speaking somewhat loudly, bade him go inside, when the master exclaimed, "Holy Father! A man of whom I know nothing has been made my substitute. If the commissioners and your Holiness are persuaded that I can no longer fill my office, I will return to Florence to rest, to be near the great prince who so often has desired my presence, and to finish my days in my own house. I beg leave of your Holiness to depart." The Pope sought to pacify the master with kind words and bade him to come to Araceli on the following day to talk the matter over. His Holiness assembled the commissioners, who claimed the building was in danger of being ruined. The Pope sent one of them to examine the structure and to require Nanni Bigio to show where the errors might be found, for it was he who had made these accusations.

All the reports were found to be false and malignant, and Nanni was dismissed with few compliments. Michelangelo indeed has brought the building to such a state that the work has now a fair prospect of being completed. By all this we see that God, the protector of the good, has extended his hand over the fabric and the master, even to his death. Pope Pius IV, who survived Michelangelo, commanded that nothing should be altered, while Pius V, his successor, continued, with even greater authority, to command that the designs of Michelangelo should be followed exactly. When Piero Ligorio, who was directing the building, presumed to propose certain changes, he was dismissed with little honor. Pope Pius V was indeed as zealous for the honor of the edifice as for the glory of the Christian faith. When Vasari went to pay his respects, in 1565, the pontiff spoke of nothing but the regard that was to be paid to the designs of Michelangelo, and he commanded Vasari to go to Bishop Ferratino and to direct that prelate to guide himself by the records and memoranda which Vasari would give him, to the end that no presumptuous person should ever be able to alter a single point of those arrangements made by the admirable genius of Michelangelo. On this occasion, which was witnessed by Messer Giovambattista Altoviti, Ferratino solemnly promised to observe every order and arrangement left by Michelangelo.

To return to Michelangelo, I have to relate that about a year before his death, Vasari secretly prevailed upon Duke Cosimo to use his influence with the Pope to the end that, since Michelangelo was now much debilitated, His Holiness should keep a watch over him, have him visited daily and take measures that, in case of any sudden accident such as may easily happen to the very old, the plans for Saint Peter's, or for the sacristy, the library, or the façade of San Lorenzo might not be lost, as so frequently happens.

In Lent of this year, Leonardo, Michelangelo's nephew, resolved to go to Rome. Perhaps he sensed that his kinsman was near the end of his life. Michelangelo was already suffering from a slow fever and he had his doctor, Messer Federigo Donato, write Leonardo to hasten his coming. But the malady increased, in spite of the care of those around him. Still in perfect self-possession, the master at length made his will in three clauses. He left his soul to God, his body to the earth, and his goods to his nearest relatives. He recommended his attendants to think upon the sufferings of Christ, and departed to a better life on February 17, 1564.

Michelangelo found his greatest pleasure in the labor of art. He was a born genius and his studies were unremitting. He dissected the human frame and examined every part: the articulation of joints, the muscles, the nerves, and the veins. Of animals also, particularly of horses, he made exhaustive study. These labors enabled him to complete his works with inimitable perfection and to give them a grace, a beauty, and an animation that surpass even the antique. He has overcome the difficulties of art with so much facility that no trace of labor may be seen.

Michelangelo's powers were so great that his sublime ideas were often inexpressible. He spoiled many works because of this. Shortly before his death he burned a large number of designs, sketches, and cartoons so that none might see the labors he endured in his resolution to achieve perfection. I have, myself, some drawings by his hand which were found in Florence, and these, although they give evidence of his great genius, yet prove that the hammer of Vulcan was necessary to bring Minerva from the head of Jupiter. He used to make figures nine, ten, even twelve heads high, simply to increase their grace. He would say that the artist must have his measuring tools in the eye, rather than in the hand, as it is the eye that judges. He used the same idea in architectural designs.

None will marvel that Michelangelo was a lover of solitude, devoted as he was to art, and, therefore, never alone or without food for contemplation.

Whoever thinks this solitude merely eccentricity is wrong. To produce works of merit, the artist must be free from cares and anxieties. Art does not permit wandering of the mind. Our artist did, nevertheless, prize the society of learned and distinguished men, more especially the illustrious Cardinal Ippolito de' Medici, who loved him greatly. He had a host of friends, but above all the rest, he loved Messer Tommaso de' Cavalieri, a Roman gentleman, still young and much inclined to the arts. For him, to help him in his drawing, he made superb cartoons, beautiful heads in red and black chalk and the *Ganymede* (carried to heaven by the bird of Jove), the *Tityus,* the *Phaethon* (falling from the chariot of the sun into the river Po), and also a Bacchanalia of Children, all most admirable. He also made a portrait of Messer Tommaso in a cartoon the size of life—he, who never painted the likeness of anyone before and after! The friendships of Michelangelo were all for deserving and noble persons. Messer Tommaso induced him to make drawings for his friends: an Annunciation for the Cardinal di Cesis, which was afterward painted by Marcello da Mantua, and another Annunciation, also painted by Marcello, the design for which is preserved like a jewel by Duke Cosimo. The duke has a statue ten feet high, representing Victory with a captive. He has, besides, a group of four captives, merely roughhewn, that show how Michelangelo extracted statues from the stone. The method is to take a figure of wax, lay it in a vessel of water and gradually emerge it, and then note the most salient part. Just so, the highest parts were extracted first from the marble.

Michelangelo loved the society of artists, especially of Jacopo Sansovino, Ill Rosso, Pontormo, Daniele da Volterra, and the Aretine, Giorgio Vasari, to whom he showed infinite kindness. Those who say he would not teach others are wrong. I have been present many times when he assisted his intimates or any who asked his counsels. It is true he was unfortunate in those whom he took into his house. His disciples were wholly unable to imitate their master. Even in his old age, had he found a disciple to his mind, he would have written a treatise on anatomy, in his desire to help artists, who are frequently misled by a lack of knowledge of anatomy. But he distrusted his ability to write, although in his letters he expressed himself well and tersely. He enjoyed reading our Italian poets, particularly Dante. Like Petrarch, he was fond of writing madrigals and of making sonnets. Michelangelo sent a large number of these verses to the most illustrious Marchesana di Pescara, and received replies both in verse and prose from that lady, of whose genius he was as much enamored as she of his. Michelangelo designed for her a Pietà with two angels of infinite beauty, a figure of Christ on the Cross, and one of Our Saviour at the Well with the Woman of Samaria. He delighted in the reading of the Scriptures, like the good Christian that he was, and honored the writings of Fra Girolamo Savonarola. He was an ardent admirer of beauty for art, and knew how to select the most beautiful, but he was not liable to the undue influence of beauty. This his whole life has proved. In all things he was most moderate. He ate frugally at the close of the day's work. Though rich, he lived like a poor man and rarely had a guest at his table. He would accept no presents for fear of being under an obligation.

This master, as I said at the beginning, was certainly sent by God as an example of what an artist could be. I, who can thank God for unusual happiness, count it among the greatest of my blessings that I was born while Michelangelo still lived, was found worthy to have him for my master, and was accepted as his trusted friend.

Michelangelo was followed to his tomb by all the artists and by his numerous friends. The Pope expressed his intention of commanding that a monument should be erected to his memory in Saint Peter's.

Michelangelo's nephew Leonardo did not arrive in Rome until it was all over, though he traveled post haste. When Duke Cosimo heard of his death, he resolved that, since he had not been able to do the master honor in his lifetime, Michelangelo's body should be brought to Florence and his obsequies solemnized with all possible splendor. But Michelangelo's body had to be smuggled out of Rome in a sort of bale, such as merchants use, to prevent a tumult in the city.

A committee of four artists of the Academy of Painters and Sculptors of Florence was chosen to make all the arrangements. Agnolo Bronzino and Giorgio Vasari, painters, and the sculptors Benvenuto Cellini and Bartolommeo Ammanato formed the committee. First they decided to ask the duke if the funeral could be held in the church of San Lorenzo, where the greater part of Michelangelo's Florentine works were. Also, they requested that the distinguished Messer Benedetto Varchi pronounce the funeral oration. The duke most readily and graciously consented.

Leonardo Buonarroti directed the secret removal of his uncle's body from Rome and brought it to Florence, where it arrived on Saturday, March 11. The next day all the painters, sculptors, and architects assembled quietly, bearing only a pall of velvet rich with gold embroidery. This they placed over the coffin and the bier. At nightfall they gathered silently around the corpse. The oldest and most distinguished masters each took a torch, while the younger artists at the same moments raised the bier. Blessed was he who could get a shoulder under it! All desired the glory of having borne to earth the remains of the greatest man ever known to the arts!

A rumor had spread that the body of Michelangelo had come and was to be carried to Santa Croce. The news passed from mouth to mouth and the church was filled in the twinkling of an eye. It was with difficulty that the bearers made their way to the sacristy to place the body in the receptacle destined to receive it. Although the priests, the black-clad mourners, and the wax tapers are, without doubt, imposing and grand in funeral ceremonies, still the sight of so many artists gathered with so much affection around the corpse was also a very grand and imposing spectacle.

The number of artists in Florence, and they were all present, was very great, if I may say so without offence to other cities, Florence is the seat of art as Athens was of science. But there were also so many citizens that the place could hold no more. Nothing was heard but the praise of Michelangelo. True art has this power.

When the remains, with this magnificent attendance, had been carried to Santa Croce, the monks performed the customary ceremonies for the dead. The prorector [of the Academy] by virtue of his office, who wished to gratify the people, and, as he afterward confessed, to see him for himself, resolved to have the cerements taken off. This was done, and though the master had been dead nearly twenty-five days, we were tempted to think he lay in a sweet and quiet sleep. The features were exactly as in life except for their pallor, and the face and cheeks were firm to the touch, as though but a few days had passed since his death. So great a concourse hastened to look upon the corpse that the tomb was not closed without great difficulty, and, if it had been day instead of night, we must have left it open many hours to satisfy the general wish. Early next morning many verses, both in Latin and in dialect [Italian] were appended to the tomb, and this was continued for some time.

But to come to the obsequies. These were deferred until July 14. The three men of the committee (for Benvenuto Cellini, the fourth, had been indisposed from the first and had taken no part in the matter), chose the sculptor Zanobi Lastricati, as their chairman. His fellow artists agreed that such a man as Michelangelo should be honored by works of spirit and beauty rather than by costly ceremonies. Thus would they honor Art by art. Although this was their intention, the magnificence of the ceremonial was the equal of any ever held by those academicians in true splendor.

A catafalque was erected in the central nave of San Lorenzo. It was surmounted by a figure of Fame and decorated with symbolical sculpture and paintings from the life of Michelangelo. In the picture which faced the high altar was a Latin inscription, the meaning of which was as follows:

The Academy of Painters, Sculptors, and Architects, by favor of the Duke Cosimo de' Medici, their chief, the supreme protector of these arts, admiring the extraordinary genius of Michelangelo Buonarroti, and acknowledging the benefits received from his divine works, have dedicated this monument, erected by their own hands, and consecrated with all the affection of their hearts, to the eminence and genius of the greatest painter, sculptor, and architect that ever lived.

Not a surface in the church but was decorated, or draped in black, except only the pulpit from which Varchi pronounced the funeral oration. This was Donatello's pulpit, in bronze and marble. Whatever decoration the artists might have attempted must have proved less beautiful. The church, adorned by numerous lights, was thronged with an incalculable number of people, who abandoned every other care to behold that honorable solemnity.

The decorations were left for several weeks to allow the whole city time to examine the ornaments. The multitude of verses and epitaphs in Latin and Italian are not repeated here, because they would fill a book by themselves and have, besides, been printed by others. After all the honors described above, the duke commanded that sepulture should be given the master in Santa Croce. His excellency gave to Leonardo, Michelangelo's nephew, all the marble for the tomb. The able sculptor Battista Lorenzi was commissioned to construct it after the designs of Giorgio Vasari. His excellency, that nothing may be wanting to the honor of so great a man, proposes to place Michelangelo's bust, with an inscription, in the cathedral, where there are busts and names of many other distinguished Florentines.

BALDASSARE CASTIGLIONE

Count Baldassare Castiglione (1478–1529), an Italian statesman, served the duke of Milan, and from 1504 to 1508 was a member of the court of the duke of Urbino. Himself a model courtier, Castiglione is famous for his work, *The Book of the Courtier,* which reports the conversations held in the court of Urbino, supposedly in March, 1507. Besides being a minute analysis of courtly virtues, including intellectual accomplishments as well as etiquette, Castiglione's work is a vivid rendition of the atmosphere and life of such a court, and suggests the new interests of the changing world in which it had its basis.

The book enjoyed an enormous vogue throughout Europe, for with the rise of the commercial towns in Italy and the attendant incursion of strong princes the feudal lord and knight had a new vocation. Attaching himself to the court of a powerful prince he joined to the traditional virtues of the knight the new and many-sided qualities of the courtier. The courtier's virtues were those of the graceful knight, the artful speaker, the patron of the arts gifted in his own right, the loyal friend, the passionate and Platonic lover.

The following translation from the Italian is by L. E. Opdycke (New York, Charles Scribner's Sons, 1903).

BOOK OF THE COURTIER

[Book I]

[Count Ludovico da Canossa said:] . . . I believe that there exists in everything its own perfection, although concealed; and that this can be determined through rational discussion by any having knowledge of the thing in hand. And since, as I have said, the truth often lies concealed, and I do not profess to have this knowledge, I can only praise the kind of Courtier that I most esteem, and approve him who seems to me nearest right, according to my poor judgment; the which you will follow if you find it good, or you will hold to your own if it differs from mine. Nor shall I at all insist that mine is better than yours; not only because you may think one thing and I another, but I myself may sometimes think one thing, and sometimes another.

I wish, then, that this Courtier of ours should be nobly born and of gentle race; because it is far less unseemly for one of ignoble birth to fail in worthy deeds, than for one of noble birth, who, if he strays from the path of his predecessors, stains his family name, and not only fails to achieve but loses what has been achieved already; for noble birth is like a bright lamp that manifests and makes visible good and evil deeds, and kindles and stimulates to virtue both by fear of shame and by hope of praise. And since this splendour of nobility does not illumine the deeds of the humbly born, they lack that stimulus and fear of shame, nor do they feel any obligation to advance beyond what their predecessors have done; while to the nobly born it seems a reproach not to reach at least the goal set them by their ancestors. And thus it nearly always happens that both in the profession of arms and in other worthy pursuits the most famous men have been of noble birth, because nature has implanted in everything that hidden seed which gives a certain force and quality of its own essence to all things that are derived from it, and makes them like itself: as we see not only in the breeds of horses and of other animals, but also in trees, the shoots of which nearly always resemble the trunk; and if they sometimes degenerate, it arises from poor cultivation. And so it is with men who if rightly trained are nearly always like those from whom they spring, and often better; but if there be no one to give them proper care, they become like savages and never reach perfection.

It is true that, by favour of the stars or of nature, some men are endowed at birth with such graces that they seem not to have been born, but rather as if some god had formed them with his very hands and adorned them with every excellence of mind and body. So too there are many men so foolish and rude that one cannot but think that nature brought them into the world out of contempt or mockery. Just as these can usually accomplish little even with constant diligence and good training, so with slight pains those others reach the highest summit of excellence. And to give you an instance: you see my lord Don Ippolito d'Este, Cardinal of Ferrara, who has enjoyed such fortune from his birth, that his person, his aspect, his words and all his movements are so disposed and imbued with this grace, that—although he is young—he exhibits among the most aged prelates such weight of character that he seems fitter to teach than to be taught; likewise in conversation with men and women of every rank, in games, in pleasantry and in banter, he has a certain sweetness and manners so gracious, that whoso speaks with him or even sees him, must needs remain attached to him forever.

But to return to our subject: I say that there is a middle state between perfect grace on the one hand and senseless folly on the other; and those who are not thus perfectly endowed by nature, with study and toil can in great part polish and amend their natural defects. Besides his noble birth, then, I would have the Courtier favoured in this regard also, and endowed by nature not only with talent and beauty of person and feature, but with a certain grace and (as we say) air that shall make him at first sight pleasing and agreeable to all who see him; and I would have this an ornament that should dispose and unite all his actions, and in his outward aspect give promise of whatever is worthy the society and favour of every great lord.

Here, without waiting longer, my lord Gaspar Pallavicino said:

In order that our game may have the form prescribed, and that we may not seem to slight the privilege given us to contradict, I say that this nobility of birth does not appear to me so essential in the Courtier; and if I thought I were saying what was new to any of us, I should cite instances of many men born of the noblest blood who have been full of vices; and on the other hand, of many men among the humbly born who by their virtue have made their posterity illustrious. And if what you just said be true, namely that there is in everything this occult influence of the original seed, then we should all be in the same case, because we had the same origin, nor would any man be more noble than another. But as to our differences and grades of eminence and obscurity, I believe there are many other causes: among which I rate fortune to be chief; for we see her holding sway in all mundane affairs, often amusing herself by lifting to heaven whom she pleases (although wholly without merit), and burying in the depths those most worthy to be exalted.

I quite agree with what you say as to the good fortune of those endowed from birth with advantages of mind and body: but this is seen as well among the humbly born as among the nobly born, since nature has no such subtle distinctions as these; and often, as I said, the highest gifts of nature are found among the most obscure. Therefore, since this nobility of birth is won neither by talent nor by strength nor by craft, and is rather the merit of our predecessors than our own, it seems to me too extravagant to maintain that if our Courtier's parents be humbly born, all his good qualities are spoiled, and that all those other qualifications that you mentioned do not avail to raise him to the summit of perfection; I mean talent, beauty of feature, comeliness of person, and that grace which makes him always charming to everyone at first sight. . . ."

[Count Ludovico said:] But to come to some details, I am of opinion that the principal and true profession of the Courtier ought to be that of arms; which I would have him follow actively above all else, and be known among others as bold and strong, and loyal to whomsoever he serves. And he will win a reputation for these good qualities by exercising them at all times and in all places, since one may never fail in this without severest censure. And just as among women, their fair name once sullied never recovers its first lustre, so the reputation of a gentleman who bears arms, if once it be in the least tarnished with cowardice or other disgrace, remains forever infamous before the world and full of ignominy. Therefore the more our Courtier excels in this art, the more he will be worthy of praise; and yet I do not deem essential in him that perfect knowledge of things and those other qualities that befit a commander; since this would be too wide a sea, let us be content, as we have said, with perfect loyalty and unconquered courage, and that he be always seen to possess them. For the courageous are often recognized even more in small things than in great; and frequently in perils of importance and where there are many spectators, some men are to be found who, although their hearts be dead within them, yet, moved by shame or by the presence of others, press forward almost with their eyes shut, and do their duty God knows how. While on occasions of little moment, when they think they can avoid putting themselves in danger without being detected, they are glad to keep safe. But those who, even when they do not expect to be observed or seen or recognized by anyone, show their ardour and neglect nothing, however paltry, that may be laid to their charge,—they have that strength of mind which we seek in our Courtier.

Not that we would have him look so fierce, or go about blustering, or say that he has taken his cuirass to wife, or threaten with those grim scowls that we have often seen in Berto; because to such men as this, one might justly say that which a brave lady jestingly said in gentle company to one whom I will not name at present; who, being invited by her out of compliment to dance, refused not only that, but to listen to the music, and many other entertainments proposed to him,—saying always that such silly trifles were not his business; so that at last the lady said, "What is your business, then?" He replied with a sour look, "To fight." Then the lady at once said, "Now that you are in no war and out of fighting trim, I should think it were a good thing to have yourself well oiled, and to stow yourself with all your battle harness in a closet until you be needed, lest you grow more rusty than you are"; and so, amid much laughter from the bystanders, she left the discomfited fellow to his silly presumption.

Therefore let the man we are seeking, be very bold, stern, and always among the first, where the enemy are to be seen; and in every other place, gentle, modest, reserved, above all things avoiding ostentation and that impudent self-praise by which men ever excite hatred and disgust in all who hear them. . . .

I think that what is chiefly important and necessary for the Courtier, in order to speak and write well, is knowledge; for he who is ignorant and has nothing in his mind that merits being heard, can neither say it nor write it.

Next he must arrange in good order what he has to say or write; then express it well in words, which (if I do not err) ought to be precise, choice, rich and rightly formed, but above all, in use even among the masses; because such words as these make the grandeur and pomp of speech, if the speaker has good sense and carefulness, and knows how to choose the words most expressive of his meaning, and to exalt them, to mould them like wax to his will, and to arrange them in such position and order that they shall at a glance show and make known their dignity and splendour, like pictures placed in good and proper light.

And this I say as well of writing as of speaking: in which however some things are required that are not needful in writing,—such as a good voice, not too thin and soft like a woman's, nor yet so stern and rough as to smack of the rustic's,—but sonorous, clear, sweet and well sounding, with distinct enunciation, and with proper bearing and gestures; which I think consist in certain movements of the whole body, not affected or violent, but tempered by a calm face and with a play of the eyes that shall give an effect of grace, accord with the words, and as far as possible express also, together with the gestures, the speaker's intent and feeling.

But all these things would be vain and of small moment, if the thoughts expressed by the words were not beautiful, ingenious, acute, elegant and grave,—according to the need.

Then my lord Morello said:

If this Courtier speaks with so much elegance and grace, I doubt if anyone will be found among us who will understand him.

Nay, he will be understood by everyone, replied the Count, because facility is no impediment to elegance.

Nor would I have him speak always of grave matters, but of amusing things, of games, jests and waggery, according to the occasion; but sensibly of everything, and with readiness and lucid fullness: and in no place let him show vanity or childish folly. And again when he is speaking on an obscure or difficult subject, I would have him carefully explain his meaning with precision of both word and thought, and make every ambiguity clear and plain with a certain touch of unpedantic care. Likewise, where there is occasion, let him know how to speak with dignity and force, to arouse those emotions that are part of our nature, and to kindle them or to move them according to the need. Sometimes, with that simple candour that makes it seem as if nature herself were speaking, let him know how to soften them, and as it were to intoxicate them with sweetness, and so easily withal that the listener shall think that with very little effort he too could reach that excellence, and when he tries, shall find himself very far behind.

In such fashion would I have our Courtier speak and write; and not only choose rich and elegant words from every part of Italy, but I should even praise him for sometimes using some of those French and Spanish terms that are already accepted by our custom. . . .

I would have him more than passably accomplished in letters, at least in those studies that are called the humanities, and conversant not only with the Latin language but with the Greek, for the sake of the many different things that have been admirably written therein. Let him be well versed in the poets, and not less in the orators and historians, and also proficient in writing verse and prose, especially in this vulgar tongue of ours; for besides the enjoyment he will find in it, he will by this means never lack agreeable entertainment with ladies, who are usually fond of such things. And if other occupations or want of study prevent his reaching such perfection as to render his writings worthy of great praise, let him be careful to suppress them so that others may not laugh at him, and let him show them only to a friend whom he can trust: because they will at least be of this service to him, that the exercise will enable him to judge the work of others. For it very rarely happens that a man who is not accustomed to write, however learned he may be, can ever quite appreciate the toil and industry of writers, or taste the sweetness and excellence of style, and those latent niceties that are often found in the ancients.

[Book IV]

[The Lord Ottaviano, Doge of Genoa, said:] . . . To pursue these gentlemen's discourse, which I wholly approve and confirm, I say that of the things that we call good, there are some which simply and in themselves are always good, like temperance, fortitude, health, and all the virtues that bestow tranquillity upon the mind; others which are good in various respects and for the object to which they tend, like law, liberality, riches, and other like things. Hence I think that the perfect Courtier, such as Count Ludovico and messer Federico have described, may be a truly good thing and worthy of praise, not however simply and in himself, but in respect to the end to which he may be directed. For indeed if by being nobly born, graceful, agreeable, and expert in so many exercises, the Courtier brought forth no other fruit than merely being what he is, I should not deem it right for a man to devote so much study and pains to acquiring this perfection of Courtiership, as anyone must who wishes to attain it. Nay, I should say that many of those accomplishments that have been ascribed to him (like dancing, merrymaking, singing and playing) were follies and vanities, and in a man of rank worthy rather of censure than of praise: for these elegances, devices, mottoes, and other like things that pertain to discourse about women and love, although perhaps many other men think the contrary, often serve only to effeminate the mind, to corrupt youth, and to reduce it to great wantonness of living; whence then it comes to pass that the Italian name is brought into opprobrium, and but few are to be found who dare, I will not say to die, but even to run into danger.

And surely there are countless other things, which, if industry and study were spent upon them, would be of much greater utility in both peace and war than this kind of Courtiership in itself merely; but if the Courtier's actions are directed to that good end to which they ought, and which I have in mind, methinks they are not only not harmful or vain, but very useful and deserving of infinite praise.

I think then that the aim of the perfect Courtier, which has not been spoken of till now, is so to win for himself, by means of the accomplishments ascribed to him by these gentlemen, the favour and mind of the prince whom he serves, that he may be able to say, and always shall say, the truth about everything which it is fitting for the prince to know, without fear or risk of giving offence thereby; and that when he sees his prince's mind inclined to do something wrong, he may be quick to oppose, and gently to make use of the favour acquired by his good accomplishments, so as to banish every bad intent and lead his prince into the path of virtue. And thus, possessing the goodness which these gentlemen have described, together with readiness of wit and pleasantness, and shrewdness and knowledge of letters and many other things,—the Courtier will in every case be able deftly to show the prince how much honour and profit accrue to him and his from justice, liberality, magnanimity, gentleness, and the other virtues that become a good prince; and on the other hand how much infamy and loss proceed from the vices opposed to them. Therefore I think that just as music, festivals, games, and the other pleasant accomplishments are as it were the flower, in like manner to lead or help one's prince towards right, and to frighten him from wrong, are the true fruit of Courtiership. . . .

. . . Since princes are to-day so corrupted by evil customs and by ignorance and mistaken self-esteem, and since it is so difficult to give them knowledge of the truth and lead them on to virtue, and since men seek to enter into their favour by lies and flatteries and such vicious means,—the Courtier, by the aid of those gentle qualities that Count Ludovico and messer Federico have given him, can with ease and should try to gain the good will and so charm the mind of his prince, that he shall win free and safe indulgence to speak of everything without being irksome. And if he be such as has been said, he will accomplish this with little trouble, and thus be able always to disclose the truth about all things with ease; and also to instil goodness into his prince's mind little by little, and to teach continence, fortitude, justice, temperance, by giving a taste of how much sweetness is hidden by the little bitterness that at first sight appears to him who withstands vice; which is always hurtful and displeasing, and accompanied by infamy and blame, just as virtue is profitable, blithe and full of praise. And thereto he will be able to incite his prince by the example of the famous captains and other eminent men to whom the ancients were wont to make statues of bronze and of marble and sometimes of gold, and to erect the same in public places, both for the honour of these men and as a stimulus to others, so that they might be led by worthy emulation to strive to reach that glory too.

In this way the Courtier will be able to lead his prince along the thorny path of virtue, decking it as with shady leafage and strewing it with lovely flowers to relieve the tedium of the weary journey to one whose strength is slight; and now with music, now with arms and horses, now with verses, now with love talk, and wit with all those means whereof these gentlemen have told, to keep his mind continually busied with worthy pleasures, yet always impressing upon him also, as I have said, some virtuous practice along with these allurements, and playing upon him with salutary craft; like cunning doctors, who often anoint the edge of the cup with a sweet cordial, when they wish to give some bitter-tasting medicine to sick and over-delicate children.

If, therefore, the Courtier put the veil of pleasure to such a use, he will reach his aim in every time and place and exercise, and will deserve much greater praise and reward than for any other good work that he could do in the world. For there is no good thing that is of such universal advantage as a good prince, nor any evil so universally noxious as a bad prince: hence, too, there is no punishment so harsh and cruel as to be a sufficient penalty for those wicked courtiers who use their gentle and pleasant ways and fine accomplishments to a bad end, and therewith seek their prince's favour, in order to corrupt him and entice him from the path of virtue and lead him into vice; for such as these may be said to taint with deadly poison not a single cup from which one man alone must drink, but the public fountain used by all men. . . .

. . . As in the other arts, so too in virtue it is necessary to have a master, who by instruction and good reminders shall arouse and awake in us those moral virtues whereof we have the seed enclosed and buried in our soul, and like a good husbandman shall cultivate them and open the way for them by freeing us from the thorns and tares of appetite, which often so overshadow and choke our minds as not to let them blossom or bring forth those happy fruits which alone we should desire to have spring up in the human heart.

In this sense, then, justice and shame, which you say Jove sent upon earth to all men, are natural in each one of us. But just as a body without eyes, however strong it be, often fails if it moves towards any object, so the root of these virtues potentially engendered in our minds often comes to naught if it be not helped by cultivation. For if it is to ripen into action and perfect character, nature alone is not enough, as has been said, but there is need of studied practice and of reason, to purify and clear the soul by lifting the dark veil of ignorance, from which nearly all the errours of men proceed,—because if good and evil were well perceived and understood, everyone would always prefer good and shun evil. Thus virtue may almost be said to be a kind of prudence and wit to prefer the good, and vice a kind of imprudence and ignorance which lead us to judge falsely; for men never prefer evil deeming it to be evil, but are deceived by a certain likeness that it bears to good.

Then my lord Gaspar replied:

There are, however, many who know well that they are doing evil, and yet do it; and this because they have more thought for the present pleasure which they feel, than for the chastisement which they fear must come upon them: like thieves, homicides, and other such men.

My lord Ottaviano said:

True pleasure is always good, and true suffering always evil; therefore these men deceive themselves in taking false pleasure for true, and true suffering for false; hence by false pleasures they often run into true sufferings. Therefore that art which teaches how to discern the true from the false, may well be learned; and the faculty whereby we choose that which is truly good and not that which falsely seems so, may be called true wisdom and more profitable to human life than any other, because it dispels the ignorance from which, as I have said, all evils spring. . . .

. . . Just as in heaven the sun and moon and other stars show the world as in a mirrour some likeness of God, so on earth a much liker image of God is found in those good princes who love and revere Him, and show their people the shining light of His justice and a reflection of His divine reason and mind; and with such as these God shares His righteousness, equity, justice and goodness, and those other happy blessings which I know not how to name, but which display to the world much clearer proof of divinity than the sun's light, or the continual revolving of the heavens and the various coursing of the stars.

Accordingly men have been placed by God under the ward of princes, who for this reason ought to take diligent care of them, in order to render Him an account of them like good stewards to their lord, and ought to love them, and regard them as personal to themselves every good and evil thing that happens to them, and provide for their happiness above every other thing. Therefore the prince ought not only to be good, but also to make others good, like that square used by architects, which not only is straight and true itself, but also makes straight and true all things to which it is applied. And a very great proof that the prince is good is when his people are good, because the prince's life is law and preceptress to his subjects, and upon his behaviour all the others must needs depend; nor is it fitting for an ignorant man to teach, nor for an unordered man to give orders, nor for one who falls to raise up others.

Hence if the prince would perform these duties rightly, he must devote every study and diligence to wisdom; then he must set before himself and follow steadfastly in everything the law of reason (unwritten on paper or metal, but graven upon his own mind), to the end that it may be not only familiar to him, but ingrained in him, and abide with him as a part of himself; so that day and night, in every place and time, it may admonish him and speak inwardly to his heart, freeing him from those disturbances that are felt by intemperate minds, which—because they are oppressed on the one hand as it were by the very deep sleep of ignorance, and on the other by the travail which they suffer from their perverse and blind desires—are tossed by relentless fury, as a sleeper sometimes is by strange and dreadful visions.

. . . My lord Gaspar said:

I remember that in discussing the accomplishments of the Courtier last evening, these gentlemen desired that he should be in love; and since, by reviewing what has thus far been said, we might conclude that a Courtier who has to allure his prince to virtue by his worth and authority, must almost of necessity be old (because knowledge very rarely comes before years, and especially in those things that are learned by experience),—I do not know how becoming it is for him (being advanced in age) to be in love. . . .

. . . Messer Pietro [Bembo said:]

I say, then, that according to the definition of the ancient sages love is naught but a certain desire to enjoy beauty; and as desire longs only for things that are perceived, perception must needs always precede desire, which by its nature wishes good things, but in itself is blind and does not perceive them. Therefore nature has so ordained that to every faculty of perception there is joined a certain faculty of appetite; and since in our soul there are three modes of perceiving, that is, by sense, by reason, and by intellect: from sense springs appetite, which we have in common with the brutes; from reason springs choice, which is peculiar to man; from the intellect, by which man is able to commune with the angels, springs will. Thus, just as sense perceives only things that are perceptible by the senses, appetite desires the same only; and just as intellect is directed solely to the contemplation of things intellectual, the will feeds only upon spiritual benefits. Being by nature rational and placed as a mean between these two extremes, man can at pleasure (by descending to sense or mounting to intellect) turn his desires now in the one direction and now in the other. In these two ways, therefore, it is possible to desire beauty, which universal name applies to all things (whether natural or artificial) that are framed in good proportion and due measure according to their nature.

But speaking of the beauty we have in mind, which is only that which is seen in the bodies and especially in the faces of men, and which excites this ardent desire that we call love,—we will say that it is an effluence of divine goodness, and that although it is diffused like the sun's light upon all created things, yet when it finds a face well proportioned and framed with a certain pleasant harmony of various colours embellished by lights and shadows and by an orderly distance and limit of outlines, it infuses itself therein and appears most beautiful, and adorns and illumines that object whereon it shines with grace and wonderful splendour, like a sunbeam falling upon a beautiful vase of polished gold set with precious gems. Thus it agreeably attracts the eyes of men, and entering thereby, it impresses itself upon the soul, and stirs and delights her with a new sweetness throughout, and by kindling her it excites in her a desire for its own self.

Then, being seized with desire to enjoy this beauty as something good, if the soul allows herself to be guided by the judgment of sense, she runs into very grievous errours, and judges that the body wherein the beauty is seen is the chief cause thereof; and hence, in order to enjoy that beauty, she deems it necessary to join herself as closely to that body as she can; which is false: and accordingly, whoever thinks to enjoy the beauty by possessing the body deceives himself, and is moved, not by true perception through reasonable choice, but by false opinion through sensual appetite: wherefore the pleasure also that results therefrom is necessarily false and vicious.

Hence all those lovers who satisfy their unchaste desires with the women whom they love, run into one of two errours: for as soon as they have attained the end desired, they either not only feel satiety and tedium, but hate the beloved object as if appetite repented its errour and perceived the deceit practised upon it by the false judgment of sense, which made it believe evil to be good; or else they remain in the same desire and longing, like those who have not truly attained the end they sought. . . .

Such lovers as these, therefore, love most unhappily; for either they never attain their desires (which is great unhappiness), or if they do attain thereto, they find they have attained their woe, and finish their miseries with other miseries still greater; because even in the beginning and midst of their love naught else is ever felt but anguish, torments, sorrows, sufferings, toils. So that to be pale, melancholy, in continual tears and sighs, to be sad, to be ever silent or lamenting, to long for death, in short, to be most unhappy, are the conditions that are said to befit lovers.

The cause, then, of this havoc in the minds of men is chiefly sense, which is very potent in youth, because the vigour of flesh and blood at that period gives to it as much strength as it takes away from reason, and hence easily leads the soul to follow appetite. For, finding herself plunged into an earthly prison and deprived of spiritual contemplation by being set the task of governing the body, the soul cannot of herself clearly comprehend the truth; wherefore, in order to have perception of things, she must needs go begging first notions from the senses, and so she believes them and bows before them and allows herself to be guided by them, especially when they have so much vigour that they almost force her; and as they are fallacious, they fill her with errours and false opinions.

Hence it nearly always happens that young men are wrapped in this love which is sensual and wholly rebellious to reason, and thus they become unworthy to enjoy the graces and benefits which love bestows upon its true subjects; nor do they feel any pleasures in love beyond those which the unreasoning animals feel, but anguish far more grievous.

This premise being admitted then,—and it is most true,—I say that the contrary happens to those who are of maturer age. For if such as these (when the soul is already less weighed down by bodily heaviness and when the natural heat begins to become tepid) are inflamed by beauty and turn thereto a desire guided by rational choice,—they are not deceived, and possess beauty perfectly. Therefore their possession of it always brings them good; because beauty is good, and hence true love of beauty is most good and holy, and always works for good in the mind of those who restrain the perversity of sense with the bridle of reason; which the old can do much more easily than the young.

Hence it is not beyond reason to say further that the old can love without blame and more happily than the young; taking this word old, however, not in the sense of decrepit, nor when the bodily organs have already become so weak that the soul cannot perform its functions through them, but when our knowledge is at its true prime.

I will not refrain from saying also this: which is, that I think that although sensual love is evil at every age, yet in the young it deserves excuse, and is perhaps in a measure permitted. For although it gives them anguish, dangers, toils, and those woes that have been told, still there are many who, to win the favour of the ladies of their love, do worthy acts, which (although not directed to a good end) are intrinsically good; and thus from that mass of bitterness they extract a little sweet, and through the adversities which they endure they at last perceive their errour. Hence, just as I deem those youths divine who control their appetites and love in reason, so I excuse those who allow themselves to be overcome by sensual love, to which they are so strongly inclined by human fraility: provided they show therein gentleness, courtesy and worth, and the other noble qualities of which these gentlemen have told; and provided that when they are no longer of youthful age, they abandon it altogether, shunning this sensual desire as it were the lowest round of the ladder by which true love can be attained. . . .

Look at the state of this great fabric of the world, which was made by God for the health and preservation of every created thing. The round firmament, adorned with so many heavenly lights, and the earth in the centre, surrounded by the elements and sustained by its own weight; the sun, which in its revolving illumines the whole, and in winter approaches the lowest sign, then little by little mounts to the other side; the moon, which derives her light from it, according as it approaches her or withdraws from her; and the five other stars, which separately travel the same course. These things have such influence upon one another through the linking of an order thus precisely framed, that if they were changed for an instant, they could not hold together, and would wreck the world; they have also such beauty and grace that human wit cannot imagine anything more beautiful.

Think now of the shape of man, which may be called a little world; wherein we see every part of the body precisely composed with skill, and not by chance; and then the whole form together so beautiful that we could hardly decide whether more utility or more grace is given to the human features and the rest of the body by all the members, such as the eyes, nose, mouth, ears, arms, breast, and other parts withal. The same can be said of all the animals. Look at the feathers of birds, the leaves and branches of trees, which are given them by nature to preserve their being, and yet have also very great loveliness.

Leave nature, and come to art. What thing is so necessary in ships as the prow, the sides, the yards, the masts, the sails, the helm, the oars, the anchors and the cordage? Yet all these things have so much comeliness, that it seems to him who looks upon them that they are thus devised as much for beauty as for use. Columns and architraves support lofty galleries and palaces, yet they are not on that account less pleasing to the eyes of him who looks upon them, than useful to the buildings. When men first began to build, they set that middle ridge in their temples and houses, not in order that the buildings might have more grace, but to the end that the water might flow off conveniently on either side; yet to utility soon was added comeliness, so that if a temple were built under a sky where no hail or rain falls, it would not seem able to have any dignity or beauty without the ridge.

Much praise is therefore bestowed, not only upon other things, but upon the world, by saying that it is beautiful. We praise when we say: "Beautiful sky, beautiful earth, beautiful sea, beautiful rivers, beautiful lands, beautiful woods, trees, gardens; beautiful cities, beautiful churches, houses, armies." In short, this gracious and sacred beauty gives highest ornament to everything; and we may say that the good and the beautiful are in a way one and the same thing, and especially in the human body; of whose beauty I think the most immediate cause is beauty of the soul, which (as partaker of true divine beauty) brightens and beautifies whatever it touches, and especially if the body wherein it dwells is not of such base material that it cannot impress thereon its quality. Therefore beauty is the true trophy of the soul's victory, when with power divine she holds sway over material nature, and by her light overcomes the darkness of the body.

. . . Bembo laughed and said: . . . "It often happens also that our sight deceives us like our other senses, and accounts a face beautiful which in truth is not beautiful; and since in some women's eyes and whole aspect a certain wantonness is seen depicted, together with unseemly blandishments,—many (who like such manner because it promises them ease in attaining what they desire) call it beauty: but in truth it is disguised immodesty, unworthy a name so honoured and so sacred."

Messer Pietro Bembo was silent, and those gentlemen still urged him to speak further of this love and of the mode of enjoying beauty truly; and he at last said:

"Methinks I have shown clearly enough that old men can love more happily than young, which was my thesis; therefore it does not become me to go further."

Count Ludovico replied:

"You have better shown the unhappiness of youths than the happiness of old men, whom as yet you have not taught what road to follow in this love of theirs, but have only told them to be guided by reason; and by many it is thought impossible for love to abide with reason."

Bembo still sought to put an end to his discourse, but my lady Duchess begged him to speak; and he began anew thus:

"Too unhappy would human nature be, if our soul (wherein such ardent desire can spring up easily) were forced to feed it solely upon that which is common to her with the beasts, and could not direct it to that other nobler part which is peculiar to herself. Therefore, since so indeed it pleases you, I have no wish to avoid discoursing upon this noble subject. And as I feel myself unworthy to speak of Love's most sacred mysteries, I pray him so to inspire my thought and tongue that I may be able to show this excellent Courtier how to love beyond the manner of the vulgar crowd; and since from boyhood up I have dedicated my whole life to him, so now also may my words comport with this intent and with his praise.

"I say, then, that as in youth human nature is so greatly prone to sense, the Courtier may be allowed to love sensually while he is young. But if afterwards in maturer years he chances still to be kindled with this amorous desire, he must be very wary and take care not to deceive himself by allowing himself to be led into those calamities which in the young merit more compassion than blame, and, on the contrary, in the old more blame than compassion.

"Therefore when the gracious aspect of some fair woman meets his view, accompanied with such sweet behaviour and gentle manners that he, as an adept in love, feels that his spirit accords with hers: as soon as he finds that his eyes lay hold upon her image and carry it to his heart; and that his soul begins to contemplate her with pleasure and to feel that influence within which stirs and warms it little by little, and that those quick spirits which shine out through the eyes continually add fresh tinder to the fire;—he ought at his first stage to provide a speedy cure, and arouse his reason, and therewith, arm the fortress of his heart, and so shut the way to sense and appetite that they cannot enter there by force or trickery. Thus, if the flame is extinguished, the danger is extinguished also; but if it survives or grows, then the Courtier, feeling himself caught, must resolve on shunning wholly every stain of vulgar love, and thus enter on the path of divine love, with reason for guide. And first he must consider that the body wherein this beauty shines is not the fountain whence it springs, but rather that beauty (being an incorporeal thing and, as we have said, a heavenly beam) loses much of its dignity when it finds itself joined to vile and corruptible matter; for the more perfect it is the less it partakes thereof, and is most perfect when wholly separate therefrom. And he must consider that just as one cannot hear with the palate or smell with the ears, so too can beauty in no wise be enjoyed, nor can the desire which it excites in our minds be satisfied, by means of touch, but by that sense of which this beauty is the very object, namely, the power of vision.

"Therefore let him shun the blind judgment of sense, and with his eyes enjoy the splendour of his lady, her grace, her amorous sparkle, the laughs, the ways and all the other pleasant ornaments of her beauty. Likewise with his hearing let him enjoy the sweetness of her voice, the concord of her words, the harmony of her music (if this beloved be a musician). Thus will he feed his soul on sweetest food by means of these two senses—which have little of the corporeal and are ministers of reason—without passing in his desire for the body to any appetite less than seemly.

"Next let him obey, please and honour his lady with all reverence, and hold her dearer than himself, and prefer her convenience and pleasures to his own, and love in her not less the beauty of mind than that of body. Therefore let him take care not to leave her to fall into any kind of error, but by admonition and good advice let him always seek to lead her on to modesty, to temperance, to true chastity, and see to it that no thoughts find place in her except those that are pure and free from every stain of vice; and by thus sowing virtue in the garden of her mind, he will gather fruits of fairest behaviour too, and will taste them with wonderful delight. And this will be the true engendering and manifesting of beauty in beauty, which by some is said to be the end of love.

"In such fashion will our Courtier be most acceptable to his lady, and she will always show herself obedient, sweet and affable to him, and as desirous of pleasing him as of being loved by him; and the wishes of both will be most virtuous and harmonious, and they themselves will thus be very happy."

Here my lord Morello said:

"To engender beauty in beauty, forsooth, would be to beget a beautiful child in a beautiful woman; and pleasing him in this would seem to me a much clearer token that she loved her lover than treating him with the affability of which you speak."

Bembo laughed, and said:

"You must not go beyond bounds, my lord Morello; nor does a woman give small token of her love when she gives her lover her beauty, which is so precious a thing, and by the ways that are the avenues to her soul (that is, sight and hearing) sends the glances of her eyes, the image of her face, her voice, her words, which strike home to the lover's heart and give him proof of her love."

My lord Morello said:

"Glances and words may be, and often are, false proofs; therefore he who has not better pledge of love is, in my judgment far from sure; and truly I quite expected you to make this lady of yours a little more courteous and generous to the Courtier than my lord Magnifico made his; but methinks that both of you are in like case with those judges who pronounce sentence against their friends for the sake of appearing wise."

Bembo said:

"I am very willing that this lady should be much more courteous to my unyouthful Courtier, than my lord Magnifico's is to the youthful Courtier;

and with reason, for my Courtier will desire only seemly things, and therefore the lady can grant him all of them without blame; while my lord Magnifico's lady, who is not so sure of the youthful Courtier's modesty, ought to grant him only seemly things, and to refuse him the unseemly. Hence my Courtier, to whom is granted what he asks, is more happy than the other, to whom part is granted and part refused.

"And to the end that you may still better understand that rational love is happier than sensual, I say that the same things ought sometimes to be refused in sensual love and granted in rational love, because they are unseemly in the one and seemly in the other. Thus, to please her worthy lover, besides granting him pleasant smiles, familiar and secret discourse, and leave to joke and jest with her and to touch her hand, the lady may in reason even go so far as kissing without blame, which is not permitted in sensual love according to my lord Magnifico's rules. For since the kiss is the union of body and soul, there is danger lest the sensual lover incline more in the direction of the body than in that of the soul; while the rational lover perceives that although the mouth is part of the body, yet it gives issue to words, which are interpreters of the soul, and to that inward breath which is itself even called soul. Hence a man delights to join his mouth to that of his beloved in a kiss, not in order to arouse any unseemly desire in him, but because he feels that bond to be the opening of a passage between their souls, which, being each drawn by desire for the other, pour themselves each into the other's body by turn, and so commingle that each has two souls, and a single soul (thus composed of these two) rules as it were over two bodies. Hence the kiss may be oftener said to be a joining of soul than of body, because it has such power over the soul that it draws her to itself and separates her from the body. On this account all chaste lovers desire to kiss as a joining of the soul; and thus the divinely enamoured Plato says that in kissing the soul came to his lips to escape his body. And since the separation of the soul from things material, and its complete union with things spiritual, may be denoted by the kiss, Solomon, in his divine book of the Song, says: 'Let him kiss me with the kiss of his mouth,' to express desire that his soul might be so transported with divine love to the contemplation of celestial beauty, that by joining closely therewith she might forsake the body."

Everyone gave closest heed to Bembo's discourse; and he, having made a little pause and seeing that no one else spoke said:

"As you have made me begin to teach our unyouthful Courtier happy love, I fain would lead him a little farther; for it is very dangerous to stop at this stage, seeing that the soul is very prone to the senses, as has many times been said; and although reason and argument choose well and perceive that beauty does not spring from the body, and although they therefore put a bridle upon unseemly desires, still, always contemplating beauty in the body often perverts sound judgment. And even if no other evil flowed therefrom, absence from the beloved object brings much suffering with it, because the influence of her beauty gives the lover wonderful delight when she is present, and by warming his heart weakens and melts certain dormant and frozen forces in his soul, which (being nourished by the warmth of love) spread and blossom about his heart, and send forth through the eyes those spirits that are very subtle vapours made of the purest and brightest part of the blood, which receive the image of her beauty and fashion it with a thousand various ornaments. Hence the soul delights, and trembles with awe and yet rejoices, and as in a stupor feels not only pleasure, but that fear and reverence which we are wont to have for sacred things, and speaks of being in paradise.

"Therefore the lover who considers beauty in the body only, loses this blessing and felicity as soon as his beloved lady by her absence leaves his eyes without their splendour, and his soul consequently widowed of its blessing. Because, her beauty being far away, that amorous influence does not warm his heart as it did in her presence; wherefore his pores become arid and dry, and still the memory of her beauty stirs a little those forces of his soul, so that they seek to scatter abroad the spirits; and these, finding the ways shut, have no exit, and yet seek to issue forth; and thus hemmed in by those goads, they sting the soul and give it keenest suffering, as in the case of children when the teeth begin to come through the tender gums. And from this proceed the tears, the sighs, the anguish and the torments of lovers, because the soul is ever in affliction and travail, and becomes almost raging until her dear beauty appears to it again; and then it suddenly is calmed and breathes, and all intent upon that beauty it feeds on sweetest food, nor would ever part from so delightful a spectacle.

"Hence, to escape the torment of this absence and to enjoy beauty without suffering, there is need that the Courtier should, with the aid of reason, wholly turn his desire from the body to the beauty alone, and contemplate it in itself simple and pure, as far as he can, and fashion it in his imagination apart from all matter; and thus make it lovely and dear to his soul, and enjoy it there, and have it with him day and night, in every time and place, without fear of ever losing it; bearing always in mind that the body is something very different from beauty, and not only does not enhance it, but diminishes its perfection.

"In this wise will our unyouthful Courtier be beyond all the bitterness and calamities that the young nearly always feel: such as jealousies, suspicions, disdainings, angers, despairings, and certain furies full of madness whereby they are often led into such error that some of them not only beat the women whom they love, but deprive themselves of life. He will do no injury to the husband, father, brothers or kinsfolk of his beloved lady; he will put no infamy upon her; he will never be forced to bridle his eyes and tongue with such difficulty in order not to disclose his desires to others, or to endure suffering at partings or absences;—because he will always carry his precious treasure with him shut up in his heart, and also by force of his imagination he will inwardly fashion her beauty much more beautiful than in fact it is.

"But besides these blessings the lover will find another much greater still, if he will employ his love as a step to mount to one much higher; which he will succeed in doing if he continually considers within himself how narrow a restraint it is to be always occupied in contemplating the beauty of one body only; and therefore, in order to escape such close bounds as these, in his thought he will little by little add so many ornaments, that by heaping all beauties together he will form an universal concept, and will reduce the multitude of these beauties to the unity of that single beauty which is spread over human nature at large. In this way he will no longer contemplate the particular beauty of one woman, but that universal beauty which adorns all bodies; and thus, bewildered by this greater light, he will not heed the lesser, and glowing with a purer flame, he will esteem lightly that which at first he so greatly prized.

"This stage of love, although it be very noble and such as few attain, still cannot be called perfect; for since the imagination is merely a corporeal faculty and has no perception except through those means that are furnished it by the senses, it is not wholly purged of material darkness; and hence, although it considers this universal beauty in the abstract and intrinsically, yet it does not discern that beauty very clearly or without some ambiguity, because of the likeness which phantoms bear to substance. Thus those who attain this love are like tender birds beginning to put on feathers, which, although with their frail wings they lift themselves a little in flight, yet dare not go far from their nest or trust themselves to the winds and open sky.

"Therefore when our Courtier shall have reached this goal, although he may be called a very happy lover by comparison with those who are plunged in the misery of sensual love, still I would have him not rest content, but press boldly on following along the lofty path after the guide who leads him to the goal of true felicity. And thus, instead of going outside himself in thought (as all must needs do who choose to contemplate bodily beauty only), let him have recourse to himself, in order to contemplate that beauty which is seen by the eyes of the mind, which begin to be sharp and clear when those of the body lose the flower of their loveliness. Then the soul, —freed from vice, purged by studies of true philosophy, versed in spiritual life, and practised in matters of the intellect, devoted to the contemplation of her own substance,—as if awakened from deepest sleep, opens those eyes which all possess but few use, and sees in herself a ray of that light which is the true image of the angelic beauty communicated to her, and of which she then communicates a faint shadow to the body. Grown blind to things earthly, the soul thus becomes very keen-sighted to things heavenly; and sometimes, when the motive forces of the body are absorbed by earnest contemplation or fettered by sleep, being unhampered by them, she is conscious of a certain far-off perfume of true angelic beauty, and ravished by the splendour of that light, she begins to kindle and pursues it so eagerly that she almost becomes phrensied with desire to unite herself to that beauty, thinking that she has found God's footstep, in the contemplation of which she seeks to rest as in her beatific end. And thus, glowing this most happy flame, she rises to her noblest part, which is the intellect; and here, no longer darkened by the gloomy night of things earthly, she sees the divine beauty; but still she does not yet quite enjoy it perfectly, because she contemplates it in her own particular intellect only, which cannot be capable of the vast universal beauty.

"Wherefore, not well content with this boon, love gives the soul a greater felicity; for just as from the particular beauty of one body it guides her to the universal beauty of all bodies, so in the highest stage of perfection it guides her from the particular to the universal intellect. Hence the soul, kindled by the most sacred fire of true divine love, flies to unite herself with the angelic nature, and not only quite forsakes sense, but has no longer need of reason's discourse; for, changed into an angel, she understands all things intelligible, and without veil or cloud views the wide sea of pure divine beauty, and receives it into herself, and enjoys that supreme felicity of which the senses are incapable.

"If, then, the beauties which with these dim eyes of ours we daily see in corruptible bodies (but which are naught but dreams and faintest shadows of beauty) seem to us so fair and gracious that they often kindle most ardent fire in us, and of such delight that we deem no felicity able to equal that which we sometimes feel at a single glance coming to us from a woman's beloved eyes,—what happy wonder, what blessed awe, shall we think it that which fills the souls that attain to the vision of divine beauty! What sweet flame, what delightful burning, must that be thought which springs from the fountain of supreme and true beauty!—which is the source of every other beauty, which never waxes nor wanes: ever fair, and of its own self most simple in every part alike; like only to itself, and partaking of none other; but fair in such wise that all other fair things are fair because they derive their beauty from it.

"This is that beauty identical with highest good, which by its light calls and attracts all things to itself, and not only gives intellect to the intellectual, reason to the rational, sense and desire for life to the sensual, but to plants also and to stones communicates motion and that natural instinct of their quality, as an imprint of itself.

"Therefore this love is a much greater and happier than the others, as the cause that moves it is more excellent; and hence, just as material fire refines gold, so does this most sacred fire in our souls destroy and consume that which is mortal there, and quickens and beautifies that celestial part which at first, by reason of the senses, was dead and buried in them. This is the Pyre whereon the poets write that Hercules was burned on the crest of Mount Œta, and by such burning became divine and immortal after death. This is the Burning Bush of Moses, the Cloven Tongues of fire, the Fiery Chariot of Elias, which doubles grace and felicity in the souls of those who are worthy to behold it, when they leave this earthly baseness and take flight towards heaven.

"Let us, then, direct all the thoughts and forces of our soul to this most sacred light, which shows us the way that leads to heaven; and following after it, let us lay aside the passions wherewith we were clothed at our fall, and by the stairway that bears the shadow of sensual beauty on its lowest step, let us mount to the lofty mansion where dwells the heavenly, lovely and true beauty, which lies hidden in the inmost secret recesses of God, so that profane eyes cannot behold it. Here we shall find a most happy end to our desires, true rest from our toil, certain cure for our miseries, most wholesome medicine for our diseases, safest refuge from the boisterous storms of this life's tempestuous sea.

"What mortal tongue, then, O most holy Love, can praise thee worthily? Most fair, most good, most wise, thou springest from the union of beauty and goodness and divine wisdom, and abidest in that union, and by that union returnest to that union as in a circle. Sweetest bond of the universe, joining things celestial to things terrestrial, thou with benignant sway inclinest the supernal powers to rule the lower powers, and turning the minds of mortals to their origin, joinest them thereto. Thou unitest the elements in concord, movest nature to produce—and that which is born, to the perpetuation of life. Thou unitest things that are separate, givest perfection to the imperfect, likeness to the unlike, friendship to the unfriendly, fruit to the earth, tranquillity to the sea, vital light to the heavens.

"Thou art father of true pleasure, of grace, of peace, of gentleness and good will, enemy to rustic savagery and sloth—in short, the beginning and the end of every good. And since thou delightest to inhabit the flower of beautiful bodies and beautiful souls, and thence sometimes to display thyself a little to the eyes and minds of those who are worthy to behold thee, methinks that now thy abode is here among us.

"Deign, then, O Lord, to hear our prayers, pour thyself upon our hearts, and with the splendour of thy most holy fire illumine our darkness and, like a trusted guide, in this blind labyrinth show us the true path. Correct the falseness of our senses, and after our long pursuit of vanities give us true and solid good; make us to inhale those spiritual odours that quicken the powers of the intellect, and to hear the celestial harmony with such accord that there may no longer be room in us for any discord of passion; fill us at that inexhaustible fountain of content which ever delights and never satiates, and gives a taste of true beatitude to all who drink of its living and limpid waters; with the beams of thy light purge our eyes of misty ignorance, to the end that they may no longer prize mortal beauty, and may know that the things which first they seemed to see, are not, and that those which they saw not, really are.

"Accept our souls, which are offered thee in sacrifice; burn them in that living flame which consumes all mortal dross, to the end that, being wholly separated from the body, they may unite with divine beauty by a perpetual and very sweet bond, and that we, being severed from ourselves, may, like true lovers, be able to transform ourselves into the beloved, and rising above the earth may be admitted to the angels' feast, where, fed on ambrosia and immortal nectar, we may at last die a most happy and living death, as died of old those ancient fathers whose souls thou, by the most glowing power of contemplation, didst ravish from the body and unite with God."

DESIDERIUS ERASMUS

ESIDERIUS ERASMUS of Rotterdam (1466–1536) became a priest at the insistence of his guardians; but his real enthusiasm was for letters. A constant traveler in Europe, he was especially welcome in England, where he made the acquaintance of Colet the Oxford humanist, and of a good many other dignitaries. It was in Thomas More's house in 1509 that he wrote *The Praise of Folly,* his most famous, if not his most important work. While lecturing at Cambridge, he completed his work on the New Testament, on the *Letters of Jerome,* and other books. His translation of the New Testament from the Greek shook the authority of the Vulgate version and raised a storm among the clergy.

Erasmus seems to have begun his association with Johann Froben's press in Basel in 1513. Froben printed his work, and from 1521 to 1529 Erasmus was editor of the press, which became in his hands the foremost in Europe, both in the value of the works published and in the quality of the printing.

In his own time Erasmus was denounced by partisans of both sides as a trimmer in the great questions of the Reformation. His criticisms of ecclesiastical abuses could have put him in the camp of Luther. They did contribute much to the movement but his respect for tradition and his dislike of the new evangelical fanaticism led him finally to oppose Luther.

At no point did he desire to overthrow orthodox theology; he was merely convinced that religion was less a matter of ceremony or dogma than of morality. A Catholic and humanist, Erasmus was concerned to write the teachings of classical and Christian antiquity into one conception of religion as a way of life. If Luther's religion appealed to the common man, Erasmus found his audience among the learned men of Europe.

Among Erasmus' works are the *Colloquies,* the *Adages* from the Greek, the *Manual of a Christian Knight,* and his anti-Lutheran *De libero arbitrio,* a graceful defense of free will. We quote here from *The Praise of Folly,* in the translation from the Latin of Hoyt H. Hudson (Princeton University Press, 1941).

THE PRAISE OF FOLLY

HOWEVER mortal folk may commonly speak of me (for I am not ignorant how ill the name of Folly sounds, even to the greatest fools), I am she—the only she, I may say—whose divine influence makes gods and men rejoice. One great and sufficient proof of this is that the instant I stepped up to speak to this crowded assembly, all faces at once brightened with a fresh and unwonted cheerfulness, all of you suddenly unbent your brows, and with frolic and affectionate smiles you applauded; so that as I look upon all present about me, you seem flushed with nectar, like gods in Homer, not without some nepenthe, also; whereas a moment ago you were sitting moody and depressed, as if you had come out of the cave of Trophonius. Just as it commonly happens, when the sun first shows his splendid golden face to the earth or when, after a bitter winter, young spring breathes mild west winds, that a new face comes over everything, new color and a sort of youthfulness appear; so at the mere sight of me, you straightway take on another aspect. . . .

. . . What can be dearer or more precious than life? And the beginning and first principle of life is owed to whom else but me? Not the spear of "potent-fathered" Pallas, not the shield of "cloud-compelling" Jove, procreates the children of men or multiplies their race. Even he, the father of gods and king of men, who shakes all heaven by a nod, is obliged to lay aside his three-pronged thunder and that Titanic aspect by which, when he pleases, he scares all the gods, and assume another character in the slavish manner of an actor, if he wishes to do what he never refrains from doing, that is to say, to beget children. . . . And why not speak to you still more frankly, as is my fashion? I beg to inquire whether the head, whether the face, the breast, the hand, or the ear—all of them accounted honorable members—generates gods and men? I judge not; nay, rather that foolish, even silly, part which cannot be named without laughter, is the propagator of the human race. This is at last that sacred spring from which all things derive existence, most truly than from the elemental tetrad of Pythagoras.

Now tell me, what man, by heaven, could wish to stick his head into the halter of marriage if, as your wiseacres have the habit of doing, he first weighed with himself the inconveniences of wedded life? Or what woman would ever admit her husband to her person, if she had heard or thought about the dangerous pains of childbirth and the irksomeness of bringing up a child? But since you owe your existence to the marriage-bed, and marriage is owing to Anoia, a servant of mine, you can see how vastly indebted you are to me! Then, too, would a woman who has gone through all this, wish to make a second venture, if the power and influence of my Lethe did not attend her? And in spite of what Lucretius claims, Venus herself would not deny that without the addition of my presence her strength would be enfeebled and ineffectual. So it is that from this brisk and silly little game of mine come forth the haughty philosophers (to whose places those who are vulgarly called monks have now succeeded), and kings in their scarlet, pious priests, and triply most holy popes; also, finally, that assembly of the gods of the poets, so numerous that Olympus, spacious as it is, can hardly accommodate the crowd.

But let it be accounted a little thing that the seedplot and source of existence are mine, if I do not show that whatever is profitable in any life is also of my giving. For what about it? Can life be called life at all if you take away pleasure? . . . You applaud! I knew that none of you is so wise—or rather so foolish—no, I prefer to say so wise—as to err on that point. Even the famous Stoics do not really scorn pleasure, but they studiously dissemble and attack it in public with a thousand reproaches, only to the end that, with other people scared off, they may enjoy it more liberally. But let them tell me, by Jove, what part of life is not sad, unpleasant, graceless, flat, and burdensome, unless you have pleasure added to it, that is, a seasoning of folly? As proof of this, there is extant that lovely tribute to me by Sophocles, who can never be sufficiently praised, "To know nothing affords the happiest life." . . .

In sum, no society, no union in life, could be either pleasant or lasting without me. A people does not for long tolerate its prince, or a master tolerate his servant, a handmaiden her mistress, a teacher his student, a friend his friend, a wife her husband, a landlord his tenant, a partner his partner, or a boarder his fellow-boarder, except as they mutually or by turns are mistaken, on occasion flatter, on occasion wisely wink, and otherwise soothe themselves with sweetness of folly. . . .

For what is so foolish as to be satisfied with yourself? Or to admire yourself? Yet on the other hand, if you are displeased with yourself, what can you do that is pleasing or graceful or seemly? Take this ingredient from life, and at once the orator, like his style, will be flat and cold, the musician will be as sour as his notes, the actor, with all his mimicry, will be hissed from the stage, the painter as well as his pictures will be cheap, and the poor doctor will famish among his poor medicines. Without self-love, though you may be a handsome Nireus, you will appear like Thersites; you will seem a Nestor, though a Phaon; a sow instead of Minerva, tongue-tied instead of eloquent, a gawk instead of a man of the world. That is how necessary it is to capture your own fancy, and to appreciate your own value by a bit of self-applause, before you can be held in price by others. Finally, since the better part of happiness is to wish to be what you are, why certainly my Philautia reaches that end by a short cut;

so that no one is ashamed of his own looks, no one regrets his own temperament, or feels shame for his race, his locality, his profession, or his fatherland.
An Irishman does not want to change places with an Athenian, or a Scythian
with a dweller in the Fortunate Isles. Oh, the singular foresight of nature, who,
in spite of such differences of condition, equalizes all things! Where she has
withheld something of her bounties, there she is wont to add a little more
self-love; but I have made a foolish saying, for self-love is itself the greatest
bounty of nature.

May I not affirm, indeed, that you will find no great exploit undertaken, no
important arts invented, except at my prompting? As, for instance, is not the
war the seed-plot and fountain of renowned actions? Yet what is more foolish
than to enter upon a conflict for I know not what causes, wherein each side
reaps more of loss than of gain? As for those who fall, as was said of the
Megarians, "no particulars." And when armored ranks engage each other and
bugles bray with harsh accord, of what use are those wise men, who, exhausted
by studies, scarce maintain any life in their thin, cold blood? The day belongs
to stout, gross fellows; the littler wit they have, the bolder they are—unless,
forsooth, you prefer a soldier like Demosthenes, who, since he agreed with
the poetic sentiment of Archilochus, dropped his shield and ran, as cowardly
in warfare as he was consummate in eloquence. But wise planning, they say,
is of most importance in war. Yes, on the part of a general, I grant; yet is it
military, not philosophical, wisdom. Far otherwise: this famous game of war
is played by parasites, panders, bandits, assassins, peasants, sots, bankrupts,
and such other dregs of mankind; never by philosophers, with their candles
of wisdom. . . .

Come, then, and suppose a man could look from a high tower, as the poets
say Jove is in the habit of doing. To how many calamities would he see the
life of man subject! How painful, how messy, man's birth! How irksome his
rearing—his childhood exposed to so many hurts, his youth beset by so many
problems! Then age is a burden; the certainty of death is inexorable. Diseases
infest life's every way; accidents threaten, troubles assail without warning;
there is nothing that is not tainted with gall. Nor can I recite all those evils
which man suffers at the hands of man; poverty is in this class, and imprisonment, infamy, shame, tortures, snares, treachery, slander, litigation, fraud.
But you see I am engaged in "counting the sand." For what offenses men have
deserved these things, or what angry god compelled them to be born to such
miseries, it is no business of mine to discuss at the moment. But if one ponders
upon the evils I speak of, will not one approve the example, pitiable as it is,
set by the Milesian virgins? And yet who are the people that, merely because
of weariness of life, have hastened their fate? Were they not the people who

lived next door to wisdom? Among them, to pass over such as Diogenes, Xenocrates, Cato, Cassius, and Brutus, there was even Chiron, who, though he had the privilege of being immortal, took the option of death. You will observe, I am sure, what would happen if men generally became wise: there would be need for some fresh clay and for another potter like Prometheus. . . .

The fact is that the more ways a man is deluded, the happier he is, if Folly is any judge. Only let him remain in that kind of madness which is peculiarly my own, and which is so widespread that I do not know whether out of the whole world of mortals it is possible to find one who is wise at all times of day, and who is not subject to some extravagance. It may be only that a man seeing a pumpkin believes it is a woman, and others give him the epithet of "mad," simply because so few people share his belief. But when another man swears roundly that his wife (whom he holds in common with many others) is a Penelope, only more virtuous, and thus flatters himself in the key of C-major, happily deluded; nobody calls him mad, because they see that this happens to other husbands here and there.

To this order belong the fellows who renounce everything else in favor of hunting wild game, and protest they feel an ineffable pleasure in their souls whenever they hear the raucous blast of the horns and the yelping of the hounds. Even the dung of the dogs, I am sure, smells like cinnamon to them. And what is so sweet as a beast being butchered? . . .

. . . Then what shall I say of the people who so happily fool themselves with forged pardons for sins, measuring out time to be spent in purgatory as if with an hour-glass, and figuring its centuries, years, months, days, and hours as if from a mathematical table, beyond possibility of error? Or I might speak of those who will promise themselves any and every thing, relying upon certain charms or prayers devised by some pious impostor either for his soul's sake or for money, to bring them wealth, reputation, pleasure, plenty, good health, long life, and a green old age, and at last a seat next to Christ's in heaven— but they do not wish to get it too soon. That is to say, when the pleasures of this life have finally failed them, willy-nilly, though they struggled tooth and nail to hold on to them, then it is time for the bliss of heaven to arrive.

I fancy that I see some merchant or soldier or judge laying down one small coin from his extensive booty and expecting that the whole cesspool of his life will be at once purified. He conceives that just so many perjuries, so many lustful acts, so many debauches, so many fights, murders, frauds, lies and so many breaches of faith, are bought off as by contract; and so bought off that with a clean slate he may start from scratch upon a new round of sins. And who are more foolish, yet who more happy, than those who promise themselves something more than the highest felicity if they daily recite those seven verses of the *Psalms?* The seven, I mean, which some devil, a playful one, but blabbing rather than crafty, is believed to have pointed out to St. Bernard after he had been duped by the saint's trick. Things like that are so foolish, you know, that I am almost ashamed of them myself; yet they stand approved not only by the common people but even by teachers of religion. And is it not almost as bad when the several countries each lay claim to a particular saint of their own, and then assign particular powers respectively to the various saints and observe for each one his own peculiar rites of worship? One saint assists in time of toothache, another is propitious to women in travail, another recovers stolen goods, a fourth stands by with help in a shipwreck, and still another keeps the sheep in good repair; and so of the rest, though it would take too long to specify all of them. . . .

And now I see that it is not only in individual men that nature has implanted self-love. She implants a kind of it as a common possession in the various races, and even cities. By this token the English claim, besides a few other things, good looks, music, and the best eating as their special properties. The Scots flatter themselves on the score of high birth and royal blood, not to mention their dialectical skill. Frenchmen have taken all politeness for their province; though the Parisians, brushing all others aside, also award themselves the prize for knowledge of theology. The Italians usurp *belles lettres* and eloquence; and they all flatter themselves upon the fact that they alone, of all mortal men, are not barbarians. In this particular point of happiness the Romans stand highest, still dreaming pleasantly of ancient Rome. The Venetians are blessed with a belief in their own nobility. The Greeks, as well as being the founders of the learned disciplines, vaunt themselves upon their titles to the famous heroes of old. The Turks, and that whole rabble of the truly barbarous, claim praise for their religion, laughing at Christians as superstitious. And what is much more pleasant, the Jews still are awaiting their own Messiah, and even today hold on to their Moses with might and main. Spaniards yield to no one in martial reputation. Germans take pride in their great stature and their knowledge of magic. . . .

You would never believe what sport and entertainment your mortal manikins provide daily for the gods. These gods, you know, set aside their sober forenoon hours for composing quarrels and giving ear to prayers. But after that, when they are well moistened with nectar and have no desire for the transaction of business, they seek out some promontory of heaven and, sitting there with faces bent downward, they watch what mortal men are adoing. There is no show like it, Good God, what a theater! How various the action of fools! (I may say that now and then I take a seat alongside the gods of the poets.) Here is a fellow dying for love of a sweet young thing, and the less he is loved in return, the more helplessly he is in love. This one marries a dowry, not a wife. This one prostitutes his own wife. The jealousy of another keeps watch like Argus. Here is a man in mourning, but mercy me, what fool things he says and does! Hiring mourners as if they were actors, to play a comedy of grief! Another man squeezes out a tear at the tomb of his mother-in-law. This one spends on his belly whatever he can scrape together by hook or crook, but presently he will be just as hungry again. Another finds nothing better than sleep and idleness. There are those who get themselves into a stew working at what is other people's business, while they neglect their own. There is also the broker, who accounts himself rich on other people's money, but is on the way to bankruptcy. Another thinks that the happy life consists in living like a pauper in order that his heir may be wealthy. Another, for the sake of a small and uncertain profit, sails the seven seas, exposing his life, which no money could pay for, to the hazard of waves and winds. This one prefers seeking riches in war to passing a safe and quiet life at home. Some decide that they can most conveniently attain to wealth by courting and fawning upon childless old men. There are even those who prefer to do the same to rich old women. Both kinds furnish rare sport to the gods who are spectators, because they are usually cheated by the parties they set out to catch.

But the most foolish and sordid of all are your merchants, in that they carry on the most sordid business of all and this by the most sordid methods; for on occasion they lie, they perjure themselves, they steal, they cheat, they impose on the public. Yet they make themselves men of importance—because they have gold rings on their fingers. Nor do they lack for flattering friars who admire them and call them Right Honorable in public, with the purpose, surely, that some little driblet from the ill-gotten gains may flow to themselves. Elsewhere you will see certain Pythagoreans, in whose eyes all things are common—to such a degree, in fact, that whatever they light upon that is lying around loose they carry off with a tranquil spirit, as if it passed to them by inheritance. There are others who are rich only in wishes; they build beautiful air-castles and conceive that doing so is enough for happiness. Some delight in passing for wealthy men away from home, though they starve meanly enough in their own houses. One man hastens to put into circulation what money he has; his neighbor hoards his up through thick and thin. This one pushes forward as a candidate for public honors; that one finds his pleasure by his fireside. A good many people bring suits which are destined never to end; once and again they eagerly strive to outdo each other—in enriching the judge who sets the postponements and the advocate who colludes with him. One burns with zeal for revolutions; another is toiling upon his Grand Scheme. This man leaves wife and children at home and sets out on a pilgrimage to

Jerusalem, Rome, or the shrine of St. James, where he has no particular business. In sum, if you might look down from the moon, as Menippus did of old, upon the numberless agitations among mortal men, you would think you were seeing a swarm of flies or gnats, quarreling among themselves, waging wars, setting snares for each other, robbing, sporting, wantoning, being born, growing old, and dying. . . .

Among men of learned professions, the lawyers may claim first place for themselves, nor is there any other class quite so self-satisfied; for while they industriously roll up the stone of Sisyphus by dint of weaving together six hundred laws in the same breath, no matter how little to the purpose, and by dint of piling glosses upon glosses and opinions upon opinions, they contrive to make their profession seem the most difficult of all. . . .

Near these march the scientists, reverenced for their beards and the fur on their gowns, who teach that they alone are wise while the rest of mortal men flit about as shadows. How pleasantly they dote, indeed, while they construct their numberless worlds, and measure the sun, moon, stars, and spheres as with thumb and line. They assign causes for lightning, winds, eclipses, and other inexplicable things, never hesitating a whit, as if they were privy to the secrets of nature, artificer of things, or as if they visited us fresh from the council of the gods. Yet all the while nature is laughing grandly at them and their conjectures. For to prove that they have good intelligence of nothing, this is a sufficient argument: they can never explain why they disagree with each other on every subject. Thus knowing nothing in general, they profess to know all things in particular; though they are ignorant even of themselves, and on occasion do not see the ditch or the stone lying across their path, because many of them are blear-eyed or absent-minded. . . .

Perhaps it were better to pass over the theologians in silence, and not to move such a Lake Camarina, or to handle such an herb *Anagyris foetida,* as that marvellously supercilious and irascible race. For they may attack me with six hundred arguments, in squadrons, and drive me to make a recantation; which if I refuse, they will straightway proclaim me an heretic. . . .

They are protected by a wall of scholastic definitions, arguments, corollaries, implicit and explicit propositions; they have so many hideaways that they could not be caught even by the net of Vulcan; for they slip out on their distinctions, by which also they cut through all knots as easily as with a double-bitted axe from Tenedos; and they abound with newly-invented terms and prodigious vocables. Furthermore, they explain as pleases them the most arcane matters, such as by what method the world was founded and set in order, through what conduits original sin has been passed down along the generations, by what means, in what measure, and how long the perfect Christ was in the Virgin's womb, and how accidents subsist in the Eucharist without their subject.

But those are hackneyed. Here are questions worthy of the great and (as some call them) illuminated theologians, questions to make them prick up their ears—if ever they chance upon them. Whether divine generation took place at a particular time? Whether there are several sonships in Christ? Whether this is a possible proposition: God the Father hates the Son? Whether God could have taken upon Himself the likeness of a woman? Or of a devil? Of an ass? Of a gourd? Of a piece of flint? Then how would that gourd have preached, performed miracles, or been crucified? Also, what would Peter have consecrated if he had administered the sacrament while Christ's body hung upon the Cross? Also whether at that moment Christ could be said to be a man? And whether after the resurrection it will be forbidden to eat and drink? (Now, while there is time, they are providing against hunger and thirst!) These finespun trifles are numberless, with others even more subtle, having to do with instants of time, notions, relations, accidents, quiddities, entities, which no one can perceive with his eyes unless, like Lynceus, he can see in blackest darkness things that are not there.

We must put in also those hard sayings, contradictions indeed, compared to which the Stoic maxims which were called paradoxes seem the merest simplicity. For instance: it is less of a crime to cut the throats of a thousand men than to set a stitch on a poor man's shoe on the Lord's day; it is better to choose that the universe should perish, body, boots, and breeches (as the saying is), than that one should tell a single lie, however inconsequential. The methods our scholastics pursue only render more subtle these subtlest of subtleties; for you will escape from a labyrinth more quickly than from the tangles of Realists, Nominalists, Thomists, Albertists, Occamists, Scotists— I have not named them all, but the chief ones only. But in all these sects there is so much learning and so much difficulty that I should think the apostles themselves must needs have the help of some other spirit if they were to try disputing on these topics with our new generation of theologues. . . .

In my poor judgment Christians would be wiser if instead of their gross unwieldy battalions of soldiers, with which for some time now they have been warring without any particular favor from Mars, they would send against the Turks and Saracens these brawling Scotists and stubborn Occamists and invincible Albertists, along with the whole band of Sophists. Then, I am bold to think, they would witness a battle which would be the merriest ever fought, and a victory such as was never seen before. Who is so phlegmatic that the shrewdness of these fighters would not excite him? Who so stupid that such sophistries would not quicken him? Who so quick-sighted that they would not throw a mist before his eyes? . . .

Coming nearest to these in felicity are the men who generally call themselves "the religious" and "monks"—utterly false names both, since most of
them keep as far away as they can from religion and no people are more in
evidence in every sort of place. But I do not see how anything could be more
dismal than these monks if I did not succor them in many ways. For though
people as a whole so detest this race of men that meeting one by accident is
supposed to be bad luck, yet they flatter themselves to the queen's taste. For
one thing, they reckon it the highest degree of piety to have no contact with
literature, and hence they see to it that they do not know how to read. For another, when with asinine voices they bray out in church those psalms they
have learned, by rote rather than by heart, they are convinced that they are
anointing God's ears with the blandest of oil. Some of them make a good
profit from their dirtiness and mendicancy, collecting their food from door
to door with importunate bellowing; nay, there is not an inn, public conveyance,
or ship where they do not intrude, to the great disadvantage of the other common beggars. Yet according to their account, by their very dirtiness, ignorance,
want of manners, and insolence, these delightful fellows are representing to
us the lives of the apostles. . . .

In short, all orders take remarkable care that nothing in their way of life
shall be consistent; nor is it so much their concern to be like Christ as to be
unlike each other. Thus a great part of their felicity derives from their various
names. Those of one order delight to call themselves Cordeliers, but among
them some are Coletes, some Minors, some Minims, some Crutched. Again,
there are the Benedictines and the Bernardines; the Bridgetines and the Au-
gustinians; the Williamists and the Jacobines; as if it were not enough to be
called Christians. . . .

In truth I am glad to get away from these actors and dissemblers, who are
as ungrateful for my benefits as they are false in their pretensions to piety. And
at this point it pleases me to touch upon kings and nobles of the court, by whom
I am worshipped sincerely and, as becomes gentlemen, frankly. And indeed,
if they had so much as half an ounce of sound wisdom, what life were more
dismal than theirs or more to be avoided? For let a person weigh in his mind
how heavy a burden rests on the shoulders of anyone wishing to act the true
prince, and he will not conclude that sovereignty is a thing worth using perjury
and parricide to gain. He will consider that one who grasps the helm of great
affairs must further the public, not his private, interest and give his mind to
nothing except as it concerns the general good; he must not deviate a finger's
breadth from the laws of which he is author and executor; he must himself
be warrant for the integrity of all officials and magistrates; he is one person
who is exposed to all eyes, and like a favorable star he has power, by the good
influence of his conduct, to bring salvation in human affairs; or like a fatal

comet he may bring destruction in his train. The vices of other men are not so deeply felt or so widely communicated. A prince is in such a position that if he lapses ever so slightly from honesty, straightway a dangerous and vital infection spreads to many people. Then the lot of princes brings with it a host of things which tend to lead them from righteousness, such as pleasure, liberty, adulation, and excess; so that he must endeavor more earnestly and watch more vigilantly lest, beguiled by these, he fail of his duty. Finally, to say nothing of treasons, hatred, and other perils or dreads, there stands above his own crown that true King who will call him to account for even the least of his trespasses; and the accounting will be more severe as the empire he ruled was the more mighty. I say that if the prince weighed these things, and many more like them, within himself—and he would do so, were he wise—I am afraid he could neither sleep nor eat in any joy.

But as it is, with my assistance, kings leave all these concerns to the gods, take care of themselves nicely, and grant no hearing to anyone unless he knows how to speak pleasant things, because solicitude must not get a foothold in their minds. They believe they have played the part of a sovereign to the hilt if they diligently go hunting, feed some fine horses, sell dignities and offices at a profit to themselves, and daily devise new measures by which to drain away the wealth of citizens and sweep it into their own exchequer. All this, of course, is done in due form, under new-found names, so that even when most unjust it shall carry some appearance of equity; and they take care to add a little sweetening so that in any event they may secure for themselves the hearts of the people. . . .

Now what shall I say about the noble courtiers? Though nothing is more venal, more servile, more witless, or more contemptible than most of them, yet they desire to seem the foremost of created things. Here is one point, however, in which they are as modest as one could wish: they are satisfied to carry about on their bodies gold, gems, scarlet, and the other insignia of wisdom and the virtues, but the reality of these they leave for the use of others. They find themselves abundantly happy in being allowed to speak of the king as "our master," in having learned how to turn a compliment in three words, and in knowing how to repeat on occasion those courteous titles of Your Grace, Your Lordship, and Your Majesty; in having cast off shame beyond other men, and in flattering handsomely. For these are the arts which truly become the nobleman and courtier. . . .

Our popes, cardinals, and bishops for some time now have earnestly copied the state and practice of princes, and come near to beating them at their own game. Let a bishop but consider what his alb, the white emblem of sincerity, should teach him, namely, a life in every way blameless; and what is signified on his part by the two-horned miter, the two peaks bound by the same knot—I suppose it is a perfect knowledge of the Old and New Testaments; what is meant by covering his hands with gloves, a clean administration of the sacrament and one unsullied by any taint of human concerns; what the crozier symbolizes, most watchful care of the flock put under his charge; what is indicated by the cross that is carried before him, to wit, a victory over all carnal affections. If he would contemplate these and other lessons of the sort, I say, would he not lead a sad and troubled life? But as it is, they do well enough by way of feeding themselves; as for the other, the care of the sheep, they delegate that to Christ himself, or else refer it to their suffragans, as they call them, or other deputies. Nor do they keep in mind the name they bear, or what the word "bishop" means—labor, vigilance, solicitude. Yet in raking in moneys they truly play the bishop, overseeing everything—and overlooking nothing.

In a similar way the cardinals, if they considered the fact that they have succeeded to the places of the apostles, would see that the same works are required of them as were performed by their predecessors; that they are not lords, but stewards, of spiritual things, and that shortly they are to render an exact account of what they hold in trust. Yes, let them too philosophize a bit concerning their vestments, and question themselves in this fashion: "What does the whiteness of this upper garment mean? Is it not a notable and singular purity of heart? What the crimson lower garment? Is it not a burning love of God? What, again, that outer rober flowing down in broad folds and spreading over the mule of his Exalted Reverence, though it would suffice to cover a camel? Is it not charity ample enough to embrace all men in its helpfulness, by way of teaching, exhorting, chastising, admonishing, ending wars, resisting wicked princes, and freely spending blood—not money alone—for the flock of Christ? And wherefore all this money, anyway, for those who hold the places of the needy apostles?" If they would weigh these things, I repeat, they would not be so ambitious for the post, and would willingly give it up, or at least they would lead a toilsome and watchful life of the sort lived by those ancient apostles.

As to these Supreme Pontiffs who take the place of Christ, if they tried to emulate His life, I mean His poverty, labors, teaching, cross, and contempt for safety, if even they thought upon the title of Pope—that is, Father—or the addition "Most Holy," who on earth would be more afflicted? Who would purchase that seat at the price of every resource and effort? Or who defend it, when purchased, by the sword, by poison, or by anything else? Were wisdom to descend upon them, how it would inconvenience them! Wisdom, did I say? Nay, even a grain of salt would do it—a grain of that salt which is spoken of by Christ. It would lose them all that wealth and honor, all those possessions, triumphal progresses, offices, dispensations, tributes, and indulgences; it would lose them so many horses, mules, and retainers; so many pleasures. . . .

And so it comes about—by my doing, remember—that scarcely any kind of men live more softly or less oppressed with care; believing that they are amply acceptable to Christ if with a mystical and almost theatrical finery, with ceremonies, and with those titles of Beatitude and Reverence and Holiness, along with blessing and cursing, they perform the office of bishops. To work miracles is primitive and old-fashioned, hardly suited to our times; to instruct the people is irksome; to interpret the Holy Scriptures is pedantry; to pray is otiose; to shed tears is distressing and womanish; to live in poverty is sordid; to be beaten in war is dishonorable and less than worthy of one who will hardly admit kings, however great, to kiss his sacred foot; and finally, to die is unpleasant, to die on the cross a disgrace.

There remain only those weapons and sweet benedictions of which Paul speaks, and the popes are generous enough with these: interdictions, excommunications, re-excommunications, anathematizations, pictured damnations, and the terrific lightning-bolt of the bull, which by its mere flicker sinks the souls of men below the floor of hell. And these most holy fathers in Christ, and vicars of Christ, launch it against no one with more spirit than against those who, at the instigation of the devil, try to impair or to subtract from the patrimony of Peter. Although this saying of Peter's stands in the Gospel, "We have left all and followed Thee," yet they give the name of his patrimony to lands, towns, tribute, imposts, and moneys. On behalf of these things, inflamed by zeal for Christ, they fight with fire and sword, not without shedding of Christian blood; and then they believe they have defended the bride of Christ in apostolic fashion, having scattered what they are pleased to designate as "her enemies." As if the church had any enemies more pestilential than impious pontiffs who by their silence allow Christ to be forgotten, who enchain Him by mercenary rules, adulterate His teaching by forced interpretations, and crucify Him afresh by their scandalous life!

Now the Christian church was founded on blood, strengthened by blood, and augmented by blood; yet nowadays they carry on Christ's cause by the sword just as if He who defends His own by His own means had perished. And although war is so cruel a business that it befits beasts and not men, so frantic that poets feign it is sent with evil purpose by the Furies, so pestilential that it brings with it a general blight upon morals, so iniquitous that it is usually conducted by the worst bandits, so impious that it has no accord with Christ, yet our popes, neglecting all their other concerns, make it their only task. Here you will see feeble old men assuming the strength of youth, not shocked by the expense or tired out by the labor, not at all discouraged, if only they may upset laws, religion, peace, and all humane usages, and turn them heels over head. Learned sycophants will be found who will give to this manifest madness the names of zeal, piety, and fortitude, devising a way whereby it is possible for a man to whip out his sword, stick it into the guts of his brother, and nonetheless dwell in that supreme charity which, according to Christ's precept, a Christian owes to his neighbor. . . .

Come, now that I have "put on the lion's skin," I shall show this also, that the happiness of Christians, which they pursue with so much travail, is nothing else but a kind of madness and folly. Let these words give no offense; instead, keep your mind on the point. To begin with, Christians come near to agreeing with Platonists in this, that the soul is sunk and shackled by corporeal bonds, being so clogged by the grossness of the body that but little can it contemplate and enjoy things as they truly are. Hence Plato defined philosophy as "a study of death," because it leads the mind away from visible and bodily things, and certainly death does the same. And thus as long as the soul uses the bodily organs aright, so long it is called sane, but when with its bonds broken it attempts to make good its liberty, planning, as it were, escape from its prison, then it is called mad. . . .

. . . Since there is so great contrariety between the pious and the vulgar, it comes about that each appears to the other to be mad—though in my opinion, to be sure, the word is more correctly applied to the pious than to the others. This will become clearer if I briefly demonstrate, as I promised to do, that their *summum bonum* [1] itself is no other than a kind of insanity. First, let us suppose that Plato was dreaming of something very like it when he wrote that "the madness of lovers is the happiest state of all." Now he who loves intensely no longer lives in himself but in whatever he loves, and the more he can depart from himself and enter into the other, the happier he is. And when a mind yearns toward travelling out of the body, and does not rightly use its own bodily organs, you doubtless, and with accuracy, call the state of it madness. Otherwise, what do they mean by those common phrases, "he is not at home," and "to come to yourself," and "he is himself again"? Furthermore, so far as the love is more perfect the madness is greater and more delightful. Of what sort, then, is that future life with those who dwell on high, toward which pious hearts aspire with such fervor? First the spirit, as conqueror and the more vital, will overmaster and absorb the body, and this it will do the more easily in that now it is in its own realm, so to speak, and also because already, during life, it has cleansed and lightened the body in preparation for this change. Then the spirit itself will be absorbed in marvellous wise by that supreme spirit, more potent than its infinity of parts. Thus the whole man will be outside of himself, nor will he be happy for any other reason than that,

[1] [*Highest good.*]

so placed outside of himself, he shall have some ineffable portion in that *summum bonum* which draws all things unto itself. And although this happiness arrives at its perfection only when souls, joined to their former bodies, shall be clothed with immortality, yet because the earthly life of pious folk is nothing but a contemplation and kind of shadowing of that other, they sometimes feel a foretaste and a glow of the reward to come. Although this is as but the least little drop in comparison with that flowing fountain of eternal happiness, yet it far surpasses any bodily pleasure, yes, even if all mortal delights were brought together into one. By so much does the spiritual excel over the corporeal, and the invisible over the visible. This surely is what the prophet has promised: "Eye hath not seen, nor ear heard, neither have entered into the heart of man the things which God hath prepared for them that love Him." And this truly is the portion of Folly, that "good part" which "shall not be taken away" by the transformation of life, but will be perfected.

Hence those who are permitted to have a foretaste of this—and it comes to but few—suffer something very like to madness. They say things that are not quite coherent, and this not in the ordinary way of men, but they make a sound without meaning, and suddenly they change the whole aspect of their faces; now cheerful, now downcast, they will weep, then laugh, and then sigh; in brief, they are truly outside themselves. When presently they return to themselves they say that they do not know where they have been, whether in the body or out of it, waking or sleeping; they do not remember what they have heard, seen, spoken, or done; and yet through a cloud, or as in a dream, they know one thing, that they were at their happiest while they were thus out of their wits. So they are sorry to come to themselves again and would prefer, of all good things, nothing but to be mad always with this madness. And this is a tiny little taste of that future happiness.

But indeed I have long since forgotten myself and run out of bounds. If anything I have said shall seem too saucy or too glib, stop and think: 'tis Folly, and a woman, that has spoken. But of course you will also remember that Greek proverb, "Even a foolish man will often speak a word in season," unless, perhaps, you assume that this does not extend to women. I see that you are expecting a peroration, but you are just too foolish if you suppose that after I have poured out a hodgepodge of words like this I can recall anything that I have said. There is an old saying, "I hate a pot-companion with a memory." Here is a new one: "I hate a hearer that remembers anything."

And so farewell. . . . Applaud . . . live . . . drink . . . O most distinguished initiates of Folly!

THOMAS MORE

THOMAS MORE (1478–1535) was born in London and studied two years at Oxford during the period of humanist influence. His later career as a lawyer did not prevent the continued development of his interest in humanism which brought him the friendship of Colet and Erasmus. More was Speaker of the House of Commons in 1523 and, by now high in the favor of King Henry VIII, became Lord Chancellor on the fall of Cardinal Wolsey in 1529. More was recurrently at odds with Henry VIII, however, over the latter's quarrels with the pope. Upon Henry's second marriage, to Anne Boleyn, Pope Clement VII excommunicated the English king, whereupon Parliament declared the king to be the "only supreme head in earth of the Church of England." Persistent in his opposition to Henry's marriage and to schism within the Church, More retired from the court in 1532. His continued disfavor with the rulers, his loyalty to the Roman Catholic Church, and his refusal to subscribe to the Act of Supremacy led to his imprisonment in the Tower where he was beheaded for treason in 1535. He is today one of the martyrs of the Catholic Church and was canonized in 1935.

More's most famous work, *Utopia,* was published in Latin in 1516 and in English translation in 1551. The *Utopia* is the account of a traveler (Raphael); the first part deals with criticisms of existing conditions in Europe and England; the second part is a description of Utopia (literally, *Nowhere*), an imaginary state where ideal principles are realized. More's numerous works include the *Apology of Sir Thomas More,* the *Dialogue of Comfort against Tribulation,* and *The Life of John Picus, Earl of Mirandula.*

The following is from the Robinson translation from Latin of 1551.

UTOPIA

The First Book of the Communication of Raphael Hythloday, Concerning the Best State of a Commonwealth

THE MOST VICTORIOUS and triumphant king of England, Henry the eighth of that name, in all royal virtues a prince most peerless, had of late in controversy with Charles, the right high and mighty king of Castile, weighty matters and of great importance; for the debatement and final determination whereof the king's majesty sent me ambassador into Flanders, joined in commission with Cuthbert Tunstall, a man doubtless out of comparison and whom the king's majesty of late, to the great rejoicing of all men, did prefer to the office of Master of the Rolls. . . .

There met us at Bruges (for thus it was before agreed) they whom their prince had for that matter appointed commissioners, excellent men all. . . . After that we had once or twice met, and upon certain points or articles could not fully and thoroughly agree, they for a certain space took their leave of us and departed to Brussels, there to know their prince's pleasure.

I, in the meantime (for so my business lay), went straight thence to Antwerp. While I was there abiding, oftentimes among others but which to me was more welcome than any other, did visit me one Peter Giles, a citizen of Antwerp; a man there in his country of honest reputation, and also preferred to high promotions, worthy truly of the highest, for it is hard to say whether the young man be in learning or in honesty more excellent. . . .

Upon a certain day when I had heard the divine service in our Lady's Church—which is the fairest, the most gorgeous, and curious church of building in all the city, and also most frequented of people—and, the service being done, was ready to go home to my lodging, I chanced to espy this foresaid Peter talking with a certain stranger, a man well stricken in age, with a black sun-burned face, a long beard, and a cloak cast homely about his shoulders, whom by his favour and apparel forthwith I judged to be a mariner. But the said Peter, seeing me, came unto me and saluted me. And as I was about to answer him: See you this man? sayeth he (and therewith he pointed to the man that I saw him talking with before). I was minded, quoth he, to bring him straight home to you.

He should have been very welcome to me, said I, for your sake.

Nay, quoth he, for his own sake, if you knew him; for there is no man this day living that can tell you of so many strange and unknown peoples and countries as this man can. And I know well that you be very desirous to hear of such news.

Then I conjectured not far amiss, quoth I, for even at the first sight I judged him to be a mariner.

Nay, quoth he, there ye were greatly deceived. He hath sailed indeed, not as the mariner Palinurus, but as the expert and prudent prince Ulysses; yea, rather as the ancient and sage philosopher Plato. For this same Raphael Hythloday (for this is his name) is very well learned in the Latin tongue, but profound and excellent in the Greek language, wherein he ever bestowed more study than in the Latin, because he had given himself wholly to the study of philosophy; whereof he knew that there is nothing extant in Latin that is to any purpose, saving a few of Seneca's and Cicero's doings. His patrimony that he was born unto he left to his brethren (for he is a Portuguese born), and for the desire that he had to see and know the far countries of the world, he joined himself in company with Amerigo Vespucci, and in the three last voyages of those four that be now in print and abroad in every man's hands, he continued still in his company, saving that in the last voyage he came not home again with him. For he made such means and shift, what by entreatance, and what by importune suit, that he got licence of Master Amerigo (though it were sore against his will) to be one of the twenty-three which in the end of the last voyage were left in the country of Gulike. He was therefore left behind for his mind sake, as one that took more thought and care for travelling than dying, having customarily in his mouth these sayings: He that hath no grave is covered with the sky, and, The way to heaven out of all places is of like length and distance. Which fantasy of his (if God had not been his better friend) he had surely bought full dear. But after the departing of Master Vespucci, when he had travelled through and about many countries with five of his companions Gulikians, at the last by marvellous chance he arrived in Taprobane, from whence he went to Calicut, where he chanced to find certain of his country ships, wherein he returned again into his country, nothing less than looked for.

All this when Peter had told me, I thanked him for his gentle kindness that he had vouchsafed to bring me to the speech of that man whose communication he thought should be to me pleasant and acceptable. And therewith I turned me to Raphael; and when we had hailed each other and had spoken those common words that be customarily spoken at the first meeting and acquaintance of strangers, we went thence to my house, and there in my garden, upon a bench covered with green turves, we sat down talking together. There he told us how that, after the departing of Vespucci, he and his fellows that tarried behind in Gulike began by little and little, through fair and gentle speech, to win the love and favour of the people of that country, insomuch that within short space they did dwell amongst them not only harmless, but also occupying with them very familiarly. He told us also that they were in high reputation and favour with a certain great man (whose name and country is now quite out of my remembrance) which of his mere liberality did bear the costs and charges of him and his five companions; and besides that gave them a trusty guide to conduct them in their journey (which by water was in boats and by land in wagons) and to bring them to other princes with very friendly commendations.

Thus after many days' journeys, he said, they found towns and cities and weal-publics, full of people governed by good and wholesome laws. For under the line equinoctial, and on both sides of the same as far as the sun doth extend his course, lieth, quoth he, great and wide deserts and wildernesses, parched, burned, and dried up with continual and intolerable heat.

All things be hideous, terrible, loathsome, and unpleasant to behold; all things out of fashion and comeliness, inhabited with wild beasts and serpents, or at the least wise with people that be no less savage, wild and noisome than the very beasts themselves be. But a little farther beyond that, all things begin by little and little to wax pleasant; the air soft, temperate, and gentle; the ground covered with green grass; less wildness in the beasts. At the last shall ye come again to people, cities, and towns wherein is continual intercourse and occupying of merchandise and chaffare, not only among themselves and with their borderers, but also with merchants of far countries, both by land and water. There I had occasion, said he, to go to many countries on every side. For there was no ship ready to any voyage or journey, but I and my fellows were into it very gladly received. The ships that they found first were made plain, flat, and broad in the bottom, troughwise. The sails were made of great rushes, or of wickers, and in some places of leather. Afterwards, they found ships with ridged keels and sails of canvas, yea, and shortly after, having all things like ours. . . .

But what he told us that he saw in every country where he came, it were very long to declare. Neither it is my purpose at this time to make rehearsal thereof. But peradventure in another place I will speak of it, chiefly such things as shall be profitable to be known, as in special be those decrees and ordinances that he marked to be well and wisely provided and enacted among such peoples as do live together in a civil policy and good order. For of such things did we busily inquire and demand of him, and he likewise very willingly told us of the same. But as for monsters, because they be no news, of them we were nothing inquisitive. For nothing is more easy to be found than be barking Scyllas, ravening Celaenos, and Laestrygons, devourers of people and such like great and incredible monsters. But to find citizens ruled by good and wholesome laws, that is an exceeding rare and hard thing. But as he marked many fond and foolish laws in those new found lands, so he rehearsed divers acts and constitutions whereby these our cities, nations, countries, and kingdoms may take example to amend their faults, enormities, and errors. Whereof in another place (as I said) I will entreat.

Now at this time I am determined to rehearse only that he told us of the manners, customs, laws, and ordinances of the Utopians. But first I will repeat our former communication by the occasion and (as I might say) the drift whereof he was brought into the mention of that weal-public. For, when Raphael had very prudently touched divers things that be amiss, some here and some there, yea, very many on both parts; and again had spoken of such wise laws and prudent decrees as be established and used, both here among us and also there among them, as a man so perfect and expert in the laws and customs of every several country, as though into what place soever he came guestwise there he had led all his life: then Peter, much marvelling at the man: Surely, Master Raphael, quoth he, I wonder greatly why you get you not into some king's court. For I am sure there is no prince living, that would not be very glad of you, as a man not only able highly to delight him with your profound learning and this your knowledge of countries and peoples, but also meet to instruct him with examples and help him with counsel. And thus doing, you shall bring yourself in a very good case, and also be of ability to help all your friends and kinsfolk.

As concerning my friends and kinsfolk, quoth he, I pass not greatly for them. For I think I have sufficiently done my part towards them already. For these things that other men do not depart from until they be old and sick, yea, which they be then very loath to leave when they can no longer keep, those very same things did I, being not only lusty and in good health, but also in the flower of my youth, divide among my friends and kinsfolk. Which I think with this my liberality ought to hold them contented, and not to require nor to look that besides this I should for their sakes give myself in bondage unto kings.

Nay, God forbid that, quoth Peter, it is not my mind that you should be in bondage to kings, but as a retainer to them at your pleasure. Which surely I think is the nighest way that you can devise how to bestow your time fruitfully, not only for the private commodity of your friends and for the general profit of all sorts of people but also for the advancement of yourself to a much wealthier state and condition than you be now in.

To a wealthier condition, quoth Raphael, by that means that my mind standeth clean against? Now I live at liberty after mine own mind and pleasure, which I think very few of these great states and peers of realms can say. Yea, and there be enough of them that sue for great men's friendships, and therefore think it no great hurt if they have not me, nor three or four such other as I am.

Well, I perceive plainly, friend Raphael, quoth I, that you be desirous neither of riches nor of power; and truly I have in no less reverence and estimation a man of your mind than any of them all that be so high in power and authority. But you shall do as it becometh you: yea, and according to this wisdom, to this high and free courage of yours, if you can find in your heart so to appoint and dispose yourself that you may apply your wit and diligence to the profit of the weal-public, though it be somewhat to your own pain and hindrance. And this shall you never so well do, nor with so great profit perform, as if you be of some great prince's council, and put into his head (as I doubt not but you will) honest opinions and virtuous persuasions. For from the prince, as from a perpetual well-spring, cometh among the people the flood of all that is good or evil. But in you is so perfect learning that, without any experience, and again so great experience that without any learning you may well be any king's counsellor.

You be twice deceived, Master More, quoth he, first in me and again in the thing itself. For neither is in me the ability that you force upon me, and if it were never so much, yet in disquieting mine own quietness I should nothing further the weal-public. For, first of all, the most part of all princes have more delight in warlike matters and feats of chivalry (the knowledge whereof I neither have nor desire) than in the good feats of peace, and employ much more study how by right or by wrong to enlarge their dominions, than how well and peaceable to rule and govern that they have already. Moreover, they that be counsellors to kings, every one of them either is of himself so wise indeed that he needeth not, or else he thinketh himself so wise that he will not, allow another man's counsel, saving that they do shamefully and flatteringly give assent to the fond and foolish sayings of certain great men, whose favours, because they be in high authority with their prince, by assentation and flattery they labour to obtain. And verily it is naturally given to all men to esteem their own inventions best. So both the raven and the ape think their own young ones fairest. Then if a man in such a company, where some disdain and have despite at other men's inventions and some count their own best, if among such men (I say) a man should bring forth anything that he hath read done in times past or that he hath seen done in other places, there the hearers fare as though the whole existimation of their wisdom were in jeopardy to be overthrown, and that ever after they should be counted for very dizzards, unless they could in other men's inventions pick out matter to reprehend and find fault at. If all other poor helps fail, then this is their extreme refuge. These things, say they, pleased our forefathers and ancestors; would God we could be so wise as they were. And as though they had wittily concluded the matter, and with this answer stopped every man's mouth, they sit down again. As who should say it were a very dangerous matter if a man in any point should be found wiser than his forefathers were. And yet be we content to suffer the best and wittiest of their decrees to lie unexecuted: but if in anything a better order might have been taken than by them was, there we take fast hold, finding therein many faults. Many times have I chanced upon such proud, lewd, overthwart, and wayward judgments, yea, and once in England.

I pray you, sir, quoth I, have you been in our country?

Yea forsooth, quoth he, and there I tarried for the space of four or five months together, not long after the insurrection that the western English-men made against their kind, which by their own miserable and pitiful slaughter was suppressed and ended. In the mean season I was much bound and beholden to the right reverend father, John Morton, Archbishop and Cardinal of Canterbury, and at that time also Lord Chancellor of England: a man, Master Peter (for Master More knoweth already that I will say), not more honourable for his authority than for his prudence and virtue. He was of a mean stature, and though stricken in age, yet bare he his body upright. In his face did shine such an amiable reverence as was pleasant to behold; gentle in communication, yet earnest, and sage. He had great delight many times with rough speech to his suitors, to prove, but without harm, what prompt wit and what bold spirit were in every man. In the which, as in a virtue much agreeing with his nature so that therewith were not joined impudency, he took great delectation. And the same person, as apt and meet to have an administration in the weal-public, he did lovingly embrace. In his speech he was fine, eloquent, and pithy. In the law he had profound knowledge, in wit he was incomparable, and in memory wonderful excel-lent. These qualities, which in him were by nature singular, he by learning and use had made perfect. The king put much trust in his counsel, the weal-public also, in a manner, leaned unto him when I was there. For even in the chief of his youth he was taken from school into the court, and there passed all his time in much trouble and business, being continually tumbled and tossed in the waves of divers misfortunes and adversities. And so by many and great dangers he learned the experience of the world, which so being learned cannot easily be forgotten.

It chanced on a certain day, when I sat at his table, there was also a certain layman cunning in the laws of your realm. Who, I cannot tell whereof taking occasion, began diligently and earnestly to praise that strait and rigorous justice which at that time was there executed upon felons, who, as he said, were for the most part twenty hanged together upon one gallows. And, seeing so few escaped punishment, he said he could not choose but greatly wonder and marvel how and by what evil luck it should so come to pass that thieves, nevertheless, were in every place so rife and so rank.

Nay, sir, quoth I (for I durst boldly speak my mind before the cardinal), marvel nothing hereat: for this punishment of thieves passeth the limits of justice, and is also very hurtful to the weal-public. For it is too extreme and cruel a punishment for theft, and yet not sufficient to refrain and withhold men from theft. For simple theft is not so great an offence that it ought to be punished with death. Neither there is any punishment so horrible that it can keep them from stealing which have no other craft whereby to get their living. Therefore in this point not you only but also the most part of the world be like evil schoolmasters, which be readier to beat than to teach their scholars. For great and horrible punishments be appointed for thieves, whereas much rather provision should have been made that there were some means whereby they might get their living, so that no man should be driven to this extreme necessity, first to steal and then to die.

Yes, quoth he, this matter is well enough provided for already. There be handicrafts, there is husbandry to get their living by, if they would not willingly be nought.

Nay, quoth I, you shall not escape so: for, first of all, I will speak nothing of them that come home out of the wars maimed and lame, as not long ago out of Blackheath field and a little before that out of the wars in France; such, I say, as put their lives in jeopardy for the weal-public's or the king's sake, and by reason of weakness and lameness be not able to occupy their old crafts, and be too aged to learn new: of them I will speak nothing, forasmuch as wars have their ordinary recourse. But let us consider those things that chance daily before our eyes.

First there is a great number of gentlemen which cannot be content to live idle themselves, like dors, of that which others have laboured for: their tenants, I mean, whom they poll and shave to the quick by raising their rents (for this only point of frugality do they use, men else, through their lavish and prodigal spending, able to bring themselves to very beggary); these gentlemen, I say, do not only live in idleness themselves, but also carry about with them at their tails a great flock or train of idle and loitering serving-men, which never learned any craft whereby to get their livings. These men, as soon as their master is dead, or be sick themselves, be incontinent thrust out of doors. For gentlemen had rather keep idle persons than sick men, and many times the dead man's heir is not able to maintain so great a house and keep so many serving-men as his father did. Then in the mean season they that be thus destitute of service either starve for hunger or manfully play the thieves. For what would you have them to do? When they have wandered abroad so long, until they have worn threadbare their apparel and also impaired their health, then gentlemen, because of their pale and sickly faces and patched coats, will not take them into service. And husbandmen dare not set them a-work; knowing well enough that he is nothing meet to do true and faithful service to a poor man with a spade and a mattock for small wages and hard fare, which being daintily and tenderly pampered up in idleness and pleasure, was wont with a sword and a buckler by his side to jet through the street with a bragging look and to think himself too good to be any man's mate. Nay, by Saint Mary, sir, quoth the lawyer, not so. For this kind of men must we make most of. For in them, as men of stouter stomachs, bolder spirits, and manlier courages than handicraftsmen and plowmen be, doth consist the whole power, strength, and puissance of our army, when we must fight in battle.

Forsooth, sir, as well you might say, quoth I, that for war's sake you must cherish thieves; for surely you shall never lack thieves while you have them. No, nor thieves be not the most false and faint-hearted soldiers, nor soldiers be not the cowardliest thieves: so well these two crafts agree together. But this fault, though it be much used among you, yet is it not peculiar to you only, but common also almost to all nations.

Yet France besides this is troubled and infected with a much sorer plague. The whole realm is filled and besieged with hired soldiers in peace time (if that be peace) which be brought in under the same colour and pretence that hath persuaded you to keep these idle serving-men. For these wise fools and very archdolts thought the wealth of the whole country herein to consist, if there were ever in a readiness a strong and sure garrison, specially of old practised soldiers, for they put no trust at all in men unexercised. And therefore they must be forced to seek for war, to the end they may ever have practised soldiers and cunning manslayers, lest (as it is prettily said of Sallust) their hands and their minds, through idleness or lack of exercise, should wax dull. But how pernicious and pestilent a thing it is to maintain such beasts the Frenchmen by their own harms have learned, and the examples of the Romans, Carthaginians, Syrians, and of many other countries do manifestly declare. For not only the empire but also the fields and cities of all these by divers occasions have been overrunned and destroyed of their own armies beforehand had in a readiness. Now how unnecessary a thing this is hereby it may appear, that the French soldiers, which from their youth have been practised and inured in feats of arms, do not crack nor advance themselves to have very often got the upper hand and mastery of your new-made and unpractised soldiers. But in this point I will not use many words, lest perchance I may seem to flatter you. No, nor those same handicraftsmen of yours in cities, nor yet the rude and uplandish plowmen of the country, are not supposed to be greatly afraid of your gentlemen's idle serving-men, unless it be such as be not of body or stature correspondent to their strength and courage, or else whose bold stomachs be discouraged through poverty.

Thus you may see that it is not to be feared lest they should be effeminated if they were brought up in good crafts and laboursome works whereby to get their livings, whose stout and sturdy bodies (for gentlemen vouchsafe to corrupt and spill none but picked and chosen men) now, either by reason of rest and idleness be brought to weakness, or else by too easy and womanly exercises be made feeble and unable to endure hardness. Truly, howsoever the case standeth, this, methinketh, is nothing available to the weal-public, for war sake, which you never have but when you will yourselves, to keep and maintain an innumerable flock of that sort of men that be so troublesome and noyous in peace, whereof you ought to have a thousand times more regard, than of war. But yet this is not only the necessary cause of stealing. There is another, which, as I suppose, is proper and peculiar to you Englishmen alone.

What is that? quoth the cardinal.

Forsooth, my lord, quoth I, your sheep that were wont to be so meek and tame and so small eaters, now, as I hear say, be become so great devourers and so wild, that they eat up and swallow down the very men themselves. They consume, destroy, and devour whole fields, houses, and cities. For look in what parts of the realm doth grow the finest and therefore dearest wool, there noblemen and gentlemen, yea and certain abbots, holy men no doubt, not contenting themselves with the yearly revenues and profits that were wont to grow to their forefathers and predecessors of their lands, nor being content that they live in rest and pleasure nothing profiting, yea, much annoying the weal-public, leave no ground for tillage. They enclose all into pastures; they throw down houses; they pluck down towns, and leave nothing standing but only the church to be made a sheep-house. And as though you lost no small quantity of ground by forests, chases, lands, and parks, those good holy men turn all dwelling places and all glebeland into desolation and wilderness. Therefore that one covetous and insatiable cormorant and very plague of its native country may compass about and enclose many thousand acres of ground together within one pale or hedge, the husbandmen be thrust out of their own, or else either by covin and fraud or by violent oppression they be put besides it, or by wrongs and injuries they be so wearied, that they be compelled to sell all. By one means, therefore, or by other, either by hook or crook, they must needs depart away, poor, silly, wretched souls, men, women, husbands, wives, fatherless children, widows, woeful mothers with their young babes, and their whole household small in substance and much in number, as husbandry requireth many hands. Away they trudge, I say, out of their known and accustomed houses, finding no place to rest in. All their household stuff, which is very little worth though it might well abide the sale, yet being suddenly thrust out they be constrained to sell it for a thing of nought. And when they have wandered abroad till that be spent, what can they then else do but steal, and then justly pardy be hanged, or else go about a-begging? And yet then also they be cast in prison as vagabonds, because they go about and work not, whom no man will set a-work, though they never so willingly proffer themselves thereto.

For one shepherd or herdman is enough to eat up that ground with cattle, to the occupying whereof about husbandry many hands were requisite. And this is also the cause why victuals be now in many places dearer. Yea, besides this the price of wool is so risen, that poor folks, which were wont to work it and make cloth thereof, be now able to buy none at all. And by this means very many be forced to forsake work and to give themselves to idleness. For after that so much ground was enclosed for pasture an infinite multitude of sheep died of the rot, such vengeance God took of their inordinate and insatiable covetousness, sending among the sheep that pestiferous murrain which much more justly should have fallen on the sheepmasters' own heads. And though the number of sheep increase never so fast, yet the price falleth not one mite, because there be so few sellers; for they be almost all come into a few rich men's hands, whom no need forceth to sell before they lust, and they lust not before they may sell as dear as they lust.

Now the same cause bringeth in like dearth of the other kinds of cattle, yea, and that so much the more because that after farms plucked down and husbandry decayed there is no man that passeth for the breeding of young store. For these rich men bring not up the young ones of great cattle as they do lambs. But first they buy them abroad very cheap, and afterward, when they be fatted in their pastures, they sell them again exceeding dear. And therefore (as I suppose) the whole incommodity hereof is not yet felt; for yet they make dearth only in those places where they sell. But when they shall fetch them away from thence where they be bred faster than they can be brought up, then shall there also be felt great dearth, store beginning there to fail where the ware is bought. Thus the unreasonable covetousness of a few hath turned that thing to the utter undoing of your island, in the which thing the chief felicity of your realm did consist. For this great dearth of victuals causeth men to keep as little houses and as small hospitality as they possibly may, and to put away their servants; whither, I pray you, but a-begging, or else (which these gentle bloods and stout stomachs will sooner set their minds unto) a-stealing?

Now to amend the matter, to this wretched beggary and miserable poverty is joined great wantonness, importunate superfluity, and excessive riot. For not only gentlemen's servants, but also handicraftsmen, yea, and almost the plowmen of the country, with all other sorts of people use much strange and proud newfangleness in their apparel, and too much prodigal riot and sumptuous fare at their table. Now bawds, queans, whores, harlots, strumpets, brothel-houses, stews; and yet another stews, wine-taverns, ale-houses, and tippling houses, with so many naughty, lewd, and unlawful games, as dice, cards, tables, tennis, bowls, quoits, do not all these send the haunters of them straight a-stealing, when their money is gone? Cast out these pernicious abominations; make a law that they which plucked down farms and towns of husbandry shall re-edify them, or else yield and uprender the possession thereof to such as will go to the cost of building them anew. Suffer not these rich men to buy up all to engross and forestall, and with their monopoly to keep the market alone as please them. Let not so many be brought up in idleness; let husbandry and tillage be restored; let clothworking be renewed, that there may be honest labours for this idle sort to pass their time in profitably, which hitherto either poverty hath caused to be thieves, or else now be either vagabonds or idle serving men, and shortly will be thieves.

Doubtless unless you find a remedy for these enormities you shall in vain advance yourselves of executing justice upon felons. For this justice is more beautiful in appearance and more flourishing to the shew than either just or profitable. For by suffering your youth wantonly and viciously to be brought up, and to be infected, even from their tender age, by little and little with vice, then, a God's name, to be punished when they commit the same faults after being come to man's state, which from their youth they were ever like to do; in this point, I pray you, what other thing do you than make thieves and then punish them?

Now as I was thus speaking, the lawyer began to make himself ready to answer, and was determined with himself to use the common fashion and trade of disputers, which be more diligent in rehearsing than answering, as thinking the memory worthy of the chief praise. Indeed, sir, quoth he, you have said well, being but a stranger and one that might rather hear something of these matters, than have any exact or perfect knowledge of the same, as I will incontinent by open proof make manifest and plain. For first I will rehearse in order all that you have said; then I will declare wherein you be deceived through lack of knowledge in all our fashions, manners, and customs; and last of all I will answer your arguments, and confute them every one. First therefore I will begin where I promised. Four things you seemed to me—

Hold your peace, quoth the cardinal, for it appeareth that you will make no short answer, which make such a beginning. Wherefore at this time you shall not take the pains to make your answer, but keep it to your next meeting, which I would be right glad that it might be even tomorrow next, unless either you or master Raphael have any earnest let. But now, Master Raphael,

I would very gladly hear of you, why you think theft not worthy to be punished with death, or what other punishment you can devise more expedient to the weal-public. For I am sure you are not of that mind, that you would have theft escape unpunished. For if now the extreme punishment of death cannot cause them to leave stealing, then if ruffians and robbers should be sure of their lives, what violence, what fear, were able to hold their hands from robbing which would take the mitigation of the punishment as a very provocation to the mischief?

Surely, my lord, quoth I, I think it not right nor justice that the loss of money should cause the loss of man's life. For mine opinion is, that all the goods in the world are not able to countervail man's life. But if they would thus say, that the breaking of justice and the transgression of the laws is recompensed with this punishment, and not the loss of the money, then why may not this extreme and rigorous justice well be called plain injury? For so cruel governance, so strict rules and unmerciful laws be not allowable, that if a small offence be committed, by and by the sword should be drawn. Nor so stoical ordinances are to be borne withal, as to count all offences of such equality, that the killing of a man or the taking of his money from him were both a matter, and the one no more heinous offence than the other, between the which two, if we have any respect to equity, no similitude or equality consisteth. God commandeth us that we shall not kill. And be we then so hasty to kill a man for taking a little money? And if any man would understand killing by this commandment of God to be forbidden after no larger wise than man's constitutions define killing to be lawful, then why may it not likewise by man's constitutions be determined after what sort whoredom, fornication, and perjury may be lawful? For whereas, by the permission of God, no man hath power to kill neither himself nor yet any other man, then if a law make by the consent of men concerning slaughter of men ought to be of such strength, force, and virtue, that they which contrary to the commandment of God have killed those whom this constitution of man commanded to be killed, be clean quit and exempt out of the bonds and danger of God's commandment, shall it not then, by this reason follow that the power of God's commandment shall extend no further than man's law doth define and permit? And so shall it come to pass, that in like manner man's constitutions in all things shall determine how far the observation of all God's commandments shall extend. To be short, Moses' law, though it were ungentle and sharp, as a law that was given to bondmen, yea, and them very obstinate, stubborn, and stiff-necked, yet it punished theft by the purse and not with death. And let us not think that God in the new law of clemency and mercy, under the which He ruleth us with fatherly gentleness, as His dear children, hath given us greater scope and licence to the execution of cruelty one upon another.

Now ye have heard the reasons whereby I am persuaded that this punishment is unlawful. Furthermore, I think there is nobody that knoweth not how unreasonable, yea, how pernicious a thing it is to the weal-public that a thief and an homicide or murderer should suffer equal and like punishment. For the thief, seeing that man that is condemned for theft in no less jeopardy nor judged to no less punishment than him that is convict of manslaughter, through this cogitation only he is strongly and forcibly provoked, and in a manner constrained, to kill him whom else he would have but robbed. For the murder being once done, he is in less fear and in more hope that the deed shall not be betrayed or known, seeing the party is now dead and rid out of the way, which only might have uttered and disclosed it. But if he chance to be taken and descried, yet he is in no more danger and jeopardy than if he had committed but single felony. Therefore while we go about with such cruelty to make thieves afraid, we provoke them to kill good men.

Now as touching this question, what punishment were more commodious and better, that truly in my judgment is easier to be found than what punishment might be worse. For why should we doubt that to be a good and a profitable way for the punishment of offenders, which we know did in times past so long please the Romans, men in the administration of a weal-public most expert, politic, and cunning? Such as among them were convict of great and heinous trespasses, them they condemned into stone quarries, and into mines to dig metal, there to be kept in chains all the days of their life. But as concerning this matter, I allow the ordinance of no nation so well as that which I saw while I travelled abroad about the world, used in Persia among the people that commonly be called the Polylerites, whose land is both large and ample and also well and wittily governed, and the people in all conditions free and ruled by their own laws, saving that they pay a yearly tribute to the great king of Persia. But because they be far from the sea, compassed and enclosed almost round about with high mountains, and do content themselves with the fruits of their own land, which is of itself very fertile and fruitful, for this cause neither they go to other countries, nor other come to them. And according to the old custom of the land they desire not to enlarge the bounds of their dominions; and those that they have by reason of the high hills be easily defended, and the tribute which they pay to their chief lord and king setteth them quit and free from warfare. Thus their life is commodious rather than gallant, and may better be called happy or wealthy than notable or famous. For they be not known as much as by name, I suppose, saving only to their next neighbours and borderers.

They that in this land be attainted and convict of felony, make restitution of that which they stole to the right owner, and not (as they do in other lands) to the king, whom they think to have no more right to the thief-stolen thing than the thief himself hath. But if the thing be lost or made away, then the value of it is paid of the goods of such offenders, which else remaineth all whole to their wives and children. And they themselves be condemned to be common labourers; and, unless the theft be very heinous, they be neither locked in prison nor fettered in gyves, but be untied and go at large, labouring in the common works. They that refuse labour, or go slowly and slackly to their work, be not only tied in chains, but also pricked forward with stripes; but being diligent about their work they live without check or rebuke. Every night they be called in by name, and be locked in their chambers. Beside their daily labour, their life is nothing hard or incommodious. Their fare is indifferent good, borne at the charges of the weal-public, because they be common servants to the commonwealth. But their charges in all places of the land are not borne alike, for in some parts that which is bestowed upon them is gathered of alms. And though that way be uncertain, yet the people be so full of mercy and pity, that none is found more profitable or plentiful. In some places certain lands be appointed hereunto, of the revenues whereof they be maintained; and in some places every man giveth a certain tribute for the same use and purpose.

Again, in some parts of the land these serving-men (for so be these damned persons called) do no common work, but as every private man needeth labourers, so he cometh into the market-place and there hireth some of them for meat and drink and a certain limited wages by the day, somewhat cheaper than he should hire a free man. It is also lawful for them to chastise the sloth of these serving-men with stripes. By this means they never lack work, and besides the gaining of their meat and drink, everyone of them bringeth daily something into the common treasury. All and every one of them be apparelled in one colour. Their heads be not polled or shaven, but rounded a little above the ears, and the tip of the one ear is cut off. Every one of them may take meat and drink of their friends, and also a coat of their own colour; but to receive money is death, as well to the giver as to the receiver. And no less jeopardy it is for a free man to receive money of a serving-man for any manner of cause, and likewise for serving-men to touch weapons. The serving-men of every several shire be distinct and known from other by their several and distinct badges which to cast away is death, as it is also to be seen out of the precinct of their own shire, or to talk with a serving-man of another shire. And it is no less danger to them for to intend to run away than to do it indeed. Yea, and to conceal such an enterprise in a serving-man is death, in a free man servitude. Of the contrary part, to him that openeth and uttereth such counsels be decreed large gifts, to a free man a great sum of money, to a serving-man freedom, and, to them both, forgiveness and pardon of that they were of counsel in that pretence. So that it can never be so good for them to go forward in their evil purpose, as by repentance, to turn back.

This is the law and order in this behalf, as I have shewed you. Wherein what humanity is used, how far it is from cruelty, and how commodious it is, you do plainly perceive, forasmuch as the end of their wrath and punishment intendeth nothing else but the destruction of vices and saving of men, with so using and ordering them that they cannot choose but be good, and what harm soever they did before, in the residue of their life to make amends for the same. Moreover it is so little feared that they should turn again to their vicious conditions, that wayfaring men will for their safeguard choose them to their guides before any other, in every shire changing and taking new; for if they would commit robbery they have nothing about them meet for that purpose. They may touch no weapons; money found about them should betray the robbery. They should be no sooner taken with the manner, but forthwith they should be punished. Neither they can have any hope at all to scape away by fleeing. For how should a man that in no part of his apparel is like other men fly privily and unknown, unless he would run away naked? Howbeit, so also fleeing he should be described by the rounding of his head and his ear mark. But it is a thing to be doubted that they will lay their heads together and conspire against the weal-public. No, no, I warrant you. For the serving-men of one shire alone could never hope to bring to pass such an enterprise without soliciting, enticing, and alluring the serving-men of many other shires to take their parts. Which thing is to them so impossible, that they may not as much as speak or talk together or salute one another. No, it is not to be thought that they would make their own countrymen and companions of their counsel in such a matter, which they know well should be jeopardy to the concealer thereof and great commodity and goodness to the opener and detector of the same. Whereas, on the other part, there is none of them all hopeless or in despair to recover again his former state of freedom by humble obedience, by patient suffering, and by giving good tokens and likelihood of himself, that he will ever after that live like a true and an honest man. For every year divers of them be restored to their freedom through the commendation of their patience.

When I had thus spoken, saying moreover that I could see no cause why this order might not be had in England with much more profit than the justice which the lawyer so highly praised, Nay, quoth the lawyer, this could never be so stablished in England but that it must needs bring the weal-public into great jeopardy and hazard. And, as he was thus saying, he shaked his head and made wry mouth, and so he held his peace. And all that were there present with one assent agreed to his saying.

Well, quoth the cardinal, yet it were hard to judge without a proof whether this order would do well here or no. But when the sentence of death is given, if then the king should command execution to be deferred and spared, and would prove this order and fashion, taking away the privileges of all sanctuaries, if then the proof should declare the thing to be good and profitable, then it were well done that it were stablished; else the condemned and reprieved persons may as well and as justly be put to death after this proof as when they were first cast. Neither any jeopardy can in the mean space grow hereof. Yea, and methinketh that these vagabonds may very well be ordered after the same fashion against whom we have hitherto made so many laws and so little prevailed.

When the cardinal had thus said, then every man gave great praise to my sayings, which a little before they had disallowed. But most of all was esteemed that which was spoken of vagabonds, because it was the cardinal's own addition. I cannot tell whether it were best to rehearse the communication that followed, for it was not very sad; but yet you shall hear it, for there was no evil in it, and partly it pertained to the matter before said.

There chanced to stand by a certain jesting parasite or scoffer, which would seem to resemble and counterfeit the fool. But he did in such wise counterfeit, that he was almost the very same indeed that he labored to represent. He so studied with words and sayings brought forth so out of time and place to make sport and move laughter, that he himself was oftener laughed at than his jests were. Yet the foolish fellow brought out now and then such indifferent and reasonable stuff, that he made the proverb true, which saith: He that shooteth oft, at the last shall hit the mark. So that when one of the company said that through my communication a good order was found for thieves, and that the cardinal also had well provided for vagabonds, so that only remained some good provision to be made for them that through sickness and age were fallen into poverty and were become so impotent and unwieldy that they were not able to work for their living: Tush, quoth he, let me alone with them; you shall see me do well enough with them. For I had rather than any good that this kind of people were driven somewhere out of my sight, they have so sore troubled me many times and oft when they have with their lamentable tears begged money of me; and yet they could never to my mind so tune their song that thereby they ever got of me one farthing. For evermore the one of these two chanced: either that

I would not, or else that I could not because I had it not. Therefore now they be waxed wise; for when they see me go by, because they will not lose their labour, they let me pass and say not one word to me. So they look for nothing of me, no, in good sooth, no more than if I were a priest or a monk. But I will make a law, that all these beggars shall be distributed and bestowed into houses of religion. The men shall be made lay brethren, as they call them, and the women nuns.

Hereat the cardinal smiled, and allowed it in jest, yea, and all the residue in good earnest. But a certain friar, graduate in divinity, took such pleasure and delight in this jest of priests and monks, that he also being else a man of grisly and stern gravity, began merrily and wantonly to jest and taunt. Nay, quoth he, you shall not so be rid and dispatched of beggars unless you make some provision also for us friars.

Why, quoth the jester, that is done already, for my lord himself set a very good order for you when he decreed that vagabonds should be kept strait, and set to work; for you be the greatest and veriest vagabonds that be.

This jest also, when they saw the cardinal not disprove it, every man took it gladly, saving only the friar. For he (and that no marvel) being thus touched on the quick, and hit on the gall, so fret, so fumed, and chafed at it, and was in such a rage, that he could not refrain himself from chiding, scolding, railing, and reviling. He called the fellow ribald, villain, javel, backbiter, slanderer, and the child of perdition, citing therewith terrible threatenings out of Holy Scripture.

Then the jesting scoffer began to play the scoffer indeed, and verily he was good at that, for he could play a part in that play, no man better. Patient yourself, good master friar, quoth he, and be not angry, for Scripture saith: In your patience you shall save your souls.

Then the friar (for I will rehearse his own very words): No, gallows wretch, I am not angry, quoth he, or at the least wise I do not sin; for the Psalmist saith, Be you angry, and sin not. Then the cardinal spake gently to the friar, and desired him to quiet himself.

No, my lord, quoth he, I speak not but of a good zeal as I ought, for holy men had a good zeal. Wherefore it is said: The zeal of thy house hath eaten me. And it is sung in the church. The scorners of Elisha, while he went up into the house of God, felt the zeal of the bald, as peradventure this scorning villain ribald shall feel.

You do it, quoth the cardinal, perchance of a good mind and affection; but methinketh you should do, I cannot tell whether more holily, certes more wisely, if you would not set your wit to a fool's wit, and with a fool take in hand a foolish contention.

No, forsooth, my lord, quoth he, I should not do more wisely. For Solomon the wise saith: Answer a fool according to his folly, like as I do now, and do shew him the pit that he shall fall into if he take not heed. For if many scorners of Elisha, which was but one bald man, felt the zeal of the bald, how much more shall one scorner of many friars feel, among whom be many bald men? And we have also the pope's bulls, whereby all that mock and scorn us be excommunicate, suspended, and accursed.

The cardinal, seeing that none end would be made, sent away the jester by a privy beck, and turned the communication to another matter. Shortly after, when he was risen from the table, he went to hear his suitors, and so dismissed us.

Look, Master More, with how long and tedious a tale I have kept you, which surely I would have been ashamed to have done, but that you so earnestly desired me, and did after such a sort give ear unto it as though you would not that any parcel of that communication should be left out. Which though I have done somewhat briefly, yet could I not choose but rehearse it for the judgment of them which, when they had disproved and disallowed my sayings, yet incontinent, hearing the cardinal allow them, did themselves also approve the same, so impudently flattering him, that they were nothing ashamed to admit, yet, almost in good earnest, his jester's foolish inventions, because that he himself by smiling at them did seem not to disprove them. So that hereby you may right well perceive how little the courtiers would regard and esteem me and my sayings.

I ensure you, Master Raphael, quoth I, I took great delectation in hearing you; all things that you said were spoken so wittily and so pleasantly. And methought myself to be in the meantime not only at home in my country, but also through the pleasant remembrance of the cardinal, in whose house I was brought up of a child, to wax a child again. And, friend Raphael, though I did bear very great love towards you before, yet seeing you do so earnestly favour this man, you will not believe how much my love towards you is now increased. But yet, all this notwithstanding, I can by no means change my mind, but that I must needs believe that you, if you be disposed and can find in your heart to follow some prince's court, shall with your good counsels greatly help and further the commonwealth. Wherefore there is nothing more appertaining to your duty, that is to say to the duty of a good man. For whereas your Plato judgeth that weal-publics shall by this means attain perfect felicity, either if philosophers be kings, or else if kings give themselves to the study of philosophy, how far, I pray you, shall commonwealths then be from this felicity, if philosophers will vouchsafe to instruct kings with their good counsel?

They be not so unkind, quoth he, but they would gladly do it, yea, many have done it already in books that they have put forth, if kings and princes would be willing and ready to follow good counsel. But Plato doubtless did well foresee unless kings themselves would apply their minds to the study of philosophy, that else they would never thoroughly allow the counsel of philosophers, being themselves before, even from their tender age, infected and corrupt with perverse and evil opinions. Which thing Plato himself proved true in King Dionysius. If I should propose to any king wholesome decrees, doing my endeavour to pluck out of his mind the pernicious original causes of vice and naughtiness, think you not that I should forthwith either be driven away or else made a laughing-stock? Well, suppose I were the French king, and there sitting in his council while in that most secret consultation, the king himself there being present in his own person, they beat their brains, and search the very bottoms of their wits to discuss by what craft and means the king may still keep Milan and draw to him again fugitive Naples; and then how to conquer the Venetians, and how to bring under his jurisdiction all Italy; then how to win the dominion of Flanders, Brabant, and of all Burgundy with divers other lands whose kingdoms he hath long ago in mind and purpose invaded. Here while one counselleth to conclude a league of peace with the Venetians, so long to endure as shall be thought meet and expedient for their purpose, and to make them also of their counsel, yea, and besides that to give them part of the prey which afterward, when they have brought their purpose about after their own minds, they may require and claim again, another thinketh best to hire the Germans. Another would have the favour of the Swiss won with money. Another's advice is to appease the puissant power of the emperor's majesty with gold as with a most pleasant and acceptable sacrifice. While another giveth counsel to make peace with the king of Aragon, and to restore unto him his own kingdom of Navarre as a full assurance of peace. Another cometh in with his five eggs, and adviseth to hook in the king of Castile with some hope of affinity or alliance, and to bring to their part certain peers of his court for great pensions. While they all stay at the chiefest doubt of all, what to do in the mean time with England; and yet agree all in this to make peace with the Englishmen, and with most sure and strong bonds to bind that weak and feeble friendship, so that they must be called friends, and had in suspicion as enemies; and that therefore the Scots must be had in a readiness, as it were in a standing, ready at all occasions, in aunters the Englishmen should stir never so little, incontinent to set upon them. And moreover privily and secretly (for openly it may not be done by the truce that is taken), privily, therefore, I say, to make much of some peer of England that is banished his country, which must claim title to the crown of the realm and affirm himself just inheritor thereof, that by this subtle means they may hold to them the king, in whom else they have but small trust and affiance. Here, I say, where so great and high matters be in consultation, where so many noble and wise men counsel their king only to war, here if I, silly man, should rise up and will them to turn over the leaf, and learn a new lesson, saying that my counsel is not to meddle with Italy but to tarry still at home and that the kingdom of France alone is almost greater than that it may well be governed of one man, so that the king should not need to study how to get more; and then should propose unto them the decrees of the people that be called the Achorians, which be situate over against the island of Utopia on the southeast side.

These Achorians once made war in their king's quarrel for to get him another kingdom which he laid claim unto and advanced himself right inheritor to the crown thereof by the title of an old alliance. At the last, when they had got it, and saw that they had even as much vexation and trouble in keeping it as they had in getting it, and that either their new conquered subjects by sundry occasions were making daily insurrections to rebel against them, or else that other countries were continually with divers inroads and foragings invading them, so that they were ever fighting either for them or against them, and never could break up their camps: seeing themselves in the mean season pilled and impoverished, their money carried out of the realm, their own men killed to maintain the glory of another nation; when they had no war, peace nothing better than war, by reason that their people in war had so inured themselves to corrupt and wicked manners, that they had taken a delight and pleasure in robbing and stealing; that through manslaughter they had gathered boldness to mischief; that their laws were had in contempt, and nothing set by or regarded; that their king, being troubled with the charge and governance of two kingdoms, could not nor was not able perfectly to discharge his office towards them both: seeing again, that all these evils and troubles were endless, at the last (they) laid their heads together, and like faithful and loving subjects gave to their king free choice and liberty to keep still the one of these two kingdoms, whether he would, alleging that he was not able to keep both, and that they were more than might well be governed of half a king, forasmuch as no man would be content to take him for his muleteer that keepeth another man's mules besides his. So this good prince was constrained to be content with his old kingdom and to give over the new to one of his friends. Who shortly after was violently driven out.

Furthermore if I should declare unto them that all this busy preparance to war, whereby so many nations for his sake should be brought into a troublesome hurly-burly, when all his coffers were emptied, his treasures wasted, and his people destroyed, should at the length through some mis-chance be in vain and to none effect, and that therefore it were best for him to content himself with his own kingdom of France as his forefathers and predecessors did before him, to make much of it, to enrich it, and to make it as flourishing as he could, to endeavour himself to love his subjects and again to be beloved of them, willingly to live with them, peaceably to govern them, and with other kingdoms not to meddle, seeing that which he hath already is even enough for him, yea, and more than he can well turn him to: this mine advice, Master More, how think you it would be heard and taken?

So God help me, not very thankfully, quoth I.

Well, let us proceed then, quoth he. Suppose that some king and his council were together whetting their wits and devising what subtle craft they might invent to enrich the king with great treasures of money. First one counselleth to raise and enhance the valuation of money when the king must pay any, and again to call down the value of coin to less than it is worth when he must receive or gather any. For thus great sums shall be paid with a little money, and where little is due much shall be received. Another counselleth to feign war, that when under this colour and pretence the king hath gathered great abundance of money, he may, when it shall please him, make peace with great solemnity and holy ceremonies, to blind the eyes of the poor community as taking pity and compassion forsooth upon man's blood, like a loving and a merciful prince. Another putteth the king in remembrance of certain old and moth-eaten laws that of long time have not been put in execution, which because no man can remember that they were made, every man hath transgressed. The fines of these laws he counselleth the king to require, for there is no way so profitable nor more honourable as the which hath a shew and colour of justice. Another ad-viseth him to forbid many things under great penalties and fines, specially such things as is for the people's profit not be used, and afterward to dis-pense for money with them, which by this prohibition sustain loss and damage. For by this means the favour of the people is won, and profit riseth two ways. First by taking forfeits of them whom covetousness of gains hath brought in danger of this statute, and also by selling privileges and licences, which the better that the prince is, forsooth the dearer he selleth them, as one that is loath to grant to any private person anything that is against the profit of his people, and therefore may sell none but at an exceeding dear price.

Another giveth the king counsel to endanger unto his grace the judges of the realm, that he may have them ever on his side, and that they may in every matter dispute and reason for the king's right; yea, and further to call them into his palace and to require them there to argue and discuss his matters in his own presence. So there shall be no matter of his so openly wrong and unjust wherein one or other of them, either because he will have something to allege and object, or that he is ashamed to say that which is said already, or else to pick a thank with his prince, will not find some hold open to set a snare in, wherewith to take the contrary part in a trip. Thus while the judges cannot agree amongst themselves, reasoning and arguing of that which is plain enough and bringing the manifest truth in doubt, in the mean season the king may take a fit occasion to understand the law as shall most make for his advantage, whereunto all other, for shame or for fear, will agree. Then the judges may be bold to pronounce on the king's side, for he that giveth sentence for the king cannot be without a good excuse. For it shall be sufficient for him to have equity on his part, or the bare words of the law, or a writhen and wrested understanding of the same, or else (which with good and just judges is of greater force than all laws be) the king's indisputable prerogative.

To conclude, all the counsellors agree and consent together with the rich Crassus, that no abundance of gold can be sufficient for a prince which must keep and maintain an army. Furthermore that a king, though he would, can do nothing unjustly; for all that all men have, yea, also the men themselves, be all his. And that every man hath so much of his own as the king's gentleness hath not taken from him. And that it shall be most for the king's advantage that his subjects have very little or nothing in their possession, as whose safeguard doth herein consist, that his people do not wax wanton and wealthy through riches and liberty, because where these things be, there men be not wont patiently to obey hard, unjust, and unlawful commandments; whereas, on the other part, need and poverty doth hold down and keep under stout courages, and maketh them patient perforce, taking from them bold and rebelling stomachs.

Here again, if I should rise up and boldly affirm that all these counsels be to the king dishonour and reproach, whose honour and safety is more and rather supported and upholden by the wealth and riches of his people than by his own treasures; and if I should declare that the commonalty chooseth their king for their own sake, and not for his sake, to the intent that through his labour and study they might all live wealthily safe from wrongs and injuries; and that therefore the king ought to take more care for the wealth of his people than for his own wealth, even as the office and duty of a shepherd is, in that he is a shepherd, to feed his sheep rather than himself.

For as touching this, that they think the defense and maintenance of peace to consist in the poverty of the people the thing itself sheweth that they be far out of the way. For where shall a man find more wrangling, quarrelling, brawling, and chiding than among beggars? Who be more desirous of new mutations and alterations, than they that be not content with the present state of their life? Or, finally, who be bolder stomached to bring all in a hurly-burly (thereby trusting to get some windfall) than they that have now nothing to lose? And if any king were so smally regarded and so lightly esteemed, yea, so behated of his subjects, that other ways he could not keep them in awe, but only by open wrongs, by polling and shaving and by bringing them to beggary, surely it were better for him to forsake his kingdom than to hold it by this means, whereby though the name of a king be kept, yet the majesty is lost. For it is against the dignity of a king to have rule over beggars, but rather over rich and wealthy men. Of this mind was the hardy and courageous Fabricius when he said that he had rather be a ruler of rich men than be rich himself. And, verily, one man to live in pleasure and wealth while all others weep and smart for it, that is the part, not of a king, but of a jailer. To be short, as he is a foolish physician that cannot cure his patient's disease unless he cast him in another sickness, so he that cannot amend the lives of his subjects but by taking from them the wealth and commodity of life, he must needs grant that he knoweth not the feat how to govern men. But let him rather amend his own life, renounce unhonest pleasures, and forsake pride; for these be the chief vices that cause him to run in the contempt or hatred of his people. Let him live of his own, hurting no man. Let him do cost not above his power. Let him restrain wickedness. Let him prevent vices and take away the occasions of offences by well ordering his subjects, and not by suffering wickedness to increase, afterwards to be punished. Let him not be too hasty in calling again laws which a custom hath abrogated, specially such as have been long forgotten and never lacked nor needed. And let him never, under the cloak and pretence of transgression, take such fines and forfeits as no judge will suffer a private person to take as unjust and full of guile.

Here if I should bring forth before them the law of the Macarians, which be not far distant from Utopia, whose king the day of his coronation is bound by a solemn oath that he shall never at any time have in his treasury above a thousand pound of gold and silver. They say a very good king, which took more care for the wealth and commodity of his country than for the enriching of himself, made this law to be a stop and a bar to kings from heaping and hoarding up so much money as might impoverish their people. For he foresaw that this sum of treasure would suffice to support the king in battle against his own people if they should chance to rebel, and also to maintain his wars against the invasions of his foreign enemies. Again, he perceived the same stock of money to be too little and insufficient to encourage and enable him wrongfully to take away other men's good, which was the chief cause why the law was made. Another cause was this: He thought that by this provision his people should not lack money wherewith to maintain their daily occupying and chaffare. And seeing the king could not choose but lay out and bestow all that came in above the prescript sum of his stock, he thought he would seek no occasions to do his subjects injury. Such a king shall be feared of evil men and loved of good men. These, and such other information, if I should use among men wholly inclined and given to the contrary part, how deaf hearers think you should I have?

Deaf hearers doubtless, quoth I, and in good faith no marvel. And to be plain with you, truly I cannot allow that such communication shall be used, or such counsel given, as you be sure shall never be regarded nor received. For how can so strange information be profitable, or how can they be beaten into their heads whose minds be already prevented with clean contrary persuasions? This school philosophy is not unpleasant among friends in familiar communication, but in the councils of kings, where great matters be debated and reasoned with great authority, these things have no place.

That is it which I meant, quoth he, when I said philosophy had no place among kings.

Indeed, quoth I, this school philosophy hath not, which thinketh all things meet for every place. But there is another philosophy more civil, which knoweth, as ye would say, her own stage, and thereafter, ordering and behaving herself in the play that she hath in hand, playeth her part accordingly with comeliness, uttering nothing out of due order and fashion. And this is the philosophy that you must use. Or else whiles a comedy of Plautus is playing, and the vile bondmen scoffing and trifling among themselves, if you should suddenly come upon the stage in a philosopher's apparel, and rehearse out of *Octavia* the place wherein Seneca disputeth with Nero, had it not been better for you to have played the dumb person, than, by rehearsing that which served neither for the time nor place, to have made such a tragical comedy or gallimaufry? For by bringing in other stuff that nothing appertaineth to the present matter, you must needs mar and pervert the play that is in hand, though the stuff that you bring be much better. What part soever you have taken upon you, play that as well as you can and make the best of it. And do not therefore disturb and bring out of order the whole matter because that another which is merrier and better cometh to your remembrance.

So the case standeth in a commonwealth, and so it is in the consultations of kings and princes. If evil opinions and naughty persuasions cannot be utterly and quite plucked out of their hearts, if you cannot even as you would remedy vices which use and custom hath confirmed, yet for this cause you must not leave and forsake the commonwealth. You must not forsake the ship in a tempest because you cannot rule and keep down the winds. No, nor you must not labour to drive into their heads new and strange information which you know well shall be nothing regarded with them that be of clean contrary minds. But you must with a crafty wile and a subtle train study and endeavour yourself, as much as in you lieth, to handle the matter wittily and handsomely for the purpose; and that which you cannot turn to good, so to order it that it be not very bad. For it is not possible for all things to be well unless all men were good, which I think will not be yet this good many years.

By this means, quoth he, nothing else will be brought to pass, but whiles that I go about to remedy the madness of others I should be even as mad as they. For if I would speak such things that be true I must needs speak such things; but as for to speak false things, whether that be a philosopher's part or no I cannot tell, truly it is not my part. Howbeit, this communication of mine, though peradventure it may seem unpleasant to them, yet can I not see why it should seem strange or foolishly newfangled. If so be that I should speak those things that Plato feigneth in his weal-public, or that the Utopians do in theirs, these things, though they were (as they be indeed) better, yet they might seem spoken out of place, forasmuch as here amongst us every man hath his possessions several to himself, and there all things be common. But what was in my communication contained that might not, and ought not, in any place to be spoken? Saving that to them which have thoroughly decreed and determined with themselves to run headlong the contrary way it cannot be acceptable and pleasant, because it calleth them back and sheweth them the jeopardies. Verily, if all things that evil and vicious manners have caused to seem inconvenient and nought should be refused as things unmeet and reproachful, then we must among Christian people wink at the most part of all those things which Christ taught us and so straitly forbade them to be winked at, that those things also which He whispered in the ears of his disciples He commanded to be proclaimed in open houses. And yet the most part of them is more dissident from the manners of the world nowadays than my communication was.

But preachers, sly and wily men, following your counsel (as I suppose) because they saw men evil willing to frame their manners to Christ's rule, they have wrested and wried His doctrine, and like a rule of lead have applied it to men's manners, that by some means, at the least way, they might agree together. Whereby I cannot see what good they have done, but that men may more securely be evil. And I truly should prevail even as little in king's councils. For either I must say otherways than they say, and then I were as good to say nothing; or else I must say the same that they say, and (as Mitio saith in Terence), help to further their madness. For that crafty wile and subtle train of yours, I cannot perceive to what purpose it serveth, wherewith you would have me to study and endeavour myself, if all things cannot be made good yet to handle them wittily and handsomely for the purpose, that as far forth as is possible they may not be very evil. For there is no place to dissemble in nor to wink in. Naughty counsels must be openly allowed and very pestilent decrees must be approved. He shall be counted worse than a spy, yea, almost as evil as a traitor, that with a faint heart doth praise evil and noisome decrees.

Moreover, a man can have no occasion to do good, chancing into the company of them which will sooner pervert a good man than be made good themselves, through whose evil company he shall be marred, or else, if he remain good and innocent, yet the wickedness and folly of others shall be imputed to him and laid in his neck. So that it is impossible with that crafty wile and subtle train to turn anything to better. Wherefore Plato by a goodly similitude declareth why wise men refrain to meddle in the commonwealth. For when they see the people swarm into the streets, and daily wet to the skin with rain, and yet cannot persuade them to go out of the rain and to take their houses, knowing well that if they should go out to them they should nothing prevail nor win aught by it but with them be wet also in the rain, they do keep themselves within their houses, being content that they be safe themselves, seeing they cannot remedy the folly of the people.

Howbeit, doubtless, Master More (to speak truly as my mind giveth me) where possessions be private, where money beareth all the stroke, it is hard and almost impossible that there the weal-public may justly be governed and prosperously flourish. Unless you think thus: that justice is there executed where all things come into the hands of evil men, or that prosperity there flourisheth where all is divided among a few, which few, nevertheless, do not lead their lives very wealthily, and the residue live miserably, wretchedly, and beggarly. Wherefore when I consider with myself and weigh in my mind the wise and godly ordinances of the Utopians, among whom with very few laws all things be so well and wealthily ordered that virtue is had in price and estimation, and yet, all things being there common, every man hath abundance of everything. Again, on the other part, when I compare with them so many nations ever making new laws, yet none of them all well and sufficiently furnished with laws, where every man calleth that he hath gotten his own proper and private goods, where so many new laws daily made be not sufficient for every man to enjoy, defend, and know from another man's that which he calleth his own; which thing the infinite controversies in the law, daily rising, never to be ended, plainly declare to be true: these things (I say) when I consider with myself, I hold well with Plato, and do nothing marvel that he would make no laws for them that refused those laws whereby all men should have and enjoy equal portions of wealths and commodities.

For the wise man did easily foresee this to be the one and only way to the wealth of a commonalty, if equality of all things should be brought in and stablished. Which, I think, is not possible to be observed where every man's good be proper and peculiar to himself. For where every man under certain titles and pretences draweth and pluketh to himself as much as he can, so that a few divide among themselves all the whole riches, be there never so much abundance and store, there to the residue is left lack and poverty. And for the most part it chanceth that this latter sort is more worthy to enjoy that state of wealth than the other be, because the rich men be covetous, crafty, and unprofitable. On the other part the poor be lowly, simple, and by their daily labour more profitable to the commonwealth than to themselves. Thus I do fully persuade myself that no equal and just distribution of things can be made, nor that perfect wealth shall ever be among men, unless this propriety be exiled and banished. But so long as it shall continue, so long shall remain among the most and best part of men the heavy and inevitable burden of poverty and wretchedness. Which, as I grant that it may be somewhat eased, so I utterly deny that it can wholly be taken away. For if there were a statute made that no man should possess above a certain measure of ground, and that no man should have in his stock above a prescript and appointed sum of money, if it were by certain laws decreed that neither the king should be of too great power, neither the people too haut and wealthy, and that offices should not be obtained by inordinate suit, or by bribes and gifts, that they should neither be bought nor sold, nor that it should be needful for the officers to be at any cost or charge in their offices (for so occasion is given to them by fraud and ravin to gather up their money again, and by reason of gifts and bribes the offices be given to rich men, which should rather have been executed of wise men) by such laws, I say, like as sick bodies that be desperate and past cure be wont with continual good cherishing to be kept and botched up for a time, so these evils also might be lightened and mitigated. But that they may be perfectly cured, and brought to a good and upright state, it is not to be hoped for, whiles every man is master of his own to himself. Yea, and whiles you go about to do your cure of one part you shall make bigger the sore of another part, so the help on one causeth another's harm, forasmuch as nothing can be given to any one unless it be taken from another.

But I am of a contrary opinion, quoth I, for methinketh that men shall never there live wealthily where all things be common. For how can there be abundance of goods or of anything where every man withdraweth his hand from labour? Whom the regard of his own gains driveth not to work, but the hope that he hath in other men's travails maketh him slothful. Then when they be pricked with poverty, and yet no man can by any law or right defend that for his own which he hath gotten with the labour of his own hands, shall not there of necessity be continual sedition and bloodshed? Specially the authority and reverence of magistrates being taken away, which, what place it may have with such men among whom is no difference, I cannot devise.

I marvel not, quoth he, that you be of this opinion. For you conceive in your mind either none at all, or else a very false image and similitude of this thing. But if you had been with me in Utopia and had presently seen their fashions and laws, as I did which lived there five years and more, and would never have come thence but only to make that new land known here, then doubtless you would grant that you never saw people well ordered but only there.

Surely, quoth Master Peter, it shall be hard for you to make me believe that there is better order in that new land than is here in these countries that we know. For good wits be as well here as there, and I think our commonwealths be ancienter than theirs. Wherein long use and experience hath found out many things commodious for man's life, besides that many things here among us have been found by chance which no wit could ever have devised.

As touching the ancientness, quoth he, of commonwealths, then you might better judge, if you had read the histories and chronicles of that land, which if we may believe, cities were there before men were here. Now what thing soever hitherto by wit hath been devised or found by chance, that might be as well there as here. But I think verily, though it were so that we did pass them in wit, yet in study, in travail, and in laboursome endeavour they far pass us. For (as their chronicles testify) before our arrival there they never heard anything of us whom they call the ultra-equinoctials; saving that once about 1200 years ago, a certain ship was lost by the isle of Utopia which was driven thither by tempest. Certain Romans and Egyptians were cast on land, which after that never went thence. Mark now what profit they took of this one occasion through diligence and earnest travail. There was no craft nor science within the empire of Rome whereof any profit could rise, but they either learned it of these strangers, or else of them taking occasion to search for it, found it out. So great profit was it to them that ever any went thither from hence. But if any like chance before this hath brought any man from thence hither, that is as quite out of remembrance as this also perchance in time to come shall be forgotten, that ever I was there. And like as they quickly, almost at the first meeting, made their own whatsoever is among us wealthily devised, so I suppose it would be long before we would receive anything that among them is better instituted than among us. And this, I suppose, is the chief cause why their commonwealths be wiselier governed and do flourish in more wealth than ours, though we neither in wit nor riches be their inferiors.

Therefore, gentle Master Raphael, quoth I, I pray you and beseech you describe unto us the island. And study not to be short, but declare largely in order their grounds, their rivers, their cities, their people, their manners, their ordinances, their laws, and, to be short, all things that you shall think us desirous to know. And you shall think us desirous to know whatsoever we know not yet.

There is nothing, quoth he, that I will do gladlier. For all these things I have fresh in mind. But the matter requireth leisure.

Let us go in, therefore, quoth I, to dinner; afterward we will bestow the time at our pleasure.

Content, quoth he, be it.

VII THE REFORMATION AND NATIONAL CHURCHES

JOHN WYCLIFFE

JOHN WYCLIFFE (c.1320–84), born in Yorkshire, studied and taught religion at Oxford and served as minister at Fillingham, Ludgershall, and Lutterworth. Wycliffe participated in the discussions between the English Crown and the Holy See at Bruges in 1374, where he emerged as a champion of national independence by attacking the papacy for its attempt to collect tribute promised it by King John a century and a half before. This position enabled him to enjoy lifelong protection against the papal denunciations which his religious principles aroused. His sermons and those of his followers opposed many of the basic dogmas of the Church. Priests and sacraments he subordinated to the Christian individual's direct relation to God, and he conceived of the true church not as the Roman Church but as the body of all who were destined for salvation. The Bible, not the Church, was for him the primary source of Christian doctrine. In 1380 and 1382 Wycliffe was declared a heretic; he withdrew to Lutterworth, where he was not molested, and died there in 1384. The followers of Wycliffe, the Lollards, suffered persecution long after his death.

Wycliffe's many sermons and dogmatic treatises influenced the leaders of the Reformation through their impact on John Hus. His most important literary endeavor was the supervision of the first complete translation of the Bible into English.

The following selections are taken from H. Gee and W. J. Hardy, *Documents Illustrative of English Church History* (Macmillan, 1896); H. Bettenson, *Documents of the Christian Church* (Oxford University Press, 1943); and B. J. Kidd, *Documents Illustrative of the History of the Church* (Macmillan, 1941), Vol. III.

❧

WYCLIFFE PROPOSITIONS CONDEMNED AT LONDON, 1382

HERETICAL CONCLUSIONS REPUGNANT TO THE CHURCH'S DETERMINA-
TION . . .

3. THAT CHRIST is not in the Sacrament of the altar essentially, truly, and really, in His own corporal presence. 4. That if bishop or priest be in mortal sin he cannot ordain, consecrate, or baptize. 5. That if a man be properly repentant all outward confession is superfluous or useless for him. 6. To affirm constantly that it was not set down in the Gospel that Christ ordained the Mass. 8. That if the pope be an abandoned or evil man, and so a member of the Devil, he has not power over the faithful of Christ granted him by any, save perhaps by Caesar. 9. That after Urban VI no one is to be regarded as pope, but we must live like the Greeks under our own laws. 10. To assert that it is contrary to Holy Scripture that ecclesiastical men should have temporal possessions.

ERRONEOUS CONCLUSIONS REPUGNANT TO THE CHURCH'S DETERMINA-
TION . . .

11. That no prelate ought to excommunicate any unless he first knows that he is excommunicated by God. 12. That if he excommunicates he is thereby a heretic or excommunicate. 13. That a prelate excommunicating a clerk who has appealed to the king and the council of the realm is thereby a traitor to God, king, and realm. 14. That those who cease to preach or hear the Word of God or the Gospel preached on account of the excommunication of men are excommunicate, and on the day of judgment will be held traitors to God. 15. To assert that it is lawful to any deacon or priest to preach the Word of God without the authority of the Apostolic See, or a catholic bishop, or some other [authority] sufficiently sure. 16. To assert that no one is civil lord, bishop, or prelate while he is in mortal sin. 17. That temporal lords can at their will take away temporal goods from ecclesiastics habitually sinful, or that the public may at their will correct sinful lords. 18. That tithes are pure alms, and that parishioners can withhold them for the sins of their curates, and confer them at pleasure on others. 19. That special prayers restricted to one person by prelates or religious do no more avail the same person, other things being equal, than general prayers. 20. That the very fact of a man entering any private religion [i.e. religious house] makes him more foolish and unfit for performing God's commandment. 21. That holy men endowing private religions, as well of

possessioners as of mendicants, have sinned in so endowing. 22. That the religious living in private religions are not of the Christian religion. 23. That friars are bound to get their living by the labour of their hands and not by mendicancy. 24. That he who gives alms to friars or a preaching friar is excommunicate, and he who takes them.

WYCLIFFE AND LOLLARD PROPOSITIONS CONDEMNED AT COUNCIL OF CONSTANCE, 1415

28. THAT THE CONFIRMATION of young men, the ordination of clerics, the consecration of places are reserved for the Pope and bishops on account of the desire for temporal gain and honour. 30. That the excommunication of the Pope or of any prelate is not to be feared, because it is the censure of antichrist. 34. That all of the order of mendicants are heretics. 35. That the Roman Church is the synagogue of Satan, and the Pope is not the next and immediate vicar of Christ and the Apostles. 42. That it is fatuous to believe in the indulgences of the Pope and the bishops. 43. That all oaths made to corroborate human contracts and civil business are unlawful.

HUS PROPOSITIONS CONDEMNED AT CONSTANCE

1. THAT THE CHURCH is the whole body of all the predestinate. 9. That Peter never was, and is not, the head of the Church. 10. That if the Vicar of Christ imitates the life of Christ, he is His Vicar. 12. That the Papacy took its origin from the Imperial power. 17. That Cardinals are not true successors of the Apostles unless they live like the Apostles. 18. That heretics should be censured by the Church, but not handed over [to the secular power] to be burnt.

JOHN HUS

John Hus (c.1369–1415), born in Husinec of peasant parents, was a Bohemian supporter of Wycliffe. Already distinguished as rector of the University of Prague, Hus came into special prominence from 1403 on as preacher in the Czech language in Bethlehem chapel. He opposed the university's condemnation of Wycliffe, attacked the sale of indulgences (authorized by Pope John XXIII) in the streets of Prague, and in general advocated practices which, had they been fully carried out, would have led to the establishment of a national church. Though he was excommunicated, the people still flocked to Hus' chapel; he therefore left the city of Prague to save her from the interdict. Under the protection of the Emperor Sigismund's safe-conduct, Hus voluntarily attended the Council of Constance in Germany in 1414, only to be placed on trial for heresy. His persistent refusal to retract his statements led to the burning of his books on June 24, 1415. On July 6, before Emperor Sigismund and the full council, he was sentenced, and on the same day burned at the stake; his ashes were thrown into the Rhine. The council decreed that the remains of Wycliffe should be dug up and burned. Hus' martyrdom provoked a national and religious revolution in Bohemia.

The selections that follow are from Hus' most important work, *The Church*, translated by David S. Schaff from the Latin edition of 1715 (verbally identical with the original printed edition of 1558), *Historia et Monumenta J. Hus,* Vol. I (New York, Charles Scribner's Sons, 1915).

THE CHURCH

. . . For the reason that believing is an act of faith, that is, to put trust in—*fidere*—therefore know that to believe that which is necessary for a man to secure blessedness is to adhere firmly and without wavering to the truth spoken as by God. For this truth, because of its certitude, a man ought to expose his life to the danger of death. And, in this way, every Christian is expected to believe explicitly and implicitly all the truth which the Holy Spirit has put in Scripture, and in this way a man is not bound to believe the sayings of the saints which are apart from Scripture, nor should he believe papal bulls, except in so far as they speak out of Scripture, or in so far as what they say is founded in Scripture simply. But a man may believe bulls as probable, for both the pope and his curia make mistakes from ignorance of the truth. And, with reference to this ignorance, it can be substantiated that the pope makes mistakes and may be deceived. Lucre deceives the pope, and he is deceived through ignorance. How far, however, faith ought to be placed in the letters of princes, the instruments of notaries, and the descriptions of men, experience, which is the teacher of things, teaches. For she teaches that these three often make mistakes. Of one kind is the faith which is placed in God. He cannot deceive or be deceived; of another is the faith placed in the pope, who may deceive and be deceived. Of one kind is the faith placed in holy Scripture; and another, faith in a bull thought out in a human way. For to holy Scripture exception may not be taken, nor may it be gainsaid; but it is proper at times to take exception to bulls and gainsay them when they either commend the unworthy or put them in authority, or savor of avarice, or honor the unrighteous or oppress the innocent, or implicitly contradict the commands or counsels of God. . . .

To this the conclusion follows, namely: "To be subject to the Roman pontiff is necessary for salvation for every human being." But there is no other such pontiff except the Lord Jesus Christ himself, our pontiff. This is so because the humanity of Christ is not subject to any other pontiff as of necessity to salvation, inasmuch as God hath exalted him and given him a name which is to be the most worthy above every other name, that at the name of Jesus every knee should bow and every power bend in obedience to him "of things in heaven," that is, the angels; "things on the earth," that is, all men; and "of things in hell," that is, the devils. And it is also so because Christ's mother was a human being; John the Baptist also, Peter the apostle, and other saints now in heaven and for none of these was it necessary for salvation to be subject to any other Roman pontiff besides Christ, seeing that they are already saved, persons whom no Roman pontiff can loose or bind. . . .

When we have kept all his precepts, and shall have humbled our souls before this High Priest—knowing that it is possible that our pontiffs may be thieves and robbers—this Bishop of our souls will not fail us in things necessary to salvation, but will pasture, guard, and feed his sheep as a truly good Shepherd. . . .

The . . . doctors lay down in their writing that

the pope is head of the Roman Church and the college of cardinals the body, and that they are very successors and princes of the apostle Peter and the college of Christ's other apostles in ecclesiastical office for the purpose of discerning and defining all Catholic and Church matters, correcting and purging all errors in respect to them and, in all these matters, to have the care of all the churches and of all the faithful of Christ. For in order to govern the Church throughout the whole world it is fitting there should always continue to be such manifest and true successors in the office of Peter, the prince of the apostles, and of the college of the other apostles of Christ. And such successors cannot be found or procured on the earth other than the pope, the existing head, and the college of cardinals, the existing body, of the aforesaid Roman Church.

These follies, long drawn out, which, I think, proceeded for the most part from the brain of Stanislaus, overcome and terrified by the Roman curia, involve many points. And in regard to these, I note that in their writing the church is taken to mean all Christian pilgrims. They seem to admit this when they say that "the body of the clergy in the kingdom of Bohemia, not only with the whole body of clergy in the world but also with the whole body of Christendom, always feels and believes as the faith dictates, just as the Roman Church does." Or, secondly, these doctors call the pope, together with his cardinals, alone the Roman Church, when they say that they believe just as the Roman Church believes and not otherwise, the pope being the head of this Roman Church and the cardinals the body. In these ways only, so far as I can see, do the doctors designate the church in their writing.

I assume that the pope stands for that spiritual bishop who, in the highest way and in the most similar way, occupies the place of Christ, just as Peter did after the ascension. But if any person whatsoever is to be called pope—whom the Western Church accepts as Roman bishop—appointed to decide as the final court ecclesiastical cases and to teach the faithful whatever he wishes, then there is an abuse of the term, because according to this view, it would be necessary in cases to concede that the most unlettered layman or a female, or a heretic and antichrist, may be pope. This is plain, for Constantine II, an unlettered layman, was suddenly ordained a priest and through ambition made pope and then was deposed and all the things which he ordained were declared invalid, about A.D. 707. And the same is plain from the case of Gregory, who was unlettered and consecrated another in addition to himself. And as the people were displeased with the act, a third pope was superinduced. Then these quarrelling among themselves, the emperor came to Rome and elected another as sole pope. As for a female, it is plain in the case of Agnes, who was called John Anglicus, and of her Castrensis, 5:3, writes:

A certain woman sat in the papal chair two years and five months, following Leo. She is said to have been a girl, called Agnes, of the nation of Mainz, was led about by her paramour in a man's dress in Athens and named John Anglicus. She made such progress in different studies that, coming to Rome, she read the trivium to an audience of great teachers. Finally, elected pope, she was with child by her paramour, and, as she was proceeding from St. Peter's to the Lateran, she had the pains of labor in a narrow street between the Colosseum and St. Clement's and gave birth to a child. Shortly afterward she died there and was buried. For this reason it is said that all the popes avoid this street. Therefore, she is not put down in the catalogue of popes.

As for a heretic occupying the papal chair we have an instance in Liberius, of whom Castrensis writes, IV [Rolls Ser., 5:158], that at Constantius's command he was exiled for three years because he wished to favor the Arians. At the counsel of the same Constantius, the Roman clergy ordained Felix pope who, during the sessions of a synod, condemned and cast out two Arian presbyters, Ursacius and Valens, and when this became known, Liberius was recalled from exile, and being wearied by his long exile and exhilarated by the reoccupation of the papal chair, he yielded to heretical depravity; and when Felix was cast down, Liberius with violence held the church of Peter and Paul and St. Lawrence so that the clergy and priests who favored Felix were murdered in the church, and Felix was martyred, Liberius not preventing.

As for antichrist occupying the papal chair, it is evident that a pope living contrary to Christ, like any other perverted person, is called by common consent antichrist. In accordance with John 2:22, many are become antichrists. And the faithful will not dare to deny persistently that it is possible for the man of sin to sit in the holy place. Of him the Savior prophesied when he said: "When ye see the abomination of desolation, which is spoken of by Daniel, standing in the holy place," Matt. 24:15. The apostle also says: "Let no man beguile you in any wise, for it will not be except the falling away come first and the man of sin be revealed, the son of perdition; he that opposeth and exalteth himself against all that is called God or is worshipped; so that he sitteth in the temple of God setting himself forth as God," II Thess. 2:3-4. And it is apparent from the *Chronicles* how the papal dignity has sunk. . . .

No pope is the most exalted person of the catholic church but Christ himself; therefore no pope is the head of the catholic church besides Christ. The conclusion is valid reasoning from description to the thing described. Inasmuch as the head of the church is the capital or chief person of the church, yea, inasmuch as the head is a name of dignity and of office—dignity in view of predestination, and office in view of the administration of the whole church—it follows that no one may reasonably assert of himself or of another without revelation that he is the head of a particular holy church, although if he live well he ought to hope that he is a member of the holy catholic church, the bride of Christ. Therefore, we should not contend in regard to the reality of the incumbency whether any one, whoever he may be, living with us is the head of a particular holy church but, on the ground of his works, we ought assume that, if he is a superior, ruling over a particular holy church, then he is the superior in that particular church, and this ought to be assumed of the Roman pontiff, unless his works gainsay it, for the Savior said: "Beware of false prophets which come unto you in sheep's clothing but inwardly they are ravening wolves. By their fruits ye shall know them," Matt. 7:15. Also John 10:38: "Believe the works." . . .

Obedience, like humility, is of three kinds: namely, of the greater to the less—which is the highest form of obedience;—of an equal to an equal—which is the intermediate form;—and of the less to the greater—which is the lowest form. To the last the first definition of obedience applies—namely, that obedience is the subjection of one's own will to the will of a superior in things lawful and right. And it may be defined thus: obedience is an act of the will of a rational creature by virtue of which he voluntarily and intelligently submits himself to his superior: and such obedience is related to what is good, just as disobedience is related to what is evil. In both cases, however, it pertains to the rational creature and his subjection. And secondly, it refers fundamentally to activity, suffering, silence or any other activity of this sort to which the command is directed. . . .

Hence, as all sin is disobedience and as disobedience is related to sin, and as every good man obeys God, so every sinner is disobedient. But obedience may be in the understanding and the will—in the understanding, which discerns that obedience ought to be rendered in given cases; and in the will, which yields consent to him who commands. But its results are shown in certain powers within and in an external effect. . . .

Hence, whenever obedience is rendered to man rather than God, as Adam obeyed Eve, then it is always evil obedience, so that every one obeying evilly is

disobedient to God; and so it is that the same man may be obedient and disobedient, with respect to the different persons commanding or to different
commands. And it does not follow that, because a beloved man is disobedient,
therefore he is not obedient, but it does follow that the man is not obedient
with respect to whom he is disobedient or with respect to whose commands he
is disobedient. And it is clear that to obey in one's brotherhood is to fulfil the
will of the one giving commands, and this is well, as when a man or a created
spirit living in grace fulfils the lawful will of the one giving commands. But
to obey is bad when either living in sin one fulfils the will of a superior as to
a given command, as when one who lives in luxury, fasts from respect to the
command; or, secondly, when one fulfils a bad command against God. In view
of these things it is clear that it is impossible for a rational creature to be virtuous morally unless he is obedient to his God. . . .

Clerical inferiors, and much more laics, may sit in judgment on the works
of their superiors. From this it follows that the judgment by discreet and hidden arbitrament in the court of conscience is one thing, and the judgment in
virtue of the empowered jurisdiction in the court of the church is another. By
the first way the inferior ought chiefly to examine and judge himself, as it is
written: "If we would judge ourselves, we would not be judged," I Cor. 11:31.
And again, in the same way, he ought to judge all things pertaining to his
salvation as it is written: "He that is spiritual judgeth all things," I Cor. 2:15.
The laic also ought to examine and judge the works of his superior, as the
apostle judged the works of Peter, when he corrected him and said: "When I
saw that they walked not uprightly according to the truth of the Gospel, I said
unto Cephas before them all, If thou, who art a Jew, livest as do the Gentiles
and not as do the Jews, how compellest thou the Gentiles to walk as do the
Jews?" Gal. 2:14. Secondly, the laic ought to examine and judge his superior
for the purpose of fleeing, for Christ said: "Beware of false prophets which
come unto you in sheep's clothing, but inwardly they are ravening wolves,"
Matt. 7:15. Thirdly, he ought to examine and judge that the superior may attend to spiritual offices and bodily nourishment or other good works to be
done. For not otherwise should clergymen ever be chosen by laics as their
curates and confessors and the dispensers of their alms.

Therefore, it is lawful for the rich of this world with diligent scrutiny to
examine by what and what kind of superiors they shall administer their alms
and in what way they shall administer them, guarding against rapacious
wolves, because according to the apostle, in Acts 20:29, and according to Chrysostom, in *Imperfecto,* Homily 20, it is clear that in this way they seek more the
money of those subject to them than their salvation, and this is at variance with
the apostle, who says: "I seek not yours, but you," II Cor. 12:14. And looking

ahead with prophetic vision and seeing such false apostles, he affirmed, "I know that after my departing rapacious wolves shall enter in among you, not sparing the flock," Acts 20:29. And because this wolfishness is clearly discerned in the robbing of temporal things and in the infliction of punishments for the very purpose of plundering temporal goods more abundantly, he declares that he had himself pursued the opposite course. No man's gold and silver, he says, or vestments have I coveted, as ye yourselves know, because for those things that were needful for me and for those that were with me these hands have ministered.

Therefore, subjects living piously in Christ ought to pay heed to the life of the apostles and see to it whether their superiors live conformably to the apostles. For, if in their spiritual ministry they are out of accord with the apostles, if they are busy in exacting money, spurn evangelical poverty and incline to the world, nay, if they evidently sow offences, then they know by their works that they have departed from the religion of Jesus Christ the Lord. Therefore, O ye who love Christ's law from the heart, first note their works and see if they [the superiors] incline to the world, second give heed to their commands, whether they savor of avarice or the gain of this world, and third consult holy Scripture whether they command in accordance with Christ's counsel. And in the light of this counsel believe them; or disbelieve them, if they command contrary to this counsel. But let not curates say to laics, "What concern is it of yours to take note of our life or works," for did not our Savior say: "Do not according to their works"? Matt. 23. And afterwards he exposed the works of the prelates to the multitude that they might know them and to their advantage avoid them. Yea, much more to the prelates, who say, "What concern is it of yours to take note of our life and works?" it is pertinent for laics to reply: "What concern is it of yours that ye should receive our alms?" for the apostle says: "We command you in the name of Jesus Christ that ye withdraw yourselves from every brother that walketh disorderly and not after the tradition which they received of us, for ye yourselves know how ye ought to imitate us, for we behaved not ourselves disorderly among you, neither did we eat bread for naught at any man's hands, but in labor and travail, for even when we were with you, this we commanded you, If any man will not work, neither let him eat." II Thess. 3:6, 10.

It is clear how inferiors ought to examine and judge intelligently and reasonably in respect to the commands and works of superiors, for otherwise they would be in peril of eternal death, if they did not judge wisely about these things, how far they ought to believe their superiors, how far follow them, and in what things they ought intelligently to obey them according to the Lord's law.

POPE PIUS II

Pius II (1405–64), pope (1458–64), born near Siena in Italy, was named Enea Silvio de' Piccolomini and generally called Aeneas Sylvius. After studying at Siena and Florence, he became secretary to the bishop of Fermo, in which capacity he attended with his patron the Council of Basel (1431–49), where he was befriended by a number of churchmen and supported the anti-papal conciliar position on the governance of the Roman Catholic Church. Piccolomini, as a well-known humanist, was appointed court poet and, in 1442, secretary to the chancery at Vienna by the Holy Roman Emperor Frederick III. In 1445, however, he went to Rome in submission to Pope Eugene IV. The next year he took holy orders. His rise in the priesthood was rapid. Abandoning his earlier disorderly mode of life, he devoted himself to his ecclesiastical functions as bishop of Trieste (1447–50) and of Siena (1450–58). Having been made a cardinal by Pope Calixtus III in 1456, he was elected to succeed that pontiff two years later, taking the name Pius II. The main political efforts of his pontificate were to unite Christendom against the Turks, who in 1453 had conquered Constantinople; to combat Gallicanism within the Roman Catholic Church; to weaken the Bohemian king, George of Podebrad, a follower of John Hus; and to limit the powers of ecumenical church councils *vis-à-vis* the papacy. Only in the last of these undertakings was he successful. A worldly man of superior literary talents, the author of histories of the Council of Basel, of the reign of Frederick III, and of Bohemia, Pius II is unique as the only pope to leave an autobiography, the *Memoirs,* which are the chief source of information about his life.

The following selection has been taken from *The Commentaries of Pius II,* translated by F. A. Gragg, in *Smith College Studies in History,* Vol. XXII (October, 1936–January, 1937).

THE ELECTION OF A POPE

1458

Ten days after Calixtus's death the other eighteen cardinals entered the conclave, while the whole city waited in suspense for the outcome; though indeed it was common talk that Aeneas, Cardinal of Siena, would be pope, since no one was held in highter esteem.

The conclave was held in the apostolic palace at St. Peter's, where two halls and two chapels were set apart for it. In the larger chapel were constructed cells in which the cardinals might eat and sleep; the smaller, called the chapel of San Niccolò, was reserved for discussion and the election of the pope. The halls were places where all might walk about freely.

On the day of their entrance nothing was done about the election. On the next day certain capitulations were announced, which they agreed should be observed by the new pope, and each swore that he would abide by them, should the lot fall on him. On the third day, after Mass, when they came to the scrutiny, it was found that Filippo, Cardinal of Bologna, and Aeneas, Cardinal of Siena, had an equal number of votes, five apiece. No one else had more than three. On that ballot, whether from strategy or dislike, no one voted for Guillaume, Cardinal of Rouen.

The cardinals were accustomed, after the result of the scrutiny was announced, to sit and talk together in case any wished to change his mind and transfer the vote he had given one to another (a method called "by accession"), for in this way they more easily reach an agreement. This procedure was omitted after the first scrutiny, owing to the opposition of those who had received no votes and therefore could not now be candidates for accession. They adjourned for luncheon, and then there were many private conferences. The richer and more influential members of the college summoned the rest and sought to gain the papacy for themselves or their friends. They begged, promised, threatened, and some, shamelessly casting aside all decency, pleaded their own causes and claimed the papacy as their right. Among these were Guillaume, Cardinal of Rouen, Pietro, Cardinal of San Marco, and Giovanni, Cardinal of Pavia; nor did the Cardinal of Lerida neglect his own interests. Each had a great deal to say for himself. Their rivalry was extraordinary, their energy unbounded. They took no rest by day nor sleep by night. Rouen, however, did not fear these men so much as he did Aeneas and the Cardinal of Bologna, towards whom he saw the majority of the votes inclining. But he was especially afraid of Aeneas, whose silence he had no doubt would prove far more effective than the barkings of the rest. Therefore he would summon now some, now others, and upbraid them as follows: "What is Aeneas to you? Why do you think him worthy of the papacy? Will you give us a lame, poverty-stricken pope? How shall a destitute pope restore a destitute Church, or an ailing pope an ailing Church? He has but recently come from Germany. We do not know him. Perhaps he will even transfer the Curia thither. And look at his writing! Shall we set a poet in Peter's place? Shall we govern the Church by the laws of the heathen? Or do you think Filippo of Bologna is to be preferred?—a stiff-necked fellow, who has not the wit to rule himself, and will not listen to those who show him the right course. I am the senior cardinal. You know I am not without wisdom. I am learned in pontifical law and can boast of royal blood.

I am rich in friends and resources with which I can succour the impoverished Church. I hold also not a few ecclesiastical benefices, which I shall distribute among you and the others, when I resign them." He would then add many entreaties, and if they had no effect he would resort to threats. If anyone brought up his past simony as an indication that in his hands the papacy would be for sale, he did not deny that his past life had been tainted with that stain but swore that in the future his hands should be clean. He was supported by Alain, Cardinal of Avignon, who lent him every assistance in his power, not so much because he was a Frenchman riding with a Frenchman as because, at the elevation of Guillaume, he expected to obtain his house in Rome, the church of Rouen, and the vice-chancellorship.

Not a few were won over by Rouen's splendid promises and were caught like flies by their gluttony. And the tunic of Christ without Christ was being sold.

Many cardinals met in the privies as being a secluded and retired place. Here they agreed as to how they might elect Guillaume pope, and they bound themselves by written pledges and by oath. Guillaume trusted them and was presently promising benefices and preferment and dividing provinces among them. A fit place for such a pope to be elected! For where could one more appropriately enter into a foul covenant then in the privies? Guillaume could certainly count on the two Greeks, the Cardinals of Genoa, San Sisto, Avignon, Colonna, and Pavia. The vice-chancellor and the Cardinals of Bologna, Orsini, and Sant' Anastasia were doubtful and seemed likely to accede to him if pushed a little. Indeed they had almost given him definite grounds for hope. Since it now appeared that eleven were agreed, they did not doubt that they would at once get the twelfth. For when it has come to this point, someone is always at hand to say, "I too make you pope," to win the favour that utterance always brings. They thought therefore that the thing was as good as done and were only waiting for daylight to go to the scrutiny.

Some time after midnight the Cardinal of Bologna went hurriedly to Aeneas's cell and, waking him, said, "Look here, Aeneas! Don't you know that we already have a pope? Some of the cardinals have met in the privies and decided to elect Guillaume. They are only waiting for daylight. I advise you to get up and go and offer him your vote before he is elected, for fear that if he is elected with you against him, he will make trouble for you. I intend to take care not to fall into the old trap. I know what it means to have the pope your enemy. I have had experience with Calixtus, who never gave me a friendly look because I had not voted for him. It seems to me expedient to curry favour beforehand with the man who is going to be pope. I offer you the advice I am taking myself."

Aeneas answered, "Filippo, away with you and your advice! No one shall persuade me to vote for a man I think utterly unworthy to be the successor of St. Peter. Far from me be such a sin! I will be clean of that crime and my conscience shall not prick me. You say it is hard not to have the pope well disposed to you. I have no fears on that score. I know he will not murder me because I have not voted for him. 'But,' you say, 'he will not love you, will not make you presents, will not help you. You will feel the pinch of poverty.' Poverty is not hard for one accustomed to it. I have led a life of indigence heretofore; what matter if I die indigent? He will not take from me the Muses, who are all the sweeter in humble fortunes. But I am not the man to believe that God will allow the Church, His Bride, to perish in the hands of the Cardinal of Rouen. For what is more alien to the profession of Christ than that His Vicar should be a slave in simony and lewdness? The divine mercy will not endure that this palace, which has been the dwelling of so many Holy Fathers, shall become a den of thieves or a brothel of whores. The apostleship is bestowed by God, not by men. Those who have conspired to commit the papacy to Rouen are men; and men's schemes are vain—who does not know it? Well has their conspiracy been made in the privies! Their plots too will have to retire, and, like the Arian heresy, their most foul contrivings will end in a most foul place. Tomorrow will show that the Bishop of Rome is chosen by God not by men. As for you, if you are a Christian, you will not choose as Christ's Vicar him whom you know to be a limb of the devil." With these words he frightened Filippo from going over to Rouen.

Next Aeneas went at daybreak to Rodrigo, the vice-chancellor, and asked whether he had sold himself to Rouen. "What would you have me do?" he answered. "The thing is settled. Many of the cardinals have met in the privies and decided to elect him. It is not for my advantage to remain with a small minority out of favor with a new pope. I am joining the majority, and I have looked out for my own interests. I shall not lose the chancellorship; I have a note from Rouen assuring me that. If I do not vote for him, the others will elect him anyway, and I shall be stripped of my office." Aeneas said to him, "You young fool! Will you then put an enemy of your nation in the Apostle's chair? and will you put faith in the note of a man who is faithless? You will have the note; Avignon will have the chancellorship. For what has been promised you has been promised him also and solemnly affirmed. Will faith be kept with him or with you? Will a Frenchman be more friendly to a Frenchman or to a Catalan? Will he be more

concerned for a foreigner or for his own countryman? Take care, you inexperienced boy! Take care, you fool! And if you have no thought for the
Church of Rome, if you have no regard for the Christian religion, and
despise God, for whom you are preparing such a vicar, at least take thought
for yourself, for you will find yourself among the hindmost, if a Frenchman
is pope."

The vice-chancellor listened patiently to these words of his friend and
completely abandoned his purpose.

After this Aeneas, meeting the Cardinal of Pavia, said to him, "I hear that
you too are with those who have decided to elect Rouen. Is this true?" He
replied, "You have heard correctly, I have agreed to give him my vote so that
I may not be left alone. For his victory is already certain; so many have
declared for him." Aeneas said, "I thought you a different man from what I
find you. Only see how much you have degenerated from your ancestors!
Your father's brother (or was he your mother's?), Branda, Cardinal of
Piacenza, when the papacy was beyond the mountains in Germany (for
John XXIII, when he appointed the Council of Constance, had carried the
Roman Curia across the Alps), never rested till he brought the Holy See
back to Italy. It was owing to his diplomacy, devotion, and genius that on
the withdrawal of the contestants for the papacy, Martin V, a Roman of the
house of Colonna, was elected pope. Branda brought the Apostolic Curia
back from Germany to Italy; you, his nephew, are going to transfer it from
Italy to France. But Rouen will prefer his own nation to Italy, and a Frenchman will be off to France with the supreme office. You say, 'He is under
oath. He will not go outside this province, without the decree of the senate,
and if he wishes to go we will not consent.' What cardinal will dare oppose
him when he is once seated on the apostolic throne? You will be the first,
when you have secured some rich benefice, to say, 'Go where you will, Holy
Father.' And what is our Italy without the Bishop of Rome? We still have
the Apostleship though we have lost the Imperium, and in this one light we
see light. Shall we be deprived of this with your sympathy, persuasion, help?
A French pope will either go to France—and then our dear country is
bereft of its splendour; or he will stay among us—and Italy, the queen of
nations, will serve a foreign master, while we shall be the slaves of the
French. The kingdom of Sicily will come into the hands of the French. The
French will possess all the cities and strongholds of the Church. You might
have taken warning from Calixtus, during whose papacy there was nothing
the Catalans did not get. After trying the Catalans, are you so eager to try
the French? You will soon be sorry if you do! You will see the college filled
with Frenchmen and the papacy will never again be wrested from them.

Are you so dull that you do not realize that this will lay a yoke upon your nation forever? And what shall I say of this man's life? Are you not ashamed to entrust Christ's office to a slippery fellow who would sell his own soul? A fine bridegroom you are planning for the bride of Christ. You are trusting a lamb to a wolf. Where is your conscience? your zeal for justice, your common sense? Have you so far fallen below your true self? I suppose we have not often heard you say that it would be the Church's ruin if it fell into Rouen's hands? and that you would rather die than vote for this very man? what is the reason for this change? Has he suddenly been transformed from a demon to an angel of light? Or have you been changed from an angel of light to the devil, that you love his lust and filth and greed? What has become of your love for your country and your continual protestations that you preferred Italy above all other nations? I used to think that if everyone else fell away from devotion to her, you never would. You have failed me; nay, more, you have failed yourself and Italy, your country, unless you come to your senses."

The cardinal of Pavia was stunned by these words and, overcome alike with grief and shame, he burst into tears. Then, stifling his sobs, he said, "I am ashamed, Aeneas. But what am I to do? I have given my promise. If I do not vote for Rouen I shall be charged with treachery." Aeneas answered, "So far as I can see, it has come to the point where you will be guilty of treachery whichever way you turn. You now have to choose whether you prefer to betray Italy, your country, and the Church, or the Bishop of Rouen." Convinced by these arguments, Pavia decided it was less shameful to fail Rouen.

When Pietro, Cardinal of San Marco, learned of the conspiracy of the French and had lost hope of getting the papacy himself, actuated alike by patriotism and hatred of Rouen, he began to go to the Italian cardinals, urging and warning them not to abandon their country; and he did not rest till he had gathered all the Italians except Colonna in the cell of the Cardinal of Genoa, revealed the conspiracy that had been made in the privies, and showed them that the Church would be ruined and Italy a slave forever if Rouen should obtain the papacy. He implored them individually to show themselves men, to consult for the good of Mother Church and unhappy Italy, to put aside their enmities for one another and choose an Italian rather than a foreigner for pope. If they listened to him, they would prefer Aeneas to all others. There were present seven cardinals: Genoa, Orsini, Bologna, San Marco, Pavia, Siena, and Sant' Anastasia. All approved Pavia's words except Aeneas, who thought himself unworthy of so exalted an office.

The next day they went as usual to Mass, and then began the scrutiny. A golden chalice was placed on the altar, and three cardinals, the Bishop of Ruthen, the Presbyter of Rouen, and the Deacon of Colonna, were set to watch it and see that there should be no cheating. The other cardinals took their seats, and then, rising in order of rank and age, each approached the altar and deposited in the chalice a ballot on which was written the name of his choice for pope. When Aeneas came up to put in his ballot, Rouen, pale and trembling, said, "Look, Aeneas! I commend myself to you"—certainly a rash thing to say when it was not allowable to change what he had written. But ambition overcame prudence. Aeneas said, "Do you commend yourself to a worm like me?" and without another word he dropped his ballot in the cup and went back to his place.

When all had voted, a table was placed in the middle of the room and the three cardinals mentioned above turned out upon it the cupful of votes. Then they read aloud the ballots one after another and noted down the names written on them. And there was not a single cardinal who did not likewise make notes of those named, that there might be no possibility of trickery. This proved to be to Aeneas's advantage, for when the votes were counted and the teller, Rouen, announced that Aeneas had eight, though the rest said nothing about another man's loss, Aeneas did not allow himself to be defrauded. "Look more carefully at the ballots," he said to the teller, "for I have nine votes." The others agreed with him. Rouen said nothing, as if he had merely made a mistake.

This was the form of the ballot: the voter wrote with his own hand, "I, Peter (or John or whatever his name was), choose for pope Aeneas, Cardinal of Siena, and Jaime, Cardinal of Lisbon"; for it is permitted to vote for one or two or more, on the understanding that the one first named is the one preferred, but if he does not have enough votes to be elected, the next is to be counted in his place, that any agreement may more easily be reached. But a thing advantageous in itself some men pervert to base ends, as Latino Orsini did on that day. He named seven in the hope that those he named might be influenced by that good turn either to accede to him in that scrutiny or to vote for him another; although he who has the reputation of a cheat does not gain much by tricks.

When the result of the scrutiny was made known, it was found, as we have said before, that nine cardinals (Genoa, Orsini, Lerida, Bologna, San Marco, Santi Quattro Coronati, Zamora, Pavia and Portugal) had voted for Aeneas; the Cardinal of Rouen had only six votes, and the rest were far behind. Rouen was petrified when he saw himself so far outstripped by Aeneas, and all the rest were amazed, for never within the memory of man had anyone polled as many as nine votes by scrutiny. Since no one had received enough votes for election, they decided to resume their seats and try the method that is called "by accession," to see if perhaps it might be possible to elect a pope that day. And here again Rouen indulged in empty hopes. All sat pale and silent in their places, as if entranced. For some time no one spoke, no one opened his lips, no one moved any part of his body except the eyes, which kept glancing all about. It was a strange silence and a strange sight, men sitting there like their own statues; no sound to be heard, no movement to be seen. They remained thus for some moments, those inferior in rank waiting for their superiors to begin the accession. Then Rodrigo, the vice-chancellor, rose and said, "I accede to the Cardinal of Siena," an utterance which was like a dagger in Rouen's heart, so pale did he turn. A silence followed, and each man, looking at his neighbour, began to indicate his sentiments by gestures. By this time it looked as if Aeneas would be pope, and some, fearing this result, left the conclave, pretending physical needs, but really with the purpose of escaping the fate of that day. Those who thus withdrew were the Cardinals of Ruthen, and San Sisto. However, as no one followed them, they soon returned. Then Jacopo, Cardinal of Sant' Anastasia, said, "I accede to the Cardinal of Siena." At this all appeared even more stunned, like people in a house shaken by unprecedented earthquakes, and lost the power of speech. Aeneas now lacked but one vote, for twelve would elect a pope. Realizing this, Cardinal Prospero Colonna thought that he must get for himself the glory of announcing the pope. He rose and was about to pronounce his vote, with the customery dignity, when he was seized by the Cardinals of Nicaea and Rouen and sharply rebuked for wishing to accede to Aeneas. When he persisted his intention, they tried to get him out of the room by force, resorting even to such means to snatch the papacy from Aeneas. But Prospero, who, though he had voted for the Cardinal of Rouen on his ballot, was nevertheless bound to Aeneas by ties of old friendship, paid no attention to their abuse and empty threats. Turning to the other cardinals, he said, "I too accede to the Cardinal of Siena and I make him pope." When they heard this, the courage of the opposition failed and all their machinations were shattered.

All the cardinals immediately fell at Aeneas's feet and saluted him as pope. Then they resumed their seats and ratified his election without a dissenting vote. At this point Bessarion, Cardinal of Nicaea, speaking for himself and for the others who had voted for the Cardinal of Rouen, said, "Your Holiness, we approve your election, which we do not doubt is of God. We thought before and still think that you are worthy of this office. The reason we did not vote for you was your infirmity. We thought your gout the one thing against you, for the Church needs an active man who has the physical strength to take long journeys and meet the dangers which we fear threaten us from the Turks. You, on the contrary, need rest. It was this consideration that won us to the side of the Cardinal of Rouen. If you were physically strong, there is no one we should have preferred. But, since God is satisfied, we must needs be satisfied too. God Himself, who has chosen you, will make good the defect in your feet and will not punish our ignorance. We revere you as pope, we elect you again, so far as in our power, and we will serve you faithfully."

Aeneas answered, "Your Eminence of Nicaea, your opinion of us, as we understand it, is much higher than our own, when you attribute to us no defect except that in our feet. We are not ignorant that our imperfection is more general, and we realize that our failings, which might justly have caused us to be rejected as pope, are almost innumerable. As to any virtues, which might raise us to this post, we know of none; and we should declare ourselves utterly unworthy and should refuse the honour offered us if we did not fear the judgment of Him who has called us. For what is done by two-thirds of the sacred college, that is surely of the Holy Ghost, which may not be resisted. Therefore we obey the divine summons, and we praise you, your Eminence of Nicaea, and those who voted with you. If, following the dictates of your conscience, you thought you ought not to be elected as being inadequate, you will still be welcomed by us, who attribute our calling not to this man or that but to the whole college and to God Himself, from whom cometh every good and perfect gift."

With these words he took off the garments he was wearing and put on the white tunic of Christ. When asked by what name he wished to be called, he answered, "Pius," and he was at once addressed as Pius II. Then, after swearing to observe the capitulations that had been announced in the college two days before, he took his place by the altar and was again reverenced by the cardinals, who kissed his feet, hands, and cheek. After that the election of a pope was proclaimed to the people from a high window, and it was announced that he who had been Cardinal of Siena was now Pope Pius II.

The attendants of the cardinals in the conclave plundered Aeneas's cell and meanly carried off all the plate (though it was very modest), his clothes, and his books; and the infamous rabble not only pillaged his house in the city but actually demolished it, taking away even the blocks of marble. Other cardinals, too, suffered losses, for while the people were waiting in suspense, various rumours got about, and as now this cardinal, now that, was reported elected, the crowd would rush to their houses and plunder them. The Cardinal of Genoa, whose name was mistaken for Siena, lost part of his possessions. Though many names were mentioned, none was received with enthusiasm except that of the Cardinal of Siena. When the cry arose that Rouen or Genoa or Lerida (for there were reports of them too) had been elected, all cast down their eyes and cursed the college. Only their personal friends were pleased; the rest shared the general sorrow. But when it was certain that Aeneas had been seated on Peter's throne, there was no one who did not rejoice. You might have seen not men only but the very animals and the buildings of the city exulting. Everywhere was heard laughter and expressions of joy and the cries of men shouting, "Siena! Siena! O happy Siena! Viva Siena!" Though the city was under arms and no one seemed to have confidence in anything but the sword, presently, when the people were told that the papacy had fallen to Aeneas, the aspect of the capital was completely changed. What had a little time before been the city of Mars all at once became the city, I will not say of Venus, the mother of that ancient Trojan Aeneas, but of Peace and Quiet, and joy and tranquillity reigned everywhere.

Meantime the new pope, after taking a little refreshment, was escorted to the basilica of St. Peter and conducted to the high altar, under which lie the bodies of the blessed Apostles. Shortly after, he took his seat according to custom on the high throne and in the apostolic chair itself. There the cardinals and bishops and after them many of the people kissed his feet and reverenced him on his throne as Christ's Vicar. Then after a brief interval, when evening was coming on, they escorted him back to the palace. At nightfall fires blazed at every crossroad and on every tower; singing could be heard; neighbours called to neighbours; everywhere horns and trumpets blared, and there was no spot in all the city which did not share in the general rejoicing. The older men said they had never seen such enthusiasm among the Roman populace.

The next night in a procession that reached from Hadrian's mausoleum to the Church of St. Peter the chief citizens of Rome on horseback and carrying lighted tapers went to the palace to greet the pope.

MARTIN LUTHER

MARTIN LUTHER (1483–1546) was born in Saxony, the son of a miner. In
1501 he entered the University of Erfurt intending to study jurisprudence. He distinguished himself in his studies, although remaining
singularly untouched by the humanistic tendencies active in the university. Following a frightening vision and the death of a friend he abandoned the law and
entered the Augustinian order, of which he was ordained a priest in 1505. In
1510–11 he went to Rome as an emissary of his Order, and there the splendor as
well as the corruption of the capital of Christendom depressed him profoundly.
Returning to Germany, he became a vicar of his order, supervising eleven monasteries, and professor at Wittenberg.

In 1517 the Dominican John Tetzel traveled through Germany, selling papal
indulgences and advertising that the purchase of an indulgence would release
from Purgatory the soul of a departed relative. Angered that the instruments of
salvation should be sold, and that people already poverty-stricken should be prevailed upon by such promises, Luther attacked indulgences in his famous Ninety-
five Theses, which he nailed to the door of the Castle Church in Wittenberg.

The posting of the Ninety-five Theses was the beginning of Luther's break with
the Church. Although he had envisaged no schism, before he was done he had
broken his monastic vows and denounced the Pope as Antichrist, and had been in
turn excommunicated by Leo X and banned by the Holy Roman Emperor Charles
V. Aside from its religious significance, the Lutheran movement was the occasion
for widespread disorder and revolution in Germany, despite Luther's own opposition to political rebellion.

Luther hoped to exercise his influence primarily through the written and spoken
word. He translated the Bible into German, giving a standard form to the language
and making religion available outside the Church organization. His voluminous
writings include the *Address to the Christian Nobility of the German Nation*
(1520), which argues, among other things, for the independence of the civil from
the ecclesiastical power; *On Christian Liberty* (1520), the basis of his "program"
of reformation; *The Babylonian Captivity of the Church;* and the *De servo arbitrio,*
a reply to the *De libero arbitrio* of Erasmus. In 1525 he wrote an *Exhortation to
Peace* in which he made both the aristocrats and the lower classes responsible for
the Peasant War, and followed it up with a tract *Against the Thievish, Murderous
Hordes of Peasants.*

The following selections from the *Address* and *On Christian Liberty* are from the
translations from the German by C. A. Buchheim and R. S. Grignon, respectively.

ADDRESS
TO THE CHRISTIAN NOBILITY
OF THE GERMAN NATION

INTRODUCTION

The grace and might of God be with you, Most Serene Majesty! most gracious, well beloved gentlemen!

It is not out of mere arrogance and perversity that I, a single poor man, have taken upon me to address your lordships. The distress and misery that oppress all the Christian estates, more especially in Germany, have led not only myself, but every one else, to cry aloud and to ask for help, and have now forced me too, to cry out and to ask, if God would give His Spirit to any one, to reach a hand to His wretched people. Councils have often put forward some remedy, but through the cunning of certain men it has been adroitly frustrated, and the evils have become worse; whose malice and wickedness I will now, by the help of God, expose, so that, being known, they may henceforth cease to be so obstructive and injurious. God has given us a young and noble sovereign, and by this has roused hope in many hearts: now it is right that we too should do what we can, and make good use of time and grace.

The first thing that we must do is to consider the matter with great earnestness, and, whatever we attempt, not to trust in our own strength and wisdom alone, even if the power of all the world were ours; for God will not endure that a good work should be begun, trusting to our own strength and wisdom. He destroys it; it is all useless: as we read in the xxxiii Psalm. "There is no king saved by the multitude of an host: a mighty man is not delivered by much strength." And I fear it is for that reason, that those beloved Princes, the Emperors Frederick, the First and the Second, and many other German Emperors were, in former times, so piteously spurned and oppressed by the Popes, though they were feared by all the world. Perchance they trusted rather in their own strength than in God; therefore they could not but fall: and how would the sanguinary tyrant Julius II have risen so high in our own days, but, that, I fear, France, the Germans and Venice trusted to themselves? The children of Benjamin slew forty-two thousand Israelites, for this reason, that these trusted to their own strength.

That it may not happen thus to us and to our noble Emperor Charles, we must remember that in this matter we wrestle not against flesh and blood, but against the rulers of the darkness of this world, who may fill the world with war and bloodshed, but cannot themselves be overcome thereby. We must renounce all confidence in our natural strength, and take the matter in hand with humble trust in God; we must seek God's help with earnest prayer, and have nothing before our eyes but the misery and wretchedness of Christendom, irrespective of what punishment the wicked may deserve. If we do not act thus, we may begin the game with great pomp; but when we are well in it, the spirits of evil will make such confusion that the whole world will be immersed in blood, and yet nothing be done. Therefore let us act in the fear of God, and prudently. The greater the might of the foe, the greater is the misfortune, if we do not act in the fear of God, and with humility. As Popes and Romanists have hitherto, with the Devil's help, thrown Kings into confusion, so will they still do, if we attempt things with our own strength and skill, without God's help.

THE THREE WALLS OF THE ROMANISTS

The romanists have, with great adroitness, drawn three walls round themselves, with which they have hitherto protected themselves, so that no one could reform them, whereby all Christendom has fallen terribly.

Firstly, if pressed by the temporal power, they have affirmed and maintained that the temporal power has no jurisdiction over them, but on the contrary that the spiritual power is above the temporal.

Secondly, if it were proposed to admonish them with the Scriptures, they objected that no one may interpret the Scriptures but the Pope.

Thirdly, if they are threatened with a Council, they pretend that no one may call a Council but the Pope.

Thus they have secretly stolen our three rods, so that they may be unpunished, and entrenched themselves behind these three walls, to act with all wickedness and malice, as we now see. And whenever they have been compelled to call a Council, they have made it of no avail, by binding the Princes beforehand with an oath to leave them as they were. Besides this they have given the Pope full power over the arrangement of the Council, so that it is all one, whether we have many Councils, or no Councils, for in any case they deceive us with pretences and false tricks. So grievously do they tremble for their skin before a true, free Council; and thus they have overawed Kings and Princes, that these believe they would be offending God, if they were not to obey them in all such knavish, deceitful artifices.

Now may God help us, and give us one of those trumpets, that overthrew the walls of Jericho, so that we may blow down these walls of straw and paper, and that we may set free our Christian rods, for the chastisement of sin, and expose the craft and deceit of the devil, so that we may amend ourselves by punishment and again obtain God's favour.

THE FIRST WALL

Let us, in the first place, attack the first wall.

It has been devised, that the Pope, bishops, priests and monks are called the Spiritual Estate; princes, lords, artificers and peasants, are the Temporal Estate; which is a very fine, hypocritical device. But let no one be made afraid by it; and that for this reason: That all Christians are truly of the Spiritual Estate, and there is no difference among them, save of office alone. As St. Paul says, we are all one body, though each member does its own work, to serve the others. This is because we have one baptism, one gospel, one faith, and are all Christians alike; for baptism, gospel and faith, these alone make Spiritual and Christian people.

As for the unction by a pope or a bishop, tonsure, ordination, consecration, clothes differing from those of laymen—all this may make a hypocrite or an anointed puppet, but never a Christian, or a spiritual man. Thus we are all consecrated as priests by baptism, as St. Peter says: "Ye are a royal priesthood, a holy nation"; and in the book of Revelations: "and hast made us unto our God, kings and priests." For, if we have not a higher consecration in us than Pope or bishop can give, no priest could ever be made by the consecration of Pope or bishop; nor could he say the mass, or preach, or absolve. Therefore the bishop's consecration is just as if in the name of the whole congregation he took one person out of the community, each member of which has equal power, and commanded him to exercise this power for the rest; in the same way as if ten brothers, co-heirs as king's sons, were to choose one from among them to rule over their inheritance; they would, all of them, still remain kings and have equal power, although one is ordered to govern.

And to put the matter even more plainly; if a little company of pious Christian laymen were taken prisoners and carried away to a desert, and had not among them a priest consecrated by a bishop, and were there to agree to elect one of them, married or unmarried, and were to order him to baptize, to celebrate the mass, to absolve and to preach; this man would as truly be a priest, as if all the bishops and all the Popes had consecrated him. That is why in cases of necessity every man can baptize and absolve, which would not be possible if we were not all priests. This great grace and virtue of baptism and of the Christian Estate, they have almost destroyed and made us forget by their ecclesiastical law. In this way the Christians used to choose their bishops and priests out of the community; these being afterwards confirmed by other bishops, without the pomp that we have now. So was it that St. Augustine, Ambrose, Cyprian, were bishops.

Since then the temporal power is baptized as we are, and has the same faith and gospel, we must allow it to be priest and bishop, and account its office an office that is proper and useful to the Christian community. For whatever issues from baptism may boast that it has been consecrated priest, bishop, and Pope, although it does not beseem every one to exercise these offices. For, since we are all priests alike no man may put himself forward, or take upon himself, without our consent and election, to do that which we have all alike power to do. For, if a thing is common to all, no man may take it to himself without the wish and command of the community. And if it should happen that a man were appointed to one of these offices and deposed for abuses, he would be just what he was before. Therefore a priest should be nothing in Christendom but a functionary; as long as he holds his office, he has precedence of others; if he is deprived of it, he is a peasant and a citizen like the rest. Therefore a priest is verily no longer a priest after deposition. But now they have invented *characteres indelebiles*,[1] and pretend that a priest after deprivation still differs from a simple layman. They even imagine that a priest can never be anything but a priest, that is, that he can never become a layman. All this is nothing but mere talk and ordinance of human invention.

It follows then, that between layman and priests, princes and bishops, or as they call it, between spiritual and temporal persons, the only real difference is one of office and function, and not of estate: for they are all of the same Spiritual Estate, true priests, bishops and Popes, though their functions are not the same: just as among priests and monks every man has not the same functions. And this St. Paul says and St. Peter; "we being many are one body in Christ, and every one members one of another." Christ's body is not double or twofold, one temporal, the other spiritual. He is one head, and he has one body.

We see then that just as those that we call spiritual, or priests, bishops or popes, do not differ from other Christians in any other or higher degree, but in that they are to be concerned with the word of God, and the sacraments— that being their work and office—in the same way the temporal authorities hold the sword and the rod in their hands to punish the wicked and to protect the good. A cobbler, a smith, a peasant, every man has the office and function of his calling, and yet all alike are consecrated priests and bishops, and every man in his office must be useful and beneficial to the rest, that so many kinds of work may all be united into one community: just as the members of the body all serve one another.

[1] [That is, distinctive attributes not subject to change.]

Now see, what a Christian doctrine is this: that the temporal authority is not above the clergy, and may not punish it. This is, as if one were to say, the hand may not help, though the eye is in grievous suffering. Is it not unnatural, not to say unchristian, that one member may not help another, or guard it against harm? Nay, the nobler the member, the more the rest are bound to help it. Therefore I say: forasmuch as the temporal power has been ordained by God for the punishment of the bad, and the protection of the good, therefore we must let it do its duty throughout the whole Christian body, without respect of persons: whether it strike popes, bishops, priests, monks, or nuns. If it were sufficient reason for fettering the temporal power that it is inferior among the offices of Christianity to the offices of priest or confessor, or to the spiritual estate—if this were so, then we ought to restrain tailors, cobblers, masons, carpenters, cooks, servants, peasants, and all secular workmen, from providing the Pope, or bishops, priests and monks, with shoes, clothes, houses or victuals, or from paying them tithes. But if these laymen are allowed to do their work without restraint, what do the Romanist scribes mean by their laws? They mean that they withdraw themselves from the operation of temporal Christian power, simply in order that they may be free to do evil, and thus fulfill what St. Peter said: "There shall be false teachers among you, . . . and through covetousness shall they with feigned words make merchandise of you."

Therefore the temporal Christian power must exercise its office without let or hindrance, without considering whom it may strike, whether pope, or bishop, or priest: whoever is guilty let him suffer for it. Whatever the ecclesiastical law says in opposition to this, is merely the invention of Romanist arrogance. For this is what St. Paul says to all Christians: "Let every soul" (I presume including the Popes) "be subject unto the higher powers: for he beareth not the sword in vain: for he is the minister of God, a revenger to execute wrath upon him that doeth evil." Also St. Peter: "Submit yourselves to every ordinance of man for the Lord's sake . . . for so is the will of God." He has also said, that men would come, who should despise government; as has come to pass through ecclesiastical law.

Now I imagine, the first paper wall is overthrown, inasmuch as the temporal power has become a member of the Christian body, and although its work relates to the body, yet does it belong to the spiritual estate. Therefore it must do its duty without let or hindrance upon all members of the whole body, to punish or urge, as guilt may deserve, or need may require, without respect of Pope, bishops or priests; let them threaten or excommunicate as they will. That is why a guilty priest is deprived of his priesthood before being given over to the secular arm; whereas this would not be right, if the secular sword had not authority over him already by divine ordinance.

It is, indeed, past bearing that the spiritual law should esteem so highly the liberty, life and property of the clergy, as if laymen were not as good spiritual Christians, or not equally members of the Church. Why should your body, life, goods, and honour be free and not mine, seeing that we are equal as Christians, and have received alike baptism, faith, spirit and all things? If a priest is killed, the country is laid under an interdict: why not also if a peasant is killed? Whence comes all this difference among equal Christians? Simply from human laws and inventions.

It can have been no good spirit that devised these exceptions, and made sin to go unpunished. For, if as Christ and the Apostles bid us, it is our duty to oppose the evil one, and all his works and words, and to drive him away as well as may be; how then should we look on in silence, when the Pope and his followers are guilty of devilish works and words? Are we for the sake of men to allow the commandments and the truth of God to be defeated, which at our baptism we vowed to support with body and soul? Truly we should have to answer for all souls that are thus led away into error.

Therefore it must have been the archdevil himself who said, as we read in the ecclesiastical law: If the Pope were so perniciously wicked, as to be dragging souls in crowds to the devil, yet he could not be deposed. This is the accursed and devilish foundation on which they build a Rome, and think that the whole world is to be allowed to go to the devil, rather than they should be opposed in their knavery. If a man were to escape punishment simply because he is above the rest, then no Christian might punish another, since Christ has commanded each of us to esteem himself the lowest and the humblest.

Where there is sin, there remains no avoiding the punishment, as St. Gregory says: We are all equal, but guilt makes one subject to another. Now see how they deal with Christendom, depriving it of its freedom without any warrant from the Scriptures, out of their own wickedness, whereas God and the Apostles made them subject to the secular sword; so that we must fear that it is the work of Antichrist, or a sign of his near approach.

THE SECOND WALL

The second wall is even more tottering and weak: that they alone pretend to be considered masters of the Scriptures; although they learn nothing of them all their life, they assume authority, and juggle before us with impudent words, saying that the Pope cannot err in matters of faith, whether he be evil or good; albeit they cannot prove it by a single letter. That is why the canon law contains so many heretical and unchristian, nay, unnatural laws; but of these we need not speak now. For whereas they imagine the Holy Ghost never leaves them, however unlearned and wicked they may be, they grow bold enough to decree whatever they like. But were this true, where were the need and use of the Holy Scriptures? Let us burn them, and content ourselves with the unlearned gentlemen at Rome, in whom the Holy Ghost dwells, who however can dwell in pious souls only. If I had not read it, I could never have believed that the Devil should have put forth such follies at Rome and find a following.

But not to fight them with our own words, we will quote Scriptures. St. Paul says: "If anything be revealed to another that sitteth by, let the first hold his peace." What would be the use of this commandment, if we were to believe him alone that teaches or has the highest seat? Christ Himself says: "And they shall be all taught of God." Thus it may come to pass that the Pope and his followers are wicked and not true Christians, and not being taught by God, have no true understanding, whereas a common man may have true understanding. Why should we then not follow him? Has not the Pope often erred? Who could help Christianity, in case the Pope errs, if we do not rather believe another, who has the Scriptures for him?

Therefore it is a wickedly devised fable, and they cannot quote a single letter to confirm it, that it is for the Pope alone to interpret the Scriptures or to confirm the interpretation of them: they have assumed the authority of their own selves. And though they say that this authority was given to St. Peter when the keys were given to him, it is plain enough that the keys were not given to St. Peter alone, but to the whole community. Besides, the keys were not ordained for doctrine or authority, but for sin, to bind or loose; and what they claim besides this is mere invention. But what Christ said to St. Peter: "I have prayed for thee, that thy faith fail not," cannot relate to the Pope, inasmuch as there have been many Popes without faith, as they are themselves forced to acknowledge. Nor did Christ pray for Peter alone, but for all the Apostles and all Christians, as He says, "Neither pray I for these alone, but for them also which shall believe on me through their word." Is not this plain enough?

Only consider the matter. They must needs acknowledge that there are pious Christians among us, that have the true faith, spirit, understanding, word, and mind of Christ; why then should we reject their word and understanding, and follow a Pope who has neither understanding nor Spirit? Surely this were to deny our whole faith and the Christian Church. Moreover, if the article of our faith is right: *I believe in the Holy Christian Church,* the Pope cannot alone be right; else we must say: *I believe in the Pope of Rome,* and reduce the Christian Church to one man, which is a devilish and damnable heresy. Besides that, we are all priests, as I have said, and have all one faith, one gospel, one sacrament; how then should we not have the power of discerning and judging what is right or wrong in matters of faith? What becomes of St. Paul's words: "But he that is spiritual judgeth all things, yet he himself is judged of no man"; and also, "we having the same spirit of faith." Why then should we not perceive as well as an unbelieving Pope, what agrees, or disagrees with our faith?

By these and many other texts we should gain courage and freedom, and should not let the spirit of liberty (as St. Paul has it) be frightened away by the inventions of the Popes; we should boldly judge what they do and what they leave undone, by our own understanding, and not their own. Did not Abraham in old days have to obey his Sarah, who was in stricter bondage to him than we are to any one on earth? Thus too Balaam's ass was wiser than the prophet. If God spoke by an ass against a prophet, why should He not speak by a pious man against the Pope? Besides, St. Paul withstood St. Peter as being in error. Therefore it behoves every Christian to aid the faith by understanding and defending it, and by condemning all errors.

THE THIRD WALL

The third wall falls of itself, as soon as the first two have fallen; for if the Pope acts contrary to the Scriptures, we are bound to stand by the Scriptures, to punish and to constrain him, according to Christ's commandment; "Moreover if thy brother shall trespass against thee, go and tell him his fault between thee and him alone: if he shall hear thee, thou hast gained thy brother. But if he will not hear thee, then take with thee one or two more, that in the mouth of two or three witnesses every word may be established. And if he shall neglect to hear them, tell it unto the church: but if he neglect to hear the church, let him be unto thee as an heathen man and a publican." Here each member is commanded to take care for the other; much more then should we do this, if it is a ruling member of the community that does evil, which by its evil doing, causes great harm and offence to the others. If then I am to accuse him before the church, I must collect the church together. Moreover they can show nothing in the Scriptures giving the Pope sole power to call and confirm councils; they have nothing but their own laws; but these hold good only so long as they are not injurious to Christianity and the laws of God. Therefore, if the Pope deserves punishment, these laws cease to bind us, since Christendom would suffer, if he were not punished by a council. Thus we read, that the council of the Apostles was not called by St. Peter, but by all the Apostles and the elders. But if the right to call it had lain with St. Peter alone, it would not have been a Christian council, but a heretical *conciliabulum*.[2] Moreover the

2 [The Latin word itself implies an illegitimate or heretical council.]

most celebrated Nicene Council was neither called nor confirmed by the Bishop of Rome, but by the Emperor Constantine; and after him many other Emperors have done the same, and yet the councils called by them were accounted most Christian. But if the Pope alone had the power, they must all have been heretical. Moreover if I consider the councils that the Pope has called, I do not find that they produced any notable results.

Therefore when need requires and the Pope is a cause of offence to Christendom, in these cases whoever can best do so, as a faithful member of the whole body, must do what he can to procure a true free council. This no one can do so well as the temporal authorities, especially since they are fellow-Christians, fellow-priests, sharing one spirit, and one power in all things; and since they should exercise the office that they have received from God without hindrance, whenever it is necessary and useful that it should be exercised. Would it not be most unnatural, if a fire were to break out in a city, and every one were to keep still and let it burn on and on, whatever might be burnt, simply because they had not the mayor's authority, or because the fire perhaps broke out at the mayor's house? Is not every citizen bound in this case to rouse and call in the rest? How much more should this be done in the spiritual city of Christ, if a fire of offence breaks out, either at the Pope's government or wherever it may! The like happens if an enemy attacks a town. The first to rouse up the rest earns glory and thanks. Why then should not he earn glory that announces the coming of our enemies from hell, and rouses and summons all Christians?

But as for their boasts of their authority, that no one must oppose it, this is idle talk. No one in Christendom has any authority to do harm, or to forbid others to prevent harm being done. There is no authority in the Church but for reformation. Therefore if the Pope wished to use his power to prevent the calling of a free council, so as to prevent the reformation of the Church, we must not respect him or his power; and if he should begin to excommunicate and fulminate, we must despise this as the ravings of a madman, and trusting in God, excommunicate and repel him, as best we may. For this his usurped power is nothing; he does not possess it, and he is at once overthrown by a text from the Scriptures. For St. Paul says to the Corinthians, "That God has given us authority for edification and not for destruction." Who will set this text at naught? It is the power of the Devil and of Antichrist that prevents what would serve for the reformation of Christendom. Therefore we must not follow it, but oppose it with our body, our goods and all that we have. And even if a miracle were to happen in favour of the Pope, against the temporal power, or if some were to be stricken by a plague, as they sometimes boast has happened: all this is to be held as having been done by the Devil, for our want of faith in God, as was foretold by Christ: "There shall arise false Christs, and false prophets, and shall shew great signs and wonders; insomuch that, if it were possible, they shall deceive the very elect"; and St. Paul tells the Thessalonians that the coming of Antichrist shall be "after the working of Satan with all power and signs and lying wonders."

Therefore let us hold fast to this: that Christian power can do nothing against Christ, as St. Paul says: "for we can do nothing against Christ, but for Christ." But, if it does anything against Christ, it is the power of Antichrist and the Devil, even if it rained and hailed wonders and plagues. Wonders and plagues prove nothing, especially in these latter evil days, of which false wonders are foretold in all the Scriptures. Therefore we must hold fast to the words of God with an assured faith; then the Devil will soon cease his wonders.

And now I hope we have laid the false, lying spectre with which the Romanists have long terrified and stupefied our consciences. And we have shown that, like all the rest of us, they are subject to the temporal sword; that they have no authority to interpret the Scriptures by force without skill; and that they have no power to prevent a council, or to pledge it in accordance with their pleasure, or to bind it beforehand, and deprive it of its freedom; and that if they do this, they are verily of the fellowship of Antichrist and the Devil, and have nothing of Christ but the name.

OF THE MATTERS TO BE CONSIDERED IN THE COUNCILS

Let us now consider the matters which should be treated in the councils, and with which popes, cardinals, bishops, and all learned men should occupy themselves day and night, if they loved Christ and His Church. But if they do not so, the people at large and the temporal powers must do so, without considering the thunders of their excommunications. For an unjust excommunication is better than ten just absolutions, and an unjust absolution is worse than ten just excommunications. Therefore let us rouse ourselves, fellow-Germans, and fear God more than man, that we be not answerable for all the poor souls that are so miserably lost through the wicked, devilish government of the Romanists, through which also the dominion of the Devil grows day by day; if indeed this hellish government can grow any worse, which for my part I can neither conceive nor believe.

1. It is a distressing and terrible thing to see that the head of Christendom, who boasts of being the Vicar of Christ and the successor of St. Peter, lives in a worldly pomp that no king or emperor can equal: so that in him that calls himself most holy and most spiritual, there is more worldliness than in the world itself. He wears a triple crown, whereas the mightiest kings only wear one crown. If this resembles the poverty of Christ and St. Peter, it is a new sort of resemblance. They prate of its being heretical to object to this; nay, they

will not even hear how unchristian and ungodly it is. But I think that if he should have to pray to God with ears, he would have to lay down his crowns; for God will not endure any arrogance. His office should be nothing else than to weep and pray constantly for Christendom, and to be an example of all humility.

However this may be, this pomp is a stumbling-block, and the Pope, for the very salvation of his soul, ought to put it off; for St. Paul says: "Abstain from all appearance of evil" (1 Thess. v, 21); and again: "Provide things honest in the sight of all men." (2 Cor. viii, 21.) A simple mitre would be enough for the Pope: wisdom and sanctity should raise him above the rest; the crown of pride he should leave to Antichrist, as his predecessors did for some hundreds of years. They say: He is the ruler of the world. This is false; for Christ, whose vice-gerent and vicar he claims to be, said to Pilate: "My kingdom is not of this world." (John xviii, 36.) But no vice-gerent can have a wider dominion than his Lord. Nor is he a vice-gerent of Christ in His glory, but of Christ crucified, as St. Paul says: "For I determined not to know anything among you, save Jesus Christ, and him crucified" (Phil. ii, 5, 7). Again (1 Cor. i.): "We preach Christ crucified." Now they make the Pope a vice-gerent of Christ exalted in heaven, and some have let the Devil rule them so thoroughly, that they have maintained that the Pope is above the angels in heaven, and has power over them; which is precisely the true work of the true Antichrist.

2. What is the use in Christendom of the people called "Cardinals"? I will tell you. In Italy and Germany there are many rich convents, endowments, fiefs and benefices, and as the best way of getting these into the hands of Rome, they created cardinals, and gave them the sees, convents, and prelacies, and thus destroyed the service of God. That is why Italy is almost a desert now: the convents are destroyed, the sees consumed, the revenues of the prelacies and of all the churches drawn to Rome; towns are decayed; the country and the people ruined, while there is no more any worship of God or preaching; why? Because the cardinals must have all the wealth. No Turk could have thus desolated Italy and overthrown the worship of God.

Now that Italy is sucked dry, they come to Germany and begin very quietly; but we shall see, that Germany is soon to be brought into the same state as Italy. We have a few cardinals already. What the Romanists mean thereby the drunken Germans are not to see until they have lost everything—bishoprics, convents, benefices, fiefs, even to their last farthing. Antichrist must take the riches of the earth, as it is written. They begin by taking off the cream of the bishoprics, convents, and fiefs; and as they do not dare destroy everything as they have done in Italy, they employ such holy cunning to join together ten or twenty prelacies, and take such a portion of each, annually, that the total amounts to a considerable sum. The priory of Würzburg gives one thousand guilders, those of Bamberg, Mayence, Treves and others also contribute. In this way they collect one thousand or ten thousand guilders, in order that a cardinal may live at Rome in a state like that of a wealthy monarch.

After we have gained this, we will create thirty or forty cardinals on one day, and give one St. Michael's Mount near Bamberg, and likewise the see of Würzburg, to which belongs some rich benefices, until the churches and the cities are desolated; and then we shall say: We are the vicars of Christ, the shepherds of Christ's flocks; those mad, drunken Germans must submit to it. I advise, however, that there be made fewer cardinals, or that the Pope should have to support them out of his own purse. It would be amply sufficient, if there were twelve, and if each of them had an annual income of one thousand guilders. What has brought us Germans to such a pass, that we have to suffer this robbery and this destruction of our property by the Pope? If the kingdom of France has resisted it, why do we Germans suffer ourselves to be fooled and deceived? It would be more endurable, if they did nothing but rob us of our property; but they destroy the church and deprive Christ's flock of their good shepherds, and overthrow the service and word of God. Even if there were no cardinals at all, the Church would not perish; for they do nothing for the good of Christendom; all they do is to bargain and traffic in prelacies and bishoprics; which any robber could do as well.

3. If we took away ninety-nine parts of the Pope's court and only left one hundredth, it would still be large enough to answer questions on matters of belief. Now there is such a swarm of vermin at Rome, all called Papal, that Babylon itself never saw the like. There are more than three thousand Papal secretaries alone; but who shall count the other office-bearers, since there are so many offices that we can scarcely count them, and all waiting for German benefices, as wolves wait for a flock of sheep? I think Germany now pays more to the Pope, than it formerly paid the Emperors; nay, some think more than three hundred thousand guilders are sent from Germany to Rome every year, for nothing whatever; and in return we are scoffed at and put to shame. Do we still wonder why princes, noblemen, cities, foundations, convents and people are poor? We should rather wonder that we have anything left to eat.

Now that we have got well into our game, let us pause awhile and show that the Germans are not such fools, as not to perceive or understand this Romish trickery. I do not here complain, that God's commandments and Christian justice are despised at Rome; for the state of things in Christendom, especially at Rome, is too bad for us to complain of such high matters. Nor do I even complain that no account is taken of natural or secular justice and reason. The mischief lies still deeper. I complain that they do not observe their own fabricated canon law, though this is in itself rather mere tyranny, avarice and worldly pomp, than a law. This we shall now show.

Long ago the Emperors and Princes of Germany allowed the Pope to claim the *annates* from all German benefices; that is, half of the first year's income from every benefice. The object at this confession was that the Pope should collect a fund with all this money, to fight against the Turks and infidels, and to protect Christendom, so that the nobility should not have to bear the burden of the struggle alone, and that the priests should also contribute. The Popes have made such use of this good simple piety of the Germans, that they have taken this money for more than one hundred years, and have now made of it a regular tax and duty; and not only have they accumulated nothing, but they have founded out of it many posts and offices at Rome, which are paid by it yearly, as out of a settled rent.

Whenever there is any pretence of fighting the Turks, they send out some commission for collecting money, and often send out indulgences under the same pretext of fighting the Turks. They think we Germans will always remain such great and inveterate fools, that we will go on giving money to satisfy their unspeakable greed, though we see plainly that neither *annates* nor absolution money, nor any other—not one farthing—goes against the Turks, but all goes into the bottomless sack. They lie and deceive, form and make covenants with us of which they do not mean to keep one jot. And all this is done in the holy name of Christ and St. Peter.

This being so, the German nation, the bishops and princes, should remember that they are Christians, and should defend the people, who are committed to their government and protection in temporal and spiritual affairs, from these ravenous wolves in sheep's clothing, that profess to be shepherds and rulers; and since the *annates* are so shamefully abused, and the covenants concerning them not carried out, they should not suffer their lands and people to be so piteously and unrighteously flayed and ruined; but by an imperial or a national law they should either retain the *annates* in the country, or abolish them altogether. For since they do not keep to the covenants, they have no rights to the *annates;* therefore bishops and princes are bound to punish this thievery and robbery, or prevent it, as justice demands. And herein should we assist and strengthen the Pope, who is perchance too weak to prevent this scandal by himself; or, if he wishes to protect or support it, restrain and oppose him as a wolf and tyrant; for he has no authority to do evil or to protect evildoers. Even if it were proposed to collect any such treasure for use against the Turks, we should be wise in future, and remember that the German nation is more fitted to take charge of it than the Pope, seeing that the German nation by itself is able to provide men enough, if the money is forthcoming. This matter of the *annates* is like many other Romish pretexts. . . .

TWENTY-SEVEN ARTICLES RESPECTING THE REFORMATION OF THE
CHRISTIAN ESTATE

25. The Universities also require a good, sound Reformation. I must say this, let it vex whom it may. The fact is that whatever the Papacy has ordered or instituted is only designed for the propagation of sin and error. What are the Universities, as at present ordered, but as the Book of Maccabees says: "Schools of 'Greek fashion' and 'heathenish manners.'" full of dissolute living, where very little is taught of the Holy Scriptures and of the Christian faith, and the blind heathen teacher, Aristotle, rules even further than Christ. Now, my advice would be that the books of Aristotle, the "Physics," the "Metaphysics," "Of the Soul," "Ethics," which have hitherto been considered the best, be altogether abolished, with all others that profess to treat of nature, though nothing can be learned from them, either of natural or of spiritual things. Besides, no one has been able to understand his meaning, and much time has been wasted, and many noble souls vexed, with much useless labour, study, and expense. I venture to say that any potter has more knowledge of natural things than is to be found in these books. My heart is grieved to see how many of the best Christians this accursed, proud, knavish heathen has fooled and led astray with his false words. God sent him as a plague for our sins.

Does not the wretched man in his best book, "Of the Soul," teach that the soul dies with the body; though many have tried to save him with vain words, as if we had not the Holy Scriptures to teach us fully of all things, of which Aristotle had not the slightest perception. Yet this dead heathen has conquered, and has hindered and almost suppressed the books of the living God; so that, when I see all this misery, I cannot but think that the evil spirit has introduced this study.

Then there is the "Ethics," which is accounted one of the best, though no book is more directly contrary to God's will and the Christian virtues. Oh, that such books could be kept out of the reach of all Christians! Let no one object that I say too much, or speak without knowledge. My friend, I know of what I speak. I know Aristotle as well as you or men like you. I have read him with more understanding than St. Thomas or Scotus; which I may say without arrogance, and can prove if need be. It matters not that so many great minds have exercised themselves in these matters for many hundred years. Such objections do not affect me as they might have done once; since it is plain as day that many more errors have existed for many hundred years in the world and the Universities.

I would, however, gladly consent that Aristotle's books of Logic, Rhetoric and Poetic should be retained; or they might be usefully studied in a condensed form, to practise young people in speaking and preaching; but the notes and comments should be abolished, and just as Cicero's Rhetoric is read without note or comment, Aristotle's Logic should be read without such long commentaries. But now neither speaking nor preaching are taught out of them, and they are used only for disputation and confusion. Besides this there are languages, Latin, Greek and Hebrew, the Mathematics, History; but this I leave to men of higher understanding; if they seriously strive after reform, all these things will come of themselves. And truly it is an important matter! for it concerns the teaching and training of Christian youths and of our noble people, in whom Christianity still abides. Therefore I think that Pope and Emperor could have no better task than the reformation of the Universities, just as there is nothing more devilishly mischievous than an unreformed University.

Physicians I would leave to reform their own faculty; Lawyers and Theologians I take under my charge, and say firstly, that it would be right to abolish the canon law entirely, from beginning to end, more especially the decretals. We are taught quite sufficiently in the Bible how we ought to act; all this study only prevents the study of the Scriptures, and for the most part it is tainted with covetousness and pride. And even though there were some good in it, it should nevertheless be destroyed, for the Pope having the canon law in *scrinio pectoris*,[3] all further study is useless and deceitful. At the present time the canon law is not to be found in the books, but in the whims of the Pope and his sycophants. You may have settled a matter in the best possible way according to the canon law, but the Pope has his *scrinium pectoris,* to which all law must bow in all the world. Now this *scrinium* is oftentimes directed by some knave, and the devil himself, whilst it boasts that it is directed by the Holy Ghost. This is the way they treat Christ's poor people, imposing many laws and keeping none; forcing others to keep them, or to free themselves by money.

Therefore since the Pope and his followers have cancelled the whole canon law, despising it and setting their own will above all the world, we should follow them and reject the books. Why should we study them to no purpose? We should never be able to know the Pope's caprice, which has now become the canon law. Let it fall then in God's name, after having risen in the devil's name. Let there be henceforth no *doctor decretorum,* but let them all be *doctores scrinii papalis,* that is, the Pope's sycophants. They say that there is no better temporal government than among the Turks, though they have no canon nor civil law, but only their Koran; we must at least own that there is no worse government than ours with its canon and civil law, for no estate lives according to the Scriptures, or even according to natural reason.

The civil law, too, good God! what a wilderness it is become! It is, indeed,

---

[3] [The *scrinium* was the Papal Archive. This phrase means: *stored within himself.*]

much better, more skilful and more honest than the canon law, of which nothing is good but the name. Still there is far too much of it. Surely good governors, judging according to the Scriptures, would be law enough, as St. Paul says: "Is it so, that there is not a wise man among you? No, not one that shall be able to judge between his brethren?" (1 Cor. vi, 5.) I think also that the common law and usage of the country should be preferred to the law of the Empire, and that the law of the Empire should only be used in cases of necessity. And would to God that, as each land has its own peculiar character and nature, they could all be governed by their own simple laws, just as they were governed before the law of the Empire was devised, and as many are governed even now! Elaborate and far-fetched laws are only burdensome to the people, and a hindrance rather than a help to business. But I hope that others have thought of this, and considered it to more purpose than I could.

Our worthy Theologians have saved themselves much trouble and labour by leaving the Bible alone and only reading the Sentences. I should have thought that young Theologians might begin by studying the Sentences and that Doctors should study the Bible. Now they invert this: the Bible is the first thing they study; this ceases with the Bachelor's degree; the Sentences are the last, and these they keep for ever with the Doctors' degree; and this too under such sacred obligation that one that is not a priest may read the Bible, but a priest must read the Sentences; so that, as far as I can see, a married man might be a Doctor in the Bible, but not in the Sentences. How should we prosper so long as we act so perversely, and degrade the Bible, the holy word of God? Besides this, the Pope orders with many stringent words that his laws be read and used in schools and courts; while the law of the Gospel is but little considered. The result is that in schools and courts the Gospel lies dusty on the shelf, so that the Pope's mischievous laws may alone be in force.

Since, then, we hold the name and title of teachers of the Holy Scriptures, we should verily be forced to act according to our title, and to teach the Holy Scriptures and nothing else. Although, indeed, it is a proud, presumptuous title, for a man to proclaim himself teacher of the Scriptures, still it could be suffered, if the works confirmed the title. But as it is, under the rule of the Sentences, we find among Theologians more human and heathenish fallacies than true holy knowledge of the Scriptures. What then are we to do? I know not, except to pray humbly to God to give us Doctors of Theology. Doctors of Arts, of Medicine, of Law, of the Sentences, may be made by Popes, Emperors and the Universities; but of this we may be certain, a Doctor of the Holy Scriptures can be made by none but the Holy Ghost, as Christ says: "They shall all be taught of God." (John vi, 45.) Now the Holy Ghost does not consider red caps or brown, or any other pomp; nor whether we are young or old, layman or priest, monk or secular, virgin or married; nay, he once spoke by an ass against the prophet that rode on it. Would to God we were worthy of having such Doctors given us, be they laymen or priests, married or virgin! but now they try to force the Holy Ghost to enter into Popes, Bishops or Doctors, though there is no sign to show that He is in them.

We must also lessen the number of theological books, and choose the best; for it is not the number of books that make the learned man; nor much reading, but good books often read, however few, make a man learned in the Scriptures and pious. Even the Father should only be read for a short time as an introduction to the Scriptures. As it is, we read nothing else, and never get from them into the Scriptures, as if one should be gazing at the signposts and never follow the road. These good Fathers wished to lead us into the Scriptures by their writings, whereas we lead ourselves out by them, though the Scriptures are our vineyard in which we should all work and exercise ourselves.

Above all, in schools of all kinds the chief and most common lesson should be the Scriptures, and for young boys the Gospel; and would to God each town had also a girl's school in which girls might be taught the Gospel for an hour daily, either in German or Latin! In truth, schools, monasteries and convents, were founded for this purpose, and with good Christian intentions; as we read concerning St. Agnes, and other saints; then were there holy virgins and martyrs; and in those times it was well with Christendom; but now it has been turned into nothing but praying and singing. Should not every Christian be expected by his ninth or tenth year to know all the holy Gospels, containing as they do his very name and life? A spinner or a seamstress teaches her daughter her trade, while she is young, but now even the most learned Prelates and Bishops do not know the Gospel.

Oh, how badly we treat all these poor young people that are entrusted to us for discipline and instruction! and a heavy reckoning shall we have to give for it that we keep them from the word of God; their fate is that described by Jeremiah: "Mine eyes do fail with tears, my bowels are troubled, my liver is poured upon the earth, for the destruction of the daughter of my people; because the children and the sucklings swoon in the streets of the city. They say to their mothers, Where is corn and wine? when they swooned as the wounded in the streets of the city, when their soul is poured out into their mothers' bosom." (Lamen. ii, 11, 12.) We do not perceive all this misery, how the young folk are being pitifully corrupted in the midst of Christendom, all for want of the Gospel, which we should read and study with them.

However, if the high schools studied the Scriptures diligently we should not send every one to them, as we do now, when nothing is considered but numbers, and every man wishes to have a Doctor's title; we should only send the aptest pupils, well prepared in the lower schools. This should be seen to by princes or the magistrates of the towns, and they should take care none but apt pupils be sent. But where the Holy Scriptures are not the rule, I advise no one to send his child. Everything must perish where God's word is not studied unceasingly; and so we see what manner of men there are now in the high schools, and all this is the fault of no one but of the Pope, the Bishops and the Prelates, to whom the welfare of the young has been entrusted. For the High Schools should train men simply to be of good understanding in the Scriptures, fit to become bishops and priests, and to stand at our head against heretics and the Devil and all the world. But where do we find this? I greatly fear the High Schools are nothing but great gates of hell, unless they diligently study the Holy Scriptures and teach them to the young people. . . .

ON CHRISTIAN LIBERTY

CHRISTIAN FAITH has appeared to many an easy thing; nay, not a few even reckon it among the social virtues, as it were; and this they do, because they have not made proof of it experimentally, and have never tasted of what efficacy it is. For it is not possible for any man to write well about it, or to understand well what is rightly written, who has not at some time tasted of its spirit, under the pressure of tribulation. While he who has tasted of it, even to a very small extent, can never write, speak, think, or hear about it sufficiently. For it is a living fountain, springing up unto eternal life, as Christ calls it in the 4th chapter of St. John.

Now, though I cannot boast of my abundance, and though I know how poorly I am furnished, yet I hope that, after having been vexed by various temptations, I have attained some little drop of faith, and that I can speak of this matter, if not with more elegance, certainly with more solidity than those literal and too subtle disputants who have hitherto discoursed upon it, without understanding their own words. That I may open, then, an easier way for the ignorant—for these alone I am trying to serve—I first lay down these two propositions, concerning spiritual liberty and servitude.

A Christian man is the most free lord of all, and subject to none; a Christian man is the most dutiful servant of all, and subject to every one.

Although these statements appear contradictory, yet when they are found to agree together, they will be highly serviceable to my purpose. They are both the statements of Paul himself, who says: "Though I be free from all men, yet have I made myself servant unto all," and: "Owe no man anything, but to love one another." Now love is by its own nature dutiful and obedient to the beloved object. Thus even Christ, though Lord of all things, was yet made of a woman; made under the law; at once free and a servant; at once in the form of God and in the form of a servant.

Let us examine the subject on a deep and less simple principle. Man is composed of a twofold nature, a spiritual and a bodily. As regards the spiritual nature, which they name the soul, he is called the spiritual, inward, new man; as regards the bodily nature, which they name the flesh, he is called the fleshly, outward, old man. The Apostle speaks of this: "Though our outward man perish, yet the inward man is renewed day by day." The result of this diversity is, that in the Scriptures opposing statements are made concerning the same man; the fact being that in the same man these two men are opposed to one another; the flesh lusting against the spirit, and the spirit against the flesh.

We first approach the subject of the inward man, that we may see by what means a man becomes justified, free, and a true Christian; that is, a spiritual, new, and inward man. It is certain that absolutely none among outward things, under whatever name they may be reckoned, has any weight in producing a state of justification and Christian liberty, nor, on the other hand, an unjustified state and one of slavery. This can be shown by an easy course of argument.

What can it profit the soul, that the body should be in good condition, free, and full of life; that it should eat, drink, and act according to its pleasure; when even the most impious slaves of every kind of vice are prosperous in these matters? Again, what harm can ill-health, bondage, hunger, thirst, or any other outward evil, do to the soul, when even the most pious of men, and the freest in the purity of their conscience, are harassed by these things? Neither of these states of things has to do with the liberty or the slavery of the soul.

And so it will profit nothing that the body should be adorned with sacred vestments, or dwell in holy places, or be occupied in sacred offices, or pray, fast, and abstain from certain meats, or do whatever works can be done through the body and in the body. Something widely different will be necessary for the justification and liberty of the soul, since the things I have spoken of can be done by any impious person, and only hypocrites are produced by devotion to these things. On the other hand, it will not at all injure the soul that the body should be clothed in profane raiment, should dwell in profane places, should eat and drink in the ordinary fashion, should not pray aloud, and should leave undone all the things abovementioned, which may be done by hypocrites.

And, to cast everything aside, even speculations, meditations, and whatever things can be performed by the exertions of the soul itself, are of no profit. One thing, and one alone, is necessary for life, justification, and Christian liberty; and that is the most holy word of God, the Gospel of Christ, as He says: "I am the resurrection and the life; he that believeth in me shall not die eternally"; and also "If the Son shall make you free, ye shall be free indeed"; and "Man shall not live by bread alone, but by every word that proceedeth out of the mouth of God."

Let us therefore hold it for certain and firmly established, that the soul can do without everything, except the word of God, without which none at all of its wants are provided for. But, having the word, it is rich and wants for nothing; since that is the word of life, of truth, of light, of peace, of justification, of salvation, of joy, of liberty, of wisdom, of virtue, of grace, of glory, and of every good thing. It is on this account that the prophet in a whole psalm, and in many other places, sighs for and calls upon the word of God with so many groanings and words.

Again, there is no more cruel stroke of the wrath of God than when He sends a famine of hearing His words; just as there is no greater favour from Him than the sending forth of His word, as it is said: "He sent his word and healed them, and delivered them from their destructions." Christ was sent for no other office than that of the word, and the order of apostles, that of bishops, and that of the whole body of the clergy, have been called and instituted for no object but the ministry of the word.

But you will ask:—"What is this word, and by what means is it to be used, since there are so many words of God?" I answer, the Apostle Paul explains what it is, namely, the Gospel of God, concerning His son, incarnate, suffering, risen, and glorified through the Spirit, the sanctifier. To preach Christ is to feed the soul, to justify it, to set it free, and to save it, if it believes the preaching. For faith alone, and the efficacious use of the word of God, bring salvation. "If thou shalt confess with thy mouth the Lord Jesus, and shalt believe in thine heart that God hath raised him from the dead, thou shalt be saved." And again: "Christ is the end of the law for righteousness to every one that believeth"; and "The just shall live by faith." For the word of God cannot be received and honoured by any works, but by faith alone. Hence it is clear that, as the soul needs the word alone for life and justification, so it is justified by faith alone and not by any works. For if it could be justified by any other means, it would have no need of the word, nor consequently of faith.

But this faith cannot consist at all with works; that is, if you imagine that you can be justified by those works, whatever they are, along with it. For this would be to halt between two opinions, to worship Baal, and to kiss the hand to him, which is a very great iniquity, as Job says. Therefore, when you begin to believe, you learn at the same time that all that is in you is utterly guilty, sinful, and damnable; according to that saying: "All have sinned, and come short of the glory of God." And also: "There is none righteous, no, not one; they are all gone out of the way; they are together become unprofitable; there is none that doeth good, no, not one." When you have learnt this, you will know that Christ is necessary for you, since He has suffered and risen again for you, that, believing on Him, you might by this faith become another man, all your sins being remitted, and you being justified by the merits of another, namely, of Christ alone.

Since then this faith can reign only in the inward man, as it is said: "With the heart man believeth unto righteousness"; and since it alone justifies, it is evident that by no outward work of labour can the inward man be at all justified, made free, and saved; and that no works whatever have any relation to him. And so, on the other hand, it is solely by impiety and incredulity of heart that he becomes guilty, and a slave of sin, deserving condemnation; not by any outward sin or work. Therefore the first care of every Christian ought to be, to lay aside all reliance on works, and strengthen his faith alone more and more, and by it grow in the knowledge, not of works, but of Christ Jesus, who has suffered and risen again for him; as Peter teaches, when he makes no other work to be a Christian one. Thus Christ, when the Jews asked Him what they should do that they might work the works of God, rejected the multitude of works, with which He saw that they were puffed up, and commanded them one thing only, saying: "This is the work of God, that ye believe on him whom He hath sent, for him hath God the Father sealed."

Hence a right faith in Christ is an incomparable treasure, carrying with it universal salvation, and preserving from all evil, as it is said: "He that believeth not shall be damned." Isaiah, looking to this treasure, predicted: "The consumption decreed shall overflow with righteousness. For the Lord God of hosts shall make a consumption, even determined, in the midst of the land." As if he said:—"Faith, which is the brief and complete fulfilling of the law, will fill those who believe with such righteousness, that they will need nothing else for justification." Thus too Paul says: "For with the heart man believeth unto righteousness."

But you ask how it can be the fact that faith alone justifies, and affords without works so great a treasure of good things, when so many works, ceremonies, and laws are prescribed to us in the Scriptures. I answer: before all things bear in mind what I have said, that faith alone without works justifies, sets free, and saves, as I shall show more clearly below.

Meanwhile it is to be noted, that the whole Scripture of God is divided into two parts, precepts and promises. The precepts certainly teach us what is good, but what they teach is not forthwith done. For they show us what we ought to do, but do not give us the power to do it. They were ordained, however, for the purpose of showing man to himself; that through them he may learn his own impotence for good, and may despair of his own strength. For this reason they are called the Old Testament, and are so.

For example: "thou shalt not covet," is a precept by which we are all convicted of sin; since no man can help coveting, whatever efforts to the contrary he may make. In order therefore that he may fulfil the precept, and not covet, he is constrained to despair of himself, and to seek elsewhere and through another the help which he cannot find in himself; as it is said: "O Israel, thou hast destroyed thyself; but in me is thine help." Now what is done by this one precept, is done by all; for all are equally impossible of fulfilment by us.

Now when a man has through the precepts been taught his own impotence, and become anxious by what means he may satisfy the law—for the law must be satisfied, so that no jot or tittle of it may pass away; otherwise he must be hopelessly condemned—then, being truly humbled and brought to nothing in in his own eyes, he finds in himself no resource for justification and salvation.

Then comes in that other part of Scripture, the promises of God, which declare the glory of God, and say: "If you wish to fulfil the law, and, as the law requires, not to covet, lo! believe in Christ, in whom are promised to you grace, justification, peace, and liberty." All these things you shall have, if you believe, and shall be without them, if you do not believe. For what is impossible for you by all the works of the law, which are many and yet useless, you shall fulfil in an easy and summary way through faith; because God the Father has made everything to depend on faith, so that whosoever has it, has all things, and he who has it not, has nothing. "For God hath concluded them all in unbelief, that He might have mercy upon all." Thus the promises of God give that which the precepts exact, and fulfil what the law commands; so that all is of God alone, both the precepts and their fulfilment. He alone commands. He alone also fulfils. Hence the promises of God belong to the New Testament; nay, are the New Testament.

Now since these promises of God are words of holiness, truth, righteousness, liberty, and peace, and are full of universal goodness; the soul, which cleaves to them with a firm faith, is so united to them, nay, thoroughly absorbed by them, that it not only partakes in, but is penetrated and saturated by, all their virtue. For if the touch of Christ was healing how much more does that most tender spiritual touch, nay, absorption of the word, communicate to the soul all that belongs to the word. In this way, therefore, the soul, through faith alone, without works, is from the word of God justified, sanctified, endued with truth, peace, and liberty, and filled with every good thing, and is truly made the child of God; as it is said: "To them gave he power to become the sons of God, even to them that believe on his name."

From all this it is easy to understand why faith has such great power, and why no good works, nor even all good works put together, can compare with it; since no work can cleave to the word of God, or be in the soul. Faith alone and the word reign in it; and such as is the word, such is the soul made by it; just as iron exposed to fire glows like fire, on account of its union with the fire. It is clear then that to a Christian man his faith suffices for everything, and that he has no need of works for justification. But if he has no need of works, neither has he need of the law; and, if he has no need of the law, he is certainly free from the law, and the saying is true: "The law is not made for a righteous man." This is that Christian liberty, our faith, the effect of which is, not that we should be careless or lead a bad life, but that no one should need the law or works for justification and salvation.

Let us consider this as the first virtue of faith; and let us look also to the second. This also is an office of faith, that it honours with the utmost veneration and the highest reputation him in whom it believes, inasmuch as it holds him to be truthful and worthy of belief. For there is no honour like that reputation of truth and righteousness, with which we honour him, in whom we believe. What higher credit can we attribute to any one than truth and righteousness, and absolute goodness? On the other hand, it is the greatest insult to brand any one with the reputation of falsehood and unrighteousness, or to suspect him of these, as we do when we disbelieve him. . . .

Thus the soul, in firmly believing the promises of God, holds Him to be true and righteous; and it can attribute to God no higher glory than the credit of being so. The highest worship of God is to ascribe to Him truth, righteousness, and whatever qualities we must ascribe to one in whom we believe. In doing this the soul shows itself prepared to do His whole will; in doing this it hallows His name, and gives itself up to be dealt with as it may please God. For it cleaves to His promises, and never doubts that He is true, just, and wise, and will do, dispose, and provide for all things in the best way. Is not such a soul, in this its faith, most obedient to God in all things? What commandment does there remain which has not been amply fulfilled by such an obedience? What fulfilment can be more full than universal obedience? Now this is not accomplished by works, but by faith alone.

On the other hand, what greater rebellion, impiety, or insult to God can there be, than not to believe His promises? What else is this, than either to make God a liar, or to doubt His truth—that is, to attribute truth to ourselves, but to God falsehood and levity? In doing this, is not a man denying God and setting himself up as an idol in his own heart? What then can works, done in such a state of impiety, profit us, were they even angelic or apostolic works? Rightly hath God shut up all—not in wrath nor in lust—but in unbelief; in order that those who pretend that they are fulfilling the law by works of purity and benevolence (which are social and human virtues), may not presume that they will therefore be saved; but, being included in the sin of unbelief, may either seek mercy, or be justly condemned. . . .

The third incomparable grace of faith is this, that it unites the soul to Christ, as the wife to the husband; by which mystery, as the Apostle teaches, Christ and the soul are made one flesh. Now if they are one flesh, and if a true marriage—nay, by far the most perfect of all marriages—is accomplished between them (for human marriages are but feeble types of this one great marriage), then it follows that all they have becomes theirs in common, as well good things as evil things; so that whatsoever Christ possesses, that the believing soul may take to itself and boast of as its own, and whatever belongs to the soul, that Christ claims as his.

If we compare these possessions, we shall see how inestimable is the gain. Christ is full of grace, life, and salvation; the soul is full of sin, death, and condemnation. Let faith step in, and then sin, death, and hell will belong to Christ, and grace, life, and salvation to the soul. For, if he is a husband, he must needs take to himself that which is his wife's, and, at the same time, impart to his wife that which is his. For, in giving her his own body and himself, how can he but give her all that is his? And, in taking to himself the body of his wife, how can he but take to himself all that is hers?

In this is displayed the delightful sight, not only of communion, but of a prosperous warfare, of victory, salvation, and redemption. For since Christ is God and man, and is such a person as neither has sinned, nor dies, nor is condemned,—nay, cannot sin, die or be condemned; and since his righteousness, life, and salvation are invincible, eternal, and almighty; when, I say, such a person, by the wedding-ring of faith, takes a share in the sins, death, and hell of his wife, nay, makes them his own, and deals with them no otherwise than as if they were his, and as if he himself had sinned; and when he suffers, dies, and descends to hell, that he may overcome all things, since sin, death, and hell cannot swallow him up, they must needs be swallowed up by him in stupendous conflict. For his righteousness rises above the sins of all men; his life is more powerful than all death; his salvation is more unconquerable than all hell.

Thus the believing soul, by the pledge of its faith in Christ, becomes free from all sin, fearless of death, safe from hell, and endowed with the eternal righteousness, life, and salvation of its husband Christ. Thus he presents to himself a glorious bride, without spot or wrinkle, cleansing her with the washing of water by the word; that is, by faith in the word of life, righteousness, and salvation. Thus he betroths her unto himself "in faithfulness, in righteousness, and in judgment, and in lovingkindness, and in mercies. . . ."

From all this you will again understand, why so much importance is attributed to faith, so that it alone can fulfil the law, and justify without any works. For you see that the first commandment, which says, "Thou shalt worship one God only," is fulfilled by faith alone. If you were nothing but good works from the soles of your feet to the crown of your head, you would not be worshipping God, nor fulfilling the first commandment, since it is impossible to worship God, without ascribing to Him the glory of truth and of universal goodness, as it ought in truth to be ascribed. Now this is not done by works, but only by faith of heart. It is not by working, but by believing, that we glorify God and confess Him to be true. On this ground faith is the sole righteousness of a Christian man, and the fulfilling of all the commandments. For to him who fulfils the first, the task of fulfilling all the rest is easy.

Works, since they are irrational things, cannot glorify God; although they may be done to the glory of God, if faith be present. But at present we are enquiring, not into the quality of the works done, but into him who does them, who glorifies God, and brings forth good works. This is faith of heart, the head and the substance of all our righteousness. Hence that is a blind and perilous doctrine which teaches that the commandments are fulfilled by works. The commandments must have been fulfilled, previous to any good works, and good works follow their fulfilment, as we shall see. . . .

Let it suffice to say this concerning the inner man and its liberty, and concerning that righteousness of faith, which needs neither laws nor good works; nay, they are even hurtful to it, if any one pretends to be justified by them.

And now let us turn to the other part, to the outward man. Here we shall give an answer to all those who, taking offence at the word of faith and at what I have asserted, say: "If faith does everything, and by itself suffices for justification, why then are good works commanded? Are we then to take our ease and do no works, content with faith?" Not so, impious men, I reply; not so. That would indeed really be the case, if we were thoroughly and completely inner and spiritual persons; but that will not happen until the last day, when the dead shall be raised. As long as we live in the flesh, we are but beginning and making advances in that which shall be completed in a future life. On this account the Apostle calls that which we have in this life, the first-fruits of the Spirit. In future we shall have the tenths, and the fulness of the Spirit. To this part belongs the fact I have stated before, that the Christian is the servant of all and subject to all. For in that part in which he is free, he does no works, but in that in which he is a servant, he does all works. Let us see on what principle this is so.

Although, as I have said, inwardly, and according to the spirit, a man is amply enough justified by faith, having all that he requires to have, except that this very faith and abundance ought to increase from day to day, even till the future life; still he remains in this mortal life upon earth, in which it is necessary that he should rule his own body, and have intercourse with men. Here then works begin; here he must not take his ease; here he must give heed to exercise his body by fastings, watchings, labour, and other moderate discipline, so that it may be subdued to the spirit, and obey and conform itself to the inner man and faith, and not rebel against them nor hinder them, as is its nature to do if it is not kept under. For the inner man, being conformed to God, and created after the image of God through faith, rejoices and delights itself in Christ, in whom such blessings have been conferred on it; and hence has only this task before it, to serve God with joy and for nought in free love.

In doing this he offends that contrary will in his own flesh, which is striving to serve the world, and to seek its own gratification. This the spirit of faith cannot and will not bear; but applies itself with cheerfulness and zeal to keep it down and restrain it; as Paul says: "I delight in the law of God after the inward man; but I see another law in my members, warring against the law of my mind, and bringing me into captivity to the law of sin." And again: "I keep under my body, and bring it into subjection, lest that by any means, when I have preached to others, I myself should be a castaway." And: "They that are Christ's have crucified the flesh with the affections and lusts."

These works, however, must not be done with any notion that by them a man can be justified before God—for faith, which alone is righteousness before God, will not bear with this false notion—but solely with this purpose, that the body may be brought into subjection, and be purified from its evil lusts, so that our eyes may be turned only to purging away those lusts. For when the soul has been cleansed by faith and made to love God, it would have all things to be cleansed in like manner; and especially its own body, so that all things might unite with it in the love and praise of God. Thus it comes that, from the requirements of his own body, a man cannot take his ease, but is compelled on its account to do many good works, that he may bring it into subjection. Yet these works are not the means of his justification before God; he does them out of disinterested love to the service of God; looking to no other end than to do what is well-pleasing to Him whom he desires to obey most dutifully in all things.

On this principle every man may easily instruct himself in what measure, and with what distinctions, he ought to chasten his own body. He will fast, watch, and labour, just as much as he sees to suffice for keeping down the wantonness and concupiscence of the body. But those who pretend to be justified by works are looking, not to the mortification of their lusts, but only to the works themselves; thinking that, if they can accomplish as many works and as great ones as possible, all is well with them, and they are justified. Sometimes they even injure their brain, and extinguish nature, or at least make it useless. This is enormous folly, and ignorance of Christian life and faith, when a man seeks, without faith, to be justified and saved by works.

To make what we have said more easily understood, let us set it forth under a figure. The works of a Christian man, who is justified and saved by his faith out of the pure and unbought mercy of God, ought to be regarded in the same light as would have been those of Adam and Eve in Paradise, and of all their posterity, if they had not sinned. Of them it is said: "The Lord God took the man, and put him into the garden of Eden to dress it and to keep it." Now Adam had been created by God just and righteous, so that he could not have needed to be justified and made righteous by keeping the garden and working in it; but, that he might not be unemployed, God gave him the business of keeping and cultivating Paradise. These would have indeed been works of perfect freedom, being done for no object but that of pleasing God, and not in order to obtain justification, which he already had to the full, and which would have been innate in us all.

So it is with the works of a believer. Being by his faith replaced afresh in Paradise and created anew, he does not need works for his justification, but that he may not be idle, but may keep his own body and work upon it. His works are to be done freely, with the sole object of pleasing God. Only we are not yet fully created anew in perfect faith and love; these require to be increased, not however through works, but through themselves.

A bishop, when he consecrates a church, confirms children, or performs any other duty of his office, is not consecrated as bishop by these works; nay, unless he had been previously consecrated as bishop, not one of those works would have any validity; they would be foolish, childish, and ridiculous. Thus a Christian, being consecrated by his faith, does good works; but he is not by these works made a more sacred person, or more a Christian. That is the effect of faith alone; nay, unless he were previously a believer and a Christian, none of his works would have any value at all, they would really be impious and damnable sins.

True then are these two sayings: Good works do not make a good man, but a good man does good works. Bad works do not make a bad man, but a bad man does bad works. Thus it is always necessary that the substance or person should be good before any good works can be done, and that good works should follow and proceed from a good person. As Christ says: "A good tree cannot bring forth evil fruit, neither can a corrupt tree bring forth good fruit."

Now it is clear that the fruit does not bear the tree, nor does the tree grow on the fruit; but, on the contrary, the trees bear the fruit and the fruit grows on the trees.

As then trees must exist before their fruit, and as the fruit does not make the tree either good or bad, but, on the contrary, a tree of either kind produces fruit of the same kind; so must first the person of the man be good or bad, before he can do either a good or a bad work; and his works do not make him bad or good, but he himself makes his works either bad or good.

We may see the same thing in all handicrafts. A bad or good house does not make a bad or good builder, but a good or bad builder makes a good or bad house. And in general, no work makes the workman such as it is itself; but the workman makes the work such as he is himself. Such is the case too with the works of men. Such as the man himself is, whether in faith or in unbelief, such is his work; good if it be done in faith, bad if in unbelief. But the converse is not true—that, such as the work is, such the man becomes in faith or in unbelief. For as works do not make a believing man, so neither do they make a justified man; but faith, as it makes a man a believer and justified, so also it makes his works good.

Since, then, works justify no man, but a man must be justified before he can do any good work, it is most evident that it is faith alone which, by the mere mercy of God through Christ, and by means of His word, can worthily and sufficiently justify and save the person; and that a Christian man needs no work, no law, for his salvation; for by faith he is free from all law, and in perfect freedom does gratuitously all that he does, seeking nothing either of profit or of salvation—since by the grace of God he is already saved and rich in all things through his faith—but solely that which is well-pleasing to God.

So too no good work can profit an unbeliever to justification and salvation; and on the other hand no evil work makes him an evil and condemned person, but that unbelief, which makes the person and the tree bad, makes his works evil and condemned. Wherefore, when any man is made good or bad, this does not arise from his works, but from his faith or unbelief, as the wise man says: "The beginning of sin is to fall away from God"; that is, not to believe, Paul says: "He that cometh to God must believe"; and Christ says the same thing: "Either make the tree good, and his fruit good; or else make the tree corrupt, and his fruit corrupt." As much as to say: He who wishes to have good fruit, will begin with the tree, and plant a good one; even so he who wishes to do good works must begin, not by working, but by believing, since it is this which makes the person good. For nothing makes the person good but faith, nor bad but unbelief.

It is certainly true that, in the sight of men, a man becomes good or evil by his works; but here "becoming" means that it is thus shown and recognized who is good or evil; as Christ says: "By their fruits ye shall know them." But all this stops at appearances and externals; and in this matter very many deceive themselves, when they presume to write and teach that we are to be justified by good works, and meanwhile make no mention even of faith, walking in their own ways, ever deceived and deceiving, going from bad to worse, blind leaders of the blind, wearying themselves with many works, and yet never attaining to true righteousness; of whom Paul says: "Having a form of godliness, but denying the power thereof; ever learning, and never able to come to the knowledge of the truth. . . ."

Here is the truly Christian life; here is faith really working by love; when a man applies himself with joy and love to the works of that freest servitude, in which he serves others voluntarily and for nought; himself abundantly satisfied in the fulness and riches of his own faith. . . .

Thus from faith flow forth love and joy in the Lord, and from love a cheerful, willing, free spirit, disposed to serve our neighbour voluntarily, without taking any account of gratitude or ingratitude, praise or blame, gain or loss. Its object is not to lay men under obligations, nor does it distinguish between friends and enemies, or look to gratitude or ingratitude, but most freely and willingly spends itself and its goods, whether it loses them through ingratitude, or gains good will. For thus did its Father, distributing all things to all men abundantly and freely; making His sun to rise upon the just and the unjust. Thus too the child does and endures nothing, except from the free joy with which it delights through Christ in God, the giver of such great gifts. . . .

Finally, for the sake of those to whom nothing can be stated so well but that they misunderstand and distort it, we must add a word, in case they can understand even that. There are very many persons, who, when they hear of this liberty of faith, straightway turn it into an occasion of licence. They think that everything is now lawful for them, and do not choose to show themselves free men and Christians in any other way than by their contempt and reprehension of ceremonies, of traditions, of human laws; as if they were Christians merely because they refuse to fast on stated days, or eat flesh when others fast, or omit the customary prayers; scoffing at the precepts of men, but utterly passing over all the rest that belongs to the Christian religion. On the other hand, they are most pertinaciously resisted by those who strive after salvation solely by their observance of and reverence for ceremonies; as if they would be saved merely because they fast on stated days, or abstain from flesh, or make formal prayers; talking loudly of the precepts of the Church and of the Fathers, and not caring a straw about those things which belong to our genuine faith. Both these parties are plainly culpable, in that, while they neglect matters which are of weight and necessary for salvation, they contend noisily about such as are without weight and not necessary.

How much more rightly does the Apostle Paul teach us to walk in the middle path, condemning either extreme, and saying: "Let not him that eateth despise him that eateth not; and let not him which eateth not judge him that eateth." You see here how the Apostle blames those who, not from religious feeling, but in mere contempt, neglect and rail at ceremonial observances; and teaches them not to despise, since this "knowledge puffeth up." Again he teaches the pertinacious upholders of these things not to judge their opponents. For neither party observes towards the other that charity which edifieth. In this matter we must listen to Scripture, which teaches us to turn aside neither to the right hand nor to the left, but to follow those right precepts of the Lord which rejoice the heart. For just as a man is not righteous, merely because he serves and devotes himself to works and ceremonial rites, so neither will he be accounted righteous, merely because he neglects and despises them.

It is not from works that we are set free by the faith of Christ, but from the belief in works, that is, from foolishly presuming to seek justification through works. Faith redeems our consciences, makes them upright and preserves them, since by it we recognise the truth that justification does not depend on our works, although good works neither can nor ought to be wanting to it; just as we cannot exist without food and drink and all the functions of this mortal body. Still it is not on them that our justification is based, but on faith; and yet they ought not on that account to be despised or neglected. Thus in this world we are compelled by the needs of this bodily life; but we are not hereby justified. "My kingdom is not hence, nor of this world," says Christ; but He does not say: "My kingdom is not here, nor in this world." Paul too says: "Though we walk in the flesh, we do not war after the flesh"; and: "The life which I now live in the flesh I live by the faith of the Son of God." Thus our doings, life, and being, in works and ceremonies, are done from the necessities of this life, and with the motive of governing our bodies; but yet we are not justified by these things, but by the faith of the Son of God. . . .

Since, then, we cannot live in this world without ceremonies and works; since the hot and inexperienced period of youth has need of being restrained and protected by such bonds; and since every one is bound to keep under his own body by attention to these things; therefore the minister of Christ must be prudent and faithful in so ruling and teaching the people of Christ in all these matters that no root of bitterness may spring up among them, and so many be defiled, as Paul warned the Hebrews; that is, that they may not lose the faith, and begin to be defiled by a belief in works, as the means of justification. This is a thing which easily happens, and defiles very many, unless faith be constantly inculcated along with works. It is impossible to avoid this evil, when faith is passed over in silence, and only the ordinances of men are taught, as has been done hitherto by the pestilent, impious, and soul-destroying traditions of our pontiffs, and opinions of our theologians. An infinite number of souls have been drawn down to hell by these snares, so that you may recognise the work of Antichrist. . . .

Hence in the Christian life ceremonies are to be not otherwise looked upon than builders and workmen look upon those preparations for building or working which are not made with any view of being permanent or anything in themselves, but only because without them there could be no building and no work. When the structure is completed, they are laid aside. Here you see that we do not contemn these preparations, but set the highest value on them; a belief in them we do contemn, because no one thinks that they constitute a real and permanent structure. If anyone were so manifestly out of his senses as to have no other object in life but that of setting up these preparations with all possible expense, diligence, and perseverance, while he never thought of the structure itself, but pleased himself and made his boast of these useless preparations and props; should we not all pity his madness, and think that, at the cost thus thrown away, some great building might have been raised?

JOHN CALVIN

JOHN CALVIN (1509–64) was a Frenchman, born in Picardy and reared by aristocratic foster parents. He studied scholastic philosophy in Paris, and later law at Bourges and Orleans, where he came under the influence of Protestant teachers. Returning to Paris, he studied the classics, Hebrew, and the Greek Testament.

By 1534 Calvin's heretical opinions were conspicuous enough to make his leaving France advisable. In 1536 he stopped in Geneva, which was already evangelical. His moralism was so extreme that he was expelled in 1538 by the town council. Calvin's reputation grew, however, and in 1541 he was recalled to Geneva to take charge of the troubled affairs of the city. He immediately instituted the theocracy which in a short time made of Geneva the center of the Protestant world. The austere puritanical regime attempted to regulate minutely the daily lives of the citizens; the basis of Calvinist rule was literal interpretation of the Bible, the power of decision being delegated to clerical authority and elders chosen by the town council. The system was copied by John Knox in Scotland and has exerted great influence in that country and North America.

The ideal which Calvin attempted to impose on Geneva was uncompromisingly otherworldly. "There is no medium between these two extremes, either the earth must become vile in our estimation, or it must retain our immoderate love. Wherefore if we have any concern about eternity, we must use our most diligent efforts to extricate ourselves from these fetters." Such a regime had its limitations, of course. "As I see that we cannot forbid men all diversions," Calvin admitted, "I confine myself to those that are really bad."

In contrast with the mystical Luther, Calvin was legalistic and rationalistic. It was Calvin rather than Luther who institutionalized the Reformation, and his theocracy contrasts starkly with Luther's pietistic version of the religious life.

Calvin's major work is the *Institutes of the Christian Religion* (1536, Basel); it came to occupy a place in informed Protestant opinion similar to that of the *Summa* within the Catholic world.

The following translation is by John Allen (Philadelphia, Presbyterian Board of Christian Education, 1928).

INSTITUTES OF THE CHRISTIAN RELIGION

GOD'S PRESERVATION AND SUPPORT OF THE WORLD BY HIS POWER, AND HIS GOVERNMENT OF EVERY PART OF IT BY HIS PROVIDENCE

TO REPRESENT GOD as a Creator only for a moment, who entirely finished all his work at once, were frigid and jejune; and in this it behoves us especially to differ from the heathen, that the presence of the Divine power may appear to us no less in the perpetual state of the world than in its first origin. For although the minds even of impious men, by the mere contemplation of earth and heaven, are constrained to rise to the Creator, yet faith has a way peculiar to itself to assign to God the whole praise of creation. To which purpose is that assertion of an Apostle before cited, that it is only "through faith that we understand the worlds were framed by the word of God"; because, unless we proceed to his providence, we have no correct conception of the meaning of this article, "that God is the Creator"; however we may appear to comprehend it in our minds, and to confess it with our tongues. The carnal sense, when it has once viewed the power of God in the creation, stops there; and when it proceeds the furthest, it only examines and considers the wisdom, and power, and goodness, of the Author in producing such a work, which spontaneously present themselves to the view even of those who are unwilling to observe them. In the next place, it conceives of some general operation of God in preserving and governing it, on which the power of motion depends. Lastly, it supposes that the vigour originally infused by God into all things is sufficient for their sustentation. But faith ought to penetrate further. When it has learned that he is the Creator of all things, it should immediately conclude that he is also their perpetual governor and preserver; and that not by a certain universal motion, actuating the whole machine of the world, and all its respective parts, but by a particular providence sustaining, nourishing, and providing for every thing which he has made. . . .

But as we know that the world was made chiefly for the sake of mankind, we must also observe this end in the government of it. The Prophet Jeremiah exclaims, "I know that the way of man is not in himself: it is not in man that walketh to direct his steps." And Solomon: "Man's goings are of the Lord: how can a man then understand his own way?" Now, let them say that man is actuated by God according to the bias of his nature, but that he directs that influence according to his own pleasure. If this could be asserted with truth, man would have the free choice of his own ways. That, perhaps, they will deny, because he can do nothing independently of the power of God. But since it is evident that both the Prophet and Solomon ascribe to God choice and appointment, as well as power, this by no means extricates them from the difficulty. But Solomon, in another place, beautifully reproves this temerity of men, who predetermine on an end for themselves, without regard to God, as though they were not led by his hand: "The preparation of the heart in man," says he, "and the answer of the tongue, is from the Lord." It is, indeed, a ridiculous madness for miserable men to resolve on undertaking any work independently of God, whilst they cannot even speak a word but what he chooses. Moreover, the Scripture, more fully to express that nothing is transacted in the world but according to his destination, shows that those things are subject to him which appear most fortuitous. For what would you be more ready to attribute to chance, than when a limb broken off from a tree kills a passing traveller? But very different is the decision of the Lord, who acknowledges that he has delivered him into the hand of the slayer. Who, likewise, does not leave lots to the blindness of fortune? Yet the Lord leaves them not, but claims the disposal of them himself. He teaches us that it is not by any power of their own that lots are cast into the lap and drawn out; but the only thing which could be ascribed to chance, he declares to belong to himself. To the same purpose is another passage from Solomon: "The poor and the deceitful man meet together: the Lord enlighteneth the eyes of them both." For although the poor and the rich are blended together in the world, yet, as their respective conditions are assigned to them by Divine appointment, he suggests that God, who enlightens all, is not blind, and thus exhorts the poor to patience; because those who are discontented with their lot, are endeavouring to shake off the burden imposed on them by God. Thus also another Prophet rebukes profane persons, who attribute it to human industry, or to fortune, that some men remain in obscurity, and others rise to honours: "Promotion cometh neither from the east, nor from the west, nor from the south. But God is the Judge; he putteth down one, and setteth up another." Since God cannot divest himself of the office of a judge, hence he reasons, that it is from the secret counsel of God, that some rise to promotion, and others remain in contempt. . . .

THE PROPER APPLICATION OF THIS DOCTRINE TO RENDER IT USEFUL TO US

. . . Those who have learned this modesty, will neither murmur against God on account of past adversities, nor charge him with the guilt of their crimes, like Agamemnon, in Homer, who says, "The blame belongs not to me, but to Jupiter and Fate." Nor will they, as if hurried away by the Fates, under the influence of despair, put an end to their own lives, like the young man whom Plautus introduces as saying, "The condition of our affairs is inconstant; men are governed by the caprice of the Fates; I will betake myself to a precipice, and there destroy my life and every thing at once." Nor will they excuse their flagitious actions by ascribing them to God, after the example of another young man introduced by the same poet, who says, "God was the cause: I believe it was the Divine will. For had it not been so, I know it would not have happened." But they will rather search the Scripture, to learn what is pleasing to God, that by the guidance of the Spirit they may strive to attain it; and at the same time, being prepared to follow God whithersoever he calls them, they will exhibit proofs in their conduct that nothing is more useful than a knowledge of this doctrine. Some profane men foolishly raise such a tumult with their absurdities, as almost, according to a common expression, to confound heaven and earth together. They argue in this manner: If God has fixed the moment of our death, we cannot avoid it; therefore all caution against it will be but lost labour. One man dares not venture himself in a way which he hears is dangerous, lest he should be assassinated by robbers; another sends for physicians, and wearies himself with medicines, to preserve his life; another abstains from the grosser kinds of food, lest he should injure his valetudinary constitution; another dreads to inhabit a ruinous house; and men in general exert all their faculties in devising and executing methods by which they may attain the object of their desires. Now, either all these things are vain remedies employed to correct the will of God, or life and death, health and disease, peace and war, and other things which, according to their desires or aversions, men industriously study to obtain or to avoid, are not determined by his certain decree. Moreover they conclude, that the prayers of the faithful are not only superfluous, but perverse, which contain petitions that the Lord will provide for those things which he has already decreed from eternity. In short, they supersede all deliberations respecting futurity, as opposed to the providence of God, who, without consulting men, has decreed whatever he pleased. And what has already happened they impute to the Divine providence in such a manner as to overlook the person, who is known to have committed any particular act. Has an assassin murdered a worthy citizen? they say he has executed the counsel of God. Has any one been guilty of theft or fornication? because he has done what was foreseen and ordained by the Lord, he is the minister of his providence. Has a son, neglecting all remedies, carelessly waited the death of his father? it was impossible for him to resist God, who had decreed this event from eternity. Thus by these persons all crimes are denominated virtues, because they are subservient to the ordination of God. . . .

The same persons inconsiderately and erroneously ascribe all past events to the absolute providence of God. For since all things which come to pass are dependent upon it, therefore, say they, neither thefts, nor adulteries, nor homicides, are perpetrated without the intervention of the Divine will. Why, therefore, they ask, shall a thief be punished for having pillaged him whom it has pleased the Lord to chastise with poverty? Why shall a homicide be punished for having slain him whose life the Lord had terminated? If all such characters are subservient to the Divine will, why shall they be punished? But I deny that they serve the will of God. For we cannot say, that he who is influenced by a wicked heart, acts in obedience to the commands of God, while he is only gratifying his own malignant passion. That man obeys God, who, being instructed in his will, hastens whither God calls him. Where can we learn his

will, but in his word? Therefore in our actions we ought to regard the will of
God, which is declared in his word. God only requires of us conformity to his
precepts. If we do any thing contrary to them, it is not obedience, but con-
tumacy and transgression. But it is said, if he would not permit it, we should
not do it. This I grant. But do we perform evil actions with the design of
pleasing him? He gives us no such command. We precipitate ourselves into
them, not considering what is his will, but inflamed with the violence of our
passions, so that we deliberately strive to oppose him. In this manner even by
criminal actions we subserve his righteous ordination; because, in the infinite
greatness of his wisdom, he well knows how to use evil instruments for the
accomplishment of good purposes. . . .

MAN, IN HIS PRESENT STATE DESPOILED OF FREEDOM OF WILL, AND SUB-
JECTED TO A MISERABLE SLAVERY

Since we have seen that the domination of sin, from the time of its subjuga-
tion of the first man, not only extends over the whole race, but also exclusively
possesses every soul, it now remains to be more closely investigated, whether we
are despoiled of all freedom, and, if any particle of it yet remain, how far its
power extends. But, that we may the more easily discover the truth of this
question, I will first set up by the way a mark, by which our whole course
must be regulated. The best method of guarding against error is to consider
the dangers which threaten us on every side. For when man is declared to be
destitute of all rectitude, he immediately makes it an occasion of slothfulness;
because he is said to have no power of himself for the pursuit of righteousness,
he totally neglects it, as though it did not at all concern him. On the other
hand, he cannot arrogate any thing to himself, be it ever so little, without God
being robbed of his honour, and himself being endangered by presumptuous
temerity. Therefore, to avoid striking on either of these rocks, this will be the
course to be pursued—that man, being taught that he has nothing good left
in his possession, and being surrounded on every side with the most miserable
necessity, should, nevertheless, be instructed to aspire to the good of which he
is destitute, and to the liberty of which he is deprived; and should be roused
from indolence with more earnestness, than if he were supposed to be possessed of the greatest strength. The necessity of the latter is obvious to every
one. The former, I perceive, is doubted by more than it ought to be. For this
being placed beyond all controversy, that man must not be deprived of any
thing that properly belongs to him, it ought also to be manifest how important
it is that he should be prevented from false boasting. For if he was not even
then permitted to glory in himself, when by the Divine beneficence he was
decorated with the noblest ornaments, how much ought he now to be hum-

bled, when, on account of his ingratitude, he has been hurled from the summit of glory to the abyss of ignominy! At that time, I say, when he was exalted to the most honourable eminence, the Scripture attributes nothing to him, but that he was created after the image of God; which certainly implies that his happiness consisted not in any goodness of his own, but in a participation of God. What, then, remains for him now, deprived of all glory, but that he acknowledge God, to whose beneficence he could not be thankful, when he abounded in the riches of his favour? and that he now, at least, by a confession of his poverty, glorify him, whom he glorified not by an acknowledgment of his blessings? It is also no less conducive to our interests than to the Divine glory, that all the praise of wisdom and strength be taken away from us; so that they join sacrilege to our fall, who ascribe to us any thing more than truly belongs to us. For what else is the consequence, when we are taught to contend in our own strength, but that we are lifted into the air on a reed, which being soon broken, we fall to the ground. Though our strength is placed in too favourable a point of view, when it is compared to a reed. For it is nothing but smoke, whatever vain men have imagined and pretended concerning it. Wherefore it is not without reason, that that remarkable sentence is so frequently repeated by Augustine, that free will is rather overthrown than established even by its own advocates. It was necessary to premise these things for the sake of some, who, when they hear that human power is completely subverted in order that the power of God may be established in man, inveterately hate this whole argument, as dangerous and unprofitable; which yet appears to be highly useful to us, and essential to true religion. . . .

This being admitted will place it beyond all doubt, that man is not possessed of free will for good works, unless he be assisted by grace, and that special grace which is bestowed on the elect alone in regeneration. For I stop not to notice those fanatics, who pretend that grace is offered equally and promiscuously to all. But it does not yet appear, whether he is altogether deprived of power to do good, or whether he yet possesses some power, though small and feeble; which of itself can do nothing, but by the assistance of grace does also perform its part. Lombard, in order to establish this notion, informs us that two sorts of grace are necessary to qualify us for the performance of good works. One he calls operative, by which we efficaciously will what is good; the other cooperative, which attends as auxiliary to a good will. This division I dislike, because, while he attributes an efficacious desire of what is good to the grace of God, he insinuates that man has of his own nature antecedent, though ineffectual, desires after what is good; as Bernard asserts that a good will is the work of God, but yet allows that man is self-impelled to desire such a good will. But this is very remote from the meaning of Augustine, from whom, however,

Lombard would be thought to have borrowed this division. The second part of it offends me by its ambiguity, which has produced a very erroneous interpretation. For they have supposed that we cooperate with the second sort of Divine grace, because we have it in our power either to frustrate the first sort by rejecting it, or to confirm it by our obedience to it. The author of the treatise "On the Vocation of the Gentiles" expresses it thus—that those who have the use of reason and judgment are at liberty to depart from grace, that they may be rewarded for not having departed, and that what is impossible without the cooperation of the Spirit, may be imputed to their merits, by whose will it might have been prevented. These two things I have thought proper to notice as I proceed, that the reader may perceive how much I dissent from the sounder schoolmen. For I differ considerably more from the later sophists, as they have departed much further from the judgment of antiquity. However, we understand from this division, in what sense they have ascribed free will to man. For Lombard at length pronounces, that we are not therefore possessed of free will, because we have an equal power to do or to think either good or evil, but only because we are free from constraint. And this liberty is not diminished, although we are corrupt, and the slaves of sin, and capable of doing nothing but sin.

Then man will be said to possess free will in this sense, not that he has an equally free election of good and evil, but because he does evil voluntarily, and not by constraint. That, indeed, is very true; but what end could it answer to decorate a thing so diminutive with a title so superb? Egregious liberty indeed, if man be not compelled to serve sin, but yet is such a willing slave, that his will is held in bondage by the fetters of sin. I really abominate contentions about words, which disturb the Church without producing any good effect; but I think that we ought religiously to avoid words which signify any absurdity, particularly when they lead to a pernicious error. How few are there, pray, who, when they hear free will attributed to man, do not immediately conceive, that he has the sovereignty over his own mind and will, and is able by his innate power to incline himself to whatever he pleases? But it will be said, all danger from these expressions will be removed, if the people are carefully apprized of their signification. But on the contrary, the human mind is naturally so prone to falsehood, that it will sooner imbibe error from one single expression, than truth from a prolix oration; of which we have a more certain experiment than could be wished in this very word. For neglecting that explanation of the fathers, almost all their successors have been drawn into a fatal self-confidence, by adhering to the original and proper signification of the word. . . .

But I am obliged to repeat here, what I premised in the beginning of this chapter—that he who feels the most consternation, from a consciousness of his own calamity, poverty, nakedness, and ignominy, has made the greatest proficiency in the knowledge of himself. For there is no danger that man will divest himself of too much, provided he learns that what is wanting in him may be recovered in God. But he cannot assume to himself even the least particle beyond his just right, without ruining himself with vain confidence, and incurring the guilt of enormous sacrilege, by transferring to himself the honour which belongs to God. And whenever our minds are pestered with this cupidity, to desire to have something of our own, which may reside in ourselves rather than in God, we may know that this idea is suggested by the same counsellor, who excited in our first parents the desire of resembling "gods, knowing good and evil." . . .

ETERNAL ELECTION, OR GOD'S PREDESTINATION OF SOME TO SALVATION, AND OF OTHERS TO DESTRUCTION

The covenant of life not being equally preached to all, and among those to whom it is preached not always finding the same reception, this diversity discovers the wonderful depth of the Divine judgment. Nor is it to be doubted that this variety also follows, subject to the decision of God's eternal election. If it be evidently the result of the Divine will, that salvation is freely offered to some, and others are prevented from attaining it,—this immediately gives rise to important and difficult questions, which are incapable of any other explication, than by the establishment of pious minds in what ought to be received concerning election and predestination—a question, in the opinion of many, full of perplexity; for they consider nothing more unreasonable, than that, of the common mass of mankind, some should be predestinated to salvation, and others to destruction. But how unreasonably they perplex themselves will afterwards appear from the sequel of our discourse. Besides, the very obscurity which excites such dread, not only displays the utility of this doctrine, but shows it to be productive of the most delightful benefit. We shall never be clearly convinced as we ought to be, that our salvation flows from the fountain of God's free mercy, till we are acquainted with his eternal election, which illustrates the grace of God by this comparison, that he adopts not all promiscuously to the hope of salvation, but gives to some what he refuses to others. Ignorance of this principle evidently detracts from the Divine glory, and diminishes real humility. But according to Paul, what is so necessary to be known, never can be known, unless God, without any regard to works, chooses those whom he has decreed. "At this present time also, there is a remnant according to the election of grace. And if by grace, then it is no more of works; otherwise, grace is no more grace. But if it be of works, then it is no more grace; otherwise, work is no more work." If we need to be recalled to the origin of election, to prove that we obtain salvation from no other source than the mere goodness of God, they who desire to extinguish this principle, do all they can to obscure what ought to be magnificently and loudly celebrated, and to pluck humility by the roots. In ascribing the salvation of the remnant of the people to the election of grace, Paul clearly testifies, that it is then only known that God saves whom he will of his mere good pleasure, and does not dispense a reward to which there can be no claim. They who shut the gates to prevent any one from presuming to approach and taste this doctrine, do no less injury to man than to God; for nothing else will be sufficient to produce in us suitable humility, or to impress us with a due sense of our great obligations to God. Nor is there any other basis for solid confidence, even according to the authority of Christ, who, to deliver us from all fear, and render us invincible amidst so many dangers, snares, and deadly conflicts, promises to preserve in safety all whom the Father has committed to his care. Whence we infer, that they who know not themselves to be God's peculiar people will be tortured with continual anxiety; and therefore, that the interest of all believers, as well as their own, is very badly consulted by those who, blind to the three advantages we have remarked, would wholly remove the foundation of our salvation. And hence the Church rises to our view, which otherwise, as Bernard justly observes, could neither be discovered nor recognized among creatures, being in two respects wonderfully concealed in the bosom of a blessed predestination, and in the mass of a miserable damnation. But before I enter on the subject itself, I must address some preliminary observations to two sorts of persons. The discussion of predestination—a subject of itself rather intricate—is made very perplexed, and therefore dangerous, by human curiosity, which no barriers can restrain from wandering into forbidden labyrinths, and soaring beyond its sphere, as if determined to leave none of the Divine secrets unscrutinized or unexplored. As we see multitudes every where guilty of this arrogance and presumption, and among them some who are not censurable in other respects, it is proper to admonish them of the bounds of their duty on this subject. First, then, let them remember that when they inquire into predestination, they penetrate the inmost recesses of Divine wisdom, where the careless and confident intruder will obtain no satisfaction to his curiosity, but will enter a labyrinth from which he will find no way to depart. For it is unreasonable that man should scrutinize with impunity those things which the Lord has determined to be hidden in himself; and investigate, even from eternity, that sublimity of wisdom which God would have us to adore and not comprehend,

to promote our admiration of his glory. The secrets of his will which he determined to reveal to us, he discovers in his word; and these are all that he
foresaw would concern us or conduce to our advantage. . . .

Predestination, by which God adopts some to the hope of life, and adjudges
others to eternal death, no one, desirous of the credit of piety, dares absolutely
to deny. But it is involved in many cavils, especially by those who make foreknowledge the cause of it. We maintain, that both belong to God; but it is
preposterous to represent one as dependent on the other. When we attribute
foreknowledge to God, we mean that all things have ever been, and perpetually remain, before his eyes, so that to his knowledge nothing is future or past,
but all things are present; and present in such a manner, that he does not
merely conceive of them from ideas formed in his mind, as things remembered by us appear present to our minds, but really beholds and sees them as
if actually placed before him. And this foreknowledge extends to the whole
world, and to all the creatures. Predestination we call the eternal decree of
God, by which he has determined in himself, what he would have to become
of every individual of mankind. For they are not all created with a similar
destiny; but eternal life is foreordained for some, and eternal damnation for
others. Every man, therefore, being created for one or the other of these ends,
we say, he is predestinated either to life or to death. This God has not only
testified in particular persons, but has given a specimen of it in the whole
posterity of Abraham, which should evidently show the future condition of
every nation to depend upon his decision. . . .

THE TRUE CHURCH AND THE NECESSITY OF OUR UNION WITH HER, BEING THE MOTHER OF ALL THE PIOUS

. . . Here we must regard both the secret election of God, and his internal
vocation; because he alone "knoweth them that are his"; and keeps them enclosed under his "seal," to use the expression of Paul; except that they bear his
impression, by which they may be distinguished from the reprobate. But
because a small and contemptible number is concealed among a vast multitude,
and a few grains of wheat are covered with a heap of chaff, we must leave to
God alone the knowledge of his Church whose foundation is his secret election.
Nor is it sufficient to include in our thoughts and minds the whole multitude
of the elect, unless we conceive of such a unity of the Church, into which we
know ourselves to be truly ingrafted. For unless we are united with all the
other members under Christ our Head, we can have no hope of the future
inheritance. Therefore the Church is called *Catholic,* or universal; because
there could not be two or three churches, without Christ being divided, which
is impossible. But all the elect of God are so connected with each other in Christ,

that as they depend upon one head, so they grow up together as into one body, compacted together like members of the same body; being made truly one, as living by one faith, hope, and charity, through the same Divine Spirit, being called not only to the same inheritance of eternal life, but also to a participation of one God and Christ. Therefore, though the melancholy desolation which surrounds us, seems to proclaim that there is nothing left of the Church, let us remember that the death of Christ is fruitful, and that God wonderfully preserves his Church as it were in hiding-places; according to what he said to Elijah: "I have reserved to myself seven thousand men, who have not bowed the knee to Baal."

This article of the creed, however, relates in some measure to the external Church, that every one of us may maintain a brotherly agreement with all the children of God, may pay due deference to the authority of the Church, and, in a word, may conduct himself as one of the flock. Therefore we add *The Communion of Saints*—a clause which, though generally omitted by the ancients, ought not to be neglected, because it excellently expresses the character of the Church; as though it had been said that the saints are united in the fellowship of Christ on this condition, that whatever benefits God confers upon them, they should mutually communicate to each other. This destroys not the diversity of grace, for we know that the gifts of the Spirit are variously distributed; nor does it disturb the order of civil polity, which secures to every individual the exclusive enjoyment of his property, as it is necessary for the preservation of the peace of society that men should have peculiar and distinct possessions. . . .

Here are three things, therefore, worthy of our observation. First, that whatever holiness may distinguish the children of God, yet such is their condition as long as they inhabit a mortal body, that they cannot stand before God without remission of sins. Secondly, that this benefit belongs to the Church; so that we cannot enjoy it unless we continue in its communion. Thirdly, that it is dispensed to us by the ministers and pastors of the Church, either in the preaching of the gospel, or in the administration of the sacraments; and that this is the principal exercise of the power of the keys, which the Lord has conferred on the society of believers. Let every one of us, therefore, consider it as his duty, not to seek remission of sins any where but where the Lord has placed it. Of public reconciliation, which is a branch of discipline, we shall speak in its proper place. . . .

ON CIVIL GOVERNMENT

Having already stated that man is the subject of two kinds of government, and having sufficiently discussed that which is situated in the soul, or the inner man, and relates to eternal life,—we are, in this chapter, to say something of the other kind, which relates to civil justice, and the regulation of the external conduct. For, though the nature of this argument seems to have no connection with the spiritual doctrine of faith which I have undertaken to discuss, the sequel will show that I have sufficient reason for connecting them together, and, indeed, that necessity obliges me to it; especially since, on the one hand, infatuated and barbarous men madly endeavour to subvert this ordinance established by God; and, on the other hand, the flatterers of princes, extolling their power beyond all just bounds, hesitate not to oppose it to the authority of God himself. Unless both these errors be resisted, the purity of the faith will be destroyed. Besides, it is of no small importance for us to know what benevolent provision God has made for mankind in this instance, that we may be stimulated by a greater degree of pious zeal to testify our gratitude. In the first place, before we enter on the subject itself, it is necessary for us to recur to the distinction which we have already established, lest we fall into an error very common in the world, and injudiciously confound together these two things, the nature of which is altogether different. For some men when they hear that the gospel promises a liberty which acknowledges no king or magistrate among men, but submits to Christ alone, think they can enjoy no advantage of their liberty, while they see any power exalted above them. They imagine, therefore, that nothing will prosper, unless the whole world be modelled in a new form, without any tribunals, or laws, or magistrates, or any thing of a similar kind, which they consider injurious to their liberty. But he who knows how to distinguish between the body and the soul, between this present transitory life and the future eternal one, will find no difficulty in understanding, that the spiritual kingdom of Christ and civil government are things very different and remote from each other. Since it is a Jewish folly, therefore, to seek and include the kingdom of Christ under the elements of this world, let us, on the contrary, considering what the Scripture clearly inculcates, that the benefit which is received from the grace of Christ is spiritual; let us, I say, remember to confine within its proper limits all this liberty which is promised and offered to us in him. For why is it that the same apostle, who, in one place, exhorts to "stand fast in the liberty wherewith Christ hath made us free, and be not entangled again with the yoke of bondage," in another, enjoins servants to "care not for" their servile condition; except that spiritual liberty may very well consist with civil servitude? In this sense we are likewise to understand him in these passages: "There is neither Jew nor Greek, there is neither bond nor free, there is neither male nor female." Again: "There is neither Greek nor Jew, circumcision nor uncircumcision, Barbarian, Scythian, bond nor free: but Christ is all, and in all"; in which he signifies, that it is of no importance, what is our condition among men, or under the laws of what nation we live, as the kingdom of Christ consists not in these things.

Yet this distinction does not lead us to consider the whole system of civil government as a polluted thing, which has nothing to do with Christian men. Some fanatics, who are pleased with nothing but liberty, or rather licentiousness without any restraint, do indeed boast and vociferate, That since we are dead with Christ to the elements of this world, and, being translated into the kingdom of God, sit among the celestials, it is a degradation to us, and far beneath our dignity, to be occupied with those secular and impure cares which relate to things altogether uninteresting to a Christian man. Of what use, they ask, are laws without judgments and tribunals? But what have judgments to do with a Christian man? And if it be unlawful to kill, of what use are laws and judgments to us? But as we have just suggested that this kind of government is distinct from that spiritual and internal reign of Christ, so it ought to be known that they are in no respect at variance with each other. For that spiritual reign, even now upon earth, commences within us some preludes of the heavenly kingdom, and in this mortal and transitory life affords us some prelibations of immortal and incorruptible blessedness; but this civil government is designed, as long as we live in this world, to cherish and support the external worship of God, to preserve the pure doctrine of religion, to defend the constitution of the Church, to regulate our lives in a manner requisite for the society of men, to form our manners to civil justice, to promote our concord with each other, and to establish general peace and tranquillity; all which I confess to be superfluous, if the kingdom of God, as it now exists in us, extinguishes the present life. But if it is the will of God, that while we are aspiring towards our true country, we be pilgrims on the earth, and if such aids are necessary to our pilgrimage, they who take them from man deprive him of his human nature. They plead that there should be so much perfection in the Church of God, that its order would suffice to supply the place of all laws; but they foolishly imagine a perfection which can never be found in any community of men. For since the insolence of the wicked is so great, and their iniquity so obstinate that it can scarcely be restrained by all the severity of the laws, what may we expect they would do, if they found themselves at liberty to perpetrate crimes with impunity, whose outrages even the arm of power cannot altogether prevent?

But for speaking of the exercise of civil polity, there will be another place more suitable. At present we only wish it to be understood, that to entertain a thought of its extermination, is inhuman barbarism; it is equally as necessary to mankind as bread and water, light and air, and far more excellent. For it not only tends to secure the accommodations arising from all these things, that men may breathe, eat, drink, and be sustained in life, though it comprehends all these things while it causes them to live together, yet, I say, this is not its only tendency; its objects also are, that idolatry, sacrileges against the name of God, blasphemies against his truth, and other offences against religion, may not openly appear and be disseminated among the people; that the public tranquillity may not be disturbed; that every person may enjoy his property without molestation; that men may transact their business together without fraud or injustice; that integrity and modesty may be cultivated among them; in short, that there may be a public form of religion among Christians, and that humanity may be maintained among men. Nor let any one think it strange that I now refer to human polity the charge of the due maintenance of religion, which I may appear to have placed beyond the jurisdiction of men. For I do not allow men to make laws respecting religion and the worship of God now, any more than I did before; though I approve of civil government, which provides that the true religion which is contained in the law of God, be not violated, and polluted by public blasphemies, with impunity. But the perspicuity of order will assist the readers to attain a clearer understanding of what sentiments ought to be entertained respecting the whole system of civil administration, if we enter on a discussion of each branch of it. These are three: The magistrate, who is the guardian and conservator of the laws: The laws, according to which he governs: The people, who are governed by the laws, and obey the magistrate. Let us, therefore, examine, first, the function of a magistrate, whether it be a legitimate calling and approved by God, the nature of the duty, and the extent of the power; secondly, by what laws Christian government ought to be regulated; and lastly, what advantage the people derive from the laws, and what obedience they owe to the magistrate.

The Lord has not only testified that the function of magistrates has his approbation and acceptance, but has eminently commended it to us, by dignifying it with the most honourable titles. We will mention a few of them. When all who sustain the magistracy are called "gods," it ought not to be considered as an appellation of trivial importance; for it implies, that they have their command from God, that they are invested with his authority, and are altogether his representatives, and act as his vicegerents. This is not an invention of mine, but the interpretation of Christ, who says, "If he called them gods, unto whom the word of God came, and the Scripture cannot be broken." What is the meaning of this, but that their commission has been given to them by God, to serve him in their office, and, as Moses and Jehoshaphat said to the judges whom they appointed, to "judge not for man, but for the Lord?" To the same purpose is the declaration of the wisdom of God by the mouth of Solomon: "By me kings reign, and princes decree justice. By me princes rule, and nobles, even all the judges of the earth." This is just as if it had been affirmed, that the authority possessed by kings and other governors over all things upon earth is not a consequence of the perverseness of men, but of the providence and holy ordinance of God, who has been pleased to regulate human affairs in this manner; forasmuch as he is present, and also presides among them, in making laws and in executing equitable judgments. This is clearly taught by Paul, when he enumerates governments (ὁ προϊστάμενος) among the gifts of God, which being variously distributed according to the diversity of grace, ought to be employed by the servants of Christ to the edification of the Church. For though in that place he is properly speaking of the council of elders, who were appointed in the primitive Church to preside over the regulation of the public discipline, the same office which in writing to the Corinthians he calls κυβερνήσεις, "governments," yet, as we see that civil government tends to promote the same object, there is no doubt that he recommends to us every kind of just authority. But he does this in a manner much more explicit, where he enters on a full discussion of that subject. For he says, "There is no power but of God; the powers that be are ordained of God. Rulers are ministers of God, revengers to execute wrath upon him that doeth evil. Do that which is good, and thou shalt have praise of the same." This is corroborated by the examples of holy men; of whom some have been kings, as David, Josiah, Hezekiah; some have been viceroys, as Joseph and Daniel; some have held civil offices in a commonwealth, as Moses, Joshua, and the Judges; whose functions God declared to be approved by him. Wherefore no doubt ought now to be entertained by any person that civil magistracy is a calling not only holy and legitimate, but far the most sacred and honourable in human life. . . .

And for private men, who have no authority to deliberate on the regulation of any public affairs, it would surely be a vain occupation to dispute which would be the best form of government in the place where they live. Besides, this could not be simply determined, as an abstract question, without great impropriety, since the principle to guide the decision must depend on circumstances. And even if we compare the different forms together, without their circumstances, their advantages are so nearly equal, that it will not be easy to discover of which the utility preponderates. The forms of civil government are considered to be of three kinds: Monarchy, which is the dominion of one person, whether called a king, or a duke, or any other title; Aristocracy, or the dominion of the principal persons of a nation; and Democracy, or popular government, in which the power resides in the people at large. It is true that the transition is easy from monarchy to despotism; it is not much more difficult from aristocracy to oligarchy, or the faction of a few; but it is most easy of all from democracy to sedition. Indeed, if these three forms of government, which are stated by philosophers, be considered in themselves, I shall by no means deny, that either aristocracy, or a mixture of aristocracy and democracy, far excels all others; and that indeed not of itself, but because it very rarely happens that kings regulate themselves so that their will is never at variance with justice and rectitude; or, in the next place, that they are endued with such penetration and prudence, as in all cases to discover what is best. The vice or imperfection of men therefore renders it safer and more tolerable for the government to be in the hands of many, that they may afford each other mutual assistance and admonition, and that if any one arrogate to himself more than is right, the many may act as censors and masters to restrain his ambition. This has always been proved by experience, and the Lord confirmed it by his authority, when he established a government of this kind among the people of Israel, with a view to preserve them in the most desirable condition, till he exhibited in David a type of Christ. And as I readily acknowledge that no kind of government is more happy than this, where liberty is regulated with becoming moderation, and properly established on a durable basis, so also I consider those as the most happy people, who are permitted to enjoy such a condition; and if they exert their strenuous and constant efforts for its preservation and retention, I admit that they act in perfect consistence with their duty. And to this object the magistrates likewise ought to apply their greatest diligence, that they suffer not the liberty, of which they are constituted guardians, to be in any respect diminished, much less to be violated: if they are inactive and unconcerned about this, they are perfidious to their office, and traitors to their country. But if those, to whom the will of God has assigned another form of government, transfer this to themselves so as to be tempted to desire a revolution, the very thought will be not only foolish and useless, but altogether criminal. If we limit not our views to one city, but look round and take a comprehensive survey of the whole world, or at least extend our observations to distant lands, we shall certainly find it to be a wise arrangement of Divine Providence that various countries are governed by different forms of civil polity; for they are admirably held together with a certain inequality, as the elements are combined in very unequal proportions. All these remarks, however, will be unnecessary to those who are satisfied with the will of the Lord. For if it be his pleasure to appoint kings over kingdoms, and senators or other magistrates over free cities, it is our duty to be obedient to any governors whom God has established over the places in which we reside.

Here it is necessary to state in a brief manner the nature of the office of magistracy, as described in the word of God; and wherein it consists. If the Scripture did not teach that this office extends to both tables of the law, we might learn it from heathen writers; for not one of them has treated of the office of magistrates, of legislation, and civil government, without beginning with religion and Divine worship. And thus they have all confessed that no government can be happily constituted, unless its first object be the promotion of piety and that all laws are preposterous which neglect the claims of God, and merely provide for the interests of men. Therefore, as religion holds the first place among all the philosophers, and as this has always been regarded by the universal consent of all nations, Christian princes and magistrates ought to be ashamed of their indolence, if they do not make it the object of their most serious care. We have already shown that this duty is particularly enjoined upon them by God; for it is reasonable that they should employ their utmost efforts in asserting and defending the honour of him, whose vicegerents they are, and by whose favour they govern. And the principal commendations given in the Scripture to the good kings are for having restored the worship of God when it had been corrupted or abolished, or for having devoted their attention to religion, that it might flourish in purity and safety under their reigns. On the contrary, the sacred history represents it as one of the evils arising from anarchy, or a want of good government, that when "there was no king in Israel, every man did that which was right in his own eyes." These things evince the folly of those who would wish magistrates to neglect all thoughts of God, and to confine themselves entirely to the administration of justice among men; as though God appointed governors in his name to decide secular controversies, and disregarded that which is of far greater importance— the pure worship of himself according to the rule of his law. But a rage for universal innovation, and a desire to escape with impunity, instigate men of turbulent spirits to wish that all the avengers of violated piety were removed out of the world. With respect to the second table, Jeremiah admonishes kings in the following manner: "Execute ye judgment and righteousness, and deliver the spoiled out of the hand of the oppressor; and do not wrong, do not violence to the stranger, the fatherless, nor the widow, neither shed innocent blood." To the same purpose is the exhortation in the eighty-second psalm: "Defend the poor and fatherless: do justice to the afflicted and needy: deliver the poor and needy: rid them out of the hand of the wicked." And Moses "charged the judges" whom he appointed to supply his place, saying, "Hear the causes between your brethren, and judge righteously between every man and his brother, and the stranger that is with him: ye shall not respect persons in judgment; but ye shall hear the small as well as the great; ye shall not be afraid of the face of man; for the judgment is God's." I forbear to remark the directions given by him in another place respecting their future kings: "He shall not multiply horses to himself;

neither shall he greatly multiply to himself silver and gold; his heart shall not be lifted up above his brethren; he shall read in the law all the days of his life"; also that judges show no partiality, nor take bribes, with similar injunctions, which abound in the Scriptures; because, in describing the office of magistrates in this treatise, my design is not so much to instruct magistrates themselves, as to show to others what magistrates are, and for what end God has appointed them. We see, therefore, that they are constituted the protectors and vindicators of the public innocence, modesty, probity, and tranquillity, whose sole object it ought to be to promote the common peace and security of all. Of these virtues, David declares that he will be an example, when he shall be exalted to the royal throne. "I will set no wicked thing before mine eyes. I will not know a wicked person. Whoso privily slandereth his neighbour, him will I cut off: him that hath a high look and a proud heart will I not suffer. Mine eyes shall be upon the faithful of the land, that they may dwell with me: he that walketh in a perfect way, he shall serve me." But as they cannot do this, unless they defend good men from the injuries of the wicked, and aid the oppressed by their relief and protection, they are likewise armed with power for the suppression of crimes, and the severe punishment of malefactors, whose wickedness disturbs the public peace. For experience fully verifies the observation of Solon: "That all states are supported by reward and punishment; and that when these two things are removed, all the discipline of human societies is broken and destroyed." For the minds of many lose their regard for equity and justice, unless virtue be rewarded with due honour; nor can the violence of the wicked be restrained, unless crimes are followed by severe punishments. And these two parts are included in the injunction of the prophet to kings and other governors, to "execute judgment and righteousness." *Righteousness* means the care, patronage, defence, vindication, and liberation of the innocent: *judgment* imports the repression of the audacity, the coercion of the violence, and the punishment of the crimes, of the impious.

But here, it seems, arises an important and difficult question. If by the law of God all Christians are forbidden to kill, and the prophet predicts respecting the Church, that "they shall not hurt nor destroy in all my holy mountain, saith the Lord," how can it be compatible with piety for magistrates to shed blood? But if we understand, that in the infliction of punishments, the magistrate does not act at all from himself, but merely executes the judgments of God, we shall not be embarrassed with his scruple. The law of the Lord commands, "Thou shalt not kill"; but that homicide may not go unpunished, the legislator himself puts the sword into the hands of his ministers, to be used against all homicides. *To hurt* and *to destroy* are incompatible with the character of the godly; but to avenge the afflictions of the righteous at the command of God, is neither *to hurt* nor *to destroy*. Therefore it is easy to conclude that in this respect magistrates are not subject to the common law; by which, though the Lord binds the hands of men, he does not bind his own justice, which he exercises by the hands of magistrates. So, when a prince forbids all his subjects to strike or wound any one, he does not prohibit his officers from executing that justice which is particularly committed to them. I sincerely wish that this consideration were constantly in our recollection, that nothing is done here by the temerity of men, but every thing by the authority of God, who commands it, and under whose guidance we never err from the right way. For we can find no valid objection to the infliction of public vengeance, unless the justice of God be restrained from the punishment of crimes. But if it be unlawful for us to impose restraints upon him, why do we calumniate his ministers? Paul says of the magistrate, that "He beareth not the sword in vain; for he is the minister of God, a revenger to execute wrath upon him that doeth evil." Therefore, if princes and other governors know that nothing will be more acceptable to God than their obedience, and if they desire to approve their piety, justice, and integrity before God, let them devote themselves to this duty. This motive influenced Moses, when, knowing himself to be destined to become the liberator of his people by the power of the Lord, "he slew the Egyptian"; and when he punished the idolatry of the people by the slaughter of three thousand men in one day. The same motive actuated David, when, at the close of his life, he commanded his son Solomon to put to death Joab and Shimei. Hence, also it is enumerated among the virtues of a king, to "destroy all the wicked of the land, that he may cut off all wicked doers from the city of the Lord." The same topic furnishes the eulogium given to Solomon: "Thou lovest righteousness, and hatest wickedness. . . ." There ought not, however, to be any excessive or unreasonable severity, nor ought any cause to be given for considering the tribunal as a gibbet prepared for all who are accused. For I am not an advocate for unnecessary cruelty, nor can I conceive the possibility of an equitable sentence being pronounced without mercy; of which Solomon affirms, that "mercy and truth preserve the king; and his throne is upholden by mercy." Yet it behoves the magistrate to be on his guard against both these errors; that he do not, by excessive severity, wound rather than heal; or, through a superstitious affectation of clemency, fall into a mistaken humanity, which is the worst kind of cruelty, by indulging a weak and ill-judged lenity, to the detriment of multitudes. For it is a remark not without foundation, that was anciently applied to the government of Nerva, that it is bad to live under a prince who permits nothing, but much worse to live under one who permits every thing. . . .

It now remains for us, as we proposed, in the last place, to examine what advantage the common society of Christians derives from laws, judgments, and magistrates; with which is connected another question—what honour private persons ought to render to magistrates, and how far their obedience ought to extend. . . .

The first duty of subjects towards their magistrates is to entertain the most honourable sentiments of their function, which they know to be a jurisdiction delegated to them from God, and on that account to esteem and reverence them as God's ministers and vicegerents. For there are some persons to be found, who show themselves very obedient to their magistrates, and have not the least wish that there were no magistrates for them to obey, because they know them to be so necessary to the public good; but who, nevertheless, consider the magistrates themselves as no other than necessary evils. But something more than this is required of us by Peter, when he commands us to "honour the king"; and by Solomon, when he says, "Fear thou the Lord and the king"; for Peter, under the term *honour,* comprehends a sincere and candid esteem; and Solomon, by connecting the king with the Lord, attributes to him a kind of sacred veneration and dignity. . . .

But the most remarkable and memorable passage of all is in the Prophecy of Jeremiah, which, though it is rather long, I shall readily quote, because it most clearly decides the whole question: "I have made the earth, the man and the beast that are upon the ground, by my great power and by my outstretched arm, and have given it unto whom it seemed meet unto me. And now I have given all these lands into the hand of Nebuchadnezzar, the king of Babylon, my servant. And all nations shall serve him, and his son, and his son's son, until the very time of his land come. And it shall come to pass, that the nation and kingdom which will not serve the same king of Babylon, that nation will I punish with the sword, and with the famine, and with the pestilence. Therefore serve the king of Babylon and live." We see what great obedience and honour the Lord required to be rendered to that pestilent and cruel tyrant, for no other reason than because he possessed the kingdom; and it was by the heavenly decree that he was seated on the throne of the kingdom, and exalted to that regal majesty, which it was not lawful to violate. If we have this constantly present to our eyes and impressed upon our hearts, that the most iniquitous kings are placed on their thrones by the same decree by which the authority of all kings is established, those seditious thoughts will never enter our minds, that a king is to be treated according to his merits, and that it is not reasonable for us to be subject to a king who does not on his part perform towards us those duties which his office requires. . . .

But in the obedience which we have shown to be due to the authority of governors, it is always necessary to make one exception, and that is entitled to our first attention,—that it do not seduce us from obedience to him, to whose will the desires of all kings ought to be subject, to whose decrees all their commands ought to yield, to whose majesty all their sceptres ought to submit. And, indeed, how preposterous it would be for us, with a view to satisfy men, to incur the displeasure of him on whose account we yield obedience to men! The Lord, therefore, is the King of kings; who, when he has opened his sacred mouth, is to be heard alone, above all, for all, and before all; in the next place, we are subject to those men who preside over us; but no otherwise than in him. If they command any thing against him, it ought not to have the least attention; nor, in this case, ought we to pay any regard to all that dignity attached to magistrates; to which no injury is done when it is subjected to the unrivalled and supreme power of God. On this principle Daniel denied that he had committed any crime against the king in disobeying his impious decree; because the king had exceeded the limits of his office, and had not only done an injury to men, but, by raising his arm against God, had degraded his own authority. On the other hand, the Israelites are condemned for having been too submissive to the impious edict of their king. For when Jeroboam had made his golden calves, in compliance with his will, they deserted the temple of God and revolted to new superstitions. Their posterity conformed to the decrees of their idolatrous kings with the same facility. The prophet severely condemns them for having "willingly walked after the commandment": so far is any praise from being due to the pretext of humility, with which courtly flatterers excuse themselves and deceive the unwary, when they deny that it is lawful for them to refuse compliance with any command of their kings; as if God had resigned his right to mortal men when he made them rulers of mankind; or as if earthly power were diminished by being subordinated to its author, before whom even the principalities of heaven tremble with awe. I know what great and present danger awaits this constancy, for kings cannot bear to be disregarded without the greatest indignation; and "the wrath of a king," says Solomon, "is as messengers of death." But since this edict has been proclaimed by that celestial herald, Peter, "We ought to obey God rather than men,"—let us console ourselves with this thought, that we truly perform the obedience which God requires of us, when we suffer any thing rather than deviate from piety. And that our hearts may not fail us, Paul stimulates us with another consideration—that Christ has redeemed us at the immense price which our redemption cost him, that we may not be submissive to the corrupt desires of men, much less be slaves to their impiety.

SEBASTIAN CASTELLIO

SEBASTIAN CASTELLIO (1515–63), a Frenchman, was a native of Savoy. He early became a humanist scholar and student of the Bible. In flight from the Inquisition, he became a friend of Calvin at Strasbourg and was made principal of the College of Geneva. Castellio's studies led to some untraditional interpretations of Biblical material and to a break with Calvin, who prevented his ordination as a minister. Castellio went to Basel in 1544, living for years in great poverty. While supporting his family by doing odd jobs, he continued his work and was subsequently made Professor of Greek at the University of Basel. He died on the verge of a trial for heresies.

Castellio translated the Bible twice: the first translation was an annotated Latin version whose dedication to Edward VI of England requested toleration in religion, and the second was a French version whose dedication to Henry II of France asked for caution in the era of religious controversy. *Concerning Heretics,* most of which is attributed to Castellio, was published in protest against Calvin's execution of Servetus at Geneva for his rejection of infant baptism and the doctrine of the Trinity. It attempts to find sanction for greater leniency to supposed heretics and defends the free conscience.

The following selections are from *Concerning Heretics* and two other works. The translation of the Bible into French was published in 1555; the *Counsel to France,* published in French in 1562 under the pseudonym "Martin Bellius," exhorts Catholics and Huguenots to end their civil strife. All are taken from Roland H. Bainton's translation and edition of Castellio, *Concerning Heretics* (New York, Columbia University Press, "Records of Civilization" Series, 1935).

PREFACE TO
THE FRENCH TRANSLATION
OF THE BIBLE

To THE MOST VALIANT AND VICTORIOUS Prince Henry of Valois, the second of that name, by the grace of God most Christian King of France from Sebastian Castellio, his subject, greeting.

When night falls upon the battle field the combatants wait for the day lest by chance friends be killed instead of enemies, for it is better to spare one's enemies than to kill some of one's friends. Likewise also in the day time, when the hand to hand combat begins the artillery ceases for fear of the aforesaid mischance. Here I should like to point a moral if your Majesty will deign to listen. The world today is embroiled in great disturbance principally touching the question of religion. There never were so many calamities and evils, from which we may well perceive the night of ignorance. If not all are enveloped, at least many are. If it were day there would never be such diverse and even contrary judgments about the same color. Or if it is day, at least the good and the evil are so confused in the matter of religion that if one wishes to disentangle those who are at variance as to the truth there is danger lest the wheat be rooted out with the tares. That would be an irreparable loss. Hitherto the world has always made this mistake. The prophets, the apostles, so many thousands of martyrs, and even the Son of God were put to death under color of religion. An account must be given for all this blood by those who have been striking at random in the night of ignorance. . . . Believe me, your Majesty, the world today is neither better nor wiser nor more enlightened than formerly. It were better, therefore, in view of so much doubt and confusion to wait before shooting until the dawn, or until things are better disentangled, lest in the darkness and confusion we do that of which afterwards we shall have to say, "I did not intend to."

COUNSEL TO FRANCE IN HER DISTRESS

To THE CATHOLICS. And first I address you, Catholics, you who say that you have the ancient true and Catholic faith and religion, consider closely your case for a moment. It is high time that you did. Recall how you have treated the Evangelicals. You have pursued and imprisoned them and left them to be consumed of lice and rot in foul dungeons in hideous darkness and the shadow of death, and then you have roasted them alive at a slow fire to prolong their torture. And for what crime? Because they did not believe in the pope, the mass, purgatory, and other things, which are so far from being based on Scripture that even the very names are not to be found there. Is that a good and just cause for burning men alive? Do you call yourselves Catholics and profess to maintain the Catholic faith contained in the sacred Scriptures and yet hold as heretics and burn alive those who wish to believe only that which is contained in the Scriptures? Wait now and weigh this carefully. Here is a point of great importance. Answer now, for you will have to answer some day, whether you like it or not, before the just Judge whose name you bear. Answer this one question which undoubtedly will be asked of you at the judgment day. Would you wish that this be done unto you? . . . You well know whether the wrong you have done to your brothers is small. It is so small indeed that they have preferred to endure all that your cruelty (I must call it by its proper name) could invent than to go counter to their conscience as you require, and this is a sign that to force the conscience of a man is worse than cruelly to take his life. . . .

To the Evangelicals. I turn now to you, Evangelicals. Formerly you suffered persecution for the Evangel with patience. You loved your enemies and returned good for evil. You blessed those that cursed you, and offered no resistance save flight in case of necessity, and this you did in accord with the command of the Lord. How does it happen that some of you are now so changed? . . . Has the Lord changed His commandment? . . . and ordered you to return evil for evil? Or have you turned your backs on His commandment? . . . What else can one infer when you convert all resources even to the substance of the poor into battle axes, and massacre your enemies at the edge of the sword until roads and byways, yes, houses and temples, are stained with the blood of those for whom Christ died as much as for you, and who are baptized in His name as are you? What more can I say than that you compel them to attend your sermons, and you even force brothers to take arms against brothers and those of their own religion contrary to conscience? You examine men as to your doctrine and are not content that they should agree on the main points of religion, which are clear and evident in sacred Scripture. . . . Here are the three remedies which you employ: to shed blood, to force consciences, and to condemn as infidels those who do not agree with your doctrine. I am at a loss to discover what has become of your intelligence if you do not see that in these three points you follow your enemies, those whom you commonly call Antichrist. I know well that some of you reply, "We are right and they are wrong." . . . But rationalize as much as you please before men and draw as many fine distinctions as you please, nevertheless we know well, and I call your own consciences to witness, that you are doing to others what you would not have done unto you. . . .

To both the Catholics and the Evangelicals. When Jesus disputed with the Jews, though they were highly opinionated, he was sometimes able to reduce them to silence with a single word. . . . The world is not more obstinate today. I am sure, therefore, that this case can be settled by a single word of evident truth and none will be able to gainsay it. We need only ask those who force consciences, "Would you like to have yours forced?" and immediately their own conscience, which is worth more than a thousand witnesses, will convict and make them dumb. . . . And do not begin to excuse yourselves and say as someone once did, "If I were an adulterer I should not wish to be punished, but it does not follow that if I were the judge I should not punish an adulterer." To which I reply, "If you were an adulterer and you were punished, you would admit that you had been done no injustice. So, also, a thief when punished confesses that he deserves it, or if his mouth denies it, his conscience, whether he will or no, confesses and gives him the lie." Here we see the invincible force of truth and rectitude which cannot be extinguished in the heart of a man, no matter how bad he is. The case of one whose conscience is forced and who is persecuted for the faith is precisely the reverse. Though he may be constrained to confess with his mouth that no wrong is done, yet in his heart he will always say, "You have done me an injustice, and you would not have wished the like done to you." See how we ought to understand this rule, "Do not unto others what you would not that they do unto you." This is a rule, so true, so just, so natural, and so written by the finger of God in the hearts of all men that there is no one so degenerate, so estranged from discipline and enlightenment, but that he will confess this rule to be right and reasonable the moment it is proposed to him. Hence we can easily see that when the Truth judges us it will be in accord with this rule. And in fact Christ, who is the Truth, has confirmed it when He not only forbade us to do to others what we would not have done unto us, but, even more, commanded that we should do unto others as we would that they do unto us. . . .

Take the case of a man who has scruples against going to Mass or hearing a minister whom he considers a heretic or supporting by money and arms a church which he regards as heretical against one which he holds as Catholic, and you tell him that if he does not comply he will be banished, or disinherited or miserably put to death. What do you want him to do? Advise him, for he is in extreme anguish like a piece of bread roasted on the end of a knife. If it moves forward it is burned and if backward it is pierced. So the poor man, if he does what you desire he will be damned for going against his conscience; if he withstands you he will lose goods and life. . . . I ask you, you Inquisitors . . . you who egg on princes . . . what advice would you give to such a man? Would you counsel him to go against his conscience? Then he will lose his soul. Or would you advise him to follow his conscience? Then he will be put to death. . . . If a sick man does not wish to eat meat, will you ram it down his throat, or if a donkey will not drink, will you drown him to make him drink?

CONCERNING HERETICS

MARTIN BELLIUS to Duke Christoph of Württemberg, Greeting. Most Illustrious Prince, suppose you had told your subjects that you would come to them at some uncertain time and had commanded them to make ready to go forth clad in white garments to meet you whenever you might appear. What would you do if, on your return, you discovered that they had taken no thought for the white robes but instead were disputing among themselves concerning your person? Some were saying that you were in France, others that you were in Spain; some that you would come on a horse, others in a chariot; some were asserting that you would appear with a great equipage, others that you would be unattended. Would this please you?

Suppose further that the controversy was being conducted not merely by words but by blows and swords, and that one group wounded and killed the others who did not agree with them. "He will come on a horse," one would say.

"No, in a chariot," another would retort.

"You lie."

"You're the liar. Take that." He punches him.

"And take that in the belly." The other stabs.

Would you, O Prince, commend such citizens? Suppose, however, that some did their duty and followed your command to prepare the white robes, but the others oppressed them on that account and put them to death. Would you not rigorously destroy such scoundrels?

But what if these homicides claimed to have done all this in your name and in accord with your command, even though you had previously expressly forbidden it? Would you not consider that such outrageous conduct deserved to be punished without mercy? Now I beg you, most Illustrious Prince, to be kind enough to hear why I say these things.

Christ is the Prince of this world who on His departure from the earth foretold to men that He would return some day at an uncertain hour, and He commanded them to prepare white robes for His coming, that is to say, that they should live together in a Christian manner, amicably, without controversy and contention, loving one another. But consider now, I beg you, how well we discharge our duty.

How many are there who show the slightest concern to prepare the white robe? Who is there who bends every effort to live in this world in a saintly, just, and religious manner in the expectation of the coming of the Lord? For nothing is there so little concern. The true fear of God and charity are fallen and grown cold. Our life is spent in contention and in every manner of sin. We dispute, not as to the way by which we may come to Christ, which is to correct our lives, but rather as to the state and office of Christ, where He now is and what He is doing, how He is seated at the right hand of the Father, and how He is one with the Father; likewise with regard to the Trinity, predestination, free will; so, also, of God, the angels, the state and souls after this life and other like things, which do not need to be known for salvation by faith (for the publicans and sinners were saved without this knowledge), nor indeed can they be known before the heart is pure (for to see these things is to see God Himself, who cannot be seen save by the pure in heart, as the text says, "Blessed are the pure in heart for they shall see God"). Nor if these are known do they make a man better, as Paul says, "Though I understand all mysteries and have not love it profiteth me nothing." This perverse curiosity engenders worse evils. Men are puffed up with knowledge or with a false opinion of knowledge and look down upon others. Pride is followed by cruelty and persecution so that now scarcely anyone is able to endure another who differs at all from him. Although opinions are almost as numerous as men, nevertheless there is hardly any sect which does not condemn all others and desire to reign alone. Hence arise banishments, chains, imprisonments, stakes, and gallows and this miserable rage to visit daily penalties upon those who differ from the mighty about matters hitherto unknown, for so many centuries disputed, and not yet cleared up.

If, however, there is someone who strives to prepare the white robe, that is, to live justly and innocently, then all others with one accord cry out against him if he differ from them in anything, and they confidently pronounce him a heretic on the ground that he seeks to be justified by works. Horrible crimes of which he never dreamed are attributed to him and the common people are prejudiced by slander until they consider it a crime merely to hear him speak. Hence arises such cruel rage that some are so incensed by calumny as to be infuriated when the victim is first strangled instead of being burned alive at a slow fire. . . .

Sins of the heart, such as infidelity, heresy, envy, hate, etc., are to be punished by the sword of the Spirit which is the Word of God. If anyone disturbs the commonwealth by an assault under color of religion, the magistrate may punish such an one not on the score of religion, but because he has done damage to bodies and goods, like any other criminal. If anyone conducts himself amiss in the Church, both in his life and in his doctrine, the Church should use the spiritual sword, which is excommunication, if he will not be admonished. Then, if after excommunication, he perseveres in his evil design to the point of disturbing the peace, the Christian magistrate may see to it that he no longer trouble the Church with his heresies and blasphemies which are plainly contrary to the Word of God. Of such a character is the teaching of those who deny the creation of the world, the immortality of souls and the resurrection, as well as of those who repudiate the office of the magistrate in order that they may the better disturb the state to their hearts' content without reproof. These men thrive on disturbance, to which the Spirit of God is utterly alien. If they continue to disobey princes and magistrates, they may be punished, but not with the death penalty, as St. Augustine teaches, especially in the case of those who admit one true God, the source of all good, but err obstinately in the understanding of some passages of Scripture. The good magistrate will content himself with punishing them by a fine or some similar penalty. Then, if they continue, he may banish them from the land. This is the extreme penalty. If they come back they may be imprisoned if they do not amend. This . . . is the way in which emperors and magistrates punished the heretics in the early Church, as you may read in the present book, which is both useful and necessary in these last days in which not only those who have never properly known the truth, but even those who glory in it, nevertheless thirst for the blood of any who contradict them and try to stop bloodshed for the sake of religion. Hereby the persecutors show how far they are from the clemency of Christ and His apostles, from the mercy of the doctors of the primitive Church who begged the princes and magistrates not to kill and burn the heretics, as you may read in this book. Follow St. Augustine, Chrysostom, and Jerome and the other doctors so long as they follow Scripture, as Augustine himself advises us to do, and, on the contrary, avoid those who urge that we kill and burn any for the faith. Certainly they are of the nature of the devil and of Antichrist, who desire the death of poor souls, whereas true Christians desire that sinners and adversaries of the truth turn and live. Beware of false doctors and the writings of those who cannot suffer the assertion that heretics should not be killed lest their souls be destroyed. These doctors make simple people believe that those who object to coercion do so in order the more readily to disseminate their poison. But the same may be said of these doctors. That is just what they have done. May the Lord cause them to recognize their blindness and ill will.

RICHARD HOOKER

RICHARD HOOKER (c.1553–1600), an Englishman, entered Oxford at about fifteen and later taught there for some twenty years, until shortly after his ordination. His appointment to the post of Master of the Temple in London marked for Hooker the beginning of ecclesiastical controversy. His Anglican sermons were given in the morning; he was followed later in the day by Walter Travers, of Presbyterian tendencies. Out of the issues raised in this situation grew Hooker's major work, *Of the Laws of Ecclesiastical Polity,* a contribution to the literature of the English language as well as to theology and political theory. The first four parts appeared about 1592, the fifth in 1597, and the last three posthumously. Beginning with a justification of the episcopal organization and traditions of the English Church, Hooker develops a philosophic defense of the authority of reason as equal and parallel to that of Scripture. His work remains the classic defense of the Church of England.

The following brief selections touch on the position of Anglicanism with respect to the Roman Church on the one hand and Continental Protestantism on the other; on the role of private religious judgment; and on the relation between church and state, a central problem in the Anglican viewpoint. It should be mentioned that Book VIII, from which the last selection is taken, though generally accepted as the work of Hooker, was left unrevised by him and has come down in edited form.

OF THE LAWS
OF ECCLESIASTICAL POLITY

[Book II]

VIII. Two opinions . . . there are concerning sufficiency of Holy Scripture, each extremely opposite unto the other, and both repugnant unto truth. The schools of Rome teach Scripture to be so unsufficient, as if, except traditions were added, it did not contain all revealed and supernatural truth, which absolutely is necessary for the children of men in this life to know that they may in the next be saved. Others justly condemning this opinion grow likewise unto a dangerous extremity, as if Scripture did not only contain all things

in that kind necessary, but all things simply, and in such sort that to do anything according to any other law were not only unnecessary but even opposite
unto salvation, unlawful and sinful. Whatsoever is spoken of God or things
appertaining to God otherwise than as the truth is; though it seem an honour,
it is an injury. And as incredible praises given unto men do often abate and
impair the credit of their deserved commendation; so we must likewise take
great heed, lest in attributing unto Scripture more than it can have, the in-
credibility of that do cause even those things which indeed it hath most abundantly to be less reverently esteemed. I therefore leave it to themselves to consider, whether they have in this first point or not overshot themselves . . .

[Book IV]

VIII. They which measure religion by dislike of the church of Rome think
every man so much the more sound, by how much he can make the corruptions
thereof to seem more large. And therefore some there are, namely the Arians
in reformed churches of Poland, which imagine the canker to have eaten so
far into the very bones and marrow of the church of Rome, as if it had not
so much as a sound belief, no not concerning God himself, but that the very
belief of the Trinity were a part of antichristian corruption; and that the wonderful providence of God did bring to pass that the bishop of the see of Rome
should be famous for his triple crown; a sensible mark whereby the world
might know him to be that mystical beast spoken of in the Revelation, to be
that great and notorious Antichrist in no one respect so much as in this, that
he maintaineth the doctrine of the Trinity. Wisdom therefore and skill is
requisite to know, what parts are sound in that church, and what corrupted.

Neither is it to all men apparent which complain of unsound parts, with what
kind of unsoundness every such part is possessed. They can say, that in doctrine, in discipline, in prayers, in sacraments, the church of Rome hath (as
it hath indeed) very foul and gross corruptions; the nature whereof notwithstanding because they have not for the most part exact skill and knowledge
to discern, they think that amiss many times which is not; and the salve of
reformation they mightily call for, but where and what the sores are which
need it, as they wot full little, so they think it not greatly material to search.
Such men's contentment must be wrought by stratagem; the usual method
of art is not for them. . . .

XIII. . . . The church of England is grievously charged with forgetfulness
of her duty, which duty had been to frame herself unto the pattern of their
example that went before her in the work of reformation. . . .

XIV. To leave reformed churches . . . and their actions for Him to judge of, in whose sight they are as they are; and our desire is that they may even in His sight be found such as we ought to endeavour by all means that our own may likewise be; somewhat we are enforced to speak by way of simple declaration concerning the proceedings of the church of England in these affairs, to the end that men whose minds are free from those partial constructions, whereby the only name of difference from some other churches is thought cause sufficient to condemn ours, may the better discern whether that we have done be reasonable, yea or no. The church of England being to alter her received laws concerning such orders, rites, and ceremonies, as had been in former times an hindrance unto piety and religious service of God, was to enter into consideration first, that the change of laws, especially concerning matter of religion, must be warily proceeded in. Laws, as all other things human, are many times full of imperfection; and that which is supposed behoveful unto men, proveth oftentimes most pernicious. The wisdom which is learned by tract of time, findeth the laws that have been in former ages established, needful in later to be abrogated. Besides, that which sometime is expedient doth not always so continue: and the number of needless laws unabolished doth weaken the force of them that are necessary. But true withal it is, that alteration though it be from worse to better hath in it inconveniences, and those weighty; unless it be in such laws as have been made upon special occasions, which occasions ceasing, laws of that kind do abrogate themselves. But when we abrogate a law as being ill made, the whole cause for which it was made still remaining, do we not herein revoke our very own deed, and upbraid ourselves with folly, yea, all that were makers of it with oversight and with error? . . .

. . . What exception can there be taken against the judgment of St. Augustine, who saith, "That of things harmless, whatsoever there is which the whole Church doth observe throughout the world, to argue for any man's immunity from observing the same, it were a point of most insolent madness?" And surely odious it must needs have been for one Christian church to abolish that which all had received and held for the space of many ages, and that without any detriment unto religion so manifest and so great, as might in the eyes of unpartial men appear sufficient to clear them from all blame of rash and inconsiderate proceeding, if in fervour of zeal they had removed such things. Whereas contrariwise, so reasonable moderation herein used hath freed us from being deservedly subject unto that bitter kind of obloquy, whereby as the church of Rome doth under the colour of love towards those things which be harmless, maintain extremely most hurtful corruptions; so we peradventure might be upbraided, that under colour of hatred towards those things that are corrupt, we are on the other side as extreme even against most harmless ordinances. And as they are obstinate to retain that, which no man of any conscience is able well to defend; so we might be reckoned fierce and violent to tear away that, which if our own mouths did condemn, our consciences would storm and repine thereat. The Romans having banished Tarquinius the Proud, and taken a solemn oath that they never would permit any man more to reign, could not herewith content themselves or think that tyranny was thoroughly extinguished, till they had driven one of their consuls to depart the city, against whom they found not in the world what to object, saving only that his name was Tarquin, and that the commonwealth could not seem to have recovered perfect freedom, as long as a man of so dangerous a name was left remaining. For the church of England to have done the like in casting out of papal tyranny and superstition; to have shewed greater willingness of accepting the very ceremonies of the Turk Christ's professed enemy, than of the most indifferent things which the church of Rome approveth; to have left not so much as the names which the church of Rome doth give unto things innocent; to have ejected whatsoever that Church doth make account of, be it never so harmless in itself, and of never so ancient continuance, without any other crime to charge it with, than only that it hath been the hap thereof to be used by the church of Rome, and not to be commanded in the word of God: this kind of proceeding might haply have pleased some few men, who having begun such a course themselves must needs be glad to see their example followed by us. But the Almighty which giveth wisdom and inspireth with right understanding whomsoever it pleaseth him, he foreseeing that which man's wit had never been able to reach unto, namely, what tragedies the attempt of so extreme alteration would raise in some part of the Christian world, did for the endless good of his Church (as we cannot choose but interpret it) use the bridle of his provident restraining hand, to stay those eager affections in some, and to settle their resolution upon a course more calm and moderate: lest as in other most ample and heretofore most flourishing dominions it hath since fallen out, so likewise if in ours it had come to pass, that the adverse part being enraged, and betaking itself to such practices as men are commonly wont to embrace, when they behold things brought to desperate extremities, and no hope left to see any other end, than only the utter oppression and clean extinguishment of one side; by this mean Christendom flaming in all parts of greatest importance at once, they all had wanted that comfort of mutual relief, whereby they are now for the time sustained (and not the least by this our church which they so much impeach) till mutual combustions, bloodsheds, and wastes (because no other inducement will serve) may enforce them through very faintness, after the experience of so endless miseries, to enter on all sides at the length into such consultation, as may tend to the best re-establishment of the whole Church of Jesus Christ. To the singular good whereof it cannot but serve as a profitable direction to teach men what is most likely to prove available, when they shall quietly consider the trial that hath been thus long had of both kinds of reformation; as well this moderate kind which the church of England hath taken, as that other more extreme and rigorous which certain churches elsewhere have better liked. In the meanwhile it may be, that suspense of judgment and exercise of charity were safer and seemlier for Christian men, than the hot pursuit of these controversies, wherein they that are most fervent to dispute be not always the most able to determine. But who are on this side, and who against him, our Lord in his good time shall reveal. . . .

[Book V]

I. . . . We agree that pure and unstained religion ought to be the highest of all cares appertaining to public regiment: as well in regard of that aid and protection which they who faithfully serve God confess they receive at his merciful hands; as also for the force which religion hath to qualify all sorts of men, and to make them in public affairs the more serviceable, governors the apter to rule with conscience, inferiors for conscience' sake the willinger to obey. It is no peculiar conceit, but a matter of sound consequence, that all duties are by so much the better performed, by how much the men are more religious from whose abilities the same proceed. For if the course of politic affairs cannot in any good sort go forward without fit instruments, and that which fitteth them be their virtues, let Polity acknowledge itself indebted to Religion; godliness being the chiefest top and wellspring of all true virtues, even as God is of all good things. . . .

X. Now where the word of God leaveth the Church to make choice of her own ordinances, if against those things which have been received with great reason, or against that which the ancient practice of the Church hath continued time out of mind, or against such ordinances as the power and authority of that Church under which we live hath itself devised for the public good, or against the discretion of the Church in mitigating sometimes with favourable equity that rigour which otherwise the literal generality of ecclesiastical laws hath judged to be more convenient and meet; if against all this it should be free for men to reprove, to disgrace, to reject at their own liberty what they see done and practised according to order set down; if in so great variety of ways as the wit of man is easily able to find out towards any purpose, and in so great liking as all men especially have unto those inventions whereby some one shall seem to have been more enlightened from above than many thousands, the Church did give every man license to follow what himself imagineth that "God's Spirit doth reveal" unto him, or what he supposeth that God is likely to have revealed to some special person whose virtues deserve to be highly esteemed: what other effect could hereupon ensue, but the utter confusion of his Church under pretence of being taught, led, and guided by his Spirit? The gifts and graces whereof do so naturally all tend unto common peace, that where such singularity is, they whose hearts it possesseth ought to suspect it the more, inasmuch as if it did come of God, and should for that cause prevail with others, the same God which revealeth it to them, would also give them power of confirming it unto others, either with miraculous operation, or with strong and invincible remonstrance of sound Reason, such as whereby it might appear that God would indeed have all men's judgments give place unto it; whereas now the error and unsufficiency of their arguments do make it on the contrary side against them a strong presumption, that God hath not moved their hearts to think such things as he hath not enabled them to prove.

[Book VIII]

I. It was not thought fit in the Jews' commonwealth, that the exercise of supremacy ecclesiastical should be denied unto him, to whom the exercise of chiefty civil did appertain; and therefore their kings were invested with both. . . .

According to the pattern of which example, the like power in causes ecclesiastical is by the laws of this realm annexed unto the crown. And there are which imagine, that kings, being mere lay persons, do by this means exceed the lawful bounds of their calling. Which thing to the end that they may persuade, they first make a necessary separation perpetual and personal between the Church and commonwealth. Secondly, they so tie all kind of power ecclesiastical unto the Church, as if it were in every degree their only right which are by proper spiritual function termed Church-governors, and might not to Christian princes any wise appertain.

To lurk under shifting ambiguities and equivocations of words in matters of principal weight is childish. A church and a commonwealth we grant are things in nature the one distinguished from the other. A commonwealth is one way, and a church another way, defined. In their opinion the church and the commonwealth are corporations, not distinguished only in nature and definition, but in subsistence perpetually severed; so that they that are of the one can neither appoint nor execute in whole nor in part the duties which belong unto them which are of the other, without open breach of the law of God, which hath divided them, and doth require that being so divided they should distinctly and severally work, as depending both upon God, and not hanging one upon the other's approbation for that which either hath to do.

We say that the care of religion being common unto all societies politic, such societies as do embrace the true religion have the name of the Church given unto every of them for distinction from the rest; so that every body politic hath some religion, but the Church that religion which is only true. Truth of religion is that proper difference whereby a church is distinguished from other politic societies of men. We here mean true religion in gross, and not according to every particular: for they which in some particular points of religion do swerve from the truth, may nevertheless most truly, if we compare them to men of an heathenish religion, be said to hold and profess that religion which is true. For which cause, there being of old so many politic societies established throughout the world, only the commonwealth of Israel, which had the truth of religion, was in that respect the Church of God: and the Church of Jesus Christ is every such politic society of men, as doth in religion hold that truth which is proper to Christianity. As a politic society it doth maintain religion; as a church, that religion which God hath revealed by Jesus Christ.

With us therefore the name of a church importeth only a society of men, first united into some public form of regiment, and secondly distinguished from other societies by the exercise of Christian religion. With them on the other side the name of the Church in this present question importeth not only a multitude of men so united and so distinguished, but also further the same divided necessarily and perpetually from the body of the commonwealth: so that even in such a politic society as consisteth of none but Christians, yet the Church of Christ and the commonwealth are two corporations, independently each subsisting by itself.

We hold, that seeing there is not any man of the Church of England but the same man is also a member of the commonwealth; nor any man a member of the commonwealth, which is not also of the Church of England; therefore as in a figure triangular the base doth differ from the sides thereof, and yet one and the selfsame line is both a base and also a side; a side simply, a base if it chance to be the bottom and underlie the rest: so, albeit properties and actions of one kind do cause the name of a commonwealth, qualities and functions of another sort the name of a Church to be given unto a multitude, yet one and the selfsame multitude may in such sort be both, and is so with us, that no person appertaining to the one can be denied to be also of the other. Contrariwise, unless they against us should hold, that the Church and the commonwealth are two, both distinct and separate societies, of which two, the one comprehendeth always persons not belonging to the other; that which they do they could not conclude out of the difference between the Church and the commonwealth; namely, that bishops may not meddle with the affairs of the commonwealth, because they are governors of another corporation, which is the Church; nor kings with making laws for the Church, because they have government not of this corporation, but of another divided from it, the commonwealth; and the walls of separation between these two must for ever be upheld. They hold the necessity of personal separation, which clean excludeth the power of one man's dealing in both; we of natural, which doth not hinder but that one and the same person may in both bear a principal sway. . . .

Wherefore to end this point, I conclude: First, that under dominions of infidels, the Church of Christ, and their commonwealth, were two societies independent. Secondly, that in those commonwealths where the bishop of Rome beareth sway, one society is both the Church and the commonwealth; but the bishop of Rome doth divide the body into two diverse bodies, and doth not suffer the Church to depend upon the power of any civil prince or potentate. Thirdly, that within this realm of England the case is neither as in the one, nor as in the other of the former two: but from the state of pagans we differ, in that with us one society is both the Church and commonwealth, which with them it was not; as also from the state of those nations which subject themselves to the bishop of Rome, in that our Church hath dependency upon the chief in our commonwealth, which it hath not under him. In a word, our estate is according to the pattern of God's own ancient elect people, which people was not part of them the commonwealth, and part of them the Church of God, but the selfsame people whole and entire were both under one chief Governor, on whose supreme authority they did all depend.

IGNATIUS OF LOYOLA

I GNATIUS OF LOYOLA (1491–1556), a Spaniard, was of noble birth and grew up in the household of a courtier. He became a soldier of the Emperor Charles V and, during a long convalescence from a serious battle wound, turned to religious meditation. His recovery found him determined to become a soldier of Christ. After austere preparation, he made an unsuccessful effort to enter Palestine. Realizing the handicaps of trying to serve the Church without an education, he studied at Barcelona, Alcala, Salamanca, and finally at Paris. At Paris he met a group of scholarly and pious men, from whom were to come advisers to the Council of Trent and the first members of the Society of Jesus. The Jesuits sprang from a religious fraternity that Ignatius founded among these friends at Paris. The Society's original group of seven intended to go to Palestine and model their lives on the pattern of Jesus, but their journey was prevented by the Turkish wars. The group was ordained, and the pope officially recognized the order in 1540. Ignatius served as its head from 1541 until his death. He was a leading figure in the Catholic Counter-Reformation, which stressed internal revivification of the Church through austerity and piety. In 1622 he was canonized.

Ignatius formulated and rewrote the organizational plans for the Jesuit Order— called in their final form the *Constitutions*. His *Spiritual Exercises* was also composed over a period of time. Originally written in rough Spanish, it was twice translated into Latin during his lifetime. The book reflects Ignatius's deep concern for orthodoxy and his major emphasis on patterning one's life after that of Christ. The following selection is taken from a translation published by Burns and Oates (4th ed., 1908).

SPIRITUAL EXERCISES

RULES FOR THINKING WITH THE CHURCH

In order to think truly, as we ought, in the church militant, the following rules are to be observed.

I. Laying aside all private judgment, we ought to keep our minds prepared and ready to obey in all things the true Spouse of Christ our Lord, which is our Holy Mother, the Hierarchical Church.

II. The second is to praise confession made to a priest, and the reception of the Most Holy Sacrament, once a year, and what is much better once a month, and much better still every eight days, always with the requisite and due dispositions.

III. The third is to praise the frequent hearing of Mass, also hymns, psalms, and long prayers, both in and out of the church, and likewise the hours ordained at fixed times for all the Divine Office, for prayers of any kind, and all the canonical hours.

IV. The fourth, to praise greatly religious orders, and a life of virginity and continency, and not to praise the married state as much as any of these.

V. The fifth is to praise the vows of religion, of Obedience, Poverty, and Chastity, and vows to perform other works of perfection and supererogation; and it is to be noticed that as a vow is made in matters more nearly approaching evangelical perfection, so in matters which depart from it a vow ought not to be made, *v.g.,* to become a merchant or to enter the marriage state, &c.

VI. The sixth is to praise the relics of saints, showing veneration to the relics, and praying to the saints, and to praise likewise the Stations, pilgrimages, indulgences, jubilees, Bulls of the *Cruciata,* and candles lighted in churches.

VII. The seventh is to praise the precepts with regard to fasts and abstinences, as those of Lent, Ember days, Vigils, Fridays, and Saturdays; likewise not only interior but also exterior penances.

VIII. To praise the building and the ornaments of churches; and also images, and to venerate them according to what they represent.

IX. Finally, to praise all the precepts of the Church, keeping our minds ready to seek reasons to defend, never to impugn them.

X. We ought to be very ready to approve and praise the constitutions, recommendations, and habits of life of our superiors; because, although they may not be or may not have been praiseworthy, still to speak against them in public discourse, or before the lower classes, would give rise to murmurs and scandals, rather than be of any use, and thus the people would be irritated against their temporal or spiritual superiors. Nevertheless, as on the one hand it is hurtful to speak ill before the people concerning superiors in their absence, so on the other it may be useful to speak of their bad habits to those who can apply a remedy.

XI. The eleventh is to praise positive and scholastic theology: for as it rather belongs to the positive doctors, as St. Jerome, St. Augustine, St. Gregory, etc. to stir up the affections to the love and service of God our Lord in all things: so it rather belongs to the scholastic doctors, as St. Thomas, St. Bonaventure, and the Master of the Sentences, etc., to define and explain for our times what is necessary for salvation, and more to attack and to expose all errors and fallacies; because the scholastic doctors being of later date can avail themselves not only of the right understanding of the Holy Scriptures, and of the writings of the holy positive doctors, but being themselves illuminated and enlightened by the Divine Power, they can be helped by the Councils, Canons, and Constitutions of our Holy Mother the Church.

XII. We ought to guard against making comparisons between the living and the blessed who have passed away, for no slight error is committed in this, as for example, in saying: He knows more than St. Augustine; He is as great or greater than St. Francis; He is another St. Paul in virtue and holiness, &c.

XIII. To attain the truth in all things, we ought always to hold that we believe what seems to us white to be black, if the Hierarchical Church so defines it; believing that between Christ our Lord the Bridegroom and the Church His Bride there is one and the same Spirit, which governs and directs us to the salvation of our souls; for our Holy Mother the Church is guided and ruled by the same Spirit and Lord that gave the Ten Commandments.

XIV. Although it is very true that no one can be saved without being predestined, and without having faith and grace, we must be very careful in our manner of speaking and treating of all this subject.

XV. We ought not habitually to speak much of Predestination; but if sometimes mention be made of it in any way, we must so speak that the common people may not fall into error, as happens sometimes when they say: "It is already fixed whether I am to be saved or damned, and there cannot be any other result whether I do good or ill"; and, becoming slothful in consequence, they neglect works conducive to their salvation, and to the spiritual profit of their souls.

XVI. In the same way it is to be noticed that we must take heed lest by speaking much with great earnestness on Faith, without any distinction or explanation, occasion be given to the people to become slothful and sluggish in good works, whether it be before or after that faith is formed in charity.

XVII. In like manner we ought not to speak or to insist on the doctrine of Grace so strongly, as to give rise to that poisonous teaching that takes away free-will. Therefore, we may treat of Faith and Grace, as far as we may with the help of God, for the greater praise of His Divine Majesty; but not in such a way, especially in these dangerous times of ours, that works or free-will receive any detriment, or come to be accounted for nothing.

XVIII. Although it is above all things praiseworthy to greatly serve God our Lord out of pure love, yet we ought much to praise the fear of His Divine Majesty, because not only is filial fear a pious and most holy thing, but even servile fear, when a man does not rise to anything better and more useful, is of great help to him to escape from mortal sin; and, after he has escaped from it, he easily attains to filial fear, which is altogether acceptable and pleasing to God our Lord, because it is inseparable from Divine love.

THE COUNCIL OF TRENT

HE COUNCIL OF TRENT, divided into three periods under three different popes, began in 1545 and ended in 1563. Its original convocation was due in large part to the efforts of the Emperor Charles V, a loyal Catholic. After many delays it assembled in the capital of the Italian Tyrol, which was imperial territory; but Charles and Pope Paul III had opposing conceptions of the proper mode of procedure. The pope thought in terms of condemning the Protestant heresy and emphasizing doctrine; Charles insisted that the internal reform of ecclesiastical abuses should be given prior consideration, the problems of dogma to be deferred until he could get Protestant representatives to attend. The papal party had its way, and the emperor's plan for reconciliation with the Protestants was superseded.

From the beginning, as a result of the many parties represented, numerous differences of opinion existed. Voting was by individuals instead of nations, so that the Italian delegates, constituting a majority of two thirds, influenced the proceedings in the papal behalf. Nevertheless, the council emerged with a reaffirmation and systematization of Catholic doctrine and practice, enacting certain regulations for the reform of ecclesiastical life, establishing an Index of prohibited books, and strengthening the Inquisition. Though the varied results often met inevitable opposition among the secular national powers, the council on the whole achieved a unified front against Protestantism and fortified the ranks of the orthodox faithful.

The first of the following brief selections is from the *History of the Council of Trent* by Paolo Sarpi (1552–1623), a Venetian church reformer and scientist. Attacking the pope's authority in secular matters, Sarpi became a high official in Venice. Himself a Catholic ecclesiastic, he pressed for toleration of Protestantism and for an independent Venetian church. The translation from the Italian is that of N. Brent, 1640. The other two selections are taken from J. Waterworth, *Canons and Decrees of the Council of Trent* (1848).

PAOLO SARPI'S HISTORY OF THE COUNCIL OF TRENT

18 January, 1546. The Imperialists said that the points of doctrine could not be touched with hope of any fruit, because it was first necessary to remove the transgressions, from whence the heresies arose, by a good reformation, enlarging themselves very much in this field, and concluding that so long as the scandal which the world receiveth, by the deformation of the clergy, ceaseth not, nothing that they can say or preach will ever be believed, all being persuaded that deeds ought to be regarded, and not words. And that they ought not to take example by the ancient councils, because in them either there was not corruption of manners, or that was not cause of heresy; and in fine, that to defer the treaty of reformation, was to show themselves incorrigible. Some few others thought fit to begin with doctrine, and then to pass to reformation, alleging that faith is the ground and foundation of Christian life; that no man begins to build from the roof, but from the foundations; that it is a greater sin to err in faith than in other human actions; and that the point of rooting out heresies was put first in the Pope's bulls. A third opinion was, that the points of reformation and faith might ill be separated, because there was no doctrine without abuse, nor abuse which drew not after it the bad interpretation and bad sense of some doctrine. Therefore it was necessary to handle them at the same time, for that the world having their eyes fixed upon this council and expecting a remedy as well in matters of faith as manners, it would be satisfied better by handling them both together, than one after another, especially if, according to the proposition of the Cardinal of Monte, divers deputations were made, and one handled this matter, and the other that, which should be done quickly, considering that the time present, when Christendom had peace, was precious, and not to be lost, not knowing what impediments the time to come might bring. And the rather, because they should study to make the Council as short as they could, that the churches the less while might remain deprived of their pastors, and for many other respects, intimating that which might arise in length of time, to the distaste of the pope and court of Rome. Some others, among whom were the Frenchmen, demanded, that that of the peace might be the first: that they should write unto the emperor, the most Christian king, and other princes, giving them thanks for the convocation of the council, for continuance whereof that they would establish peace, and help the work forward, by sending their ambassadors and prelates; and likewise should write friendly to the Lutherans, inviting them charitably to come at the Council, and join themselves with the rest of Christendom.

PROCEEDINGS OF THE COUNCIL

ON SCRIPTURE AND TRADITION

THE SACRED AND HOLY, œcumenical, and general Synod of Trent, lawfully assembled in the Holy Ghost, the same three legates of the Apostolic See presiding therein,—keeping this always in view, that, errors being removed, the purity itself of the Gospel be preserved in the Church; which (Gospel), before promised through the prophets in the holy Scriptures, our Lord Jesus Christ,

the Son of God, first promulgated with His own mouth, and then commanded
to be preached by His Apostles to every creature, as the fountain of all, both
saving truth, and moral discipline; and seeing clearly that this truth and discipline are contained in the written books, and the unwritten traditions which,
received by the Apostles from the mouth of Christ himself, or from the Apostles themselves, the Holy Ghost dictating, have come down even unto us,
transmitted as it were from hand to hand; (the Synod) following the examples
of the orthodox Fathers, receives and venerates with an equal affection of piety,
and reverence, all the books both of the Old and of the New Testament—seeing
that one God is the author of both—as also the said traditions, as well those
appertaining to faith as to morals, as having been dictated, either by Christ's
own word of mouth, or by the Holy Ghost, and preserved in the Catholic
Church by a continuous succession. . . .

ON JUSTIFICATION

Canon I. If any one saith, that man may be justified before God by his own
works, whether done through the teaching of human nature, or that of the
law, without the grace of God through Jesus Christ; let him be anathema.

Canon II. If any one saith, that the grace of God, through Jesus Christ, is
given only for this, that man may be able more easily to live justly, and to
merit eternal life, as if, by free will without grace, he were able to do both,
though hardly indeed and with difficulty; let him be anathema.

Canon III. If any one saith, that without the prevenient inspiration of the
Holy Ghost, and without his help, man can believe, hope, love, or be penitent
as he ought, so as that the grace of Justification may be bestowed upon him;
let him be anathema.

Canon IV. If any one saith, that man's free will moved and excited by God,
by assenting to God exciting and calling, nowise cooperates towards disposing
and preparing itself for obtaining the grace of Justification; that it cannot
refuse its consent, if it would, but that, as something inanimate, it does nothing
whatever and is merely passive; let him be anathema.

Canon V. If any one saith, that since Adam's sin, the free will of man is
lost and extinguished; or, that it is a thing with only a name, yea a name without a reality, a figment, in fine, introduced into the Church by Satan; let him
be anathema.

Canon VI. If any one saith, that it is not in man's power to make his ways
evil, but that the works that are evil God worketh as well as those that are
good, not permissively only, but properly, and of Himself, in such wise that
the treason of Judas is no less His own proper work than the vocation of Paul;
let him be anathema.

Canon VII. If any one saith, that all works done before Justification, in whatsoever way they be done, are truly sins, or merit the hatred of God; or that the more earnestly one strives to dispose himself for grace, the more grievously he sins: let him be anathema.

Canon VIII. If any one saith, that the fear of hell,—whereby, by grieving for our sins, we flee unto the mercy of God, or refrain from sinning,—is a sin, or makes sinners worse; let him be anathema.

Canon IX. If any one saith, that by faith alone the impious is justified; in such wise as to mean, that nothing else is required to cooperate in order to the obtaining the grace of Justification, and that it is not in any way necessary, that he be prepared and disposed by the movement of his own will; let him be anathema.

Canon XV. If any one saith, that a man, who is born again and justified, is bound of faith to believe that he is assuredly in the number of the predestinate; let him be anathema.

Canon XXIII. If any one saith, that a man once justified can sin no more, nor lose grace, and that therefore he that falls and sins was never truly justified; or, on the other hand, that he is able, during his whole life, to avoid all sins, even those that are venial,—except by a special privilege from God, as the Church holds in regard of the Blessed Virgin; let him be anathema.

Canon XXIV. If any one saith, that the justice received is not preserved and also increased before God through good works; but that the said works are merely the fruits and signs of Justification obtained, but not a cause of the increase thereof; let him be anathema.

THE VERONESE INQUISITION

For a painting of "The Supper at the House of Simon," Paolo Veronese (1528–88) was called before the court of the Inquisition at Venice. The mere existence of an Inquisition trial hardly means that procedures of this kind were taken for granted, or that the Inquisition sitting at Venice did not have its own characteristics adapted to local and contemporary circumstances. But the basic opposition of outlooks cannot be obscured. In the following piece the questions are such as would be expected from the post-Trentine Catholic revival of the later sixteenth century and that Veronese's answers would be made by any man who mirrored the humanistic interests of an increasingly secularized age—views that the pre-Reformation Catholic Church had itself once supported. Evidence, incidentally, indicates that, despite the verdict rendered, the picture was never "corrected."

The selection is taken from F. M. Crawford, *Salve Venetia* (New York, 1906), II, 29–34.

REPORT OF THE SITTING OF THE TRIBUNAL OF THE INQUISITION ON SATURDAY, JULY EIGHTEENTH, 1573

This day, July eighteenth, 1573. Called to the Holy Office before the sacred tribunal, Paolo Galliari Veronese, residing in the parish of Saint Samuel, and being asked as to his name and surname, replied as above.

Being asked as to his profession:

Answer. I paint and make figures.

Question. Do you know the reasons why you have been called here?

A. No.

Q. Can you imagine what those reasons may be?

A. I can well imagine.

Q. Say what you think about them.

A. I fancy that it concerns what was said to me by the reverend fathers, or rather by the prior of the monastery of San Giovanni e Paolo, whose name I did not know, but who informed me that he had been here, and that your

Most Illustrious Lordships had ordered him to cause to be placed in the picture a Magdalen instead of the dog; and I answered him that very readily I would do all that was needful for my reputation and for the honour of the picture; but that I did not understand what this figure of the Magdalen could be doing here. . . .

Q. In this Supper . . . what signifies the figure of him whose nose is bleeding?

A. He is a servant who has a nose-bleed from some accident.

Q. What signify those armed men dressed in the fashion of Germany, with halberds in their hands?

A. It is necessary here that I should say a score of words.

Q. Say them.

A. We painters use the same license as poets and madmen, and I represented those halberdiers, the one drinking, the other eating at the foot of the stairs, but both ready to do their duty, because it seemed to me suitable and possible that the master of the house, who as I have been told was rich and magnificent, should have such servants.

Q. And the one who is dressed as jester with a parrot on his wrist, why did you put him into the picture?

A. He is there as an ornament, as it is usual to insert such figures.

Q. Who are the persons at the table of Our Lord?

A. The twelve apostles.

Q. What is Saint Peter doing, who is the first?

A. He is carving the lamb, in order to pass it to the other table.

Q. What is he doing who comes next?

A. He holds a plate to see what Saint Peter will give him.

Q. Tell us what the third is doing.

A. He is picking his teeth with his fork.

Q. And who are really the persons whom you admit to have been present at this Supper?

A. I believe that there was only Christ and His Apostles; but when I have some space left in a picture I adorn it with figures of my own invention.

Q. Did some person order you to paint Germans, buffoons, and other similar figures in this picture?

A. No, but I was commissioned to adorn it as I thought proper; now it is very large and can contain many figures.

Q. Should not the ornaments which you were accustomed to paint in pictures be suitable and in direct relation to the subject, or are they left to your fancy, quite without discretion or reason?

A. I paint my pictures with all the considerations which are natural to my intelligence, and according as my intelligence understands them.

Q. Does it seem suitable to you, in the Last Supper of our Lord, to represent buffoons, drunken Germans, dwarfs, and other such absurdities?

A. Certainly not.

Q. Then why have you done it?

A. I did it on the supposition that those people were outside the room in which the Supper was taking place.

Q. Do you not know that in Germany and other countries infested by heresy, it is habitual, by means of pictures full of absurdities, to vilify and turn to ridicule the things of the Holy Catholic Church, in order to teach false doctrine to ignorant people who have no common sense?

A. I agree that it is wrong, but I repeat what I have said, that it is my duty to follow the examples given me by my masters.

Q. Well, what did your masters paint? Things of this kind, perhaps?

A. In Rome, in the Pope's Chapel, Michel Angelo has represented Our Lord, His Mother, St. John, St. Peter, and the celestial court; and he has represented all these personages nude, including the Virgin Mary, and in various attitudes not inspired by the most profound religious feeling.

Q. Do you not understand that in representing the Last Judgment, in which it is a mistake to suppose that clothes are worn, there was no reason for painting any? But in these figures what is there that is not inspired by the Holy Spirit? There are neither buffoons, dogs, weapons, nor other absurdities. Do you think therefore, according to this or that view, that you did well in so painting your picture, and will you try to prove that it is a good and decent thing?

A. No, my most Illustrious Sirs; I do not pretend to prove it, but I had not thought that I was doing wrong; I had never taken so many things into consideration. I had been far from imagining such a great disorder, all the more as I had placed these buffoons outside the room in which Our Lord was sitting.

These things having been said, the judges pronounced that the aforesaid Paolo should be obliged to correct his picture within the space of three months from the date of the reprimand, according to the judgments and decision of the Sacred Court, and altogether at the expense of the said Paolo.

Et ita decreverunt omni melius modo. (And so they decided everything for the best!)

VIII

THE DEVELOPMENT OF MODERN SCIENCE

FRANCIS BACON

FRANCIS BACON (1561–1626) was born in London, the youngest son of Sir Nicholas Bacon, Queen Elizabeth's Lord Keeper of the Great Seal. He attended Trinity College, Cambridge, then still dominated by traditional modes of thought. Bacon, however, was influenced by the writings of Peter Ramus, a humanist opponent of scholastic logic. After a short period of foreign travel, Bacon entered Gray's Inn, one of the Inns of Court where English barristers are trained; he was admitted to the bar in 1582. He entered Parliament in 1595 and became a private counselor to the Earl of Essex; but Bacon offered his legal services to the crown at the trial of Essex for rebellion against the Queen and contributed heavily to Essex's conviction. Bacon's advancement under Elizabeth was slow, but he began to realize his ambitions after James I took the throne in 1603. Within ten years he was Attorney General; in 1617 he became Lord Keeper of the Great Seal, and in 1618 Lord Chancellor with the title of Baron Verulam. Later he was made Viscount St. Albans. He did nothing to dissuade King James from pursuing an uncompromising policy with Parliament, and Bacon's political enemies finally used the fact of his taking bribes in the Chancery Courts to bring about his downfall. He admitted the facts but declared that the gifts did not sway his judgment. Found guilty, fined, and deprived of office, Bacon spent only a few days in the Tower, had his sentence remitted, and evaded his fine. But his political power was broken, and he spent the rest of his life in retirement.

Bacon's literary and philosophical output was great even during his political career. His *Essays* (1597) established his literary fame. The *Advancement of Learning* (1605), which offers a detailed criticism of medieval science, and the *Novum Organum* (1620), which proposed a method of inductive inquiry in opposition to scholastic a priorism, are the two completed parts of a projected *Instauratio Magna*.

The general disgust with the old learning and the ideal of useful knowledge, of a science humanized with a new and practical aim of power over nature, had their most outspoken exponent in Bacon. In the *Novum Organum* (*New Method* or *Logic*) he writes (1620): "The method of discovery and proof according to which the most general principles are first established, and then intermediate axioms are tried and proved by them, is the parent of error and the curse of all science." Bacon was equally scornful of what he called the "delicate learning" of humanism. With regard to the humanists' reliance on ancient authorities, Bacon says that Greek wisdom "has the characteristic property of boys: it can talk, but it cannot generate; for it is fruitful of controversies but barren of works." Bacon's writings on scientific method impressed many of his contemporaries, including Leibniz and Boyle, and Macaulay expressed a view widespread in the nineteenth century when he declared that the Baconian philosophy "performed the wonders of subsequent scientific progress." Nonetheless, though his writings on logic contain some valuable reminders, Bacon had no sound grasp of the mathematical-experimental method which characterizes the modern sciences of nature. He underrated the role of bold conjectures in the conduct of inquiry, while at the same time his own thought was controlled by an unwarranted theory concerning the constitution of nature. His writings have had in fact little influence upon the practice of the great contributors to scientific progress. He himself failed to appreciate the work of such men as Copernicus, Kepler, and Gilbert, and in many ways his conception of scientific method was a continuation of the scholasticism he thought he was attacking.

But if Bacon neither initiated nor formulated the method of the new science, he did perform an important mission. He recognized the immense possibilities for human welfare of a science freed from ancient superstitions and authoritarian dogmas. He saw clearly the boundless power men could exercise over nature if only they would first learn to obey her rather than their unconfirmed prejudices. He filled his readers with the great hope that men could master their destiny, and he gave them courage for the struggle against tradition and for a more adequate interpretation of nature.

The following selection summarizes Bacon's criticism of the learning of his time.

$$\mathcal{C}$$

NOVUM ORGANUM

Aphorisms—Book I

I. Man, as the minister and interpreter of nature, does and understands as much as his observations on the order of nature, either with regard to things or the mind, permit him, and neither knows nor is capable of more.

II. The unassisted hand and the understanding left to itself possess but little power. Effects are produced by the means of instruments and helps, which the understanding requires no less than the hand; and as instruments either promote or regulate the motion of the hand, so those that are applied to the mind prompt or protect the understanding.

III. Knowledge and human power are synonymous, since the ignorance of the cause frustrates the effect; for nature is only subdued by submission, and that which in contemplative philosophy corresponds with the cause in practical science becomes the rule.

IX. The sole cause and root of almost every defect in the sciences is this, that while we falsely admire and extol the powers of the human mind, we do not search for its real helps.

XI. As the present sciences are useless for the discovery of effects, so the present system of logic is useless for the discovery of the sciences.

XII. The present system of logic rather assists in confirming and rendering inveterate the errors founded on vulgar notions than in searching after truth, and is therefore more hurtful than useful.

XIII. The syllogism is not applied to the principles of the sciences, and is of no avail in intermediate axioms, as being very unequal to the subtilty of nature. It forces assent, therefore, and not things.

XIX. There are and can exist but two ways of investigating and discovering truth. The one hurries on rapidly from the senses and particulars to the most general axioms, and from them, as principles and their supposed indisputable truth, derives and discovers the intermediate axioms. This is the way now in use. The other constructs its axioms from the senses and particulars, by ascending continually and gradually, till it finally arrives at the most general axioms, which is the true but unattempted way.

XXXIX. Four species of idols beset the human mind, to which (for distinction's sake) we have assigned names, calling the first Idols of the Tribe, the second Idols of the Den, the third Idols of the Market, the fourth Idols of the Theatre.

XL. The formation of notions and axioms on the foundation of true induction is the only fitting remedy by which we can ward off and expel these idols. It is, however, of great service to point them out; for the doctrine of idols bears the same relation to the interpretation of nature as that of the confutation of sophisms does to common logic.

XLI. The idols of the tribe are inherent in human nature and the very tribe or race of man; for man's sense is falsely asserted to be the standard of things; on the contrary, all the perceptions both of the senses and the mind bear reference to man and not to the universe, and the human mind resembles those uneven mirrors which impart their own properties to different objects, from which rays are emitted and distort and disfigure them.

XLII. The idols of the den are those of each individual; for everybody (in addition to the errors common to the race of man) has his own individual den or cavern, which intercepts and corrupts the light of nature, either from his own peculiar and singular disposition, or from his education and intercourse with others, or from his reading, and the authority acquired by those whom he reverences and admires, or from the different impressions produced on the mind, as it happens to be preoccupied and predisposed, or equable and tranquil, and the like; so that the spirit of man (according to its several dispositions), is variable, confused, and as it were actuated by chance; and Heraclitus said well that men search for knowledge in lesser worlds, and not in the greater or common world.

XLIII. There are also idols formed by the reciprocal intercourse and society of man with man, which we call idols of the market, from the commerce and association of men with each other; for men converse by means of language, but words are formed at the will of the generality, and there arises from a bad and unapt formation of words a wonderful obstruction to the mind. Nor can the definitions and explanations with which learned men are wont to guard and protect themselves in some instances afford a complete remedy,—words still manifestly force the understanding, throw everything into confusion, and lead mankind into vain and innumerable controversies and fallacies.

LIX. The idols of the market are the most troublesome of all, those namely which have entwined themselves round the understanding from the associations of words and names. For men imagine that their reason governs words, whilst, in fact, words react upon the understanding; and this has rendered philosophy and the sciences sophistical and inactive. Words are generally formed in a popular sense, and define things by those broad lines which are most obvious to the vulgar mind; but when a more acute understanding, or more diligent observation is anxious to vary those lines, and to adapt them more accurately to nature, words oppose it. Hence the great and solemn disputes of learned men often terminate in controversies about words and names, in regard to which it would be better (imitating the caution of mathematicians) to proceed more advisedly in the first instance, and to bring such disputes to a regular issue by definitions. Such definitions, however, cannot remedy the evil in natural and material objects, because they consist themselves of words, and these words produce others; so that we must necessarily have recourse to particular instances, and their regular series and arrangement, as we shall mention when we come to the mode and scheme of determining notions and axioms.

LX. The idols imposed upon the understanding by words are of two kinds. They are either the names of things which have no existence (for as some objects are from inattention left without a name, so names are formed by fanciful imaginations which are without an object), or they are the names of actual objects, but confused, badly defined, and hastily and irregularly abstracted from things. Fortune, the *primum mobile,* the planetary orbits, the element of fire, and the like fictions, which owe their birth to futile and false theories, are instances of the first kind. And this species of idols is removed with greater facility, because it can be exterminated by the constant refutation or the desuetude of the theories themselves. The others, which are created by vicious and unskilful abstraction, are intricate and deeply rooted. Take some word for instance, as moist, and let us examine how far the different significations of this word are consistent. It will be found that the word moist is nothing but a confused sign of different actions admitting of no settled and defined uniformity. For it means that which easily diffuses itself over another body; that which is indeterminable and cannot be brought to a consistency; that which yields easily in every direction; that which is easily divided and dispersed; that which is easily united and collected; that which easily flows and is put in motion; that which easily adheres to, and wets another body; that which is easily reduced to a liquid state though previously solid. When, therefore, you come to predicate or impose this name, in one sense flame is moist, in another air is not moist, in another fine powder is moist, in another glass is moist, so that it is quite clear that this notion is hastily abstracted from water only, and common ordinary liquors, without any due verification of it.

There are, however, different degrees of distortion and mistake in words. One of the least faulty classes is that of the names of substances, particularly of the less abstract and more defined species (those then of chalk and mud are good, of earth, bad); words signifying actions are more faulty, as to generate, to corrupt, to chance; but the most faulty are those denoting qualities (except the immediate objects of sense), as heavy, light, rare, dense. Yet in all of these there must be some notions a little better than others, in proportion as a greater or less number of things come before the senses.

LXI. The idols of the theatre are not innate, nor do they introduce themselves secretly into the understanding, but they are manifestly instilled and cherished by the fictions of theories and depraved rules of demonstration. To attempt however, or undertake their confutation would not be consistent with our declarations. For since we neither agree in our principles nor our demonstrations, all argument is out of the question. And it is fortunate that the ancients are left in possession of their honours. We detract nothing from them, seeing our whole doctrine relates only to the path to be pursued. The lame (as they say) in the path outstrip the swift who wander from it, and it is clear that the very skill and swiftness of him who runs not in the right direction must increase his aberration.

Our method of discovering the sciences is such as to leave little to the acuteness and strength of wit, and indeed rather to level wit and intellect. For as in the drawing of a straight line, or accurate circle by the hand, much depends on its steadiness and practice, but if a ruler or compass be employed there is little occasion for either; so it is with our method. Although, however, we enter into no individual confutations, yet a little must be said, first, of the sects and general divisions of these species of theories; secondly, something further to show that there are external signs of their weakness; and, lastly, we must consider the causes of so great a misfortune, and so long and general a unanimity in error, that we may thus render the access to truth less difficult, and that the human understanding may the more readily be purified, and brought to dismiss its idols.

LXII. The idols of the theatre, or of theories, are numerous, and may, and perhaps will, be still more so. For unless men's minds had been now occupied for many ages in religious and theological considerations, and civil governments (especially monarchies), had been averse to novelties of that nature even in theory (so that men must apply to them with some risk and injury to their own fortunes, and not only without reward, but subject to contumely and envy), there is no doubt that many other sects of philosophers and theorists would have been introduced, like those which formerly flourished in such diversified abundance amongst the Greeks. For as many imaginary theories of the heavens can be deduced from the phenomena of the sky, so it is even more easy to found many dogmas upon the phenomena of philosophy—and the plot of this our theatre resembles those of the poetical, where the plots which are invented for the stage are more consistent, elegant, and pleasurable than those taken from real history.

In general, men take for the groundwork of their philosophy either too much from a few topics, or too little from many; in either case their philosophy is founded on too narrow a basis of experiment and natural history, and decides on too scanty grounds. For the theoretic philosopher seizes various common circumstances by experiment, without reducing them to certainty or examining and frequently considering them, and relies for the rest upon meditation and the activity of his wit.

There are other philosophers who have diligently and accurately attended to a few experiments, and have thence presumed to deduce and invent systems of philosophy, forming everything to conformity with them.

A third set, from their faith and religious veneration, introduce theology and traditions; the absurdity of some among them having proceeded so far as to seek and derive the sciences from spirits and genii. There are, therefore, three sources of error and three species of false philosophy; the sophistic, empiric, and superstitious.

CV. In forming axioms, we must invent a different form of induction from that hitherto in use; not only for the proof and discovery of principles (as they are called), but also of minor, intermediate, and, in short, every kind of axioms. The induction which proceeds by simple enumeration is puerile, leads to uncertain conclusions, and is exposed to danger from one contradictory instance, deciding generally from too small a number of facts, and those only the most obvious. But a really useful induction for the discovery and demonstration of the arts and sciences, should separate nature by proper rejections and exclusions, and then conclude for the affirmative, after collecting a sufficient number of negatives. Now this has not been done, nor even attempted, except perhaps by Plato, who certainly uses this form of induction in some measure, to sift definitions and ideas. But much of what has never yet entered the thoughts of man must necessarily be employed in order to exhibit a good and legitimate mode of induction or demonstration, so as even to render it essential for us to bestow more pains upon it than have hitherto been bestowed on syllogisms. The assistance of induction is to serve us not only in the discovery of axioms, but also in defining our notions. Much indeed is to be hoped from such an induction as has been described.

CVI. In forming our axioms from induction, we must examine and try whether the axiom we derive be only fitted and calculated for the particular instances from which it is deduced, or whether it be more extensive and general. If it be the latter, we must observe, whether it confirm its own extent and generality by giving surety, as it were, in pointing out new particulars, so that we may neither stop at actual discoveries, nor with a careless grasp catch at shadows and abstract forms, instead of substances of a determinate nature: and as soon as we act thus, well authorized hope may with reason, be said to beam upon us.

GALILEO GALILEI

G ALILEO (1564–1642), born in Pisa, the eldest son of a cultivated but impoverished Florentine noble, studied first medicine and then science in his native city. At twenty-six he was appointed professor of mathematics at the University of Pisa. In 1592 he accepted a professorship in Padua. He remained there for eighteen years, during which time he achieved his most sensational triumphs. He constructed a telescope (1609), through which he discovered Jupiter's moons, the phases of Venus, and spots on the surface of the sun; he then publicly declared himself a Copernican. In 1610 he accepted the post of mathematician at the court of the grand duke of Tuscany, where he came under the censorship of the Church. Although Galileo was well received by Pope Paul V when he visited Rome in 1615 to explain his astronomical views, the next year Copernicus' work was declared heretical by the Inquisition. Galileo thereafter taught the heliocentric theory only as a hypothesis, but his writings made his real acceptance of the Copernican view evident. He was summoned to Rome and forced by the Inquisition to abjure his Copernican views; forbidden to teach, he went into seclusion at his estate in Arcetri, near Florence, where he continued his work.

Galileo's most brilliant literary work is his *Dialogue on the Two Chief Systems of the World* (1632), an implicit defense of the Copernican against the Ptolemaic system. His *Sidereal Messenger* (1610) presents his findings with the telescope, *The Assayer* (1623) his famous distinction between primary and secondary qualities. The *Dialogues concerning Two New Sciences* (1638), his most important work, contains the foundations upon which all subsequent work in dynamics was to be erected.

The first of the following selections is from *The Assayer* (*Il Saggiatore*), originally a series of letters to Virginio Cesarini, chamberlain to Urban VIII.

The second selection, from Galileo's letter of 1615 to the Grand Duchess of Tuscany, has been taken from *Discoveries and Opinions of Galileo* (New York: Anchor Books, 1954). It is followed by a part of the transcript from the record of Galileo's trial.

The last selection, from the First Dialogue of the *Dialogue Concerning the Two Great World-Systems,* has, like the first, been translated from the Italian of Galileo's *Opere,* Vols. V–VII (Florence 1895–98).

THE ASSAYER

IN ACCORDANCE with the promise which I made to Your Excellency, I shall certainly state my ideas concerning the proposition "Motion is the cause of heat," explaining in what way it appears to me to be true. But first it will be necessary for me to say a few words concerning that which we call "heat," for

I strongly suspect that the commonly held conception of the matter is very far from the truth, inasmuch as heat is generally believed to be a true accident, affection, or quality which actually resides in the material which we feel to be heated.

Now, whenever I conceive of any material or corporeal substance, I am necessarily constrained to conceive of that substance as bounded and as possessing this or that shape, as large or small in relationship to some other body, as in this or that place during this or that time, as in motion or at rest, as in contact or not in contact with some other body, as being one, many, or few—and by no stretch of imagination can I conceive of any corporeal body apart from these conditions. But I do not at all feel myself compelled to conceive of bodies as necessarily conjoined with such further conditions as being red or white, bitter or sweet, having sound or being mute, or possessing a pleasant or unpleasant fragrance. On the contrary, were they not escorted by our physical senses, perhaps neither reason nor understanding would ever, by themselves, arrive at such notions. I think, therefore, that these tastes, odors, colors, etc., so far as their objective existence is concerned, are nothing but mere names for something which resides exclusively in our sensitive body (*corpo sensitivo*), so that if the perceiving creature were removed, all of these qualities would be annihilated and abolished from existence. But just because we have given special names to these qualities, different from the names we have given to the primary and real properties, we are tempted into believing that the former really and truly exist as well as the latter.

An example, I believe, will clearly explain my concept. Suppose I pass my hand, first over a marble statue, then over a living man. So far as the hand, considered in itself, is concerned, it will act in an identical way upon each of these objects; that is, the primary qualities of motion and contact will similarly affect the two objects, and we would use identical language to describe this in each case. But the living body, which I subject to this experiment, will feel itself affected in various ways, depending upon the part of the body I happen to touch; for example, should it be touched on the sole of the foot or the kneecap, or under the armpit, it will feel, in addition to simple contact, a further affection to which we have given a special name: we call it "tickling." This latter affection is altogether our own, and is not at all a property of the hand itself. And it seems to me that he would be gravely in error who would assert that the hand, in addition to movement and contact, intrinsically possesses another and different faculty which we might call the "tickling faculty," as though tickling were a resident property of the hand *per se*. Again, a piece of paper or a feather, when gently rubbed over any part of our body whatsoever, will in itself act everywhere in an identical way; it will, namely, move and contact. But we, should we be touched between the eyes, on the tip of the nose, or under the nostrils, will feel an almost intolerable titillation—while if touched in other places, we will scarcely feel anything at all. Now this titillation is completely ours and not the feather's, so that if the living, sensing body were removed, nothing would remain of the titillation but an empty name. And I believe that many other qualities, such as taste, odor, color, and so on, often predicated of natural bodies, have a similar and no greater existence than this.

A solid body and, so to speak, one that is sufficiently heavy, when moved and applied against any part of my body whatsoever, will produce in me the sensation which we call "touch." Although this sense is to be found in every part of the body, it appears principally to reside in the palm of the hand, and even more so in the fingertips, with which we can feel the minutest differences of roughness, texture, and softness and hardness—differences which the other parts of the body are less capable of distinguishing. Some amongst these tactile sensations are more pleasing than others, depending upon the differences of configuration of tangible bodies; that is to say, in accordance with whether they are smooth or irregular, sharp or dull, flexible or rigid. And the sense of touch, being more material than the other senses and being produced by the mass of the material itself, seems to correspond to the element of earth.

Since certain material bodies are continually resolving themselves into tiny particles, some of the particles, because they are heavier than air, will descend; and some of them, because they are lighter than air, will ascend. From this, perhaps, two further senses are born, for certain of the particles penetrate two parts of our body which are effectively more sensitive than the skin, which is incapable of feeling the incursion of materials which are too fine, subtle, or flexible. The descending particles are received by the upper surface of the tongue, and penetrating, they blend with its substance and moisture. Thus our tastes are caused, pleasant or harsh in accordance with variations in the contact of diversely shaped particles, and depending upon whether they are few or many, and whether they have high or low velocity. Other particles ascend, and entering the nostrils they penetrate the various nodes (*mammilule*) which are the instruments of smell; and these particles, in like manner through contact and motion, produce savoriness or unsavoriness—again depending upon whether the particles have this or that shape, high or low velocity, and whether they are many or few. It is remarkable how providently the tongue and nasal passages are situated and disposed, the former stretched beneath to receive the ingression of descending particles, and the latter so arranged as to receive those which ascend. The arrangement whereby the sense of taste is excited in us is perhaps analogous to the way in which fluids descend through the air, and the stimulation of the sense of smell may be compared to the manner in which flames ascend in it.

There remains the element of air, which corresponds to the sense of sound. Sounds come to us indiscriminately, from above and below and from either side, since we are so constituted as to be equally disposed to every direction of the air's movement; and the ear is so situated as to accommodate itself in the highest possible degree to any position in space. Sounds, then, are produced in us and felt when (without any special quality of harmoniousness or dissonance) there is a rapid vibration of air, forming minutely small waves, which move certain cartilages of a certain drum which is in our ear. The various external ways in which this wave-motion of the air is produced are manifold, but can in large part be reduced to the vibrating of bodies which strike the air and form the waves which spread out with great velocity. High frequencies give rise to high tones; low frequencies give rise to low tones. But I cannot believe that there exists in external bodies anything, other than their size, shape, or motion (slow or rapid), which could excite in us our tastes, sounds, and odors. And indeed I should judge that, if ears, tongues, and noses be taken away, the number, shape, and motion of bodies would remain, but not their tastes, sounds, and odors. The latter, external to the living creature, I believe to be nothing but mere names, just as (a few lines back) I asserted tickling and titillation to be, if the armpit or the sensitive skin inside the nose were removed. As to the comparison between the four senses which we have mentioned and the four elements, I believe that the sense of sight, most excellent and noble of all the senses, is like light itself. It stands to the others in the same measure of comparative excellence as the finite stands to the infinite, the gradual to the instantaneous, the divisible to the indivisible, the darkness to the light. Of this sense, and all that pertains to it, I can pretend to understand but little; yet a great deal of time would not suffice for me to set forth even this little bit that I know, or (to put it more exactly) for me to sketch it out on paper. Therefore I shall ponder it in silence.

I return to my first proposition, having now shown how some affections, often reputed to be indwelling properties of some external body, have really no existence save in us, and apart from us are mere names. I confess myself to be very much inclined to believe that heat, too, is of this sort, and that those materials which produce and make felt in us the sense of heat and to which we give the general name "fire" consist of a multitude of tiny particles of such and such a shape, and having such and such a velocity. These, when they encounter our body, penetrate it by means of their extreme subtlety; and it is their contact, felt by us in their passage through our substance, which is the affection we call "heat." It will be pleasantly warm or unpleasantly hot depending upon the number and the velocity (greater or lesser) of these pricking, penetrating particles—pleasant if by their penetration our necessary perspiring is facilitated, unpleasant if their penetrating effects too great a division and dissolution of our substance. In sum, the operation of fire, considered in itself, is nothing but movement, or the penetration of bodies by its extreme subtlety, quickly or slowly, depending upon the number and velocity of tiny corpuscles of flame (*ignicoli*) and upon the greater or lesser density of the bodies concerned. Many bodies dissolve in such a manner that the major part of them becomes transformed into further corpuscles of flame; and this dissolution continues as further dissolvable material is encountered. But that there exists in fire, apart from shape, number, movement, penetration, and contact, some further quality which we call "heat," I cannot believe. And I again judge that heat is altogether subjective, so that if the living, sensitive body be removed, what we call heat would be nothing but a simple word. Since it is the case that this affection is produced in us by passage of tiny corpuscles of flame through our substance and their contact with it, it is obvious that once this motion ceases, their operation upon us will be null. It is thus that we perceive that a quantity of fire, retained in the pores and pits of a piece of calcified stone, does not heat—even if we hold it in the palm of our hand— because the flame remains stationary in the stone. But should we swish the stone in water where, because of its weight, it has greater propensity for movement and where the pits of the stone open somewhat, the corpuscles of flame will escape and, encountering our hand, will penetrate it, so that we will feel heat. Since, in order for heat to be stimulated in us, the mere presence of corpuscles of flame is not by itself sufficient, and since movement is required in addition, it is with considerable reason that I declare motion to be the cause of heat.

This or that movement by which a scantling or other piece of wood is burned up or by which lead and other metals are melted will continue so long as the corpuscles of flame, moved either by their own velocity or (if this be insufficient) aided by a strong blast from a bellows, continue to penetrate the body in question; the former will resolve itself into further corpuscles of flame or into ash; the latter will liquify and be rendered fluid like water. From a common-sense point of view, to assert that that which moves a stone, piece of iron, or a stick, is what *heats* it, seems like an extreme vanity. But the friction produced when two hard bodies are rubbed together, which either reduces them to fine flying particles or permits the corpuscles of flame contained in them to escape, can finally be analyzed as motion. And the particles, when they encounter our body and penetrate and tear through it, are felt, in their motion and contact, by the living creature, who thus feels those pleasant or unpleasant affections which we call "heat," "burning," or "scorching."

Perhaps while this pulverizing and attrition continue, and remain confined to the particles themselves, their motion will be temporary and their operation will be merely that of heating. But once we arrive at the point of ultimate and maximum dissolution into truly indivisible atoms, light itself may be created, with an instantaneous motion or (I should rather say) an instantaneous diffusion and expansion, capable—I do not know if by the atoms' subtlety, rarity, immateriality, or by different and as yet unspecifiable conditions—capable, I say, of filling vast spaces.

But I should not like, Your Excellency, inadvertently to engulf myself in an infinite ocean without the means to find my way back to port. Nor should I like, while removing one doubt, to give birth to a hundred more, as I fear might in part be the case even in this timid venture from shore. Therefore, I shall await a more opportune moment to re-embark.

LETTER TO MADAME CHRISTINA OF LORRAINE, GRAND DUCHESS OF TUSCANY

Concerning the Use of Biblical Quotations in Matters of Science

Galileo Galilei
to
The Most Serene
Grand Duchess Mother:

Some years ago, as Your Serene Highness well knows, I discovered in the heavens many things that had not been seen before our own age. The novelty of these things, as well as some consequences which followed from them in contradiction to the physical notions commonly held among academic philosophers, stirred up against me no small number of professors—as if I had placed these things in the sky with my own hands in order to upset nature and overturn the sciences. They seemed to forget that the increase of known truths stimulates the investigation, establishment, and growth of the arts; not their diminution or destruction.

Showing a greater fondness for their own opinions than for truth, they sought to deny and disprove the new things which, if they had cared to look for themselves, their own senses would have demonstrated to them. To this end they hurled various charges and published numerous writings filled

with vain arguments, and they made the grave mistake of sprinkling these
with passages taken from places in the Bible which they had failed to understand properly, and which were ill suited to their purposes.

Persisting in their original resolve to destroy me and everything mine by
any means they can think of, these men are aware of my views in astronomy
and philosophy. They know that as to the arrangement of the parts of the
universe, I hold the sun to be situated motionless in the center of the revolution of the celestial orbs while the earth rotates on its axis and revolves about
the sun. They know also that I support this position not only by refuting the
arguments of Ptolemy and Aristotle, but by producing many counter-
arguments; in particular, some which relate to physical effects whose causes
can perhaps be assigned in no other way. In addition there are astronomical
arguments derived from many things in my new celestial discoveries that
plainly confute the Ptolemaic system while admirably agreeing with and
confirming the contrary hypothesis. . . .

In order to facilitate their designs, they seek so far as possible (at least
among the common people) to make this opinion seem new and to belong
to me alone. They pretend not to know that its author, or rather its restorer
and confirmer, was Nicholas Copernicus; and that he was not only a
Catholic, but a priest and a canon. He was in fact so esteemed by the church
that when the Lateran Council under Leo X took up the correction of the
church calendar, Copernicus was called to Rome from the most remote parts
of Germany to undertake its reform. . . .

I hope to show that I proceed with much greater piety than they do, when
I argue not against condemning this book, but against condemning it in the
way they suggest—that is, without understanding it, weighing it, or so much
as reading it. For Copernicus never discusses matters of religion or faith, nor
does he use arguments that depend in any way upon the authority of sacred
writings which he might have interpreted erroneously. He stands always
upon physical conclusions pertaining to the celestial motions, and deals with
them by astronomical and geometrical demonstrations, founded primarily
upon sense experiences and very exact observations. He did not ignore the
Bible, but he knew very well that if his doctrine were proved, then it could
not contradict the Scriptures when they were rightly understood. . . .

The reason produced for condemning the opinion that the earth moves
and the sun stands still is that in many places in the Bible one may read
that the sun moves and the earth stands still. Since the Bible cannot err, it
follows as a necessary consequence that anyone takes an erroneous and

heretical position who maintains that the sun is inherently motionless and the earth movable.

With regard to this argument, I think in the first place that it is very pious to say and prudent to affirm that the holy Bible can never speak untruth—whenever its true meaning is understood. But I believe nobody will deny that it is often very abstruse, and may say things which are quite different from what its bare words signify. Hence in expounding the Bible if one were always to confine oneself to the unadorned grammatical meaning, one might fall into error. Not only contradictions and propositions far from true might thus be made to appear in the Bible, but even grave heresies and follies. Thus it would be necessary to assign to God feet, hands, and eyes, as well as corporeal and human affections, such as anger, repentance, hatred, and sometimes even the forgetting of things past and ignorance of those to come. These propositions uttered by the Holy Ghost were set down in that manner by the sacred scribes in order to accommodate them to the capacities of the common people, who are rude and unlearned. For the sake of those who deserve to be separated from the herd, it is necessary that wise expositors should produce the true senses of such passages, together with the special reasons for which they were set down in these words. This doctrine is so widespread and so definite with all theologians that it would be superfluous to adduce evidence for it.

Hence I think that I may reasonably conclude that whenever the Bible has occasion to speak of any physical conclusion (especially those which are very abstruse and hard to understand), the rule has been observed of avoiding confusion in the minds of the common people which would render them contumacious toward the higher mysteries. Now the Bible, merely to condescend to popular capacity, has not hesitated to obscure some very important pronouncements, attributing to God himself some qualities extremely remote from (and even contrary to) His essence. Who, then, would positively declare that this principle has been set aside, and the Bible has confined itself rigorously to the bare and restricted sense of its words, when speaking but casually of the earth, of water, of the sun, or of any other created thing? Especially in view of the fact that these things in no way concern the primary purpose of the sacred writings, which is the service of God and the salvation of souls—matters infinitely beyond the comprehension of the common people.

This being granted, I think that in discussions of physical problems we ought to begin not from the authority of scriptural passages, but from sense-experiences and necessary demonstrations; for the holy Bible and the phenomena of nature proceed alike from the divine Word, the former as the dictate of the Holy Ghost and the latter as the observant executrix of God's commands. It is necessary for the Bible, in order to be accommodated to the understanding of every man, to speak many things which appear to differ from the absolute truth so far as the bare meaning of the words is concerned. But Nature, on the other hand, is inexorable and immutable; she never transgresses the laws imposed upon her, or cares a whit whether her abstruse reasons and methods of operation are understandable to men. For that reason it appears that nothing physical which sense-experience sets before our eyes, or which necessary demonstrations prove to us, ought to be called in question (much less condemned) upon the testimony of biblical passages which may have some different meaning beneath their words. For the Bible is not chained in every expression to conditions as strict as those which govern all physical effects; nor is God any less excellently revealed in Nature's actions than in the sacred statements of the Bible. . . .

From this I do not mean to infer that we need not have an extraordinary esteem for the passages of Holy Scripture. On the contrary, having arrived at any certainties in physics, we ought to utilize these as the most appropriate aids in the true exposition of the Bible and in the investigation of those meanings which are necessarily contained therein, for these must be concordant with demonstrated truths. I should judge that the authority of the Bible was designed to persuade men of those articles and propositions which, surpassing all human reasoning, could not be made credible by science, or by any other means than through the very mouth of the Holy Spirit.

Yet even in those propositions which are not matters of faith, this authority ought to be preferred over that of all human writings which are supported only by bare assertions or probable arguments, and not set forth in a demonstrative way. This I hold to be necessary and proper to the same extent that divine wisdom surpasses all human judgment and conjecture.

But I do not feel obliged to believe that that same God who has endowed us with senses, reason, and intellect has intended to forgo their use and by some other means to give us knowledge which we can attain by them. He would not require us to deny sense and reason in physical matters which are set before our eyes and minds by direct experience or necessary demonstrations. This must be especially true in those sciences of which but the faintest trace (and that consisting of conclusions) is to be found in the Bible. Of astronomy, for instance, so little is found that none of the planets except Venus are so much as mentioned, and this only once or twice under the name of "Lucifer." If the sacred scribes had had any intention of teaching

people certain arrangements and motions of the heavenly bodies, or had
they wished us to derive such knowledge from the Bible, then in my opinion
they would not have spoken of these matters so sparingly in comparison
with the infinite number of admirable conclusions which are demonstrated
in that science. Far from pretending to teach us the constitution and motions
of the heavens and the stars, with their shapes, magnitudes, and distances,
the authors of the Bible intentionally forebore to speak of these things,
though all were quite well known to them. Such is the opinion of the holiest
and most learned Fathers, and in St. Augustine we find the following
words:

"It is likewise commonly asked what we may believe about the form and
shape of the heavens according to the Scriptures, for many contend much
about these matters. But with superior prudence our authors have forborne
to speak of this, as in no way furthering the student with respect to a blessed
life—and, more important still, as taking up much of that time which should
be spent in holy exercises. What is it to me whether heaven, like a sphere,
surrounds the earth on all sides as a mass balanced in the center of the
universe, or whether like a dish it merely covers and overcasts the earth?
Belief in Scripture is urged rather for the reason we have often mentioned;
that is, in order that no one, through ignorance of divine passages, finding
anything in our Bibles or hearing anything cited from them of such a nature
as may seem to oppose manifest conclusions, should be induced to suspect
their truth when they teach, relate, and deliver more profitable matters.
Hence let it be said briefly, touching the form of heaven, that our authors
knew the truth but the Holy Spirit did not desire that men should learn
things that are useful to no one for salvation." . . .

From these things it follows as a necessary consequence that, since the
Holy Ghost did not intend to teach us whether heaven moves or stands still,
whether its shape is spherical or like a discus or extended in a plane, nor
whether the earth is located at its center or off to one side, then so much the
less was it intended to settle for us any other conclusion of the same kind.
And the motion or rest of the earth and the sun is so closely linked with
the things just named, that without a determination of the one, neither side
can be taken in the other matters. Now if the Holy Spirit has purposely
neglected to teach us propositions of this sort as irrelevant to the highest
goal (that is, to our salvation), how can anyone affirm that it is obligatory to
take sides on them, and that one belief is required by faith, while the other
side is erroneous? Can an opinion be heretical and yet have no concern with
the salvation of souls? Can the Holy Ghost be asserted not to have intended teaching us something that does concern our salvation? I would say

here something that was heard from an ecclesiastic of the most eminent degree: "That the intention of the Holy Ghost is to teach us how one goes to heaven, not how heaven goes." . . .

This granted, and it being true that two truths cannot contradict one another, it is the function of wise expositors to seek out the true senses of scriptural texts. These will unquestionably accord with the physical conclusions which manifest sense and necessary demonstrations have previously made certain to us. Now the Bible, as has been remarked, admits in many places expositions that are remote from the signification of the words for reasons we have already given. Moreover, we are unable to affirm that all interpreters of the Bible speak by divine inspiration, for if that were so there would exist no differences between them about the sense of a given passage. Hence I should think it would be the part of prudence not to permit anyone to usurp scriptural texts and force them in some way to maintain any physical conclusion to be true, when at some future time the senses and demonstrative or necessary reasons may show the contrary. Who indeed will set bounds to human ingenuity? Who will assert that everything in the universe capable of being perceived is already discovered and known? Let us rather confess quite truly that "Those truths which we know are very few in comparison with those which we do not know." . . .

I do not wish to place in the number of such lay writers some theologians whom I consider men of profound learning and devout behavior, and who are therefore held by me in great esteem and veneration. Yet I cannot deny that I feel some discomfort which I should like to have removed, when I hear them pretend to the power of constraining others by scriptural authority to follow in a physical dispute that opinion which they think best agrees with the Bible, and then believe themselves not bound to answer the opposing reasons and experiences. In explanation and support of this opinion they say that since theology is queen of all the sciences, she need not bend in any way to accommodate herself to the teachings of less worthy sciences which are subordinate to her; these others must rather be referred to her as to their supreme empress, changing and altering their conclusions according to her statutes and decrees. They add further that if in the inferior sciences any conclusion should be taken as certain in virtue of demonstrations or experiences, while in the Bible another conclusion is found repugnant to this, then the professors of that science should themselves undertake to undo their proofs and discover the fallacies in their own experiences, without bothering the theologians and exegetes. For, they say, it does not become the dignity of theology to stoop to the investigation of fallacies in the subordinate sciences; it is sufficient for her merely to determine the truth of a given conclusion with absolute authority, secure in her inability to err. . . .

First, I question whether there is not some equivocation in failing to specify the virtues which entitle sacred theology to the title of "queen." It might deserve the name by reason of including everything that is learned from all the other sciences and establishing everything by better methods and with profounder learning. It is thus, for example, that the rules for measuring fields and keeping accounts are much more excellently contained in arithmetic and in the geometry of Euclid than in the practices of surveyors and accountants. Or theology might be queen because of being occupied with a subject which excels in dignity all the subjects which compose the other sciences, and because her teachings are divulged in more sublime ways.

That the title and authority of queen belongs to theology in the first sense, I think will not be affirmed by theologians who have any skill in the other sciences. None of these, I think, will say that geometry, astronomy, music, and medicine are much more excellently contained in the Bible than they are in the books of Archimedes, Ptolemy, Boethius, and Galen. Hence it seems likely that regal pre-eminence is given to theology in the second sense; that is, by reason of its subject and the miraculous communication of divine revelation of conclusions which could not be conceived by men in any other way, concerning chiefly the attainment of eternal blessedness.

Let us grant then that theology is conversant with the loftiest divine contemplation, and occupies the regal throne among the sciences by dignity. But acquiring the highest authority in this way, if she does not descend to the lower and humbler speculations of the subordinate sciences and has no regard for them because they are not concerned with blessedness, then her professors should not arrogate to themselves the authority to decide on controversies in professions which they have neither studied nor practiced. Why, this would be as if an absolute despot, being neither a physician or an architect but knowing himself free to command, should undertake to administer medicines and erect buildings according to his whim—at grave peril of his poor patients' lives, and the speedy collapse of his edifices. . . .

If, in order to banish the opinion in question from the world, it were sufficient to stop the mouth of a single man—as perhaps those men persuade themselves who, measuring the minds of others by their own, think it impossible that this doctrine should be able to continue to find adherents—then that would be very easily done. But things stand otherwise. To carry out such a decision it would be necessary not only to prohibit the book of Copernicus and the writings of other authors who follow the same opinion, but to ban the whole science of astronomy. Furthermore, it would be necessary to forbid men to look at the heavens, in order that they might not see Mars and Venus sometimes quite near the earth and sometimes very distant, the variation being so great that Venus is forty times and Mars sixty times as large at one time as another. And it would be necessary to prevent Venus being seen round at one time and forked at another, with very thin horns; as well as many other sensory observations which can never be reconciled with the Ptolemaic system in any way, but are very strong arguments for the Copernican. And to ban Copernicus now that his doctrine is daily reinforced by many new observations and by the learned applying themselves to the reading of his book, after this opinion has been allowed and tolerated for those many years during which it was less followed and less confirmed, would seem in my judgment to be a contravention of truth, and an attempt to hide and suppress her the more as she revealed herself the more clearly and plainly. Not to abolish and censure his whole book, but only to condemn as erroneous this particular proposition, would (if I am not mistaken) be a still greater detriment to the minds of men, since it would afford them occasion to see a proposition proved that it was heresy to believe. And to prohibit the whole science would be but to censure a hundred passages of holy Scripture which teach us that the glory and greatness of Almighty God are marvelously discerned in all his works and divinely read in the open book of heaven. For let no one believe that reading the lofty concepts written in that book leads to nothing further than the mere seeing of the splendor of the sun and the stars and their rising and setting, which is as far as the eyes of brutes and of the vulgar can penetrate. Within its pages are couched mysteries so profound and concepts so sublime that the vigils, labors, and studies of hundreds upon hundreds of the most acute minds have still not pierced them, even after continual investigations for thousands of years. . . . Likewise, that which presents itself to mere sight is as nothing in comparison with the high marvels that the ingenuity of learned men discovers in the heavens by long and accurate observation. . . .

But finally let us grant to these gentlemen even more than they demand; namely, let us admit that we must subscribe entirely to the opinion of wise theologians. Then, since this particular dispute does not occur among the ancient Fathers, it must be undertaken by the wise men of this age. After first hearing the experiences, observations, arguments, and proofs of philosophers and astronomers on both sides—for the controversy is over physical problems and logical dilemmas, and admits of no third alternative—they will be able to determine the matter positively, in accordance with the dictates of divine inspiration. But as to those men who do not scruple to hazard the majesty and dignity of holy Scripture to uphold the reputation of their own vain fancies, let them not hope that a decision such as this is to be made without minutely airing and discussing all the arguments on both sides. Nor need we fear this from men who will make it their whole business to examine most attentively the very foundations of this doctrine, and who will do so only in a holy zeal for the truth, the Bible, and the majesty, dignity, and authority in which every Christian wants to see these maintained.

THE TRIAL OF GALILEO

Accusation

WE, Gaspar, of the title of Holy Cross of Jerusalem, Borgia, brother Felix Certinus of the title of St. Anastatia, surnamed of Asculum.

Guidus, of the title of St. Mary of the People, Bentivolus, brother Desiderius Scaglia, of the title of St. Charles, surnamed of Cremona.

Brother Antonius Barbarinus, surnamed of St. Onuphrius, Laudivius Zacchis, of the title of St. Peter, in vinculis, surnamed of St. Sixtus.

Berlingerius, of the title of St. Augustin Gyposius.

Fabricius of St. Lawrence.

Francis of St. Lawrence.

Martin, of the new St. Mary and Ginethis, Deacons, by the mercy of God, Cardinals of the Holy Roman Catholic Church, and specially deputed by the Holy Apostolical seat as Inquisitors General against heretical perverseness throughout the whole Christian common-wealth.

Whereas you, Galileo, son of the late Vincent Galileo of Florence, being 70 years of age, had a charge brought against you in the year 1615, in this Holy Office, that you held as true, an erroneous opinion held by many; namely, *that the Sun is the centre of the World, and immoveable,* and that the *Earth* moves even with a *diurnal motion:* also that you had certain scholars into whom you instilled the same doctrine: also that you maintained a correspondence on this point, with certain Mathematicians of Germany: also that you published certain Epistles, treating of the *solar spots,* in which you explained the same doctrine, *as true,* because you answered to the objections, which from time to time were brought against you, taken from the Holy Scripture, by glossing over the said Scripture according to *your own sense;* and that afterwards when a copy of a writing in the form of an Epistle, written by you to a certain late scholar of yours, was presented to you, (it following the hypothesis of Copernicus) you stood up for, and defended certain propositions in it, which are against the true sense, and authority of Holy Scripture.

This Holy Tribunal, desiring, therefore, to provide against the inconveniences and mischiefs which have issued hence, and increased to the danger of our Holy Faith; agreeably to the mandate of Lord N——— and the very eminent Doctors, Cardinals of this supreme and universal inquisition: to propositions respecting the immobility of the Sun, and the motion of the Earth, have been adopted and pronounced, as under.

That the Sun is the centre of the World, and immoveable, in respect of local motion, is an absurd proposition, false in philosophy and formally heretical; seeing it is expressly contrary to Holy Scripture.

That the Earth is not the centre of the World, nor immoveable, but moves even with a diurnal motion, is also an absurd proposition, false in Philosophy, and considered Theologically, is at least an error in Faith.

But whereas we have thought fit in the interim to proceed gently with you, it has been agreed upon in the Holy Congregation held before D. N. on the 25th day of Feb. 1616, that the most Eminent Lord Cardinal Bellarmine should enjoin you entirely to recede from the aforesaid false doctrine; and, on your refusal, it was commanded by the Commissary of the Holy Office, that you should recant the said false doctrine, and should not teach it to others, nor defend it, nor dispute concerning it: to which command if you would not submit, that you should be cast into prison: and in order to put in execution the same decree, on the following day you were gently admonished in the Palace before the abovesaid most eminent Lord Cardinal Bellarmine, and afterwards by the same Lord Cardinal: and by the Commissary of the Holy Office, a notary and witnesses being present, entirely to desist from the said erroneous opinion; and that thereafter it should not be permitted you to defend it, or teach it in any manner, either by speaking, or writing; and whereas you promised obedience, you were at that time dismissed.

And to the end, such a *pernicious doctrine* may be entirely extirpated away, and spread no farther, to the grievous detriment of the Catholic verity, a decree was issued by the Holy Congregation *indicis,* prohibiting the printing of books, which treat of such sort of doctrine, which was therein pronounced false, and altogether contrary to Holy and Divine Scripture. And the same book has since appeared at Florence, published in the year last past, the inscription of which, shewed that you were its author, as the title was, *"A Dialogue of Galileo Galilei,"* concerning the two principal systems of the World, the Ptolemaic and the Copernican, as the Holy Congregation, recognizing from the expression of the aforesaid book, that the false opinion concerning the motion of the Earth, and the immobility of the Sun prevailed daily more and more: the aforesaid book, was diligently examined, when we openly discovered the transgression of the aforesaid command, before injoined you; seeing that in the same book you had resumed and defended the aforesaid opinion already condemned, and in your presence declared to be erroneous, because in the said book by various circumlocutions, you earnestly endeavour to persuade, that it is left by you undecided, and at the least probable which must necessarily be a grievous error, since an opinion can by no means be probable, which hath already been declared and adjudged contrary to divine Scripture.

Wherefore you have by our authority been summoned to this our Holy Office, in which being examined you have on oath acknowledged the said book was written and printed by you. And have also confessed, that about ten or twelve years ago, after the injunction had been given you as above, that the said book was begun to be written by you. Also that you petitioned for licence to publish it, but without signifying to those who gave you such licence, that it had been prohibited you, not by any means to maintain, defend, or teach such doctrine.

You likewise confessed, that the writing of the aforesaid book was so composed in many places, that the reader might think, that arguments adduced on the false part, calculated rather to perplex the understanding by their weight, than be easily resolved; excusing yourself, by saying you had fallen into an error so foreign from your intention, (as you declared) because you had handled the subject in the form of a dialogue, and because of the natural complacence which every one hath in maintaining his own arguments, and in shewing himself more acute than others in defending even false propositions by ingenious deductions, and of apparent probability.

And, when a time was assigned you for making your defence, you produced a certificate under the hand-writing of the most eminent Lord Cardinal Bellarmine, procured as you said, in order to defend yourself against the calumnies of our enemies, who everywhere gave it out, that you had abjured, and had been punished by the Holy Office: in which certificate it is said, that you had not abjured, nor had been punished, but only that a declaration had been filed against you, drawn up by the said Lord, and formally issued by the Holy Congregation *Indicis,* in which it is declared that the doctrine concerning the motion of the Earth, and the immobility of the Sun, is contrary to the Holy Scriptures, and therefore can neither be defended or maintained. Wherefore seeing no mention was then made of two particulars of the mandate; namely, *(docere & quovis modo) teaching, and by any means,* we judge that in the course of fourteen or sixteen years they had slipped out of your memory, and for the same reason you were silent respecting the mandate, when you petitioned for a licence to print your book, and yet this was said by you not to maintain, or obstinately persist in your error, but as proceeding from vain ambition, and not perverseness. But this very certificate produced in your defence, rather tends to make your excuse look worse, because in it is declared, that the aforesaid opinion is contrary to the Holy Scripture, and yet you have dared to treat of it as a matter of dispute, and defend, and teach it as probable: nor does the licence itself favour you, seeing it was deceitfully and artfully extorted by you, as you did not produce the mandate imposed upon you.

And whereas it appeared to us, that the whole truth was not expressed by you, respecting your intention: we have judged it necessary to come to a more accurate examination of the business, in which (without prejudice to those things which you have confessed, and which have been brought against you as above, respecting your said intention) you have answered as a penitent, and good Catholic. Wherefore we having maturely considered the merits of your cause, together with your abovesaid confessions, and defence, and are come to the underwritten definitive sentence against you.

Having invoked the most holy name of our Lord Jesus Christ, and of his most glorious mother the ever blessed Virgin Mary, we, by this our definitive sentence, by the advice and judgment of the most Reverend Masters of Holy Theology, and the Doctors of both Laws, our Counsellors respecting the cause and causes controverted before us, between the magnificent Charles Sincerus, Dr. of both Laws, Fiscal Procurator of this Holy Office on the one part, and you, Galileo Galilei defendant, question examined, and having confessed, as above on the other part, we say, judge and declare, by the present processional writing, you, the abovesaid Galileo, on account of those things, which have been adduced in the written process, and which you have confessed, as above, that you have rendered yourself liable to the suspicion of heresy by this office, that is, you have believed and maintained a false doctrine, and contrary to the Holy and Divine Scriptures, namely, that the Sun is the centre of the orb of the Earth, and that it does not move from the East to the West, and that the Earth moves and is not the centre of the World; and that this position may be held and defended as a probable opinion, after it had been declared and defined to be contrary to Holy Scriptures, and consequently that you have incurred all the censures and penalties of the Holy Canons, and other Constitutions general and particular, enacted and promulgated against such delinquents from which it is our pleasure to absolve you, on condition that first, with sincere heart and faith unfeigned, you abjure, execrate, and detest the above errors and heresies, and every other error and heresy, contrary to the Catholic and Apostolical Roman Church, in our presence, in that formula which is hereby exhibited to you.

But that your grievous and pernicious error and transgression may not remain altogether unpunished, and that you may hereafter be more cautious, serving as an example to others, that they may abstain from the like offences, we decree, that the book of the Dialogue of Galileo, be prohibited by public edict, *and we condemn yourself to the prison of this Holy Office, to a time to be limited by our discretion; and we enjoin under the title of salutary penitence, that during three years to come you recite once a week the seven penitential Psalms,* reserving to ourselves the power of moderating, changing, or taking away entirely, or in part, the aforesaid penalties and penitences.

And so we say, pronounce, and by our sentence declare, enact, condemn, and reserve, by this and every other better mode or formula, by which of right we can and ought.

So we, the underwritten Cardinals pronounce, F. Cardinal de Asculo, G. Cardinal Bentivolus, F. Cardinal de Cremona, Fr. Antony Cardinal S. Onuphrii, B. Cardinal Gypsius, F. Cardinal Verospius, M. Cardinal Ginettus.

The Abjuration of Galileo

I, GALILEO GALILEI, son of the late Vincent Galileo, a Florentine, of the age of 70, appearing personally in judgment, and being on my knees in the presence of you, most eminent and most reverend Lords Cardinals of the Universal Christian Commonwealth, Inquisitors General against heretical depravity, having before my eyes the holy Gospels, on which I now lay my hands, swear that I have always believed, and now believe, and God helping, that I shall for the future always believe, whatever the Holy Catholic and Apostolic Roman Church holds, preaches, and teaches. But because this Holy Office had enjoined me by precept, entirely to relinquish the false dogma which maintains that the Sun is the centre of the world, and immoveable, and that the Earth is not the centre, and moves; not to hold, defend, or teach by any means, or by writing, the aforesaid false doctrine; and after it had been notified to me that the aforesaid doctrine is repugnant to the Holy Scripture, I have written and printed a book, in which I treat of the same doctrine already condemned, and adduce reasons with great efficacy in favour of it, not offering any solution of them; therefore I have been adjudged and vehemently suspected of heresy, namely, that I maintained and believed that the Sun is the centre of the world, and immoveable, and that the Earth is not the centre, and moves.

Therefore, being willing to take out of the minds of your eminences, and of every Catholic Christian, this vehement suspicion of right conceived against me, I with sincere heart, and faith unfeigned, abjure, execrate, and detest the aforesaid errors and heresies, and generally every other sect contrary to the above said Holy Church; and I swear that I will never any more hereafter say or assert, by speech or writing, any thing through which the like suspicion may be had of me; but if I shall know any one heretical, or suspected of heresy, I will denounce him to this Holy Office, or to the Inquisitor, and Ordinary of the place in which I shall be. I moreover swear and promise, that I will fulfil and observe entirely all the penitences which have been imposed upon me, or which shall be imposed by this Holy Office. But if it shall happen that I shall go contrary (which God avert) to any of my words, promises, protestations, and oaths, I subject myself to all the penalties and punishments, which, by the Holy Canons, and other Constitutions, general and particular, have been enacted and promulgated against such delinquents: So help me God, and his Holy Gospels, on which I now lay my hands.

I, the aforesaid Galileo Galilei, have abjured, sworn, promise, and have bound myself as above, and in the fidelity of those with my own hands, and have subscribed to this present writing of my abjuration, which I have recited word by word. At Rome, in the Convent of Minerva, this 22d of June, of the year 1633.

I, Galileo Galilei, have abjured as above, with my own hand.

DIALOGUE CONCERNING THE TWO GREAT WORLD-SYSTEMS

Simplicius. However perspicacious his genius may have been, Aristotle was not one to depend upon it more than seemed advisable; and in his philosophizing, he judged that sense-experience must be preferred to any argument whatsoever, fabricated by the mind of man. He said that whoever would deny his senses ought, as punishment, to be deprived of them. . . . So let us proceed to the specific reasons and the sensory experiences which (how well Aristotle put it!) must be preferred to what may be supplied by human reason.

Sagredo. What has been said, then, should enable us to consider which of the two general arguments, that of Aristotle or that of Salviatus, has the greater probability. Aristotle's would persuade us that sublunary bodies are generable, corruptible, etc.; and that they are, therefore, different indeed from celestial bodies, which are impassible—that is to say, ingenerable, incorruptible, and so forth. . . . Salviatus, who supposes that the integral parts of the world are arranged in a perfect order, . . . deems the Earth itself to be a celestial body, endowed with all the prerogatives which the latter possess. His argument, it seems to me, is much more in accord with things than Aristotle's. But be so good, Simplicius, as to produce all those particular reasons, experiments, and observations, natural as well as astronomical, on the basis of which others may remain persuaded that the Earth is different from celestial bodies, that it is immobile and located in the center of the world, and that it is otherwise prohibited from being as mobile as a planet like Jupiter or the Moon. And let Salviatus, on his part, be kind enough to answer them, point for point.

Simp. Well, to begin with, here are two powerful demonstrations which prove the Earth to be altogether different from celestial bodies. First. Bodies which are generable, corruptible, alterable, etc., are different from those which are ingenerable, incorruptible, inalterable, etc. But the Earth is generable, corruptible, alterable, etc.; and heavenly bodies are not. Therefore, the Earth is different from heavenly bodies!

Sagr. With your first argument, you merely bring back to the table that which stood there all day long, and which we just eliminated a moment back.

Simp. Just a moment, sir! Listen to the rest of it, and you shall see how really different the two sorts of bodies are. In my first argument, the minor premise was set forth *a priori*. I should like now to prove it *a posteriori*—watch if they are not the same. Since the major premise is too obviously true, I shall prove the minor premise as follows. Sensory experience shows us how on Earth there is continual generation, corruption, and change. But neither our own senses, nor the records of antiquity, have ever once witnessed these as taking place in celestial bodies. Hence the heavens are inalterable and the Earth is alterable, etc.

I base my second argument on a principal and essential property. A body which is obscure and deprived of light is different from a luminous, resplendent body. The Earth is dark and without light, but the heavenly bodies are full of light and brilliant. Therefore, they are different. Answer these arguments first, before we accumulate too many, and then I shall bring forward some others.

Salviatus. As to the first one, the force of which you derive from experience, I should like you to produce for me more distinctly those alterations which you see taking place on Earth but not in the heavens, and on the basis of which you claim Earth to be alterable and the heavens not.

Simp. I see on Earth the continual generation and decay of animals and plants; and I see the rising up of winds and rains, storms and tempests. In sum, the face of the Earth is in perpetual metamorphosis. Yet none of these mutations is to be discerned in celestial bodies: *their* constitutions and configurations exactly conform to what they have been from time immemorial, with neither the generation of anything new, nor the corruption of anything old.

Salv. But, if you rest content with these visible things, or rather, to express myself more clearly, with what you have experienced, it would be necessary for you to call China and America heavenly bodies. For surely, you have never observed in them those alterations which you have seen here in Italy. So if it is a question of your apprehension of them, America and China are inalterable.

Simp. Of course, I have never seen such alterations in those places with my senses: but I have heard unquestionable reports of them. Besides, part and whole have the same nature; and since those countries are as much a part of the Earth as Italy is, they must necessarily be as alterable as Italy.

Salv. Why is it, though, that you are reduced to placing faith in other men's reports? Why can't you, with your own eyes, observe and witness what takes place there?

Simp. Because those countries are not exposed to my eyes. Besides, they are so remote that our vision cannot come to comprehend similar mutations there.

Salv. Look, how you have discovered the fallacy of your own argument unintentionally! For if you assert that changes, which may be seen in parts of the Earth near to us, cannot, because of the great distance, be discerned in America, how much less could we discern them in the Moon, which is many hundred times more distant! And if you believe that there are changes which take place in Mexico on the basis of reports which have come from there, what reports have come from the Moon to signify that there are no alterations there? Now, simply because you have never seen any alterations in the heavens (owing to the great distance), and because you have never heard reports of any (since there are none), you ought not to argue that there are in fact no alterations in Heaven. It is not the same thing as arguing that alterations exist on Earth from your having seen and understood them. You can well argue that.

Simp. I shall show you mutations which have taken place on Earth which are so vast that, if similar mutations had taken place on the Moon, they would have been observed from here below. We know, from the most antique records, that in the Straits of Gibraltar, Abile and Calpe were once connected; and that they, together with smaller mountains, held back the sea. But, from some cause or other, these mountains were separated. Thus an opening was made for the waters of the sea, which flowed in to such an extent that our entire Mediterranean Sea was formed. If we but consider the size of that sea, and how different the aspect of land and water must now appear if seen from afar, there can be no doubt that such a mutation would have been observable to someone then in the Moon. A similar alteration, had it taken place in the Moon, would have to be perceivable to us inhabitants of the Earth. Yet there is no record of any such thing having ever been seen there; and there remains, then, no basis for challenging our ability to claim that no celestial body is alterable, and so on.

Salv. I would not be so audacious as to declare that such vast mutations have taken place in the Moon; but I am not at all sure that they *could* not have occurred. Such a mutation would be represented only by some variation between the light and dark parts of the Moon, and I do not know if there are, on Earth, careful moon-specialists who, over a long sequence of years, have gathered information exact enough to convince us that no such mutation has ever occurred on the Moon's surface. I have not yet been able to gather very detailed descriptions of the configuration of the Moon. Some say it represents a human face. Others say it is like the muzzle of a lion, and still others maintain that it is Cain, with a bundle of thorns on his back. So, to assert that "Heaven is inalterable because the alterations discerned on Earth are not discernible in the Moon or in other celestial bodies" is to prove nothing at all.

Sagr. There still remains in my mind some vague doubt concerning Simplicius's first argument, and I would like to have it removed. So I should want to ask whether the Earth was generable and corruptible before the Mediterranean inundation, or whether it only became so afterwards?

Simp. There is no doubt that it was generable and corruptible even before. That was only a vast mutation which could have been observed from the Moon.

Sagr. Ah, but if the Earth, even before that inundation, was generable and corruptible, why cannot the Moon be so as well, even though there has been no similar mutation there? Why should that which made no difference in the Earth necessarily make any difference in the Moon?

Salv. A very clever point. But I suspect that Simplicius has somewhat altered the meaning of the texts of Aristotle and the other Peripatetics. For they declare and maintain that the heavens are inalterable because the generation and corruption of no star has ever been seen. Yet a star is a lesser part of heaven than a city is of Earth; and countless cities have been destroyed in such a manner that no vestige of them now remains.

Sagr. I certainly disagree with you: *I* thought that Simplicius twisted his exposition of the text in order not to burden his Master and his fellow disciples with a still more distorted notion. But how silly to say "the heavens are inalterable because no stars are generated or destroyed there!" Indeed! Has anyone ever seen a *terrestrial* globe corrupted and another one regenerated? And is it not accepted by all philosophers that there be few stars in heaven smaller than the Earth, and a great, great many much larger than the Earth? The corruption of a star in heaven would surely not be a smaller event than the destruction of the whole terrestrial globe. So if, in order truly to introduce generability and corruptibility into the universe, it is necessary that bodies as vast as stars be destroyed and regenerated, you may as well forget the whole idea. For I assure you, the destruction neither of the terrestrial globe nor of any body which is an integral part of the world will ever be seen. As though, after having been observed for several centuries in a row, these bodies should dissolve in such a way as to leave no trace behind!

Salv. But to give superabundant satisfaction to Simplicius and to disabuse him, if possible, of error, I say that we have in our century such new events and discoveries that Aristotle, were he alive today, would change his opinions. That he would do so may be gathered from his own manner of philosophizing. Thus, when he writes that he deems the heavens to be inalterable, etc., because neither the generation of any new thing nor the corruption of any old thing has ever been seen there, he seems implicitly to leave it understood that if he should see such an event he would assert the contrary; and that he would prefer, as is proper, sensory experience to natural reason. For had he not wished to value his senses, he would never have argued that the heavens are inalterable from the fact that he had never, with his senses, seen any change there.

Simp. Aristotle bases his principle fundamentally on *a priori* argument, showing that, from his own principles of nature, the inalterability of the heavens necessarily follows and is manifestly and clearly the case. Afterwards he establishes the same proposition *a posteriori, i.e.,* by means of the senses and by means of the traditions of antiquity.

Salv. What you are speaking about is the method he used to write down his doctrine; but I still do not believe that he used the same method in his actual inquiries. I feel certain that he first procured what observations and experiments he could by means of the senses, in order, wherever possible, to be sure of his conclusions. Afterwards he would have sought out the means by which to demonstrate them; this is common practice in the demonstrative sciences. The reason for the latter step is as follows: when our conclusion is true we can, with the analytic method, easily connect it with certain already demonstrated propositions or with principles already known *per se* to be true. But if the conclusion is false, we might proceed to infinity without ever connecting it with any known truth, but only with propositions either known to be false or else impossible or patently absurd. . . . But even if it were the case that, in Aristotle's procedure, *a priori* argument preceded *a posteriori* sensation, instead of conversely, it is sufficient that Aristotle himself preferred—as has often been said—the experience of his senses to all argumentation. Besides, we have already examined how much force your *a priori* arguments possess.

Now to return to the matter at hand. I assert that the things discovered in the skies during our own era have been, and are, such as to give sufficient satisfaction to any philosopher. For in individual bodies, and throughout the entire expanse of heaven, we have seen and we continue to see happenings which are similar to what is called amongst us generation and corruption. Many excellent astronomers have observed the generation and destruction of many comets in regions high above the Moon's sphere. Furthermore, there are the two new stars of 1572 and 1604: without contradiction, they are high above all the planets. And thanks to the telescope, dense and dark materials, similar to fogs over the Earth, may be seen produced and dissolved across the very face of the Sun. And these [spots] are so vast that they are not merely larger than your Mediterranean Sea, but all of Africa and Asia as well! Now, if Aristotle were to see all this, Simplicius, what do you believe he would say and how do you think he would act? . . .

Sagr. Those who have wished to make human capacity for understanding the measure of what Nature knows and can do, have always struck me as extraordinarily brash. On the contrary, the most speculative spirit cannot fully comprehend any natural effect, however small it be. The vain presumption that everything is understood can come only from having understood nothing at all. For if someone were to have experienced perfect knowledge of just one thing, and to have truly tasted what knowledge is made of, he would recognize that he has not understood even one of all the infinitely many other things.

Salv. Your argument is quite conclusive indeed; and for confirmation we have the experience of those who understand, or have understood, some thing. The more knowledge they possess, the more they recognize and freely confess themselves to know little. He whom the oracle pronounced to be the wisest of the Greeks, openly declared that he was aware that he knew nothing.

Simp. If Socrates declared himself to be the most ignorant while the oracle declared him to be the wisest, then I must point out that either Socrates or the oracle was a liar.

Salv. Neither conclusion follows, for both statements could be true. The oracle judged Socrates to be wise above all other men, whose wisdom is limited. Socrates claimed to know nothing with respect to absolute knowledge, which is infinite. With respect to infinity, any finite thing, be it large or small, is as nothing (to arrive at infinity, for example, it does not matter whether we add together thousands, tens, or units). Socrates understood well enough that the extent of his wisdom was nothing in comparison with the infinite wisdom which he lacked. Still, since there is some wisdom found in men, and this not equally distributed amongst all, Socrates could have had a greater share than all the others, and the response of the oracle would thence be verified.

Sagr. I seem to understand that point very well. Amongst men, Simplicius, there is the power to act, but it is not shared equally by all. There is no doubt that the power of an emperor is far greater than that of an ordinary person —but neither the one nor the other counts as anything in comparison with divine omnipotence. Amongst men, we find some who understand agriculture better than most others do. But to know how to plant a grape-seed in a hole—what has that to do with knowing how to make it take root, or how to draw nourishment to it, or how to select this part as good for making leaves, that for the vines, another for the clusters, another for the grapes, another for the skins! These are the workings of Nature, in all her wisdom. And yet this is only one of all the innumerable things which Nature does; and in just this one thing, we may recognize infinite wisdom. Can we not conclude that divine wisdom is infinitely infinite?

Salv. Here is another example. Would we not say that the knowledge of how to discover a beautiful statue in a piece of marble has raised the genius of Michelangelo high, high above the common wit of other men? And his work is only the imitation of a single pose and disposition of the outside parts of the external members of an immobile man. What is this, though, compared to a man made by Nature, composed of all the external and internal members, all the muscles, tendons, nerves, and bones which serve so many different motions? And what shall we say of the senses, the will, and the intellect? Can we not with good reason say that the fabrication of a statue, by an interval of infinity, falls short of the formation not only of a living man, but even of the vilest worm? . . .

Simp. Either I am not a man who understands, or else your discourse is manifestly inconsistent. You reckon understanding to be one of the greatest gifts—if not, indeed, the greatest—which have been given to man who is made by Nature. But a moment ago, you said of Socrates that his understanding was as nothing. So you must say that Nature has not understood how to make an understanding that understands!

Salv. Very sharply put! And in order to reply to your objection, I must have recourse to a philosophical distinction. Now, understanding may be interpreted in two different ways, *intensively* and *extensively*. Extensively, that is to say, with respect to the infinite number of intelligible things, the human understanding is as nothing. Even if it well understood a thousand propositions, a thousand is like zero in comparison with infinity. But intensively, that is to say, in terms of knowing some one thing perfectly, I assert that there are some propositions of which the human understanding is as absolutely certain as Nature is. I mean the sciences of pure mathematics— geometry and arithmetic. The divine intellect may well know infinitely more such propositions than we, because it knows them all. But of those few that the human intellect does know, I believe our knowledge is equal to divine knowledge, so far as objective certainty is concerned. For we have come to understand the necessity of these propositions, and there can be no greater certainty than that.

Simp. This appears very bold to me, very rash.

Salv. These are common notions and are far from being tainted by audacity or presumptuousness. Nor do they in any way detract from the majesty of divine wisdom, any more than it would diminish God's omnipotence to assert that He cannot undo what has once been done. But I suspect, Simplicius, that you take umbrage at my words because, as you hear them, you feel them to be somewhat equivocal. Therefore, in order better to express myself, I shall say that the truth which mathematical demonstration gives us is the same truth that divine wisdom apprehends. I grant you that the manner in which God knows the infinity of propositions is utterly more excellent than is the manner by means of which we know the few that we do. We proceed by argumentation, and advance from conclusion to conclusion, while God [apprehends] through a simple, sudden intuition. . . . To conclude, then, the manner and number of propositions known to human intellect is infinitely surpassed by divine intellect. Nonetheless, I would not dishonor it. For when I consider how many, and how marvelous, are the things that human intellect has understood, discovered, and invented, I clearly know and do acknowledge that the mind of man is the work of God. And that is one of His most excellent ones.

RENÉ DESCARTES

R ENÉ DESCARTES (1596–1650) was born at La Haye in Touraine, France, of a noble family. He received a solid foundation in scholastic methods at the excellent Jesuit College of La Flèche; but he also prepared himself for his subsequent career by intense early study of mathematics. After completing his formal education at the University of Poitiers he spent several years in secluded study, and then joined the army of Prince Maurice of Nassau and later that of the elector of Bavaria. He lived in Paris for a time, arranged his finances to provide him with a comfortable income, and settled in Holland in 1628 to work out the details of his universal mathematics and philosophical methodology. His views were widely known and taught and bitterly attacked by both Catholic and Protestant theologians as leading to skeptical unbelief, though Descartes himself continued to profess Catholicism. His international reputation established, Descartes went to Stockholm in 1649 to instruct Queen Christina; but the climate was too harsh for his poor health, and he died within a year.

Descartes united geometry and algebra into the single discipline of analytical geometry for a universal mathematics of nature. *Le Monde* presents his conviction that the cosmic order is created by a First Cause (God) out of an initial chaos according to mechanical laws. A group of essays published in 1637 included his well-known *Discourse on Method*, which outlines his dualistic philosophy with its emphasis on the radical division between matter and spirit. *Dioptrics, Meteors,* and *Geometry* offer more concrete illustrations of his method. *Meditations* (1640) and *Principles of Philosophy* (1644) give fuller accounts of his ideas. *Passions of the Soul* (1649) is his chief work on psychology and ethics.

Descartes's philosophy had a great appeal for his contemporaries. It provided them with an apparently infallible method for achieving certainty. It gave full scope for the application of mathematical methods to all domains of material existence. And it supplied a plausible distinction on the strength of which matters of religious interest could be exempted from the dominion of a universal mechanics. Descartes could profess his Catholicism without hypocrisy and at the same time he could boast "Give me extension and motion and I will construct the world." But the Church was not convinced that his philosophy presented no dangers, and Descartes's writings were placed on the Index in 1663.

Descartes's conception of his universal mathematics made it applicable not only to inorganic materials but also to biological and psychological phenomena. He stimulated the further application of mathematical methods to phases of nature not previously investigated in that manner. And this aspect of Descartes's influence was to prove of immense importance for the sciences of man and society.

The following selections are from the John Veitch translation of the *Discourse on Method* (Chicago, Open Court, 1908), which was taken from the original French and collated with the subsequent Latin version. They describe Descartes's intellectual development, the essential features of his method, and his attempt to supply a mechanical explanation for physiological facts.

❧

DISCOURSE ON METHOD

Part I

GOOD SENSE is, of all things among men, the most equally distributed; for every one thinks himself so abundantly provided with it, that those even who are the most difficult to satisfy in everything else, do not usually desire a larger measure of this quality than they already possess. And in this it is not likely that all are mistaken: the conviction is rather to be held as testifying that the power of judging aright and of distinguishing Truth from Error, which is properly what is called Good Sense or Reason, is by nature equal in all men; and that the diversity of our opinions, consequently, does not arise from some being endowed with a larger share of Reason than others, but solely from this, that we conduct our thoughts along different ways, and do not fix our attention on the same objects. For to be possessed of a vigorous mind is not enough; the prime requisite is rightly to apply it. The greatest minds, as they are capable of the highest excellencies, are open likewise to the greatest aberrations; and those who travel very slowly may yet make far greater progress, provided they keep always to the straight road, than those who, while they run, forsake it.

For myself, I have never fancied my mind to be in any respect more perfect than those of the generality; on the contrary, I have often wished that I were equal to some others in promptitude of thought, or in clearness and distinctness of imagination, or in fulness and readiness of memory. And besides these, I know of no other qualities that contribute to the perfection of the mind; for as to the Reason or Sense, inasmuch as it is that alone which constitutes us men, and distinguishes us from the brutes, I am disposed to believe that it is to be found complete in each individual; and on this point to adopt the common opinion of philosophers, who say that the difference of greater and less holds only among the *accidents,* and not among the *forms* or *natures* of *individuals* of the same *species.*

I will not hesitate, however, to avow my belief that it has been my singular good fortune to have very early in life fallen in with certain tracks which have conducted me to considerations and maxims, of which I have formed a Method that gives me the means, as I think, of gradually augmenting my knowledge, and of raising it by little and little to the highest point which the mediocrity of my talents and the brief duration of my life will permit me to reach. For I have already reaped from it such fruits that, although I have been accustomed to think lowly enough of myself, and although when I look with the eye of a philosopher at the varied courses and pursuits of mankind at large, I find scarcely one which does not appear vain and useless, I nevertheless derive the highest satisfaction from the progress I conceive myself to have already made in the search after truth, and cannot help entertaining such expectations of the future as to believe that if, among the occupations of men as men, there is any one really excellent and important, it is that which I have chosen.

After all, it is possible I may be mistaken; and it is but a little copper and glass, perhaps, that I take for gold and diamonds. I know how very liable we are to delusion in what relates to ourselves, and also how much the judgments of our friends are to be suspected when given in our favour. But I shall endeavour in this Discourse to describe the paths I have followed, and to delineate my life as in a picture, in order that each one may be able to judge of them for himself, and that in the general opinion entertained of them, as gathered from current report, I myself may have a new help towards instruction to be added to those I have been in the habit of employing.

My present design, then, is not to teach the Method which each ought to follow for the right conduct of his reason, but solely to describe the way in which I have endeavoured to conduct my own. They who set themselves to give precepts must of course regard themselves as possessed of greater skill than those to whom they prescribe; and if they err in the slightest particular, they subject themselves to censure. But as this Tract is put forth merely as a history, or, if you will, as a tale, in which, amid some examples worthy of imitation, there will be found, perhaps, as many more which it were advisable not to follow, I hope it will prove useful to some without being hurtful to any, and that my openness will find some favour with all.

From my childhood, I have been familiar with letters; and as I was given to believe that by their help a clear and certain knowledge of all that is useful in life might be acquired, I was ardently desirous of instruction. But as soon as I had finished the entire course of study, at the close of which it is customary to be admitted into the order of the learned, I completely changed my opinion.

For I found myself involved in so many doubts and errors, that I was convinced I had advanced no farther in all my attempts at learning, than the discovery at every turn of my own ignorance. And yet I was studying in one of the most celebrated Schools in Europe, in which I thought there must be learned men, if such were anywhere to be found. I had been taught all that others learned there; and not contented with the sciences actually taught us, I had, in addition, read all the books that had fallen into my hands, treating of such branches as are esteemed the most curious and rare. I knew the judgment which others had formed of me; and I did not find that I was considered inferior to my fellows, although there were among them some who were already marked out to fill the places of our instructors. And, in fine, our age appeared to me as flourishing, and as fertile in powerful minds as any preceding one. I was thus led to take the liberty of judging of all other men by myself, and of concluding that there was no science in existence that was of such a nature as I had previously been given to believe.

I still continued, however, to hold in esteem the studies of the Schools. I was aware that Languages taught in them are necessary to the understanding of the writings of the ancients; that the grace of Fable stirs the mind; that the memorable deeds of History elevate it; and, if read with discretion, aid in forming the judgment; that the perusal of all excellent books is, as it were, to interview with the noblest men of past ages, who have written them, and even a studied interview, in which are discovered to us only their choicest thoughts; that Eloquence has incomparable force and beauty; that Poesy has its ravishing graces and delights; that in the Mathematics there are many refined discoveries eminently suited to gratify the inquisitive, as well as further all the arts and lessen the labour of man; that numerous highly useful precepts and exhortations to virtue are contained in treatises on Morals; that Theology points out the path to heaven; that Philosophy affords the means of discoursing with an appearance of truth on all matters, and commands the admiration of the more simple; that Jurisprudence, Medicine, and the other Sciences, secure for their cultivators honours and riches; and, in fine, that it is useful to bestow some attention upon all, even upon those abounding the most in superstition and error, that we may be in a position to determine their real value, and guard against being deceived.

But I believed that I had already given sufficient time to Languages, and likewise to the reading of the writings of the ancients, to their Histories and Fables. For to hold converse with those of other ages and to travel, are almost the same thing. It is useful to know something of the manners of different nations, that we may be able to form a more correct judgment regarding our own, and be prevented from thinking that everything contrary to our customs is ridiculous and irrational,—a conclusion usually come to by those whose experience has been limited to their own country. On the other hand, when too much time is occupied in travelling, we become strangers to our native country; and the over curious in the customs of the past are generally ignorant of those of the present. Besides, fictitious narratives lead us to imagine the possibility of many events that are impossible; and even the most faithful histories, if they do not wholly misrepresent matters, or exaggerate their importance to render the account of them more worthy of perusal, omit, at least, almost always the meanest and least striking of the attendant circumstances; hence it happens that the remainder does not represent the truth, and that such as regulate their conduct by examples drawn from this source, are apt to fall into the extravagances of the knight-errants of Romance, and to entertain projects that exceed their powers.

I esteemed Eloquence highly, and was in raptures with Poesy; but I thought that both were gifts of nature rather than fruits of study. Those in whom the faculty of Reason is predominant, and who most skilfully dispose their thoughts with a view to render them clear and intelligible, are always the best able to persuade others of the truth of what they lay down, though they should speak only in the language of Lower Brittany, and be wholly ignorant of the rules of Rhetoric; and those whose minds are stored with the most agreeable fancies, and who can give expression to them with the greatest embellishment and harmony, are still the best poets, though unacquainted with the Art of Poetry.

I was especially delighted with the Mathematics, on account of the certitude and evidence of their reasonings: but I had not as yet a precise knowledge of their true use; and thinking that they but contributed to the advancement of the mechanical arts, I was astonished that foundations, so strong and solid, should have had no loftier superstructure reared on them. On the other hand, I compared the disquisitions of the ancient Moralists to very towering and magnificent palaces with no better foundation than sand and mud: they laud the virtues very highly, and exhibit them as estimable far above anything on earth; but they give us no adequate criterion of virtue, and frequently that which they designate with so fine a name is but apathy, or pride, or despair, or parricide.

I revered our Theology, and aspired as much as any one to reach heaven: but being given assuredly to understand that the way is not less open to the most ignorant than to the most learned, and that the revealed truths which lead to heaven are above our comprehension, I did not presume to subject them to the impotency of my Reason; and I thought that in order competently to undertake their examination, there was need of some special help from heaven, and of being more than man.

Of Philosophy I will say nothing, except that when I saw that it had been cultivated for many ages by the most distinguished men, and that yet there is not a single matter within its sphere which is not still in dispute, and nothing, therefore, which is above doubt, I did not presume to anticipate that my success would be greater in it than that of others; and further, when I considered the number of conflicting opinions touching a single matter that may be upheld by learned men, while there can be but one true, I reckoned as well-nigh false all that was only probable.

As to the other Sciences, inasmuch as these borrow their principles from Philosophy, I judged that no solid superstructures could be reared on foundations so infirm; and neither the honour nor the gain held out by them was sufficient to determine me to their cultivation: for I was not, thank heaven, in a condition which compelled me to make merchandise of Science for the bettering of my fortune; and though I might not profess to scorn glory as a Cynic, I yet made very slight account of that honour which I hoped to acquire only through fictitious titles. And, in fine, of false Sciences I thought I knew the worth sufficiently to escape being deceived by the professions of an alchemist, the predictions of an astrologer, the impostures of a magician, or by the artifices and boasting of any of those who profess to know things of which they are ignorant.

For these reasons, as soon as my age permitted me to pass from under the control of my instructors, I entirely abandoned the study of letters, and resolved no longer to seek any other science than the knowledge of myself, or of the great book of the world. I spent the remainder of my youth in travelling, in visiting courts and armies, in holding intercourse with men of different dispositions and ranks, in collecting varied experience, in proving myself in the different situations into which fortune threw me, and, above all, in making such reflection on the matter of my experience as to secure my improvement. For it occurred to me that I should find much more truth in the reasonings of each individual with reference to the affairs in which he is personally interested, and the issue of which must presently punish him if he has judged amiss, than in those conducted by a man of letters in his study, regarding speculative matters that are of no practical moment, and followed by no consequences to himself, farther, perhaps, than that they foster his vanity the better the more remote they are from common sense; requiring, as they must in this case, the exercise of greater ingenuity and art to render them probable. In addition, I had always a most earnest desire to know how to distinguish the true from the false, in order that I might be able clearly to discriminate the right path in life, and proceed in it with confidence.

It is true that, while busied only in considering the manners of other men, I found here, too, scarce any ground for settled conviction, and remarked hardly less contradiction among them than in the opinions of the philosophers. So that the greatest advantage I derived from the study consisted in this, that, observing many things which, however extravagant and ridiculous to our apprehension, are yet by common consent received and approved by other great nations, I learned to entertain too decided a belief in regard to nothing of the truth of which I had been persuaded merely by example and custom: and thus I gradually extricated myself from many errors powerful enough to darken our Natural Intelligence, and incapacitate us in great measure from listening to Reason. But after I had been occupied several years in thus study-ing the book of the world, and in essaying to gather some experience, I at length resolved to make myself an object of study, and to employ all the powers of my mind in choosing the paths I ought to follow; an undertaking which was accompanied with greater success than it would have been had I never quitted my country or my books.

Part II

I was then in Germany, attracted thither by the wars in that country, which have not yet been brought to a termination; and as I was returning to the army from the coronation of the Emperor, the setting in of winter arrested me in a locality where, as I found no society to interest me, and was besides fortunately undisturbed by any cares or passions, I remained the whole day in seclusion, with full opportunity to occupy my attention with my own thoughts. Of these one of the very first that occurred to me was, that there is seldom so much perfection in works composed of many separate parts, upon which different hands have been employed, as in those completed by a single master. Thus it is observable that the buildings which a single architect has planned and executed, are generally more elegant and commodious than those which several have attempted to improve, by making old walls serve for purposes for which they were not originally built. Thus also, those ancient cities which, from being at first only villages, have become, in course of time, large towns, are usually but ill laid out compared with the regularly constructed towns which a pro-fessional architect has freely planned on an open plain; so that although the several buildings of the former may often equal or surpass in beauty those of the latter, yet when one observes their indiscriminate juxtaposition, there a large one and here a small, and the consequent crookedness and irregularity of the streets, one is disposed to allege that chance rather than any human will guided by reason, must have led to such an arrangement. And if we consider that nevertheless there have been at all times certain officers whose duty it was to see that private buildings contributed to public ornament, the difficulty of reaching high perfection with but the materials of others to operate on, will be readily acknowledged. In the same way I fancied that those nations which, starting from a semi-barbarous state and advancing to civilisation by slow degrees, have had their laws successively determined, and, as it were, forced upon them simply by experience of the hurtfulness of particular crimes and disputes, would by this process come to be possessed of less perfect institutions than those which, from the commencement of their association as communities, have followed the appointments of some wise legislator. It is thus quite certain that the constitution of the true religion, the ordinances of which are derived from God, must be incomparably superior to that of every other. And, to speak of human affairs, I believe that the past preeminence of Sparta was due not to the goodness of each of its laws in particular, for many of these were very strange, and even opposed to good morals, but to the circumstance that, originated by a single individual, they all tended to a single end. In the same way I thought that the sciences contained in books (such of them at least as are made up of probable reasonings, without demonstrations), composed as they are of the opinions of many different individuals massed together, are farther removed from truth than the simple inferences which a man of good sense using his natural and unprejudiced judgment draws respecting the matters of his experience. And because we have all to pass through a state of infancy to manhood, and have been of necessity, for a length of time, governed by our desires and preceptors (whose dictates were frequently conflicting, while neither perhaps always counselled us for the best), I further concluded that it is almost impossible that our judgments can be so correct or solid as they would have been, had our Reason been mature from the moment of our birth, and had we always been guided by it alone.

It is true, however, that it is not customary to pull down all the houses of a town with a single design of rebuilding them differently, and thereby rendering the streets more handsome; but it often happens that a private individual takes down his own with the view of erecting it anew, and that people are even sometimes constrained to this when their houses are in danger of falling from age, or when the foundations are insecure. With this before me by way of example, I was persuaded that it would indeed be preposterous for a private individual to think of reforming a state by fundamentally changing it throughout, and overturning it in order to set it up amended; and the same I thought was true of any similar project for reforming the body of the Sciences, or the order of teaching them established in the Schools: but as for the opinions which up to that time I had embraced, I thought that I could not do better than resolve at once to sweep them wholly away, that I might afterwards be in a position to admit either others more correct, or even perhaps the same when they had undergone the scrutiny of Reason. I firmly believed that in this way I should much better succeed in the conduct of my life, than if I built only upon old foundations, and leant upon principles which, in my youth, I had taken upon trust. For although I recognised various difficulties in this undertaking, these were not, however, without remedy, nor once to be compared with such as attend the slightest reformation in public affairs. Large bodies, if once overthrown, are with great difficulty set up again, or even kept erect when once seriously shaken, and the fall of such is always disastrous. Then if there are any imperfections in the constitutions of states (and that many such exist the diversity of constitutions is alone sufficient to assure us), custom has without doubt materially smoothed their inconveniences, and has even managed to steer altogether clear of, or insensibly corrected a number which sagacity could not have provided against with equal effect; and, in fine, the defects are almost always more tolerable than the change necessary for their removal; in the same manner that highways which wind among mountains, by being much frequented, become gradually so smooth and commodious, that it is much better to follow them than to seek a straighter path by climbing over the tops of rocks and descending to the bottoms of precipices.

Hence it is that I cannot in any degree approve of those restless and busy meddlers who, called neither by birth nor fortune to take part in the management of public affairs, are yet always projecting reforms; and if I thought that this Tract contained ought which might justify the suspicion that I was a victim of such folly, I would by no means permit its publication. I have never contemplated anything higher than the reformation of my own opinions, and basing them on a foundation wholly my own. And although my own satisfaction with my work has led me to present here a draft of it, I do not by any means therefore recommend to every one else to make a similar attempt. Those whom God has endowed with a larger measure of genius will entertain, perhaps, designs still more exalted; but for the many I am much afraid lest even the present undertaking be more than they can safely venture to imitate. The single design to strip one's self of all past beliefs is one that ought not to be taken by every one. The majority of men is composed of two classes, for neither of which would this be at all a befitting resolution: in the *first* place, of those who with more than a due confidence in their own powers, are precipitate in their judgments and want the patience requisite for orderly and circumspect thinking; whence it happens, that if men of this class once take the liberty to doubt of their accustomed opinions, and quit the beaten highway, they will never be able to thread the byeway that would lead them by a shorter course, and will lose themselves and continue to wander for life; in the *second* place, of those who, possessed of sufficient sense or modesty to determine that there are others who excel them in the power of discriminating between truth and error, and by whom they may be instructed, ought rather to content themselves with the opinions of such than trust for more correct [opinions] to their own Reason.

For my own part, I should doubtless have belonged to the latter class, had I received instruction from but one master, or had I never known the diversities of opinion that from time immemorial have prevailed among men of the greatest learning. But I had become aware, even so early as during my college life, that no opinion, however absurd and incredible, can be imagined, which has not been maintained by some one of the philosophers; and afterwards in the course of my travels I remarked that all those whose opinions are decidedly repugnant to ours are not on that account barbarians and savages, but on the contrary that many of these nations make an equally good, if not a better, use of their Reason than we do. I took into account also the very different character which a person brought up from infancy in France or Germany exhibits, from that which, with the same mind originally, this individual would have possessed had he lived always among the Chinese or with savages, and the circumstance that in dress itself the fashion which pleased us ten years ago, and which may again, perhaps, be received into favour before ten years have gone, appears to us at this moment extravagant and ridiculous. I was thus led to infer that the ground of our opinions is far more custom and example than any certain knowledge. And, finally, although such be the ground of our opinions, I remarked that a plurality of suffrages is no guarantee of truth where it is at all of difficult discovery, as in such cases it is much more likely that it will be found by one than by many. I could, however, select from the crowd no one whose opinions seemed worthy of preference, and thus I found myself constrained, as it were, to use my own Reason in the conduct of my life.

But like one walking alone and in the dark, I resolved to proceed so slowly and with such circumspection, that if I did not advance far, I would at least guard against falling. I did not even choose to dismiss summarily any of the opinions that had crept into my belief without having been introduced by

Reason, but first of all took sufficient time carefully to satisfy myself of the general nature of the task I was setting myself, and ascertain the true Method by which to arrive at the knowledge of whatever lay within the compass of my powers.

Among the branches of Philosophy, I had, at an earlier period, given some attention to Logic, and among those of the Mathematics to Geometrical Analysis and Algebra,—three arts or Sciences which ought, as I conceived, to contribute something to my design. But, on examination, I found that, as for Logic, its syllogisms and the majority of its other precepts are of avail rather in the communication of what we already know, or even as the Art of Lully, in speaking without judgment of things of which we are ignorant, than in the investigation of the unknown; and although this Science contains indeed a number of correct and very excellent precepts, there are, nevertheless, so many others, and these either injurious or superfluous, mingled with the former, that it is almost quite as difficult to effect a severance of the true from the false as it is to extract a Diana or a Minerva from a rough block of marble. Then as to the Analysis of the ancients and the Algebra of the moderns, besides that they embrace only matters highly abstract, and, to appearance, of no use, the former is so exclusively restricted to the consideration of figures, that it can exercise the Understanding only on condition of greatly fatiguing the Imagination; and, in the latter, there is so complete a subjection to certain rules and formulas, that there results an art full of confusion and obscurity calculated to embarrass, instead of a science fitted to cultivate the mind. By these considerations I was induced to seek some other Method which would comprise the advantages of the three and be exempt from their defects. And as a multitude of laws often only hampers justice, so that a state is best governed when, with few laws, these are rigidly administered; in like manner, instead of the great number of precepts of which Logic is composed, I believed that the four following would prove perfectly sufficient for me, provided I took the firm and unwavering resolution never in a single instance to fail in observing them.

The *first* was never to accept anything for true which I did not clearly know to be such; that is to say, carefully to avoid precipitancy and prejudice, and to comprise nothing more in my judgment than what was presented to my mind so clearly and distinctly as to exclude all ground of doubt.

The *second,* to divide each of the difficulties under examination into as many parts as possible, and as might be necessary for its adequate solution.

The *third,* to conduct my thoughts in such order that, by commencing with objects the simplest and easiest to know, I might ascend by little and little, and, as it were, step by step, to the knowledge of the more complex; assigning in thought a certain order even to those objects which in their own nature do not stand in a relation of antecedence and sequence.

And the *last,* in every case to make enumerations so complete, and reviews so general, that I might be assured that nothing was omitted.

The long chains of simple and easy reasonings by means of which geometers are accustomed to reach the conclusions of their most difficult demonstrations, had led me to imagine that all things, to the knowledge of which man is competent, are mutually connected in the same way, and that there is nothing so far removed from us as to be beyond our reach, or so hidden that we cannot discover it, provided only we abstain from accepting the false for the true, and always preserve in our thoughts the order necessary for the deduction of one truth from another. And I had little difficulty in determining the objects with which it was necessary to commence, for I was already persuaded that it must be with the simplest and easiest to know, and, considering that of all those who have hitherto sought truth in the Sciences, the mathematicians alone have been able to find any demonstrations, that is, any certain and evident reasons, I did not doubt but that such must have been the rule of their investigations. I resolved to commence, therefore with the examination of the simplest objects, not anticipating, however, from this any other advantage than that to be found in accustoming my mind to the love and nourishment of truth, and to a distaste for all such reasonings as were unsound. But I had no intention on that account of attempting to master all the particular Sciences commonly denominated Mathematics: but observing that, however, different their objects, they all agree in considering only the various relations or proportions subsisting among those objects, I thought it best for my purpose to consider these proportions in the most general form possible, without referring them to any objects in particular, except such as would most facilitate the knowledge of them, and without by any means restricting them to these, that afterwards I might thus be the better able to apply them to every other class of objects to which they are legitimately applicable. Perceiving further, that in order to understand these relations I should sometimes have to consider them one by one, and sometimes only to bear them in mind, or embrace them in the aggregate, I thought that, in order the better to consider them individually, I should view them as subsisting between straight lines, than which I could find no objects more simple, or capable of being more distinctly represented to my imagination and senses; and on the other hand, that in order to retain them in the memory, or embrace an aggregate of many, I should express them by certain characters the briefest possible. In this way I believed that I could borrow all that was best both in Geometrical Analysis and in Algebra, and correct all the defects of the one by help of the other.

And, in point of fact, the accurate observance of these few precepts gave me, I take the liberty of saying, such ease in unravelling all the questions embraced in these two sciences, that in the two or three months I devoted to their examination, not only did I reach solutions of questions I had formerly deemed exceedingly difficult, but even as regards questions of the solution of which I continued ignorant, I was enabled, as it appeared to me, to determine the means whereby, and the extent to which, a solution was possible; results attributable to the circumstance that I commenced with the simplest and most general truths, and that thus each truth discovered was a rule available in the discovery of subsequent ones. Nor in this perhaps shall I appear too vain, if it be considered that, as the truth on any particular point is one, whoever apprehends the truth, knows all that on that point can be known. The child, for example, who has been instructed in the elements of Arithmetic, and has made a particular addition, according to rule, may be assured that he has found, with respect to the sum of the numbers before him, all that in this instance is within the reach of human genius. Now, in conclusion, the Method which teaches adherence to the true order, and an exact enumeration of all the conditions of the thing sought, includes all that gives certitude to the rules of Arithmetic.

But the chief ground of my satisfaction with this Method, was the assurance I had of thereby exercising my reason in all matters, if not with absolute perfection, at least with the greatest attainable by me: besides, I was conscious that by its use my mind was becoming gradually habituated to clearer and more distinct conceptions of its objects; and I hoped, also, from not having restricted this Method to any particular matter, to apply it to the difficulties of the other Sciences, with no less success than to those of Algebra. I should not, however, on this account have ventured at once on the examination of all the difficulties of the Sciences which presented themselves to me, for this would have been contrary to the order prescribed in the Method, but observing that the knowledge of such is dependent on principles borrowed from Philosophy, in which I found nothing certain, I thought it necessary first of all to endeavour to establish its principles. And because I observed, besides, that an inquiry of this kind was of all others of the greatest moment, and one in which precipitancy and anticipation in judgment were most to be dreaded, I thought that I ought not to approach it till I had reached a more mature age (being at that time but twenty-three), and had first of all employed much of my time in preparation for the work, as well by eradicating from my mind all the erroneous opinions I had up to that moment accepted, as by amassing variety of experience to afford materials for my reasonings, and by continually exercising myself in my chosen Method with a view to increased skill in its application.

Part V

I would here willingly have proceeded to exhibit the whole chain of truths which I deduced from these primary; but as with a view to this it would have been necessary now to treat of many questions in dispute among the learned, with whom I do not wish to be embroiled, I believe that it will be better for me to refrain from this exposition, and only mention in general what these truths are, that the more judicious may be able to determine whether a more special account of them would conduce to the public advantage. I have ever remained firm in my original resolution to suppose no other principle than that of which I have recently availed myself in demonstrating the existence of God and of the soul, and to accept as true nothing that did not appear to me more clear and certain than the demonstrations of the geometers had formerly appeared; and yet I venture to state that not only have I found means to satisfy myself in a short time on all the principal difficulties which are usually treated of in Philosophy, but I have also observed certain laws established in nature by God in such a manner, and of which he has impressed on our minds such notions, that after we have reflected sufficiently upon these, we cannot doubt that they are accurately observed in all that exists or takes place in the world: and farther, by considering the concatenation of these laws, it appears to me that I have discovered many truths more useful and more important than all I had before learned, or even had expected to learn.

But because I have essayed to expound the chief of these discoveries in a Treatise which certain considerations prevent me from publishing, I cannot make the results known more conveniently than by here giving a summary of the contents of this Treatise. It was my design to comprise in it all that, before I set myself to write it, I thought I knew of the nature of material objects. But like the painters who, finding themselves unable to represent equally well on a plain surface all the different faces of a solid body, select one of the chief, on which alone they make the light fall, and throwing the rest into the shade, allow them to appear only in so far as they can be seen while looking at the principal one; so, fearing lest I should not be able to comprise in my discourse all that was in my mind, I resolved to expound singly, though at considerable length, my opinions regarding light; then to take the opportunity of adding something on the sun and the fixed stars, since light almost wholly proceeds from them; on the heavens, since they transmit it; on the planets, comets, and earth, since they reflect it; and particularly on all the bodies that are upon the earth, since they are either coloured, or transparent, or luminous; and finally on man, since he is the spectator of these objects. Further, to enable me to cast this variety of subjects somewhat into the shade, and to express my judgment regarding them with greater freedom, without being necessitated to adopt or refute the opinions of the learned, I resolved to leave all the people here to their disputes, and to speak only of what would happen in a new world, if God were now to create somewhere in the imaginary spaces matter sufficient to compose one, and were to agitate variously and confusedly the different parts of this matter, so that there resulted a chaos as disordered as the poets ever feigned, and after that did nothing more than lend his ordinary concurrence to nature, and allow her to act in accordance with the laws which he had established. On this supposition, I, in the first place, described this matter, and essayed to represent it in such a manner that to my mind there can be nothing clearer and more intelligible, except what has been recently said regarding God and the soul; for I even expressly supposed that it possessed none of those forms or qualities which are so debated in the Schools, nor in general anything the knowledge of which is not so natural to our minds that no one can so much as imagine himself ignorant of it. Besides, I have pointed out what are the laws of nature; and, with no other principle upon which to found my reasonings except the infinite perfection of God, I endeavoured to demonstrate all those about which there could be any room for doubt, and to prove that they are such, that even if God had created more worlds, there could have been none in which these laws were not observed. Thereafter, I showed how the greatest part of the matter of this chaos must, in accordance with these laws, dispose and arrange itself in such a way as to present the appearance of heavens; how in the meantime some of its parts must compose an earth and some planets and comets, and others a sun and fixed stars. And, making a digression at this stage on the subject of light, I expounded at considerable length what the nature of that light must be which is found in the sun and the stars, and how thence in an instant of time it traverses the immense spaces of the heavens, and how from the planets and comets it is reflected towards the earth. To this I likewise added much respecting the substance, the situation, the motions, and all the different qualities of these heavens and stars; so that I thought I had said enough respecting them to show that there is nothing observable in the heavens or stars of our system that must not, or at least may not, appear precisely alike in those of the system which I described. I came next to speak of the earth in particular, and to show how, even though I had expressly supposed that God had given no weight to the matter of which it is composed, this should not prevent all its parts from tending exactly to its centre; how with water and air on its surface, the disposition of the heavens and heavenly bodies, more especially of the moon, must cause a flow and ebb, like in all its circumstances to that observed in our seas, as also a certain current both of water and air from east to west, such

as is likewise observed between the tropics; how the mountains, seas, fountains, and rivers might naturally be formed in it, and the metals produced
in the mines, and the plants grow in the fields; and in general, how all the
bodies which are commonly denominated mixed or composite might be
generated: and, among other things in the discoveries alluded to, inasmuch
as besides the stars, I knew nothing except fire which produces light, I spared
no pains to set forth all that pertains to its nature,—the manner of its production and support, and to explain how heat is sometimes found without light,
and light without heat; to show how it can induce various colours upon different bodies and other diverse qualities; how it reduces some to a liquid state
and hardens others; how it can consume almost all bodies, or convert them
into ashes and smoke; and finally, how from these ashes, by the mere intensity
of its action, it forms glass: for as this transmutation of ashes into glass appeared to me as wonderful as any other in nature, I took a special pleasure
in describing it.

I was not, however, disposed, from these circumstances, to conclude that this
world had been created in the manner I described; for it is much more likely
that God made it at the first such as it was to be. But this is certain, and an
opinion commonly received among theologians, that the action by which he
now sustains it is the same with that by which he originally created it; so that
even although he had from the beginning given it no other form than that
of chaos, provided only he had established certain laws of nature, and had
lent it his concurrence to enable it to act as it is wont to do, it may be believed,
without discredit to the miracle of creation, that, in this way alone, things
purely material might, in course of time, have become such as we observe
them at present; and their nature is much more easily conceived when they
are beheld coming in this manner gradually into existence, than when they are
only considered as produced at once in a finished and perfect state.

From the description of inanimate bodies and plants, I passed to animals,
and particularly to man. But since I had not as yet sufficient knowledge to
enable me to treat of these in the same manner as of the rest, that is to say, by
deducing effects from their causes, and by showing from what elements and
in what manner Nature must produce them, I remained satisfied with the
supposition that God formed the body of man wholly like to one of ours, as
well in the external shape of the members as in the internal conformation of
the organs, of the same matter with that I had described, and at first placed
in it no Rational Soul, nor any other principle, in room of the Vegetative or
Sensitive Soul, beyond kindling in the heart one of those fires without light,
such as I had already described, and which I thought was not different from
the heat in hay that has been heaped together before it is dry, or that which

causes fermentation in new wines before they are run clear of the fruit. For, when I examined the kind of functions which might, as consequences of this supposition, exist in this body, I found precisely all those which may exist in us independently of all power of thinking, and consequently without being in any measure owing to the soul; in other words, to that part of us which is distinct from the body, and of which it has been said above that the nature distinctively consists in thinking,—functions in which the animals void of Reason may be said wholly to resemble us; but among which I could not discover any of those that, as dependent on thought alone, belong to us as men, while, on the other hand, I did afterwards discover these as soon as I supposed God to have created a Rational Soul, and to have annexed it to this body in a particular manner which I described.

But, in order to show how I there handled this matter, I mean here to give the explication of the motion of the heart and arteries, which, as the first and most general motion observed in animals, will afford the means of readily determining what should be thought of all the rest. And that there may be less difficulty in understanding what I am about to say on this subject, I advise those who are not versed in Anatomy, before they commence the perusal of these observations, to take the trouble of getting dissected in their presence the heart of some large animal possessed of lungs (for this is throughout sufficiently like the human), and to have shewn to them its two ventricles or cavities: in the first place, that in the right side, with which correspond two very ample tubes, viz., the hollow vein (*vena cava*), which is the principal receptacle of the blood, and the trunk of the tree, as it were, of which all the other veins in the body are branches; and the arterial vein (*vena arteriosa*), inappropriately so denominated, since it is in truth only an artery, which, taking its rise in the heart, is divided, after passing out from it, into many branches which presently disperse themselves all over the lungs; in the second place, the cavity in the left side, with which correspond in the same manner two canals in size equal to or larger than the preceding, viz., the venous artery (*arteria venosa*), likewise inappropriately thus designated, because it is simply a vein which comes from the lungs, where it is divided into many branches, interlaced with those of the arterial vein, and those of the tube called the windpipe, through which the air we breathe enters; and the great artery which, issuing from the heart, sends its branches all over the body. I should wish also that such persons were carefully shewn the eleven pellicles which, like so many small valves, open and shut the four orifices that are in these two cavities, viz., three at the entrance of the hollow vein, where they are disposed in such a manner as by no means to prevent the blood which it contains from flowing into the right ventricle of the heart, and yet exactly to prevent its flowing out; three at the entrance to the arterial vein, which, arranged in a manner exactly the opposite of the former, readily permit the blood contained in this cavity to pass into the lungs, but hinder that contained in the lungs from returning to this cavity; and, in like manner, two others at the mouth of the venous artery, which allow the blood from the lungs to flow into the left cavity of the heart, but preclude its return; and three at the mouth of the great artery, which suffer the blood to flow from the heart, but prevent its reflux. Nor do we need to seek any other reason for the number of these pellicles beyond this that the orifice of the venous artery being of an oval shape from the nature of its situation, can be adequately closed with two, whereas the others being round are more conveniently closed with three. Besides, I wish such persons to observe that the grand artery and the arterial vein are of much harder and firmer texture than the venous artery and the hollow vein; and that the two last expand before entering the heart, and there form, as it were, two pouches denominated the auricles of the heart, which are composed of a substance similar to that of the heart itself; and that there is always more warmth in the heart than in any other part of the body; and, finally, that this heat is capable of causing any drop of blood that passes into the cavities rapidly to expand and dilate, just as all liquors do when allowed to fall drop by drop into a highly heated vessel.

For, after these things, it is not necessary for me to say anything more with a view to explain the motion of the heart, except that when its cavities are not full of blood, into these the blood of necessity flows,—from the hollow vein into the right, and from the venous artery into the left; because these two vessels are always full of blood, and their orifices, which are turned towards the heart, cannot then be closed. But as soon as two drops of blood have thus passed, one into each of the cavities, these drops which cannot but be very large, because the orifices through which they pass are wide, and the vessels from which they come full of blood, are immediately rarefied, and dilated by the heat they meet with. In this way they cause the whole heart to expand, and at the same time press home and shut the five small valves that are at the entrances of the two vessels from which they flow, and thus prevent any more blood from coming down into the heart, and becoming more and more rarefied, they push open the six small valves that are in the orifices of the other two vessels, through which they pass out, causing in this way all the branches of the arterial vein and of the grand artery to expand almost simultaneously with the heart—which immediately thereafter begins to contract, as do also the arteries, because the blood that has entered them has cooled, and the six small valves close, and the five of the hollow vein and of the venous artery open anew and allow a passage to other two drops of blood, which cause the heart and the arteries again to expand as before. And, because the blood which thus enters into the heart passes through these two pouches called auricles, it thence happens that their motion is the contrary of that of the heart, and that when it expands they contract. But lest those who are ignorant of the force of mathematical demonstrations, and who are not accustomed to distinguish true reasons from mere verisimilitudes, should venture, without examination, to deny what has been said, I wish it to be considered that the motion which I have now explained follows as necessarily from the very arrangement of the parts, which may be observed in the heart by the eye alone, and from the heat which may be felt with the fingers, and from the nature of the blood as learned from experience, as does the motion of a clock from the power, the situation, and shape of its counterweights and wheels.

But if it be asked how it happens that the blood in the veins, flowing in this way continually into the heart, is not exhausted, and why the arteries do not become too full, since all the blood which passes through the heart flows into them, I need only mention in reply what has been written by a physician [1] of England, who has the honour of having broken the ice on this subject, and of having been the first to teach that there are many small passages at the extremities of the arteries, through which the blood received by them from the heart passes into the small branches of the veins, whence it again returns to the heart; so that its course amounts precisely to a perpetual circulation. Of this we have abundant proof in the ordinary experience of surgeons, who, by binding the arm with a tie of moderate straitness above the part where they open the vein, cause the blood to flow more copiously than it would have done without any ligature; whereas quite the contrary would happen were they to bind it below; that is, between the hand and the opening, or were to make the ligature above the opening very tight. For it is manifest that the tie, moderately straitened, while adequate to hinder the blood already in the arm from returning towards the heart by the veins, cannot on that account prevent new blood from coming forward through the arteries, because these are situated below the veins, and their coverings, from their great consistency, are more difficult to compress; and also that the blood which comes from the heart tends to pass through them to the hand with greater force than it does to return from the hand to the heart through the veins. And since the latter current escapes from the arm by the opening made in one of the veins, there must of necessity be certain passages below the ligature, that is, towards the extermities of the arm, through which it can come thither from the arteries. This physician likewise abundantly establishes what he has advanced respecting the motion of the blood, from the existence of certain pellicles, so disposed in various places

[1] [William Harvey (1578–1657).]

along the course of the veins, in the manner of small valves, as not to permit the blood to pass from the middle of the body towards the extremities, but only to return from the extremities to the heart; and farther, from experience which shows that all the blood which is in the body may flow out of it in a very short time through a single artery that has been cut, even although this had been closely tied in the immediate neighbourhood of the heart, and cut between the heart and the ligature, so as to prevent the supposition that the blood flowing out of it could come from any other quarter than the heart.

But there are many other circumstances which evince that what I have alleged is the true cause of the motion of the blood: thus, in the first place, the difference that is observed between the blood which flows from the veins, and that from the arteries, can only arise from this, that being rarefied, and, as it were, distilled by passing through the heart, it is thinner, and more vivid, and warmer immediately after leaving the heart, in other words, when in the arteries, than it was a short time before passing into either, in other words, when it was in the veins; and if attention be given, it will be found that this difference is very marked only in the neighbourhood of the heart; and is not so evident in parts more remote from it. In the next place, the consistency of the coats of which the arterial vein and the great artery are composed, sufficiently shows that the blood is impelled against them with more force than against the veins. And why should the left cavity of the heart and the great artery be wider and larger than the right cavity and the arterial vein, were it not that the blood of the venous artery, having only been in the lungs after it has passed through the heart, is thinner, and rarefies more readily, and in a higher degree, than the blood which proceeds immediately from the hollow vein? And what can physicians conjecture from feeling the pulse unless they know that according as the blood changes its nature it can be rarefied by the warmth of the heart, in a higher or lower degree, and more or less quickly than before? And if it be inquired how this heat is communicated to the other members, must it not be admitted that this is effected by means of the blood, which, passing through the heart, is there heated anew, and thence diffused over all the body? Whence it happens, that if the blood be withdrawn from any part, the heat is likewise withdrawn by the same means; and although the heart were as hot as glowing iron, it would not be capable of warming the feet and hands as at present, unless it continually sent thither new blood. We likewise perceive from this, that the true use of respiration is to bring sufficient fresh air into the lungs, to cause the blood which flows into them from the right ventricle of the heart, where it has been rarefied and, as it were, changed into vapours, to become thick, and to convert it anew into blood, before it flows into the left cavity, without which process it would be unfit for the nourishment of the fire that is there. This receives confirmation from the circumstance, that it is observed of animals destitute of lungs that they have also but one cavity in the heart, and that in children who cannot use them while in the womb, there is a hole through which the blood flows from the hollow vein into the left cavity of the heart, and a tube through which it passes from the arterial vein into the grand artery without passing through the lung. In the next place, how could digestion be carried on in the stomach unless the heart communicated heat to it through the arteries, and along with this certain of the more fluid parts of the blood, which assist in the dissolution of the food that has been taken in? Is not also the operation which converts the juice of food into blood easily comprehended, when it is considered that it is distilled by passing and repassing through the heart perhaps more than one or two hundred times in a day? And what more need be adduced to explain nutrition, and the production of the different humours of the body, beyond saying, that the force with which the blood, in being rarefied, passes from the heart towards the extremities of the arteries, causes certain of its parts to remain in the members at which they arrive, and there occupy the place of some others expelled by them; and that according to the situation, shape, or smallness of the pores with which they meet, some rather than others flow into certain parts, in the same way that some sieves are observed to act, which, by being variously perforated, serve to separate different species of grain? And, in the last place, what above all is here worthy of observation, is the generation of the animal spirits, which are like a very subtle wind, or rather a very pure and vivid flame which, continually ascending in great abundance from the heart to the brain, thence penetrates through the nerves into the muscles, and gives motion to all the members; so that to account for other parts of the blood which, as most agitated and penetrating, are the fittest to compose these spirits, proceeding towards the brain, it is not necessary to suppose any other cause, than simply, that the arteries which carry them thither proceed from the heart in the most direct lines, and that, according to the rules of Mechanics, which are the same with those of Nature, when many objects tend at once to the same point where there is not sufficient room for all (as is the case with the parts of the blood which flow forth from the left cavity of the heart and tend towards the brain), the weaker and less agitated parts must necessarily be driven aside from that point by the stronger which alone in this way reach it.

I had expounded all these matters with sufficient minuteness in the Treatise which I formerly thought of publishing. And after these, I had shewn what must be the fabric of the nerves and muscles of the human body to give the animal spirits contained in it the power to move the members, as when we see heads shortly after they have been struck off still move and bite the earth, although no longer animated; what changes must take place in the brain to produce waking, sleep, and dreams, how light, sounds, odours, tastes, heat, and all the other qualities of external objects impress it with different ideas by means of the senses; how hunger, thirst, and the other internal affections can likewise impress upon it divers ideas; what must be understood by the common sense (*sensus communis*) in which these ideas are received, by the memory which retains them, by the fantasy which can change them in various ways, and out of them compose new ideas, and which, by the same means, distributing the animal spirits through the muscles, can cause the members of such a body to move in as many different ways, and in a manner as suited, whether to the objects that are presented to its senses or to its internal affections, as can take place in our own case apart from the guidance of the will. Nor will this appear at all strange to those who are acquainted with the variety of movements performed by the different automata, or moving machines fabricated by human industry, and that with help of but few pieces compared with the great multitude of bones, muscles, nerves, arteries, veins, and other parts that are found in the body of each animal. Such persons will look upon this body as a machine made by the hands of God, which is incomparably better arranged, and adequate to movements more admirable than is any machine of human invention. And here I specially stayed to show that, were there such machines exactly resembling in organs and outward form an ape or any other irrational animal, we could have no means of knowing that they were in any respect of a different nature from these animals; but if there were machines bearing the image of our bodies, and capable of imitating our actions as far as it is morally possible, there would still remain two most certain tests whereby to know that they were not therefore really men. Of these the first is that they could never use words or other signs arranged in such a manner as is competent to us in order to declare our thoughts to others: for we may easily conceive a machine to be so constructed that it emits vocables, and even that it emits some correspondent to the action upon it of external objects which cause a change in its organs; for example, if touched in a particular place it may demand what we wish to say to it; if in another it may cry out that it is hurt, and such like; but not that it should arrange them variously so as appositely to reply to what is said in its presence, as men of the lowest grade of intellect can do. The second test is, that although such machines might execute many things with equal or perhaps greater perfection than any of us, they would, without doubt, fail in certain others from which it could be discovered that they did not act from knowledge, but solely from the disposition of their organs: for while Reason is an universal instrument that is alike availaable on every occasion, these organs, on the contrary, need a particular arrangement for each particular action; whence it must be morally impossible that there should exist in any machine a diversity of organs sufficient to enable it to act in all the occurrences of life, in the way in which our reason enables us to act. Again, by means of these two tests we may likewise know the difference between men and brutes. For it is highly deserving, of remark, that there are no men so dull and stupid, not even idiots, as to be incapable of joining together different words, and thereby constructing a declaration by which to make their thoughts understood; and that on the other hand, there is no other animal, however perfect or happily circumstanced, which can do the like. Nor does this inability arise from want of organs: for we observe that magpies and parrots can utter words like ourselves, and are yet unable to speak as we do, that is, so as to show that they understand what they say; in place of which men born deaf and dumb, and thus not less, but rather more than the brutes, destitute of the organs which others use in speaking, are in the habit of spontaneously inventing certain signs by which they discover their thoughts to those who, being usually in their company, have leisure to learn their language. And this proves not only that the brutes have less Reason than man, but that they have none at all: for we see that very little is required to enable a person to speak; and since a certain inequality of capacity is observable among animals of the same species, as well as among men, and since some are more capable of being instructed than others, it is incredible that the most perfect ape or parrot of its species, should not in this be equal to the most stupid infant of its kind, or at least to one that was crack-brained, unless the soul of brutes were of a nature wholly different from ours. And we ought not to confound speech with the natural movements which indicate the passions, and can be imitated by machines as well as manifested by animals; nor must it be thought with certain of the ancients, that the brutes speak, although we do not understand their language. For if such were the case, since they are endowed with many organs analogous to ours, they could as easily communicate their thoughts to us as to their fellows. It is also very worthy of remark, that, though there are many animals which manifest more industry than we in certain of their actions, the same animals are yet observed to show none at all in many others: so that the circumstance that they do better than we does not prove that they are endowed with mind, for it would thence follow that they possessed greater Reason than any of us, and could surpass us in all things; on the contrary, it rather proves that they are destitute of Reason, and that it is Nature which acts in them according to the disposition of their organs: thus it is seen, that a clock composed only of wheels and weights can number the hours and measure time more exactly than we with all our skill.

I had after this described the Reasonable Soul, and shewn that it could by no means be educed from the power of matter, as the other things of which I had spoken, but that it must be expressly created; and that it is not sufficient that it be lodged in the human body exactly like a pilot in a ship, unless perhaps to move its members, but that it is necessary for it to be joined and united more closely to the body, in order to have sensations and appetites similar to ours, and thus constitute a real man. I here entered, in conclusion, upon the subject of the soul at considerable length, because it is of the greatest moment: for after the error of those who deny the existence of God, an error which I think I have already sufficiently refuted, there is none that is more powerful in leading feeble minds astray from the straight path of virtue than the supposition that the soul of the brutes is of the same nature with our own; and consequently that after this life we have nothing to hope for or fear, more than flies and ants; in place of which, when we know how far they differ we much better comprehend the reasons which establish that the soul is of a nature wholly independent of the body, and that consequently it is not liable to die with the latter; and, finally, because no other causes are observed capable of destroying it, we are naturally led thence to judge that it is immortal.

ISAAC NEWTON

Isaac Newton (1642–1727) was born at Woolsthorpe in Lincolnshire, England. His widowed mother planned to make a country squire of him, and he was given the customary grammar school education. But the boy consistently neglected the chores required of him and showed instead a strong liking for mechanical contrivances; finally he was permitted to enter Trinity College, Cambridge. Here he rapidly revealed unusual gifts for mathematics, and won the interest and the friendship of Isaac Barrow, the first Lucasian Professor of Mathematics at the university. From Barrow, himself groping toward the methods of the differential calculus, Newton acquired a strong interest in optics, in the general problem of drawing tangents to curves, and in theology.

In 1664 he obtained his B.A., and on the outbreak of the Great Plague returned to Woolsthorpe, the scene of the famous alleged incident of the falling apple; although the story may be apocryphal, there is no question that most of his great ideas suggested themselves during the two years of enforced seclusion at Woolsthorpe. He then returned to Cambridge, and in 1699 succeeded Barrow as Lucasian Professor of Mathematics. He was presently made Fellow of the Royal Society and became involved in various controversies over his researches on such topics as the compound nature of white light and the force required to keep planets in orbit. His important works began to achieve recognition, and many honors were bestowed on him, including the presidency of the Royal Society, which he retained until his death twenty-four years later. He was made Warden, and later Master, of the Mint, with a comfortable salary; in 1705 he was knighted. Newton's duties as a Treasury official consumed much of his energy, but in his later years he gave free rein to his theological interests.

Newton's major work is the *Philosophiae Naturalis Principia Mathematica* (1687), which realized Descartes's dream of a universal mathematical science of nature, at least in astronomy and dynamics; it came to be regarded as the authoritative model of scientific method. In 1704 he published his *Opticks,* his most well-known work in the eighteenth century. His later religious works, such as *Two Notable Corruptions of Scripture* and *Observations on the Prophecies of Daniel and the Apocalypse of St. John,* reveal Newton's belief in the necessary existence of God behind the orderly world machine.

The following selections aim to explain Newton's achievements in his *Principia* and the character of his mathematical experimental method. The first is taken from Roger Cotes's *Preface to the Second Edition of Newton's Principia* (1713); the second from a widely read book by one of his editors, Henry Pemberton's *A View of Sir Isaac Newton's Philosophy* (1728); and the third is comprised of excerpts from Newton's *Principia.*

THE PREFACE OF MR. ROGER COTES,
TO THE SECOND EDITION OF
[PRINCIPIA MATHEMATICA],
SO FAR AS IT RELATES TO
THE INVENTIONS AND DISCOVERIES
THEREIN CONTAINED

THOSE WHO HAVE TREATED of natural philosophy may be nearly reduced to three classes. Of these, some have attributed to the several species of things specific and occult qualities, on which, in a manner unknown, they make the operations of the several bodies to depend. The sum of the doctrine of the schools derived from Aristotle and the Peripatetics is herein contained. They affirm that the several effects of bodies arise from the particular natures of those bodies; but whence it is that bodies derive those natures they do not tell us, and therefore they tell us nothing. And being entirely employed in giving names to things, and not in searching into things themselves, we may say, that they have invented a philosophical way of speaking, but not that they have made known to us true philosophy.

Others, therefore, by laying aside that useless heap of words, thought to employ their pains to better purpose. These supposed all matter homogeneous, and that the variety of forms which is seen in bodies arises from some very plain and simple affections of the component particles; and by going on from simple things to those which are more compounded, they certainly proceed right, if they attribute no other properties to those primary affections of the particles than nature has done. But when they take a liberty of imagining at pleasure unknown figures and magnitudes, and uncertain situations and motions of the parts; and, moreover, of supposing occult fluids, freely pervading the pores of bodies, endued with an all-performing subtilty, and agitated with occult motions; they now run out into dreams and chimeras, and neglect the true constitution of things; which certainly is not to be expected from fallacious conjectures, when we can scarcely reach it by the most certain observations. Those who fetch from hypotheses the foundation on which they build their speculations, may form, indeed, an ingenious romance; but a romance it will still be.

There is left, then, the third class, which profess experimental philosophy. These, indeed, derive the causes of all things from the most simple principles possible; but, then, they assume nothing as a principle that is not proved by phænomena. They frame no hypotheses, nor receive them into philosophy otherwise than as questions whose truth may be disputed. They proceed, therefore, in a twofold method, synthetical and analytical. From some select phænomena they deduce by analysis the forces of nature, and the more simple laws of forces; and from thence by synthesis shew the constitution of the rest. This is that incomparably best way of philosophizing which our renowned author most justly embraced before the rest, and thought alone worthy to be cultivated and adorned by his excellent labours. Of this he has given us a most illustrious example by the explication of the System of the World, most happily deduced from the theory of gravity. That the virtue of gravity was found in all bodies, others suspected or imagined before him; but he was the only and the first philosopher that could demonstrate it from appearances, and make it a solid foundation to the most noble speculations. . . .

Since, then, all bodies, whether upon earth or in the heavens, are heavy, so far as we can make any experiments or observations concerning them, we must certainly allow that gravity is found in all bodies universally; and in like manner, as we ought not to suppose that any bodies can be otherwise than extended, moveable, or impenetrable, so we ought not to conceive that any bodies can be otherwise than heavy. The extension, mobility, and impenetrability of bodies become known to us only by experiments; and in the very same manner their gravity becomes known to us. All bodies we can make any observations upon are extended, moveable, and impenetrable; and thence we conclude all bodies, and those we have no observations concerning, to be extended, and moveable, and impenetrable. So all bodies we can make observations on we find to be heavy; and thence we conclude all bodies, and those we have no observations of, to be heavy also. If any one should say that the bodies of the fixed stars are not heavy, because their gravity is not yet observed, they may say, for the same reason, that they are neither extended, nor moveable, nor impenetrable, because these affections of the fixed stars are not yet observed. In short, either gravity must have a impenetrability, must not. And if the nature of things is not rightly explained by the gravity of bodies, it will not be rightly explained by their extension, mobility and impenetrability.

Some, I know, disapprove this conclusion, and mutter something about occult qualities. They are continually cavilling with us, that gravity is an occult property; and occult causes are to be quite banished from philosophy.

But to this the answer is easy: that those are, indeed, occult causes whose existence is occult; and imagined, but not proved; but not those whose real existence is clearly demonstrated by observations. Therefore gravity can by no means be called an occult cause of the celestial motions, because it is plain from the phænomena that such a virtue does really exist. Those rather have recourse to occult causes who set imaginary vortices, of a matter entirely fictitious, and imperceptible by our senses, to direct those motions.

But shall gravity be therefore called an occult cause, and thrown out of philosophy, because the cause of gravity is occult, and not yet discovered? Those who affirm this should be careful not to fall into an absurdity that may overturn the foundations of all philosophy; for causes use to proceed in a continued chain from those that are more compounded to those that are more simple: when we are arrived at the most simple cause, we can go no farther. Therefore no mechanical account or explanation of the most simple cause is to be expected or given; for if it could be given, the cause were not the most simple. The most simple causes will you, then, call occult, and reject them? Then you must reject those that immediately depend upon them, and those which depend upon these last, till philosophy is quite cleared and disencumbered of all causes.

Some there are who say that gravity is præternatural, and call it a perpetual miracle; therefore they would have it rejected, because præternatural causes have no place in physics. It is hardly worth while to spend time in answering this ridiculous objection, which overturns all philosophy; for either they will deny gravity to be in bodies, which cannot be said, or else they will therefore call it præternatural, because it is not produced by the other affections of bodies, and therefore not by mechanical causes. But certainly there are primary affections of bodies; and these, because they are primary, have no dependance on the others. Let them consider whether all these are not in like manner præternatural, and in like manner to be rejected; and then what kind of philosophy we are like to have.

Some there are who dislike this celestial physics, because it contradicts the opinions of Descartes, and seems hardly to be reconciled with them. Let these enjoy their own opinion; but let them act fairly, and not deny the same liberty to us which they demand for themselves. Since the Newtonian Philosophy appears true to us, let us have the liberty to embrace and retain it, and to follow causes proved by phænomena, rather than causes only imagined, and not yet proved. The business of true philosophy is to derive the natures of things from causes truly existent; and to enquire after those laws on which the Great Creator actually chose to found this most beautiful frame of the world; not those by which he might have done the same, had he so pleased. It is reasonable enough to suppose that, from several causes somewhat differing from each other, the same effect may arise; but the true cause will be that from which it truly and actually does arise: the others have no place in true philosophy. The same motion of the hour-hand in a clock may be occasioned either by a weight hung or a spring shut up within; but if a certain clock should be really moved with a weight, we should laugh at a man that would suppose it moved by a spring, and from that principle, suddenly taken up without farther examination, should go about to explain the motion of the index; for certainly the way he ought to have taken should have been actually to look into the inward parts of the machine, that he might find the true principle of the proposed motion. The like judgment ought to be made of those philosophers who will have the heavens to be filled with a most subtile matter, which is perpetually carried round in vortices; for if they could explain the phænomena ever so accurately by their hypotheses, we could not yet say that they have discovered true philosophy, and the true causes of the celestial motions, unless they could either demonstrate that those causes do actually exist, or, at least, that no other do exist. Therefore if it be made clear that the attraction of all bodies is a property actually existing *in rerum natura,*[1] and if it be also shewn how the motions of the celestial bodies may be solved by that property, it would be very impertinent for any one to object that these motions ought to be accounted for by vortices, even though we should ever so much allow such an explication of those motions to be possible. But we allow no such thing; for the phænomena can by no means be accounted for by vortices, as our author has abundantly proved from the cleared reasons. So that men must be strangely fond of chimeras who can spend their time so idly as in patching up a ridiculous figment, and setting it off with new comments of their own.

If the bodies of the planets and comets are carried round the sun in vortices, the bodies so carried, and the parts of the vortices next surrounding them, must be carried with the same velocity and the same direction, and have the same density, and the same *vis inertiæ*[2] answering to the bulk of the matter. But it is certain the planets and comets, when in the very same parts of the heavens, are carried with various velocities and various directions;

---

[1] [*In the nature of things.*]

[2] [That property of matter by which it tends when at rest to remain so, and when in motion to continue in rectilinear motion.]

therefore it necessarily follows that those parts of the celestial fluid which are at the same distances from the sun must revolve at the same time with different velocities in different directions; for one kind of velocity and direction is required for the motion of the planets, and another for that of the comets. But, since this cannot be accounted for, we must either say that all the celestial bodies are not carried about by vortices, or else that their motions are derived not from one and the same vortex, but from several distinct ones, which fill and pervade the spaces round about the sun.

But if several vortices are contained in the same space, and are supposed to penetrate each other, and to revolve with different motions, then, because these motions must agree with those of the bodies carried about by them, which are perfectly regular, and performed in conic sections which are sometimes very eccentric, and sometimes nearly circles, one may reasonably ask, how it comes to pass that these vortices remain entire, and have suffered no manner of perturbation in so many ages from the actions of the conflicting matter? Certainly, if these fictitious motions are more compounded and more hard to be accounted for than the true motions of the planets and comets, it seems to no purpose to admit them into philosophy, since every cause ought to be more simple than its effect. Allowing men to indulge their own fancies, suppose any man should affirm that the planets and comets are surrounded with atmospheres like our earth, which hypothesis seems more reasonable than that of vortices. Let him then affirm that these atmospheres, by their own nature, move about the sun, and describe conic sections, which motion is much more easily conceived than that of the vortices penetrating each other. Lastly, that the planets and comets are carried about the sun by these atmospheres of their's; and then applaud his own sagacity in discovering the causes of the celestial motions. He that rejects this fable, must also reject the other; for two drops of water are not more like than this hypothesis of atmospheres, and that of vortices.

Galileo has shewn, that when a stone projected moves in a parabola, its deflexion into that curve from its rectilinear path is occasioned by the gravity of the stone towards the earth; that is, by an occult quality. But, now, somebody more cunning than he may come to explain the cause after this manner. He will suppose a certain subtile matter, not discernible by our sight, our touch, or any other of our senses, which fills the spaces which are near and contiguous to the superficies of the earth; and that this matter is carried with different directions, and various, and often contrary motions, describing parabolic curves. Then see how easily he may account for the deflexion of the stone above spoken of. The stone, says he, floats in this subtile fluid, and, following its motion, cannot chuse but describe the same figure. But the fluid moves in parabolic curves, and therefore the stone must move in a parabola of course. Would not the acuteness of this philosopher be thought very extraordinary, who could deduce the appearances of nature from mechanical causes, matter, and motion, so clearly that the meanest man may understand it? Or, indeed, should not we smile to see this new Galileo taking so much mathematical pains to introduce occult qualities into philosophy, from whence they have been so happily excluded? But I am ashamed to dwell so long upon trifles.

The sum of the matter is this: the number of the comets is certainly very great; their motions are perfectly regular, and observe the same laws with those of the planets. The orbits in which they move are conic sections, and those very eccentric. They move every way towards all parts of the heavens, and pass through the planetary regions with all possible freedom; and their motion is often contrary to the order of the signs. These phænomena are most evidently confirmed by astronomical observations, and cannot be accounted for by vortices. Nay, indeed, they are utterly irreconcileable with the vortices of the planets. There can be no room for the motions of the comets, unless the celestial spaces be entirely cleared of that fictitious matter. . . . Without all doubt, this world, so diversified with that variety of forms and motions we find in it, could arise from nothing but the perfectly free will of GOD directing and presiding over all.

From this Fountain it is that those laws, which we call the laws of Nature, have flowed; in which there appear many traces, indeed, of the most wise contrivance, but not the least shadow of necessity. These, therefore, we must not seek from uncertain conjectures, but learn them from observations and experiments. He who thinks to find the true principles of physics and the laws of natural things by the force alone of his own mind, and the internal light of his reason, must either suppose that the world exists by necessity, and by the same necessity follows the laws proposed; or, if the order of Nature was established by the will of GOD, that himself, a miserable reptile, can tell what was fittest to be done. All sound and true philosophy is founded on the appearances of things, which, if they draw us ever so much against our wills to such principles as most clearly manifest to us the most excellent counsel and supreme dominion of the Allwise and Almighty Being, those principles are not therefore to be laid aside, because some men may perhaps dislike them. They may call them, if they please, miracles or occult qualities; but names maliciously given ought not to be a disadvantage to the things themselves; unless they will say, at last, that all philosophy ought to be founded in atheism. Philosophy must not be corrupted in complaisance to these men; for the order of things will not be changed.

Fair and equal judges will therefore give sentence in favour of this most excellent method of philosophy, which is founded on experiments and observations. To this method it is hardly to be said or imagined what light, what splendor, hath accrued from this admirable work of our illustrious author, whose happy and sublime genius, resolving the most difficult problems, and reaching to discoveries of which the mind of man was thought incapable before, is deservedly admired by all those who are somewhat more than superficially versed in these matters. The gates are now set open; and by his means we may freely enter into the knowledge of the hidden secrets and wonders of natural things. He has so clearly laid open and set before our eyes the most beautiful frame of the System of the World, that, if King Alphonsus were now alive, he would not complain for want of the graces either of simplicity or of harmony in it. Therefore we may now more nearly behold the beauties of Nature, and entertain ourselves with the delightful contemplation; and, which is the best and most valuable fruit of philosophy, be thence incited the more profoundly to reverence and adore the great Maker and Lord of all. He must be blind, who, from the most wise and excellent contrivances of things, cannot see the infinite wisdom and goodness of their Almighty Creator; and he must be mad and senseless who refuses to acknowledge them.

A VIEW OF SIR ISAAC NEWTON'S PHILOSOPHY
BY HENRY PEMBERTON

. . . But what surprising advancements in the knowledge of nature may be made by pursuing the true course in philosophical inquiries; when those searches are conducted by a genius equal to so divine a work, will be best understood by considering Sir Isaac Newton's discoveries. That my reader may apprehend as just a notion of these, as can be conveyed to him, by the brief account, which I intend to lay before him; I have set apart this introduction for explaining, in the fullest manner I am able, the principles, whereon Sir Isaac Newton proceeds. For without a clear conception of these, it is impossible to form any true idea of the singular excellence of the inventions of this great philosopher.

The principles then of this philosophy are: upon no consideration to indulge conjectures concerning the powers and laws of nature, but to make it our endeavour with all diligence to search out the real and true laws, by which the constitution of things is regulated. The philosopher's first care must be to distinguish, what he sees to be within his power, from what is beyond his reach; to assume no greater degree of knowledge, than what he finds himself possessed of; but to advance by slow and cautious steps; to search gradually into natural causes; to secure to himself the knowledge of the most immediate cause of each appearance, before he extends his views farther to causes more remote. This is the method, in which philosophy ought to be cultivated; which does not pretend to so great things, as the more airy speculations; but will perform abundantly more: we shall not perhaps seem to the unskilful to know so much, but our real knowledge will be greater. And certainly it is no objection against this method, that some others promise, what is nearer to the extent of our wishes: since this, if it will not teach us all we could desire to be informed of, will however give us some true light into nature; which no other can do. Nor has the philosopher any reason to think his labour lost, when he finds himself stopt at the cause first discovered by him, or at any other more remote cause, short of the original: for if he has but sufficiently proved any one cause; he has entered so far into the real constitution of things, has laid a safe foundation for others to work upon, and has facilitated their endeavours in the search after yet more distant causes; and besides, in the mean time he may apply the knowledge of these intermediate causes to *many useful purposes*. Indeed the being able to make practical deductions from natural causes, constitutes the great distinction between the true philosophy and the false. Causes assumed upon conjecture, must be so loose and undefined, that nothing particular can be collected from them. But those causes, which are brought to light by a strict examination of things, will be more distinct. Hence it appears to have been no unuseful discovery, that the ascent of water in pumps is owing to the pressure of the air by its weight or spring; though the causes, which make the air gravitate, and render it elastic, be unknown: for notwithstanding we are ignorant of the original, whence these powers of the air are derived; yet we may receive much advantage from the bare knowledge of these powers. If we are but certain of the degree of force, wherewith they act, we shall know the extent of what is to be expected from them; we shall know the greatest height, to which it is possible by pumps to raise water; and shall thereby be prevented from making any useless efforts towards improving these instruments beyond the limits prescribed to them by nature; whereas without so much knowledge as this, we might probably have wasted in attempts of this kind much time and labour. . . . It is confessed by all, that Galileo greatly improved philosophy, by shewing, as we shall relate hereafter, that the power in bodies, which we call gravity, occasions them to move downwards with a velocity equably accelerated; and that when any body is thrown forwards, the same power obliges it to describe in its motion that line, which is called by geometers a parabola: yet we are ignorant of the cause, which makes bodies gravitate. But although we are unacquainted with the spring, whence this power in nature is derived, nevertheless we can estimate its effects. When a Body falls perpendicularly, it is known, how long time it takes in descending from any height whatever: and if it be thrown forward, we know the real path, which it describes; we can determine in what direction, and with what degree of swiftness it must be projected, in order to its striking against any object desired; and we can also ascertain the very force, wherewith it will strike. Sir Isaac Newton has further taught, that this power of gravitation extends up to the moon, and causes that planet to gravitate as much towards the earth, as any of the bodies, which are familiar to us, would, if placed at the same distance: he has proved likewise, that all the planets gravitate towards the sun, and towards one another; and that their respective motions follow from this gravitation. All this he has demonstrated upon indisputable geometrical principles, which cannot be rendered precarious for want of knowing what it is, which causes these Bodies thus mutually to gravitate: any more than we can doubt of the propensity in all the bodies about us, to descend towards the earth; or can call in question the fore-mentioned propositions of Galileo, which are built upon that principle. And as Galileo has shewn more fully, than was known before, what effects were produced in the motion of bodies by their gravitation towards the earth; so Sir Isaac Newton, by this his invention, has much advanced our knowledge in the celestial motions. By discovering that the moon gravitates towards the sun, as well as towards the earth; he has laid open those intricacies in the moon's motion, which no astronomer, from observations only, could ever find out: and one kind of heavenly bodies, the comets, have their motion now clearly ascertained; whereof we had before no true knowledge at all.

Doubtless it might be expected, that such surprising success should have silenced, at once, every cavil. But we have seen the contrary. For because this philosophy professes modestly to keep within the extent of our faculties, and is ready to confess its imperfections, rather than to make any fruitless attempts to conceal them, by seeking to cover the defects in our knowledge with the vain ostentation of rash and groundless conjectures; hence has been taken an occasion to insinuate that we are led to miraculous causes, and the occult qualities of the schools.

But the first of these accusations is very extraordinary. If by calling these causes miraculous nothing more is meant than only, that they often appear to us wonderful and surprising, it is not easy to see what difficulty can be raised from thence; for the works of nature discover every where such proofs of the unbounded power, and the consummate wisdom of their author, that the more they are known, the more they will excite our admiration: and it is too manifest to be insisted on, that the common sense of the word miraculous can have no place here, when it implies what is above the ordinary course of things. The other imputation, that these causes are occult upon the account of our not perceiving what produces them, contains in it great ambiguity. That something relating to them lies hid, the followers of this philosophy are ready to acknowledge, nay desire it should be carefully remarked, as pointing out proper subjects for future inquiry. But this is very different from the proceeding of the schoolmen in the causes called by them occult. For as their occult qualities were understood to operate in a manner occult, and not apprehended by us; so they were obtruded upon us for such original and essential properties in bodies, as made it vain to seek any farther cause; and a greater power was attributed to them, than any natural appearances authorized. For instance, the rise of water in pumps was ascribed to a certain abhorrence of vacuum, which they thought fit to assign to nature. And this was so far a true observation, that the water does move, contrary to its usual course, into the space, which otherwise would be left void of any sensible matter; and, that the procuring such a vacuity was the apparent cause of the water's ascent. But while we were not in the least informed how this power, called an abhorrence of a vacuum, produced the visible effects; instead of making any advancement in the knowledge of nature, we only gave an artificial name to one of her operations: and when the speculation was pushed so beyond what any appearances required, as to have it concluded, that this abhorrence of a vacuum was a power inherent in all matter, and so unlimited as to render it impossible for a vacuum to exist at all; it then became a much greater absurdity, in being made the foundation of a most ridiculous manner of reasoning; as at length evidently appeared, when it came to be discovered, that this rise of the water followed only from the pressure of the air, and extended itself no farther, than the power of that cause. The scholastic style in discoursing of these occult qualities, as if they were essential differences in the very substances, of which bodies consisted, was certainly very absurd; by reason it tended to discourage all farther inquiry. But no such ill consequences can follow from the considering of any natural causes, which confessedly are not traced up to their first original. How shall we ever come to the knowledge of the several original causes of things, otherwise than by storing up all intermediate causes which we can discover? Are all the original and essential properties of matter so very obvious, that none of them can escape our first view? This is not probable. It is much more likely, that, if some of the essential properties are discovered by our first observations, a stricter examination should bring more to light.

But in order to clear up this point concerning the essential properties of matter, let us consider the subject a little distinctly. We are to conceive, that the matter, out of which the universe of things is formed, is furnished with certain qualities and powers, whereby it is rendered fit to answer the purposes, for which it was created. But every property, of which any particle of this matter is in itself possessed, and which is not barely the consequence of the union of this particle with other portions of matter, we may call an essential property: whereas all other qualities or attributes belonging to bodies, which depend on their particular frame and composition, are not essential to the matter, whereof such bodies are made; because the matter of these bodies will be deprived of those qualities, only by the dissolution of the body, without working any change in the original constitution of one single particle of this mass of matter. *Extension* we apprehend to be one of these essential properties, and *impenetrability* another. These two belong universally to all matter; and are the principal ingredients in the idea, which this word matter usually excites in the mind. Yet as the idea, marked by this name, is not purely the creature of our own understandings, but is taken for the representation of a certain substance without us; if we should discover, that every part of the substance, in which we find these two properties, should likewise be endowed universally with any other essential qualities; all these, from the time they come to our notice, must be united under our general idea of matter. How many such properties there are actually in all matter we know not; those, of which we are at present apprized, have been found out only by our observations on things; how many more a farther search may bring to light, no one can say; nor are we certain, that we are provided with sufficient methods of perception to discern them all. Therefore, since we have no other way of making discoveries in nature, but by gradual inquiries into the properties of bodies; our first step must be to admit without distinction all the properties, which we observe; and afterwards we must endeavour, as far as we are able, to distinguish between the qualities, wherewith the very substances themselves are indued, and those appearances, which result from the structure only of compound bodies. Some of the properties, which we observe in things, are the attributes of particular bodies only; others universally belong to all, that fall under our notice. Whether some of the qualities and powers of particular bodies, be derived from different kinds of matter entering their composition, cannot, in the present imperfect state of our knowledge, absolutely be decided; though we have not yet any reason to conclude, but that all the bodies, with which we converse, are framed out of the very same kind of matter, and that their distinct qualities are occasioned only by their structure; through the variety whereof the general powers of matter are caused to produce different effects. On the other hand, we should not hastily conclude, that whatever is found to appertain to all matter, which falls under our examination, must for that reason only be an essential property thereof, and not be derived from some unseen disposition in the frame of nature. Sir Isaac Newton has found reason to conclude, that *gravity* is a property universally belonging to all the perceptible bodies in the universe, and to every particle of matter, whereof they are composed. *But yet he no where asserts this property to be essential to matter.* And he was so far from having any design of establishing it as such, that, on the contrary, he has given some hints worthy of himself at a cause for it; and expressly says, that he proposed those hints to shew that he had no such intention.

It appears from hence, that it is not easy to determine, what properties of Bodies are essentially inherent in the matter, out of which they are made, and what depend upon their frame and composition. But certainly whatever properties are found to belong either to any particular systems of matter or universally to all, must be considered in philosophy; because philosophy will be otherwise imperfect. Whether those properties can be deduced from some other appertaining to matter, either among those, which are already known, or among such as can be discovered by us, is afterwards to be sought for the farther improvement of our knowledge. But this inquiry cannot properly have place in the deliberation about admitting any property of matter or bodies into philosophy; for that purpose it is only to be considered, whether the existence of such a property has been justly proved or not. Therefore to decide what causes of things are rightly received into natural philosophy, requires only a distinct and clear conception of what kind of reasoning is to be allowed of as convincing, when we argue upon the works of nature.

The proofs in natural philosophy cannot be so absolutely conclusive, as in the mathematics. For the subjects of that science are purely the ideas of our own minds. They may be represented to our senses by material objects, but they are themselves the arbitrary productions of our own thoughts; so that as the mind can have a full and adequate knowledge of its own ideas, the reasoning in geometry can be rendered perfect. But in natural knowledge the subject of our contemplation is without us, and not so compleatly to be known: therefore our method of arguing must fall a little short of absolute perfection. It is only here required to steer a just course between the conjectural method of proceeding, against which I have so largely spoke; and demanding so rigorous a proof, as will reduce all philosophy to mere scepticism, and exclude all prospect of making any progress in the knowledge of nature.

NEWTON'S PRINCIPIA

Preface

SINCE THE ANCIENTS (as we are told by *Pappus*), made great account of the science of mechanics in the investigation of natural things; and the moderns, laying aside substantial forms and occult qualities, have endeavoured to subject the phænomena of nature to the laws of mathematics, I have in this treatise cultivated mathematics so far as it regards philosophy. The ancients considered mechanics in a twofold respect; as rational, which proceeds accurately by demonstration; and practical. To practical mechanics all the manual arts belong, from which mechanics took its name. But as artificers do not work with perfect accuracy, it comes to pass that mechanics is so distinguished from geometry, that what is perfectly accurate is called geometrical; what is less so, is called mechanical. But the errors are not in the art, but in the artificers. He that works with less accuracy is an imperfect mechanic; and if any could work with perfect accuracy, he would be the most perfect mechanic of all; for the description of right lines and circles, upon which geometry is founded, belongs to mechanics. Geometry does not teach us to draw these lines, but requires them to be drawn; for it requires that the learner should first be taught to describe these accurately, before he enters upon geometry; then it shows how by these operations problems may be solved. To describe right lines and circles are problems, but not geometrical problems. The solution of these problems is required from mechanics; and by geometry the use of them, when so solved, is shown; and it is the glory of geometry that from those few principles, brought from without, it is able to produce so many things. Therefore geometry is founded in mechanical practice, and is nothing but that part of universal mechanics which accurately proposes and demonstrates the art of measuring. But since the manual arts are chiefly conversant in the moving of bodies, it comes to pass that geometry is commonly referred to their magnitudes, and mechanics to their motion. In this sense rational mechanics will be the science of motions resulting from any forces whatsoever, and of the forces required to produce any motions, accurately proposed and demonstrated. This part of mechanics was cultivated by the ancients in the five powers which relate to manual arts, who considered gravity (it not being a manual power), no otherwise than as it moved weights by those powers. Our design not respecting arts, but philosophy, and our subject not manual but natural powers, we consider chiefly those things which relate to gravity, levity, elastic force, the resistance of fluids, and the like forces, whether attractive or impulsive; and therefore we offer this work as the mathematical principles of philosophy; for all the difficulty of philosophy seems to consist in this—from the phænomena of motions to investigate the forces of nature, and then from these forces to demonstrate the other phænomena; and to this end the general propositions in the first and second book are directed. In the third book we give an example of this in the explication of the System of the World; for by the propositions mathematically demonstrated in the former books, we in the third derive from the celestial phænomena the forces of gravity with which bodies tend to the sun and the several planets. Then from these forces, by other propositions which are also mathematical, we deduce the motions of the planets, the comets, the moon, and the sea. I wish we could derive the rest of the phænomena of nature by the same kind of reasoning from mechanical principles; for I am induced by many reasons to suspect that they may all depend upon certain forces by which the particles of bodies, by some causes hitherto unknown, are either mutually impelled towards each other, and cohere in regular figures, or are repelled and recede from each other; which forces being unknown, philosophers have hitherto attempted the search of nature in vain; but I hope the principles here laid down will afford some light either to this or some truer method of philosophy. . . .

Book III

RULES OF REASONING IN PHILOSOPHY

Rule I. *We are to admit no more causes of natural things than such as are both true and sufficient to explain their appearances.*

To this purpose the philosophers say that Nature does nothing in vain, and more is in vain when less will serve; for Nature is pleased with simplicity, and affects not the pomp of superfluous causes.

Rule II. *Therefore to the same natural effects we must, as far as possible, assign the same causes.*

As to respiration in a man and in a beast; the descent of stones in Europe and in America; the light of our culinary fire and of the sun; the reflection of light in the earth, and in the planets.

Rule III. *The qualities of bodies, which admit neither intension nor remission of degrees, and which are found to belong to all bodies within the reach of our experiments, are to be esteemed the universal qualities of all bodies whatsoever.*

For since the qualities of bodies are only known to us by experiments, we are to hold for universal all such as universally agree with experiments and such as are not liable to diminution can never be quite taken away. We are certainly not to relinquish the evidence of experiments for the sake of dreams and vain fictions of our own devising; nor are we to recede from the analogy of Nature, which uses to be simple, and always consonant to itself. We no other way know the extension of bodies than by our senses, nor do these reach it in all bodies; but because we perceive extension in all that are sensible, therefore we ascribe it universally to all others also. That abundance of bodies are hard, we learn by experience; and because the hardness of the whole arises from the hardness of the parts, we therefore justly infer the hardness of the undivided particles not only of the bodies we feel but of all others. That all bodies are impenetrable, we gather not from reason, but from sensation. The bodies which we handle we find impenetrable, and thence conclude impenetrability to be an universal property of all bodies whatsoever. That all bodies are moveable, and endowed with certain powers (which we call the *vires inertiæ*) of persevering in their motion, or in their rest, we only infer the like properties observed in the bodies which we have seen. The extension, hardness, impenetrability, mobility, and *vis inertiæ* of the whole, result from the extension, hardness, impenetrability, mobility, and *vires inertiæ* of the parts; and thence we conclude the least particles of all bodies to be also all extended, and hard, and impenetrable, and moveable, and endowed with their proper *vires inertiæ*. And this is the foundation of all philosophy. Moreover, that the divided but contiguous particles of bodies may be separated from one another, is matter of observation; and, in the particles that remain undivided, our minds are able to distinguish yet lesser parts, as is mathematically demonstrated. But whether the parts so distinguished, and not yet divided, may, by the powers of Nature, be actually divided and separated from one another, we cannot certainly determine. Yet, had we the proof of but one experiment that any undivided particle, in breaking a hard and solid body, suffered a division, we might by virtue of this rule conclude that the undivided as well as the divided particles may be divided and actually separated to infinity.

Lastly, if it universally appears, by experiments and astronomical observations, that all bodies about the earth gravitate towards the earth, and that in proportion to the quantity of matter which they severally contain; that the moon likewise, according to the quantity of its matter, gravitates towards the earth; that, on the other hand, our sea gravitates towards the moon; and all the planets mutually one towards another; and the comets in like manner towards the sun; we must, in consequence of this rule, universally allow that all bodies whatsoever are endowed with a principle of mutual gravitation. For the argument from the appearances concludes with more force for the universal gravitation of all bodies than for their impenetrability; of which, among those in the celestial regions, we have no experiments, nor any manner of observation. Not that I affirm gravity to be essential to bodies: by their *vis insita* I mean nothing but their *vis inertiæ*. This is immutable. Their gravity is diminished as they recede from the earth.

Rule IV. *In experimental philosophy we are to look upon propositions collected by general induction from phænomena as accurately or very nearly true, notwithstanding any contrary hypotheses that may be imagined, till such time as other phænomena occur, by which they may either be made more accurate, or liable to exceptions.*

This rule must follow, that the argument of induction may not be evaded by hypotheses.

GENERAL SCHOLIUM

. . . Hitherto we have explained the phænomena of the heavens and of our sea by the power of gravity, but have not yet assigned the cause of this power. This is certain, that it must proceed from a cause that penetrates to the very centres of the sun and planets, without suffering the least diminution of its force; that [it] operates not according to the quantity of the surfaces of the particles upon which it acts (as mechanical causes use to do), but according to the quantity of the solid matter which they contain, and propagates its virtue on all sides to immense distances, decreasing always in the duplicate proportion of the distances. Gravitation towards the sun is made up out of the gravitations towards the several particles of which the body of the sun is composed; and in receding from the sun decreases accurately in the duplicate proportion of the distances as far as the orb of Saturn, as evidently appears from the quiescence of the aphelions of the planets; nay, and even to the remotest aphelions of the comets, if those aphelions are also quiescent. But hitherto I have not been able to discover the cause of those properties of gravity from phænomena, and I frame no hypotheses; for whatever is not deduced from the phænomena is to be called an hypothesis; and hypotheses, whether metaphysical or physical, whether of occult qualities or mechanical, have no place in experimental philosophy. In this philosophy particular propositions are inferred from the phænomena, and afterwards rendered general by induction. Thus it was that the impenetrability, the mobility, and the impulsive force of bodies, and the laws of motion and of gravitation, were discovered. And to us it is enough that gravity does really exist, and act according to the laws which we have explained, and abundantly serves to account for all the motions of the celestial bodies, and of our sea. . . .

BLAISE PASCAL

BLAISE PASCAL (1623–62), French philosopher, scientist, and mystic, early in life showed a rare gift for mathematics and has come to be regarded as the founder of probability theory. At the age of sixteen he wrote a treatise on conic sections and two years later invented a calculating machine. Pascal, like the other members of his family, was strongly and favorably impressed by the Augustinian doctrines of Jansenism which appeared to support the determinism to which he was inclined both by scientific commitment and emotional predilection. Even in science, his method was synthetic rather than rationally analytic as was Descartes's. Distinguishing between the analytical "spirit of geometry" and the intuitive "spirit of finesse," Pascal insisted that the latter develops insights into spiritual and emotional truths which the former is incapable of comprehending. Convinced of the impotence of reason to solve and explain man's spiritual problems and hopes, impatient with those who claim to provide rational proofs for the existence of God, Pascal exalted faith and intuitive revelation.

These selections are taken from *The Living Thoughts of Pascal,* edited by François Mauriac (New York and Toronto: Longmans, Green and Co., 1940).

FRAGMENT OF A TREATISE ON VACUUM

Concerning Authority in the Matter of Philosophy

THE RESPECT that we bear to antiquity is at the present day carried to such a point on subjects in which it ought to have less weight, that oracles are made of all its thoughts and mysteries, even of its obscurities; that novelties can no longer be advanced without peril, and that the text of an author* suffices to destroy the strongest reasons. . . .

Not that it is my intention to correct one error by another, and not to esteem the ancients at all because others have esteemed them too much.

I do not pretend to banish their authority in order to exalt reasoning alone, although others have sought to establish their authority alone to the prejudice of reasoning. . . .

In matters in which we only seek to know what the authors have written, as in history, geography, jurisprudence, languages . . . and especially in theology; and in fine in all those which have for their principle either simple facts or divine or human institutions, we must necessarily have recourse to

* Aristotle.

their books, since all that we can know of them is therein contained; hence it is evident that we can have full knowledge of them, and that it is not possible to add anything hereto.

If it is in question to know who was the first king of the French; in what spot geographers place the first meridian; what words are used in a dead language, and all things of this nature; what other means than books can guide us to them? And who can add anything new to what they teach us, since we wish only to know what they contain?

Authority alone can enlighten us on these. But the subject in which authority has the principal weight is theology, because there she is inseparable from truth, and we know it only through her: so that to give full certainty to matter incomprehensible to reason, it suffices to show them in the sacred books; as to show the uncertainty of the most probable things, it is only necessary to show that they are not included therein; since its principles are superior to nature and reason, and since, the mind of man being too weak to attain them by its own efforts, he cannot reach these lofty conceptions if he be not carried thither by an omnipotent and superhuman power.

It is not the same with subjects that fall under the senses and under reasoning; authority here is useless; it belongs to reason alone to know them. They have their separate rights: there the one has all the advantage, here the other reigns in turn. But as subjects of this kind are proportioned to the grasp of the mind, it finds full liberty to extend them; its inexhaustible fertility produces continually, and its inventions may be multiplied altogether without limit and without interruption.

It is thus that geometry, arithmetic, music, physics, medicine, architecture, and all the sciences that are subject to experiment and reasoning, should be augmented in order to become perfect. The ancients found them merely outlined by those who preceded them; and we shall leave them to those who will come after us in a more finished state than we received them.

As their perfection depends on time and pains, it is evident that although our pains and time may have acquired less than their labors separate from ours, both joined together must nevertheless have more effect than each one alone.

The clearing up of this difference should make us pity the blindness of those who bring authority alone as proof in physical matters, instead of reasoning or experiments; and inspire us with horror for the wickedness of others who make use of reasoning alone in theology, instead of the authority of the Scripture and the Fathers. We must raise the courage of those timid people who dare invent nothing in physics, and confound the insolence of those rash persons who produce novelties in theology. Nevertheless the misfortune of the age is such, that we see many new opinions in theology, unknown to all antiquity, maintained with obstinacy and received with applause; whilst those that are produced in physics, though small in number, should, it seems, be convicted of falsehood as soon as they shock already received opinions in the slightest degree; as if the respect that we have for the ancient philosophers were a duty, and that which we bear to the most ancient of the Fathers solely a matter of courtesy! I leave it to judicious persons to remark the importance of this abuse which perverts the order of the sciences with so much injustice. . . .

Let us divide our credulity and suspicion with more justice, and limit this respect we have for the ancients. As reason gives it birth, she ought also to measure it; and let us consider that if they had continued in this restraint of not daring to add anything to the knowledge which they had received, or if those of their times had made the like difficulty in receiving the novelties which they offered them, they would have deprived themselves and their posterity of the fruit of their inventions.

As they only made use of that which had been bequeathed to them as a means whereby to gain more, and as this happy daring opened to them the way to great things, we should take that which they acquired in the same manner, and by their example make of it the means and not the end of our study, and thus strive while imitating to surpass them.

For what is more unjust than to treat our ancestors with more deference than they showed to those who preceded them, and to have for them that inviolable respect which they have only merited from us because they had not the like for those who possessed the same advantage over them? . . . .

The secrets of nature are concealed; although she is continually working, we do not always discover her effects: time reveals them from age to age, and although always alike in herself she is not always alike known.

The experiments that give us the knowledge of these secrets are multiplied continually; and as they are the sole principles of physics, the consequences are multiplied in proportion.

It is in this manner that we may at the present day adopt different sentiments and new opinions, without despising *the ancients and* without ingratitude, since the first knowledge which they have given us has served as a stepping-stone to our own, and since in these advantages we are indebted to them for our ascendency over them; because being raised by their aid to a certain degree, the slightest effort causes us to mount still higher, and with less pains and less glory we find ourselves above them. Thence it is that we are enabled to discover things which it was impossible for them to perceive. Our view is more extended, and although they knew as well as we all that they could observe in nature, they did not, nevertheless, know it so well, and we see more than they.

Yet it is marvellous in what manner their sentiments are revered. It is made a crime to contradict them and an act of treason to add to them, as though they had left no more truths to be known.

Is not this to treat unworthily the reason of man and to put it on a level with the instinct of animals, since we take away the principal difference between them, which is that the effects of reason accumulate without ceasing, whilst instinct remains always in the same state? The cells of the bees were as correctly measured a thousand years ago as to-day, and each formed a hexagon as exactly the first time as the last. It is the same with all that the animals produce by the occult impulse. Nature instructs them in proportion as necessity impels them; but this fragile science is lost with the wants which give it birth: as they received it without study, they have not the happiness of preserving it; and every time it is given them it is new to them, since nature having for her object nothing but the maintenance of animals in a limited order of perfection, she inspires them with this necessary science always the same, lest they may fall into decay, and does not permit them to add to it, less they should exceed the limits that she has prescribed to them. It is not the same with man, who is formed only for infinity. He is ignorant at the earliest age of his life; but he is instructed unceasingly in his progress; for he derives advantage, not only from his own experience, but also from that of his predecessors; since he always retains in his memory the knowledge which he himself has once acquired, and since he has that of the ancients ever present in the books which they have bequeathed to him. And as he preserves this knowledge, he can also add to it easily; so that men are at the present day in some sort in the same condition in which those ancient philosophers would have been found, could they have survived till the present time, adding to the knowledge which they possessed that which their studies would have acquired by the aid of so many centuries. Thence it is that by an especial prerogative, not only does each man advance from day to day in the sciences, but all mankind together make continual progress in proportion as the world grows older, since the same things happen in the succession of men as in the different ages of single individuals. So that the whole succession of men, during the course of many ages, should be considered as a single man who subsists forever and learns continually, whence we see with what injustice we respect antiquity in philosophers; for as old age in this universal man ought not to be sought in the times nearest his birth, but in those the most remote from it. Those whom we call ancient were really new in all things, and properly constituted the infancy of mankind; and as we have joined to their knowledge the experience of the centuries which have followed them, it is in ourselves that we should find this antiquity that we revere in others.

They should be admired for the results which they derived from the very few principles they possessed, and they should be excused for those in which they failed rather from the lack of the advantage of experience than the strength of reasoning. . . .

Thus it is that, in respect to vacuum, they had a right to say that nature would not suffer it, since all their experiments had always made them remark that she abhorred, and could not suffer it. But if the modern experiments had been known to them, perhaps they would have found cause for affirming what they found cause for denying, for the reason that vacuum had not yet appeared. Thus, in the judgment they formed that nature would not suffer vacuum, they only heard nature spoken of in the condition in which they knew her.

Thus it is that, without contradicting them, we can affirm the contrary of what they say; and, whatever authority, in fine, this antiquity may have, truth should always have more, although newly discovered, since she is always older than all the opinions that we have had of her, and it would be showing ourselves ignorant of her nature to imagine that she may have begun to be at the time when she began to be known.

THE ART OF PERSUASION
(Of the Geometrical Spirit)

THE ART OF PERSUASION has a necessary relation to the manner in which men are led to consent to that which is proposed to them, and to the conditions of things which it is sought to make them believe.

No one is ignorant that there are two avenues by which opinions are received into the soul, which are its two principal powers: the understanding and the will. The more natural is that of the understanding, for we should never consent to any but demonstrated truths; but the more common, though the one contrary to nature, is that of the will; for all men are almost led to believe not of proof, but by attraction. This way is base, ignoble, and irrelevant: every one therefore disavows it. Each one professes to believe and even to love nothing but what he knows to be worthy of belief and love.

I do not speak here of divine truths, which I shall take care not to comprise under the art of persuasion, because they are infinitely superior to nature: God alone can place them in the soul and in such a way as it pleases him. I know that he has desired that they should enter from the heart into the mind, and not from the mind into the heart, to humiliate that proud power of reasoning that pretends to the right to be the judge of the things that the will chooses; and to cure this infirm will which is wholly corrupted by its filthy attachments. . . .

I speak only of the truths within our reach; and it is of them that I say that the mind and the heart are as doors by which they are received into the soul, but that very few enter by the mind, whilst they are brought in in crowds by the rash caprices of the will, without the counsel of the reason.

These powers have each their principles and their mainsprings of action.

Those of the mind are truths which are natural and known to all the world, as that the whole is greater than its part, besides several particular maxims that are received by some and not by others, but which as soon as they are admitted are as powerful, although false, in carrying away belief, as those the most true.

Those of the will are certain desires natural and common to all mankind, as the desire of being happy, which no one can avoid having, besides several particular objects which each one follows to please us are as powerful, although pernicious in fact, in causing the will to act, as though they made its veritable happiness.

So much for that which regards the powers that lead us to consent.

But as for the qualities of things which should persuade us they are very different.

Some are drawn, by a necessary consequence, from common principles and admitted truths. These may be infallibly persuasive; for in showing the harmony which they have with acknowledged principles there is an inevitable necessity of conviction, and it is impossible that they shall not be received into the soul as it has been enabled to class them among the principles which it has already admitted.

There are some which have a close connection with the objects of our satisfaction; and these again are received with certainty, for as soon as the soul has been made to perceive that a thing can conduct it to that which it loves supremely, it must inevitably embrace it with joy.

But those which have this double union both with admitted truths and with the desires of the heart, are so sure of their effect that there is nothing that can be more so in nature.

As, on the contrary, that which does not accord either with our belief or with our pleasures is importunate, false, and absolutely alien to us.

In all these positions, there is no room for doubt. But there are some wherein the things which it is sought to make us believe are well established upon truths which are known, but which are at the same time contrary to the pleasures that interest us most. And these are in great danger of showing, by an experience which is only too common, what I said at the beginning—that this imperious soul, which boasted of acting only by reason, follows by a rash and shameful choice the desires of a corrupt will, whatever resistance may be opposed to it by the too enlightened mind.

Then it is that a doubtful balance is made between truth and pleasure, and that the knowledge of the one and the feeling of the other stir up a combat the success of which is very uncertain, since, in order to judge it, it would be necessary to know all that passes in the innermost spirit of the man, of which the man himself is scarcely ever conscious.

It appears from this, that whatever it may be of which we wish to persuade men, it is necessary to have regard to the person whom we wish to persuade, of whom we must know the mind and the heart, what principles he acknowledges, what things he loves; and then observe in the thing in question what affinity it has with the acknowledged principles, or with the objects so delightful by the pleasure which they give him.

So that the art of persuasion consists as much in that of pleasing as in that of convincing, so much more are men governed by caprice than by reason!

Now, of these two methods, the one of convincing, the other of pleasing, I shall only give here the rules of the first; and this in case we have granted the principles, and remain firm in avowing them: otherwise I do not know whether there could be an art for adapting proofs to the inconstancy of our caprices.

But the manner of pleasing is incomparably more difficult, more subtle, more useful, and more admirable; therefore, if I do not treat of it, it is because I am not capable of it; and I feel myself so far disproportionate to the task, that I believe the thing absolutely impossible.

Not that I do not believe that there may be as sure rules for pleasing as for demonstrating, and that he who knows perfectly how to comprehend and to practice them will as surely succeed in making himself beloved by princes and by people of all conditions, as in demonstrating the elements of geometry to those who have enough imagination to comprehend its hypotheses. But I consider, and it is, perhaps, my weakness that makes me believe it, that it is impossible to reach this. At least I know that if any are capable of it, they are certain persons whom I know, and that no others have such clear and such abundant light on this matter.

The reason of this extreme difficulty comes from the fact that the principles of pleasure are not firm and stable. They are different in all mankind, and variable in every particular with such a diversity that there is no man more different from another than from himself at different times. A man has other pleasures than a woman; a rich man and a poor man have different enjoyments; a prince, a warrior, a merchant, a citizen, a peasant, the old, the young, the well, the sick, all vary; the least accidents change them.

Now there is an art, and it is that which I give, for showing the connection of truths with their principles, whether of truth or of pleasure, provided that the principles which have once been avowed remain firm, and without being ever contradicted.

But as there are few principles of this kind, and as, apart from geometry, which deals only with very simple figures, there are hardly any truths upon which we always remain agreed, and still fewer objects of pleasure which we do not change every hour, I do not know whether there is a means of giving fixed rules for adapting discourse to the inconstancy of our caprices.

This art, which I call the *art of persuading,* and which, properly speaking, is simply the process of perfect methodical proofs, consists of three essential parts: of defining the terms of which we should avail ourselves by clear definitions; of proposing principles or evident axioms to prove the thing in question; and of always mentally substituting in the demonstrations the definition in the place of the thing defined.

The reason of this method is evident, since it would be useless to propose what it is sought to prove, and to undertake the demonstration of it, if all the terms which are not intelligible had not first been clearly defined; and since it is necessary in the same manner that the demonstration should be preceded by the demand for the evident principles that are necessary in demonstrating mentally, to substitute the definitions in the place of the things defined, as otherwise there might be an abuse of the different meanings that are encountered in the terms. It is easy to see that, by observing this method, we are sure of convincing, since the terms all being understood, and perfectly exempt from ambiguity by the definitions, and the principles being granted, if in the demonstration we always mentally substitute the definitions for the things defined, the invincible force of the conclusions cannot fail of having its whole effect.

Thus, never can a demonstration in which these conditions have been observed be subject to the slightest doubt; and never can those have force in which they are wanting.

The difference between the mathematical and the intuitive mind. In the one the principles are palpable, but removed from ordinary use; so that for want of habit it is difficult to turn one's mind in that direction: but if one turns it thither ever so little, one sees the principles fully, and one must have a quite inaccurate mind who reasons wrongly from principles so plain that it is almost impossible they should escape notice.

But in the intuitive mind the principles are found in common use, and are before the eyes of everybody. One has only to look, and no effort is necessary; it is only a question of good eyesight, but it must be good, for the principles are so subtle and so numerous, that it is almost impossible but that some escape notice. Now the omission of one principle leads to error; thus one must have very clear sight to see all the principles, and in the next place an accurate mind not to draw false deductions from known principles.

All mathematicians would then be intuitive if they had clear sight, for they do not reason incorrectly from principles known to them; and intuitive minds would be mathematical if they could turn their eyes to the principles of mathematics to which they are unused.

The reason, therefore, that some intuitive minds are not mathematical is that they cannot at all turn their attention to the principles of mathematics. But the reason that mathematicians are not intuitive is that they do not see what is before them, and that, accustomed to the exact and plain principles of mathematics, and not reasoning till they have well inspected and arranged their principles, they are lost in matters of intuition where the principles do not allow of such arrangement. They are scarcely seen; they are felt rather than seen; there is the greatest difficulty in making them felt by those who do not of themselves perceive them. These principles are so fine and so numerous that a very delicate and very clear sense is needed to perceive them, and to judge rightly and justly when they are perceived without the most part being able to demonstrate them in order as in mathematics; because the principles are not known to us in the same way, and because it would be an endless matter to undertake it. We must see the matter at once, at one glance, and not by a process of reasoning, at least to a certain degree. And thus it is rare that mathematicians are intuitive, and that men of intuition are mathematicians, because mathematicians wish to treat matters of intuition mathematically, and make themselves ridiculous, wishing to begin with definitions and then with axioms, which is not the way to proceed in this kind of reasoning. Not that the mind does not do so, but it does it tacitly, naturally, and without technical rules; for the expression of it is beyond all men, and only a few can feel it.

Intuitive minds, on the contrary, being thus accustomed to judge at a single glance, are so astonished when they are presented with propositions of which they understand nothing, and the way to which is through definitions and axioms so sterile, and which they are not accustomed to see thus in detail, that they are repelled and disheartened.

But dull minds are never either intuitive or mathematical.

Mathematicians, who are only mathematicians have exact minds, provided all things are explained to them by means of definitions and axioms; otherwise they are inaccurate and insufferable, for they are only right when the principles are quite clear.

And men of intuition who are only intuitive cannot have the patience to reach to first principles of things speculative and conceptual, which they have never seen in the world, and which are altogether out of the common.

There are different kinds of right understanding; some have right understanding in a certain order of things, and not in others, where they go astray. Some draw conclusions well from a few premises, and this displays an acute judgment.

Others draw conclusions well where there are many premises.

For example, the former easily learn hydrostatics, where the premises are few, but the conclusions are so fine that only the greatest acuteness can reach them.

And in spite of that these persons would perhaps not be great mathematicians, because mathematics contain a great number of premises, and there is perhaps a kind of intellect that can search with ease a few premises to the bottom; and cannot in the least penetrate those matters in which there are many premises.

There are then two kinds of intellect: the one able to penetrate acutely and deeply into the conclusions of given premises, and this is the precise intellect; the other able to comprehend a great number of premises without confusing them, and this is the mathematical intellect. The one has force and exactness, the other comprehension. Now the one quality can exist without the other; the intellect can be strong and narrow, and can also be comprehensive and weak.

Those who are accustomed to judge by feeling do not understand the process of reasoning, for they would understand at first sight, and are not used to seek for principles. And others, on the contrary, who are accustomed to reason from principles, do not at all understand matters of feeling, seeking principles, and being unable to see at a glance.

Mathematics, Intuition. True eloquence makes light of eloquence, true morality makes light of morality; that is to say, the morality of the judgment, which has no rules, makes light of the morality of the intellect.

For it is to judgment that perception belongs, as science belongs to intellect. Intuition is part of judgment, mathematics of intellect.

To make light of philosophy is to be a true philosopher.

The lust of the flesh, the lust of the eyes, pride, &c. There are three orders of things: the flesh, the spirit, and the will. The carnal are the rich and kings; they have the body as their object. Inquirers and scientists; they have the mind as their object. The wise; they have righteousness as their object.

God must reign over all, and all men must be brought back to Him. In things of the flesh lust reigns specially; in intellectual matters, inquiry specially, in wisdom, pride specially. Not that a man cannot boast of wealth or knowledge, but it is not the place for pride; for in granting to a man that he is learned, it is easy to convince him that he is wrong to be proud. The proper place for pride is in wisdom, for it cannot be granted to a man that he has made himself wise, and that he is wrong to be proud; for that is right. Now God alone gives wisdom, and this is why *Qui gloriatur, in Domino glorietur.**

* "He that glorieth, may glory in the lord." St. Paul, Ad Cor., I. 31.

IX THE ELABORATION OF THE SOVEREIGN STATE

CARDINAL RICHELIEU

A RMAND JEAN DU PLESSIS, DUC DE RICHELIEU (1585–1642), was born into a French family of the lesser nobility. He became bishop of Luçon at twenty-one and was chosen to represent the clergy of Poitou in the Estates-General of 1614. The queen-regent, Marie de' Medici, employed him as one of her chief advisers; Richelieu was banished from court with her in 1617 by the young king Louis XIII. In 1622 a reconciliation took place and Richelieu secured both a cardinal's hat and a seat in the council of state; he became chief minister to the king in 1624, a position which he held until his death. He worked unceasingly and successfully to perfect the machinery of monarchical absolutism, and to establish the power of France in Europe. During the Thirty Years War he supported not only Bourbons against Hapsburgs, but also Protestants against Catholics and the German princes against their emperor. Although Richelieu died in 1642, the Peace of Westphalia (1648) was a victory for his policies. Richelieu also established the French Academy and rebuilt the Sorbonne. His written works include his *Mémoires* and the *Testament politique,* a summary and justification of his career.

POLITICAL TESTAMENT

Part I

CHAPTER I: SUCCINCT NARRATION OF
   ALL THE GREAT ACTS OF THE KING
   UP UNTIL THE PEACE OF THE YEAR——

WHEN YOUR MAJESTY decided to grant me entry into his councils and considerable responsibility in the management of his affairs, I can truthfully say that the Huguenots shared control of the State with him, that the great nobles behaved as if they were not his subjects, and the powerful governors of the provinces as if they were sovereign in their jurisdictions.

I may say that their bad example was so prejudicial to the kingdom that the most orderly groups were aware of their own shortcomings and in certain cases diminished your legitimate authority as much as they possibly could in order to increase their own beyond the bounds of reason.

I may say that each gauged his merit by his audacity; that instead of esteeming the benefits that they received from Your Majesty at their proper worth they evaluated them only in the light of the disorderliness of their ambitions, and that the most enterprising were considered the wisest, and were often the happiest.

I may say further that foreign alliances were scorned, that private interests received preference over public interests, in short, the prestige of the crown was diminished, and so very different from what it should have been, owing to the failings of those then principally responsible for the conduct of your affairs, that it was almost impossible to perceive it.

It was no longer possible without losing everything to tolerate the actions of those to whom Your Majesty had entrusted the helm of your ship of state, and moreover, it was not possible to change this all at once without violating the laws of prudence which forbid jumping from one extreme to the other.

The poor state of your affairs seemed to force you into hurried decisions, without choice of time or means, and yet both choices had to be made, in order to profit from the change that your wisdom saw necessary to make.

The best minds did not think it possible to pass all the reefs that appeared in such uncertain times without being wrecked. There were many people at court who accused those who wanted to do so of foolhardiness; and knowing that princes readily blame on those near to them the unfortunate outcome of courses which they have been advised to follow, so few people foresaw success from the changes it was rumored I wished to make that many regarded my fall as certain even before your majesty had raised me to power.

Despite all the difficulties which I pointed out to Your Majesty, knowing what kings can accomplish when they make good use of their power I made bold to promise that you would have reason to be satisfied with your State and that within a brief period of time your wisdom and the grace of God would change the face of this kingdom.

I promised Your Majesty to apply myself to devote all my labors and all the authority that you were pleased to give me in order to ruin the Huguenot party and to humble the pride of the great nobles, to bring all your subjects to their duty and to raise your repute in foreign lands to the estate which it deserved.

I called to your attention the fact that to attain such an end your confidence was absolutely necessary and that although in the past all those who had served you thought there was no better or more certain way of winning and keeping your confidence than by separating you from the Queen your mother, I took the opposite course and did everything within my power to maintain between Your Majesties the close relations so important to your reputations and so beneficial to the well being of the kingdom.

And thus the success of the good plans which it pleased God to give me for the guidance of this state will justify to future centuries the firmness with which I steadfastly carried out this design. Your Majesty will bear witness that I did everything I possibly could to prevent the guile of many evil intentioned men from becoming powerful enough to divide that which being united by nature should also have been united by grace. If after having for several years successfully resisted their maneuvers their malice finally prevailed it is a source of deep consolation to me that Your Majesty was often heard to say that when I had the glory of the Queen your mother uppermost in my mind she was working for my ruin. . . .

The Huguenots lost no opportunity to increase their strength; in 1624 they seized certain ships which the Duke of Nevers was readying against the Turk and subsequently prepared a strong force against Your Majesty.

Although the fleet had been sadly neglected up until that time and although it did not have a single ship the navy fought with such daring and courage with whatever vessels it could secure from your subjects, twenty from Holland and seven *roberges* [1] from England, that it defeated the fleet of the people of La Rochelle. . . .

In the same manner the Isle of Ré which had some time before been so unfairly seized by the people of La Rochelle was taken. Four or five thousand men whom they had brought in to defend it were routed and Soubise who was the commander was forced to flee to Oléron; from there your supporters drove him not only from Oléron but also from the kingdom itself.

This victory drove those rebels into a peace so glorious for Your Majesty that the most critical were extremely satisfied and all avowed that there had never been anything like it before.

The kings your predecessors had in the past accepted peace from their subjects rather than granting it to them. Although they never hesitated to fight a single war, in every one they were losers in the treaties which they made with their subjects; and although at that time Your Majesty had many other matters at hand you laid down the terms of peace, keeping Fort Louis as a citadel at La Rochelle as well as the islands of Ré and d'Oléron as two other strong points. . . .

At the same time Your Majesty protected the Duke of Savoy from the oppression of the Spaniards who had openly attacked him, and though they

---

[1] [A type of English war vessel.]

had one of the largest armies seen in Italy for many years and though it was commanded by the Duke of Feria, they were prevented from seizing Veruë, which your armies, joined with those of the Duke of Savoy, defended with such glory that they were forced with shame to lift the siege.

The Spaniards having shortly thereafter taken all the passes of Grisons and having fortified the best positions of all the valleys of this area, Your Majesty, being unable by negotiation to save his old allies from this invasion in which these unjust usurpers were strengthened all the more since the Pope supported them in the vain hope of securing some advantage for religion, obtained by force of arms what he could not obtain by force of reason.

By this means Your Majesty would have forever freed this nation from the tyranny of the House of Austria, had not Fargis, your Ambassador in Spain, concluded, at the solicitation of the Cardinal de Berule (as he later confessed), without your knowledge and contrary to the express orders of Your Majesty, an extremely disadvantageous treaty, to which you finally adhered in order to please the Pope, who claimed to be in no way involved in this matter. . . .

If it was of exceptional prudence to have engaged the forces of the enemies of your state, for ten years, with the forces of your allies, placing your hand to your purse and not to arms, it is still another instance of combined wisdom and courage to have entered into open warfare when your allies could no longer stand alone, showing that in husbanding the exertions of the kingdom, you did as those stewards who, having been careful in amassing money, know when to spend it to secure themselves against greater losses.

To have made a number of simultaneous attacks in different places, which neither the Romans nor the Ottomans ever did, might have seemed to many people proof of very great imprudence and daring. And while this may have been proof of your power, it was strong proof of your judgment, since it was necessary so to occupy your enemies in all regions that they could be invincible in none. . . .

There are several things that should be noted in this war.

The first is that Your Majesty entered the war only when you could no longer avoid so doing. . . . This is all the more to Your Majesty's glory inasmuch as, being at peace, you were several times called upon by your allies to take up arms, without wishing to do so, and inasmuch as during the war your enemies frequently suggested a separate peace, without your ever being willing to heed them, because you would not separate yourself from the interests of your allies. . . .

The second remark worthy of great consideration on this subject is that Your Majesty never wished, in order to secure himself against the peril of war, to expose Christendom to the peril of the arms of the Ottomans, which were often offered to him.

Your Majesty was not unaware that you could justly accept such aid, but this knowledge was nevertheless not strong enough to bring you to a decision hazardous to the faith, while advantageous toward enabling you to have peace.

The example of some of your predecessors, and of various Princes of the House of Austria, which particularly affects to appear as religious before God when it is to its own interests,—this example was not strong enough to bring you to do that which history teaches us was several times practised by others.

The third circumstance to cause astonishment in this war, is the great number of armies and the sums of money necessary to carry it on.

As the greatest princes of the earth have always hesitated to undertake two wars simultaneously, posterity will find it hard to believe that this kingdom was capable of supporting, at its own expense, three land armies and two fleets, without counting those of its allies, to the support of which it contributed not a little. . . .

If I add that these various undertakings did not prevent this Crown from fortifying, at the same time, all the frontiers so perfectly, that instead of being open at all points to its enemies as previously, those enemies can now regard them only with astonishment, I touch another point of no less significance to posterity, since, placing this kingdom in a state of security forever, it will derive as much benefit therefrom as Your Majesty in the past had labor and troubles.

JACQUES BOSSUET

JACQUES BÉNIGNE BOSSUET (1627–1704), an important French churchman, preacher, administrator, orator, and educator, was educated by the Jesuits and early came under the influence of Descartes's philosophy. As the most eloquent preacher of his generation, he enjoyed great favor and exercised much influence at the court of Louis XIV. In the years 1660 to 1669 he rapidly rose to high ecclesiastical office, and in 1669 he was made a bishop. In 1670 he was put in charge of the education of the heir to the throne; in 1681 he became bishop of Meaux.

Bossuet's chief interests throughout his career were to restore the unity of the Christian church, especially in France, by persuading the Protestants of the futility of their cardinal principle of private judgment, and to uphold and solidify the centralized monarchy of Louis XIV. At the same time he defended the liberties of the French church, and supported the king in his quarrel with the papacy over the royal appointment of French bishops. He wrote at that time the "Four Propositions" of Gallicanism, which were burned in Rome but which long remained a fundamental part of French law. For his royal pupil, Bossuet wrote his great *Discours sur l'histoire universelle,* still regarded as a classical expression of the Providential interpretation of history, and *Politique tirée de l'écriture sainte.* Bossuet also achieved recognition as a controversialist (against Fénelon) and as a funeral orator (upon the deaths of Queen Henrietta of England, her daughter, and Condé).

Bossuet retained from his early study of Descartes an overriding intellectual preference for everything that expressed uniformity, regularity, rationality, symmetry, stability, clarity, and order—the geometrical virtues—which are hallmarks of Cartesian thought, of French classicism, and of the political organization that Louis XIV sought to establish.

The selection that follows is from the French of *Politics Drawn from the Very Words of Holy Scripture,* the edition used being Volume XXXVI of the *Oeuvres de Bossuet, Evêque de Meaux, revues sur les manuscrits originaux* . . . (Versailles, J. A. Lebel, 1818). Bossuet made his own French translations of biblical passages from the Latin text of the Vulgate, and it has been thought best to translate them directly into English from Bossuet's French; hence the wording of such passages will be found to vary from that of the standard English versions of the Bible.

POLITICS DRAWN FROM THE VERY WORDS
OF HOLY SCRIPTURE

TO MONSEIGNEUR LE DAUPHIN:

God is the King of Kings: it is His prerogative to teach them and to guide them as His ministers. Listen, then, my lord, to the lessons He gives to them in His Scriptures, and learn from Him the rules and examples upon which they ought to model their conduct.

Besides the other advantages of the scriptures, they have this one as well, that they recount the history of the world from its first origin and so make us see, better than all other works of history, the first principles on which governments have been constructed.

No work of history better reveals the good and the evil that are in the human heart; what upholds and what overthrows kingdoms; what religion can do to establish them and what impiety can do to destroy them.

The other virtues and vices are also portrayed in their true colors in the scriptures, and one sees nowhere else more clearly what are their true consequences.

There one sees the government of a people [the Hebrews] whose legislator was God Himself; one sees the abuses He repressed and the laws He established; these comprise the finest and the most just polity that ever was.

All that Sparta, all that Athens, all that Rome—to go back to the source, all that Egypt—and the best regulated states have had that was most wisely conceived was nothing by comparison with the wisdom that is contained in the law of God, from which all other laws have drawn whatever is best in them.

Therefore there has never been a more perfect constitution for a state than that under which God's people lived.

Moses, who composed it, was instructed by all the divine and human wisdom that can adorn a great and noble genius; and inspiration did nothing but bring to the last degree of perfection and certitude that which had been marked out by the customs and the knowledge of the wisest of all empires and of its greatest ministers, such as the patriarch Joseph, who like Moses was divinely inspired.

Two great kings of this nation, David and Solomon, one a warrior, the other a man of peace, both preeminent in the art of reigning, will provide you not only with examples from their lives but also with precepts, the former in his divine poems, the latter in the proverbs which eternal wisdom dictated to him.

Jesus Christ will teach you, in His own words and in those of His apostles, all the things that make a state happy: His gospel makes men all the more fit to be good citizens on this earth in that it teaches them to make themselves thereby worthy to become citizens of Heaven.

Finally, God, by Whom kings rule, forgets nothing that could teach them how to rule well. The ministers of princes and those who, under their authority, have a part in the government of states and in the administration of justice, will find in His words the lessons which God alone can give them. It is part of Christian morality to model the magistracy upon His laws, for God wishes to decide everything, that is to say, to give decisions for all ranks and conditions of men—and even more especially to him to whom all the others are subject.

This, my lord, is the greatest of all the undertakings one could propose to mankind, and they cannot be too attentive to the laws according to which they are to be judged by a sentence that will be eternal and irrevocable. Those who believe that piety is a weakness in politics will be confounded, for the one which you will see [in these pages] is truly divine.

Book I. On the Principles of Human Society

ARTICLE THREE: IN ORDER TO FORM THE NATIONS AND UNITE THE PEOPLES
IT WAS NECESSARY TO ESTABLISH A GOVERNMENT

Proposition 1. Among men all tends toward division and partiality.

It is not enough that men inhabit the same country or speak the same language because, having become intractable by reason of the violence of their passions and incompatible by reason of their different humors, they could not be united except by submitting all together to a single government which would rule them all.

Lacking that, Abraham and Lot could not suffer one another and were constrained to separate. . . . [Gen. 13:6-7, 9.]

If Abraham and Lot, two just men, and so closely related besides, could not agree with one another over their servants, what disorder would not prevail among the wicked?

Proposition 2. Only the authority of a government can put a brake on the passions and on the violence that has become natural to man.

. . . Justice has no other support but authority and the subordination of powers.

This order is the restraint of license. When each does what he will, and has no other rule than his own desires, all becomes confusion. A Levite violated what was most holy in God's law. The scriptures give as the cause:

"It was in those days that there was no king in Israel, and each man did as he would." [Judg. 17:6.] . . .

Proposition 4. In a well-regulated government each individual renounces the right to occupy by force that which pleases him.

Take government away and the earth with all its goods is as much the common property of men as air and light. God said to all men, "Increase and multiply and fill up the earth." [Gen. 1:28; 9:7.] He gave to all of them without distinction "all the grass that bears its seed on the earth, and all the woods which grow there." [Gen. 1:29.] According to this original law of nature, no one has any right to anything whatsoever, and all is fair booty for everyone.

In a well-regulated government no private individual has a right to occupy anything. Abraham, when he was in Palestine, even had to ask the rulers of the land for a plot of land in which to bury his wife, Sarah. . . .

Thus originates the right of property; and in general every right ought to come from the public authority, without its being permitted to invade or to attack anything by force.

Proposition 5. Through government each individual becomes stronger.

The reason is that each man is sustained by the others. All the forces of the nation flow together into a single force, and the sovereign magistrate has the right to collect them. . . . [Num. 32:6, 14, 17–18.] Thus the sovereign magistrate has in his hand all the forces of the nation which submits to his orders. "We will do," the whole people told Joshua, "everything that you command, and we will go wherever you send us. Death to him who resists your words and will not be obedient to all your orders! Only be firm, and act with vigor." [Josh. 1:16, 18.]

All force is given into the hands of the sovereign magistrate; each one contributes to strengthen it at the expense of his own power, and renounces his own life in the event that he should disobey. Everyone gains; for there reappears in the person of this supreme magistrate more force than that which was given up when he was acknowledged, for we find there all the force of the nation gathered up together to protect us.

Thus an individual is secure against oppression and violence because he has an invincible defender in the person of the prince, one who is incomparably more strong than all those among the people who might undertake to oppress him. . . .

The prince, by virtue of his office, is thus for every individual "a shelter in which to take refuge from wind and tempest and an overhanging rock under which he finds shade in a dry and burning land. Justice establishes peace; there is nothing more pleasing than to see men living in tranquillity:

each one is in safety in his tent and enjoys rest and abundance." [Isa. 32:2, 17–18.] These are the natural fruits of a regular government.

In relying wholly on his own force, each man finds himself too weak to assert his most legitimate claims by reason of the multitude of rivals against whom he must be on guard. But under a legitimate power each one finds himself strong by entrusting all force to the magistrate whose interest it is to enforce peace so that he himself may be secure.

In a regular government widows, orphans, wards, even the infants in the cradle, are strong. Their property is safeguarded, the public assumes the care of their education, their rights are defended, and their cause is the magistrate's own affair. All the scriptures charge him to do justice to the poor and to the weak, to the widow, to the orphan, and to the ward. [Deut. 10:18; Ps. 81:3; et alibi.]

Thus it is with reason that St. Paul urges us "to pray untiringly and with fervor for kings and for all those who are endowed with public office so that we may pass our lives in tranquillity in all piety and chastity." [I Tim. 2:1–2.]

From all this it follows that there is no worse condition than anarchy, that is to say, the state where there is no government nor any authority. Where everyone tries to do as he pleases no one does as he wishes; where there is no master everyone is master; where everyone is master everyone is a slave. . . .

ARTICLE FOUR: CONCERNING THE LAWS

Proposition 1. Laws must be combined with government in order to bring it to its perfection.

This is to say that it is not sufficient for the prince or for the sovereign magistrate to settle cases according to the circumstances [on each occasion]; but that it is necessary to establish general rules of conduct so that government will be constant and uniform: and these are what are called laws.

Proposition 2. Outline of the original principles of all laws.

All laws are founded on the first law of all, which is that of nature, that is to say, on right reason and on natural equity. The laws ought to regulate things human and divine, public and private, and they were instituted by nature according to what St. Paul says: "That the Gentiles who have not the law, doing naturally that which is enjoined by the law, make a law for themselves and show the workings of the law written in their hearts by the testimony of their consciences and by their private thoughts that accuse or else defend themselves one against another." [Rom. 2:14–15.]

The laws must establish sacred and profane jurisprudence, public as well as private rights, in a word, the strict observance of divine and human things among the citizens, together with punishments and rewards.

Thus before all else it is necessary to regulate the worship of God. This is where Moses began, and he laid this foundation of Israelite society. At the head of the Decalogue we find this fundamental precept: "I am the Lord, thou shalt have no other God beside Me," and so on. [Exod. 20:2-6, etc.]

Then come the precepts that concern society. "Thou shalt not kill, thou shalt not steal," and the others. . . . Such is the general order of all legislation.

Proposition 6. The law is sacred and inviolable.

In order to understand perfectly the nature of the law one must observe that all those who have spoken well about it have regarded it, in its origin, as a pact and solemn treaty by which men, by the authority of princes, agree together concerning that which is needful for establishing their society.

By this I do not mean to say that the authority of the laws depends upon the consent and agreement of the peoples, but only that the prince (who, in any case, has by his nature no other interest than that of the public) is aided by the wisest heads of the nation and is supported by the experience of past ages.

This truth, which is unchanging among all men, is admirably explained in the scriptures. God assembles His people, causes to be propounded before them all the laws by which He established sacred and profane jurisprudence, the public and private law of the nation, and makes them all agree to it in His presence. . . . [Deut. 24:2, 9-15.]

Moses received this contract in the name of the whole people who had given their consent to it. . . . [Deut. 5:5.]

The whole people explicitly agreed to the contract. "The Levites said in a loud voice: 'Cursed be he who does not abide firmly in all the words of this law, and who does not fulfill them'; and the whole people answered: 'Amen, so shall it be.' " [Deut. 27:14, 26.]

I must observe that God had no need of the consent of men to legitimate His law, for He was their creator and could oblige them to do what pleased Him; nevertheless, to make the obligation more solemn and more strong He obliged them to accept the law by an express and voluntary contract.

Proposition 7. The law is considered to have a divine origin.

The treaty of which I have just been speaking had a double effect: it united the people to God, and it united the people among themselves.

The people could not unite among themselves in an inviolable society if the contract of union had not been made in their midst in the presence of a superior power, such as that of God, the natural protector of human society, and the ineluctable avenger of all violations of the law.

But when men assume an obligation to God, promising Him to keep, both toward Him and among themselves, all the articles of the law that He proposes to them, then the agreement is inviolable, authorized by a power to whom all is subordinate.

It is for this reason that all peoples have wished to claim a divine origin for their laws, and those whose laws had no such origin have pretended that they have had it. . . .

Proposition 8. There are fundamental laws that cannot be changed; it is even very dangerous to change unnecessarily those which are not fundamental.

It is written, principally concerning these fundamental laws, that when they are violated, "all the foundations of the earth are shaken" [Ps. 81:5], after which there can only ensue the fall of empires.

In general, laws are not laws if they are not in some sense inviolable. To mark their solidity and permanence Moses ordained "that they shall all be written clearly and legibly on stone." [Deut. 27:8.] Joshua carried out this injunction. [Josh. 8:32.]

The other civilized peoples subscribe to this maxim. "Let an edict be made and let it be written according to the inviolable law of the Medes and Persians, Ahasuerus was told by the wise men of his council who were always near his person. These wise men knew the laws and jurisprudence of the ancients." [Esther 1:13, 19.] Such attachment to the laws and to ancient maxims strengthens the bonds of society and makes states immortal.

One loses one's veneration for the laws when one sees them too often changed. It is then that nations seem to totter as if out of their senses and made drunk by wine, in the prophets' manner of speaking. [Isa. 19:14.] Dizziness seizes them and their fall is certain: "because the peoples have violated the laws, altered the public polity and broken the most solemn compacts." [Isa. 24:5.] Their condition is that of a restless sick person who does not know what to do with his limbs. . . .

Book II. Concerning Authority: That Royal and Hereditary Rule Is the Best Government

ARTICLE ONE: BY WHOM AUTHORITY HAS BEEN EXERCISED SINCE THE BEGINNING OF THE WORLD

Proposition 8. Monarchical government is the best.

If it is the most natural it is consequently the most durable, and hence the strongest.

It is also the one most hostile to internal strife, which is the most radical defect in states and the most certain cause of their ruin; this we see from these words which have already been cited: "Every kingdom divided against itself will be laid waste: any city or any family divided against itself will not endure." [Matt. 12:25.]

We have seen that our Lord followed, in this sentence, the natural evolution of government, and seems to have wished to assign to kingdoms and to cities the same means of achieving unity as that established by nature in families.

Indeed, it is natural that when families find it well to unite in order to form a political body they should organize as though by themselves under the form of government most suitable for them.

When men form states they seek to unite themselves, and they are never more united than when they are under a single chief. They are never stronger, moreover, for then everything goes harmoniously. . . .

CONCLUSION

We have, then, established, by the scriptures:

That royalty has its origin in the divinity itself

That God, therefore, visibly exerted [royal authority] over men from the origins of the world

That He continued this supernatural and miraculous exercise of power over the people of Israel up to the time when kings were established

That He then chose [for them] a hereditary monarchical state as being the most natural and the most durable

That the exclusion of the sex that is born to obey was according to the nature of sovereign power

Thus we have found that by the order of divine Providence the constitution of this kingdom was from its origin the most closely in conformity with God's will as it is declared in His scriptures.

Yet we have not forgotten that there appear in antiquity other forms of government concerning which God has prescribed nothing to the human race; consequently each people ought to observe, as divinely ordained, the form of government established in its country, for God is a God of peace and desires tranquillity in human affairs.

But since we write in a monarchical state, and for a prince in the line of succession to so great a kingdom, we shall henceforth apply all the teachings that we shall draw from the scriptures to the form of government under which we live; although by the things that will be said about this state it will be easy to determine what is applicable to the others.

FRANÇOIS FÉNELON

FRANÇOIS DE SALIGNAC DE LA MOTHE FÉNELON (1651–1715), distinguished French theologian and writer, was Archbishop of Cambrai and tutor to a grandson of Louis XIV, the Duke of Burgundy, for whom he wrote his best-known work, *Télémaque* (1699). After a lengthy theological quarrel with Bossuet, Fénelon fell from royal favor and was obliged to retire to Cambrai, where he devoted himself to his ecclesiastical functions. Regarded in his own lifetime as a man of scintillating charm and profound sincerity, Fénelon became a severe critic of what he regarded as the frivolity and irresponsibility of the policies of Louis XIV during the period of French defeat and decline in the second half of the reign.

Among Fénelon's other writings were a treatise on the education of girls (1687), which Madame de Maintenon used as a manual for her fashionable school at Saint-Cyr, and the *Lettre à l'Académie*. The *Lettre à Louis XIV,* from which the following selection is taken, was probably written in 1694.

LETTER TO LOUIS XIV

THE PERSON, Sire, who takes the liberty of writing this letter to you, has no interest in this world. He does not write it because of dissatisfaction, ambition, or any desire to take part in great affairs. He loves you without being known to you; he sees God in your person. With all your power, you are unable to give him any good that he wishes, and there is no evil which he would not willingly suffer in order to bring you to understand the truths that are necessary to your salvation. If he speaks boldly to you, do not be surprised, for the truth is free and strong. You are hardly accustomed to hearing it. Persons inured to flattery may easily sense irritation, bitterness, or intemperance where there is merely pure truth. It is to betray it not to reveal it to you in all its fullness. God is witness that the person who speaks to you does so with his heart full of zeal, respect, fidelity, and emotion for all that concerns your true interests.

You were born, Sire, with an upright and equitable heart; but those who reared you gave you as knowledge of government merely distrust, jealousy, aversion to virtue, fear of all clear merit, a taste for supple and cringing men, arrogance, and concern merely for your own interests.

For thirty years, your principal ministers have shaken and overthrown all the ancient maxims of the state in order to increase your authority beyond all bounds, because it had become theirs since it was in their hands. They no longer spoke of the state or the rules; they spoke merely of the king and his pleasure. They perpetually increased your revenues and your expenses. They exalted you as high as the heavens, in order to efface, they said, the grandeur of all your predecessors together, that is to say, in order to impoverish all France so as to introduce a monstrous and incurable extravagance into the court. They wished to raise you above the ruins of all the social classes in the state, as though you might become great by ruining all your subjects on whom your greatness is founded. It is true that you have been perhaps overly jealous of your authority in foreign affairs, but essentially each minister has been the master throughout his branch of the administration. You believed that you were governing because you regulated the limits between those who governed. They paraded their power before the public, and it was felt only too well. They have been harsh, haughty, unjust, violent and dishonest. They have known no rule of conduct in domestic or foreign affairs but to threaten, crush, and annihilate all that opposed them. They consulted you only in order to remove all your scruples that might cause them embarrassment. They accustomed you to receiving endless, extravagant praises which approached idolatry, and which for the sake of your honor, you should have rejected with indignation. They rendered your name odious and the French nation unbearable to all our neighbors. They did not retain a single ally, since they only desired slaves. They have caused more than twenty years of bloody wars. . . .

The strangest result of these bad counsels is the long duration of the league formed against you. The allies prefer waging a losing war to concluding peace with you, because they are convinced by their own experience that this peace will not be a true one, that you will observe it no more than the others, and that you will merely use it to crush each of your neighbors separately and without difficulty as soon as they are disunited. Thus, the more you are victorious, the more they fear you and cling together in order to avoid the slavery with which they believe themselves threatened. Not being able to conquer you, they hope at least to exhaust you in the course of time. In a word, they no longer hope for security with you except by rendering you powerless to injure them. Put yourself, Sire, in their place for a moment, and observe the fruits of preferring your advantages to justice and good faith.

But your people, whom you should love as your children and who thus far have been so enamored of you, are dying of hunger. Cultivation of the land is almost abandoned; the cities and the countryside are depopulated; all crafts languish and no longer support the workers. All commerce has been decimated. You have consequently destroyed half the real power within your state, in order to win and defend vain conquests abroad. Instead of squeezing money from the poor people, you should give them alms and nourishment. All France is but a great poorhouse without provisions. The magistrates are degraded and overworked. The nobility, whose entire wealth depends on royal decrees, live only on gifts from the state. You are annoyed by the mob of people who beg and murmur. It is you, Sire, who called down on yourself all these difficulties; for, since the realm is in ruins, you have everything in your hands, and no one can continue to live without your gifts. Such is this great realm, so flourishing under a king who daily is described to us as the delight of the people, and who would truly be this if flattering advice had not corrupted him.

Even the people (one must tell all) who loved you so, and who had every confidence in you, are beginning to lose their affection, their trust, and even their respect for you. Your victories and conquests delight them no longer; they are full of bitterness and despair. Sedition is slowly appearing in all places. They believe that you have no pity for their ills, and that you love only your power and your glory. If the king, they say, felt the tenderness of a father toward his people, would he not rather employ his glory toward giving them bread and letting them breathe again after so many troubles, instead of retaining strongholds on the frontier as a cause of further war? What answer is there to that, Sire? Uprisings of the people, unknown for so long, are becoming frequent. Even Paris, so near to you, is not untouched by them. The magistrates are obliged to tolerate the insolence of the subordinate, and to pass them money secretly in order to appease them; thus are paid those who should be punished. You are reduced to the shameful and deplorable extremity of either leaving sedition unpunished and thus allowing it to increase, or ordering the inhuman massacre of the very people whom you have reduced to despair by squeezing from them, through taxes for this war, the bread that they try to earn by the sweat of their brows.

But while they lack bread, you yourself lack money and refuse to recognize the extremity to which you are reduced. Because you have always been fortunate, you are unable to imagine that some day you might be otherwise. You fear to open your eyes; you fear being forced to diminish the least part of your glory. This glory, which hardens your heart, is dearer to you than justice, your own tranquility, the preservation of your people who daily perish from maladies caused by famine, and even your own eternal salvation, which is incompatible with such worship of glory.

That, Sire, is the position in which you are. You live as though you have a fatal blindfold over your eyes; you delude yourself with your daily successes which determine nothing. And since you never consider the totality of affairs from the standpoint of general policy, they decline imperceptibly into ruin. While you are assaulting positions and taking the battlefields and cannon of your enemy in fierce combat, you do not dream that you are fighting on ground which is sinking beneath your feet, and that you will fall in spite of your victories.

Everyone sees this, but no one dares bring it to your attention. Perhaps you will see it too late. True courage consists of undeceiving yourself and making firm decisions according to necessity. You willingly lend an ear, Sire, only to those who delude you with vain hopes. The men whom you know to be most trustworthy are those whom you fear and most avoid. Since you are king, you should seek the truth, urge men to tell it to you without alteration, and encourage those who are too timid. On the contrary, you only wish to avoid going to the heart of any matter; but God will eventually be able to lift the veil which covers your eyes, and will reveal to you what you avoid seeing. For long He has held His upraised arm over you, but He is slow to strike you because He pities a prince who has been plagued by flatterers all his life. Moreover, your enemies are also His. But He is fully capable of separating His cause which is just from yours which is not, and will humiliate you in order to convert you, for you may be Christian only in humiliation. You do not love God; you do not even fear Him with the fear of a slave; it is hell and not God that you fear. Your religion consists only of superstitions and petty, superficial practices. You are like the Jews of whom God said: *while they honor me with their lips, their heart is far from me.* You are scrupulous about bagatelles and hardened to terrible wrongs. You love only your glory and your comforts. You view everything in terms of yourself, as though you were God on earth and all others had been created merely to be sacrificed to you. On the contrary, it is you whom God has placed on earth solely for your people. But alas! You understand nothing of these truths. How could you appreciate them? You do not know God; you do not love Him; you do not pray to Him from the heart, and you do nothing to comprehend Him.

You have an archbishop who is corrupt, scandalous, incorrigible, base, wicked, cunning, an enemy of all virtue, and who causes all upright men to grieve. You have accommodated yourself to him because he seeks only to please you with his flattery. For more than twenty years he has enjoyed your confidence while prostituting his honor. You give over upright men to him; you allow him to tyrannize over the church, and no virtuous prelate is treated as well as he.

As for your confessor, he is not vicious, but he fears solid virtue, and cares only for irreverent and loose persons. And he is jealous of his authority which you have raised beyond all bounds. Never before have royal confessors alone made bishops and decided all matters of conscience. You alone in France, Sire, are unaware that he knows nothing, that his mind is limited and vulgar, and that he continually indulges in stratagems with grossness of spirit. Even the Jesuits are contemptuous of him, and are indignant to see him so readily reward the ridiculous ambitions of his family. You have made a minister of state of a monk. He is not a good judge of men nor of anything else. He is the dupe of all who flatter him and give him petty gifts. He has no doubts or hesitations concerning any difficult question. An upright and learned man would not dare to decide them alone. But as for him, he only fears having to deliberate with men who know the rules. He proceeds boldly without fearing to lead you astray, and will always incline toward laxity and keeping you in ignorance. That is to say, he will tend toward decisions in conformity with the rules only when he fears to scandalize you. Thus, it is one blind man leading another, and as Jesus Christ said, *they shall both fall into the ditch.*

Your archbishop and your confessor have caused your difficulties in the affair of the *régale* and your unfortunate relations with Rome. They allowed you to permit the fraud of M. de Louvois against the Order of Saint-Lazare, and would have let you die in this injustice if M. de Louvois had lived longer than you.

It was hoped, Sire, that your council would keep you from going so far astray, but your council has neither the strength nor the vigor to do good. At least Mme de M——— and M. le D de B——— [Madame de Maintenon and M. le Duc de Beauvilliers] should avail themselves of your confidence in them in order to undeceive you, but their weakness and timidity dishonor them and disgust everyone. France is in desperate straits; what do they await to speak frankly to you? That all should be lost? They must not love you, for one must be willing to offend those whom one loves, in preference to flattering them or betraying them with silence. What is their worth, if they do not show you that you should make restitution of the lands which are not yours, prefer the lives of your people to a false glory, redress the wrongs that you have done to the church, and seek to become a true Christian before you are surprised by death? I know well that to speak with such Christian liberty is to risk the loss of royal favor; but is your favor dearer to them than your salvation? I also know well that one should pity you, console you, comfort you, and speak to you with zeal, kindness, and respect; but after all one must speak the truth. Woe, woe to those who do not speak it, and woe to you if you are not worthy of hearing it! It is scandalous that they have fruitlessly held your confidence for so long. They should withdraw if you are too sensitive and wish only flatterers around you. Perhaps you ask, Sire, what they should say to you. Here it is. They should point out to you that you must humble yourself under the powerful hand of God if you do not wish that He humble you, that you should seek peace and expiate through this humiliation all the glory which you have made your idol, that you should reject the unjust counsel of flattering politicians, and that finally, for the sake of the state, you must immediately return to your enemies the conquests which you may not retain without injustice. Are you so happy in your misfortune that God must terminate the successes which have blinded you, and compel you to make the restitutions which are necessary to your salvation, and which you could never bring yourself to make in a state of undisturbed triumph?

The person who tells you these truths, Sire, far from being opposed to your interest, would give his life to see you as God wishes you, and does not cease to pray for you.

COUNT DE SAINT-SIMON

LOUIS DE ROUVROI, DUC DE SAINT-SIMON (1675–1755), French courtier and mem-
oirist, thought not in favor with Louis XIV, resided at the court of Versailles after his resignation from the army in 1702. Until his retirement from
affairs in 1723, he served without distinction in the regency of the Duke of Orleans,
formed after the death of Louis XIV in 1715; as special ambassador to Spain
(1722–23), he ineffectually negotiated to obtain a bride for the young Louis XV.
Saint-Simon's extensive *Mémoirs* of the reign of Louis XIV, written with indifference to conventional standards of grammar and style, reveal their author as a
passionate partisan of his own social caste, the old aristocracy against which
Louis XIV had warred politically. Scornful of the bourgeois ministers, resentful
of the late king, proud of his own lineage, Saint-Simon was nevertheless capable
of perceptive insight into character, which he used to draw an astute picture of
the royal court during the second and unhappy half of the reign of Louis XIV.

DESCRIPTION OF LOUIS XIV

LET ME TOUCH NOW upon some other incidents in his career, and upon some
points in his character.

He early showed a disinclination for Paris. The troubles that had taken
place during the minority made him regard the place as dangerous; he
wished, too, to render himself venerable by hiding himself from the eyes
of the multitude; all these considerations fixed him at St. Germains soon
after the death of the Queen, his mother. It was to that place he began to
attract the world by fêtes and gallantries, and by making it felt that he
wished to be often seen.

His love for Madame de la Vallière, which was at first kept secret, occasioned frequent excursions to Versailles, then a little card castle, which
had been built by Louis XIII—annoyed, and his suite still more so, at being
frequently obliged to sleep in a wretched inn there, after he had been out
hunting in the forest of Saint Leger. That monarch rarely slept at Versailles
more than one night, and then from necessity; the King, his son, slept there,
so that he might be more in private with his mistress; pleasures unknown to
the hero and just man, worthy son of Saint Louis, who built the little
chateau.

These excursions of Louis XIV by degrees gave birth to those immense buildings he erected at Versailles; and their convenience for a numerous court, so different from the apartments at St. Germains, led him to take up his abode there entirely shortly after the death of the Queen. He built an infinite number of apartments, which were asked for by those who wished to pay their court to him; whereas at St. Germains nearly everybody was obliged to lodge in the town, and the few who found accommodation at the chateau were strangely inconvenienced.

The frequent fêtes, the private promenades at Versailles, the journeys, were means on which the King seized in order to distinguish or mortify the courtiers, and thus render them more assiduous in pleasing him. He felt that of real favours he had not enough to bestow; in order to keep up the spirit of devotion, he therefore unceasingly invented all sorts of ideal ones, little preferences and petty distinctions, which answered his purpose as well.

He was exceedingly jealous of the attention paid him. Not only did he notice the presence of the most distinguished courtiers, but those of inferior degree also. He looked to the right and to the left, not only upon rising but upon going to bed, at his meals, in passing through his apartments, or his gardens of Versailles, where alone the courtiers were allowed to follow him; he saw and noticed everybody; not one escaped him, not even those who hoped to remain unnoticed. He marked well all absentees from the court, found out the reason of their absence, and never lost an opportunity of acting towards them as the occasion might seem to justify. With some of the courtiers (the most distinguished), it was a demerit not to make the court their ordinary abode; with others 'twas a fault to come but rarely; for those who never or scarcely ever came it was certain disgrace. When their names were in any way mentioned, "I do not know them," the King would reply haughtily. Those who presented themselves but seldom were thus characterized: "They are people I never see"; these decrees were irrevocable. He could not bear people who liked Paris.

Louis XIV took great pains to be well informed of all that passed everywhere in the public places, in the private houses, in society and familiar intercourse. His spies and tell-tales were infinite. He had them of all species; many who were ignorant that their information reached him; others who knew it; others who wrote to him direct, sending their letters through channels he indicated; and all these letters were seen by him alone, and always before everything else; others who sometimes spoke to him secretly in his cabinet, entering by the back stairs. These unknown means ruined an infinite number of people of all classes, who never could discover the cause; often ruined them very unjustly; for the King, once prejudiced, never altered his opinion, or so rarely, that nothing was more rare. He had, too, another fault, very dangerous for others and often for himself, since it deprived him of good subjects. He had an excellent memory; in this way, that if he saw a man who, twenty years before, perhaps, had in some manner offended him, he did not forget the man, though he might forget the offence. This was enough, however, to exclude the person from all favour. The representations of a minister, of a general, of his confessor even, could not move the King. He would not yield.

The most cruel means by which the King was informed of what was passing—for many years before anybody knew it—was that of opening letters. The promptitude and dexterity with which they were opened passes understanding. He saw extracts from all the letters in which there were passages that the chiefs of the post office, and then the minister who opened it, thought ought to go before him; entire letters, too, were sent to him, when their contents seemed to justify the sending. Thus the chiefs of the post, nay, the principal clerks were in a position to suppose what they pleased and against whom they pleased. A word of contempt against the King or the government, a joke, a detached phrase was enough. It is incredible how many people, justly or unjustly, were more or less ruined, always without resource, without trial, and without knowing why. The secret was imprenetrable; for nothing ever cost the King less than profound silence and dissimulation.

This last talent he pushed almost to falsehood, but never to deceit, pluming himself upon keeping his word—therefore he scarcely ever gave it. The secrets of others he kept as religiously as his own. He was even flattered by certain confessions and certain confidences; and there was no mistress, minister, or favourite, who could have wormed them out, even though the secret regarded themselves.

We know, amongst many others, the famous story of a woman of quality, who after having been separated a year from her husband, found herself in the family way just as he was on the point of returning from the army, and who, not knowing what else to do, in the most urgent manner begged a private interview of the King. She obtained it, and confided to him her position, as to the worthiest man in his realm, as she said. The King counselled her to profit by her distress, and live more wisely for the future, and immediately promised to retain her husband on the frontier as long as was necessary, and to forbid his return under any pretext, and in fact he gave orders the same day to Louvois, and prohibited the husband not only all leave of absence, but forbade him to quit for a single day the post he was to command all the winter. The officer who was distinguished, and who had neither wished nor asked to be employed all the winter upon the frontier, and Louvois, who had in no way thought of it, were equally surprised and vexed. They were obliged, however, to obey to the letter, and without asking why; and the King never mentioned the circumstances until many years afterwards, when he was quite sure nobody could find out either husband or wife, as in fact they never could, or even obtain the most vague or the most uncertain suspicion.

JEAN BAPTISTE COLBERT

J EAN BAPTISTE COLBERT (1619–83), the son of a draper of Rheims, secured a
place in the office of Le Tellier, the French war secretary, and rose to become
Cardinal Mazarin's most trusted assistant. When Mazarin died in 1661, Colbert became chief economic adviser to King Louis XIV, then starting his personal
rule. Colbert instituted an orderly system of finance which helped establish the
power of the French state in its period of fully developed absolutism. French
mercantilism is still called Colbertism, and many of the achievements of the reign
of Louis XIV are now credited to Colbert. His plans were broad, and they led to
the development of a great Navy, the establishment of a shipbuilding industry,
acquisition of a colonial empire, the development of new industries and the
extension of old ones, the use of government pensions for artists, and the improvement of the French Academy and Academy of Sciences. When Louis XIV opened
his wars, however, Colbert had to resort to increasing taxes, the sale of offices, and
borrowing; as a result he died an unpopular figure in France. Colbert's administrative correspondence illustrates his basic views and methods.

The following selections are translated from the French texts in Pierre Clément,
Lettres, instructions et mémoires de Colbert (1863), Vol. II.

LETTERS

TO M. ROUILLÉ, INTENDANT AT AIX

March 29, 1679. From all you write me concerning monies, the greatest irregularity is found in the three-sous in use in Marseille, which provides certain and constant proof of the great quantity thereof which the merchants
are shipping to the Levant. If you reread the letter I wrote you on this matter, you will perceive that it has never been my thought suddenly to prohibit
this export; but you may be sure that this may be considerably diminished,
especially if you look carefully into what the English and the Dutch do in this
trade; they never bring money there except when, following the example of
the French (especially the merchants of Marseille, in whose hands the entire

the French (especially the merchants of Marseille, in whose hands the entire trade lies), they introduced some false monies in the Levant, to which procedure the people of Marseille are only too accustomed. Thus these foreigners also take money there because, in the beginning, there is very considerable profit. But, aside from this reason, they would only carry commodities they have grown or manufactured. The merchants of Marseille are people who do not look ahead, who think only of the small immediate profit they can make, and who heedlessly abuse the full liberty thus far given them to transport all the money they wish to the Levant, contrary and prejudicial to the universal and fundamental law of all states which, under penalty of death, prohibits the export of gold and silver; these merchants have never been willing to take the slightest trouble either to found their own manufactures or to make use of those established in the kingdom for commerce. What I asked you to think and work toward in my letter of the 3rd of this month was to seek means of obliging them to begin to look for manufactures, in order steadily to diminish the export of this money. Among the means you will have to induce them to do this, you could even inform them that, the King being determined to prevent this export, His Majesty will have his warships stop and search vessels going to the Levant, and will punish the merchants who have shipped money on these vessels under the strict provisions of his laws.

Please be informed that you should treat this matter as the most important of all those to which you will have to give your attention during the time you remain in this province. . . .

April 20, 1679. In reply to your letter of the 8th of this month, in all I have written you concerning the Levant trade and the export of money involved therein, you did not find that I claimed that it was possible to carry on the Levant trade without shipping money there, because I do not believe in going to extremes, but only that it was necessary, by creating various obstacles to this practice, to induce the merchants, and in greater number than at present, to turn to the manufacture of goods which could be shipped to the Levant, in order in like proportion to reduce the trade of the English and the Dutch who bring in their manufactured goods, and to diminish the export of money. . . .

TO M. DAGUESSEAU, INTENDANT AT TOULOUSE

January 28, 1682. I am in complete agreement with you that it is absolutely impossible for a single inspector to do all that is necessary with respect to the regulations for manufactures throughout the province of Languedoc. But I cannot agree with you on choosing persons from the province for these positions or on naming as many as you say, as it is difficult, not to say impossible, for a native of the province to see to the execution of these regulations, and for everything not to turn into a matter of favors, of individual friendships or enmities.

In short, I am not convinced that this procedure could yield any good result, but I believe that two or three good outsiders could be appointed inspector, men who would have no connections with the province and who would report to you each month as to what went on within their purview. You could rigorously enforce the thorough and punctual observance of these regulations, and you could even consider previously with some of the leading merchants the provisions of these regulations, and secure their opinion as to changes to be made. In which it would be necessary for you to proceed with the greatest caution, because all merchants generally want complete freedom with respect to their trade, and especially in manufactured goods the length, width and quality of which they always wish to change and reduce for considerations of a small profit that they make; this tends to the complete ruin of manufactures, the principle of which, in a state as prosperous and great as this, is to produce goods always the same in quality, length and width.

To attain this degree of conformity, which is the principle of all forms of trade, it is necessary to override the motives of small private interests which do not deserve consideration among the general motives of the good of the state. . . .

LETTERS PATENT OF LOUIS XIV

Vincennes, August, 1664

LOUIS, ETC. As one of the most considerable advantages of the peace it has pleased God to grant us is the restoration of all kinds of trade in this kingdom, and to enable commerce to do without recourse to foreigners for things necessary for the use and convenience of our subjects, we have hitherto neglected nothing that would bring them this advantage, through all means we have judged suitable to the success of this great plan. And among these means is the restoration of the manufacture of tapestries in the style of those of Flanders, previously introduced in our good city of Paris, and in others of this kingdom, through the initiative of the late King Henry the Great our well honored ancestor, and this means rightly appearing to us to be of very great importance; and our dear and well beloved Sieur Colbert, councillor in all our councils, superintendent and director general of all our buildings arts and manufactures of France, having informed us that the restoration of this production and manufacture of the said tapestries could not be better begun, nor could this work be entrusted to anyone more capable of bringing it to a successful conclusion than Louis Hinard, tapestry maker and merchant and bourgeois of our said city of Paris, known as one of the ablest not only in the said manufacture, but also in the commerce in this type of goods, if it pleased us to grant him permission to establish the said manufacture in our city of Beauvais, or in any other city of our province of Picardy he may wish and consider the most suitable, said permission to be enjoyed by him, by his successors and assigns, for such time and under such obligations as are carried by the articles and provisions he has presented to us for this purpose.

For these reasons, . . . we have granted permission to the said Hinard to establish the said factory and manufacture of all types of high and low warp tapestry of scenes and persons. We desire that the said Hinard, his successors and assigns shall enjoy the said permission and establishment for thirty years; and this to the exclusion and prohibition of all others, subject to 10,000 livres fine, confiscation of their goods, houses, shops, looms and other things used by them in manufacturing, together with all costs, damages, and interest, and all to the profit of the said Hinard.

And inasmuch as the cost and expenditures necessary to the foundation of this establishment may be beyond the capacity and resources of the said Hinard, we desire that the capital, houses, and property necessary to the said establishment be provided, and if need be constructed, at our expense, up to two thirds, or up to 30,000 livres; and we desire that there be placed on the doors and facades of the said houses and buildings a plaque bearing our arms and this inscription, *Manufacture royale de tapisseries.*[1] In addition to the said sum of 30,000 livres, and always better to aid the said establishment, we shall deliver and pay to the said Hinard and his associates another sum of 30,000 livres, as a loan to be employed by them for the purchase of supplies of wool, chemicals, dyes, and other goods and things necessary for the said manufacture, which sum the said Hinard and his associates will undertake to repay us without interest within the period and by the end of six years. So doing, the said Hinard and associates shall be held and obliged to maintain in the said manufacture, the first year of the said establishment, one hundred workers, French or foreign, and to add a like number of one hundred in each of the said first six years. And, in order to enable them to bring from foreign countries the largest number of workers possible, we shall pay the said Hinard and associates from our funds, the sum of 20 livres for each of the said workers. And, as there is nothing more important than to train many French apprentices, the said Hinard and associates shall be obliged to keep them at all times to at least the number of fifty; and to assist in their maintenance and feeding we shall pay, also from our funds, for each of the said apprentices, the sum of 30 livres for each year of their apprenticeship. Which apprentices, having completed

[1] [*Royal Tapestry Factory.*]

six years of apprenticeship and having served two years as journeymen, shall be reputed masters. We likewise desire that foreign workers who shall have worked for the time and period of eight years shall be reputed naturalized subjects and French nationals, subject to the provision that they shall permanently maintain their residence in this kingdom.

And, because it is our intention that both the said Hinard and associates and the said workers shall be able to go about their work with the least interruption, we desire that they shall all be and remain exempted from all *tailles,* levies for military supplies and other taxes, both regular and extraordinary, from all payments on the debts and all watch and ward duties of the said city, quartering soldiers, etc. To the said Hinard we grant the right and privilege of having legal cases concerning him tried in royal courts.

And, because it is necessary to the said establishment that the said Hinard and associates be able easily to maintain on the premises of the said establishment all the workers and other persons there employed by them, we permit them to bring to and install in the said premises as many painters, dyers, beer brewers, bakers, masters and journeymen as they wish, and who shall enjoy the same privileges and exemptions as the said tapestry workers. We desire that the wool and chemicals for dyeing purchased by the said Hinard and associates and their agents within the area of the Five Big Farms, be loaded and transported by them to the said establishment without being subject to the payment of any duties. . . . To which end we permit the said persons to place and carry upon their carts, horses, boats and other means of transportation of both the said wool and chemicals and the tapestries which shall be manufactured by them, a covering in our arms and colors; in producing and weaving the said tapestries they shall mark them with the mark given them by the said superintendent [Colbert], no other person being able to use the said mark for other tapestries, or copy the designs in which these have been made, subject to 10,000 livres fine and confiscation. . . . We desire that the said tapestries be transported, sold and marketed by the said Hinard and associates, either within this kingdom or in foreign countries, subject to their paying the sum of 20 livres for each tapestry twenty ells in length; and they shall pay no duties on those sold within the area of the Five Big Farms. . . .

THE FRENCH WEST INDIA COMPANY

LIKE THE Dutch, British, and French East India companies, and many others, the French West India Company was established by the state and granted state support and the right of monopoly in the hope that it would lead to increase in trade, more and stronger colonies, an enlarged merchant marine, and a supply of needed raw materials. In 1664, when the French West India Company was founded, France held fourteen islands in the West Indies, which were under the actual ownership of individual French proprietors. The trade of these islands, however, was very largely carried on by the Dutch. Colbert hoped, by establishment of a state monopoly over the trade of the islands, to exclude the Dutch and divert their trade and profits to French hands. He believed that a single company would prove more efficient than the various proprietors and chartered companies previously in the field. Thus the islands were repossessed, with compensation to their owners, and the Company of the Cape Verdes and Senegal, the Company of New France (Canada), and the Cayenne Company were either suppressed or absorbed into the new West India Company.

The Company's early years were marked by difficulties both for itself and for its colonists, who were cut off from the more than one hundred Dutch ships which each year had brought them supplies. War between France and England broke out in 1666, and the Dutch soon entered as France's allies. Wartime necessities led to relaxation of the prohibitions against both private trading and the Dutch, but following the return of peace in 1667 the policy of excluding the Dutch was gradually resumed. Colbert began to encourage independent trade, however, urging the Company more and more to concentrate on the slave trade and leave general commerce to private individuals. French trade with the West Indies increased greatly, although the Company failed to show profits. In December, 1674, Colbert had it dissolved, the king taking back all the rights and privileges he had granted it. This should not, however, be taken to indicate either the failure of the scheme or a change of heart on the part of Colbert in the direction of free trade. It was merely that the Company had accomplished its assigned task: to exclude the Dutch and build up French trade with the colonies. It was no longer needed, and hence its work could be left to private individuals.

The following selection was translated from the French text of the Edict as given by Moreau de Saint-Méry, *Loix et constitutions des colonies françoises de l'Amérique sous le vent* (1784), Vol. I.

❧

EDICT PROVIDING FOR THE ESTABLISHMENT OF A COMPANY OF THE WEST INDIES

To Conduct All the Trade in the Islands and the Mainland of North America, and Other Countries, the Concessions, Powers, Authorities, Rights, Exemptions and Privileges Therein Contained. . . .
[*May 28, 1664*]

LOUIS, ETC. GREETINGS. The peace which this state now enjoys having given us the opportunity to apply ourselves to the restoration of trade, we have recognized that colonial trade and navigation are the only and true means of raising commerce to the brilliant position it holds in foreign lands; to achieve this and to stimulate our subjects to form powerful companies we have promised them such great advantages that there is reason to hope that all those who take interest in the glory of the State, and who wish to profit by honorable and legitimate means will willingly participate; with much joy we have already given recognition to this through the company formed several months ago for the mainland of America, otherwise called *France Equinoxiale;* but as it is not sufficient for these companies to take possession of the lands which we grant them, and have them cleared and cultivated by the people they send there at great expense, if they do not equip themselves to carry on the commerce through which the Frenchmen who live in the said countries deal with the native inhabitants, giving them in exchange for the products which grow in their countries the goods which they need, it is also absolutely necessary, in order to carry on this trade, to provide numerous ships to carry each day the goods which are to be sold in the said countries, and bring back to France those which they export, which has not so far been done by the companies heretofore formed.

Having recognized that the land of Canada has been abandoned by the investors of the Company which was formed in 1628, for lack of having sent annually some small help; and that in the islands of America, where the fertility of the land attracted a great many Frenchmen, those of the Company to whom we granted them in 1642, instead of applying themselves to the advancement of these colonies and establishing in this great extent of land a commerce which would have been very advantageous to them, were content to sell the said islands to various individuals, who, having applied themselves only to cultivating the land, have subsisted since that time only through the help of foreigners, with the result that so far they only have profited from the courage of the Frenchmen who first discovered and settled the said islands, and from the work of several thousand persons who cultivated the said lands.

It is for these considerations that we have withdrawn from the investors in the said Company of Canada the concession of this country granted them by the late King our most honored lord and father, of glorious memory, which they ceded to us voluntarily by act of their assembly of February 24, 1663, and that we have resolved to repossess all the islands of America sold to the said individuals by the said Company, reimbursing their proprietors the purchase price and for the improvements they have made; but, as our intention in repossessing the said islands has been to place them in the hands of one company which could own them all, succeed in peopling them, and carry on the trade which foreigners now conduct, we have considered at the same time that it would be to our glory and the greatness and advantage of the State to create a powerful company to handle all the trade of the West Indies, to which we wish to grant all the said islands; that of Cayenne, and all the mainland of America from the Amazon river to the Orinoco, Canada, Acadia, the Islands of Newfoundland, and the other islands and mainlands from the north of the said land of Canada to Virginia and Florida, together with all the coast of Africa, from the Cape Verdes to the Cape of Good Hope, whether the said lands belong to us, being or having heretofore been inhabited by Frenchmen, or the said company establish itself there, driving out or subjecting the savages or natives of the country, or the other nations of Europe which are not in our alliance; in order that the Company be able, when it shall have established strong colonies in the said countries, to rule and govern them by a single design and develope considerable trade, both with the Frenchmen who already live there and those who settle there hereafter and with the Indians and other native inhabitants of the said countries, from which it could draw great benefits.

For this result we have thought it fit to employ the said Company of the Mainland of America, which Company already being composed of many shareholders and equipped with numerous ships, could easily prepare itself to form that of the West Indies, and, strengthening itself with all those of our subjects who wish to participate, undertake this great and praiseworthy enterprise. . . .

Art. I. As, in the establishment of the said colonies, we consider principally the glory of God, in securing the salvation of the Indians and savages, to whom we wish to make known the true religion, the said Company now established under the name of *Company of the West Indies,* will be obliged to introduce into the lands granted above, the number of clergy necessary for preaching the Holy Gospel, and instructing these peoples in the faith of the Catholic, Apostolic and Roman religion; and also to build churches and provide parish-priests and priests (whom it shall nominate) to conduct the Divine Services at the usual days and hours, and administer the sacraments to the inhabitants; the said Company will be obliged to support these churches, parish-priests and priests decently and with honor. . . .

Art. II. The said Company shall be composed of all those of our subjects who wish to participate, of whatever rank and station they be, without their thereby detracting from the nobility and privileges we bestow upon them, foreigners and subjects of any Prince or State may likewise enter the said Company.

Art. IV. Those who invest from ten to twenty thousand pounds in the said Company, be they French or foreign, may attend the general assemblies and vote and those who invest twenty thousand *livres* or more, may be elected Directors General, each in turn, or according to an order to be decided upon by the said Company, and those who have invested twenty thousand *livres* in the said Company, shall receive the rights of *bourgeois* in the cities of the Kingdom in which they reside.

Art. V. Foreigners who shall invest the sum of twenty thousand *livres* in the said Company shall be reputed French and native born during the time they live [in France] and have shares for the said twenty thousand *livres* in the said company; and after the expiration of twenty years, they shall enjoy the said privilege incommutably without the need of any other letters of naturalization; and their relatives, although foreigners, may succeed them in all the possessions they shall have in this kingdom, declaring to them that in this regard we renounce from this moment all rights of escheat.

Art. VII. Shareholders in the said Company may sell, give and transfer the shares they hold to whom and as it shall seem well to them. . . .

Art. XI. Neither the properties of said Company, nor the shares and portions which belong to the shareholders, may be seized for our affairs, for any cause, pretext or occasion whatever, nor even the shares which belong to foreigners for reason or under pretext of war, reprisal or otherwise, which we might have against the Princes and States of which they are subjects. . . .

Art. XV. The Company alone will carry on all the trade and navigation in the said lands granted, during forty years, to the exclusion of all other of our subjects who do not participate in it; and to this end we forbid all our said subjects who do not belong to the said Company to trade there, under penalty of confiscation of their vessels and goods, applicable to the profit of the said Company, with the exception of fishing, which shall be free to all our said subjects.

Art. XVI. And to enable the said Company to meet the great expenses it will be obliged to make for the support of the colonies, and of the great number of ships it will send to the said lands granted, we promise the said Company to have it paid for each voyage of the said vessels which take supplies and cargo in the ports of France, . . . 30 *livres* for each ton of goods they bring to the said countries, and 40 *livres* for each ton of goods they bring back and discharge . . . in the ports of the kingdom. . . .

Art. XVII. Goods coming from the said countries brought to France by vessels of the said Company to be transported by sea or land to foreign lands, shall pay no duties on import or export. . . .

Art. XVIII. Goods declared to be consumed in the kingdom, on which import duties have been paid, and which the Company wishes to send to foreign lands, shall pay no export duties, any more than sugars refined in France in the refineries which the Company will establish, which we likewise exempt from all export duties, provided that they are shipped on French vessels to be transported out of the kingdom.

Art. XIX. The said Company will be likewise exempted from all import and export duties on munitions of war, provisions and other things necessary for the victualling and arming of the ships it will equip, also on all woods, ropes, tar, cast iron cannons, and other things which it will import from foreign lands for the construction of ships it will build in France.

Art. XX. There shall belong to the said Company in all lordship, property and justice all the lands it may conquer and settle during the said forty years in the expanse of the said countries above stated and granted, and also the islands of America called the Antilles. . . .

Art. XXI. All which countries, islands and lands, posts and forts which may have been constructed and established there by our subjects we have given, granted and bestowed, do give, grant and bestow upon the said Company, to enjoy in perpetuity in full lordship, property, and justice, reserving to ourselves no other right nor duty than only fealty and liege homage, which the said Company will be obliged to render us and to our successor Kings, at each change of King, with a gold crown of the weight of thirty *marcs*. . . .

Art. XXIII. In its capacity as lord of the said islands and lands, the said Company will enjoy seignorial rights now established over the inhabitants of the said lands and islands. . . .

Art. XXIV. The said Company may sell or enfief land, whether in the said islands, the mainland of America or elsewhere in the said countries granted, at whatever rates, rents and seignorial duties it shall judge desirable, and to such persons as it shall find fitting.

Art. XXV. The said company will possess all mines and mineral deposits, capes, gulfs, ports, harbors, rivers, streams, islands and islets within the extent of the said countries granted, without being obliged to pay us, for the said mines or mineral deposits, any dues of sovereignty. . . .

Art. XXVI. The said Company may build forts in all places it shall judge necessary for the defense of the said country, have cannon cast with our coat of arms, above which it may place that which we grant it hereafter, make powder, cast balls, forge arms and recruit warriors in the Kingdom to send to the said country. . . .

Art. XXVII. The said Company may also create such governors as it shall judge fitting, whether on the mainland, by provinces or separate departments, or in the said islands, which governors shall be nominated and presented by the Directors of the said Company, so that our confirmation may be sent them, and the said Company may remove them whenever it shall deem it well. . . .

Art. XXVIII. The said Company may arm and equip for war such number of vessels as it shall deem fitting for the defense of the said countries and the security of the said commerce, on which vessels it may place as many cast iron cannons as it thinks advisable, fly the white flag with the coat of arms of France, and appoint such captains, officers, soldiers and sailors as it shall find necessary, without the said ships being employable by us, either on the occasion of a war or otherwise, without the consent of the said Company.

Art. XXIX. If any prizes are taken by the ships of the said Company from the enemies of the State in the waters of the countries granted they shall belong to it [the Company]. . . .

Art. XXX. The said Company may negotiate peace and alliances in our name, with the Kings and Princes of the countries where it wishes to establish its settlements and trade, and agree with them on the provisions of the said treaties, which shall be approved by us, and, in case of insult, declare war on them, attack them, and defend itself by force of arms.

Art. XXXI. In case the said Company should be disturbed in the possession of the said lands and in commerce by the enemies of our State, we promise to defend it and aid with our arms and our ships, at our cost and expense.

Art. XXXIII. The said Company, as Lord High Justice of all the said countries, may establish there judges and officials wherever necessary, . . . and depose and remove them when it shall deem it advisable, which [judges] shall have cognizance in all matters of justice, police, commerce and navigation, civil as well as criminal. . . .

Art. XXXIV. The judges established in all the said places shall be obliged to judge according to the laws and ordinances of the Kingdom, and the officials to conform to the Custom of the Provostship and Viscounty of Paris, according to which the inhabitants may contract, without there being able to be introduced any other Custom, in order to avoid diversity.

Art. XXXV. And further to aid the inhabitants of the said countries granted, and bring our subjects to settle there, we desire that those who move to the said countries should enjoy the same liberties and immunities as if they remained resident in this kingdom, and that those who are born of them and savages converted to the Catholic, Apostolic and Roman faith should be counted and reputed native born French subjects, and as such capable of all inheritances, gifts, legacies and other conveyances without being obliged to obtain any letters of naturalization, and that artisans who shall have practiced their arts and crafts in the said countries for ten consecutive years, on presenting certificates of the officials of the places in which they have resided, attested by the governors and certified by the Directors of the said Company, shall be reputed masters in all cities of our kingdom where they wish to settle, without any exception.

Art. XXXVI. We permit the said Company to draw up and decree such statutes and regulations as it shall deem necessary for the conduct and direction of its affairs, in Europe as well as in the said countries granted, which statutes and regulations we will confirm by letters patent, in order that the shareholders in the said Company may be obliged to observe them according to their forms and terms. . . .

Art. XLI. After the expiration of the said forty years, if it is not judged fitting to continue the privilege [monopoly] of commerce, all the lands or islands which the Company shall have conquered, inhabited or settled, together with the seignorial duties and rents owed by the said inhabitants, shall belong to it in perpetuity in full property, lordship and justice, to deal with and dispose of as shall seem fitting to it, as of its own heirdom; as also the forts, arms and munitions, furnishings, implements, ships and goods it has in the said countries, without its being therein disturbed, nor can we repossess the said lands and islands, for any cause, occasion or pretext whatsoever, which we have renounced from this time forth, subject to the condition that the said Company may not sell the said lands to any foreigners without our express permission.

Art. XLII. And, to make known to the said Company that we wish to aid it by all measures, contribute from our own funds to its establishment and to the purchase of vessels and goods which it needs to send to the said countries, we promise to furnish the tenth of all the capital gathered by the said Company, and this during four years, after which the said Company will return us the said sums without any interest; and in case it suffer any loss during the said four years, proving it by the accounts, we consent that this be charged against the funds we shall have advanced, unless we wish to leave the tenth thus advanced by us in the funds of the said Company, for yet another four years, all without any interest, for there to be made at the end of the said eight years a general accounting of all the properties of the said Company; and in case there prove to be a loss of capital funds, we consent that the said loss be charged to the said tenth, and to the extent of this. . . .

THOMAS MUN

THOMAS MUN (1571–1641) has been called the founder of English mercantilism. This is quite incorrect, but it would be true to say that Mun played an important role in changing the emphasis of English mercantilism from bullionism to trade.

It was as a director of the British East India Company that Mun entered the field of economic thought. The Company had been under severe attack by bullionist mercantilists such as Gerard de Malynes for exporting gold and silver to the East in the course of its trade. Mun pointed out, in *A Discourse of Trade, from England into the East-Indies* (1621), that the net result of the Indian trade was actually an influx of precious metals. This position of modified bullionism was expanded in *England's Treasure by Foreign Trade,* published posthumously in 1664. Mun emphasized the importance of the total balance of trade, including the so-called invisible items. Hence he urged the diversification of manufactures and commercial services as the best means of securing more bullion: the limitation of luxury and unnecessary imports, rather than the prohibition of export of gold and silver, as the best means of preventing its flight from England.

ENGLAND'S TREASURE BY FOREIGN TRADE

CHAPTER II: THE MEANS TO ENRICH THIS KINGDOM, AND TO ENCREASE OUR TREASURE

ALTHOUGH A KINGDOM may be enriched by gifts received, or by purchase taken from some other nations, yet these are things uncertain and of small consideration when they happen. The ordinary means therefore to encrease our wealth and treasure is by foreign trade, wherein we must ever observe this rule; to sell more to strangers yearly than we consume of theirs in value. For suppose that when this kingdom is plentifully served with the cloth, lead, tin, iron, fish and other native commodities, we do yearly export the overplus to foreign countries to the value of twenty two hundred thousand pounds; by which means we are enabled beyond the seas to buy and bring in foreign wares for our use and consumptions, to the value of twenty hundred thousand pounds; by this order duly kept in our trading, we may rest assured that the kingdom shall be enriched yearly two hundred thousand pounds, which must be brought to us in so much treasure; because that part of our stock which is not returned to us in wares must necessarily be brought home in treasure.

For in this case it cometh to pass in the stock of a kingdom, as in the estate of a private man; who is supposed to have one thousand pounds yearly revenue and two thousand pounds of ready money in his chest: if such a man through excess shall spend one thousand five hundred pounds per annum, all his ready money will be gone in four years; and in the like time his said money will be doubled if he take a frugal course to spend but five hundred pounds per annum; which rule never faileth likewise in the commonwealth, but in some cases (of no great moment) which I will hereafter declare, when I shall shew by whom and in what manner this ballance of the kingdom's account ought to be drawn up yearly, or so often as it shall please the state to discover how much we gain or lose by trade with foreign nations. But first I will say something concerning those ways and means which will encrease our exportations and diminish our importations of wares; which being done, I will then set down some other arguments both affirmative and negative to strengthen that which is here declared, and thereby to shew that all the other means which are commonly supposed to enrich the kingdom with treasure are altogether insufficient and meer fallacies.

CHAPTER III: THE PARTICULAR WAYS AND MEANS TO ENCREASE THE EXPORTATION OF OUR COMMODITIES, AND TO DECREASE OUR CONSUMPTION OF FOREIGN WARES

The revenue or stock of a kingdom by which it is provided of foreign wares is either natural or artificial. The natural wealth is so much only as can be spared from our own use and necessities to be exported unto strangers. The artificial consists in our manufactures and industrious trading with foreign commodities, concerning which I will set down such particulars as may serve for the cause we have in hand.

1. First, although this realm be already exceeding rich by nature, yet might it be much encreased by laying the waste grounds (which are infinite) into such employments as should no way hinder the present revenues of other manured lands, but hereby to supply our selves and prevent the importations of hemp, flax, cordage, tobacco, and divers other things which now we fetch from strangers to our great impoverishing.

2. We may likewise diminish our importations, if we would soberly refrain from excessive consumption of foreign wares in our diet and rayment, with such often change of fashions as is used. so much the more to encrease the waste and charge; which vices at this present are more notorious amongst us than in former ages. Yet might they easily be amended by enforcing the observation of such good laws as are strictly practised in other countries against the said excesses; where likewise by commanding their own manufactures to

be used, they prevent the coming in of others, without prohibition, or offence to strangers in their mutual commerce.

3. In our exportations we must not only regard our own superfluities, but also we must consider our neighbours necessities, that so upon the wares which they cannot want, nor yet be furnished thereof elsewhere, we may (besides the vent of the materials) gain so much of the manufacture as we can, and also endeavour to sell them dear, so far forth as the high price cause not a less vent in the quantity. But the superfluity of our commodities which strangers use, and may also have the same from other nations, or may abate their vent by the use of some such like wares from other places, and with little inconvenience; we must in this case strive to sell as cheap as possible we can, rather than to lose the utterance of such wares. For we have found of late years by good experience, that being able to sell our cloth cheap in Turkey, we have greatly encreased the vent thereof, and the Venetians have lost as much in the utterance of theirs in those countries, because it is dearer. And on the other side a few years past, when by the excessive price of wools our cloth was exceeding dear, we lost at the least half our clothing for foreign parts, which since is no otherwise (well neer) recovered again than by the great fall of price for wools and cloth. We find that twenty five in the hundred less in the price of these and some other wares, to the loss of private mens revenues, may raise above fifty upon the hundred in the quantity vented to the benefit of the public. For when cloath is dear, other nations do presently practise clothing, and we know they want neither art nor materials to this performance. But when by cheapness we drive them from this employment, and so in time obtain our dear price again, then do they also use their former remedy. So that by these alterations we learn, that it is in vain to expect a greater revenue of our wares than their condition will afford, but rather it concerns us to apply our endeavours to the times with care and diligence to help our selves the best we may, by making our cloth and other manufactures without deceit, which will encrease their estimation and use.

4. The value of our exportations likewise may be much advanced when we perform it ourselves in our own ships, for then we get not only the price of our wares as they are worth here, but also the merchants gains, the charges of ensurance, and fraight to carry them beyond the seas. As for example, if the Italian merchants should come hither in their own shipping to fetch our corn, our red herrings or the like, in this case the kingdom should have ordinarily but 25 s. for a quarter of wheat, and 20 s. for a barrel of red herrings, whereas if we carry these wares ourselves into Italy upon the said rates, it is likely that we shall obtain fifty shillings for the first, and forty shillings for the last, which is a great difference in the utterance or vent of the kingdom's stock. And al-

though it is true that the commerce ought to be free to strangers to bring in and carry out at their pleasure, yet nevertheless in many places the exportation of victuals and munition are either prohibited, or at least limited to be done only by the people and shipping of those places where they abound.

5. The frugal expending likewise of our own natural wealth might advance much yearly to be exported unto strangers; and if in our rayment we will be prodigal, yet let this be done with our own materials and manufactures, as cloth, lace, imbroideries, cutworks and the like, where the excess of the rich may be the employment of the poor, whose labours notwithstanding of this kind, would be more profitable for the common wealth, if they were done to the use of strangers.

6. The fishing in his majesty's seas of England, Scotland and Ireland is our natural wealth, and would cost nothing but labour, which the Dutch bestow willingly, and thereby draw yearly a very great profit to themselves by serving many places of Christendom with our fish, for which they return and supply their wants both of foreign wares and money, besides the multitude of mariners and shipping, which hereby are maintained, whereof a long discourse might be made to shew the particular manage of this important business. Our fishing plantation likewise in New-England, Virginia, Groenland, the Summer Islands and the New-foundland, are of the like nature, affording much wealth and employments to maintain a great number of poor, and to encrease our decaying trade.

7. A staple or magazine for foreign corn, indico, spices, raw-silks, cotton wool or any other commodity whatsoever, to be imported will encrease shipping, trade, treasure, and the king's customs, by exporting them again where need shall require, which course of trading hath been the chief means to raise Venice, Genoa, the Low-Countries, with some others; and for such a purpose England stands most commodiously, wanting nothing to this performance but our own diligence and endeavour.

8. Also we ought to esteem and cherish those trades which we have in remote or far countries, for besides the encrease of shipping and mariners thereby, the wares also sent thither and received from thence are far more profitable unto the kingdom than by our trades near at hand; as for example; suppose pepper to be worth here two shillings the pound constantly, if then it be brought from the Dutch at Amsterdam, the merchant may give there twenty pence the pound, and gain well by the bargain; but if he fetch this pepper from the East Indies, he must not give above three pence the pound at the most, which is a mighty advantage, not only in that part which serveth for our own use, but also for that great quantity which (from hence) we transport yearly unto divers other nations to be sold at a higher price: whereby it

is plain, that we make a far greater stock by gain upon these Indian commodities, than those nations do where they grow, and to whom they properly appertain, being the natural wealth of their countries. But for the better understanding of this particular, we must ever distinguish between the gain of the kingdom, and the profit of the merchant; for although the kingdom payeth no more for this pepper than is before supposed, nor for any other commodity bought in foreign parts more than the stranger receiveth from us for the same, yet the merchant payeth not only that price, but also the fraight, ensurance, customs and other charges which are exceeding great in these long voyages; but yet all these in the kingdom's accompt are but commutations among our selves, and no privation of the kingdom's stock, which being duly considered, together with the support also of our other trades in our best shipping to Italy, France, Turkey, the East countries and other places, by transporting and venting the wares which we bring yearly from the East Indies; it may well stir up our utmost endeavours to maintain and enlarge this great and noble business, so much importing the public wealth, strength, and happiness. Neither is there less honour and judgement by growing rich (in this manner) upon the stock of other nations, than by an industrious encrease of our own means, especially when this latter is advanced by the benefit of the former, as we have found in the East Indies by sale of much of our tin, cloth, lead and other commodities, the vent whereof doth daily encrease in those countries which formerly had no use of our wares.

9. It would be very beneficial to export money as well as wares, being done in trade only, it would encrease our treasure; but of this I write more largely in the next chapter to prove it plainly.

10. It were policy and profit for the state to suffer manufactures made of foreign materials to be exported custom-free, as velvets and all other wrought silks, fustians, thrown silks and the like, it would employ very many poor people, and much encrease the value of our stock yearly issued into other countries, and it would (for this purpose) cause the more foreign materials to be brought in, to the improvement of his majesty's customs. I will here remember a notable encrease in our manufacture of winding and twisting only of foreign raw silk, which within 35. years to my knowledge did not employ more than 300. people in the city and suburbs of London, where at this present time it doth set on work above fourteen thousand souls, as upon diligent enquiry hath been credibly reported unto his majesty's commissioners for trade. And it is certain, that if the said foreign commodities might be exported from hence, free of custom, this manufacture would yet encrease very much, and decrease as fast in Italy and in the Netherlands. But if any man alledge the Dutch proverb, Live and let others live; I answer, that the Dutchmen notwithstand-

ing their own proverb, do not only in these kingdoms, encroach upon our livings, but also in other foreign parts of our trade (where they have power) they do hinder and destroy us in our lawful course of living, hereby taking the bread out of our mouth, which we shall never prevent by plucking the pot from their nose, as of late years too many of us do practise to the great hurt and dishonour of this famous nation; we ought rather to imitate former times in taking sober and worthy courses more pleasing to God and suitable to our ancient reputation.

11. It is needful also not to charge the native commodities with too great customs, lest by indearing them to the strangers use, it hinder their vent. And especially foreign wares brought in to be transported again should be favoured, for otherwise that manner of trading (so much importing the good of the common-wealth) cannot prosper nor subsist. But the consumption of such foreign wares in the realm may be the more charged, which will turn to the profit of the kingdom in the ballance of the trade, and thereby also enable the king to lay up the more treasure out of his yearly incomes, as of this particular I intend to write more fully in its proper place, where I shall shew how much money a prince may conveniently lay up without the hurt of his subjects.

12. Lastly, in all things we must endeavour to make the most we can of our own, whether it be natural or artificial; and forasmuch as the people which live by the arts are far more in number than they who are masters of the fruits, we ought the more carefully to maintain those endeavours of the multitude, in whom doth consist the greatest strength and riches both of king and kingdom: for where the people are many, and the arts good, there the traffic must be great, and the country rich. The Italians employ a greater number of people, and get more money by their industry and manufactures of the raw silks of the kingdom of Sicilia, than the king of Spain and his subjects have by the revenue of this rich commodity. But what need we fetch the example so far, when we know that our own natural wares do not yield us so much profit as our industry? For iron oar in the mines is of no great worth, when it is compared with the employment and advantage it yields being digged, tried, transported, bought, sold, cast into ordnance, muskets, and many other instruments of war for offence and defence, wrought into anchors, bolts, spikes, nayles and the like, for the use of ships, houses, carts, coaches, ploughs, and other instruments for tillage. Compare our fleece-wools with our cloth, which requires shearing, washing, carding, spinning, weaving, fulling, dying, dressing and other trimmings, and we shall find these arts more profitable than the natural wealth, whereof I might instance other examples, but I will not be more tedious, for if I would amplify upon this and the other particulars before witness, I might find matter sufficient to make a large

volume, but my desire in all is only to prove what I propound with brevity and plainness.

CHAPTER IV: THE EXPORTATION OF OUR MONEYS IN TRADE OF MERCHAN-
DIZE IS A MEANS TO ENCREASE OUR TREASURE

This position is so contrary to the common opinion, that it will require many and strong arguments to prove it before it can be accepted of the multitude, who bitterly exclaim when they see any monies carried out of the realm; affirming thereupon that we have absolutely lost so much treasure, and that this is an act directly against the long continued laws made and confirmed by the wisdom of this kingdom in the high court of parliament, and that many places, nay Spain itself which is the fountain of money, forbids the exportation thereof, some cases only excepted. To all which I might answer, that Venice, Florence, Genoa, the Low Countries and divers other places permit it, their people applaud it, and find great benefit by it; but all this makes a noise and proves nothing, we must therefore come to those reasons which concern the business in question.

First, I will take that for granted which no man of judgement will deny, that we have no other means to get treasure but by foreign trade, for mines we have none which do afford it, and how this money is gotten in the managing of our said trade I have already shewed, that it is done by making our commodities which are exported yearly to over-ballance in value the foreign wares which we consume; so that it resteth only to shew how our monies may be added to our commodities, and being jointly exported may so much the more encrease our treasure.

We have already supposed our yearly consumptions of foreign wares to be for the value of twenty hundred thousand pounds, and our exportations to exceed that two hundred thousand pounds, which sum we have thereupon affirmed is brought to us in treasure to ballance the accompt. But now if we add three hundred thousand pounds more in ready money unto our former exportations in wares, what profit can we have (will some men say) although by this means we should bring in so much ready money more than we did before, seeing that we have carried out the like value.

To this the answer is, that when we have prepared our exportations of wares, and sent out as much of every thing as we can spare or vent abroad: It is not therefore said that then we should add our money thereunto to fetch in the more money immediately, but rather first to enlarge our trade by enabling us to bring in more foreign wares, which being sent out again will in due time much encrease our treasure.

For although in this manner we do yearly multiply our importations to the maintenance of more shipping and mariners, improvement of his majesty's customs and other benefits: yet our consumption of those foreign wares is no more than it was before; so that all the said encrease of commodities brought in by the means of our ready money sent out as is afore written, doth in the end become an exportation unto us of a far greater value than our said monies were, which is proved by three several examples following.

1. For I suppose that 100000. £ being sent in our shipping to the East countries, will buy there one hundred thousand quarters of wheat clear aboard the ships, which being after brought into England and housed, to export the same at the best time for vent thereof in Spain or Italy, it cannot yield less in those parts than two hundred thousand pounds to make the merchant but a saver, yet by this reckoning we see the kingdom hath doubled that treasure.

2. Again this profit will be far greater when we trade thus in remote countries, as for example, if we send one hundred thousand pounds into the East Indies to buy pepper there, and bring it hither, and from hence send it for Italy or Turkey, it must yield seven hundred thousand pounds at least in those places, in regard of the excessive charge which the merchant disburseth in those long voyages in shipping wages, victuals, insurance, interest, customs, imposts, and the like, all which notwithstanding the king and the kingdom gets.

3. But where the voyages are short and the wares rich, which therefore will not employ much shipping, the profit will be far less. As when another hundred thousand pounds shall be employed in Turkey in raw silks, and brought hither to be after transported from hence into France, the Low Countries, or Germany, the merchant shall have good gain, although he sell it there but for one hundred and fifty thousand pounds: and thus take the voyages altogether in their medium, the monies exported will be returned unto us more than trebled. But if any man will yet object, that these returns come to us in wares, and not really in money as they were issued out.

The answer is (keeping our first ground) that if our consumption of foreign wares be no more yearly than is already supposed, and that our exportations be so mightily encreased by this manner of trading with ready money as is before declared: it is not then possible but that all the overballance or difference should return either in money or in such wares as we must export again, which, as is already plainly shewed, will be still a greater means to encrease our treasure.

For it is in the stock of the kingdom as in the estates of private men, who having store of wares, do not therefore say that they will not venture out or trade with their money (for this were ridiculous) but do also turn that into wares whereby they multiply their money, and so by a continual and orderly change of one into the other grow rich, and when they please turn all their estates into treasure; for they that have wares cannot want money.

Neither is it said that money is the life of trade, as if it could not subsist without the same; for we know that there was great trading by way of commutation or barter when there was little money stirring in the world. The Italians and some other nations have such remedies against this want, that it can neither decay nor hinder their trade, for they transfer bills of debt, and have banks both public and private, wherein they do assign their credits from one to another daily for very great sums with ease and satisfaction by writings only, whilst in the mean time the mass of treasure which gave foundation to these credits is employed in foreign trade as a merchandize, and by the said means they have little other use of money in those countries more than for their ordinary expences. It is not therefore the keeping of our money in the kingdom, but the necessity and use of our wares in foreign countries, and our want of their commodities that causeth the vent and consumption on all sides, which makes a quick and ample trade. If we were once poor, and now having gained some store of money by trade with resolution to keep it still in the realm; shall this cause other nations to spend more of our commodities than formerly they have done, whereby we might say that our trade is quickened and enlarged? No verily, it will produce no such good effect: but rather according to the alteration of times by their true causes we may expect the contrary; for all men do consent that plenty of money in a kingdom doth make the native commodities dearer, which as it is to the profit of some private men in their revenues, so it is directly against the benefit of the public in the quantity of the trade; for as plenty of money makes wares dearer, so dear wares decline their use and consumption, as hath been already plainly shewed in the last chapter upon that particular of our cloth; and although this is a very hard lesson for some great landed men to learn, yet I am sure it is a true lesson for all the land to observe, lest when we have gained some store of money by trade, we lose it again by not trading with our money. I knew a prince in Italy (of famous memory) Ferdinando the first, great duke of Tuscany, who being very rich in treasure, endeavoured therewith to enlarge his trade by issuing out to his merchants great sums of money for very small profit; I myself had forty thousand crowns of him gratis for a whole year, although he knew that I would presently send it away in specie for the parts of Turkey to be employed in wares for his countries, he being well assured that in this course of trade it would return again (according to the old saying) with a duck in the mouth. This noble and industrious prince by his care and diligence to countenance and favour merchants in their affairs, did so encrease the practice thereof, that there is scarce a nobleman or gentleman in all his dominions that doth not merchandize either by himself or in partnership with others, whereby within these thirty years the trade to his port of Leghorn is so much encreased, that of a poor little town (as I myself knew it) it is now become a fair and strong city, being one of the most famous places for trade in all Christendom. And yet it is worthy our observation, that the multitude of ships and wares which come thither from England, the Low Countries, and other places, have little or no means to make their returns from thence but only in ready money, which they may and do carry away freely at all times, to the incredible advantage of the said great Duke of Tuscany and his subjects, who are much enriched by the continual great concourse of merchants from all the states of the neighbour princes, bringing them plenty of money daily to supply their wants of the said wares. And thus we see that the current of merchandize which carries away their treasure, becomes a flowing stream to fill them again in a greater measure with money.

There is yet an objection or two as weak as all the rest: that is, if we trade with our money we shall issue out the less wares; as if a man should say, those countries which heretofore had occasion to consume our cloth, lead, tin, iron, fish, and the like, shall now make use of our monies in the place of those necessaries, which were most absurd to affirm, or that the merchant had not rather carry out wares by which there is ever some gain expected, than to export money which is still but the same without any encrease.

But on the contrary there are many countries which may yield us very profitable trade for our money, which otherwise afford us no trade at all, because they have no use of our wares, as namely the East Indies for one in the first beginning thereof, although since by industry in our commerce with those nations we have brought them into the use of much of our lead, cloth, tin, and other things, which is a good addition to the former vent of our commodities.

Again, some men have alledged that those countries which permit money to be carried out, do it because they have few or no wares to trade withall: but we have great store of commodities, and therefore their action ought not to be our example.

To this the answer is briefly, that if we have such a quantity of wares as doth fully provide us of all things needful from beyond the seas: why should we then doubt that our monies sent out in trade, must not necessarily come back again in treasure; together with the great gains which it may procure in such manner as is before set down? And on the other side, if those nations which send out their monies do it because they have but few wares of their own, how come they then to have so much treasure as we ever see in those places which suffer it freely to be exported at all times and by whomsoever? I answer, even by trading with their monies; for by what other means can they get it, having no mines of gold or silver?

Thus may we plainly see, that when this weighty business is duly considered in this end, as all our human actions ought well to be weighed, it is found much contrary to that which most men esteem thereof, because they search no further than the beginning of the work, which misinforms their judgements, and leads them into error: for if we only behold the actions of the husbandman in the seed-time when he casteth away much good corn into the ground, we will rather account him a mad man than a husbandman: but when we consider his labours in the harvest which is the end of his endeavours, we find the worth and plentiful encrease of his actions.

CHAPTER XX: THE ORDER AND MEANS WHEREBY WE MAY DRAW UP THE BALLANCE OF OUR FOREIGN TRADE

Now, that we have sufficiently proved the ballance of our foreign trade to be the true rule of our treasure; it resteth that we shew by whom and in what manner the said ballance may be drawn up at all times, when it shall please the state to discover how we prosper or decline in this great and weighty business, wherein the officers of his majesty's customs are the only agents to be employed, because they have the accounts of all the wares which are issued out or brought into the kingdom; and although (it is true) they cannot exactly set down the cost and charges of other mens goods bought here or beyond the seas; yet nevertheless, if they ground themselves upon the book of rates, they shall be able to make such an estimate as may well satisfy this enquiry: for it is not expected that such an account can possibly be drawn up to a just ballance, it will suffice only that the difference be not over-great.

First therefore, concerning our exportations, when we have valued their first cost, we must add twenty five per cent. thereunto for the charges here, for fraight of ships, ensurance of the adventure, and the merchants gain; and for our fishing trades, which pay no custom to his majesty, the value of such exportations may be easily esteem'd by good observations which have been made, and may continually be made, according to the increase or decrease of those affairs, the present estate of this commodity being valued at one hundred and forty thousand pounds issued yearly. Also we must add to our exportations all the monies which are carried out in trade by licence from his majesty.

Secondly, for our importations of foreign wares, the custom-books serve only to direct us concerning the quantity, for we must not value them as they are rated here, but as they cost us with all charges laden into our ships beyond the seas, in the respective places where they are bought: for the merchants

gain, the charges of ensurance, fraight of ships, customs, imposts, and other
duties here, which do greatly indear them unto our use and consumption, are
notwithstanding but commutations amongst ourselves, for the stranger hath
no part thereof: wherefore our said importations ought to be valued at twenty
five per cent. less than they are rated to be worth here. And although this may
seem to be too great allowance upon many rich commodities, which come but
from the Low Countries and other places near hand, yet will it be found reasonable, when we consider it in gross commodities, and upon wares laden in
remote countries, as our pepper, which cost us, with charges, but four pence
the pound in the East Indies, and it is here rated at twenty pence the pound:
so that when all is brought into a medium, the valuation ought to be made as
aforewritten. And therefore, the order which hath been used to multiply the
full rates upon wares inwards by twenty, would produce a very great error in
the ballance, for in this manner the ten thousand bags of pepper, which this
year we have brought hither from the East Indies, should be valued at very near
two hundred and fifty thousand pounds, whereas all this pepper in the kingdom's accompt, cost not above fifty thousand pounds, because the Indians
have had no more of us, although we paid them extraordinary dear prices for
the same. All the other charges (as I have said before) is but a change of
effects amongst ourselves, and from the subject to the king, which cannot
impoverish the commonwealth. But it is true, that whereas nine thousand bags
of the said pepper are already shipped out for divers foreign parts; these and
all other wares, foreign or domestic, which are thus transported outwards,
ought to be cast up by the rates of his majesty's custom-money, multiplied by
twenty, or rather by twenty five (as I conceive) which will come nearer the
reckoning, when we consider all our trades to bring them into a medium.

Thirdly, we must remember, that all wares exported or imported by strangers
(in their shipping) be esteemed by themselves, for what they carry out, the
kingdom hath only the first cost and the custom: and what they bring in, we
must rate it as it is worth here, the custom, impost, and petty charges only
deducted.

Lastly, there must be good notice taken of all the great losses which we receive at sea in our shipping either outward or homeward bound: for the value
of the one is to be deducted from our exportations, and the value of the other
is to be added to our importations: for to lose and to consume doth produce
one and the same reckoning. Likewise if it happen that his majesty doth make
over any great sums of money by exchange to maintain a foreign war, where
we do not feed and cloth the soldiers, and provide the armies, we must deduct
all this charge out of our exportations or add it to our importations; for this
expence doth either carry out or hinder the coming in of so much treasure.

And here we must remember the great collections of money which are supposed to be made throughout the realm yearly from our recusants by priests and Jesuits, who secretly convey the same unto their colleges, cloysters and nunneries beyond the seas, from whence it never returns to us again in any kind; therefore if this mischief cannot be prevented, yet it must be esteemed and set down as a clear loss to the kingdom, except (to ballance this) we will imagine that as great a value may perhaps come in from foreign princes to their pensioners here for favours or intelligence, which some states account good policy, to purchase with great liberality; the receipt whereof notwithstanding is plain treachery.

There are yet some other petty things which seem to have reference to this ballance, of which the said officers of his majesty's customs can take no notice, to bring them into the accompt. As namely, the expences of travellers, the gifts to ambassadors and strangers, the fraud of some rich goods not entred into the customhouse, the gain which is made here by strangers by change and re-change, interest of money, ensurance upon English mens goods and their lives: which can be little when the charges of their living here is deducted; besides that the very like advantages are as amply ministred unto the English in foreign countries, which doth counterpoize all these things, and therefore they are not considerable in the drawing up of the said ballance.

CHAPTER XXI: THE CONCLUSION UPON ALL THAT HATH BEEN SAID, CONCERNING THE EXPORTATION OR IMPORTATION OF TREASURE

The sum of all that hath been spoken, concerning the enriching of the kingdom, and the encrease of our treasure by commerce with strangers, is briefly thus. That it is a certain rule in our foreign trade, in those places where our commodities exported are overballanced in value by foreign wares brought into this realm, there our money is undervalued in exchange; and where the contrary of this is performed, there our money is overvalued. But let the merchants exchange be at a high rate, or at a low rate, or at the *par pro pari*,[1] or put down altogether; let foreign princes enhance their coins, or debase their standards, and let his majesty do the like, or keep them constant as they now stand; let foreign coins pass current here in all payments at higher rates than they are worth at the Mint; let the statute for employments by strangers stand in force or be repealed; let the meer exchanger do his worst; let princes oppress, lawyers extort, usurers bite, prodigals waste, and lastly let merchants carry out what money they shall have occasion to use in traffic. Yet all these actions can work no other effects in the course of trade than is declared in this discourse. For so much treasure only will be brought in or carried out of a commonwealth, as the foreign trade doth over or under ballance in value. And

---

[1] [That is, *equal for equal.*]

this must come to pass by a necessity beyond all resistance. So that all other courses (which tend not to this end) howsoever they may seem to force money into a kingdom for a time, yet are they (in the end) not only fruitless but also hurtful: they are like to violent floods which bear down their banks, and suddenly remain dry again for want of waters.

Behold then the true form and worth of foreign trade, which is, the great revenue of the king, the honour of the kingdom, the noble profession of the merchant, the school of our arts, the supply of our wants, the employment of our poor, the improvements of our lands, the nursery of our mariners, the walls of the kingdoms, the means of our treasure, the sinews of our wars, the terror of our enemies. For all which great and weighty reasons, do so many well governed states highly countenance the profession, and carefully cherish the action, not only with policy to encrease it, but also with power to protect it from all foreign injuries: because they know it is a principal in reason of state to maintain and defend that which doth support them and their estates.

THE HAT ACT OF 1732

THE HAT ACT of 1732 is illustrative of the so-called "Colonial Compact," the mercantilist concept of the relations which should exist between mother country and colonies. The colonies were to serve as sources of raw materials and as markets for the home land. In turn, they were to be protected and given every aid and encouragement to stimulate their legitimate industries. James I, for example, was willing to destroy by force of arms tobacco cultivation in England, securing a monopoly to colonial planters in return for higher import duties. As the colonial population increased, and the colonial economy became more diversified, industries rose in the New World to compete with those of the Old. The terms of the "Colonial Compact" were thereby violated, and an effort was made to maintain them.

When colonial merchants and manufacturers began to take advantage of the plentiful supply of beaver to develop a growing hat trade, English producers protested strongly, and secured the passage of the act which follows. The text was taken from Pickering's *Statutes at Large*, 5 George II C. 22.

AN ACT TO PREVENT THE EXPORTATION OF HATS OUT OF ANY OF HIS MAJESTY'S COLONIES OR PLANTATIONS IN AMERICA
And to Restrain the Number of Apprentices Taken by the Hat-makers in the Said Colonies or Plantations, and for the Better Encouraging the Making Hats in GREAT BRITAIN

WHEREAS *the art and mystery of making hats in* Great Britain *hath arrived to great perfection, and considerable quantities of hats manufactured in this kingdom have heretofore been exported to his Majesty's plantations or colonies in* America, *who have been wholly supplied with hats from Great Britain; and whereas great quantities of hats have of late years been made, and the said manufacture is daily increasing in the* British *plantations in* America, *and is from thence exported to foreign markets, which were heretofore supplied from Great Britain, and the hat-makers in the said plantations take many apprentices for very small terms, to the discouragement of the said trade, and debasing the said manufacture:* wherefore for preventing the said ill practices for the future, and for promoting and encouraging the trade of making hats in *Great*

Britain, be it enacted by the King's most excellent majesty, by and with the advice and consent of the lords spiritual and temporal and commons in this present parliament assembled, and by the authority of the same, That from and after the twenty ninth day of *September* in the year of our Lord one thousand seven hundred and thirty two, no hats or felts whatsoever, dyed or undyed, finished or unfinished, shall be shipt, loaden or put on board any ship or vessel in any place or parts within any of the *British* plantations, upon any pretence whatsoever, by any person or persons whatsoever, and also that no hats or felts, either dyed or undyed, finished or unfinished, shall be loaden upon any horse, cart or other carriage, to the intent or purpose to be exported, transported, shipped off, carried or conveyed out of any of the said *British* plantations to any other of the *British* plantations, or to any other place whatsoever, by any person or persons whatsoever.

II. And be it further enacted by the authority aforesaid, That all and every the offender and offenders, offence and offences against this act, shall be subject and liable to the penalties and forfeitures herein after mentioned, that is to say, The said hats or felts dyed or undyed, finished or unfinished, so exported, transported, shipped off, carried, conveyed or loaden contrary to the true intent and meaning of this act, shall be forfeited, and that every of the offender and offenders therein shall likewise forfeit and pay the sum of five hundred pounds, for every such offence committed; and every master, mariner, porter, carter, waggoner, boatman, or other person whatsoever knowing such offence, and wittingly aiding and assisting therein, shall forfeit and pay the sum of forty pounds; which said several penalties and forfeitures shall and may be recovered by action of debt, bill, plaint or information in any of his Majesty's courts of record in *Great Britain,* or in such of the said plantations wherein such offence shall be committed (in which suit no essoin,[1] protection or wager of law, or more than one imparlance shall be allowed) and shall go and be applied, one moiety to the use of his Majesty, his heirs and successors, and the other moiety to him, her or them, that shall sue for the same.

III. And be it further enacted by the authority aforesaid, That it shall and may be lawful to and for any person or persons to seize, take, secure and convey to his Majesty's next warehouse all such hats and felts dyed or undyed, finished or unfinished, as he or they shall happen to see, find, know or discover to be laid on board in any ship, vessel or boat, or to be brought, carried or laid on shore, at or near the sea, or in any navigable river or water, to the intent or purpose to be exported or conveyed out of the said plantations, contrary to the

---

[1] [Excuse for non-appearance in court; protection: writ temporarily excusing one from a legal action; wager of law: acquittal by defendant's oath of innocence, when twelve others swear they believe his oath true. Imparlance: continuance or postponement of an action.]

true intent and meaning of this act, or to be laden upon any horse, cart or other carriage to the intent or purpose to be exported, conveyed or carried into any other of the said plantations, or into any other part or place whatsoever, contrary to the true intent and meaning hereof; and that such person or persons, that shall happen so to seize, take or secure any of the commodities aforesaid, shall be indemnified for so doing to all intents and purposes.

IV. *And to the intent and purpose that this act may more effectually be put in execution, for preventing the growing mischiefs that daily do or may arise to this kingdom, from the exportation of such goods as aforesaid, or any of them, out of the* British *plantations, should the same still be suffered to be sent from thence to supply other plantations and foreign markets, that are or have been supplied from* Great Britain: be it further enacted by the authority aforesaid, That if any commissioner or commissioners, or other officer or officers of the customs of any port or place within the *British* plantations, or any farmer or farmers of the revenue of the customs arising in the plantations, or any officer or officers imployed in the management of the said revenue, shall, from and after the said twenty ninth day of *September* one thousand seven hundred and thirty two, take or suffer to be taken any entry outward, or sign any cocket,[2] warrant or sufferance for the shipping or exporting any hats or felts dyed or undyed, finished or unfinished, or shall wittingly and willingly permit, contrive or suffer the same to be done, directly or indirectly, contrary to the true intent and meaning of this act, that then and in every such case, such commissioner or commissioners, farmer or farmers, officer or officers so signing such cocquet, warrant or sufferance, or passing such entry for the same, or any wise conniving thereat, contrary to the true intent and meaning hereof, shall for every such offence or neglect, forfeit his office, and shall moreover for every such offence forfeit the sum of five hundred pounds, to be recovered and applied in manner and form as aforesaid.

V. And be it further enacted by the authority aforesaid, That every offence committed against this act shall and may be inquired of, tried, heard and determined, in the county where any such goods shall be so laden or put on board as aforesaid, or else in the county or place either in *Great Britain* or the plantations where such offender shall happen to be apprehended or arrested for such offence, or where any of the goods aforesaid shall happen to be seized, taken or brought in; and that the said trial shall be in such manner and form, and in such effect to all intents and purposes as if the same offence had been wholly done and committed in the same county or place where the same shall be tried by virtue and in pursuance of this act.

VI. And be it further enacted by the authority aforesaid, That if any action,

---

2 [A customs certificate.]

bill, plaint or information, shall be commenced or prosecuted against any person for what he shall do in pursuance of this act, such person so sued shall and may file common bail or enter into a common appearance, and plead the general issue, not guilty, and, upon issue joined, may give this act and the special matter in evidence; and if the plaintiff or prosecutor shall become nonsuit, or suffer discontinuance, or if a verdict pass against him, or if upon demurrer judgment pass against him, the defendant shall recover treble costs, and damages.

VII. And it is hereby further enacted by the authority aforesaid, That no person residing in any of his Majesty's plantations in *America* shall, from and after the said twenty ninth day of *September* one thousand seven hundred and thirty two, make or cause to be made, any felt or hat of or with any wool or stuff whatsoever, unless he shall have first served as an apprentice in the trade or art of felt-making during the space of seven years at the least; neither shall any felt-maker or hat-maker in any of the said plantations imploy, retain or set to work, in the said art or trade, any person as a journeyman or hired servant, other than such as shall have lawfully served an apprenticeship in the said trade for the space of seven years; nor shall any felt-maker or hat-maker in any of the said plantations have, take or keep above the number of two apprentices at one time, or take any apprentice for any less term than seven years, upon pain to forfeit and pay the sum of five pounds for every month that he shall continue offending in the premisses contrary to the true meaning of this act, of which one moiety shall go and be applied to the use of his Majesty, his heirs and successors, and the other moiety thereof to such person or persons as will sue for the same by action of debt, bill, plaint or information, to be commenced, brought or prosecuted in any court in the said plantations, wherein no essoin, protection or wager of law, or more than one imparlance shall be admitted or allowed for the defendant.

VIII. And be it further enacted by the authority aforesaid, That no person or persons inhabiting in the said plantations, from and after the said twenty ninth day of *September* one thousand seven hundred and thirty two, shall retain or set on work, in the said art of hat or felt making, any black or negro, upon pain to forfeit and pay the sum of five pounds for every month wherein such person or persons shall so offend, contrary to the meaning of this act; and to be recovered and applied in manner, and to the uses aforesaid.

IX. Provided always, That nothing in this act contained shall extend to charge any person or persons lawfully exercising the said art, with any penalty or forfeiture for setting or using his or their own son or sons to the making or working hats or felts in his or their own house or houses, so as every such son or sons be bound by indenture of apprenticeship, for the term of seven years at the least, which term shall not be to expire before he shall be of the full age of twenty one years; any thing herein contained to the contrary notwithstanding.

X. Provided also, and be it enacted by the authority aforesaid, That every felt-maker residing in the said plantations, who at the beginning of this present session of parliament was a maker or worker of hats or felts, and being an housholder, and likewise all such as were at the beginning of this present session apprentices, covenant servants, or journeymen in the same art or mystery of felt-making so as such apprentices serve or make up their respective apprenticeships, shall and may continue and exercise the trade or art of making hats and felts in the said plantations, although the same persons were not bound apprentices to the same art for the term of seven years; any thing in this act to the contrary notwithstanding.

XI. And be it further enacted by the authority aforesaid, That this present act shall be deemed, and is hereby declared to be a public act, of which all judges and justices are to take notice without special pleading the same.

X ABSOLUTISM AND CONSTITUTIONALISM: THE BRITISH EXPERIENCE

JAMES I OF ENGLAND

U PON THE DEATH of Elizabeth, James VI (1566–1625), king of Scotland, as-
scended the English throne as James I and thereby united England and Scotland under a common ruler. This first of the Stuarts to sit on the throne of
England was a devout Anglican and a convinced absolute monarch, resting his
authority on divine right. The *Trew Law of Free Monarchies,* published in 1598,
was James's own statement of this position.

The background of this work was James's recurrent conflict with a recalcitrant
Scottish nobility, and the unhappy treatment he and his mother (Mary, Queen
of Scots) had suffered at the hands of the Calvinists. By a "free" monarchy James
meant one free of foreign interference and domestic strife. Typical of divine
right theorists, he insisted that the only alternative to the rule of a monarch by
divine right and legitimate inheritance was anarchy. This was the position of the
Stuarts in the English Civil Wars, when they held persistently to the doctrine that
the office of king was beyond the reach of rational inquiry or civil rebellion.

THE TREW LAW OF FREE MONARCHIES; OR,
THE RECIPROCK AND MUTUALL DUETIE
BETWIXT A FREE KING AND HIS
NATURALL SUBJECTS

As THERE IS NOT a thing so necessarie to be knowne by the people of any land,
next the knowledge of their God, as the right knowledge of their alleageance,
according to the forme of governement established among them, especially in
a *Monarchie* (which forme of governement, as resembling the Divinitie, ap-
proacheth nearest to perfection, as all the learned and wise men from the
beginning have agreed upon; Unitie being the perfection of all things,) So
hath the ignorance, and (which is worse) the seduced opinion of the multitude
blinded by them, who thinke themselves able to teach and instruct the igno-
rants, procured the wracke and overthrow of sundry flourishing Commonwealths; and heaped heavy calamities, threatning utter destruction upon others.
And the smiling successe, that unlawfull rebellions have oftentimes had against
Princes in aages past (such hath bene the misery, and iniquitie of the time)
hath by way of practise strengthened many in their errour: albeit there
cannot be a more deceiveable argument; then to judge ay the justnesse of the

cause by the event thereof; as hereafter shall be proved more at length. And among others, no Commonwealth, that ever hath bene since the beginning, hath had greater need of the trew knowledge of this ground, then this our so long disordered, and distracted Commonwealth hath: the misknowledge hereof being the onely spring, from whence have flowed so many endlesse calamities, miseries, and confusions, as is better felt by many, then the cause thereof well knowne, and deepely considered. The naturall zeale therefore, that I beare to this my native countrie, with the great pittie I have to see the so-long disturbance thereof for lacke of the trew knowledge of this ground (as I have said before) hath compelled me at last to breake silence, to discharge my conscience to you my deare country men herein, that knowing the ground from whence these your many endlesse troubles have proceeded, as well as ye have already too-long tasted the bitter fruites thereof, ye may by knowledge, and eschewing of the cause escape, and divert the lamentable effects that ever necessarily follow thereupon. I have chosen then onely to set downe in this short Treatise, the trew grounds of the mutuall duetie, and alleageance betwixt a free and absolute *Monarche,* and his people; not to trouble your patience with answering the contrary propositions, which some have not bene ashamed to set downe in writ, to the poysoning of infinite number of simple soules, and their owne perpetuall, and well deserved infamie: For by answering them, I could not have eschewed whiles to pick, and byte wel saltly their persons; which would rather have bred contentiousnesse among the readers (as they had liked or misliked) then sound instruction of the trewth: Which I protest to him that is the searcher of all hearts, is the onely marke that I shoote at herein.

First then, I will set downe the trew grounds, whereupon I am to build, out of the Scriptures, since *Monarchie* is the trew paterne of Divinitie, as I have already said: next, from the fundamental Lawes of our owne Kingdome, which nearest must concerne us: thirdly, from the law of Nature, by divers similitudes drawne out of the same: and will conclude syne by answering the most waighty and appearing incommodities that can be objected.

The Princes duetie to his Subjects is so clearly set downe in many places of the Scriptures, and so openly confessed by all the good Princes, according to their oath in their Coronation, as not needing to be long therein, I shall as shortly as I can runne through it.

Kings are called Gods by the prophetical King *David,* because they sit upon God his Throne in the earth, and have the count of their administration to give unto him. Their office is, *To minister Justice and Judgement to the people,* as the same *David* saith: *To advance the good, and punish the evill,* as he likewise saith: *To establish good Lawes to his people, and procure obe-*

dience to the same, as divers good Kings of *Judah* did: *To procure the peace of the people,* as the same *David* saith: *To decide all controversies that can arise among them* as *Salomon* did: *To be the Minister of God for the weale of them that doe well, and as the minister of God, to take vengeance upon them that doe evill,* as S. *Paul* saith. And finally, *As a good Pastour, to goe out and in before his people* as is said in the first of *Samuel: That through the Princes prosperitie, the peoples peace may be procured,* as *Jeremie* saith.

And therefore in the Coronation of our owne Kings, as well as of every Christian *Monarche* they give their Oath, first to maintaine the Religion presently professed within their countrie, according to their lawes, whereby it is established, and to punish all those that should presse to alter, or disturbe the profession thereof; And next to maintaine all the lovable and good Lawes made by their predecessours: to see them put in execution, and the breakers and violators thereof, to be punished, according to the tenour of the same: And lastly, to maintaine the whole countrey, and every state therein, in all their ancient Priviledges and Liberties, as well against all forreine enemies, as among themselves: And shortly to procure the weale and flourishing of his people, not onely in maintaining and putting to execution the olde lovable lawes of the countrey, and by establishing of new (as necessitie and evill manners will require) but by all other meanes possible to fore-see and prevent all dangers, that are likely to fall upon them, and to maintaine concord, wealth, and civilitie among them, as a loving Father, and careful watchman, caring for them more then for himselfe, knowing himselfe to be ordained for them, and they not for him; and therefore countable to that great God, who placed him as his lieutenant over them, upon the perill of his soule to procure the weale of both soules and bodies, as farre as in him lieth, of all them that are committed to his charge. And this oath in the Coronation is the clearest, civill, and fundamentall Law, whereby the Kings office is properly defined.

By the Law of Nature the King becomes a naturall Father to all his Lieges at his Coronation: And as the Father of his fatherly duty is bound to care for the nourishing, education, and vertuous government of his children; even so is the king bound to care for all his subjects. As all the toile and paine that the father can take for his children, will be thought light and well bestowed by him, so that the effect thereof redound to their profite and weale; so ought the Prince to doe towards his people. As the kindly father ought to foresee all inconvenients and dangers that may arise towards his children, and though with the hazard of his owne person presse to prevent the same; so ought the King towards his people. As the fathers wrath and correction upon any of his children that offendeth, ought to be by a fatherly chastisement seasoned with pitie, as long as there is any hope of amendment in them;

so ought the King towards any of his Lieges that offend in that measure. And shortly, as the Fathers chiefe joy ought to be in procuring his childrens welfare, rejoycing at their weale, sorrowing and pitying at their evill, to hazard for their safetie, travell for their rest, wake for their sleepe; and in a word, to thinke that his earthly felicitie and life standeth and liveth more in them, nor in himselfe; so ought a good Prince thinke of his people.

As to the other branch of this mutuall and reciprock band, is the duety and alleageance that the Lieges owe to their King: the ground whereof, I take out of the words of *Samuel*, dited [spoken] by Gods Spirit, when God had given him commandment to heare the peoples voice in choosing and annointing them a King. And because that place of Scripture being well understood, is so pertinent for our purpose, I have insert herein the very words of the Text.

9 *Now therefore hearken to their voice: howbeit yet testifie unto them, and shew them the maner of the King, that shall raigne over them.*

10 *So Samuel* tolde all the wordes of the Lord unto the people that asked a King of him.

11 *And he said, This shall be the maner of the King that shall raigne over you: he will take your sonnes, and appoint them to his Charets, and to be his horsemen, and some shall runne before his Charet.*

12 *Also, hee will make them his captaines over thousands, and captaines over fifties, and to eare* [plow] *his ground, and to reape his harvest, and to make instruments of warre and the things that serve for his Charets:*

13 *Hee will also take your daughters, and make them Apothicaries, and Cookes, and Bakers.*

14 *And hee will take your fields, and your vineyards, and your best Olive trees, and give them to his servants.*

15 *And he will take the tenth of your seed, and of your Vineyards, and gave it to his Eunuches, and to his servants.*

16 *And he will take your men servants, and your maid-servants, and the chiefe of your young men, and your asses, and put them to his worke.*

17 *He will take the tenth of your sheepe: and ye shall be his servants.*

18 *And ye shall cry out at that day, because of your King, whom ye have chosen you: and the Lord God will not heare you at that day.*

19 *But the people would not heare the voice of* Samuel, *but did say: Nay, but there shalbe a King over us.*

20 *And we also will be all like other Nations, and our King shall judge us, and goe out before us, and fight our battels. . . .*

First, God commandeth Samuel to doe two things: the one, to grant the people their suit in giving them a king; the other, to forewarne them, what some kings will doe unto them, that they may not thereafter in their grudging and murmuring say, when they shal feele the snares here fore-spoken; We would never have had a king of God, in case when we craved him, hee had let us know how wee would have beene used by him, as now we finde but overlate. And this is meant by these words:

Now therefore hearken unto their voice: howbeit yet testifie unto them, and shew them the maner of the King that shall rule over them. . . .

And as unto the next point (which is his forewarning them, that, weary as they will, they shall not have leave to shake off the yoke, which God thorow [through] their importunity hath laid upon them) it is expressed in these words:

18 *And yee shall crie out at that day, because of your King whom yee have chosen you: and the Lord will not heare you at that day.*

As he would say; When ye shall finde these things in proofe that now I forewarne you of, although you shall grudge and murmure, yet it shal not be lawful to you to cast it off, in respect it is not only the ordinance of God, but also your selves have chosen him unto you, thereby renouncing for ever all priviledges, by your willing consent out of your hands, whereby in any time hereafter ye would claime, and call backe unto your selves againe that power, which God shall not permit you to doe. And for further taking away of all excuse, and retraction of this their contract, after their consent to under-lie this yoke with all the burthens that hee hath declared unto them, he craves their answere, and consent to his proposition: which appeareth by their answere, as it is expressed in these words:

19 *Nay, but there shall be a king over us.* 20 *And we also will be like all other nations: and our king shall judge us, and goe out before us and fight our battels.*

As if they would have said; All your speeches and hard conditions shall not skarre us, but we will take the good and evill of it upon us, and we will be content to beare whatsoever burthen it shal please our King to lay upon us, as well as other nations doe. And for the good we will get of him in fighting our battels, we will more patiently beare any burden that shall please him to lay on us.

Now then, since the erection of this Kingdome and Monarchie among the Jewes, and the law thereof may, and ought to bee a paterne to all Christian and well founded Monarchies, as beeing founded by God himselfe, who by his Oracle, and out of his owne mouth gave the law thereof: what liberty can broiling spirits, and rebellious minds claime justly to against any Christian Monarchie; since they can claime to no greater libertie on their part, nor the people of God might have done, and no greater tyranny was ever executed by any Prince or tyrant, whom they can object, nor was here fore-warned to the people of God, (and yet all rebellion countermanded unto them) if tyrannizing over mens persons, sonnes, daughters and servants; redacting [reducing] noble houses, and men, and women of noble blood, to slavish and servile offices; and extortion, and spoile of their lands and goods to the princes owne private use and commoditie, and of his courteours, and servants, may be called a tyrannie?

And that this proposition grounded upon the Scripture, may the more clearly appeare to be trew by the practise oft prooved in the same booke, we never reade, that ever the Prophets perswaded the people to rebell against the Prince, how wicked soever he was. . . .

And under the Evangel, that king, whom *Paul* bids the *Romanes obey* and serve *for conscience sake,* was *Nero* that bloody tyrant, an infamie to his aage, and a monster to the world, being also an idolatrous persecuter, as the King of *Babel* was. If then Idolatrie and defection from God, tyranny over their people, and persecution of the Saints, for their profession sake, hindered not the Spirit of God to command his people under all highest paine to give them all due and heartie obedience for conscience sake, giving to *Caesar* that which was *Caesars,* and to God that which was Gods, as Christ saith; and that this practise throughout the booke of God agreeth with this lawe, which he made in the erection of that Monarchie (as is at length before deduced) what shamelesse presumption is it to any Christian people now adayes to claime to that unlawfull libertie, which God refused to his owne peculiar and chosen people? Shortly then to take up in two or three sentences, grounded upon all these arguments, out of the lawe of God, the duetie, and alleageance of the people to their lawfull king, their obedience, I say, ought to be to him, as to Gods Lieutenant in earth, obeying his commands in all thing, except directly against God, as the commands of Gods Minister, acknowledging him a Judge set by God over them, having power to judge them, but to be judged onely by God, whom to onely hee must give count of his judgement; fearing him as their Judge, loving him as their father; praying for him as their protectour; for his continuance, if he be good; for his amendment, if he be wicked; following and obeying his lawfull commands, eschewing and flying his fury in his unlawfull, without resistance, but by sobbes and teares to God, according to that sentence used in the primitive Church in the time of the persecution.

Preces, & Lachrymae sunt arma Ecclesiae.[1]

Now, as for the describing the allegeance, that the lieges owe to their native King, out of the fundamentall and civill Lawe, especially of this contrey, as I promised, the ground must first be set downe of the first maner of establishing the Lawes and forme of governement among us; that the ground being first right laide, we may thereafter build rightly thereupon. Although it be trew (according to the affirmation of those that pryde themselves to be the scourges of Tyrants) that in the first beginning of King's rising among the Gentiles, in that time of the first aage, divers commonwealths and societies of men choosed out one among themselves, who for his vertues and valour, being more eminent then the rest, was chosen out by them, and set up in that roome, to maintaine the weakest in their right, to throw downe oppressours, and to foster and continue the societie among men; which could not otherwise, but by vertue of that unitie be wel done: yet these examples are nothing pertinent to us; because our Kingdome and divers other Monarchies are not in that case, but had their beginning in a farre contrary fashion.

For as our Chronicles beare witnesse, this Ile, and especially our part of it, being scantily inhabited, but by very few, and they as barbarous and scant of civilitie, as number, there comes our first King *Fergus,* with a great number with him, out of *Ireland,* which was long inhabited before us, and making himself master of the countrey, by his owne friendship, and force, as well of the *Irelandmen* that came with him, as of the countrey-men that willingly fell to him, hee made himselfe King and Lord, as well of the whole landes, as of the whole inhabitants within the same. Thereafter he and his successours, a long while after their being Kinges, made and established their lawes from time to time, and as the occasion required. So the trewth is directly contrarie in our state to the false affirmation of such seditious writers, as would perswade us, that the Lawes and state of our countrey were established before the admitting of a king: where by the countrarie ye see it plainely prooved, that a wise king comming in among barbares, first established the estate and forme of government, and thereafter made lawes by himselfe, and his successours according thereto.

The kings therefore in *Scotland* were before any estates or rankes of men within the same, before any Parliaments were holden, or lawes made: and by them was the land distributed (which at the first was whole theirs) states erected and decerned, [decreed] and formes of government devised and established: And so it followes of necessitie, that the kings were the authors and makers of the Lawes, and not the Lawes of the kings. And to proove

---

[1] [*Prayers and tears are the weapons of the Church.*]

this my assertion more clearly, it is evident by the rolles of our Chancellery (which containe our eldest and fundamentall Lawes) that the King is *Dominus omnium bonorum*,[2] and *Dominus directus totius Dominij*,[3] the whole subjects being but his vassals, and from him holding all their lands as their over-lord, who according to good services done unto him, chaungeth their holdings from tacke to few, from ward to blanch,[4] erecteth new Baronies, and uniteth olde, without advice or authoritie of either Parliament or any other subalterin judiciall seate; So as if wrong might bee admitted in play (albeit I grant wrong should be wrong in all persons) the King might have a better colour for his pleasure, without further reason, to take the land from his lieges, as overlord of the whole, and doe with it as pleaseth him, since all that they hold is of him, then, as foolish writers say, the people might unmake the king, and put an other in his roome: But either of them as unlawful, and against the ordinance of God, ought to be alike odious to be thought, much lesse put in practise.

And according to these fundamentall Lawes already alledged, we daily see that in the Parliament (which is nothing else but the head Court of the king and his vassals) the lawes are but craved by his subjects, and onely made by him at their rogation, [supplication] and with their advice: For albeit the king make daily statutes and ordinances, enjoyning such paines thereto as hee thinkes meet, without any advice of Parliament or estates; yet it lies in the power of no Parliament, to make any kinde of Lawe or Statute, without his Scepter be to it, for giving it the force of a Law: And although divers changes have beene in other countries of the blood Royall, and kingly house, the kingdome being reft by conquest from one to another, as in our neighbour countrey in *England,* (which was never in ours) yet the same ground of the kings right over all the land, and subjects thereof remaineth alike in all other free Monarchies, as well as in this: For when the Bastard of *Normandie* came into *England,* and made himselfe king, was it not by force, and with a mighty army? Where he gave the Law, and tooke none, changed the Lawes, inverted the order of governement, set downe the strangers his followers in many of the old possessours roomes, as at this day well appeareth a great part of the Gentlemen in *England,* beeing come of the *Norman* blood, and their old Lawes, which to this day they are ruled by, are written in his language, and not in theirs: And yet his successours have with great happinesse enjoyed the Crowne to this day; Whereof the like was also done by all them that conquested them before.

And for conclusion of this point, that the king is over-lord over the whole lands, it is likewise daily proved by the Law of our hoordes, of want of Heires,

---

[2] [*Lord of all goods.*]   [3] [*Immediate Lord of the whole realm.*]   [4] [Kinds of land tenure.]

and of Bastardies: For if a hoord be found under the earth, because it is no more in the keeping or use of any person, it of the law pertains to the king. If a person, inheritour of any lands or goods, dye without any sort of heires, all his lands and goods returne to the king. And if a bastard die unrehabled without heires of his bodie (which rehabling onely lyes in the kings hands) all that hee hath likewise returnes to the king. And as ye see it manifest, that the King is over-Lord of the whole land: so is he Master over every person that inhabiteth the same, having power over the life and death of every one of them: For although a just Prince will not take the life of any of his subjects without a cleare law; yet the same lawes whereby he taketh them, are made by himselfe, or his predecessours; and so the power flowes alwaies from him selfe; as by daily experience we see, good and just Princes will from time to time make new lawes and statutes, adjoyning the penalties to the breakers thereof, which before the law was made, had beene no crime to the subject to have committed. Not that I deny the old definition of a King, and of a law; which makes the king to bee a speaking law, and the Law a dumbe king: for certainely a king that governes not by his lawe, can neither be countable to God for his administration, nor have a happy and established raigne: For albeit it be trew that I have at length prooved, that the King is above the law, as both the author and giver of strength thereto; yet a good king will not onely delight to rule his subjects by the lawe, but even will conforme himselfe in his owne actions thereunto, alwaies keeping that ground, that the health of the common-wealth be his chiefe lawe: And where he sees the lawe doubtsome or rigorous, hee may interpret or mitigate the same, lest otherwise *Summum ius* bee *summa iniuria:* [5] And therefore generall lawes, made publikely in Parliament, may upon knowen respects to the King by his authoritie bee mitigated, and suspended upon causes onely knowen to him.

As likewise, although I have said, a good king will frame all his actions to be according to the Law; yet is hee not bound thereto but of his good will, and for good example-giving to his subjects: For as in the law of abstaining from eating of flesh in *Lenton,* the king will, for examples sake, make his owne house to observe the Law; yet no man will thinke he needs to take a licence to eate flesh. And although by our Lawes, the bearing and wearing of hag-buts, and pistolets be forbidden, yet no man can find any fault in the King, for causing his traine to use them in any raide upon the Borderers, or other malefactours or rebellious subjects. So as I have alreadie said, a good King, although hee be above the Law, will subject and frame his actions thereto, for examples sake to his subjects, and of his owne free-will, but not as subject or bound thereto.

[5] [Lest otherwise *supreme right* be *supreme injury.*]

Since I have so clearly prooved then out of the fundamentall lawes and practise of this country, what right & power a king hath over his land and subjects, it is easie to be understood, what alleageance & obedience his lieges owe unto him; I meane alwaies of such free Monarchies as our king is, and not of elective kings, and much lesse of such sort of governors, as the dukes of *Venice* are, whose Aristocratick and limited government, is nothing like to free Monarchies; although the malice of some writers hath not beene ashamed to mis-know any difference to be betwixt them. And if it be not lawfull to any particular Lordes tenants or vassals, upon whatsoever pretext, to controll and displace their Master, and overlord (as is clearer nor the Sunne by all Lawes of the world) how much lesse may the subjects and vassals of the great over-lord the KING controll or displace him? And since in all inferiour judgements in the land, the people may not upon any respects displace their Magistrates, although but subaltern: for the people of a borough, cannot displace their Provost before the time of their election: nor in Ecclesiasticall policie the flocke can upon any pretence displace the Pastor, nor judge of him: yea even the poore Schoolemaster cannot be displaced by his schollers: If these, I say (whereof some are but inferiour, subaltern, and temporall Magistrates, and none of them equall in any sort to the dignitie of a King) cannot be displaced for any occasion or pretext by them that are ruled by them: how much lesse is it lawfull upon any pretext to controll or displace the great Provost, and great Schoole-master of the whole land: except by inverting the order of all Law and reason, the commanded may be made to command their commander, the judged to judge their Judge, and they that are governed, to governe their time about their Lord and governour.

And the agreement of the Law of nature in this our ground with the Lawes and constitutions of God, and man, already alledged, will by two similitudes easily appeare. The King towards his people is rightly compared to a father of children, and to a head of a body composed of divers members: For as fathers, the good Princes, and Magistrates of the people of God acknowledged themselves to their subjects. And for all other well ruled Common-wealths, the stile of *Pater patriae* [6] was ever, and is commonly used to Kings. And the proper office of a King towards his Subjects, agrees very wel with the office of the head towards the body, and all members thereof; For from the head, being the seate of Judgement proceedeth the care and foresight of guiding, and preventing all evill that may come to the body or any part thereof. The head cares for the body, so doeth the King for his people. As the discourse and direction flowes from the head, and the execution according thereunto belongs to the rest of the members, every one according to their office: so it is betwixt a wise Prince, and his people. As the judgement comming from the

[6] [*Father of his country.*]

head may not onely imploy the members, every one in their owne office, as long as they are able for it; but likewise in case any of them be affected with any infirmitie must care and provide for their remedy, incase it be curable, and if otherwise, gar [completely] cut them off for feare of infecting of the rest: even so is it betwixt the Prince, and his people. And as there is ever hope of curing any diseased member by the direction of the head, as long as it is whole; but by the contrary, if it be troubled, all the members are partakers of that paine, so is it betwixt the Prince and his people.

And now first for the fathers part (whose naturall love to his children I described in the first part of this my discourse, speaking of the dutie that Kings owe to their Subjects) consider, I pray you what dutie his children owe to him & whether upon any pretext whatsoever, it wil not be thought monstrous and unnaturall to his sons, to rise up against him, to control him at their appetite, and when they thinke good to sley him or to cut him off, and adopt to themselves any other they please in his roome: Or can any pretence of wickednes or rigor on his part be a just excuse for his children to put hand into him? And although wee see by the course of nature, that love useth to descend more then to ascend, in case it were trew, that the father hated and wronged the children never so much, will any man, endued with the least sponke of reason, thinke it lawfull for them to meet him with the line? Yea, suppose the father were furiously following his sonnes with a drawen sword, is it lawfull for them to turne and strike againe, or make any resistance but by flight? I thinke surely, if there were no more but the example of bruit beasts & unreasonable creatures, it may serve well enough to qualifie and prove this my argument. We reade often the pietie that the Storkes have to their olde and decayed parents: And generally wee know, that there are many sorts of beasts and fowles, that with violence and many bloody strokes will beat and banish their yong ones from them, how soone they perceive them to be able to fend themselves; but wee never read or heard of any resistance on their part, except among the vipers; which prooves such persons, as ought to be reasonable creatures, and yet unnaturally follow this example, to be endued with their viperous nature.

And for the similitude of the head and the body, it may very well fall out that the head will be forced to garre cut off some rotten members (as I have already said) to keep the rest of the body in integritie: but what state the body can be in, if the head, for any infirmitie that can fall to it, be cut off, I leave it to the readers judgement.

So as (to conclude this part) if the children may upon any pretext that can be imagined, lawfully rise up against their Father, cut him off, & choose any other whom they please in his roome; and if the body for the weale of it, may for any infirmitie that can be in the head, strike it off, then I cannot deny that the people may rebell, controll, and displace, or cut off their king at their owne pleasure, and upon respects mooving them. And whether these similitudes represent better the office of a King, or the offices of Masters or Deacons of crafts, or Doctors in Physicke (which jolly comparisons are used by such writers as maintaine the contrary proposition) I leave it also to the readers discretion.

And in case any doubts might arise in any part of this treatise, I will (according to my promise) with the solution of foure principall and most weightie doubts, that the adversaries may object, conclude this discourse. And first it is casten up by divers, that employ their pennes upon Apologies for rebellions and treasons, that every man is borne to carry such a naturall zeale and duety to his common-wealth, as to his mother; that seeing it so rent and deadly wounded, as whiles it will be by wicked and tyrannous Kings, good Citizens will be forced, for the naturall zeale and duety they owe to their owne native countrey, to put their hand to worke for freeing their common-wealth from such a pest.

Whereunto I give two answeres: First, it is a sure Axiome in *Theologie;* that evill shoud not be done, that good may come of it: The wickednesse therefore of the King can never make them that are ordained to be judged by him, to become his Judges. And if it be not lawfull to a private man to revenge his private injury upon his private adversary (since God hath onely given the sword to the Magistrate) how much lesse is it lawfull to the people, or any part of them (who all are but private men, the authoritie being alwayes with the Magistrate, as I have already proved) to take upon them the use of the sword, whom to it belongs not, against the publicke Magistrate, whom to onely it belongeth.

Next, in place of relieving the common-wealth out of distresse (which is their onely excuse and colour) they shall heape double distresse and desolation upon it; and so their rebellion shall procure the contrary effects that they pretend it for: For a king cannot be imagined to be so unruly and tyrannous, but the common-wealth will be kept in better order, notwithstanding thereof, by him, then it can be by his way-taking. For first, all sudden mutations are perillous in common-wealths, hope being thereby given to all bare men to set up themselves, and flie with other mens feathers, the reines being loosed to all the insolencies that disordered people can commit by hope of impunitie, because of the loosenesse of all things.

And next, it is certaine that a king can never be so monstrously vicious, but hee will generally favour justice, and maintaine some order, except in the particulars, wherein his inordinate lustes and passions carry him away; where by the contrary, no King being, nothing is unlawfull to none: And so the olde opinion of the Philosophers prooves trew, That better it is to live in a Common-wealth, where nothing is lawfull, then where all things are lawfull to all men; the Common-wealth at that time resembling an undanted [untamed] young horse that hath casten his rider: For as the divine Poet Du Bartas sayth, *Better it were to suffer some disorder in the estate, and some spots in the Common-wealth, then in pretending to reforme, utterly to over-throw the Republicke.*

The second objection they ground upon the curse that hangs over the common-wealth, where a wicked king reigneth: and, say they, there cannot be a more acceptable deed in the sight of God, nor more dutiful to their common-weale, then to free the countrey of such a curse, and vindicate to them their libertie, which is naturall to all creatures to crave.

Whereunto for answere, I grant indeed, that a wicked king is sent by God for a curse to his people, and a plague for their sinnes: but that it is lawfull to them to shake off that curse at their owne hand, which God hath laid on them, that I deny, and may so do justly. Will any deny that the king of *Babel* was a curse to the people of God, as was plainly forespoken and threatened unto them in the prophecie of their captivtie? And what was *Nero* to the Christian Church in his time? And yet *Jeremy* and *Paul* (as yee have else heard) commanded them not onely to obey them, but heartily to pray for their welfare.

It is certaine then (as I have already by the Law of God sufficiently proved) that patience, earnest prayers to God, and amendment of their lives, are the onely lawful means to move God to relieve them of that heavie curse. As for vindicating to themselves their owne libertie, what lawfull power have they to revoke to themselves againe those priviledges, which by their owne consent before were so fully put out of their hands? For if a Prince cannot justly bring backe againe to himself the priviledges once bestowed by him or his predecessors upon any state or ranke of his subjects; how much lesse may the subjects reave out of the princes hand that superioritie, which he and his Predecessors have so long brooked over them?

But the unhappy iniquitie of the time, which hath oft times given over good success to their treasonable attempts, furnisheth them the ground of their third objection: For, say they, the fortunate successe that God hath so oft given to such enterprises, prooveth plainely by the practise, that God favoured the justnesse of their quarrell.

To the which I answere, that it is trew indeed, that all the successe of battels, as well as other wor[l]dly things, lyeth onely in Gods hand: And therefore it is that in the Scripture he takes to himselfe the style of God of Hosts. But upon that generall to conclude, that hee ever gives victory to the just quarrell, would proove the *Philistims,* and divers other neighbour enemies of the people of God to have oft times had the just quarrel against the people of God, in respect of the many victories they obtained against them. And by that same argument they had also just quarrell against the Arke of God: For they wan it in the field, and kept it long prisoner in their countrey. As likewise by all good Writers, as well Theologues, as other, Duels and singular combats are disallowed; which are onely made upon pretence, that God will kith [show] thereby the justice of the quarrel: For wee must consider that the innocent partie is not innocent before God: And therefore God will make oft times them that have the wrong side revenge justly his quarrell; and when he hath done, cast his scourge in the fire, as he oft times did to his owne people, stirring up and strengthening their enemies, while they were humbled in his sight, and then delivered them in their hands. So God, as the great Judge may justly punish his Deputie, and for his rebellion against him stir up his rebels to meet him with the like: And when it is done, the part of the instrument is no better than the divels part is in tempting and torturing such as God committeth to him as his hangman to doe: Therefore, as I said in the beginning, it is oft times a very deceiveable argument, to judge of the cause by the event.

And the last objection is grounded upon the mutuall paction and adstipulation (as they call it) betwixt the King and his people, at the time of his coronation: For there, say they, there is a mutuall paction, and contract bound up, and sworne betwixt the king, and the people: Whereupon it followeth, that if the one part of the contract or the Indent bee broken upon the Kings side, the people are no longer bound to keep their part of it, but are thereby freed of their oath: For (say they) a contract betwixt two parties, of all Law frees the one partie, if the other breake unto him.

As to this contract alledged made at the coronation of a King, although I deny any such contract to bee made then, especially containing such a clause irritant as they alledge; yet I confesse, that a king at his coronation, or at the entry to his kingdome, willingly promiseth to his people, to discharge honorably and trewly the office given him by God over them: But presuming that thereafter he breaks his promise unto them never so inexcusable; the question is, who should bee judge of the breake, giving unto them, this contract were made unto them never so sicker, according to their alleageance. I thinke no man that hath but the smallest entrance into the civill Law, will doubt that of all Law, either civil or municipal of any nation, a contract cannot be thought broken by the one partie, and so the other likewise to be freed therefro, except that first a lawfull triall and cognition be had by the ordinary Judge of the breakers thereof: Or else every man may be both party and Judge in his owne cause; which is absurd once to be thought. Now in this contract (I say) betwixt the king and his people, God is doubtles the only Judge, both because to him onely the king must make count of his administration (as is oft said before) as likewise by the oath in the coronation. God is made judge and revenger of the breakers: For in his presence, as only judge of oaths, all oaths ought to be made. Then since God is the onely Judge betwixt the two parties contractors, the cognition and revenge must onely appertaine to him: It followes therefore of necessitie, that God must first give sentence upon the King that breaketh, before the people can thinke themselves freed of their oath. What justice then is it, that the partie shall be both judge and partie, usurping upon himselfe the office of God, may by this argument easily appeare: And shall it lie in the hands of headlesse multitude, when they please to weary off subjection, to cast off the yoake of governement that God hath laid upon them, to judge and punish him, whomby they should be judged and punished, and in that case, wherein by their violence they kythe [show] themselves to be most passionate parties, to use the office of an ungracious Judge or Arbiter? Nay, to speak trewly of that case, as it stands betwixt the king and his people, none of them ought to judge of the others break: For considering rightly the two parties at the time of their mutuall promise, the king is the one party, and the whole people in one body are the other party. And therfore since it is certaine, that a king, in case so it should fal out, that his people in one body had rebelled against him, hee should not in that case, as thinking himselfe free of his promise and oath, become an utter enemy, and practise the wreake of his whole people and native country: although he ought justly to punish the principall authors and bellowes of that universall rebellion: how much lesse then ought the people (that are alwaies subject unto him, and naked of all authoritie on their part) presse to judge and over-throw him? otherwise the people, as the one partie contracters, shall no sooner challenge the king as breaker, but hee assoone shall judge them as breakers: so as the victors making the tyners the traitors (as our proverbe is) the partie shall aye become both judge and partie in his owne particular, as I have alreadie said.

And it is here likewise to be noted, that the duty and alleageance, which the people sweareth to their prince, is not only bound to themselves, but likewise to their lawfull heires and posterity, the lineall succession of crowns being begun among the people of God, and happily continued in divers christian common-wealths: So as no objection either of heresie, or whatsoever private statute or law may free the people from their oath-giving to their king, and his succession, established by the old fundamentall lawes of the kingdome: For, as hee is there heritable over-lord, and so by birth, not by any right in the coronation, commeth to his crowne; it is a like unlawful (the crowne ever standing full) to displace him that succeedeth thereto, as to eject the former: For at the very moment of the expiring of the king reigning, the nearest and lawful heire entreth in his place: And so to refuse him or intrude another, is not to holde out uncomming in, but to expell and put out their righteous King. And I trust at this time whole *France* acknowledgeth the superstitious rebellion of the liguers, who upon pretence of heresie, by force of armes held so long out, to the great desolation of their whole countrey, their native and righteous king from possessing of his owne crowne and naturall kingdome.

Not that by all this former discourse of mine, and Apologie for kings, I meane that whatsoever errors and intollerable abominations a sovereigne prince commit, hee ought to escape all punishment, as if thereby the world were only ordained for kings, & they without controlment to turne it upside down at their pleasure: but by the contrary, by remitting them to God (who is their onely ordinary Judge) I remit them to the sorest and sharpest schoolemaster that can be devised for them: for the further a king is preferred by God above all other ranks & degrees of men, and the higher that his seat is above theirs, the greater is his obligation to his maker. And therfore in case he forget him-selfe (his unthankfulnes being in the same measure of height) the sadder and sharper will his correction be; and according to the greatnes of the height he is in, the weight of his fall wil recompense the same: for the further that any person is obliged to God, his offence becomes and growes so much the greater, then it would be in any other. *Joves* thunderclaps light oftner and sorer upon the high & stately oakes, then on the low and supple willow trees: and the highest bench is sliddriest [most slippery] to sit upon. Neither is it ever heard that any king forgets himselfe towards God, or in his vocation; but God with the greatness of the plague revengeth the greatness of his ingratitude: Neither thinke I by the force and argument of this my discourse so to perswade the people, that none will hereafter be raised up, and rebell against wicked Princes. But remitting to the justice and providence of God to stirre up such scourges as pleaseth him, for punishment of wicked kings (who made the very vermine and filthy dust of the earth to bridle the insolencie of proud *Pharaoh*) my onely purpose and intention in this treatise is to perswade, as farre as lieth in me, by these sure and infallible grounds, all such good Christian readers, as beare not onely the naked name of a Christian, but kith the fruites thereof in their daily forme of life, to keep their hearts and hands free from such monstrous and unnaturall rebellions, whensoever the wickednesse of a Prince shall procure the same at Gods hands: that, when it shall please God to cast scourges of princes, and instruments of his fury in the fire, ye may stand up with cleane handes, and unspotted consciences, having prooved your selves in all your actions trew Christians toward God, and dutifull subjects towards your King, having remitted the judgement and punishment of all his wrongs to him, whom to onely of right it appertaineth.

But craving at God, and hoping that God shall continue his blessing with us, in not sending such fearefull desolation, I heartily wish our kings behaviour so to be, and continue among us, as our God in earth, and loving Father, endued with such properties as I described a King in the first part of this Treatise. And that ye (my deare countreymen, and charitable readers) may presse by all means to procure the prosperitie and welfare of our King; that as hee must on the one part thinke all his earthly felicitie and happinesse grounded upon your weale, caring more for himselfe, for your sake then for his owne, thinking himself onely ordained for your weale; such holy and happy emulation may arise betwixt him and you, as his care for your quietnes, and your care for his honour and preservation, may in all your actions daily strive together, that the Land may thinke themselves blessed with such a King, and the king may thinke himselfe most happy in ruling over so loving and obedient subjects.

"AN AGREEMENT OF THE PEOPLE" AND DEBATES IN CROMWELL'S ARMY COUNCIL

THE PURITAN REVOLUTION produced in 1653 the first written constitution of modern times—the "Instrument of Government." The forerunner of this document was the more radical *Agreement of the People,* which had been drawn up by the group of Independents known as the Levellers, led by John Lilburne (1614?–1657) and Richard Overton (fl. 1646) and devoted to the ideal of constitutional government.

Leveller agitation reached its peak in 1647. The Levellers were the radicals of the Puritan Revolution, representing the small property owners, the farmers, tradesmen, and artisans. Their leaders were recruited from the rank and file of Cromwell's army. As representatives of soldier committees formed to move Cromwell from what they considered a temporizing policy with regard to both king and Parliament, they found occasion to voice their protest and to gain some share in the formulation of policy. The views of the Levellers were developed in their discussions and controversies in the Army Council with their superior officers, men such as Cromwell and his son-in-law Ireton (1611–51) who were members of the landed gentry and revolutionaries of a more moderate stamp.

Such radical proposals went beyond the traditional practice of the English and shocked the upholders of the supreme power of Parliament. It is not surprising that, when it came down to principles, the discussion between the Levellers and the moderates should turn about the relation between "natural" and "civil" rights. Ireton, for example, insisted that the right to vote was granted to an individual largely by the law and by virtue of his participation as a citizen, and he was irked by the appeal to an abstract natural right. The Levellers, on the other hand, could not make their peace with an unjust law, and while they were ready to admit—when it was expedient—that the rights for which they were struggling were peculiarly those of Englishmen, they maintained that they were "birthrights" which no society and no law might disregard. The controversy between them was never settled in the terms in which it was argued. The final form of *An Agreement of the People* conceded to the people's Representative "the highest and final judgment concerning all natural or civil things." It was Cromwell's direct coercion, rather than philosophic discussion, which ended the effective career of these seventeenth-century advocates of popular government as the basis for the radically democratic program of the lower-middle class.

In the debates from which selections follow, invited civilians are present in support of the Levellers. The debates are concerned with *An Agreement of the People,* which embodied the Leveller's postrevolutionary proposals. Selections from the texts of this agreement (drawn up principally by Lilburne) precede the passages from the debates and are taken from A. S. P. Woodhouse, *Puritanism and Liberty* (London, J. M. Dent and Sons, 1938). The first selection is the preamble to the Second Agreement, dated Friday, December 10, 1648. The debates, which have been preserved almost verbatim, are selected from *The Clarke Papers,* edited by C. H. Firth, (4 vols., Camden Society Publications, 1891–1901).

AN AGREEMENT OF THE PEOPLE

HAVING by our late labours and hazards made it appear to the world at how high a rate we value our just freedom, and God having so far owned our cause as to deliver the enemies thereof into our hands, we do now hold ourselves bound, in mutual duty to each other, to take the best care we can for the future, to avoid both the danger of returning into a slavish condition and the chargeable remedy of another war. For as it cannot be imagined that so many of our countrymen would have opposed us in this quarrel if they had understood their own good, so may we safely promise to ourselves, that when our common rights and liberties shall be cleared, their endeavours will be disappointed, that seek to make themselves our masters. Since therefore our former oppressions, and not-yet-ended troubles, have been occasioned either by want of frequent national meetings in council, or by the undue or unequal constitution thereof, or by rendering those meetings ineffectual, we are fully agreed and resolved to provide that hereafter our Representatives be neither left for uncertainty for time, nor be unequally constituted, nor made useless to the ends for which they are intended. And in order whereunto we declare and agree:

I. That the people of England, being at this very day unequally distributed by counties, cities, and boroughs, for the election of their deputies in Parliament, ought to be more indifferently proportioned, according to the number of the inhabitants; the circumstances whereof, for number, place, and manner, are to be set down before the end of this present Parliament.

II. That to prevent the many inconveniences apparently arising from the long continuance of the same persons in authority, this present Parliament be dissolved upon the last day of September, which shall be in the year of our Lord 1648.

III. That the people do of course choose themselves a Parliament once in two years, *viz.,* upon the first Thursday in every second March, after the manner as shall be prescribed before the end of this Parliament, to begin to sit upon the first Thursday in April following, at Westminster (or such other place as shall be appointed from time to time by the preceding Representatives), and to continue till the last day of September then next ensuing, and no longer.

IV. That the power of this, and all future Representatives of this nation is inferior only to theirs who choose them, and doth extend, without the consent or concurrence of any other person or persons, to the enacting, altering, and repealing of laws; to the erecting and abolishing of offices and courts; to the appointing, removing, and calling to account magistrates and officers of all degrees; to the making war and peace; to the treating with foreign states; and generally to whatsoever is not expressly or impliedly reserved by the represented to themselves.

Which are as followeth:

1. That matters of religion, and the ways of God's worship, are not at all entrusted by us to any human power, because therein we cannot remit or exceed a tittle of what our consciences dictate to be the mind of God, without wilful sin; nevertheless the public way of instructing the nation (so it be not compulsive) is referred to their discretion.

2. That the matter of impressing and constraining any of us to serve in the wars is against our freedom, and therefore we do not allow it in our representatives; the rather because money (the sinews of war) being always at their disposal, they can never want numbers of men apt enough to engage in any just cause.

3. That after the dissolution of this present Parliament, no person be at any time questioned for anything said or done in reference to the late public differences, otherwise than in execution of the judgments of the present representatives, or House of Commons.

4. That in all laws made, or to be made, every person may be bound alike, and that no tenure, estate, charter, degree, birth, or place, do confer any exemption from the ordinary course of legal proceedings, whereunto others are subjected.

5. That as the laws ought to be equal, so they must be good, and not evidently destructive to the safety and well-being of the people.

These things we declare to be our native rights, and therefore are agreed and resolved to maintain them with our utmost possibilities against all opposition whatsoever, being compelled thereunto not only by the examples of our ancestors, whose blood was often spent in vain for the recovery of their freedoms, suffering themselves, through fraudulent accommodations, to be still deluded of the fruit of their victories, but also by our own woeful experience, who, having long expected, and dearly earned, the establishment of these certain rules of government, are yet made to depend for the settlement of our peace and freedom upon him that intended our bondage and brought a cruel war upon us.

THE DEBATES

DEBATE OF OCTOBER 29, 1647

Major Rainborough: I desire we may come to that end we all strive after. I humbly desire you will fall upon that which is the engagement of all, which is the rights and freedoms of the people, and let us see how far we have made sure to them a right and freedom, and if anything be tendered as to that [in this paper]. And when that engagement is gone through, then, let us consider of those [things only] that are of greater weight.

(*The paper called the Agreement read. Then the first article read by itself.*)

Ireton: The exception that lies in it is this. It is said, they are to be distributed according to the number of the inhabitants: "The people of England," &c. And this doth make me think that the meaning is, that every man that is an inhabitant is to be equally considered, and to have an equal voice in the election of those representatives, the persons that are for the general Representative; and if that be the meaning, then I have something to say against it. But if it be only that those people that by the civil constitution of this kingdom, which is original and fundamental, and beyond which I am sure no memory of record does go—

[*Cowling, interrupting*]: Not before the Conquest.

[*Ireton*]: But before the Conquest it was so. If it be intended that those that by that constitution that was before the Conquest, that hath been beyond memory, such persons that have been before [by] that constitution [the electors], should be [still] the electors, I have no more to say against it.

Colonel Rainborough objected: That others might have given their hands to it.

Captain Denne denied that those that were set of their regiment were their hands.

Ireton [asked]: Whether those men whose hands are to it, or those that brought it, do know so much of the matter as [to know] whether they mean that all that had a former right of election [are to be electors], or [that] those that had no right before are to come in.

Cowling: In the time before the Conquest. Since the Conquest the greatest part of the kingdom was in vassalage.

Petty: We judge that all inhabitants that have not lost their birthright should have an equal voice in elections.

Rainborough: I desired that those that had engaged in it [might be included]. For really I think that the poorest he that is in England hath a life to live, as the greatest he; and therefore truly, sir, I think it's clear, that every man that is to live under a government ought first by his own consent to put himself under that government; and I do think that the poorest man in England is not at all bound in a strict sense to that government that he hath not had a voice to put himself under; and I am confident that, when I have heard the reasons against it, something will be said to answer those reasons, insomuch that I should doubt whether he was an Englishman or no, that should doubt of these things.

Ireton: That's [the meaning of] this, ["according to the number of the inhabitants"]?

Give me leave to tell you, that if you make this the rule I think you must fly for refuge to an absolute natural right, and you must deny all civil right; and I am sure it will come to that in the consequence. This, I perceive, is pressed as that which is so essential and due: the right of the people of this kingdom, and as they are the people of this kingdom, distinct and divided from other people, and that we must for this right lay aside all other considerations; this is so just, this is so due, this is so right to them. And that those that they do thus choose must have such a power of binding all, and loosing all, according to those limitations, this is pressed as so due, and so just, as [it] is argued, that it is an engagement paramount [to] all others: and you must for it lay aside all others; if you have engaged any otherwise, you must break it. [We must] so look upon these as thus held out to us; so it was held out by the gentleman that brought it yesterday. For my part, I think it is no right at all. I think that no person hath a right to an interest or share in the disposing of the affairs of the kingdom, and in determining or choosing those that shall determine what laws we shall be ruled by here—no person hath a right to this, that hath not a permanent fixed interest in this kingdom, and those persons together are properly the represented of this kingdom, and consequently are [also] to make up the representers of this kingdom, who taken together do comprehend whatsoever is of real or permanent interest in the kingdom. And I am sure otherwise I cannot tell what any man can say why a foreigner coming in amongst us—or as many as will coming in amongst us, or by force or otherwise settling themselves here, or at least by our permission having a being here—why they should not as well lay claim to it as any other. We talk of birthright. Truly [by] birthright there is thus much claim. Men may justly have by birthright, by their very being born in England, that we should not seclude them out of England, that we should not refuse to give them air and place and ground, and the freedom of the highways and other things, to live amongst us—not any man that is born here, though by his birth there come nothing at all (that is part of the permanent interest of this kingdom) to him. That I think is due to a man by birth. But that by a man's being born here he shall have a share in that power that shall dispose of the lands here, and of all things here, I do not think it a sufficient ground. I am sure if we look upon that which is the utmost (within [any] man's view) of what was originally the constitution of this kingdom, upon that which is most radical and fundamental, and which if you take away, there is no man hath any land, any goods, [or] any civil interest, that is this: that those that choose the representers for the making of laws by which this state and kingdom are to be governed, are the persons who, taken together, do comprehend the local interest of this kingdom; that is, the persons in whom all land lies, and those in corporations in whom all trading lies. This is the most fundamental constitution of this kingdom and [that] which if you do not allow, you allow none at all. This constitution hath limited and determined it that only those shall have voices in elections. It is true, as was said by a gentleman near me, the meanest man in England ought to have [a voice in the election of the government he lives under—but only if he has some local interest]. I say this: that those that have the meanest local interest—that man that hath but forty shillings a year, he *hath* as great voice in the election of a knight for the shire as he that hath ten thousand a year, or more if he had never so much; and therefore there is that regard had to it. But this [local interest], still the constitution of this government hath had an eye to (and what other government hath not an eye to this?). It doth not relate to the interest of the kingdom if it do not lay the foundation of the power that's given to the representers, in those who have a permanent and a local interest in the kingdom, and who taken all together do comprehend the whole [interest of the kingdom]. There is all the reason and justice that can be, [in this]: if I will come to live in a kingdom, being a foreigner to it, or live in a kingdom, having no permanent interest in it, [and] if I will desire as a stranger, or claim as one freeborn here, the air, the free passage of highways, the protection of laws, and all such things—if I will either desire them or claim them, [then] I (if I have no permanent interest in that kingdom) must submit to those laws and those rules [which they shall choose], who, taken together, do comprehend the whole interest of the kingdom. And if we shall go to take away this, we shall plainly go to take away all property and interest that any man hath either in land by inheritance, or in estate by possession, or anything else—[I say], if you take away this fundamental part of the civil constitution.

Rainborough: Truly, sir, I am of the same opinion I was, and am resolved to keep it till I know reason why I should not. I confess my memory is bad, and therefore I am fain to make use of my pen. I remember that, in a former speech [which] this gentleman brought before this [meeting], he was saying that in some cases he should not value whether [there were] a king or no king, whether lords or no lords, whether a property or no property. For my part I differ in that. I do very much care whether [there be] a king or no king, lords or no lords, property or no property; and I think, if we do not all take care, we shall all have none of these very shortly. But as to this present business. I do hear nothing at all that can convince me, why any man that is born in England ought not to have his voice in election of burgesses. It is said that if a man have not a permanent interest, he can have no claim; and [that] we must be no freer than the laws will let us be, and that there is no [law in any] chronicle will let us be freer than that we [now] enjoy. Something was said to this yesterday. I do think that the main cause why Almighty God gave men reason, it was that they should make use of that reason, and that they should improve it for that end and purpose that God gave it them. And truly, I think that half a loaf is better than none if a man be anhungry: [this gift of reason without other property may seem a small thing], yet I think there is nothing that God hath given a man that any [one] else can take from him. And therefore I say, that either it must be the Law of God or the law of man that must prohibit the meanest man in the kingdom to have this benefit as well as the greatest. I do not find anything in the Law of God, that a lord shall choose twenty burgesses, and a gentleman but two, or a poor man shall choose none: I find no such thing in the Law of Nature, nor in the Law of Nations. But I do find that all Englishmen must be subject to English laws, and I do verily believe that there is no man but will say that the foundation of all laws lies in the people, and if [it lie] in the people, I am to seek for this exemption.

And truly I have thought something [else]: in what a miserable distressed condition would many a man that hath fought for the Parliament in this quarrel, be! I will be bound to say that many a man whose zeal and affection to God and this kingdom hath carried him forth in this cause, hath so spent his estate that, in the way the state [and] the Army are going, he shall not hold up his head, if when his estate is lost, and not worth forty shillings a year, a man shall not have any interest. And there are many other ways by which [the] estates men have (if that be the rule which God in his providence does use) do fall to decay. A man, when he hath an estate, hath an interest in making laws, [but] when he hath none, he hath no power in it; so that a man cannot lose that which he hath for maintenance of his family but he must [also] lose that which God and nature hath given him! And therefore I do [think], and am still of the same opinion, that every man born in England cannot, ought not, neither by the Law of God nor the Law of Nature, to be exempted from the choice of those who are to make laws for him to live under, and for him, for aught I know, to lose his life under. And therefore I think there can be no great stick in this.

Truly I think that there is not this day reigning in England a greater fruit or effect of tyranny than this very thing would produce. Truly I know nothing free but only the knight of the shire, nor do I know anything in a parliamentary way that is clear from the height and fulness of tyranny, but only [that]. As for this of corporations [which you also mentioned], it is as contrary to freedom as may be. For, sir, what is it? The King he grants a patent under the Broad Seal of England to such a corporation to send burgesses, he grants to [such] a city to send burgesses. When a poor base corporation from the King['s grant] shall send two burgesses, when five hundred men of estate shall not send one, when those that are to make their laws are called by the King, or cannot act [but] by such a call, truly I think that the people of England have little freedom.

Ireton: I think there was nothing that I said to give you occasion to think that I did contend for this, that such a corporation [as that] should have the electing of a man to the Parliament: I think I agreed to this matter, that all should be equally distributed. But the question is, whether it should be distributed to all persons, or whether the same persons that are the electors [now] should be the electors still, and it [be] equally distributed amongst *them*. I do not see anybody else that makes this objection; and if nobody else be sensible of it I shall soon have done. Only I shall a little crave your leave to represent the consequences of it, and clear myself from one thing that was misrepresented by the gentleman that sat next me. I think, if the gentleman remember himself, he cannot but remember that what I said was to this effect: that if I saw the hand of God leading so far as to destroy King, and destroy Lords, and destroy property, and [leave] no such thing at all amongst us, I should acquiesce in it; and so I did not care, if no king, no lords, or no property [should] be, in comparison of the tender care that I have of the honour of God, and of the people of God, whose [good] name is so much concerned in this Army. This I did deliver [so], and not absolutely.

All the main thing that I speak for, is because I would have an eye to property. I hope we do not come to contend for victory—but let every man consider with himself that he do not go that way to take away all property. For here is the case of the most fundamental part of the constitution of the kingdom, which if you take away, you take away all by that. Here men of this and this quality are determined to be the electors of men to the Parliament, and they are all those who have any permanent interest in the kingdom, and who, taken together, do comprehend the whole [permanent, local] interest of the kingdom. I mean by permanent [and] local, that [it] is not [able to be removed] anywhere else. As for instance, he that hath a freehold, and that freehold cannot be removed out of the kingdom; and so there's a [freeman of a] corporation, a place which hath the privilege of a market and trading, which if you should allow to all places equally, I do not see how you could preserve any peace in the kingdom, and that is the reason why in the constitution we have but some few market towns. Now those people [that have freeholds] and those [that] are the freemen of corporations, were looked upon by the former constitution to comprehend the permanent interest of the kingdom. For [first], he that hath his livelihood by his trade, and by his freedom of trading in such a corporation, which he cannot exercise in another, he is tied to that place, [for] his livelihood depends upon it. And secondly, that man hath an interest, hath a permanent interest there, upon which he may live, and live a freeman without dependence. These [things the] constitution [of] this kingdom hath looked at. Now I wish we may all consider of what right you will challenge that all the people should have right to elections. Is it by the right of nature? If you will hold forth that as your ground, then I think you must deny all property too, and this is my reason. For thus: by that same right of nature (whatever it be) that you pretend, by which you can say, one man hath an equal right with another to the choosing of him that shall govern him—by the same right of nature, he hath the same [equal] right in any goods he sees—meat, drink, clothes—to take and use them for his sustenance. He hath a freedom to the land, [to take] the ground, to exercise it, till it; he hath the [same] freedom to anything that any one doth account himself to have any propriety in. Why now I say then, if you, against the most fundamental part of [the] civil constitution (which I have now declared), will plead the Law of Nature, that a man should (paramount [to] this, and contrary to this) have a power of choosing those men that shall determine what shall be law in this state, though he himself have no permanent interest in the state, [but] whatever interest he hath he may carry about with him—if this be allowed, [because by the right of nature] we are free, we are equal, one man must have as much voice as another, then show me what step or difference [there is], why [I may not] by the same right [take your property, though not] of necessity to sustain nature. It is for my better being, and [the better settlement of the kingdom]? Possibly not for it, neither: possibly I may not have so real a regard to the peace of the kingdom as that man who hath a permanent interest in it. He that is here to-day, and gone to-morrow, I do not see that he hath such a permanent interest. Since you cannot plead to it by anything but the Law of Nature, [or for anything] but for the end of better being, and [since] that better being is not certain, and [what is] more, destructive to another; upon these grounds, if you do, paramount [to] all constitutions, hold up this Law of Nature, I would fain have any man show me their bounds, where you will end, and [why you should not] take away all property.

Rainborough: I shall now be a little more free and open with you than I was before. I wish we were all true-hearted, and that we did all carry ourselves with integrity. If I did mistrust you I would [not] use such asseverations. I think it doth go on mistrust, and things are thought too [readily] matters of reflection, that were never intended. For my part, as I think, *you* forgot something that was in *my* speech, and you do not only yourselves believe that [some] men are inclining to anarchy, but you would make all men believe that. And, sir, to say because a man pleads that every man hath a voice [by right of nature], that therefore it destroys [by] the same [argument all property—this is to forget the Law of God]. That there's a property, the Law of God says it; else why [hath] God made that law, *Thou shalt not steal?* I am a poor man, therefore I must be [op]pressed: if I have no interest in the kingdom, I must suffer by all their laws be they right or wrong. Nay thus: a gentleman lives in a country and hath three or four lordships, as some men have (God knows how they got them); and when a Parliament is called he must be a Parliament-man; and it may be he sees some poor men, they live near this man, he can crush them—I have known an invasion to make sure he hath turned the poor men out of doors; and I would fain know whether the potency of [rich] men do not this, and so keep them under the greatest tyranny that was [ever] thought of in the world. And therefore I think that to that it is fully answered: God hath set down that thing as to propriety with this law of his, *Thou shalt not steal.* And for my part I am against any such thought, and, as for yourselves, I wish you would not make the world believe that we are for anarchy.

Cromwell: I know nothing but this, that they that are the most yielding have the greatest wisdom; but really, sir, this is not right as it should be. No man says that you have a mind to anarchy, but [that] the consequence of this rule tends to anarchy, must end in anarchy; for where is there any bound or limit set if you take away this [limit], that men that have no interest but the interest of breathing [shall have no voice in elections]? Therefore I am confident on 't, we should not be so hot one with another.

Rainborough: I know that some particular men we debate with [believe we] are for anarchy. . . . To the thing itself—property [in the franchise]. I would fain know how it comes to be the property [of some men, and not of others]. As for estates and those kind of things, and other things that belong to men, it will be granted that they are property; but I deny that that is a property, to a lord, to a gentleman, to any man more than another in the kingdom of England. If it be a property, it is a property by a law—neither do I think that there is very little property in this thing by the law of the land, because I think that the law of the land in that thing is the most tyrannical law under heaven. And I would fain know what we have fought for. [For our laws and liberties?] And this is the old law of England—and that which enslaves the people of England—that they should be bound by laws in which they have no voice at all! [With respect to the divine law which says *Honour thy father and thy mother*] the great dispute is, who is a right father and a right mother? I am bound to know who is my father and mother; and—I take it in the same sense you do—I would have a distinction, a character whereby God commands me to honour [them]. And for my part I look upon the people of England so, that wherein they have not voices in the choosing of their [governors—their civil] fathers and mothers—they are not bound to that commandment.

Petty: I desire to add one word concerning the word *property*. It is for something that anarchy is so much talked of. For my own part I cannot believe in the least that it can be clearly derived from that paper. 'Tis true, that somewhat may be derived in the paper against the King, the power of the King, and somewhat against the power of the Lords; and the truth is when I shall see God going about to throw down King and Lords and property, then I shall be contented. But I hope that they may live to see the power of the King and the Lords thrown down, that yet may live to see property preserved. And for this of changing the Representative of the nation, of changing those that choose the Representative, making of them more full, taking more into the number than formerly, I had verily thought we had all agreed in it that more should have chosen—all that had desired a more equal representation than we now have. For now those only choose who have forty shillings freehold. A man may have a lease for one hundred pounds a year, a man may have a lease for three lives, [but he has no voice]. But [as] for this [argument], that it destroys all right [to property] that every Englishman that is an inhabitant of England should choose and have a voice in the representatives, I suppose it is, [on the contrary], the only means to preserve all property. For I judge every man is naturally free; and I judge the reason why men [chose representatives] when they were in so great numbers that every man could not give his voice [directly], was that they who were chosen might preserve property [for all]; and therefore men agreed to come into some form of government that they might preserve property, and I would fain know, if we were to begin a government, [whether you would say], "You

have not forty shillings a year, therefore you shall not have a voice." Whereas
before there was a government every man had such a voice, and afterwards,
and for this very cause, they did choose representatives, and put themselves
into forms of government that they may preserve property, and therefore it is
not to destroy it, [to give every man a voice].

Ireton: I think we shall not be so apt to come to a right understanding in
this business, if one man, and another man, and another man do speak their
several thoughts and conceptions to the same purpose, as if we do consider
where the objection lies, and what the answer is which is made to it; and
therefore I desire we may do so. To that which this gentleman spake last.
The main thing that he seemed to answer was this: that he would make it
appear that the going about to establish this government, [or] such a government, is not a destruction of property, nor does not tend to the destruction of
property, because the people's falling into a government is for the preservation
of property. What weight there [is in it] lies in this: since there is a falling
into a government, and government is to preserve property, therefore this
cannot be against property. The objection does not lie in that, the making of
the representation more equal, but [in] the introducing of men into an
equality of interest in this government, who have no property in this kingdom,
or who have no local permanent interest in it. For if I had said that I would
not wish at all that we should have any enlargement of the bounds of those
that are to be the electors, then you might have excepted against it. But [what
I said was] that I would not go to enlarge it beyond all bounds, so that upon
the same ground you may admit of so many men from foreign states as
would outvote you. The objection lies still in this. I do not mean that I would
have it restrained to that proportion [that now obtains], but to restrain it
still to men who have a local, a permanent interest in the kingdom, who
have such an interest that they may live upon it as freemen, and who have
such an interest as is fixed upon a place, and is not the same equally everywhere. If a man be an inhabitant upon a rack rent for a year, for two years, or
twenty years, you cannot think that man hath any fixed or permanent interest. That man, if he pay the rent that his land is worth, and hath no advantage
but what he hath by his land, is as good a man, may have as much interest, in
another kingdom as here. I do not speak of not enlarging this [representation]
at all, but of keeping this to the most fundamental constitution in this kingdom, that is, that no person that hath not a local and permanent interest in
the kingdom should have an equal dependence in election [with those that
have]. But if you go beyond this law, if you admit any man that hath a
breath and being, I did show you how this will destroy property. It may come
to destroy property thus. You may have such men chosen, or at least the

major part of them, [as have no local and permanent interest]. Why may not those men vote against all property? [Again] you may admit strangers by this rule, if you admit them once to inhabit, and those that have interest in the land may be voted out of their land. It may destroy property that way. But here is the rule that you go by. You infer this to be the right of the people, of every inhabitant, because man hath such a right in nature, though it be not of necessity for the preserving of his being; [and] therefore you are to overthrow the most fundamental constitution for this. By the same rule, show me why you will not, by the same right of nature, make use of anything that any man hath, [though it be not] for the necessary sustenance of men. Show me what you will stop at; wherein you will fence any man in a property by this rule.

Rainborough: I desire to know how this comes to be a property in some men, and not in others.

Colonel [Nathaniel] Rich: I confess [there is weight in] that objection that the Commissary-General last insisted upon; for you have five to one in this kingdom that have no permanent interest. Some men [have] ten, some twenty servants, some more, some less. If the master and servant shall be equal electors, then clearly those that have no interest in the kingdom will make it their interest to choose those that have no interest. It may happen, that the majority may by law, not in a confusion, destroy property; there may be a law enacted, that there shall be an equality of goods and estate. I think that either of the extremes may be urged to inconveniency; that is, [that] men that have no interest as to estate should have no interest as to election [and that they should have an equal interest]. But there may be a more equitable division and distribution than that he that hath nothing should have an equal voice; and certainly there may be some other way thought of, that there may be a representative of the poor as well as the rich, and not to exclude all. I remember there were many workings and revolutions, as we have heard, in the Roman Senate; and there was never a confusion that did appear (and that indeed *was* come to) till the state came to know this kind of distribution of election. That is how the people's voices were bought and sold, and that by the poor; and thence it came that he that was the richest man, and [a man] of some considerable power among the soldiers, and one they resolved on, made himself a perpetual dictator. And if we strain too far to avoid monarchy in kings [let us take heed] that we do not call for emperors to deliver us from more than one tyrant.

Rainborough: I should not have spoken again. I think it is a fine gilded pill. But there is much danger, and it may seem to some that there is some kind of remedy [possible]. I think that we are better as we are [if it can be really proved] that the poor shall choose many [and] still the people be in the same case, be over-voted still. [But of this, and much else, I am unsatisfied], and therefore truly, sir, I should desire to go close to the business; and the [first] thing that I am unsatisfied in is how it comes about that there is such a propriety in some freeborn Englishmen, and not [in] others. . . .

Ireton: In the beginning of your speech you seem to acknowledge [that] by law, by civil constitution, the propriety of having voices in election was fixed in certain persons. So then your exception of your argument does not prove that by civil constitution they have no such propriety, but your argument does acknowledge [that] by civil [constitution they have such] propriety. You argue against this law [only] that this law is not good.

Wildman: Unless I be very much mistaken we are very much deviated from the first question. Instead of following the first proposition to inquire what is just, I conceive we look to prophecies, and look to what may be the event, and judge of the justness of a thing by the consequence. I desire we may recall [ourselves to the question] whether it be right or no. I conceive all that hath been said against it will be reduced to this [question of consequences], and [to] another reason—that it is against a fundamental law, that every person [choosing] ought to have a permanent interest, because it is not fit that those should choose Parliaments that have no lands to be disposed of by Parliament.

Ireton: If you will take it by the way, it is not fit that the representees should choose [as] the representers, or the persons who shall make the law in the kingdom, [those] who have not a permanent fixed interest in the kingdom. [The reason is the same in the two cases.]

Wildman: Sir, I do so take it; and I conceive that that is brought in for the same reason: that foreigners might [otherwise not only] come to have a voice in our elections as well as the native inhabitants, [but to be elected].

Ireton: That is upon supposition that these [foreigners] should be all inhabitants.

Wildman: I shall begin with the last first. The case is different with the native inhabitant and [the] foreigner. If a foreigner shall be admitted to be an inhabitant in the nation, so he will submit to that form of government as the natives do, he hath the same right as the natives but in this particular. Our case is to be considered thus, that we have been under slavery. That's acknowledged by all. Our very laws were made by our conquerors; and whereas it's spoken much of chronicles, I conceive there is no credit to be given to any of them; and the reason is because those that were our lords, and made us their vassals, would suffer nothing else to be chronicled. We are now engaged for our freedom. That's the end of Parliaments: not to constitute what is already [established, but to act] according to the just rules of government. Every person in England hath as clear a right to elect his representative as the greatest person in England. I conceive that's the undeniable maxim of government: that all government is in the free consent of the people. If [so], then upon that account there is no person that is under a just government, or hath justly his own, unless he by his own free consent be put under that government. This he cannot be unless he be consenting to it, and therefore, according to this maxim, there is never a person in England [but ought to have a voice in elections]. If [this], as that gentleman says, be true, there are no laws that in this strictness and rigour of justice [any man is bound to], that are not made by those who[m] he doth consent to. And therefore I should humbly move, that if the question be stated—which would soonest bring things to an issue —it might rather be thus: Whether any person can justly be bound by law, who doth not give his consent that such persons shall make laws for him?

Ireton: Let the question be so: Whether a man can be bound to any law that he doth not consent to? And I shall tell you, that he may and ought to be [bound to a law] that he doth not give a consent to, nor doth not choose any [to consent to]; and I will make it clear. If a foreigner come within this kingdom, if that stranger will have liberty [to dwell here] who hath no local interest here, he, as a man, it's true, hath air, [the passage of highways, the protection of laws, and all] that by nature; we must not expel [him from] our coasts, give him no being amongst us, nor kill him because he comes upon our land, comes up our stream, arrives at our shore. It is a piece of hospitality, of humanity, to receive that man amongst us. But if that man be received to a being amongst us, I think that man may very well be content to submit himself to the law of the land; that is, the law that is made by those people that have a property, a fixed property, in the land. I think, if any man will receive protection from this people though [neither] he nor his ancestors, not any betwixt him and Adam, did ever give concurrence to this constitution, I think this man ought to be subject to those laws, and to be bound by those laws, so long as he continues amongst them. That is my opinion. A man ought to be subject to a law, that did not give his consent, but with this reservation, that if this man do think himself unsatisfied to be subject to this law he may go into another kingdom. And so the same reason doth extend, in my understanding, [to] that man that hath no permanent interest in the kingdom. If he hath money, his money is as good in another place as here; he hath nothing that doth locally fix him to this kingdom. If that man will live in this kingdom, or trade amongst us, that man ought to subject himself to the law made by the people who have the interest of this kingdom in them. And yet I do acknowledge that which you take to be so general a maxim, that in every kingdom, within every land, the original of power of making laws, of determining what shall be law in the land, does lie in the people—[but by the people is meant those] that are possessed of the permanent interest in the land. But whoever is extraneous to this, that is, as good a man in another land, that man ought to give such a respect to the property of men that live in the land. They do not determine [that I shall live in this land]. Why should I have any interest in determining what shall be the law of this land?

Major [William] Rainborough: I think if it can be made to appear that it is a just and reasonable thing, and that it is for the preservation of all the [native] freeborn men, [that they should have an equal voice in election]—I think it ought to be made good unto them. And the reason is: that the chief end of this government is to preserve persons as well as estates, and if any law shall take hold of my person it is more dear than my estate.

Colonel Rainborough: I do very well remember that the gentleman in the window [said] that, if it were so, there were no propriety to be had, because five parts of [the nation], the poor people, are now excluded and would then come in. So one on the other side said [that], if [it were] otherwise, then rich men [only] shall be chosen. Then, I say, the one part shall make hewers of wood and drawers of water of the other five, and so the greatest part of the nation be enslaved. Truly I think we are still where we were; and I do not hear any argument given but only that it is the present law of the kingdom. I say still, what shall become of those many [men] that have laid out themselves for the Parliament of England in this present war, that have ruined themselves by fighting, by hazarding all they had? They are Englishmen. They have now nothing to say for themselves.

Rich: I should be very sorry to speak anything here that should give offence, or that may occasion personal reflection[s] that we spoke against just now. I did not urge anything so far as was represented, and I did not at all urge that there should be a consideration [had of rich men], and that [a] man that is [poor] shall be without consideration, [or that] he deserves to be made poore[r] and not to live [in independence] at all. But all that I urged was this: that I think it worthy consideration, whether they should have an equality in their interest. However, I think we have been a great while upon this point, and if we be as long upon all the rest, it were well if there were no greater difference than this.

Mr. [Hugh] Peter: I think that this [matter of the franchise] may be easily agreed on—that is, there may be a way thought of. I think you would do well to set up all night [if thereby you could effect it], but I think that three or four might be thought of in this company [to form a committee]. You will be forced [only] to put characters upon electors or elected; therefore I do suppose that if there be any here that can make up a Representative to your mind,

the thing is gained. But I would fain know whether that will answer the
work of your meeting. The question is, whether you can state any one question
for [removing] the present danger of the kingdom, whether any one question
or no will dispatch the work.

Sir, I desire, [if it be possible], that some question may be stated to finish
the present work, to cement us [in the points] wherein lies the distance; and
if the thoughts [be] of the commonwealth [and] the people's freedom, I think
that's soon cured. I desire that all manner of plainness may be used, that we
may not go on with the lapwing and carry one another off the nest. There is
something else that must cement us where the awkwardness of our spirits lies.

Rainborough: For my part, I think we cannot engage one way or other in
the Army if we do not think of the people's liberties. If we can agree where
the liberty and freedom of the people lies, that will do all.

Ireton: I cannot consent so far. As I said before: when I see the hand of
God destroying King, and Lords, and Commons too, [or] any foundation
of human constitution, when I see God hath done it, I shall, I hope, comfortably acquiesce in it. But first, I cannot give my consent to it, because it is
not good. And secondly, as I desire that this Army should have regard to
engagements wherever they are lawful, so I would have them have regard to
this [as well]: that they should not bring that scandal upon the name of God
[and the Saints], that those that call themselves by that name, those whom God
hath owned and appeared with—that we should represent ourselves to the
world as men so far from being of that peaceable spirit which is suitable to
the Gospel, as we should have bought peace of the world upon such terms—
[as] we would not have peace in the world but upon such terms—as should
destroy all property. If the principle upon which you move this alteration,
or the ground upon which you press that we should make this alteration, do
destroy all kind of property or whatsoever a man hath by human constitution,
[I cannot consent to it]. The Law of God doth not give me property, nor the
Law of Nature, but property is of human constitution. I have a property and
this I shall enjoy. Constitution founds property. If either the thing itself that
you press or the consequence [of] that you press [do destroy property], though
I shall acquiesce in having no property, yet I cannot give my heart or hand
to it; because it is a thing evil in itself and scandalous to the world, and I desire
this Army may be free from both.

Sexby: I see that though liberty were our end, there is a degeneration from
it. We have engaged in this kingdom and ventured our lives, and it was all
for this: to recover our birthrights and privileges as Englishmen; and by the
arguments urged there is none. There are many thousands of us soldiers that
have ventured our lives; we have had little propriety in the kingdom as to

our estates, yet we have had a birthright. But it seems now, except a man hath a fixed estate in this kingdom, he hath no right in this kingdom. I wonder we were so much deceived. If we had not a right to the kingdom, we were mere mercenary soldiers. There are many in my condition, that have as good a condition [as I have]; it may be little estate they have at present, and yet they have as much a [birth] right as those two [2] who are their lawgivers, as any in this place. I shall tell you in a word my resolution. I am resolved to give my birthright to none. Whatsoever may come in the way, and [whatsoever may] be thought, I will give it to none. If this thing [be denied the poor], that with so much pressing after [they have sought, it will be the greatest scandal]. There was one thing spoken to this effect: that if the poor and those in low condition [were given their birthright it would be the destruction of this kingdom]. I think this was but a distrust of Providence. I do think the poor and meaner of this kingdom—I speak as in relation [to the condition of soldiers], in which we are—have been the means of the preservation of this kingdom. I say, in their stations, and really I think to their utmost possibility; and their lives have not been [held] dear for purchasing the good of the kingdom. [And now they demand the birthright for which they fought.] Those that act to this end are as free from anarchy or confusion as those that oppose it, and they have the Law of God and the law of their conscience [with them]. But truly I shall only sum up [in] this. I desire that we may not spend so much time upon these things. We must be plain. When men come to understand these things, they will not lose that which they have contended for. That which I shall beseech you is to come to a determination of this question.

Ireton: I am very sorry we are come to this point, that from reasoning one to another we should come to express our resolutions. I profess for my part, what I see is good for the kingdom, and becoming a Christian to contend for, I hope through God I shall have strength and resolution to do my part towards it. And yet I will profess direct contrary in some kind to what that gentleman said. For my part, rather than I will make a disturbance to a good constitution of a kingdom wherein I may live in godliness and honesty, and peace and quietness, I will part with a great deal of my birthright. I will part with my own property rather than I will be the man that shall make a disturbance in the kingdom for my property; and therefore if all the people in this kingdom, or [the] representative[s] of them all together, should meet and should give away my property I would submit to it, I would give it away. But that gentleman, and I think every Christian, ought to bear that spirit, to carry that in him, that he will not make a public disturbance upon a private prejudice.

[2] [The reference is probably to Cromwell and Ireton.]

Now let us consider where our difference lies. We all agree that you should have a Representative to govern, and this Representative to be as equal as you can [make it]. But the question is, whether this distribution can be made to all persons equally, or whether [only] amongst those equals that have the interest of England in them. That which I have declared [is] my opinion [still]. I think we ought to keep to that [constitution which we have now], both because it is a civil constitution—it is the most fundamental constitution that we have—and [because] here is so much justice and reason and prudence [in it]—as I dare confidently undertake to demonstrate—that there are many more evils that will follow in case you do alter [it] than there can [be] in the standing of it. But I say but this in the general, that I do wish that they that talk of birthrights—we any of us when we talk of birthrights—would consider what really our birthright is.

If a man mean by birthright, whatsoever I can challenge by the Law of Nature (suppose there were no constitution at all, no civil law and [no] civil constitution), [and] that *that* I am to contend for against constitution; [then] you leave no property, nor no foundation for any man to enjoy anything. But if you call that your birthright which is the most fundamental part of your constitution, then let him perish that goes about to hinder you or any man of the least part of your birthright, or will [desire to] do it. But if you will lay aside the most fundamental constitution, which is as good, for aught you can discern, as anything you can propose—at least it is a constitution, and I will give you consequence for consequence of good upon [that] constitution as you [can give] upon your birthright [without it]—and if you merely upon pretence of a birthright, of the right of nature, which is only true as for [your being, and not for] your better being; if you will upon that ground pretend that this constitution, the most fundamental constitution, the thing that hath reason and equity in it, shall not stand in your way, [it] is the same principle to me, say I, [as if] but for your better satisfaction you shall take hold of anything that a[nother] man call his own.

Rainborough: Sir, I see that it is impossible to have liberty but all property must be taken away. If it be laid down for a rule, and if you will say it, it must be so. But I would fain know what the soldier hath fought for all this while? He hath fought to enslave himself, to give power to men of riches, men of estates, to make him a perpetual slave. We do find in all presses that go forth none must be pressed that are freehold men. When these gentlemen fall out among themselves they shall press the poor scrubs to come and kill [one another for] them.

Ireton: I confess I see so much right in the business that I am not easily satisfied with flourishes. If you will [not] lay the stress of the business upon

the consideration of reason, or right relating to anything of human constitution, or anything of that nature, but will put it upon consequences, I will
show you greater ill consequences—I see enough to say that, to my apprehensions, I can show you greater ill consequences to follow upon that alteration which you would have, by extending [voices] to all that have a being
in this kingdom, than [any] that [can come] by this [present constitution],
a great deal. That [that you urge of the present constitution] is a particular
ill consequence. This [that I object against your proposal] is a general ill
consequence, and this is as great as that or any [ill consequence] else [what-
soever], though I think you will see that the validity of that argument must
be that for one ill [that] lies upon that which now is, I can show you a thousand upon this [that you propose].

Give me leave [to say] but this one word. I [will] tell you what the soldier
of the kingdom hath fought for. First, the danger that we stood in was that
one man's will must be a law. The people of the kingdom must have this
right at least, that they should not be concluded [but] by the Representative
of those that had the interest of the kingdom. So[m]e men fought in this,
because they were immediately concerned and engaged in it. Other men who
had no other interest in the kingdom but this, that they should have the benefit
of those laws made by the Representative, yet [fought] that they should have
the benefit of this Representative. They thought it was better to be concluded
by the common consent of those that were fixed men, and settled men, that
had the interest of this kingdom [in them]. "And from that way," [said they],
"I shall know a law and have a certainty." Every man that was born [in the
country, that] is a denizen in it, that hath a freedom, he was capable of trading
to get money, to get estates by; and therefore this man, I think, had a great
deal of reason to build up such a foundation of interest to himself: that is, that
the will of one man should not be a law, but that the law of this kingdom
should be by choice of persons to represent, and that choice to be made by, the
generality of the kingdom. Here was a right that induced men to fight, and
those men that had this interest, though this be not the utmost interest that
other men have, yet they had *some* interest. Now [tell me] why we should
go to plead whatsoever we can challenge by the right of nature against whatsoever any man can challenge by constitution. I do not see where that man
will stop, as to point of property, [so] that he shall not use [against other
property] that right he hath [claimed] by the Law of Nature against that
constitution. I desire any man to show me where there is a difference. I have
been answered, "Now we see liberty cannot stand without [destroying] property." Liberty may be had and property not be destroyed. First, the liberty of
all those that have the permanent interest in the kingdom, *that* is provided

for [by the constitution]. And [secondly, by an appeal to the Law of Nature] liberty cannot be provided for in a general sense, if property be preserved. For if property be preserved [by acknowledging a natural right in the possessor, so] that I am not to meddle with such a man's estate, his meat, his drink, his apparel, or other goods, then the right of nature destroys liberty. By the right of nature I am to have sustenance rather than perish; yet property destroys it for a man to have [this] by the right of nature, [even] suppose there be no human constitution. . . .

THOMAS HOBBES

T HOMAS HOBBES (1588–1679) was educated at Magdalen College, Oxford, and became a private tutor to the Cavendish family (the earls of Devonshire). As a student he visited France where he met leaders in the "new learning" and members of the Cartesian circle. He was also the friend of Francis Bacon. From 1640 to 1651 he lived on the Continent, where for a time he was tutor to Charles II. Hobbes had to flee from the opposition of the parliamentarians in England to his work on political science. What most alienated Hobbes's contemporaries was not his alleged materialism but his attack on the division between temporal and spiritual authority: the state power or sovereign must be absolute. Hobbes lived peacefully in England from 1651 to the Restoration, and as a result was criticized later for lack of loyalty to the royalists. Charles II accepted Hobbes, but he was involved in religious and scientific controversies until his death.

Hobbes's most famous work is the *Leviathan* (1651), which presents his theory of the social contract: the egoism natural to man is the root of social conflict, so a contract is established whereby men accept a common superior and sovereign power, which will protect them from themselves and from each other and make possible the satisfaction of certain human desires. Hobbes's many other writings include: *De cive* (1642); *De homine*; *De corpore politico* (1650); and *Behemoth*, a history of the British civil war.

Hobbes was a prolific writer on other themes. In his late eighties he made translations (still widely used) of the *Iliad* and *Odyssey*. In 1641 he published a number of objections to Descartes's metaphysics. The *Leviathan*, from which selections follow, was published in 1651 with the title *Leviathan, or the Matter, Forme, and Power of a Commonwealth Ecclesiastical and Civil*.

LEVIATHAN

THE INTRODUCTION

NATURE, the art whereby God hath made and governs the world, is by the *art* of man, as in many other things, so in this also imitated, that it can make an artificial animal. For seeing life is but a motion of limbs, the beginning whereof is in some principal part within; why may we not say, that all *automata* (engines that move themselves by springs and wheels as doth a watch) have an artificial life? For what is the *heart*, but a *spring;* and the *nerves*, but so many *strings;* and the *joints*, but so many *wheels*, giving motion to the whole body, such as was intended by the artificer? *Art* goes yet further, imitating that rational and most excellent work of nature, *man*. For by art is created that great LEVIATHAN called a COMMONWEALTH, or STATE, in Latin CIVITAS, which is but an artificial man; though of greater stature and strength than the natural, for whose protection and defense it was intended; and in which the *sovereignty* is an artificial *soul*, as giving life and motion to the whole body; the *magistrates*, and other *officers* of judicature and execution, artificial *joints; reward* and *punishment*, by which fastened to the seat of the sovereignty every joint and member is moved to perform his duty, are the *nerves*, that do the same in the body natural; the *wealth* and *riches* of all the particular members, are the *strength; salus populi*, the *people's safety*, its *business; counsellors*, by whom all things needful for it to know are suggested unto it, are the *memory; equity*, and *laws*, an artificial *reason* and *will; con-cord, health; sedition, sickness;* and *civil war, death.* Lastly, the *pacts* and *covenants*, by which the parts of this body politic were at first made, set together, and united, resemble that *fiat*, or the *let us make man*, pronounced by God in the creation.

To describe the nature of this artificial man, I will consider

First, the *matter* thereof, and the *artificer;* both which is *man*.

Secondly, *how*, and by what *covenants* it is made; what are the *rights* and just *power* or *authority* of a *sovereign;* and what it is that *preserveth* or *dissolveth* it.

Thirdly, what is a *Christian commonwealth*.

Lastly, what is the *kingdom of darkness*. . . .

CHAPTER X: OF POWER, WORTH, DIGNITY, HONOUR, AND WORTHINESS

The Power *of a man,* to take it universally, is his present means, to obtain some future apparent good; and is either *original* or *instrumental*.

Natural power, is the eminence of the faculties of body, or mind: as extraordinary strength, form, prudence, arts, eloquence, liberality, nobility. *Instrumental* are those powers, which acquired by these, or by fortune, are means and instruments to acquire more: as riches, reputation, friends, and the secret working of God, which men call good luck. For the nature of power, is in this point, like to fame, increasing as it proceeds; or like the motion of heavy bodies, which the further they go, make still the more haste.

The greatest of human powers, is that which is compounded of the powers of most men, united by consent, in one person, natural, or civil, that has the use of all their powers depending on his will; such as is the power of a commonwealth: or depending on the wills of each particular; such as is the power of a faction or of divers factions leagued. Therefore to have servants, is power; to have friends, is power: for they are strengths united. . . .

I put for a general inclination of all mankind, a perpetual and restless desire of power after power, that ceaseth only in death. And the cause of this, is not always that a man hopes for a more intensive delight, than he has already attained to; or that he cannot be content with a moderate power: but because he cannot assure the power and means to live well, which he hath present, without the acquisition of more.

CHAPTER XIII: OF THE NATURAL CONDITION OF MANKIND AS CONCERNING THEIR FELICITY, AND MISERY

Nature hath made men so equal, in the faculties of the body, and mind; as that though there be found one man sometimes manifestly stronger in body, or of quicker mind than another; yet when all is reckoned together, the difference between man, and man, is not so considerable, as that one man can thereupon claim to himself any benefit, to which another may not pretend, as well as he. For as to the strength of body, the weakest has strength enough to kill the strongest, either by secret machination, or by confederacy with others, that are in the same danger with himself.

And as to the faculties of the mind, setting aside the arts grounded upon words, and especially that skill of proceeding upon general, and infallible rules, called science; which very few have, and but in few things; as being not a native faculty, born with us; nor attained, as prudence, while we look after somewhat else, I find yet a greater equality amongst men, than that of strength. For prudence, is but experience; which equal time, equally bestows on all men, in those things they equally apply themselves unto. That which may perhaps make such equality incredible, is but a vain conceit of one's own wisdom, which almost all men think they have in a greater degree, than the vulgar; that is, than all men but themselves, and a few others, whom by fame, or for concurring with themselves, they approve. For such is the nature of men, that howsoever they may acknowledge many others to be more witty, or more eloquent, or more learned; yet they will hardly believe there be many so wise as themselves; for they see their own wit at hand, and other men's at a distance. But this proveth rather that men are in that point equal, than unequal. For there is not ordinarily a greater sign of the equal distribution of any thing, than that every man is contented with his share.

From this equality of ability, ariseth equality of hope in the attaining of our ends. And therefore if any two men desire the same thing, which nevertheless they cannot both enjoy, they become enemies; and in the way to their end, which is principally their own conservation, and sometimes their delectation only, endeavour to destroy, or subdue one another. And from hence it comes to pass, that where an invader hath no more to fear, than another man's single power; if one plant, sow, build, or possess a convenient seat, others may probably be expected to come prepared with forces united, to dispossess, and deprive him, not only of the fruit of his labour, but also of his life, or liberty. And the invader again is in the like danger of another.

And from this diffidence of one another, there is no way for any man to secure himself, so reasonable, as anticipation; that is, by force, or wiles, to master the persons of all men he can, so long, till he see no other power great enough to endanger him: and this is no more than his own conservation requireth, and is generally allowed. Also because there be some, that taking pleasure in contemplating their own power in the acts of conquest, which they pursue farther than their security requires; if others, that otherwise would be glad to be at ease within modest bounds, should not by invasion increase their power, they would not be able, long time, by standing only on their defence, to subsist. And by consequence, such augmentation of dominion over men being necessary to a man's conservation, it ought to be allowed him.

Again, men have no pleasure, but on the contrary a great deal of grief, in keeping company, where there is no power able to over-awe them all. For every man looketh that his companion should value him, as the same rate he sets upon himself: and upon all signs of contempt, or undervaluing, naturally endeavours, as far as he dares, (which amongst them that have no common power to keep them in quiet, is far enough to make them destroy each other), to extort a greater value from his contemners, by damage; and from others, by the example.

So that in the nature of man, we find three principal causes of quarrel. First, competition; second, diffidence; thirdly, glory.

The first, maketh men invade for gain; the second, for safety; and the third, for reputation. The first use violence, to make themselves masters of other men's persons, wives, children, and cattle; the second, to defend them; the third, for trifles, as a word, a smile, a different opinion, and any other sign of undervalue, either direct in their persons, or by reflection in their kindred, their friends, their nation, their profession, or their name.

Hereby it is manifest, that during the time men live without a common power to keep them all in awe, they are in that condition which is called war; and such a war, as is of every man, against every man. For WAR, consisteth not in battle only, or the act of fighting; but in a tract of time, wherein the will to contend by battle is sufficiently known: and therefore the notion of *time,* is to be considered in the nature of war; as it is in the nature of weather. For as the nature of foul weather, lieth not in a shower or two of rain; but in an inclination thereto of many days together: so the nature of war, consisteth not in actual fighting; but in the known disposition thereto, during all the time there is no assurance to the contrary. All other time is PEACE.

Whatsoever therefore is consequent to a time of war, where every man is enemy to every man; the same is consequent to the time, wherein men live without other security, than what their own strength, and their own invention shall furnish them withal. In such condition, there is no place for industry; because the fruit thereof is uncertain: and consequently no culture of the earth; no navigation, nor use of the commodities that may be imported by sea; no commodious building; no instruments of moving, and removing, such things as require much force; no knowledge of the face of the earth; no account of time; no arts; no letters; no society; and which is worst of all, continual fear, and danger of violent death; and the life of man, solitary, poor, nasty, brutish, and short.

It may seem strange to some man, that has not well weighed these things; that nature should thus dissociate, and render men apt to invade, and destroy one another: and he may therefore, not trusting to this inference, made from the passions, desire perhaps to have the same confirmed by experience. Let him therefore consider with himself, when taking a journey, he arms himself, and seeks to go well accompanied; when going to sleep, he locks his doors; when even in his house he locks his chests; and this when he knows there be laws, and public officers, armed, to revenge all injuries shall be done him; what opinion he has of his fellow-subjects, when he rides armed; of his fellow citizens, when he locks his doors; and of his children, and servants, when he locks his chests. Does he not there as much accuse mankind by his actions, as I do by my words? But neither of us accuse man's nature in it. The desires, and other passions of man, are in themselves no sin. No more are the actions, that proceed from those passions, till they know a law that forbids them: which till laws be made they cannot know: nor can any law be made, till they have agreed upon the person that shall make it.

It may peradventure be thought, there was never such a time, nor condition of war as this; and I believe it was never generally so, over all the world: but there are many places, where they live so now. For the savage people in many places of America, except the government of small families, the concord whereof dependeth on natural lust, have no government at all; and live at this day in that brutish manner, as I said before. Howsoever, it may be perceived what manner of life there would be, where there were no common power to fear, by the manner of life, which men that have formerly lived under a peaceful government, use to degenerate into, in a civil war.

But though there had never been any time, wherein particular men were in a condition of war one against another; yet in all times, kings, and persons of sovereign authority, because of their independency, are in continual jealousies, and in the state and posture of gladiators; having their weapons pointing, and their eyes fixed on one another; that is, their forts, garrisons, and guns upon the frontiers of their kingdoms; and continual spies upon their neighbours; which is a posture of war. But because they uphold thereby, the industry of their subjects; there does not follow from it, that misery, which accompanies the liberty of particular men.

To this war of every man, against every man, this also is consequent; that nothing can be unjust. The notions of right and wrong, justice and injustice have there no place. Where there is no common power, there is no law: where no law, no injustice. Force, and fraud, are in war the two cardinal virtues. Justice, and injustice are none of the faculties neither of the body, nor mind. If they were, they might be in a man that were alone in the world, as well as his senses, and passions. They are qualities, that relate to men in society, not in solitude. It is consequent also to the same condition, that there be no propriety, no dominion, no *mine* and *thine* distinct; but only that to be every man's, that he can get; and for so long, as he can keep it. And thus much for the ill condition, which man by mere nature is actually placed in; though with a possibility to come out of it, consisting partly in the passions, partly in his reason.

The passions that incline men to peace, are fear of death; desire of such things as are necessary to commodious living; and a hope by their industry to obtain them. And reason suggesteth convenient articles of peace, upon which men may be drawn to agreement. These articles, are they, which otherwise are called the Laws of Nature: whereof I shall speak more particularly in the two following chapters.

CHAPTER XIV: OF THE FIRST AND SECOND NATURAL LAWS, AND OF CONTRACTS

The RIGHT OF NATURE, which writers commonly call *jus naturale*, is the liberty each man hath, to use his own power, as he will himself, for the preservation of his own nature; that is to say, of his own life; and consequently, of doing anything, which in his own judgment, and reason, he shall conceive to be the aptest means thereunto.

By LIBERTY, is understood, according to the proper signification of the word, the absence of external impediments: which impediments, may oft take away part of a man's power to do what he would; but cannot hinder him from using the power left him, according as his judgment, and reason shall dictate to him.

A LAW OF NATURE, *lex naturalis,* is a precept or general rule, found out by reason, by which a man is forbidden to do that, which is destructive of his life, or taketh away the means of preserving the same; and to omit that, by which he thinketh it may be best preserved. For though they that speak of this subject, use to confound *jus,* and *lex, right* and *law:* yet they ought to be distinguished; because RIGHT, consisteth in liberty to do, or to forbear; whereas LAW, determineth, and bindeth to one of them: so that law, and right, differ as much, as obligation, and liberty; which in one and the same matter are inconsistent.

And because the condition of man, as hath been declared in the precedent chapter, is a condition of war of every one against every one; in which case every one is governed by his own reason; and there is nothing he can make use of, that may not be a help unto him, in preserving his life against his enemies; it followeth, that in such a condition, every man has a right to every thing; even to one another's body. And therefore, as long as this natural right of every man to every thing endureth, there can be no security to any man, how strong or wise soever he be, of living out the time, which nature ordinarily alloweth men to live. And consequently it is a precept, or general rule of reason, *that every man, ought to endeavour peace, as far as he has hope of obtaining it; and when he cannot obtain it, that he may seek, and use, all helps, and advantages of war.* The first breach of which rule, containeth the first, and fundamental law of nature; which is, *to seek peace, and follow it.* The second, the sum of the right of nature; which is, *by all means we can, to defend ourselves.*

From this fundamental law of nature, by which men are commanded to endeavour peace, is derived this second law; *that a man be willing, when others are so too, as far forth, as for peace, and defence of himself he shall think it necessary, to lay down this right to all things; and be contented with so much liberty against other men, as he would allow other men against himself.* For as long as every man holdeth this right, of doing any thing he liketh; so long are all men in the condition of war. But if other men will not lay down their right, as well as he; then there is no reason for anyone, to divest himself of his: for that were to expose himself to prey, which no man is bound to, rather than to dispose himself to peace. This is that law of the Gospel; *whatsoever you require that others should do to you, that do ye to them.* And that law of all men, *quod tibi fieri non vis, alteri ne feceris.*[1]

To *lay down* a man's *right* to any thing, is to *divest* himself of the *liberty,* of hindering another of the benefit of his own right to the same. For he that renounceth, or passeth away his right, giveth not to any other man a right which he had not before; because there is nothing to which every man had not right by nature: but only standeth out of his way, that he may enjoy his own original right, without hindrance from him; not without hindrance from another. So that the effect which redoundeth to one man, by another man's defect of right, is but so much diminution of impediments to the use of his own right original.

Right is laid aside, either by simply renouncing it; or by transferring it to another. By *simply* RENOUNCING; when he cares not to whom the benefit thereof redoundeth. By TRANSFERRING; when he intendeth the benefit thereof to some certain person, or persons. And when a man hath in either manner abandoned, or granted away his right; then is he said to be OBLIGED, or BOUND, not to hinder those, to whom such right is granted, or abandoned, from the benefit of it: and that he *ought,* and it is his DUTY, not to make void that voluntary act of his own: and that such hindrance is INJUSTICE, and INJURY, as being *sine jure;* [2] the right being before renounced, or transferred. So that *injury,* or *injustice,* in the controversies of the world, is somewhat like to that, which in the disputations of scholars is called *absurdity.* For as it is there called an absurdity, to contradict what one maintained in the beginning: so in the world, it is called injustice, and injury, voluntarily to undo that, which from the beginning he had voluntarily done. The way by which a man either simply renounceth, or transferreth his right, is a declaration, or signification, by some voluntary and sufficient sign, or signs, that he doth so renounce, or transfer; or hath so renounced, or transferred the same, to him that accepteth it. And these signs are either words only, or actions only; or, as it happeneth most often, both words, and actions. And the same are the BONDS, by which men are bound, and obliged: bonds, that have their strength, not from their own nature, for nothing is more easily broken than a man's word, but from fear of some evil consequence upon the rupture.

Whensoever a man transferreth his right, or renounceth it; it is either in consideration of some right reciprocally transferred to himself; or for some

---

[1] [*What you would not have done unto you, do not unto others.*]
[2] [*Without right.*]

other good he hopeth for thereby. For it is a voluntary act: and of the voluntary acts of every man, the object is some *good to himself*. And therefore there be some rights, which no man can be understood by any words, or other signs, to have abandoned, or transferred. As first a man cannot lay down the right of resisting them, that assault him by force, to take away his life; because he cannot be understood to aim thereby, at any good to himself. The same may be said of wounds, and chains, and imprisonment; both because there is no benefit consequent to such patience; as there is to the patience of suffering another to be wounded, or imprisoned: as also because a man cannot tell, when he seeth men proceed against him by violence, whether they intend his death or not. And lastly the motive, and end for which this renouncing, and transferring of right is introduced, is nothing else but the security of a man's person, in his life, and in the means of so preserving life, as not to be weary of it. And therefore if a man by words, or other signs, seem to despoil himself of the end, for which those signs were intended; he is not to be understood as if he meant it, or that it was his will; but that he was ignorant of how such words and actions were to be interpreted.

The mutual transferring of right, is that which men call CONTRACT. . . .

. . . One of the contractors, may deliver the thing contracted for on his part, and leave the other to perform his part at some determinate time after, and in the mean time be trusted; and then the contract on his part, is called PACT, or COVENANT: or both parts may contract now, to perform hereafter: in which cases, he that is to perform in time to come, being trusted, his performance is called *keeping of promise,* or faith; and the failing of performance, if it be voluntary, *violation of faith.*

When the transferring of right, is not mutual: but one of the parties transferreth, in hope to gain thereby friendship, or service from another, or from his friends; or in hope to gain the reputation of charity, or magnanimity; or to deliver his mind from the pain of compassion; or in hope of reward in heaven; this is not contract, but GIFT, FREE-GIFT, GRACE: which words signify one and the same thing. . . .

Words alone, if they be of the time to come, and contain a bare promise, are an insufficient sign of a free gift, and therefore not obligatory. For if they be of the time to come, as *to-morrow I will give,* they are a sign I have not given yet, and consequently that my right is not transferred, but remaineth till I transfer it by some other act. But if the words be of the time present, or past, as, *I have given,* or, *do give to be delivered to-morrow,* then is my to-morrow's right given away to-day; and that by the virtue of the words, though there were no other argument of my will. . . .

If a covenant be made, wherein neither of the parties perform presently, but trust one another; in the condition of mere nature, which is a condition of war of every man against every man, upon any reasonable suspicion, it is void: but if there be a common power set over them both, with right and force sufficient to compel performance, it is not void. For he that performeth first, has no assurance the other will perform after; because the bonds of words are too weak to bridle men's ambition, avarice, anger, and other passions, without the fear of some coercive power; which in the condition of mere nature, where all men are equal, and judges of the justness of their own fears, cannot possibly be supposed. And therefore he which performeth first, does but betray himself to his enemy; contrary to the right, he can never abandon, of defending his life, and means of living.

But in a civil estate, where there is a power set up to constrain those that would otherwise violate their faith, that fear is no more reasonable; and for that cause, he which by the covenant is to perform first, is obliged so to do.

The cause of fear, which maketh such a covenant invalid, must be always something arising after the covenant made; as some new fact, or other sign of the will not to perform: else it cannot make the covenant void. For that which could not hinder a man from promising, ought not to be admitted as a hindrance of performing.

He that transferreth any right, transferreth the means of enjoying it, as far as lieth in his power. As he that selleth land, is understood to transfer the herbage, and whatsoever grows upon it: nor can he that sells a mill turn away the stream that drives it. And they that give to a man the right of government in sovereignty, are understood to give him the right of levying money to maintain soldiers; and of appointing magistrates for the administration of justice.

To make covenants with brute beasts, is impossible; because not understanding our speech, they understand not, nor accept of any translation of right; nor can translate any right to another: and without mutual acceptation, there is no covenant.

To make covenant with God, is impossible, but by mediation of such as God speaketh to, either by revelation supernatural, or by his lieutenants that govern under him, and in his name: for otherwise we know not whether our covenants be accepted, or not. And therefore they that vow anything contrary to any law of nature, vow in vain; as being a thing unjust to pay such vow. And if it be a thing commanded by the law of nature, it is not the vow, but the law that binds them.

The matter, or subject of a covenant, is always something that falleth under deliberation; for to covenant, is an act of the will; that is to say, an act, and the last act of deliberation; and is therefore always understood to be something to come; and which is judged possible for him that covenanteth, to perform.

And therefore, to promise that which is known to be impossible, is no covenant. But if that prove impossible afterwards, which before was thought possible, the covenant is valid, and bindeth, though not to the thing itself, yet to the value; or, if that also be impossible, to the unfeigned endeavour of performing as much as is possible: for to more no man can be obliged.

Men are freed of their covenants two ways; by performing; or by being forgiven. For performance, is the natural end of obligation; and forgiveness, the restitution of liberty; as being a retransferring of that right, in which the obligation consisted.

Covenants entered into by fear, in the condition of mere nature, are obligatory. For example, if I covenant to pay a ransom, or service, for my life, to an enemy; I am bound by it: for it is a contract, wherein one receiveth the benefit of life; the other is to receive money, or service for it; and consequently, where no other law, as in the condition of mere nature, forbiddeth the performance, the covenant is valid. Therefore prisoners of war, if trusted with the payment of their ransom, are obliged to pay it: and if a weaker prince, make a disadvantageous peace with a stronger, for fear; he is bound to keep it; unless, as hath been said before, there ariseth some new, and just cause of fear, to renew the war. And even in commonwealths, if I be forced to redeem myself from a thief by promising him money, I am bound to pay it, till the civil law discharge me. For whatsoever I may lawfully do without obligation, the same I may lawfully covenant to do through fear: and what I lawfully covenant, I cannot lawfully break.

A former covenant, makes void a later. For a man that hath passed away his right to one man to-day, hath it not to pass to-morrow to another: and therefore the later promise passeth no right, but is null.

A covenant not to defend myself from force, by force, is always void. For, as I have showed before, no man can transfer, or lay down his right to save himself from death, wounds, imprisonment, the avoiding whereof is the only end of laying down any right; and therefore the promise of not resisting force, in no covenant transferreth any right; nor is obliging. For though a man may covenant thus, *unless I do so, or so, kill me*; he cannot covenant thus, *unless I do so, or so, I will not resist you, when you come to kill me*. For man by nature chooseth the lesser evil, which is danger of death in resisting; rather than the greater, which is certain and present death in not resisting. And this is granted to be true by all men, in that they lead criminals to execution, and prison, with armed men, notwithstanding that such criminals have consented to the law, by which they are condemned. . . .

The force of words, being, as I have formerly noted, too weak to hold men to the performance of their covenants; there are in man's nature, but two imaginable helps to strengthen it. And those are either a fear of the consequence of breaking their word; or a glory, or pride in appearing not to need to break it. This latter is a generosity too rarely found to be presumed on, especially in the pursuers of wealth, command, or sensual pleasure; which are the greatest part of mankind. The passion to be reckoned upon, is fear; whereof there be two very general objects: one, the power of spirits invisible; the other, the power of those men they shall therein offend. Of these two, though the former be the greater power, yet the fear of the latter is commonly the greater fear. The fear of the former is in every man, his own religion: which hath place in the nature of man before civil society. The latter hath not so; at least not place enough, to keep men to their promises; because in the condition of mere nature, the inequality of power is not discerned, but by the event of battle. So that before the time of civil society, or in the interruption thereof by war, there is nothing can strengthen a covenant of peace agreed on, against the temptations of avarice, ambition, lust, or other strong desire, but the fear of that invisible power, which they every one worship as God; and fear as a revenger of their perfidy. All therefore that can be done between two men not subject to civil power, is to put one another to swear by the God he feareth. . . .

CHAPTER XV: OF OTHER LAWS OF NATURE

From that law of nature, by which we are obliged to transfer to another, such rights, as being retained, hinder the peace of mankind, there followeth a third; which is this, *that men perform their covenants made:* without which, covenants are in vain, and but empty words; and the right of all men to all things remaining, we are still in the condition of war.

And in this law of nature, consisteth the fountain and original of JUSTICE. For where no covenant hath preceded, there hath no right been transferred, and every man has right to every thing; and consequently, no action can be unjust. But when a covenant is made, then to break it is *unjust:* and the definition of INJUSTICE, is no other than *the not performance of covenant.* And whatsoever is not unjust, is *just.*

But because covenants of mutual trust, where there is a fear of not performance on either part, as hath been said in the former chapter, are invalid; though the original of justice be the making of covenants; yet injustice actually there can be none, till the cause of such fear be taken away; which while men are in the natural condition of war, cannot be done. Therefore before the names of just, and unjust can have place, there must be some coercive power, to compel men equally to the performance of their covenants, by the terror of some punishment, greater than the benefit they expect by the breach of their covenant; and to make good that propriety, which by mutual contract men acquire, in recompense of the universal right they abandon: and such power there is none before the erection of a commonwealth. And this is also to be gathered out of the ordinary definition of justice in the Schools: for they say, that *justice is the constant will of giving to every man his own*. And therefore where there is no *own,* that is no propriety, there is no injustice; and where is no coercive power erected, that is, where there is no commonwealth, there is no propriety; all men having right to all things: therefore where there is no commonwealth, there nothing is unjust. So that the nature of justice, consisteth in keeping of valid covenants: but the validity of covenants begins not but with the constitution of a civil power, sufficient to compel men to keep them: and then it is also that propriety begins.

The fool hath said in his heart, there is no such thing as justice; and sometimes also with his tongue; seriously alleging, that every man's conservation, and contentment, being committed to his own care, there could be no reason, why every man might not do what he thought conduced thereunto: and therefore also to make, or not make; keep, or not keep covenants, was not against reason, when it conduced to one's benefit. He does not therein deny, that there be covenants; and that they are sometimes broken, sometimes kept; and that such breach of them may be called injustice, and the observance of them justice: but he questioneth, whether injustice, taking away the fear of God, for the same fool hath said in his heart there is no God, may not sometimes stand with that reason, which dictateth to every man his own good; and particularly then, when it conduceth to such a benefit, as shall put a man in a condition, to neglect not only the dispraise, and revilings, but also the power of other men. The kingdom of God is gotten by violence: but what if it could be gotten by unjust violence? were it against reason so to get it, when it is impossible to receive hurt by it? and if it be not against reason, it is not against justice; or else justice is not to be approved for good. From such reasoning as this, successful wickedness hath obtained the name of virtue: and some that in all other things have disallowed the violation of faith; yet have allowed it, when it is for the getting of a kingdom. And the heathen that believed, that Saturn was deposed by his son Jupiter, believed nevertheless the same Jupiter to be the avenger of injustice: somewhat like to a piece of law in Coke's *Commentaries on Littleton;* where he says, if the right heir of the crown be attainted of treason; yet the crown shall descend to him, and *eo instante* [3] the attainder be void: from which instances a man will be very prone to infer; that when the heir apparent of a kingdom, shall kill him that is in possession, though his father; you may call it injustice, or by what other name you will; yet it can never be against reason, seeing all the voluntary actions of men tend to the benefit of

[3] [*At that moment.*]

themselves; and those actions are most reasonable, that conduce most to their ends. This specious reasoning is nevertheless false.

For the question is not of promises mutual, where there is no security of performance on either side; as when there is no civil power erected over the parties promising; for such promises are no covenants: but either where one of the parties has performed already; or where there is a power to make him perform; there is the question whether it be against reason, that is, against the benefit of the other to perform, or not. And I say it is not against reason. For the manifestation whereof, we are to consider; first, that when a man doth a thing, which notwithstanding any thing can be foreseen, and reckoned on, tendeth to his own destruction, howsoever some accident which he could not expect, arriving may turn it to his benefit; yet such events do not make it reasonably or wisely done. Secondly, that in a condition of war, wherein every man to every man, for want of a common power to keep them all in awe, is an enemy, there is no man who can hope by his own strength, or wit, to defend himself from destruction, without the help of confederates; where every one expects the same defense by the confederation, that any one else does: and therefore he which declares he thinks it reason to deceive those that help him, can in reason expect no other means of safety, than what can be had from his own single power. He therefore that breaketh his covenant, and consequently declareth that he thinks he may with reason do so, cannot be received into any society, that unite themselves for peace and defense, but by the error of them that receive him; nor when he is received, be retained in it, without seeing the danger of their error; which errors a man cannot reasonably reckon upon as the means of his security: and therefore if he be left, or cast out of society, he perisheth; and if he live in society, it is by the errors of other men, which he could not foresee, nor reckon upon; and consequently against the reason of his preservation; and so, as all men that contribute not to his destruction, forbear him only out of ignorance of what is good for themselves.

As for the instance of gaining the secure and perpetual felicity of heaven, by any way; it is frivolous: there being but one way imaginable; and that is not breaking, but keeping of covenant.

And for the other instance of attaining sovereignty by rebellion; it is manifest, that though the event follow, yet because it cannot reasonably be expected, but rather the contrary; and because by gaining it so, others are taught to gain the same in like manner, the attempt thereof is against reason. Justice therefore, that is to say, keeping of covenant, is a rule of reason, by which we are forbidden to do any thing destructive to our life; and consequently a law of nature.

There be some that proceed further; and will not have the law of nature, to be those rules which conduce to the preservation of man's life on earth; but to the attaining of an eternal felicity after death; to which they think the breach of covenant may conduce; and consequently be just and reasonable; such are they that think it a work of merit to kill, or depose, or rebel against, the sovereign power constituted over them by their own consent. But because there is no natural knowledge of man's estate after death; much less of the reward that is then to be given to breach of faith; but only a belief grounded upon other men's saying, that they know it supernaturally, or that they know those, that knew them, that knew others, that knew it supernaturally; breach of faith cannot be called a precept of reason, or nature.

Others, that allow for a law of nature, the keeping of faith, do nevertheless make exception of certain persons; as heretics, and such as use not to perform their covenant to others: and this also is against reason. For if any fault of a man, be sufficient to discharge our covenant made; the same ought in reason to have been sufficient to have hindered the making of it. . . .

As justice dependeth on antecedent covenant; so does GRATITUDE depend on antecedent grace; that is to say, antecedent free gift: and is the fourth law of nature; which may be conceived in this form, *that a man which receiveth benefit from another of mere grace, endeavour that he which giveth it, have no reasonable cause to repent him of his good will.* For no man giveth, but with intention of good to himself; because gift is voluntary; and of all voluntary acts, the object is to every man his own good; of which if men see they shall be frustrated, there will be no beginning of benevolence, or trust; nor consequently of mutual help; nor of reconciliation of one man to another; and therefore they are to remain still in the condition of *war;* which is contrary to the first and fundamental law of nature, which commandeth men to *seek peace.* The breach of this law, is called *ingratitude;* and hath the same relation to grace, that injustice hath to obligation by covenant.

A fifth law of nature, is COMPLAISANCE; that is to say, *that every man strive to accommodate himself to the rest.* For the understanding whereof, we may consider, that there is in men's aptness to society, a diversity of nature, rising from their diversity of affections; not unlike to that we see in stones brought together for building of an edifice. For as that stone which by the asperity, and irregularity of figure, takes more room from others, than itself fills; and for the hardness, cannot be easily made plain, and thereby hindereth the building, is by the builders cast away as unprofitable, and troublesome: so also, a man that by asperity of nature, will strive to retain those things which to himself are superfluous, and to others necessary; and for the stubbornness of his passions, cannot be corrected, is to be left, or cast out of society, as cumbersome thereunto. For seeing every man, not only by right, but also by necessity of nature, is supposed to endeavour all he can, to obtain that which is necessary for his conservation; he that shall oppose himself against it, for things superfluous, is guilty of the war that thereupon is to follow; and therefore doth that, which is contrary to the fundamental law of nature, which commandeth *to seek peace.* The observers of this law, may be called SOCIABLE the Latins call them *commodi;* the contrary, *stubborn, insociable, froward, intractable.*

A sixth law of nature, is this *that upon caution of the future time, a man ought to pardon the offences past of them that repenting, desire it.* For PARDON, is nothing but granting of peace; which though granted to them that persevere in their hostility, be not peace, but fear; yet not granted to them that give caution of the future time, is sign of an aversion to peace; and therefore contrary to the law of nature.

A seventh is, *that in revenges,* that is, retribution of evil for evil, *men look not at the greatness of the evil past, but the greatness of the good to follow.* Whereby we are forbidden to inflict punishment with any other design, than for correction of the offender, or direction of others. For this law is consequent to the next before it, that commandeth pardon, upon security of the future time. Besides, revenge without respect to the example, and profit to come, is a triumph, or glorying in the hurt of another, tending to no end; for the end is always somewhat to come; and glorying to no end, is vainglory, and contrary to reason, and to hurt without reason, tendeth to the introduction of war; which is against the law of nature; and is commonly styled by the name of *cruelty.*

And because all signs of hatred, or contempt, provoke to fight; insomuch as most men choose rather to hazard their life, than not to be revenged; we may in the eighth place, for a law of nature, set down this precept, *that no man by deed, word, countenance, or gesture, declare hatred, or contempt of another.* The breach of which law, is commonly called *contumely.*

The question who is the better man, has no place in the condition of mere nature; where, as has been shewn before, all men are equal. The inequality that now is, has been introduced by the laws civil. I know that Aristotle in the first book of his *Politics,* for a foundation of his doctrine, maketh men by nature, some more worthy to command, meaning the wiser sort, such as he thought himself to be for his philosophy; others to serve, meaning those that had strong bodies, but were not philosophers as he; as if master and servant were not introduced by consent of men, but by difference of wit: which is not only against reason; but also against experience. For there are very few so foolish, that had not rather govern themselves, than be governed by others: nor when the wise in their own conceit, contend by force, with them who distrust their own wisdom, do they always, or often, or almost at any time, get the victory. If nature therefore have made men equal, that equality is to be acknowledged: or if nature have made men unequal; yet because men that think themselves equal, will not enter into conditions of peace, but upon equal terms, such equality must be admitted. And therefore for the ninth law of nature, I put this, *that every man acknowledge another for his equal by nature.* The breach of this precept is *pride.*

On this law, dependeth another, *that at the entrance into conditions of peace, no man require to reserve to himself any right, which he is not content should be reserved to every one of the rest.* As it is necessary for all men that seek peace, to lay down certain rights of nature; that is to say, not to have liberty to do all they list: so is it necessary for man's life, to retain some; as right to govern their own bodies; enjoy air, water, motion, ways to go from place to place; and all things else, without which a man cannot live, or not live well. If in this case, at the making of peace, men require for themselves, that which they would not have to be granted to others, they do contrary to the precedent law, that commandeth the acknowledgment of natural equality, and therefore also against the law of nature. The observers of this law, are those we call *modest,* and the breakers *arrogant* men. The Greeks call the violation of this law πλεονεξία; that is, a desire of more than their share. . . .

And because, though men be never so willing to observe these laws, there may nevertheless arise questions concerning a man's action; first, whether it were done, or not done; secondly, if done, whether against the law, or not against the law; the former whereof, is called a question *of fact;* the latter a question *of right,* therefore unless the parties to the question, covenant mutually to stand to the sentence of another, they are as far from peace as ever. This other to whose sentence they submit is called an ARBITRATOR. And therefore it is of the law of nature, *that they that are at controversy, submit their right to the judgment of an arbitrator.*

And seeing every man is presumed to do all things in order to his own benefit, no man is a fit arbitrator in his own cause; and if he were never so fit; yet equity allowing to each party equal benefit, if one be admitted to be judge, the other is to be admitted also; and so the controversy, that is, the cause of war, remains, against the law of nature.

For the same reason no man in any cause ought to be received for arbitrator, to whom greater profit, or honour, or pleasure apparently ariseth out of the victory of one party, than of the other: for he hath taken, though an unavoidable bribe, yet a bribe; and no man can be obliged to trust him. And thus also the controversy, and the condition of war remaineth, contrary to the law of nature.

And in a controversy of *fact,* the judge being to give more credit to one, than to the other, if there be no other arguments, must give credit to a third; or to a third and fourth; or more: for else the question is undecided, and left to force, contrary to the law of nature.

These are the laws of nature, dictating peace, for a means of the conservation of men in multitudes; and which only concern the doctrine of civil society. There be other things tending to the destruction of particular men; as drunkenness, and all other parts of intemperance; which may therefore also be reckoned amongst those things which the law of nature hath forbidden; but are not necessary to be mentioned, nor are pertinent enough to this place.

And though this may seem too subtle a deduction of the laws of nature, to be taken notice of by all men; whereof the most part are too busy in getting food, and the rest too negligent to understand; yet to leave all men inexcusable, they have been contracted into one easy sum, intelligible even to the meanest capacity; and that is, *Do not that to another, which thou wouldst not have done to thyself;* which sheweth him, that he has no more to do in learning the laws of nature, but, when weighing the actions of other men with his own, they seem too heavy, to put them into the other part of the balance, and his own into their place, that his own passions, and self-love, may add nothing to the weight; and then there is none of these laws of nature that will not appear unto him very reasonable.

The laws of nature oblige *in foro interno;* that is to say, they bind to a desire they should take place: but *in foro externo;* [4] that is, to the putting them in act, not always. For he that should be modest, and tractable, and perform all he promises, in such time, and place, where no man else should do so, should but make himself a prey to others, and procure his own certain ruin, contrary to the ground of all laws of nature, which tend to nature's preservation. And again, he that having sufficient security, that others shall observe the same laws towards him, observes them not himself, seeketh not peace, but war; and consequently the destruction of his nature by violence.

And whatsoever laws bind *in foro interno,* may be broken, not only by a fact contrary to the law, but also by a fact according to it, in case a man think it contrary. For though his action in this case, be according to the law; yet his purpose was against the law; which, where the obligation is *in foro interno,* is a breach.

The laws of nature are immutable and eternal; for injustice, ingratitude, arrogance, pride, iniquity, acception of persons, and the rest, can never be made lawful. For it can never be that war shall preserve life, and peace destroy it.

The same laws, because they oblige only to a desire, and endeavour, I mean

[4] [These phrases refer to the *internal* and *external forum,* or *tribunal.*]

an unfeigned and constant endeavour, are easy to be observed. For in that they require nothing, but endeavour, he that endeavoureth their performance, fulfilleth them, and he that fulfilleth the law, is just.

And the science of them, is the true and only moral philosophy. For moral philosophy is nothing else but the science of what is *good,* and *evil,* in the conversation, and society of mankind. *Good,* and *evil,* are names that signify our appetites, and aversions; which in different tempers, customs, and doctrines of men, are different: and divers men, differ not only in their judgment, on the senses of what is pleasant, and unpleasant to the taste, smell, hearing, touch, and sight; but also of what is conformable, or disagreeable to reason, in the actions of common life. Nay, the same man, in divers times, differs from himself; and one time praiseth, that is, calleth good, what another time he dispraiseth, and calleth evil: from whence arise disputes, controversies, and at last war. And therefore so long as a man is in the condition of mere nature, which is a condition of war, his private appetite is the measure of good, and evil: and consequently all men agree on this, that peace is good, and therefore also the way, or means of peace, which, as I have shewed before, are *justice, gratitude, modesty, equity, mercy,* and the rest of the laws of nature, are good; that is to say; *moral virtues;* and their contrary *vices,* evil. Now the science of virtue and vice, is moral philosophy; and therefore the true doctrine of the laws of nature, is the true moral philosophy. But the writers of moral philosophy, though they acknowledge the same virtues and vices; yet not seeing wherein consisted their goodness; nor that they come to be praised, as the means of peaceable, sociable, and comfortable living, place them in a mediocrity of passions: as if not the cause, but the degree of daring, made fortitude; or not the cause, but the quantity of a gift, made liberality.

These dictates of reason, men used to call by the name of laws, but improperly: for they are but conclusions, or theorems concerning what conduceth to the conservation and defense of themselves; whereas law, properly, is the word of him, that by right hath command over others. But yet if we consider the same theorems, as delivered in the word of God, that by right commandeth all things; then are they properly called laws. . . .

CHAPTER XVIII: OF THE RIGHTS OF SOVEREIGNS BY INSTITUTION

A *commonwealth* is said to be *instituted,* when a *multitude* of men do agree, and *covenant, every one, with every one,* that to whatsoever *man,* or *assembly of men,* shall be given by the major part, the *right* to *present* the person of them all, that is to say, to be their *representative;* every one, as well he that *voted for it,* as he that *voted against it,* shall *authorize* all the actions and judgments, of that man, or assembly of men, in the same manner, as if they were his own, to the end, to live peaceably amongst themselves, and be protected against other men.

From this institution of a commonwealth are derived all the *rights,* and *faculties* of him, or them, on whom sovereign power is conferred by the consent of the people assembled.

First, because they covenant, it is to be understood, they are not obliged by former covenant to anything repugnant hereunto. And consequently they that have already instituted a commonwealth, being thereby bound by covenant, to own the actions, and judgments of one, cannot lawfully make a new covenant, amongst themselves, to be obedient to any other, in any thing whatsoever, without his permission. And therefore, they that are subject to a monarch, cannot without his leave cast off monarchy, and return to the confusion of a disunited multitude; nor transfer their person from him that beareth it, to another man, or other assembly of men: for they are bound, every man to every man, to own, and be reputed author of all, that he that already is their sovereign, shall do, and judge fit to be done: so that any one man dissenting, all the rest should break their covenant made to that man, which is injustice: and they have also every man given the sovereignty to him that beareth their person; and therefore if they depose him, they take from him that which is his own, and so again it is injustice. Besides, if he that attempteth to depose his sovereign, be killed, or punished by him for such attempt, he is author of his own punishment, as being by the institution, author of all his sovereign shall do: and because it is injustice for a man to do anything, for which he may be punished by his own authority, he is also upon that title, unjust. And whereas some men have pretended for their disobedience to their sovereign, a new covenant, made, not with men, but with God; this also is unjust: for there is no covenant with God, but by mediation of somebody that representeth God's person; which none doth but God's lieutenant, who hath the sovereignty under God. But this pretence of covenant with God, is so evident a lie, even in the pretenders' own consciences, that it is not only an act of an unjust, but also of a vile and unmanly disposition.

Secondly, because the right of bearing the person of them all, is given to him they make sovereign, by covenant only of one to another, and not of him to any of them; there can happen no breach of covenant on the part of the sovereign; and consequently none of his subjects, by any pretence of forfeiture, can be freed from his subjection. That he which is made sovereign maketh no covenant with his subjects beforehand, is manifest; because either he must make it with the whole multitude, as one party to the covenant; or he must make a several covenant with every man. With the whole, as one party, it is impossible; because as yet they are not one person: and if he make so many several covenants as there be men, those covenants after he hath the sovereignty are void; because what act soever can be pretended by any one of them for breach thereof, is the act both of himself, and of all the rest, because done in the person, and by the right of every one of them in particular. Besides, if any one, or more of them, pretend a breach of the covenant made by the sovereign at his institution; and others, or one other of his subjects, or himself alone, pretend there was no such breach, there is in this case, no judge to decide the controversy; it returns therefore to the sword again; and every man recovereth the right of protecting himself by his own strength, contrary to the design they had in the institution. It is therefore in vain to grant sovereignty by way of precedent covenant. The opinion that any monarch receiveth his power by covenant, that is to say, on condition, proceedeth from want of understanding this easy truth, that covenants being but words and breath, have no force to oblige, contain, constrain, or protect any man, but what it has from the public sword; that is, from the untied hands of that man, or assembly of men that hath the sovereignty, and whose actions are avouched by them all, and performed by the strength of them all, in him united. But when an assembly of men is made sovereign; then no man imagineth any such covenant to have passed in the institution; for no man is so dull as to say, for example, the people of Rome made a covenant with the Romans, to hold the sovereignty on such or such conditions; which not performed, the Romans might lawfully depose the Roman people. That men see not the reason to be alike in a monarchy, and in a popular government, proceedeth from the ambition of some, that are kinder to the government of an assembly, whereof they may hope to participate, than of monarchy, which they despair to enjoy.

Thirdly, because the major part hath by consenting voices declared a sovereign; he that dissented must now consent with the rest; that is, be contented to avow all the actions he shall do, or else justly be destroyed by the rest. For if he voluntarily entered into the congregation of them that were assembled, he sufficiently declared thereby his will, and therefore tacitly covenanted, to stand to what the major part should ordain: and therefore if he refuse to stand thereto, or make protestation against any of their decrees, he does contrary to his covenant, and therefore unjustly. And whether he be of the congregation, or not; and whether his consent be asked, or not, he must either submit to their decrees, or be left in the condition of war he was in before; wherein he might without injustice be destroyed by any man whatsoever.

Fourthly, because every subject is by this institution author of all the actions, and judgments of the sovereign instituted; it follows, that whatsoever he doth, it can be no injury to any of his subjects; nor ought he to be by any of them accused of injustice. For he that doth anything by authority from another, doth therein no injury to him by whose authority he acteth: but by this institution of a commonwealth, every particular man is author of all the sovereign doth: and consequently he that complaineth of injury from his sovereign, complaineth of that whereof he himself is author; and therefore ought not to accuse any man but himself; no nor himself of injury; because to do injury to one's self, is impossible. It is true that they that have sovereign power may commit iniquity, but not injustice, or injury in the proper signification.

Fifthly, and consequently to that which was said last, no man that hath sovereign power can justly be put to death, or otherwise in any manner by his subjects punished. For seeing every subject is author of the actions of his sovereign; he punisheth another for the actions committed by himself.

And because the end of this institution, is the peace and defense of them all; and whosoever has right to the end, has right to the means; it belongeth of right, to whatsoever man, or assembly that hath the sovereignty, to be judge both of the means of peace and defense, and also of the hindrances, and disturbances of the same; and to do whatsoever he shall think necessary to be done, both beforehand, for the preserving of peace and security, by prevention of discord at home, and hostility from abroad; and, when peace and security are lost, for the recovery of the same. And therefore,

Sixthly, it is annexed to the sovereignty, to be judge of what opinions and doctrines are averse, and what conducing to peace; and consequently, on what occasions, how far, and what men are to be trusted withal, in speaking to multitudes of people; and who shall examine the doctrines of all books before they be published. For the actions of men proceed from their opinions; and in the well-governing of opinions, consisteth the well-governing of men's actions, in order to their peace, and concord. And though in matter of doctrine, nothing ought to be regarded but the truth; yet this is not repugnant to regulating the same by peace. For doctrine repugnant to peace, can no more be true, than peace and concord can be against the law of nature. It is true, that in a commonwealth, whereby the negligence, or unskilfulness of governors, and teachers, false doctrines are by time generally received; the contrary truths may be generally offensive. Yet the most sudden, and rough bursting in of a new truth, that can be, does never break the peace, but only sometimes awake the war. For those men that are so remissly governed, that they dare take up arms to defend, or introduce an opinion, are still in war; and their condition not peace, but only a cessation of arms for fear of one another; and they live, as it were, in the precincts of battle continually. It belongeth therefore to him that hath the sovereign power, to be judge, or constitute all judges of opinions and doctrines, as a thing necessary to peace; thereby to prevent discord and civil war.

Seventhly, is annexed to the sovereignty, the whole power of prescribing the rules, whereby every man may know, what goods he may enjoy, and what actions he may do, without being molested by any of his fellow-subjects; and this is it men call *propriety*. For before constitution of sovereign power, as hath already been shown, all men had right to all things; which necessarily causeth war: and therefore this propriety, being necessary to peace, and depending on sovereign power, is the act of that power, in order to the public peace. These rules of propriety, or *meum* and *tuum*,[5] and of *good, evil, lawful,* and *unlawful* in the actions of subjects, are the civil laws; that is to say, the laws of each commonwealth in particular; though the name of civil law be now restrained to the ancient civil laws of the city of Rome; which being the head of a great part of the world, her laws at that time were in these parts the civil law.

Eighthly, is annexed to the sovereignty, the right of judicature; that is to say, of hearing and deciding all controversies, which may arise concerning law, either civil, or natural; or concerning fact. For without the decision of controversies, there is no protection of one subject, against the injuries of another; the laws concerning *meum* and *tuum* are in vain; and to every man remaineth, from the natural and necessary appetite of his own conservation, the right of protecting himself by his private strength, which is the condition of war, and contrary to the end for which every commonwealth is instituted.

Ninthly, is annexed to the sovereignty, the right of making war and peace with other nations, and commonwealths; that is to say, of judging when it is for the public good, and how great forces are to be assembled, armed, and paid for that end; and to levy money upon the subjects, to defray the expenses thereof. For the power by which the people are to be defended, consisteth in their armies; and the strength of an army, in the union of their strength under one command; which command the sovereign instituted, therefore hath; because the command of the *militia,* without other institution, maketh him that hath it sovereign. And therefore whosoever is made general of an army, he that hath the sovereign power is always generalissimo.

Tenthly, is annexed to the sovereignty, the choosing of all counsellors, ministers, magistrates, and officers, both in peace and war. For seeing the sovereign is charged with the end, which is the common peace and defense, he is understood to have power to use such means, as he shall think most fit for his discharge.

Eleventhly, to the sovereign is committed the power of rewarding with

[5] [*Mine* and *yours.*]

riches, or honour, and of punishing with corporal or pecuniary punishment, or with ignominy, every subject according to the law he hath formerly made; or if there be no law made, according as he shall judge most to conduce to the encouraging of men to serve the commonwealth, or deterring of them from doing disservice to the same.

Lastly, considering what value men are naturally apt to set upon themselves; what respect they look for from others; and how little they value other men; from whence continually arise amongst them, emulation, quarrels, factions, and at last war, to the destroying of one another, and diminution of their strength against a common enemy; it is necessary that there be laws of honour, and a public rate of the worth of such men as have deserved, or are able to deserve well of the commonwealth; and that there be force in the hands of some or other, to put those laws in execution. But it hath already been shown, that not only the whole *militia,* or forces of the commonwealth; but also the judicature of all controversies, is annexed to the sovereignty. To the sovereign therefore it belongeth also to give titles of honour; and to appoint what order of place, and dignity, each man shall hold; and what signs of respect, in public or private meetings, they shall give to one another.

These are the rights, which make the essence of sovereignty; and which are the marks, whereby a man may discern in what man, or assembly of men, the sovereign power is placed, and resideth. For these are incommunicable, and inseparable. The power to coin money; to dispose of the estate and persons of infant heirs; to have præemption in markets; and all other statute prerogatives, may be transferred by the sovereign; and yet the power to protect his subjects be retained. But if he transfer the *militia,* he retains the judicature in vain, for want of execution of the laws: or if he grant away the power of raising money; the *militia* is in vain; or if he give away the government of doctrines, men will be frighted into rebellion with the fear of spirits. And so if we consider any one of the said rights, we shall presently see, that the holding of all the rest will produce no effect, in the conservation of peace and justice, the end for which all commonwealths are instituted. And this division is it, whereof it is said, a *kingdom divided in itself cannot stand:* for unless this division precede, division into opposite armies can never happen. If there had not first been an opinion received of the greatest part of England, that these powers were divided between the King, and the Lords, and the House of Commons, the people had never been divided and fallen into this civil war; first between those that disagreed in politics; and after between the dissenters about the liberty of religion; which have so instructed men in this point of sovereign right, and there be few now in England that do not see, that these rights are inseparable, and will be so generally acknowledged at the next return of peace; and so continue, till their miseries are forgotten; and no longer, except the vulgar be better taught than they have hitherto been.

And because they are essential and inseparable rights, it follows necessarily, that in whatsoever words any of them seem to be granted away, yet if the sovereign power itself be not in direct terms renounced, and the name of sovereign no more given by the grantees to him that grants them, the grant is void: for when he has granted all he can, if we grant back the sovereignty, all is restored, as inseparably annexed thereunto.

This great authority being indivisible, and inseparably annexed to the sovereignty, there is little ground for the opinion of them, that say of sovereign kings, though they be *singulis majores,* of greater power than every one of their subjects, yet they be *universis minores,* of less power than them all together. For if by *all together,* they mean not the collective body as one person, then *all together,* and *every one,* signify the same; and the speech is absurd. But if by *all together,* they understand them as one person, which person the sovereign bears, then the power of all together, is the same with the sovereign's power; and so again the speech is absurd: which absurdity they see well enough, when the sovereignty is in an assembly of the people; but in a monarch they see it not; and yet the power of sovereignty is the same in whomsoever it be placed.

And as the power, so also the honour of the sovereign, ought to be greater, than that of any, or all the subjects. For in the sovereignty is the fountain of honour. The dignities of lord, earl, duke, and prince are his creatures. As in the presence of the master, the servants are equal, and without any honour at all; so are the subjects, in the presence of the sovereign. And though they shine some more, some less, when they are out of his sight; yet in his presence, they shine no more than the stars in the presence of the sun.

But a man may here object, that the condition of subjects is very miserable; as being obnoxious to the lusts, and other irregular passions of him, or them that have so unlimited a power in their hands. And commonly they that live under a monarch, think it the fault of monarchy; and they that live under the government of democracy, or other sovereign assembly, attribute all the inconvenience to that form of commonwealth; whereas the power in all forms, if they be perfect enough to protect them, is the same: not considering that the state of man can never be without some incommodity or other; and that the greatest, that in any form of government can possibly happen to the people in general, is scarce sensible, in respect to the miseries, and horrible calamities, that accompany a civil war, or that dissolute condition of masterless men, without subjection to laws, and a coercive power to tie their hands from rapine and revenge: nor considering that the greatest pressure of sovereign governors, proceedeth not from any delight, or profit they can expect in the damage or weakening of their subjects, in whose vigour consisteth their own strength and glory; but in the restiveness of themselves, that unwillingly contributing to their own defense, make it necessary for their governors to draw from them what they can in time of peace, that they may have means on any emergent occasion, or sudden need, to resist, or take advantage on their enemies. For all men are by nature provided of notable multiplying glasses, that is their passions and self-love, through which, every little payment appeareth a great grievance; but are destitute of those prospective glasses, namely moral and civil science, to see afar off the miseries that hang over them, and cannot without such payment be avoided. . . .

CHAPTER XXI: OF THE LIBERTY OF SUBJECTS

Liberty, or freedom, signifieth, properly, the absence of opposition; by opposition, I mean external impediments of motion; and may be applied no less to irrational, and inanimate creatures, than to rational. For whatsoever is so tied, or environed, as it cannot move but within a certain space, which space is determined by the opposition of some external body, we say it hath not liberty to go further. And so of all living creatures, whilst they are imprisoned, or restrained, with walls, or chains; and of the water whilst it is kept in by banks, or vessels, that otherwise would spread itself into a larger space, we use to say, they are not at liberty, to move in such manner, as without those external impediments they would. But when the impediment of motion, is in the constitution of the thing itself, we use not to say; it wants the liberty; but the power to move; as when a stone lieth still, or a man is fastened to his bed by sickness.

And according to this proper, and generally received meaning of the word, a FREEMAN, *is he, that in those things, which by his strength and wit he is able to do, is not hindered to do what he has a will to.* But when the words *free,* and *liberty,* are applied to any thing but bodies, they are abused; for that which is not subject to motion is not subject to impediment: and therefore, when it is said, for example, the way is free, no liberty of the way is signified, but of those that walk in it without stop. And when we say a gift is free, there is not meant any liberty of the gift, but of the giver, that was not bound by any law or covenant to give it. So when we *speak freely,* it is not the liberty of voice, or pronunciation, but of the man, whom no law hath obliged to speak otherwise than he did. Lastly, from the use of the word *free-will,* no liberty can be inferred of the will, desire, or inclination, but the liberty of the man; which consisteth in this, that he finds no stop, in doing what he has the will, desire, or inclination to do.

Fear and liberty are consistent; as when a man throweth his goods into the sea for *fear* the ship should sink, he doth it nevertheless very willingly, and may refuse to do it if he will; it is therefore the action of one that was *free:* so a man sometimes pays his debt, only for *fear* of imprisonment, which because nobody hindered him from detaining, was the action of a man at *liberty.* And generally all actions which men do in commonwealths, for *fear* of the law, are actions, which the doers had *liberty* to omit.

Liberty, and *necessity* are consistent: as in the water, that hath not only *liberty,* but a *necessity* of descending by the channel; so likewise in the actions which men voluntarily do: which, because they proceed from their will, proceed from *liberty;* and yet, because every act of man's will, and every desire, and inclination proceedeth from some cause, and that from another cause, in a continual chain, whose first link is in the hand of God the first of all causes, proceed from *necessity.* So that to him that could see the connexion of those causes, the *necessity* of all men's voluntary actions, would appear manifest. And therefore God, that seeth, and disposeth all things, seeth also that the liberty of man in doing what he will, is accompanied with the *necessity* of doing that which God will, and no more, nor less. For though men may do many things, which God does not command, nor is therefore author of them; yet they can have no passion, nor appetite to anything, of which appetite God's will is not the cause. And did not his will assure the *necessity* of man's will, and consequently of all that on man's will dependeth, the *liberty* of men would be a contradiction, and impediment to the omnipotence and *liberty* of God. And this shall suffice, as to the matter in hand, of that natural *liberty,* which only is properly called *liberty.*

But as men, for the attaining of peace, and conservation of themselves thereby, have made an artificial man, which we call a commonwealth; so also have they made artificial chains, called *civil laws,* which they themselves, by mutual covenants, have fastened at one end, to the lips of that man, or assembly, to whom they have given the sovereign power; and at the other end to their own ears. These bonds, in their own nature but weak, may nevertheless be made to hold, by the danger, though not by the difficulty of breaking them.

In relation to these bonds only it is, that I am to speak now, of the *liberty* of *subjects.* For seeing there is no commonwealth in the world, wherein there be rules enough set down, for the regulating of all the actions, and words of men; as being a thing impossible: it followeth necessarily, that in all kinds of actions by the laws praetermitted, men have the liberty, of doing what their own reasons shall suggest, for the most profitable to themselves. For if we take liberty in the proper sense, for corporal liberty; that is to say, freedom from chains and prison; it were very absurd for men to clamour as they do, for the liberty they so manifestly enjoy. Again, if we take liberty, for an exemption from laws, it is no less absurd, for men to demand as they do, that liberty, by which all other men may be masters of their lives. And yet, as absurd as it is, this is it they demand; not knowing that the laws are of no power to protect them, without a sword in the hands of a man, or men, to cause those laws to be put in execution. The liberty of a subject, lieth therefore only in those things, which in regulating their actions, the sovereign hath praetermitted: such as is the liberty to buy, and sell, and otherwise contract with one another; to choose their own abode, their own diet, their own trade of life, and institute their children as they themselves think fit; and the like.

Nevertheless we are not to understand, that by such liberty, the sovereign power of life and death, is either abolished, or limited. For it has been already shown, that nothing the sovereign representative can do to a subject, on what pretence soever, can properly be called injustice, or injury; because every subject is author of every act the sovereign doth; so that he never wanteth right to any thing, otherwise, than as he himself is the subject of God, and bound thereby to observe the laws of nature. And therefore it may, and doth often happen in commonwealths, that a subject may be put to death, by the command of the sovereign power; and yet neither do the other wrong; as when Jephtha caused his daughter to be sacrificed: in which, and the like cases, he that so dieth, had liberty to do the action, for which he is nevertheless, without injury put to death. And the same holdeth also in a sovereign prince, that putteth to death an innocent subject. For though the action be against the law of nature, as being contrary to equity, as was the killing of Uriah, by David; yet it was not an injury to Uriah, but to God. Not to Uriah, because the right to do what he pleased was given him by Uriah himself: and yet to God, because David was God's subject, and prohibited all iniquity by the law of nature. . . .

The liberty, whereof there is so frequent and honourable mention, in the histories, and philosophy of the ancient Greeks, and Romans, and in the writings, and discourse of those that from them have received all their learning in the politics, is not the liberty of particular men; but the liberty of the commonwealth: which is the same with that which every man then should have, if there were no civil laws, nor commonwealth at all. And the effects of it also be the same. For as amongst masterless men, there is perpetual war, of every man against his neighbor; no inheritance, to transmit to the son, nor to expect from the father; no propriety of goods, or lands; no security; but a full and absolute liberty in every particular man: so in states, and commonwealths not dependent on one another, every commonwealth, not every man, has an absolute liberty, to do what it shall judge, that is to say, what that man, or assembly that representeth it, shall judge most conducing to their benefit. But withal, they live in the condition of a perpetual war, and upon the confines of battle, with their frontiers armed, and cannons planted against their neighbors round about. The Athenians, and Romans were free; that is, free commonwealths: not that any particular men had the liberty to resist their own representative; but that their representative had the liberty to resist, or invade other people. There is written on the turrets of the city of Lucca in great characters at this day, the word LIBERTAS; yet no man can thence infer, that a particular man has more liberty, or immunity from the service of the commonwealth there, than in Constantinople. Whether a commonwealth be monarchical, or popular, the freedom is still the same.

But it is an easy thing, for men to be deceived, by the specious name of liberty; and for want of judgment to distinguish, mistake that for their private inheritance, and birth-right, which is the right of the public only. And when the same error is confirmed by the authority of men in reputation for their writings on this subject, it is no wonder if it produce sedition, and change of government. In these western parts of the world, we are made to receive our opinions concerning the institution, and rights of commonwealths, from Aristotle, Cicero, and other men, Greeks and Romans, that living under popular states, derived those rights, not from the principles of nature, but transcribed them into their books, out of the practice of their own common-wealths, which were popular; as the grammarians describe the rules of language, out of the practice of the time; or the rules of poetry, out of the poems of Homer and Virgil. And because the Athenians were taught, to keep them from desire of changing their government, that they were freemen, and all that lived under monarchy were slaves; therefore Aristotle puts it down in his *Politics, (lib. 6. cap. ii.) In democracy,* LIBERTY *is to be supposed: for it is commonly held, that no man is* FREE *in any other government.* And as Aristotle; so Cicero, and other writers have grounded their civil doctrine, on the opinions of the Romans, who were taught to hate monarchy, at first, by them that having deposed their sovereign; shared amongst them the sovereignty of Rome; and afterwards by their successors. And by reading of these Greek, and Latin authors, men from their childhood have gotten a habit, under a false show of liberty, of favouring tumults, and of licentious controlling the actions of their sovereigns, and again of controlling those controllers; with the effusion of so much blood, as I think I may truly say, there was never any thing so dearly bought, as these western parts have bought the learning of the Greek and Latin tongues.

To come now to the particulars of the true liberty of a subject; that is to say, what are the things, which though commanded by the sovereign, he may nevertheless, without injustice, refuse to do; we are to consider, what rights we pass away, when we make a commonwealth; or, which is all one, what liberty we deny ourselves, by owning all the actions, without exception, of the man, or assembly, we make our sovereign. For in the act of our *submission*, consisteth both our *obligation*, and our *liberty*; which must therefore be inferred by arguments taken from thence; there being no obligation on any man, which ariseth not from some act of his own; for all men equally, are by nature free. And because such arguments, must either be drawn from the express words, *I authorize all his actions*, or from the intention of him that submitteth himself to his power, which intention is to be understood by the end for which he so submitteth; the obligation, and liberty of the subject, is to be derived, either from those words, or others equivalent; or else from the end of the institution of sovereignty, namely, the peace of the subjects within themselves, and their defense against a common enemy.

First therefore, seeing sovereignty by institution, is by covenant of every one to every one; and sovereignty by acquisition, by covenants of the vanquished to the victor, or child to the parent; it is manifest, that every subject has liberty in all those things, the right whereof cannot by covenant be transferred. I have shewn before in the 14th chapter, that covenants, not to defend a man's own body, are void. Therefore,

If the sovereign command a man, though justly condemned, to kill, wound, or maim himself; or not to resist those that assault him; or to abstain from the use of food, air, medicine, or any other thing, without which he cannot live; yet hath that man the liberty to disobey.

If a man be interrogated by the sovereign, or his authority, concerning a crime done by himself, he is not bound, without assurance of pardon, to confess it; because no man . . . can be obliged by covenant to accuse himself.

Again, the consent of a subject to sovereign power, is contained in these words, *I authorize, or take upon me, all his actions;* in which there is no restriction at all, of his own former natural liberty: for by allowing him to *kill* me, I am not bound to kill myself when he commands me. It is one thing to say, *kill me, or my fellow, if you please;* another thing to say, *I will kill myself, or my fellow.* It followeth therefore, that

No man is bound by the words themselves, either to kill himself, or any other man; and consequently, that the obligation a man may sometimes have, upon the command of the sovereign to execute any dangerous, or dishonourable office, dependeth not on the words of our submission; but on the intention, which is to be understood by the end thereof. When therefore our refusal to obey, frustrates the end for which the sovereignty was ordained; then there is no liberty to refuse: otherwise there is.

Upon this ground, a man that is commanded as a soldier to fight against the enemy, though his sovereign have right enough to punish his refusal with death, may nevertheless in many cases refuse, without injustice; as when he substituteth a sufficient soldier in his place: for in this case he deserteth not the service of the commonwealth. And there is allowance to be made for natural timorousness; not only to women, of whom no such dangerous duty is expected, but also to men of feminine courage. When armies fight, there is on one side, or both, a running away; yet when they do it not out of treachery, but fear, they are not esteemed to do it unjustly, but dishonourably. For the same reason, to avoid battle, is not injustice, but cowardice. But he that inrolleth himself a soldier, or taketh imprest money, taketh away the excuse of a timorous nature; and is obliged, not only to go to the battle, but also not to run from it, without his captain's leave. And when the defense of the commonwealth, required at once the help of all that are able to bear arms, every one is obliged; because otherwise the institution of the commonwealth, which they have not the purpose, or courage to preserve, was in vain.

To resist the sword of the commonwealth, in defense of another man, guilty, or innocent, no man hath liberty; because such liberty, takes away from the sovereign, the means of protecting us; and is therefore destructive of the very essence of government. But in case a great many men together, have already resisted the sovereign power unjustly, or committed some capital crime, for which every one of them expecteth death, whether have they not the liberty then to join together, and assist, and defend one another? Certainly they have: for they but defend their lives, which the guilty man may as well do, as the innocent. There was indeed injustice in the first breach of their duty; their bearing of arms subsequent to it, though it be to maintain what they have done, is no new unjust act. And if it be only to defend their persons, it is not unjust at all. But the offer of pardon taketh from them, to whom it is offered, the plea of self-defense, and maketh their perseverance in assisting, or defending the rest, unlawful.

As for other liberties, they depend on the silence of the law. In cases where the sovereign has prescribed no rule, there the subject hath the liberty to do, or forbear, according to his own discretion. And therefore such liberty is in some places more, and in some less; and in some times more, in other times less, according as they that have the sovereignty shall think most convenient. As for example, there was a time, when in England a man might enter into his own land, and dispossess such as wrongfully possessed it, by force. But in after times, that liberty of forcible entry, was taken away by a statute made, by the king, in parliament. And in some places of the world, men have the liberty of many wives: in other places, such liberty is not allowed.

If a subject have a controversy with his sovereign, of debt, or of right of possession of lands or goods, or concerning any service required at his hands, or concerning any penalty, corporal, or pecuniary, grounded on a precedent law; he hath the same liberty to sue for his right, as if it were against a subject; and before such judges, as are appointed by the sovereign. For seeing the sovereign demandeth by force of a former law, and not by virtue of his power; he declareth thereby, that he requireth no more, than shall appear to be due by that law. The suit therefore is not contrary to the will of the sovereign; and consequently the subject hath the liberty to demand the hearing of his cause; and sentence, according to that law. But if he demand, or take anything by pretence of his power; there lieth, in that case, no action of law; for all that is done by him in virtue of his power, is done by the authority of every subject, and consequently he that brings an action against the sovereign, brings it against himself.

If a monarch, or sovereign assembly, grant a liberty to all, or any of his subjects, which grant standing, he is disabled to provide for their safety, the grant is void; unless he directly renounce, or transfer the sovereignty to another. For in that he might openly, if it had been his will, and in plain terms, have renounced, or transferred it, and did not; it is to be understood it was not his will, but that the grant proceeded from ignorance of the repugnancy between such a liberty and the sovereign power; and therefore the sovereignty is still retained; and consequently all those powers, which are necessary to the exercising thereof; such as are the power of war, and peace, of judicature, of appointing officers, and councillors, of levying money, and the rest named in the 18th chapter.

The obligation of subjects to the sovereign, is understood to last as long, and no longer, than the power lasteth, by which he is able to protect them. For the right men have by nature to protect themselves, when none else can protect them, can by no covenant be relinquished. The sovereignty is the soul of the commonwealth; which once departed from the body, the members do no more receive their motion from it. The end of obedience is protection; which, wheresoever a man seeth it, either in his own, or in another's sword, nature applieth his obedience to it, and his endeavour to maintain it. And though sovereignty, in the intention of them that make it, be immortal; yet it is in its own nature, not only subject to violent death, by foreign war; but also through the ignorance, and passions of men, it hath in it, from the very institution, many seeds of a natural mortality, by intestine discord.

If a subject be taken prisoner in war; or his person or his means of life be within the guards of the enemy, and hath his life and corporal liberty given him, on condition to be subject to the victor, he hath liberty to accept the condition; and having accepted it, is the subject of him that took him; because he had no other way to preserve himself. The case is the same, if he be detained on the same terms, in a foreign country. But if a man be held in prison, or bonds, or is not trusted with the liberty of his body; he cannot be understood to be bound by covenant to subjection; and therefore may, if he can, make his escape by any means whatsoever.

If a monarch shall relinquish the sovereignty, both for himself, and his heirs; his subjects return to the absolute liberty of nature; because, though nature may declare who are his sons, and who are the nearest of his kin; yet it dependeth on his own will, as hath been said in the precedent chapter, who shall be his heir. If therefore he will have no heir, there is no sovereignty, nor subjection. The case is the same, if he die without known kindred, and without declaration of his heir. For then there can no heir be known, and consequently no subjection be due.

If the sovereign banish his subject; during the banishment, he is not subject. But he that is sent on a message, or hath leave to travel, is still subject; but it is, by contract between sovereigns, not by virtue of the covenant of subjection. For whosoever entereth into another's dominion, is subject to all the laws thereof; unless he have a privilege of the amity of the sovereigns, or by special licence.

If a monarch subdued by war, render himself subject to the victor; his subjects are delivered from their former obligation, and become obliged to the victor. If he be held prisoner, or have not the liberty of his own body; he is not understood to have given away the right of sovereignty; and therefore his subjects are obliged to yield obedience to the magistrates formerly placed, governing not in their own name, but in his. For, his right remaining, the question is only of the administration; that is to say, of the magistrates and officers; which, if he have not means to name, he is supposed to approve those, which he himself had formerly appointed.

JAMES HARRINGTON

JAMES HARRINGTON (1611–77), an English political writer, is important for his work *The Commonwealth of Oceana* (1656), a Utopian treatise obviously dealing with the problems of contemporary England. Although Harrington supported a republican form of government under aristocratic auspices, he was personally loyal to Charles I during his captivity and until his execution. His book is addressed to Oliver Cromwell; its Utopian form was adopted, perhaps, in an attempt to avoid the censorship.

Harrington's analysis of political events introduced the idea that the form of government possible for a country depends upon the distribution of property, especially real estate; hence government requires the coincidence of economic and political powers. Harrington's ideas were not as influential during the Puritan Revolution as they became during and after the American Revolution. The practical devices which he suggested, such as a written constitution, the use of elections by ballot, and the separation of powers, were all incorporated into the structure of American government. The French Revolution, at least in its first phase, came under his influence also; and in England, by the nineteenth century, democratic reformers had succeeded in getting some of his practical ideas established.

Harrington was one of the most characteristic of those who used classic models as instruments for the criticism of contemporary society. He admired Hobbes but spent most of his time criticizing from the point of view of a social economist that thinker's narrowly legalistic approach. He looked up to Machiavelli as the very image among modern writers of that "ancient prudence" which governed for the common good, and it was this ideal he hoped to restore.

THE COMMONWEALTH OF OCEANA

. . . GOVERNMENT (to define it *de jure,* or according to ancient prudence) is an art whereby a civil society of men is instituted and preserved upon the foundation of common right or interest; or, to follow Aristotle and Livy, it is the empire of laws, and not of men.

And government (to define it *de facto,* or according to modern prudence) is an art whereby some man, or some few men, subject a city or a nation, and rule it according to his or their private interest; which, because the laws in such cases are made according to the interest of a man, or of some families, may be said to be the empire of men, and not of laws.

The former kind is that which Machiavel (whose books are neglected) is the only politician that has gone about to retrieve; and that Leviathan (who would have his book imposed upon the universities) goes about to destroy. For "it is," says he, "another error of Aristotle's politics that in a well-ordered commonwealth not men should govern, but the laws. What man that has his natural senses, though he can neither write nor read, does not find himself governed by them he fears, and believes can kill or hurt him when he obeys not? Or, who believes that the law can hurt him, which is but words and paper, without the hands and swords of men?" I confess that the magistrate upon his bench is that to the law which a gunner upon his platform is to his cannon. Nevertheless, I should not dare to argue with a man of any ingenuity after this manner. A whole army, though they can neither write nor read, are not afraid of a platform, which they know is but earth or stone; nor of a cannon, which, without a hand to give fire to it, is but cold iron; therefore a whole army is afraid of one man. But of this kind is the ratiocination of Leviathan, as I shall show in divers places that come in my way, throughout his whole politics, or worse; as where he says, "Of Aristotle and of Cicero, of the Greeks, and of the Romans, who lived under popular States, that they derived those rights not from the principles of Nature, but transcribed them into their books out of the practice of their own commonwealths, as grammarians describe the rules of language out of poets." Which is as if a man should tell famous Harvey that he transcribed his circulation of the blood not out of the principles of Nature, but out of the anatomy of this or that body. . . .

Government, according to the ancients, and their learned disciple Machiavel, the only politician of later ages, is of three kinds: the government of one man, or of the better sort, or of the whole people; which, by their more learned names, are called monarchy, aristocracy, and democracy. These they hold, through their proneness to degenerate, to be all evil. For whereas they that govern should govern according to reason, if they govern according to passion they do that which they should not do. Wherefore, as reason and passion are two things, so government by reason is one thing, and the corruption of government by passion is another thing, but not always another government: as a body that is alive is one thing, and a body that is dead is another thing, but not always another creature, though the corruption of one comes at length to be the generation of another. The corruption then of monarchy is called tyranny; that of aristocracy, oligarchy; and that of democracy, anarchy. But legislators, having found these three governments at the best to be naught, have invented another, consisting of a mixture of them all, which only is good. This is the doctrine of the ancients.

But Leviathan is positive that they are all deceived, and that there is no other government in Nature than one of the three; as also that the flesh of them cannot stink, the names of their corruptions being but the names of men's fancies, which will be understood when we are shown which of them was *Senatus Populusque Romanus*.[1]

To go my own way, and yet to follow the ancients, the principles of government are twofold: internal, or the goods of the mind; and external, or the goods of fortune. The goods of the mind are natural or acquired virtues, as wisdom, prudence, and courage, &c. The goods of fortune are riches. There be goods also of the body, as health, beauty, strength; but these are not to be brought into account upon this score, because if a man or an army acquires victory or empire, it is more from their discipline, arms, and courage than from their natural health, beauty, or strength, in regard that a people conquered may have more of natural strength, beauty and health, and yet find little remedy. The principles of government then are in the goods of the mind, or in the goods of fortune. To the goods of the mind answers authority; to the goods of fortune, power or empire. Wherefore Leviathan, though he be right where he says that "riches are power," is mistaken where he says that "prudence, or the reputation of prudence, is power"; for the learning or prudence of a man is no more power than the learning or prudence of a book or author, which is properly authority. A learned writer may have authority though he has no power; and a foolish magistrate may have power, though he

---

1 [*The Senate and the Roman People*. This formula (often abbreviated as SPQR) was used to express the ultimate source of Roman authority.]

has otherwise no esteem or authority. The difference of these two is observed by Livy in Evander, of whom he says that he governed rather by the authority of others than by his own power.

To begin with riches, in regard that men are hung upon these, not of choice as upon the other, but of necessity and by the teeth; forasmuch as he who wants bread is his servant that will feed him, if a man thus feeds a whole people, they are under his empire.

Empire is of two kinds, domestic and national, or foreign and provincial. Domestic empire is founded upon dominion.

Dominion is property, real or personal; that is to say, in lands, or in money and goods.

Lands, or the parts and parcels of a territory, are held by the proprietor or proprietors, lord or lords of it, in some proportion; and such (except it be in a city that has little or no land, and whose revenue is in trade) as is the proportion or balance of dominion or property in land, such is the nature of the empire.

If one man be sole landlord of a territory, or overbalance the people, for example, three parts in four, he is Grand Seignior; for so the Turk is called from his property, and his empire is absolute monarchy.

If the few or a nobility, or a nobility with the clergy, be landlords, or overbalance the people to the like proportion, it makes the Gothic balance (to be shown at large in the second part of this discourse), and the empire is mixed monarchy, as that of Spain, Poland, and late of Oceana.

And if the whole people be landlords, or hold the lands so divided among them that no one man, or number of men, within the compass of the few or aristocracy, overbalance them, the empire (without the interposition of force) is a commonwealth.

If force be interposed in any of these three cases, it must either frame the government to the foundation, or the foundation to the government; or holding the government not according to the balance, it is not natural, but violent; and therefore if it be at the devotion of a prince, it is tyranny; if at the devotion of the few, oligarchy; or if in the power of the people, anarchy. Each of which confusions, the balance standing otherwise, is but of short continuance, because against the nature of the balance, which, not destroyed, destroys that which opposes it.

But there be certain other confusions, which, being rooted in the balance, are of longer continuance, and of worse consequence; as, first, where a nobility holds half the property, or about that proportion, and the people the other half; in which case, without altering the balance there is no remedy but the one must eat out the other, as the people did the nobility in Athens, and the nobility the people in Rome. Secondly, when a prince holds about half the dominion, and the people the other half (which was the case of the Roman emperors, planted partly upon their military colonies, and partly upon the senate and the people), the government becomes a very shambles, both of the princes and the people. Somewhat of this nature are certain governments at this day, which are said to subsist by confusion. In this case, to fix the balance, is to entail misery; but in the three former, not to fix it, is to lose the government. Wherefore it being unlawful in Turkey that any should possess land but the Grand Seignior, the balance is fixed by the law, and that empire firm. Nor, though the kings often sell, was the throne of Oceana known to shake, until the statute of alienations broke the pillars, by giving way to the nobility to sell their estates. While Lacedemon held to the division of land made by Lycurgus, it was immovable; but, breaking that, could stand no longer. This kind of law fixing the balance in lands is called Agrarian, and was first introduced by God himself, who divided the land of Canaan to His people by lots, and is of such virtue, that wherever it has held that government has not altered, except by consent; as in that unparalleled example of the people of Israel, when being in liberty they would needs choose a king. But without an Agrarian law, government, whether monarchical, aristocratical, or popular, has no long lease.

As for dominion, personal or in money, it may now and then stir up a Melius or a Manlius, which, if the commonwealth be not provided with some kind of dictatorian power, may be dangerous, though it has been seldom or never successful; because to property producing empire, it is required that it should have some certain root or foothold, which, except in land, it cannot have, being otherwise as it were upon the wing.

Nevertheless, in such cities as subsist mostly by trade, and have little or no land, as Holland and Genoa, the balance of treasure may be equal to that of land in the cases mentioned.

But Leviathan, though he seems to skew at antiquity, following his furious master Carneades, has caught hold of the public sword, to which he reduces all manner and matter of government; as, where he affirms this opinion [that any monarch receives his power by covenant, that is to say, upon conditions] "to proceed from the not understanding this easy truth, that covenants being but words and breath, have no power to oblige, contain, constrain, or protect any man, but what they have from the public sword." But as he said of the law, that without this sword it is but paper, so he might have thought of this sword, that without a hand it is but cold iron. The hand which holds this sword is the militia of a nation; and the militia of a nation is either an army in the field, or ready for the field upon occasion. But an army is a beast that has a great belly, and must be fed: wherefore this will come to what pastures you have, and what pastures you have will come to the balance of property, without which the public sword is but a name or mere spitfrog. Wherefore, to set that which Leviathan says of arms and of contracts a little straighter, he that can graze this beast with the great belly, as the Turk does his Timariots, may well deride him that imagines he received his power by covenant, or is obliged to any such toy: it being in this case only that covenants are but words and breath. But if the property of the nobility, stocked with their tenants and retainers, be the pasture of that beast, the ox knows his master's crib; and it is impossible for a king in such a constitution to reign otherwise than by covenant; or if he break it, it is words that come to blows.

"But," says he, "when an assembly of men is made sovereign, then no man imagines any such covenant to have part in the institution." But what was that by Publicola of appeal to the people, or that whereby the people had their tribunes? "Fie," says he, "nobody is so dull as to say that the people of Rome made a covenant with the Romans, to hold the sovereignty on such or such conditions, which, not performed, the Romans might depose the Roman people." In which there be several remarkable things; for he holds the commonwealth of Rome to have consisted of one assembly, whereas it consisted of the senate and the people; that they were not upon covenant, whereas every law enacted by them was a covenant between them; that the one assembly was made sovereign, whereas the people, who only were sovereign, were such from the beginning as appears by the ancient style of their covenants or laws—"The senate has resolved, the people have decreed;" that a council being made sovereign, cannot be made such upon conditions, whereas the Decemvirs being a council that was made sovereign, was made such upon conditions; that all conditions or covenants making a sovereign, the sovereign being made, are void; whence it must follow that, the Decemviri being made, were ever after the lawful government of Rome, and that it was unlawful for the commonwealth of Rome to depose the Decemvirs; as also that Cicero, if he wrote otherwise out of his commonwealth, did not write out of nature. But to come to others that see more of this balance.

You have Aristotle full of it in divers places, especially where he says, that "immoderate wealth, as where one man or the few have greater possessions than the equality or the frame of the commonwealth will bear, is an occasion of sedition, which ends for the greater part in monarchy; and that for this cause the ostracism has been received in divers places, as in Argos and Athens. But that it were better to prevent the growth in the beginning, than, when it has got head, to seek the remedy of such an evil."

Machiavel has missed it very narrowly and more dangerously; for, not fully perceiving that if a commonwealth be galled by the gentry it is by their over-balance, he speaks of the gentry as hostile to popular governments, and of popular governments as hostile to the gentry; and makes us believe that the people in such are so enraged against them, that where they meet a gentleman they kill him: which can never be proved by any one example, unless in civil war, seeing that even in Switzerland the gentry are not only safe, but in honour. But the balance, as I have laid it down, though unseen by Machiavel, is that which interprets him, and that which he confirms by his judgment in many others as well as in this place, where he concludes, "That he who will go about to make a commonwealth where there be many gentlemen, unless he first destroys them, undertakes an impossibility. And that he who goes about to introduce monarchy where the condition of the people is equal, shall never bring it to pass, unless he cull out such of them as are the most turbulent and ambitious, and make them gentlemen or noblemen, not in name but in effect; that is, by enriching them with lands, castles and treasures, that may gain them power among the rest, and bring in the rest to dependence upon themselves, to the end that, they maintaining their ambition by the prince, the prince may maintain his power by them."

Wherefore, as in this place I agree with Machiavel, that a nobility or gentry, overbalancing a popular government, is the utter bane and destruction of it; so I shall show in another, that a nobility or gentry, in a popular government, not overbalancing it, is the very life and soul of it. . . .

So much for the principles of power, whether national or provincial, domestic or foreign; being such as are external, and founded in the goods of fortune.

I come to the principles of authority, which are internal, and founded upon the goods of the mind. These the legislator that can unite in his government with those of fortune, comes nearest to the work of God, whose government consists of heaven and earth; which was said by Plato, though in different words, as, when princes should be philosophers, or philosophers princes, the world would be happy. And says Solomon: "There is an evil which I have seen under the sun, which proceeds from the ruler [enimvero neque nobilem, neque ingenuum, nec libertinum quidem armis præponere, regia utilitas est]. Folly is set in great dignity, and the rich [either in virtue and wisdom, in the goods of the mind, or those of fortune upon that balance which gives them a sense of the national interest] sit in low places. I have seen servants upon horses, and princes walking as servants upon the earth." Sad complaints, that the principles of power and of authority, the goods of the mind and of fortune, do not meet and twine in the wreath or crown of empire! Wherefore, if we have anything of piety or of prudence, let us raise ourselves out of the mire of private interest to the contemplation of virtue, and put a hand to the removal of "this evil from under the sun;" this evil against which no government that is not secured can be good; this evil from which the government that is secure must be perfect. Solomon tells us, that the cause of it is from the ruler, from those principles of power, which, balanced upon earthly trash, exclude the heavenly treasures of virtue, and that influence of it upon government which is authority. We have wandered the earth to find out the balance of power; but to find out that of authority we must ascend, as I said, nearer heaven, or to the image of God, which is the soul of man.

The soul of man (whose life or motion is perpetual contemplation or thought) is the mistress of two potent rivals, the one reason, the other passion, that are in continual suit; and, according as she gives up her will to these or either of them, is the felicity or misery which man partakes in this mortal life.

For, as whatever was passion in the contemplation of a man, being brought forth by his will into action, is vice and the bondage of sin; so whatever was reason in the contemplation of a man, being brought forth by his will into action, is virtue and the freedom of soul.

Again, as those actions of a man that were sin acquire to himself repentance or shame, and affect others with scorn or pity, so those actions of a man that are virtue acquire to himself honour, and upon others authority.

Now government is no other than the soul of a nation or city: wherefore that which was reason in the debate of a commonwealth being brought forth by the result, must be virtue; and forasmuch as the soul of a city or nation is the sovereign power, her virtue must be law. But the government whose law is virtue, and whose virtue is law, is the same whose empire is authority, and whose authority is empire.

Again, if the liberty of a man consists in the empire of his reason, the absence whereof would betray him to the bondage of his passions, then the liberty of a commonwealth consists in the empire of her laws, the absence whereof would betray her to the lust of tyrants. And these I conceive to be the principles upon which Aristotle and Livy (injuriously accused by Leviathan for not writing out of Nature) have grounded their assertion, "that a commonwealth is an empire of laws and not of men." But they must not carry it so. "For," says he, "the liberty, whereof there is so frequent and honourable mention in the histories and philosophy of the ancient Greeks and Romans, and the writings and discourses of those that from them have received all their learning in the politics, is not the liberty of particular men, but the liberty of the commonwealth." He might as well have said that the estates of particular men in a commonwealth are not the riches of particular men, but the riches of the commonwealth; for equality of estates causes equality of power, and equality of power is the liberty, not only of the commonwealth, but of every man. But such a man would never be thus irreverent with the greatest authors, and positive against all antiquity, without some certain demonstration of truth—and what is it? Why, "there is written on the turrets of the city of Lucca in great characters at this day the word LIBERTAS; yet no man can thence infer that a particular man has more liberty or immunity from the service of the commonwealth there than in Constantinople. Whether a commonwealth be monarchical or popular, the freedom is the same." The mountain has brought forth, and we have a little equivocation! For to say that a Lucchese has no more liberty or immunity from the laws of Lucca than a Turk has from those of Constantinople; and to say that a Lucchese has no more liberty or immunity by the laws of Lucca, than a Turk has by those of Constantinople, are pretty different speeches. The first may be said of all governments alike; the second scarce of any two; much less of these, seeing it is known that, whereas the greatest Bashaw is a tenant, as well of his head as of his estate, at the will of his lord, the meanest Lucchese that has land is a freeholder of both, and not to be controlled but by the law, and that framed by every private man to no other end (or they may thank themselves) than to protect the liberty of every private man, which by that means comes to be the liberty of the commonwealth.

But seeing they that make the laws in commonwealths are but men, the main question seems to be, how a commonwealth comes to be an empire of laws, and not of men? Or how the debate or result of a commonwealth is so sure to be according to reason; seeing they who debate, and they who resolve, be but men? "And as often as reason is against a man, so often will a man be against reason."

This is thought to be a shrewd saying, but will do no harm; for be it so that reason is nothing but interest, there be divers interests, and so divers reasons.

At first, There is private reason, which is the interest of a private man.

Secondly, There is reason of State, which is the interest (or error, as was said by Solomon) of the ruler or rulers, that is to say, of the prince, of the nobility, or of the people.

Thirdly, There is that reason, which is the interest of mankind, or of the whole. "Now if we see even in those natural agents that want sense, that as in themselves they have a law which directs them in the means whereby they tend to their own perfection, so likewise that another law there is, which touches them as they are sociable parts united into one body; a law which binds them each to serve to others' good, and all to prefer the good of the whole, before whatsoever their own particular; as when stones, or heavy things, forsake their ordinary wont or centre, and fly upwards, as if they heard themselves commanded to let go the good they privately wish, and to relieve the present distress of Nature in common." There is a common right, law of

Nature, or interest of the whole, which is more excellent, and so acknowledged to be by the agents themselves, than the right or interest of the parts only. "Wherefore, though it may be truly said that the creatures are naturally carried forth to their proper utility or profit, that ought not to be taken in too general a sense; seeing divers of them abstain from their own profit, either in regard of those of the same kind, or at least of their young."

Mankind then must either be less just than the creature, or acknowledge also his common interest to be common right. And if reason be nothing else but interest, and the interest of mankind be the right interest, then the reason of mankind must be right reason. Now compute well; for if the interest of popular government come the nearest to the interest of mankind, then the reason of popular government must come the nearest to right reason.

But it may be said that the difficulty remains yet; for be the interest of popular government right reason, a man does not look upon reason as it is right or wrong in itself, but as it makes for him or against him. Wherefore, unless you can show such orders of a government as, like those of God in Nature, shall be able to constrain this or that creature to shake off that inclination which is more peculiar to it, and take up that which regards the common good or interest, all this is to no more end than to persuade every man in a popular government not to carve himself of that which he desires most, but to be mannerly at the public table, and give the best from himself to decency and the common interest. But that such orders may be established as may, nay must, give the upper hand in all cases to common right or interest, notwithstanding the nearness of that which sticks to every man in private, and this in a way of equal certainty and facility, is known even to girls, being no other than those that are of common practice with them in divers cases. For example, two of them have a cake yet undivided, which was given between them: that each of them therefore might have that which is due, "divide," says one to the other, "and I will choose; or let me divide, and you shall choose." If this be but once agreed upon, it is enough; for the divident, dividing unequally, loses, in regard that the other takes the better half; wherefore she divides equally, and so both have right. "O the depth of the wisdom of God!" and yet "by the mouths of babes and sucklings has He set forth His strength;" that which great philosophers are disputing upon in vain, is brought to light by two harmless girls, even the whole mystery of a commonwealth, which lies only in dividing and choosing. Nor has God (if His works in Nature be understood) left so much to mankind to dispute upon as who shall divide and who choose, but distributed them for ever into two orders, whereof the one has the natural right of dividing, and the other of choosing. For example:

A commonwealth is but a civil society of men: let us take any number of men (as twenty) and immediately make a commonwealth. Twenty men (if they be not all idiots, perhaps if they be) can never come so together but there will be such difference in them, that about a third will be wiser, or at least less foolish than all the rest; these upon acquaintance, though it be but small, will be discovered, and, as stags that have the largest heads, lead the herd; for while the six, discoursing and arguing one with another, show the eminence of their parts, the fourteen discover things that they never thought on; or are cleared in divers truths which had formerly perplexed them. Wherefore, in matter of common concernment, difficulty, or danger, they hang upon their lips, as children upon their fathers; and the influence thus acquired by the six, the eminence of whose parts are found to be a stay and comfort to the fourteen, is the authority of the fathers. Wherefore this can be no other than a natural aristocracy diffused by God throughout the whole body of mankind to this end and purpose; and therefore such as the people have not only a natural but a positive obligation to make use of as their guides; as where the people of Israel are commanded to "take wise men, and understanding, and known among their tribes, to be made rulers over them." The six then approved of, as in the present case, are the senate, not by hereditary right, or in regard of the greatness of their estates only, which would tend to such power as might force or draw the people, but by election for their excellent parts, which tends to the advancement of the influence of their virtue or authority that leads the people. Wherefore the office of the senate is not to be commanders, but counsellors of the people; and that which is proper to counsellors is first to debate, and afterward to give advice in the business whereupon they have debated, whence the decrees of the senate are never laws, nor so called; and these being maturely framed, it is their duty to propose in the case of the people. Wherefore the senate is no more than the debate of the commonwealth. But to debate, is to discern or put a difference between things that, being alike, are not the same; or it is separating and weighing this reason against that, and that reason against this, which is dividing.

The senate then having divided, who shall choose? Ask the girls: for if she that divided must have chosen also, it had been little worse for the other in case she had not divided at all, but kept the whole cake to herself, in regard that being to choose too she divided accordingly. Wherefore if the senate have any farther power than to divide, the commonwealth can never be equal. But in a commonwealth consisting of a single council, there is no other to choose than that which divided; whence it is, that such a council fails not to scramble—that is, to be factious, there being no other dividing of the cake in that case but among themselves.

Nor is there any remedy but to have another council to choose. The wisdom of the few may be the light of mankind; but the interest of the few is not the profit of mankind, nor of a commonwealth. Wherefore, seeing we have granted interest to be reason, they must not choose lest it put out their light. But as the council dividing consists of the wisdom of the commonwealth, so the assembly or council choosing should consist of the interest of the commonwealth: as the wisdom of the commonwealth is in the aristocracy, so the interest of the commonwealth is in the whole body of the people. And whereas this, in case the commonwealth consist of a whole nation, is too unwieldy a body to be assembled, this council is to consist of such a representative as may be equal, and so constituted, as can never contract any other interest than that of the whole people; the manner whereof, being such as is best shown by exemplification, I remit to the model. But in the present case, the six dividing, and the fourteen choosing, must of necessity take in the whole interest of the twenty.

Dividing and choosing in the language of a commonwealth is debating and resolving; and whatsoever, upon debate of the senate, is proposed to the people, and resolved by them, is enacted by the authority of the fathers, and by the power of the people, which concurring, make a law. . . .

By what has been shown in reason and experience, it may appear, that though commonwealths in general be governments of the senate proposing, the people resolving, and the magistracy executing, yet some are not so good at these orders as others, through some impediment or defect in the frame, balance, or capacity of them, according to which they are of divers kinds.

The first division of them is into such as are single, as Israel, Athens, Lacedemon, &c.; and such as are by leagues, as those of the Acheans, Etolians, Lycians, Switz, and Hollanders.

The second (being Machiavel's) is into such as are for preservation, as Lacedemon and Venice, and such as are for increase, as Athens and Rome; in which I can see no more than that the former takes in no more citizens than are necessary for defence, and the latter so many as are capable of increase.

The third division (unseen hitherto) is into equal and unequal, and this is the main point, especially as to domestic peace and tranquillity; for to make a commonwealth unequal, is to divide it into parties, which sets them at perpetual variance, the one party endeavouring to preserve their eminence and inequality, and the other to attain to equality; whence the people of Rome derived their perpetual strife with the nobility and senate. But in an equal commonwealth there can be no more strife than there can be overbalance in equal weights; wherefore the commonwealth of Venice, being that which of all others is the most equal in the constitution, is that wherein there never happened any strike between the senate and the people.

An equal commonwealth is such a one as is equal both in the balance or foundation, and in the superstructure; that is to say, in her Agrarian law, and in her rotation.

An equal Agrarian is a perpetual law, establishing and preserving the balance of dominion by such a distribution, that no one man or number of men, within the compass of the few or aristocracy, can come to overpower the whole people by their possessions in lands.

As the Agrarian answers to the foundation, so does rotation to the superstructures.

Equal rotation is equal vicissitude in government, or succession to magistracy conferred for such convenient terms, enjoying equal vacations, as take in the whole body by parts, succeeding others, through the free election or suffrage of the people.

The contrary, whereunto is prolongation of magistracy, which, trashing the wheel of rotation, destroys the life or natural motion of a commonwealth.

The election or suffrage of the people is most free, where it is made or given in such a manner that it can neither oblige nor disoblige another, nor through fear of an enemy, or bashfulness towards a friend, impair a man's liberty.

Wherefore, says Cicero, the tablet or ballot of the people of Rome (who gave their votes by throwing tablets or little pieces of wood secretly into urns marked for the negative or affirmative) was a welcome constitution to the people, as that which, not impairing the assurance of their brows, increased the freedom of their judgment. I have not stood upon a more particular description of this ballot, because that of Venice exemplified in the model is of all others the most perfect.

An equal commonwealth (by that which has been said) is a government established upon an equal Agrarian, arising into the superstructures or three orders, the senate debating and proposing, the people resolving, and the magistracy executing, by an equal rotation through the suffrage of the people given by the ballot. For though rotation may be without the ballot, and the ballot without rotation, yet the ballot not only as to the ensuing model includes both, but is by far the most equal way; for which cause under the name of the ballot I shall hereafter understand both that and rotation too.

Now having reasoned the principles of an equal commonwealth, I should come to give an instance of such a one in experience, if I could find it; but if this work be of any value, it lies in that it is the first example of a commonwealth that is perfectly equal. . . .

But there be who say (and think it a strong objection) that, let a commonwealth be as equal as you can imagine, two or three men when all is done will govern it; and there is that in it which, notwithstanding the pretended sufficiency of a popular State, amounts to a plain confession of the imbecility of that policy, and of the prerogative of monarchy; forasmuch as popular governments in difficult cases have had recourse to dictatorian power, as in Rome.

To which I answer, that as truth is a spark to which objections are like bellows, so in this respect our commonwealth shines; for the eminence acquired by suffrage of the people in a commonwealth, especially if it be popular and equal, can be ascended by no other steps than the universal acknowledgment of virtue: and where men excel in virtue, the commonwealth is stupid and unjust, if accordingly they do not excel in authority. Wherefore this is both the advantage of virtue, which has her due encouragement, and of the commonwealth, which has her due services. These are the philosophers which Plato would have to be princes, the princes which Solomon would have to be mounted, and their steeds are those of authority, not empire; or, if they be buckled to the chariot of empire, as that of the dictatorian power, like the chariot of the sun, it is glorious for terms and vacations or intervals. And as a commonwealth is a government of laws and not of men, so is this the principality of virtue, and not of man; if that fail or set in one, it rises in another who is created his immediate successor. And this takes away that vanity from under the sun, which is an error proceeding more or less from all other rulers under heaven but an equal commonwealth. . . .

But let a commonwealth be equal or unequal, it must consist, as has been shown by reason and all experience, of the three general orders; that is to say, of the senate debating and proposing, of the people resolving, and of the magistracy executing. Wherefore I can never wonder enough at Leviathan, who, without any reason or example, will have it that a commonwealth consists of a single person, or of a single assembly; nor can I sufficiently pity those "thousand gentlemen, whose minds, which otherwise would have wavered, he has framed [as is affirmed by himself] into a conscientious obedience [for so he is pleased to call it] of such a government."

But to finish this part of the discourse, which I intend for as complete an epitome of ancient prudence, and in that of the whole art of politics, as I am able to frame in so short a time:

The two first orders, that is to say, the senate and the people, are legislative, whereunto answers that part of this science which by politicians is entitled "of laws"; and the third order is executive, to which answers that part of the same science which is styled "of the frame and course of courts or judicatories." A word to each of these will be necessary.

And first for laws: they are either ecclesiastical or civil, such as concern religion or government.

Laws, ecclesiastical, or such as concern religion, according to the universal course of ancient prudence, are in the power of the magistrate; but, according to the common practice of modern prudence, since the Papacy, torn out of his hands.

But, as a government pretending to liberty, and yet suppressing liberty of conscience (which, because religion not according to a man's conscience can to him be none at all, is the main), must be a contradiction, so a man that, pleading for the liberty of private conscience, refuses liberty to the national conscience, must be absurd.

A commonwealth is nothing else but the national conscience. And if the conviction of a man's private conscience produces his private religion, the conviction of the national conscience must produce a national religion. . . . And for Rome, if Cicero, in his most excellent book "De Natura Deorum," overthrew the national religion of that commonwealth, he was never the farther from being consul. But there is a meanness and poorness in modern prudence, not only to the damage of civil government, but of religion itself; for to make a man in manner of religion, which admits not of sensible demonstrations (*jurare in verba magistri* [2]), engage to believe no otherwise than is believed by my Lord Bishop, or Goodman Presbyter, is a pedantism that has made the sword to be a rod in the hands of schoolmasters; by which means, whereas the Christian religion is the farthest of any from countenancing war, there never was a war of religion but since Christianity, for which we are beholden to the Pope; for the Pope not giving liberty of conscience to princes and commonwealths, they cannot give that to their subjects which they have not themselves, whence both princes and subjects, either through his instigation or their own disputes, have introduced that execrable custom, never known in the world before, of fighting for religion, and denying the magistrate to have any jurisdiction concerning it, whereas the magistrate's losing the power of religion loses the liberty of conscience, which in that case has nothing to protect it. But if the people be otherwise taught, it concerns them to look about them, and to distinguish between the shrieking of the lapwing and the voice of the turtle.

To come to civil laws: if they stand one way and the balance another, it is the case of a government which of necessity must be new modelled; wherefore your lawyers, advising you upon the like occasions to fit your government to their laws, are no more to be regarded than your tailor if he should desire you to fit your body to his doublet. There is also danger in the plausible pretence of reforming the law, except the government be first good, in which case it is a good tree, and (trouble not yourselves overmuch) brings not forth evil fruit; otherwise, if the tree be evil, you can never reform the fruit, or if a root that is naught bring forth fruit of this kind that seems to be good, take

---

[2] [*To swear to the words of a master.*]

the more heed, for it is the ranker poison. It was nowise probable, if Augustus had not made excellent laws, that the bowels of Rome could have come to be so miserably eaten out by the tyranny of Tiberius and his successors. The best rule as to your laws in general is, that they be few. Rome, by the testimony of Cicero, was best governed under those of the twelve tables; and by that of Tacitus, *Plurimæ leges, corruptissima respublica.*[3] You will be told, that where the laws be few, they leave much to arbitrary power; but where they be many, they leave more, the laws in this case, according to Justinian and the best lawyers, being as litigious as the suitors. Solon made few, Lycurgus fewer laws; and commonwealths have the fewest at this day of all other governments.

Now to conclude this part with a word *de judiciis,* or of the constitution or course of courts; it is a discourse not otherwise capable of being well managed but by particular examples, both the constitution and course of courts being divers in different governments, but best beyond compare in Venice, where they regard not so much the arbitrary power of their courts as the constitution of them, whereby that arbitrary power being altogether unable to retard or do hurt to business, produces and must produce the quickest despatch, and the most righteous dictates of justice that are perhaps in human nature. The manner I shall not stand in this place to describe, because it is exemplified at large in the judicature of the people of Oceana. And thus much of ancient prudence, and the first branch of this preliminary discourse.

[3] [*The state with most laws is most corrupt.*]

JOHN LOCKE

John Locke (1632–1704) was educated at Christ Church, Oxford, where he later lectured. He studied medicine and, though he practiced the profession little, served as physician to his patron, the Earl of Shaftesbury, through whose influence Locke obtained several diplomatic and civil posts, such as secretary to the Board of Trade. He became involved in Whig politics and the shifting fortunes of Shaftesbury's life and went into exile in the Netherlands with him, losing the position at Oxford. Locke returned to England when the Glorious Revolution put William of Orange and Mary on the British throne in 1688, and he subsequently filled several important public offices. He served on the Board of Trade from 1696 to 1700 when he retired because of his health.

Locke's most famous work is the *Essay concerning Human Understanding* (1690), in which he subjects the human mind to an analysis of the effects of environmental influences. He denied the existence of innate ideas, arguing that all ideas come from experience which the mind combines. His *Two Treatises of Government* (1690) present a theory of politics based on natural rights and social contract. *Some Thoughts concerning Education* (1693) emphasizes moral and physical development rather than the inculcation of knowledge. *The Reasonableness of Christianity* (1695) is famous as a religious treatise.

Locke's influence was powerful in America and France; early American political documents often read like paraphrases of his writings. In England, constitutional lawyers as well as religious and secularist philosophers were influenced by Locke, though it was not until the nineteenth century that his classic formulation of the moral basis of popular government was echoed widely in his native country.

Of Civil Government is the second of *Two Treatises of Government,* which appeared in 1690, and which Locke prefaced with these words: "These . . . I hope are sufficient to establish the Throne of our great Restorer, our present King *William;* to make good his title, in the Consent of the People; which being the only one of all lawful Governments, he has more fully and clearly, than any Prince in *Christendom;* and to justify to the World the People of *England,* whose love of their just and natural Rights, with their Resolution to preserve them, saved the Nation when it was on the very birth of Slavery and Ruin." Such a justification rested first on Locke's refutation of the doctrine of absolute monarchy, and the first *Treatise* is devoted to an attack upon Sir Robert Filmer's defense of that form of government.

OF CIVIL GOVERNMENT

CHAPTER I

. . . I think it may not be amiss to set down what I take to be political power. That the power of a magistrate over a subject may be distinguished from that of a father over his children, a master over his servant, a husband over his wife, and a lord over his slave. All which distinct powers happening sometimes together in the same man, if he be considered under these different relations, it may help us to distinguish these powers one from another, and show the difference betwixt a ruler of a commonwealth, a father of a family, and a captain of a galley.

Political power, then, I take to be a right of making laws, with penalties of death, and consequently all less penalties for the regulating and preserving of property, and of employing the force of the community in the execution of such laws, and in the defence of the commonwealth from foreign injury, and all this only for the public good.

CHAPTER II: OF THE STATE OF NATURE

To understand political power aright, and derive it from its original, we must consider what estate all men are naturally in, and that is, a state of perfect freedom to order their actions, and dispose of their possessions and persons as they think fit, within the bounds of the law of Nature, without asking leave or depending upon the will of any other man.

A state also of equality, wherein all the power and jurisdiction is reciprocal, no one having more than another, there being nothing more evident than that creatures of the same species and rank, promiscuously born to all the same advantages of Nature, and the use of the same faculties, should also be equal one amongst another, without subordination or subjection, unless the lord and master of them all should, by any manifest declaration of his will, set one above another, and confer on him, by an evident and clear appointment, an undoubted right to dominion and sovereignty. . . .

But though this be a state of liberty, yet it is not a state of licence; though man in that state have an uncontrollable liberty to dispose of his person or possessions, yet he has not liberty to destroy himself, or so much as any creature in his possession, but where some nobler use than its bare preservation calls for it. The state of Nature has a law of Nature to govern it, which obliges every one, and reason, which is that law, teaches all mankind who will but consult it, that being all equal and independent, no one ought to harm another in his life, health, liberty or possessions; for men being all the workmanship of one omnipotent and infinitely wise Maker; all the servants of one sovereign Master, sent into the world by His order and about His business; they are His property, whose workmanship they are made to last during His, not one another's pleasure. And, being furnished with like faculties, sharing all in one community of Nature, there cannot be supposed any such subordination among us that may authorise us to destroy one another, as if we were made for one another's uses, as the inferior ranks of creatures are for ours. Every one as he is bound to preserve himself, and not to quit his station wilfully, so by the like reason, when his own preservation comes not in competition, ought he as much as he can to preserve the rest of mankind, and not unless it be to do justice on an offender, take away or impair the life, or what tends to the preservation of the life, the liberty, health, limb, or goods of another.

And that all men may be restrained from invading others' rights, and from doing hurt to one another, and the law of Nature be observed, which willeth the peace and preservation of all mankind, the execution of the law of Nature is in that state put into every man's hands, whereby every one has a right to punish the transgressors of that law to such a degree as may hinder its violation. For the law of Nature would, as all other laws that concern men in this world, be in vain if there were nobody that in the state of Nature had a power to execute that law, and thereby preserve the innocent and restrain offenders; and if any one in the state of Nature may punish another for any evil he has done, every one may do so. For in that state of perfect equality, where naturally there is no superiority of jurisdiction of one over another, what any may do in prosecution of that law, every one must needs have a right to do.

And thus, in the state of Nature, one man comes by a power over another, but yet no absolute or arbitrary power to use a criminal, when he has got him in his hands, according to the passionate heats or boundless extravagancy of his own will, but only to retribute to him so far as calm reason and conscience dictate, what is proportionate to his transgression, which is so much as may serve for reparation and restrain. For these two are the only reasons why one man may lawfully do harm to another, which is that we call punishment. In transgressing the law of Nature, the offender declares himself to live by another rule than that of reason and common equity, which is that measure God has set to the actions of men for their mutual security, and so he becomes dangerous to mankind; the tie which is to secure them from injury and violence being slighted and broken by him, which being a trespass against the whole species, and the peace and safety of it, provided for by the law of Nature, every man upon this score, by the right he hath to preserve mankind in general, may restrain, or where it is necessary, destroy things noxious to them, and so may bring such evil on any one who hath transgressed that law, as may make him repent the doing of it, and thereby deter him, and, by his example, others from doing the like mischief. And in this case, and upon this ground, every man hath a right to punish the offender, and be executioner of the law of Nature.

I doubt not but this will seem a very strange doctrine to some men; but before they condemn it, I desire them to resolve me by what right any prince or state can put to death or punish an alien for any crime he commits in their country? It is certain their laws, by virtue of any sanction they receive from the promulgated will of the legislature, reach not a stranger. They speak not to him, nor, if they did, is he bound to hearken to them. The legislative authority by which they are in force over the subjects of that commonwealth hath no power over him. Those who have the supreme power of making laws in England, France, or Holland are, to an Indian, but like the rest of the world—men without authority. And therefore, if by the law of Nature every man hath not a power to punish offences against it, as he soberly judges the case to require, I see not how the magistrates of any community can punish an alien of another country, since, in reference to him, they can have no more power than what every man naturally may have over another.

Besides the crime which consists in violating the laws, and varying from the right rule of reason, whereby a man so far becomes degenerate, and declares himself to quit the principles of human nature and to be a noxious creature, there is commonly injury done, and some person or other, some other man, receives damages by his transgression; in which case, he who hath received any damage has (besides the right of punishment common to him, with other men) a particular right to seek reparation from him that hath done it. And any other person who finds it just may also join with him that is injured, and assist him in recovering from the offender so much as may make satisfaction for the harm he hath suffered.

From these two distinct rights (the one of punishing the crime, for restraint and preventing the like offence, which right of punishing is in everybody, the other of taking reparation, which belongs only to the injured party) comes it to pass that the magistrate, who by being magistrate hath the common right of punishing put into his hands, can often, where the public good demands not the execution of the law, remit the punishment of criminal offences by his own authority, but yet cannot remit the satisfaction due to any private man for the damage he has received. That he who hath suffered the damage has a right to demand in his own name, and he alone can remit. The damnified person has this power of appropriating to himself the goods or service of the offender by right of self-preservation, as every man has a power to punish the crime to prevent its being committed again, by the right he has of preserving all mankind, and doing all reasonable things he can in order to that end. And thus it is that every man in the state of Nature has a power to kill a murderer, both to deter others from doing the like injury (which no reparation can compensate) by the example of the punishment that attends it from everybody, and also to secure men from the attempts of a criminal who, having renounced reason, the common rule and measure God hath given to mankind, hath, by the unjust violence and slaughter he hath committed upon one, declared war against all mankind, and therefore may be destroyed as a lion or a tiger, one of those wild savage beasts with whom men can have no society nor security. And upon this is grounded that great law of Nature, "Whoso sheddeth man's blood, by man shall his blood be shed." And Cain was so fully convinced that every one had a right to destroy such a criminal, that, after the murder of his brother, he cries out, "Every one that findeth me shall slay me," so plain was it writ in the hearts of all mankind.

By the same reason may a man in the state of Nature punish the lesser breaches of that law, it will, perhaps, be demanded, with death? I answer: Each transgression may be punished to that degree, and with so much severity, as will suffice to make it an ill bargain to the offender, give him cause to repent, and terrify others from doing the like. Every offence that can be committed in the state of Nature may, in the state of Nature, be also punished equally, and as far forth, as it may, in a commonwealth. For though it would be beside my present purpose to enter here into the particulars of the law of Nature, or its measures of punishment, yet it is certain there is such a law, and that too as intelligible and plain to a rational creature and a studier of that law as the positive laws of commonwealths, nay, possibly plainer; as much as reason is easier to be understood than the fancies and intricate contrivances of men, following contrary and hidden interests put into words; for truly so are a great part of the municipal laws of countries, which are only so far right as they are founded on the law of Nature, by which they are to be regulated and interpreted.

To this strange doctrine—viz., That in the state of Nature every one has the executive power of the law of Nature—I doubt not but it will be objected that it is unreasonable for men to be judges in their own cases, that self-love will make men partial to themselves and their friends; and, on the other side, ill-nature, passion, and revenge will carry them too far in punishing others, and hence nothing but confusion and disorder will follow, and that therefore God hath certainly appointed government to restrain the partiality and violence of men. I easily grant that civil government is the proper remedy for the inconveniences of the state of Nature, which must certainly be great where men may be judges in their own case, since it is easy to be imagined that he who was so unjust as to do his brother an injury will scarce be so just as to condemn himself for it. But I shall desire those who make this objection to remember that absolute monarchs are but men; and if government is to be the remedy of those evils which necessarily follow from men being judges in their own cases, and the state of Nature is therefore not to be endured, I desire to know what kind of government that is, and how much better it is than the state of

Nature, where one man commanding a multitude has the liberty to be judge in his own case, and may do to all his subjects whatever he pleases without the least question or control of those who execute his pleasure? and in whatsoever he doth, whether led by reason, mistake, or passion, must be submitted to? which men in the state of Nature are not bound to do one to another. And if he that judges, judges amiss in his own or any other case, he is answerable for it to the rest of mankind.

It is often asked as a mighty objection, where are, or ever were, there any men in such a state of Nature? To which it may suffice as an answer at present, that since all princes and rulers of "independent" governments all through the world are in a state of Nature, it is plain the world never was, nor never will be, without numbers of men in that state. I have named all governors of "independent" communities, whether they are, or are not, in league with others; for it is not every compact that puts an end to the state of Nature between men, but only this one of agreeing together mutually to enter into one community, and make one body politic; other promises and compacts men may make one with another, and yet still be in the state of Nature. The promises and bargains for truck, etc., between the two men in Soldania, in or between a Swiss and an Indian, in the woods of America, are binding to them, though they are perfectly in a state of Nature in reference to one another for truth, and keeping of faith belongs to men as men, and not as members of society.

To those that say there were never any men in the state of Nature, I will not only oppose the authority of the judicious Hooker, where he says, "the laws which have been hitherto mentioned"—*i.e.,* the laws of Nature—"do bind men absolutely, even as they are men, although they have never any settled fellowship, never any solemn agreement amongst themselves what to do or not to do; but for as much as we are not by ourselves sufficient to furnish ourselves with competent store of things needful for such a life as our Nature doth desire, a life fit for the dignity of man, therefore to supply those defects and imperfections which are in us, as living single and solely by ourselves, we are naturally induced to seek communion and fellowship with others; this was the cause of men uniting themselves as first in politic societies." But I, moreover, affirm that all men are naturally in that state, and remain so till, by their own consents, they make themselves members of some politic society, and I doubt not, in the sequel of this discourse, to make it very clear.

CHAPTER III: OF THE STATE OF WAR

The state of war is a state of enmity and destruction; and therefore declaring by word or action, not a passionate and hasty, but sedate, settled design upon another man's life puts him in a state of war with him against whom he has declared such an intention, and so has exposed his life to the other's power to be taken away by him, or any one that joins with him in his defence, and espouses his quarrel; it being reasonable and just I should have a right to destroy that which threatens me with destruction; for by the fundamental law of Nature, man being to be preserved as much as possible, when all cannot be preserved, the safety of the innocent is to be preferred, and one may destroy a man who makes war upon him, or has discovered an enmity to his being, for the same reason that he may kill a wolf or a lion, because they are not under the ties of the common law of reason, have no other rule but that of force and violence, and so may be treated as a beast of prey, those dangerous and noxious creatures that will be sure to destroy him whenever he falls into their power.

And hence it is that he who attempts to get another man into his absolute power does thereby put himself into a state of war with him; it being to be understood as a declaration of a design upon his life. For I have reason to conclude that he who would get me into his power without my consent would use me as he pleased when he had got me there, and destroy me too when he had a fancy to it; for nobody can desire to have me in his absolute power unless it be to compel me by force to that which is against the right of my freedom—*i.e.,* make me a slave. To be free from such force is the only security of my preservation, and reason bids me look on him as an enemy to my preservation who would take away that freedom which is the fence to it; so that he who makes an attempt to enslave me thereby puts himself into a state of war with me. He that in the state of Nature would take away the freedom that belongs to any one in that state must necessarily be supposed to have a design to take away everything else, that freedom being the foundation of all the rest; as he that in the state of society would take away the freedom belonging to those of that society or commonwealth must be supposed to design to take away from them everything else, and so be looked on as in a state of war.

This makes it lawful for a man to kill a thief who has not in the least hurt him, nor declared any design upon his life, any farther than by the use of force, so to get him in his power as to take away his money, or what he pleases, from him; because using force, where he has no right to get me into his power, let his pretence be what it will, I have no reason to suppose that he who would take away my liberty would not, when he had me in his power, take away everything else. And, therefore, it is lawful for me to treat him as one who has put himself into a state of war with me—*i.e.,* kill him if I can; for to that hazard does he justly expose himself whoever introduces a state of war, and is aggressor in it.

And here we have the plain difference between the state of Nature and the state of war, which however some men have confounded, are as far distant as a state of peace, goodwill, mutual assistance, and preservation; and a state of enmity, malice, violence and mutual destruction are one from another. Men living together according to reason without a common superior on earth, with authority to judge between them, is properly the state of Nature. But force, or a declared design of force upon the person of another, where there is no common superior on earth to appeal to for relief, is the state of war; and it is the want of such an appeal gives a man the right of war even against an aggressor, though he be in society and a fellow-subject. Thus, a thief whom I cannot harm, but by appeal to the law, for having stolen all that I am worth, I may kill when he sets on me to rob me but of my horse or coat, because the law, which was made for my preservation, where it cannot interpose to secure my life from present force, which if lost is capable of no reparation, permits me my own defence and the right of war, a liberty to kill the aggressor, because the aggressor allows not time to appeal to our common judge, nor the decision of the law, for remedy in a case where the mischief may be irreparable. Want of a common judge with authority puts all men in a state of Nature; force without right upon a man's person makes a state of war both where there is, and is not, a common judge.

But when the actual force is over, the state of war ceases between those that are in society and are equally on both sides subject to the judge; and, therefore, in such controversies, where the question is put, "Who shall be judge?" it cannot be meant who shall decide the controversy; every one knows what Jephtha here tells us, that "the Lord the Judge" shall judge. Where there is no judge on earth the appeal lies to God in Heaven. That question then cannot mean who shall judge, whether another hath put himself in a state of war with me, and whether I may, as Jephtha did, appeal to Heaven in it? Of that I myself can only judge in my own conscience, as I will answer it at the great day to the Supreme Judge of all men.

CHAPTER IV: OF SLAVERY

The natural liberty of man is to be free from any superior power on earth, and not to be under the will or legislative authority of man, but to have only the law of Nature for this rule. The liberty of man in society is to be under no other legislative power but that established by consent in the commonwealth, nor under the dominion of any will, or restraint of any law, but what that legislative shall enact according to the trust put in it. Freedom, then, is not what Sir Robert Filmer tells us: "A liberty for every one to do what he lists, to live as he pleases, and not to be tied by any laws"; but freedom of men under government is to have a standing rule to live by, common to every one of that society, and made by the legislative power erected in it. A liberty to follow my own will in all things where that rule prescribes not, not to be subject to the inconstant, uncertain, unknown, arbitrary will of another man, as freedom of nature is to be under no other restraint but the law of Nature.

This freedom from absolute, arbitrary power is so necessary to, and closely joined with, a man's preservation, that he cannot part with it but by what forfeits his preservation and life together. For a man, not having the power of his own life, cannot by compact or his own consent enslave himself to any one, nor put himself under the absolute, arbitrary power of another to take away his life when he pleases. Nobody can give more power than he has himself, and he that cannot take away his own life cannot give another power over it. Indeed, having by his fault forfeited his own life by some act that deserves death, he to whom he has forfeited it may, when he has him in his power, delay to take it, and make use of him to his own service; and he does him no injury by it. For, whenever he finds the hardship of his slavery outweigh the value of his life, it is in his power, by resisting the will of his master, to draw on himself the death he desires. . . .

CHAPTER V: OF PROPERTY

Whether we consider natural reason, which tells us that men, being once born, have a right to their preservation, and consequently to meat and drink and such other things as Nature affords for their subsistence, or "revelation," which gives us an account of those grants God made of the world to Adam, and to Noah and his sons, it is very clear that God, as King David says, "has given the earth to the children of men," given it to mankind in common. But, this being supposed, it seems to some a very great difficulty how any one should ever come to have a property in anything, I will not content myself to answer, that, if it be difficult to make out "property" upon a supposition that God gave the world to Adam and his posterity in common, it is impossible that any man but one universal monarch should have any "property" upon a supposition that God gave the world to Adam and his heirs in succession, exclusive of all the rest of his posterity; but I shall endeavour to show how men might come to have a property in several parts of that which God gave to mankind in common, and that without any express compact of all the commoners.

God, who hath given the world to men in common, hath also given them reason to make use of it to the best advantage of life and convenience. The earth and all that is therein is given to men for the support and comfort of their being. And though all the fruits it naturally produces, and beasts it

feeds, belong to mankind in common, as they are produced by the spontaneous hand of Nature, and nobody has originally a private dominion exclusive
of the rest of mankind in any of them, as they are thus in their natural state,
yet being given for the use of men, there must of necessity be a means to
appropriate them some way or other before they can be of any use, or at all
beneficial, to any particular men. The fruit or venison which nourishes the
wild Indian, who knows no enclosure, and is still a tenant in common, must
be his, and so his—*i.e.,* a part of him, that another can no longer have any
right to it before it can do him any good for the support of his life.

Though the earth and all inferior creatures be common to all men, yet
every man has a "property" in his own "person." This nobody has any right
to but himself. The "labour" of his body and the "work" of his hands, we
may say, are properly his. Whatsoever, then, he removes out of the state that
Nature hath provided and left it in, he hath mixed his labour with it, and
joined to it something that is his own, and thereby makes it his property. It
being by him removed from the common state Nature placed it in, it hath
by this labour something annexed to it that excludes the common right of
other men. For this "labour" being the unquestionable property of the labourer, no man but he can have a right to what that is once joined to, at
least where there is enough, and as good left in common for others.

He that is nourished by the acorns he picked up under an oak, or the apples
he gathered from the trees in the wood, has certainly appropriated them to
himself. Nobody can deny but the nourishment is his. I ask, then, when did
they begin to be his? when he digested? or when he ate? or when he boiled?
or when he brought them home? or when he picked them up? And it is plain,
if the first gathering made them not his, nothing else could. That labour put
a distinction between them and common. That added something to them
more than Nature, the common mother of all, had done, and so they became
his private right. And will any one say he had no right to those acorns or
apples he thus appropriated because he had not the consent of all mankind
to make them his? Was it a robbery thus to assume to himself what belonged
to all in common? If such a consent as that was necessary, man had starved,
notwithstanding the plenty God had given him. We see in commons, which
remain so by compact, that it is the taking any part of what is common, and
removing it out of the state Nature leaves it in, which begins the property,
without which the common is of no use. And the taking of this or that part
does not depend on the express consent of all the commoners. Thus, the grass
my horse has bit, the turfs my servant has cut, and the ore I have digged in
any place, where I have a right to them in common with others, become my
property without the assignation or consent of anybody. The labour that was

mine, removing them out of that common state they were in, hath fixed my property in them.

By making an explicit consent of every commoner necessary to any one's appropriating to himself any part of what is given in common, children or servants could not cut the meat which their father or master had provided for them in common without assigning to every one his peculiar part. Though the water running in the fountain be every one's, yet who can doubt but that in the pitcher is his only who drew it out? His labour hath taken it out of the hands of Nature where it was common, and belonged equally to all her children, and hath thereby appropriated it to himself. . . .

It will, perhaps, be objected to this, that if gathering the acorns or other fruits of the earth, etc., makes a right to them, then any one may engross as much as he will. To which I answer, Not so. The same law of Nature that does by this means give us property, does also bound that property too. "God has given us all things richly." Is the voice of reason confirmed by inspiration? But how far has He given it us—"to enjoy"? As much as any one can make use of to any advantage of life before it spoils, so much he may by his labour fix a property in. Whatever is beyond this is more than his share, and belongs to others. Nothing was made by God for man to spoil or destroy. And thus considering the plenty of natural provisions there was a long time in the world, and the few spenders, and to how small a part of that provision the industry of one man could extend itself and engross it to the prejudice of others, especially keeping within the bounds set by reason of what might serve for his use, there could be then little room for quarrels or contentions about property so established.

But the chief matter of property being now not the fruits of the earth and the beasts that subsist on it, but the earth itself, as that which takes in and carries with it all the rest, I think it is plain that property in that too is acquired as the former. As much land as a man tills, plants, improves, cultivates, and can use the product of, so much is his property. He by his labour does, as it were, enclose it from the common. Nor will it invalidate his right to say everybody else has an equal title to it, and therefore he cannot appropriate, he cannot enclose, without the consent of all his fellow-commoners, all mankind. God, when He gave the world in common to all mankind, commanded man also to labour, and the penury of his condition required it of him. God and his reason commanded him to subdue the earth—*i.e.,* improve it for the benefit of life and therein lay out something upon it that it was his own, his labour. He that, in obedience to this command of God, subdued, tilled, and sowed any part of it, thereby annexed to it something that was his property, which another had no title to, nor could without injury take from him.

Nor was this appropriation of any parcel of land, by improving it, any prejudice to any other man, since there was still enough and as good left, and more
than the yet unprovided could use. So that, in effect, there was never the less
left for others because of his enclosure for himself. For he that leaves as much
as another can make use of does as good as take nothing at all. Nobody could
think himself injured by the drinking of another man, though he took a good
draught, who had a whole river of the same water left him to quench his
thirst. And the case of land and water, where there is enough of both, is
perfectly the same.

God gave the world to men in common, but since He gave it them for
their benefit and the greatest conveniences of life they were capable to draw
from it, it cannot be supposed He meant it should always remain common and
uncultivated. He gave it to the use of the industrious and rational (and labour
was to be his title of it); not to the fancy or covetousness of the quarrelsome
and contentious. He that had as good left for his improvement as was already
taken up needed not complain, ought not to meddle with what was already
improved by another's labour; if he did it is plain he desired the benefit of
another's pains, which he had no right to, and not the ground which God
had given him, in common with others, to labour on, and whereof there was
as good left as that already possessed, and more than he knew what to do with,
or his industry could reach to.

It is true, in land that is common in England or any other country, where
there are plenty of people under government who have money and commerce,
no one can enclose or appropriate any part without the consent of all his
fellow-commoners; because this is left common by compact—*i.e.,* by the law
of the land, which is not to be violated. And, though it be common in respect
of some men, it is not so to all mankind, but is the joint propriety of this
country, or this parish. Besides, the remainder, after such enclosure, would
not be as good to the rest of the commoners as the whole was, when they could
all make use of the whole; whereas in the beginning and first peopling of
the great common of the world it was quite otherwise. The law man was
under was rather for appropriating. God commanded, and his wants forced
him to labour. That was his property, which could not be taken from him
wherever he had fixed it. And hence subduing or cultivating the earth and
having dominion, we see, are joined together. The one gave title to the other.
So that God, by commanding to subdue, gave authority so far to appropriate.
And the condition of human life, which requires labour and materials to work
on, necessarily introduce private possessions.

The measure of property Nature well set, by the extent of men's labour and the conveniency of life. No man's labour could subdue or appropriate all, nor could his enjoyment consume more than a small part; so that it was impossible for any man, this way, to entrench upon the right of another or acquire to himself a property to the prejudice of his neighbour, who would still have room for as good and as large a possession (after the other had taken out his) as before it was appropriated. Which measure did confine every man's possession to a very moderate proportion, and such as he might appropriate to himself without injury to anybody in the first ages of the world, when men were more in danger to be lost, by wandering from their company, in the then vast wilderness of the earth than to be straitened for want of room to plant in.

The same measure may be allowed still, without prejudice to anybody, full as the world seems. For, supposing a man or family, in the state they were at first, peopling of the world by the children of Adam or Noah, let him plant in some inland vacant places of America. We shall find that the possessions he could make himself, upon the measures we have given, would not be very large, nor, even to this day, prejudice the rest of mankind or give them reason to complain or think themselves injured by this man's encroachment, though the race of men have now spread themselves to all the corners of the world, and do infinitely exceed the small number was at the beginning. Nay, the extent of ground is of so little value without labour that I have heard it affirmed that in Spain itself a man may be permitted to plough, sow and reap, without being disturbed, upon land he has no other title to, but only his making use of it. But, on the contrary, the inhabitants think themselves beholden to him who, by his industry on neglected, and consequently waste land, has increased the stock of corn, which they wanted. But be this as it will, which I lay no stress on, this I dare boldly affirm, that the same rule of property—viz., that every man should have as much as he could make use of, would hold still in the world, without straitening anybody, since there is land enough in the world to suffice double the inhabitants, had not the invention of money, and the tacit agreement of men to put a value on it, introduced (by consent) larger possessions and a right to them; which, how it has done, I shall by and by show more at large.

This is certain, that in the beginning, before the desire of having more than men needed had altered the intrinsic value of things, which depends only on their usefulness to the life of man, or had agreed that a little piece of yellow metal, which would keep without wasting or decay, should be worth a great piece of flesh or a whole heap of corn, though men had a right to appropriate by their labour, each one to himself, as much of the things of

Nature as he could use, yet this could not be much, nor to the prejudice of others, where the same plenty was still left, to those who would use the same industry.

Before the appropriation of land, he who gathered as much of the wild fruit, killed, caught, or tamed as many of the beasts as he could—he that so employed his pains about any of the spontaneous products of Nature as any way to alter them from the state Nature put them in, by placing any of his labour on them, did thereby acquire a propriety in them; but if they perished in his possession without their due use—if the fruits rotted or the venison putrefied before he could spend it, he offended against the common law of Nature, and was liable to be punished: he invaded his neighbour's share, for he had no right farther than his use called for any of them, and they might serve to afford him conveniencies of life.

The same measures governed the possession of land, too. Whatsoever he tilled and reaped, laid up and made use of before it spoiled, that was his peculiar right; whatsoever he enclosed, and could feed and make use of, the cattle and product was also his. But if either the grass of his enclosure rotted on the ground, or the fruit of his planting perished without gathering and laying up, this part of the earth, notwithstanding his enclosure, was still to be looked on as waste, and might be the possession of any other. Thus, at the beginning, Cain might take as much ground as he could till and make it his own land, and yet leave enough to Abel's sheep to feed on: a few acres would serve for both their possessions. But as families increased and industry enlarged their stocks, their possessions enlarged with the need of them; but yet it was commonly without any fixed property in the ground they made use of till they incorporated, settled themselves together, and built cities, and then, by consent, they came in time to set out the bounds of their distinct territories and agree on limits between them and their neighbours, and by laws within themselves settled the properties of those of the same society. . . .

Nor is it so strange as, perhaps, before consideration, it may appear, that the property of labour should be able to overbalance the community of land, for it is labour indeed that puts the difference of value on everything; and let any one consider what the difference is between an acre of land planted with tobacco or sugar, sown with wheat or barley, and an acre of the same land lying in common without any husbandry upon it, and he will find that the improvement of labour makes the far greater part of the value. I think it will be but a very modest computation to say, that of the products of the earth useful to the life of man, nine-tenths are the effects of labour. Nay, if we will rightly estimate things as they come to our use, and cast up the several expenses about them—what in them is purely owing to Nature and what to labour—we shall find that in most of them ninety-nine hundredths are wholly to be put on the account of labour. . . .

The greatest part of things really useful to the life of man, and such as the necessity of subsisting made the first commoners of the world look after, as it doth the Americans now, are generally things of short duration, such as, if they are not consumed by use, will decay and perish of themselves; gold, silver, and diamonds are things that fancy or agreement hath put the value on, more than real use and the necessary support of life. Now of those good things which nature hath provided in common, every one had a right, as hath been said, to as much as he could use, and property in all that he could effect with his labour; all that his industry could extend to, to alter from the state nature had put it in, was his. He that gathered a hundred bushels of acorns or apples had thereby a property in them; they were his goods as soon as gathered. He was only to look that he used them before they spoiled, else he took more than his share and robbed others. And indeed it was a foolish thing, as well as dishonest, to hoard up more than he could make use of. If he gave away a part to anybody else so that it perished not uselessly in his possession, these he also made use of. And if he also bartered away plums that would have rotted in a week for nuts that would last good for his eating a whole year, he did no injury; he wasted not the common stock, destroyed no part of the portion of the goods that belonged to others, so long as nothing perished uselessly in his hands. Again, if he would give his nuts for a piece of metal, pleased with its colour, or exchange his sheep for shells, or wool for a sparkling pebble or a diamond, and keep those by him all his life, he invaded not the right of others; he might heap as much of these durable things as he pleased; the exceeding of the bounds of his just property not lying in the largeness of his possession, but the perishing of anything uselessly in it.

And thus came in the use of money—some lasting thing that men might keep without spoiling, and that by mutual consent men would take in exchange for the truly useful but perishable supports of life.

And as different degrees of industry were apt to give men possessions in different proportions, so this invention of money gave them the opportunity to continue and enlarge them; for supposing an island, separate from all possible commerce with the rest of the world, wherein there were but a hundred families, but there were sheep, horses, and cows, with other useful animals, wholesome fruits, and land enough for corn for a hundred thousand times as many, but nothing in the island, either because of its commonness or perishableness, fit to supply the place of money; what reason could anyone have there to enlarge his possessions beyond the use of his family and a plentiful supply to its consumption, either in what their own industry produced or they could barter for like perishable, useful commodities with others? Where there is not something both lasting and scarce, and so valuable to be hoarded up, there men will not be apt to enlarge their possessions of land were it ever so rich, ever so free for them to take. For, I ask, what would a man value ten thousand or a hundred thousand acres of excellent land, ready cultivated and well stocked, too, with cattle, in the middle of the inland parts of America where he had no hopes of commerce with other parts of the world to draw money to him by the sale of the product? It would not be worth the enclosing, and we should see him give up again to the wild common of nature whatever was more than would supply the conveniences of life to be had there for him and his family. . . .

But since gold and silver, being little useful to the life of man, in proportion to food, raiment, and carriage, has its value only from the consent of men—whereof labour yet makes in great part the measure—it is plain that the consent of men have agreed to a disproportionate and unequal possession of the earth—I mean out of the bounds of society and compact; for in governments the laws regulate it; they having, by consent, found out and agreed in a way how a man may, rightfully and without injury, possess more than he himself can make use of by receiving gold and silver, which may continue long in a man's possession without decaying for the overplus, and agreeing those metals should have a value. . . .

CHAPTER VI: OF PATERNAL POWER

. . . Though I have said above . . . "That all men by nature are equal," I cannot be supposed to understand all sorts of "equality." Age or virtue may give men a just precedency. Excellency of parts and merit may place others above the common level. Birth may subject some, and alliance or benefits others, to pay an observance to those to whom Nature, gratitude, or other respects, may have made it due; and yet all this consists with the equality which all men are in, in respect of jurisdiction or dominion one over another, which was the equality I there spoke of as proper to the business in hand, being that equal right that every man hath to his natural freedom, without being subjected to the will or authority of any other man.

Children, I confess, are not born in this full state of equality, though they are born to it. Their parents have a sort of rule and jurisdiction over them when they come into the world, and for some time after, but it is but a temporary one. The bonds of this subjection are like the swaddling clothes they are wrapt up in and supported by in the weakness of their infancy. Age and reason as they grow up loosen them, till at length they drop quite off, and leave a man at his own free disposal.

Adam was created a perfect man, his body and mind in full possession of their strength and reason, and so was capable from the first instance of his being to provide for his own support and preservation, and govern his actions according to the dictates of the law of reason God had implanted in him. From him the world is peopled with his descendants, who are all born infants, weak and helpless, without knowledge or understanding. But to supply the defects of this imperfect state till the improvement of growth and age had removed them, Adam and Eve, and after them all parents were, by the law of Nature, under an obligation to preserve, nourish and educate the children they had begotten, not as their own workmanship, but the workmanship of their own Maker, the Almighty, to whom they were to be accountable for them.

The law that was to govern Adam was the same that was to govern all his posterity, the law of reason. But his offspring having another way of entrance into the world, different from him, by a natural birth, that produced them ignorant, and without the use of reason, they were not presently under that law. For nobody can be under a law that is not promulgated to him; and this law being promulgated or made known by reason only, he that is not come to the use of his reason cannot be said to be under this law; and Adam's children being not presently as soon as born under this law of reason, were not presently free. For law, in its true notion, is not so much the limitation as the direction of a free and intelligent agent to his proper interest, and prescribes no farther than is for the general good of those under that law. Could they be happier without it, the law, as a useless thing, would of itself vanish; and that ill deserves the name of confinement which hedges us in only from bogs and precipices. So that, however it may be mistaken, the end of law is not to abolish or restrain, but to preserve and enlarge freedom. For in all the states of created beings, capable of laws, where there is no law there is no freedom. For liberty is to be free from restraint and violence from others, which cannot be where there is no law; and is not, as we are told, "a liberty for every man to do what he lists." For who could be free, when every other man's humour might domineer over him? But a liberty to dispose and order freely as he lists his person, actions, possessions, and his whole property within the allowance of those laws under which he is, and therein not to be subject to the arbitrary will of another, but freely follow his own. . . .

The freedom then of man, and liberty of acting according to his own will, is grounded on his having reason, which is able to instruct him in that law he is to govern himself by, and make him know how far he is left to the freedom of his own will. To turn him loose to an unrestrained liberty, before he has reason to guide him, is not the allowing him the privilege of his nature to be free, but to thrust him out amongst brutes, and abandon him to a state as wretched and as much beneath that of a man as theirs. This is that which puts the authority into the parents' hands to govern the minority of their children. . . .

CHAPTER VII: OF POLITICAL OR CIVIL SOCIETY

. . . But how a family, or any other society of men, differ from that which is properly political society, we shall best see by considering wherein political society itself consists.

Man being born, as has been proved, with a title to perfect freedom and an uncontrolled enjoyment of all the rights and privileges of the law of Nature, equally with any other man, or number of men in the world, hath by nature a power not only to preserve his property—that is, his life, liberty, and estate, against the injuries and attempts of other men, but to judge of and punish the breaches of that law in others, as he is persuaded the offence deserves, even with death itself, in crimes where the heinousness of the fact, in his opinion, requires it. But because no political society can be, nor subsist, without having in itself the power to preserve the property, and in order thereunto punish the offences of all those of that society, there, and there only, is political society where every one of the members hath quitted this natural power, resigned it up into the hands of the community in all cases that exclude him not from appealing for protection to the law established by it. And thus all private judgment of every particular member being excluded, the community comes to be umpire, and by understanding indifferent rules and men authorised by the community for their execution, decides all the differences that may happen between any members of that society concerning any matter of right, and punishes those offences which any member hath committed against the society with such penalties as the law has established; whereby it is easy to discern who are, and are not, in political society together. Those who are united into one body, and have a common established law and judicature to appeal to, with authority to decide controversies between them and punish offenders, are in civil society one with another; but those who have no such common appeal, I mean on earth, are still in the state of Nature, each being where there is no other, judge for himself and executioner; which is, as I have before showed it, the perfect state of Nature.

And thus the commonwealth comes by a power to set down what punishment shall belong to the several transgressions they think worthy of it, committed amongst the members of that society (which is the power of making laws), as well as it has the power to punish any injury done unto any of its members by any one that is not of it (which is the power of war and peace); and all this for the preservation of the property of all the members of that society, as far as is possible. But though every man entered into society has quitted his power to punish offences against the law of Nature in prosecution of his own private judgment, yet with the judgment of offences which he has given up to the legislative, in all cases where he can appeal to the magistrate, he has given up a right to the commonwealth to employ his force for the execution of the judgments of the commonwealth whenever he shall be called to it, which, indeed, are his own judgments, they being made by himself or his representative. And herein we have the original of the legislative and executive power of civil society, which is to judge by standing laws how far offences are to be punished when committed within the commonwealth; and also by occasional judgments founded on the present circumstances of the fact, how far injuries from without are to be vindicated, and in both these to employ all the force of all the members when there shall be need.

Wherever, therefore, any number of men so unite into one society as to quit every one his executive power of the law of Nature, and to resign it to the public, there and there only is a political or civil society. And this is done wherever any number of men, in the state of Nature, enter into society to make one people one body politic under one supreme government: or else when any one joins himself to, and incorporates with any government already made. For hereby he authorises the society, or which is all one, the legislative thereof, to make laws for him as the public good of the society shall require, to the execution whereof his own assistance (as to his own decrees) is due. And this puts men out of a state of Nature into that of a commonwealth, by setting up a judge on earth with authority to determine all the controversies and redress the injuries that may happen to any member of the commonwealth, which judge is the legislative or magistrates appointed by it. And wherever there are any number of men, however associated, that have no such decisive power to appeal to, there they are still in the state of Nature.

And hence it is evident that absolute monarchy, which by some men is counted for the only government in the world, is indeed inconsistent with civil society, and so can be no form of civil government at all. For the end of civil society being to avoid and remedy those inconveniencies of the state of Nature which necessarily follow from every man's being judge in his own case, by setting up a known authority to which every one of that society may appeal upon any injury received, or controversy that may arise, and which every one of the society ought to obey. Wherever any persons are who have not such an authority to appeal to, and decide any difference between them there, those persons are still in the state of Nature. And so is every absolute prince in respect of those who are under his dominion.

For he being supposed to have all, both legislative and executive, power in himself alone, there is no judge to be found, no appeal lies open to any one, who may fairly and indifferently, and with authority decide, and from whence relief and redress may be expected of any injury or inconveniency that may be suffered from him, or by his order. So that such a man, however entitled, Czar, or Grand Signior, or how you please, is as much in the state of Nature, with all under his dominion, as he is with the rest of mankind. For wherever any two men are, who have no standing rule and common judge to appeal to on earth, for the determination of controversies of right betwixt them, there they are still in the state of Nature, and under all the inconveniencies of it, with only this woeful difference to the subject, or rather slave of an absolute prince. That whereas, in the ordinary state of Nature, he has a liberty to judge of his right, according to the best of his power to maintain it; but whenever his property is invaded by the will and order of his monarch, he has not only no appeal, as those in society ought to have, but, as if he were degraded from the common state of rational creatures, is denied a liberty to judge of, or defend his right, and so is exposed to all the misery and inconveniencies that a man can fear from one, who being in the unrestrained state of Nature, is yet corrupted with flattery and armed with power.

For he that thinks absolute power purifies men's blood, and corrects the baseness of human nature, need read but the history of this, or any other age, to be convinced to the contrary. . . .

CHAPTER VIII: OF THE BEGINNING OF POLITICAL SOCIETIES

Men being, as has been said, by nature all free, equal and independent, no one can be put out of this estate and subjected to the political power of another without his own consent, which being done by agreeing with other men, to join and unite into a community for their comfortable, safe, and peaceable living, one amongst another, in a secure enjoyment of their properties, and a greater security against any that are not of it. This any number of men may do, because it injures not the freedom of the rest; they are left, as they were, in the liberty of the state of Nature. When any number of men have so consented to make one community or government, they are thereby presently incorporated, and make one body politic, wherein the majority have a right to act and conclude the rest.

For, when any number of men have, by the consent of every individual, made a community, they have thereby made that community one body, with a power to act as one body, which is only by the will and determination of the majority. For that which acts any community, being only the consent of the individuals of it, and it being one body, must move one way, it is necessary the body should move that way whither the greater force carries it, which is the consent of the majority, or else it is impossible it should act or continue one body, one community, which the consent of every individual that united into it agreed that it should; and so every one is bound by that consent to be concluded by the majority. And therefore we see that in assemblies empowered to act by positive laws where no number is set by that positive law which empowers them, the act of the majority passes for the act of the whole, and of course determines as having, by the law of Nature and reason, the power of the whole.

And thus every man, by consenting with others to make one body politic under one government, puts himself under an obligation to every one of that society to submit to the determination of the majority, and to be concluded by it; or else this original compact, whereby he with others incorporates into one society, would signify nothing, and be no compact if he be left free and under no other ties than he was in before in the state of Nature. For what appearance would there be of any compact? What new engagement if he were no farther tied by any decrees of the society than he himself thought fit and did actually consent to? This would be still as great a liberty as he himself had before his compact, or any one else in the state of Nature, who may submit himself and consent to any acts of it if he thinks fit.

For if the consent of the majority shall not in reason be received as the act of the whole, and conclude every individual, nothing but the consent of every individual can make anything to be the act of the whole, which, considering the infirmities of health and avocations of business, which in a number though much less than that of a commonwealth, will necessarily keep many away from the public assembly; and the variety of opinions and contrariety of interests which unavoidably happen in all collections of men, it is next impossible ever to be had. And, therefore, if coming into society be upon such terms, it will be only like Cato's coming into the theatre, *tantum ut exiret*.[2] Such a constitution as this would make the mighty leviathan of a shorter duration than the feeblest creatures, and not let it outlast the day it was born in, which cannot be supposed till we can think that rational creatures should desire and constitute societies only to be dissolved. For where the majority cannot conclude the rest, there they cannot act as one body, and consequently will be immediately dissolved again. . . .

Every man being, as has been showed, naturally free, and nothing being able to put him into subjection to any earthly power, but only his own consent, it is to be considered what shall be understood to be a sufficient declaration of a man's consent to make him subject to the laws of any government. There is a common distinction of an express and a tacit consent, which will concern our present case. Nobody doubts but an express consent of any man, entering into any society, makes him a perfect member of that society, a subject of that government. The difficulty is, what ought to be looked upon as a tacit consent,

[2] [*Only to go out again.* Cato (234–149 B.C.), a Roman statesman, held puritanical views on the theater.]

and how far it binds—*i.e.,* how far any one shall be looked on to have consented, and thereby submitted to any government, where he has made no expressions of it at all. And to this I say, that every man that hath any possession or enjoyment of any part of the dominions of any government doth hereby give his tacit consent, and is as far forth obliged to obedience to the laws of that government, during such enjoyment, as any one under it, whether this his possession be of land to him and his heirs for ever, or a lodging only for a week; or whether it be barely travelling freely on the highway; and, in effect, it reaches as far as the very being of any one within the territories of that government.

To understand this the better, it is fit to consider that every man when he at first incorporates himself into any commonwealth, he, by his uniting himself thereunto, annexes also, and submits to the community those possessions which he has, or shall acquire, that do not already belong to any other government. For it would be a direct contradiction for any one to enter into society with others for the securing and regulating of property, and yet to suppose his land, whose property is to be regulated by the laws of the society, should be exempt from the jurisdiction of that government to which he himself, and the property of the land, is a subject. By the same act, therefore, whereby any one unites his person, which was before free, to any commonwealth, by the same he unites his possessions, which were before free, to it also; and they become, both of them, person and possession, subject to the government and dominion of that commonwealth as long as it hath a being. Whoever therefore, from thenceforth, by inheritance, purchase, permission, or otherwise, enjoys any part of the land so annexed to, and under the government of that commonweal, must take it with the condition it is under—that is, of submitting to the government of the commonwealth, under whose jurisdiction it is, as far forth as any subject of it.

But since the government has a direct jurisdiction only over the land and reaches the possessor of it (before he has actually incorporated himself in the society) only as he dwells upon and enjoys that, the obligation any one is under by virtue of such enjoyment to submit to the government begins and ends with the enjoyment; so that whenever the owner, who has given nothing but such a tacit consent to the government will, by donation, sale or otherwise, quit the said possession, he is at liberty to go and incorporate himself into any other commonwealth, or agree with others to begin a new one *in vacuis locis,* in any part of the world they can find free and unpossessed; whereas he that has once, by actual agreement and any express declaration, given his consent to be of any commonweal, is perpetually and indispensably obliged to be, and remain unalterably a subject to it, and can never be again in the liberty of the state of Nature, unless by any calamity the government he was under comes to be dissolved.

But submitting to the laws of any country, living quietly and enjoying privileges and protection under them, makes not a man a member of that society; it is only a local protection and homage due to and from all those who, not being in a state of war, come within the territories belonging to any government, to all parts whereof the force of its law extends. But this no more makes a man a member of that society, a perpetual subject of that commonwealth, than it would make a man a subject to another in whose family he found it convenient to abide for some time, though, whilst he continued in it, he were obliged to comply with the laws and submit to the government he found there. And thus we see that foreigners, by living all their lives under another government, and enjoying the privileges and protection of it, though they are bound, even in conscience, to submit to its administration as far forth as any denizen, yet do not thereby come to be subjects or members of that commonwealth. Nothing can make any man so but his actually entering into it by positive engagement and express promise and compact. This is that which, I think, concerning the beginning of political societies, and that consent which makes any one a member of any commonwealth.

CHAPTER IX: OF THE ENDS OF POLITICAL SOCIETY AND GOVERNMENT

If man in the state of Nature be so free as has been said, if he be absolute lord of his own person and possessions, equal to the greatest and subject to nobody, why will he part with his freedom, this empire, and subject himself to the dominion and control of any other power? To which it is obvious to answer, that though in the state of Nature he hath such a right, yet the enjoyment of it is very uncertain and constantly exposed to the invasion of others; for all being kings as much as he, every man his equal, and the greater part no strict observers of equity and justice, the enjoyment of the property he has in this state is very unsafe, very insecure. This makes him willing to quit this condition which, however free, is full of fears and continual dangers; and it is not without reason that he seeks out and is willing to join in society with others who are already united, or have a mind to unite for the mutual preservation of their lives, liberties and estates, which I call by the general name—property.

The great and chief end, therefore, of men uniting into commonwealths, and putting themselves under government, is the preservation of their property; to which in the state of Nature there are many things wanting.

Firstly, there wants an established, settled, known law, received and allowed by common consent to be the standard of right and wrong, and the common measure to decide all controversies between them. For though the law of Nature be plain and intelligible to all rational creatures, yet men, being biased by their interest, as well as ignorant for want of study of it, are not apt to allow of it as a law binding to them in the application of it to their particular cases.

Secondly, in the state of Nature there wants a known and indifferent judge, with authority to determine all differences according to the established law. For every one in that state being both judge and executioner of the law of Nature, men being partial to themselves, passion and revenge is very apt to carry them too far, and with too much heat in their own cases, as well as negligence and unconcernedness, make them too remiss in other men's.

Thirdly, in the state of Nature there often wants power to back and support the sentence when right, and to give it due execution. They who by any injustice offended will seldom fail where they are able by force to make good their injustice. Such resistance many times makes the punishment dangerous and frequently destructive to those who attempt it.

Thus mankind, notwithstanding all the privileges of the state of Nature, being but in an ill condition while they remain in it are quickly driven into society. Hence it comes to pass, that we seldom find any number of men live any time together in this state. The inconveniencies that they are therein exposed to by the irregular and uncertain exercise of the power every man has of punishing the transgressions of others, make them take sanctuary under the established laws of government, and therein seek the preservation of their property. It is this makes them so willingly give up every one his single power of punishing to be exercised by such alone as shall be appointed to it amongst them, and by such rules as the community, or those authorised by them to that purpose, shall agree on. And in this we have the original right and rise of both the legislative and executive power as well as of the governments and societies themselves.

For in the state of Nature to omit the liberty he has of innocent delights, a man has two powers. The first is to do whatsoever he thinks fit for the preservation of himself and others within the permission of the law of Nature; by which law, common to them all, he and all the rest of mankind are one community, make up one society distinct from all other creatures, and were it not for the corruption and viciousness of degenerate men, there would be no need of any other, no necessity that men should separate from this great and natural community, and associate into lesser combinations. The other power a man has in the state of Nature is the power to punish the crimes committed against that law. Both these he gives up when he joins in a private, if I may so call it, or particular political society, and incorporates into any commonwealth separate from the rest of mankind.

The first power—viz., of doing whatsoever he thought fit for the preservation of himself and the rest of mankind, he gives up to be regulated by laws made by the society, so far forth as the preservation of himself and the rest of that society shall require; which laws of the society in many things confine the liberty he had by the law of Nature.

Secondly, the power of punishing he wholly gives up, and engages his natural force, which he might before employ in the execution of the law of Nature, by his own single authority, as he thought fit, to assist the executive power of the society as the law thereof shall require. For being now in a new state, wherein he is to enjoy many conveniencies from the labour, assistance, and society of others in the same community, as well as protection from its whole strength, he is to part also with as much of his natural liberty, in providing for himself, as the good, prosperity, and safety of the society shall require, which is not only necessary but just, since the other members of the society do the like.

But though men when they enter into society give up the equality, liberty, and executive power they had in the state of Nature into the hands of the society, to be so far disposed of by the legislative as the good of the society shall require, yet it being only with an intention in every one the better to preserve himself, his liberty and property (for no rational creature can be supposed to change his condition with an intention to be worse), the power of the society or legislative constituted by them can never be supposed to extend farther than the common good, but is obliged to secure every one's property by providing against those three defects above mentioned that made the state of Nature so unsafe and uneasy. And so, whoever has the legislative or supreme power of any commonwealth, is bound to govern by established standing laws, promulgated and known to the people, and not by extemporary decrees, by indifferent and upright judges, who are to decide controversies by those laws; and to employ the force of the community at home only in the execution of such laws, or abroad to prevent or redress foreign injuries and secure the community from inroads and invasion. And all this to be directed to no other end but the peace, safety, and public good of the people.

CHAPTER XI: OF THE EXTENT OF THE LEGISLATIVE POWER

The great end of men's entering into society being the enjoyment of their properties in peace and safety, and the great instrument and means of that being the laws established in that society, the first and fundamental positive law of all commonwealths is the establishing of the legislative power, as the first and fundamental natural law which is to govern even the legislative itself is the preservation of the society and (as far as will consist with the public good) of every person in it. This legislative is not only the supreme power of the commonwealth, but sacred and unalterable in the hands where the community have once placed it. Nor can any edict of anybody else, in what form soever conceived, or by what power soever backed, have the force and obligation of a law which has not its sanction from that legislative which the public has chosen and appointed; for without this the law could not have that which is absolutely necessary to its being a law, the consent of the society, over whom nobody can have a power to make laws but by their own consent and by authority received from them; and therefore all the obedience, which by the most solemn ties any one can be obliged to pay, ultimately terminates in this supreme power, and is directed by those laws which it enacts. Nor can any oaths to any foreign power whatsoever, or any domestic subordinate power, discharge any member of the society from his obedience to the legislative, acting pursuant to their trust, nor oblige him to any obedience contrary to the laws so enacted or farther than they do allow, it being ridiculous to imagine one can be tied ultimately to obey any power in the society which is not the supreme.

Though the legislative, whether placed in one or more, whether it be always in being or only by intervals, though it be the supreme power in every commonwealth, yet, first, it is not, nor can possibly be, absolutely arbitrary over the lives and fortunes of the people. For it being but the joint power of every member of the society given up to that person or assembly which is legislator, it can be no more than those persons had in a state of Nature before they entered into society, and gave it up to the community. For nobody can transfer to another more power than he has in himself, and nobody has an absolute arbitrary power over himself, or over any other, to destroy his own life, or take away the life or property of another. A man, as has been proved, cannot subject himself to the arbitrary power of another; and having, in the state of Nature, no arbitrary power over the life, liberty, or possession of another, but only so much as the law of Nature gave him for the preservation of himself and the rest of mankind, this is all he doth, or can give up to the commonwealth, and by it to the legislative power, so that the legislative can have no more than this. Their power in the utmost bounds of it is limited to the public good of the society. It is a power that hath no other end but preservation, and therefore can never have a right to destroy, enslave, or designedly to impoverish the subjects; the obligations of the law of Nature cease not in society, but only in many cases are drawn closer, and have, by human laws, known penalties annexed to them to enforce their observation. Thus the law of Nature stands as an eternal rule to all men, legislators as well as others. The rules that they make for other men's actions must, as well as their own and other men's actions, be conformable to the law of Nature—*i.e.,* to the will of God, of which that is a declaration, and the fundamental law of Nature being the preservation of mankind, no human sanction can be good or valid against it.

Secondly, the legislative or supreme authority cannot assume to itself a power to rule by extemporary arbitrary decrees, but is bound to dispense justice and decide the rights of the subject by promulgated standing laws, and known authorised judges. For the law of Nature being unwritten, and so nowhere to be found but in the minds of men, they who, through passion or interest, shall miscite or misapply it, cannot so easily be convinced of their mistake where there is no established judge; and so it serves not as it ought, to determine the rights and fence the properties of those that live under it, especially where every one is judge, interpreter, and executioner of it too, and that in his own case; and he that has right on his side, having ordinarily but his own single strength, hath not force enough to defend himself from injuries or punish delinquents. To avoid these inconveniencies which disorder men's properties in the state of Nature, men unite into societies that they may have the united strength of the whole society to secure and defend their properties, and may have standing rules to bound it by which every one may know what is his. To this end it is that men give up all their natural power to the society they enter into, and the community put the legislative power into such hands as they think fit, with this trust, that they shall be governed by declared laws, or else their peace, quiet, and property will still be at the same uncertainty as it was in the state of Nature.

Absolute arbitrary power, or governing without settled standing laws, can neither of them consist with the ends of society and government, which men would not quit the freedom of the state of Nature for, and tie themselves up under, were it not to preserve their lives, liberties, and fortunes, and by stated rules of right and property to secure their peace and quiet. It cannot be supposed that they should intend, had they a power so to do, to give any one or more an absolute arbitrary power over their persons and estates, and put a force into the magistrate's hand to execute his unlimited will arbitrarily upon them; this were to put themselves into a worse condition than the state of Nature, wherein they had a liberty to defend their right against the injuries of others, and were upon equal terms of force to maintain it, whether invaded by a single man or many in combination. Whereas by supposing they have given up themselves to the absolute arbitrary power and will of a legislator, they have disarmed themselves, and armed him to make a prey of them when he pleases; he being in a much worse condition that is exposed to the arbitrary power of one man who has the command of a hundred thousand than he that is exposed to the arbitrary power of a hundred thousand single men, nobody being secure, that his will who has such a command is better than that of other men, though his force be a hundred thousand times stronger. And, therefore, whatever form the commonwealth is under, the ruling power ought to govern by declared and received laws, and not by extemporary dictates

and undetermined resolutions, for then mankind will be in a far worse condition than in the state of Nature if they shall have armed one or a few men with
the joint power of a multitude, to force them to obey at pleasure the exorbitant
and unlimited decrees of their sudden thoughts, or unrestrained, and till that
moment, unknown wills, without having any measures set down which may
guide and justify their actions. For all the power the government has, being
only for the good of the society, as it ought not to be arbitrary and at pleasure,
so it ought to be exercised by established and promulgated laws, that both
the people may know their duty, and be safe and secure within the limits of
the law, and the rulers, too, kept within their due bounds, and not be tempted
by the power they have in their hands to employ it to purposes, and by such
measures as they would not have known, and own not willingly.

Thirdly, the supreme power cannot take from any man any part of his
property without his own consent. For the preservation of property being the
end of government, and that for which men enter into society, it necessarily
supposes and requires that the people should have property, without which
they must be supposed to lose that by entering into society which was the end
for which they entered into it; too gross an absurdity for any man to own.
Men, therefore, in society having property, they have such a right to the goods,
which by the law of the community are theirs, that nobody hath a right to
take them, or any part of them, from them without their own consent; without this they have no property at all. For I have truly no property in that which
another can by right take from me when he pleases against my consent. Hence
it is a mistake to think that the supreme or legislative power of any commonwealth can do what it will, and dispose of the estates of the subject arbitrarily,
or take any part of them at pleasure. This is not much to be feared in governments where the legislative consists wholly or in part in assemblies which are
variable, whose members upon the dissolution of the assembly are subjects
under the common laws of their country, equally with the rest. But in governments where the legislative is in one lasting assembly, always in being, or in
one man as in absolute monarchies, there is danger still, that they will think
themselves to have a distinct interest from the rest of the community, and so
will be apt to increase their own riches and power by taking what they think
fit from the people. For a man's property is not at all secure, though there
be good and equitable laws to set the bounds of it between him and his fellow-
subjects, if he who commands those subjects have power to take from any
private man what part he pleases of his property, and use and dispose of it as
he thinks good.

But government, into whosesoever hands it is put, being as I have before
showed, entrusted with this condition, and for this end, that men might have

and secure their properties, the prince or senate, however it may have power to make laws for the regulating of property between the subjects one amongst another, yet can never have a power to take to themselves the whole, or any part of the subjects' property, without their own consent; for this would be in effect to leave them no property at all. And to let us see that even absolute power, where it is necessary, is not arbitrary by being absolute, but is still limited by that reason, and confined to those ends which required it in some cases to be absolute, we need look no farther than the common practice of martial discipline. For the preservation of the army, and in it of the whole commonwealth, requires an absolute obedience to the command of every superior officer, and it is justly death to disobey or dispute the most dangerous or unreasonable of them; but yet we see that neither the sergeant that could command a soldier to march up to the mouth of a cannon, or stand in a breach where he is almost sure to perish, can command that soldier to give him one penny of his money; nor the general that can condemn him to death for deserting his post, or not obeying the most desperate orders, cannot yet with all his absolute power of life and death dispose of one farthing of that soldier's estate, or seize one jot of his goods; whom yet he can command anything, and hang for the least disobedience. Because such a blind obedience is necessary to that end for which the commander has his power—viz., the preservation of the rest, but the disposing of his goods has nothing to do with it.

It is true governments cannot be supported without great charge, and it is fit every one who enjoys his share of the protection should pay out of his estate his proportion for the maintenance of it. But still it must be with his own consent—i.e., the consent of the majority, giving it either by themselves or their representatives chosen by them; for if any one shall claim a power to lay and levy taxes on the people by his own authority, and without such consent of the people, he thereby invades the fundamental law of property, and subverts the end of government. For what property have I in that which another may by right take when he pleases to himself?

Fourthly. The legislative cannot transfer the power of making laws to any other hands, for it being but a delegated power from the people, they who have it cannot pass it over to others. The people alone can appoint the form of the commonwealth, which is by constituting the legislative, and appointing in whose hands that shall be. And when the people have said, "We will submit, and be governed by laws made by such men, and in such forms," nobody else can say other men shall make laws for them; nor can they be bound by any laws but such as are enacted by those whom they have chosen and authorised to make laws for them.

These are the bounds which the trust that is put in them by the society and the law of God and Nature have set to the legislative power of every common-wealth, in all forms of government. First: They are to govern by promulgated established laws, not to be varied in particular cases, but to have one rule for rich and poor, for the favourite at Court, and the countryman at plough. Secondly: These laws also ought to be designed for no other end ultimately but the good of the people. Thirdly: They must not raise taxes on the prop-erty of the people without the consent of the people given by themselves or their deputies. And this properly concerns only such governments where the legislative is always in being, or at least where the people have not reserved any part of the legislative to deputies, to be from time to time chosen by them-selves. Fourthly: Legislative neither must nor can transfer the power of mak-ing laws to anybody else, or place it anywhere but where the people have.

CHAPTER XII: THE LEGISLATIVE, EXECUTIVE, AND FEDERATIVE POWER OF THE COMMONWEALTH

The legislative power is that which has a right to direct how the force of the commonwealth shall be employed for preserving the community and the mem-bers of it. Because those laws which are constantly to be executed, and whose force is always to continue, may be made in a little time, therefore there is no need that the legislative should be always in being, not having always business to do. And because it may be too great temptation to human frailty, apt to grasp at power, for the same persons who have the power of making laws to have also in their hands the power to execute them, whereby they may exempt themselves from obedience to the laws they make, and suit the law, both in its making and execution, to their own private advantage, and thereby come to have a distinct interest from the rest of the community, contrary to the end of society and government. Therefore in well-ordered commonwealths, where the good of the whole is so considered as it ought, the legislative power is put into the hands of divers persons who, duly assembled, have by themselves, or jointly with others, a power to make laws, which when they have done, being separated again, they are themselves subject to the laws they have made; which is a new and near tie upon them to take care that they make them for the public good.

But because the laws that are at once, and in a short time made, have a constant and lasting force, and need a perpetual execution, or an attendance thereunto, therefore it is necessary there should be a power always in being which should see to the execution of the laws that are made, and remain in force. And thus the legislative and executive power come often to be separated.

There is another power in every commonwealth which one may call natural, because it is that which answers to the power every man naturally had before he entered into society. For though in a commonwealth the members of it are distinct persons, still, in reference to one another, and, as such, are governed by the laws of the society, yet, in reference to the rest of mankind, they make one body, which is, as every member of it before was, still in the state of Nature with the rest of mankind, so that the controversies that happen between any man of the society with those that are out of it are managed by the public, and an injury done to a member of their body engages the whole in the reparation of it. So that under this consideration the whole community is one body in the state of Nature in respect of all other states or persons out of its community.

This, therefore, contains the power of war and peace, leagues and alliances, and all the transactions with all persons and communities without the commonwealth, and may be called federative if any one pleases. So the thing be understood, I am indifferent as to the name.

These two powers, executive and federative, though they be really distinct in themselves . . . are hardly to be separated and placed at the same time in the hands of distinct persons. For both of them requiring the force of the society for their exercise, it is almost impracticable to place the force of the commonwealth in distinct and not subordinate hands, or that the executive and federative power should be placed in persons that might act separately, whereby the force of the public would be under different commands, which would be apt some time or other to cause disorder and ruin.

CHAPTER XIII: OF THE SUBORDINATION OF THE POWERS OF THE COMMON-
WEALTH

Though in a constituted commonwealth standing upon its own basis and acting according to its own nature—that is, acting for the preservation of the community, there can be but one supreme power, which is the legislative, to which all the rest are and must be subordinate, yet the legislative being only a fiduciary power to act for certain ends, there remains still in the people a supreme power to remove or alter the legislative, when they find the legislative act contrary to the trust reposed in them. For all power given with trust for the attaining an end being limited by that end, whenever that end is manifestly neglected or opposed, the trust must necessarily be forfeited, and the power devolve into the hands of those that gave it, who may place it anew where they shall think best for their safety and security. And thus the community perpetually retains a supreme power of saving themselves from the attempts and designs of anybody, even of their legislators, whenever they shall be so foolish or so wicked as to lay and carry on designs against the liberties and properties of the subject. For no man or society of men having a power to deliver up their preservation, or consequently the means of it, to the absolute will and arbitrary dominion of another, whenever any one shall go about to bring them into such a slavish condition, they will always have a right to preserve what they have not a power to part with, and to rid themselves of those who invade this fundamental, sacred, and unalterable law of self-preservation for which they entered into society. And thus the community may be said in this respect to be always the supreme power, but not as considered under any form of government, because this power of the people can never take place till the government be dissolved.

In all cases whilst the government subsists, the legislative is the supreme power. For what can give laws to another must needs be superior to him, and since the legislative is no otherwise legislative of the society but by the right it has to make laws for all the parts, and every member of the society prescribing rules to their actions, and giving power of execution where they are transgressed, the legislative must needs be the supreme, and all other powers in any members or parts of the society derived from and subordinate to it. . . .

It is not necessary—no, nor so much as convenient—that the legislative should be always in being; but absolutely necessary that the executive power should, because there is not always need of new laws to be made, but always need of execution of the laws that are made. . . .

If the legislative, or any part of it, be of representatives, chosen for that time by the people, which afterwards return into the ordinary state of subjects, and have no share in the legislative but upon a new choice, this power of choosing must also be exercised by the people, either at certain appointed seasons, or else when they are summoned to it; and, in this latter case, the power of convoking the legislative is ordinarily placed in the executive, and has one of these two limitations in respect of time:—that either the original constitution requires their assembling and acting at certain intervals; and then the executive power does nothing but ministerially issue directions for their electing and assembling according to due forms; or else it is left to his prudence to call them by new elections when the occasions or exigencies of the public require the amendment of old or making of new laws, or the redress or prevention of any inconveniencies that lie on or threaten the people.

It may be demanded here, what if the executive power, being possessed of the force of the commonwealth, shall make use of that force to hinder the meeting and acting of the legislative, when the original constitution or the public exigencies require it? I say, using force upon the people, without authority, and contrary to the trust put in him that does so, is a state of war with the people, who have a right to reinstate their legislative in the exercise of their power. For having erected a legislative with an intent they should exercise the power of making laws, either at certain set times, or when there is need of it, when they are hindered by any force from what is so necessary to the society, and wherein the safety and preservation of the people consists, the people have a right to remove it by force. In all states and conditions the true remedy of force without authority is to oppose force to it. The use of force without authority always puts him that uses it into a state of war as the aggressor, and renders him liable to be treated accordingly. . . .

CHAPTER XVIII: OF TYRANNY

As usurpation is the exercise of power which another hath a right to, so tyranny is the exercise of power beyond right, which nobody can have a right to; and this is making use of the power any one has in his hands, not for the good of those who are under it, but for his own private, separate advantage. When the governor, however entitled, makes not the law, but his will, the rule, and his commands and actions are not directed to the preservation of the properties of his people, but the satisfaction of his own ambition, revenge, covetousness, or any other irregular passion.

If one can doubt this to be truth or reason because it comes from the obscure hand of a subject, I hope the authority of a king will make it pass with him. King James, in his speech to the Parliament, 1603, tells them thus: "I will ever prefer the weal of the public and of the whole commonwealth, in making of good laws and constitutions, to any particular and private ends of mine, thinking ever the wealth and weal of the commonwealth to be my greatest weal and worldly felicity—a point wherein a lawful king doth directly differ from a tyrant; for I do acknowledge that the special and greatest point of difference that is between a rightful king and an usurping tyrant is this—that whereas the proud and ambitious tyrant doth think his kingdom and people are only ordained for satisfaction of his desires and unreasonable appetites, the righteous and just king doth, by the contrary, acknowledge himself to be ordained for the procuring of the wealth and property of his people." And again, in his speech to the Parliament, 1609, he hath these words: "The king binds himself, by a double oath, to the observation of the fundamental laws of his kingdom— tacitly, as by being a king, and so bound to protect, as well the people as the laws of his kingdom; and expressly by his oath at his coronation; so as every just king, in a settled kingdom, is bound to observe that paction made to his people, by his laws, in framing his government agreeable thereunto, according to that paction which God made with Noah after the deluge: 'Hereafter, seed-time, and harvest, and cold, and heat, and summer, and winter, and day, and night, shall not cease while the earth remaineth.' And therefore a king, governing in a settled kingdom, leaves to be a king, and degenerates into a tyrant, as soon as he leaves off to rule according to his laws." And a little after: "There-

fore, all kings that are not tyrants, or perjured, will be glad to bound themselves within the limits of their laws, and they that persuade them the contrary are vipers, pests, both against them and the commonwealth." Thus, that
learned king, who well understood the notions of things, makes the difference
betwixt a king and a tyrant to consist only in this: that one makes the laws
the bounds of his power and the good of the public the end of his government;
the other makes all give way to his own will and appetite.

It is a mistake to think this fault is proper only to monarchies. Other forms
of government are liable to it as well as that; for wherever the power that is
put in any hands for the government of the people and the preservation of their
properties is applied to other ends, and made use of to impoverish, harass, or
subdue them to the arbitrary and irregular commands of those that have it,
there it presently becomes tyranny, whether those that thus use it are one or
many. Thus we read of the thirty tyrants at Athens, as well as one at Syracuse;
and the intolerable dominion of the Decemviri at Rome was nothing better.

Wherever law ends, tyranny begins, if the law be transgressed to another's
harm; and whosoever in authority exceeds the power given him by the law,
and makes use of the force he has under his command to compass that upon
the subject which the law allows not, ceases in that to be a magistrate, and
acting without authority may be opposed, as any other man who by force
invades the right of another. This is acknowledged in subordinate magistrates.
He that hath authority to seize my person in the street may be opposed as a
thief and a robber if he endeavours to break into my house to execute a writ,
notwithstanding that I know he has such a warrant and such a legal authority
as will empower him to arrest me abroad. And why this should not hold in
the highest, as well as in the most inferior magistrate, I would gladly be informed. Is it reasonable that the eldest brother, because he has the greatest part
of his father's estate, should thereby have a right to take away any of his
younger brothers' portions? Or that a rich man, who possessed a whole country, should from thence have a right to seize, when he pleased, the cottage and
garden of his poor neighbour? The being rightfully possessed of great power
and riches, exceedingly beyond the greatest part of the sons of Adam, is so
far from being an excuse, much less a reason for rapine and oppression, which
the endamaging another without authority is, that it is a great aggravation
of it. For exceeding the bounds of authority is no more a right in a great than
a petty officer, no more justifiable in a king than a constable. But so much
the worse in him as that he has more trust put in him, is supposed, from the advantage of education and counsellors, to have better knowledge and less reason
to do it, having already a greater share than the rest of his brethren.

May the commands, then, of a prince be opposed? May he be resisted, as often as any one shall find himself aggrieved, and but imagine he has not right done him? This will unhinge and overturn all polities, and instead of government and order, leave nothing but anarchy and confusion.

To this I answer: That force is to be opposed to nothing but to unjust and unlawful force. Whoever makes any opposition in any other case draws on himself a just condemnation, both from God and man; and so no such danger or confusion will follow, as is often suggested. . . .

If either these illegal acts have extended to the majority of the people, or if the mischief and oppression has light only on some few, but in such cases as the precedent and consequences seem to threaten all, and they are persuaded in their consciences that their laws, and with them, their estates, liberties, and lives are in danger, and perhaps their religion too, how they will be hindered from resisting illegal force used against them I cannot tell. This is an inconvenience, I confess, that attends all governments whatsoever, when the governors have brought it to this pass, to be generally suspected of their people, the most dangerous state they can possibly put themselves in; wherein they are the less to be pitied, because it is so easy to be avoided. . . .

CHAPTER XIX: OF THE DISSOLUTION OF GOVERNMENT

He that will, with any clearness, speak of the dissolution of government, ought in the first place to distinguish between the dissolution of the society and the dissolution of the government. That which makes the community, and brings men out of the loose state of Nature into one politic society, is the agreement which every one has with the rest to incorporate and act as one body, and so be one distinct commonwealth. The usual, and almost only way whereby this union is dissolved, is the inroad of foreign force making a conquest upon them. For in that case (not being able to maintain and support themselves as one entire and independent body) the union belonging to that body, which consisted therein, must necessarily cease, and so every one return to the state he was in before, with a liberty to shift for himself and provide for his own safety, as he thinks fit, in some other society. Whenever the society is dissolved, it is certain the government of that society cannot remain. Thus conquerors' swords often cut up governments by the roots, and mangle societies to pieces, separating the subdued or scattered multitude from the protection of and dependence on that society which ought to have preserved them from violence. The world is too well instructed in, and too forward to allow of this way of dissolving of governments, to need any more to be said of it; and there wants not much argument to prove that where the society is dissolved, the government cannot remain; that being as impossible as for the frame of a house to subsist when the materials of it are scattered and displaced by a whirlwind, or jumbled into a confused heap by an earthquake.

Besides this overturning from without, governments are dissolved from within:

First. When the legislative is altered, civil society being a state of peace amongst those who are of it, from whom the state of war is excluded by the umpirage which they have provided in their legislative for the ending all differences that may arise amongst any of them; it is in their legislative that the members of a commonwealth are united and combined together into one coherent living body. This is the soul that gives form, life, and unity to the commonwealth; from hence the several members have their mutual influence, sympathy, and connection; and therefore when the legislative is broken, or dissolved, dissolution and death follows. For the essence and union of the society consisting in having one will, the legislative, when once established by the majority, has the declaring and, as it were, keeping of that will. The constitution of the legislative is the first and fundamental act of society, whereby provision is made for the continuation of their union under the direction of persons and bonds of laws, made by persons authorised thereunto, by the consent and appointment of the people, without which no one man, or number of men, amongst them can have authority of making laws that shall be binding to the rest. When any one, or more, shall take upon them to make laws whom the people have not appointed so to do, they make laws without authority, which the people are not therefore bound to obey; by which means they come again to be out of subjection, and may constitute to themselves a new legislative, as they think best, being in full liberty to resist the force of those who, without authority, would impose anything upon them. Every one is at the disposure of his own will, when those who had, by the delegation of the society, the declaring of the public will, are excluded from it, and others usurp the place who have no such authority or delegation.

This being usually brought about by such in the commonwealth, who misuse the power they have, it is hard to consider it aright, and know at whose door to lay it, without knowing the form of government in which it happens. Let us suppose, then, the legislative placed in the concurrence of three distinct persons:—First, a single hereditary person having the constant, supreme, executive power, and with it the power of convoking and dissolving the other two within certain periods of time. Secondly, an assembly of hereditary nobility. Thirdly, an assembly of representatives chosen, *pro tempore*, by the people. Such a form of government supposed, it is evident:

First, that when such a single person or prince sets up his own arbitrary will in place of the laws which are the will of the society declared by the legislative, then the legislative is changed. For that being, in effect, the legislative whose rules and laws are put in execution, and required to be obeyed, when other laws are set up, and other rules pretended and enforced than what the legislative, constituted by the society, have enacted, it is plain that the legislative is changed. Whoever introduces new laws, not being thereunto authorised, by the fundamental appointment of the society, or subverts the old, disowns and overturns the power by which they were made, and so sets up a new legislative.

Secondly, when the prince hinders the legislative from assembling in its due time, or from acting freely, pursuant to those ends for which it was constituted, the legislative is altered. For it is not a certain number of men—no, nor their meeting, unless they have also freedom of debating and leisure of perfecting what is for the good of the society, wherein the legislative consists; when these are taken away, or altered, so as to deprive the society of the due exercise of their power, the legislative is truly altered. For it is not names that constitute governments, but the use and exercise of those powers that were intended to accompany them; so that he who takes away the freedom, or hinders the acting of the legislative in its due seasons, in effect takes away the legislative, and puts an end to the government.

Thirdly, when, by the arbitrary power of the prince, the electors or ways of election are altered without the consent and contrary to the common interest of the people, there also the legislative is altered. For if others than those whom the society hath authorised thereunto do choose, or in another way than what the society hath prescribed, those chosen are not the legislative appointed by the people.

Fourthly, the delivery also of the people into the subjection of a foreign power, either by the prince or by the legislative, is certainly a change of the legislative, and so a dissolution of the government. For the end why people entered into society being to be preserved one entire, free, independent society, to be governed by its own laws, this is lost whenever they are given up into the power of another.

Why, in such a constitution as this, the dissolution of the government in these cases is to be imputed to the prince is evident, because he, having the force, treasure, and offices of the State to employ, and often persuading himself or being flattered by others, that, as supreme magistrate, he is incapable of control; he alone is in a condition to make great advances towards such changes under pretence of lawful authority, and has it in his hands to terrify or suppress opposers as factious, seditious, and enemies to the government; whereas no other part of the legislative, or people, is capable by themselves to attempt any alteration of the legislative without open and visible rebellion, apt enough to be taken notice of, which, when it prevails, produces effects very little different from foreign conquest. Besides, the prince, in such a form of government, having the power of dissolving the other parts of the legislative, and thereby rendering them private persons, they can never, in opposition to him, or without his concurrence, alter the legislative by a law, his consent being necessary to give any of their decrees that sanction. But yet so far as the other parts of the legislative any way contribute to any attempt upon the government, and do either promote, or not, what lies in them, hinder such designs, they are guilty, and partake in this, which is certainly the greatest crime men can be guilty of one towards another.

There is one way more whereby such a government may be dissolved, and that is: When he who has the supreme executive power neglects and abandons that charge, so that the laws already made can no longer be put in execution; this is demonstratively to reduce all to anarchy, and so effectively to dissolve the government. For laws not being made for themselves, but to be, by their execution, the bonds of the society to keep every part of the body politic in its due place and function; when that totally ceases, the government visibly ceases, and the people become a confused multitude without order or connection. Where there is no longer the administration of justice for the securing of men's rights, nor any remaining power within the community to direct the force, or provide for the necessities of the public, there certainly is no government left. Where the laws cannot be executed it is all one as if there were no laws, and a government without laws is, I suppose, a mystery in politics inconceivable to human capacity, and inconsistent with human society.

In these, and the like cases, when the government is dissolved, the people are at liberty to provide for themselves by erecting a new legislative differing from the other by the change of persons, or form, or both, as they shall find it most for their safety and good. For the society can never, by the fault of another, lose the native and original right it has to preserve itself, which can only be done by a settled legislative and a fair and impartial execution of the laws made by it. But the state of mankind is not so miserable that they are not capable of using this remedy till it be too late to look for any. To tell people they may provide for themselves by erecting a new legislative, when, by oppression, artifice, or being delivered over to a foreign power, their old one is gone, is only to tell them they may expect relief when it is too late, and the evil is past cure. This is, in effect, no more than to bid them first be slaves, and then to take care of their liberty, and, when their chains are on, tell them they may act like free men. This, if barely so, is rather mockery than relief, and men can never be secure from tyranny if there be no means to escape it till they are perfectly under it; and, therefore, it is that they have not only a right to get out of it, but to prevent it.

There is, therefore, secondly, another way whereby governments are dissolved, and that is, when the legislative, or the prince, either of them act contrary to their trust.

For the legislative acts against the trust reposed in them when they endeavour to invade the property of the subject, and to make themselves, or any part of the community, masters or arbitrary disposers of the lives, liberties, or fortunes of the people.

The reason why men enter into society is the preservation of their property; and the end while they choose and authorise a legislative is that there may be laws made, and rules set, as guards and fences to the properties of all the society, to limit the power and moderate the dominion of every part and member of the society. For since it can never be supposed to be the will of the society that the legislative should have a power to destroy that which every one designs to secure by entering into society, and for which the people submitted themselves to legislators of their own making: whenever the legislators endeavour to take away and destroy the property of the people, or to reduce them to slavery under arbitrary power, they put themselves into a state of war with the people, who are thereupon absolved from any farther obedience, and are left to the common refuge which God hath provided for all men against force and violence. Whensoever, therefore, the legislative shall transgress this fundamental rule of society, and either by ambition, fear, folly, or corruption, endeavour to grasp themselves, or put into the hands of any other, an absolute power over the lives, liberties, and estates of the people, by this breach of trust they forfeit the power the people had put into their hands for quite contrary ends, and it devolves to the people, who have a right to resume their original liberty, and by the establishment of a new legislative (such as they shall think fit), provide for their own safety and security, which is the end for which they are in society. What I have said here concerning the legislative in general holds true also concerning the supreme executor, who having a double trust put in him, both to have a part in the legislative and the supreme execution of the law, acts against both, when he goes about to set up his own arbitrary will as the law of the society. He acts also contrary to his trust when he employs the force, treasure, and offices of the society to corrupt the representatives and gain them to his purposes, when he openly pre-engages the electors, and prescribes, to their choice, such whom he has, by solicitation, threats, promises, or otherwise, won to his designs, and employs them to bring in such who have promised beforehand what to vote and what to enact. Thus to regulate candidates and electors, and new model the ways of election, what is it but to cut up the government by the roots, and poison the very fountain of public security? For the people having reserved to themselves the choice of their representatives as the fence to their properties, could do it for no other end but that they might always be freely chosen, and so chosen, freely act and advise as the necessity of the commonwealth and the public good should, upon examination and mature debate, be judged to require. This, those who give their votes before they hear the debate, and have weighed the reasons on all sides, are not capable of doing. To prepare such an assembly as this, and endeavour to set up the declared abettors of his own will, for the true representatives of the people, and the law-makers of the society, is certainly as great a breach of trust, and as perfect a declaration of a design to subvert the government, as is possible to be met with. To which, if one shall add rewards and punishments visibly employed to the same end, and all the arts of perverted law made use of to take off and destroy all that stand in the way of such a design, and will not comply and consent to betray the liberties of their country, it will be past doubt what is doing. What power they ought to have in the society who thus employ it contrary to the trust went along with it in its first institution, is easy to determine; and one cannot but see that he who has once attempted any such thing as this cannot any longer be trusted.

To this, perhaps, it will be said that the people being ignorant and always discontented, to lay the foundation of government in the unsteady opinion and uncertain humour of the people, is to expose it to certain ruin; and no government will be able long to subsist if the people may set up a new legislative whenever they take offence at the old one. To this I answer, quite the contrary. People are not so easily got out of their old forms as some are apt to suggest. They are hardly to be prevailed with to amend the acknowledged faults in the frame they have been accustomed to. And if there be any original defects, or adventitious ones introduced by time or corruption, it is not an easy thing to get them changed, even when all the world sees there is an opportunity for it. This slowness and aversion in the people to quit their old constitutions has in the many revolutions which have been seen in this kingdom, in this and former ages, still kept us to, or after some interval of fruitless attempts, still brought us back again to our old legislative of king, lords and commons; and whatever provocations have made the crown be taken from some of our princes' heads, they never carried the people so far as to place it in another line.

But it will be said this hypothesis lays a ferment for frequent rebellion. To which I answer:

First: no more than any other hypothesis. For when the people are made miserable, and find themselves exposed to the ill usage of arbitrary power, cry up their governors as much as you will for sons of Jupiter, let them be sacred and divine, descended or authorised from Heaven; give them out for whom or what you please, the same will happen. The people generally ill treated, and contrary to right, will be ready upon any occasion to ease themselves of a burden that sits heavy upon them. They will wish and seek for the opportunity, which in the change, weakness, and accidents of human affairs, seldom delays long to offer itself. He must have lived but a little while in the world, who has not seen examples of this in his time; and he must have read very little who cannot produce examples of it in all sorts of governments in the world.

Secondly: I answer, such revolutions happen not upon every little mismanagement in public affairs. Great mistakes in the ruling part, many wrong and inconvenient laws, and all the slips of human frailty will be borne by the people without mutiny or murmur. But if a long train of abuses, prevarications, and artifices, all tending the same way, make the design visible to the people, and they cannot but feel what they lie under, and see whither they are going, it is not to be wondered that they should then rouse themselves, and endeavour to put the rule into such hands which may secure to them the ends for which government was at first erected, and without which, ancient names and specious forms are so far from being better, that they are much worse than the state of Nature or pure anarchy; the inconveniencies being all as great and as near, but the remedy farther off and more difficult.

Thirdly: I answer, that this power in the people of providing for their safety anew by a new legislative when their legislators have acted contrary to their trust by invading their property, is the best fence against rebellion, and the probablest means to hinder it. For rebellion being an opposition, not to persons, but authority, which is founded only in the constitutions and laws of the government: those, whoever they be, who, by force, break through, and, by force, justify their violation of them, are truly and properly rebels. For when men, by entering into society and civil government, have excluded force, and introduced laws for the preservation of property, peace, and unity amongst themselves, those who set up force again in opposition to the laws, do *rebellare* —that is, bring back again the state of war, and are properly rebels, which they who are in power, by the pretence they have to authority, the temptation of force they have in their hands, and the flattery of those about them being likeliest to do, the properest way to prevent the evil is to show them the danger and injustice of it who are under the greatest temptation to run into it.

In both the forementioned cases, when either the legislative is changed, or the legislators act contrary to the end for which they were constituted, those who are guilty are guilty of rebellion. For if any one by force takes away the established legislative of any society, and the laws by them made, pursuant to their trust, he thereby takes away the umpirage which every one had consented to for a peaceable decision of all their controversies, and a bar to the state of war amongst them. They who remove or change the legislative take away this decisive power, which nobody can have but by the appointment and consent of the people, and so destroying the authority which the people did, and nobody else can set up, and introducing a power which the people hath not authorised, actually introduce a state of war, which is that of force without authority; and thus by removing the legislative established by the society, in whose decisions the people acquiesced and united as to that of their own will, they untie the knot, and expose the people anew to the state of war. And if those, who by force take away the legislative, are rebels, the legislators themselves, as has been shown, can be no less esteemed so, when they who were set up for the protection and preservation of the people, their liberties and properties shall by force invade and endeavour to take them away; and so they putting themselves into a state of war with those who made them the protectors and guardians of their peace, are properly, and with the greatest aggravation, *rebellantes,* rebels.

But if they who say it lays a foundation for rebellion mean that it may occasion civil wars or intestine broils to tell the people they are absolved from obedience when illegal attempts are made upon their liberties or properties, and may oppose the unlawful violence of those who were their magistrates when they invade their properties, contrary to the trust put in them, and that, therefore, this doctrine is not to be allowed, being so destructive to the peace of the world; they may as well say, upon the same ground, that honest men may not oppose robbers or pirates, because this may occasion disorder or bloodshed. If any mischief come in such cases, it is not to be charged upon him who defends his own right, but on him that invades his neighbour's. If the innocent honest man must quietly quit all he has for peace sake to him who will lay violent hands upon it, I desire it may be considered what a kind of peace there will be in the world which consists only in violence and rapine, and which is to be maintained only for the benefit of robbers and oppressors. Who would not think it an admirable peace betwixt the mighty and the mean, when the lamb, without resistance, yielded his throat to be torn by the imperious wolf? Polyphemus's den gives us a perfect pattern of such a peace. Such a government wherein Ulysses and his companions had nothing to do but quietly to suffer themselves to be devoured. And no doubt Ulysses, who was a prudent man, preached up passive obedience, and exhorted them to a quiet submission by representing to them of what concernment peace was to mankind, and by showing the inconveniencies might happen if they should offer to resist Polyphemus, who had now the power over them.

The end of government is the good of mankind; and which is best for mankind, that the people should be always exposed to the boundless will of tyranny, or that the rulers should be sometimes liable to be opposed when they grow exorbitant in the use of their power, and employ it for the destruction, and not the preservation, of the properties of their people?

Nor let any one say that mischief can arise from hence as often as it shall please a busy head or turbulent spirit to desire the alteration of the government. It is true such men may stir whenever they please, but it will be only to their own just ruin and perdition. For till the mischief be grown general, and the ill designs of the rulers become visible, or their attempts sensible to the greater part, the people, who are more disposed to suffer than right themselves by resistance, are not apt to stir. The examples of particular injustice or oppression of here and there an unfortunate man moves them not. But if they universally have a persuasion grounded upon manifest evidence that designs are carrying on against their liberties, and the general course and tendency of things cannot but give them strong suspicions of the evil intention of their governors, who is to be blamed for it? Who can help it if they, who might avoid it, bring themselves into this suspicion? Are the people to be blamed if they have the sense of rational creatures, and can think of things no otherwise than as they find and feel them? And is it not rather their fault who put things in such a posture that they would not have them thought as they are? I grant that the pride, ambition, and turbulency of private men have sometimes caused great disorders in commonwealths, and factions have been fatal to states and kingdoms. But whether the mischief hath oftener begun in the people's wantonness, and a desire to cast off the lawful authority of their rulers, or in the rulers' insolence and endeavours to get and exercise an arbitrary power over their people, whether oppression or disobedience gave the first rise to the disorder, I leave it to impartial history to determine. This I am sure, whoever, either ruler or subject, by force goes about to invade the rights of either prince or people, and lays the foundation for overturning the constitution and frame of any just government, he is guilty of the greatest crime I think a man is capable of, being to answer for all those mischiefs of blood, rapine, and desolation, which the breaking to pieces of governments bring on a country; and he who does it is justly to be esteemed the common enemy and pest of mankind, and is to be treated accordingly.

That subjects or foreigners attempting by force on the properties of any people may be resisted with force is agreed on all hands; but that magistrates doing the same thing may be resisted, hath of late been denied; as if those who had the greatest privileges and advantages by the law had thereby a power to break those laws by which alone they were set in a better place than their brethren; whereas their offence is thereby the greater, both as being ungrateful for the greater share they have by the law, and breaking also that trust which is put into their hands by their brethren.

Whosoever uses force without right—as every one does in society who does it without law—puts himself into a state of war with those against whom he so uses it, and in that state all former ties are cancelled, all other rights cease, and every one has a right to defend himself, and to resist the aggressor. This is so evident that Barclay himself—that great assertor of the power and sacredness of kings—is forced to confess that it is lawful for the people, in some cases, to resist their king, and that, too, in a chapter wherein he pretends to show that the Divine law shuts up the people from all manner of rebellion. Whereby it is evident, even by his own doctrine, that since they may, in some cases, resist, all resisting of princes is not rebellion. . . .

To conclude. The power that every individual gave the society when he entered into it can never revert to the individuals again, as long as the society lasts, but will always remain in the community; because without this there can be no community—no commonwealth, which is contrary to the original agreement; so also when the society hath placed the legislative in any assembly of men, to continue in them and their successors, with direction and authority for providing such successors, the legislative can never revert to the people whilst that government lasts; because, having provided a legislative with power to continue for ever, they have given up their political power to the legislative, and cannot resume it. But if they have set limits to the duration of their legislative, and made this supreme power in any person or assembly only temporary; or else when, by the miscarriages of those in authority, it is forfeited; upon the forfeiture of their rulers, or at the determination of the time set, it reverts to the society, and the people have a right to act as supreme, and continue the legislative in themselves or place it in a new form, or new hands, as they think good.

XI THE ENLIGHTENMENT: BACKGROUND AND IDEALS

JOHN LOCKE

THE NAME of Locke was, with Newton's, preeminent in the Enlightenment. The philosophers of that period, especially in France, looked up to Locke for having done for human nature what Newton had done for the physical world. These thinkers had most in mind Locke's epoch-making work, the *Essay concerning Human Understanding* (1690). To men like Voltaire in pre-Revolutionary France it seemed that Locke had liberated the human mind from the trammels of supernatural authority by demonstrating that all ideas were primarily derived from man's experience and circumstances. Although not without ambiguities, his implication was that neither innate flaws in human nature (e.g. original sin) nor accident of birth (e.g. lowly birth) were responsible for what a man came to be in life.

The influence of Locke's ideas in psychology is impossible to measure. There are few modern students of theory of knowledge, of education, and of character formation who have not, directly or indirectly been affected by the *Essay concerning Human Understanding*. The following selection is taken from A. C. Fraser's edition (Oxford, Clarendon Press, 1894).

AN ESSAY CONCERNING
HUMAN UNDERSTANDING

Book I: Of Innate Notions

CHAPTER I: INTRODUCTION

1. Since it is the *understanding* that sets man above the rest of sensible beings, and gives him all the advantage and dominion which he has over them; it is certainly a subject, even for its nobleness, worth our labour to inquire into. The understanding, like the eye, whilst it makes us see and perceive all other things, takes no notice of itself; and it requires art and pains to set it at a distance and make it its own object. But whatever be the difficulties that lie in the way of this inquiry; whatever it be that keeps us so much in the dark to ourselves; sure I am that all the light we can let in upon our minds, all the acquaintance we can make with our own understandings, will not only be very pleasant, but bring us great advantage, in directing our thoughts in the search of other things.

2. This, therefore, being my purpose—to inquire into the original, cer-

tainty, and extent of human knowledge, together with grounds and degrees of belief, opinion, and assent—I shall not at present meddle with the physical consideration of the mind; or trouble myself to examine wherein its essence consists; or by what motions of our spirits or alterations of our bodies we come to have any sensation by our organs, or any *ideas* in our understandings; and whether those *ideas* do in their formation, any or all of them, depend on matter or not. These are speculations which, however curious and entertaining, I shall decline, as lying out of my way in the design I am now upon. It shall suffice to my present purpose, to consider the discerning faculties of a man, as they are employed about the objects which they have to do with. And I shall imagine I have not wholly misemployed myself in the thoughts I shall have on this occasion, if, in this historical, plain method, I can give any account of the ways whereby our understandings come to attain those notions of things we have, and can set down any measures of the certainty of our knowledge; or the grounds of those persuasions which are to be found amongst men, so various, different, and wholly contradictory; and yet asserted somewhere or other with such assurance and confidence that he that shall take a view of the opinions of mankind, observe their opposition, and at the same time consider the fondness and devotion wherewith they are embraced, the resolution and eagerness wherewith they are maintained, may perhaps have reason to suspect, that either there is no such thing as truth at all, or that mankind hath no sufficient means to attain a certain knowledge of it.

5. For though the comprehension of our understandings comes exceeding short of the vast extent of things, yet we shall have cause enough to magnify the bountiful Author of our being, for that proportion and degee of knowledge he has bestowed on us, so far above all the rest of the inhabitants of this our mansion. Men have reason to be well satisfied with what God hath thought fit for them, since he hath given them (as St. Peter says) πάντα πρὸς ζωὴν καὶ εὐσέβειαν, whatsoever is necessary for the conveniences of life and information of virtue; and has put within the reach of their discovery, the comfortable provision for this life, and the way that leads to a better. How short soever their knowledge may come of an universal or perfect comprehension of whatsoever is, yet it secures their great concernments, that they have light enough to lead them to the knowledge of their Maker, and the sight of their own duties. Men may find matter sufficient to busy their heads and employ their hands with variety, delight and satisfaction, if they will not boldly quarrel with their own constitution, and throw away the blessings their hands are filled with, because they are not big enough to grasp every-

thing. We shall not have much reason to complain of the narrowness of our minds, if we will but employ them about what may be of use to us; for of that they are very capable. And it will be an unpardonable as well as childish peevishness, if we undervalue the advantages of our knowledge, and neglect to improve it to the ends for which it was given us, because there are some things that are set out of the reach of it. It will be no excuse to an idle and untoward servant, who would not attend his business by candlelight, to plead that he had not broad sunshine. The Candle that is set up in us shines bright enough for all our purposes. The discoveries we can make with this ought to satisfy us; and we shall then use our understandings right, when we entertain all objects in that way and proportion that they are suited to our faculties, and upon those grounds they are capable of being proposed to us; and not peremptorily or intemperately require demonstration, and demand certainty, where probability only is to be had, and which is sufficient to govern all our concernments. If we will disbelieve everything, because we cannot certainly know all things, we shall do muchwhat as wisely as he who would not use his legs, but sit still and perish because he had no wings to fly.

CHAPTER II: NO INNATE PRINCIPLES IN THE MIND

1. It is an established opinion amongst some men, that there are in the understanding certain *innate principles;* some primary notions, κοιναὶ ἔννοιαι, characters, as it were stamped upon the mind of man; which the soul receives in its very first being, and brings into the world with it. It would be sufficient to convince unprejudiced readers of the falseness of this supposition, if I should only show (as I hope I shall in the following parts of this Discourse) how men, barely by the use of their natural faculties, may attain to all the knowledge they have, without the help of any innate impressions; and may arrive at certainty, without any such original notions or principles. For I imagine any one will easily grant that it would be impertinent to suppose the ideas of colours innate in a creature to whom God hath given sight, and a power to receive them by the eyes from external objects; and no less unreasonable would it be to attribute several truths to the impressions of nature, and innate characters, when we may observe in ourselves faculties fit to attain as easy and certain knowledge of them as if they were originally imprinted on the mind.

2. There is nothing more commonly taken for granted than that there are certain principles, both *speculative* and *practical* (for they speak of both), universally agreed upon by all mankind: which therefore, they argue, must needs be the constant impressions which the souls of men

receive in their first beings, and which they bring into the world with them, as necessarily and really as they do any of their inherent faculties.

4. But, which is worse, this argument of universal consent, which is made use of to prove innate principles, seems to me a demonstration that there are none such: because, there are none to which all mankind give an universal assent. I shall begin with the speculative, and instance in those magnified principles of demonstration, "Whatsoever is, is," and "It is impossible for the same thing to be and not to be"; which of all others, I think have the most allowed title to innate. But yet I take liberty to say, that these propositions are so far from having an universal assent, that there are a great part of mankind to whom they are not so much as known.

6. To avoid this it is usually answered, that all men know and assent to them, *when they come to the use of reason;* and this is enough to prove them innate. I answer:

7. Doubtful expressions, that have scarce any signification, go for clear reasons to those who, being prepossessed, take not the pains to examine even what they themselves say. For, to apply this answer with any tolerable sense to our present purpose, it must signify one of these two things: either that as soon as men come to the use of reason these supposed native inscriptions come to be known and observed by them; or else, that the use and exercise of men's reason assists them in the discovery of these principles, and certainly makes them known to them.

CHAPTER III: NO INNATE PRACTICAL PRINCIPLES

1. If those speculative Maxims, whereof we discoursed in the foregoing chapter, have not an actual universal assent from all mankind, as we there proved, it is much more visible concerning *practical* Principles, that they come short of an universal reception: and I think it will be hard to instance any one moral rule which can pretend to so general and ready an assent as, "What is, is," or to be so manifest a truth as this, that "It is impossible for the same thing to be and not to be." Whereby it is evident that they are further removed from a title to be innate; and the doubt of their being native impressions on the mind is stronger against those moral principles than the others. Not that it brings their truth at all in question. They are equally true, though not equally evident. Those speculative maxims carry their own evidence with them: but moral principles require reasoning and discourse, and some exercise of the mind, to discover the certainty of their truth. They lie not open as natural characters engraven on the mind; which, if any such were, they must needs be visible by themselves, and by their own light be certain and known to everybody. But this is no derogation to

their truth and certainty; no more than it is to the truth or certainty of the three angles of a triangle being equal to two right ones: because it is not so evident as "The whole is bigger than a part," nor so apt to be assented to at first hearing. It may suffice that these moral rules are capable of demonstration; and therefore it is our own fault if we come not to a certain knowledge of them. But the ignorance wherein many men are of them, and the slowness of assent wherewith others receive them, are manifest proofs that they are not innate, and such as offer themselves to their view without searching.

2. Whether there be any such moral principles, wherein all men do agree, I appeal to any who have been but moderately conversant in the history of mankind and looked abroad beyond the smoke of their own chimneys. Where is that practical truth that is universally received, without doubt or question as it must be if innate? *Justice,* and keeping of contracts, is that which most men seem to agree in. This is a principle which is thought to extend itself to the dens of thieves, and the confederacies of the greatest villains; and they who have gone furthest towards the putting off of humanity itself, keep faith and rules of justice one with another. I grant that outlaws themselves do this one amongst another: but it is without receiving these as the innate laws of nature. They practise them as rules of convenience within their own communities: but it is impossible to conceive that he embraces justice as a practical principle, who acts fairly with his fellow highwayman, and at the same time plunders or kills the next honest man he meets with. Justice and truth are the common ties of society; and therefore even outlaws and robbers, who break with all the world besides, must keep faith and rules of equity amongst themselves; or else they cannot hold together. But will any one say, that those that live by fraud or rapine have innate principles of truth and justice which they allow and assent to?

Book II: Of Ideas

CHAPTER II: OF SIMPLE IDEAS OF SENSE

1. The better to understand the nature, manner, and extent of our knowledge, one thing is carefully to be observed concerning the ideas we have; and that is, that some of them are *simple* and some *complex.*

Though the qualities that affect our senses are, in the things themselves so united and blended, that there is no separation, no distance between them; yet it is plain, the ideas they produce in the mind enter by the senses simple and unmixed. For, though the sight and touch often take in from the same object, at the same time, different ideas—as a man sees at once motion and colour; the hand feels softness and warmth in the same piece of wax: yet the simple ideas thus united in the same subject, are as perfectly distinct as those that come in by different senses. The coldness and hardness which a man feels in a piece of ice being as distinct ideas in the mind as the smell and whiteness of a lily; or as the taste of sugar, and smell of a rose. And there is nothing can be plainer to a man than the clear and distinct perception he has of those simple ideas; which, being each in itself uncompounded, contains in it nothing but *one uniform appearance* of conception in the mind, and is not distinguishable into different ideas.

2. These simple ideas, the materials of all our knowledge, are suggested and furnished to the mind only by those two ways above mentioned, viz. sensation and reflection. When the understanding is once stored with these simple ideas, it has the power to repeat, compare, and unite them, even to an almost infinite variety, and so can make at pleasure new complex ideas. But it is not in the power of the most exalted wit or enlarged understanding, by any quickness or variety of thought, to *invent* or *frame* one new simple idea in the mind, not taken in by the ways before mentioned: nor can any force of the understanding *destroy* those that are there, the dominion of man in this little world of his own understanding being muchwhat the same as it is in the great world of visible things; wherein his power, however managed by art and skill, reaches no farther than to compound and divide the materials that are made to his hand; but can do nothing towards the making the least particle of new matter, or destroying one atom of what is already in being. The same inability will every one find in himself, who shall go about to fashion in his understanding one simple idea, not received in by his senses from external objects, or by reflection from the operations of his own mind about them.

3. This is the reason why it is not possible for any one to imagine any other qualities in bodies, howsoever constituted, whereby they can be taken notice of, besides sounds, tastes, smells, visible and tangible qualities. And had mankind been made but with four senses, the qualities then which are the objects of the fifth sense had been as far from our notice, imagination, and conception, as now any belonging to a sixth, seventh, or eighth sense can possibly be. I have here followed the common opinion of man's having but five senses, though perhaps, there may be justly counted more; but either supposition serves equally to my present purpose.

Book IV: Of Knowledge, Certain and Probable

CHAPTER I: OF KNOWLEDGE IN GENERAL

1. Since the mind, in all its thoughts and reasonings, hath no other immediate object but its own ideas, which it alone does or can contemplate, it is evident that our knowledge is only conversant about them.

2. *Knowledge* then seems to me to be nothing but *the perception of the connection of and agreement, or disagreement and repugnancy, of any of our ideas*. In this alone it consists. Where this perception is, there is knowledge, and where it is not, there, though we may fancy, guess, or believe, yet we always come short of knowledge. For when we know that white is not black, what do we else but perceive, that these two ideas do not agree? When we possess ourselves with the utmost security of the demonstration that the three angles of a triangle are equal to two right ones, what do we more but perceive, that equality to two right ones does necessarily agree to, and is inseparable from, the three angles of a triangle?

CHAPTER II: OF THE DEGREES OF OUR KNOWLEDGE

1. All our knowledge consisting, as I have said, in the view the mind has of its own ideas, which is the utmost light and greatest certainty we, with our faculties, and in our way of knowledge, are capable of, it may not be amiss to consider a little the degree of its evidence. The different clearness of our knowledge seems to me to lie in the different way of perception the mind has of the agreement or disagreement of any of its ideas. For if we will reflect on our own ways of thinking, we will find, that sometimes the mind perceives the agreement or disagreement of two ideas immediately by themselves, without the intervention of any other: and this I think we may call *intuitive knowledge*. For in this the mind is at no pains of proving or examining, but perceives the truth as the eye doth light, only by being directed towards it. Thus the mind perceives that *white* is not *black*, that a *circle* is not a *triangle*, that *three* are more than *two* and equal to *one and two*. Such kinds of truths the mind perceives at the first sight of the ideas together, by bare intuition; without the intervention of any other idea: and this kind of knowledge is the clearest and most certain that human frailty is capable of. This part of knowledge is irresistible, and like bright sunshine, forces itself immediately to be perceived, as soon as ever the mind turns its view that way; and leaves no room for hesitation, doubt, or examination but the mind is presently filled with the

clear light of it. It is on this intuition that depends all the certainty and evidence of all our knowledge; which certainty every one finds to be so great, that he cannot imagine, and therefore not require, a greater: for a man cannot conceive himself capable of a greater certainty than to know that any idea in his mind is such as he perceives it to be; and that two ideas, wherein he perceives a difference, are different and not precisely the same. He that demands a greater certainty than this, demands he knows not what, and shows only that he has a mind to be a sceptic, without being able to do so. Certainty depends so wholly on this intuition, that in the next degree of knowledge, which I call demonstrative, this intuition is necessary in all the connections of the intermediate ideas, without which we cannot attain knowledge and certainty.

2. The next degree of knowledge is, where the mind perceives the agreement or disagreement of any ideas, but not immediately. The reason why the mind cannot always perceive presently the agreement or disagreement of two ideas, is because those ideas, concerning whose agreement or disagreement the inquiry is made, cannot by the mind be so put together as to show it. In this case then, when the mind cannot so bring its ideas together as by their immediate comparison, and as it were juxtaposition or application one to another, to perceive their agreement or disagreement, it is fain, *by the intervention of other ideas* (one or more, as it happens) to discover the agreement or disagreement which it searches; and this is that which we call *reasoning*.

CHAPTER X: OF THE KNOWLEDGE OF THE EXISTENCE OF A GOD

1. Though God has given us no innate ideas of himself; though he has stamped no original characters on our minds, wherein we may read his being; yet having furnished us with those faculties our minds are endowed with, he hath not left himself without witness; since we have sense, perception, and reason, and cannot want a clear proof of him, as long as we carry *ourselves* about us. But, though this be the most obvious truth that reason discovers, and though its evidence be (if I mistake not) equal to mathematical certainty: yet it requires thought and attention; and the mind must apply itself to a regular deduction of it from some part of our intuitive knowledge, or else we shall be as uncertain and ignorant of this as of other propositions, which are in themselves capable of clear demonstration. To show, therefore, that there is a God, and *how we may come* by this certainty, I think we need go no further than *ourselves,* and that undoubted knowledge we have of our own existence.

2. This, I think I may take for a truth, which every one's certain knowl-

edge assures him of, beyond the liberty of doubting, viz. that he is *something that actually exists*. If any one pretends to be so sceptical as to deny his own existence (for really to doubt of it is manifestly impossible), let him for me enjoy his beloved happiness of being nothing, until hunger or some other pain convince him of the contrary.

3. In the next place, man knows, by an intuitive certainty, that bare *nothing can no more produce any real being, than it can be equal to two right angles*. If a man knows not that nonentity, or the absence of all being, cannot be equal to two right angles, it is impossible he should know any demonstration in Euclid. If, therefore, we know there is some real being, and that nonentity cannot produce any real being, it is an evident demonstration, that *from eternity there has been something;* since what was not from eternity had a beginning; and what had a beginning must be produced by something else.

4. Next, it is evident, that what had its being and beginning from another, must also have all that which is in and belongs to its being from another too. All the powers it has must be owing to and received from the same source. This eternal source, then, of all being must also be the source and original of all power; and so *this eternal Being must be also the most powerful.*

5. Again, a man finds in himself perception and knowledge. We have then got one step further; and we are certain now that there is not only some being, but some knowing, intelligent being in the world. There was a time, then, when there was no knowing being, and when knowledge began to be; or else there has been also a *knowing being from eternity.* If it be said, there was a time when no being had any knowledge, when that eternal being was void of all understanding; I reply, that then it was impossible there should ever have been any knowledge; it being as impossible that things wholly void of knowledge, and operating blindly, and without any perception, should produce a knowing being, as it is impossible that a triangle should make itself three angles bigger than two right ones. For it is as repugnant to the idea of senseless matter, that it should put into itself sense, perception, and knowledge, as it is repugnant to the idea of a triangle, that it should put into itself greater angles than two right ones.

6. Thus, from the consideration of ourselves, and what we infallibly find in our own constitutions, our reason leads us to the knowledge of this certain and evident truth—*that there is an eternal, most powerful, and most knowing Being;* which whether any one will please to call God, it matters not. The thing is evident; and from this idea duly considered, will easily

be deduced all those other attributes, which we ought to ascribe to this eternal Being.

7. How far the *idea* of a most perfect being, which a man may frame in his mind, does or does not prove the *existence* of a God, I will not here examine. For in the different make of men's tempers and application of their thoughts, some arguments prevail more on one, and some on another, for the confirmation of the same truth. But yet, I think, this I may say, that it is an ill way of establishing this truth, and silencing atheists, to lay the whole stress of so important a point as this upon that sole foundation: and take some men's having that idea of God in their minds (for it is evident some men have none, and some worse than none, and the most very different), for the only proof of a Deity.

8. It being, then, unavoidable for all rational creatures to conclude that *something* has existed from eternity, let us next see *what kind of thing* that must be.

9. There are but two sorts of being in the world that man knows or conceives.

First, Such as are purely material, without sense, perception, or thought, as the clippings of our beards, and parings of our nails.

Secondly, Sensible, thinking, perceiving beings, such as we find ourselves to be. Which, if you please, we will hereafter call *cogitative* and *incogitative* beings; which to our present purpose, if for nothing else, are perhaps better terms than material and immaterial.

10. If, then, there must be something eternal, let us see what sort of being it must be. And to that it is very obvious to reason, that it must necessarily be a cogitative being. For it is as impossible to conceive that ever bare incogitative matter should produce a thinking intelligent being, as that nothing should of itself produce matter. Let us suppose any parcel of matter eternal, great or small, we shall find it, in itself, able to produce nothing. For example: let us suppose the matter of the next pebble we meet with eternal, closely united, and the parts firmly at rest together; if there were no other being in the world, must it not eternally remain so, a dead inactive lump? Is it possible to conceive it can add motion to itself, being purely matter, or produce anything? Matter, then, by its own strength cannot produce in itself so much as motion: the motion it has must also be from eternity, or else be produced, and added to matter by some other being more powerful than matter; matter, as is evident, having not power to produce motion in itself. But let us suppose motion eternal too: yet matter, *incogitative* matter and motion, whatever changes it might produce of figure and bulk, could never produce thought: knowledge will still be as

far beyond the power of motion and matter to produce, as matter is beyond the power of nothing or nonentity to produce. So that, if we will suppose *nothing* first or eternal, matter can never begin to be: if we suppose bare matter without motion, eternal, motion can never begin to be: if we suppose only matter and motion first, or eternal, thought can never begin to be.

11. If, therefore it be evident, that something necessarily must exist from eternity, it is also as evident, that that something must necessarily be a cogitative being: for it is as impossible that incogitative matter should produce a cogitative being, as that nothing, or the negation of all being, should produce a positive being or matter.

12. Though this discovery of the *necessary existence of an eternal Mind* does sufficiently lead us into the knowledge of God; since it will hence follow, that all other knowing beings that have a beginning must depend on him, and have no other ways of knowledge or extent of power than what he gives them; and, therefore, if he made those, he made also the less excellent pieces of this universe—all inanimate beings, whereby his omniscience, power, and providence will be established, and all his other attributes necessarily follow: yet, to clear up this a little further, we will see what doubts can be raised against it.

13. First, Perhaps it will be said, that, though it be as clear as demonstration can make it, that there must be an eternal Being, and that Being must also be knowing: yet it does not follow but that thinking Being may also be material. There being no way to avoid the demonstration that there is an eternal knowing Being, men, devoted to matter, would willingly have it granted that this knowing being is material; and then, letting slide out of their minds, or the discourse, the demonstration whereby an eternal *knowing* Being was proved necessarily to exist, would argue all to be matter, and so deny a God, that is, an eternal cogitative Being: whereby they are so far from establishing that they destroy their own hypothesis.

14. But now let us see how they can satisfy themselves, or others, that this eternal thinking Being is material. I would ask them, whether they imagine that all matter, *every particle of matter,* thinks. This, I suppose, they will scarcely say; since then there would be as many eternal thinking beings as there are particles of matter, and so an infinity of gods. And yet, if they will not allow matter as matter, that is, every particle of matter, to be as well cogitative as extended, they will have as hard a task to make out to their own reasons a cogitative being out of incogitative particles, as an extended being out of unextended parts, if I may so speak.

15. If all matter does not think, I next ask, whether it be *only one atom* that does so. This has as many absurdities as the other; for then this atom

of matter must be alone eternal or not. If this alone be eternal, then this alone, by its powerful thought or will, made all the rest of matter. And so we have the creation of matter by a powerful thought, which is that the materialists stick at; for if they suppose one single thinking atom to have produced all the rest of matter, they cannot ascribe that pre-eminency to it upon any other account than that of its thinking, the only supposed difference. To suppose all matter eternal, and yet one small particle in knowledge and power infinitely above all the rest, is without any the least appearance of reason to frame an hypothesis. Every particle of matter, as matter, is capable of all the same figures and motions of any other; and I challenge any one, in his thoughts, to add anything else to one above another.

16. If then neither one peculiar atom alone can be this eternal thinking being; nor all matter, as matter, i.e. every particle of matter, can be it; it only remains, that it is some certain *system* of matter, duly put together, that is this thinking eternal Being. This is that which, I imagine, is that notion which men are aptest to have of God; who would have him a material being as most readily suggested to them by the ordinary conceit they have of themselves and other men, which they take to be material thinking beings. But this imagination, however more natural, is no less absurd than the other. For unthinking particles of matter, however put together can have nothing thereby added to them, but a new relation of position, which it is impossible should give thought and knowledge to them.

18. Secondly, Others would have matter to be eternal, notwithstanding that they allow an eternal, cogitative, immaterial Being. This, though it take not away the being of a God, yet since it denies one and the first great piece of his workmanship, the creation, let us consider it a little. Matter must be allowed eternal: Why? because you cannot conceive how it can be made out of nothing: why do you not also think yourself eternal? You will answer, perhaps, Because, about twenty or forty years since, you began to be. But if I ask you, what that *you* is, which began then to be, you can scarce tell me. The matter whereof you are made began not then to be: for if it did, then it is not eternal: but it began to be put together in such a fashion and frame as makes up your body; but yet that frame of particles is not you, it makes not that thinking thing you are (for I have now to do with one who allows an eternal, immaterial, thinking Being, but would have unthinking matter eternal too); therefore, when did that thinking thing begin to be? If it did never begin to be, then have you always been a thinking thing from eternity; the absurdity whereof I need not confute,

till I meet with one who is so void of understanding as to own it. If, therefore, you can allow a thinking thing to be made out of nothing (as all things that are not eternal must be) why also can you not allow it possible for a material being to be made out of nothing by an equal power, but that you have the experience of the one in view, and not of the other?

19. But you will say, Is it not impossible to admit of the making anything out of nothing, since we cannot possibly conceive it? I answer, No. Because it is not reasonable to deny the power of an infinite Being, because we cannot comprehend its operations. We do not deny other effects upon this ground, because we cannot possibly conceive the manner of their production. For example: my right hand writes, whilst my left hand is still: What causes rest in one, and motion in the other? Nothing but my will— a thought of my mind; my thought only changing, the right hand rests, and the left hand moves. This is matter of fact, which cannot be denied: explain this and make it intelligible, and then the next step will be to understand creation.

IMMANUEL KANT

IMMANUEL KANT (1724–1804) was born in Königsberg of a family of Scottish descent. He was influenced at an early age by pietism and entered the Collegium Fredericianum at the age of ten with a view to studying theology. His taste, however, was for the Latin classics, and he was considered one of the most promising classical scholars of the college. During his university career he was satisfied neither by theology nor by classics, and turned to mathematics and physics. Plagued by poverty, he was obliged to earn his living for nine years as a private tutor. In 1755 he qualified as *Privatdocent,* and for fifteen years he remained in this position, failing twice to obtain a professorship despite his growing fame.

At first he lectured only on physics, but gradually his speculations extended to cover every aspect of philosophical inquiry. In 1770 he obtained the chair of logic and metaphysics. Eleven years later the *Kritik der reinen Vernunft* (*Critique of the Pure Reason*) appeared; in 1783 he published the *Prologomena* to it. In spite of its difficulty, and its opposition to prevailing systems, the *Kritik* found a wide audience in Germany. In 1780 appeared the *Kritik der praktischen Vernunft* (*Critique of the Practical Reason*); in 1785 followed the *Grundlegung zur Metaphysik der Sitten* (*Fundamental Principles of the Metaphysic of Morals*); in 1790 the *Kritik der Urteilskraft* (*Critique of Judgment*); *Zum ewigen Frieden* (*Perpetual Peace*) in 1795; in 1798 his completed *Metaphysics of Morals;* and a host of other works.

In 1792 Kant was required by the government to cease writing and lecturing on religious subjects, for the tendency of his work to undermine Christianity in favor of moral rationalism had unsettled the orthodox. This incident depressed him, and he gradually gave up his lectures until in 1797 he ceased his public activities altogether.

It is impossible even to indicate here the nature and significance of Kant's philosophical thought; suffice it to say that it forms the most far-reaching and complete system of modern times.

We reproduce here, in translation from the German, *What is Enlightenment?* (1784) and major portions of *Perpetual Peace* (1795), translated by Mary C. Smith (London, George Allen and Unwin, 1903).

WHAT IS ENLIGHTENMENT?

ENLIGHTENMENT IS man's emergence from his self-imposed nonage. Nonage is the inability to use one's own understanding without another's guidance. This nonage is self-imposed if its cause lies not in lack of understanding but in indecision and lack of courage to use one's own mind without another's guidance. *Dare to know!* (*Sapere aude.*) "Have the courage to use your own understanding," is therefore the motto of the enlightenment.

Laziness and cowardice are the reasons why such a large part of mankind gladly remain minors all their lives, long after nature has freed them from external guidance. They are the reasons why it is so easy for others to set themselves up as guardians. It is so comfortable to be a minor. If I have a book that thinks for me, a pastor who acts as my conscience, a physician who prescribes my diet, and so on—then I have no need to exert myself. I have no need to think, if only I can pay; others will take care of that disagreeable business for me. Those guardians who have kindly taken supervision upon themselves see to it that the overwhelming majority of mankind—among them the entire fair sex—should consider the step to maturity, not only as hard, but as extremely dangerous. First, these guardians make their domestic cattle stupid and carefully prevent the docile creatures from taking a single step without the leading-strings to which they have fastened them. Then they show them the danger that would threaten them if they should try to walk by themselves. Now this danger is really not very great; after stumbling a few times they would, at last, learn to walk. However, examples of such failures intimidate and generally discourage all further attempts.

Thus it is very difficult for the individual to work himself out of the nonage which has become almost second nature to him. He has even grown to like it, and is at first really incapable of using his own understanding because he has never been permitted to try it. Dogmas and formulas, these mechanical tools designed for reasonable use—or rather abuse—of his natural gifts, are the fetters of an everlasting nonage. The man who casts them off would make an uncertain leap over the narrowest ditch, because he is not used to such free movement. That is why there are only a few men who walk firmly, and who have emerged from nonage by cultivating their own minds.

It is more nearly possible, however, for the public to enlighten itself; indeed, if it is only given freedom, enlightenment is almost inevitable. There will always be a few independent thinkers, even among the self-appointed guardians of the multitude. Once such men have thrown off the yoke of nonage, they will spread about them the spirit of a reasonable appreciation of man's value and of his duty to think for himself. It is especially to be noted that the public which was earlier brought under the yoke by these men afterwards forces these very guardians to remain in submission, if it is so incited by some of its guardians who are themselves incapable of any enlightenment. That shows how pernicious it is to implant prejudices: they will eventually revenge themselves upon their authors or their authors' descendants. Therefore, a public can achieve enlightenment only slowly. A revolution may bring about the end of a personal despotism or of avaricious and tyrannical oppression, but never a true reform of modes of thought. New prejudices will serve, in place of the old, as guide lines for the unthinking multitude.

This enlightenment requires nothing but *freedom*—and the most innocent of all that may be called "freedom": freedom to make public use of one's reason in all matters. Now I hear the cry from all sides: "Do not argue!" The officer says: "Do not argue—drill!" The tax collector: "Do not argue—pay!" The pastor: "Do not argue—believe!" Only one ruler in the world says: "Argue as much as you please, and about what you please, but obey!" We find restrictions on freedom everywhere. But which restriction is harmful to enlightenment? Which restriction is innocent, and which advances enlightenment? I reply: the public use of one's reason must be free at all times, and this alone can bring enlightenment to mankind.

On the other hand, the private use of reason may frequently be narrowly restricted without especially hindering the progress of enlightenment. By "public use of one's reason" I mean that use which a man, as *scholar,* makes of it before the reading public. I call "private use" that use which a man makes of his reason in a civic post that has been entrusted to him. In some affairs affecting the interest of the community a certain [governmental] mechanism is necessary in which some members of the community remain passive. This creates an artificial unanimity which will serve the fulfillment of public objectives, or at least keep these objectives from being destroyed. Here arguing is not permitted: one must obey. Insofar as a part of this machine considers himself at the same time a member of a universal community—a world society of citizens—(let us say that he thinks of himself as a scholar rationally addressing his public through his writings) he may indeed argue, and the affairs with which he is associated in part as a passive member will not suffer. Thus it would be very unfortunate if an officer on duty and under orders from his superiors should want to criticize the appropriateness or utility of his orders. He must obey. But as a scholar he could not rightfully be prevented from taking notice of the mistakes in the military service and from submitting his views to his public for its judgment. The citizen cannot refuse to pay the taxes levied upon him; indeed, impertinent censure of such taxes could be punished as a scandal that might cause general disobedience. Nevertheless, this man does not violate the duties of a citizen if, as a scholar, he publicly expresses his objections to the impropriety or possible injustice of such levies. A pastor, too, is bound to preach to his congregation in accord with the doctrines of the church which he serves, for he was ordained on that condition. But as a scholar he has full freedom, indeed the obligation, to communicate to his public all his carefully examined and constructive thoughts concerning errors in that doctrine and his proposals concerning improvement of religious dogma and church institutions. This is nothing that could burden his conscience. For what he teaches in pursuance of his office as representative of the church, he represents as something which he is not free to teach as he sees it. He speaks as one who is employed to speak in the name and under the orders of another. He will say: "Our church teaches this or that; these are the proofs which it employs." Thus he will benefit his congregation as much as possible by presenting doctrines to which he may not subscribe with full conviction. He can commit himself to teach them because it is not completely impossible that they may contain hidden truth. In any event, he has found nothing in the doctrines that contradicts the heart of religion. For if he believed that such contradictions existed he would not be able to administer his office with a clear conscience. He would have to resign it. Therefore the use which a scholar makes of his reason before the congregation that employs him is only a private use, for, no matter how sizable, this is only a domestic audience. In view of this he, as preacher, is not free and ought not to be free, since he is carrying out the orders of others. On the other hand, as the scholar who speaks to his own public (the world) through his writings, the minister in the public use of his reason enjoys unlimited freedom to use his own reason and to speak for himself. That the spiritual guardians of the people should themselves be treated as minors is an absurdity which would result in perpetuating absurdities.

But should a society of ministers, say a Church Council, . . . have the right to commit itself by oath to a certain unalterable doctrine, in order to secure perpetual guardianship over all its members and through them over the people? I say that this is quite impossible. Such a contract, concluded to keep all further enlightenment from humanity, is simply null and void even if it should be confirmed by the sovereign power, by parliaments, and the most solemn treaties. An epoch cannot conclude a pact that will commit succeeding ages, prevent them from increasing their significant insights, purging themselves of errors, and generally progressing in enlightenment. That would be a crime against human nature whose proper destiny lies precisely in such progress. Therefore, succeeding ages are fully entitled to repudiate such decisions as unauthorized and outrageous. The touchstone of all those decisions that may be made into law for a people lies in this question: Could a people impose such a law upon itself? Now it might be possible to introduce a certain order for a definite short period of time in expectation of a better order. But, while this provisional order continues, each citizen (above all, each pastor acting as a scholar) should be left free to publish his criticisms of the faults of existing institutions. This should continue until public understanding of these matters has gone so far that, by uniting the voices of many (although not necessarily all) scholars, reform proposals could be brought before the sovereign to protect those congregations which had decided according to their best lights upon an altered religious order, without, however, hindering those who want to remain true to the old institutions. But to agree to a perpetual religious constitution which is not to be publicly questioned by anyone would be, as it were, to annihilate a period of time in the progress of man's improvement. This must be absolutely forbidden.

A man may postpone his own enlightenment, but only for a limited period of time. And to give up enlightenment altogether, either for oneself or one's descendants, is to violate and to trample upon the sacred rights of man. What a people may not decide for itself may even less be decided for it by a monarch, for his reputation as a ruler consists precisely in the way in which he unites the will of the whole people within his own. If he only sees to it that all true or supposed [religious] improvement remains in step with the civic order, he can for the rest leave his subjects alone to do what they find necessary for the salvation of their souls. Salvation is none of his business; it *is* his business to prevent one man from forcibly keeping another from determining and promoting his salvation to the best of his ability. Indeed, it would be prejudicial to his majesty if he meddled in these matters and supervised the writings in which his subjects seek to bring their [religious] views into the open, even when he does this from his own highest insight, because then he exposes himself to the reproach: *Caesar non est supra grammaticos.*[3] It is worse when he debases his sovereign power so far as to support the spiritual despotism of a few tyrants in his state over the rest of his subjects.

When we ask, Are we now living in an enlightened age? the answer is, No, but we live in an age of enlightenment. As matters now stand it is still far from true that men are already capable of using their own reason in religious matters confidently and correctly without external guidance. Still, we have some obvious indications that the field of working toward the goal [of religious truth] is now being opened. What is more, the hindrances against

---

[3] [*Caesar is not above grammarians.*]

general enlightenment or the emergence from self-imposed nonage are gradually diminishing. In this respect this is the age of the enlightenment and the century of Frederick [the Great].

A prince ought not to deem it beneath his dignity to state that he considers it his duty not to dictate anything to his subjects in religious matters, but to leave them complete freedom. If he repudiates the arrogant word "tolerant," he is himself enlightened; he deserves to be praised by a grateful world and posterity as that man who was the first to liberate mankind from dependence, at least on the government, and let everybody use his own reason in matters of conscience. Under his reign, honorable pastors, acting as scholars and regardless of the duties of their office, can freely and openly publish their ideas to the world for inspection, although they deviate here and there from accepted doctrine. This is even more true of every other person not restrained by any oath of office. This spirit of freedom is spreading beyond the boundaries [of Prussia] even where it has to struggle against the external hindrances established by a government that fails to grasp its true interest. [Frederick's Prussia] is a shining example that freedom need not cause the least worry concerning public order or the unity of the community. When one does not deliberately attempt to keep men in barbarism, they will gradually work out of that condition by themselves.

I have emphasized the main point of the enlightenment—man's emergence from his self-imposed nonage—primarily in religious matters, because our rulers have no interest in playing the guardian to their subjects in the arts and sciences. Above all, nonage in religion is not only the most harmful but the most dishonorable. But the disposition of a sovereign ruler who favors freedom in the arts and sciences goes even further: he knows that there is no danger in permitting his subjects to make public use of their reason and to publish their ideas concerning a better constitution, as well as candid criticism of existing basic laws. We already have a striking example [of such freedom], and no monarch can match the one whom we venerate.

But only the man who is himself enlightened, who is not afraid of shadows, and who commands at the same time a well disciplined and numerous army as guarantor of public peace—only he can say what [the sovereign of] a free state cannot dare to say: "Argue as much as you like, and about what you like, but obey!" Thus we observe here as elsewhere in human affairs, in which almost everything is paradoxical, a surprising and unexpected course of events: a large degree of civic freedom appears to be of advantage to the intellectual freedom of the people, yet at the same time it establishes insurmountable barriers. A lesser degree of civic freedom, however, creates room to let that free spirit expand to the limits of its capacity. Nature, then, has carefully cultivated the seed within the hard core—namely the urge for and the vocation of free thought. And this free thought gradually reacts back on the modes of thought of the people, and men become more and more capable of acting in freedom. At last free thought acts even on the fundamentals of government and the state finds it agreeable to treat man, who is now more than a machine, in accord with his dignity.

PERPETUAL PEACE

WE NEED NOT try to decide whether this satirical inscription [*i.e.,* "Perpetual Peace"] (once found on a Dutch innkeeper's signboard above the picture of a churchyard) is aimed at mankind in general, or at the rulers of states in particular, unwearying in their love of war, or perhaps only at the philosophers who cherish the sweet dream of perpetual peace. The author of the present sketch would make one stipulation, however. The practical politician stands upon a definite footing with the theorist: with great self-complacency he looks down upon him as a mere pedant whose empty ideas can threaten no danger to the state (starting as it does from principles derived from experience), and who may always be permitted to knock down his eleven skittles at once without a worldly-wise statesman needing to disturb himself. Hence, in the event of a quarrel arising between the two, the practical statesman must always act consistently, and not scent danger to the state behind opinions ventured by the theoretical politician at random and publicly expressed. With which saving clause (*clausula salvatoria*) the author will herewith consider himself duly and expressly protected against all malicious misinterpretation.

First Section

CONTAINING THE PRELIMINARY ARTICLES OF PERPETUAL PEACE
BETWEEN STATES

1. No treaty of peace shall be regarded as valid, if made with the secret reservation of material for a future war.

For then it would be a mere truce, a mere suspension of hostilities, not peace. A peace signifies the end of all hostilities and to attach to it the epithet "eternal" is not only a verbal pleonasm, but matter of suspicion. The causes of a future war existing, although perhaps not yet known to the high contracting parties themselves, are entirely annihilated by the conclusion of peace, however acutely they may be ferreted out of documents in the public archives. There may be a mental reservation of old claims to be thought out at a future time, which are, none of them, mentioned at this stage, because both parties are too much exhausted to continue the war, while the evil intention remains of using the first favourable opportunity for further hostilities. Diplomacy of this kind only Jesuitical casuistry can justify: it is beneath the dignity of a ruler, just as acquiescence in such processes of reasoning is beneath the dignity of his minister, if one judges the facts as they really are.

If, however, according to present enlightened ideas of political wisdom, the true glory of a state lies in the uninterrupted development of its power by every possible means, this judgment must certainly strike one as scholastic and pedantic.

2. No state having an independent existence—whether it be great or small—shall be acquired by another through inheritance, exchange, purchase or donation.

For a state is not a property (*patrimonium*), as may be the ground on which its people are settled. It is a society of human beings over whom no one but itself has the right to rule and to dispose. Like the trunk of a tree, it has its own roots, and to graft it on to another state is to do away with its existence as a moral person, and to make of it a thing. Hence it is in contradiction to the idea of the original contract without which no right over a people is thinkable. Everyone knows to what danger the bias in favour of these modes of acquisition has brought Europe (in other parts of the world it has never been known). The custom of marriage between states, as if they were individuals, has survived even up to the most recent times, and is regarded partly as a new kind of industry by which ascendency may be acquired through family alliances, without any expenditure of strength; partly as a device for territorial expansion. Moreover, the hiring out of the troops of one state to another to fight against an enemy not at war with their native country is to be reckoned in this connection; for the subjects are in this way used and abused at will as personal property.

3. Standing armies (miles perpetuus) *shall be abolished in course of time.*

For they are always threatening other states with war by appearing to be in constant readiness to fight. They incite the various states to outrival one another in the number of their soldiers, and to this number no limit can be set. Now, since owing to the sums devoted to this purpose, peace at last becomes even more oppressive than a short war, these standing armies are themselves the cause of wars of aggression, undertaken in order to get rid of this burden. To which we must add that the practice of hiring men to kill or to be killed seems to imply a use of them as mere machines and instruments in the hand of another (namely, the state) which cannot easily be reconciled with the right of humanity in our own person. The matter stands quite differently in the case of voluntary periodical military exercise on the part of citizens of the state, who thereby seek to secure themselves and their country against attack from without.

The accumulation of treasure in a state would in the same way be regarded by other states as a menace of war, and might compel them to anticipate this by striking the first blow. For of the three forces, the power of arms, the power of alliance and the power of money, the last might well become the most reliable instrument of war, did not the difficulty of ascertaining the amount stand in the way.

4. No national debts shall be contracted in connection with the external affairs of the state.

This source of help is above suspicion, where assistance is sought outside or within the state, on behalf of the economic administration of the country (for instance, the improvement of the roads, the settlement and support of new colonies, the establishment of granaries to provide against seasons of scarcity, and so on). But, as a common weapon used by the Powers against one another, a credit system under which debts go on indefinitely increasing and are yet always assured against immediate claims (because all the creditors do not put in their claim at once) is a dangerous money power. This ingenious invention of a commercial people in the present century is, in other words, a treasure for the carrying on of war which may exceed the treasures of all the other states taken together, and can only be exhausted by a threatening deficiency in the taxes—an event, however, which will long be kept off by the very briskness of commerce resulting from the reaction of this system on industry and trade. The ease, then, with which war may be waged, coupled with the inclination of rulers towards it—an inclination which seems to be implanted in human nature—is a great obstacle in the way of perpetual peace. The prohibition of this system must be laid down as a preliminary article of perpetual peace, all the more necessarily because the final inevitable bankruptcy of the state in question must involve in the loss many who are innocent; and this would be a public injury to these states. Therefore other nations are at least justified in uniting themselves against such an one and its pretensions.

5. No state shall violently interfere with the constitution and administration of another.

For what can justify it in so doing? The scandal which is here presented to the subjects of another state? The erring state can much more serve as a

warning by exemplifying the great evils which a nation draws down on itself through its own lawlessness. Moreover, the bad example which one free
person gives another (as *scandalum acceptum*) does no injury to the latter. In
this connection, it is true, we cannot count the case of a state which has become
split up through internal corruption into two parts, each of them representing
by itself an individual state which lays claim to the whole. Here the yielding
of assistance to one faction could not be reckoned as interference on the
part of a foreign state with the constitution of another, for here anarchy
prevails. So long, however, as the inner strife has not yet reached this stage
the interference of other powers would be a violation of the rights of an
independent nation which is only struggling with internal disease. It would
therefore itself cause a scandal, and make the autonomy of all states insecure.

6. *No state at war with another shall countenance such modes of hostility
as would make mutual confidence impossible in a subsequent state of peace:
such are the employment of assassins* (percussores) *or of poisoners* (venefici),
breaches of capitulation, the instigating and making use of treachery (per-
duellio) *in the hostile state.*

These are dishonourable stratagems. For some kind of confidence in the
disposition of the enemy must exist even in the midst of war, as otherwise
peace could not be concluded, and the hostilities would pass into a war of
extermination (*bellum internecinum*). War, however, is only our wretched
expedient of asserting a right by force, an expedient adopted in the state of
nature, where no court of justice exists which could settle the matter in dispute.
In circumstances like these, neither of the two parties can be called an unjust
enemy, because this form of speech presupposes a legal decision: the issue of
the conflict—just as in the case of the so-called judgments of God—decides
on which side right is. Between states, however, no punitive war (*bellum
punitivum*) is thinkable, because between them a relation of superior and
inferior does not exist. Whence it follows that a war of extermination, where
the process of annihilation would strike both parties at once and all right as
well, would bring about perpetual peace only in the great graveyard of the
human race. Such a war then, and therefore also the use of all means which
lead to it, must be absolutely forbidden. That the methods just mentioned do
inevitably lead to this result is obvious from the fact that these infernal arts,
already vile in themselves, on coming into use, are not long confined to the
sphere of war. Take, for example, the use of spies (*uti exploratoribus*). Here
only the dishonesty of others is made use of; but vices such as these, when
once encouraged, cannot in the nature of things be stamped out and would be

carried over into the state of peace, where their presence would be utterly destructive to the purpose of that state.

Although the laws stated are, objectively regarded (*i.e.,* in so far as they affect the action of rulers), purely prohibitive laws (*leges prohibitivæ*), some of them (*leges strictæ*) are strictly valid without regard to circumstances and urgently require to be enforced. Such are Nos. 1, 5, 6. Others, again, (like Nos. 2, 3, 4) although not indeed exceptions to the maxims of law, yet in respect of the practical application of these maxims allow subjectively of a certain latitude to suit particular circumstances. The enforcement of these *leges latæ* may be legitimately put off, so long as we do not lose sight of the ends at which they aim. This purpose of reform does not permit of the deferment of an act of restitution (as, for example, the restoration to certain states of freedom of which they have been deprived in the manner described in article 2) to an infinitely distant date—as Augustus used to say, to the "Greek Kalends," a day that will never come. This would be to sanction non-restitution. Delay is permitted only with the intention that restitution should not be made too precipitately and so defeat the purpose we have in view. For the prohibition refers here only to the *mode of acquisition* which is to be no longer valid, and not to the *fact of possession* which, although indeed it has not the necessary title of right, yet at the time of so-called acquisition was held legal by all states, in accordance with the public opinion of the time.

Second Section

CONTAINING THE DEFINITIVE ARTICLES OF A PERPETUAL PEACE BETWEEN STATES

A state of peace among men who live side by side is not the natural state (*status naturalis*), which is rather to be described as a state of war: that is to say, although there is not perhaps always actual open hostility, yet there is a constant threatening that an outbreak may occur. Thus the state of peace must be *established*. For the mere cessation of hostilities is no guarantee of continued peaceful relations, and unless this guarantee is given by every individual to his neighbour—which can only be done in a state of society regulated by law—one man is at liberty to challenge another and treat him as an enemy.

FIRST DEFINITIVE ARTICLE OF PERPETUAL PEACE

1. The civil constitution of each state shall be republican.

The only constitution which has its origin in the idea of the original contract, upon which the lawful legislation of every nation must be based, is the republican. It is a constitution, in the first place, founded in accordance with the principle of the freedom of the members of society as human beings: secondly, in accordance with the principle of the dependence of all, as subjects, on a common legislation: and, thirdly, in accordance with the law of the equality of the members as citizens. It is then, looking at the question of right, the only constitution whose fundamental principles lie at the basis of every form of civil constitution. And the only question for us now is, whether it is also the one constitution which can lead to perpetual peace.

Now the republican constitution apart from the soundness of its origin, since it arose from the pure source of the concept of right, has also the prospect of attaining the desired result, namely, perpetual peace. And the reason is this. If, as must be so under this constitution, the consent of the subjects is required to determine whether there shall be war or not, nothing is more natural than that they should weigh the matter well, before undertaking such a bad business. For in decreeing war, they would of necessity be resolving to bring down the miseries of war upon their country. This implies: they must fight themselves; they must hand over the costs of the war out of their own property; they must do their poor best to make good the devastation which it leaves behind; and finally, as a crowning ill, they have to accept a burden of debt which will embitter even peace itself, and which they can never pay off on account of the new wars which are always impending. On the other hand, in a government where the subject is not a citizen holding a vote (*i.e.,* in a constitution which is not republican), the plunging into war is the least serious thing in the world. For the ruler is not a citizen, but the owner of the state, and does not lose a whit by the war, while he goes on enjoying the delights of his table or sport, or of his pleasure palaces and gala days. He can therefore decide on war for the most trifling reasons, as if it were a kind of pleasure party. Any justification of it that is necessary for the sake of decency he can leave without concern to the diplomatic corps who are always only too ready with their services.

The following remarks must be made in order that we may not fall into the common error of confusing the republican with the democratic constitution. The forms of the state (*civitas*) may be classified according to either of two principles of division:—the difference of the persons who hold the supreme authority in the state, and the manner in which the people are governed by their ruler whoever he may be. The first is properly called the form of sovereignty (*forma imperii*), and there can be only three constitutions differing in this respect: where, namely, the supreme authority belongs to only one, to several individuals working together, or to the whole people constituting the civil society. Thus we have autocracy or the sovereignty of a monarch, aristocracy or the sovereignty of the nobility, and democracy or the sovereignty of the people. The second principle of division is the form of government (*forma regiminis*), and refers to the way in which the state makes use of its supreme power: for the manner of government is based on the constitution, itself the act of that universal will which transforms a multitude into a nation. In this respect the form of government is either republican or despotic. Republicanism is the political principle of severing the executive power of the government from the legislature. Despotism is that principle in pursuance of which the state arbitrarily puts into effect laws which it has itself made: consequently it is the administration of the public will, but this is identical with the private will of the ruler. Of these three forms of a state, democracy, in the proper sense of the word, is of necessity despotism, because it establishes an executive power, since all decree regarding—and, if need be, against—any individual who dissents from them. Therefore the "whole people," so-called, who carry their measure are really not all, but only a majority: so that here the universal will is in contradiction with itself and with the principle of freedom.

Every form of government in fact which is not representative is really no true constitution at all, because a law-giver may no more be, in one and the same person, the administrator of his own will, than the universal major premise of a syllogism may be, at the same time, the subsumption under itself of the particulars contained in the minor premise. And, although the other two constitutions, autocracy and aristocracy, are always defective in so far as they leave the way open for such a form of government, yet there is at least always a possibility in these cases, that they may take the form of a government in accordance with the spirit of a representative system. Thus Frederick the Great used at least to *say* that he was "merely the highest servant of the state." The democratic constitution, on the other hand, makes this impossible, because under such a government every one wishes to be master. We may therefore say that the smaller the staff of the executive—that is to say, the number of rulers—and the more real, on the other hand, their representation of the people, so much the more is the government of the state in accordance with a possible republicanism; and it may hope by gradual reforms to raise itself to that standard. For this reason, it is more difficult under an aristocracy than under a monarchy—while under a democracy it is impossible except by a violent revolution—to attain to this, the one perfectly lawful constitution. The kind of government, however, is of infinitely more importance to the people than the kind of constitution, although the greater or less aptitude of a people for this ideal greatly depends upon such external form. The form of government, however, if it is to be in accordance with the idea of right, must embody the representative system in which alone a republican form of administration is possible and without which it is despotic and violent, be the constitution what it may. None of the ancient so-called republics were aware of this, and they necessarily slipped into absolute despotism which, of all despotisms, is most endurable under the sovereignty of one individual.

SECOND DEFINITIVE ARTICLE OF PERPETUAL PEACE

2. *The law of nations shall be founded on a federation of free states.*

Nations, as states, may be judged like individuals who, living in the natural states of society—that is to say, uncontrolled by external law—injure one another through their very proximity. Every state, for the sake of its own security, may—and ought to—demand that its neighbour should submit itself to conditions, similar to those of the civil society where the right of every individual is guaranteed. This would give rise to a federation of nations which, however, would not have to be a State of nations. That would involve a contradiction. For the term "state" implies the relation of one who rules to those who obey— that is to say, of lawgiver to the subject people: and many nations in one state would constitute only one nation, which contradicts our hypothesis, since here we have to consider the right of one nation against another, in so far as they are so many separate states and are not to be fused into one.

The attachment of savages to their lawless liberty, the fact that they would rather be at hopeless variance with one another than submit themselves to a legal authority constituted by themselves, that they therefore prefer their senseless freedom to a reason-governed liberty, is regarded by us with profound contempt as barbarism and uncivilisation and the brutal degradation of humanity. So one would think that civilised races, each formed into a state by itself, must come out of such an abandoned condition as soon as they possibly can. On the contrary, however, every state thinks rather that its majesty (the "majesty" of a people is an absurd expression) lies just in the very fact that it is subject to no external legal authority: and the glory of the ruler consists in this, that, without his requiring to expose himself to danger, thousands stand at his command ready to let themselves be sacrificed for a matter of no concern to them. The difference between the savages of Europe and those of America lies chiefly in this, that, while many tribes of the latter have been entirely devoured by their enemies, Europeans know a better way of using the vanquished than by eating them; and they prefer to increase through them the number of their subjects, and so the number of instruments at their command for still more widely spread war.

The depravity of human nature shows itself without disguise in the unrestrained relations of nations to each other, while in the law-governed civil state much of this is hidden by the check of government. This being so, it is astonishing that the word "right" has not yet been entirely banished from the politics of war as pedantic, and that no state has yet ventured publicly to advocate this point of view. For Hugo Grotius, Puffendorf, Vattel and others—Job's comforters, all of them—are always quoted in good faith to justify an attack, although their codes, whether couched in philosophical or diplomatic terms, have not—nor can have—the slightest legal force, because states, as such, are under no common external authority; and there is no instance of a state having ever been moved by argument to desist from its purpose, even when this was backed up by the testimony of such great men. This homage which every state renders—in words at least—to the idea of right, proves that, although it may be slumbering, there is, notwithstanding, to be found in man a still higher natural moral capacity by the aid of which he will in time gain the mastery over the evil principle in his nature, the existence of which he is unable to deny. And he hopes the same of others; for otherwise the word "right" would never be uttered by states who wish to wage war, unless to deride it like the Gallic Prince who declared:—"The privilege which nature gives the strong is that the weak must obey them."

The method by which states prosecute their rights can never be by process of law—as it is where there is an external tribunal—but only by war. Through this means, however, and its favourable issue, victory, the question of right is never decided. A treaty of peace makes, it may be, an end to the war of the moment, but not to the conditions of war which at any time may afford a new pretext for opening hostilities; and this we cannot exactly condemn as unjust, because under these conditions everyone is his own judge. Notwithstanding, not quite the same rule applies to states according to the law of nations as holds good of individuals in a lawless condition according to the law of nature, namely, "that they ought to advance out of this condition." This is so, because, as states, they have already within themselves a legal constitution, and have therefore advanced beyond the stage at which others, in accordance with their ideas of right, can force them to come under a wider legal constitution. Meanwhile, however, reason, from her throne of the supreme law-giving moral power, absolutely condemns war as a morally lawful proceeding, and makes a state of peace, on the other hand, an immediate duty. Without a compact between the nations, however, this state of peace cannot be established or assured. Hence there must be an alliance of a particular kind which we may call a covenant of peace (*foedus pacificum*), which would differ from a treaty of peace (*pactum pacis*) in this respect, that the latter merely puts an end to one war, while the former would seek to put an end to war for ever. This alliance does not aim at the gain of any power whatsoever of the state, but merely at the preservation and security of the freedom of the state for itself and of other allied states at the same time. The latter do not, however, require, for this reason, to submit themselves like individuals in the state of nature to public laws and coercion. The practicability or objective reality of this idea of federation which is to extend gradually over all states and so lead to perpetual peace can be shewn. For, if Fortune ordains that a powerful and enlightened people should form a republic—which by its very nature is inclined to perpetual peace—this would serve as a centre of federal union for other states wishing to join, and thus secure conditions of freedom among the states in accordance with the idea of the law of nations. Gradually, through different unions of this kind, the federation would extend further and further.

It is quite comprehensible that a people should say:—"There shall be no war among us, for we shall form ourselves into a state, that is to say, constitute for ourselves a supreme legislative, administrative and judicial power which will settle our disputes peaceably." But if this state says:—"There shall be no war between me and other states, although I recognise no supreme law-giving power which will secure me my rights and whose rights I will guarantee;" then it is not at all clear upon what grounds I could base my confidence in my right, unless it were the substitute for that compact on which civil society is based—namely, free federation which reason must necessarily connect with the idea of the law of nations, if indeed any meaning is to be left in that concept at all.

There is no intelligible meaning in the idea of the law of nations as giving a right to make war; for that must be a right to decide what is just, not in accordance with universal, external laws limiting the freedom of each individual, but by means of one-sided maxims applied by force. We must then understand by this that men of such ways of thinking are quite justly served, when they destroy one another, and thus find perpetual peace in the wide grave which covers all the abominations of acts of violence as well as the authors of such deeds. For states, in their relation to one another, there can be, according to reason, no other way of advancing from that lawless condition which unceasing war implies, than by giving up their savage lawless freedom, just as individual men have done, and yielding to the coercion of public laws. Thus they can form a society of nations (*civitas gentium*), one, too, which will be ever increasing and would finally embrace all the peoples of the earth. States, however, in accordance with their understanding of the law of nations, by no means desire this, and therefore reject in practice (*in hypothesi*) what is correct in theory (*in thesi*). Hence, instead of the positive idea of a world-republic, if all is not to be lost, only the negative substitute for it, a federation averting war, maintaining its ground and ever extending over the world may stop the current of this tendency to war and shrinking from the control of law. But even then there will be a constant danger that this propensity may break out.

THIRD DEFINITIVE ARTICLE OF PERPETUAL PEACE

3. The rights of men, as citizens of the world, shall be limited to the conditions of universal hospitality.

We are speaking here, as in the previous articles, not of philanthropy, but of right; and in this sphere hospitality signifies the claim of a stranger entering foreign territory to be treated by its owner without hostility. The latter may send him away again, if this can be done without causing his death; but, so long as he conducts himself peaceably, he must not be treated as an enemy. It is not a right to be treated as a guest to which the stranger can lay claim —a special friendly compact on his behalf would be required to make him for a given time an actual inmate—but he has a right of visitation. This right to present themselves to society belongs to all mankind in virtue of our common right of possession on the surface of the earth on which, as it is a globe, we cannot be infinitely scattered, and must in the end reconcile ourselves to existence side by side: at the same time, originally no one individual had more right than another to live in any one particular spot. Uninhabitable portions of the surface, ocean and desert, split up the human community, but in such a way that ships and camels—"the ship of the desert"—make it possible for men to come into touch with one another across these unappropriated regions and to take advantage of our common claim to the face of the earth with a view to a possible intercommunication. The inhospitality of the inhabitants of certain sea coasts—as, for example, the coast of Barbary—in plundering ships in neighbouring seas or making slaves of shipwrecked mariners; or the behaviour of the Arab Bedouins in the deserts, who think that proximity to nomadic tribes constitutes a right to rob, is thus contrary to the law of nature. This right to hospitality, however—that is to say, the privilege of strangers arriving on foreign soil—does not amount to more than what is implied in a permission to make an attempt at intercourse with the original inhabitants. In this way far distant territories may enter into peaceful relations with one another. These relations may at last come under the public control of law, and thus the human race may be brought nearer the realisation of a cosmopolitan constitution.

Let us look now, for the sake of comparison, at the inhospitable behaviour of the civilised nations, especially the commercial states of our continent. The injustice which they exhibit on visiting foreign lands and races—this being equivalent in their eyes to conquest—is such as to fill us with horror. America, the negro countries, the Spice Islands, the Cape etc. were, on being discovered, looked upon as countries which belonged to nobody; for the native inhabitants were reckoned as nothing. In Hindustan, under the pretext of intending to establish merely commercial depots, the Europeans introduced foreign troops; and, as a result, the different states of Hindustan were stirred up to far-spreading wars. Oppression of the natives followed, famine, insurrection, perfidy and all the rest of the litany of evils which can afflict mankind.

China and Japan (Nippon), which had made an attempt at receiving guests of this kind, have now taken a prudent step. Only to a single European people, the Dutch, has China given the right of access to her shores (but not of entrance into the country), while Japan has granted both these concessions; but at the same time they exclude the Dutch, who enter as if they were prisoners, from social intercourse with the inhabitants. The worst, or from the standpoint of ethical judgment the best, of all this is that no satisfaction is derived from all this violence, that all these trading companies stand on the verge of ruin, that the Sugar Islands, that seat of the most horrible and deliberate slavery, yield no real profit, but only have their use indirectly and for no very praiseworthy object—namely, that of furnishing men to be trained as sailors for the men-of-war and thereby contributing to the carrying on of war in Europe. And this has been done by nations who make a great ado about their piety, and who, while they are quite ready to commit injustice, would like, in their orthodoxy, to be considered among the elect.

The intercourse, more or less close, which has been everywhere steadily increasing between the nations of the earth, has now extended so enormously that a violation of right in one part of the world is felt all over it. Hence the idea of a cosmopolitan right is no fantastical, high-flown notion of right, but a complement of the unwritten code of law—constitutional as well as international law—necessary for the public rights of mankind in general and thus for the realisation of perpetual peace. For only by endeavouring to fulfil the conditions laid down by this cosmopolitan law can we flatter ourselves that we are gradually approaching that ideal.

JEAN A. N. C. DE CONDORCET

THE MARQUIS DE CONDORCET (1743–94), mathematician, philosopher, and revolutionary, was educated at the Jesuit College in Rheims and at the College of Navarre, where he displayed an extraordinary talent for mathematics. In 1769 he became a member of the Academy of Sciences, to which he contributed voluminously. He also belonged to the French Academy, and to many other academies, for he was enthusiastic and gifted in more than one direction.

Probably under the influence of his friends D'Alembert, Turgot, and Voltaire, he became interested in social questions. He supported the American Revolution with all his heart, his principal writings on the subject being *The Influence of the American Revolution on Europe,* the *Lettre d'un citoyen des États-Unis sur les affaires présentes,* the *Lettres d'un bourgeois de Newhaven à un citoyen de Virginie,* and *Reflexions sur l'esclavage des nègres.*

When the Revolution broke out in France, Condorcet labored for the triumph of middle-class democracy. He was first a member of the municipality of Paris (1790), then a representative of Paris in the Legislative Assembly. He was made one of the secretaries of that body, in which capacity he drew up most of its addresses. He was especially interested in educational questions, and presented a bold scheme for the organization of a system of state education which is still the basis of French schooling. After the flight of the king, he was one of the first to declare for a republic. Elected to the Convention, he found his proposed constitution rejected. His criticism of the adopted constitution, as well as his objections to the Convention's assumption of judicial functions for the trial of Louis XVI, his denunciation of the arrest of the Girondists, and of the violent conduct of the Jacobins in general, led to his being accused of conspiring against the Republic. Mme Vernet gave him asylum, and he was prevailed upon by his wife and friends to write the work for which he is best known, *The Progress of the Human Mind.* This work, though composed under dire circumstances, rests on Condorcet's belief in human perfectability and in the certain progress of history toward national and class equality.

Fearing that harm would come to Mme Vernet if he took advantage of her kindness any longer, Condorcet left without her knowledge and wandered the countryside. Captured at Clamat by a member of the revolutionary tribunal of that town, he was thrown into a cell, and next morning was found dead.

The eighteenth century is often conceived of, too simply, as the "age of reason" and the Enlightenment is similarly oversimplified. Just a few men, for example —Turgot was among them—had any worked-out theory of human progress, and Condorcet's similar essay is in one sense exceptional. On the other hand, there can be little doubt that the general mood of the Enlightenment was progressive and rested on the belief that the accumulation of knowledge, the spread of toleration and free discussion, and the use of general happiness as a test of government would bring the fulfillment of man's best potentialities.

In Condorcet's theory of progress the methods by which science, from one point of view, arrives at its conclusions and the ideal of open-minded scientists patiently pursuing truth are taken as models for the conduct of an enlightened political community. His work, however, was only a sketch, written without books for reference and in the shadow of the guillotine maintained in the name of Reason. Nevertheless, it registers the belief that flowered in the eighteenth century that systematic critical inquiry as free as possible from prejudice is essential to the liberation of man from ignorance and tyranny.

This selection has been translated from the French, *Esquisse d'un tableau historique du progrès de l'esprit.*

❧

THE PROGRESS OF THE HUMAN MIND

NINTH EPOCH: FROM THE TIME OF DESCARTES, TO THE FORMATION OF THE FRENCH REPUBLIC

And now we arrive at the period when philosophy, the most general and obvious effects of which we have before remarked, obtained an influence on the thinking class of men, and these on the people and their governments, that, ceasing any longer to be gradual, produced a revolution in the entire mass of certain nations, and gave thereby a secure pledge of the general revolution one day to follow that shall embrace the whole human species.

After ages of error, after wandering in all the mazes of vague and defective theories, writers upon politics and the law of nations at length arrived at the knowledge of the true rights of man, which they deduced from this simple principle: that *he is a being endowed with sensation, capable of reasoning upon and understanding his interests, and of acquiring moral ideas.*

They saw that the maintenance of his rights was the only object of political union, and that the perfection of the social art consisted in preserving them with the most entire equality, and in their fullest extent. They perceived that the means of securing the rights of the individual, consisting of general rules to be laid down in every community, the power of choosing these means, and determining these rules, could vest only in the majority of the community; and that for this reason, as it is impossible for any individual in this choice to follow the dictates of his own understanding, without subjecting that of others, the will of the majority is the only principle which can be followed by all, without infringing upon the common equality.

Each individual may enter into a previous engagement to comply with the will of the majority, which by this engagement becomes unanimity; he can however bind nobody but himself, nor can he bind himself except so far as the majority shall not violate his individual rights, after having recognised them.

Such are at once the rights of the majority over individuals, and the limits of these rights; such is the origin of that unanimity, which renders the engagement of the majority binding upon all; a bond that ceases to operate when, by the change of individuals, this species of unanimity ceases to exist. There are objects, no doubt, upon which the majority would pronounce perhaps oftener in favour of error and mischief, than in favour of truth and happiness; still the majority, and the majority only, can decide what are the objects which cannot properly be referred to its own decision; it can alone determine as to the individuals whose judgement it resolves to prefer to its own, and the method which these individuals are to pursue in the exercise of their judgement; in fine, it has also an indispensable authority of pronouncing whether the decisions of its officers have or have not wounded the rights of all.

From these simple principles men discovered the folly of former notions respecting the validity of contracts between a people and its magistrates, which it was supposed could only be annulled by mutual consent, or by a violation of the conditions by one of the parties; as well as of another opinion, less servile, but equally absurd, that would chain a people for ever to the provisions of a constitution when once established, as if the right of changing it were not the security of every other right, as if human institutions, necessarily defective, and capable of improvement as we become enlightened, were to be condemned to an eternal monotony. Accordingly the governors of nations saw themselves obliged to renounce that false and subtle policy, which, forgetting that all men derive from nature an equality of rights, would sometimes measure the extent of those which it might think proper to grant by the size of territory, the temperature of the climate, the national character, the wealth of the people, the state of commerce and industry; and sometimes cede them in unequal portions among the different classes of society, according to their birth, their fortune, or their profession, thereby creating contrary interests and jarring powers, in order afterwards to apply correctives, which, but for these institutions, would not be wanted, and which, after all, are inadequate to the end.

It was now no longer practicable to divide mankind into two species, one destined to govern, the other to obey, one to deceive, the other to be dupes: the doctrine was obliged universally to be acknowledged, that all have an equal right to be enlightened respecting their interests, to share in the acquisition of truth, and that no political authorities appointed by the people for the benefit of the people, can be entitled to retain them in ignorance and darkness. . . .

Hitherto we have exhibited the state of philosophy only among men by whom it has in a manner been studied, investigated, and perfected. It remains to mark its influence on the general opinion, and to show, that, while it arrived at the certain and infallible means of discovering and recognising truth, reason at the same time detected the delusions into which it had so often been led by a respect for authority or a misguided imagination, and undermined those prejudices in the mass of individuals which had so long been the scourge, at once corrupting and inflicting calamity upon the human species.

The period at length arrived when men no longer feared openly to avow the right, so long withheld, and even unknown, of subjecting every opinion to the test of reason, or, in other words, of employing, in their search after truth, the only means they possess for its discovery. Every man learned, with a degree of pride and exultation, that nature had not condemned him to see with the eyes and to conform his judgement to the caprice of another. The superstitions of antiquity accordingly disappeared; and the debasement of reason to the shrine of supernatural faith, was as rarely to be found in society as in the circles of metaphysics and philosophy.

A class of men speedily made their appearance in Europe, whose object was less to discover and investigate truth, than to disseminate it; who, pursuing prejudice through all the haunts and asylums in which the clergy, the schools, governments, and privileged corporations had placed and protected it, made it their glory rather to eradicate popular errors, than add to the stores of human knowledge; thus aiding indirectly the progress of mankind, but in a way neither less arduous, nor less beneficial.

In England, Collins and Bolingbroke, and in France, Bayle, Fontenelle, Montesquieu, and the respective disciples of these celebrated men, combated on the side truth with all the weapons that learning, wit and genius were able to furnish: assuming every shape, employing every tone, from the sublime and pathetic to pleasantry and satire, from the most laboured investigation to an interesting romance or a fugitive essay; accommodating truth to those eyes that were too weak to bear its effulgence; artfully caressing prejudice, the more easily to strangle it; never aiming a direct blow at errors, never attacking more than one at a time, nor even that one in all its fortresses; sometimes soothing the enemies of reason, by pretending to require in religion but a partial toleration, in politics but a limited freedom; siding with despotism, when their hostilities were directed against the priesthood, and with priests, when their object was to unmask the despot; sapping the principle of both these pests of human happiness, striking at the root of both these baneful trees, while apparently wishing for the reform only of glaring abuses and seemingly confining themselves to lopping off the exuberant branches; sometimes representing to the partisans of liberty, that superstition, which covers despotism as with a coat of mail, is the first victim which ought to be sacrificed, the first chain that ought to be broken; and sometimes denouncing it to tyrants as the true enemy of their power, and alarming them with recitals of its hypocritical conspiracies and its sanguinary vengeance. These writers, meanwhile, were uniform in their vindication of freedom of thinking and freedom of writing, as privileges upon which depended the salvation of mankind. They declaimed, without cessation or weariness, against the crimes both of fanatics and tyrants, exposing every feature of severity, of cruelty, of oppression, whether in religion, in administration, in manners, or in laws; commanding kings, soldiers, magistrates and priests, in the name of truth and of nature, to respect the blood of mankind; calling upon them, with energy, to answer for the lives still profusely sacrificed in the field of battle or by the infliction of punishments, or else to correct this inhuman policy, this murderous insensibility; and lastly, in every place, and upon every occasion, rallying the friends of mankind with the cry of *reason, toleration, and humanity!* . . .

While we thus take a general view of the human species, we may prove that the discovery of true methods in all the sciences; the extent of the theories they include; their application to all the objects of nature, and all the wants of man; the lines of communication established between them; the great number of those who cultivate them; and, lastly, the multiplication of printing presses, are sufficient to assure us, that none of them will hereafter descend below the point to which it has been carried. We may shew that the principles of philosophy, the maxims of liberty, the knowledge of the true rights of man, and his real interests, are spread over too many nations, and in each of those nations direct the opinions of too great a number of enlightened men, for them ever to fall again into oblivion.

What fear can be entertained when we find that the two languages the most universally extended, are, likewise, the languages of two peoples who possess the most extended liberty; who have best known its principles. So that no confederacy of tyrants, nor any possible combination of policy, can prevent the rights of reason, as well as those of liberty, from being openly defended in both languages.

But if it be true, as every prospect assures us, that the human race shall not again relapse into its ancient barbarity; if every thing ought to assure us against that pusillanimous and corrupt system which condemns man to eternal oscillations between truth and falsehood, liberty and servitude, we must, at the same time, perceive that the light of information is spread over a small part only of our globe; and the number of those who possess real instruction, seems to vanish in the comparison with the mass of men consigned over to ignorance and prejudice. We behold vast countries groaning under slavery, and presenting nations, in one place, degraded by the vices of civilization, so corrupt as to impede the progress of man; and in others, still vegetating in the infancy of its early age. We perceive that the exertions of these last ages have done much for the progress of the human mind, but little for the perfection of the human species; much for the glory of man, somewhat for his liberty, but scarcely any thing yet for his happiness. In a few directions, our eyes are struck with a dazzling light; but thick darkness still covers an immense horizon. The mind of the philosopher reposes with satisfaction upon a small number of objects, but the spectacle of the stupidity, the slavery, the extravagance, and the barbarity of man, afflicts him still more strongly. The friend of humanity cannot receive unmixed pleasure but by abandoning himself to the endearing hope of the future. . . .

TENTH EPOCH: FUTURE PROGRESS OF MANKIND

If man can predict, almost with certainty, those appearances of which he understands the laws; if, even when the laws are unknown to him, experience of the past enables him to foresee, with considerable probability, future appearances; why should we suppose it a chimerical undertaking to delineate with some degree of truth, the picture of the future destiny of mankind from the results of its history? The only foundation of faith in the natural sciences is the principle, that the general laws, known or unknown, which regulate the phenomena of the universe, are regular and constant; and why should this principle, applicable to the other operations of nature, be less true when applied to the development of the intellectual and moral faculties of man? In short, as opinions formed from experience, relative to the same class of objects, are the only rule by which men of soundest understanding are governed in their conduct, why should the philosopher be proscribed from supporting his conjectures upon a similar basis, provided he attribute to them no greater certainty than the number, the consistency, and the accuracy of actual observations shall authorise?

Our hopes, as to the future condition of the human species, may be reduced to three points: the destruction of inequality between different nations; the progress of equality in one and the same nation; and lastly, the real improvement of man.

Will not every nation one day arrive at the state of civilization attained by those people who are most enlightened, most free, most exempt from prejudices, as the French, for instance, and the Anglo-Americans? Will not the slavery of countries subjected to kings, the barbarity of African tribes, and the ignorance of savages gradually vanish? Is there upon the face of the globe a single spot the inhabitants of which are condemned by nature never to enjoy liberty, never to exercise their reason?

Does the difference of knowledge, of means, and of wealth, observable hitherto in all civilized nations, between the classes into which the people constituting those nations are divided; does that inequality, which the earliest progress of society has augmented, or, to speak more properly, produced, belong to civilization itself, or to the imperfections of the social order? Must it not continually weaken, in order to give place to that actual equality, the chief end of the social art, which, diminishing even the effects of the natural difference of the faculties, leaves no other inequality subsisting but what is useful to the interest of all, because it will favour civilization, instruction, and industry, without drawing after it either dependence, humiliation or poverty? In a word, will not men be continually verging towards that state, in which all will possess the requisite knowledge for conducting themselves in the common affairs of the life by their own reason, and of maintaining that reason uncontaminated by prejudices; in which they will understand their rights, and exercise them according to their opinion and their conscience; in which all will be able, by the development of their faculties, to procure the certain means of providing for their wants; lastly, in which folly and wretchedness will be accidents, happening only now and then, and not the habitual lot of a considerable portion of society?

In fine, may it not be expected that the human race will be meliorated by new discoveries in the sciences and the arts, and, as an unavoidable consequence, in the means of individual and general prosperity; by farther progress in the principles of conduct, and in moral practice; and lastly, by the real improvement of our faculties, moral, intellectual and physical, which may be the result either of the improvement of the instruments which increase the power and direct the exercise of those faculties, or of the improvement of our natural organization itself?

In examining the three questions we have enumerated, we shall find the strongest reasons to believe, from past experience, from observation of the progress which the sciences and civilization have hitherto made, and from the analysis of the march of the human understanding, and the development of its faculties, that nature has fixed no limits to our hopes. . . .

The different causes of equality we have enumerated do not act distinctly and apart; they unite, they incorporate, they support one another; and from their combined influence results an action proportionably forcible, sure, and constant. If instruction become more equal, industry thence acquires greater equality, and from industry the effect is communicated to fortunes; and equality of fortunes necessarily contributes to that of instruction, while equality of nations, like that established between individuals, have also a mutual operation upon each other.

In fine, instruction, properly directed, corrects the natural inequality of the faculties, instead of strengthening it, in like manner as good laws remedy the natural inequality of the means of subsistence; or as, in societies whose institutions shall have effected this equality, liberty, though subjected to a regular government, will be more extensive, more complete, than in the independence of savage life. Then has the social art accomplished its end, that of securing and extending for all the enjoyment of the common rights which impartial nature has bequeathed to all.

The advantages that must result from the state of improvement, of which I have proved we may almost entertain the certain hope, can have no limit but the absolute perfection of the human species, since, in proportion as different kinds of equality shall be established as to the various means of providing for our wants, as to a more universal instruction, and a more entire liberty, the more real will be this equality, and the nearer will it approach towards embracing everything truly important to the happiness of mankind.

It is then by examining the progression and the laws of this perfection, that we can alone arrive at the knowledge of the extent or boundary of our hopes.

It has never yet been supposed, that all the facts of nature, and all the means of acquiring precision in the computation and analysis of those facts, and all the connections of objects with each other, and all the possible combinations of ideas, can be exhausted by the human mind. The mere relations of magnitude, the combinations, quantity and extent of this idea alone, form already a system too immense for the mind of man ever to grasp the whole of it; a portion, more vast than that which he may have penetrated, will always remain unknown to him. It has, however, been imagined, that, as man can know a part only of the objects which the nature of his intelligence permits him to investigate, he must at length reach the point at which, the number and complication of those he already knows having absorbed all his powers, farther progress will become absolutely impossible.

But, in proportion as facts are multiplied, man learns to class them, and reduce them to more general facts, at the same time that the instruments and methods for observing them, and registering them with exactness, acquire a new precision: in proportion as relations more multifarious between a greater number of objects are discovered, man continues to reduce them to relations of a wider denomination, to express them with greater simplicity, and to present them in a way which may enable a given strength of mind, with a given quantity of attention, to take in a greater number than before: in proportion as the understanding embraces more complicated combinations, a simple mode of announcing these combinations renders them more easy to be treated. Hence it follows that truths, the discovery of which was accompanied with the most laborious efforts, and which at first could not be comprehended but by men of the severest attention, will after a time be unfolded and proved in methods that are not above the efforts of an ordinary capacity. And thus should the methods that led to new combinations be exhausted, should their applications to questions, still unresolved, demand exertions greater than the time or the powers of the learned can bestow, more general methods, means more simple would soon come to their aid, and open a farther career to genius. The energy, the real extent of the human intellect may remain the same; but the instruments which it can employ will be multiplied and improved; but the language which fixes and determines the idea will acquire more precision and compass; and it will not be here, as in the science of mechanics, where, to increase the force, we must diminish the velocity; on the contrary the methods by which genius will arrive at the discovery of new truths, augment at once both the force and the rapidity of its operations.

In a word, these changes being themselves the necessary consequences of additional progress in the knowledge of truths of detail, and the cause which produces a demand for new resources, producing at the same time the means of supplying them, it follows that the actual mass of truths appertaining to the sciences of observation, calculation and experiment, may be perpetually augmented, and that without supposing the faculties of man to possess a force and activity, and a scope of action greater than before.

By applying these general reflections to the different sciences, we might exhibit, respecting each, examples of this progressive improvement, which would remove all possibility of doubts as to the certainty of the further improvement that may be expected. . . .

If we pass to the progress of the arts, those arts particularly the theory of which depends on these very same sciences, we shall find that it can have no inferior limits; that their processes are susceptible of the same improvement, the same simplifications, as the scientific methods; that instruments, machines, looms, will add every day to the capabilities and skill of man—will augment at once the excellence and precision of his works, while they will diminish the time and labour necessary for executing them; and that then will disappear the obstacles that still oppose themselves to the progress in question, accidents which will be foreseen and prevented; and, lastly, the unhealthiness at present attendant upon certain operations, habits and climates. . . .

Thus, not only the same species of ground will nourish a greater number of individuals, but each individual, with a less quantity of labour, will labour more successfully, and be surrounded with greater conveniences.

It may, however, be demanded, whether, amidst this improvement in industry and happiness, where the wants and faculties of men will continually become better proportioned, each successive generation possess more various stores, and of consequence in each generation the number of individuals be greatly increased; it may, I say, be demanded, whether these principles of improvement and increase may not, by their continual operation, ultimately lead to degeneracy and destruction? Whether the number of inhabitants in the universe at length exceeding the means of existence, there will not result a continual decay of happiness and population, and a progress towards barbarism, or at least a sort of oscillation between good and evil? Will not this oscillation, in societies arrived at this epoch, be a perennial source of periodical calamity and distress? In a word, do not these considerations point out the limit at which all farther improvement will become impossible, and consequently the perfectibility of man arrive at a period which in the immensity of ages it may attain, but which it can never pass?

There is, doubtless, no individual that does not perceive how very remote from us will be this period: but must it one day arrive? It is equally impossible to pronounce on either side respecting an event, which can only be realized at an epoch when the human species will necessarily have acquired a degree of knowledge, of which our short-sighted understandings can scarcely form an idea. And who shall presume to foretell to what perfection the art of converting the elements of life into substances fitted for our use, may, in a progression of ages, be brought?

But supposing the affirmative, supposing it actually to take place, there would result from it nothing alarming, either to the happiness of the human race, or its indefinite perfectibility; if we consider, that prior to this period the progress of reason will have walked hand in hand with that of the sciences; that the absurd prejudices of superstition will have ceased to infuse into morality a harshness that corrupts and degrades, instead of purifying and exalting it; that men will then know, that the duties they may be under relative to propagation will consist not in the question of giving *existence* to a greater number of beings, but *happiness;* will have for their object, the general welfare of the human species; of the society in which they live; of the family to which they are attached; and not the puerile idea of encumbering the earth with useless and wretched mortals. Accordingly, there might then be a limit to the possible mass of provision, and of consequence to the greatest possible population, without that premature destruction, so contrary to nature and to social prosperity, of a portion of the beings who may have received life, being the result of those limits.

As the discovery, or rather the accurate solution of the first principles of metaphysics, morals, and politics, is still recent; and as it has been preceded by the knowledge of a considerable number of truths of detail, the prejudice, that they have thereby arrived at their highest point of improvement, becomes easily established in the mind; and men suppose that nothing remains to be done, because there are no longer any gross errors to destroy, or fundamental truths to establish.

But it requires little penetration to perceive how imperfect is still the development of the intellectual and moral faculties of man; how much farther the sphere of his duties, including therein the influence of his actions upon the welfare of his fellow-creatures and of the society to which he belongs, may be extended by a more fixed, a more profound and more accurate observation of that influence; how many questions still remain to be solved, how many social ties to be examined, before we can ascertain the precise catalogue of the individual rights of man, as well as of the rights which the social state confers upon the whole community with regard to each member. Have we even ascertained with any precision the limits of these rights, whether as they exist between different societies, or in any single society, over its members, in cases of division and hostility; or, in fine, the rights of individuals, their spontaneous unions in the case of a primitive formation, or their separations when separation becomes necessary?

If we pass on to the theory which ought to direct the application of these principles, and serve as the basis of the social art, do we not see the necessity of acquiring an exactness of which first truths, from their general nature, are not susceptible? Are we so far advanced as to consider justice, or a proved and acknowledged utility, and not vague, uncertain, and arbitrary views of pretended political advantages, as the foundation of all institutions of law? Among the variety, almost infinite, of possible systems, in which the general principles of equality and natural rights should be respected, have we yet fixed upon the precise rules of ascertaining with certainty those which best secure the preservation of these rights, which afford the freest scope for their exercise and enjoyment, which promote most effectually the peace and welfare of individuals, and the strength, repose, and prosperity of nations?

The application of the arithmetic of combinations and probabilities to these sciences, promises an improvement by so much the more considerable, as it is the only means of giving to their results an almost mathematical precision, and of appreciating their degree of certainty or probability. The facts upon which these results are built may, indeed, without calculation, and by a glance only, lead to some general truths; teach us whether the effects produced by such a cause have been favourable or the reverse: but if these facts have neither been counted nor estimated; if these effects have not been the object of an exact admeasurement, we cannot judge of the quantity of good or evil they contain: if the good or evil nearly balance each other, nay, if the difference be not considerable, we cannot pronounce with certainty to which side the balance inclines. . . .

There is another species of progress, appertaining to the sciences in question, equally important; I mean, the improvement of their language, at present so vague and so obscure. To this improvement must they owe the advantage of becoming popular, even in their first elements. Genius can triumph over these inaccuracies, as over other obstacles; it can recognize the features of truth, in spite of the mask that conceals or disfigures them. But how is the man who can devote but a few leisure moments to instruction to do this? how is he to acquire and retain the most simple truths, if they be disguised by an inaccurate language? The fewer ideas he is able to collect and combine, the more requisite it is that they be just and precise. . . .

What is the object of the improvement of laws and public institutions, consequent upon the progress of these sciences, but to reconcile, to approximate, to blend and unite into one mass the common interest of each individual with the common interest of all? What is the end of the social art, but to destroy the opposition between these two apparently jarring sentiments? And will not the constitution and laws of that country best accord with the intentions of reason and nature where the practice of virtue shall be least difficult, and the temptations to deviate from her paths least numerous and least powerful?

What vicious habit can be mentioned, what practice contrary to good faith, what crime even, the origin and first cause of which may not be traced in the legislation, institutions, and prejudices of the country in which we observe such habit, such practice, or such crime to be committed?

In short, does not the well-being, the prosperity, resulting from the progress that will be made by the useful arts, in consequence of their being founded upon a sound theory, resulting, also, from an improved legislation, built upon the truths of the political sciences, naturally dispose men to humanity, to benevolence, and to justice? Do not all the observations, in fine, which we proposed to develop in this work prove, that the moral goodness of man, the necessary consequence of his organization, is, like all his other faculties, susceptible of an indefinite improvement? and that nature has connected, by a chain which cannot be broken, truth, happiness, and virtue?

Among those causes of human improvement that are of most importance to the general welfare, must be included, the total annihilation of the prejudices which have established between the sexes an inequality of rights, fatal even to the party which it favours. In vain might we search for motives by which to justify this principle, in difference of physical organization, of intellect, or of moral sensibility. It had at first no other origin but abuse of strength, and all the attempts which have since been made to support it are idle sophisms. . . .

The people being more enlightened, and having resumed the right of disposing for themselves of their blood and their treasure, will learn by degrees to regard war as the most dreadful of all calamities, the most terrible of all crimes. . . .

All the causes which contribute to the improvement of the human species, all the means we have enumerated that insure its progress, must, from their very nature, exercise an influence always active, and acquire an extent for ever increasing. The proofs of this have been exhibited, and from their development in the work itself they will derive additional force: accordingly we may already conclude, that the perfectibility of man is indefinite. Meanwhile we have hitherto considered him as possessing only the same natural faculties, as endowed with the same organization. How much greater would be the certainty, how much wider the compass of our hopes, could we prove that these natural faculties themselves, that this very organization, are also susceptible of melioration? And this is the last question we shall examine.

The organic perfectibility or deterioration of the classes of the vegetable, or species of the animal kingdom, may be regarded as one of the general laws of nature.

This law extends itself to the human race; and it cannot be doubted that the progress of the sanative art, that the use of more wholesome food and more comfortable habitations, that a mode of life which shall develop the physical powers by exercise, without at the same time impairing them by excess; in fine, that the destruction of the two most active causes of deterioration, penury and wretchedness on the one hand, and enormous wealth on the other, must necessarily tend to prolong the common duration of man's existence, and secure him a more constant health and a more robust constitution. It is manifest that the improvement of the practice of medicine, become more efficacious in consequence of the progress of reason and the social order, must in the end put a period to transmissible or contagious disorders, as well as to those general maladies resulting from climate, ailments, and the nature of certain occupations. Nor would it be difficult to prove that this hope might be extended to almost every other malady, of which it is probable we shall hereafter discover the most remote causes. Would it even be absurd to suppose this quality of melioration in the human species as susceptible of an indefinite advancement; to suppose that a period must one day arrive when death will be nothing more than the effect either of extraordinary accidents, or of the flow and gradual decay of the vital powers; and that the duration of the middle space, of the interval between the birth of man and this decay, will itself have no assignable limit? Certainly man will not become immortal; but may not the distance between the moment in which he draws his first breath, and the common term when, in the course of nature, without malady, without accident, he finds it impossible any longer to exist, be necessarily protracted? . . .

But may not our physical faculties, the force, the sagacity, the acuteness of the senses, be numbered among the qualities, the individual improvement of which it will be practicable to transmit? An attention to the different breeds of domestic animals must lead us to adopt the affirmative of this question, and a direct observation of the human species itself will be found to strengthen the opinion.

Lastly, may we not include in the same circle the intellectual and moral faculties? May not our parents, who transmit to us the advantages or defects of their conformation, and from whom we receive our features and shape, as well as our propensities to certain physical affections, transmit to us also that part of organization upon which intellect, strength of understanding, energy of soul or moral sensibility depend? Is it not probable that education, by improving these qualities, will at the same time have an influence upon, will modify and improve this organization itself? Analogy, an investigation of the human faculties, and even some facts appear to authorise these conjectures, and thereby to enlarge the boundary of our hopes.

Such are the questions with which we shall terminate the last division of our work. And how admirably calculated is this view of the human race, emancipated from its chains, released alike from the dominion of chance, as well as from that of the enemies of its progress, and advancing with a firm and indeviate step in the paths of truth, to console the philosopher lamenting the errors, the flagrant acts of injustice, the crimes with which the earth is still polluted? It is the contemplation of this prospect that rewards him for all his efforts to assist the progress of reason and the establishment of liberty. He dares to regard these efforts as a part of the eternal chain of the destiny of mankind; and in this persuasion he finds the true delight of virtue, the pleasure of having performed a durable service, which no vicissitude will ever destroy in a fatal operation calculated to restore the reign of prejudice and slavery. This sentiment is the asylum into which he retires, and to which the memory of his persecutors cannot follow him: he unites himself in imagination with man restored to his rights, delivered from oppression, and proceeding with rapid strides in the path of happiness: he forgets his own misfortunes while his thoughts are thus employed; he lives no longer to adversity, calumny and malice, but becomes the associate of these wiser and more fortunate beings whose enviable condition he so earnestly contributed to produce.

XII THE ENLIGHTENMENT: KNOWLEDGE AND MORALITY

VOLTAIRE

Voltaire (1694–1778) was born François Marie Arouet, the son of a notary. While he had less genius than cleverness, he approached being a cult in his own time, the symbol for all of Europe of the battle against the privileged orthodoxy of Church and state.

Voltaire was early instructed by his sponsor, the abbé de Chateauneuf, in belles-lettres and deism. At ten he went to the Jesuit Collège Louis-le-Grand, where he seems to have received a good education, though he himself, of course, deplored it. At seventeen he began the study of law, but soon he was introduced into the famous "court of Sceau," the coterie of the Duchesse du Maine, and in 1716 he was exiled for having helped her to compose lampoons on the Regent. After his return he was sent to the Bastille because of further libels. It was there that he altered his name. Why he chose Voltaire is not certain, but opinion has tended to believe it an anagram on Arouet le jeune (l.j.).

His first play, *Oedipe,* was produced in 1718 and was a great success. First the Regent, and then the Duke of Richelieu became his patrons; but in 1725 an exchange of insults with the Chevalier de Rohan led to his being bastinadoed, imprisoned, and finally packed off to England at his own request. Voltaire was never a good courtier.

England made a deep impression on him, and when he returned three years later it was as the champion of English toleration and Newtonian thought. In 1733 appeared his *Lettres philosophiques sur les Anglais* and the *Temple du goût.* The latter was a satire on contemporary French literature, the former an attack on all the institutions of France. The *Lettres* were burned, and Voltaire took refuge with the Marquise du Châtelet at Cirey. Eventually, he returned to court and was rewarded by the appointment to the post of historiographer-royal, once jointly held by Racine and Boileau. In 1749, however, he accepted the long-proffered invitation of Frederick of Prussia. The vicissitudes of his three-year visit were great and became notorious; at any rate, Voltaire was finally arrested by Frederick in response to various Voltairean offenses; and upon his release he was refused permission to reenter France. He settled near Geneva, where he wrote *Candide.* Buying the estate of Ferney there, whence he became known to Europe as the squire of Ferney, he opened his full attack on superstition and tyranny.

After twenty-eight years he returned to Paris with his new tragedy *Irène.* He was received with wild acclaim by the people and the Academy, if not by the court.

Voltaire was an immensely prolific writer. His works are usually divided into eight categories: his fifty or sixty plays; his poems proper; his prose romances, undoubtedly his best works (including *Candide, L'Homme aux quarante écus* and *Zadig*); his historical writings, the best known of which is the *Siècle de Louis XIV;* his philosophical works, especially the *Dictionnaire philosophique,* which consists mainly of his articles for the *Encyclopédie;* his criticism and miscellaneous writings; some work in physics; and the huge correspondence.

The first selection from Voltaire is from his *Philosophical Dictionary,* translated from the French by H. I. Woolf (New York, Alfred A. Knopf, 1924). The *Essay on Toleration* was translated by Joseph McCabe (New York, G. P. Putnam's Sons, 1912).

℘

NATURAL LAW

B: What is natural law?

A: The instinct which makes us feel justice.

B: What do you call just and unjust?

A: What appears such to the entire universe.

B: The universe is composed of many heads. It is said that in Lacedæmon were applauded thefts for which people in Athens were condemned to the mines.

A: Abuse of words, logomachy, equivocation; theft could not be committed at Sparta, when everything was common property. What you call "theft" was the punishment for avarice.

B: It was forbidden to marry one's sister in Rome. It was allowed among the Egyptians, the Athenians and even among the Jews, to marry one's sister on the father's side. It is but with regret that I cite that wretched little Jewish people, who should assuredly not serve as a rule for anyone, and who (putting religion aside) was never anything but a race of ignorant and fanatic brigands. But still, according to their books, the young Thamar, before being ravished by her brother Amnon, says to him:—"Nay, my brother, do not thou this folly, but speak unto the king; for he will not withhold me from thee."

A: Conventional law and all that, arbitrary customs, fashions that pass: the essential remains always. Show me a country where it was honourable to rob me of the fruit of my toil, to break one's promise, to lie in order to hurt, to calumniate, to assassinate, to poison, to be ungrateful towards a benefactor, to beat one's father and one's mother when they offer you food.

B: Have you forgotten that Jean-Jacques, one of the fathers of the modern Church, has said that "the first man who dared enclose and cultivate a piece of land" was the enemy "of the human race," that he should have been exterminated, and that "the fruits of the earth are for all, and that the land belongs to none"?[1] Have we not already examined together this lovely proposition which is so useful to society?

A: Who is this Jean-Jacques? he is certainly not either John the Baptist, nor John the Evangelist, nor James the Greater, nor James the Less; it must

---

[1] [Rousseau, *Discourse on the Origin of Inequality*, 2.]

be some Hunnish wit who wrote that abominable impertinence or some poor joker *bufo magro* who wanted to laugh at what the entire world regards as most serious. For instead of going to spoil the land of a wise and industrious neighbour, he had only to imitate him; and every father of a family having followed this example, behold soon a very pretty village formed. The author of this passage seems to me a very unsociable animal.

B: You think then that by outraging and robbing the good man who has surrounded his garden and chicken-run with a live hedge, he has been wanting in respect towards the duties of natural law?

A: Yes, yes, once again, there is a natural law, and it does not consist either in doing harm to others, or in rejoicing thereat.

B: I imagine that man likes and does harm only for his own advantage. But so many people are led to look for their own interest in the misfortune of others, vengeance is so violent a passion, there are such disastrous examples of it; ambition, still more fatal, has inundated the world with so much blood, that when I retrace for myself the horrible picture, I am tempted to avow that man is a very devil. In vain have I in my heart the notion of justice and injustice; an Attila courted by St. Leo, a Phocas flattered by St. Gregory with the most cowardly baseness, an Alexander VI sullied with so many incests, so many murders, so many poisonings, with whom the weak Louis XII, who is called "the good," makes the most infamous and intimate alliance; a Cromwell whose protection Cardinal Mazarin seeks, and for whom he drives out of France the heirs of Charles I, Louis XIV's first cousins, etc., etc.; a hundred like examples set my ideas in disorder, and I know no longer where I am.

A: Well, do storms stop our enjoyment of to-day's beautiful sun? Did the earthquake which destroyed half the city of Lisbon stop your making the voyage to Madrid very comfortably? If Attila was a brigand and Cardinal Mazarin a rogue, are there not princes and ministers who are honest people? Has it not been remarked that in the war of 1701, Louis XIV's council was composed of the most virtuous men? The Duc de Beauvilliers, the Marquis de Torci, the Maréchal de Villars, Chamillart lastly who passed for being incapable, but never for dishonest. Does not the idea of justice subsist always? It is upon that idea that all laws are founded. The Greeks called them "daughters of heaven," which only means daughters of nature. Have you no laws in your country?

B: Yes, some good, some bad.

A: Where, if it was not in the notions of natural law, did you get the idea, that every man has within himself, when his mind is properly made? You must have obtained it there, or nowhere.

B: You are right, there is a natural law; but it is still more natural to many people to forget it.

A: It is natural also to be one-eyed, hump-backed, lame, deformed, unhealthy; but one prefers people who are well made and healthy.

B: Why are there so many one-eyed and deformed minds?

A: Peace! But go to the article on "Power."

ON TOLERATION

WHETHER INTOLERANCE IS OF NATURAL AND HUMAN LAW

Natural law is that indicated to men by nature. You have reared a child; he owes you respect as a father, gratitude as a benefactor. You have a right to the products of the soil that you have cultivated with your own hands. You have given or received a promise; it must be kept.

Human law must in every case be based on natural law. All over the earth the great principle of both is: Do not unto others what you would that they do not unto you. Now, in virtue of this principle, one man cannot say to another: "Believe what I believe, and what thou canst not believe, or thou shalt perish." Thus do men speak in Portugal, Spain, and Goa. In some other countries they are now content to say: "Believe, or I detest thee; believe, or I will do thee all the harm I can. Monster, thou sharest not my religion, and therefore hast no religion; thou shalt be a thing of horror to thy neighbours, thy city, and thy province."

If it were a point of human law to behave thus, the Japanese should detest the Chinese, who should abhor the Siamese; the Siamese, in turn, should persecute the Thibetans, who should fall upon the Hindoos. A Mogul should tear out the heart of the first Malabarian he met; the Malabarian should slay the Persian, who might massacre the Turk; and all of them should fling themselves against the Christians, who have so long devoured each other.

The supposed right of intolerance is absurd and barbaric. It is the right of the tiger; nay, it is far worse, for tigers do but tear in order to have food, while we rend each other for paragraphs. . . .

WHETHER IT IS USEFUL TO MAINTAIN THE PEOPLE IN SUPERSTITION

Such is the weakness, such the perversity, of the human race that it is better, no doubt, for it to be subject to all conceivable superstitions, provided they be not murderous, than to live without religion. Man has always needed a curb; and, although it was ridiculous to sacrifice to fauns or naiads, it was much more reasonable and useful to worship these fantastic images of the deity than to sink into atheism. A violent atheist would be as great a plague as a violent superstitious man.

When men have not sound ideas of the divinity, false ideas will take their place; just as, in ages of impoverishment, when there is not sound money, people use bad coin. The pagan feared to commit a crime lest he should be punished by his false gods; the Asiatic fears the chastisement of his pagoda. Religion is necessary wherever there is a settled society. The laws take care of known crimes; religion watches secret crime.

But once men have come to embrace a pure and holy religion, superstition becomes, not merely useless, but dangerous. We must not feed on acorns those to whom God offers bread.

Superstition is to religion what astrology is to astronomy—the mad daughter of a wise mother. These daughters have too long dominated the earth. . . .

There remain, it is true, a few bigoted fanatics in the suburbs; but the disease, like vermin, attacks only the lowest of the populace. Every day reason penetrates farther into France, into the shops of merchants as well as the mansions of lords. We must cultivate the fruits of reason, the more willingly since it is now impossible to prevent them from developing. France, enlightened by Pascal, Nicole, Arnaud, Bossuet, Descartes, Gassendi, Bayle, Fontenelle, etc., cannot be ruled as it was ruled in earlier times.

If the masters of error—the grand masters—so long paid and honoured for brutalising the human species, ordered us to-day to believe that the seed must die in order to germinate; that the earth stands motionless on its foundations—that it does not travel round the sun; that the tides are not a natural effect of gravitation; that the rainbow is not due to the refraction and reflection of light, etc., and based their decrees on ill-understood passages of Scripture, we know how they would be regarded by educated men. Would it be too much to call them fools? And if these masters employed force and persecution to secure the ascendancy of their insolent ignorance, would it be improper to speak of them as wild beasts?

The more the superstitions of the monks are despised, the more the bishops and priests are respected; while they do good, the monkish superstitions from Rome do nothing but evil. And of all these superstitions, is not the most dangerous that of hating one's neighbour on account of his opinions? And is it not evident that it would be even more reasonable to worship the sacred navel, the sacred prepuce, and the milk and dress of the Virgin Mary, than to detest and persecute one's brother?

OF UNIVERSAL TOLERATION

One does not need great art and skilful eloquence to prove that Christians ought to tolerate each other—nay, even to regard all men as brothers. Why, you say, is the Turk, the Chinese, or the Jew my brother? Assuredly; are we not all children of the same father, creatures of the same God?

But these people despise us and treat us as idolaters. Very well; I will tell them that they are quite wrong. It seems to me that I might astonish, at least, the stubborn pride of a Mohammedan or a Buddhist priest if I spoke to them somewhat as follows:

This little globe, which is but a point, travels in space like many other globes; we are lost in the immensity. Man, about five feet high, is certainly a small thing in the universe. One of these imperceptible beings says to some of his neighbours, in Arabia or South Africa: "Listen to me, for the God of all these worlds has enlightened me. There are nine hundred million little ants like us on the earth, but my ant-hole alone is dear to God. All the others are eternally reprobated by him. Mine alone will be happy."

They would then interrupt me, and ask who was the fool that talked all this nonsense. I should be obliged to tell them that it was themselves. I would then try to appease them, which would be difficult.

I would next address myself to the Christians, and would venture to say to, for instance, a Dominican friar—an inquisitor of the faith: "Brother, you are aware that each province in Italy has its own dialect, and that people do not speak at Venice and Bergamo as they do at Florence. The Academy of La Crusca has fixed the language. Its dictionary is a rule that has to be followed, and the grammar of Matei is an infallible guide. But do you think that the consul of the Academy, or Matei in his absence, could in conscience cut out the tongues of all the Venetians and the Bergamese who persisted in speaking their own dialect?"

The inquisitor replies: "The two cases are very different. In our case it is a question of your eternal salvation. It is for your good that the heads of the inquisition direct that you shall be seized on the information of any one person, however infamous or criminal; that you shall have no advocate to defend you; that the name of your accuser shall not be made known to you; that the inquisitor shall promise you pardon and then condemn you; and that you shall then be subjected to five kinds of torture, and afterwards either flogged or sent to the galleys or ceremoniously burned. On this Father Ivonet, Doctor Chucalon, Zanchinus, Campegius, Royas, Telinus, Gomarus, Diabarus, and Gemelinus are explicit, and this pious practice admits of no exception."

I would take the liberty of replying: "Brother, possibly you are right. I am convinced that you wish to do me good. But could I not be saved without all that?"

It is true that these absurd horrors do not stain the face of the earth every day; but they have often done so, and the record of them would make up a volume much larger than the gospels which condemn them. Not only is it cruel to persecute, in this brief life, those who differ from us, but I am not sure if it is not too bold to declare that they are damned eternally. It seems to me that it is not the place of the atoms of a moment, such as we are, thus to anticipate the decrees of the Creator. Far be it from me to question the principle, "Out of the Church there is no salvation." I respect it, and all that it teaches; but do we really know all the ways of God, and the full range of his mercies? May we not hope in him as much as fear him? Is it not enough to be loyal to the Church? Must each individual usurp the rights of the Deity, and decide, before he does, the eternal lot of all men?

When we wear mourning for a king of Sweden, Denmark, England, or Prussia, do we say that we wear mourning for one who burns eternally in hell? There are in Europe forty million people who are not of the Church of Rome. Shall we say to each of them: "Sir, seeing that you are infallibly damned, I will neither eat, nor deal, nor speak with you"?

What ambassador of France, presented in audience to the Sultan, would say in the depths of his heart: "His Highness will undoubtedly burn for all eternity because he has been circumcised"? If he really believed that the Sultan is the mortal enemy of God, the object of his vengeance, could he speak to him? Ought he to be sent to him? With whom could we have intercourse? What duty of civil life could we ever fulfil if we were really convinced that we were dealing with damned souls?

Followers of a merciful God, if you were cruel of heart; if, in worshipping him whose whole law consisted in loving one's neighbour as oneself, you had burdened this pure and holy law with sophistry and unintelligible disputes; if you had lit the fires of discord for the sake of a new word or a single letter of the alphabet; if you had attached eternal torment to the omission of a few words or ceremonies that other peoples could not know, I should say to you:

"Transport yourselves with me to the day on which all men will be judged, when God will deal with each according to his works. I see all the dead of former ages and of our own stand in his presence. Are you sure that our Creator and Father will say to the wise and virtuous Confucius, to the lawgiver Solon, to Pythagoras, to Zaleucus, to Socrates, to Plato, to the divine Antonines, to the good Trajan, to Titus, the delight of the human race, to Epictetus, and to so many other model men: "Go, monsters, go and submit to a chastisement infinite in its intensity and duration; your torment shall be as eternal as I. And you, my beloved, Jean Chatel, Ravaillac, Damiens, Cartouche, etc. [assassins in the cause of the Church], who have died with the prescribed formulæ, come and share my empire and felicity for ever."

You shrink with horror from such sentiments; and, now that they have escaped me, I have no more to say to you.

CLAUDE ADRIEN HELVÉTIUS

CLAUDE ADRIEN HELVÉTIUS (1715–71) was one of the more extreme of the *philosophes*. Undistinguished in his studies, he was royally provided for by his family, who purchased for him a share in the financial syndicate (the *Ferme Générale*) which collected many royal taxes. Thus equipped with an income of 100,000 *livres* a year, Helvétius dabbled in literature, interested himself in agricultural improvement and the development of rural industry (he lived eight months of the year on his country estate), and contributed to the support of needy artists and writers. In 1751 he sold his interest in the *Ferme Générale* because he felt that its profits were too large to be morally or socially defensible.

He had long been friendly with Diderot, D'Alembert, and their collaborators on the staff of the *Encyclopédie*, from whom he may have acquired his education in political and social theory. He made himself representative of the most avantgarde tendencies of the Encyclopedists, and went much further than the deists in his hostility to all forms of religion. He was associated with them in the public mind, however, and in 1758 his publication of *De l'esprit*, a reckless attack on orthodox ideas and institutions intended to rival Montesquieu's *L'esprit des lois*, brought down upon him and his friends the wrath of the entire Establishment. His book was condemned and suppressed along with the *Encyclopédie*, and he managed to escape severe punishment only by making public a series of retractions and apologies. His friends criticized the book as severely as anyone. The virulence of the attacks on it caused it to be widely read; it was translated into most of the languages of Europe.

Helvétius published nothing further in his lifetime, but his posthumous treatise *De l'homme* (1772) presented his ideas in still less guarded language; but by then they seemed a good deal less shocking. His ideas have not been much more politely received since his time than they were then. His utilitarian ideas, as well as his practical reforms, however, were an influence on Bentham and John Stuart Mill.

The following selections have been taken from W. Hooper's translation of this work from the French: *A Treatise on Man; His Intellectual Faculties and His Education* (2 vols., London, 1810).

A TREATISE ON MAN

Section I. The Education Necessarily Different in Different Men Is Perhaps the Cause of That Inequality of Understandings Hitherto Attributed to the Unequal Perfection of Their Organs

CHAPTER I: NO TWO PERSONS RECEIVE THE SAME EDUCATION

I still learn; my instruction is not yet finished: when will it be? When I shall be no longer sensible; at my death. The course of my life is properly nothing more than a long course of education.

What is necessary in order that two individuals should receive precisely the same education? That they should be in precisely the same positions and the same circumstances. Now such an hypothesis is impossible: it is therefore evident, that no two persons can receive the same instructions.

But why put off the term of our education to the utmost period of life? Why not confine it to the time expressly set apart for instruction, that is, to the period of infancy and adolescence?

I am content to confine it to that period; and I will prove in like manner, that it is impossible for two men to acquire precisely the same ideas.

CHAPTER II: OF THE MOMENT AT WHICH EDUCATION BEGINS

It is at the very instant a child receives motion and life that it receives its first instruction: it is sometimes even in the womb where it is conceived, that it learns to distinguish between sickness and health. The mother however delivered, the child struggles and cries; hunger grips it, it feels a want, and that want opens its lips, makes it seize, and greedily suck the nourishing breast. When some months have passed, its sight is distinct, its organs are fortified, it becomes by degrees susceptible of all impressions; then the senses of seeing, hearing, tasting, touching, smelling, in a word, all the inlets to the mind are set open; then all the objects of nature rush thither in crowds, and engrave an infinity of ideas in the memory. In these first moments what can be true instructors of infancy? The various sensations it feels: these are so many instructions it receives.

If two children have the same preceptor, if they are taught to distinguish their letters, to read and repeat their catechism, &c. they are supposed to receive the same education. The philosopher judges otherwise: according to him, the true preceptors of a child are the objects that surround him; these are the instructors to whom he owes almost all his ideas. . . .

Section II. All Men, Commonly Well Organized, Have an Equal Aptitude to Understanding

CHAPTER IV: HOW THE MIND ACTS

All the operations of the mind are reducible to the observing of the resemblances and differences, the agreements and disagreements that objects have among themselves and with respect to us. The justness of the mind or judgment depends on the greater or less attention with which its observations are made.

Would I know the relations certain objects have to each other? What must I do? I place before my eyes, or present to my memory two or more of these objects; and then I compare them. But what is this comparison? *It is an alternate and attentive observation of the different impressions which these objects, present, or absent, make on me.*[1] This observation made, I judge, that is, I make an exact report of the impressions I have received.

Am I, for example, anxious to distinguish between two shades of the same color, that are almost indistinguishable; I examine a long time and successively two pieces of cloth tinged with these two shades. *I compare them,* that is, *I regard them alternately.* I am very attentive to the different impressions the reflected rays of these two patterns make on my eyes, and I at last determine, that one of them is of a deeper color than the other; that is to say, I make an exact report of the impressions I have received. Every other judgment would be false. All judgment therefore is nothing more than a *recital of the two sensations, either actually proved, or preserved in my memory.*[2]

When I observe the relation objects have to me, I am in like manner attentive to the impressions I receive. These impressions are either agreeable or disagreeable. Now in either case what is judgment? *To tell what I feel.*

[1] If the memory, the preserver of impressions received, makes me perceive, in the absence of the objects, nearly the same sensations that they excite in me when present, it is indifferent, with regard to the question here discussed, whether the objects of which I form a judgment, be presented to my eyes, or my memory.

[2] There can be no judgment without memory: as I have proved in the preceding chapter.

Am I struck on the head? Is the pain violent? The simple recital of what I feel forms my judgment.

I shall only add one word to what I have here said, which is, that with regard to the judgments formed of the relations which objects have to each other, or to us, there is a difference, which though of little importance in appearance, deserves however to be remarked.

When we are to judge of the relation which objects bear to each other, we must have at least two of them before our eyes. But when we judge of the relation an object has to ourselves, it is evident, as every object can excite a sensation, that one alone is sufficient to produce a judgment.

From this observation I conclude, that every assertion concerning the relation of objects to each other, supposes a comparison of those objects; every comparison a trouble; every trouble an efficacious motive to take it. But on the contrary, when we are to observe the relation of an object to ourselves, that is to say, a sensation, that sensation, if it be lively, becomes itself the efficacious motive to excite our attention.

Every sensation of this kind, therefore, invariably produces a judgment. I shall not stop longer at this observation, but repeat, agreeably to what I have said above, that in every case, to *judge* is to *feel*.

This being settled, all the operations of the mind are reduced to mere sensations. Why then admit in man a faculty of judging distinct from the faculty of sensation. But this is the general opinion: I own it; and it even ought to be so. We say, I perceive, and I compare; there is therefore in man a faculty of judging and comparing, distinct from the faculty of sensation. This method of reasoning is sufficient to impose on the greatest part of mankind. However, to show its fallacy, it is only necessary to fix a clear idea to the word *compare*. When this word is properly elucidated, it will be found to express no one real operation of the mind; that the business of comparing, as I have before said, is nothing else than *rendering ourselves attentive to the different impressions excited in us by objects actually before our eyes, or present to our memory;* and consequently, that all judgment is nothing more *than the pronouncing upon sensations experienced.*

But if the judgment formed from the comparison of material objects be nothing more than mere sensations, is it the same with every other sort of judgment?

CHAPTER V: OF SUCH JUDGMENTS AS RESULT FROM THE COMPARISON OF IDEAS THAT ARE ABSTRACTED, COLLECTIVE, &C.

The words weakness, strength, smallness, greatness, crime, &c. do not represent any substance, that is, any body; how then can the judgments resulting from the comparison of such words, or ideas, be reduced to mere sensations? I answer, that as these words do not represent any ideas, it is impossible, so long as we do not apply them to any sensible and particular object, to form any judgment about them. But when they are applied by design, or imperceptibly, to some determinate object, then the word *great* will express a relation, that is, a certain difference or resemblance observed between objects present to our sight, or to our memory. Now the judgment formed of ideas, that by this application become material, will be, as I have repeatedly said, nothing more than the pronouncing of sensations felt. . . .

Every idea whatever may therefore, in its ultimate analysis, be always reduced to material facts or sensations. Some obscurity is thrown on discussions of this kind by the vague significations of a certain number of words, and the trouble that is sometimes necessary to deduce clear ideas from them. Perhaps it is as difficult to analyze some of these expressions, and to reduce them, if I may so say, to their constituent ideas, as it is in chemistry to decompose certain bodies. However, let us but apply the method and attention necessary in this decomposition, and we shall not fail of success.

What is here said will be sufficient to convince the discerning reader, that every idea and every judgment may be reduced to a sensation. It would be therefore unnecessary, in order to explain the different operations of the mind, to admit a faculty of judging and comparing distinct from the faculty of sensation. But what, it may be asked, is the principle or motive that makes us compare objects with each other, and gives us the necessary attention to observe their relations? Interest, which is in like manner, as I am going to show, an effect of corporeal sensibility.

CHAPTER VI: WHERE THERE IS NO INTEREST THERE IS NO COMPARISON OF OBJECTS WITH EACH OTHER

All comparison of objects with each other supposes attention, all attention a trouble, and all trouble a motive for exerting it. If there could exist a man without desire, he would not compare any objects, or pronounce any judgment; but he might still judge of the immediate impressions of objects on himself, supposing their impressions to be strong. Their strength becoming a motive to attention, would carry with it a judgment. It would not be the same if the sensation were weak; he would then have no knowledge or remembrance of the judgment it had occasioned. A man surrounded by an infinity of objects, must necessarily be affected by an infinity of sensations, and consequently form an infinity of judgments; but he forms them unknown to himself. Why? Because these judgments are of the same nature with the sensations. If they make an impression that is effaced as soon as made, the judgments formed on these impressions are of the same sort; they leave no remembrance. There is in fact no man who does not, without perceiving it, make every day an infinity of reasonings, of which he is not conscious. I will take, for example, those that attend almost all the rapid motions of our bodies.

When in the dance, Vestris makes a capriole rather than an entrechat, when Moté in the fencing-school thrusts tierce rather than quart, if there be no effect without a cause, Vestris and Moté must be determined by reasons too rapid, if I may so say, to be perceived. So the motion I make with my hand when a body is going to strike my eye, may be reduced to nearly the same; experience tells me, that my hand can resist without pain the blow of a body that would deprive me of sight: my eyes moreover are dearer to me than my hand: I ought therefore to expose my hand to save my eyes. There is no person that would not use the same reasoning in the same situation; but this habitual reasoning is not so rapid, but that we perceive the moment we have put the hand before the eye, the action and the cause of action. Now how many sensations are there of the nature of these habitual reasonings? How many weak sensations that do not fix our attention, or produce in us either consciousness or remembrance?

There are moments when the strongest sensations are, in some measure, imperceptible. I fight, and am wounded. I continue the combat, and perceive not my wound. Why? Because the love of preservation, rage, and the motion given to my blood, render me insensible to the stroke that at another time would have fixed all my attention.

There are moments on the contrary, when we are sensible of the slightest impressions; that is, when the passions of fear, ambition, avarice, envy, &c. concentrate all our attention on an object. Am I concerned in a conspiracy? There is not a gesture, not a look that can escape the restless and suspicious eyes of my accomplices. Am I a painter? Every remarkable effect of the light strikes me. Am I a jeweller? There is not a flaw in a diamond that I do not perceive. Am I envious? There is no defect in a great character that my piercing eye does not discern. In like manner those passions that by fixing all my attention on certain objects, render me susceptible of the keenest sensations, with regard to them, make me at the same time insensible to every other sort of sensation. . . .

For the rest, the consciousness or unconsciousness of such impressions, change not their nature; it is therefore true, as I have already said, that all our sensations carry with them a judgment, whose existence, though unnoticed when they fix not our attention, is however not the less real.

It results from the contents of this chapter, that all judgments formed by comparing objects with each other, suppose an interest in us to compare them. Now that interest, necessarily founded on our love of happiness, cannot be anything else than the effect of bodily sensibility; because there all our pleasures, and all our pains have their source. This question being discussed, I conclude that corporeal pains and pleasures are the unknown principles of all human actions.

CHAPTER VII: CORPOREAL SENSIBILITY IS THE SOLE CAUSE OF OUR ACTIONS, OUR THOUGHTS, OUR PASSIONS, AND OUR SOCIABILITY

Action

It is to clothe himself and adorn his mistress, or his wife, to procure them amusements, to support himself and his family, in a word to enjoy the pleasures attached to the gratification of bodily desires that the artisan and the peasant thinks, contrives, and labors. Corporeal sensibility is therefore the sole mover of man,[3] he is consequently susceptible, as I am going to prove, but of two sorts of pleasures and pains, the one are present bodily pains and pleasures, the other are the pains and pleasures of foresight or memory.

[3] What is called intellectual pain, or pleasure, may be always referred to some bodily pain or pleasure. . . .

Born without ideas, without vice, and without virtue, everything in man, even his humanity, is an acquisition: it is to his education he owes this sentiment. Among all the various ways of inspiring him with it, the most efficacious is to accustom him from childhood, in a manner from the cradle to ask himself when he beholds a miserable object, by what chance he is not exposed in like manner to the inclemency of the seasons, to hunger, cold, poverty, &c. When the child has been used to put himself in the place of the wretched, that habit gained, he becomes the more touched with their misery, as in deploring their fate it is for human nature in general, and for himself in particular, that he is concerned. An infinity of different sentiments then mix with the first sentiment, and their assemblage composes the total sentiment of pleasure felt by a noble soul in succoring the distressed: a sentiment that he is not always in a situation to analyze.

We relieve the unfortunate,

1. To avoid the bodily pain of seeing them suffer.

2. To enjoy an example of gratitude, which produces in us at least a confused hope of distant utility.

3. To exhibit an act of power, whose exercise is always agreeable to us, because it always recalls to the mind the images of pleasures attached to that power.

4. Because the idea of happiness is constantly connected, in a good education, with the idea of beneficence, and this beneficence in us conciliating the esteem and affection of men, may like riches be regarded as a power, or means of avoiding pains and procuring pleasures.

In this manner, as from an affinity of different sentiments, is made up the total sentiment of the pleasure we feel in the exercise of beneficence.

I have here said enough, to furnish a man of discernment with the means of decomposing, in like manner, every other kind of pleasure, called intellectual, and reducing it to mere sensation.

Pain

I know but two sorts of pain, that which we feel, and that which we foresee. I die of hunger; I feel a present pain. I foresee that I shall soon die of hunger. I feel a pain by foresight, the strength of whose impression is in proportion to the proximity and severity of the pain. The criminal who is going to the scaffold, feels yet no torment, but the foresight that constitutes his present punishment, is begun.

Remorse

Remorse is nothing more than a foresight of bodily pain, to which some crime has exposed us: and is consequently the effect of bodily sensibility. We tremble at the description of the flames, the wheels, the fiery scourges, which the heated imagination of the painter or the poet represents. Is a man without fear, and above the law? he feels no remorse from the commission of a wicked action; provided, however, that he have not previously contracted a virtuous habit; for then he will not pursue a contrary conduct, without feeling an uneasiness, a secret inquietude, to which is also given the name of remorse. Experience tells us, that every action which does not expose us to legal punishment, or to dishonor, is an action, performed in general without remorse. Solon and Plato loved women and even boys, and avowed it. Theft was not punished in Sparta: and the Lacedæmonians robbed without remorse. The princes of the East can, with impunity, load their subjects with taxes, and they do it effectually. The inquisitor can with impunity burn any person who does not think as he does, on certain metaphysical points, and it is without remorse that he gluts his vengeance by hideous torments, for the slight offence that is given to his vanity by the contradiction of a Jew or an Infidel. Remorse, therefore, owes its existence to the fear of punishment or of shame, which is always reducible, as I have already said to a bodily sensation.

Friendship

From bodily sensibility flow in like manner, the tears that bathe the urn of my friend. I lament the loss of the man whose conversation relieved me from disquietude, from that disagreeable sensation of the soul, which actually produces bodily pain: I deplore him who exposed his life and fortune to save me from sorrow and destruction; who was incessantly employed in promoting my felicity, and increasing it by every sort of pleasure. When a man enters into himself, when he examines the bottom of his soul, he perceives nothing in all these sentiments but the development of bodily pain and pleasure. What cannot this pain produce? It is by this medium that the magistrate enchains vice, and disarms the assassin.

Pleasure

There are two sorts of pleasures, as there are two sorts of pains: the one is the present bodily pleasure, the other is that of foresight. Does a man love fine slaves and beautiful paintings? If he discovers a treasure he is transported. He does not, however, yet feel any bodily pleasure, you will say. It is true; but he gains at that moment, the means of procuring the objects of his desires. Now this foresight of an approaching pleasure, is in fact an actual pleasure: for without the love of fine slaves and paintings, he would have been entirely unconcerned at the discovery of the treasure.

The pleasures of foresight, therefore, constantly suppose the existence of the pleasures of the senses. It is the hopes of enjoying my mistress to-morrow that makes me happy to-day. Foresight or memory converts into an actual enjoyment the acquisition of every means proper to procure pleasure. From what motive in fact, do I feel an agreeable sensation every time I obtain a new degree of esteem, of importance, riches, and above all, of power? It is because I esteem power as the most sure means of increasing my happiness.

Power

Men love themselves: they all desire to be happy, and think their happiness would be complete, if they were invested with a degree of power sufficient to procure them every sort of pleasure. The love of power therefore takes its source from the love of pleasure.

Suppose a man absolutely insensible. But, it will be said, he must then be without ideas, and consequently a mere statue. Be it so: but allow that he may exist, and even think. Of what consequence would the sceptre of a monarch be to him? None. In fact, what could the most immense power add to the felicity of a man without feeling.

If power be so coveted by the ambitious, it is as the mean of acquiring pleasure. Power is like gold, a money. The effect of power, and of a bill of exchange is the same. If I be in possession of such a bill, I receive at London or Paris a hundred thousand crowns, and consequently all the pleasures that sum can procure. Am I in possession of a letter of authority or command? I draw in like manner from my fellow-citizens, a like quantity of provisions or pleasures. The effects of riches and power are in a manner the same: for riches are power.

In a country where money is unknown, in what manner can taxes be paid?

In kind, that is, in corn, wine, cattle, fowls, &c.—How can commerce be carried on? By exchange. Money therefore is to be regarded as a portable merchandise, which it is agreed, for the facility of commerce, to take in exchange for all other sorts of merchandise. Can it be the same with the dignities and honors with which polished nations recompense the services rendered their country? Why not? What are honors? A money that is in like manner the representative of every kind of provision and pleasure. Suppose a country where the honorary money is not current; suppose the people to be too free, and too haughty, to suffer a very great inequality in the ranks and authority of the people: in what manner must the nation recompense great actions, and such as are useful to the nation? By natural riches and pleasures, that is, by transferring a certain quantity of corn, beer, hay, wine, &c. to the granary and cellar of the hero: by giving him so many acres of land to till, or so many handsome slaves. It was by the possession of Briseis, that the Greeks recompenced the valor of Achilles. What among the Scandinavians, the Saxons, the Scythians, the Celts, the Samnites, and the Arabs, was the recompence of courage, of talents and virtues? Sometimes a fine woman, and sometimes a banquet, where feasting on delicate viands, and quaffing delicious liquors, the warriors with transport listened to the songs of the bards.

It is therefore evident, that if money and honors be, among most polished nations, the rewards of virtuous actions, they are in that case the representative of the same possessions, and the same pleasures that poor and free nations grant to their heroes, and for the acquisition of which those heroes expose themselves to the greatest dangers. Therefore on the supposition, that these dignities and honors were not the representatives of wealth or pleasures, that they were nothing more than empty titles,[4] those titles being estimated according to their real value, would presently cease to be the objects of desire. To enter a breach, a crown piece, the representative of a pint of brandy, and the enjoyment of a trull must be given to the soldier. The warriors of antiquity, and those of the present day are the same. Men have not changed

_____

[4] If in despotic nations the spring of glory be commonly very weak, it is, because glory there confers no sort of power, because all power is absorbed in despotism; because in these countries a hero, covered with glory, is not secure from the intrigues of a villainous courtier; because he has no certain property in his effects, or his liberty; because, in short, he is liable, at the pleasure of his sovereign, to be thrown into a prison, to be deprived of his wealth and honors, and even of life itself.

Why does the Englishman behold, in the greatest part of foreign noblemen, nothing more than gaudy valets and victims adorned with garlands? Because a peasant in England, is in fact greater than an officer of state in another country: the peasant is free; he can be virtuous with impunity; and sees nothing above him but the law.

It is the desire of glory that must be the most powerful principle of action in poor republics; and it is the love of money, founded on the love of luxury, that in despotic countries is the principle of action, and the moving power in nations subject to that sort of government.

their nature, and they will always perform nearly the same actions for the same rewards. If a man be supposed indifferent to pleasure and pain, he will be without action: unsusceptible of remorse, or friendship, or, in short, of the love of riches or of power: for when we are insensible to pleasure itself, we must be insensible to the means of acquiring it. What we seek in riches and power, is the means of avoiding bodily pains, and procuring bodily pleasures. If the acquisition of gold and power be always a pleasure, it is because foresight and memory convert into an actual pleasure all the means of obtaining it.

The general conclusion of this chapter, is, that in man all is sensation: a truth of which I shall give a fresh proof, by showing that his sociability is nothing more than a consequence of the same sensations.

CHAPTER VIII: OF SOCIABILITY

Man is by nature a devourer of fruits and of flesh; but he is weak, unarmed, and consequently exposed to the voracity of animals stronger than himself. Man, therefore, to avoid the fury of the tiger and the lion, was forced to unite with man. The object of this union was to attack and kill other animals, either to feed on them, or to prevent their consuming the fruits and herbs that served him for nourishment. In the meantime mankind multiplied, and to support themselves, they were obliged to cultivate the earth; but to induce them to this, it became necessary to stipulate, that the harvest should belong to the husbandman. For this purpose the inhabitants made agreements or laws among themselves. These laws strengthened the bonds of a union, that, founded on their wants, was the immediate effect of corporeal sensibility.[5] But cannot this sociability be regarded as an innate quality,[6] a species of amiable morality? All that we learn from experience on this head, is, that in man, as in other animals, sociability is the effect of want. If the desire of defending themselves makes the grazing animals as horses, bulls, &c. assemble in herds; that of chasing, attacking, and conquering their prey, forms in like manner a society of carnivorous animals, such as foxes and wolves.

Interest and want are the principles of all sociability. It is, therefore, these principles alone (of which few writers have given clear ideas) that unite men among themselves: and the force of their union is always in proportion to that of habit and want. From the moment the young savage, or the young bear, is able to provide for his nourishment and his defense, the one quits the hut, and the other the den of his parents. The eagle, in like manner, drives away her

---

[5] Because man is sociable, people have concluded that he is good. But they have deceived themselves. Wolves form societies, but they are not good. . . .

[6] That curiosity, which certain writers regard as an innate principle, is the desire in us of being happy, and of improving our condition: it is no other than the development of corporeal sensibility.

young ones from the nest, the moment they have sufficient strength to dart upon their prey, and live without her aid.

The bond that attaches children to their parents, and parents to their children, is less strong than is commonly imagined. A too great strength in this bond would be even fatal to societies. The first regard of a citizen should be for the laws, and the public prosperity; I speak it with regret, filial affection should be in man subordinate to the love of patriotism. If this last affection do not take place of all others, where shall we find a measure of virtue and vice? It would then be no more, and all morality would be abolished.

For what reason, in fact, has justice and the love of God been recommended to men, above all things? On account of the danger to which a too great love of their parents would expose them. If the excess of this passion were sanctioned; if it were declared the principal attachment, a son would then have a right to rob his neighbor, or plunder the public treasury, to supply the wants, and promote the comforts of his father. Every family would form a little nation, and these nations having opposite interests, would be continually at war with each other.

Every writer, who to give us a good opinion of his own heart, founds the sociability of man on any other principle, than that of bodily and habitual wants, deceives weak minds, and gives them a false idea of morality.

Nature, no doubt, designed that gratitude and habit should form in man a sort of gravitation, by which they should be impelled to a love of their parents: but it has also designed that man should have, in the natural desire of independence, a repulsive power, which should diminish the too great force of that gravitation. Thus the daughter joyfully leaves the house of her mother to go to that of her husband; and the son quits with pleasure his native spot, for an employment in India, an office in a distant country, or merely for the pleasure of travelling.

Notwithstanding the pretended force of sentiment, friendship, and habit, mankind change at Paris, every day, the part of the town, their acquaintance and their friends. Do men seek to make dupes? They exaggerate the force of sentiment and friendship, they represent sociability as *an innate affection or principle*. Can they, in reality, forget that there is but one principle of this kind, which is corporeal sensibility? It is to this principle alone, that we owe our self-love, and the powerful love of independence: if men were, as it is said, drawn toward each other by a strong and mutual attraction, would the heavenly Legislator have commanded them to love each other, and to honor their parents? Would he not have left this point to nature, which, without the aid of any law, obliges men to eat and drink when they are hungry and thirsty, to open their eyes to the light, and keep their hands out of the fire.

Travellers do not inform us that the love which mankind bear to their fellows, is so common as pretended. The sailor, escaped from a wreck, and cast on an unknown coast, does not run with open arms to embrace the first man he meets. On the contrary, he hides himself in a thicket, where he observes the manners of the inhabitants, and then presents himself trembling before them.

But if an European vessel chance to approach an unknown island, do not the savages, it is said, run in crowds towards the ship? They are, without doubt, amazed at the sight, they are struck with the novelty of our dress, our arms and implements. The appearance excites their curiosity. But what desire succeeds to this first sensation? That of possessing the objects of their admiration. They become less gay and more thoughtful; are busied in contriving means to obtain, by force or fraud, the objects of their desires: for that purpose they watch the favorable opportunity to rob, plunder, and massacre the Europeans, who, in their conquests of Mexico and Peru, gave them early examples of similar injustice and cruelty.

The conclusion of this chapter is, that the principles of morality and politics, like those of all other sciences, ought to be established on a great number of facts and observations. Now, what is the result of the observations hitherto made on morality? That the love of men for their brethren is the effect of the necessity of mutual assistance, and of an affinity of wants, dependent on that corporeal sensibility, which I regard as the principle of our actions, our virtues, and our vices. . . .

CHAPTER XXIII: THERE IS NO TRUTH NOT REDUCIBLE TO A FACT

Almost all philosophers agree, that the most sublime truths once simplified and reduced to their plainest terms, may be converted into facts, and in that case present nothing more to the mind than this proposition, *white is white, and black is black*. The apparent obscurity of certain truths lies not therefore in the truths themselves, but in the confused manner of representing them, and the impropriety of the words used in expressing them. Can they be reduced to simple facts? If every fact can be equally well perceived by every man organized in the common manner, there is no truth which he cannot comprehend. Now if all men can conceive the same truths, they must all have essentially the same aptitude to understanding.

But is it quite certain that every truth may be reduced to those clear propositions above-mentioned? I shall add only one proof to what the philosophers have already given: I deduce it from the perfectibility of the human mind or understanding; experience demonstrates that the understanding is capable of it. Now what does this perfectibility suppose? Two things:

The one, that every truth is essentially comprehensible by every mind.

The other, that every truth may be clearly represented.

The capacity that all men have to learn a trade proves this. If the most sublime discoveries of the ancient mathematicians are at this day comprised in the elements of geometry, and are understood by every student in that science, it is because those discoveries are reduced to facts.

Truths being once brought to this point of simplicity, if there be some among them that men of ordinary capacity cannot comprehend, it is then, they may say, that borne up by experience, like the eagle, who alone among the feathered race can soar above the clouds and gaze upon the sun, the man of genius alone can raise himself to the intellectual regions, and there sustain the resplendence of a new truth. Now nothing is more contrary to experience. Does a man of genius discover a truth, and represent it clearly? At the instant all men of ordinary capacity seize it, and make it their own. The genius is an adventurous chief, who penetrates the region of discoveries: he lays open the road, and men of common capacity rush in crowds after him. They have therefore the force necessary to follow him, otherwise genius would there penetrate alone. Now to the present day its only privilege is to make the first track.

But if there be a period when the highest truths are attainable by common minds, when is that period? When freed from the obscurity of words, and reduced to propositions more or less simple, they pass from the empire of genius to that of the sciences. Till then, like those souls who are said to wander in the celestial abodes, waiting till they can animate a body, and appear before the light, the truths yet unknown wander in the regions of discoveries, waiting for some genius to seize, and transport them to this terrestrial sphere. Once descended to the earth, and perceived by superior minds, they become common property.

. . . When the discoveries of genius are metamorphosed into sciences, each discovery deposited in their temple becomes a public property; the temple is open to all. Whoever desires to learn, learns, and is sure to make nearly so many feet of science per day. The time fixed for apprenticeship is a proof of this. If the greatest part of arts, at the degree of perfection to which they are now carried, may be regarded as the produce of the discoveries of a hundred men of genius placed end to end; to exercise those arts it is necessary therefore that the workman unite them in himself, and know how properly to apply the ideas of those hundred men of genius: what can be a stronger proof of the perfectibility of the human mind, and of its aptitude to comprehend every sort of truth?

If from the arts I pass to the sciences, it will be equally apparent that the truths, whose discoveries formerly deified their inventor, are now quite common. The system of Newton is taught everywhere.

It is with the author of a new truth as with an astronomer, whom curiosity or the desire of glory calls up to his observatory. He points his glass to the heavens, and in the immensity of space beholds a new star or satellite. He calls his friends; they go up and looking through the telescope, behold the same star: for with organs nearly the same, men must discover the same objects.

If there were ideas that ordinary men could not attain, there would be truths discovered in the process of ages, that could not be comprehended but by two or three men equally organized. The rest of the human race would be subject in this respect to an invincible ignorance. The discovery of the square of the hypotenuse being equal to the square of the other two sides of a triangle, could not be known but to another Pythagoras: the human mind could not be susceptible of perfectibility; in a word, there would be truths reserved for certain men only. Experience, on the contrary, shows us, that the most sublime discoveries, clearly represented, are conceivable by all. Hence arise that astonishment and shame we perceive when we say, *there is nothing more plain than that truth; how was it possible I did not perceive it before?* This is doubtless sometimes the language of envy, as in the case of Christopher Columbus. When he departed for America, the courtiers said, *nothing is more ridiculous than such an enterprise:* and at his return, *nothing was more easy than such a discovery.* Though this be frequently the language of envy, is it never that of the heart? Is it not with the utmost sincerity, when suddenly struck by the evidence of a new idea, and presently accustomed to regard it as trivial, that we think we always knew it?

If we have a clear idea of the expression of a truth, and not only have it in our memory, but have also habitually present to our remembrance all the ideas of the comparison from which it results, and if we be not blinded by any interest or superstition, that truth being presently reduced to the plainest terms, that is, to this simple proposition, that *white is white, and black is black,* is conceived almost as soon as proposed.

In fact, if the systems of Locke and Newton, without being yet carried to the last degree of perspicuity, are nevertheless generally taught and understood, men of a common organization can therefore comprehend the ideas of those of the greatest genius. Now to conceive their ideas is to have the same aptitude to understanding. But if men can attain those truths, and if their knowledge in general be constantly in proportion to the desire they have to learn, does it follow that all can equally attain to truths hitherto unknown? This objection deserves to be considered.

CHAPTER XXIV: THE UNDERSTANDING NECESSARY TO COMPREHEND THE
TRUTHS ALREADY KNOWN, IS SUFFICIENT TO DISCOVER THOSE THAT
ARE UNKNOWN

A truth is always the result of just comparisons of the resemblances or differences, the agreements or disagreements, between different objects. When a
master would explain to his scholars the principles of a science, and demonstrate the truths already known, he places before their eyes the objects of the
comparison from which those truths are to be deduced.

But when a new truth is to be sought, the inventor must in like manner
have before his eyes the objects of comparison from which the truth is to be
deduced: But what shall present them to him? Chance; the common mother
of all inventions. It appears therefore, that the mind of man, whether it follow
the demonstration of a truth, or whether it discover it, has in both cases, the
same objects to compare, and the same relations to observe; in short, the same
operations to perform. The understanding necessary to comprehend truths
already known, is therefore sufficient to discover those that are unknown. Few
men indeed attain the latter; but this is the effect of the different situations in
which they are placed, and that series of circumstances to which is given the
name of chance; or of the desire, more or less cogent, that men have to distinguish themselves, and consequently their greater or less passion for glory.

The passions can do all things. There is no girl so stupid that love will not
make witty. What means does it not furnish her with, to deceive the vigilance
of her parents, to see and converse with her lover? The most stupid frequently
become the most inventive.

A man without passions is incapable of that degree of attention to which a
superior judgment is annexed: a superiority that is, perhaps, less the effect of
an extraordinary effort than of habitual attention. . . .

*Section V. Of the Errors and Contradictions of Those, Whose
Principles Differing from Mine, Refer the Unequal Degrees
of Understandings, to the Unequal Degrees of Perfection
in the Organs of the Senses*

CHAPTER II: OF THE UNDERSTANDING AND OF TALENTS

What is in man the understanding? The assemblage of his ideas. To what
sort of understanding do we give the name of talent? To an understanding
concentred in one subject; that is to say, to a large assemblage of ideas of the
same kind.

Now, if there be no innate ideas, (as M. Rousseau allows in several parts of his work,) understanding and talent must be acquisitions in us, and both of them, as I have already said, have therefore for generating principles:

1. Corporeal sensibility; without which we can receive no sensations.

2. Memory; that is, the faculty of recollecting sensations received.

3. An interest to induce us to compare our sensations with each other; that is, to observe with attention the resemblances and differences, and agreements and disagreements that various objects have with each other.

It is this interest that fixes the attention, and that in men, organized in the common manner, is the productive principle of their understanding.

The talents, regarded by some as the effect of a particular disposition to a particular sort of understanding, are, in reality, nothing more than the produce of the attention applied to ideas of a certain sort. I compare the mass of human knowledge to the keys of an organ. The several talents are the stops, and the attention, put in action by interest, is the hand, that can indifferently apply itself to one or other of the stops.

In short, if we acquire even the sentiment of self-love, and if we cannot love ourselves, without having previously felt the sensation of corporeal pleasure and pain, all then in us is acquisition.

Our understanding, our talents, our vices and virtues, our prejudices and characters, necessarily formed by the assemblage of our ideas and sentiments, are not therefore the effect of our several temperaments. Our passions themselves are not dependent on them. I shall cite the people of the North as a proof of this truth. Their phlegmatic temperament we are told, is the particular effect of their climate and nourishment; yet are they as susceptible of pride, envy, ambition, avarice, and superstition, as the more sanguine [7] and bilious inhabitants of the South? When we look into history, we see nations change their characters on a sudden, without any change in the nature of their climates, or in their nourishment. . . .

CHAPTER III: OF THE GOODNESS OF MAN IN THE CRADLE

I love you, O my fellow citizens! and my chief desire is to be useful to you. I doubtless desire your approbation; but shall I owe your esteem and applause to a lie? A thousand others will deceive you; I shall not be their accomplice. Some will say you are good, and flatter the desire you have to think yourselves so: believe them not. Others will say you are wicked, and in like manner will say false. You are neither the one nor the other.

No individual is born good or bad. Men are the one or the other, according as a similar or opposite interest unites or divides them. Philosophers suppose

---

[7] This fact clearly proves that the passions above-mentioned are not the effects of the diversity of temperaments but, as I have said, of the love of power.

men to be born in a state of war. A common desire to possess the same things arms them from the cradle, say they, against each other.

The state of war, without doubt, closely follows the instant of their birth. The peace between them is of short duration. They are not however both enemies. Goodness or badness is an incident to them; it is the consequence of their good or bad laws. What we call in man his goodness or moral sense, is his benevolence to others; and that benevolence is always proportionate to the utility they are of to him. I prefer my countrymen to strangers, and my friends to my countrymen. The prosperity of my friend is reflected on me. If he becomes more rich and powerful, I participate in his riches and power. Benevolence to others is therefore the effect of love for ourselves. Now if self-love, as I have proved in the fourth section, be the necessary effect of the faculty of sensation our love for others, whatever the Shaftesburians may say, is in like manner the effect of the same faculty.

What in fact is that original goodness or moral sense, so much boasted of by the English? What clear idea can we form of such a sense,[8] and on what fact do we found its existence? On the goodness of men? But there are also persons who are envious and liars, *omnis homo mendax*.[9] Will they say in consequence, that those men have in them an immoral sense of envy, and a lying

---

[8] If they admit a moral sense, why not an algebraic or chemical sense? Why should we create a sixth sense in man? Is it to give him clearer ideas of morality? But what is morality? *The science of the means invented by men to live together in the most happy manner possible.* This science, if those in power do not oppose its progress, will advance in proportion as the people acquire more knowledge. Men would have morality to be the work of God; but it makes every where a part of the legislation of the people: now legislation is the work of man. If God be esteemed the author of morality, it is because he is the author of human reason, and morality the offspring of that reason. To identify God and morality is idolatry; it is to deify the work of men. They have made compacts; morality is nothing more than the collection of these compacts. The true object of this science is the happiness of the majority. *Salus populi suprema lex esto* [*Let the safety of the people be the supreme law*]. If the morality of mankind produces so often a contrary effect, it is because the powerful direct all its precepts to their particular advantage; it is because they constantly repeat, *Salus gubernantium suprema lex esto* [*Let the safety of the rulers be the supreme law*]. It is in short, because the morality of most nations is now nothing more than a collection of the means employed, and the precepts dictated by the powerful to secure their authority, and to be unjust with impunity.

But can such precepts be respected? Yes, when they are consecrated by edicts, by absurd laws, and above all, by the dread of power. It is then they acquire a legal authority while that power continues.

There is then nothing more difficult than to recall morality to its true object. For which reason we find a wise legislation, and a pure morality in those countries only where, as in England, the people have a part in the administration, where the nation is the sovereign; and where the laws, constantly established in favor of the people in power, are necessarily conformable to the interest of the majority.

According to this summary idea of the science of morality, it is evident, that like others, it is the produce of experience and meditation, and not of *a moral sense;* that it may, like other sciences, be daily improved; and that nothing authorizes man to suppose he has a sixth sense, of which it is impossible to form any clear idea.

[9] [*Every man is a liar.*]

sense. Nothing is more absurd than this theological philosophy of Shaftesbury; and yet the greatest part of the English are as fond of it as the French were formerly of their music. It is not the same with other nations. No stranger can understand the one or bear the other. It is a web on the eye of the English. It must be taken away before they can see clearly.

According to their philosophy, the man indifferent and seated at his ease, desires the happiness of others: but as being indifferent, he does not, and cannot desire any thing. The states of desire and indifference are contradictory. Perhaps the state of perfect indifference is even impossible. Experience teaches us that man is born neither good nor bad: that his happiness is not necessarily connected with the misery of others: that on the contrary, from a good education, the idea of my own happiness will be always more or less closely connected in my memory with that of my fellow-citizens; and that the desire of the one will produce in me the desire of the other: whence it follows, that the love of his neighbor is in every individual the effect of the love of himself. The most clamorous declaimers for original goodness have not moreover been always the greatest benefactors to humanity.

When the welfare of England was at stake, the idle Shaftesbury, that ardent apostle of the beauty of morality, would not, we are told, even go to the parliament-house to save it. It was not the sense of the beauty of morality, but the love of glory and of their country that formed Horatius Cocles, Brutus, and Scaevola. The English philosophers will in vain tell me that beauty of morality is a sense that is developed with the human foetus, and in a certain time, renders man compassionate to the misfortune of his brethren. I can form an idea of my five senses, and of the organs by which they are produced; but I confess I have no more idea of a moral sense, than of a moral castle and elephant.

How long will men continue to use words that are void of meaning, and that not conveying any clear and determinate idea, ought to be forever banished to the schools of theology. Do they mean by this moral sense that sentiment of compassion felt at the sight of an unhappy object? But to compassionate another man's miseries, we must first know what he suffers, and for that purpose must have felt pain. A compassion on report supposes also a knowledge of misery. Which are the evils moreover that in general we are most sensible of? Those which we suffer with the most impatience, and the remembrance of which is consequently the most habitually present to us. Compassion therefore is not an innate sentiment.

What do I feel at the presence of an unhappy person? A strong emotion. What produces it? The remembrance of pains to which men are subject, and to which I myself am exposed: such an idea troubles me, makes me uneasy, and as long as the unfortunate person is present I am afflicted. When I have assisted him, and see him no more, a calm takes place insensibly in my mind; for in proportion as he is distant from me, the remembrance of the miseries that his presence recalled, insensibly vanishes: when therefore I was afflicted at his presence, it was for myself I was afflicted. Which in fact are the evils I commiserate most. They are, as I have already said, not only those I have felt, but those I may still feel: those evils being most present to my memory, strike me most forcibly. My affliction for the miseries of an unhappy person, is always in proportion to the fear I have of being afflicted with the same miseries. I would, if it were possible, destroy in him the very root of his misfortune, and thereby free myself at the same time from the fear of suffering in the same manner. The love of others is therefore never anything else in man than an effect of the love of himself, and consequently of his corporeal sensibility. In vain does M. Rousseau repeat incessantly *that all men are good, and all the first movements of nature right.* The necessity of laws proves the contrary. What does this necessity imply? That the different interests of men render them good or bad; and that the only method to form virtuous citizens, is to unite the interest of the individual with that of the public. . . .

A proof that humanity is nothing more in man than the effect of the misfortunes he has known either by himself or by others is, that of all the ways to render him humane and compassionate, the most efficacious is to habituate him from his most tender age to put himself in the place of the miserable. Some have in consequence treated compassion as a weakness: let him call it so if they please; this weakness will always be in my eyes the first of virtues, because it always contributes the most to the happiness of humanity.

I have proved that compassion is not either a moral sense, or an innate sentiment, but the pure effect of self-love. What follows? That it is this same love, differently modified, according to the different education we receive, and the circumstances, and situations in which chance has placed us, which renders us humane or obdurate: that man is not born compassionate, but that all may and will become so when the laws, the form of government, and their education lead them to it.

O! you, to whom heaven has entrusted the legislative power, let your administration be gentle, your laws sagacious, and you will have subjects humane, valiant, and virtuous! But if you alter either those laws, or that wise administration, those virtuous citizens will expire without posterity, and you will be surrounded by wicked men only; for the laws will make them such. Man, by nature indifferent to evil, will not give himself up to it without a motive: the happy man is humane; he is the couching lion.

Unhappy is the prince who confides in the original goodness of characters;

M. Rousseau supposes its existence; experience denies it: whoever consults that, will learn that the child kills flies, beats his dog, and strangles his sparrow; that the child, born without any humanity, has all the vices of the man.

The man in power is often unjust; the sturdy child is the same: when he is not restrained by the presence of his master, he appropriates by force, like the man in power, the sweetmeat or plaything of his companion. He does that for a coral or a doll which he would do at a mature age for a title or a scepter. The uniformity in the manner of acting at those two ages made M. de la Mothe say, *It is because the child is already a man, that the man is still a child.*

The original goodness of characters cannot be maintained by any argument. I will even add, that in man, goodness and humanity cannot be the work of nature, but of education only.

CHAPTER IV: THE MAN OF NATURE CANNOT BUT BE CRUEL

What does the prospect of nature present to us? A multitude of beings destined to devour each other. Man in particular, say the anatomists, has the tooth of a carnivorous animal; he ought therefore to be voracious, and consequently cruel and bloody. Flesh, moreover, is his most wholesome nourishment, and the most comfortable to his organization: his preservation, like that of almost all the species of animals, is connected with the destruction of others.

Men dispersed among the vast forests are at first hunters; when they become more numerous, and are forced to find their nourishment within a smaller space, necessity makes them shepherds; when still more multiplied, they become at last husbandmen. Now in all these several situations, man is born a destroyer of animals, either by eating their flesh, or by defending against them the fruits, grain, or pulse, necessary to his subsistence.

The man of nature is his own butcher, and his own cook; his hands are always imbrued in blood; habituated to murder, he must be deaf to the cry of pity. If the stag at bay affects me; if his tears excite mine, this object so affecting by its novelty, is agreeable to the savage whom habit has rendered obdurate.

The most pleasing melody to an inquisitor are the groans of torture: he laughs by the side of the fire in which the heretic is burning. This inquisitor, an authorized assassin of the law, preserves, even in the bosom of cities, the ferocity of the man of nature; he is a man of blood. The nearer we return to that state, the more we accustom ourselves to murder, the less it costs. Why is the lowest of the butchering tribe, in default of an executioner, obliged to perform his functions? Because his profession renders him void of compassion.

He whom a good education has not accustomed to see, in the misfortunes of others, to what he is himself exposed, will be always obdurate, and often sanguinary. The common people are so; they have not the understanding to be humane. It is curiosity, they say, that carries them to Tyburn or the Greve: yes, the first time; if they go again, it is cruelty. They are moved and weep at executions; and so does the man of education at a tragedy, but yet the representation is agreeable to him.

He that maintains the original goodness of men, designs to deceive them. Must there be in morals, as well as in religion, so many hypocrites, and so few that are sincere? Can the regard with which a reciprocal fear inspires two persons, nearly equal in force, be taken for a natural goodness in human nature, when even the polished man, not restrained by that fear, becomes cruel and sanguinary? . . .

Let me not be accused of denying the existence of good men: I know there are such, who tenderly sympathize in the miseries of their fellow-creatures: but the humanity of these is the effect of their education, not their nature. . . .

DENIS DIDEROT

ENIS DIDEROT (1713–84), like most of the bitterest enemies of Catholicism, at the time, was educated by the Jesuits. Evading his parents' conventional plans for him, he went to Paris, where he became a translator and the inspiration of the philosophic circle who dined weekly at the Baron d'Holbach's. He was, indeed, a prodigious talker, reputedly, as good a talker as he was a prose stylist.

His famous *Lettre sur les aveugles* (1749) introduced him to the world; in it Diderot pointed out the dependence of men's ideas on their five senses. The militant philosophers were quick to pick up and exploit the atheism in his work; and the authorities threw Diderot into prison.

When he emerged, he entered upon the production of the *Encyclopédie*. For twenty years he labored at the monumental work, bringing it out finally despite poverty, persecution, and the desertion of his co-workers. Besides this, he managed to write a great many fugitive pieces, among them plays, his influential essays on dramatic poetry, and the art criticisms of the *Salons*. His masterpiece, perhaps, is the witty satire *Le Neveu de Rameau,* which was introduced to Europe through Goethe's translation. In that work is the clearest evidence of his differences with many of his colleagues who had presumed that the growth of knowledge and of control over circumstance would necessarily increase man's rationality and social well-being. His dissent from his friends' views can also be found in the following selections from Diderot's *Refutation of Helvétius' Treatise on Man* taken from the *Œuvres complètes,* edited by J. Assézat and M. Tourneux (Paris, Garnier, 1875–77) and translated by Stephen J. Gendzier.

REFUTATION OF HELVETIUS' TREATISE ON MAN

[Book I]

IN SPITE OF all the faults that I have found in your work, do not believe that I scorn it. There are a hundred beautiful, very beautiful pages that are filled with fine and true observations, and everything that offends me I could correct with a stroke of the pen.

Instead of asserting that education and education alone makes men what they are, merely say that *you are more than half inclined to believe it.*

Say that *often* our works, sacrifices, pains, pleasures, vices, virtues, passions, tastes, and the love of glory, the desire for public esteem, all these

have a purpose which is related to sensual feelings, and nobody will contradict you.

Say that the diversity of the human constitution as well as the variety
of diets, climates, and foods have *less influence* upon our talents than is
generally thought, and we will agree.

Say that laws, mores, and governments are the *principal causes* of diversity
among nations, and if society is not sufficient to make all individuals the
same, it does level a great mass of men. And we will bow our head before
the experience of past centuries which has taught that Demosthenes, who
was not merely a product of Greece, may one day appear under the icy
sky of the frigid zone or under the fiery sun of the torrid zone.

Your logic is not as rigorous as it could be. You state your conclusions
exclusively in terms of general laws or precepts, but for all that you are
nevertheless a great moralist, a very subtle observer of human nature, a great
thinker, an excellent writer, and even a rare genius. Please try to be satisfied with this glory and let your friends be gratified by this praise.

The difference between you and Rousseau is that the principles of
Rousseau are false and his conclusions true, while your principles are true
and your conclusions false. Rousseau's disciples exaggerate his principles,
and they are extravagantly foolish. Your disciples can temper your conclusions and become very sensible people.

You are sincere when picking up your pen; Rousseau is only sincere
when he puts his down: he is the first person to be taken in by his own
sophistry. Rousseau believes that the man of nature is good; and you believe that there are only good social laws which can correct the original
corruption of nature.

Rousseau fancies that everything is for the best in the forests and everything for the worst in the cities. You think that everything is rather bad
in the cities, while it is certainly for the worst in the forest.

Rousseau writes against the theater and produces a comedy; praises the
uncivilized man and composes a treatise on education. His philosophy, if
there is one, is made of shreds and patches; yours is of one piece. Perhaps
I would prefer to be him than you, but I would prefer to have written
your work than his.

If I had his eloquence and your sagacity, I would be worth more than
both of you.

CHAPTER VI

To feel is to judge. This assertion, as it is stated, does not seem absolutely true to me. The stupid person feels, but he may not judge. The per-

son who is completely deprived of a good memory feels, but does not judge: judgment implies the comparison of two ideas. The difficulty consists in knowing how this comparison is made, because it presupposes the existence of two ideas present in the mind. Helvétius would have cut an extraordinary knot if he had clearly explained to us how we have two ideas which are present in the mind at one and the same time, or how we compare two ideas which are not present in the mind at one and the same time.

Perhaps I was out of temper when I read this sixth chapter, but here is my observation, which will remain unchanged regardless of whether it is good or bad. It follows from the entire metaphysical system of the author that judgments or the comparison of objects in relation to one another implies an interest in comparing them. Now this interest necessarily arises from the desire to be happy, and this desire originates in corporeal sensibility. This is a rather farfetched conclusion: it applies more readily to animals than to men. His method is to proceed abruptly from corporeal sensibility, that is, from the fact that I am not a plant, a stone, or a metal, to a love of happiness; and from a love of happiness to a personal interest; from personal interest to attention; and from attention to a comparison of our ideas. I do not know how to accept such generalizations. I am a man and need causes which are appropriate to men. The author adds that in advancing or retreating two steps he could proceed from corporeal sensibility to bodily organization, from this organization to the state of being or existence, and he might have said: I exist, I exist in this form; I feel, I judge; I want to be happy because I feel; it is in my interest to compare ideas, since I want to be happy. How can I profit from such a succession of assumptions which are equally applicable to a dog, a weasel, an oyster, or a camel? If Jean-Jacques denies this syllogism, he is wrong; if he find it frivolous, he would be quite right.

Descartes had said: "I think, therefore I am."

Helvétius wants us to say: "I feel, therefore I want to feel agreeably."

I prefer Hobbes who claims that in order to draw a conclusion which leads us somewhere, it would be necessary to say: "I feel, I think, I judge, therefore a part of organized matter like myself can feel, think, and judge."

As a matter of fact, if after this first deductive step, you make another, you are carried quite far. . . .

To feel is to think, or you do not think if you have not felt. . . . Are these two propositions so different that after having found the first, you can consider the second a wonderful discovery?

Yes, if proceeding from the single phenomenon of corporeal sensibility, the general property of matter or the result of bodily organization, he had clearly deduced all the operations of understanding, then he would have done something new, difficult, and profound.

I will esteem even more the person who, by experiment or observation, will rigorously demonstrate either that corporeal sensibility belongs as essentially to matter as impenetrability, or who will deduce it uncontrovertibly from bodily organization.

I urge all physicists and chemists to inquire into the nature of animal, sensible, and living matter.

I see clearly in the growth of the egg and in other operations of nature that matter which is apparently inert, but actually organized, passes by purely physical means from the inert state to the state of sensibility and life, but the necessary agent of this transition escapes my understanding.

Our notions of matter, organization, movement, heat, body, sensibility, and life must still be rather incomplete.

You must agree that organization or the co-ordination of inert parts does not at all lead to or cause sensibility, and the general sensibility of the molecules of matter is only a supposition that derives its cogency from the difficulties it brushes aside, which is not a satisfactory philosophic argument. But let us return to our author.

Is it really true that corporeal pain and pleasure are the only motivating factors for either men or animals?

Without doubt, you must be organized and feel as we do in order to act, but it seems to me that these are essential and primary conditions, the givens or the *sine qua non,* but the immediate and intimate motives of our aversions and desires are another thing.

Without alkali and sand, there would not be glass, but are these elements the cause of transparency?

Without waste land and arms you do not cultivate the earth, but are these the farmer's motives when he cultivates the earth?

To take necessary conditions for primary causes is to lay oneself open to puerile paralogisms and insignificant conclusions.

If I said: You must be in order to feel, you must feel in order to be an animal or a man, you must be an animal or a man in order to be miserly, ambitious, and jealous; therefore, jealousy, ambition, and avarice have the following primary causes: organization, sensibility, and existence . . . could you prevent yourself from laughing? And why? It is because I would take the condition of every animal action in general for the motive of the action of an individual of the species of animal called man.

All that I do, assuredly I do to feel pleasure or for fear of feeling pain, but the words *to feel* have they only one accepted meaning?

Is there only physical pleasure in possessing a beautiful woman? Is there only physical pain in losing her by death or by inconstancy?

Is not the distinction between the physical and the mental as substantial as that between an animal who feels and an animal who reasons?

Do we not sometimes combine and at other times divorce feeling from thinking in all those activities which constitute the happiness or misfortune of our life, a happiness or misfortune which presupposes the condition of corporeal sensibility; in other words, one must not be a cabbage?

Therefore, it is very important not to make *feeling* and *judging* two perfectly identical processes.

CHAPTER VII

Here is his title: *Corporeal sensibility is the sole cause of our actions, our thoughts, our passions, and our sociability.*

Notice carefully that he does not say a primary, essential condition, as impenetrability is related to movement, which is incontestable, but the cause, the sole cause, which seems to me almost as obviously false. . . .

It is to clothe himself and adorn his wife or his mistress . . . that the peasant labors. Is the act of adorning his wife or his mistress that of an animal who feels or of a man who judges? When people improve their looks, it is sometimes to arouse corporeal pleasure in others, yet when people who are in love want to experience pleasure, their sprucing up is also a superfluous affectation. . . .

Remorse is nothing more than a foresight of bodily pain to which some crime has exposed us. Yes, that is perhaps the remorse of the scoundrel, but do you not know of any other kind?

There are pains and pleasures which derive from opinion alone and which can enrapture or grieve us without any bodily reactions. I have often preferred an attack of the gout to a slight indication of contempt.

I must walk to go to Sainte-Anne street in order to chat with a certain philosopher whom I like, or to converse more sweetly with a lady in the neighborhood. But do I go only because I have feet? These two actions are without doubt reducible in the last analysis to corporeal sensibility, but as a condition and not as a cause, goal, or motive. . . .

Discuss [Helvétius] the nature of friendship, and when, after having disfigured it by making it only pain or bodily pleasure, do not be astonished if people regard you as an atrocious man or as an absurd reasoner. . . .

You still speak about the pleasures of possessing fine slaves and beautiful paintings, but how do you speak about them? About the possession of a slave: like a gourmand who devours a plover; about a beautiful painting, like a physicist who gazes at the solar spectrum. They are nevertheless very different types of pleasures.

In order to caress a slave or admire a painting, you must feel, I agree, but it is like saying that you must exist.

Without the love of fine slaves and paintings, this man would have been entirely indifferent to the discovery of a treasure. This is false in every sense.

When you are happy today about the prospect of enjoying your mistress tomorrow, is this bodily pleasure? You confuse the pleasure of expectation with the pleasure of actual sensual enjoyment, as you have confused real pain with the foresight of pain. What do you experience when you are dying of hunger? Stomach contractions with a peculiar and acute sensation from the organs of deglutition. What do these symptoms have in common with the hunger that you foresee with your anxiety, agitation, and despair? There is hardly any relationship between these two pains, and your attention is so fixed upon the harm or pain which threatens you that all corporeal sensations are suspended. It is no longer you that you perceive, but the image of a man in the throes of death, sinking fast, and dying in a horrible coma: a frightening image of the state you will be in within the next three days. If you saw a man dying of hunger, you would not hesitate to say that this man is dying of hunger. If you saw a man who was threatened with death from hunger, would you suspect it? Never. Hunger is a need, this need when not satisfied becomes an illness: will you say that the illness and the fear of falling ill are the same thing? Hunger exists in the throat, the œsophagus, the stomach, and all along the intestinal tract. The fear of starvation, as well as all other fears, exist in the understanding.

To undermine a soldier, you must offer him a crown piece, the equivalent of a pint of brandy, or the enjoyment of a camp follower. This is not always true. There are soldiers who would refuse the crown piece which was the equivalent of only a pint of brandy, or a night with a camp follower: witness the fellow who was in danger of being killed like the ten other soldiers who had preceded him in action during the famous siege of Lille [1708] which was so well defended by Boufflers. When he was offered the 100 louis promised to anyone who would reveal the maneuvers of the besieging army, he answered: *My captain, take back your 100 louis, this is not done for money.* The man who truly understands the meaning of honor can not be bribed. He who was given Briseis in recompense for the danger he braved, did not risk death to have Briseis. Achilles, what would you choose: Briseis without fighting or victory without Briseis? Achilles answers: I want to fight, I want to conquer.

CHAPTER XV

Do men have different opinions on the same question? This is always due to the fact that either they do not understand each other, or they do not have the same objects in mind, or they do not give to the question itself the necessary interest. This is not all, for there is perhaps an even more abundant source of their arguments than those previously mentioned.

However well organized two heads may be, it is impossible for the same ideas to be equally evident in one as in the other. I do not think that this principle can be refuted.

Therefore, it is impossible for the same reasoning to be equally obvious to both.

One line of reasoning, which is tied in with the chain of ideas of one of the disputants, will appear logically conclusive to him. Because the other disputant would have to admit that there are several errors in his own chain of ideas which do not tie in or even contradict this line of reasoning, he is naturally inclined to think it false. . . .

All men are born with equality of understanding. All men are born without understanding; they have it neither false nor just: it is the experience of the things of life which disposes them toward justness or falseness.

He who has always made bad use of his senses will have false understanding.

He who is mediocrely educated and thinks he knows everything, will have false understanding.

He who is carried away by self-sufficiency and hastiness, will be hurried in his judgments and have false understanding.

He who attaches too much or too little importance to certain things will have false understanding.

He who dares pronounce himself on a question which exceeds the capacity of his natural talent will have false understanding.

There is nothing so rare as logic: an infinity of men lack it, almost all women have none at all.

He who is subject to prejudices will have false understanding.

He who is obstinate out of vanity, out of a desire to be different, or out of inclination for paradoxes, will have false understanding.

And he who trusts his reason too much and he who trusts it too little will have false understanding.

All interests, prejudices, passions, vices, and virtues are capable of perverting the understanding.

Therefore I conclude that equality of understanding is in every respect a creation of the mind. . . .

[Book II]
Section V

CHAPTER II

Is man good or evil at birth. If you call good, only the person who does good, and evil, only the person who does evil, then certainly man at birth is neither good nor evil. I say as much of understanding and stupidity.

But does not man at birth bring with him certain organic and natural tendencies to say and do foolish things, to harm himself and his fellowmen, to listen to or neglect the advice of his parents, to be industrious or lazy, just or angry, to respect or scorn laws? It can only be doubted by the person who in his lifetime has never seen two children and who has never heard them crying from the cradle. Man is born nothing, but each man is born with an aptitude for something.

CHAPTER IV

There are good men, but the humanity in them is not natural, it is the effect of education. Always? I don't believe anything of the sort. Regardless of the education you might have given a wild man who observes the death convulsions of a capuchin friar he has just killed, I find it difficult to believe that he would have made a sensitive and compassionate individual.

You can not give to a man what nature has refused; perhaps you can destroy what it has provided. However, education can improve the gifts of nature.

Corporeal sensibility is the only gift that nature has bestowed upon us. But is this sensibility which is diffused throughout the human body apportioned equally to all of its parts? This is not true and could not be so.

If the amount of corporeal sensibility is limited in the brain and in the sympathetic nervous system, then there will be little imagination, compassion, and benevolence.

Is the degree of corporeal sensibility the same in all individuals? This is not true and could not be so.

Can you therefore obtain the same results from a machine whose spring is too strong and from another with one that is too weak?

NOTES

In almost all the author's reasoning, the premises are true and the conclusions false, but the premises have a great deal of insight and sagacity.

It is difficult to find his reasoning satisfactory, but it is easy to rectify his findings and substitute a sound conclusion for an erroneous one which generally sins only by excessive generalization. It is merely a question of limiting his statements.

He says: Education does everything. *Say:* Education does a great deal.

He says: The organization of the human body does nothing. *Say:* The organization of the human body does less than one thinks.

He says: Our pains and pleasures resolve themselves into sensual pains and pleasures. *Say:* Rather often.

He says: All those people who understand a truth would have been able to discover it. *Say:* Some people.

He says: There are no truths which can not be brought within the understanding of everyone. *Say:* There are few truths of this type.

He says: Personal concern and interest compensate perfectly for a deficiency in bodily organization. *Say:* More or less, according to the deficiency.

He says: Chance makes men of genius. *Say:* It places them in favorable circumstances.

He says: There is nothing that you can not succeed in doing with an intent mind and some work. *Say:* You can succeed in doing many things.

He says: Education is the only cause of differences between minds. *Say:* It is one of the main causes.

He says: You can make nothing of one man that you can not make of another. *Say:* Sometimes this seems true.

He says: Climate does not influence the human mind. *Say:* People give it too much credit.

He says: It is legislation and government which alone make a nation stupid or enlightened. *Say:* I concede this for the masses, but there was a Sa'dī and there were some great doctors under the Caliphs.

He says: Character depends entirely upon circumstances. *Say:* I believe that they modify it.

He says: You can give a man any temperament you desire; and regardless of the one that he has received from nature, he has neither more nor less of an aptitude for genius. *Say:* Temperament is not always an invincible obstacle for the progress of the mind.

He says: Women are capable of the same education as men. *Say:* They can be educated better than they are.

He says: Everything which emanates from man can be resolved in the last analysis into corporeal sensibility. *Say:* As a necessary condition, but not as a cause or a motive.

He says: It often takes greater effort to understand an experiment than to discover the truth. *Say:* But this does not prove that genius is equally distributed.

He says: Men who are equally well organized are equally adaptable to all things. *Say:* To many things.

He says: The alleged scale which divides the minds of men is imaginary and unreal. *Say:* The difference in men's minds is less than people assume.

And so on with all his assertions, which are neither absolutely true nor absolutely false.

. . . I recommend the reading of [*The Treatise on Man*] to all my countrymen, and especially to the heads of State, so that they may at last know all the influence that good legislation can have upon the brilliance and happiness of their empires, and the necessity of better education; and in order that they may rid themselves of a prejudice which simply reveals their ineptitude: that scholars and philosophers are only seditious subjects and would only be bad ministers. I recommend [this book] to parents so that they may not despair too easily of their children; and to men who are vain because of their talents, so that they may know that the distance which separates them from the common man is not so great as their pride has persuaded them; and to all authors so that they may be astonished by the peculiar absurdity into which a solid mind can be led if too strongly possessed by its own opinions: let them become more prudent by his example. . . .

DAVID HUME

D AVID HUME (1711–76) was born in Edinburgh and attended the university there. What his course of study was is not clear, but he had begun early to read both Cicero and Seneca and the English philosophers since Hobbes. After trying first law and then business, he set out for France in the middle of 1734. At La Flèche he wrote the *Treatise of Human Nature,* returning to London in 1739 to arrange for its publication. The book was scarcely noticed; but it remains the most complete exposition of his fundamental philosophical ideas. He extended and impressively refined Locke's empirical psychology and theory of knowledge.

In 1741–42 he published his *Essays Moral and Political,* which was immediately successful but his *Philosophical Essays* (afterwards entitled *An Enquiry concerning Human Understanding*) received little more favor than his first book.

He returned in 1751 to Edinburgh, and the following twelve years were full of literary activity. He published first his *Political Discourses,* which were popular in England and abroad; revised the third book of the *Treatise* into the *Enquiry concerning the Principles of Morals;* and wrote the *Dialogues concerning Natural Religion,* which he was prevailed upon not to publish (charges of heresy were already being leveled against him). During this period he wrote his very popular *History of England,* which, although it became more and more irascibly anti-Whig as it proceeded, was nevertheless an early attempt at a comprehensive secular treatment of a specific culture for he included social and literary aspects of English life. In 1757 appeared the *Four Dissertations:* The Natural History of Religion, Of the Passions, Of Tragedy, and Of the Standard of Taste.

This selection from Hume's *Enquiry concerning the Principles of Morals* reveals his persistent attempt to demonstrate that moral knowledge, like all other knowledge, is neither logically certain nor universal in application but has its source in human desires and in the "conventions" or regularized habits of behavior of a particular society. Usefulness, not reason, is the test of the worth of a moral or political idea.

℘

AN ENQUIRY CONCERNING THE PRINCIPLES OF MORALS

OF THE GENERAL PRINCIPLES OF MORALS

Disputes with men, pertinaciously obstinate in their principles, are, of all others, the most irksome; except, perhaps, those with persons, entirely disingenuous, who really do not believe the opinions they defend, but engage in the controversy, from affectation, from a spirit of opposition, or from a desire of showing wit and ingenuity, superior to the rest of mankind. The same blind adherence to their own arguments is to be expected in both; the same contempt of their antagonists; and the same passionate vehemence, in inforcing sophistry and falsehood. And as reasoning is not the source, whence either disputant derives his tenets; it is in vain to expect, that any logic, which speaks not to the affections, will ever engage him to embrace sounder principles.

Those who have denied the reality of moral distinctions, may be ranked among the disingenuous disputants; nor is it conceivable, that any human creature could ever seriously believe, that all characters and actions were alike entitled to the affection and regard of everyone. The difference, which nature has placed between one man and another, is so wide, and this difference is still so much farther widened, by education, example, and habit, that, where the opposite extremes come at once under our apprehension, there is no scepticism so scrupulous, and scarce any assurance so determined, as absolutely to deny all distinction between them. Let a man's insensibility be ever so great, he must often be touched with the images of Right and Wrong; and let his prejudices be ever so obstinate, he might observe, that others are susceptible of like impressions. The only way, therefore, of converting an antagonist of this kind, is to leave him to himself. For, finding that nobody keeps up the controversy with him, it is probable he will, at last, of himself, from mere weariness, come over to the side of common sense and reason.

There has been a controversy started of late, much better worth examination, concerning the general foundation of Morals; whether they be derived from Reason, or from Sentiment; whether we attain the knowledge of them by a chain of argument and induction, or by an immediate feeling and finer internal sense; whether, like all sound judgement of truth and falsehood, they should be the same to every rational intelligent being; or whether, like the perception of beauty and deformity, they be founded entirely on the particular fabric and constitution of the human species.

The ancient philosophers, though they often affirm, that virtue is nothing but conformity to reason, yet in general, seem to consider morals as deriving their existence from taste and sentiment. On the other hand, our modern enquirers, though they also talk much of the beauty of virtue, and deformity of vice, yet have commonly endeavoured to account for these distinctions by metaphysical reasonings, and by deductions from the most abstract principles of the understanding. Such confusion reigned in these subjects, that an opposition of the greatest consequence could prevail between one system and another, and even in the parts of almost each individual system; and yet nobody, till very lately, was ever sensible of it. The elegant Lord Shaftesbury, who first gave occasion to remark this distinction, and who, in general, adhered to the principles of the ancients, is not, himself, entirely free from the same confusion.

It must be acknowledged, that both sides of the question are susceptible of specious arguments. Moral distinctions, it may be said, are discernible by pure *reason:* else, whence the many disputes that reign in common life, as well as in philosophy, with regard to this subject: the long chain of proofs often produced on both sides; the examples cited, the authorities appealed to, the analogies employed, the fallacies detected, the inferences drawn, and the several conclusions adjusted to their proper principles. Truth is disputable; not taste: what exists in the nature of things is the standard of our judgement; what each man feels within himself is the standard of sentiment. Propositions in geometry may be proved, systems in physics may be converted; but the harmony of verse, the tenderness of passion, the brilliancy of wit, must give immediate pleasure. No man reasons concerning another's beauty; but frequently concerning the justice or injustice of his actions. In every criminal trial the first object of the prisoner is to disprove the facts alleged, and deny the actions imputed to him: the second to prove, that, even if these actions were real, they might be justified, as innocent and lawful. It is confessedly by deductions of the understanding, that the first point is ascertained: how can we suppose that a different faculty of the mind is employed in fixing the other?

On the other hand, those who would resolve all moral determinations into *sentiment,* may endeavour to show, that it is impossible for reason ever to draw conclusions of this nature. To virtue, say they, it belongs to be *amiable,* and vice *odious.* This forms their very nature or essence. But can reason or argumentation distribute these different epithets to any subjects, and pronounce beforehand, that this must produce love, and that hatred? Or what other reason can we ever assign for these affections, but the original fabric and formation of the human mind, which is naturally adapted to receive them?

The end of all moral speculations is to teach us our duty; and, by proper representations of the deformity of vice and beauty of virtue, beget correspondent habits, and engage us to avoid the one, and embrace the other. But is this ever to be expected from inferences and conclusions of the understanding, which of themselves have no hold of the affections or set in motion the active powers of men? They discover truths: but where the truths which they discover are indifferent, and beget no desire or aversion, they can have no influence on conduct and behaviour. What is honourable, what is fair, what is becoming, what is noble, what is generous, takes possession of the heart, and animates us to embrace and maintain it. What is intelligible, what is evident, what is probable, what is true, procures only the cool assent of the understanding; and gratifying a speculative curiosity, puts an end to our researches.

Extinguish all the warm feelings and prepossessions in favour of virtue, and all disgust or aversion to vice: render men totally indifferent towards these distinctions; and morality is no longer a practical study, nor has any tendency to regulate our lives and actions.

These arguments on each side (and many more might be produced) are so plausible, that I am apt to suspect, they may, the one as well as the other, be solid and satisfactory, and that *reason* and *sentiment* concur in almost all moral determinations and conclusions. The final sentence, it is probable, which pronounces characters and actions amiable or odious, praise-worthy or blame-able; that which stamps on them the mark of honour or infamy, approbation or censure; that which renders morality an active principle and constitutes virtue our happiness, and vice our misery: it is probable, I say, that this final sentence depends on some internal sense or feeling, which nature has made universal in the whole species. For what else can have an influence of this nature? But in order to pave the way for such a sentiment, and give a proper discernment of its object, it is often necessary, we find, that much reasoning should precede, that nice distinctions be made, just conclusions drawn, distant comparisons formed, complicated relations examined, and general facts fixed and ascertained. Some species of beauty, especially the natural kinds, on their first appearance, command our affection and approbation; and where they fail of this effect, it is impossible for any reasoning to redress their influence, or adapt them better to our taste and sentiment. But in many orders of beauty, particularly those of the finer arts, it is requisite to employ much reasoning, in order to feel the proper sentiment; and a false relish may frequently be corrected by argument and reflection. There are just grounds to conclude, that moral beauty partakes much of this latter species, and demands the assistance of our intellectual faculties, in order to give it a suitable influence on the human mind.

But though this question, concerning the general principles of morals, be curious and important, it is needless for us, at present, to employ further care in our researches concerning it. For if we can be so happy, in the course of this enquiry, as to discover the true origin of morals, it will then easily appear how far either sentiment or reason enters into all determinations of this nature. In order to attain this purpose, we shall endeavour to follow a very simple method: we shall analyse that complication of mental qualities, which form what, in common life, we call Personal Merit: we shall consider every attribute of the mind, which renders a man an object either of esteem and affection, or of hatred and contempt; every habit or sentiment or faculty, which, if ascribed to any person, implies either praise or blame, and may enter into any panegyric or satire of his character and manners. The quick sensibility, which, on this head, is so universal among mankind, gives a philosopher sufficient assurance, that he can never be considerably mistaken in framing the catalogue, or incur any danger of misplacing the objects of his contemplation: he needs only enter into his own breast for a moment, and consider whether or not he should desire to have this or that quality ascribed to him, and whether such or such an imputation would proceed from a friend or an enemy. The very nature of language guides us almost infallibly in forming a judgement of this nature; and as every tongue possesses one set of words which are taken in a good sense, and another in the opposite, the least acquaintance with the idiom suffices, without any reasoning, to direct us in collecting and arranging the estimable or blameable qualities of men. The only object of reasoning is to discover the circumstances on both sides, which are common to these qualities; to observe that particular in which the estimable qualities agree on the one hand, and the blameable on the other; and thence to reach the foundation of ethics, and find those universal principles, from which all censure or approbation is ultimately derived. As this is a question of fact, not of abstract science, we can only expect success, by following the experimental method, and deducing general maxims from a comparison of particular instances. The other scientific method, where a general abstract principle is first established, and is afterwards branched out into a variety of inferences and conclusions, may be more perfect in itself, but suits less the imperfection of human nature, and is a common source of illusion and mistake in this as well as in other subjects. Men are now cured of their passion for hypotheses and systems in natural philosophy, and will hearken to no arguments but those which are derived from experience. It is full time they should attempt a like reformation in all moral disquisitions; and reject every system of ethics, however subtle or ingenious, which is not founded on fact and observation.

We shall begin our enquiry on this head by the consideration of the social virtues, Benevolence and Justice. The explication of them will probably give us an opening by which the others may be accounted for.

OF BENEVOLENCE

Part I. It may be esteemed, perhaps, a superfluous task to prove, that the benevolent or softer affections are estimable; and wherever they appear, engage the approbation and good-will of mankind. The epithets *sociable, good-natured, humane, merciful, grateful, friendly, beneficent,* or their equivalents, are known in all languages, and universally express the highest merit, which *human nature* is capable of attaining. Where these amiable qualities are attended with birth and power and eminent abilities, and display themselves in the good government or useful instruction of mankind, they seem even to raise the possessors of them above the rank of *human nature,* and make them approach in some measure to the divine. Exalted capacity, undaunted courage, prosperous success; these may only expose a hero or politician to the envy and ill-will of the public: but as soon as the praises are added of humane and beneficent; when instances are displayed of lenity, tenderness or friendship; envy itself is silent, or joins the general voice of approbation and applause. . . .

But I forget, that it is not my present business to recommend generosity and benevolence, or to paint, in their true colours, all the genuine charms of the social virtues. These, indeed, sufficiently engage every heart, on the first apprehension of them; and it is difficult to abstain from some sally of panegyric, as often as they occur in discourse or reasoning. But our object here being more the speculative, than the practical part of morals, it will suffice to remark (what will readily, I believe, be allowed) that no qualities are more intitled to the general good-will and approbation of mankind than beneficence and humanity, friendship and gratitude, natural affection and public spirit, or whatever proceeds from a tender sympathy with others, and a generous concern for our kind and species. These wherever they appear, seem to transfuse themselves, in a manner, into each beholder, and to call forth, in their own behalf, the same favourable and affectionate sentiments, which they exert on all around.

Part II. We may observe that, in displaying the praises of any humane, beneficent man, there is one circumstance which never fails to be amply insisted on, namely, the happiness and satisfaction, derived to society from his intercourse and good offices. To his parents, we are apt to say, he endears himself by his pious attachment and duteous care still more than by the connexions of nature. His children never feel his authority, but when employed for their advantage. With him, the ties of love are consolidated by beneficence and friendship. The ties of friendship approach, in a fond observance of each obliging office, to those of love and inclination. His domestics and dependents have in him a sure resource; and no longer dread the power of fortune, but so far as she exercises it over him. From him the hungry receive food, the naked clothing, the ignorant and slothful skill and industry. Like the sun, an inferior minister of providence he cheers, invigorates, and sustains the surrounding world.

If confined to private life, the sphere of his activity is narrower; but his influence is all benign and gentle. If exalted into a higher station, mankind and posterity reap the fruit of his labours.

As these topics of praise never fail to be employed, and with success, where we would inspire esteem for any one; may it not thence be concluded, that the utility, resulting from the social virtues, forms, at least, a *part* of their merit, and is one source of that approbation and regard so universally paid to them?

When we recommend even an animal or a plant as *useful* and *beneficial,* we give it an applause and recommendation suited to its nature. As, on the other hand, reflection on the baneful influence of any of these inferior beings always inspires us with the sentiment of aversion. The eye is pleased with the prospect of cornfields and loaded vineyards; horses grazing, and flocks pasturing: but flies the view of briars and brambles, affording shelter to wolves and serpents.

A machine, a piece of furniture, a vestment, a house well contrived for use and conveniency, is so far beautiful, and is contemplated with pleasure and approbation. An experienced eye is here sensible to many excellencies, which escape persons ignorant and uninstructed.

Can anything stronger be said in praise of a profession, such as merchandise or manufacture, than to observe the advantages which it procures to society; and is not a monk and inquisitor enraged when we treat his order as useless or pernicious to mankind?

The historian exults in displaying the benefit arising from his labours. The writer of romance alleviates or denies the bad consequences ascribed to his manner of composition.

In general, what praise is implied in the simple epithet *useful!* What reproach in the contrary! . . .

Upon the whole, then, it seems undeniable, *that* nothing can bestow more merit on any human creature than the sentiment of benevolence in an eminent degree; and *that a part,* at least, of its merit arises from its tendency to promote the interests of our species, and bestow happiness on human society. We carry our view into the salutary consequences of such a character and disposition; and whatever has so benign an influence, and forwards so desirable an end, is beheld with complacency and pleasure. The social virtues are never regarded without their beneficial tendencies, nor viewed as barren and unfruitful. The happiness of mankind, the order of society, the harmony of families, the mutual support of friends, are always considered as the result of their gentle dominion over the breasts of men.

How considerable a *part* of their merit we ought to ascribe to their utility, will better appear from future disquisitions; as well as the reason, why this circumstance has such a command over our esteem and approbation.

OF JUSTICE

Part I. That justice is useful to society, and consequently that part of its merit, at least, must arise from that consideration, it would be a superfluous undertaking to prove. That public utility is the *sole* origin of justice, and that reflections on the beneficial consequences of this virtue are the *sole* foundation of its merit; this proposition, being more curious and important, will better deserve our examination and enquiry.

Let us suppose that nature has bestowed on the human race such profuse *abundance* of all *external* conveniences, that, without any uncertainty in the event, without any care or industry on our part, every individual finds himself fully provided with whatever his most voracious appetites can want, or luxurious imagination wish or desire. His natural beauty, we shall suppose, surpasses all acquired ornaments: the perpetual clemency of the seasons renders useless all clothes or covering: the raw herbage affords him the most delicious fare; the clear fountain, the richest beverage. No laborious occupation required: no tillage: no navigation. Music, poetry, and contemplation form his sole business: conversation, mirth, and friendship his sole amusement.

It seems evident that, in such a happy state, every other social virtue would flourish, and receive tenfold increase; but the cautious, jealous virtue of justice would never once have been dreamed of. For what purpose make a partition of goods, where every one has already more than enough? Why give rise to property, where there cannot possibly be any injury? Why call this object *mine,* when upon the seizing of it by another, I need but stretch out my hand to possess myself to what is equally valuable? Justice, in that case, being totally useless, would be an idle ceremonial, and could never possibly have place in the catalogue of virtues.

We see, even in the present necessitous condition of mankind, that, wherever any benefit is bestowed by nature in an unlimited abundance, we leave it always in common among the whole human race, and make no subdivisions of right and property. Water and air, though the most necessary of all objects, are not challenged as the property of individuals; nor can any man commit injustice by the most lavish use and enjoyment of these blessings. In fertile extensive countries, with few inhabitants, land is regarded on the same footing. And no topic is so much insisted on by those, who defend the liberty of the seas, as the unexhausted use of them in navigation. Were the advantages, procured by navigation, as inexhaustible, these reasoners had never had any adversaries to refute; nor had any claims ever been advanced of a separate, exclusive dominion over the ocean.

It may happen, in some countries, at some periods, that there be established a property in water, none in land; if the latter be in greater abundance than can be used by the inhabitants, and the former be found, with difficulty, and in very small quantities.

Again; suppose, that, though the necessities of the human race continue the same as at present, yet the mind is so enlarged, and so replete with friendship and generosity, that every man has the utmost tenderness for every man, and feels no more concern for his own interest than for that of his fellows; it seems evident, that the use of justice would, in this case, be suspended by such an extensive benevolence, nor would the divisions and barriers of property and obligation have ever been thought of. Why should I bind another, by a deed or promise, to do me any good office, when I know that he is already prompted, by the strongest inclination, to seek my happiness, and would, of himself, perform the desired service; except the hurt, he thereby receives, be greater than the benefit accruing to me? in which case, he knows, that from my innate humanity and friendship, I should be the first to oppose myself to his imprudent generosity. Why raise land-marks between my neighbour's field and mine, when my heart has made no division between our interests; but shares all his joys and sorrows with the same force and vivacity as if originally my own? Every man, upon this supposition, being a second self to another, would trust all his interests to the discretion of every man; without jealousy, without partition, without distinction. And the whole human race would form only one family; where all would lie in common, and be used freely, without regard to property; but cautiously too, with as entire regard to the necessities of each individual, as if our own interests were most intimately concerned.

In the present disposition of the human heart, it would, perhaps, be difficult to find complete instances of such enlarged affections; but still we may observe, that the case of families approaches towards it; and the stronger the mutual benevolence is among the individuals, the nearer it approaches; till all distinction of property be, in a great measure, lost and confounded among them. Between married persons, the cement of friendship is by the laws supposed so strong as to abolish all division of possessions; and has often, in reality, the force ascribed to it. And it is observable, that, during the ardour of new enthusiasms, when every principle is inflamed into extravagance, the community of goods has frequently been attempted; and nothing but experience of its inconveniences, from the returning or disguised selfishness of men, could make the imprudent fanatics adopt anew the ideas of justice and of separate property. So true is it, that this virtue derives its existence entirely from its necessary *use* to the intercourse and social state of mankind.

To make this truth more evident, let us reverse the foregoing suppositions; and carrying everything to the opposite extreme, consider what would be the effect of these new situations. Suppose a society to fall into such want of all common necessaries, that the utmost frugality and industry cannot preserve the greater number from perishing, and the whole from extreme misery; it will readily, I believe, be admitted, that the strict laws of justice are suspended, in such a pressing emergence, and give place to the stronger motives of necessity and self-preservation. Is it any crime, after a shipwreck, to seize whatever means or instrument of safety one can lay hold of, without regard to former limitations of property? Or if a city besieged were perishing with hunger; can we imagine, that men will see any means of preservation before them, and lose their lives, from a scrupulous regard to what, in other situations, would be the rules of equity and justice? The use and tendency of that virtue is to procure happiness and security, by preserving order in society: but where the society is ready to perish from extreme necessity, no greater evil can be dreaded from violence and injustice; and every man may now provide for himself by all the means, which prudence can dictate, or humanity permit. The public, even in less urgent necessities, opens granaries, without the consent of proprietors; as justly supposing, that the authority of magistracy may, consistent with equity, extend so far: but were any number of men to assemble, without the tie of laws or civil jurisdiction; would an equal partition of bread in a famine, though effected by power and even violence, be regarded as criminal or injurious?

Suppose likewise, that it should be a virtuous man's fate to fall into the society of ruffians, remote from the protection of laws and government; what conduct must he embrace in that melancholy situation? He sees such a desperate rapaciousness prevail; such a disregard to equity, such contempt of order, such stupid blindness to future consequences, as must immediately have the most tragical conclusion, and must terminate in destruction to the greater number, and in a total dissolution of society to the rest. He, meanwhile, can have no other expedient than to arm himself, to whomever the sword he seizes, or the buckler, may belong. To make provision of all means of defence and security: And his particular regard to justice being no longer of use to his own safety or that of others, he must consult the dictates of self-preservation alone, without concern for those who no longer merit his care and attention.

When any man, even in political society, renders himself by his crimes, obnoxious to the public, he is punished by the laws in his goods and person; that is, the ordinary rules of justice are, with regard to him, suspended for a moment, and it becomes equitable to inflict on him, for the *benefit* of society, what otherwise he could not suffer without wrong or injury.

The rage and violence of public war; what is it but a suspension of justice among the warring parties, who perceive, that this virtue is now no longer of any *use* or advantage to them? The laws of war, which then succeed to those of equity and justice, are rules calculated for the *advantage* and *utility* of that particular state, in which men are now placed. And were a civilized nation engaged with barbarians, who observed no rules even of war, the former must also suspend their observance of them, where they no longer serve to any purpose; and must render every action or rencounter as bloody and pernicious as possible to the first aggressors.

Thus, the rules of equity or justice depend entirely on the particular state and condition in which men are placed, and owe their origin and existence to that utility, which results to the public from their strict and regular observance. Reverse, in any considerable circumstance, the condition of men: Produce extreme abundance or extreme necessity: Implant in the human breast perfect moderation and humanity, or perfect rapaciousness and malice: By rendering justice totally *useless,* you thereby totally destroy its essence, and suspend its obligation upon mankind.

The common situation of society is a medium amidst all these extremes. We are naturally partial to ourselves, and to our friends; but are capable of learning the advantage resulting from a more equitable conduct. Few enjoyments are given from the open and liberal hand of nature; but by art, labour, and industry, we can extract them in great abundance. Hence the ideas of property become necessary in all civil society: Hence justice derives its usefulness to the public: And hence alone arises its merit and moral obligation.

These conclusions are so natural and obvious, that they have not escaped even the poets, in their descriptions of the felicity attending the golden age or the reign of Saturn. The seasons, in that first period of nature, were so temperate, if we credit these agreeable fictions, that there was no necessity for men to provide themselves with clothes, and houses, as a security against the violence of heat and cold: The rivers flowed with wine and milk: The oaks yielded honey; and nature spontaneously produced her greatest delicacies. Nor were these the chief advantages of that happy age. Tempests were not alone removed from nature; but those more furious tempests were unknown to human breasts, which now cause such uproar, and engender such confusion. Avarice, ambition, cruelty, selfishness, were never heard of: Cordial affection, compassion, sympathy, were the only movements with which the mind was yet acquainted. Even the punctilious distinction of *mine* and *thine* was banished from among that happy race of mortals, and carried with it the very notion of property and obligation, justice and injustice.

This *poetical* fiction of the *golden age* is, in some respects, of a piece with the *philosophical* fiction of the *state of nature;* only that the former is represented as the most charming and most peaceable condition, which can possibly be imagined; whereas the latter is painted out as a state of mutual war and violence, attended with the most extreme necessity. On the first origin of mankind, we are told, their ignorance and savage nature were so prevalent, that they could give no mutual trust, but must each depend upon himself and his own force or cunning for protection and security. No law was heard of: No rule of justice known: No distinction of property regarded: Power was the only measure of right; and a perpetual war of all against all was the result of men's untamed selfishness and barbarity.

Whether such a condition of human nature should ever exist, or if it did, could continue so long as to merit the appellation of a *state,* may justly be doubted. Men are necessarily born in a family-society, at least; and are trained up by their parents to some rule of conduct and behaviour. But this must be admitted, that, if such a state of mutual war and violence was ever real, the suspension of all laws of justice, from their absolute inutility, is a necessary and infallible consequence. . . .

Part II. . . . The dilemma seems obvious: As justice evidently tends to promote public utility and to support civil society, the sentiment of justice is either derived from our reflecting on that tendency, or like hunger, thirst, and other appetites, resentment, love of life, attachment to offspring, and other passions, arises from a simple original instinct in the human breast, which nature has implanted for like salutary purposes. If the latter be the case, it follows, that property, which is the object of justice, is also distinguished by a simple original instinct, and is not ascertained by any argument or reflection. But who is there that ever heard of such an instinct? Or is this a subject in which new discoveries can be made? We may as well expect to discover, in the body, new senses, which had before escaped the observation of all mankind.

But farther, though it seems a very simple proposition to say, that nature, by an instinctive sentiment, distinguishes property, yet in reality we shall find, that there are required for that purpose ten thousand different instincts, and these employed about objects of the greatest intricacy and nicest discernment. For when a definition of *property* is required, that relation is found to resolve itself into any possession acquired by occupation, by industry, by prescription, by inheritance, by contract, &c. Can we think that nature, by an original instinct, instructs us in all these methods of acquisition?

These words too, inheritance and contract, stand for ideas infinitely complicated; and to define them exactly, a hundred volumes of laws, and a thousand volumes of commentators, have not been found sufficient. Does nature, whose instincts in men are all simple, embrace such complicated and artificial objects, and create a rational creature, without trusting anything to the operation of his reason?

But even though all this were admitted, it would not be satisfactory. Positive laws can certainly transfer property. It is by another original instinct, that we recognize the authority of kings and senates, and mark all the boundaries of their jurisdiction? Judges too, even though their sentence be erroneous and illegal, must be allowed, for the sake of peace and order, to have decisive authority, and ultimately to determine property. Have we original innate ideas of praetors and chancellors and juries? Who sees not, that all these institutions arise merely from the necessities of human society?

All birds of the same species in every age and country, built their nests alike: In this we see the force of instinct. Men, in different times and places, frame their houses differently: Here we perceive the influence of reason and custom. A like inference may be drawn from comparing the instinct of generation and the institution of property.

How great soever the variety of municipal laws, it must be confessed, that their chief out-lines pretty regularly concur; because the purposes, to which they tend, are everywhere exactly similar. In like manner, all houses have a roof and walls, windows and chimneys; though diversified in their shape, figure, and materials. The purposes of the latter, directed to the conveniences of human life, discover not more plainly their origin from reason and reflection, than do those of the former, which point all to a like end.

I need not mention the variations, which all the rules of property receive from the finer turns and connexions of the imagination, and from the subtilties and abstractions of law-topics and reasonings. There is no possibility of reconciling this observation to the notion of original instincts.

What alone will beget a doubt concerning the theory, on which I insist, is the influence of education and acquired habits, by which we are so accustomed to blame injustice, that we are not, in every instance, conscious of any immediate reflection on the pernicious consequences of it. The views the most familiar to us are apt, for that very reason, to escape us; and what we have very frequently performed from certain motives, we are apt likewise to continue mechanically, without recalling, on every occasion, the reflections, which first determined us. The convenience, or rather necessity, which leads to justice is so universal, and everywhere points so much to the same rules, that the habit takes place in all societies; and it is not without some scrutiny, that we are able to ascertain its true origin. The matter, however, is not so obscure, but that even in common life we have every moment recourse to the principle of public utility, and ask, *What must become of the world, if such practices prevail? How could society subsist under such disorders?* Were the distinction or separation of possessions entirely useless, can any one conceive, that it ever should have obtained in society?

Thus we seem, upon the whole, to have attained a knowledge of the force of that principle here insisted on, and can determine what degree of esteem or moral approbation may result from reflections on public interest and utility. The necessity of justice to the support of society is the sole foundation of that virtue; and since no moral excellence is more highly esteemed, we may conclude that this circumstance of usefulness has, in general, the strongest energy, and most entire command over our sentiments. It must, therefore, be the source of a considerable part of the merit ascribed to humanity, benevolence, friendship, public spirit, and other social virtues of that stamp; as it is the sole source of the moral approbation paid to fidelity, justice, veracity, integrity, and those other estimable and useful qualities and principles. It is entirely agreeable to the rules of philosophy, and even of common reason; where any principle has been found to have a great force and energy in one instance, to ascribe to it a like energy in all similar instances. This indeed is Newton's chief rule of philosophizing. . . .

CONCERNING MORAL SENTIMENT

If the foregoing hypothesis be received, it will now be easy for us to determine the question first started, concerning the general principles of morals; and though we postpone the decision of that question, lest it should then involve us in intricate speculations, which are unfit for moral discourses, we may resume it at present, and examine how far either *reason* or *sentiment* enters into all decisions of praise or censure.

One principal foundation of moral praise being supposed to lie in the usefulness of any quality or action, it is evident that *reason* must enter for a considerable share in all decisions of this kind; since nothing but that faculty can instruct us in the tendency of qualities and actions, and point out their beneficial consequences to society and to their possessor. In many cases this is an affair liable to great controversy: doubts may arise; opposite interests may occur; and a preference must be given to one side, from very nice views, and a small overbalance of utility. This is particularly remarkable in questions with regard to justice; as is, indeed, natural to suppose, from that species of utility which attends this virtue. Were every single instance of justice, like that of benevolence, useful to society; this would be a more simple state of the case, and seldom liable to great controversy. But as single instances of justice are often pernicious in their first and immediate tendency, and as the advantage to society results only from the observance of the general rule, and from the concurrence and combination of several persons in the same equitable conduct; the case here becomes more intricate and involved. The various circumstances of society; the various consequences of any practice; the various interests which may be proposed; these, on many occasions, are doubtful, and subject to great discussion and inquiry. The object of municipal laws is to fix all the questions with regard to justice: the debates of civilians; the reflections of politicians; the precedents of history and public records, are all directed to the same purpose. And a very accurate *reason* or *judgement* is often requisite, to give the true determination, amidst such intricate doubts arising from obscure or opposite utilities.

But though reason, when fully assisted and improved, be sufficient to instruct us in the pernicious or useful tendency of qualities and actions; it is not alone sufficient to produce any moral blame or approbation. Utility is only a tendency to a certain end; and were the end totally indifferent to us, we should feel the same indifference towards the means. It is requisite *a sentiment* should here display itself, in order to give a preference to the useful above the pernicious tendencies. This sentiment can be no other than a feeling for the happiness of mankind, and a resentment of their misery; since these are the different ends which virtue and vice have a tendency to promote. Here therefore *reason* instructs us in the several tendencies of actions, and *humanity* makes a distinction in favour of those which are useful and beneficial.

This partition between the faculties of understanding and sentiment, in all moral decisions, seems clear from the preceding hypothesis. But I shall suppose that hypothesis false: it will then be requisite to look out for some other theory that may be satisfactory; and I dare venture to affirm that none such will ever be found, so long as we suppose reason to be the sole source of morals. To prove this, it will be proper to weigh the five following considerations.

I. It is easy for a false hypothesis to maintain some appearance of truth, while it keeps wholly in generals, makes use of undefined terms, and employs comparisons, instead of instances. This is particularly remarkable in that philosophy, which ascribes the discernment of all moral distinctions to reason alone, without the concurrence of sentiment. It is impossible that, in any particular instance, this hypothesis can so much as be rendered intelligible, whatever specious figure it may make in general declamations and discourses. Examine the crime of *ingratitude,* for instance, which has place, wherever we observe good-will, expressed and known, together with good-offices performed, on the one side, and a return of ill-will or indifference, with ill-offices or neglect on the other: anatomize all these circumstances, and examine, by your reason alone, in what consists the demerit or blame. You never will come to any issue or conclusion.

Reason judges either of *matter of fact* or of *relations.* Enquire then, *first,* where is that matter of fact which we here call *crime;* point it out; determine the time of its existence; describe its essence or nature; explain the sense or faculty to which it discovers itself. It resides in the mind of the person who is ungrateful. He must, therefore, feel it, and be conscious of it. But nothing is there, except the passion of ill-will or absolute indifference. You cannot say that these, of themselves, always, and in all circumstances, are crimes. No, they are only crimes when directed towards persons who have before expressed and displayed good-will towards us. Consequently, we may infer, that the crime of ingratitude is not any particular individual *fact;* but arises from a complication of circumstances, which, being presented to the spectator, excites the *sentiment* of blame, by the particular structure and fabric of his mind.

This representation, you say, is false. Crime, indeed, consists not in a particular *fact,* of whose reality we are assured by *reason;* but it consists in certain *moral relations,* discovered by reason, in the same manner as we discover by reason the truths of geometry or algebra. But what are the relations, I ask, of which you here talk? In the case stated above, I see first good-will and good-offices in one person; then ill-will and ill-offices in the other. Between these, there is a relation of *contrariety.* Does the crime consist in that relation? But suppose a person bore me ill-will or did me ill-offices; and I, in return, were indifferent towards him, or did him good-offices. Here is the same relation of *contrariety;* and yet my conduct is often highly laudable. Twist and turn this matter as much as you will, you can never rest the morality on relation; but must have recourse to the decisions of sentiment.

When it is affirmed that two and three are equal to the half of ten, this relation of equality I understand perfectly. I conceive, that if ten be divided into two parts, of which one has as many units as the other; and if any of these parts be compared to two added to three, it will contain as many units as that compound number. But when you draw thence a comparison to moral relations, I own that I am altogether at a loss to understand you. A moral action, a crime, such as ingratitude, is a complicated object. Does the morality consist in the relation of its parts to each other? How? After what manner? Specify the relation: be more particular and explicit in your propositions, and you will easily see their falsehood.

No, say you, the morality consists in the relation of actions to the rule of right; and they are denominated good or ill, according as they agree or disagree with it. What then is this rule of right? In what does it consist? How is it determined? By reason, you say, which examines the moral relations of actions. So that moral relations are determined by the comparison of action to a rule. And that rule is determined by considering the moral relations of objects. Is not this fine reasoning?

All this is metaphysics, you cry. That is enough; there needs nothing more to give a strong presumption of falsehood. Yes, reply I, here are metaphysics surely; but they are all on your side, who advance on abstruse hypothesis, which can never be made intelligible, nor quadrate with any particular instance or illustration. The hypothesis which we embrace is plain. It maintains that morality is determined by sentiment. It defines virtue to be *whatever mental action or quality gives to a spectator the pleasing sentiment of approbation;*

and vice the contrary. We then proceed to examine a plain matter of fact, to wit, what actions have this influence. We consider all the circumstances in which these actions agree, and thence endeavour to extract some general observations with regard to these sentiments. If you call this metaphysics, and find anything abstruse here, you need only conclude that your turn of mind is not suited to the moral sciences.

II. When a man, at any time, deliberates concerning his own conduct (as, whether he had better, in a particular emergency, assist a brother or a benefactor), he must consider these separate relations, with all the circumstances and situations of the persons, in order to determine the superior duty and obligation; and in order to determine the proportion of lines in any triangle, it is necessary to examine the nature of that figure, and the relation which its several parts bear to each other. But notwithstanding this appearing similarity in the two cases, there is, at bottom, an extreme difference between them. A speculative reasoner concerning triangles or circles considers the several known and given relations of the parts of these figures, and thence infers some unknown relation, which is dependent on the former. But in moral deliberations we must be acquainted beforehand with all the objects, and all their relations to each other; and from a comparison of the whole, fix our choice or approbation. No new fact to be ascertained; no new relation to be discovered. All the circumstances of the case are supposed to be laid before us, ere we can fix any sentence of blame or approbation. If any material circumstance be yet unknown or doubtful, we must first employ our inquiry or intellectual faculties to assure us of it; and must suspend for a time all moral decision or sentiment. While we are ignorant whether a man were aggressor or not, how can we determine whether the person who killed him be criminal or innocent? But after every circumstance, every relation is known, the understanding has no further room to operate, nor any object on which it could employ itself. The approbation or blame which then ensues, cannot be the work of the judgement, but of the heart; and is not a speculative proposition or affirmation, but an active feeling or sentiment. In the disquisitions of the understanding, from known circumstances and relations, we infer some new and unknown. In moral decisions, all the circumstances and relations must be previously known; and the mind, from the contemplation of the whole, feels some new impression of affection or disgust, esteem or contempt, approbation or blame.

Hence the great difference between a mistake of *fact* and one of *right;* and hence the reason why the one is commonly criminal and not the other. When Oedipus killed Laius, he was ignorant of the relation, and from circumstances, innocent and involuntary, formed erroneous opinions concerning the action

which he committed. But when Nero killed Agrippina, all the relations between himself and the person, and all the circumstances of the fact, were
previously known to him; but the motive of revenge, or fear, or interest,
prevailed in his savage heart over the sentiments of duty and humanity. And
when we express that detestation against him to which he himself, in a little
time, became insensible, it is not that we see any relations, of which he was
ignorant; but that, for the rectitude of our disposition, we feel sentiments
against which he was hardened from flattery and a long perseverance in the
most enormous crimes. In these sentiments then, not in a discovery of relations
of any kind, do all moral determination consist. Before we can pretend to
form any decision of this kind, everything must be known and ascertained on
the side of the object or action. Nothing remains but to feel, on our part, some
sentiment of blame or approbation; whence we pronounce the action criminal or virtuous.

III. This doctrine will become still more evident, if we compare moral
beauty with natural, to which in many particulars it bears so near a resemblance.
It is on the proportion, relation, and position of parts, that all natural beauty
depends; but it would be absurd thence to infer, that the perception of beauty,
like that of truth in geometrical problems, consists wholly in the perception of
relations, and was performed entirely by the understanding or intellectual
faculties. In all the sciences, our mind from the known relations investigates
the unknown. But in all decisions of taste or external beauty, all the relations
are beforehand obvious to the eye; and we thence proceed to feel a sentiment
of complacency or disgust, according to the nature of the object, and disposition of our organs.

Euclid has fully explained all the qualities of the circle; but has not in any
proposition said a word of its beauty. The reason is evident. The beauty is not
a quality of the circle. It lies not in any part of the line, whose parts are
equally distant from a common centre. It is only the effect which that figure
produces upon the mind, whose peculiar fabric of structure renders it susceptible of such sentiments. In vain would you look for it in the circle, or seek it,
either by your senses or by mathematical reasoning, in all the properties of
that figure.

Attend to Palladio and Perrault, while they explain all the parts and proportions of a pillar. They talk of the cornice, and frieze, and base, and entablature
and shaft and architrave; and give the description and position of each of these
members. But should you asked the description and position of its beauty, they
would readily reply, that the beauty is not in any of the parts or members
of a pillar, but results from the whole, when that complicated figure is presented to an intelligent mind, susceptible to those finer sensations. Till such

a spectator appear, there is nothing but a figure of such particular dimensions and proportions: from his sentiments alone arise its elegance and beauty.

Again; attend to Cicero, while he paints the crimes of a Verres or a Catiline. You must acknowledge that the moral turpitude results, in the same manner, from the contemplation of the whole, when presented to a being whose organs have such a particular structure and formation. The orator may paint rage, insolence, barbarity on the one side; meekness, suffering, sorrow, innocence on the other. But if you feel no indignation or compassion arise in you from this complication of circumstances, you would in vain ask him, in what consists the crime or villainy, which he so vehemently exclaims against? At what time, or on what subject it first began to exist? And what has a few months afterwards become of it, when every disposition and thought of all the actors is totally altered or annihilated? No satisfactory answer can be given to any of these questions, upon the abstract hypothesis of morals; and we must at last acknowledge, that the crime or immorality is no particular fact or relation, which can be the object of the understanding, but arises entirely from the sentiment of disapprobation, which, by the structure of human nature, we unavoidably feel on the apprehension of barbarity or treachery.

IV. Inanimate objects may bear to each other all the same relations which we observe in moral agents; though the former can never be the object of love or hatred, nor are consequently susceptible of merit or iniquity. A young tree, which over-tops and destroys its parent, stands in all the same relations with Nero, when he murdered Agrippina; and if morality consisted merely in relations, would no doubt be equally criminal.

V. It appears evident that the ultimate ends of human actions can never, in any case, be accounted for by *reason,* but recommend themselves entirely to the sentiments and affections of mankind, without any dependence on the intellectual faculties. Ask a man *why he uses exercise;* he will answer, *because he desires to keep his health.* If you then enquire, *why he desires health,* he will readily reply, *because sickness is painful.* If you push your enquiries farther, and desire a reason *why he hates pain,* it is impossible he can ever give any. This is an ultimate end, and is never referred to any other object.

Perhaps to your second question, *why he desires health,* he may also reply, that *it is necessary for the exercise of his calling.* If you ask, *why he is anxious on that head,* he will answer, *because he desires to get money.* If you demand *Why? It is the instrument of pleasure,* says he. And beyond this is an absurdity to ask for a reason. It is impossible there can be a progress *in infinitum;* and that one thing can always be a reason why another is desired. Something must be desirable on its own account, and because of its immediate accord or agreement with human sentiment and affection.

Now as virtue is an end, and is desirable on its own account, without fee and reward, merely for the immediate satisfaction which it conveys; it is requisite that there should be some sentiment which it touches, some internal taste or feeling, or whatever you may please to call it, which distinguishes moral good and evil, and which embraces the one and rejects the other.

Thus the distinct boundaries and offices of *reason* and of *taste* are easily ascertained. The former conveys the knowledge of truth and falsehood: the latter gives the sentiment of beauty and deformity, vice and virtue. The one discovers objects as they really stand in nature, without addition or diminution: the other has a productive faculty, and gilding or staining all natural objects with the colours, borrowed from internal sentiment, raises in a manner a new creation. Reason being cool and disengaged, is no motive to action, and directs only the impulse received from appetite or inclination, by showing us the means of attaining happiness or avoiding misery: Taste, as it gives pleasure or pain, and thereby constitutes happiness or misery, becomes a motive to action, and is the first spring or impulse to desire and volition. From circumstances and relations, known or supposed, the former leads us to the discovery of the concealed and unknown: after all circumstances and relations are laid before us, the latter makes us feel from the whole a new sentiment of blame or approbation. The standard of the one, being founded on the nature of things, is eternal and inflexible, even by the will of the Supreme Being: the standard of the other, arising from the eternal frame and constitution of animals, is ultimately derived from that Supreme Will, which bestowed on each being its peculiar nature, and arranged the several classes and orders of existence.

IMMANUEL KANT

IT IS OFTEN SAID that most modern ethical theories derive either from David Hume or Immanuel Kant. As formal moral philosophers Hume and Kant had little direct effect on the diverse movements of opinion that are called the Enlightenment. Yet their ethics are probably the most impressive achievements of the eighteenth-century philosophers.

Hume had tried to demonstrate that ethical systems were ultimately some expression, however subtle and special, of human feelings and sentiments and that they could be justified for the individual only as satisfactions of what he called "the sentiment of humanity."

Important parts of Kant's theory of ethics can be construed as attempts to answer Hume by demonstrating that an adequate account of how men come to have moral rules and of the effect rules have in satisfying individual or social needs does not establish a sufficient test of the rightness of the rules. In what way then can men establish a test of the worth of an action independent of the pleasures or satisfaction they may take from suggesting or doing what seems right?

The selections below are key passages from Kant's *Fundamental Principles of the Metaphysic of Morals* and are based, with some corrections, on Semple's translation from the German (Edinburgh, 1836).

FUNDAMENTAL PRINCIPLES OF THE
METAPHYSIC OF MORALS

TRANSITION FROM THE COMMON RATIONAL KNOWLEDGE OF MORALITY TO THE PHILOSOPHICAL

Nothing can possibly be conceived in the world, or even out of it, which can be called good without qualification, except a GOOD WILL. Intelligence, wit, judgment, and the other *talents* of the mind, however they may be named, or courage, resolution, perseverance, as qualities of temperament, are undoubtedly good and desirable in many respects. But these gifts of nature may also become extremely bad and mischievous if the will which is to make use of these gifts, and which therefore constitutes what is called *character,* is not good. It is the same with the *gifts of fortune.* Power, riches, honor, even health, and the general well-being and contentment with one's condition which is called *happiness,* inspire pride and often presumption if there is not a good will to correct the influence of these things on the mind, and with this to rectify also the whole principle of acting and adapt it to its end. . . .

A good will is good not because of what it performs or effects, nor by its aptness for attaining some proposed end, but simply by virtue of the volition; that is, it is good in itself and when considered by itself is to be esteemed much higher than all that it can bring about in pursuing any inclination, nay even in pursuing the sum total of all inclinations. It might happen that, owing to special misfortune, or to the niggardly provision of a step-motherly nature, this will should wholly lack power to accomplish its purpose. If with its greatest efforts this will should yet achieve nothing and there should remain only good will (to be sure, not a mere wish but the summoning of all means in our power), then, like a jewel, good will would still shine by its own light as a thing having its whole value in itself. Its usefulness or fruitlessness can neither add to nor detract anything from this value. . . .

We assume, as a fundamental principle, that no organ [designed] for any purpose will be found in the physical constitution of an organized being, except one which is also the fittest and best adapted for that purpose. Now if the proper object of nature for a being with reason and a will was its *preservation,* its *welfare,* in a word its happiness, then nature would have hit upon a very bad arrangement when it selected the reason of the creature to carry out this function. For all the actions which the creature has to perform with a view to this purpose, and the whole rule of its conduct would be far more surely prescribed by [its own] instinct, and that end [happiness] would have been attained by instinct far more certainly than it ever can be by reason. Should reason have been attributed to this favored creature over and above [such instinct], reason would only have served this creature for contemplating the happy constitution of its nature, for admiring it and congratulating itself thereon, and for feeling thankful for it to the beneficent cause. But [certainly nature would not have arranged it so that] such a creature should subject its desires to that weak and deceptive guidance, and meddle with nature's intent. In a word, nature would have taken care that reason should not turn into *practical* exercise, nor have the presumption, with its feeble insight, to figure out for itself a plan of happiness and the means for attaining it. In fact, we find that the more cultivated reason applies itself with deliberate purpose to enjoying life and happiness, so much more does the man lack true satisfaction. From this circumstance there arises in many men, if they are candid enough to confess it, a certain degree of *misology;* that is, hatred of reason, especially in the case of those who are most experienced in the use of reason. For, after calculating all the advantages they derive, not only from the invention of all the arts of common luxury, but even from the sciences (which then seem to them only a luxury of the intellect after all) they find that they have actually only brought more trouble upon themselves, rather than gaining in happiness. They end by envying, rather than despising, the common run of men who keep closer to the guidance of mere instinct and who do not allow their reason to have much influence on their conduct. We must admit this much; that the judgment of those, who would diminish very much the lofty eulogies on the advantages which reason gives us in regard to the happiness and satisfaction of life, or would even deny these advantages altogether, is by no means morose or ungrateful for the goodness with which the world is governed. At the root of these judgments lies the idea that the existence of world order has a different and far nobler end for which, rather than for happiness, reason is properly intended. Therefore this end must be regarded as the supreme condition to which the private ends of man must yield for the most part. . . .

Nay, it may even reduce happiness to nothing without nature failing thereby in her purpose. For reason recognizes the establishment of a good will as its highest practical destination, and is capable of only satisfying its own proper kind in attaining this purpose: the attainment of an end determined only by reason, even when such an attainment may involve many a disappointment over otherwise desirable purposes. . . .

To be beneficent when we can is a duty; besides this, there are many minds so sympathetically constituted that without any other motive of vanity or self-interest, they find a pleasure in spreading joy [about them] and can take delight in the satisfaction of others so far as it is their own work. But I maintain that in such a case, however proper, however amiable an action of this kind may be, it nevertheless has no true moral worth, but is on a level with other inclinations; e.g. the inclination to honor which, if it is happily directed to that which is actually of public utility and accordant with duty and consequently honorable, deserves praise and encouragement but not respect. For the maxim lacks the moral ingredient that such actions be done *out of duty,* not from inclination. Put the case [another way and suppose] that the mind of that philanthropist were clouded by sorrow of his own, extinguishing all sympathy with the lot of others, and that while he still has the power to benefit others in distress he is not touched by their trouble because he is absorbed with his own; suppose that he now tears himself out of this deadening insensibility, and performs the action without any inclination for it, but simply from duty; only then has his action genuine moral worth. Furthermore, if nature has put little sympathy into the heart of this or that man, if a supposedly upright man is by temperament cold and indifferent to the sufferings of others, perhaps because in respect of his own sufferings he is provided with the special gift of patience and fortitude so that he supposes or even requires that others should have the same; such a man would certainly not be the meanest product of nature. But if nature had not specially shaped him to be a philanthropist, would he not find cause in himself for attributing to himself a value far higher than the value of a good-natured temperament could be? Unquestionably. It is just in this that there is brought out the moral worth of the character which is incomparably the highest of all; namely, that he is beneficent, not from inclination, but from duty. . . .

The second proposition is: That an action done from duty derives its moral worth, *not from the purpose* which is to be attained by it, but from the maxim by which it is determined. Therefore the action does not depend on the realization of its objective, but merely on the *principle* of volition by which the action has taken place, without regard to any object of desire. . . .

The third proposition, which is a consequence of the preceding two, I would express thus: *Duty is the necessity of an action, resulting from respect for the law.* I may have an *inclination* for an object as the effect of my proposed action, but I cannot have *respect* for an object just for this reason: that it is merely an effect and not an action of will. Similarly, I cannot have respect for an inclination, whether my own or another's; I can at most, if it is my own, approve it; if it is another's I can sometimes even cherish it; that is, look on it as favorable to my own interest. Only the law itself which is connected with my will by no means as an effect but as a principle which does not serve my inclination but outweighs it, or at least in case of choice excludes my inclination from its calculation; only such a law can be an object of respect and hence a command. Now an action done from duty must wholly exclude the influence of inclination, and with it every object of the will, so that nothing remains which can determine the will objectively except the *law,* and [determine the will] subjectively except *pure respect* for this practical law, and hence [pure respect] for the maxim [1] to follow this law even to the thwarting of all my inclinations.

Thus the moral worth of an action does not consist of the effect expected from it, nor from any principle of action which needs to borrow its motive from this expected effect. . . . Therefore the pre-eminent good which we

---

[1] A maxim is the subjective principle of volition. The objective principle, that is, what would also serve all rational beings subjectively as a practical principle if reason had full power over desire; this objective principle is the practical *law.*

call moral can consist in nothing other than the *concept of law* in itself, *which is certainly only possible in a rational being,* in so far as this conception, and not the expected effect, determines the will. . . .

But what sort of law can it be the conception of which must determine the will, even without our paying any attention to the effect expected from it, in order that this will may be called good absolutely and without qualification? As I have stripped the will of every impulse which could arise from it from obedience to any law, there remains nothing but the general conformity of the will's actions to law in general. Only this conformity to law is to serve the will as a principle; that is, I am never to act in any way other than *so I could want my maxim also to become a general law.* It is the simple conformity to law in general, without assuming any particular law applicable to certain actions, that serves the will as its principle, and must so serve it, if duty is not to be a vain delusion and a chimerical notion. The common reason of men in their practical judgments agrees perfectly with this and always has in view the principle suggested here. For example, let the question be: When in distress may I make a promise with the intention of not keeping it? I readily distinguish here between the two meanings which the question may have: Whether it is prudent, or whether it is in accordance with duty, to make a false promise. The former undoubtedly may often be the case. I [may] see clearly that it is not enough to extricate myself from a present difficulty by means of this subterfuge, but that it must be carefully considered whether there may not result from such a lie a much greater inconvenience than that from which I am now freeing myself. But, since in spite of all my supposed *cunning* the consequences cannot be foreseen easily; the loss of credit may be much more injurious to me than any mischief which I seek to avoid at present. That being the case, one might consider whether it would not be more *prudent* to act according to a general maxim, and make it a habit to give no promise except with the intention of keeping it. But, it is soon clear that such a maxim is still only based on the fear of consequences. It is a wholly different thing to be truthful from a sense of duty, than to be so from apprehension of injurious consequences. In the first case, the very conceiving of the action already implies a law for me; in the second case, I must first look about elsewhere to see what results may be associated with it which would affect me. For it is beyond all doubt wicked to deviate from the principle of duty; but to be unfaithful to my maxim of prudence may often be very advantageous to me, although it is certainly wiser to abide by it. However, the shortest way, and an unerring one, to discover the answer to this question of whether a lying promise is consistent with duty, is to ask myself, "Would I be content if this maxim of extricating myself from difficulty by a false promise held good as a general law for others as well as for myself?" Would I care to say to myself, "Everyone may make a deceitful promise when he finds himself in a difficulty from which he cannot extricate himself otherwise"? Then I would presently become aware that while I can decide in favor of the lie, I can by no means decide that lying should be a general law. For under such a law there would be no promises at all, since I would state my intentions in vain in regard to my future actions to those who would not believe my allegation, or, if they did so too hastily, they would pay me back in my own coin. Hence, as soon as such a maxim was made a universal law, it would necessarily destroy itself. . . .

Thus we have arrived at the principle of moral knowledge of common human reason. Although common men no doubt do not conceive this principle in such an abstract and universal form, yet they really always have it before their eyes and use it as the standard for their decision. It would be easy to show here how, with this compass in hand, men are well able to distinguish, in every case that occurs, what is good, bad, conformable to duty or inconsistent with it. Without teaching them anything at all new, we are only, like Socrates, directing their attention to the principle they employ themselves and [showing] that we therefore do not need science and philosophy to know what we should do to be honest and good and even wise and virtuous. Indeed, we might well have understood before that the knowledge of what every man ought to do, and hence also [what he ought] to know is within the reach of every man, even the commonest. . . .

Innocence is indeed a glorious thing, only it is a pity that it cannot maintain itself well and is easily seduced. On this account even wisdom, which otherwise consists more in conduct than in knowledge, yet has need of science, not in order to learn from it, but to secure for its own precepts acceptance and permanence. In opposition to all the commands of duty that reason represents to man as so greatly deserving respect, man feels within himself a powerful counterpoise in his wants and inclinations, the entire satisfaction of which he sums up under the name of happiness. Reason issues its commands unyieldingly, without promising anything to the inclinations and with disregard and contempt, as it were, for these demands which are so impetuous and at the same time so plausible and which will not allow themselves to be suppressed by any command. Hence there arises a natural *dialectic;* that is, a disposition to argue against these strict laws of duty and to question their validity, or at least to question their purity and strictness. [There is also a disposition] to make them more accordant, if possible, with our wishes and inclinations; that is to say, to corrupt them at their very source and to destroy their value entirely, an act that even common practical reason cannot ultimately approve.

Thus the *common reason of man* is compelled to leave its proper sphere and to take a step into the field of a *practical philosophy,* but not for satisfying any desire to speculate, which never occurs to it as long as it is content to be mere sound reason. But the purpose is to secure on practical grounds information and clear instruction respecting the source of the principle [of common sense] and the correct definition of this principle as contrasted with the maxims which are based on wants and inclinations, so that common sense may escape from the perplexity of opposing claims, and not run the risk of losing all genuine moral principles through the equivocation into which it easily falls.

TRANSITION FROM POPULAR MORAL PHILOSOPHY TO THE METAPHYSIC OF MORALS

If hitherto we have drawn our concept of duty from the common use of our practical reason it is by no means to be inferred that we have treated it as an empirical concept. On the contrary, if we attend to the experience of men's conduct, we meet frequent and, as we admit ourselves, just complaints that there is not to be found a single certain example of the disposition to act from pure duty. Although many things are done *in conformity* to what duty prescribes, it is nevertheless always doubtful whether they are done strictly *out of duty* [which would have to be the case if they are to have a moral value]. Hence, in all ages there have been philosophers who have denied altogether that this disposition actually exists in human actions at all, and who have ascribed everything to a more or less refined self-love. Not that they have on that account questioned the soundness of the conception of morality; on the contrary they have spoken with sincere regret of the frailty and corruption of human nature, which though noble enough to take as its law an idea so worthy of respect, is yet too weak to follow it, and employs reason, which ought to give it the law, only for the purpose of accommodating the inclinations, whether single, or, at best, in the greatest possible harmony with one another. In fact it is absolutely impossible to ascertain by experience with complete certainty a single case in which the maxim of an action, however right in itself, rested simply on moral grounds and on the conception of duty. Sometimes it happens that with the sharpest self-examination, we can find nothing, besides the moral principle of duty, powerful enough to move us to this or that action and to such a great sacrifice; yet we cannot infer from this with certainty that it was not some really secret impulse of self-love, under the false appearance of that idea [of the moral principle of duty] that was the actual determining cause of the will. We then like to flatter ourselves by falsely taking credit for a more noble motive. In fact we can never, even by the strictest self-examination, penetrate completely [to the causes] behind the secret springs of action, since when we ask about moral worth, we are not concerned with actions but with their inward principles which we do not see. . . .

Moral concepts cannot be obtained by abstraction from any empirical and hence merely contingent knowledge. It is exactly this purity in origin that makes them worthy of serving our supreme practical principle [for right action] and, as we add anything empirical, we detract in proportion from their genuine influence and from the absolute value of actions. It is not only very necessary from a purely speculative point of view, but it is also of the greatest practical importance to derive these notions and laws from pure reason, to present them pure and unmixed, and even to determine the compass of this practical or pure rational knowledge; that is, to determine the entire faculty of pure practical reason. In doing so we must not make the principles of pure practical reason dependent on the particular nature of human reason, though in speculative philosophy this may be permitted and even necessary at times. Since moral laws ought to hold true for every rational creature we must derive them from the general concept of a rational being. Although morality has need of anthropology for its application to man, yet in this way, as in the first step, we must treat morality independently as pure philosophy; that is, metaphysics, complete in itself. . . .

Everything in nature works according to laws. Rational beings alone have the faculty for acting according to *the concept* of laws; that is, according to principles. [In other words, rational beings alone] have a will. Since deriving actions from principles requires *reason,* the will is nothing more than practical reason. If reason infallibly determines the will, then the actions of such a being that are recognized as objectively necessary are also subjectively necessary. The will is a faculty for choosing *only that* which reason, independently of inclination, recognizes as practically necessary; that is, as good. But if reason does not sufficiently determine the will by itself, if the latter is also subject to the subjective conditioning of particular impulses which do not always coincide with the objective conditions; in a word, if the will *in itself* does not completely accord with reason, as is actually the case with men, then the actions which are objectively recognized as necessary are subjectively contingent. Determining such a will according to objective laws is compulsory (Nötigung). This means that the relation of objective laws to a will not thoroughly good is conceived as the determination of the will of a rational being by principles of reason which the will, because of its nature, does not necessarily follow.

The concept of an objective principle, in so far as it is compulsory for a will, is called a command of reason and the formulation of such a command is called an IMPERATIVE. . . .

Consequently no imperative holds true for the Divine will, or in general for a *holy* will. *Ought* is out of place here because the act of willing is already necessarily in unison with the law. Therefore imperatives are only formulations for expressing the relation of the objective laws of all volition to the subjective imperfections of the will of this or that rational being; that is, the human will.

All *imperatives* command either *hypothetically* or *categorically*. . . . Since every practical law represents a possible action as good, and on this account as necessary for a subject who can determine practically by reason, all imperatives are formulations determining an action which is necessary according to the principle of a will in some respects good. If the action is good only as a means to *something else,* then the imperative is *hypothetical.* If the action is conceived as good *in itself* and consequently as necessarily being the principle of a will which of itself conforms to reason then it is *categorical.* . . .

Whatever is possible through the ability of some rational being may also be considered as a possible purpose of some will. Therefore the principles of action concerning the means needed to attain some possible purpose are really infinitely numerous. All sciences have a practical aspect consisting of problems expressing that some end is possible for us, and of imperatives directing how it may be attained. Therefore, these may, in general, be called imperatives of *skill*. There is no question as to whether the end is rational and good, but only as to what one must do in order to attain it. The precepts for the physician to make his patient thoroughly healthy, and for a poisoner to ensure certain death, are equivalent in that each serves to effect its purpose perfectly. Since in early youth it cannot be known what purposes are likely to occur to us in the course of life, parents seek to have their children taught a *great many things* and provide for their *skill* in using means for all sorts of purposes. They cannot be sure whether any particular purpose may perhaps hereafter be an objective for their pupil; it is possible that he might aim at any of them. This anxiety is so great that parents commonly neglect to form and correct their judgment on the value of the things which may be chosen as ends.

However there is *one* end which may actually be assumed to be an end for all rational beings, there is one purpose which they not only *may* have, but which we may assume with certainty that they all actually *do have* by natural necessity; that is *happiness*. The hypothetical imperative expressing the practical necessity of an action as a means for the advancement of happiness is assertorial. We are not presenting it as necessary for an uncertain and merely possible purpose, but for a purpose which we may presuppose with certainty and *a priori* for every man, because it belongs to his being. Now a man's skill in choosing the means to his own greatest well-being may be called *prudence* in the most specific sense. Thus the imperative which refers to the choice of means to one's own happiness, that is, the precept of prudence, is still hypothetical. The action is not commanded absolutely but only as a means to another purpose. Whereas, the categorical imperative directly commands a certain conduct without being conditioned by any other attainable purpose. . . . This imperative may be called the imperative of morality. . . .

The question now arises: How are all these imperatives possible? This question is to ascertain, not how the action commanded by the imperative can be carried out, but merely how the compulsion of will expressed by the imperative can be conceived. I should think that no special explanation is needed to show how an imperative related to skill is possible. Whoever wills the end, also wills, as far as reason decisively influences his conduct, the means in his power which are indispensable for achieving this end. This proposition is analytical in regard to the volition. For, in willing an object as an effect, there is already implied therein that I myself am acting as a cause, that is, I make use of the means. From the concept of the willed end, the imperative derives the concept of the actions necessary for achieving this end. . . .

If it were equally easy to give a definite concept of happiness [as of simpler ends], the imperatives of prudence would correspond exactly with those of skill, and would likewise be analytical. It could then be said that whoever wills the end also wills the indispensable means thereto which are in his power. But unfortunately the notion of happiness is so indefinite that although every man wishes to attain it, he never can say definitely and consistently what it is that he really wishes and wills. The reason is that the elements belonging to the notion of happiness are altogether empirical; that is, they must be borrowed from experience. Nevertheless, the idea of happiness implies something absolute and whole; a maximum of well-being in my present and all future circumstances. Now, it is impossible for even the most clear-sighted and most powerful being, as long as it is sup-

posedly finite, to frame for itself a definite concept of what it really wills
[when it wants to be happy]. If he wills riches, how much anxiety, envy,
and snares might not be drawn upon his shoulders thereby? If he wills
knowledge and discernment, perhaps such knowledge might only prove to
be so much sharper sight showing him much more fearfully the unavoidable evils now concealed from him, or suggesting more wants for his desires
which already give him concern enough. If he should will a long life,
who can guarantee him that it will not be a long misery? If he should at
least have health, how often has infirmity of the body restrained a man from
excesses into which perfect health would have allowed him to fall? And
so on. In short, a human being is unable with certainty to determine by
any principle what would make him truly happy, because to do so he
would have to be omniscient. Therefore, we cannot act on any definite
principles to secure happiness, but only on counsels derived from experience; e.g., the frugality, courtesy, reserve, etc., which experience teaches
us will promote well-being, for the most part. Hence it follows that the
imperatives of prudence do not command at all, strictly speaking; that is,
they cannot present actions objectively as practically *necessary,* so that
they are to be regarded as *counsels* (*consilia*) or reason rather than precepts
(*praecepta*). The problem of determining certainly and generally which
action would most promote the happiness of a rational being is completely
insoluble. Consequently, no imperative respecting happiness is possible, for
such a command should, in a strict sense, command men to do what makes
them happy. Happiness is an ideal, not of reason, but of imagination resting
solely on empirical grounds. It is vain to expect that these grounds should
define an action for attaining the totality of a series of consequences that
are really endless. However, this imperative of prudence could be an analytical proposition if we assume that the means to happiness could, with certainty, be assigned. For, this imperative is distinguished from the imperative
of skill only by this; in the latter the end is merely possible [and available
to be chosen]; in the former the end is given. However, both only prescribe
the means to an end which we assume to have been willed. It follows
that the imperative which calls for the willing of the means by him who
wills the end is analytical in both cases. Thus there is no difficulty in regard
to the possibility of this kind of imperative either.

On the other hand, the question of how the imperative of *morality* is
possible is undoubtedly the only question demanding a solution as this
imperative is not at all hypothetical, and the objective necessity it presents
cannot rest on any hypothesis, as is the case with hypothetical imperatives.
Only we must never leave out of consideration the fact that we *cannot*

determine *by any example,* i.e., empirically, whether there is any such imperative at all. Rather it is to be feared that all those apparently categorical imperatives may actually be hypothetical. For instance, when you have a precept such as: thou shalt not promise deceitfully, and it is assumed that the [normative] necessity of this is not a mere counsel to avoid some other evil, [in which case] it might mean: you shall not make a lying promise lest it become known and your credit would be destroyed. On the contrary, an action of this kind should be regarded as evil in itself so that the imperative of the prohibition is categorical. Yet we cannot show with certainty in any instance that the will is determined merely by the law without any other source of action, although this may appear to be so. It is always possible that fear of disgrace, also perhaps obscure dread of other dangers, may have a secret influence on the will. Who can prove by experience the non-existence of a cause when all that experience tells us is that we do not perceive it? In such a case the so-called moral imperative, which appears to be categorical and unconditional, would really only be a pragmatic precept, drawing our attention to our own interests, and merely teaching us to take these interests into consideration.

Therefore we shall have to investigate *a priori* the possibility of a *categorical* imperative, since, in this case, we do not have the advantage that the imperative's reality is given in experience, so that the elucidation of its possibility would be needed only for explaining it, not for establishing it. It can be discerned that the categorical imperative has the purport of a practical law. All the rest may certainly be called *principles* of the will but not laws, since whatever is merely necessary for attaining some casual purpose may be considered contingent in itself, and at any time we can be free from the precept if we give up the purpose. However, the unconditional command leaves the will no liberty to choose the opposite, and consequently only the will carries with it that necessity we require in a law. . . .

When I conceive of a hypothetical imperative at all, I do not know previously what it will contain until I am given the condition. But when I conceive of a categorical imperative I know at once what it contains. In addition to the law, the imperative contains only the necessity that the maxim conform to this law. As the maxim contains no condition restricting the maxim, nothing remains but the general statement of the law to which the maxim of the action should conform, and it is only this conformity that the imperative properly represents as necessary.

Therefore there is only one categorical imperative, namely this: *Act only on a maxim by which you can will that it, at the same time, should become a general law.* . . .

If we now watch ourselves for any transgression of duty, we shall find that we actually do not will that our maxim should be a general law in such cases. On the contrary, we will that the opposite should remain a general law. We merely take the liberty of making an *exception* in our own favor or (just for this time) in favor of our inclination. Consequently, if we considered all cases from the point of view of reason, we should find a contradiction in our own will; namely, that a certain principle is objectively necessary as a general law and yet is subjectively not general but has exceptions. In regarding our action on the one hand from the point of view of a will wholly conformed to reason, and on the other hand looking at the same action from the point of view of a will affected by inclination, there is really no contradiction but an antagonism on the part of inclination to the precept of reason which turns the universality of the principle into a mere generality, so that the principle of practical reason can meet the maxim half way. . . .

However, we cannot yet prove *a priori* that such an imperative actually exists; that there is a practical law which commands absolutely by itself and without any other impulse and that compliance with this law is duty. . . .

However, supposing that there were something *whose existence* was *in itself* of absolute value, something which, as an *end in itself,* could be a ground for definite laws, then this end and it alone, would be the ground for a possible categorical imperative, i.e., a practical law. Now I say that man, and generally every rational being, *exists* as an end in himself, *not merely as a means* for the arbitrary use of this or that will; he must always be regarded as an end in all his actions whether aimed at himself or at other rational beings. All objects of the inclinations have only a conditional value, since, but for the inclinations and their respective wants, their object would be without value. But the inclinations themselves, being sources of want, are so far from having an absolute value that instead of relishing them it must rather be the general wish of every rational being to be wholly free from them. Hence the value of any object which *can be acquired* by our action is always conditional. Beings whose existence depends not on our will but on nature have, nevertheless, if they are irrational beings, only a relative value as means and are therefore called *things;* rational beings, on the other hand, are called *persons.* Their very nature constitutes them as ends in themselves; that is, as something which must not be used merely as means. To that extent, a person is limiting freedom of action and is an object of respect. Therefore persons are not merely subjective ends whose existence is an end for us as the result of our action, but they are objective ends; that is, things whose existence in itself is an end. No other end can be substituted (as a justification) for such an end, making it *merely* serve as a means, because otherwise nothing whatever could be found that would possess *absolute value*. If all values were conditional and therefore contingent, reason would have no supreme practical principle whatever. . . .

This principle of man, and any rational creature, being *an end in itself,* which is the main limiting condition of every man's freedom of action, is not taken from experience for two reasons. First, its universal character, applying as it does to all rational beings whatever, is a fact which no experience can determine; second, because this principle does not present humanity as a subjective end of men; that is, as an object which actually we set ourselves as an end, but it [presents humanity as] an objective end which, whatever [subjective] ends we may have, is to constitute as a law the supreme limiting condition of all subjective ends. It must, therefore, derive from pure reason. In fact, according to the first principle, *the rule* and its universal character which enables [such legislation] to be some kind of law, for example, a law of nature, the *subjective* ground is the *end*. Since, according to the second principle the subject of all ends is some rational being, each being an end in itself, the third practical principle of the will follows as the ultimate prerequisite for the congruity [of will] with general practical reason; viz. the idea that *the will of every rational being is a will giving general laws.*

By virtue of this principle all maxims are rejected which cannot co-exist with the will as the general legislator. Thus the will is not being subjected simply to law, but is so subjected that it must be regarded as *giving itself the law,* and for this very reason is subject to the law of which it may consider itself the author. . . . Although a will *which is subject to laws* may be attached to such a law through interest, yet a will which is itself a supreme law-giver cannot possibly depend on any interest, since such a dependent will would still need another law which would restrict the interest of its self-love by the condition that it should be valid as general law. . . .

Looking back now on all previous efforts to discover the principle of morality, we need not wonder why they all failed. Man was seen to be bound to laws by duty, but no one realized that he is subject *only to his own general laws* and that he is only bound to act in conformity with his own will, a will designed by nature to make general laws. For, when man was conceived as being only subject to some kind of law, such a law had to be supplemented by some interest, by way either of attraction or of constraint, since it did not originate as a law from *his own* will. [In the absence of such autonomy of the will] the will was obliged by *something else* to act in some manner or other. Through this reasoning, as such entirely necessary, all labor spent in finding a supreme principle of *duty* was irrevocably lost. Its final conclusion was never that of duty, but only that of a necessity of acting from a certain interest, be it a personal or impersonal interest. The imperative had to turn out to be a conditional one and could not by any means serve as a moral command. I will therefore call this principle [of will based on no interest] the principle of *autonomy* of the will as contrasted with every other which I regard as *heteronomy*. . . .

Rational nature is distinguished from the rest of nature by setting itself an end. This end would be the content of every good will. But since the idea of an absolutely good will is not limited by any condition of attaining this or that end we must completely disregard every end *to be effected* which would make every will only relatively good. The end here must be understood to be not an end to be effected but an *independently existing end,* consequently only a negative one, i.e., one against which we must never act and therefore every act of willing must never be regarded merely as a means, but as an end as well. This end can be nothing but the subject of all possible ends, since it is also the subject of a possible absolutely good will; because such a will cannot be related to any other object without contradiction. The principle: So act toward every rational being (yourself and others), that he may for you always be an end in himself, is therefore essentially identical with this other: Act upon a maxim which is generally valid for every rational being. . . .

In this way an intelligible world (*mundus intelligibilis*) is possible as a realm of ends, by virtue of the lawmaking of all persons as members. . . . Such a realm of ends would be actually realized if maxims conforming to the canon of the categorical imperative for all rational beings *were universally followed*. But a rational being, though punctiliously following this maxim himself, cannot count upon all others being equally faithful to it, nor [can he be certain] that the realm of nature and its purposive design so accord with him as a proper member as to form a realm made possible by himself; that is, favoring his expectation of happiness. Still the law remains in full force: Act according to the maxims of a member of a merely possible realm of ends in making general law since this law commands categorically. Therein lies the paradox; that merely the dignity of man as a rational creature, in other words, respect for a mere idea, should serve as an inflexible precept without any other end or advantage. The sublime character [of this dignity] consists precisely in this independence of maxims from all such springs of action. This makes every rational subject worthy to be a law-making member of the realm of ends. Otherwise he would have to be imagined as subject only to the natural law of his wants. Although we would suppose the realm of nature and the realm of ends to be united under one ruler, so that the realm of ends thereby would no longer be a mere idea but acquire true reality, [such reality] would no doubt gain an additional strong incentive, but never any increase of its intrinsic value. For, this sole unlimited lawgiver must nonetheless always be conceived as evaluating the value of rational beings only by their disinterested behavior, as prescribed by the idea of the dignity of man alone. The essence of things is not altered by their external conditions and man must be judged by whatever constitutes his absolute value, irrespective of these [conditions], whoever be the judge, even it be the Supreme Being. . . .

Among the *rational* principles of morality, the ontological concept of *perfection,* in spite of its defects, is better than the theological concept which deduces morality from a Divine, absolutely perfect, will. The ontological concept is no doubt empty and indefinite and consequently useless for finding the highest degree [of perfection] in the boundless field of possible reality. Moreover, in attempting to distinguish specifically the reality of which we are now speaking from every other reality, it inevitably tends to go around in circles and cannot avoid presupposing tacitly the morality which this reality is to explain. Nevertheless it is better than the theological concept, not only because we cannot visualize (*anschauen*) the divine perfection and can only deduce it from our own concepts of which the most important is morality itself (and even then our explanation would involve a gross, roundabout, reasoning), but also because the remaining concept of a [divine] will, derived from the attributes of desire for glory and domination and combined with the terrible ideas of power and vengeance, would constitute the basis of a system or morals diametrically opposed to morality. . . .

TRANSITION FROM THE METAPHYSIC OF MORALS TO THE CRITIQUE OF PURE PRACTICAL REASON

The *will* is a kind of causality of living beings in so far as they are rational, and *freedom* should be that quality of this causality through which it can be an efficient cause independent of extraneous *determining* causes; just as *physical necessity* is the peculiar quality of the causality of all non-rational beings as impelled into activity by extraneous causes.

The above definition of freedom is *negative* and therefore unsuitable for understanding its essence; but it leads to a *positive* concept which is all the more ample and fruitful. Since the concept of causality implies that of law, according to which something called a cause produces something else called an effect, freedom, though not a quality of the will in so far as it depends on natural laws, is not for that reason without law, but must rather be a causality acting in accordance with immutable laws of a peculiar kind; otherwise free will would be an absurdity. Natural necessity is a heteronomy of efficient causes because every effect is possible only according to the law [of natural causality]: some [antecedent cause] determines the efficient cause to act causally. What else can freedom of the will be but autonomy; that is, the property of the will to be a law unto itself? But the proposition: the will is a law unto itself in every action, only expresses the principle of acting on no other maxim than that which can also aim to be a general law. This is precisely the formula of the categorical imperative and of the principle of ethics, so that a free will and a will subject to moral laws are one and the same. . . .

It is not enough to attribute freedom, for whatever reason, to our own will if we have not sufficient grounds for attributing the same to all rational beings. For, as morality serves us as a law only because we are *rational beings,* it must also hold true for all rational beings. As morality must be deduced simply from the quality of freedom, it must be shown that freedom is also a quality of all rational beings. It is not enough then to expound it as derived from certain supposed experiences of human nature (which indeed is quite impossible and can only be shown *a priori*), but we must prove that morality is part of the activity of any and all rational beings endowed with a will. Now I say that every being who cannot act except *under the idea of freedom* is, in practical respects, really free for just that reason. That is to say; all laws inseparably connected with freedom are as valid for this being as though his will had been shown to be free in itself and accepted by theoretical philosophy.[2] I assert that we must necessarily attribute to every rational being having a will the idea of freedom under which alone it acts. In such a being we conceive reason which is practical; that is, which acts causally in reference to its objects. We cannot possibly conceive reason consciously permitting any other quarter to direct its judgments, since then the subject would attribute the control of its judgment not to reason, but to an impulse. Reason must regard itself as the author of its principles independent of extraneous influences; consequently, it, as practical reason or as the will of a rational being, must regard itself as free. That is to say; the will [of such a being]

---

[2] I adopt this method of assuming that freedom, merely *as an idea* upon which alone rational beings base their actions, is sufficient for our purpose, in order to avoid the necessity of proving freedom in its theoretical aspect also. Even though the latter is not ascertained, a being that cannot act except under the idea of freedom is bound by the same laws as a being who is actually free. Thus we can escape here from the burden which weighs upon the theory.

cannot be a will of its own except under the idea of freedom. Therefore this idea must, practically speaking, be attributed to all rational beings. . . .

Therefore it seems as if moral law, that is, the principal of the autonomy of the will, were actually only presupposed in the idea of freedom and as if its reality and objective necessity could not be proved independently. Even then we would have gained considerably in at least determining the true principle more exactly than had previously been done. But in regard to the validity of the principle and the practical necessity of subjecting oneself to it, we would not have advanced a step. If we were asked why the universal validity of our maxim as a law must be the condition restricting our actions and on what we base the value we assign to this way of acting, a value so great that there can be no higher interest, [and if we were asked further] why by this alone a man believes to feel his own value compared with which a pleasant or unpleasant condition must be regarded as nothing, to these questions we could give no satisfactory answer.

It must be freely admitted that there appears a sort of circular reasoning here that seems impossible to escape. We assume ourselves to be free in the order of efficient causes so that we may conceive ourselves to be subject to moral laws in the order of ends. Then we consider ourselves as subject to these laws because we have conferred upon ourselves freedom of will. Freedom and law-making of will are both autonomous and are therefore correlative concepts. For this very reason one concept cannot be used to explain the other or set forth its basis, [but can be used] at best to reduce, for the sake of logic, apparently different notions of the same object to one single concept (as we reduce different fractions of equal content to their lowest denominator).

One resource remains: to inquire whether we do not occupy different positions when we think of ourselves as causes efficient *a priori* through freedom and when we consider ourselves as effects of our actions which we see before our eyes.

The remark, which needs no subtle reflection and which can presumably be made by the most average mind (though after his fashion by an obscure discernment of judgment which he calls sentiment) is that all images (*Vorstellungen*) which we get without willing them, such as those of the senses, do not enable us to know objects except as they affect us. Whatever they are in themselves remains unknown. Consequently, regardless of the closest attention and clarity of which the mind is capable, "images" of this kind allow us only to acquire knowledge of *phenomena,* never of *things in themselves.* Once this distinction has been made, (even in just observing a difference between the images or ideas we receive passively from without, and those which we actively produce ourselves), it follows that we must admit and assume behind the phenomena something else that are not phenomena; namely, the things-in-themselves, although we must resign ourselves never to being able to approach them and never to knowing what they are in themselves, but only as they affect us. This must furnish a distinction, no matter how crude, between the world of sense and the world of reason. The former can be distinguished according to the difference of sense impressions in various observers, while the second always remains the same as the basis of the distinction. Man cannot even pretend to know what he is himself from the self-knowledge he has through internal sensation. Since he does not create himself, as it were, and comes by the concept [of man] not *a priori* but empirically, it is natural that he can obtain knowledge of himself only by his inner sense, and consequently only through the phenomena of his nature and the way in which his consciousness is affected. Nevertheless, beyond the structure of his own subject, as made up of mere phenomena, he must suppose something else as the basis of these phenomena; namely, his ego, whatever its nature may be. In regard to mere perception and receptivity of the senses, man must reckon himself as belonging to the *world of sense,* but in regard to what may be pure action in him (reaching consciousness directly and not by affecting the senses), he must reckon himself as belonging to the *world of the mind,* of which, however, he has no further knowledge. . . .

Man actually finds in himself a faculty which distinguishes him from all other things, even from himself as affected by objects, and that is *reason.* Reason, being pure and spontaneous, is superior even to the mind. Though the latter is spontaneous too and does not, like the sense, merely contain images that arise when we are affected by things (and are therefore passive), reason's activity cannot produce any other concepts than those designed to *bring the impressions or images based on sense rules,* to unite them in one consciousness. Without this activity of the senses, the [mind] could not think at all, whereas reason in the form of ideas displays such pure spontaneity that it far transcends anything that the sense can offer it and so proves its most important function in distinguishing the world of sense from that of the intellect, thereby setting the limits of the intellect itself.

A rational being must regard himself *as an intelligence* (not from the viewpoint of his lower faculties) belonging, not to the world of sense, but to that of the intellect. Hence man can regard himself from two points of view and similarly can come to know laws for the exercise of his faculties and consequently laws for all his actions. *First,* so far as he belongs to the world of sense, man is himself subject to laws of nature (heteronomy);

second, so far as he belongs to the intelligible world, [man is] under laws independent of nature which are founded not on experience but on reason alone. . . .

The suspicion which we considered above is now removed. This was the suspicion that our reasoning, from freedom to autonomy and from this to moral law, was mysteriously circular and that we thought the idea of freedom was basic only because of the moral law so that we might then infer the latter from freedom and that then we could offer no explanation at all for this law, but could only [present] it by *begging a principle* which well-disposed minds would gladly concede to us, but which we could never put forward as a provable proposition. Now we see that when we conceive ourselves as free we transfer ourselves into the world of the intellect and recognize the autonomy of the will with its consequence, morality; whereas if we conceive ourselves as obliged we are considering ourselves as belonging at the same time to the world of sense and to the intellectual world. . . .

Every rational being considers himself as belonging, as an intelligence, to the world of intellect and he calls his causality a will simply as an efficient cause belonging to that world. On the other hand, he is also conscious of being a part of the world of sense in which his actions are displayed as mere phenomena of that causality. However, we cannot discern how they are possible from this causality which we do not know. Instead, these actions must be viewed as determined by other phenomena; namely, desires and inclinations belonging to the sensible world. If I were only a member of the world of the intellect, all my actions would conform perfectly to the principle of the autonomy of pure will; if I were only a part of the world of sense they would be assumed to conform wholly to the natural law of desires and inclinations, i.e., to the heteronomy of nature. (The former would rest on the supreme principle of morality, the latter on that of happiness.) Since *the world of the intellect contains the basis of the world of sense, and consequently of its laws,* and so gives law directly to my will (as belonging entirely to the world of the intellect), I, as an intelligence, must recognize myself as subject to the law of the world of the intellect. [What this means is that I am subject] to reason which contains this law of the idea of freedom, and therefore as subject to the autonomy of the will, though otherwise [I am] a being belonging to the world of sense. Consequently, I must regard the laws of the world of the intellect as imperatives and the corresponding actions as duties. . . .

The moral "ought" is then the necessary "will" of a member of an intelligible world and he conceives it as an "ought" only to the same extent that he considers himself a member of the world of sense. . . .

The concept of a world of the intellect is only a *position* outside the phenomena which reason finds itself compelled to take in order to *conceive itself as practical,* which would not be possible if the influences of the senses had a determining power over man, but which is necessary unless he is denied the consciousness of himself as an intelligence; that is, as a rational cause acting freely and through reason. This thought certainly involves the idea of an order and a system of laws different from that of the mechanism of nature which governs the sensible world, and it requires the concept of an intelligible world; that is to say, of a whole system of rational beings as things in themselves. But this thought does not in the least entitle us to consider it in terms other than those of its *formal* condition; that is, the autonomy of this intelligible world which alone can co-exist with its freedom. On the other hand, all laws that refer to an object give heteronomy, which is only found in laws of nature and can only apply to the sensible world.

But reason would be overstepping all its bounds if it undertook to *explain how* pure reason could be practical; this would be exactly the same task as explaining *how freedom is possible.*

We can explain nothing but that which we can reduce to laws, whose object can be given in some possible experience. But freedom is a mere idea, whose objective reality can never be shown through laws of nature nor, consequently, through possible experience; therefore it can never be comprehended or even visualized, because we cannot support it by any sort of example or analogy. It is valid only as a necessary hypothesis of reason in a being that believes itself conscious of a will. . . .

Freedom signifies only a something that remains when I have eliminated everything belonging to the world of sense from the actuating principles of my will, serving merely to restrict the principle of such motives as are taken from the field of sensibility by fixing its limits and showing that it does not contain everything, but that there is more beyond it; but of this "more" I know nothing. After the abstraction of all matter, i.e., knowledge of objects, there remains of pure reason which conceives this ideal nothing but the form, namely, the practical law of the universality of the maxims, and congruous with it the concept of reason in reference to a pure world of the intellect as a possible efficient cause, i.e., a cause determining the will. There must be here a total absence of impulses, unless this idea of an intelligible world is itself the impulse, or the primary interest of reason; but to make this intelligible is precisely the problem that we cannot solve.

This is the extreme limit of all moral inquiry. Yet it is of great importance to determine this limit on this account; that reason may not on the one hand search about in the world of sense to the prejudice of morals for the supreme motive and an interest comprehensible but empirical; and on the other hand so that reason my not impotently raise its wings in the empty space of transcendent concepts which we call the intelligible world without being able to move and so lose itself amidst chimeras. For the rest, the idea remains of a pure world of the intellect as a whole [comprising] all intelligences, to which we ourselves belong [insofar as we are] rational beings, although otherwise we are members of the sensible world. It is a useful and legitimate idea for the purposes of rational belief, even though all knowledge stops at its threshold. It produces in us a lively interest in the moral law by means of the magnificent ideal of a universal realm of *ends in themselves* (of rational beings) to which we can belong as members only when we carefully conduct ourselves according to the maxims of freedom as if they were laws of nature.

XIII THE ENLIGHTENMENT: RELIGION

VOLTAIRE

MEMORIES of the persecutions of the seventeenth century were very much alive in the era of the Enlightenment. In Voltaire's life fears were aroused and prejudices freshened by the trial of a French Protestant, Jean Calas, for parricide. Although not clear, then or now, whether Calas was innocent or guilty, Voltaire was convinced that religious prejudice had entered the picture. He did much for Calas's defense and the *Essay on Toleration* (1763) grew out of his efforts.

Voltaire's wit and satire have become famous and on no subject were his gifts more brilliantly displayed than in his criticisms of theology and church practices. Himself a Deist, Voltaire believed for most of his life in a divine and beneficent creator who had given man simple rules of good conduct that constituted the essence of religion. Both the horrors men had done in the name of God and the absurdity (when judged by Voltaire's common sense or work-a-day reason) of most theological claims and speculations made Voltaire the greatest polemicist of his age against traditional religion. Voltaire's call to "crush the infamous thing" must, however, be compared with the evidence that throughout the first fifty years of the eighteenth century leading Catholics had been as much concerned as the *philosophes* with measuring up to the possibilities for man's enlightenment that seemed implicit in the philosophy of Locke and Newton.

The two satiric pieces on the central Christian mysteries are taken from Voltaire's *Story of the Banishment of the Jesuits from China,* translated by Peter Gay in his book, *Voltaire's Politics: The Poet as Realist* (Princeton, 1959). The selection on *Religion* is from the *Philosophical Dictionary,* translated by H. I. Woolf (New York, Knopf, 1924).

THE STORY OF THE BANISHING OF THE JESUITS FROM CHINA

Frère Rigolet. "Our God was born in a stable, seventeen hundred and twenty-three years ago, between an ox and an ass. . . . [his mother] was not a woman, she was a girl. It is true that she was married, and that she had two other children, named James as the old gospels say, but she was a virgin none the less."

The Emperor. "What! She was a virgin, and she had children!"

Frère Rigolet. "To be sure. That is the nub of the story: it was God who gave this girl a child."

The Emperor. "I don't understand you. You have just told me that she was the mother of God. So God slept with his mother in order to be born of her?"

Frère Rigolet. "You've got it, Your Sacred Majesty; grace was already in operation. You've got it, I say; God changed himself into a pigeon to give a child to a carpenter's wife, and that child was God himself."

The Emperor. "But then we have two Gods to take into account: a carpenter and a pigeon."

Frère Rigolet. "Without doubt, Sire; but there is also a third, who is the father of these two, and whom we always paint with a majestic beard: it was this God who ordered the pigeon to give a child to the carpenter's wife, from whom the God-carpenter was born; but at bottom these three make only one. The father had engendered the son before he was in the world, the son was then engendered by the pigeon, and the pigeon proceeds from the father and the son. Now you see that the pigeon who proceeds, the carpenter who is born of the pigeon, and the father who has engendered the son of the pigeon, can only be a single God; and that a man who doesn't believe this story should be burned in this world and in the other."

The Emperor. "That is as clear as day."

ON THE TRINITY

HERE IS an incomprehensible question which for over sixteen hundred years has exercised curiosity, sophistical subtlety, bitterness, the spirit of cabal, the rage to dominate, the rage to persecute, blind and bloodthirsty fanaticism, barbaric credulity, and which has produced more horrors than the ambition of princes, which indeed has produced enough. Is Jesus Word? If he is Word, did he emanate from God, is he coeternal and consubstantial with him, or is he of a similar substance? Is he distinct from him, or not? Is he created or engendered? Can he engender in turn? Has he paternity, or productive virtue without paternity? Is the holy ghost created or engendered or produced? Does he proceed from the father, or from the son, or from both? Can he engender, can he produce? Is his hypostasis consubstantial with the hypostasis of the Father and the son? and why, having precisely the same nature, the same essence as the father and the son, can he not do the same things as these two persons who are himself? I certainly do not understand any of this; nobody has ever understood any of this, and this is the reason for which people have slaughtered one another.

RELIGION

I MEDITATED last night; I was absorbed in the contemplation of nature; I admired the immensity, the course, the harmony of these infinite globes which the vulgar do not know how to admire.

I admired still more the intelligence which directs these vast forces. I said to myself: "One must be blind not to be dazzled by this spectacle; one must be stupid not to recognize the author of it; one must be mad not to worship Him. What tribute of worship should I render Him? Should not this tribute be the same in the whole of space, since it is the same supreme power which reigns equally in all space? Should not a thinking being who dwells in a star in the Milky Way offer Him the same homage as the thinking being on this little globe where we are? Light is uniform for the star Sirius and for us; moral philosophy must be uniform. If a sentient, thinking animal in Sirius is born of a tender father and mother who have been occupied with his happiness, he owes them as much love and care as we owe to our parents. If someone in the Milky Way sees a needy cripple, if he can relieve him and if he does not do it, he is guilty toward all globes. Everywhere the heart has the same duties: on the steps of the throne of God, if He has a throne; and in the depths of the abyss, if there be an abyss."

I was plunged in these ideas when one of those genii who fill the intermundane spaces came down to me. I recognized this same aerial creature who had appeared to me on another occasion to teach me how different God's judgments were from our own, and how a good action is preferable to a controversy.

He transported me into a desert all covered with piled up bones; and between these heaps of dead men there were walks of ever-green trees, and at the end of each walk a tall man of august mien, who regarded these sad remains with pity.

"Alas! my archangel," said I, "where have you brought me?"

"To desolation," he answered.

"And who are these fine patriarchs whom I see sad and motionless at the end of these green walks? They seem to be weeping over this countless crowd of dead."

"You shall know, poor human creature," answered the genius from the intermundane spaces; "but first of all you must weep."

He began with the first pile. "These," he said, "are the twenty-three thousand Jews who danced before a calf, with the twenty-four thousand who were killed while lying with Midianitish women. The number of those massacred for such errors and offences amounts to nearly three hundred thousand.

"In the other walks are the bones of the Christians slaughtered by each other for metaphysical disputes. They are divided into several heaps of four centuries each. One heap would have mounted right to the sky; they had to be divided."

"What!" I cried, "brothers have treated their brothers like this, and I have the misfortune to be of this brotherhood!"

"Here," said the spirit, "are the twelve million Americans killed in their fatherland because they had not been baptized."

"My God! why did you not leave these frightful bones to dry in the hemisphere where their bodies were born, and where they were consigned to so many different deaths? Why assemble here all these abominable monuments to barbarism and fanaticism?"

"To instruct you."

"Since you wish to instruct me," I said to the genius, "tell me if there have been peoples other than the Christians and the Jews in whom zeal and religion wretchedly transformed into fanaticism, have inspired so many horrible cruelties."

"Yes," he said. "The Mohammedans were sullied with the same inhumanities, but rarely; and when one asked *amman,* pity, of them and offered them tribute, they pardoned. As for the other nations there had not been one right from the existence of the world which has ever made a purely religious war. Follow me now." I followed him.

A little beyond these piles of dead men we found other piles; they were composed of sacks of gold and silver, and each had its label: *Substance of the heretics massacred in the eighteenth century, the seventeenth and the sixteenth.* And so on in going back: *Gold and silver of Americans slaughtered,* etc., etc. And all these piles were surmounted with crosses, mitres, croziers, triple crowns studded with precious stones.

"What, my genius! it was then to have these riches that these dead were piled up?"

"Yes, my son."

I wept; and when by my grief I had merited to be led to the end of the green walks, he led me there.

"Contemplate," he said, "the heroes of humanity who were the world's benefactors, and who were all united in banishing from the world, as far as they were able, violence and rapine. Question them."

I ran to the first of the band; he had a crown on his head, and a little censer in his hand; I humbly asked him his name. "I am Numa Pompilius," he said to me. "I succeeded a brigand, and I had brigands to govern: I taught them virtue and the worship of God; after me they forgot both more than once; I forbade that in the temples there should be any image, because the Deity which animates nature cannot be represented. During my reign the Romans had neither wars nor seditions, and my religion did nothing but good. All the neighbouring peoples came to honour me at my funeral: that happened to no one but me."

I kissed his hand, and I went to the second. He was a fine old man about a hundred years old, clad in a white robe. He put his middle-finger on his mouth, and with the other hand he cast some beans behind him. I recognized Pythagoras. He assured me he had never had a golden thigh, and that he had never been a cock; but that he had governed the Crotoniates with as much justice as Numa governed the Romans, almost at the same time; and that this justice was the rarest and most necessary thing in the world. I learned that the Pythagoreans examined their consciences twice a day. The honest people! how far we are from them! But we who have been nothing but assassins for thirteen hundred years, we say that these wise men were arrogant.

In order to please Pythagoras, I did not say a word to him and I passed to Zarathustra, who was occupied in concentrating the celestial fire in the focus of a concave mirror, in the middle of a hall with a hundred doors which all led to wisdom. (Zarathustra's precepts are called *doors*, and are a hundred in number.) Over the principal door I read these words which are the précis of all moral philosophy, and which cut short all the disputes of the casuists: "When in doubt if an action is good or bad, refrain."

"Certainly," I said to my genius, "the barbarians who immolated all these victims had never read these beautiful words."

We then saw the Zaleucus, the Thales, the Anaximanders, and all the sages who had sought truth and practised virtue.

When we came to Socrates, I recognized him very quickly by his flat nose. "Well," I said to him, "here you are then among the number of the Almighty's confidants! All the inhabitants of Europe, except the Turks and the Tartars of the Crimea, who know nothing, pronounce your name with respect. It is revered, loved, this great name, to the point that people have wanted to know those of your persecutors. Melitus and Anitus are known because of you, just as Ravaillac is known because of Henry IV; but I know only this name of Anitus. I do not know precisely who was the scoundrel who calumniated you, and who succeeded in having you condemned to take hemlock."

"Since my adventure," replied Socrates, "I have never thought about that man; but seeing that you make me remember it, I have much pity for him. He was a wicked priest who secretly conducted a business in hides, a trade reputed shameful among us. He sent his two children to my school. The other disciples taunted them with having a father who was a currier; they were obliged to leave. The irritated father had no rest until he had stirred up all the priests and all the sophists against me. They persuaded the counsel of the five hundred that I was an impious fellow who did not believe that the Moon, Mercury and Mars were gods. Indeed, I used to think, as I think now, that there is only one God, master of all nature. The judges handed me over to the poisoner of the republics; he cut short my life by a few days: I died peacefully at the age of seventy; and since that time I pass a happy life with all these great men whom you see, and of whom I am the least."

After enjoying some time in conversation with Socrates, I went forward with my guide into a grove situated above the thickets where all the sages of antiquity seemed to be tasting sweet repose.

I saw a man of gentle, simple countenance, who seemed to me to be about thirty-five years old. From afar he cast compassionate glances on these piles of whitened bones, across which I had had to pass to reach the sages' abode. I was astonished to find his feet swollen and bleeding, his hands likewise, his side pierced, and his ribs flayed with whip cuts. "Good Heavens!" I said to him, "is it possible for a just man, a sage, to be in this state? I have just seen one who was treated in a very hateful way, but there is no comparison between his torture and yours. Wicked priests and wicked judges poisoned him; is it by priests and judges that you have been so cruelly assassinated?"

He answered with much courtesy—"*Yes.*"

"And who were these monsters?"

"*They were hypocrites.*"

"Ah! that says everything; I understand by this single word that they must have condemned you to death. Had you then proved to them, as Socrates did, that the Moon was not a goddess, and that Mercury was not a god?"

"*No, these planets were not in question. My compatriots did not know at all what a planet is; they were all arrant ignoramuses. Their superstitions were quite different from those of the Greeks.*"

"You wanted to teach them a new religion, then?"

"*Not at all; I said to them simply—'Love God with all your heart and your fellow-creature as yourself, for that is man's whole duty.' Judge if this precept is not as old as the universe; judge if I brought them a new religion. I did not stop telling them that I had come not to destroy the law but to fulfil it; I had observed all their rites; circumcised as they all were, baptized as were the most zealous among them, like them I paid the Corban; I observed the Passover as they did, eating standing up a lamb cooked with lettuces. I and my friends went to pray in the temple; my friends even frequented this temple after my death; in a word, I fulfilled all their laws without a single exception."*

"What! these wretches could not even reproach you with swerving from their laws?"

"No, without a doubt."

"Why then did they put you in the condition in which I now see you?"

"What do you expect me to say! they were very arrogant and selfish. They saw that I knew them; they knew that I was making the citizens acquainted with them; they were the stronger; they took away my life: and people like them will always do as much, if they can, to whoever does them too much justice."

"But did you say nothing, do nothing that could serve them as a pretext?"

"To the wicked everything serves as pretext."

"Did you not say once that you were come not to send peace, but a sword?"

"It is a copyist's error; I told them that I sent peace and not a sword. I have never written anything; what I said can have been changed without evil intention."

"You therefore contributed in no way by your speeches, badly reported, badly interpreted, to these frightful piles of bones which I saw on my road in coming to consult you?"

"It is with horror only that I have seen those who have made themselves guilty of these murders."

"And these monuments of power and wealth, of pride and avarice, these treasures, these ornaments, these signs of grandeur, which I have seen piled up on the road while I was seeking wisdom, do they come from you?"

"That is impossible; I and my people lived in poverty and meanness: my grandeur was in virtue only."

I was about to beg him to be so good as to tell me just who he was. My guide warned me to do nothing of the sort. He told me that I was not made to understand these sublime mysteries. Only did I conjure him to tell me in what true religion consisted.

"Have I not already told you? Love God and your fellow-creature as yourself."

"What! if one loves God, one can eat meat on Friday?"

"I always ate what was given me; for I was too poor to give anyone food."

"In loving God, in being just, should one not be rather cautious not to confide all the adventures of one's life to an unknown man?"

"That was always my practice."

"Can I not, by doing good, dispense with making a pilgrimage to St. James of Compostella?"

"I have never been in that country."

"Is it necessary for me to imprison myself in a retreat with fools?"

"As for me, I always made little journeys from town to town."

"Is it necessary for me to take sides either for the Greek Church or the Latin?"

"When I was in the world I never made any difference between the Jew and the Samaritan."

"Well, if that is so, I take you for my only master." Then he made me a sign with his head which filled me with consolation. The vision disappeared, and a clear conscience stayed with me.

JEAN JACQUES ROUSSEAU

JEAN JACQUES ROUSSEAU (1712–78) had a painful childhood, owing to the early death of his mother and the dissipations of his father. After a series of escapades for whose existence there is little authority but his own *Confessions,* he settled down with Mme de Warens, a convert to Catholicism, who had also induced him to accept her faith. She sent him to the seminarists of St. Lazare and to a music master to improve his education. He relapsed into the life of a vagabond, then returned to Mme de Warens in 1732 in Chambéry; their association came to an end when he returned from a trip to find his place in the household occupied by another lover.

Rousseau became a tutor at Lyons, but he taught badly and disliked doing it. In 1742 he went to Paris, where he became acquainted with Diderot's literary group. He contributed an article on music and an article on political economy to the Encyclopedia, though he later quarreled with the *philosophes* on both personal and theoretical grounds.

In 1749 he won the prize offered by the academy of Dijon for the best essay on the effect of the progress of civilization on morals: this was his famous *Discours sur les arts et sciences,* in which he argued for the moral superiority of a simple pastoral society.

After visiting Geneva, his birthplace, where he again became a Protestant, he spent the year 1756 at the Hermitage, his cottage outside of Paris, writing his novel *La Nouvelle Héloïse,* carrying on his love affair with Mme d'Huodetot (on which the novel is based), and quarreling with Diderot. In 1758 he published his *Lettre à d'Alembert sur les spectacles,* which irritated both Voltaire, who enjoyed giving theatricals at Ferney, and d'Alembert, who had condemned prejudice against the stage in an article in the Encyclopedia.

Rousseau, despite constant feuding with contemporaries, was never at a loss for friends and patrons, and he continued to write at a great rate. *La Nouvelle Héloïse* appeared in 1760 and was immensely popular; *Émile* appeared in 1762. It started the modern criticisms of formalistic education. It is in *Émile* also that we find the simple, pietistic "Profession du vicaire savoyard," which irritated both the Church and the *philosophes.* The book was condemned by the Parlement of Paris in 1762, and Rousseau was obliged to flee to the protection of Prussia. Geneva, too, condemned *Émile,* and Rousseau did not fail to retaliate with attacks on the council and constitution of that city. Opinion was aroused against him on all sides.

In 1765 Hume offered him asylum in England. He was lionized in London, and retired to Wootton where he wrote most of his *Confessions.* But he picked a quarrel with Hume over nothing, and in 1767 he returned to France. In his last years he wrote his *Dialogues* and his *Rêveries d'un promeneur solitaire.* It has long been suspected, but never proved, that he died a suicide.

The selection from Rousseau that follows is a notable statement of belief in the natural or innate religiosity of human beings and of the enlightened ways in which so-called religious feelings can best be satisfied. It is taken from the translation of *Émile* by Barbara Foxley (London: J. M. Dent; New York: E. P. Dutton, 1950).

و

EMILE

MY CHILD, do not look to me for learned speeches or profound arguments. I am no great philosopher, nor do I desire to be one. I have, however, a certain amount of common-sense and a constant devotion to truth. I have no wish to argue with you nor even to convince you; it is enough for me to show you, in all simplicity of heart, what I really think. Consult your own heart while I speak; that is all I ask. If I am mistaken, I am honestly mistaken, and therefore my error will not be counted to me as a crime; if you, too, are honestly mistaken, there is no great harm done. If I am right, we are both endowed with reason, we have both the same motive for listening to the voice of reason. Why should not you think as I do?

By birth I was a peasant and poor; to till the ground was my portion; but my parents thought it a finer thing that I should learn to get my living as a priest and they found means to send me to college. . . . I learned what was taught me, I said what I was told to say, I promised all that was required, and I became a priest. But I soon discovered that when I promised not to be a man, I had promised more than I could perform.

Conscience, they tell us, is the creature of prejudice, but I know from experience that conscience persists in following the order of nature in spite of all the laws of man. . . . My good youth, nature has not yet appealed to your senses; may you long remain in this happy state when her voice is the voice of innocence. Remember that to anticipate her teaching is to offend more deeply against her than to resist her teaching; you must first learn to resist, that you may know when to yield without wrong-doing.

From my youth up I had reverenced the married state as the first and most sacred institution of nature. . . .

This very resolution proved my ruin. My respect for marriage led to the discovery of my misconduct. . . . The scandal must be expiated; I was arrested, suspended, and dismissed; I was the victim of my scruples rather than of my incontinence, and I had reason to believe, from the reproaches which accompanied my disgrace, that one can often escape punishment by being guilty of a worse fault.

A thoughtful mind soon learns from such experiences. I found my former ideas of justice, honesty, and every duty of man overturned by these painful events, and day by day I was losing my hold on one or another of the opinions I had accepted.

I was in that state of doubt and uncertainty which Descartes considers essential to the search for truth. It is a state which cannot continue, it is disquieting and painful; only vicious tendencies and an idle heart can keep us in that state. . . .

I pondered, therefore, on the sad fate of mortals, adrift upon this sea of human opinions, without compass or rudder, and abandoned to their stormy passions with no guide but an inexperienced pilot who does not know whence he comes or whither he is going. I said to myself, "I love truth, I seek her, and cannot find her. Show me truth and I will hold her fast; why does she hide her face from the eager heart that would fain worship her?"

My perplexity was increased by the fact that I had been brought up in a church which decides everything and permits no doubts, so that having rejected one article of faith I was forced to reject the rest; . . .

I consulted the philosophers, I searched their books and examined their various theories; I found them all alike proud, assertive, dogmatic, professing, even in their so-called scepticism, to know everything, proving nothing, scoffing at each other. . . .

I suppose this prodigious diversity of opinion is caused, in the first place, by the weakness of the human intellect; and, in the second, by pride. . . . The one thing we do not know is the limit of the knowable. We prefer to trust to chance and to believe what is not true, rather than to own that not one of us can see what really is. A fragment of some vast whole whose bounds are beyond our gaze, a fragment abandoned by its Creator to our foolish quarrels, we are vain enough to want to determine the nature of that whole and our own relations with regard to it.

The first thing I learned from these considerations was to restrict my inquiries to what directly concerned myself, to rest in profound ignorance of everything else, and not even to trouble myself to doubt anything beyond what I required to know.

I also realised that the philosophers, far from ridding me of my vain doubts, only multiplied the doubts that tormented me and failed to remove any one of them. So I chose another guide and said, "Let me follow the Inner Light; it will not lead me so far astray as others have done, or if it does it will be my own fault, and I shall not go so far wrong if I follow my own illusions as if I trusted to their deceits."

But who am I? What right have I to decide? What is it that determines my judgments? If they are inevitable, if they are the results of the impressions I receive, I am wasting my strength in such inquiries; they would be made or not without any interference of mine. I must therefore first turn my eyes upon myself to acquaint myself with the instrument I desire to use, and to discover how far it is reliable.

I exist, and I have senses through which I receive impressions. This is the first truth that strikes me and I am forced to accept it. Have I any independent knowledge of my existence, or am I only aware of it through my sensations? This is my first difficulty, and so far I cannot solve it. For I continually experience sensations, either directly or indirectly through memory, so how can I know if the feeling of self is something beyond these sensations or if it can exist independently of them?

My sensations take place in myself, for they make me aware of my own existence; but their cause is outside me, for they affect me whether I have any reason for them or not, and they are produced or destroyed independently of me. So I clearly perceive that my sensation, which is within me, and its cause or its object, which is outside me, are different things.

Thus, not only do I exist, but other entities exist also, that is to say, the objects of my sensations; and even if these objects are merely ideas, still these ideas are not me.

But everything outside myself, everything which acts upon my senses, I call matter, and all the particles of matter which I suppose to be united into separate entities I call bodies. Thus all the disputes of the idealists and the realists have no meaning for me; their distinctions between the appearance and the reality of bodies are wholly fanciful.

I am now as convinced of the existence of the universe as of my own. I next consider the objects of my sensations, and I find that I have the power of comparing them, so I perceive that I am endowed with an active force of which I was not previously aware.

To perceive is to feel; to compare is to judge; to judge and to feel are not the same. Through sensation objects present themselves to me separately and singly as they are in nature; by comparing them I rearrange them, I shift them so to speak, I place one upon another to decide whether they are alike or different, or more generally to find out their relations. To my mind, the distinctive faculty of an active or intelligent being is the power of understanding this word "is." I seek in vain in the merely sensitive entity that intelligent force which compares and judges; I can find no trace of it in its nature. This passive entity will be aware of each object separately, it will even be aware of the whole formed by the two together, but having no power to place them side by side it can never compare them, it can never form a judgment with regard to them.

To see two things at once is not to see their relations nor to judge of their differences; to perceive several objects, one beyond the other, is not to relate them. I may have at the same moment an idea of a big stick and a little stick without comparing them, without judging that one is less than the other, just as I can see my whole hand without counting my fingers. These comparative ideas, greater, smaller, together with number ideas of one, two, etc., are certainly not sensations, although my mind only produces them when my sensations occur.

We are told that a sensitive being distinguishes sensations from each other by the inherent differences in the sensations; this requires explanation. When the sensations are different, the sensitive being distinguishes them by their differences; when they are alike, he distinguishes them because he is aware of them one beyond the other. Otherwise, how could he distinguish between two equal objects simultaneously experienced? He would necessarily confound the two objects and take them for one object, especially under a system which professed that the representative sensations of space have no extension.

When we become aware of the two sensations to be compared, their impression is made, each object is perceived, both are perceived, but for all that their relation is not perceived. If the judgment of this relation were merely a sensation, and came to me solely from the object itself, my judgments would never be mistaken, for it is never untrue that I feel what I feel.

Why then am I mistaken as to the relation between these two sticks, especially when they are not parallel? Why, for example, do I say the small stick is a third of the large, when it is only a quarter? Why is the picture, which is the sensation, unlike its model which is the object? It is because I am active when I judge, because the operation of comparison is at fault; because my understanding, which judges of relations, mingles its errors with the truth of sensations, which only reveal to me things.

Add to this a consideration which will, I feel sure, appeal to you when you have thought about it: it is this— If we were purely passive in the use of our senses, there would be no communication between them; it would be impossible to know that the body we are touching and the thing we are looking at is the same. Either we should never perceive anything outside ourselves, or there would be for us five substances perceptible by the senses, whose identity we should have no means of perceiving.

This power of my mind which brings my sensations together and compares them may be called by any name; let it be called attention, meditation, reflection, or what you will; it is still true that it is in me and not in things, that it is I alone who produce it, though I only produce it when I receive an impression from things. Though I am compelled to feel or not to feel, I am free to examine more or less what I feel.

Being now, so to speak, sure of myself, I begin to look at things outside myself, and I behold myself with a sort of shudder flung at random into this vast universe, plunged as it were into the vast number of entities, knowing nothing of what they are in themselves or in relation to me. I study them, I observe them; . . .

I believe, therefore, that there is a will which sets the universe in motion and gives life to nature. This is my first dogma, or the first article of my creed. . . .

Let us compare the special ends, the means, the ordered relations of every kind, then let us listen to the inner voice of feeling; what healthy mind can reject its evidence? Unless the eyes are blinded by prejudices, can they fail to see that the visible order of the universe proclaims a supreme intelligence? What sophisms must be brought together before we fail to understand the harmony of existence and the wonderful cooperation of every part for the maintenance of the rest? . . .

In vain do those who deny the unity of intention manifested in the relations of all the parts of this great whole, in vain do they conceal their nonsense under abstractions, coordinations, general principles, symbolic expressions; whatever they do I find it impossible to conceive of a system of entities so firmly ordered unless I believe in an intelligence that orders them. It is not in my power to believe that passive and dead matter can have brought forth living and feeling beings, that blind chance has brought forth intelligent beings, that that which does not think has brought forth thinking beings.

I believe, therefore, that the world is governed by a wise and powerful will; I see it or rather I feel it, and it is a great thing to know this. But has this same world always existed, or has it been created? Is there one source of all things? Are there two or many? What is their nature? I know not; and what concern is it of mine? When these things become of importance to me I will try to learn them; till then I abjure these idle speculations, which may trouble my peace, but cannot affect my conduct nor be comprehended by my reason.

Recollect that I am not preaching my own opinion but explaining it. Whether matter is eternal or created, whether its origin is passive or not, it is still certain that the whole is one, and that it proclaims a single intelligence; for I see nothing that is not part of the same ordered system, nothing which does not cooperate to the same end, namely, the conservation of all within the established order. This being who wills and can perform his will, this being active through his own power, this being, whoever he may be, who moves the universe and orders all things, is what I call God. To this name I add the ideas of intelligence, power, will, which I have brought together, and that of kindness which is their necessary consequence; but for all this I know no more of the being to which I ascribe them. He hides himself alike from my senses and my understanding; the more I think of him, the more perplexed I am; I know full well that he exists, and that he exists of himself alone; I know that my existence depends on his, and that everything I know depends upon him also. I see God everywhere in his works; I feel him within myself; I behold him all around me; but if I try to ponder him himself, if I try to find out where he is, what he is, what is his substance, he escapes me and my troubled spirit finds nothing.

Convinced of my unfitness, I shall never argue about the nature of God unless I am driven to it by the feeling of his relations with myself. Such reasonings are always rash; a wise man should venture on them with trembling, he should be certain that he can never sound their abysses; for the most insolent attitude towards God is not to abstain from thinking of him, but to think evil of him.

Would you believe it, dear friend, from these gloomy thoughts and apparent contradictions there was shaped in my mind the sublime idea of the soul, which all my seeking had hitherto failed to discover? While I meditated upon man's nature, I seemed to discover two distinct principles in it; one of them raised him to the study of the eternal truths, to the love of justice, and of true morality, to the regions of the world of thought, which the wise delight to contemplate; the other led him downwards to himself, made him the slave of his senses, of the passions which are their instruments, and thus opposed everything suggested to him by the former principle. When I felt myself carried away, distracted by these conflicting motives, I said, No; man is not one; I will and I will not; I feel myself at once a slave and a free man; I perceive what is right, I love it, and I do what is wrong; I am active when I listen to the voice of reason; I am passive when I am carried away by my passions; and when I yield, my worst suffering is the knowledge that I might have resisted.

The motive power of all action is in the will of a free creature; we can go no farther. It is not the word freedom that is meaningless, but the word necessity. To suppose some action which is not the effect of an active motive power is indeed to suppose effects without cause, to reason in a vicious circle. Either there is no original impulse, or every original impulse has no antecedent cause, and there is no will properly so-called without freedom. Man is therefore free to act, and as such he is animated by an immaterial substance; that is the third article of my creed. From these three you will easily deduce the rest, so that I need not enumerate them.

If man is at once active and free, he acts of his own accord; what he does freely is no part of the system marked out by Providence and it cannot be imputed to Providence. Providence does not will the evil that man does when he misuses the freedom given to him; neither does Providence prevent him doing it, either because the wrong done by so feeble a creature is as nothing in its eyes, or because it could not prevent it without doing a greater wrong and degrading his nature. Providence has made him free that he may choose the good and refuse the evil. It has made him capable of this choice if he uses rightly the faculties bestowed upon him, but it has so strictly limited his powers that the misuse of his freedom cannot disturb the general order. The evil that man does reacts upon himself without affecting the system of the world, without preventing the preservation of the human species in spite of itself. To complain that God does not prevent us from doing wrong is to complain because he has made man of so excellent a nature, that he has endowed his actions with that morality by which they are ennobled, that he has made virtue man's birthright. Supreme happiness consists in self-content; that we may gain this self-content we are placed upon this earth and endowed with freedom, we are tempted by our passions and restrained by conscience. What more could divine power itself have done on our behalf? Could it have made our nature a contradiction, and given the prize of well-doing to one who was incapable of evil? To prevent a man from wickedness, should Providence have restricted him to instinct and made him a fool? Not so, O God of my soul, I will never reproach thee that thou hast created me in thine own image, that I may be free and good and happy like my Maker!

It is the abuse of our powers that makes us unhappy and wicked. Our cares, our sorrows, our sufferings are of our own making. Moral ills are undoubtedly the work of man, and physical ills would be nothing but our vices which have made us liable to them. Has not nature made us feel our needs as a means to our preservation? Is not bodily suffering a sign that the machine is out of order and needs attention? Death. . . . Do not the wicked poison their own life and ours? Who would wish to live for ever? Death is the cure for the evils you bring upon yourself; nature would not have you suffer perpetually. How few sufferings are felt by man living in a state of primitive simplicity! His life is almost entirely free from suffering and from passion; he neither fears nor feels death; if he feels it, his sufferings make him desire it; henceforth it is no evil in his eyes. If we were but content to be ourselves we should have no cause to complain of our lot; but in the search for an imaginary good we find a thousand real ills. He who cannot bear a little pain must expect to suffer greatly. If a man injures his constitution by dissipation, you try to cure him with medicine; the ill he fears is added to the ill he feels; the thought of death makes it horrible and hastens its approach; the more we seek to escape from it, the more we are aware of it; and we go through life in the fear of death, blaming nature for the evils we have inflicted on ourselves by our neglect of her laws.

O Man! seek no further for the author of evil; thou art he. There is no evil but the evil you do or the evil you suffer, and both come from yourself. Evil in general can only spring from disorder, and in the order of the world I find a never-failing system. Evil in particular cases exists only in the mind of those who experience it; and this feeling is not the gift of nature, but the work of man himself. Pain has little power over those who, having thought little, look neither before nor after. Take away our fatal progress, take away our faults and our vices, take away man's handiwork, and all is well. . . .

Men say God owes nothing to his creatures. I think he owes them all he promised when he gave them their being. Now to give them the idea of something good and to make them feel the need of it, is to promise it to them. The more closely I study myself, the more carefully I consider, the more plainly do I read these words, "Be just and you will be happy." It is not so, however, in the present condition of things, the wicked prospers and the oppression of the righteous continues. Observe how angry we are when this expectation is disappointed. Conscience revolts and murmurs against her Creator; she exclaims with cries and groans, "Thou has deceived me."

"I have deceived thee, rash soul! Who told thee this? Is thy soul destroyed? Hast thou ceased to exist? O Brutus! O my son! let there be no stain upon the close of thy noble life; do not abandon thy hope and thy glory with thy corpse upon the plains of Philippi. Why dost thou say, 'Virtue is naught,' when thou art about to enjoy the reward of virtue? Thou art about to die! Nay, thou shalt live, and thus my promise is fulfilled."

One might judge from the complaints of impatient men that God owes them the reward before they have deserved it, that he is bound to pay for virtue in advance. Oh! let us first be good and then we shall be happy. Let us not claim the prize before we have won it, nor demand our wages before we have finished our work. "It is not in the lists that we crown the victors in the sacred games," says Plutarch, "it is when they have finished their course."

. . . . Is the soul of man in its nature immortal? I know not. My finite understanding cannot hold the infinite; what is called eternity eludes my grasp. What can I assert or deny, how can I reason with regard to what I cannot conceive? I believe that the soul survives the body for the maintenance of order; who knows if this is enough to make it eternal? However, I know that the body is worn out and destroyed by the division of its parts, but I cannot conceive a similar destruction of the conscious nature, and as I cannot imagine how it can die, I presume that it does not die. As this assumption is consoling and in itself not unreasonable, why should I fear to accept it?

I am aware of my soul; it is known to me in feeling and in thought; I know what it is without knowing its essence; I cannot reason about ideas which are unknown to me. What I do know is this, that my personal identity depends upon memory, and that to be indeed the same self I must remember that I have existed. Now after death I could not recall what I was when alive unless I also remembered what I felt and therefore what I did; and I have no doubt that this remembrance will one day form the happiness of the good and the torment of the bad. In this world our inner consciousness is absorbed by the crowd of eager passions which cheat remorse. The humiliation and disgrace involved in the practice of virtue do not permit us to realise its charm. But when, freed from the illusions of the bodily senses, we behold with joy the supreme Being and the eternal truths which flow from him; when all the powers of our soul are alive to the beauty of order and we are wholly occupied in comparing what we have done with what we ought to have done, then it is that the voice of conscience will regain its strength and sway; then it is that the pure delight which springs from self-content, and the sharp regret for our own degradation of that self, will decide by means of overpowering feeling what shall be the fate which each has prepared for himself. My good friend, do not ask me whether there are other sources of happiness or suffering; I cannot tell; that which my fancy pictures is enough to console me in this life and to bid me look for a life to come. I do not say the good will be rewarded, for what greater good can a truly good being expect than to exist in accordance with his nature? But I do assert that the good will be happy, because their maker, the author of all justice, who has made them capable of feeling, has not made them that they may suffer; moreover, they have not abused their freedom upon earth and they have not changed their fate through any fault of their own; yet they have suffered in this life and it will be made up to them in the life to come. This feeling relies not so much on man's deserts as on the idea of good which seems to me inseparable from the divine essence. I only assume that the laws of order are constant and that God is true to himself.

Do not ask me whether the torments of the wicked will endure for ever, whether the goodness of their creator can condemn them to the eternal suffering; again, I cannot tell, and I have no empty curiosity for the investigation of useless problems. How does the fate of the wicked concern me? I take little interest in it. All the same I find it hard to believe that they will be condemned to everlasting torments. If the supreme justice calls for vengeance, it claims it in this life. The nations of the world with their errors are its ministers. Justice uses self-inflicted ills to punish the crimes which have deserved them. It is in your own insatiable souls, devoured by envy, greed, and ambition, it is in the midst of your false prosperity, that the avenging passions find the due reward of your crimes. What need to seek a hell in the future life? It is here in the breast of the wicked.

When our fleeting needs are over, and our mad desires are at rest, there should also be an end of our passions and our crimes. Can pure spirits be capable of any perversity? Having need of nothing, why should they be wicked? If they are free from our gross senses, if their happiness consists in the contemplation of other beings, they can only desire what is good; and he who ceases to be bad can never be miserable. That is what I am inclined to think though I have not been at the pains to come to any decision. O God, merciful and good, whatever thy decrees may be I adore them; if thou shouldst commit the wicked to everlasting punishment, I abandon my feeble reason to thy justice; but if the remorse of these wretched beings should in the course of time be extinguished, if their sufferings should come to an end, and if the same peace shall one day be the lot of all mankind, I give thanks to thee for this. Is not the wicked my brother? How often have I been tempted to be like him? Let him be delivered from his misery and freed from the spirit of hatred that accompanied it; let him be as happy as I myself; his happiness, far from arousing my jealousy, will only increase my own.

Thus it is that, in the contemplation of God in his works, and in the study of such of his attributes as it concerned me to know, I have slowly grasped and developed the idea, at first partial and imperfect, which I have formed of this Infinite Being. But if this idea has become nobler and greater it is also more suited to the human reason. As I approach in spirit the eternal light, I am confused and dazzled by its glory, and compelled to abandon all the earthly notions which helped me to picture it to myself. God is no longer corporeal and sensible; the supreme mind which rules the world is no longer the world itself; in vain do I strive to grasp his inconceivable essence. When I think that it is he that gives life and movement to the living and moving substance which controls all living bodies; when I hear it said that my soul is spiritual and that God is a spirit, I revolt against this abasement of the divine essence; as if God and my soul were of one and the same nature! As if God were not the one and only absolute being, the only really active, feeling, thinking, willing being, from whom we derive our thought, feeling, motion, will, our freedom and our very existence! We are free because he wills our freedom, and his inexplicable substance is to our souls what our souls are to our bodies. I know not whether he has created matter, body, soul, the world itself. The idea of creation confounds me and eludes my grasp; so far as I can conceive of it I believe it; but I know that he has formed the universe and all that is, that he has made and ordered all things. No doubt God is eternal; but can my mind grasp the idea of eternity? Why should I cheat myself with meaningless words? This is what I do understand; before things were—God was; he will be when they are no more, and if all things come to an end he will still endure. That a being beyond my comprehension should give life to other things, this is merely difficult and beyond my understanding; but that Being and Nothing should be convertible terms, this is indeed a palpable contradiction, an evident absurdity.

God is intelligent, but how? Man is intelligent when he reasons, but the Supreme Intelligence does not need to reason; there is neither premise nor conclusion for him, there is not even a proposition. The Supreme Intelligence is wholly intuitive, it sees what is and what shall be; all truths are one for it, as all places are but one point and all time but one moment. Man's power makes use of means, the divine power is self-active. God can because he wills; his will is his power. God is good; this is certain; but man finds his happiness in the welfare of his kind, God's happiness consists in the love of order; for it is through order that he maintains what is, and unites each part in the whole. God is just; of this I am sure, it is a consequence of his goodness; man's injustice is not God's work, but his own; that moral justice which seems to the philosophers a presumption against Providence, is to me a proof of its existence. But man's justice consists in giving to each his due; God's justice consists in demanding from each of us an account of that which he has given us.

If I have succeeded in discerning these attributes of which I have no absolute idea, it is in the form of unavoidable deductions, and by the right use of my reason; but I affirm them without understanding them, and at bottom that is no affirmation at all. In vain do I say, God is thus. I feel it, I experience it, none the more do I understand how God can be thus.

In a word: the more I strive to envisage his infinite essence the less do I comprehend it; but it is, and that is enough for me; the less I understand, the more I adore. I abase mself, saying, "Being of beings, I am because thou art; to fix my thoughts on thee is to ascend to the source of my being. The best use I can make of my reason is to resign it before thee; my mind delights, my weakness rejoices, to feel myself overwhelmed by thy greatness."

Having thus deduced from the perception of objects of sense and from my inner consciousness, which leads me to judge of causes by my native reason, the principal truths which I require to know, I must now seek such principles of conduct as I can draw from them, and such rules as I must lay down for my guidance in the fulfilment of my destiny in this world, according to the purpose of my Maker. Still following the same method, I do not derive these rules from the principles of the higher philosophy, I find them in the depths of my heart, traced by nature in characters which nothing can efface. I need only consult myself with regard to what I wish to do; what I feel to be right is right, what I feel to be wrong is wrong; conscience is the best casuist; and it is only when we haggle with conscience that we have recourse to the subtleties of argument.

Our first duty is towards ourself; yet how often does the voice of others tell us that in seeking our good at the expense of others we are doing ill? We think we are following the guidance of nature, and we are resisting it; we listen to what she says to our senses, and we neglect what she says to our heart; the active being obeys, the passive commands. Conscience is the voice of the soul, the passions are the voice of the body. Is it strange that these voices often contradict each other? And then to which should we give heed? Too often does reason deceive us; we have only too good a right to doubt her; but conscience never deceives us; she is the true guide of man; it is to the soul what instinct is to the body; he who obeys his conscience is following nature and he need not fear that he will go astray.

My young friend, let us look within, let us set aside all personal prejudices and see whither our inclinations lead us. Do we take more pleasure in the sight of the sufferings of others or their joys? Is it pleasanter to do a kind action or an unkind action, and which leaves the more delightful memory behind it? Why do you enjoy the theatre? Do you delight in the crimes you behold? Do you weep over the punishment which overtakes the criminal? They say we are indifferent to everything but self-interest; yet we find our consolation in our sufferings in the charms of friendship and humanity, and even in our pleasures we should be too lonely and miserable if we had no one to share them with us. If there is no such thing as morality in man's heart, what is the source of his rapturous admiration of noble deeds, his passionate devotion to great men?

We only delight in injustice so long as it is to our own advantage; in every other case we wish the innocent to be protected. If we see some act of violence or injustice in town or country, our hearts are at once stirred to their depths by an instinctive anger and wrath, which bids us go to the help of the oppressed; but we are restrained by a stronger duty, and the law deprives us of our right to protect the innocent. On the other hand, if some deed of mercy or generosity meets our eye, what reverence and love does it inspire! Do we not say to ourselves, "I should like to have done that myself"? What does it matter to us that two thousand years ago a man was just or unjust?

and yet we take the same interest in ancient history as if it happened yesterday. What are the crimes of Cataline to me? I shall not be his victim. Why then have I the same horror of his crimes as if he were living now? We do not hate the wicked merely because of the harm they do to ourselves, but because they are wicked. Not only do we wish to be happy ourselves, we wish others to be happy too, and if this happiness does not interfere with our own happiness, it increases it. . . .

Cast your eyes over every nation of the world; peruse every volume of its history; in the midst of all these strange and cruel forms of worship, among this amazing variety of manners and customs, you will everywhere find the same ideas of right and justice; everywhere the same principles of morality, the same ideas of good and evil. The old paganism gave birth to abominable gods who would have been punished as scoundrels here below, gods who merely offered, as a picture of supreme happiness, crimes to be committed and lust to be gratified. But in vain did vice descend from the abode of the gods armed with their sacred authority; the moral instinct refused to admit it into the heart of man. . . .

There is therefore at the bottom of our hearts an innate principle of justice and virtue, by which, in spite of our maxims, we judge our own actions or those of others to be good or evil; and it is this principle that I call conscience.

But at this word I hear the murmurs of all the wise men so-called. Childish errors, prejudices of our upbringing, they exclaim in concert! There is nothing in the human mind but what it has gained by experience; and we judge everything solely by means of the ideas we have acquired. They go further; they even venture to reject the clear and universal agreement of all peoples, and to set against this striking unanimity in the judgment of mankind, they seek out some obscure exception known to themselves alone; as if the whole trend of nature were rendered null by the depravity of a single nation, and as if the existence of monstrosities made an end of species. But to what purpose does the sceptic Montaigne strive himself to unearth in some obscure corner of the world a custom which is contrary to the ideas of justice? To what purpose does he credit the most untrustworthy travellers while he refuses to believe the greatest writers? A few strange and doubtful customs, based on local causes, unknown to us; shall these destroy a general inference based on the agreement of all the nations of the earth, differing from each other in all else, but agreed in this? O Montaigne, you pride yourself on your truth and honesty; be sincere and truthful, if a philosopher can be so, and tell me if there is any country upon earth where it is a crime to keep one's plighted word, to be merciful, helpful, and generous, where the good man is scorned, and the traitor is held in honour.

Self-interest, so they say, induces each of us to agree for the common good. But how is it that the good man consents to this to his own hurt? Does a man go to death from self-interest? No doubt each man acts for his own good, but if there is no such thing as moral good to be taken into consideration, self-interest will only enable you to account for the deeds of the wicked; possibly you will not attempt to do more. A philosophy which could find no place for good deeds would be too detestable; you would find yourself compelled either to find some mean purpose, some wicked motive, or to abuse Socrates and slander Regulus. If such doctrines ever took root among us, the voice of nature, together with the voice of reason, would constantly protest against them, till no adherent of such teaching could plead an honest excuse for his partisanship.

. . . . The decrees of conscience are not judgments but feelings. Although all our ideas come from without, the feelings by which they are weighed are within us, and it is by these feelings alone that we perceive fitness or unfitness of things in relation to ourselves, which leads us to seek or shun these things.

To exist is to feel; our feeling is undoubtedly earlier than our intelligence, and we had feelings before we had ideas. Whatever may be the cause of our being, it has provided for our preservation by giving us feelings suited to our nature; and no one can deny that these at least are innate. These feelings, so far as the individual is concerned, are self-love, fear, pain, the dread of death, the desire for comfort. Again, if, as it is impossible to doubt, man is by nature sociable, or at least fitted to become sociable, he can only be so by means of other innate feelings, relative to his kind; for if only physical well-being were considered, men would certainly be scattered rather than brought together. But the motive power of conscience is derived from the moral system formed through this twofold relation to himself and to his fellow-men. To know good is not to love it; this knowledge is not innate in man; but as soon as his reason leads him to perceive it, his conscience impels him to love it; it is this feeling which is innate.

Conscience! Conscience! Divine instinct, immortal voice from heaven; sure guide for a creature ignorant and finite indeed, yet intelligent and free; infallible judge of good and evil, making man like to God! In thee consists the excellence of man's nature and the morality of his actions. Apart from thee, I find nothing in myself to raise me above the beasts—nothing but the sad privilege of wandering from one error to another, by the help of an unbridled understanding and a reason which knows no principle.

Thank heaven we have now got rid of all that alarming show of philosophy; we may be men without being scholars; now that we need not spend our life in the study of morality, we have found a less costly and surer guide through this vast labyrinth of human thought. But it is not enough to be aware that there is such a guide; we must know her and follow her. If she speaks to all hearts, how is it that so few give heed to her voice? She speaks to us in the language of nature, and everything leads us to forget that tongue. Conscience is timid, she loves peace and retirement; she is startled by noise and numbers; the prejudices from which she is said to arise are her worst enemies. She flees before them or she is silent; their noisy voices drown her words, so that she cannot get a hearing; fanaticism dares to counterfeit her voice and to inspire crimes in her name. She is discouraged by ill-treatment; she no longer speaks to us, no longer answers to our call; when she had been scorned so long, it is as hard to recall her as it was to banish her.

How often in the course of my inquiries have I grown weary of my own coldness of heart! How often have grief and weariness poured their poison into my first meditations and made them hateful to me! My barren heart yielded nothing but a feeble zeal and a lukewarm love of truth. I said to myself: Why should I strive to find what does not exist? Moral good is a dream, the pleasures of sense are the only real good. When once we have lost the taste for the pleasures of the soul, how hard it is to recover it! How much more difficult to acquire it if we have never possessed it!

Ever at strife between my natural feelings, which spoke of the common weal, and my reasons, which spoke of self, I should have drifted through life in perpetual uncertainty, hating evil, loving good, and always at war with myself, if my heart had not received further light, if that truth which determined my opinions had not also settled my conduct, and set me at peace with myself. Reason alone is not a sufficient foundation for virtue; what solid ground can be found? Virtue we are told is love of order. But can this love prevail over my love for my own well-being, and ought it so to prevail? Let them give me clear and sufficient reason for this preference. Their so-called principle is in truth a mere playing with words; for I also say that vice is love of order, differently understood. Wherever there is feeling and intelligence, there is some sort of moral order. The difference is this: the good man orders his life with regard to all men; the wicked orders it for self alone. The latter centres all things round himself; . . .

There is an age when the heart is still free, but eager, unquiet, greedy of a happiness which is still unknown, a happiness which it seeks in curiosity and doubt; deceived by the senses it settles at length upon the empty show of happiness and thinks it has found it where it is not. In my own case these illusions endured for a long time. Alas! too late did I become aware of them, and I have not succeeded in overcoming them altogether; they will last as long as this mortal body from which they arise. If they lead me astray, I am at least no longer deceived by them; I know them for what they are, and even when I give way to them, I despise myself; far from regarding them as the goal of my happiness, I behold in them an obstacle to it. I long for the time when, freed from the fetters of the body, I shall be myself, at one with myself, no longer torn in two, when I myself shall suffice for my own happiness. Meanwhile I am happy even in this life, for I make small account of all its evils, in which I regard myself as having little or no part, while all the real good that I can get out of this life depends on myself alone.

To raise myself so far as may be even now to this state of happiness, strength, and freedom, I exercise myself in lofty contemplation. I consider the order of the universe, not to explain it by any futile system, but to revere it without ceasing, to adore the wise Author who reveals himself in it. I hold intercourse with him; I immerse all my powers in his divine essence; I am overwhelmed by his kindness, I bless him and his gifts, but I do not pray to him. What should I ask of him—to change the order of nature, to work miracles on my behalf? Should I, who am bound to love above all things the order which he has established in his wisdom and maintained by his providence, should I desire the disturbance of that order on my own account? No, that rash prayer would deserve to be punished rather than to be granted. Neither do I ask of him the power to do right; why should I ask what he has given me already? Has he not given me conscience that I may love the right, reason that I may perceive it, and freedom that I may choose it? If I do evil, I have no excuse; I do it of my own free will; to ask him to change my will is to ask him to do what he asks of me; it is to want him to do the work while I get the wages; to be dissatisfied with my lot is to wish to be no longer a man, to wish to be other than what I am, to wish for disorder and evil. Thou source of justice and truth, merciful and gracious God, in thee do I trust, and the desire of my heart is—Thy will be done. When I unite my will with thine, I do what thou doest; I have a share in thy goodness; I believe that I enjoy beforehand the supreme happiness which is the reward of goodness.

In my well-founded self-distrust the only thing that I ask of God, or rather expect from his justice, is to correct my error if I go astray, if that error is dangerous to me. To be honest I need not think myself infallible; my opinions, which seem to me true, may be so many lies; for what man is there who does not cling to his own beliefs; and how many men are agreed in everything? The illusion which deceives me may indeed have its source in myself, but it is God alone who can remove it. I have done all I can to attain to truth; but its source is beyond my reach; is it my fault if my strength fails me and I can go no further; it is for Truth to draw near to me.

DAVID HUME

Hume's criticism of familiar "proofs" of religious truth is one of the finest literary achievements of the eighteenth century as well as an essay of extraordinary intellectual power. Written in the form of a discussion among men who have different arguments for religious faith, it challenges practically every major assumption of traditional theology. It also includes an attack on Hume's contemporaries the Deists, who believed that one could deduce from nature logical proof of the existence of a loving, rational God.

Because of its wit and the range of its argument the *Dialogues* is an attractive introduction to the continuing modern debates about the nature of religious belief that were stimulated by the criticism of the Enlightenment philosophers.

DIALOGUES CONCERNING NATURAL RELIGION

Part I

AFTER I joined the company, whom I found sitting in Cleanthes's library, Demea paid Cleanthes some compliments, on the great care which he took of my education, and on his unwearied perseverance and constancy in all his friendships. The father of Pamphilus, said he, was your intimate friend: The son is your pupil and may indeed be regarded as your adopted son; were we to judge by the pains which you bestow in conveying to him every useful branch of literature and science. You are no more wanting, I am persuaded, in prudence than in industry. I shall, therefore, communicate to you a maxim, which I have observed with regard to my own children, that I may learn how far it agrees with your practice. The method I follow in their education is founded on the saying of an ancient, "That students of philosophy ought first to learn logics, then ethics, next physics, last of all the nature of the Gods." This science of natural theology, according to him, being the most profound and abstruse of any, required the maturest judgment in its students; and none but a mind, enriched with all the other sciences, can safely be entrusted with it.

Are you so late, says Philo, in teaching your children the principles of religion? Is there no danger of their neglecting or rejecting altogether, those opinions, of which they have heard so little during the whole course of their education? It is only as a science, replied Demea, subjected to human reasoning and disputation, that I postpone the study of natural theology. To season their minds with early piety is my chief care; and by continual precept and instruction, and I hope too, by example, I imprint deeply on their tender minds an habitual reverence for all the principles of religion. While they pass through every other science, I still remark the uncertainty of each part, the eternal disputations of men, the obscurity of all philosophy, and the strange ridiculous conclusions, which some of the greatest geniuses have derived from the principles of mere human reason. Having thus tamed their mind to a proper submission and self-diffidence, I have no longer any scruple of opening to them the greatest mysteries of religion, nor apprehend any danger from that assuming arrogance of philosophy, which may lead them to reject the most established doctrines and opinions.

Your precaution, says Philo, of seasoning your children's minds with early piety, is certainly very reasonable; and no more than is requisite, in this profane and irreligious age. But what I chiefly admire in your plan of education, is your method of drawing advantage from the very principles of philosophy and learning, which, by inspiring pride and self-sufficiency, have commonly, in all ages, been found so destructive to the principles of religion. The vulgar, indeed, we may remark, who are unacquainted with science and profound enquiry, observing the endless disputes of the learned, have commonly a thorough contempt for philosophy; and rivet themselves the faster, by that means in the great points of theology, which have been taught them. Those who enter a little into study and enquiry, finding many appearances of evidence in doctrines the newest and most extraordinary, think nothing too difficult for human reason; and presumptuously breaking through all fences, profane the inmost sanctuaries of the temple. But Cleanthes will, I hope, agree with me, that, after we have abandoned ignorance, the surest remedy, there is still one expedient left to prevent this profane liberty. Let Demea's principles be improved and cultivated: Let us become thoroughly sensible of the weakness, blindness, and narrow limits of human reason: Let us duly consider its uncertainty and needless contrarieties, even in subjects of common life and practice: Let the errors and deceits of our very senses be set before us; the insuperable difficulties, which attend first principles in all systems; the contradictions, which adhere to the very ideas of matter, cause and effect, extension, space, time, motion; and in a word, quantity of all kinds, the object of the only science, that can fairly pretend to any certainty or evidence. When these topics are displayed in their full light, as they are by some philosophers and almost all divines; who can retain such confidence in this frail faculty of reason as to pay any regard to its determinations in points so sublime, so abstruse, so remote from common life and experience? When the coherence of the parts of a stone, or even that composition of parts, which renders it extended; when these familiar objects, I say, are so inexplicable, and contain circumstances so repugnant and contradictory; with what assurance can we decide concerning the origin of worlds, or trace their history from eternity to eternity?

While Philo pronounced these words, I could observe a smile in the countenances both of Demea and Cleanthes. That of Demea seemed to imply an unreserved satisfaction in the doctrines delivered: But in Cleanthes's features, I could distinguish an air of finesse; as if he perceived some raillery or artificial malice in the reasonings of Philo.

You propose then, Philo, said Cleanthes, to erect religious faith on philosophical scepticism; and you think that if certainty or evidence be expelled from every other subject of enquiry, it will all retire to these theological doctrines, and there acquire a superior force and authority. Whether your scepticism be as absolute and sincere as you pretend, we shall learn bye and bye, when the company breaks up: We shall then see, whether you go out at the door or the window; and whether you really doubt, if your body has gravity, or can be injured by its fall; according to popular opinion, derived from our fallacious senses and more fallacious experience. And this consideration, Demea, may, I think, fairly serve to abate our ill-will to this humourous sect of the sceptics. If they be thoroughly in earnest, they will not long trouble the world with their doubts, cavils, and disputes: If they be only in jest, they are, perhaps, bad railliers, but can never be very dangerous, either to the state, to philosophy, or to religion.

In reality, Philo, continued he, it seems certain, that though a man, in a flush of humour, after intense reflection on the many contradictions and imperfections of human reason, may entirely renounce all belief and opinion; it is impossible for him to persevere in this total scepticism, or make it appear in his conduct for a few hours. External objects press in upon him: Passions solicit him: His philosophical melancholy dissipates; and even the utmost violence upon his own temper will not be able, during any time, to preserve the poor appearance of scepticism. And for what reason impose on himself such a violence? This is a point in which it will be impossible for him ever to satisfy himself, consistently with his sceptical principles: So that upon the whole nothing could be more ridiculous than the principles of the ancient Pyrrhonians; if in reality they endeavoured, as is pretended, to extend throughout, the same scepticism, which they had learned from the declamations of their school, and which they ought to have confined to them.

In this view, there appears a great resemblance between the sects of the Stoics and Pyrrhonians, though perpetual antagonists: And both of them seem founded on this erroneous maxim, that what a man can perform sometimes, and in some dispositions, he can perform always, and in every disposition. When the mind, by Stoical reflections, is elevated into a sublime enthusiasm of virtue, and strongly smit with any species of honour or public good, the utmost bodily pain and sufferance will not prevail over such a high sense of duty; and it is possible, perhaps, by its means, even to smile and exult in the midst of tortures. If this sometimes may be the case in fact and reality, much more may a philosopher, in his school, or even in his closet, work himself up to such an enthusiasm and support in imagination the acutest pain or most calamitous event which he can possibly conceive. But how shall he support this enthusiasm itself? The bent of his mind relaxes, and cannot be recalled at pleasure: Avocations lead him astray: Misfortunes attack him unawares: And the *philosopher* sinks by degrees into the *plebeian*.

I allow of your comparison between the Stoics and Sceptics, replied Philo. But you may observe, at the same time, that though the mind cannot, in Stoicism, support the highest flights of philosophy, yet even when it sinks lower, it still retains somewhat of its former disposition; and the effects of the Stoic's reasoning will appear in his conduct in common life, and through the whole tenor of his actions. The ancient schools, particularly that of Zeno, produced examples of virtue and constancy which seem astonishing to present times.

> Vain Wisdom all and false Philosophy
> Yet with a pleasing sorcery could charm
> Pain, for a while, or anguish, and excite
> Fallacious Hope, or arm the obdurate breast
> With stubborn Patience, as with triple steel.

In like manner, if a man has accustomed himself to sceptical considerations on the uncertainty and narrow limits of reason, he will not entirely forget them when he turns his reflections on other subjects; but in all his philosophical principles and reasoning, I dare not say, in his common conduct, he will be found different from those, who either never formed any opinions in the case, or have entertained sentiments more favourable to human reason.

To whatever length any one may push his speculative principles of scepticism, he must act, I own, and live, and converse like other men; and for this conduct he is not obliged to give any other reason than the absolute necessity he lies under of so doing. If he ever carries his speculations farther than this necessity constrains him, and philosophises, either on natural or moral subjects, he is allured by a certain pleasure and satisfaction, which he finds in employing himself after that manner. He considered besides, that every one, even in common life, is constrained to have more or less of this philosophy; that from our earliest infancy we make continual advances in forming more general principles of conduct and reasoning; that the larger experience we acquire, and the stronger reason we are endowed with, we always render our principles the more general and comprehensive; and that what we call *philosophy* is nothing but a more regular and methodical operation of the same kind. To philosophise on such subjects is nothing essentially different from reasoning on common life; and we may only expect greater stability, if not greater truth, from our philosophy, on account of its exacter and more scrupulous method of proceeding.

But when we look beyond human affairs and the properties of the surrounding bodies; when we carry our speculations into the two eternities, before and after the present state of things; into the creation and formation of the universe; the existence and properties of spirits; the powers and operations of one universal spirit, existing without beginning and without end; omnipotent, omniscient, immutable, infinite, and incomprehensible; We must be far removed from the smallest tendency to scepticism not to be apprehensive, that we have here got quite beyond the reach of our faculties. So long as we confine our speculations to trade, or morals, or politics, or criticism, we make appeals, every moment, to common sense and experience, which strengthen our philosophical conclusions, and remove (at least, in part), the suspicion, which we so justly entertain with regard to every reasoning that is very subtile and refined. But in theological reasonings, we have not this advantage; while at the same time we are employed upon objects, which, we must be sensible, are too large for our grasp, and of all others, require most to be familiarised to our apprehension. We are like foreigners in a strange country, to whom everything must seem suspicious, and who are in danger every moment of transgressing against the laws and customs of the people with whom they live and converse. We know not how far we ought to trust our vulgar methods of reasoning in such a subject; since, even in common life and in that province which is peculiarly appropriated to them, we cannot account for them, and are entirely guided by a kind of instinct or necessity in employing them.

All sceptics pretend, that, if reason be considered in an abstract view, it furnished invincible arguments against itself, and that we could never retain any conviction or assurance, on any subject, were not the sceptical reasonings so refined and subtile, that they are not able to counterpoise the more solid and more natural arguments, derived from the senses and experience. But it is evident, whenever our arguments lose this advantage, and run wide of common life, that the most refined scepticism comes to be upon a footing with them, and is able to oppose and counterbalance them. The one has no more weight than the other. The mind must remain in suspense between them; and it is that very suspense or balance, which is the triumph of scepticism.

But I observe, says Cleanthes, with regard to you, Philo, and all speculative sceptics, that your doctrine and practice are as much at variance in the most abstruse points of theory as in the conduct of common life. Wherever evidence discovers itself, you adhere to it, nothwithstanding you pretended scepticism; and I can observe, too, some of your sect to be as decisive as those who make greater professions of certainty and assurance. In reality, would not a man be ridiculous, who pretended to reject Newton's explication of the wonderful phenomenon of the rainbow, because that explication gives a minute anatomy of the rays of light; a subject, forsooth, too refined for human comprehension? And what would you say to one who having nothing particular to object to the arguments of Copernicus and Galileo for the motion of the earth, should withhold his assent, on that general principle that these subjects were too magnificent and remote to be explained by the narrow and fallacious reason of mankind?

There is indeed a kind of brutish and ignorant scepticism, as you well observed, which gives the vulgar a general prejudice against what they do not easily understand, and makes them reject every principle which requires elaborate reasoning to prove and establish it. This species of scepticism is fatal to knowledge, not to religion; since we find, that those who make greatest profession of it, give often their assent, not only to the great truths of theism, and natural theology, but even to the most absurd tenets, which a traditional superstition has recommended to them. They firmly believe in witches; though they will not believe nor attend to the most simple proposition of Euclid. But the refined and philosophical sceptics fall into an inconsistence of an opposite nature. They push their researches into the most abstruse corners of science; and their assent attends them in every step, proportioned to the evidence which they meet with. They are even obliged to acknowledge, that the most abstruse and remote objects are those which are best explained by philosophy. Light is in reality anatomized: The true system of the heavenly bodies is discovered and ascertained. But the nourishment of bodies by food is still an inexplicable mystery: The cohesion of the parts of matter is still incomprehensible. These sceptics, therefore, are obliged, in every question, to consider each particular evidence apart, and proportion their assent to the precise degree of evidence which occurs. This is their practice in all natural, mathematical, moral, and political science.

And why not the same, I ask, in the theological and religious? Why must conclusions of this nature be alone rejected on the general presumption of the insufficiency of human reason, without any particular discussion of the evidence? Is not such an unequal conduct a plain proof of prejudice and passion?

Our senses, you say, are fallacious, our understanding erroneous, our ideas even of the most familiar objects, extension, duration, motion, full of absurdities and contradictions. You defy me to solve the difficulties, or reconcile the repugnancies, which you discover in them. I have not capacity for so great an undertaking: I have not leisure for it: I perceive it to be superfluous. Your own conduct, in every circumstance, refutes your principles; and shows the firmest reliance on all the received maxims of science, morals, prudence, and behaviour.

I shall never assent to so harsh an opinion as that of a celebrated writer, who says that the sceptics are not a sect of philosophers: They are only a sect of liars. I may, however, affirm (I hope without offence), that they are a sect of jesters or railliers. But for my part, whenever I find myself disposed to mirth and amusement, I shall certainly choose my entertainment of a less perplexing and abstruse nature. A comedy, a novel, or at most a history, seems a more natural recreation than such metaphysical subtilties and abstractions.

In vain would the sceptic make a distinction between science and common life, or between one science and another. The arguments employed in all, if just, are of a similar nature, and contain the same force and evidence. Or if there be any difference among them, the advantage lies entirely on the side of theology and natural religion. Many principles of mechanics are founded on very abstruse reasoning; yet no man, who has any pretensions to science, even no speculative sceptic, pretends to entertain the least doubt with regard to them. The Copernican system contains the most surprising paradox, and the most contrary to our natural conceptions, to appearances, and to our very senses: Yet even monks and inquisitors are now constrained to withdraw their opposition to it. And shall Philo, a man of so liberal a genius, and extensive knowledge, entertain any general undistinguished scruples with regard to the religious hypothesis, which is founded on the simplest and most obvious arguments, and, unless it meet with artificial obstacles, has such easy access and admission into the mind of man?

And here we may observe, continued he, turning himself towards Demea, a pretty curious circumstance in the history of the sciences. After the union of philosophy with the popular religion, upon the first establishment of Christianity, nothing was more usual, among all religious teachers, than declamations against reason, against the senses, against every principle, derived merely from human research and enquiry. All the topics of the ancient Academics were adopted by the Fathers; and thence propagated for several ages in every school and pulpit throughout Christendom. The Reformers embraced the same principles of reasoning, or rather declamation; and all panegyrics on the excellency of faith were sure to be interlarded with some severe strokes of satire against natural reason. A celebrated prelate too, of the Romish communion, a man of the most extensive learning, who wrote a demonstration of Christianity, has also composed a treatise, which contains all the cavils of the boldest and most determined Pyrrhonism. Locke seems to have been the first Christian, who ventured openly to assert that *faith* was nothing but a species of *reason,* that religion was only a branch of philosophy, and that a chain of arguments, similar to that which established any truth in morals, politics, or physics, was always employed in discovering all the principles of theology, natural and revealed. The ill use, which Bayle and other libertines made of the philosophical scepticism of the Fathers and first Reformers, still further propagated the judicious sentiment of Mr. Locke: And it is now, in a manner, avowed, by all pretenders to reasoning and philosophy, that atheist and sceptic are almost synonymous. And as it is certain, that no man is in earnest, when he professes the latter principle; I would fain hope that there are as few, who seriously maintain the former.

Don't you remember, said Philo, the excellent saying of Lord Bacon on the head? That a little philosophy, replied Cleanthes, makes a man an atheist: A great deal converts him to religion. That is a very judicious remark too, said Philo. But what I have in my eye is another passage, where, having mentioned David's fool, who said in his heart there is no God, this great philosopher observes, that the atheists nowadays have a double share of folly: For they are not contented to say in their hearts there is no God, but they also utter that impiety with their lips, and are thereby guilty of multiplied indiscretion and imprudence. Such people though they were ever so much in earnest, cannot, methinks, be very formidable.

But though you should rank me in this class of fools, I cannot forbear communicating a remark that occurs to me from the history of the religions and irreligious scepticism with which you have entertained us. It appears to me, that there are strong symptoms of priestcraft in the whole progress of this affair. During ignorant ages, such as those which followed the dissolution of the ancient schools, the priests perceived, that atheism, deism, or heresy of any kind, could only proceed from the presumptuous questioning of received opinions, and from a belief that human reason was equal to everything. Education had then a mighty influence over the minds of men, and was almost equal in force to those suggestions of the senses and common understanding, by which the most determined sceptic must allow himself to be governed. But at present, when the influence of education is much diminished, and men, from a more open commerce of the world, have learned to compare the popular principles of different nations and ages, our sagacious divines have changed their whole system of philosophy, and talk the language of Stoics, Platonists, and Peripatetics, not that of Pyrrhonians and Academics. If we distrust human reason, we have now no other principle to lead us into religion. Thus sceptics in one age, dogmatists in another; whichever system best suits the purpose of these reverend gentlemen, in giving them an ascendant over mankind, they are sure to make it their favourite principle and established tenet.

It is very natural, said Cleanthes, for men to embrace those principles, by which they find they can best defend their doctrines; nor need we have any recourse to priestcraft to account for so reasonable an expedient. And surely, nothing can afford a stronger presumption, that any set of principles are true, and ought to be embraced, than to observe, that they tend to the confirmation of true religion, and serve to confound the cavils of atheists, libertines and freethinkers of all denominations.

Part IV

It seems strange to me, said Cleanthes, that you Demea, who are so sincere in the cause of religion, should still maintain the mysterious, incomprehensible nature of the Deity, and should insist so strenuously, that he has no manner of likeness or resemblance to human creatures. The Deity, I can readily allow, possesses many powers and attributes, of which we can have no comprehension: But if our ideas, so far as they go, be not just and adequate, and correspondent to his real nature, I know not what there is in this subject worth insisting on. Is the name, without any meaning, of such mighty importance? Or how do you Mystics, who maintain the absolute incomprehensibility of the Deity, differ from sceptics or atheists, who assert, that the first cause of All is unknown and unintelligible? Their temerity must be very great, if, after rejecting the production by a mind; I mean, a mind resembling the human (for I know of no other), they pretend to assign, with certainty, any other specific, intelligible cause: And their conscience must be very scrupulous indeed, if they refuse to call the universal, unknown cause a God or Deity; and to bestow on him as many sublime eulogies and unmeaning epithets, as you shall please to require of them.

Who could imagine, replied Demea, that Cleanthes, the calm, philosophi-

cal Cleanthes, would attempt to refute his antagonists, by affixing a nick-
name to them; and like the common bigots and inquisitors of the age,
have recourse to invective and declamation, instead of reasoning? Or does he
not perceive, that these topics are easily retorted, and that *anthropomorphite*
is an appellation as invidious, and implies as dangerous consequences, as the
epithet of *mystic,* with which he has honoured us? In reality, Cleanthes, consider what it is you assert, when you represent the Deity as similar to a
human mind and understanding. What is the soul of man? A composition
of various faculties, passions, sentiments, ideas; united, indeed into one self or
person, but still distinct from each other. When it reasons, the ideas, which are
the parts of its discourse, arrange themselves in a certain form or order; which
is not preserved entire for a moment, but immediately gives place to another
arrangement. New opinions, new passions, new affections, new feelings arise,
which continually diversify the mental scene, and produce in it the greatest
variety, and most rapid succession imaginable. How is this compatible with
that perfect immutability and simplicity, which all true theists ascribe to
the Deity? By the same act, say they, he sees past, present and future: His
love and his hatred, his mercy and his justice are one individual operation:
He is entire in every point of space; and complete in every instance of duration. No succession, no change, no acquisition, no diminution. What he is
implies not in it any shadow of distinction or diversity. And what he is,
this moment, he ever has been, and ever will be, without any new judgment, sentiment, or operation. He stands fixed in one simple, perfect, state;
nor can you ever say, with any propriety, that this act of his is different from
that other, or that this judgment or idea has been lately formed, and will
give place, by succession, to any different judgment or idea.

I can readily allow, said Cleanthes, that those who maintain the perfect
simplicity of the supreme Being, to the extent in which you have explained
it, are complete *mystics,* and chargeable with all the consequences which I
have drawn from their opinion. They are, in a word, atheists, without knowing it. For though it be allowed, that the Deity possesses attributes, of which
we have no comprehension; yet ought we never to ascribe to him any attributes, which are absolutely incompatible with that intelligent nature, essential to him. A mind, whose acts and sentiments and ideas are not distinct
and successive; one that is wholly simple, and totally immutable; is a mind
which has no thought, no reason, no will, no sentiment, no love, no hatred;
or in a word, is no mind at all. It is an abuse of terms to give it that appellation; and we may as well speak of limited extension without figure, or of
number without composition.

Pray consider, said Philo, whom you are at present inveighing against. You are honouring with the appellation of atheist all the sound, orthodox divines almost, who have treated of this subject; and you will, at last, be, yourself, found, according to your reckoning, the only sound theist in the world. But if idolaters be atheists, as I think may justly be asserted, and Christian theologians the same; What becomes of the argument, so much celebrated, derived from the universal consent of mankind?

But because I know you are not much swayed by names and authorities, I shall endeavour to show you, a little more distinctly, the inconveniences of that anthropomorphism, which you have embraced; and shall prove, that there is no ground to suppose a plan of the world to be formed in the divine mind, consisting of distinct ideas, differently arranged; in the same manner as an architect forms in his head the plan of a house which he intends to execute.

It is not easy, I own, to see, what is gained by this supposition, whether we judge of the matter by *reason* or by *experience*. We are still obliged to mount higher, in order to find the cause of this cause, which you had assigned as satisfactory and conclusive.

If *reason* (I mean abstract reason, derived from enquiries *a priori*) be not alike mute with regard to all questions concerning cause and effect; this sentence at least it will venture to pronounce, That a mental world or universe of ideas requires a cause as much as does a material world or universe of objects; and if similar in its arrangement must require a similar cause. For what is there in this subject, which should occasion a different conclusion or inference? In an abstract view, they are entirely alike; and no difficulty attends the one supposition, which is not common to both of them.

Again, when we will needs force *experience* to pronounce some sentence, even on these subjects, which lie beyond her sphere; neither can she perceive any material difference in this particular, between these two kinds of worlds, but finds them to be governed by similar principles, and to depend upon an equal variety of causes in their operations. We have specimens in miniature of both of them. Our own mind resembles the one: A vegetable or animal body the other. Let experience, therefore, judge from these samples. Nothing seems more delicate with regard to its causes than thought; and as these causes never operate in two persons after the same manner, so we never find two persons, who think exactly alike. Nor indeed does the same person think exactly alike at any two different periods of time. A difference of age, of the disposition of his body, of weather, of food, of company, of books, of passions; any of these particulars or others more minute, are sufficient to alter the curious machinery of thought, and communicate to it very different movements and operations. As far as we can judge, vegetables and animal bodies are not more delicate in their motions, nor depend upon a greater variety or more curious adjustment of springs and principles.

How therefore shall we satisfy ourselves concerning the cause of that Being, whom you suppose the Author of nature, or according to your system of anthropomorphism, the ideal world, into which you trace the material? Have we not the same reason to trace that ideal world into another ideal world, or new intelligent principle? But if we stop, and go no farther; why go so far? Why not stop at the material world? How can we satisfy ourselves without going on *ad infinitum?* And, after all, what satisfaction is there in that infinite progression? Let us remember the story of the Indian philosopher and his elephant. It was never more applicable than to the present subject. If the material world rests upon a similar ideal world, this ideal world must rest upon some other; and so on, without end. It were better, therefore, never to look beyond the present material world. By supposing it to contain the principle of its order within itself, we really assert it to be God; and the sooner we arrive at that divine Being so much the better. When you go one step beyond the mundane system you only excite an inquisitive humour, which it is impossible ever to satisfy.

To say, that the different ideas, which compose the reason of the supreme Being, fall into order, of themselves, and by their own nature, is really to talk without any precise meaning. If it has a meaning, I would fain know, why it is not as good sense to say that the parts of the material world fall into order, of themselves, and by their own nature? Can the one opinion be intelligible, while the other is not so?

We have, indeed, experience of ideas, which fall into order, of themselves, and without any *known* cause: But I am sure, we have a much larger experience of matter, which does the same; as in all instances of generation and vegetation, where the accurate analysis of the cause exceeds all human comprehension. We have also experience of particular systems of thought and of matter, which have no order; of the first, in madness, of the second, in corruption. Why then should we think, that order is more essential to one than the other? And if it requires a cause in both, what do we gain by your system, in tracing the universe of objects into a similar universe of ideas? The first step, which we make, leads us on forever. It were, therefore, wise in us, to limit all our enquiries to the present world, without looking farther. No satisfaction can ever be attained by these speculations, which so far exceed the narrow bounds of human understanding.

It was usual with the Peripatetics, you know, Cleanthes, when the cause of any phenomenon was demanded, to have recourse to their *faculties* or *occult qualities,* and to say, for instance, that bread nourished by its nutritive faculty, and senna purged by its purgative: But it has been discovered, that this subterfuge was nothing but the disguise of ignorance; and that these philosophers, though less ingenuous, really said the same thing with the sceptics or the vulgar, who fairly confessed, that they knew not the cause of these phenomena. In like manner, when it is asked, what cause produced order in the ideas of the supreme Being, can any other reason be assigned by you, anthropomorphites, than that it is a *rational* faculty, and that such is the nature of the Deity? But why a similar answer will not be equally satisfactory in accounting for the order of the world, without having recourse to any such intelligent Creator as you insist on, may be difficult to determine. It is only to say, that *such is* the nature of material objects, and that they are all originally possessed of a *faculty* of order and proportion. These are only more learned and elaborate ways of confessing our ignorance; nor has the one hypothesis any real advantage above the other, except in its greater conformity to vulgar prejudices.

You have displayed this argument with great emphasis, replied Cleanthes: You seem not sensible, how easy it is to answer it. Even in common life, if I assign a cause for any event; is it any objection, Philo, that I cannot assign the cause of that cause, and answer every new question which may incessantly be started? And what philosophers could possibly submit to so rigid a rule? philosophers, who confess ultimate causes to be totally unknown, and are sensible, that the most refined principles, into which they trace the phenomena, are still to them as inexplicable as these phenemona themselves are to the vulgar. The order and arrangement of nature, the curious adjustment of final causes, the plain use and intention of every part and organ; all these bespeak in the clearest language an intelligent cause or Author. The heavens and the earth join in the same testimony: The whole chorus of nature raises one hymn to the praises of its Creator: You alone, or almost alone, disturb this general harmony. You start abstruse doubts, cavils and objections: You ask me, what is the cause of this cause? I know not; I care not; that concerns not me. I have found a Deity; and here I stop my enquiry. Let those go farther who are wiser or more enterprising.

I pretend to be neither, replied Philo: And for that very reason, I should never perhaps have attempted to go so far; especially when I am sensible, that I must at last be contented to sit down with the same answer, which, without farther trouble, might have satisfied me from the beginning. If I am still to remain in utter ignorance of causes, and can absolutely give an explication of nothing, I shall never esteem it any advantage to shove off for a moment a difficulty, which, you acknowledge, must immediately, in its full force, recur upon me. Naturalists indeed very justly explain particular effects by more general causes; though these general causes themselves should remain in the end totally inexplicable: But they never surely thought it satisfactory to explain a particular effect by a particular cause, which was no more to be accounted for than the effect itself. An ideal system, arranged of itself, without a precedent design, is not a whit more explicable than a material one, which attains its order in a like manner; nor is there any more difficulty in the latter supposition than in the former.

Part V

BUT TO SHOW you still more inconveniences, continued Philo, in your anthropomorphism; please to take a new survey of your principles. *Like effects prove like causes.* This is the experimental argument; and this, you say too, is the sole theological argument. Now it is certain, that the liker the effects are, which are seen, and the liker the causes, which are inferred, the stronger is the argument. Every departure on either side diminishes the probability, and renders the experiment less conclusive. You cannot doubt of this principle: Neither ought you to reject its consequences.

All the new discoveries in astronomy, which prove the immense grandeur and magnificence of the works of nature, are so many additional arguments for a Deity, according to the true system of theism: But according to your hypothesis of experimental theism, they become so many objections, by removing the effect still farther from all resemblance to the effects of human art and contrivance. For if Lucretius, even following the old system of the world could exclaim:

> Quis regere immensi summam, quis habere profundi
> Indu manu validas potis est moderanter habenas?
> Quis pariter coelos omnes convertere? et omnes
> Ignibus aetheriis terras suffire feraces?
> Omnibus inque locis esse omni tempore praesto? [1]

If *Tully* esteemed this reasoning so natural, as to put it into the mouth of his Epicurean: *Quibus enim oculis animi intueri potuit vester Plato fabricam illam tanti operis, qua construi a Deo atque aedificari mundum facit? quae molitio? quae ferramenta? qui vectes? quae machinae? qui ministri tanti muneris fuerunt? quemadmodum autem obedire et parere voluntati architecti aer, ignis, aqua, terra potuerunt?* [2] If this argument, I say, had any

---

[1] *De Rerum Natura.* Who can rule the sun, who hold in his hand with controlling force the strong reins, of the immeasurable deep? Who can at once make all the different heavens to roll and warm with ethereal fires all the fruitful earths, or be present in all places at all times?

[2] *De Natura Deorum.* For with what eyes could your Plato see the construction of so vast

force in former ages; how much greater must it have at present; when the bounds of nature are so infinitely enlarged, and such a magnificent scene is opened to us? It is still more unreasonable to form our idea of so unlimited a cause from our experience of the narrow productions of human design and invention.

The discoveries by microscopes, as they open a new universe in miniature, are still objections, according to you; arguments, according to me. The farther we push our researches of this kind, we are still led to infer the universal cause of All to be vastly different from mankind, or from any object of human experience and observation.

And what say you to the discoveries in anatomy, chemistry, botany? . . . These surely are no objections, replied Cleanthes: They only discover new instances of art and contrivance. It is still the image of mind reflected on us from innumerable objects. Add, a mind *like the human,* said Philo. I know of no other, replied Cleanthes. And the liker the better, insisted Philo. To be sure, said Cleanthes.

Now, Cleanthes, said Philo, with an air of alacrity and truimph, mark the consequences. *First,* By this method of reasoning, you renounce all claim to infinity in any of the attributes of the Deity. For as the cause ought only to be proportioned to the effect, and the effect, so far as it falls under our cognisance, is not infinite; what pretensions have we, upon your suppositions, to ascribe that attribute to the divine Being? You will still insist, that, by removing him so much from all similarity to human creatures, we give into the most arbitrary hypothesis, and at the same time weaken all proofs of his existence.

Secondly, You have no reason, on your theory, for ascribing perfection to the Deity, even in his finite capacity; or for supposing him free from every error, mistake, or incoherence in his undertakings. There are many inexplicable difficulties in the works of nature, which, if we allow a perfect Author to be proved *a priori,* are easily solved, and become only seeming difficulties, from the narrow capacity of man, who cannot trace infinite relations. But according to your method of reasoning, these difficulties become all real; and perhaps will be insisted on, as new instances of likeness to human art and contrivance. At least, you must acknowledge, that it is impossible for us to tell, from our limited views, whether this system contains any great faults, or deserves any considerable praise, if compared to other possible, and even real systems. Could a peasant, if the *Aeneid* were read to him,

---

a work which, according to him, God was putting together and building? What materials, what tools, what bars, what machines, what servants were employed in such gigantic work? How could the air, fire, water, and earth pay obedience and submit to the will of the architect?

pronounce that poem to be absolutely faultless, or even assign to it its proper rank among the productions of human wit; he, who had never seen any other production?

But were this world ever so perfect a production, it must still remain uncertain, whether all the excellencies of the work can justly be ascribed to the workman. If we survey a ship, what an exalted idea must we form of the ingenuity of the carpenter, who framed so complicated, useful, and beautiful a machine? And what surprise must we entertain, when we find him a stupid mechanic, who imitated others, and copied an art, which, through a long succession of ages, after multiplied trials, mistakes, corrections, deliberations, and controversies, had been gradually improving? Many worlds might have been botched and bungled, throughout an eternity, ere this system was struck out: Much labour lost: Many fruitless trials made: And a slow, but continued improvement carried on during infinite ages in the art of world-making. In such subjects, who can determine, where the truth; nay, who can conjecture where the probability, lies; amidst a great number of hypotheses which may be proposed, and a still greater number which may be imagined?

And what shadow of an argument, continued Philo, can you produce, from your hypothesis, to prove the unity of the Deity? A great number of men join in building a house or ship, in rearing a city, in framing a commonwealth: Why may not several Deities combine in contriving and framing a world? This is only so much greater similarity to human affairs. By sharing the work among several, we may so much farther limit the attributes of each, and get rid of that extensive power and knowledge, which must be supposed in one Deity, and which, according to you, can only serve to weaken the proof of his existence. And if such foolish, such vicious creatures as man can yet often unite in framing and executing one plan; how much more those Deities or Daemons, whom we may suppose several degrees more perfect?

To multiply causes, without necessity, is indeed contrary to true philosophy: But this principle applies not to the present case. Were one Deity antecedently proved by your theory, who were possessed of every attribute requisite to the production of the universe; it would be needless, I own (though not absurd) to suppose any other Deity existent. But while it is still a question, whether all these attributes are united in one subject, or dispersed among several independent Beings: By what phenomena in nature can we pretend to decide the controversy? Where we see a body raised in a scale, we are sure that there is in the opposite scale, however concealed from sight, some counterpoising weight equal to it: But it is still allowed to doubt, whether that weight be an aggregate of several distinct bodies, or one uni-form united mass. And if the weight requisite very much exceeds any thing which we have ever seen conjoined in any single body, the former supposi-tion becomes still more probable and natural. An intelligent Being of such vast power and capacity, as is necessary to produce the universe, or, to speak in the language of ancient philosophy, so prodigious an animal, exceeds all analogy, and even comprehension.

But farther, Cleanthes; men are mortal, and renew their species by genera-tion; and this is common to all living creatures. The two great sexes of male and female, says Milton, animate the world. Why must this circum-stance, so universal, so essential, be excluded from those numerous and limited Deities? Behold then the theogony of ancient times brought back upon us.

And why not become a perfect anthropomorphite? Why not assert the Deity or Deities to be corporeal, and to have eyes, a nose, mouth, ears, etc. Epi-curus maintained, that no man had ever seen reason but in a human figure; therefore the gods must have a human figure. And this argument, which is deservedly so much ridiculed by Cicero, becomes, according to you, solid and philosophical.

In a word, Cleanthes, a man, who follows your hypothesis, is able, per-haps, to assert or conjecture, that the universe, sometime, arose from some-thing like design: But beyond that position he cannot ascertain one single circumstance, and is left afterwards to fix every point of his theology, by the utmost licence of fancy and hypothesis. This world, for aught he knows, is very faulty and imperfect, compared to a superior standard; and was only the first rude essay of some infant Deity, who afterwards abandoned it, ashamed of his lame performance; it is the work only of some dependent, inferior Deity; and is the object of derision to his superiors; it is the pro-duction of old age and dotage in some superannuated Deity; and ever since his death, has run on at adventures, from the first impulse and active force, which it received from him . . . You justly give signs of horror, Demea, at these strange suppositions: But these, and a thousand more of the same kind, are Cleanthes's suppositions, not mine. From the moment the attri-butes of the Deity are supposed finite, all these have place. And I cannot, for my part, think, that so wild and unsettled a system of theology is, in any respect, preferable to none at all.

These suppositions I absolutely disown, cried Cleanthes: They strike me, however, with no horror; especially, when proposed in that rambling way in which they drop from you. On the contrary, they give me pleasure, when I see that, by the utmost indulgence of your imagination, you never get rid of the hypothesis of design in the universe; but are obliged, at every turn, to have recourse to it. To this concession I adhere steadily; and this I regard as a sufficient foundation for religion.

Part VI

It MUST BE a slight fabric, indeed, said Demea, which can be erected on so tottering a foundation. While we are uncertain, whether there is one Deity or many; whether the Deity or Deities, to whom we owe our existence, be perfect or imperfect, subordinate or supreme, dead or alive; what trust or confidence can we repose in them? What devotion or worship address to them? What veneration or obedience pay them? To all the purposes of life, the theory of religion becomes altogether useless: And even with regard to speculative consequences, its uncertainty, according to you, must render it totally precarious and unsatisfactory.

To render it still more unsatisfactory, said Philo, there occurs to me another hypothesis, which must acquire an air of probability from the method of reasoning so much insisted on by Cleanthes. That like effects arise from like causes: This principle he supposes the foundation of all religion. But there is another principle of the same kind, no less certain, and derived from the same source of experience; that where several known circumstances are *observed* to be similar, the unknown will also be *found* similar. Thus, if we see the limbs of a human body, we conclude, that it is also attended with a human head, though hid from us. Thus, if we see, through a chink in a wall, a small part of the sun, we conclude, that, were the wall removed, we should see the whole body. In short, this method of reasoning is so obvious and familiar, that no scruple can ever be made with regard to its solidity.

Now if we survey the universe, so far as it falls under our knowledge, it bears a great resemblance to an animal or organized body, and seems actuated with a like principle of life and motion. A continual circulation of matter in it produces no disorder: A continual waste in every part is incessantly repaired: The closest sympathy is perceived throughout the entire system: And each part or member, in performing its proper offices, operates both to its own preservation and to that of the whole. The world, therefore, I infer, is an animal, and the Deity is the Soul of the world, actuating it, and actuated by it.

You have too much learning, Cleanthes, to be at all surprised at this opinion, which, you know, was maintained by almost all the theists of antiquity, and chiefly prevails in their discourses and reasonings. For though sometimes the ancient philosophers reason from final causes, as if they thought the world the workmanship of God; yet it appears rather their favourite notion to consider it as his body, whose organization renders it subservient to him. And it must be confessed, that as the universe resembles more a human body than it does the works of human art and contrivance; if our limited analogy could ever, with any propriety, be extended to the whole of nature, the inference seems juster in favour of the ancient than the modern theory.

There are many other advantages too, in the former theory, which recommended it to the ancient theologians. Nothing more repugnant to all their notions, because nothing more repugnant to common experience, than mind without body; a mere spiritual substance, which fell not under their senses nor comprehension, and of which they had not observed one single instance throughout all nature. Mind and body they knew, because they felt both: An order, arrangement, organization, or internal machinery in both they likewise knew, after the same manner: And it could not but seem reasonable to transfer this experience to the universe, and to suppose the divine mind and body to be also coeval, and to have, both of them, order and arrangement naturally inherent in them, and inseparable from them.

Here therefore is a new species of anthropomorphism, Cleanthes, on which you may deliberate; and a theory which seems not liable to any considerable difficulties. You are too much superior surely to *systematical prejudices,* to find any more difficulty in supposing an animal body to be, originally, of itself, or from unknown causes, possessed of order and organization, than in supposing a similar order to belong to mind. But the *vulgar prejudice,* that body and mind ought always to accompany each other, ought not, one should think, to be entirely neglected; since it is founded on *vulgar experience,* the only guide which you profess to follow in all these theological inquiries. And if you assert, that our limited experience is an unequal standard, by which to judge of the unlimited extent of nature; you entirely abandon your own hypothesis, and must thenceforward adopt our mysticism, as you call it, and admit of the absolute incomprehensibility of the divine nature.

This theory, I own, replied Cleanthes, has never before occurred to me, though a pretty natural one; and I cannot readily, upon so short an examination and reflection, deliver any opinion with regard to it. You are very scrupulous, indeed, said Philo; were I to examine any system of yours, I should not have acted with half that caution and reserve, in starting objections and difficulties to it. However, if any thing occur to you, you will oblige us by proposing it.

Why then, replied Cleanthes, it seems to me that, though the world does, in many circumstances, resemble an animal body; yet is the analogy also effective in many circumstances, the most material: No organs of sense; no seat of thought or reason; no one precise origin of motion and action. In short, it seems to bear a stronger resemblance to a vegetable than to an animal; and your inference would be so far inconclusive in favour of the soul of the world.

But in the next place, your theory seems to imply the eternity of the world; and that is a principle which, I think, can be refuted by the strongest reasons and probabilities. I shall suggest an argument to this purpose, which I believe, has not been insisted on by any writer. Those, who reason from the late origin of arts and sciences, though their inference wants not force, may perhaps be refuted by considerations derived from the nature of human society, which is in continual revolution between ignorance and knowledge, liberty and slavery, riches and poverty; so that it is impossible for us, from our limited experience, to foretell with assurance what events may or may not be expected. Ancient learning and history seem to have been in great danger of entirely perishing after the inundation of the barbarous nations; and had these convulsions continued a little longer, or been a little more violent, we should not probably have now known what passed in the world a few centuries before us. Nay, were it not for the superstition of the Popes, who preserved a little jargon of Latin, in order to support the appearance of an ancient and universal church, that tongue must have been utterly lost: In which case, the Western world, being totally barbarous, would not have been in a fit disposition for receiving the Greek language and learning, which was conveyed to them after the sacking of Constantinople. When learning and books had been extinguished, even the mechanical arts would have fallen considerably to decay; and it is easily imagined, that fable or tradition might ascribe to them a much later origin than the true one. This vulgar argument, therefore, against the eternity of the world, seems a little precarious.

But here appears to be the foundation of a better argument. Lucullus was the first that brought cherry-trees from Asia to Europe; though that tree thrives so well in many European climates, that it grows in the woods without any culture. Is it possible, that, throughout a whole eternity, no European had ever passed into Asia and thought of transplanting so delicious a fruit into his own country? Or if the tree was once transplanted and propagated, how could it ever afterwards perish? Empires may rise and fall; liberty and slavery succeed alternately; ignorance and knowledge give place to each other; but the cherry-tree will still remain in the woods of Greece, Spain and Italy, and will never be affected by the revolutions of human society.

It is not two thousand years since vines were transplanted into France; though there is no climate in the world more favourable to them. It is not three centuries since horses, cows, sheep, swine, dogs, corn, were known in America. Is it possible, that, during the revolutions of a whole eternity, there never arose a Columbus, who might open the communication between Europe and that continent? We may as well imagine, that all men would wear stockings for ten thousand years, and never have the sense to think of garters to tie them. All these seem convincing proofs of the youth, or rather infancy, of the world; as being founded on the operation of principles more constant and steady than those by which human society is governed and directed. Nothing less than a total convulsion of the elements will ever destroy all the European animals and vegetables, which are now to be found in the Western world.

And what argument have you against such convulsions? replied Philo. Strong and almost incontestable proofs may be traced over the whole earth, that every part of this globe has continued for many ages entirely covered with water. And though order were supposed inseparable from matter, and inherent in it; yet may matter be susceptible of many and great revolutions, through the endless periods of eternal duration. The incessant changes, to which every part of it is subject, seem to intimate some such general trans-formations; though at the same time, it is observable, that all the changes and corruptions, of which we have ever had experience, are but passages from one state of order to another; nor can matter ever rest in total de-formity and confusion. What we see in the parts, we may infer in the whole; at least, that is the method of reasoning on which you rest your whole theory. And were I obliged to defend any particular system of this nature (which I never willingly should do), I esteem none more plausible than that which ascribes an eternal, inherent principle of order to the world; though attended with great and continual revolutions and alterations. This at once solves all difficulties; and if the solution, by being so general, is not entirely com-plete and satisfactory, it is, at least, a theory, that we must, sooner or later, have recourse to, whatever system we embrace. How could things have been as they are, were there not an original, inherent principle of order somewhere, in thought or in matter? And it is very indifferent to which of these we give the preference. Chance has no place, on any hypothesis, scepti-cal or religious. Every thing is surely governed by steady, inviolable laws. And were the inmost essence of things laid open to us, we should then discover a scene, of which, at present, we can have no idea. Instead of admir-ing the order of natural beings, we should clearly see, that it was absolutely impossible for them, in the smallest article, ever to admit of any other disposition.

Were any one inclined to revive the ancient Pagan Theology, which maintained, as we learn from Hesiod, that this globe was governed by 30,000 Deities, who arose from the unknown powers of nature: You would naturally object, Cleanthes, that nothing is gained by this hypothesis, and that it is as easy to suppose all men and animals, beings more numerous, but less perfect, to have sprung immediately from a like origin. Push the same inference a step farther; and you will find a numerous society of Deities as explicable as one universal Deity, who possesses, within himself, the powers and perfections of the whole society. All these systems, then, of scepticism, polytheism, and theism, you must allow, on your principles, to be on a like footing, and that no one of them has any advantages over the others. You may thence learn the fallacy of your principles.

XIV THE ENLIGHTENMENT: POLITICS AND ECONOMICS

FREDERICK THE GREAT

THAT THE TENETS and ideals of the Enlightenment were not the exclusive property of those who believed in liberal constitutional government is indicated by the term "enlightened despotism," applied to the efforts of such rulers as Frederick II (king of Prussia, 1740–86), Catherine II (empress of Russia, 1762–96), and Joseph II of Austria (Holy Roman emperor, 1765–90). France's failure to temper despotism with sufficient enlightenment was directly related to the outbreak of the great Revolution in 1789.

The best example of the enlightened despot of the eighteenth century is Frederick the Great. Born in 1712, the eldest son of Frederick William I, he was given a very severe military education, but thanks to his mother, acquired a taste for literature and music and a knowledge of French. After a few attempts to escape his father's rigorous rule, he settled down to his duties, all the while maintaining a correspondence with Voltaire and other French men of letters. Two of his best-known works were composed during this period: the *Considérations sur l'état présent du corps politique de l'Europe* and the *Anti-Macchiavel,* the former calling for a third power in Europe, obviously Prussia, the latter enunciating the principle that the king is only the first servant of his people.

It was in this spirit that he ruled when he came to the throne. He tolerated every form of religious opinion, abolished the use of torture, and maintained justice, and even allowed free access to his presence to all citizens with grievances. The greatest results of Frederick's concern for legal reform were the *Codex Fridericianus* (1747), by which the Prussian judicial body was established, and the *Allgemeines preussisches Landrecht,* which combined the two systems of German and Roman law with the law of nature. This, the first of the modern German codes, came into effect only in 1796. Frederick instituted no fundamental reorganization of society, however, and acquired much of his glory through conquest.

In 1741 he invaded Silesia, to which he had a claim. Having gained a good deal of territory, and having concluded an alliance with France against Maria Theresa of Austria, he invaded Bohemia. His victories made him the most conspicuous sovereign of his day. He filled public offices with capable, conscientious men, promoted education, established colonies, encouraged science (though not literature, since he considered German a boorish language) and industry.

Maria Theresa was still concerned to regain Silesia; and Frederick, discovering her plans, formed an alliance with England and invaded Saxony, thus opening the Seven Years' War (1756–63), which he won in the face of the opposition of all the powers of Europe. Prussia came into its own as the equal of Austria, and her eminence produced the first national feelings in Germany.

That Frederick's labors were undertaken in an enlightened if not liberal spirit is shown by his writings, of which the following essay, privately printed in 1777 and translated in 1789 by Thomas Holcroft, will serve as an example.

AN ESSAY ON FORMS OF GOVERNMENT

WE ARE ASTONISHED at imagining the human race so long existing in a brutal state, and without forming itself into societies. Reasons are accordingly suggested, such as might induce people like these to unite in bodies. It must have been the violence and pillage which existed, among neighbouring hordes, that could have first inspired such savage families with the wish of uniting, that they might secure their possessions by mutual defence. Hence laws took birth, which taught those societies to prefer the general to individual good. From that time, no person durst seize on the effects of another, because of the dread of chastisement. The life, the wife, and the wealth of a neighbour were sacred; and, if the whole society were attacked, it was the duty of the whole to assemble for its defence. The grand truth,—"That we should do unto others as they should do unto us"—became the principle of laws, and of the social compact. Hence originated the love of our country, which was regarded as the asylum of happiness.

But, as these laws could neither be maintained nor executed, unless some one should incessantly watch for their preservation, magistrates arose, out of this necessity, whom the people elected, and to whom they subjected themselves. Let it be carefully remembered that the preservation of the laws was the sole reason which induced men to allow of, and to elect, a superior; because this is the true origin of sovereign power. The magistrate, thus appointed, was the first servant of the state. When rising states had any thing to fear from their neighbours, the magistrate armed the people, and flew to the defence of the citizens.

That general instinct, in men, which leads them to procure for themselves the greatest possible happiness, occasioned the creation of various forms of government. Some imagined that, by confiding themselves to the guidance of a few sages, they should find this great happiness; hence the aristocratic form. Others preferred an oligarchy. Athens, and most of the Grecian republics, chose a democratical government. Persia, and the east, bowed beneath despotism. The Romans, for a time, had kings; but, weary of the tyranny of the Tarquins, they changed the monarchy into an aristocracy. Presently tired of the severity of the Patricians, who oppressed them by usury, the people left the city, and did not return to Rome till the senate had first approved the tribunes, elected by Plebeians for their defence against the power of the great. The people afterward rendered their authority almost supreme. Those who seized violently on government, and who, following the guidance of the passions and of caprice, reversed the laws and overturned those fundamental principles which had been established for the preservation of society, were denominated tyrants.

But, however sage the legislators, and those who first assembled the people in bodies were, however good their intentions might be, not one of these governments is found to have maintained its perfect integrity. And why? Because men are imperfect, consequently so are their works: because the citizens, employed by the prince, were blinded by individual interest, which always overthrows the general good and, in fine, because there is no stability on earth.

In aristocracies, the abuse which the principal members of the society make of their authority is the general cause of succeeding revolutions. The Roman democracy was destroyed by the people themselves. The blind multitude of the Plebeians suffered themselves to be corrupted by ambitious citizens, by whom they were afterward deprived of their liberty, and enslaved. This is what England has to dread, if the lower house of parliament should not prefer the true interest of the nation to that infamous corruption by which it is degraded.

As to monarchical government, of this there are various forms. The ancient feudal government, which some ages since was almost general in Europe, was established by the conquest of the Barbarians. The general of a horde rendered himself sovereign of the conquered country, and divided its provinces among his principal officers; who, it is true, were subject to the lord paramount, and who supplied him with troops when required; but, as some of these vassals became equally powerful with their chief, this formed state within state; and hence a series of civil wars, which were the misfortune of the whole. In Germany, these vassals are become independent; in France, England, and Spain, they are suppressed. The only example that remains, of that abominable form of government, is the republic of Poland.

In Turkey, the sovereign is despotic: he may with impunity commit the most atrocious cruelties; but it also often happens, by a vicissitude common to barbarous nations, or from a just retribution, that he in his turn is strangled.

With respect to the true monarchical government, it is the best or the worst of all others, accordingly as it is administered.

We have remarked that men granted pre-eminence to one of their equals, in expectation that he should do them certain services. These services consisted in the maintenance of the laws; a strict execution of justice; an employment of his whole powers to prevent any corruption of manners; and defending the state against its enemies. It is the duty of this magistrate to pay attention to agriculture; it should be his care that provisions for the nation should be in abundance, and that commerce and industry should be encouraged. He is a perpetual sentinel, who must watch the acts and the conduct of the enemies of the state. His foresight and prudence should form timely alliances, which should be made with those who might most conduce to the interest of the association.

By this short abstract, the various branches of knowledge, which each article in particular requires, will be perceived. To this must be added a profound study of the local situation of the country, which it is the magistrate's duty to govern, and a perfect knowledge of the genius of the nation; for the sovereign who sins through ignorance is as culpable as he who sins through malice: the first is the guilt of idleness, the latter of a vicious heart; but the evil that results to society is the same.

Princes and monarchs, therefore, are not invested with supreme authority that they may, with impunity, riot in debauchery and voluptuousness. They are not raised by their fellow citizens in order that their pride may pompously display itself, and contemptuously insult simplicity of manners, poverty and wretchedness. Government is not intrusted to them that they may be surrounded by a crowd of useless people, whose idleness engenders every vice.

The ill administration of monarchical government originates in various causes, the source of which is in the character of the sovereign. Thus a prince addicted to women suffers himself to be governed by his mistresses, and his favourites, who abuse the ascendancy they have over his mind, commit injustice, protect the most vicious, sell places, and are guilty of other similar acts of infamy. If the prince, through debility, should abandon the helm of the state to mercenary hands, I mean to ministers, in that case, each having different views, no one proceeds on general plans: the new minister fritters away what he finds already established, however excellent that may be, to acquire the character of novelty, and execute his own schemes, generally to the detriment of the public good. His successors do the like; they destroy and overturn with equal want of understanding, that they may be supposed to possess originality. Hence that succession of change and variation which allows no project time to take root; hence confusion, disorder, and every vice of a bad administration. Prevaricators have a ready excuse; they shelter their turpitude under these perpetual changes.

Men attach themselves to that which appertains to them, and the state does not appertain to these ministers, for which reason they have not its real good at heart; business is carelessly executed, and with a kind of stoic indifference; and hence results the decay of justice, and the ill administration of the finances and the military. From a monarchy, as it was, the government degenerates into a true aristocracy, in which ministers and generals conduct affairs, according to their own fancies. There is no longer any comprehensive system; each pursues his own plans, and the central point, the point of unity, is lost. As all the wheels of a watch correspond to effect the same purpose, which is that of measuring time, so ought the springs of government to be regulated, that all the different branches of administration may equally concur to the greatest good of the state; an important object, of which we ought never to lose sight.

We may add, the personal interest of ministers and generals usually occasions them to counteract each other without ceasing, and sometimes to impede the execution of the best plans, because they had not been conceived by themselves. But the evil is at its utmost, when perverse minds are able to persuade the sovereign that his welfare and the public good are two things. The monarch then becomes the enemy of his people, without knowing why; is severe, rigorous, and inhuman, from mistake; for, the principle on which he acts being false, the consequences must necessarily be the same.

The sovereign is attached by indissoluble ties to the body of the state; hence it follows that he, by repercussion, is sensible of all the ills which afflict his subjects; and the people, in like manner, suffer from the misfortunes which affect their sovereign. There is but one general good, which is that of the state. If the monarch lose his provinces, he is no longer able as formerly to assist his subjects. If misfortune have obliged him to contract debts, they must be liquidated by the poor citizens; and, in return, if the people are not numerous, and if they are oppressed by poverty, the sovereign is destitute of all resource. These are truths so incontestable that there is no need to insist on them further.

I once more repeat, the sovereign represents the state; he and his people form but one body, which can only be happy as far as united by concord. The prince is to the nation he governs what the head is to the man; it is his duty to see, think, and act for the whole community, that he may procure it every advantage of which it is capable. If it be intended that a monarchical should excel a republican government, sentence is pronounced on the sovereign. He must be active, possess integrity, and collect his whole powers, that he may be able to run the career he has commenced. Here follow my ideas concerning his duties.

He ought to procure exact and circumstantial information of the strength and weakness of his country, as well relative to pecuniary resources as to population, finance, trade, laws, and the genius of the nation whom he is appointed to govern. If the laws are good they will be clear in their definitions; otherwise, chicanery will seek to elude their spirit to its advantage, and arbitrarily and irregularly determine the fortunes of individuals. Lawsuits ought to be as short as possible, to prevent the ruin of the appellants, who consume in useless expences what is justly and duly their right. This branch of government cannot be too carefully watched, that every possible barrier may be opposed to the avidity of judges and counsellors. Every person is kept within the limits of their duty, by occasional visits into the provinces. Whoever imagines himself to be injured will venture to make his complaints to the commission; and those who are found to be prevaricators ought to be severely punished. It is perhaps superfluous to add that the penalty ought never to exceed the crime; that violence never ought to supersede law; and that it were better the sovereign should be too merciful than too severe.

As every person who does not proceed on principle is inconsistent in his conduct, it is still more necessary that the magistrate who watches over the public good should act from a determinate system of politics, war, finance, commerce, and law. Thus, for example, a people of mild manners ought not to have severe laws, but such as are adapted to their character. The basis of such systems ought always to be correspondent to the greatest good society can receive. Their principles ought to be conformable to the situation of the country, to its ancient customs, if they are good, and to the genius of the nation.

As an instance, it is a known truth, in politics, that the most natural allies, and consequently the best, are those whose interests concur, and who are not such near neighbours as to be engaged in any contest respecting frontiers. It sometimes happens that strange accidents give place to extraordinary alliances. We have seen, in the present times, nations that had always been rivals, and even enemies, united under the same banners. But these are events that rarely take birth, and which never can serve as examples. Such connections can be no more than momentary; whereas the other kind, which are contracted from a unity of interests, are alone capable of exertion. In the present situation of Europe, when all her princes are armed, and among whom preponderating powers rise up capable of crushing the feeble, prudence requires alliances should be formed with other powers, as well to secure aid, in case of attack, as to repress the dangerous projects of enemies, and to sustain all just pretensions, by the succour of such allies, in opposition to those by whom they are controverted.

Nor is this sufficient. It is necessary to have among our neighbours, especially among our enemies, eyes and ears which shall be open to receive, and report with fidelity, what they have seen and heard. Men are wicked. Care must especially be taken not to suffer surprise, because whatever surprises intimidates and terrifies, which never happens when preparations are made, however vexatious the event may be which there is reason to expect.

European politics are so fallacious that the most sage may become dupes, if they are not always alert, and on their guard.

The military system ought, in like manner, to rest on good principles, which from experience are known to be certain. The genius of the nation ought to be understood; of what it is capable, and how far its safety may be risked by leading it against the enemy. The warlike customs of the Greeks and Romans are interdicted, in these ages. The discovery of gunpowder has entirely changed the mode of making war. A superiority of fire at present decides the day. Discipline, rules, and tactics have all been changed, in order that they may conform to this new custom; and the recent and enormous abuse of numerous trains of artillery, which incumber armies, obliges others, in like manner, to adopt this method; as well to maintain themselves in their posts as to attack the foe in those which they shall occupy, should reasons of importance so require. . . .

There are states which, from their situation and constitution, must be maritime powers: such are England, Holland, France, Spain, and Denmark. They are surrounded by the sea, and the distant colonies which they possess oblige them to keep a marine, to maintain communication and trade between the mother country and these detached members. There are other states, such as Austria, Poland, Prussia, and even Russia, some of which may well do without shipping; and others that would commit an unpardonable fault, in politics, were they to divide their forces by employing a part of their troops at sea, of the services of which they indispensably stand in need by land.

The number of troops which a state maintains ought to be in proportion to the troops maintained by its enemies. Their force should be equal, or the weakest is in danger of being oppressed. It perhaps may be objected that a king ought to depend on the aid of his allies. The reasoning would be good were allies what they ought to be; but their zeal is only lukewarm; and he who shall depend upon another as upon himself will most certainly be deceived. If frontiers permit them to be defended by fortresses, there must be no neglect in building, nor any expense spared to bring them to perfection. Of this France has given an example, and she has found the advantage of it on different occasions.

But neither politics nor the army can prosper if the finances are not kept in the greatest order, and if the prince himself be not a prudent economist. Money is like the wand of the necromancer, for by its aid miracles are performed. Grand political views, the maintenance of the military, and the best conceived plans for the ease of the people, will all remain in a lethargic state, if not animated by money. The economy of the sovereign is the more useful to the public good, because if he have not sufficient funds in reserve, either to supply the expenses of war, without loading his people with extraordinary taxes, or to succour citizens in times of public calamity, all these burthens will fall on the subjects, who will be without the resources, in such unhappy times, of which they will then stand in the most need.

No government can exist without taxation, which is equally necessary to the republic and to the monarchy. The sovereign who labours in the public cause must be paid by the public; the judge the same, that he may have no need to prevaricate. The soldier must be supported that he may commit no violence, for want of having whereon to subsist. In like manner, it is necessary that those persons who are employed in collecting the finances should receive such salaries as may not lay them under any temptation to rob the public. These various expenses demand very considerable sums, and to these must still be added money that should only be laid apart to serve for extraordinary exigences. This money must all be necessarily levied on the people; and the grand art consists in levying so as not to oppress. That taxes may be equally and not arbitrarily laid on, surveys and registers should be made, by which, if the people are properly classed, the money will be proportionate to the income of the persons paying. This is a thing so necessary that it would be an unpardonable fault, in finance, if ill-imposed taxes should disgust the husbandman with his labours. Having performed his duties, it is afterward necessary he and his family should live in a certain degree of ease. Far from oppressing the nursing fathers of the state, they ought to be encouraged in the cultivation of the lands; for in this cultivation the true riches of a country consists. . . .

Excise is another species of taxes, levied on cities, and this must be managed by able persons; otherwise, those provisions which are most necessary to life, such as bread, small beer, meat, &c, will be overloaded; and the weight will fall on the soldier, the labourer, and the artizan. The result will be, unhappily to the people, that the price of labour will be raised; consequently merchandize will become so dear as not to be saleable in foreign markets. . . . To obviate such inconveniences, the sovereign ought frequently to remember the condition of the poor, to imagine himself in the place of the peasant or the manufacturer, and then to say, "Were I born one among the class of citizens whose labours constitute the wealth of the state, what should I require from the king?" The answer which, on such a supposition, good sense would suggest it is his duty to put in practice.

In most of the kingdoms of Europe there are provinces in which the peasants are attached to the glebe, or are serfs to their lords. This, of all conditions, is the most unhappy, and that at which humanity most revolts.

No man certainly was born to be the slave of his equal. We reasonably detest such an abuse; and it is supposed that nothing more than will is wanting to abolish so barbarous a custom. But this is not true; it is held on ancient tenures, and contracts made between the landholders and the colonists. Tillage is regulated according to the service performed by the peasantry; and whoever should suddenly desire to abolish this abominable administration would entirely overthrow the mode of managing estates, and must be obliged, in part, to indemnify the nobility for the losses which their rents must suffer.

The state of manufactures and of trade, an article no less important, next presents itself. For the country to be preserved in prosperity, it is indubitably necessary that the balance of trade should be in its favour. If it pay more for importation than it gains by exportation, the result will be that it will be annually impoverished. Let us suppose a purse in which there are a hundred ducats, from which let us daily take one, and put none in, and every body will allow that in a hundred days the purse will be empty. The means to avoid incurring any such loss are to work up all raw materials of which the country is in possession, and to manufacture foreign raw materials, that the price of labour may be gained, in order to procure a foreign market.

Three things are to be considered in respect to commerce: first the surplus of native products which are exported; next the products of foreign states, which enrich those by whom they are carried; and thirdly foreign merchandize, which home consumption obliges the state to import. The trade of any kingdom must be regulated according to these three articles, for of these only is it susceptible, according to the nature of things. England, Holland, France, Spain, and Portugal, have possessions in the two Indies, and more extensive resources for their merchant ships than other kingdoms. To profit by such advantages as we are in possession of, and to undertake nothing beyond our strength, is the advice of wisdom. . . .

We shall now speak of another article, which perhaps is equally interesting. There are few countries in which the people are all of one religious opinion; they often totally differ. There are some who are called sectaries. The question then is started—Is it requisite that the people should all think alike, or may each one be allowed to think as he pleases? Gloomy politicians will tell us every body ought to be of the same opinion, that there may be no division among the citizens. The priests will add whoever does not think like me is damned, and it is by no means proper that my king should be the king of the damned. The inevitable deduction is they must be destroyed in this world, that they may be the more prosperous in the next.

To this it is answered that all the members of one society never thought alike; that, among Christian nations, the majority are Anthropomorphites; that, among the Catholics, most of the people are idolaters, for I shall never be persuaded that a clown is capable of distinguishing between *Latria* and *Hyperdulia*. He simply and really adores the image he invokes. Therefore there are a number of heretics in all Christian sects. What is more, each man believes that which appears to him to be truth. A poor wretch may be constrained to pronounce a certain form of prayer, although he inwardly refuse his consent. His persecutor consequently has gained nothing. But, if we revert to the origin of all society, it will be found evident that the sovereign has no right to interfere in the belief of the subject. Would it not be madness to imagine men who have said to another man, their equal, "We raise you to be our superior, because we are in love with slavery; and we bestow on you the power of directing our thoughts, according to your will?" On the contrary, they have said, "We have need of you for the maintenance of those laws which we are willing to obey, and that we may be wisely governed and defended; but we also require that you should respect our freedom." This is the sentence pronounced, and it is without appeal. Nay, tolerance is itself so advantageous, to the people among whom it is established, that it constitutes the happiness of the state. As soon as there is that perfect freedom of opinion, the people are all at peace; whereas persecution has given birth to the most bloody civil wars, and such as have been the most inveterate and the most destructive. The least evil that results from persecution is to occasion the persecuted to emigrate. The population of France has suffered in certain provinces, and those provinces still are sensible to the revocation of the edict of Nantes.

Such are in general the duties imposed upon a prince, from which, in order that he may never depart, he ought often to recollect he himself is but a man, like the least of his subjects. If he be the first general, the first minister of the realm, it is not that he should remain the shadow of authority, but that he should fulfill the duties of such titles. He is only the first servant of the state, who is obliged to act with probity and prudence; and to remain as totally disinterested as if he were each moment liable to render an account of his administrations to his fellow citizens.

Thus he is culpable, if he be prodigal of the money of the people, dispersing the produce of the taxes in luxury, pomp, or licentiousness. It is for him to watch over morals, which are the guardians of the laws, and to improve the national education, and not pervert it by ill examples. One of the most important objects is the preservation of good morals, in all their purity; to which the sovereign may greatly contribute, by distinguishing and rewarding those citizens who have performed virtuous actions, and testifying his contempt for such as are so depraved as not to blush at their own disorders. The prince ought highly to disapprove of every dishonest act, and refuse distinctions to men who are incorrigible.

There is another interesting object which ought not to be lost sight of, and which, if neglected, would be of irreparable prejudice to good morality; which is that princes are liable too highly to notice persons who are possessed of no other merit than that of great wealth. Honours, so undeservedly bestowed, confirm the people in the vulgar prejudice that wealth, only, is necessary to gain respect. Interest and cupidity will then break forth from the curb by which they are restrained. Each will wish to accumulate riches; and, to acquire these, the most iniquitous means will be employed. Corruption increases, takes root, and becomes general. Men of abilities and virtue are despised, and the public honour none but the bastards of Midas, who dazzle by their excessive dissipation and their pomp. To prevent national manners from being perverted to an excess so horrible, the prince ought to be incessantly attentive to distinguish nothing but personal merit, and to show his contempt for that opulence which is destitute of morals and of virtue.

As the sovereign is properly the head of a family of citizens, the father of his people, he ought on all occasions to be the last refuge of the unfortunate; to be the parent of the orphan, and the husband of the widow; to have as much pity for the lowest wretch as for the greatest courtier; and to shed his benefactions over those who, deprived of all other aid, can only find succour in his benevolence.

Such, according to the principles which we established at the beginning of this Essay, is the most accurate conception we can form of the duties of a sovereign, and the only manner which can render monarchical government good and advantageous. Should the conduct of many princes be found different, it must be attributed to their having reflected but little on their institution, and its derivatory duties. They have borne a burthen with the weight and importance of which they were unacquainted, and have been misled from the want of knowledge; for in our times ignorance commits more faults than vice. Such a sketch of sovereignty will perhaps appear to the censorious the archetype of the Stoics; an ideal sage, who never existed except in imagination, and to whom the nearest approach was Marcus Aurelius. We wish this feeble Essay were capable of forming men like Aurelius; it would be the highest reward we could possibly expect, at the same time that it would conduce to the good of mankind.

BARON DE MONTESQUIEU

CHARLES LOUIS DE SECONDAT, baron de la Brède et de Montesquieu (1689–1755) was born at the château of La Brède and educated for the law at the Oratorian school of Juilly and at Bordeaux. In 1716 his uncle died, leaving him the title "Montesquieu," a sizable fortune, and his important judicial office in the parliament of Bordeaux.

During the twelve years he held this office, he contributed papers on philosophy, politics, and natural science to the Bordeaux Academy; and in 1721 his popular satiric *Lettres persanes* appeared: this was perhaps the first major work of the *philosophes* and is one of the more notable of the eighteenth-century attempts to use other cultures as a basis for criticism of European life.

The reputation he acquired through this book procured him entry into the literary society of Paris, and in 1726 he sold the life-tenure of his office and went to live in Paris. After some difficulties over the possible subversive intent of the *Lettres,* he was elected to the Academy in 1728.

He then undertook a tour of Europe, including England, for which his admiration never diminished. Having returned to La Brède, he published, in 1734, the *Considérations sur les causes de la grandeur et de la décadence des Romains,* which was to be the most widely read of his works in his own time, and, apart from Bossuet and Vico, one of the first modern essays in the philosophy of history.

The *Esprit des lois* appeared in 1748; it was well received, although it was put on the Index, and the Sorbonne considered a regular censure of it. For a generation after Montesquieu's death, the book remained the authority of the moderate reform party; but, in general, his work has been more popular in England than in France, not merely because of his Anglophilia, but because of his notion of mixed government and his style of thought, which have been considered more English than French. Even the *philosophes* who shared his admiration for the English clung principally to the idea of reform through an enlightened, but still absolute, monarch.

The selection from the *Persian Letters* is from John Davidson's translation (London, 1892) and the excerpt from the *Spirit of the Laws* comes from the translation of Thomas Nugent (London, G. Bell and Sons, 1902).

THE PERSIAN LETTERS

Letter XXIV

WE HAVE NOW been a month at Paris, and all the time constantly moving about. There is much to do before one can get settled, find out the people with whom one has business, and procure the many requisites which are all wanted at the same time. . . .

You must not yet expect from me an exhaustive account of the manners and customs of the Europeans: I have myself but a faint notion of them yet, and have hardly had time to recover from my astonishment.

The King of France is the most powerful of European potentates. He has no mines of gold like his neighbor, the King of Spain; but he is much wealthier than that prince, because his riches are drawn from a more inexhaustible source, the vanity of his subjects. He has undertaken and carried on great wars, without any other supplies than those derived from the sale of titles of honor; and it is by a prodigy of human pride that his troops are paid, his towns fortified and his fleets equipped.

Then again, the king is a great magician, for his dominion extends to the minds of his subjects; he makes them think what he wishes. If he has only a million crowns in his exchequer, and has need of two millions, he has only to persuade them that one crown is worth two, and they believe it. If he has a costly war on hand, and is short of money, he simply suggests to his subjects that a piece of paper is coin of the realm, and they are straightway convinced of it. He has even succeeded in persuading them that his touch is a sovereign cure for all sorts of diseases, so great is the power and influence he has over their minds.

What I have told you of this prince need not astonish you: there is another magician more powerful still, who is master of the king's mind, as absolutely as the king is master of the minds of his subjects. This magician is called the Pope. Sometimes he makes the king believe that three are no more than one; that the bread which he eats is not bread; the wine which he drinks is not wine; and a thousand things of like nature.

And, to keep him in practice, and prevent him from losing the habit of belief, he gives him, now and again, as an exercise, certain articles of faith. Some two years ago he sent him a large document which he called *Constitution,* and wished to enforce belief in all that it contained upon this prince and his subjects under heavy penalties. He succeeded in the case of the king, who set the example of immediate submission; but some of his subjects revolted, and declared that they would not believe a single word of what was contained in this document. The women are the prime movers in this rebellion, which divides the court, the kingdom, and every family in the land, because the document prohibits them from reading a book which all the Christians assert is of divine origin: it is, indeed, their Koran. The women, enraged at this affront to their sex, exert all their power against the *Constitution;* and they have brought over to their side all the men who are not anxious about their privilege in the matter. And truly, the Mufti does not reason amiss. By the great Hali! he must have been instructed in the principles of our holy religion, because, since women are inferior creatures compared to us, and may not, according to our prophets, enter into Paradise, why should they meddle with a book which is only designed to teach the way thither?

Some things of a miraculous nature have been told me of the king, which I am certain will appear to you hardly credible.

It is said, that, while he was making war against such of his neighbors as had leagued against him, there were in his kingdom an infinite number of invisible foes surrounding him on all sides. They add, that, during a thirty years' search, in spite of the indefatigable exertions of certain dervishes who are in his confidence, not one of these has ever been discovered. They live with him, in his court and in his capital, among his troops, among his legislators; and yet it is believed that he will have the mortification of dying without having discovered them. They exist, as it were, in general, but not in particular: they constitute a body without members. Beyond a doubt, heaven wishes to punish this prince for his severity to the vanquished, in afflicting him with invisible enemies of a spirit and a destiny superior to his own.

I will continue to write you, and acquaint you with matters differing widely from the Persian character and genius. We tread, indeed, the same earth; but it seems incredible, remembering in the presence of the men of this country those of the country in which you are.

Paris, the 4th of the second moon of
  Rebiab, 1712

Letter XXVII

THE KING OF FRANCE is old. We have no examples in our histories of such a long reign as his. It is said that he possesses in a very high degree the faculty of making himself obeyed: he governs with equal ability his family, his court, and his kingdom: he has often been heard to say, that, of all existing governments, that of the Turks, or that of our august Sultan, pleased him best: such is his high opinion of Oriental statecraft.

I have studied his character, and I have found certain contradictions which I cannot reconcile. For example, he has a minister who is only eighteen years old, and a mistress who is fourscore; he loves his religion, and yet he cannot abide those who assert that it ought to be strictly observed; although he flies from the noises of cities, and is inclined to be reticent, from morning till night he is engaged in getting himself talked about; he is fond of trophies and victories, but he has as great a dread of seeing a good general at the head of his own troops, as at the head of an army of his enemies. It has never I believe happened to any one but himself, to be burdened with more wealth than even a prince could hope for, and yet at the same time steeped in such poverty as a private person could ill brook.

He delights to reward those who serve him; but he pays as liberally the assiduous indolence of his courtiers, as the labours in the field of his captains; often the man who undresses him, or who hands him his serviette at table, is preferred before him who has taken cities and gained battles; he does not believe that the greatness of a monarch is compatible with restriction in the distribution of favors; and, without examining into the merits of a man, he will heap benefits upon him, believing that his selection makes the recipient worthy; accordingly, he has been known to bestow a small pension upon a man who had run off two leagues from the enemy, and a good government on another who had gone four.

Above all, he is magnificent in his building; there are more statues in his palace gardens than there are citizens in a large town. His bodyguard is as strong as that of the prince before whom all the thrones of the earth tremble; his armies are as numerous, his resources as great, and his finances as inexhaustible.

Paris, the 7th of the moon of
Maharram, 1713

THE SPIRIT OF THE LAWS

Book I: Of Laws in General

I. OF THE RELATION OF LAWS TO DIFFERENT BEINGS

Laws, in their most general signification, are the necessary relations arising from the nature of things. In this sense all beings have their laws: the Deity His laws, the material world its laws, the intelligences superior to man their laws, the beasts their laws, man his laws.

They who assert that a blind fatality produced the various effects we behold in this world talk very absurdly; for can any thing be more unreasonable than to pretend that a blind fatality could be productive of intelligent beings?

There is, then, a prime reason; and laws are the relations subsisting between it and different beings, and the relations of these to one another.

God is related to the universe, as Creator and Preserver; the laws by which He created all things are those by which He preserves them. He acts according to these rules, because He knows them; He knows them, because He made them; and He made them, because they are in relation of His Wisdom and power.

Since we observe that the world, though formed by the motion of matter, and void of understanding, subsists through so long a succession of ages, its motions must certainly be directed by invariable laws; and could we imagine another world, it must also have constant rules, or it would inevitably perish.

Thus the creation, which seems an arbitrary act, supposes laws as invariable as those of the fatality of the Atheists. It would be absurd to say that the Creator might govern the world without those rules, since without them it could not subsist.

These rules are a fixed and invariable relation. In bodies moved, the motion is received, increased, diminished, or lost, according to the relations of the quantity of matter and velocity; each diversity is uniformity, each change is constancy.

Particular intelligent beings may have laws of their own making, but they have some likewise which they never made. Before there were intelligent beings, they were possible; they had therefore possible relations, and consequently possible laws. Before laws were made, there were relations of possible justice. To say that there is nothing just or unjust but what is commanded or forbidden by positive laws, is the same as saying that before the describing of a circle all the radii were not equal.

We must therefore acknowledge relations of justice antecedent to the positive law by which they are established: as, for instance, if human societies existed, it would be right to conform to their laws; if there were intelligent beings that had received a benefit of another being, they ought to show their gratitude; if one intelligent being had created another intelligent being, the latter ought to continue in its original state of dependence; if one intelligent being injures another, it deserves a retaliation; and so on.

But the intelligent world is far from being so well governed as the physical. For though the former has also its laws, which of their own nature are invariable, it does not conform to them so exactly as the physical world. This is because, on the one hand, particular intelligent beings are of a finite nature, and consequently liable to error; and on the other, their nature requires them to be free agents. Hence they do not steadily conform to their primitive laws; and even those of their own instituting they frequently infringe.

Whether brutes be governed by the general laws of motion, or by a particular movement, we cannot determine. Be that as it may, they have not a more intimate relation to God than the rest of the material world; and sensation is of no other use to them than in the relation they have either to other particular beings or to themselves.

By the allurement of pleasure they preserve the individual, and by the same allurement they preserve their species. They have natural laws, because they are united by sensation; positive laws they have none, because they are not connected by knowledge. And yet they do not invariably conform to their natural laws; these are better observed by vegetables, that have neither understanding nor sense.

Brutes are deprived of the high advantages which we have; but they have some which we have not. They have not our hopes, but they are without our fears; they are subject like us to death, but without knowing it; even most of them are more attentive than we to self-preservation, and do not make so bad a use of their passions.

Man, as a physical being, is like other bodies governed by invariable laws. As an intelligent being, he incessantly transgresses the laws established by God, and changes those of his own instituting. He is left to his private direction, though a limited being, and subject, like all finite intelligences, to ignorance and error: even his imperfect knowledge he loses; and as a sensible creature, he is hurried away by a thousand impetuous passions. Such a being might every instant forget his Creator; God has therefore reminded him of his duty by the laws of religion. Such a being is liable every moment to forget himself; philosophy has provided against this by the laws of morality. Formed to live in society, he might forget his fellow-creatures; legislators have, therefore, by political and civil laws, confined him to his duty.

II. OF THE LAWS OF NATURE

Antecedent to the above-mentioned laws are those of nature, so called, because they derive their force entirely from our frame and existence. In order to have a perfect knowledge of these laws, we must consider man before the establishment of society: the laws received in such a state would be those of nature.

The law which, impressing on our minds the idea of a Creator, inclines us towards Him, is the first in importance, though not in order, of natural laws. Man in a state of nature would have the faculty of knowing, before he had acquired any knowledge. Plain it is that his first ideas would not be of a speculative nature; he would think of the preservation of his being, before he would investigate its origin. Such a man would feel nothing in himself at first but impotency and weakness; his fears and apprehensions would be excessive; as appears from instances (were there any necessity of proving it) of savages found in forests, trembling at the motion of a leaf, and flying from every shadow.

In this state every man, instead of being sensible of his equality, would fancy himself inferior. There would, therefore, be no danger of their attacking one another; peace would be the first law of nature.

The natural impulse or desire which Hobbes attributes to mankind of subduing one another is far from being well founded. The idea of empire and dominion is so complex, and depends on so many other notions, that it could never be the first which occurred to the human understanding.

Hobbes inquires, "For what reason go men armed, and have locks and keys to fasten their doors, if they be not naturally in a state of war?" But is it not obvious that he attributes to mankind before the establishment of society what can happen but in consequence of this establishment, which furnishes them with motives for hostile attacks and self-defence?

Next to a sense of his weakness man would soon find that of his wants. Hence another law of nature would prompt him to seek for nourishment.

Fear, I have observed, would induce men to shun one another; but the marks of this fear being reciprocal, would soon engage them to associate. Besides, this association would quickly follow from the very pleasure one animal feels at the approach of another of the same species. Again, the attraction arising from the difference of sexes would enhance this pleasure, and the natural inclination they have for each other would form a third law.

Besides the sense or instinct which man possesses in common with brutes, he has the advantage of acquired knowledge; and thence arises a second tie, which brutes have not. Mankind have, therefore, a new motive of uniting; and a fourth law of nature results from the desire of living in society.

III. OF POSITIVE LAWS

As soon as man enters into a state of society he loses the sense of his weakness; equality ceases, and then commences the state of war.

Each particular society begins to feel its strength, whence arises a state of war between different nations. The individuals likewise of each society become sensible of their force; hence the principal advantages of this society they endeavor to convert to their own emolument, which constitutes a state of war between individuals.

These two different kinds of states give rise to human laws. Considered as inhabitants of so great a planet, which necessarily contains a variety of nations, they have laws relating to their mutual intercourse, which is what we call the law of nations. As members of a society that must be properly supported, they have laws relating to the governors and the governed, and this we distinguish by the name of politic law. They have also another sort of laws, as they stand in relation to each other; by which is understood the civil law.

The law of nations is naturally founded on this principle, that different nations ought in time of peace to do one another all the good they can, and in time of war as little injury as possible, without prejudicing their real interests.

The object of war is victory; that of victory is conquest; and that of conquest preservation. From this and the preceding principle all those rules are derived which constitute the law of nations.

All countries have a law of nations, not excepting the Iroquois themselves, though they devour their prisoners: for they send and receive ambassadors, and understand the rights of war and peace. The mischief is that their law of nations is not founded on true principles.

Besides the law of nations relating to all societies, there is a polity or civil constitution for each particularly considered. No society can subsist without a form of government. "The united strength of individuals," as Gravina [1] well observes, "constitutes what we call the body politic."

The general strength may be in the hands of a single person, or of many. Some think that nature having established paternal authority, the most natural

---

[1] [An Italian poet and jurist (1664–1718).]

government was that of a single person. But the example of paternal authority proves nothing. For if the power of a father relates to a single government, that of brothers after the death of a father, and that of cousins-german after the decease of brothers, refer to a government of many. The political power necessarily comprehends the union of several families.

Better is it to say that the government most conformable to nature is that which best agrees with the humor and disposition of the people in whose favor it is established.

The strength of individuals cannot be united without a conjunction of all their wills. "The conjunction of those wills," as Gravina again very justly observes, "is what we call the civil state."

Law in general is human reason, inasmuch as it governs all the inhabitants of the earth: the political and civil laws of each nation ought to be only the particular cases in which human reason is applied.

They should be adapted in such a manner to the people for whom they are framed that it should be a great chance if those of one nation suit another.

They should be in relation to the nature and principle of each government: whether they form it, as may be said of politic laws; or whether they support it, as in the case of civil institutions.

They should be in relation to the climate of each country, to the quality of its soil, to its situation and extent, to the principal occupation of the natives, whether husbandmen, huntsmen, or shepherds: they should have relation to the degree of liberty which the constitution will bear; to the religion of the inhabitants, to their inclinations, riches, numbers, commerce, manners, and customs. In fine, they have relations to each other, as also to their origin, to the intent of the legislator, and to the order of things on which they are established; in all of which different lights they ought to be considered.

This is what I have undertaken to perform in the following work. These relations I shall examine, since all these together constitute what I call the Spirit of Laws.

I have not separated the political from the civil institutions, as I do not pretend to treat of laws, but of their spirit; and as this spirit consists in the various relations which the laws may bear to different objects, it is not so much my business to follow the natural order of laws as that of these relations and objects.

I shall first examine the relations which laws bear to the nature and principle of each government; and as this principle has a strong influence on laws, I shall make it my study to understand it thoroughly: and if I can but once establish it, the laws will soon appear to flow thence as from their source. I shall proceed afterwards to other and more particular relations.

Book XI: Of the Laws Which Establish Political Liberty with Regard to the Constitution

I. A GENERAL IDEA

I make a distinction between the laws that establish political liberty as it relates to the constitution, and those by which it is established as it relates to the citizen. The former shall be the subject of this book; the latter I shall examine in the next.

II. DIFFERENT SIGNIFICATIONS OF THE WORD LIBERTY

There is no word that admits of more various significations, and has made more varied impressions on the human mind, than that of liberty. Some have taken it as a means of deposing a person on whom they had conferred a tyrannical authority; others for the power of choosing a superior whom they are obliged to obey; others for the right of bearing arms, and of being thereby enabled to use violence; others, in fine, for the privilege of being governed by a native of their own country, or by their own laws. A certain nation for a long time thought liberty consisted in the privilege of wearing a long beard. Some have annexed this name to one form of government exclusive of others: those who had a republican taste applied it to this species of polity; those who liked a monarchical state gave it to monarchy. Thus they have all applied the name of liberty to the government most suitable to their own customs and inclinations: and as in republics the people have not so constant and so present a view of the causes of their misery, and as the magistrates seem to act only in conformity to the laws, hence liberty is generally said to reside in republics, and to be banished from monarchies. In fine, as in democracies the people seem to act almost as they please, this sort of government has been deemed the most free, and the power of the people has been confounded with their liberty.

III. IN WHAT LIBERTY CONSISTS

It is true that in democracies the people seem to act as they please; but political liberty does not consist in an unlimited freedom. In governments, that is, in societies directed by laws, liberty can consist only in the power of doing what we ought to will, and in not being constrained to do what we ought not to will.

We must have continually present to our minds the difference between independence and liberty. Liberty is a right of doing whatever the laws permit, and if a citizen could do what they forbid he would be no longer possessed of liberty, because all his fellow-citizens would have the same power.

IV. THE SAME SUBJECT CONTINUED

Democratic and aristocratic states are not in their own nature free. Political liberty is to be found only in moderate governments; and even in these it is not always found. It is there only when there is no abuse of power. But constant experience shows us that every man invested with power is apt to abuse it, and to carry his authority as far as it will go. Is it not strange, though true, to say that virtue itself has need of limits?

To prevent this abuse, it is necessary from the very nature of things that power should be a check to power. A government may be so constituted, as no man shall be compelled to do things to which the law does not oblige him, nor forced to abstain from things which the law permits.

V. OF THE END OR VIEW OF DIFFERENT GOVERNMENTS

Though all governments have the same general end, which is that of preservation, yet each has another particular object. Increase of dominion was the object of Rome; war, that of Sparta; religion, that of the Jewish laws; commerce, that of Marseilles; public tranquillity, that of the laws of China; navigation, that of the laws of Rhodes; natural liberty, that of the policy of the Savages; in general, the pleasures of the prince, that of despotic states; that of monarchies, the prince's and the kingdom's glory; the independence of individuals is the end aimed at by the laws of Poland, thence results the oppression of the whole.

One nation there is also in the world that has for the direct end of its constitution political liberty. We shall presently examine the principles on which this liberty is founded; if they are sound, liberty will appear in its highest perfection.

To discover political liberty in a constitution, no great labor is requisite. If we are capable of seeing it where it exists, it is soon found and we need not go far in search of it.

VI. OF THE CONSTITUTION OF ENGLAND

In every government there are three sorts of power: the legislative; the executive in respect to things dependent on the law of nations; and the executive in regard to matters that depend on the civil law.

By virtue of the first, the prince or magistrate enacts temporary or perpetual laws, and amends or abrogates those that have been already enacted. By the second, he makes peace or war, sends or receives embassies, establishes the public security, and provides against invasions. By the third, he punishes criminals, or determines the disputes that arise between individuals. The latter we shall call the judiciary power, and the other simply the executive power of the state.

The political liberty of the subject is a tranquillity of mind arising from the opinion each person has of his safety. In order to have this liberty, it is requisite the government be so constituted as one man need not be afraid of another.

When the legislative and executive powers are united in the same person, or in the same body of magistrates, there can be no liberty; because apprehensions may arise, lest the same monarch or senate should enact tyrannical laws, to execute them in a tyrannical manner.

Again, there is no liberty, if the judiciary power be not separated from the legislative and executive. Were it joined with the legislative, the life and liberty of the subject would be exposed to arbitrary control; for the judge would be then the legislator. Were it joined to the executive power, the judge might behave with violence and oppression.

There would be an end of everything, were the same man or the same body, whether of the nobles or of the people, to exercise those three powers, that of enacting laws, that of executing the public resolutions, and of trying the causes of individuals.

Most kingdoms in Europe enjoy a moderate government because the prince who is invested with the two first powers leaves the third to his subjects. In Turkey, where these three powers are united in the Sultan's person, the subjects groan under the most dreadful oppression.

In the republics of Italy, where these three powers are united, there is less liberty than in our monarchies. Hence their government is obliged to have recourse to as violent methods for its support as even that of the Turks; witness the state inquisitors, and the lion's mouth into which every informer may at all hours throw his written accusations.

In what a situation must the poor subject be in those republics! The same body of magistrates are possessed, as executors of the laws, of the whole power they have given themselves in quality of legislators. They may plunder the state by their general determinations; and as they have likewise the judiciary power in their hands, every private citizen may be ruined by their particular decisions.

The whole power is here united in one body; and though there is no external pomp that indicates a despotic sway, yet the people feel the effects of it every moment.

Hence it is that many of the princes of Europe, whose aim has been levelled at arbitrary power, have constantly set out with uniting in their own persons all the branches of magistracy, and all the great offices of state.

I allow indeed that the mere hereditary aristocracy of the Italian republics does not exactly answer to the despotic power of the Eastern princes. The number of magistrates sometimes moderate the power of the magistracy; the whole body of the nobles do not always concur in the same design; and different tribunals are erected, that temper each other. Thus at Venice the legislative power is in the council, the executive in the *pregadi,* and the judiciary in the *quarantia.* But the mischief is, that these different tribunals are composed of magistrates all belonging to the same body; which constitutes almost one and the same power.

The judiciary power ought not to be given to a standing senate; it should be exercised by persons taken from the body of the people at certain times of the year, and consistently with a form and manner prescribed by law, in order to erect a tribunal that should last only so long as necessity requires.

By this method the judicial power, so terrible to mankind, not being annexed to any particular state or profession, becomes as it were, invisible. People have not then the judges continually present to their view; they fear the office, but not the magistrate.

In accusations of a deep and criminal nature, it is proper the person accused should have the privilege of choosing, in some measure, his judges, in concurrence with the law; or at least he should have a right to except against so great a number that the remaining part may be deemed his own choice.

The other two powers may be given rather to magistrates or permanent bodies, because they are not exercised on any private subject; one being no more than the general will of the state, and the other the execution of that general will.

But though the tribunals ought not to be fixed, the judgments ought; and to such a degree as to be ever conformable to the letter of the law. Were they to be the private opinion of the judge, people would then live in society, without exactly knowing the nature of their obligations.

The judges ought likewise to be of the same rank as the accused, or, in other words, his peers; to the end that he may not imagine he is fallen into the hands of persons inclined to treat him with rigor.

If the legislature leaves the executive power in possession of a right to imprison those subjects who can give security for their good behavior, there is an end of liberty; unless they are taken up, in order to answer without delay to a capital crime, in which case they are really free, being subject only to the power of the law.

But should the legislature think itself in danger by some secret conspiracy against the state, or by a correspondence with a foreign enemy, it might authorize the executive power, for a short and limited time, to imprison suspected persons, who in that case would lose their liberty only for a while, to preserve it forever.

And this is the only reasonable method that can be substituted to the tyrannical magistracy of the Ephori, and to the state inquisitors of Venice, who are also despotic.

As in a country of liberty, every man who is supposed a free agent ought to be his own governor; the legislative power should reside in the whole body of the people. But since this is impossible in large states, and in small ones is subject to many inconveniences, it is fit the people should transact by their representatives what they cannot transact by themselves.

The inhabitants of a particular town are much better acquainted with its wants and interests than with those of other places; and are better judges of the capacity of their neighbors than of that of the rest of their countrymen. The members, therefore, of the legislature should not be chosen from the general body of the nation; but it is proper that in every considerable place a representative should be elected by the inhabitants.

The great advantage of representatives is, their capacity of discussing public affairs. For this the people collectively are extremely unfit, which is one of the chief inconveniences of a democracy.

It is not at all necessary that the representatives who have received a general instruction from their constituents should wait to be directed on each particular affair, as is practised in the diets of Germany. True it is that by this way of proceeding the speeches of the deputies might with greater propriety be called the voice of the nation; but, on the other hand, this would occasion infinite delays; would give each deputy a power of controlling the assembly; and, on the most urgent and pressing occasions, the wheels of government might be stopped by the caprice of a single person.

When the deputies, as Mr. Sidney well observes, represent a body of people, as in Holland, they ought to be accountable to their constituents; but it is a different thing in England, where they are deputed by boroughs.

All the inhabitants of the several districts ought to have a right of voting at the election of a representative, except such as are in so mean a situation as to be deemed to have no will of their own.

One great fault there was in most of the ancient republics, that the people had a right to active resolutions, such as require some execution, a thing of which they are absolutely incapable. They ought to have no share in the government but for the choosing of representatives, which is within their reach. For though few can tell the exact degree of men's capacities, yet there are none but are capable of knowing in general whether the person they choose is better qualified than most of his neighbors.

Neither ought the representative body to be chosen for the executive part of government, for which it is not so fit; but for the enacting of laws, or to see whether the laws in being are duly executed, a thing suited to their abilities, and which none indeed but themselves can properly perform.

In such a state there are always persons distinguished by their birth, riches, or honors: but were they to be confounded with the common people, and to have only the weight of a single vote like the rest, the common liberty would be their slavery, and they would have no interest in supporting it, as most of the popular resolutions would be against them. The share they have, therefore, in the legislature ought to be proportioned to their other advantages in the state; which happens only when they form a body that has a right to check the licentiousness of the people, as the people have a right to oppose any encroachment of theirs.

The legislative power is therefore committed to the body of the nobles, and to that which represents the people, each having their assemblies and deliberations apart, each their separate views and interests.

Of the three powers above mentioned, the judiciary is in some measure next to nothing: there remain, therefore, only two; and as these have need of a regulating power to moderate them, the part of the legislative body composed of the nobility is extremely proper for this purpose.

The body of the nobility ought to be hereditary. In the first place it is so in its own nature; and in the next there must be a considerable interest to preserve its privileges—privileges that in themselves are obnoxious to popular envy, and of course in a free state are always in danger.

But as a hereditary power might be tempted to pursue its own particular interests, and forget those of the people, it is proper that where a singular advantage may be gained by corrupting the nobility, as in the laws relating to the supplies, they should have no other share in the legislation than the power of rejecting, and not that of resolving.

By the power of resolving I mean the right of ordaining by their own authority, or of amending what has been ordained by others. By the power of rejecting I would be understood to mean the right of annulling a resolution taken by another; which was the power of the tribunes at Rome. And though the person possessed of the privilege of rejecting may likewise have the right of approving, yet this approbation passes for no more than a declaration, that he intends to make no use of his privilege of rejecting, and is derived from that very privilege.

The executive power ought to be in the hands of a monarch, because this branch of government, having need of despatch, is better administered by one than by many: on the other hand, whatever depends on the legislative power is oftentimes better regulated by many than by a single person.

But if there were no monarch, and the executive power should be committed to a certain number of persons selected from the legislative body, there would be an end then of liberty; by reason the two powers would be united, as the same persons would sometimes possess, and would be always able to possess, a share in both.

Were the legislative body to be a considerable time without meeting, this would likewise put an end to liberty. For of two things one would naturally follow: either that there would be no longer any legislative resolutions, and then the state would fall into anarchy; or that these resolutions would be taken by the executive power, which would render it absolute.

It would be needless for the legislative body to continue always assembled. This would be troublesome to the representatives, and, moreover, would cut out too much work for the executive power, so as to take off its attention to its office, and oblige it to think only of defending its own prerogatives, and the right it has to execute.

Again, were the legislative body to be always assembled, it might happen to be kept up only by filling the places of the deceased members with new representatives; and in that case, if the legislative body were once corrupted, the evil would be past all remedy. When different legislative bodies succeed one another, the people who have a bad opinion of that which is actually sitting may reasonably entertain some hopes of the next: but were it to be always the same body, the people upon seeing it once corrupted would no longer expect any good from its laws; and of course they would either become desperate or fall into a state of indolence.

The legislative body should not meet of itself. For a body is supposed to have no will but when it is met; and besides, were it not to meet unanimously, it would be impossible to determine which was really the legislative body; the part assembled, or the other. And if it had a right to prorogue itself, it might happen never to be prorogued; which would be extremely dangerous, in case it should ever attempt to encroach on the executive power. Besides, there are seasons, some more proper than others, for assembling the legislative body: it is fit, therefore, that the executive power should regulate the time of meeting, as well as the duration of those assemblies, according to the circumstances and exigencies of a state known to itself.

Were the executive power not to have a right of restraining the encroachments of the legislative body, the latter would become despotic; for as it might arrogate to itself what authority it pleased, it would soon destroy all the other powers.

But it is not proper, on the other hand, that the legislative power should have a right to stay the executive. For as the execution has its natural limits, it is useless to confine it; besides, the executive power is generally employed in momentary operations. The power, therefore, of the Roman tribunes was faulty, as it put a stop not only to the legislation, but likewise to the executive part of government; which was attended with infinite mischief.

But if the legislative power in a free state has no right to stay the executive, it has a right and ought to have the means of examining in what manner its laws have been executed; an advantage which this government has over that of Crete and Sparta, where the Cosmi and the Ephori gave no account of their administration.

But whatever may be the issue of that examination, the legislative body ought not to have a power of arraigning the person, nor, of course, the conduct, of him who is intrusted with the executive power. His person should be sacred, because as it is necessary for the good of the state to prevent the legislative body from rendering themselves arbitrary, the moment he is accused or tried there is an end of liberty.

In this case the state would be no longer a monarchy, but a kind of republic, though not a free government. But as the person intrusted with the executive power cannot abuse it without bad counsellors, and such as have the laws as ministers, though the laws protect them as subjects, these men may be examined and punished—an advantage which this government has over that of Gnidus, where the law allowed of no such thing as calling the Amymones to an account, even after their administration; and therefore the people could never obtain any satisfaction of the injuries done them.

Though, in general, the judiciary power ought not to be united with any part of the legislative, yet this is liable to three exceptions, founded on the particular interest of the party accused.

The great are always obnoxious to popular envy; and were they to be judged by the people, they might be in danger from their judges, and would, moreover, be deprived of the privilege which the meanest subject is possessed of in a free state, of being tried by his peers. The nobility, for this reason, ought not to be cited before the ordinary courts of judicature, but before that part of the legislature which is composed of their own body.

It is possible that the law, which is clear sighted in one sense, and blind in another, might, in some cases, be too severe. But as we have already observed, the national judges are no more than the mouth that pronounces the words of the law, mere passive beings, incapable of moderating either its force or rigor. That part, therefore, of the legislative body, which we have just now observed to be a necessary tribunal on another occasion, also is a necessary tribunal in this; it belongs to its supreme authority to moderate the law in favor of the law itself, by mitigating the sentence.

It might also happen that a subject intrusted with the administration of public affairs may infringe the rights of the people, and be guilty of crimes which the ordinary magistrates either could not or would not punish. But, in general, the legislative power cannot try causes: and much less can it try this particular case, where it represents the party aggrieved, which is the people. It can only, therefore, impeach. But before what court shall it bring its impeachment? Must it go and demean itself before the ordinary tribunals, which are its inferiors, and, being composed, moreover, of men who are chosen from the people as well as itself, will naturally be swayed by the authority of so powerful an accuser? No: in order to preserve the dignity of the people and the security of the subject, the legislative part which represents the people must bring in its charge before the legislative part which represents the nobility, who have neither the same interests nor the same passions.

Here is an advantage which this government has over most of the ancient republics, where this abuse prevailed, that the people were at the same time both judge and accuser.

The executive power, pursuant of what has been already said, ought to have a share in the legislature by the power of rejecting; otherwise it would soon be stripped of its prerogative. But should the legislative power usurp a share of the executive, the latter would be equally undone.

If the prince were to have a part in the legislature by the power of resolving, liberty would be lost. But as it is necessary he should have a share in the legislature for the support of his own prerogative, this share must consist in the power of rejecting.

The change of government at Rome was owing to this, that neither the senate, who had one part of the executive power, nor the magistrates, who were intrusted with the other, had the right of rejecting, which was entirely lodged in the people.

Here, then, is the fundamental constitution of the government we are treating of. The legislative body being composed of two parts, they check one another by the mutual privilege of rejecting. They are both restrained by the executive power, as the executive is by the legislative.

These three powers should naturally form a state of repose or inaction. But as there is a necessity for movement in the course of human affairs, they are forced to move, but still in concert. . . .

XX. THE END OF THIS BOOK

I should be glad to inquire into the distribution of the three powers, in all the moderate governments we are acquainted with, in order to calculate the degrees of liberty which each may enjoy. But we must not always exhaust a subject, so as to leave no work at all for the reader. My business is not to make people read, but to make them think.

JEAN JACQUES ROUSSEAU

The Social Contract (1762) is the most radical political work of the eighteenth century and one of the most influential modern political theories. It professes to solve the most persistent problem in Western political thought, the reconciliation of freedom and authority. The difficulty of Rousseau's concept of the "general will" and of phrases like "forcing a man to be free" have made The Social Contract one of the most persistently and hotly debated books of the last two centuries. Scored by conservatives as a wild emotionalist and anarchist and attacked by liberals and democrats as a proto-totalitarian, Rousseau is still acknowledged as a thinker of extraordinary power and ingenious ideas.

Rousseau did not intend The Social Contract to be taken as a practical program, as it later was by Robespierre and others. He was interested in establishing some scheme for assessing the claims of any society that it was just or gave man freedom. Rousseau believed that justice might be found under any one of several systems of government. His principle concern was to demonstrate that the nature of the intentions behind the use of power as well as the effects or form of power must determine our judgment of a society. Although he believed that the greatest chance for justice could be found in a small, democratic, self-governing society, he saw little possibility that any society of his time could reform itself. He had, however, some hope for the island of Corsica which, he predicted, might one day astonish Europe.

These excerpts from The Social Contract come from G. D. H. Cole's translation (New York, E. P. Dutton, "Everyman's Library," 1913).

THE SOCIAL CONTRACT

[Book I]

CHAPTER I: SUBJECT OF THE FIRST BOOK

MAN IS BORN FREE; and everywhere he is in chains. One thinks himself the master of others, and still remains a greater slave than they. How did this change come about? I do not know. What can make it legitimate? That question I think I can answer.

If I took into account only force, and the effects derived from it, I should say: "As long as a people is compelled to obey, and obeys, it does well; as soon as it can shake off the yoke, and shakes it off, it does still better; for, regaining its liberty by the same right as took it away, either it is justified in resuming it, or there was no justification for those who took it away." But the social order is a sacred right which is the basis of all other rights. Nevertheless, this right does not come from nature, and must therefore be founded on conventions. Before coming to that, I have to prove what I have just asserted. . . .

CHAPTER III: THE RIGHT OF THE STRONGEST

The strongest is never strong enough to be always the master, unless he transforms strength into right, and obedience into duty. Hence the right of the strongest, which, though to all seeming meant ironically, is really laid down as a fundamental principle. But are we never to have an explanation of this phrase? Force is a physical power, and I fail to see what moral effect it can have. To yield to force is an act of necessity, not of will—at the most, an act of prudence. In what sense can it be a duty?

Suppose for a moment that this so-called "right" exists. I maintain that the sole result is a mass of inexplicable nonsense. For, if force creates right, the effect changes with the cause: every force that is greater than the first succeeds to its right. As soon as it is possible to disobey with impunity, disobedience is legitimate; and, the strongest being always in the right, the only thing that matters is to act so as to become the strongest. But what kind of right is that which perishes when force fails? If we must obey perforce, there is no need to obey because we ought; and if we are not forced to obey, we are under no obligation to do so. Clearly, the word "right" adds nothing to force: in this connection, it means absolutely nothing.

Obey the powers that be. If this means yield to force, it is a good precept, but superfluous: I can answer for its never being violated. All power comes from God, I admit; but so does all sickness: does that mean that we are forbidden to call in the doctor? A brigand surprises me at the edge of a wood: must I not merely surrender my purse on compulsion; but, even if I could withhold it, am I in conscience bound to give it up? For certainly the pistol he holds is also a power.

Let us then admit that force does not create right, and that we are obliged to obey only legitimate powers. In that case, my original question recurs.

CHAPTER IV: SLAVERY

. . . To renounce liberty is to renounce being a man, to surrender the rights of humanity and even its duties. For him who renounces everything no indemnity is possible. Such a renunciation is incompatible with man's nature; to remove all liberty from his will is to remove all morality from his acts. Finally, it is an empty and contradictory convention that sets up, on the one side, absolute authority, and, on the other, unlimited obedience. Is it not clear that we can be under no obligation to a person from whom we have the right to exact everything? Does not this condition alone, in the absence of equivalence or exchange, in itself involve the nullity of the act? For what right can my slave have against me, when all that he has belongs to me, and, his right being mine, this right of mine against myself is a phrase devoid of meaning?

Grotius and the rest find in war another origin for the so-called right of slavery. The victor having, as they hold, the right of killing the vanquished, the latter can buy back his life at the price of his liberty; and this convention is the more legitimate because it is to the advantage of both parties.

But it is clear that this supposed right to kill the conquered is by no means deducible from the state of war. Men, from the mere fact that, while they are living in their primitive independence, they have no mutual relations stable enough to constitute either the state of peace or the state of war, cannot be naturally enemies. War is constituted by a relation between things, and not between persons; and, as the state of war cannot arise out of simple personal relations, but only out of real relations, private war, or war of man with man, can exist neither in the state of nature, where there is no constant property, nor in the social state, where everything is under the authority of the laws.

Individual combats, duels and encounters, are acts which cannot constitute a state; while the private wars, authorised by the Establishments of Louis IX, King of France, and suspended by the Peace of God, are abuses of feudalism, in itself an absurd system if ever there was one, and contrary to the principles of natural right and to all good polity.

War then is a relation, not between man and man, but between State and State, and individuals are enemies only accidentally, not as men, nor even as citizens, but as soldiers; not as members of their country, but as its defenders. Finally, each State can have for enemies only other States, and not men; for between things disparate in nature there can be no real relation. . . .

CHAPTER VI: THE SOCIAL COMPACT

I suppose men to have reached the point at which the obstacles in the way of their preservation in the state of nature show their power of resistance to be greater than the resources at the disposal of each individual for his maintenance in that state. That primitive condition can then subsist no longer; and the human race would perish unless it changed its manner of existence.

But, as men cannot engender new forces, but only unite and direct existing ones, they have no other means of preserving themselves than the formation, by aggregation, of a sum of forces great enough to overcome the resistance.

These they have to bring into play by means of a single motive power, and cause to act in concert.

This sum of forces can arise only where several persons come together: but, as the force and liberty of each man are the chief instruments of his self-preservation, how can he pledge them without harming his own interests, and neglecting the care he owes to himself? This difficulty, in its bearing on my present subject, may be stated in the following terms—

"The problem is to find a form of association which will defend and protect with the whole common force the person and goods of each associate, and in which each, while uniting himself with all, may still obey himself alone, and remain as free as before." This is the fundamental problem of which the *Social Contract* provides the solution.

The clauses of this contract are so determined by the nature of the act that the slightest modification would make them vain and ineffective; so that, although they have perhaps never been formally set forth, they are everywhere the same and everywhere tacitly admitted and recognised, until, on the violation of the social compact, each regains his original rights and resumes his natural liberty, while losing the conventional liberty in favour of which he renounced it.

These clauses, properly understood, may be reduced to one—the total alienation of each associate, together with all his rights, to the whole community; for, in the first place, as each gives himself absolutely, the conditions are the same for all; and, this being so, no one has any interest in making them burdensome to others.

Moreover, the alienation being without reserve, the union is as perfect as it can be, and no associate has anything more to demand: for, if the individuals retained certain rights, as there would be no common superior to decide between them and the public, each, being on one point his own judge, would ask to be so on all; the state of nature would thus continue, and the association would necessarily become inoperative or tyrannical.

Finally, each man, in giving himself to all, gives himself to nobody; and as there is no associate over whom he does not acquire the same right as he yields others over himself, he gains an equivalent for everything he loses, and an increase of force for the preservation of what he has.

If then we discard from the social compact what is not of its essence, we shall find that it reduces itself to the following terms—

"Each of us puts his person and all his power in common under the supreme direction of the general will, and, in our corporate capacity, we receive each member as an indivisible part of the whole."

At once, in place of the individual personality of each contracting party, this act of association creates a moral and collective body, composed of as many members as the assembly contains votes, and receiving from this act its unity, its common identity, its life and its will. This public person, so formed by the union of all other persons formerly took the name of *city*,[1] and now takes that of *Republic* or *body politic;* it is called by its members *State* when passive, *Sovereign* when active, and *Power* when compared with others like itself. Those who are associated in it take collectively the name of *people*, and severally are called *citizens,* as sharing in the sovereign power, and *subjects,* as being under the laws of the State. But these terms are often confused and taken one for another: it is enough to know how to distinguish them when they are being used with precision.

CHAPTER VII: THE SOVEREIGN

This formula shows us that the act of association comprises a mutual undertaking between the public and the individuals, and that each individual, in making a contract, as we may say, with himself, is bound in a double capacity; as a member of the Sovereign he is bound to the individuals, and as a member of the State to the Sovereign. But the maxim of civil right, that no one is bound by undertakings made to himself, does not apply in this case; for there is a great difference between incurring an obligation to yourself and incurring one to a whole of which you form a part.

Attention must further be called to the fact that public deliberation, while competent to bind all the subjects to the Sovereign, because of the two different capacities in which each of them may be regarded, cannot, for the opposite reason, bind the Sovereign to itself; and that it is consequently against the nature of the body politic for the Sovereign to impose on itself a law which it cannot infringe. Being able to regard itself in only one capacity, it is in the position of an individual who makes a contract with himself; and this makes it clear that there neither is nor can be any kind of fundamental law binding on the body of the people—not even the social contract itself. This does not mean that the body politic cannot enter into undertakings with others, provided the contract is not infringed by them; for in relation to what is external to it, it becomes a simple being, an individual.

But the body politic or the Sovereign, drawing its being wholly from the sanctity of the contract, can never bind itself, even to an outsider, to do anything derogatory to the original act, for instance, to alienate any part of itself,

---

[1] The real meaning of this word has been almost wholly lost in modern times; most people mistake a town for a city, and a townsman for a citizen. They do not know that houses make a town, but citizens a city. . . .

or to submit to another Sovereign. Violation of the act by which it exists would be self-annihilation; and that which is itself nothing can create nothing.

As soon as this multitude is so united in one body, it is impossible to offend against one of the members without attacking the body, and still more to offend against the body without the members resenting it. Duty and interest therefore equally oblige the two contracting parties to give each other help; and the same men should seek to combine, in their double capacity, all the advantages dependent upon that capacity.

Again, the Sovereign, being formed wholly of the individuals who compose it, neither has nor can have any interest contrary to theirs; and consequently the sovereign power need give no guarantee to its subjects, because it is impossible for the body to wish to hurt all its members. We shall also see later on that it cannot hurt any in particular. The Sovereign, merely by virtue of what it is, is always what it should be.

This, however, is not the case with the relation of the subjects to the Sovereign, which, despite the common interest, would have no security that they would fulfil their undertakings, unless it found means to assure itself of their fidelity.

In fact, each individual, as a man, may have a particular will contrary or dissimilar to the general will which he has as a citizen. His particular interest may speak to him quite differently from the common interest: his absolute and naturally independent existence may make him look upon what he owes to the common cause as a gratuitous contribution, the loss of which will do less harm to others than the payment of it is burdensome to himself; and, regarding the moral person which constitutes the State as a *persona ficta,* because not a man, he may wish to enjoy the rights of citizenship without being ready to fulfil the duties of a subject. The continuance of such an injustice could not but prove the undoing of the body politic.

In order then that the social compact may not be an empty formula, it tacitly includes the undertaking, which alone can give force to the rest, that whoever refuses to obey the general will shall be compelled to do so by the whole body. This means nothing less than that he will be forced to be free; for this is the condition which, by giving each citizen to his country, secures him against all personal dependence. In this lies the key to the working of the political machine; this alone legitimises civil undertakings, which, without it, would be absurd, tyrannical, and liable to the most frightful abuses.

CHAPTER VIII: THE CIVIL STATE

The passage from the state of nature to the civil state produces a very remarkable change in man, by substituting justice for instinct in his conduct, and giving his actions the morality they formerly lacked. Then only, when the voice of duty takes the place of physical impulses and right of appetite, does man, who so far had considered only himself, find that he is forced to act on different principles, and to consult his reason before listening to his inclinations. Although, in this state, he deprives himself of some advantages which he got from nature, he gains in return others so great, his faculties are so stimulated and developed, his ideas so extended, his feelings so ennobled, and his whole soul so uplifted, that, did not the abuses of this new condition often degrade him below that which he left, he would be bound to bless continually the happy moment which took him from it for ever, and, instead of a stupid and unimaginative animal, made him an intelligent being and a man.

Let us draw up the whole account in terms easily commensurable. What man loses by the social contract is his natural liberty and an unlimited right to everything he tries to get and succeeds in getting; what he gains is civil liberty and the proprietorship of all he possesses. If we are to avoid mistake in weighing one against the other, we must clearly distinguish natural liberty, which is bounded only by the strength of the individual, from civil liberty, which is limited by the general will; and possession, which is merely the effect of force or the right of the first occupier, from property, which can be founded only on a positive title.

We might, over and above all this, add, to what man acquires in the civil state, moral liberty, which alone makes him truly master of himself; for the mere impulse of appetite is slavery, while obedience to a law which we prescribe to ourselves is liberty. But I have already said too much on this head, and the philosophical meaning of the word liberty does not now concern us.

. . . I shall end . . . this book by remarking on a fact on which the whole social system should rest: *i.e.* that, instead of destroying natural inequality, the fundamental compact substitutes, for such physical inequality as nature may have set up between men, an equality that is moral and legitimate, and that men, who may be unequal in strength or intelligence, become every one equal by convention and legal right.

[Book II]

CHAPTER I: THAT SOVEREIGNTY IS INALIENABLE

The first and most important deduction from the principles we have so far laid down is that the general will alone can direct the State according to the object for which it was instituted, *i.e.,* the common good: for if the clashing of particular interests made the establishment of societies necessary, the agreement of these very interests made it possible. The common element in these different interests is what forms the social tie; and, were there no point of agreement between them all, no society could exist. It is solely on the basis of this common interest that every society should be governed.

I hold then that Sovereignty, being nothing less than the exercise of the general will, can never be alienated, and that the Sovereign, who is no less than a collective being, cannot be represented except by himself: the power indeed may be transmitted, but not the will.

In reality, if it is not impossible for a particular will to agree on some point with the general will, it is at least impossible for the agreement to be lasting and constant; for the particular will tends, by its very nature, to partiality, while the general will tends to equality. It is even more impossible to have any guarantee of this agreement; for even if it should always exist, it would be the effect not of art, but of chance. The Sovereign may indeed say: "I now will actually what this man wills, or at least what he says he wills"; but it cannot say: "What he wills tomorrow, I too shall will" because it is absurd for the will to bind itself for the future, nor is it incumbent on any will to consent to anything that is not for the good of the being who wills. If then the people promises simply to obey, by that very act it dissolves itself and loses what makes it a people; the moment a master exists, there is no longer a Sovereign, and from that moment the body politic has ceased to exist.

This does not mean that the commands of the rulers cannot pass for general wills, so long as the Sovereign, being free to oppose them, offers no opposition. In such a case, universal silence is taken to imply the consent of the people. This will be explained later on.

CHAPTER II: THAT SOVEREIGNTY IS INDIVISIBLE

Sovereignty, for the same reason as makes it inalienable, is indivisible; for will either is, or is not, general; [2] it is the will either of the body of the people, or only of a part of it. In the first case, the will, when declared, is an act of Sovereignty and constitutes law: in the second, it is merely a particular will, or act of magistracy—at the most a decree.

But our political theorists, unable to divide Sovereignty in principle, divide it according to its object: into force and will; into legislative power and executive power; into rights of taxation, justice and war; into internal administration and power of foreign treaty. Sometimes they confuse all these sections, and sometimes they distinguish them; they turn the Sovereign into a fantastic being composed of several connected pieces: it is as if they were making man of

---

2 To be general, a will need not always be unanimous; but every vote must be counted: any exclusion is a breach of generality.

several bodies, one with eyes, one with arms, another with feet, and each with nothing besides. We are told that the jugglers of Japan dismember a child before the eyes of the spectators; then they throw all the members into the air one after another, and the child falls down alive and whole. The conjuring tricks of our political theorists are very like that; they first dismember the body politic by an illusion worthy of a fair, and then join it together again we know not how.

This error is due to a lack of exact notions concerning the Sovereign authority, and to taking for parts of it what are only emanations from it. Thus, for example, the acts of declaring war and making peace have been regarded as acts of Sovereignty; but this is not the case, as these acts do not constitute law, but merely the application of a law, a particular act which decides how the law applies, as we shall see clearly when the idea attached to the word *law* has been defined. . . .

CHAPTER III: WHETHER THE GENERAL WILL IS FALLIBLE

It follows from what has gone before that the general will is always right and tends to the public advantage; but it does not follow that the deliberations of the people are always equally correct. Our will is always for our own good, but we do not always see what that is; the people is never corrupted, but it is often deceived, and on such occasions only does it seem to will what is bad.

There is often a great deal of difference between the will of all and the general will; the latter considers only the common interest, while the former takes private interest into account, and is not more than a sum of particular wills: but take away from these same wills the pluses and minuses that cancel one another, and the general will remains as the sum of the differences.

If, when the people, being furnished with adequate information, held its deliberations, the citizens had no communication one with another, the grand total of the small differences would always give the general will, and the decision would always be good. But when factions arise, and partial associations are formed at the expense of the great association, the will of each of these associations becomes general in relation to its members, while it remains particular in relation to the State: it may then be said that there are no longer as many votes as there are men, but only as many as there are associations. The differences become less numerous and give a less general result. Lastly, when one of these associations is so great as to prevail over all the rest, the result is no longer a sum of small differences, but a single difference; in this case there is no longer a general will, and the opinion which prevails is purely particular.

It is therefore essential, if the general will is to be able to express itself, that there should be no partial society within the State, and that each citizen should think only his own thoughts: which was indeed the sublime and unique system established by the great Lycurgus. But if there are partial societies, it is best to have as many as possible and to prevent them from being unequal, as was done by Solon, Numa and Servius. These precautions are the only ones that can guarantee that the general will shall be always enlightened, and that the people shall in no way deceive itself.

CHAPTER IV: THE LIMITS OF THE SOVEREIGN POWER

If the state is a moral person whose life is in the union of its members, and if the most important of its cares is the care for its own preservation, it must have a universal and compelling force, in order to move and dispose each part as may be most advantageous to the whole. As nature gives each man absolute power over all his members, the social compact gives the body politic absolute power over all its members also; and it is this power which, under the direction of the general will, bears, as I have said, the name of Sovereignty.

But, besides the public person, we have to consider the private persons composing it, whose life and liberty are naturally independent of it. We are bound then to distinguish clearly between the respective rights of the citizens and the Sovereign, and between the duties the former have to fulfil as subjects, and the natural rights they should enjoy as men.

Each man alienates, I admit, by the social compact, only such part of his powers, goods and liberty as it is important for the community to control; but it must also be granted that the Sovereign is sole judge of what is important.

Every service a citizen can render the State he ought to render as soon as the Sovereign demands it; but the Sovereign, for its part, cannot impose upon its subjects any fetters that are useless to the community, nor can it even wish to do so; for no more by the law of reason than by the law of nature can anything occur without a cause.

The undertakings which bind us to the social body are obligatory only because they are mutual; and their nature is such that in fulfilling them we cannot work for others without working for ourselves. Why is it that the general will is always in the right, and that all continually will the happiness of each one, unless it is because there is not a man who does not think of "each" as meaning him, and consider himself in voting for all? This proves that equality of rights and the idea of justice which such equality creates originate in the preference each man gives to himself, and accordingly in the very nature of man. It proves that the general will, to be really such, must be general in its object as well as its essence; that it must both come from all and apply to all; and that it loses its natural rectitude when it is directed to some particular and determinate object, because in such a case we are judging of something foreign to us, and have no true principle of equity to guide us.

Indeed, as soon as a question of particular fact or right arises on a point not previously regulated by a general convention, the matter becomes contentious. It is a case in which the individuals concerned are one party, and the public the other, but in which I can see neither the law that ought to be followed nor the judge who ought to give the decision. In such a case, it would be absurd to propose to refer the question to an express decision of the general will, which can be only the conclusion reached by one of the parties and in consequence will be, for the other party, merely an external and particular will, inclined on this occasion to injustice and subject to error. Thus, just as a particular will cannot stand off for the general will, the general will, in turn, changes its nature, when its object is particular, and, as general, cannot pronounce on a man or a fact. When, for instance, the people of Athens nominated or displaced its rulers, decreed honours to one, and imposed penalties on another, and, by a multitude of particular decrees, exercised all the functions of government indiscriminately, it had in such cases no longer a general will in the strict sense; it was acting no longer as Sovereign, but as magistrate. This will seem contrary to current views; but I must be given time to expound my own.

It should be seen from the foregoing that what makes the will general is less the number of voters than the common interest uniting them; for, under this system, each necessarily submits to the conditions he imposes on others: and this admirable agreement between interest and justice gives to the common deliberations an equitable character which at once vanishes when any particular question is discussed, in the absence of a common interest to unite and identify the ruling of the judge with that of the party.

From whatever side we approach our principle, we reach the same conclusion, that the social compact sets up among the citizens an equality of such a kind, that they all bind themselves to observe the same conditions and should therefore all enjoy the same rights. Thus, from the very nature of the compact, every act of Sovereignty, *i.e.* every authentic act of the general will, binds or favours all the citizens equally; so that the Sovereign recognises only the body of the nation, and draws no distinctions between those of whom it is made up. What, then, strictly speaking, is an act of Sovereignty? It is not a convention between a superior and an inferior, but a convention between the body and each of its members. It is legitimate, because based on the social contract, and equitable, because common to all; useful, because it can have no other object than the general good, and stable, because guaranteed by the public force and the supreme power. So long as the subjects have to submit only to conventions of this sort, they obey no-one but their own will; and to ask how far the respective rights of the Sovereign and the citizens extend, is to ask up to what point the latter can enter into undertakings with themselves, each with all, and all with each.

We can see from this that the sovereign power, absolute, sacred and inviolable as it is, does not and cannot exceed the limits of general conventions, and that every man may dispose at will of such goods and liberty as these conventions leave him; so that the Sovereign never has a right to lay more charges on one subject than on another, because, in that case, the question becomes particular, and ceases to be within its competency.

When these distinctions have once been admitted, it is seen to be so untrue that there is, in the social contract, any real renunciation on the part of the individuals, that the position in which they find themselves as a result of the contract is really preferable to that in which they were before. Instead of a renunciation, they have made an advantageous exchange: instead of an uncertain and precarious way of living they have got one that is better and more secure; instead of natural independence they have got liberty, instead of the power to harm others security for themselves, and instead of their strength, which others might overcome, a right which social union makes invincible. Their very life, which they have devoted to the State, is by it constantly protected; and when they risk it in the State's defence, what more are they doing than giving back what they have received from it? What are they doing that they would not do more often and with greater danger in the state of nature, in which they would inevitably have to fight battles at the peril of their lives in defence of that which is the means of their preservation? All have indeed to fight when their country needs them; but then no one has ever to fight for himself. Do we not gain something by running, on behalf of what gives us our security, only some of the risks we should have to run for ourselves, as soon as we lost it?

CHAPTER VI: LAW

. . . I . . . give the name "Republic" to every State that is governed by laws, no matter what the form of its administration may be: for only in such a case does the public interest govern, and the *res publica* rank as a *reality*. Every legitimate government is republican; [3] what government is I will explain later on.

[3] I understand by this word, not merely an aristocracy or a democracy, but generally any government directed by the general will, which is the law. To be legitimate, the government must be, not one with the Sovereign, but its minister. In such a case even a monarchy is a Republic. This will be made clearer in the following book.

Laws are, properly speaking, only the conditions of civil association. The people, being subject to the laws, ought to be their author: the conditions of the society ought to be regulated solely by those who come together to form it. But how are they to regulate them? Is it to be by common agreement, by a sudden inspiration? Has the body politic an organ to declare its will? Who can give it the foresight to formulate and announce its acts in advance? Or how is it to announce them in the hour of need? How can a blind multitude, which often does not know what it wills, because it rarely knows what is good for it, carry out for itself so great and difficult an enterprise as a system of legislation? Of itself the people wills always the good, but of itself it by no means always sees it. The general will is always in the right, but the judgment which guides it is not always enlightened. It must be got to see objects as they are, and sometimes as they ought to appear to it; it must be shown the good road it is in search of, secured from the seductive influences of individual wills, taught to see times and spaces as a series, and made to weigh the attractions of present and sensible advantages against the danger of distant and hidden evils. The individuals see the good they reject; the public wills the good it does not see. All stand equally in need of guidance. The former must be compelled to bring their wills into conformity with their reason; the latter must be taught to know what it wills. If that is done, public enlightenment leads to the union of understanding and will in the social body: the parts are made to work exactly together, and the whole is raised to its highest power. This makes a legislator necessary.

CHAPTER VII: THE LEGISLATOR

In order to discover the rules of society best suited to nations, a superior intelligence beholding all the passions of men without experiencing any of them would be needed. This intelligence would have to be wholly unrelated to our nature, while knowing it through and through; its happiness would have to be independent of us, and yet ready to occupy itself with ours; and lastly, it would have, in the march of time, to look forward to a distant glory, and, working in one century, to be able to enjoy in the next. It would take gods to give men laws. . . .

The legislator occupies in every respect an extraordinary position in the State. If he should do so by reason of his genius, he does so no less by reason of his office, which is neither magistracy, nor Sovereignty. This office, which sets up the Republic, nowhere enters into its constitution; it is an individual and superior function, which has nothing in common with human empire; for if he who holds command over men ought not to have command over the laws, he who has command over the laws ought not any more to have it over men; or else his laws would be the ministers of his passions and would often merely serve to perpetuate his injustices: his private aims would inevitably mar the sanctity of his work.

When Lycurgus gave laws to his country, he began by resigning the throne. It was the custom of most Greek towns to entrust the establishment of their laws to foreigners. The Republics of modern Italy in many cases followed this example; Geneva did the same and profited by it.[4] Rome, when it was most prosperous, suffered a revival of all the crimes of tyranny, and was brought to the verge of destruction, because it put the legislative authority and the sovereign power into the same hands.

Nevertheless, the decemvirs themselves never claimed the right to pass any law merely on their own authority. "Nothing we propose to you," they said to the people, "can pass into law without your consent. Romans, be yourselves the authors of the laws which are to make you happy."

He, therefore, who draws up the laws has, or should have, no right of legislation, and the people cannot, even if it wishes, deprive itself of this incommunicable right, because, according to the fundamental compact, only the general will can bind the individuals, and there can be no assurance that a particular will is in conformity with the general will, until it has been put to the free vote of the people. This I have said already; but it is worth while to repeat it. . . .

CHAPTER XI: THE VARIOUS SYSTEMS OF LEGISLATION

If we ask in what precisely consists the greatest good of all, which should be the end of every system of legislation, we shall find it reduce itself to two main objects, liberty and equality—liberty, because all particular dependence means so much force taken from the body of the State, and equality, because liberty cannot exist without it.

I have already defined civil liberty; by equality, we should understand, not that the degrees of power and riches are to be absolutely identical for everybody; but that power shall never be great enough for violence, and shall always be exercised by virtue of rank and law; and that, in respect of riches, no citizen shall ever be wealthy enough to buy another, and none poor enough to be forced to sell himself: which implies, on the part of the great, moderation in goods and position, and, on the side of the common sort, moderation in avarice and covetousness.

Such equality, we are told, is an unpractical ideal that cannot actually exist.

---

[4] Those who know Calvin only as a theologian much underestimate the extent of his genius. The codification of our wise edicts, in which he played a large part, does him no less honour than his *Institute*. Whatever revolution time may bring in our religion, so long as the spirit of patriotism and liberty still lives among us, the memory of this great man will be for ever blessed.

But if its abuse is inevitable, does it follow that we should not at least make regulations concerning it? It is precisely because the force of circumstances tends continually to destroy equality that the force of legislation should always tend to its maintenance.

But these general objects of every good legislative system need modifying in every country in accordance with the local situation and the temper of the inhabitants; and these circumstances should determine, in each case, the particular system of institutions which is best, not perhaps in itself, but for the State for which it is destined. . . .

[Book III]

Before speaking of the different forms of government, let us try to fix the exact sense of the word, which has not yet been very clearly explained.

CHAPTER I: GOVERNMENT IN GENERAL

I warn the reader that this chapter requires careful reading, and that I am unable to make myself clear to those who refuse to be attentive.

Every free action is produced by the concurrence of two causes; one moral, *i. e.* the will which determines the act; the other physical, *i. e.* the power which executes it. When I walk towards an object, it is necessary first that I should will to go there, and, in the second place, that my feet should carry me. If a paralytic wills to run and an active man wills not to, they will both stay where they are. The body politic has the same motive powers; here too force and will are distinguished, will under the name of legislative power and force under that of executive power. Without their concurrence, nothing is, or should be, done.

We have seen that the legislative power belongs to the people, and can belong to it alone. It may, on the other hand, readily be seen, from the principles laid down above, that the executive power cannot belong to the generality as legislature or Sovereign, because it consists wholly of particular acts which fall outside the competency of the law, and consequently of the Sovereign, whose acts must always be laws.

The public force therefore needs an agent of its own to bind it together and set it to work under the direction of the general will, to serve as a means of communication between the State and the Sovereign, and to do for the collective person more or less what the union of soul and body does for man. Here we have what is, in the State, the basis of government, often wrongly confused with the Sovereign, whose minister it is.

What then is government? An intermediate body set up between the subjects and the Sovereign, to secure their mutual correspondence, charged with the execution of the laws and the maintenance of liberty, both civil and political.

The members of this body are called magistrates or *kings,* that is to say *governors,* and the whole body bears the name *prince.* Thus those who hold that the act, by which a people puts itself under a prince, is not a contract, are certainly right. It is simply and solely a commission, an employment, in which the rulers, mere officials of the Sovereign, exercise in their own name the power of which it makes them depositaries. This power it can limit, modify or recover at pleasure; for the alienation of such a right is incompatible with the nature of the social body, and contrary to the end of association.

I call then *government,* or supreme administration, the legitimate exercise of the executive power, and prince or magistrate the man or the body entrusted with that administration.

In government reside the intermediate forces whose relations make up that of the whole to the whole, or of the Sovereign to the State. This last relation may be represented as that between the extreme terms of a continuous proportion, which has government as its mean proportional. The government gets from the Sovereign the orders it gives the people, and, for the State to be properly balanced, there must, when everything is reckoned in, be equality between the product of power of the government taken in itself, and the product or power of the citizens, who are on the one hand sovereign and on the other subject.

Furthermore, none of these three terms can be altered without the equality being instantly destroyed. If the Sovereign desires to govern, or the magistrate to give laws, or if the subjects refuse to obey, disorder takes the place of regularity, force and will no longer act together, and the State is dissolved and falls into despotism or anarchy. Lastly, as there is only one mean proportional between each relation, there is also only one good government possible for a State. But, as countless events may change the relations of a people, not only may different governments be good for different peoples, but also for the same people at different times.

In attempting to give some idea of the various relations that may hold between these two extreme terms, I shall take as an example the number of a people, which is the most easily expressible.

Suppose the State is composed of ten thousand citizens. The Sovereign can only be considered collectively and as a body; but each member, as being a subject, is regarded as an individual: thus the Sovereign is to the subject as ten thousand to one, *i. e.* each member of the State has as his share only a tenthousandth part of the sovereign authority, although he is wholly under its control. If the people numbers a hundred thousand, the condition of the subject undergoes no change, and each equally is under the whole authority of the laws, while his vote, being reduced to one hundred thousandth part, has ten times less influence in drawing them up. The subject therefore remaining always a unit, the relation between him and the Sovereign increases with the number of the citizens. From this it follows that, the larger the State, the less the liberty.

When I say the relation increases, I mean that it grows more unequal. Thus the greater it is in the geometrical sense, the less relation there is in the ordinary sense of the word. In the former sense, the relation, considered according to quantity, is expressed by the quotient; in the latter, considered according to identity, it is reckoned by similarity.

Now, the less relation the particular wills have to the general will, that is, morals and manners to laws, the more should the repressive force be increased. The government, then, to be good, should be proportionately stronger as the people is more numerous.

On the other hand, as the growth of the State gives the depositaries of the public authority more temptations and chances of abusing their power, the greater the force with which the government ought to be endowed for keeping the people in hand, the greater too should be the force at the disposal of the Sovereign for keeping the government in hand. I am speaking, not of absolute force, but of the relative force of the different parts of the State.

It follows from this double relation that the continuous proportion between the Sovereign, the prince and the people, is by no means an arbitrary idea, but a necessary consequence of the nature of the body politic. It follows further that, one of the extreme terms, viz. the people, as subject, being fixed and represented by unity, whenever the duplicate ratio increases or diminishes, the simple ratio does the same, and is changed accordingly. From this we see that there is not a single unique and absolute form of government, but as many governments differing in nature as there are States differing in size.

If, ridiculing this system, any one were to say that, in order to find the mean proportional and give form to the body of the government, it is only necessary, according to me, to find the square root of the number of the people, I should answer that I am here taking this number only as an instance; that the relations of which I am speaking are not measured by the number of men alone, but generally by the amount of action, which is a combination of a multitude of causes; and that, further, if, to save words, I borrow for a moment the terms of geometry, I am none the less well aware that moral quantities do not allow of geometrical accuracy.

The government is on a small scale what the body politic which includes it is on a great one. It is a moral person endowed with certain faculties, active like the Sovereign and passive like the State, and capable of being resolved into other similar relations. This accordingly gives rise to a new proportion, within which there is yet another, according to the arrangement of the magistracies, till an indivisible middle term is reached, *i.e.* a single ruler or supreme magistrate, who may be represented, in the midst of this progression, as the unity between the fractional and the ordinal series.

Without encumbering ourselves with this multiplication of terms, let us rest content with regarding government as a new body within the State, distinct from the people and the Sovereign, and intermediate between them.

There is between these two bodies this essential difference, that the State exists by itself, and the government only through the Sovereign. Thus the dominant will of the prince is, or should be, nothing but the general will or the law; his force is only the public force concentrated in his hands, and, as soon as he tries to base any absolute and independent act on his own authority, the tie that binds the whole together begins to be loosened. If finally the prince should come to have a particular will more active than the will of the Sovereign, and should employ the public force in his hands in obedience to this particular will, there would be, so to speak, two Sovereigns, one rightful and the other actual, the social union would evaporate instantly, and the body politic would be dissolved.

However, in order that the government may have a true existence and a real life distinguishing it from the body of the State, and in order that all its members may be able to act in concert and fulfil the end for which it was set up, it must have a particular personality, a sensibility common to its members, and a force and will of its own making for its preservation. This particular existence implies assemblies, councils, power of deliberation and decision, rights, titles, and privileges belonging exclusively to the prince and making the office of magistrate more honourable in proportion as it is more troublesome. The difficulties lie in the manner of so ordering this subordinate whole within the whole, that it in no way alters the general constitution by affirmation of its own, and always distinguishes the particular force it possesses, which is destined to aid in its preservation, from the public force, which is destined to the preservation of the State; and, in a word, is always ready to sacrifice the government to the people, and never to sacrifice the people to the government.

Furthermore, although the artificial body of the government is the work of another artificial body, and has, we may say, only a borrowed and subordinate life, this does not prevent it from being able to act with more or less vigour or promptitude, or from being, so to speak, in more or less robust health. Finally, without departing directly from the end for which it was instituted, it may deviate more or less from it, according to the manner of its constitution.

From all these differences arise the various relations which the government ought to bear to the body of the State, according to the accidental and particular relations by which the State itself is modified, for often the government that is best in itself will become the most pernicious, if the relations in which it stands have altered according to the defects of the body politic to which it belongs.

CHAPTER II: THE CONSTITUENT PRINCIPLE IN THE VARIOUS FORMS OF GOVERNMENT

To set forth the general cause of the above differences, we must here distinguish between government and its principle, as we did before between the State and the Sovereign.

The body of the magistrate may be composed of a greater or less number of members. We said that the relation of the Sovereign to the subjects was greater in proportion as the people was more numerous, and, by a clear analogy, we may say the same of the relation of the government to the magistrates.

But the total force of the government, being always that of the State, is invariable; so that, the more of this force it expends on its own members, the less it has left to employ on the whole people.

The more numerous the magistrates, therefore, the weaker the government. This principle being fundamental, we must do our best to make it clear.

In the person of the magistrate we can distinguish three essentially different wills: first, the private will of the individual, tending only to his personal advantage; secondly, the common will of the magistrates, which is relative solely to the advantage of the prince, and may be called corporate will, being general in relation to the government, and particular in relation to the State, of which the government forms part; and, in the third place, the will of the people or the sovereign will, which is general both in relation to the State regarded as the whole, and to the government regarded as a part of the whole.

In a perfect act of legislation, the individual or particular will should be at zero; the corporate will belonging to the government should occupy a very subordinate position; and, consequently, the general or sovereign will should always predominate and should be the sole guide of all the rest.

According to the natural order, on the other hand, these different wills become more active in proportion as they are concentrated. Thus, the general will is always the weakest, the corporate will second, and the individual will strongest of all: so that, in the government, each member is first of all himself, then a magistrate, and then a citizen—in an order exactly the reverse of what the social system requires.

This granted, if the whole government is in the hands of one man, the particular and the corporate will are wholly united, and consequently the latter is at its highest possible degree of intensity. But, as the use to which the force is put depends on the degree reached by the will, and as the absolute force of the government is invariable, it follows that the most active government is that of one man.

Suppose, on the other hand, we unite the government with the legislative authority, and make the Sovereign prince also, and all the citizens so many magistrates: then the corporate will, being confounded with the general will, can possess no greater activity than that will, and must leave the particular will as strong as it can possibly be. Thus, the government, having always the same absolute force, will be at the lowest point of its relative force or activity.

These relations are incontestable, and there are other considerations which still further confirm them. We can see, for instance, that each magistrate is more active in the body to which he belongs than each citizen in that to which he belongs, and that consequently the particular will has much more influence on the acts of the government than on those of the Sovereign; for each magistrate is almost always charged with some governmental function, while each citizen, taken singly, exercises no function of Sovereignty. Furthermore, the bigger the State grows, the more its real force increases, though not in direct proportion to its growth; but, the State remaining the same, the number of magistrates may increase to any extent, without the government gaining any greater real force; for its force is that of the State, the dimension of which remains equal. Thus the relative force or activity of the government decreases, while its absolute or real force cannot increase.

Moreover, it is a certainty that promptitude in execution diminishes as more people are put in charge of it: where prudence is made too much of, not enough is made of fortune; opportunity is let slip, and deliberation results in the loss of its object.

I have just proved that the government grows remiss in proportion as the number of the magistrates increases; and I previously proved that, the more numerous the people, the greater should be the repressive force. From this it follows that the relation of the magistrates to the government should vary inversely to the relation of the subjects to the Sovereign; that is to say, the larger the State, the more should the government be tightened, so that the number of the rulers diminish in proportion to the increase of that of the people.

It should be added that I am here speaking of the relative strength of the government, and not of its rectitude: for, on the other hand, the more numerous the magistracy, the nearer the corporate will comes to the general will; while, under a single magistrate, the corporate will is, as I said, merely a particular will. Thus, what may be gained on one side is lost on the other, and the art of the legislator is to know how to fix the point at which the force and the will of the government, which are always in inverse proportion, meet in the relation that is most to the advantage of the State.

CHAPTER III: THE DIVISION OF GOVERNMENTS

We saw in the last chapter what causes the various kinds or forms of government to be distinguished according to the number of the members composing them; it remains in this to discover how the division is made.

In the first place, the Sovereign may commit the charge of the government to the whole people or to the majority of the people, so that more citizens are magistrates than are mere private individuals. This form of government is called *democracy*.

Or it may restrict the government to a small number, so that there are more private citizens than magistrates; and this is named *aristocracy*.

Lastly, it may concentrate the whole government in the hands of a single magistrate from whom all others hold their power. This third form is the most usual, and is called *monarchy*, or royal government.

It should be remarked that all these forms, or at least the first two, admit of degree, and even of very wide differences; for democracy may include the whole people, or may be restricted to half. Aristocracy, in its turn, may be restricted indefinitely from half the people down to the smallest possible number. Even royalty is susceptible of a measure of distribution. Sparta always had two kings, as its constitution provided; and the Roman Empire saw as many as eight emperors at once, without it being possible to say that the Empire was split up. Thus there is a point at which each form of government passes into the next, and it becomes clear that, under three comprehensive denominations, government is really susceptible of as many diverse forms as the State has citizens.

There are even more: for, as the government may also, in certain aspects, be subdivided into other parts, one administered in one fashion and one in another, the combination of the three forms may result in a multitude of mixed forms, each of which admits of multiplication by all the simple forms.

There has been at all times much dispute concerning the best form of government, without consideration of the fact that each is in some cases the best, and in others the worst.

If, in the different States, the number of supreme magistrates should be in inverse ratio to the number of citizens, it follows that, generally, democratic government suits small States, aristocratic government those of middle size, and monarchy great ones. This rule is immediately deducible from the principle laid down. But it is impossible to count the innumerable circumstances which may furnish exceptions.

CHAPTER IV: DEMOCRACY

He who makes the law knows better than any one else how it should be executed and interpreted. It seems then impossible to have a better constitution than that in which the executive and legislative powers are united; but this very fact renders the government in certain respects inadequate, because things which should be distinguished are confounded, and the prince and the Sovereign, being the same person, form, so to speak, no more than a government without government.

It is not good for him who makes the laws to execute them, or for the body of the people to turn its attention away from a general standpoint and devote it to particular objects. Nothing is more dangerous than the influence of private interests in public affairs, and the abuse of the laws by the government is a less evil than the corruption of the legislator, which is the inevitable sequel to a particular standpoint. In such a case, the State being altered in substance, all reformation becomes impossible. A people that would never misuse governmental powers would never misuse independence; a people that would always govern well would not need to be governed.

If we take the term in the strict sense, there never has been a real democracy, and there never will be. It is against the natural order for the many to govern and the few to be governed. It is unimaginable that the people should remain continually assembled to devote their time to public affairs, and it is clear that they cannot set up commissions for that purpose without the form of administration being changed.

In fact, I can confidently lay down as a principle that, when the functions of government are shared by several tribunals, the less numerous sooner or later acquire the greatest authority, if only because they are in a position to expedite affairs, and power thus naturally comes into their hands.

Besides, how many conditions that are difficult to unite does such a government presuppose! First, a very small State, where the people can readily be got together and where each citizen can with ease know all the rest; secondly, great simplicity of manners, to prevent business from multiplying and raising thorny problems; next, a large measure of equality in rank and fortune, without which equality of rights and authority cannot long subsist; lastly, little or no luxury—for luxury either comes of riches or makes them necessary; it corrupts at once rich and poor, the rich by possession and the poor by covetous-ness; it sells the country to softness and vanity, and takes away from the State all its citizens, to make them slaves one to another, and one and all to public opinion.

This is why a famous writer has made virtue the fundamental principle of Republics; for all these conditions could not exist without virtue. But, for want of the necessary distinctions, that great thinker was often inexact, and some-times obscure, and did not see that, the sovereign authority being everywhere the same, the same principle should be found in every well-constituted State, in a greater or less degree, it is true, according to the form of the government.

It may be added that there is no government so subject to civil wars and intestine agitations as democratic or popular government, because there is none which has so strong and continual a tendency to change to another form, or which demands more vigilance and courage for its maintenance as it is. Under such a constitution above all, the citizen should arm himself with strength and constancy, and say, every day of his life, what a virtuous Count Palatine said in the Diet of Poland: *Malo periculosam libertatem quam quietum servitium.*[5]

Were there a people of gods, their government would be democratic. So perfect a government is not for men.

CHAPTER V: ARISTOCRACY

We have here two quite distinct moral persons, the government and the Sovereign, and in consequence two general wills, one general in relation to all the citizens, the other only for the members of the administration. Thus, although the government may regulate its internal policy as it pleases, it can never speak to the people save in the name of the Sovereign, that is, of the people itself, a fact which must not be forgotten.

The first societies governed themselves aristocratically. The heads of families took counsel together on public affairs. The young bowed without question to the authority of experience. Hence such names as *priest, elders, senate,* and *gerontes.* The savages of North America govern themselves in this way even now, and their government is admirable.

But, in proportion as artificial inequality produced by institutions became predominant over natural inequality, riches or power were put before age, and aristocracy became elective. Finally, the transmission of the father's power along with his goods to his children, by creating patrician families, made gov-ernment hereditary, and there came to be senators of twenty.

There are then three sorts of aristocracy—natural, elective and hereditary. The first is only for simple peoples; the third is the worst of all governments; the second is the best, and is aristocracy properly so called.

[5] [*I prefer dangerous liberty to peaceful servitude.*]

Besides the advantage that lies in the distinction between the two powers, it presents that of its members being chosen; for, in popular government, all the citizens are born magistrates; but here magistracy is confined to a few, who become such only by election. By this means uprightness, understanding, experience and all other claims to pre-eminence and public esteem become so many further guarantees of wise government.

Moreover, assemblies are more easily held, affairs better discussed and carried out with more order and diligence, and the credit of the State is better sustained abroad by venerable senators than by a multitude that is unknown or despised.

In a word, it is the best and most natural arrangement that the wisest should govern the many, when it is assured that they will govern for its profit, and not for their own. There is no need to multiply instruments, or get twenty thousand men to do what a hundred picked men can do even better. But it must not be forgotten that corporate interest here begins to direct the public power less under the regulation of the general will, and that a further inevitable propensity takes away from the laws part of the executive power.

If we are to speak of what is individually desirable, neither should the State be so small, nor a people so simple and upright, that the execution of the laws follows immediately from the public will, as it does in a good democracy. Nor should the nation be so great that the rulers have to scatter in order to govern it and are able to play the Sovereign each in his own department, and, beginning by making themselves independent, end by becoming masters.

But if aristocracy does not demand all the virtues needed by popular government, it demands others which are peculiar to itself; for instance, moderation on the side of the rich and contentment on that of the poor; for it seems that thorough-going equality would be out of place, as it was not found even at Sparta.

Furthermore, if this form of government carries with it a certain inequality of fortune, this is justifiable in order that as a rule the administration of public affairs may be entrusted to those who are most able to give them their whole time, but not, as Aristotle maintains, in order that the rich may always be put first. On the contrary, it is of importance that an opposite choice should occasionally teach the people that the deserts of men offer claims to pre-eminence more important than those of riches.

CHAPTER VI: MONARCHY

So far, we have considered the prince as a moral and collective person, unified by the force of the laws, and the depositary in the State of the executive power. We have now to consider this power when it is gathered together into the hands of a natural person, a real man, who alone has the right to dispose of it in accordance with the laws. Such a person is called a monarch or king.

In contrast with other forms of administration, in which a collective being stands for an individual, in this form an individual stands for a collective being; so that the moral unity that constitutes the prince is at the same time a physical unity, and all the qualities, which in the other case are only with difficulty brought together by the law, are found naturally united.

Thus the will of the people, the will of the prince, the public force of the State, and the particular force of the government, all answer to a single motive power; all the springs of the machine are in the same hands, the whole moves towards the same end; there are no conflicting movements to cancel one another, and no kind of constitution can be imagined in which a less amount of effort produces a more considerable amount of action. Archimedes, seated quietly on the bank and easily drawing a great vessel afloat, stands to my mind for a skilful monarch, governing vast states from his study, and moving everything while he seems himself unmoved.

But if no government is more vigorous than this, there is also none in which the particular will holds more sway and rules the rest more easily. Everything moves towards the same end indeed, but this end is by no means that of the public happiness, and even the force of the administration constantly shows itself prejudicial to the State.

Kings desire to be absolute, and men are always crying out to them from afar that the best means of being so is to get themselves loved by their people. This precept is all very well, and even in some respects very true. Unfortunately, it will always be derided at court. The power which comes of a people's love is no doubt the greatest; but it is precarious and conditional, and princes will never rest content with it. The best kings desire to be in a position to be wicked, if they please, without forfeiting their mastery: political sermonisers may tell them to their hearts' content that, the people's strength being their own, their first interest is that the people should be prosperous, numerous and formidable; they are well aware that this is untrue. Their first personal interest is that the people should be weak, wretched, and unable to resist them. I admit that, provided the subjects remained always in submission, the prince's interest would indeed be that it should be powerful, in order that its power, being his own, might make him formidable to his neighbours; but, this interest being merely secondary and subordinate, and strength being incompatible with submission, princes naturally give the preference always to the principle that is more to their immediate advantage. This is what Samuel put strongly before the Hebrews, and what Machiavelli has clearly shown. He professed to teach kings; but it was the people he really taught. His *Prince* is the book of Republicans.

We found, on general grounds, that monarchy is suitable only for great States, and this is confirmed when we examine it in itself. The more numerous the public administration, the smaller becomes the relation between the prince and the subjects, and the nearer it comes to equality, so that in democracy the ratio is unity, or absolute equality. Again, as the government is restricted in numbers the ratio increases and reaches its *maximum* when the government is in the hands of a single person. There is then too great a distance between prince and people, and the State lacks a bond of union. To form such a bond, there must be intermediate orders, and princes, personages and nobility to compose them. But no such things suit a small State, to which all class differences mean ruin.

If, however, it is hard for a great State to be well governed, it is much harder for it to be so by a single man; and every one knows what happens when kings substitute others for themselves.

An essential and inevitable defect, which will always rank monarchical below republican government, is that in a republic the public voice hardly ever raises to the highest positions men who are not enlightened and capable, and such as to fill them with honour; while in monarchies those who rise to the top are most often merely petty blunderers, petty swindlers, and petty intriguers, whose petty talents cause them to get into the highest positions at Court, but, as soon as they have got there, serve only to make their ineptitude clear to the public. The people is far less often mistaken in its choice than the prince; and a man of real worth among the king's ministers is almost as rare as a fool at the head of a republican government. Thus, when, by some fortunate chance, one of those born governors takes the helm of State in some monarchy that has been nearly overwhelmed by swarms of "gentlemanly" administrators, there is nothing but amazement at the resources he discovers, and his coming marks an era in his country's history.

For a monarchical State to have a chance of being well governed, its population and extent must be proportionate to the abilities of its governor. It is easier to conquer than to rule. With a long enough lever, the world could be moved with a single finger; to sustain it needs the shoulders of Hercules. However small a State may be, the prince is hardly ever big enough for it. When, on the other hand, it happens that the State is too small for its ruler, in these rare cases too it is ill governed, because the ruler, constantly pursuing his great designs, forgets the interests of the people, and makes it no less wretched by misusing the talents he has, than a ruler of less capacity would make it for want of those he had not. A kingdom should, so to speak, expand or contract with each reign, according to the prince's capabilities; but, the abilities of a senate being more constant in quantity, the State can then have permanent frontiers without the administration suffering. . . .

CHAPTER IX: THE MARKS OF A GOOD GOVERNMENT

The question "What absolutely is the best government?" is unanswerable as well as indeterminate; or rather, there are as many good answers as there are possible combinations in the absolute and relative situations of all nations.

But if it is asked by what sign we may know that a given people is well or ill governed, that is another matter, and the question, being one of fact, admits of an answer.

It is not, however, answered, because every-one wants to answer it in his own way. Subjects extol public tranquillity, citizens individual liberty; the one class prefers security of possessions, the other that of person; the one regards as the best government that which is most severe, the other maintains that the mildest is the best; the one wants crimes punished, the other wants them prevented; the one wants the State to be feared by its neighbours, the other prefers that it should be ignored; the one is content if money circulates, the other demands that the people shall have bread. Even if an agreement were come to on these and similar points, should we have got any further? As moral qualities do not admit of exact measurement, agreement about the mark does not mean agreement about the valuation.

For my part, I am continually astonished that a mark so simple is not recognised, or that men are of so bad faith as not to admit it. What is the end of political association? The preservation and prosperity of its members. And what is the surest mark of their preservation and prosperity? Their numbers and population. Seek then nowhere else this mark that is in dispute. The rest being equal, the government under which, without external aids, without naturalisation or colonies, the citizens increase and multiply most, is beyond question the best. The government under which a people wanes and diminishes is the worst. Calculators, it is left for you to count, to measure, to compare.

CHAPTER XI: THE DEATH OF THE BODY POLITIC

. . . If Sparta and Rome perished, what State can hope to endure for ever? If we would set up a long-lived form of government, let us not even dream of making it eternal. If we are to succeed, we must not attempt the impossible, or flatter ourselves that we are endowing the work of man with a stability of which human conditions do not permit.

The body politic, as well as the human body, begins to die as soon as it is born, and carries in itself the causes of its destruction. But both may have a constitution that is more or less robust and suited to preserve them a longer or a shorter time. The constitution of man is the work of nature; that of the State the work of art. It is not in men's power to prolong their own lives; but it is for them to prolong as much as possible the life of the State, by giving it the best possible constitution. The best constituted State will have an end; but it will end later than any other, unless some unforeseen accident brings about its untimely destruction.

The life-principle of the body politic lies in the sovereign authority. The legislative power is the heart of the State; the executive power is its brain, which causes the movement of all the parts. The brain may become paralysed and the individual still live. A man may remain an imbecile and live; but as soon as the heart ceases to perform its functions, the animal is dead.

The State subsists by means not of the laws, but of the legislative power. Yesterday's law is not binding today; but silence is taken for tacit consent, and the Sovereign is held to confirm incessantly the laws it does not abrogate as it might. All that it has once declared itself to will it wills always, unless it revokes its declaration.

Why then is so much respect paid to old laws? For this very reason. We must believe that nothing but the excellence of old acts of will can have preserved them so long: if the Sovereign had not recognised them as throughout salutary, it would have revoked them a thousand times. This is why, so far from growing weak, the laws continually gain new strength in any well constituted State; the precedent of antiquity makes them daily more venerable: while wherever the laws grow weak as they become old, this proves that there is no longer a legislative power, and that the State is dead. . . .

CHAPTER XV: DEPUTIES OR REPRESENTATIVES

As soon as public service ceases to be the chief business of the citizens, and they would rather serve with their money than with their persons, the State is not far from its fall. When it is necessary to march out to war, they pay troops and stay home: when it is necessary to meet in council, they name deputies and stay at home. By reason of idleness and money, they end by having soldiers to enslave their country and representatives to sell it.

It is through the hustle of commerce and the arts, through the greedy self-interest of profit, and through softness and love of amenities that personal services are replaced by money payments. Men surrender a part of their profits in order to have time to increase them at leisure. Make gifts of money, and you will not be long without chains. The word *finance* is a slavish word, unknown in the city-state. In a country that is truly free, the citizens do everything with their own arms and nothing by means of money; so far from paying to be exempted from their duties, they would even pay for the privilege of fulfilling them themselves. I am far from taking the common view: I hold enforced labour to be less opposed to liberty than taxes.

The better the constitution of a State is, the more do public affairs encroach on private in the minds of the citizens. Private affairs are even of much less importance, because the aggregate of the common happiness furnishes a greater proportion of that of each individual, so that there is less for him to seek in particular cares. In a well-ordered city every man flies to the assemblies: under a bad government no one cares to stir a step to get to them, because no one is interested in what happens there, because it is foreseen that the general will will not prevail, and lastly because domestic cares are all-absorbing. Good laws lead to the making of better ones; bad ones bring about worse. As soon as any man says of the affairs of the State *What does it matter to me?* the State may be given up for lost.

The lukewarmness of patriotism, the activity of private interest, the vastness of States, conquest and the abuse of government suggest the method of having deputies or representatives of the people in the national assemblies. These are what, in some countries, men have presumed to call the Third Estate. Thus the individual interest of two orders is put first and second; the public interest occupies only the third place.

Sovereignty, for the same reason as makes it inalienable, cannot be represented; it lies essentially in the general will, and will does not admit of representation: it is either the same, or other; there is no intermediate possibility. The deputies of the people, therefore, are not and cannot be its representatives: they are merely its stewards, and can carry through no definitive acts. Every law the people has not ratified in person is null and void—is, in fact, not a law. The people of England regards itself as free; but it is grossly mistaken; it is free only during the election of members of parliament. As soon as they are elected, slavery overtakes it, and it is nothing. The use it makes of the short moments of liberty it enjoys shows indeed that it deserves to lose them.

The idea of representation is modern; it comes to us from feudal government, from that iniquitous and absurd system which degrades humanity and dishonours the name of man. In ancient republics and even in monarchies, the people never had representatives; the word itself was unknown. It is very singular that in Rome, where the tribunes were so sacrosanct, it was never even imagined that they could usurp the functions of the people, and that in the midst of so great a multitude they never attempted to pass on their own authority a single plebiscitum. We can, however, form an idea of the difficulties caused sometimes by the people being so numerous, from what happened in the time of the Gracchi, when some of the citizens had to cast their votes from the roofs of buildings.

Where right and liberty are everything, disadvantages count for nothing. Among this wise people everything was given its just value, its lictors were allowed to do what its tribunes would never have dared to attempt; for it had no fear that its lictors would try to represent it.

To explain, however, in what way the tribunes did sometimes represent it, it is enough to conceive how the government represents the Sovereign. Law being purely the declaration of the general will, it is clear that, in the exercise of the legislative power, the people cannot be represented; but in that of the executive power, which is only the force that is applied to give the law effect, it both can and should be represented. We thus see that if we looked closely into the matter we should find that very few nations have any laws. However that may be, it is certain that the tribunes, possessing no executive power, could never represent the Roman people by right of the powers entrusted to them, but only by usurping those of the senate.

In Greece, all that the people had to do, it did for itself; it was constantly assembled in the public square. The Greeks lived in a mild climate; they had no natural greed; slaves did their work for them; their great concern was with liberty. Lacking the same advantages, how can you preserve the same rights? Your severer climates add to your needs; for half the year your public squares are uninhabitable; the flatness of your languages unfits them for being heard in the open air; you sacrifice more for profit than for liberty, and fear slavery less than poverty.

What then? Is liberty maintained only by the help of slavery? It may be so. Extremes meet. Everything that is not in the course of nature has its disadvantages, civil society most of all. There are some unhappy circumstances in which we can only keep our liberty at others' expense, and where the citizen can be perfectly free only when the slave is most a slave. Such was the case with Sparta. As for you, modern peoples, you have no slaves, but you are slaves yourselves; you pay for their liberty with your own. It is in vain that you boast of this preference; I find in it more cowardice than humanity.

I do not mean by all this that it is necessary to have slaves, or that the right of slavery is legitimate: I am merely giving the reasons why modern peoples, believing themselves to be free, have representatives, while ancient peoples had none. In any case, the moment a people allows itself to be represented, it is no longer free: it no longer exists.

All things considered, I do not see that it is possible henceforth for the Sovereign to preserve among us the exercise of its rights, unless the city is very small. But if it is very small, it will be conquered? No. I will show later on how the external strength of a great people may be combined with the convenient polity and good order of a small State.[6]

---

[6] [Rousseau never carried this project to completion.]

CHAPTER XVI: THAT THE INSTITUTION OF GOVERNMENT IS NOT A
CONTRACT

The legislative power once well established, the next thing is to establish
similarly the executive power; for this latter, which operates only by particular acts, not being of the essence of the former, is naturally separate from
it. Were it possible for the Sovereign, as such, to possess the executive power,
right and fact would be so confounded that no one could tell what was law
and what was not; and the body politic, thus disfigured, would soon fall a
prey to the violence it was instituted to prevent.

As the citizens, by the social contract, are all equal, all can prescribe what
all should do, but no one has a right to demand that another shall do what he
does not do himself. It is strictly this right, which is indispensable for giving
the body politic life and movement, that the Sovereign, in instituting the government, confers upon the prince.

It has been held that this act of establishment was a contract between the
people and the rulers it sets over itself,—a contract in which conditions were
laid down between the two parties binding the one to command and the other
to obey. It will be admitted, I am sure, that this is an odd kind of contract
to enter into. But let us see if this view can be upheld.

First, the supreme authority can no more be modified than it can be alienated; to limit it is to destroy it. It is absurd and contradictory for the Sovereign
to set a superior over itself; to bind itself to obey a master would be to return
to absolute liberty.

Moreover, it is clear that this contract between the people and such and
such persons would be a particular act; and from this it follows that it can be
neither law nor an act of Sovereignty, and that consequently it would be
illegitimate.

It is plain too that the contracting parties in relation to each other would be
under the law of nature alone and wholly without guarantees of their mutual
understandings, a position wholly at variance with the civil state. He who has
force at his command being always in a position to control execution, it would
come to the same thing if the name "contract" were given to the act of one
man who said to another; "I give you all my goods, on condition that you give
me back as much of them as you please."

There is only one contract in the State, and that is the act of association,
which in itself excludes the existence of a second. It is impossible to conceive
of any public contract that would not be a violation of the first. . . .

[Book IV]

CHAPTER I: THAT THE GENERAL WILL IS INDESTRUCTIBLE

As long as several men in assembly regard themselves as a single body, they have only a single will which is concerned with their common preservation and general well-being. In this case, all the springs of the State are vigorous and simple and its rules clear and luminous; there are no embroilments or conflicts of interests; the common good is everywhere clearly apparent, and only good sense is needed to perceive it. Peace, unity and equality are the enemies of political subtleties. Men who are upright and simple are difficult to deceive because of their simplicity; lures and ingenious pretexts fail to impose upon them, and they are not even subtle enough to be dupes. When, among the happiest people in the world, bands of peasants are seen regulating affairs of State under an oak, and always acting wisely, can we help scorning the ingenious methods of other nations, which make themselves illustrious and wretched with so much art and mystery?

A State so governed needs very few laws; and, as it becomes necessary to issue new ones, the necessity is universally seen. The first man to propose them merely says what all have already felt, and there is no question of factions or intrigues or eloquence in order to secure the passage into law of what every one has already decided to do, as soon as he is sure that the rest will act with him.

Theorists are led into error because, seeing only States that have been from the beginning wrongly constituted, they are struck by the impossibility of applying such a policy to them. They make great game of all the absurdities a clever rascal or an insinuating speaker might get the people of Paris or London to believe. They do not know that Cromwell would have been put to "the bells" by the people of Berne, and the Duc de Beaufort on the treadmill by the Genevese.

But when the social bond begins to be relaxed and the State to grow weak, when particular interests begin to make themselves felt and the smaller societies to exercise an influence over the larger, the common interest changes and finds opponents: opinion is no longer unanimous; the general will ceases to be the will of all; contradictory views and debates arise; and the best advice is not taken without question.

Finally, when the State, on the eve of ruin, maintains only a vain, illusory and formal existence, when in every heart the social bond is broken, and the meanest interest brazenly lays hold of the sacred name of "public good," the general will becomes mute: all men, guided by secret motives, no more give their views as citizens than if the State had never been; and iniquitous decrees directed solely to private interest get passed under the name of laws.

Does it follow from this that the general will is exterminated or corrupted? Not at all: it is always constant, unalterable and pure; but it is subordinated to other wills which encroach upon its sphere. Each man, in detaching his interest from the common interest, sees clearly that he cannot entirely separate them; but his share in the public mishaps seems to him negligible beside the exclusive good he aims at making his own. Apart from this particular good, he wills the general good in his own interest, as strongly as any one else. Even in selling his vote for money, he does not extinguish in himself the general will, but only eludes it. The fault he commits is that of changing the state of the question, and answering something different from what he is asked. Instead of saying, by his vote, "It is to the advantage of the State," he says, "It is of advantage to this or that man or party that this or that view should prevail." Thus the law of public order in assemblies is not so much to maintain in them the general will as to secure that the question be always put to it, and the answer always given by it.

I could here set down many reflections on the simple right of voting in every act of Sovereignty—a right which no one can take from the citizens—and also on the right of stating views, making proposals, dividing and discussing, which the government is always most careful to leave solely to its members; but this important subject would need a treatise to itself, and it is impossible to say everything in a single work.

CHAPTER VI: THE DICTATORSHIP

The inflexibility of the laws, which prevents them from adapting themselves to circumstances, may, in certain cases, render them disastrous, and make them bring about, at a time of crisis, the ruin of the State. The order and slowness of the forms they enjoin require a space of time which circumstances sometimes withhold. A thousand cases against which the legislator has made no provision may present themselves, and it is a highly necessary part of foresight to be conscious that everything cannot be foreseen.

It is wrong therefore to wish to make political institutions so strong as to render it impossible to suspend their operation. Even Sparta allowed its laws to lapse.

However, none but the greatest dangers can counter-balance that of changing the public order, and the sacred power of the laws should never be arrested save when the existence of the country is at stake. In these rare and obvious cases, provision is made for the public security by a particular act entrusting it to him who is most worthy. This commitment may be carried out in either of two ways, according to the nature of the danger.

If increasing the activity of the government is a sufficient remedy, power is concentrated in the hands of one or two of its members: in this case the change is not in the authority of the laws, but only in the form of administering them. If, on the other hand, the peril is of such a kind that the paraphernalia of the laws are an obstacle to their preservation, the method is to nominate a supreme ruler, who shall silence all the laws and suspend for a moment the sovereign authority. In such a case, there is no doubt about the general will, and it is clear that the people's first intention is that the State shall not perish. Thus the suspension of the legislative authority is in no sense its abolition; the magistrate who silences it cannot make it speak; he dominates it, but cannot represent it. He can do anything, except make laws. . . .

However this important trust be conferred, it is important that its duration should be fixed at a very brief period, incapable of being ever prolonged. In the crises which lead to its adoption, the State is either soon lost, or soon saved; and, the present need passed, the dictatorship becomes either tyrannical or idle. At Rome, where dictators held office for six months only, most of them abdicated before their time was up. If their term had been longer, they might well have tried to prolong it still further, as the decemvirs did when chosen for a year. The dictator had only time to provide against the need that had caused him to be chosen; he had none to think of further projects.

CHAPTER VIII: CIVIL RELIGION

. . . Religion, considered in relation to society, which is either general or particular, may also be divided into two kinds: the religion of man, and that of the citizen. The first, which has neither temples, nor altars, nor rites, and is confined to the purely internal cult of the supreme God and the eternal obligations of morality, is the religion of the Gospel pure and simple, the true theism, what may be called natural divine right or law. The other, which is codified in a single country, gives it its gods, its own tutelary patrons; it has its dogmas, its rites, and its external cult prescribed by law; outside the single nation that follows it, all the world is in its sight infidel, foreign and barbarous; the duties and rights of man extend for it only as far as its own altars. Of this kind were all the religions of early peoples, which we may define as civil or positive divine right or law.

There is a third sort of religion of a more singular kind, which gives men two codes of legislation, two rulers, and two countries, renders them subject to contradictory duties, and makes it impossible for them to be faithful both to religion and to citizenship. Such are the religions of the Lamas and of the Japanese, and such is Roman Christianity, which may be called the religion of the priest. It leads to a sort of mixed and anti-social code which has no name.

In their political aspect, all these three kinds of religion have their defects. The third is so clearly bad, that it is waste of time to stop to prove it such. All that destroys social unity is worthless; all institutions that set man in contradiction to himself are worthless.

The second is good in that it unites the divine cult with love of the laws, and, making country the object of the citizens' adoration, teaches them that service done to the State is service done to its tutelary god. It is a form of theocracy, in which there can be no pontiff save the prince, and no priests save the magistrates. To die for one's country then becomes martyrdom; violation of its laws, impiety; and to subject one who is guilty to public execration is to condemn him to the anger of the gods: *Sacer estod*.

On the other hand, it is bad in that, being founded on lies and error, it deceives men, makes them credulous and superstitious, and drowns the true cult of the Divinity in empty ceremonial. It is bad, again, when it becomes tyrannous and exclusive, and makes a people bloodthirsty and intolerant, so that it breathes fire and slaughter, and regards as a sacred act the killing of every one who does not believe in its gods. The result is to place such a people in a natural state of war with all others, so that its security is deeply endangered.

There remains therefore the religion of man or Christianity—not the Christianity of to-day, but that of the Gospel, which is entirely different. By means of this holy, sublime, and real religion all men, being children of one God, recognise one another as brothers, and the society that unites them is not dissolved even at death.

But this religion, having no particular relation to the body politic, leaves the laws in possession of the force they have in themselves without making any addition to it; and thus one of the great bonds that unite society considered in severalty fails to operate. Nay, more, so far from binding the hearts of the citizens to the State, it has the effect of taking them away from all earthly things. I know of nothing more contrary to the social spirit.

We are told that a people of true Christians would form the most perfect society imaginable. I see in this supposition only one great difficulty: that a society of true Christians would not be a society of men.

I say further that such a society, with all its perfection, would be neither the strongest nor the most lasting: the very fact that it was perfect would rob it of its bond of union; the flaw that would destroy it would lie in its very perfection.

Every one would do his duty; the people be law-abiding, the rulers just and temperate; the magistrates upright and incorruptible; the soldiers would scorn death; there would be neither vanity nor luxury. So far, so good; but let us hear more.

Christianity as a religion is entirely spiritual, occupied solely with heavenly things; the country of the Christian is not of this world. He does his duty, indeed, but does it with profound indifference to the good or ill success of his cares. Provided he has nothing to reproach himself with, it matters little to him whether things go well or ill here on earth. If the State is prosperous, he hardly dares to share in the public happiness, for fear he may grow proud of his country's glory; if the State is languishing, he blesses the hand of God that is hard upon His people.

For the State to be peaceable and for harmony to be maintained, all the citizens without exception would have to be good Christians; if by ill hap there should be a single self-seeker or hypocrite, a Catiline or a Cromwell, for instance, he would certainly get the better of his pious compatriots. Christian charity does not readily allow a man to think hardly of his neighbours. As soon as, by some trick, he has discovered the art of imposing on them and getting hold of a share in the public authority, you have a man established in dignity; it is the will of God that he be respected: very soon you have a power; it is God's will that it be obeyed: and if the power is abused by him who wields it, it is the scourge wherewith God punishes His children. There would be scruples about driving out the usurper: public tranquillity would have to be disturbed, violence would have to be employed, and blood spilt; all this accords ill with Christian meekness; and after all, in this vale of sorrows, what does it matter whether we are free men or serfs? The essential thing is to get to heaven, and resignation is only an additional means of doing so.

If war breaks out with another State, the citizens march readily out to battle; not one of them thinks of flight; they do their duty, but they have no passion for victory; they know better how to die than how to conquer. What does it matter whether they win or lose? Does not Providence know better than they what is meet for them? Only think to what account a proud, impetuous and passionate enemy could turn their stoicism! Set over against them those generous peoples who were devoured by ardent love of glory and of their country, imagine your Christian republic face to face with Sparta or Rome: the pious Christians will be beaten, crushed and destroyed, before they know where they are, or will owe their safety only to the contempt their enemy will conceive for them. It was to my mind a fine oath that was taken by the soldiers of Fabius, who swore, not to conquer or die, but to come back victorious—and kept their oath. Christians would never have taken such an oath; they would have looked on it as tempting God.

But I am mistaken in speaking of a Christian republic; the terms are mutually exclusive. Christianity preaches only servitude and dependence. Its spirit is so favourable to tyranny that it always profits by such a *régime*. True Christians are made to be slaves, and they know it and do not much mind: this short life counts for too little in their eyes.

I shall be told that Christian troops are excellent. I deny it. Show me an instance. For my part, I know of no Christian troops. I shall be told of the Crusades. Without disputing the valour of the Crusaders, I answer that, so far from being Christians, they were the priests' soldiery, citizens of the Church. They fought for their spiritual country, which the Church had, somehow or other, made temporal. Well understood, this goes back to paganism: as the Gospel sets up no national religion, a holy war is impossible among Christians.

Under the pagan emperors, the Christian soldiers were brave; every Christian writer affirms it, and I believe it: it was a case of honourable emulation of the pagan troops. As soon as the emperors were Christian, this emulation no longer existed, and, when the Cross had driven out the eagle, Roman valour wholly disappeared.

But, setting aside political considerations, let us come back to what is right, and settle our principles on this important point. The right which the social compact gives the Sovereign over the subjects does not, we have seen, exceed the limits of public expediency. The subjects then owe the Sovereign an account of their opinions only to such an extent as they matter to the community. Now, it matters very much to the community that each citizen should have a religion. That will make him love his duty; but the dogmas of that religion concern the State and its members only so far as they have reference to morality and to the duties which he who professes them is bound to do to others. Each man may have, over and above, what opinions he pleases, without it being the Sovereign's business to take cognisance of them; for, as the Sovereign has no authority in the other world, whatever the lot of its subjects may be in the life to come, that is not its business, provided they are good citizens in this life.

There is therefore a purely civil profession of faith of which the Sovereign should fix the articles, not exactly as religious dogmas, but as social sentiments without which a man cannot be a good citizen or a faithful subject. While it can compel no one to believe them, it can banish from the State whoever does not believe them—it can banish him, not for impiety, but as an anti-social being, incapable of truly loving the laws and justice, and of sacrificing, at need, his life to his duty. If any one, after publicly recognising these dogmas, behaves as if he does not believe them, let him be punished by death: he has committed the worst of all crimes, that of lying before the law.

The dogmas of civil religion ought to be few, simple, and exactly worded, without explanation or commentary. The existence of a mighty, intelligent and beneficent Divinity, possessed of foresight and providence, the life to come, the happiness of the just, the punishment of the wicked, the sanctity of the social contract and the laws: these are its positive dogmas. Its negative dogmas I confine to one, intolerance, which is a part of the cults we have rejected.

Those who distinguish civil from theological intolerance are, to my mind, mistaken. The two forms are inseparable. It is impossible to live at peace with those we regard as damned; to love them would be to hate God who punishes them: we positively must either reclaim or torment them. Wherever theological intolerance is admitted, it must inevitably have some civil effect; and as soon as it has such an effect, the Sovereign is no longer Sovereign even in the temporal sphere: thenceforth priests are the real masters, and kings only their ministers.

Now that there is and can be no longer an exclusive national religion, tolerance should be given to all religions that tolerate others, so long as their dogmas contain nothing contrary to the duties of citizenship. But whoever dares to say: *Outside the Church is no salvation,* ought to be driven from the State, unless the State is the Church, and the prince the pontiff. Such a dogma is good only in a theocratic government; in any other, it is fatal. The reason for which Henry IV is said to have embraced the Roman religion ought to make every honest man leave it, and still more any prince who knows how to reason.

CHAPTER IX: CONCLUSION

Now that I have laid down the true principles of political right, and tried to give the State a basis of its own to rest on, I ought next to strengthen it by its external relations, which would include the law of nations, commerce, the right of war and conquest, public right, leagues, negotiations, treaties, etc. But all this forms a new subject that is far too vast for my narrow scope. I ought throughout to have kept to a more limited sphere.

JAMES MADISON

The most effective special pleading for the American Constitution, and the most probing insights into the nature of politics that grew out of the struggle for its adoption are found in *The Federalist,* a collection of eighty-five essays which appeared in the New York press from October, 1787, to May, 1788. Written under the pseudonym "Publius," it turned out subsequently that the essays had been written by Alexander Hamilton (1757–1804), James Madison (1751–1836), and John Jay (1745–1829). In these essays a marked distrust of direct democracy was exhibited and a strong inclination in favor of the constitutional checks that marked a "republican" as over against a "democratic" form of government.

Of these eighty-five essays Number 10 (the essay that follows) is probably the most important and contains the most characteristic aspects of federalist theory. It was written by Madison. Subsequently fourth President of the United States, the Virginia-born and Princeton-educated Madison was the most informed and acute political theorist of those who gathered at Philadelphia, and probably played the greatest single part in the actual framing of the Constitution.

Apart from their immediate importance as propaganda for the Constitution, the Federalist Papers are a distinguished exposition of eighteenth-century political principles, especially of the attempt to systematize federal or coordinate powers of government. They reflect the fear of both popular "passions" and monarchical absolutism, and represent a continuing fear of concentrated and centralized political power.

THE FEDERALIST No. 10

To the People of the State of New York: Among the numerous advantages promised by a well-constructed Union, none deserves to be more accurately developed than its tendency to break and control the violence of faction. The friend of popular governments never finds himself so much alarmed for their character and fate, as when he contemplates their propensity to this dangerous vice. He will not fail, therefore, to set a due value on any plan which, without violating the principles to which he is attached, provides a proper cure for it. The instability, injustice, and confusion introduced into the public councils, have, in truth, been the mortal diseases under which popular governments have everywhere perished; as they continue to be the favorite and fruitful topics from which the adversaries to liberty derive their most specious declamations. The valuable improvements made by the American constitutions on the popular models, both ancient and modern, cannot certainly be too much admired; but it would be an unwarrantable partiality, to contend that they have as effectually obviated the danger on this side, as was wished and expected. Complaints are everywhere heard from our most considerate and virtuous citizens, equally the friends of public and private faith, and of public and personal liberty, that our governments are too unstable, that the public good is disregarded in the conflicts of rival parties, and that measures are too often decided, not according to the rules of justice and the rights of the minor party, but by the superior force of an interested and overbearing majority. However anxiously we may wish that these complaints had no foundation, the evidence of known facts will not permit us to deny that they are in some degree true. It will be found, indeed, on a candid review of our situation, that some of the distresses under which we labor have been erroneously charged on the operation of our governments; but it will be found, at the same time, that other causes will not alone account for many of our heaviest misfortunes; and, particularly, for that prevailing and increasing distrust of public engagements, and alarm for private rights, which are echoed from one end of the continent to the other. These must be chiefly, if not wholly, effects of the unsteadiness and injustice with which a factious spirit has tainted our public administrations.

By a faction, I understand a number of citizens, whether amounting to a majority or minority of the whole, who are united and actuated by some common impulse of passion, or of interest, adverse to the rights of other citizens, or to the permanent and aggregate interests of the community.

There are two methods of curing the mischiefs of faction: the one, by removing its causes; the other, by controlling its effects.

There are again two methods of removing the causes of faction: the one, by destroying the liberty which is essential to its existence; the other, by giving to every citizen the same opinions, the same passions, and the same interests.

It could never be more truly said than of the first remedy, that it was worse than the disease. Liberty is to faction what air is to fire, an aliment without which it instantly expires. But it could not be less folly to abolish liberty, which is essential to political life, because it nourishes faction, than it would be to wish the annihilation of air, which is essential to animal life, because it imparts to fire its destructive agency.

The second expedient is as impracticable as the first would be unwise. As long as the reason of man continues fallible, and he is at liberty to exercise it, different opinions will be formed. As long as the connection subsists between his reason and his self-love, his opinions and his passions will have a reciprocal influence on each other; and the former will be objects to which the latter will attach themselves. The diversity in the faculties of men, from which the rights of property originate, is not less an insuperable obstacle to a uniformity of interests. The protection of these faculties is the first object of government. From the protection of different and unequal faculties of acquiring property, the possession of different degrees and kinds of property immediately results; and from the influence of these on the sentiments and views of the respective proprietors, ensues a division of the society into different interests and parties.

The latent causes of faction are thus sown in the nature of man; and we see them everywhere brought into different degrees of activity, according to the different circumstances of civil society. A zeal for different opinions concerning religion, concerning government, and many other points, as well of speculation as of practice; an attachment to different leaders ambitiously contending for pre-eminence and power; or to persons of other descriptions whose fortunes have been interesting to the human passions, have, in turn, divided mankind into parties, inflamed them with mutual animosity, and rendered them much more disposed to vex and oppress each other than to co-operate for their common good. So strong is this propensity of mankind to fall into mutual animosities, that where no substantial occasion presents itself, the most frivolous and fanciful distinctions have been sufficient to kindle their unfriendly passions and excite their most violent conflicts. But the most common and durable source of factions has been the various and unequal distribution of property. Those who hold and those who are without property have ever formed distinct interests in society. Those who are creditors, and those who are debtors, fall under a like discrimination. A landed interest, a manufacturing interest, a mercantile interest, a moneyed interest, with many lesser interests, grow up of necessity in civilized nations, and divide them into different classes, actuated by different sentiments and views. The regulation of these various and interfering interests forms the principal task of modern legislation, and involves the spirit of party and faction in the necessary and ordinary operations of the government.

No man is allowed to be a judge in his own cause, because his interest would certainly bias his judgment, and, not improbably, corrupt his integrity. With equal, nay with greater reason, a body of men are unfit to be both judges and parties at the same time; yet what are many of the most important acts of legislation, but so many judicial determinations, not indeed concerning the rights of single persons, but concerning the rights of large bodies of citizens? And what are the different classes of legislators but advocates and parties to the causes which they determine? Is a law proposed concerning private debts? It is a question to which the creditors are parties on one side and the debtors on the other. Justice ought to hold the balance between them. Yet the parties are, and must be, themselves the judges; and the most numerous party, or, in other words, the most powerful faction must be expected to prevail. Shall domestic manufactures be encouraged, and in what degree, by restrictions on foreign manufactures? are questions which would be differently decided by the landed and the manufacturing classes, and probably by neither with a sole regard to justice and the public good. The apportionment of taxes on the various descriptions of property is an act which seems to require the most exact impartiality; yet there is, perhaps, no legislative act in which greater opportunity and temptation are given to a predominant party to trample on the rules of justice. Every shilling with which they overburden the inferior number, is a shilling saved to their own pockets.

It is in vain to say that enlightened statesmen will be able to adjust these clashing interests, and render them all subservient to the public good. Enlightened statesmen will not always be at the helm. Nor, in many cases, can such an adjustment be made at all without taking into view indirect and remote considerations, which will rarely prevail over the immediate interest which one party may find in disregarding the rights of another or the good of the whole.

The inference to which we are brought is, that the *causes* of faction cannot be removed, and that relief is only to be sought in the means of controlling its *effects*.

If a faction consists of less than a majority, relief is supplied by the republican principle, which enables the majority to defeat its sinister views by regular vote. It may clog the administration, it may convulse the society; but it will be unable to execute and mask its violence under the forms of the Constitution. When a majority is included in a faction, the form of popular government, on the other hand, enables it to sacrifice to its ruling passion or interest both the public good and the rights of other citizens. To secure the public good and private rights against the danger of such a faction, and at the same time to preserve the spirit and the form of popular government, is then the great object to which our inquiries are directed. Let me add that it is the great desideratum by which this form of government can be rescued from the opprobrium under which it has so long labored, and be recommended to the esteem and adoption of mankind.

By what means is this object attainable? Evidently by one of two only. Either the existence of the same passion or interest in a majority at the same time must be prevented, or the majority, having such coexistent passion or interest, must be rendered, by their number and local situation, unable to concert and carry into effect schemes of oppression. If the impulse and the opportunity be suffered to coincide, we well know that neither moral nor religious motives can be relied on as an adequate control. They are not found to be such on the injustice and violence of individuals, and lose their efficacy in proportion to the number combined together, that is, in proportion as their efficacy becomes needful.

From this view of the subject it may be concluded that a pure democracy, by which I mean a society consisting of a small number of citizens, who assemble and administer the government in person, can admit of no cure for the mischiefs of faction. A common passion or interest will, in almost every case, be felt by a majority of the whole; a communication and concert result from the form of government itself; and there is nothing to check the inducements to sacrifice the weaker party or an obnoxious individual. Hence it is that such democracies have ever been spectacles of turbulence and contention; have ever been found incompatible with personal security or the rights of property; and have in general been as short in their lives as they have been violent in their deaths. Theoretic politicians, who have patronized this species of government, have erroneously supposed that by reducing mankind to a perfect equality in their political rights, they would, at the same time, be perfectly equalized and assimilated in their possessions, their opinions, and their passions.

A republic, by which I mean a government in which the scheme of representation takes place, opens a different prospect, and promises the cure for which we are seeking. Let us examine the points in which it varies from pure democracy, and we shall comprehend both the nature of the cure and the efficacy which it must derive from the Union.

The two great points of difference between a democracy and a republic are: first, the delegation of the government, in the latter, to a small number of citizens elected by the rest; secondly, the greater number of citizens, and greater sphere of country, over which the latter may be extended.

The effect of the first difference is, on the one hand, to refine and enlarge the public views, by passing them through the medium of a chosen body of citizens, whose wisdom may best discern the true interest of their country, and whose patriotism and love of justice will be least likely to sacrifice it to temporary or partial considerations. Under such a regulation, it may well happen that the public voice, pronounced by the representatives of the people, will be more consonant to the public good than if pronounced by the people themselves, convened for the purpose. On the other hand, the effect may be inverted. Men of factious tempers, of local prejudices, or of sinister designs, may, by intrigue, by corruption, or by other means, first obtain the suffrages, and then betray the interests, of the people. The question resulting is, whether small or extensive republics are more favorable to the election of proper guardians of the public weal; and it is clearly decided in favor of the latter by two obvious considerations:

In the first place, it is to be remarked that, however small the republic may be, the representatives must be raised to a certain number, in order to guard against the cabals of a few; and that, however large it may be, they must be limited to a certain number, in order to guard against the confusion of a multitude. Hence, the number of representatives in the two cases not being in proportion to that of the two constituents, and being proportionally greater in the small republic, it follows that, if the proportion of fit characters be not less in the large than in the small republic, the former will present a greater option, and consequently a greater probability of a fit choice.

In the next place, as each representative will be chosen by a greater number of citizens in the large than in the small republic, it will be more difficult for unworthy candidates to practise with success the vicious arts by which elections are too often carried; and the suffrages of the people being more free, will be more likely to centre in men who possess the most attractive merit and the most diffusive and established characters.

It must be confessed that in this, as in most other cases, there is a mean, on both sides of which inconveniences will be found to lie. By enlarging too much the number of electors, who render the representative too little acquainted with all their local circumstances and lesser interests; as by reducing it too much, you render him unduly attached to these, and too little fit to comprehend and pursue great and national objects. The federal Constitution forms a happy combination in this respect; the great and aggregate interests being referred to the national, the local and particular to the State legislatures.

The other point of difference is, the greater number of citizens and extent of territory which may be brought within the compass of republican than of democratic government; and it is this circumstance principally which renders factious combinations less to be dreaded in the former than in the latter. The smaller the society, the fewer probably will be the distinct parties and interests composing it; the fewer the distinct parties and interests, the more frequently will a majority be found of the same party; and the smaller the number of individuals composing a majority, and the smaller the compass within which they are placed, the more easily will they convert and execute their plans of oppression. Extend the sphere, and you take in a greater variety of parties and interests; you make it less probable that a majority of the whole will have a common motive to invade the rights of other citizens; or if such a common motive exists, it will be more difficult for all who feel it to discover their own strength, and to act in unison with each other. Besides other impediments, it may be remarked that, where there is a consciousness of unjust or dishonorable purposes, communication is always checked by distrust in proportion to the number whose concurrence is necessary.

Hence, it clearly appears, that the same advantage which a republic has over a democracy, in controlling the effects of faction, is enjoyed by a large over a small republic,—is enjoyed by the Union over the States composing it. Does the advantage consist in the substitution of representatives whose enlightened views and virtuous sentiments render them superior to local prejudices and to schemes of injustice? It will not be denied that the representation of the Union will be most likely to possess these requisite endowments. Does it consist in the greater security afforded by a greater variety of parties, against the event of any one party being able to outnumber and oppress the rest? In an equal degree does the increased variety of parties comprised within the Union, increase this security. Does it, in fine, consist in the greater obstacles opposed to the concert and accomplishment of the secret wishes of an unjust and interested majority? Here, again, the extent of the Union gives it the most palpable advantage.

The influence of factious leaders may kindle a flame within their particular States, but will be unable to spread a general conflagration through the other States. A religious sect may degenerate into a political faction in a part of the Confederacy; but the variety of sects dispersed over the entire face of it must secure the national councils against any danger from that source. A rage for paper money, for an abolition of debts, for an equal division of property, or for any other improper or wicked project, will be less apt to pervade the whole body of the Union than a particular member of it; in the same proportion as such a malady is more likely to taint a particular county or district, than an entire State.

In the extent and proper structure of the Union, therefore, we behold a republican remedy for the diseases most incident to republican government. And according to the degree of pleasure and pride we feel in being republicans, ought to be our zeal in cherishing the spirit and supporting the character of Federalists.

PUBLIUS

ADAM SMITH

ADAM SMITH (1723–93), born at Kirkcaldy, Scotland, studied mathematics and natural philosophy at Glasgow and spent seven years at Balliol College, Oxford, pursuing his interest in moral philosophy and political science. In 1748 he was invited to lecture at Edinburgh on English literature; in 1751 he became Professor of Logic at Glasgow, and in the following year Professor of Moral Philosophy. His book, the *Theory of Moral Sentiments,* published in 1759, embodied his lectures on ethics.

As early as 1752 he adopted the liberal view of commercial affairs, propounded in that year by Hume in his *Political Discourses.* In Paris in 1763, Smith made the acquaintance of Quesnay, Turgot, D'Alembert, Helvétius, and others. There has been much argument about the extent of Physiocrat influence on his thinking, but it seems that his connections with them did little more than confirm his opinions.

Upon his return he began working in earnest on his *Inquiry into the Nature and Causes of the Wealth of Nations,* which finally appeared in 1776. Our selection is from that influential work, commonly credited with having originated the science of political economy.

THE WEALTH OF NATIONS

INTRODUCTION AND PLAN OF THE WORK

THE ANNUAL LABOUR of every nation is the fund which originally supplies it with all the necessaries and conveniencies of life which it annually consumes, and which consist always either in the immediate produce of that labour, or in what is purchased with that produce from other nations.

According therefore, as this produce, or what is purchased with it, bears a greater or smaller proportion to the number of those who are to consume it, the nation will be better or worse supplied with all the necessaries and conveniencies for which it has occasion.

But this proportion must in every nation be regulated by two different circumstances; first, by the skill, dexterity, and judgment with which its labour is generally applied; and, secondly, by the proportion between the number of those who are employed in useful labour, and that of those who are not so employed. Whatever be the soil, climate, or extent of territory of any particular nation, the abundance or scantiness of its annual supply must, in that particular situation, depend upon those two circumstances.

The abundance or scantiness of this supply too seems to depend more upon the former of those two circumstances than upon the latter. Among the savage nations of hunters and fishers, every individual who is able to work, is more or less employed in useful labour, and endeavours to provide, as well as he can, the necessaries and conveniencies of life, for himself, or such of his family or tribe as are either too old, or too young, or too infirm to go a hunting and fishing. Such nations, however, are so miserably poor, that from mere want, they are frequently reduced, or, at least, think themselves reduced, to the necessity sometimes of directly destroying, and sometimes of abandoning their infants, their old people, and those afflicted with lingering diseases, to perish with hunger, or to be devoured by wild beasts. Among civilized and thriving nations, on the contrary, though a great number of people do not labour at all, many of whom consume the produce of ten times, frequently of a hundred times more labour than the greater part of those who work; yet the produce of the whole labour of the society is so great, that all are often abundantly supplied, and a workman, even of the lowest and poorest order, if he is frugal and industrious, may enjoy a greater share of the necessaries and conveniencies of life than it is possible for any savage to acquire. . . .

[Book I]

CHAPTER II: OF THE PRINCIPLE WHICH GIVES OCCASION TO THE DIVISION OF LABOUR

[The] division of labour, from which so many advantages are derived, is not originally the effect of any human wisdom, which foresees and intends that general opulence to which it gives occasion. It is the necessary, though very slow and gradual, consequence of a certain propensity in human nature which has in view no such extensive utility; the propensity to truck, barter, and exchange one thing for another.

Whether this propensity be one of those original principles in human nature, of which no further account can be given; or whether, as seems more probable, it be the necessary consequence of the faculties of reason and speech, it belongs not to our present subject to enquire. It is common to all men, and to be found in no other race of animals, which seem to know neither this nor any other species of contracts. Two greyhounds, in running down the same hare, have sometimes the appearance of acting in some sort of concert. Each turns her towards his companion, or endeavours to intercept her when his companion turns her towards himself. This, however, is not the effect of any contract, but of the accidental concurrence of their passions in the same object at that particular time. Nobody ever saw a dog make a fair and deliberate exchange of one bone for another with another dog. Nobody ever saw one animal by its gestures and natural cries signify to another, this is mine, that yours; I am willing to give this for that. When an animal wants to obtain something either of a man or of another animal, it has no other means of persuasion but to gain the favour of those whose service it requires. A puppy fawns upon its dam, and a spaniel endeavours by a thousand attractions to engage the attention of its master who is at dinner, when it wants to be fed by him. Man sometimes uses the same arts with his brethren, and when he has no other means of engaging them to act according to his inclinations, endeavours by every servile and fawning attention to obtain their good will. He has not time, however, to do this upon every occasion. In civilized society he stands at all times in need of the co-operation and assistance of great multitudes, while his whole life is scarce sufficient to gain the friendship of a few persons. In almost every other race of animals each individual, when it is grown up to maturity, is entirely independent, and in its natural state has occasion for the assistance of no other living creature. But man has almost constant occasion for the help of his brethren, and it is in vain for him to expect it from their benevolence only. He will be more likely to prevail if he can interest their self-love in his favour, and show them that it is for their own advantage to do for him what he requires of them. Whoever offers to another a bargain of any kind, proposes to do this: Give me that which I want, and you shall have this which you want, is the meaning of every such offer; and it is in this manner that we obtain from one another the far greater part of those good offices which we stand in need of. It is not from the benevolence of the butcher, the brewer, or the baker, that we expect our dinner, but from their regard to their own interest. We address ourselves, not to their humanity, but to their self-love, and never talk to them of our own necessities but of their advantages. Nobody but a beggar chuses to depend chiefly upon the benevolence of his fellow-citizens. Even a beggar does not depend upon it entirely. The charity of well-disposed people, indeed, supplies him with the whole fund of his subsistence. But though this principle ultimately provides him with all the necessaries of life which he has occasion for, it neither does nor can provide him with them as he has occasion for them. The greater part of his occasional wants are supplied in the same manner as those of other people, by treaty, by barter, and by purchase. With the money which one man gives him he purchases food. The old cloaths which another bestows upon him he exchanges for other old cloaths which suit him better, or for lodging, or for food, or for money, with which he can buy either food, cloaths, or lodging, as he has occasion.

As it is by treaty, by barter, and by purchase, that we obtain from one another the greater part of those mutual good offices which we stand in need of, so it is this same trucking disposition which originally gives occasion to the division of labour. In a tribe of hunters or shepherds a particular person makes bows and arrows, for example, with more readiness and dexterity than any other. He frequently exchanges them for cattle or for venison with his companions; and he finds at last that he can in this manner get more cattle and venison, than if he himself went to the field to catch them. From a regard to his own interest, therefore, the making of bows and arrows grows to be his chief business, and he becomes a sort of armourer. Another excels in making the frames and covers of their little huts or moveable houses. He is accustomed to be of use in this way to his neighbours, who reward him in the same manner with cattle and with venison, till at last he finds it his interest to dedicate himself entirely to this employment, and to become a sort of house-carpenter. In the same manner a third becomes a smith or a brazier; a fourth a tanner or dresser of hides or skins, the principal part of the clothing of savages. And thus the certainty of being able to exchange all that surplus part of the produce of his own labour, which is over and above his own consumption, for such parts of the produce of other men's labour as he may have occasion for, encourages every man to apply himself to a particular occupation, and to cultivate and bring to perfection whatever talent of genius he may possess for that particular species of business.

The difference of natural talents in different men is, in reality, much less than we are aware of; and the very different genius which appears to distinguish men of different professions, when grown up to maturity, is not upon many occasions so much the cause, as the effect of the division of labour. The difference between the most dissimilar characters, between a philosopher and a common street porter, for example, seems to arise not so much from nature, as from habit, custom, and education. When they came into the world, and for the first six or eight years of their existence, they were, perhaps, very much alike, and neither their parents nor playfellows could perceive any remarkable difference. About that age, or soon after, they come to be employed in very different occupations. The difference of talents comes then to be taken notice of, and widens by degrees, till at last the vanity of the philosopher is willing to acknowledge scarce any resemblance. But without the disposition to truck, barter, and exchange, every man must have procured to himself every necessary and conveniency of life which he wanted. All must have had the same duties to perform, and the same work to do, and there could have been no such difference of employment as could alone give occasion to any great difference of talents.

As it is this disposition which forms that difference of talents, so remarkable among men of different professions, so it is this same disposition which renders that difference useful. Many tribes of animals acknowledged to be all of the same species, derive from nature a much more remarkable distinction of genius, than what, antecedent to custom and education, appears to take place among men. By nature a philosopher is not in genius and disposition half so different from a street porter, as a mastiff is from a greyhound, or a greyhound from a spaniel, or this last from a shepherd's dog. Those different tribes of animals, however, though all of the same species, are of scarce any use to one another. The strength of the mastiff is not in the least supported either by the swiftness of the greyhound, or by the sagacity of the spaniel, or by the docility of the shepherd's dog. The effects of those different geniuses and talents, for want of the power or disposition to barter and exchange, cannot be brought into a common stock, and do not in the least contribute to the better accommodation and conveniency of the species. Each animal is still obliged to support and defend itself, separately and independently, and derives no sort of advantage from that variety of talents with which nature has distinguished its fellows. Among men, on the contrary, the most dissimilar geniuses are of use to one another; the different produces of their respective talents, by the general disposition to truck, barter, and exchange, being brought into a common stock, where every man may purchase whatever part of the produce of other men's talents he has occasion for.

[Book IV]

CHAPTER I: THE PRINCIPLE OF THE COMMERCIAL OR MERCANTILE SYSTEM

That wealth consists in money, or in gold and silver, is a popular notion which naturally arises from the double function of money, as the instrument of commerce, and as the measure of value. In consequence of its being the instrument of commerce, when we have money we can more readily obtain whatever else we have occasion for than by means of any other commodity. The great affair, we always find, is to get money. When that is obtained there is no difficulty in making any subsequent purchase. In consequence of its being the measure of value, we estimate that of all other commodities by the quantity of money which they will exchange for. We say of a rich man that he is worth a great deal, and of a poor man that he is worth very little money. A frugal man, or a man eager to be rich, is said to love money; and a careless, a generous, or a profuse man, is said to be indifferent about it. To grow rich is to get money; and wealth and money, in short, are, in common language, considered as in every respect synonymous.

A rich country, in the same manner as a rich man, is supposed to be abounding in money; and to heap up gold and silver in any country is supposed to be the readiest way to enrich it. For some time after the discovery of America, the first inquiry of the Spaniards, when they arrived upon any unknown coast, used to be, if there was any gold or silver to be found in the neighbourhood? By the information which they received, they judged whether it was worth while to make a settlement there, or if the country was worth the conquering. Plano Carpino, a monk, sent ambassador from the king of France to one of the sons of the famous Gengis Khan, says that the Tartars used frequently to ask him, if there was plenty of sheep and oxen in the kingdom of France? Their inquiry had the same object with that of the Spaniards. They wanted to know if the country was rich enough to be worth the conquering. Among the Tartars, as among all other nations of shepherds, who are generally ignorant of the use of money, cattle are the instruments of commerce and the measures of value. Wealth, therefore, according to them, consisted in cattle, as according to the Spaniards it consisted in gold and silver. Of the two, the Tartar notion, perhaps, was the nearest to the truth.

Mr. Locke marks a distinction between money and other movable goods. All other movable goods, he says, are of so consumable a nature, that the wealth which consists in them cannot be much depended on, and a nation which abounds in them one year may, without any exportation, but merely by their own waste and extravagance, be in great want of them the next. Money, on the contrary, is a steady friend, which, though it may travel about from hand to hand, yet if it can be kept from going out of the country, is not very liable to be wasted and consumed. Gold and silver, therefore, are, according to him, the most solid and substantial part of the movable wealth of a nation, and to multiply those metals ought, he thinks, upon that account, to be the great object of its political economy.

Others admit, that if a nation could be separated from all the world, it would be of no consequence how much or how little money circulated in it. The consumable goods which were circulated by means of this money, would only be exchanged for a greater or a smaller number of pieces: but the real wealth or poverty of the country, they allow, would depend altogether upon the abundance or scarcity of those consumable goods. But it is otherwise, they think, with countries which have connections with foreign nations, and which are obliged to carry on foreign wars, and to maintain fleets and armies in distant countries. This, they say, cannot be done, but by sending abroad money to pay them with; and a nation cannot send much money abroad, unless it has a good deal at home. Every such nation must endeavour in time of peace to accumulate gold and silver, that when occasion requires, it may have wherewithal to carry on foreign wars.

In consequence of these popular notions, all the different nations of Europe have studied, though to little purpose, every possible means of accumulating gold and silver in their respective countries. Spain and Portugal, the proprietors of the principal mines which supply Europe with those metals, have either prohibited their exportation under the severest penalties, or subjected it to a considerable duty. The like prohibition seems anciently to have made a part of the policy of most other European nations. It is even to be found, where we should least of all expect to find it, in some old Scotch acts of parliament, which forbid, under heavy penalties, the carrying gold or silver *forth of the kingdom*. The like policy anciently took place both in France and England.

When those countries became commercial, the merchants found this prohibition, upon many occasions, extremely inconvenient. They could frequently buy more advantageously with gold and silver than with any other commodity the foreign goods which they wanted, either to import into their own, or to carry to some other foreign country. They remonstrated therefore against this prohibition as hurtful to their trade.

They represented, first, that the exportation of gold and silver in order to purchase foreign goods, did not always diminish the quantity of those metals in the kingdom. That, on the contrary, it might frequently increase that quantity; because, if the consumption of foreign goods was not thereby increased in the country, those goods might be re-exported to foreign countries, and, being there sold for a large profit, might bring back much more treasure than was originally sent out to purchase them. Mr. Mun compares this operation of foreign trade to the seed time and harvest of agriculture. "If we only behold," says he, "the actions of the husbandman in the seed time, when he casteth away much good corn into the ground, we shall account him rather a madman than a husband. But when we consider his labours in the harvest, which is the end of his endeavours, we shall find the worth and plentiful increase of his actions."

They represented, secondly, that this prohibition could not hinder the exportation of gold and silver, which, on account of the smallness of their bulk in proportion to their value, could easily be smuggled abroad. That this exportation could only be prevented by a proper attention to what they called the balance of trade. That when the country exported to a greater value than it imported, a balance became due to it from foreign nations, which was necessarily paid to it in gold and silver, and thereby increased the quantity of those metals imported in the kingdom. But that when it imported to a greater value than it exported, a contrary balance became due to foreign nations, which was necessarily paid to them in the same manner, and thereby diminished that quantity. That in this case, to prohibit the exportation of those metals could not prevent it, but only by making it more dangerous, render it more expensive. That the exchange was thereby turned more against the country which

owed the balance than it otherwise might have been; the merchant who purchased a bill upon the foreign country being obliged to pay the banker who
sold it, not only for the natural risk, trouble, and expense of sending the money
thither, but for the extraordinary risk arising from the prohibition. But that
the more the exchange was against any country, the more the balance of trade
became necessarily against it; the money of that country becoming necessarily
of so much less value, in comparison with that of the country to which the
balance was due. That if the exchange between England and Holland, for
example, was five per cent against England, it would require 105 oz. of silver
in England to purchase a bill for 100 oz. of silver in Holland: that 105 oz. of
silver in England, therefore, would be worth only 100 oz. of silver in Holland,
and would purchase only a proportionate quantity of Dutch goods: but that
100 oz. of silver in Holland, on the contrary, would be worth 105 oz. in England, and would purchase a proportionate quantity of English goods: that
the English goods which were sold to Holland would be sold so much cheaper;
and the Dutch goods which were sold to England so much dearer, by the
difference of the exchange; that the one would draw so much less Dutch
money to England, and the other so much more English money to Holland as
this difference amounted to: and that the balance of trade, therefore, would
necessarily be so much more against England, and would require a greater
balance of gold and silver to be imported to Holland.

Those arguments were partly solid and partly sophistical. They were solid
so far as they asserted that the exportation of gold and silver in trade might
frequently be advantageous to the country. They were solid, too, in asserting
that no prohibition could prevent their exportation when private people found
any advantage in exporting them. But they were sophistical in supposing,
that either to preserve or to augment the quantity of those metals required
more attention of government, than to preserve or to augment the quantity
of any other useful commodities, which the freedom of trade, without any
such attention, never fails to supply in the proper quantity. They were sophistical, too, perhaps, in asserting that the high price of exchange necessarily increased, what they called, the unfavourable balance of trade, or occasioned the
exportation of a greater quantity of gold and silver. That high price, indeed,
was extremely disadvantageous to the merchants who had any money to pay
in foreign countries. They paid so much dearer for the bills which their bankers
granted them upon those countries. But though the risk arising from the
prohibition might occasion some extraordinary expense to the bankers, it
would not necessarily carry any more money out of the country. This expense
would generally be all laid out in the country, in smuggling the money out
of it, and could seldom occasion the exportation of a single sixpence beyond

the precise sum drawn for. The high price of exchange would naturally dispose the merchants to endeavour to make their exports nearly balance their imports, that they might have this high exchange to pay upon as small a sum as possible. The high price of exchange must necessarily have operated as a tax, in raising the price of foreign goods, and diminishing their consumption. It would tend, therefore, not to increase, but to diminish, what they called, the unfavourable balance of trade, and the exportation of gold and silver. . . .

A country that has no mines of its own must undoubtedly draw its gold and silver from foreign countries, in the same manner as one that has no vineyards of its own must draw its wines. It does not seem necessary, however, that the attention of government should be more turned towards the one than towards the other object. A country that has wherewithal to buy wine, will always get the wine which it has occasion for; and a country that has wherewithal to buy gold and silver, will never be in want of those metals. They are to be bought for a certain price like all other commodities, and as they are the price of all other commodities, so all other commodities are the price of those metals. We trust with perfect security that the freedom of trade, without any attention of government, will always supply us with the wine which we have occasion for; and we may trust with equal security that it will always supply us with all the gold and silver which we can afford to purchase or employ in circulating our commodities, or in other uses.

The quantity of every commodity which human industry can either purchase or produce, naturally regulates itself in every country according to effectual demand, or according to the demand of those who are willing to pay the whole rent, labour, and profits which must be paid in order to prepare and bring it to market. But no commodities regulate themselves more easily or more exactly according to this effectual demand than gold and silver; because, on account of the small bulk and great value of those metals, no commodities can be more easily transported from one place to another, from the places where they are cheap, to those where they are dear, from the places where they exceed, to those where they fall short of this effectual demand. If there were in England, for example, an effectual demand for an additional quantity of gold, a packet-boat could bring from Lisbon, or from wherever else it was to be had, 50 tons of gold, which could be coined into more than 5,000,000 of guineas. But if there were an effectual demand for grain to the same value, to import it would require, at five guineas a ton, 1,000,000 of tons of shipping, or 1,000 ships of 1,000 tons each. The navy of England would not be sufficient. . . .

It would be too ridiculous to go about seriously to prove that wealth does not consist in money, or in gold and silver, but in what money purchases, and is valuable only for purchasing. Money, no doubt, makes always a part of the national capital; but it has already been shown that it generally makes but a small part, and always the most unprofitable part of it. . . .

The importation of gold and silver is not the principal, much less the sole benefit which a nation derives from its foreign trade. Between whatever places foreign trade is carried on, they all of them derive two distinct benefits from it. It carries out that surplus part of the produce of their land and labour for which there is no demand among them, and brings back in return for it something else for which there is a demand. It gives a value to their super-fluities, by exchanging them for something else, which may satisfy a part of their wants, and increase their enjoyments. By means of it, the narrowness of the home market does not hinder the division of labour in any particular branch of art or manufacture from being carried to the highest perfection. By opening a more extensive market for whatever part of the produce of their labour may exceed the home consumption, it encourages them to improve its productive powers, and to augment its annual produce to the utmost, and thereby to increase the real revenue and wealth of the society. These great and important services foreign trade is continually occupied in performing, to all the different countries between which it is carried on. They all derive great benefit from it, though that in which the merchant resides generally derives the greatest, as he is generally more employed in supplying the wants, and carrying out the superfluities of his own, than of any other particular country. To import the gold and silver which may be wanted, into the countries which have no mines, is, no doubt, a part of the business of foreign commerce. It is, however, a most insignificant part of it. A country which carried on foreign trade merely upon this account, could scarce have occasion to freight a ship in a century.

It is not by the importation of gold and silver that the discovery of America has enriched Europe. By the abundance of the American mines, those metals have become cheaper. A service of plate can now be purchased for about a third part of the corn, or a third part of the labour, which it would have cost in the fifteenth century. With the same annual expense of labour and commodities, Europe can annually purchase about three times the quantity of plate which it could have purchased at that time. But when a commodity comes to be sold for a third part of what had been its usual price, not only those who purchased it before can purchase three times their former quantity, but it is brought down to the level of a much greater number of purchasers, perhaps to more than ten, perhaps to more than twenty times the former number. So that there may be in Europe at present not only more than three times, but more than twenty or thirty times the quantity of plate which would have been in it, even in its present state of improvement, had the discovery of the American mines never been made. So far Europe has, no doubt, gained a real conveniency, though surely a very trifling one. The cheapness of gold and silver render those metals rather less fit for the purposes of money than they were before. In order to make the same purchases, we must load ourselves with a greater quantity of them, and carry about a shilling in our pocket where a groat would have done before. It is difficult to say which is most trifling, this inconveniency, or the opposite inconveniency. Neither the one nor the other could have made any very essential change in the state of Europe. The discovery of America, however, certainly made a most essential one. By opening a new and inexhaustible market to all the commodities of Europe, it gave occasion to new divisions of labour and improvements of art, which, in the narrow circle of the ancient commerce, could never have taken place for want of a market to take off the greater part of their produce. The productive powers of labour were improved, and its produce increased in all the different countries of Europe, and together with it the real revenue and wealth of the inhabitants. The commodities of Europe were almost all new to America, and many of those of America were new to Europe. A new set of exchanges, therefore, began to take place which had never been thought of before, and which should naturally have proved as advantageous to the new, as it certainly did to the old continent. The savage injustice of the Europeans rendered an event, which ought to have been beneficial to all, ruinous and destructive to several of those unfortunate countries. . . .

I thought it necessary, though at the hazard of being tedious, to examine at full length this popular notion that wealth consists in money, or in gold and silver. Money, in common language, as I have already observed, frequently signifies wealth; and this ambiguity of expression has rendered this popular notion so familiar to us, that even they who are convinced of its absurdity, are very apt to forget their own principles, and in the course of their reasonings to take it for granted as a certain and undeniable truth. Some of the best English writers upon commerce set out with observing, that the wealth of a country consists, not in its gold and silver only, but in its lands, houses, and consumable goods of all different kinds. In the course of their reasonings, however, the lands, houses, and consumable goods seem to slip out of their memory, and the strain of their argument frequently supposes that all wealth consists in gold and silver, and that to multiply those metals is the great object of national industry and commerce.

The two principles being established, however, that wealth consisted in gold and silver, and that those metals could be brought into a country which had no mines only by the balance of trade, or by exporting to a greater value than it imported, it necessarily became the great object of political economy to diminish as much as possible the importation of foreign goods for home consumption, and to increase as much as possible the exportation of the produce of domestic industry. Its two great engines for enriching the country, therefore, were restraints upon importation and encouragements for exportation.

The restraints upon importation were of two kinds.

I. Restraints upon the importation of such foreign goods for home consumption as could be produced at home, from whatever country they were imported. II. Restraints upon the importation of goods of almost all kinds from those particular countries with which the balance of trade was supposed to be disadvantageous.

Those different restraints consisted sometimes in high duties, and sometimes in absolute prohibitions. Exportation was encouraged sometimes by drawbacks, sometimes by bounties, sometimes by advantageous treaties of commerce with foreign states, and sometimes by the establishment of colonies in distant countries.

Drawbacks were given upon two different occasions. When the home manufacturers were subject to any duty or excise, either the whole or a part of it was frequently drawn back upon their exportation; and when foreign goods liable to a duty were imported in order to be exported again, either the whole or a part of this duty was sometimes given back upon such exportation.

Bounties were given for the encouragement either of some beginning manufacturers, or of such sorts of industry of other kinds as were supposed to deserve particular favour.

By advantageous treatise of commerce, particular privileges were procured in some foreign state for the goods and merchants of the country beyond what were granted to those of other countries.

By the establishment of colonies in distant countries, not only particular privileges, but a monopoly was frequently procured for the goods and merchants of the country which established them.

The two sorts of restraints upon importation, together with these four encouragements to exportation, constitute the six principal means by which the commercial system proposes to increase the quantity of gold and silver in any country by turning the balance of trade in its favour. I shall consider each of them in a particular chapter, and without taking much further notice of their supposed tendency to bring money into the country, I shall examine chiefly what are likely to be the effects of each of them upon the annual produce of its industry. According as they tend either to increase or diminish the value of this annual produce, they must evidently tend either to increase or diminish the real wealth and revenue of the country.

CHAPTER II: OF RESTRAINTS UPON THE IMPORTATION FROM FOREIGN COUN-
TRIES OF SUCH GOODS AS CAN BE PRODUCED AT HOME

The general industry of the society never can exceed what the capital of
the society can employ. As the number of workmen that can be kept in employment by any particular person must bear a certain proportion to his
capital, so the number of those that can be continually employed by all the
members of a great society, must bear a certain proportion to the whole capital
of that society, and never can exceed that proportion. No regulation of commerce can increase the quantity of industry in any society beyond what its
capital can maintain. It can only divert a part of it into a direction into which
it might not otherwise have gone; and it is by no means certain that this
artificial direction is likely to be more advantageous to the society than that into
which it would have gone of its own accord.

Every individual is continually exerting himself to find out the most advantageous employment for whatever capital he can command. It is his own
advantage, indeed, and not that of the society, which he has in view. But the
study of his own advantage naturally, or rather necessarily leads him to prefer
that employment which is most advantageous to the society.

First, every individual endeavours to employ his capital as near home as he
can, and consequently as much as he can in the support of domestic industry;
provided always that he can thereby obtain the ordinary, or not a great deal
less than the ordinary profits of stock.

Thus, upon equal or nearly equal profits, every wholesale merchant naturally
prefers the home-trade to the foreign trade of consumption, and the foreign
trade of consumption to the carrying trade. In the home-trade his capital is
never so long out of his sight as it frequently is in the foreign trade of consumption. He can know better the character and situation of the persons whom
he trusts, and if he should happen to be deceived, he knows better the laws of
the country from which he must seek redress. In the carrying trade, the capital
of the merchant is, as it were, divided between two foreign countries, and
no part of it is ever necessarily brought home, or placed under his own immediate view and command. The capital which an Amsterdam merchant employs in carrying corn from Konnigsberg to Lisbon, and fruit and wine from
Lisbon to Konnigsberg, must generally be the one-half of it at Konnigsberg
and the other half at Lisbon. No part of it need ever come to Amsterdam. The
natural residence of such a merchant should either be at Konnigsberg or Lisbon, and it can only be some very particular circumstances which can make
him prefer the residence of Amsterdam. The uneasiness, however, which he

feels at being separated so far from his capital, generally determines him to bring part both of the Konnigsberg goods which he destines for the market of Lisbon, and of the Lisbon goods which he destines for that of Konnigsberg, to Amsterdam: and though this necessarily subjects him to a double charge of loading and unloading, as well as to the payment of some duties and customs, yet for the sake of having some part of this capital always under his own view and command, he willingly submits to this extraordinary charge; and it is in this manner that every country which has any considerable share of the carrying trade, becomes always the emporium, or general market, for the goods of all the different countries whose trade it carries on. The merchant, in order to save a second loading and unloading, endeavours always to sell in the home-market as much of the goods of all those different countries as he can, and thus, so far as he can, to convert his carrying trade into a foreign trade of consumption. A merchant, in the same manner, who is engaged in the foreign trade of consumption, when he collects goods for foreign markets, will always be glad, upon equal or nearly equal profits, to sell as great a part of them at home as he can. He saves himself the risk and trouble of exportation, when, so far as he can, he thus converts his foreign trade of consumption into a home-trade. Home is in this manner the center, if I may say so, round which the capitals of the inhabitants of every country are continually circulating, and towards which they are always tending, though by particular causes they may sometimes be driven off and repelled from it towards more distant employment. But a capital employed in the home-trade, . . . necessarily puts into motion a greater quantity of domestic industry, and gives revenue and employment to a greater number of the inhabitants of the country, than an equal capital employed in the foreign trade of consumption: and one employed in the foreign trade of consumption has the same advantage over an equal capital employed in the carrying trade. Upon equal, or only nearly equal profits, therefore, every individual naturally inclines to employ his capital in the manner in which it is likely to afford the greatest support to domestic industry, and to give revenue and employment to the greatest number of people of his own country.

Secondly, every individual who employs his capital in the support of domestic industry, necessarily endeavours so to direct that industry, that its produce may be of the greatest possible value.

The produce of industry is what it adds to the subject or materials upon which it is employed. In proportion as the value of this produce is great or small, so will likewise be the profits of the employer. But it is only for the sake of profit that any man employs a capital in the support of industry; and he will always, therefore, endeavour to employ it in the support of that industry of which the produce is likely to be of the greatest value, or to exchange for the greatest quantity either of money or of other goods.

But the annual revenue of every society is always precisely equal to the exchangeable value of the whole annual produce of its industry, or rather is precisely the same thing with that exchangeable value. As every individual, therefore, endeavours as much as he can both to employ his capital in the support of domestic industry, and so to direct that industry that its produce may be of the greatest value; every individual necessarily labours to render the annual revenue of the society as great as he can. He generally, indeed, neither intends to promote the public interest, nor knows how much he is promoting it. By preferring the support of domestic to that of foreign industry, he intends only his own security; and by directing that industry in such a manner as its produce may be of the greatest value, he intends only his own gain, and he is in this, as in many other cases, led by an invisible hand to promote an end which was no part of his intention. Nor is it always the worse for the society that it was no part of it. By pursuing his own interest he frequently promotes that of the society more effectually than when he really intends to promote it. I have never known much good done by those who affected to trade for the public good. It is an affectation, indeed, not very common among merchants, and very few words need be employed in dissuading them from it.

What is the species of domestic industry which his capital can employ, and of which the produce is likely to be of the greatest value, every individual, it is evident, can, in his local situation, judge much better than any statesman or lawgiver can do for him. The statesman, who should attempt to direct private people in what manner they ought to employ their capitals, would not only load himself with a most unnecessary attention, but assume an authority which could safely be trusted, not only to no single person, but to no council or senate whatever, and which would no-where be so dangerous as in the hands of a man who had folly and presumption enough to fancy himself fit to exercise it.

To give the monopoly of the home-market to the produce of domestic industry, in any particular art of manufacture, is in some measure to direct private people in what manner they ought to employ their capitals, and must, in almost all cases, be either a useless or a hurtful regulation. If the produce of domestic can be brought there as cheap as that of foreign industry, the regulation is evidently useless. If it cannot, it must generally be hurtful. It is the maxim of every prudent master of a family, never to attempt to make at home what it will cost him more to make than to buy. The taylor does not attempt to make his own shoes, but buys them of the shoemaker. The shoemaker does not attempt to make his own clothes, but employs a taylor. The farmer attempts to make neither the one nor the other, but employs those different artificers. All of them find it for their interest to employ their whole industry in a way in which they have some advantage over their neighbours, and to purchase with a part of its produce, or what is the same thing, with the price of a part of it, whatever else they have occasion for.

What is prudence in the conduct of every private family, can scarce be folly in that of a great kingdom. If a foreign country can supply us with a commodity cheaper than we ourselves can make it, better buy it of them with some part of the produce of our own industry, employed in a way in which we have some advantage. The general industry of the country, being always in proportion to the capital which employs it, will not thereby be diminished, no more than that of the above-mentioned artificers; but only left to find out the way in which it can be employed with the greatest advantage. It is certainly not employed to the greatest advantage, when it is thus directed towards an object which it can buy cheaper than it can make. The value of its annual produce is certainly more or less diminished, when it is thus turned away from producing commodities evidently of more value than the commodity which it is directed to produce. According to the supposition, that commodity could be purchased from foreign countries cheaper than it can be made at home. It could, therefore, have been purchased with a part only of the commodities, or, what is the same thing, with a part only of the price of the commodities, which the industry employed by an equal capital would have produced at home, had it been left to follow its natural course. The industry of the country, therefore, is thus turned away from a more, to a less advantageous employment, and the exchangeable value of its annual produce, instead of being increased, according to the intention of the lawgiver, must necessarily be diminished by every such regulation.

By means of such regulations, indeed, a particular manufacture may sometimes be acquired sooner than it could have been otherwise, and after a certain time may be made at home as cheap or cheaper than in the foreign country. But though the industry of the society may be thus carried with advantage into a particular channel sooner than it could have been otherwise, it will by no means follow that the sum total, either of its industry, or of its revenue, can ever be augmented by any such regulation. The industry of the society can augment only in proportion as its capital augments, and its capital can augment only in proportion to what can be gradually saved out of its revenue. But the immediate effect of every such regulation is to diminish its revenue, and what diminishes its revenue is certainly not very likely to augument its capital faster than it would have augmented of its own accord, had both capital and industry been left to find out their natural employments. . . .

There seem, however, to be two cases in which it will generally be advantageous to lay some burden upon foreign, for the encouragement of domestic industry.

The first is, when some particular sort of industry is necessary for the defence of the country. The defence of Great Britain, for example, depends very much upon the number of its sailors and shipping. The act of navigation, therefore, very properly endeavours to give the sailors and shipping of Great Britain the monopoly of the trade of their own country, in some cases, by absolute prohibitions, and in others by heavy burdens upon the shipping of foreign countries. . . .

The act of navigation is not favourable to foreign commerce, or to the growth of that opulence which can arise from it. The interest of a nation in its commercial relations to foreign nations is, like that of a merchant with regard to the different people with whom he deals, to buy as cheap and to sell as dear as possible. But it will be most likely to buy cheap, when by the most perfect freedom of trade it encourages all nations to bring to it the goods which it has occasion to purchase; and, for the same reason, it will be most likely to sell dear, when its markets are thus filled with the greatest number of buyers. The act of navigation, it is true, lays no burden upon foreign ships that come to export the produce of British industry. . . . But if foreigners, either by prohibitions or high duties, are hindered from coming to sell, they cannot always afford to come to buy; because coming without a cargo, they must lose the freight from their own country to Great Britain. By diminishing the number of sellers, therefore, we necessarily diminish that of buyers, and are thus likely not only to buy foreign goods dearer, but to sell our own cheaper, than if there was a more perfect freedom of trade. As defence, however, is of much more importance than opulence, the act of navigation is, perhaps, the wisest of all the commercial regulations of England.

The second case, in which it will generally be advantageous to lay some burden upon foreign for the encouragement of domestic industry, is, when some tax is imposed at home upon the produce of the latter. In this case, it seems reasonable that an equal tax should be imposed upon the like produce of the former. This would not give the monopoly of the home market to domestic industry, nor turn towards a particular employment a greater share of the stock and labour of the country, than what would naturally go to it. It would only hinder any part of what would naturally go to it from being turned away by the tax, into a less natural direction, and would leave the competition between foreign and domestic industry, after the tax, as nearly as possible upon the same footing as before it. In Great Britain, when any such tax is laid upon the produce of domestic industry, it is usual at the same time, in order to stop the clamorous complaints of our merchants and manufacturers, that they will be undersold at home, to lay a much heavier duty upon the importation of all foreign goods of the same kind. . . .

As there are two cases in which it will generally be advantageous to lay some burden upon foreign, for the encouragement of domestic industry; so there are two others in which it may sometimes be a matter of deliberation; in the one, how far it is proper to continue the free importation of certain foreign goods; and in the other, how far, or in what manner, it may be proper to restore that free importation after it has been for some time interrupted.

The case in which it may sometimes be a matter of deliberation how far it is proper to continue the free importation of certain foreign goods, is, when some foreign nation restrains by high duties or prohibitions the importation of some of our manufactures into their country. Revenge in this case naturally dictates retaliation, and that we should impose the like duties and prohibitions upon the importation of some or all of their manufacturers into ours. Nations accordingly seldom fail to retaliate in this manner. The French have been particularly forward to favour their own manufactures by restraining the importation of such foreign goods as could come into competition with them. In this consisted a great part of the policy of Mr. Colbert, who, notwithstanding his great abilities, seems in this case to have been imposed upon by the sophistry of merchants and manufacturers, who are always demanding a monopoly against their countrymen. It is at present the opinion of the most intelligent men in France that his operations of this kind have not been beneficial to his country. . . .

There may be good policy in retaliations of this kind, when there is a probability that they will procure the repeal of the high duties or prohibitions complained of. The recovery of a great foreign market will generally more than compensate the transitory inconveniency of paying dearer during a short time for some sorts of goods. To judge whether such retaliations are likely to produce such an effect, does not, perhaps, belong so much to the science of a legislator, whose deliberations ought to be governed by general principles which are always the same, as to the skill of that insidious and crafty animal, vulgarly called a statesman or politician, whose councils are directed by the momentary fluctuations of affairs. When there is no probability that any such repeal can be procured, it seems a bad method of compensating the injury done to certain classes of our people, to do another injury ourselves, not only to those classes, but to almost all the other classes of them. When our neighbours prohibit some manufacture of ours, we generally prohibit, not only the same, for that alone would seldom affect them considerably, but some other manufacture of theirs. This may no doubt give encouragement to some particular class of workmen among ourselves, and by excluding some of their rivals, may enable them to raise their price in the home-market. Those workmen, however, who suffered by our neighbours prohibition will not be benefited by ours. On the contrary, they and almost all the other classes of our citizens will thereby be obliged to pay dearer than before for certain goods. Every such law, therefore, imposes a real tax upon the whole country, not in favour of that particular class of workmen who were injured by our neighbours prohibition, but of some other class.

The case in which it may sometimes be a matter of deliberation, how far, or in what manner, it is proper to restore the free importation of foreign goods, after it has been for some time interrupted, is when particular manufactures, by means of high duties or prohibitions upon all foreign goods which can come into competition with them, have been so far extended as to employ a great multitude of hands. Humanity may in this case require that the freedom of trade should be restored only by slow gradations, and with a good deal of reserve and circumspection. Were those high duties and prohibitions taken away all at once, cheaper foreign goods of the same kind might be poured so fast into the home market, as to deprive all at once many thousands of our people of their ordinary employment and means of subsistence. The disorder which this would occasion might no doubt be very considerable. . . .

To expect, indeed, that the freedom of trade should ever be entirely restored in Great Britain, is as absurd as to expect that an Oceana or Utopia should ever be established in it. Not only the prejudices of the public, but what is much more unconquerable, the private interests of many individuals, irresistibly oppose it. Were the officers of the army to oppose with the same zeal and unanimity any reduction in the number of forces, with which master manufacturers set themselves against every law that is likely to increase the number of their rivals in the home market; were the former to animate their soldiers, in the same manner as the latter enflame their workmen, to attack with violence and outrage the proposers of any such regulation; to attempt to reduce the army would be as dangerous as it has now become to attempt to diminish in any respect the monopoly which our manufacturers have obtained against us. This monopoly has so much increased the number of some particular tribes of them, that, like an overgrown standing army, they have become formidable to the government, and upon many occasions intimidate the legislature. The member of parliament who supports every proposal for strengthening this monopoly, is sure to acquire not only the reputation of understanding trade, but great popularity and influence with an order of men whose numbers and wealth render them of great importance. If he opposes them, on the contrary, and still more if he has authority enough to be able to thwart them, neither the most acknowledged probity, nor the highest rank, nor the greatest public services, can protect him from the most infamous abuse and detraction, from personal insults, nor sometimes from real danger, arising from the insolent outrage of furious and disappointed monopolists.

The undertaker of a great manufacture, who, by the home markets being suddenly laid open to the competition of foreigners, should be obliged to abandon his trade, would no doubt suffer very considerably. That part of his capital which had usually been employed in purchasing materials and in paying his workmen, might, without much difficulty, perhaps, find another employment. But that part of it which was fixed in workhouses, and in the instruments of trade, could scarce be disposed of without considerable loss. The equitable regard, therefore, to his interest requires that changes of this kind should never be introduced suddenly, but slowly, gradually, and after a very long warning. The legislature, were it possible that its deliberations could be always directed, not by the clamorous importunity of partial interests, but by an extensive view of the general good, ought upon this very account, perhaps, to be particularly careful neither to establish any new monopolies of this kind, nor to extend further those which are already established. Every such regulation introduces some degree of real disorder into the constitution of the state, which it will be difficult afterwards to cure without occasioning another disorder. . . .

JEAN A. N. C. DE CONDORCET

WHEN THE NEWS of the American revolution (1775–83) reached French reformers a momentous change took place in their plans and hopes. The Americans had seemed to prove that the principles for which the Encyclopedists and others had struggled were practical and could be used to overthrow tyranny. In fact, the American leaders of 1776 had meant only to break politically with England. Social revolution was one of their greatest fears. The Declaration of Independence was not conceived as a proclamation of a new age of equality and freedom but as a justification for revolution on behalf of freedoms and rights, already established before 1776, that King George III seemed determined to destroy. The overwhelmingly conservative intentions of the "reluctant rebels" were almost completely ignored by the European enthusiasts for the American cause. For them, unlike the Americans, revolution in America meant a fundamental reordering of society. It was Europe, not America, that first made the American and French Revolutions one and the same in spirit.

Condorcet's essay testifies to the large European interest in the American revolution. It contributed to both Europe's misunderstanding of what America had done and to its belief that America had given the inspiration to carry through the work of the Enlightenment to a successful conclusion.

The selection from Condorcet's essay is taken from the *Oeuvres Complètes de Condorcet* (Paris, 1804). It has been translated by Stephen J. Gendzier.

THE INFLUENCE OF THE
AMERICAN REVOLUTION ON EUROPE

INTRODUCTION

The path to truth, said the poet Sa'Dī, is narrow and situated between two steep cliffs. The slightest false step can cause you to roll down the slope. You rise to your feet dazed from the fall and climb with difficulty once again to the summit. When you think you have reached it, you make one last effort, only to fall again on the other side.

America had hardly declared its independence when our politicians immediately saw that the ruin of England and the prosperity of France were to be the necessary consequences of that auspicious revolution. They seemed to view American independence with apathy when it was finally recognized and made secure; only taking it into their heads to doubt their predictions when the situation began to verify the latter half of their original statement.

Now that public opinion is beginning to stray away from this point of view, I think it timely to discuss calmly the consequences of this great event, and I am going to make an attempt to be a level-headed prophet. . . .

CHAPTER ONE: THE INFLUENCE OF THE AMERICAN REVOLUTION ON EUROPEAN VIEWS AND LEGISLATION

Montesquieu rediscovered and restored the dignity which mankind had lost.* But it is not enough that human dignity should be described in philosophical texts or implanted in the hearts of virtuous men. The uneducated or weak person must be able to see an example in a great nation.

America has given us this example. The document which proclaimed its independence is a simple and sublime exposition of these sacred rights which have so long been forgotten. In no other nation have these rights been so fully recognized and maintained in their essential integrity.

Of course, to speak the full truth, Negro slavery still exists in some of the United States. However, all enlightened men are ashamed of it and realize its danger. In the future, this stain will no longer contaminate the purity of American laws.

These wise republican leaders, who still cling to remnants of English prejudice, have not been sufficiently aware of the fact that prohibitory laws, commercial regulations, and indirect taxes all restrict and solidly prevent the free exercise of property rights. What is not at our full disposal, we cannot consider really to own.

In establishing a degree of tolerance which no other nation has witnessed, they consented to a few limitations which were demanded by the people although still contrary, if not to the exercise of personal freedom, then at least to every man's right not to have to submit to hardships caused by the mere use of his reason. Perhaps you can still find in the laws of a few states the faint remnants of a fanaticism which has been too exacerbated by long experience in the act of persecution to give way to the first concerted efforts of philosophical analysis. But if you compare these violations of man's natural rights with any other example that an enlightened person could discover in the legislation of the wisest nations of the past, and especially those nations of antiquity which are so admired yet not really understood, then you will be conscious of the fact that our opinion of America is not the product of an exaggerated enthusiasm for our age or that nation.

* Voltaire.

Moreover, if you were to justly censure the Americans, it would be for particular mistakes or for old abuses which have not been corrected because of special circumstances. And if the injustice were of sufficient importance, it would be completely abolished. The Americans are the only people who do not prescribe as rules the various Machiavellian maxims found in Europe. It is also impossible to find among their leaders the sincere or feigned belief that it is impossible to perfect the social order or to reconcile public well-being and justice.

The sight of such a great nation respecting human rights is useful to other peoples in spite of the difference in climates, mores, and constitutions. It teaches us that human rights are everywhere the same with one possible exception. In certain situations, the virtuous citizen must know how to renounce a specific privilege for the sake of peace. Yet there is no state where men cannot exercise fully all the other rights.

One must recognize that the possession of these rights has a strong influence on the general prosperity of the nation. A man who has never feared an outrage to himself acquires a more noble and gentle soul; the person whose property is always safe, finds that integrity and honesty are easy virtues; the citizen who is subject to laws, is more patriotic and courageous.

This example of America, which can be so useful to all the nations who can contemplate what is taking place in the New World, is going to be lost for the human race. Large nations scorn the example of smaller nations, and the English people, who have set such a striking example in the past century, are by their downfall going to give credence to the widespread, dangerous, and false opinion that laws can only have a transitory influence and that any body politic must break down after a short life which has had occasional moments of brilliance.

If America had been overpowered by English arms, then before long despotism would have forged chains for the mother country, and England would have experienced the fate of all states which are no longer free because the individual has been forced to become a subject instead of a citizen.

Now England should have lost its laws when it was losing its liberty. Certainly, in a peaceful monarchy, a wise legislator can sufficiently respect human rights to make the proud republican envious of the fate enjoyed by the happy subjects of the monarch. It is known that this truth, which is of consequence to the peaceful functioning of constitutions, has been proven by the French *Philosophes* precisely at the same time that they were accused of preaching sedition by newspapers, pastoral letters, and public indictments. To make an individual consent to give up his rights and status as a citizen, you must first take everything from him including his human dignity.

By a natural consequence of the respect in America for laws preserving the natural rights of mankind, all men regardless of religious beliefs, political opinions, or philosophical principles are assured of finding a place of refuge. England offers in vain the same advantage, at least to Protestants. The industries and trades of the inhabitants of the country do not offer the foreigner any means of support. The wealth of the nation drives away the poor, for there is little place left in a land where business and manufacturing have increased population. The English climate is only suitable for the peoples of a few areas in Europe. America, on the contrary, offers to young industry an alluring promise, and the poor can find easy means of gaining a livelihood. The reward for work in this country could be the accumulation of property which is secure and sufficient for one's needs. The more diversified climate is suitable to men of all countries.

But at the same time, America is separated from the European nations by a vast stretch of ocean and one must have more important reasons to cross it than the simple desire to increase one's well-being. Only the oppressed have the will power to clear that obstacle. Therefore, Europe, without having anything to fear from large emigrations, finds in America a useful restraining force to control ministers who would be tempted to govern in too offensive a manner. Oppression has to become more timorous when it is aware that a place of refuge exists for tormented people. These temporarily defeated individuals can escape persecution and then present their case before the tribune of public opinion.

Freedom of the press has been established in America and people have justly regarded this right to say and hear any kind of truth beneficial to mankind as one of the most sacred human rights.

In a country where the willow is a sacred tree and where it is forbidden by the death penalty to break one of its branches to save a drowning man, can it be said that the law does not prevent the full exercise of freedom or actually guarantee the safety of its citizens? If the absurdity of laws against the freedom of the press does not appear just as obvious, then unfortunately it is true that habits have the deadly power to accustom weak human reason to what should shock it the most.

An example of all the good that freedom of the press has done and will do in America will now be all the more useful for Europe because it is better than the English example in reassuring people against the alleged disadvantages of that liberty. More than once we have seen an American

submit peacefully to laws that he had previously attacked with fury because he disagreed with its fundamental principle or its operational meaning. This good citizen respectfully obeys the agents of public authority
without renouncing his right to enlighten them or to censure them publicly
for their mistakes and errors. We have seen public discussions destroy
prejudice and prepare public opinion to support the wisdom of certain
newly-formed laws.

We have also seen that liberty breaks up interest groups rather than encourages intrigue, and it also prevents those people with selfish interests
from forming political parties. We can conclude from these facts that
highly inflammatory and libelous statements are dangerous only insofar
as rigid laws prevent the press from being outspoken and candid.

Finally, we have seen that opinions which are widely, easily, and quickly
distributed by printed articles in a large country can offer a government
in stress a more powerful weapon than the law. We shall only cite one
example, desertion in one section of the militia. The most severe penalties
were not able to stop its occurrence because the hope of escaping punishment had removed the law's effectiveness. It was proposed that the guilty
man's name might be published in the local newspaper, and the fear of
this punishment was more efficacious than the threat of the death penalty.
We feel that such a noble and generous manner of making citizens perform their duties owes its entire success to the same right which an accused
person also enjoys, that is, the request for the same amount of publicity
when he is unjustly indicted.

The English custom of circumventing certain laws about the press by
subtle and often ridiculous interpretations have clouded the issue, for England owes even more to the freedom of the press than to its constitution
for the maintenance of the laws and the respect preserved for those human
rights which have been sanctioned by public opinion.

How is it possible to look at America where tolerance has been accepted
and practiced more extensively than in any other nation and not realize
that this principle allows men to live in harmony and brotherhood? Why
is it necessary for governments to believe that intolerance is necessary for
the peaceful functioning of the state? Can they not learn that in the long
run it is not at all dangerous to obey the voice of justice and humanity?

There was a time when fanaticism dared to assert itself openly and demand the blood of men in the name of God. Reason forced fanaticism to
hide, but it soon donned the mask of politics, and for the sake of peace, it
now demands the right to trouble the public welfare. But America has
proven that a country can be happy, even though there are neither persecu-

tors nor hypocrites in their midst. Statesmen who have had difficulty in believing this on the authority of wise men will undoubtedly believe the example before their eyes.

In observing how the Americans have based their peace and happiness upon a small number of maxims which seem to be the naive expression of what good sense would have been able to dictate to all men, people will stop praising those political machines whose complexity makes the functioning of society disorderly, violent, and distressing. In those states, so much counter-weight, allegedly for the sake of harmony, actually has the effect of bearing down heavily upon the people. Perhaps we shall become conscious of the unimportance, or even the danger of all these political subtleties which have been admired for far too long. And the same could be said of those systems in which laws are bent out of shape so that the immutable foundations of truth, reason, and justice are forced to change according to the climate, the form of government, the current prejudices, and even the local stupidities of a nation; as if it would not have been more human, more just, and more noble to look earnestly for reasonable legislation in order to disabuse the citizens of their false notions.

A state can have brave, obedient, and disciplined soldiers without recourse to the harsh military service of many European nations. In these rigid systems, subordinates are judged by the secret reports of their captains, condemned without having been heard, punished without being able to defend themselves; and under which it is also a crime to ask permission to prove one's own innocence, and still a greater crime to print that one is not guilty. We must nevertheless admit that corruption, premeditated iniquity, or tyrannical callousness are not the causes of this system of secret oppression which violates the rights of citizens and nations. It is certainly not necessary because despotism is as useless and unreliable for discipline and for the security of the state as it is unjust. How then can we account for this situation? Alas! It is only that insuperable ignorance of natural law which can excuse this sin. And the example of a free people, who have nonetheless obediently submitted to military and civil laws, will unquestionably have the power to cure us of this sinful state.

The example of the equality which prevails in the United States, and assures its peace and prosperity, can also be useful to Europe. As a matter of fact, we no longer believe that nature has divided the human race into three or four classes and that one of these classes is also condemned to work a great deal and to eat rather little. People have spoken to us so much about the advantages of commerce and trade that the nobleman is beginning to regard the banker almost as his equal, that is, provided he is rich. But our philosophy does not go far enough and we were still able to print not so long ago, a statement to the effect that the masses of a certain country are by definition taxable and liable to forced labor.

We also said recently that a sense of honor could only exist in full in certain states, and that it was necessary to debase the greater part of a nation in order to give a little more pride to the few.

But here is a story that can be read in the history of America. A young French general was entrusted with the defense of Virginia against a superior army, and he saw that the soldiers, who had been recruited from their regiments to form a special battalion, were deserting *en masse*. In order to put an end to this situation, he declared that he wanted only a select company of men to serve under him and that he would discharge from the army all soldiers whose worth, integrity, and intelligence were suspect. From that moment on, no one had the slightest idea of withdrawing from the field. A soldier who was charged with a particular mission, asked the general to promise that if he should perish while carrying out orders, that they would have published in his local newspaper the fact that he had only left his detachment under orders from his superiors. Another soldier who was unable to march because of a wound, hired a wagon at his own expense in order to follow the Army. Now we are forced to agree that a sense of honor is the same in all segments of society and acts with equal strength upon men of all classes, provided that a person is not debased by an unjust accusation or oppressed by bad laws.

This is the kind of good lesson that humanity can expect from the American example, and we would be surprised if people looked upon all these advantages as either imaginary or impossible, because they have an immediate and a tangible influence upon an individual's fate. To do so would ignore the fact that the happiness of people in society depends almost exclusively upon good laws. The nation owes its first tribute to the legislator who combines wisdom in conceiving the law with the will and the power to enact it. The second most prized benefactor must be considered that person who by his own example or guidance has indicated to each legislator the specific laws that must be passed.

CHAPTER III: THE ADVANTAGES OF THE AMERICAN REVOLUTION WHICH ARE RELATIVE TO THE PERFECTIBILITY OF THE HUMAN RACE

We have already tried to show how the example of America could be useful in the destruction of prejudices which still prevail in Europe. Equally valuable for this purpose is an understanding of the enlightenment which necessarily ensues from the freedom to discuss all the important questions relating to the happiness of mankind. But there is another useful idea which we must now discuss, although we are rather convinced that most of our readers will think it absurdly unrealistic.

America is a vast stretch of country in which millions of people live, and by a process of education are protected from prejudices and predisposed to study and reflection. There are no class distinctions and no material inducements to keep men from the natural desire of perfecting their minds and using them in useful research and coveting the glory which accrues to great creators and discoverers. Furthermore, nothing [in America] holds a part of the human race in a state of humiliation, stupidity, and misery. There is therefore every reason to hope that America within a few generations will produce as many men preoccupied with the task of adding to the storehouse of human knowledge as can be found in Europe, thereby doubly increasing human progress. This progress will include advances in the useful arts and trades as well as in the speculative sciences.

Now we must consider the benefits which have accrued to humanity as one of the effects of the revolution. Dependence upon the mother country certainly would not have extinguished the natural genius of the Americans and Mr. Franklin is the proof of this, but it would have diverted this genius toward other goals. The desire to become an important person in England would have suppressed all other feelings in the heart of an American born with energy and talent. And he would have chosen the most rapid and sure method of succeeding. The men unable to harbor such ambitious thoughts would have become discouraged and apathetic.

States which are governed by princes who are far removed from them, and the provinces of great empires which are at a considerable distance from the capital city could offer us striking proof of this assertion, and we could expand upon these examples without any fear of seeming to set ourselves up as judges or appraisers of nations and new human accomplishments.

You will perhaps be surprised to see me place on the same level of discussion: discoveries, inventions, the improvement of our understanding, and the more important subjects, such as the preservation of human rights, the maintenance of peace, and even the advantages which arise from the trade of nations.

But when I was preoccupied with how to ameliorate the fate of mankind, I was compelled to believe that there is really only one way: that is to speed the progress of human enlightenment. Any other method has only a temporary and limited effect. Even though we would grant that errors, myths, and laws arising from local prejudices and not created by reason have made the happiness of a few nations, we would also be forced to admit that everywhere this much overpraised good situation has disappeared in a short time to make room for many social disorders from which reason has not yet been able to cure the human race after several centuries. Let men become enlightened and you will soon see born, effortlessly, a common purpose to remedy our ills.